THE
AMERICAN NATION

THIRD EDITION

A History of the United States from 1865 to the Present

JOHN D. HICKS
THE UNIVERSITY OF CALIFORNIA, BERKELEY

HOUGHTON MIFFLIN COMPANY The Riverside Press Cambridge

TO

J.H., C., AND M.

*The reproduction of Grant Wood's "Stone City" on the
title page is used through the courtesy of Joslyn Memorial
and Associated American Artists Galleries.*

1958 IMPRESSION

The Riverside Press
CAMBRIDGE · MASSACHUSETTS
PRINTED IN THE U.S.A.

CONTENTS

v

Appendix

PREFACE TO THE THIRD EDITION

"THESE are the times that try men's souls." So wrote Thomas Paine in 1776, but the words were no more applicable then than they are today. Then the new United States had declared its independence, but independence had yet to be won, and the chances for success seemed none too bright. Today the United States is the leader in an equally fateful struggle. Soviet Russia and her satellites have challenged the basic freedoms upon which the American nation was founded and which most of the western nations have come to accept. The battle is joined, sometimes hot and sometimes cold, sometimes waged with bombs and bullets to restrain a ruthless aggressor; sometimes, more effectively we believe, as a battle of ideas with the minds of men as the stake. The talk of "peaceful co-existence" fools no one. The longer the truces, the less the bloodshed, the better; it is possible even that the fearful hazards of atomic warfare may serve to prevent a third world war. But the struggle to persuade mankind that the one way or the other is the better way will go on indefinitely, or until one side wins. Freedom and slavery are forever incompatible.

Can the United States survive this prolonged period of stress and strain with its ideals and principles intact? During the dark days of the Revolution it was faith in the righteousness of their cause that pulled the Patriot leaders through, faith plus works. It takes the same kind of faith today, and the same kind of works. Looking backward there is much in our history that gives us reason to hope. The new nation achieved its independence, it survived a civil war, it spread its boundaries from ocean to ocean, it fought its way through two world wars, and it emerged eventually "from isolation to leadership." It did all this without destroying its belief in the importance of the individual, in his inherent right to life, liberty, and the pursuit of happiness. Probably it faces greater perils today than ever before, perils from the ruthless enemy without, from his occasional accomplice within, from those few misguided apostles of tyranny who would use the world struggle as an excuse to sacrifice our basic freedoms. But there is reason to believe that the nation as a whole has not lost faith, that it is as willing and able as ever to work out its salvation, that the "times that try men's souls" may serve to strengthen, not destroy them.

In the making of our future, whatever it may turn out to be, our past experience will play a fundamental rôle. I offer this revision in the hope that it will help young Americans to see the problems of the present in their proper historical perspective. Necessarily in the later chapters the canvas widens; American history and world history tend to merge. Perhaps a realization of this fact will induce the interested student to read still further afield. There never was a time when Americans needed so much to know, not only the history of their own nation, but the history of all the nations of the world.

For assistance in this revision I am deeply indebted to the staff of Houghton Mifflin Company, particularly to Miss Patricia Cahir whose work on the maps and illustrations has done so much to aid in the usefulness and attractiveness of the book. Professor George E. Mowry of the University of California, Los Angeles, has read all the new material, and has offered valuable criticisms, most of which I have accepted. Mr. Albert Hoxie of Beverly Hills, California, has made helpful suggestions on the history of art. Mrs. Helen E. Burke has served faithfully as my editorial assistant, and has done practically all of the work on the bibliographies, although both she and I must acknowledge an occasional assist from her husband, Dr. Robert E. Burke, Head of the Manuscripts Division in the Bancroft Library. For a wide variety of useful comments, I am deeply obliged to numerous colleagues, students, and friends.

John D. Hicks

Berkeley, California
July 4, 1954

PREFACE TO THE FIRST EDITION

HISTORY is so alive and growing that it is hard to see how anyone can think of it as dead and dry. It is, in reality, little more than a study of the present, explained in terms of the past. History looks forward, not backward; it is dynamic, not static. Those who condemn history as a mere rattling of ancient skeletons only betray their unfamiliarity with the subject. Out of the world of yesterday the world of today has grown; out of the world of today will come the world of tomorrow. It is impossible to understand our times without a knowledge of the conditions which brought them about; and it is equally impossible to make intelligent decisions for the future if we have only an uncomprehending view of the age in which we live. At least for a democracy, history is the most practical of subjects. One overstates but little to say that any democracy will function smoothly only in proportion as its history is well-taught and well-understood.

The field of history has long since been redefined to include social and economic as well as political development, and I have done my best in this volume to give a well-rounded picture of the American nation during the last seventy-five years. I have not yielded, however, to those peda-gogical faddists who insist that political history should be stripped of its garments and consigned bare and meaningless to occasional thin chap-ters of names and dates. Just who is responsible for such a trend in an age when democracy is fighting for its life I do not know; it is hard to believe that this pernicious idea is the product merely of ignorance. Politics in a democracy is of obvious importance, and past politics throws much light on the evolving political scene. If the young people of our colleges are ever made to believe that the political life of their nation is unimportant, then our democracy will be in a sorry way indeed.

Nor have I yielded to that other group of faddists who insist that recent history is too complex to be integrated, but must be considered as a set of more or less unrelated problems, each to be pursued after the hop, skip, and jump method through a long period of time. The task of integration is indeed difficult, and I may not have done it well. But I have at least tried to recognize two important truths; first, that all his-tory is interrelated; and second, that chronology is of profound im-portance. The task of the historian is not merely to spin out fine threads of knowledge; he must weave these threads together into a pattern which, however complicated, will have meaning as a whole.

In this book as in its predecessor, *The Federal Union*, references for further reading are suggested ... throughout the text. .... This is done with the hope that students will be induced to read further in subjects that particularly interest them. "The trouble with textbooks," according to one college president, "is that they take the sport out of learning. Their authors have had all the excitement of the chase ... and leave the student only the dead quarry." This might be true if the textbook were regarded as the end rather than the beginning of wisdom. The wise teacher will assure his students that there is plenty of game still uncaught, and that the textbook merely points the way to the chase.

I would be ungracious indeed not to acknowledge the very great debt I owe to the men whose single volumes on recent American history have preceded my own. I have borrowed freely from all of them. In the main, however, this book reproduces the organization and content of a course in the subject it covers that I have given for many years past. Introduced to this field first by Professor Frederic L. Paxson, now of the University of California, my debt to him is greater than to any other scholar. It was only with his definite encouragement that I presumed to parallel his *Recent History* with a book of my own.

Acknowledgments are also due to two of my colleagues, Professor William B. Hesseltine, who read and criticized the whole manuscript, and Professor Chester V. Easum, who gave me the benefit of his advice on the section pertaining to American entrance into the World War; to Professor George E. Mowry, then of the University of North Carolina, for information gleaned from the Theodore Roosevelt papers; ... to Dr. Theodore Saloutos, my research assistant, whose suggestions with reference to recent agricultural history were particularly valuable; to two of my graduate students, Miss Anne Cochrane and Mr. James Bringe, who cheerfully performed many time-consuming tasks; and to my wife, Lucile Curtis Hicks, who took time out from her already well-filled schedule to type a large part of the manuscript.

JOHN D. HICKS

MADISON, WISCONSIN

THE

AFTERMATH OF CIVIL WAR

1865 - 1890

A long and bitterly-fought Civil War is about the most difficult experience a nation can be called upon to endure. The scars of battle are bad enough, but they are far more easily erased than the shocking damage done to the minds and spirits of the men and women who have lived through the ordeal. The Civil War in the United States ended as a military struggle soon after Lee's defeat at Appomattox, but it left in its wake a callousness toward suffering and destruction, an acceptance of ruthlessness and deceit, and a legacy of hatred and mistrust that lived on for many years to come. The period of reconstruction was strongly colored by these attitudes, and cannot be understood apart from them. The cessation of hostilities did not mean that the sections were reconciled to living with each other amicably; too many on both sides were determined to prolong the contest by political means. And so the suffering continued.

The South was hurt more by the war than the North. Except for a few engagements, the fighting had taken place on southern soil, and the toll in dead and injured in the South, when compared to the total population of the section, was much larger than in the North. Besides, the South had lost the war, and to a great extent lay at the mercy of the victorious North. Slavery, the peculiar institution of the South, and state sovereignty, the political principle by which the South had justified its action, both had to go. The South had suffered not only a defeat, but also an enforced revolution.

The reconstruction of the South was badly done. After the death of Lincoln, the government of the United States fell into the hands of crass and cruel men who scrupled at nothing in the achievement of their ends. Andrew Johnson, a Southerner who comprehended the problems of the South, was swept first out of power, then out of office, and with General Grant as an ineffective front the Radicals in Congress had their way. Out of this storm and stress emerged the "solid South." The hatreds engendered by the war grew more intense during the initial years of peace; and the "road to reunion" grew harder to find.

That the nation must inevitably travel such a road became apparent, however, as the growth of the West went on. The United States that fought the Civil War was for all practical purposes confined to the eastern half of its borders. A great new West was in the making which had had relatively little to do with the war. Its people were drawn from both North and South. It required national aid for the solving of its problems — transportation, public lands, Indians. Its weight in the balance naturally went toward an increase in national powers. Thus, with the new West a part of the nation, the spirit of nationalism was the surer to survive and grow; the South had no choice but to make terms with it.

The confidence of the nation in its future was greatly shaken by the depression that began in 1873 and lasted until nearly the end of the decade. The hard times, however, were but the growing pains of a new society. The depression years gave the American people an opportunity to take stock of themselves, to mull over the things they might have done wrong, to chart a new course for the future. They made an effort to right the worst evils of reconstruction; they attacked the frauds they saw in government and business; they gave their support to education and literature; they revived their pre-war interest in humanitarian reform.

But in politics the nation was slow to emerge from the shadow of Civil War and reconstruction. The Republican Party was the product of the tension over slavery; it thought of itself as the party of the union that had won the war; it had a record to defend on reconstruction. The Democratic Party had opposed the Republicans on slavery; it had stood out for a fuller recognition of states' rights; it, too, had a record to defend, both on war and reconstruction. Neither party was ready to face up to the new issues; both looked over their shoulders at the past. As a result American political life for a quarter century after the war was bleak indeed.

1

The Problem of the South

Post-war Problems — Conditions in the South — National Policy — The Freedmen's Bureau — "Forty acres and a mule" — The army of occupation — Private benevolence — Cotton culture — The tenant system — Lincoln's plan of reconstruction — The Wade-Davis Bill — Andrew Johnson — Johnson's plan of reconstruction.

THE generation that has come of age in the United States since the Second World War **Post-war problems** will not need to be told that the end of hostilities may precipitate problems quite as perplexing as those which mark the progress of a war itself. With the spring of 1865 the American Civil War had worn itself out, but the tardy arrival of peace introduced other difficulties more appalling, perhaps, than the nation had ever faced before. The South, after four years of warfare within its borders, was not only defeated; its whole pattern of social organization lay in hopeless ruins. How were the people of the New South to live? What was to be the status of the freedmen? When and how were the normal processes of government to be resumed? Nor were the problems of the day confined wholly, or even mainly, to the South. The government of the United States, and, indeed, the governments of the northern states also, had become accustomed to the exercise of unusual wartime prerogatives. Were these practices to become permanent, or were they to be trimmed to fit the needs of peace? A million men were under arms. How could their speedy absorption into the ordinary walks of life be best facilitated? A huge national debt, an inflated currency, an overgrown system of taxation were parts of the inevitable legacy of war. What should the new financial picture be like? Manufactures of many sorts and kinds, stimulated by war orders and war profits, had reached a phenomenal development. Could their prosperity be preserved with the nation at peace? Agriculture, too, particularly in the Northwest, had expanded abnormally. How were the farmers to find markets for their produce? Less tangible, but no less important, the peoples of North and South for full four years had unbridled their prejudices, each against the other, and had carefully nourished their hatreds. How were the two parts of the restored Union ever to become one again in spirit? How could they learn to forgive and forget?

"Reconstruction" is the label that historians have generally applied to these postwar years. The word gained **Reconstruction** currency on the eve of the Civil War, when a "reconstruction of the Union" that would satisfy the South was often suggested as an alternative to secession. It was applied during and immediately after the war to the "reconstruction" of loyal governments in states from which secessionist officials had fled. As a descriptive term it leaves much to be desired. Neither the pre-war South nor the pre-war Union could ever be rebuilt or restored. Out of the ordeal of war and its aftermath there emerged a new nation, a nation so different from the

Southern whites in defeat lamented the ruins of war and the shattering of their once cherished way of life, but the Negroes, who at last were free, thought the day of jubilee had come. The presence of northern troops, even more than the actions of government, kept war-time antagonisms alive.

BEFORE THE WAR AND SINCE THE WAR.

SLAVERY · FREEDOM

old that the term "revolution" would scarcely overstate. But "reconstruction" has the sanction of long usage, and, properly redefined, it may still be permitted to serve. In a narrow sense, "reconstruction" means the process by which state government was revived in the South; broadly speaking, it must include all the drastic transformations of the period, both North and South.

Four years of warfare had left their marks upon the South. Armies had marched, **Conditions in the South** camped, foraged, and fought in practically every southern state, and in some of them almost continuously. Sherman's exultant report of the desolation wrought by his column on the way from Atlanta to the sea speaks for itself:

We have consumed the corn and fodder in the region of country thirty miles on either side of a line from Atlanta to Savannah as also the sweet potatoes, cattle, hogs, sheep and poultry, and have carried away more than 10,000 horses and mules as well as a countless number of slaves. I

estimate the damage done to the State of Georgia and its military resources at $100,000,000; at least $20,000,000 of which has inured to our advantage and the remainder is simple waste and destruction.

As Sherman's army turned northward into South Carolina, it vented its fury upon the state that most Northerners held responsible for starting the war. Carl Schurz reported, from observations made six months later, that the countryside along the "track of Sherman's march"

looked for many miles like a broad black streak of ruin and desolation — the fences all gone; lonesome smoke stacks, surrounded by dark heaps of ashes and cinders, marking the spots where human habitations had stood; the fields along the road wildly overgrown by weeds, with here and there a sickly looking patch of cotton or corn cultivated by negro squatters.

Traveling through Virginia in October, 1865, Alexander H. Stephens wrote in his diary: "The desolation of the country from Alex-

DESOLATION IN THE SOUTH. After the war, "Wealthy families reduced to abject poverty." Woodcut, 1867.

RICHMOND LADIES. Going for government rations: "Don't you think that Yankee must feel like shrinking before such high-toned Southern ladies as we?" Drawing by A. R. Waud, 1865.

andria to near Charlottesville was horrible to behold." Around Petersburg, where the forces of Grant and Lee had fought under conditions resembling modern trench warfare, farmers were stopped in their plowing by the quantity of metal they found in the ground, and the stench of death ended only with the autumn frosts. The Shenandoah Valley was so thoroughly denuded that, in accordance with Sheridan's promise "a crow could not fly over it without carrying his rations with him." Several years after the war an English traveler in America found the Valley of the Tennessee little better:

It consists for the most part of plantations in a state of semi-ruin, and plantations of which the ruin is total and complete. . . . The trail of war is visible throughout the valley in burnt-up gin-houses, ruined bridges, mills, and factories, of which latter the gable walls only are left standing, and in large tracts of once cultivated land stripped of every vestige of fencing. The roads, long neglected, are in disorder, and having in many places become impassable, new tracks have been made through the woods and fields without much respect to boundaries. Borne down by losses, debts, and accumulating taxes, many who were once the richest among their fellows have dis-

appeared from the scene, and few have yet risen to take their places.[1]

The sight of Charleston, once the proudest city of the South, moved the war-hardened Schurz to rhetoric:

There was no shipping in the harbor except a few quartermaster's vessels and two or three small steamers. We made fast to a decaying pier constructed of palmetto-logs. There was not a human being visible on the wharf. The warehouses seemed to be completely deserted. There was no wall and no roof that did not bear eloquent marks of having been under the fire of siege guns. . . . Nothing could be more desolate and melancholy than the appearance of the lower part of the city immediately adjoining the harbor. Although the military authorities had caused the streets to be "policed" as well as possible, abundant grass had still grown up between the paving stones. The first living object that struck my view . . . was a dilapidated United States cavalry horse bearing the mark I.C. — inspected and condemned — now peacefully browsing on the grass in a Charleston street. A few cows were feeding in a vacant lot near by, surrounded by

[1] Robert Somers, *The Southern States Since the War, 1870–71* (1871), p. 114. This is typical of the great mass of travel literature on the South.

buildings gashed and shattered by shell and solid shot. The crests of the roofs and the chimneys were covered with turkey-buzzards, who evidently felt at home, and who from time to time flapped their wings and stretched their hideous necks. Proceeding higher up into the city, we passed through a part of the "burned district," looking like a vast graveyard with broken walls and tall blackened chimneys for monuments, overtopped by the picturesque ruins of the cathedral.

Many another southern city had been similarly despoiled. Columbia, the thriving pre-war capital of South Carolina, was the customary "mass of blackened chimneys and crumbling walls." The fire that destroyed it had swept eighty-four blocks, and had consumed every building for "three-fourths of a mile on each of twelve streets." Atlanta was a riot of tangled brick and mortar, charred timbers, and rubbish. "Hell has laid her egg," one Georgian observed, "and right here it hatched." Mobile, too, had suffered from fire and had fallen into "torpor and decay." Galveston was described as "a city of dogs and desolation."

The havoc that the war had wrought on the South's transportation system was one **Transpor-** of the worst of the calamities **tation** from which it suffered. Columbia, South Carolina, had been a railway center before the war, with five lines converging upon it. By the time Sherman's troops had departed, the tracks had been torn up for thirty miles in every direction. Rolling stock was left standing in the fields to be used by the homeless as dwellings. Rails were heated in the middle and twisted fantastically around trees. Similar thoroughness had characterized railroad destruction in Georgia, Mississippi, and various other parts of the South, while the wear and tear of wartime usage without adequate repairs had made the railroads outside the devastated regions almost as worthless as those within. Before the war river traffic had played a large part in moving the produce of the South. Now river channels were blocked, steamboats were destroyed, and

wharves were missing. Seaports, so essential to the trade of the pre-war South, were in similar disarray. Country roads were non-existent or worse; bridges were gone; horses, mules, oxen, carriages, wagons, and carts had all too frequently been commandeered by the troops of North or South

Property losses suffered in the states of the former Confederacy should include numerous other items. The **Southern** Confederate bonds, both state **losses from** and national, into which much **war** southern capital had gone, had ceased altogether to be of value. So also had Confederate currency. Banks were closed; factories were idle; land values had toppled to nearly nothing; business in general was shattered. Property in slaves, which before the war accounted for so much of the South's wealth, was completely wiped out. Worse still, confiscation, contrary to a common opinion, took a heavy toll from the scanty resources of the defeated states. President Johnson tried to prevent this by ordering, in an amnesty proclamation issued May 29, 1865, that no further seizures of private property be made, and his Attorney General helped still more by ruling that private property already seized must be restored to anyone who had received a presidential pardon. But it was generally agreed that the property of the Confederate government was now the property of the United States, and that all such property must be located and attached.

It was from the attempt to seize this public property that the South came to know what confiscation might mean. **Confiscation** Agents of the Treasury Department, sent South on a twenty-five per cent commission basis to locate the 150,000 bales of cotton that the Confederate government was supposed to have had on hand at the close of the war, developed a tendency to take whatever cotton they happened to find, and to turn over to the United States only such of their takings as they saw fit. "I am sure I sent some honest cotton agents South," Secretary of the Treasury McCulloch admitted ruefully, "but it sometimes seems doubtful whether any of them remained honest for long." Not only cotton, but livestock, tobacco, rice, sugar, or anything of value was seized by individuals who represented themselves as agents of the United States. The total sum realized by the Treasury from seizures was $34,000,000, a considerable part of which was later returned. But this sum represents only a fraction of the damage done. With laudable candor Secretary McCulloch reported in 1866:

Contractors, anxious for gain, were sometimes guilty of bad faith and peculation, and frequently took possession of cotton and delivered it under contracts as captured or abandoned, when in fact it was not such and they had no right to touch it. . . . Residents and others in the districts where these peculations were going on took advantage of the unsettled condition of the country, and representing themselves as agents of this department, went about robbing under such pretended authority, and thus added to the difficulties of the situation by causing unjust opprobrium and suspicion to rest upon officers engaged in the faithful discharge of their duties. Agents . . . frequently received or collected property, and sent it forward which the law did not authorize them to take. . . . Lawless men, singly and in organized bands, engaged in general plunder; every species of intrigue and peculation and theft were resorted to.

In assessing the damage done the South by the war, the personal element must not **The southern** be ignored. Perhaps a quarter **people** of a million soldiers and an untold number of civilians lost their lives because of the clash of arms. Among those who perished were a large portion of the natural leaders of the South — men who, had they lived, could have helped most during the trials of the reconstruction era. Many of the survivors were themselves immeasurably the worse for their experiences; even when they were not maimed or broken in body, men trained in the school of war could never be quite the same as if trained in the normal pursuits of peace. As for the Negroes, the boon of freedom was not without

its unfortunate consequences. Before the end of the war about 180,000 of them had been enrolled as free soldiers in the United States armies, others were merely camp-followers and refugees. The downfall of the Confederacy plunged all the rest into freedom — a state of society for which they were almost totally unprepared. As slaves, they had looked to their masters for food, shelter, and protection. As free men they had little idea how to provide such things for themselves. Freedom meant freedom from work, and the right to leave the plantation at will; that it m ght carry with it unpleasant responsibilities few of the Negroes were able to understand. Some stayed with the old masters and worked on as if nothing had happened; others wandered away to places they had never seen before. During the spring and summer of 1865 they could be found in bands like gypsies, roving the country, and emulating Sherman's "bummers" in their search for food. From one point of view the abolition of slavery had cost the South nothing. The Negroes were still there, and they could do as much work as ever before — if only they would. But the evidence compounded that most of the ex-slaves, temporarily at least, had no will to work. And with the blacks constituting nearly forty per cent of the total population, this was a frightfully serious matter.

At the present time the people of the United States, or of any other great power, if confronted with such a con- **National** dition as existed in the South of **policy** 1865, would take it for granted that the government must play the principal part in restoring the economic life of the war-stricken section. In the middle of the nineteenth century, however, there were few who would have thought of such a thing. The "less government the better" was still the dominant philosophy, not only of the Democrats, but also of the great majority of the Republicans; indeed, the doctrine of rugged individualism, whether derived from the experience of the American frontier, or from the writings of European savants, or from both, was never more universally accepted. In the main, therefore, the economic problems of the South were regarded as the concern of individuals, rather than of the government, and in their solution the government gave only incidental assistance.

The necessity of direct aid for the freedmen, however, was something that could not **The Freedmen's Bureau** easily be overlooked. The power of the national government had been used to free the slaves; hence the Negroes, now that they were free, had become in a sense the wards of the nation. The freedmen themselves were by no means unaware of this obligation. Just as their masters had cared for them in the past, so now they expected their "deliverers" to look after them. That Congress was ready to accept such responsibility, at least for a limited time, was shown by the passage in March, 1865, of an act creating the Freedmen's Bureau. This organization, which was to last for a year after the close of the war, was to be set up in the War Department under a commissioner appointed by the President, and an assistant commissioner for each of the insurrectionary states. It was authorized to distribute "such issues of provisions, clothing, and fuel" as might be necessary to relieve the "destitute and suffering refugees and freedmen and their wives and children." It had also the right to take over any land within the designated states that had been abandoned by its owners or confiscated by the United States, and to distribute it in tracts of forty acres or less, on a three-year rental basis, to "loyal refugees and freedmen."

Under the leadership of General Oliver O. Howard, an able and conscientious man, the Freedmen's Bureau went promptly to work. Its agents soon penetrated to every portion of the South, and were kept busy, for a time, distributing the bare necessities of life to hundreds of thousands of needy, white as well as black. Without this assistance there can be no doubt that many of both races would have starved to death; or, one might properly say, many more might have

starved than did. The Bureau also made a laudable effort to provide its dependents with medical care and hospitalization, but among the Negroes, who knew so little about how to take care of themselves, illness took a frightful toll. The mortality among Negro children, who in slavery times would often have been nursed through their illnesses by the plantation mistress herself, but now had to depend upon the pitifully inadequate ministrations of their parents, was particularly appalling.

The plan to distribute abandoned land to the freedmen led to an unfortunate misunderstanding. It was inferred at **"Forty acres and a mule"** first that all land "abandoned" because its owners had left it for Confederate service would be available for distribution, but President Johnson's policy permitted the pardoned owners of such property to recover it. The result was that the Bureau had comparatively little land of value to give away. The Negro, however, got the impression, often deliberately spread by unscrupulous agents, that each freedman would soon be given "forty acres of land and a mule." Some included, for good measure, a white man to do the work. With so rosy a prospect for the future, and an abundance of free rations for the present, many of the Negroes found it difficult to see why they should do more than await the day of "jubilee." For some of them this day was dated. On January 1, 1866, they believed, the redistribution of land would take place.

In noting the governmental assistance given to the South after the war, one should remember the army of occupa- **The army of occupation** tion. For several years detachments of Federal troops were not far away in any part of the South, and there were regions in which the hated "blue-bellies," as they were inelegantly termed, were very numerous. The northern army, always abundantly provided with rations, clothing, and other supplies, shared its plenty with the destitute. This was the more natural because some of the Federal troops were themselves Negroes. When the war ended, most of the whites in the Federal army had taken the first opportunity to be "mustered out," but the Negroes had shown no such eagerness, and many of them were allowed to remain in the service. This is not to say that the Federal army was dominantly Negro, but it is true that among the troops left in the South there were many Negroes. The soldiers, whether white or black, had money to spend, and the government spent still larger sums for their maintenance. Directly or indirectly, the army thus contributed an appreciable amount to the economic rehabilitation of the South.

One other item of governmental aid to the South deserves mention, and that, curiously, was given to the southern railroads. While northern troops accounted for an enormous amount of railroad destruction, it is also a fact that wherever the operations of the Federal army required the reconditioning of the railroads, that, too, was done. In those portions of the upper South that the North had long held, the railroads were ac-

tually left in better condition than they were found. At the end of the war the United States War Department even went so far as to take over and reorganize some of the bankrupt railroad companies, and then, with "loyal" boards of directors assured, to return them to their owners.

Private benevolence added a little to the aid given by the government. The Negroes, naturally, were the recipients of **Private** much such attention. Even **benevolence** before the end of the war the American Missionary Association, for example, had begun a work among them that led to expenditures after the return of peace of about $100,000 annually, mostly on Negro education. Also, the churches of the North sent a sizable army of missionaries, preachers, and teachers into the South. At first many such individuals assumed that the collapse of the Confederacy meant that the separate southern churches would also cease to exist, and that reunion under northern domination would follow immediately, with themselves in prominent positions. This failed to hap-

Reconstruction of the South. Symbolic lithograph showing contributions to industrial rehabilitation, education, labor, and the Negro, published by John Smith.

The Civil War did not alter the basic dependence of the lower South upon cotton culture. Nor did the substitution of free labor for slave labor mean that the Negroes could escape the back-breaking duties of the old plantations. Whether employed as hired laborers or as sharecroppers, they were still cotton hands. By hard experience they learned that freedom from slavery did not mean freedom from work.

pen, but the missionary zeal of the northern workers found a ready outlet in helping the Negroes adjust themselves to freedom. They induced most of the ex-slaves to separate from the churches of their former masters, and to form new churches of their own. They used northern missionary money to build and maintain Negro churches and schools, and to care for the needy. Among the most active in this respect were the agents of the Freedmen's Aid Society of the Methodist Episcopal Church, but similar work was supported by the Baptists, the Presbyterians, and many other denominations.

Philanthropy

Philanthropy, although then in its infancy, furnished another source of outside income to the South. The most notable donation of this kind came from George Peabody, who gave the income from a fund of two million dollars, or more, "to the suffering South for the good of the whole country." The Peabody Education Fund was wisely administered, and proved to be an effective aid to the establishment of better common schools in the South. The Negroes themselves were pathetically eager for book-learning, and flocked into whatever schools were provided for them. Most of them, however, showed no great proficiency beyond the elementary stages, and the wisest of their advisers were soon counseling them to seek vocational training rather than the higher learning, including Greek and Latin, that altogether too many of them craved.

Southerners were at first hopeful that a great outpouring of northern capital would aid in the rehabilitation of the South, but in this they were to be sadly disappointed.

Scarcity of capital

Northern investors did, indeed, buy southern railway securities in sufficient amounts to make possible a rapid recovery on the part of the southern railroads, and they also purchased, to their later regret, the new bond issues of the

COTTON PLANTATION.
Currier and Ives print.

THE COTTON PICKERS.
Painting by Winslow Homer, 1876.

southern states. But their southern investments went little further. The North, with its own fields of endeavor to look after — industrial expansion, agricultural extension, the building of transcontinental railroads, the development of the mining and ranching West — had little left to risk in a region where political conditions were disturbed and a racial conflict was in the making. Thrown back upon its own meager resources, the South made numerous small beginnings in the lumbering industry, in the manufacture of tobacco, in the establishment of cotton mills, in the exploitation of its resources in coal and iron, as well as in the restoration of its agricultural activities, particularly the growing of cotton, which became again, as before the war, its chief concern.

Fortunately for the South the world had need of cotton, but to restore production Cotton culture was no easy matter. Seed was lacking, tools and machinery were worn out, horses and mules were scarce,

and the labor supply was an unknown quantity. Many Southerners, convinced that without slavery the Negroes could never be induced to work, hoped to devise some scheme for sending them back to Africa or to the West Indies; and still more believed that the salvation of the South lay in replacing or supplementing Negro labor with that of immigrants from Europe or elsewhere. But the Negroes would not go and the immigrants would not come. Some of the planters attempted to revive the old plantation system on the basis of free labor. Backed with whatever money the promise of cotton enabled them to borrow in Europe or in the North, they offered the Negroes wages to return to their former duties. Such a transaction was apt to be carefully watched by the Freedmen's Bureau, which usually insisted on a written contract, with the amount of wages and the conditions of labor carefully set down. It was not the planter, however, who broke the contract, but the freedman, who rarely saw point to working after he had earned a few dollars. Delayed wages were sometimes tried, but with equally indifferent results. Other planters offered laborers a share in the annual proceeds of the plantation, but this system, likewise, proved ineffective. The freedmen resented the necessity of working in gangs, as in slavery times, and even more, the existence of anything bordering on oversight.

In the end the plantation system had to go, and in a sense the promise of "forty acres

The southern tenant system and a mule" was realized. The planters found by experience that only when they split up their land into small plots, with a Negro, or it might be a white tenant, in charge of each, could they obtain satisfactory results. Each tenant had usually to be supplied with not only his mule, but his seed, his tools, and his living until the crop was harvested; all this the landlord either furnished directly, or by obtaining credit for his tenants at one of the numerous "country stores" that sprang up all over the South. A crop lien secured both the landlord and the storekeeper against loss. As a rule the tenant turned over from a third to a half of his produce to the landlord as rental, and all the rest went to repay his debts; but by working along on his own time in his own way he at least produced a part of a crop. His status, bound as he was by his crop lien, lay somewhere between slavery and freedom, but it amounted, perhaps, to as great a change as his limited experience would permit. The first few crops after the war, with the Negroes unsettled and the Freedmen's Bureau at hand to back them up in fantastic demands, were miserable failures, but by 1869 a cotton crop worth a quarter of a billion dollars was marketed. From that time forward the acute poverty of the South began to abate.

So much attention has been focused upon the Negroes, whether slave or free, that the

The white farmer rôle of the small white farmer of the South has rarely received the prominence it deserves. Even before the Civil War white labor accounted for a con-

siderable part of the South's crop of cotton, and after the war the proportion tended to increase. In general the land worked by the whites in the time of slavery was inferior to that included in the great plantations and worked by slaves. But after the war the planters were glad to obtain tenants, white as well as black, and they often found it necessary to sell a part, or even all, of their holdings. Independent ownership was greatly stimulated by the low prices that landowners were obliged to accept. Land that had been worth from twenty to thirty dollars an acre before the war sold for from three to five dollars an acre after the war, and sometimes for less. Many of the whites who had owned poor land before, or no land at all, took advantage of this remarkable opportunity to buy. In ten years, according to the census of 1870, the number of farms in South Carolina had increased from 33,000 to 52,000; in Mississippi, from 43,000 to 68,000; in Louisiana, from 17,000 to 28,000. In the other southern states the figures, while not so striking, show the same general trend. Some of the new landowners were Negroes, but their holdings were generally very small, and most of the land that changed hands went to whites. A considerable number of Northerners were attracted into the South by the low prices of land, but most of them were unable to adjust themselves satisfactorily to the new environment.

While cotton was the best money crop of the South, it must not be forgotten that southern agriculture, both be- **Rice, sugar,** fore and after the war, produced **and tobacco** some of nearly everything that can be grown on farms. Rice culture, which had been an important activity in South Carolina and Georgia before the war, showed in those states few symptoms of revival, but in Louisiana the production of both rice and sugar cane was successfully undertaken. Tobacco-growing in the upper South made rapid headway, particularly in Kentucky, where the crop increased from 54,000,000 pounds in 1865 to 103,000,000 pounds in 1871. In the states where cotton had never been "king," and where in consequence the concentration of Negroes had been less marked, the problem of restoring normal production was far more easily solved. After the first two or three hard years, livestock and foodstuffs could be found practically anywhere in abundance.

Unfortunately, the valiant efforts of the South to work out a new economic system proved to be of far less concern to the national government than the strictly political problem. Early in the war President Lincoln had faced the necessity of deciding what to do with a seceded state after the armies of the North had conquered it. He was not much interested in theorizing about whether such a state was still in the Union, or had by the act of secession lost its legal life. He wished merely to promote the establishment within its borders of a loyal state government, and the resumption as speedily as possible of a normal relationship to the nation as a whole. As early as 1862 he appointed for each of the seceded states then occupied in considerable part by northern troops a military governor, who was expressly charged with the responsibility of reviving loyal sentiment among the state's inhabitants. Then, in December, 1863, he set forth in a presidential proclamation his plan for the re-establishment of state governments. Pardons were promised, with a few exceptions aimed mainly at high civil and military officers of the Confederacy, to all who would take a prescribed oath of allegiance to the United States, and, whenever in any state as many as one tenth of the number of persons who had voted in 1860 should take the oath, a civil government was to be inaugurated which the President bound himself to recognize "as the true government of the state." Operating under this plan, three states, Tennessee, Louisiana, and Arkansas, succeeded during the year 1864 in re-creating state governments, and were accorded presidential recognition. The President also recognized a loyal, although decidedly impotent, government in Virginia that throughout the war had maintained a

Lincoln's plan of re-construction

precarious existence at Alexandria. From these acts, and from his various utterances it was evident that he intended to use the full power of his high office to make the "road to reunion" as short and straight as possible.

Lincoln's magnanimous attitude toward the vanquished foe was not shared, however, by the majority of his party in Congress. Few of them understood as clearly as did he, the difficulties that the South had to face, and fewer still were able to view the scene with a like sense of detachment. It was natural for Northerners, and more especially northern Republicans, to hold the South responsible for the war, and to raise doubts as to whether an enemy, only recently under arms against the Union, could so speedily be trusted to maintain it. More to the point, many leading Republicans were fearful lest the return of the southern states to the fold should pave the way for the rise of the Democratic Party to power, and they were particularly aggrieved that the President should have taken into his own hands a matter so important. Congress, they maintained, should have been consulted, and a law rather than a presidential proclamation should have charted his course. As a fitting answer to his act of "executive usurpation," all senators and representatives chosen by the states that he had "reconstructed" were denied admission to Congress, and in July, 1864, by the so-called Wade-Davis Bill, a congressional substitute for the presidential plan of reconstruction was proposed.

The Wade-Davis Bill

The provisions of this bill, as a matter of fact, differed from the President's plan less than might have been expected. They provided for the appointment of a provisional governor in each conquered state, but the duties assigned him were not unlike those that the President had expected of his military governors. Each provisional governor was to take a census of the white male citizens under his jurisdiction, and to request each citizen to take an oath in support of the Constitution of the United States. In case a majority (rather than ten per cent) of those so enrolled complied with this request, the governor was to call upon the oath-bound citizens, as voters, to elect delegates to a convention, which must pledge the state (1) to deny political rights to all high-ranking civil and military officers of the Confederacy, (2) to abolish slavery, and (3) to outlaw all debts, state or Confederate, "created by or under the sanction of the usurping power." The convention might then draw up a constitution in which the three pledges were to be included, and in case this document should be approved by a majority of the voters at the polls the President, *after obtaining the consent of Congress*, was to "recognize the government so established, and none other, as the constitutional government of the state."

The fact that this measure was passed by Congress during the closing day of a session **Lincoln and** gave Lincoln the chance to de-**Congress** feat it by a pocket veto. He was far too clever a politician, however, to allow himself to be placed in the position of outright opposition to its more reasonable provisions. In a formal proclamation on the subject he declared himself unwilling as yet "to be inflexibly committed to any single plan of restoration," but he recommended the congressional plan to the people for their consideration, and described it as "one very proper plan for the loyal people of any State choosing to adopt it." What terms he might have had to make with Congress, had he lived, will never be known, but when the next session adjourned without further action on reconstruction he was not displeased. At his last cabinet meeting he spoke with regret of the tendency to treat the southern people as if they were not fellow citizens, and promised to "reanimate the States" before Congress should meet again.

It was difficult for the more radical members in Congress to conceal the relief they felt at the death of Lincoln. His "tender-heartedness" toward the South, and his determination to use the executive power to indulge it, had been their chief concern, for

they feared his strength with the country at large. Now, with a new President in office, a man relatively unknown and lacking as yet in a strong personal following, they felt certain that they could have their way. They hoped by wholesale arrests and confiscations to insure that the leaders of the Old South should not become the leaders of the New; they proposed to maintain military rule until such a time as the party they represented could be made the dominant political party of the South; and as a means to this latter end they were determined to give the freedmen the right to vote. After Lincoln's death they believed that they could count on public support for the most drastic action. They could blame the South for the assassination, and fan once more to a flame the wartime passions that Lincoln had tried to allay.

Strangely enough, Andrew Johnson (1808–1875), whose accidental succession to the Presidency so heartened the **Andrew** northern Radicals, was both a **Johnson** Southerner and a Democrat. He was not, however, of the southern ruling caste, for his North Carolina parents were as humble as the Kentucky parents of Abraham Lincoln; and Johnson, quite as much as Lincoln, was a self-made man. Unable to forget the hard and unhappy youth that poverty in the slaveholders' South had meant for him, he became a belligerent champion of the rights of the common people and a bitter enemy of the whole favored fraternity of southern aristocrats. Migrating at an early age to Greeneville, Tennessee, he worked at his trade as a tailor, and ultimately became the proprietor of a moderately prosperous tailor's shop. From his youth up he was interested in oratory, and his love of argumentation seems to have furnished the stimulus that drove him persistently forward in his quest for learning. As a highly effective rough-and-tumble debater, he drifted easily into politics — a Democratic denouncer of the aristocratic Whigs — and for ten years, beginning in 1843, he represented his district in the national House of Representatives.

Twice during the fifties he was elected governor of Tennessee, and the outbreak of the Civil War found him in the midst of his first term as a United States Senator.

Although Johnson had voted for Breckinridge in 1860, he was an ardent advocate of compromise and conciliation, and he utterly refused to become a party to the destruction of the Union. Alone among the senators from the seceding states, he remained at his desk in the Senate when his state left the Union, and gave his full support to the Union cause. While still a senator he accepted Lincoln's commission to become military governor of Tennessee, and in that capacity he worked with courage and with moderate success toward the carrying-out of Lincoln's plan of restoration. When the National Union Convention of 1864, composed of many Republicans and a few War Democrats, looked about for means of emphasizing its bipartisan character, the choice of Johnson for second place on the ticket with Lincoln seemed natural and logical. Lincoln himself insisted upon it. Had the delegates foreseen Johnson's accession to the Presidency, no doubt they would have acted differently. His obstinacy and tactlessness were not unknown, and, with the exception of his devotion to the Union, his political principles differed markedly from those of the great majority of the men who worked for him.

Probably it was Johnson's well-known dislike of the southern aristocrats that com- **Johnson and** mended him most to the Re- **the Radicals** publican Radicals. Given to intemperate utterances, he had repeatedly denounced the "slavocracy" as responsible for the chief woes of the South, including the war, and as President he ordered the arrest of many high Confederate officials whom Lincoln had been minded to leave alone. "Johnson, we have faith in you," Senator Benjamin Wade of Ohio, a leading Radical, told the President. "By the gods, there will be no trouble now in running the Government." To this remark Johnson is said to have replied: "Treason is a crime and crime must be punished. Treason must be made infamous and traitors must be impoverished."

But, as matters turned out, Johnson's vindictiveness was short-lived. Undoubtedly he planned to rebuild the South with the long-neglected lower-class whites in control, but he was soon to learn that, whatever the status of the southern aristocrat before the war, he was at the moment as penniless and as powerless as his humblest neighbor. Furthermore, Johnson as a Southerner was under no delusion as to the unpreparedness of the ex-slave for the full responsibilities of citizenship. For a time he may have toyed with the idea of Negro suffrage, but, if so, his common sense and his southern background soon led him to give it up. More important still, he was at heart as much a states' rights southern Democrat as he had ever been. Like Jackson, he was willing to go to any length to preserve the Union, but he wished to keep the powers of the national government at a minimum. To him the southern states were still states, and with them, rather than with the national government, the solution of their principal problems must lie.

Thus it soon transpired that Johnson, from the Radical point of view, was quite as untrustworthy as Lincoln. For **Johnson's** the time being he kept Lincoln's **plan of re-** cabinet intact, and inclined **construction** more and more to the advice of its more moderate members. He gradually relaxed the orders he had given for the arrest and prosecution of southern officials. He accepted as legal the loyal governments that Lincoln had recognized in Tennessee, Louisiana, Arkansas, and Virginia. And, for the seven other states of the Confederacy, he prescribed during the summer of 1865 a process of reconstruction quite as breathtaking in its generosity as Lincoln himself could have devised. For each state he appointed as provisional governor a local man, not an outsider; and, although every such official had at some time been an active opponent of secession, not one of them had fought for the North, while most of them had passively supported the Confederacy. It was the duty of each provisional governor to call a constitutional convention, the delegates to which were to be chosen by such members of the old white electorate as were now ready, and were permitted, to take the oath of allegiance to the United States. Johnson did, indeed, add a few new classes, including the owners of more than twenty thousand dollars' worth of property, to those whom Lincoln had disqualified from taking the oath, but he promised liberal pardons to those who chose to apply for them, and he did nothing to insure that even so small a number as ten per cent of the former voters must take part in the work of restoration. The constitutional conventions, so selected, were required (1) to invalidate their old ordinances of secession, (2) to abolish slavery, and (3) to repudiate all debts contracted in order to aid the Confederacy in its prosecution of the war; but otherwise they were as free as any other such conventions to write into their constitutions whatever they chose. Johnson specifically acknowledged that it was their privilege to decide who should vote and who should hold office, but he let it be known privately that, for the effect such action would have upon the northern Radicals, he hoped that Negroes who could read and write, or who owned a small amount of real estate, would be permitted to vote. With their constitutions rewritten, the states might elect their own governors, legislators, and other officers, and resume their place in the Union.

Johnson foresaw that for several months he could proceed with his plan unhampered by Congress, which, to the distress of the Radicals, could not convene without the President's call until the following December. By this time he hoped to have state governments restored throughout the South. He knew that the Radical leaders of Congress would resent deeply whatever he did, but he believed that they would find it difficult to undo a series of accomplished facts. Furthermore, he counted upon the approval of a majority of the people both in the South and in the North for what he was doing. In the former section, the easy terms he had prescribed should insure him a strong following, while in the latter he hoped to rally to his standard most of the Democrats as well as the more moderate Republicans. He took seriously the name and implications of the Union Party, which had elected him, and expected it to become, with himself at its head, a kind of party of the center, opposed only by the northern Radicals at one extreme and the southern irreconcilables at the other.

When Congress met in December, Johnson's work of restoration was far along. The provisional governors had revived the old county and municipal governments sometimes with little change of personnel. They had called constitutional conventions, and in every state but Texas the conventions had met. Unfortunately, perhaps, none of them had accepted the President's advice about allowing exceptional Negroes to vote; nor did they show any disposition to place restrictions upon the political rights of the former enemies of the Union. Furthermore, the first elections that were held showed that, for the most part, the leaders of the Confederacy were still regarded by the voters as the leaders of the South. In Mississippi, for example, an ex-Confederate brigadier-general who had not even been pardoned as yet by the President, was chosen governor; in Alabama three fourths of the members of the legislature had at one time or another fought for the Confederacy; and in Georgia the legislature chose Alexander H. Stephens, late Vice-President of the Confederate States of America, to be United States Senator. Every legislature, however, except that of Mississippi, had promptly ratified the Thirteenth Amendment, and before the end of the year the President was able to tell Congress that only in Florida and Texas was the work of restoration incomplete, and that in those states it would be finished soon.

The President's defense of what he had

done was presented in an able message to Congress, the happy phraseology of which was due to the skillful pen of George Bancroft, the historian. The meaning of the message, however, was the President's own. In it he maintained, more insistently than Lincoln had thought advisable, that the southern states, as such, had never ceased to exist, but had merely been in a state of suspended vitality. It had been his duty to assist in restoring them to their rightful energy, and this duty he had performed as "gradually and quietly" as possible. Inasmuch as he had found no constitutional warrant to do otherwise, he had left with the states themselves the problem of enfranchisement of the freedmen. As for the delegations that the restored states had sent to Congress, he believed that the adoption of the Thirteenth Amendment warranted their reception, but of this each house of Congress must judge for itself.

Bibliography

An excellent picture of post-war conditions in the South is contained in W. L. Fleming, *The Sequel of Appomattox; A Chronicle of the Reunion of the States* (1919). This is the thirty-second volume of *The Chronicles of America Series* (50 vols., 1918–21), edited by Allen Johnson. The series was resumed in 1950, under the editorship of Allan Nevins, and to date, six more volumes have been published. E. P. Oberholtzer, *A History of the United States since the Civil War* (5 vols., 1917–37), begins at this point to be useful. W. A. Dunning, *Reconstruction, Political and Economic, 1865–1877* (1907), sets a pattern for historical thinking on the problem that has only recently been challenged. This volume is the twenty-second of *The American Nation: A History* (28 vols., 1904–28), edited by A. B. Hart. These twenty-eight volumes are still unsurpassed as a general history of the United States. A useful summary of the later opinions on reconstruction is found in J. G. Randall, *The Civil War and Reconstruction* (1937). See also Charles A. and Mary R. Beard, *The Rise of American Civilization* (2 vols., 1927, new edition, 1949), II. This work presents a brilliant case for the economic interpretation of American history.

The problem of reconstruction from the Negro's point of view is presented in W. E. B. DuBois, *Black Reconstruction* (1935); also in A. A. Taylor, *The Negro in Tennessee, 1865–1880* (1941), and by the same author, *The Negro in South Carolina during Reconstruction* (1924). Also useful are two books by B. G. Brawley, *A Social History of the American Negro* (1921), and *A Short History of the American Negro* (4th edition, 1939);

G. W. Williams, *History of the Negro Race in America* (2 vols., 1882); and Vernon Lane Wharton, *The Negro in Mississippi, 1865–1890* (1947), a modern reinterpretation.

Valuable studies of a social and economic nature are M. B. Hammond, *The Cotton Industry; An Essay in American Economic History* (1897); R. P. Brooks, *The Agrarian Revolution in Georgia, 1865–1912* (1914); Meyer Jacobstein, *The Tobacco Industry in the United States* (1907); B. W. Arnold, *History of the Tobacco Industry in Virginia from 1860 to 1894* (1897). Henry Lee Swint, *The Northern Teacher in the South, 1862–1870* (1941), describes an interesting phase of carpetbag history.

On the political side of reconstruction the bibliography is enormous. Still useful among the older histories are C. H. McCarthy, *Lincoln's Plan of Reconstruction* (1901); James Ford Rhodes, *History of the United States from the Compromise of 1850* (9 vols., 1900–28); Peter J. Hamilton, *The Reconstruction Period* (1906); *Documentary History of the Reconstruction*, edited by W. L. Fleming (2 vols., 1906–07); J. W. Burgess, *Reconstruction and the Constitution, 1866–1876* (1902); and William A. Dunning, *Essays on the Civil War and Reconstruction* (1904).

The career of Andrew Johnson has been generously re-estimated. C. R. Hall, *Andrew Johnson, Military Governor of Tennessee* (1916), is an account of Johnson's work in reviving the state of Tennessee. Claude G. Bowers, *The Tragic Era; The Revolution after Lincoln* (1929), is an extremely readable but somewhat overdrawn account. George Fort Milton, *The Age of Hate;*

Andrew Johnson and the Radicals (1930); and
H. K. Beale, *The Critical Year: A Study of Andrew
Johnson and Reconstruction* (1930), are both fair
and friendly toward Johnson. Somewhat less
satisfactory are R. W. Winston, *Andrew Johnson,
Plebeian and Patriot* (1928); and L. P. Stryker,
Andrew Johnson (1929).

Monographs on reconstruction in the various
states that are important for this chapter include
J. W. Patton, *Unionism and Reconstruction in
Tennessee* (1934); Thomas B. Alexander, *Political
Reconstruction in Tennessee* (1950); T. S. Staples,
Reconstruction in Arkansas, 1862–1874 (1923);
H. J. Eckenrode *The Political History of Virginia*

during Reconstruction (1904); Willie Malvin
Caskey, *Secession and Restoration in Louisiana*
(1938); and J. R. Ficklen, *History of Reconstruction in Louisiana* (1910). See also, for the effect
of reconstruction on lower-class whites, Roger
W. Shugg, *Origins of Class Struggle in Louisiana;
A Social History of White Farmers and Laborers
during Slavery and after, 1840–1875* (1939).

For collateral reading throughout, an admirable book of *Readings in American History, 1865
to the Present*, edited by Robert C. Cotner, John
S. Ezell, and Gilbert C. Fite (1952), is particularly useful with this text.

2

Radical Reconstruction

Johnson's first message — Thaddeus Stevens — Charles Sumner — The black codes — Spirit of the South — Johnson and Congress — The Joint Committee on Reconstruction — The Fourteenth Amendment — Elections of 1866 — Impeachment of Johnson — The process of reconstruction — Negro suffrage — The Union League — The Fifteenth Amendment — "Carpetbag rule"

THE straightforwardness and good temper of Johnson's first message to Congress won much acclaim, and his Radical opponents were greatly embarrassed. It was more than could reasonably be expected, however, that Congress would permit the President to complete the process of reconstruction without legislative interference. Indeed, on the first day of the session, before the President's message had been received, the House had voted to establish a joint committee of nine representatives and six senators to inquire into the condition of the former Confederate states, and to inquire into whether they were "entitled to be represented in either House of Congress." A few days later the Senate concurred in this action, and the southern delegations were required to stand aside while this "Joint Committee on Reconstruction" conducted its investigations.

Johnson's first message

Thaddeus Stevens (1792–1868), a representative from Pennsylvania, was the elder statesman who sponsored the House resolution. A New Englander by birth and training, he had practiced law and politics in Pennsylvania, first at Gettysburg and then at Lancaster, for half a century. Early in his political career he won wide recognition for his leadership in the Anti-Masonic Party, his courageous

Thaddeus Stevens

and successful fight to save from repeal the public-school system of his state, and his opposition to a new state constitution because it limited the suffrage to whites. Meantime he had conceived, in part, perhaps, from his New England background, but in larger part, no doubt, from the unhappy experiences of such runaway slaves as chanced to cross his path, an intense dislike of slavery. As a member of the national House of Representatives during the framing of the compromise measures of 1850, and later while the secession movement was under way, he opposed with the utmost violence all concessions to the slaveholders; and after 1861, as one of the most powerful of the Republican leaders, his counsel was ever for the sternest possible prosecution of the war. His ill-temper toward the South was not bettered when in 1863 Lee's troops destroyed some ironworks near Chambersburg, Pennsylvania, in which he was financially interested, and well before the end of the war he had broken with Lincoln over reconstruction. The southern states, he held, were no longer states, but only "conquered provinces" with which Congress might deal as it chose; Lincoln's pocket veto of the Wade-Davis Bill was nothing less than "infamous." Lame from his birth, old and perilously ill, unmarried and cared for only by a faithful col-

Thaddeus Stevens, leader of the Radicals in the House of Representatives, is shown here closing the debate of March 2, 1868, on the impeachment of President Johnson. Sketched for *Harper's Weekly* by T. R. Davis, and published in the issue of March 21.

ored housekeeper, his one passion became the ruthless punishment of the South. Congressmen had already learned to fear his lashing tongue, and he proposed to destroy Johnson, whose easy terms of reconstruction he despised.

No less the enemy of Johnson than Stevens was Charles Sumner (1811–1874), the Republican senator from Massachusetts whose body still bore **Charles Sumner** the marks of Preston Brooks's assault. From his youth up Sumner had been a favored member of the Boston intelligentsia. He was a graduate of Harvard, a student of history and the classics, a friend of nearly every New Englander who had won distinction in the realm of literature, and a European traveler whose *entrée* into the highest political and intellectual circles was never denied. The soul of honor, and upright to a fault, he was vain of his own abilities, and utterly contemptuous of lesser mortals. He had always opposed slavery — the first newspaper to which he subscribed was Garrison's *Liberator* — and his scorn for all who practiced or condoned it was complete. Trained for the law, he had preferred politics, and in 1851 he was chosen by a coalition of Free-Soilers and Democrats to take the seat in the United States Senate that Webster

vacated to become Fillmore's Secretary of State. From the time of his first election to the day of his death he remained a senator, although the injuries he suffered from the Brooks assault necessitated his absence from duty for many years. Measurably recovered, but never again quite the same, he was on hand in 1863 to oppose Lincoln's plan of reconstruction, and to advance his "state-suicide" theory, that the seceding states, by their treasonous act, had ceased to exist, and that Congress had therefore precisely the same power over them that it had always exercised over the territories. A philosophic defender of the doctrine of political equality, he insisted from the beginning that Congress should make Negro suffrage a condition of reconstruction for the seceded states; and when Johnson, like Lincoln, failed to urge such a policy, he allied himself with Stevens to wreck the presidential program. His views were not shared by every member of his party in the Senate, nor were Stevens's in the House, but a less obstinate man than Johnson would have hastened to make terms with an opposition so powerful.

Unfortunately for the President, the Radical case was greatly strength- **The black** ened by the action that the **codes** southern legislatures were taking with reference to the status of the freedmen. Realizing far better than the Northerners the great gap that lay between slavery and freedom, the restored states had sought to bridge that gap by laws especially designed to fit the needs of the Negroes. "Persons of color" were invariably subjected to various regulations not required of whites. In some states, for example, they might not carry arms unless licensed to do so; they might not testify in court except in cases involving their own race; they must make annual written contracts for their labor, and if they ran away from their "masters" they must forfeit a year's wages; they must be apprenticed, if minors, to some white person, who might discipline them by means of such corporal punishment as a father might inflict upon a child; they might, if convicted of vagrancy, be assessed heavy fines, which, if unpaid, could be collected by selling the services of the vagrant for a period long enough to satisfy the claim. These "black codes," or "black laws," which at best were meant mainly to protect the Negroes from their own ignorance and helplessness, and at worst were meant to circumscribe their freedom as much as possible, were deeply resented in the North. The Thirteenth Amendment had just been adopted, and yet some of the very legislatures that had voted for it were seemingly taking steps to undermine it. Of what avail to abolish slavery if Johnson's newly established southern governments retained it in fact if not in name?

There were certain other disquieting factors about the southern situation that Radi-**The spirit of** cal politicians were quick to **the South** exploit. While Johnson's plan of reconstruction was carried through without the complete withdrawal of northern troops from the South, enough troops were withdrawn to give some of the southern states a pretext for establishing militia of their own. It was easy to say that all such actions were designed to make possible the complete subjugation of the Negro, and perhaps to lead the way in a new revolt. Radicals could point also to the prevalence of

Charles Sumner, brilliant Senator from Massachusetts, led the forces opposed to President Johnson in the United States Senate.

racial conflicts, particularly between the lower-class southern whites and the Negroes, whose long-standing hatred for one another was greatly aggravated by the fact of emancipation. Moreover, the South did not fear to show that in spirit it was neither broken nor contrite. Cordial hatred of the North, and particularly of the northern Radicals, was freely expressed; and regret that the South had failed to win was rarely well concealed. Carl Schurz, whom the President himself had sent to study conditions in the South, seemed exasperated at the failure of Southerners to recognize the "criminality" of their recent treason, and deplored their "utter absence of national feeling." Schurz's report, which throughout was most unfavorable to the South, gained wide currency, whereas a short but favorable statement on the same subject by General Grant was scarcely noticed.

The first real test of strength between the forces led by the President and those led by Stevens and Sumner came over **The** the so-called Freedmen's Bu- **Freedmen's** reau Bill. The ground for this **Bureau Bill** conflict had been carefully chosen. The Freedmen's Bureau was not a new thing, for it had been created by an act of Congress signed shortly before Lincoln's death. Hence the Radicals were proposing merely to continue an existing institution. Also, the apparent purpose of the Freedmen's Bureau was humanitarian — to provide a kind of guardianship for the Negro during the period of transition from slave labor to free labor. Its agents, with full military backing, for the Bureau was attached to the War Department and headed by an army officer, supervised the relief work carried on among the Negroes and whites; watched over the labor arrangements that freedmen made with their employers; assigned abandoned land to the freedmen, and helped them to acquire other land; in general, made sure that the work of emancipation should not be halted halfway. But the original Freedmen's Bureau Bill had provided that the Bureau should cease to exist one year after the end of the war, whereas the measure that Congress presented to President Johnson in February, 1866, proposed that the existing organization, with greatly amplified powers, should be continued for an indefinite period. In other words, Congress raised the issue: Should the Negro remain the ward of the national government working through the Freedmen's Bureau, or should he be left to the tender mercies of whatever "black laws" Johnson's restored state governments chose to pass?

Johnson met this challenge with a courageous veto. The bill, he said, proposed to **Johnson's** maintain in time of peace a **veto** military jurisdiction that could ignore at will such ordinary guaranties of the civil law as trial by jury and the right of appeal. It assumed that wartime conditions still existed, whereas in fact the country had all returned, or was returning, "to a state of peace and industry." It overstepped constitutional bounds by making the government of the United States, rather than the state governments, responsible for the care of indigents, and a favored class of indigents at that. Furthermore, it was the work of a Congress that denied representation to the eleven states most concerned, whereas in

the judgment of the President those states had been "fully restored," and were "entitled to enjoy their constitutional rights as members of the Union." If American traditions of democracy were to be maintained, then majorities, to have the right to rule, must be majorities of the whole people, not merely a part of it.

While both houses of Congress had passed the Freedmen's Bureau Bill by overwhelming majorities, the President's veto was sustained, with only a few votes to spare, in the Senate. On Washington's Birthday following, the President was serenaded at the White House, in accordance with a custom of the time, by a group of his admirers, and asked to speak. Unfortunately, he not only spoke, but let himself go in a manner not wholly becoming to the office he held. Much of what he told the crowd was strictly to the point, but he indulged also in unnecessary personalities, and asserted that such men as Thaddeus Stevens, Charles Sumner, and Wendell Phillips were as much opposed to the Union as "the Davises, the Toombses, and the Slidells."

Johnson's conduct won enthusiastic support throughout the South and among the Democrats of the North, but, **The Civil** when abundantly exaggerated **Rights Bill** by the press, it tended to solidify the Republicans behind their Radical leaders. Before long Congress presented him with an unpalatable Civil Rights Bill, which declared the freedmen to be citizens of the United States, guaranteed them the same civil status that was enjoyed by the whites, and prescribed severe penalties for all who, under state law, might discriminate against them. If Johnson could not sign the Freedmen's Bureau Bill, clearly he could not sign the Civil Rights Bill; nor did he. But this time both the Senate and the House repassed the measure by the two-thirds majorities necessary to make it a law. Congress had thus won the ascendancy. It could, if it would, take the whole policy of reconstruction out of Johnson's hands, and direct him to do whatever it wanted done. The Radicals, conscious of their advantage, presently revived in slightly different form the Freedmen's Bureau Bill, and on second trial passed it, too, over the President's veto. The new bill provided, however, that the Freedmen's Bureau should be assured of only two years' existence.

Meanwhile the joint committee that Congress had set up in December, 1865, had been hard at work on a congressional plan of reconstruction that could be substituted for the President's plan. Of the fifteen members who comprised this committee, only one senator and two representatives were Democrats, while nearly all of the remaining members, Stevens among them, were extreme Radicals. The committee soon began a spectacular sequence of hearings, in which it collected an enormous quantity of evidence, much of which was intended to prove that the loyalty of the South was far too tenuous to permit of such generous treatment as the President had accorded it. By the early summer of 1866 its deliberations had resulted in the formulation of a proposed Fourteenth Amendment to the Constitution, which, after some revision in the Senate, was duly submitted to the states for adoption.

The Joint Committee on Reconstruction

The first section of the amendment virtually restated the terms of the Civil Rights Bill. It declared that all persons born or naturalized in the United States were citizens of the United States and of the state in which they resided, and that no state might abridge in any way the "privileges or immunities" of such citizens, nor "deprive any person of life, liberty, or property, without due process of law." This clause of the amendment became in later years a matter of the greatest importance. For a time the courts showed a disposition to restrict its application to ex-slaves whose civil rights were endangered; but ultimately they held that all persons, corporations no less than individuals, were subject to its protection. One member of the committee, John A. Bingham of Ohio, ex-

The Fourteenth Amendment

plained eventually that he had formulated the statement with this later interpretation in mind, for he believed that the restriction of the Fifth Amendment to the Constitution, which denied to the national government the right to interfere with the rights of private property, should be extended also to the states, and that responsibility for its enforcement should, accordingly, be lodged with the national courts. Roscoe Conkling of New York, another member of the joint committee, confirmed Bingham's words in an argument he made before the Supreme Court in 1882:

At the time the Fourteenth Amendment was ratified, individuals and joint stock companies were appealing for congressional and administrative protection against invidious and discriminating state and local taxes. . . . That complaints of oppression in respect of property and other rights made by citizens of northern states who took up residence in the South were rife in and out of Congress, none of us can forget. . . . Those who devised the Fourteenth Amendment wrought in grave sincerity. . . . They planted in the Constitution a monumental truth to stand four square to whatever wind might blow. That truth is but the golden rule, so entrenched as to curb the many who would do to the few as they would not have the few do to them.

A second section of the Amendment dealt with the problem of Negro suffrage. This innovation, to the regret of the more extreme Radicals, was not required; instead, a state that denied the suffrage to any of its male inhabitants over twenty-one years of age, "except for participation in rebellion or other crime," would merely have its basis of representation in Congress and in the Electoral College correspondingly reduced. This was not an unreasonable position. The old "three-fifths" compromise of the Constitution, which for such purposes counted five slaves as equal to three whites, had lost its meaning, for slavery had been abolished. But with freedmen counted exactly the same as whites, the number of representatives from the southern states in Congress and the number of south-

Negro suffrage

ern votes in the Electoral College would be materially increased. If, therefore, the Negroes were denied the vote and the southern whites were not, the curious result would be to give the latter a greater weight in the Union than they had had before the war. Thus the Amendment held out an inducement to the South to permit the Negroes to vote, but the penalty for failure to do so was slight.

The third section of the amendment was designed to make ineligible for officeholding all the ex-Confederate leaders, regardless of whatever presidential pardons they might have received. Anyone who, after taking an oath of office under the United States, had aided the Confederacy might not again hold office unless Congress by a two-thirds vote of each house should remove the disability. Thaddeus Stevens was bitterly disappointed that the right to vote was not included in the disability, but, although the House dared not disagree with him, the Senate refused to take so extreme a position, and he was forced to yield the point.

Disabilities

A fourth section provided that the debt of the United States, incurred to preserve the Union, should never be questioned, and that the debt of the southern states and the Confederacy, incurred to destroy it, should never be paid. This portion of the amendment was meant to allay the fear that the Democrats, if ever they should regain control of the government, would use their power to repudiate the national debt; also, to insure that the provisions in the southern state constitutions against the payment of the Confederate debt must be observed.

A fifth section of the amendment gave Congress the power to enforce its provisions by appropriate legislation.

By the time the amendment was offered, the mid-term congressional elections of 1866 were close at hand, and Congress refused to proceed further with its work until the people had been heard from. While in general the effective portion of the press seemed to favor the Radicals, there were mutterings of discontent at the

Elections of 1866

long-continued exclusion of the South from representation in Congress, and Johnson's appeals to moderate sentiment had not been wholly in vain. As a discreet gesture of friendliness toward the South, more apparent than real, the State of Tennessee, which in July, 1866, reiterated its loyalty to the Union by ratifying the Fourteenth Amendment, was declared by act of Congress fully restored. As for the other ten states, every one of which rejected the Fourteenth Amendment as promptly as possible, all depended upon the outcome of the election. In case the Radicals were able to retain control of Congress, the President's plan would be completely overthrown; but, if the supporters of the President could only increase their numbers enough to prevent the overriding of presidential vetoes, then the President's plan might yet succeed.

A part of the President's strategy in the campaign was to emphasize the name and the history of the Union Party that had elected him to the Vice-Presidency in 1864. His friends in Congress took the lead in calling a "National Union Convention" to meet at Philadelphia in August in order to endorse his program. When the convention met, however, it was apparent that Republicans were far less in evidence than Democrats, both northern and southern. The main body of the Republicans, including many who had once been Democrats, followed the congressional leaders rather than the President. Because the President's enemies wished also to retain the Union label, there was much confusion as to party names during the election, but it was not difficult to see that the President would have to look mainly to the Democrats for his support, and that the terms "Radical" and "Republican" were rapidly becoming synonymous.

The Union Party

Johnson opened his campaign with great hope of success, but the trend of events soon turned against him. Among his most effective, but usually unseen, enemies were the northeastern industrialists who had come to

Opposition to the President

identify their growing prosperity with a continuance of Radical control of the government. They feared that the return of Southerners to the national councils might result in a revival of the old alliance between the agricultural South and the agricultural West that would imperil their interests. The agreeably high rates of the Morrill Tariff, for example, had been an impossibility until the South seceded; would the return of the South bring them down? Holders of United States bonds were frightened by the bugaboo that a revived Democracy, composed largely of northern ex-Copperheads and southern ex-Confederates, might, if it won control of the government, repudiate the war debt, or, quite as bad, pay it off in depreciated paper currency. The Radicals in Congress had also taken a benevolent attitude toward governmental assistance to railroad building, toward the rapid elimination of the income taxes and internal taxes levied during the war, and toward corporation prosperity generally. Could these policies be maintained with the South back in the Union?

Supported by such powerful vested interests, the opponents of the President made rapid headway. A congres-
Johnson's "swing around the circle" sional campaign committee, well supplied with funds, spread endless propaganda throughout the North about the "outrages" that southern whites were perpetrating upon the freedmen. Two race riots, one at Memphis in May and another at New Orleans in July, in both of which many more Negroes than whites were killed, were seized upon as evidence of what would surely happen if Johnson's plan of reconstruction were permitted to stand. When the President made a "swing around the circle" to Chicago, where he laid the cornerstone of a monument to Stephen A. Douglas, and back again by a different route to Washington, anti-Johnson demonstrations were systematically organized, which in some instances actually prevented the President from speaking, and in others goaded him into the intemperate ut-

terances for which he was famous. The Radical press made the most of his mistakes, and burlesqued his speeches so successfully that many of his former supporters were deceived and deserted him. He was repeatedly charged with drunkenness, and although all such charges were demonstrably false, such a well-known person as John Sherman complained that Johnson had "sunk the Presidential office to the level of the grog-house." [1] Thomas Nast, the cartoonist, and Petroleum V. Nasby, the favorite wit of the time, did their able best to make the President appear ridiculous. By the time the election was held, the outcome was no longer in doubt. The Radicals carried both houses of Congress by staggering majorities, and the total defeat of the President's program was assured.

When Congress reassembled in December, 1866, the triumphant Radicals took quick advantage of their victory.
The Radicals in control Confirmed in their power to pass laws over the President's veto, they meant to set up a congressional dictatorship that would reduce the President to the rôle of a well-disciplined clerk, if, indeed, it did not dispense with his services altogether. To insure that he should have no "breathing-spell" between Congresses, a new law set the fourth of March instead of the first Monday in December as the beginning date for a session of Congress. Thus, when, on the third of March next, the existing, or Thirty-Ninth, Congress should come to an end, it could rest assured that on the next day its successor, the Fortieth Congress, would be on hand to carry on. By another law, the Tenure of Office Act, Congress made it a misdemeanor, punishable by fine and imprisonment, for the President to remove civil officeholders without the consent

[1] At the time he was inaugurated Vice-President Johnson was so ill that only the insistence of Lincoln brought him to Washington. To help himself through the ordeal he took more liquor than in his weakened condition was wise, and cut a sorry spectacle. He was deeply humiliated by this incident, and although he did not become an abstainer he was never again publicly drunk.

of the Senate. The purpose of this law was to save from dismissal such Radical officials as the President had not already removed from office, and perhaps to lay a trap that might at length remove the President himself from the scene. Still another law, in utter defiance of the Constitution, sought to destroy the President's power as Commander-in-Chief of the Army. Believing that Grant, who now held the exalted rank of General, would bow to their will, the Radicals induced Congress to forbid the President to issue military orders, except through the General of the Army, or to relieve the General of his command, or assign him to duty elsewhere than in Washington, unless by his own consent or by consent of the Senate. All contrary orders were declared void, and officers who obeyed them were made subject to heavy penalties. By the same act, such militia as had been organized in any of the seceded states was declared disbanded, and its organization or use without the consent of Congress was forbidden. The scene was thus set for an era of ruthless legislative usurpation of executive prerogatives.

Even before the fourth of March the Radicals persuaded Congress to enact a new **Congressional reconstruction** plan of reconstruction far more drastic than the plan they had embodied in the Fourteenth Amendment; and a supplementary act passed after the fourth of March showed the new Congress to be in thorough accord with the old. These laws, in spite of the fact that two years had elapsed since the end of the war, were designed to undo completely all that Lincoln and Johnson had done to restore normal civil government in the ten southern states unrecognized by Congress. Military rule was to be resumed, with the South divided into five military districts and an officer of the United States Army not below the rank of brigadier-general in charge of each. Each general, duly supported by an adequate military force, must register all the legal voters, excluding all who had ever been disfranchised for disloyalty, and ad-

mitting Negroes on the same basis as whites. He must then call upon these voters to elect a constitutional convention, which should draw up a new constitution providing for Negro suffrage. If, on submission to the voters, this constitution should receive a popular majority, the general in charge should order the necessary elections to put it into effect; whereupon, if Congress should approve the new constitution, and if the legislature of the state should adopt the Fourteenth Amendment, and if as many as three-fourths of all the states should ratify the Fourteenth Amendment and so make it a part of the national Constitution, then and not until then should the representatives and senators of each restored state be considered eligible for admission to the two houses of Congress; and then, and not until then, should Federal troops be withdrawn from the state's borders. Furthermore, each of the newly chosen representatives and senators must be able to take the so-called "ironclad oath" that he had never given voluntary aid to the Confederacy.

The key to this plan of reconstruction was of course Negro suffrage. By giving the blacks the vote and by denying **Negro suffrage again** it to many whites the Radicals hoped to make sure that the southern states would long remain true to the Republican Party. They feared that, without such a provision, the Democratic Party might not only win the ascendancy in the South, but in the national government as well. Education of the Negroes in the belief that their freedom depended upon the preservation of Republican rule was well along, and the new scheme would give abundant time to complete the process.

These measures were passed over the presidential vetoes, but the President took good care to enforce their provisions as painstakingly as if he **The President and Stanton** believed in them. The Radical Congress thus found it impossible to impeach him for non-enforcement of the Reconstruction Acts, as they had hoped to do, so for a case against him they turned to the

Tenure of Office Act which he seemingly had violated. Edwin M. Stanton, whom Lincoln had appointed Secretary of War, continued under Johnson to hold that office even after he had deserted the President in all but name, and had made common cause with the Radicals. Several of Lincoln's cabinet appointees, more scrupulous than Stanton, had resigned when they could no longer support Johnson's policies, but Stanton seems to have stayed on precisely in order to act as a kind of spy, or informer. Of his close relations with the President's enemies there can be no doubt. Irritated at length beyond endurance, Johnson in August, 1867, asked Stanton to resign, and when Stanton refused, suspended him from office and named the popular General Grant as his *ad interim* successor.

When Congress met again in December, 1867, the President explained to the Senate
Attempt to remove Stanton his reasons for the suspension of Stanton, and asked that what he had done be confirmed. This action, however, the Senate promptly refused to take, whereupon Grant, in violation of an agreement he had made with Johnson, turned over his office to Stanton. Johnson had supposed that Grant would refuse to make way for Stanton, and had hoped that a court case, *Stanton vs. Grant*, would ultimately result in the Tenure of Office Act being held unconstitutional. The President did not hesitate to berate Grant roundly for his failure to live up to the bargain he had made, a course which drove the somewhat bewildered General directly into the arms of the Radicals. Thereupon the President, in defiance of the Tenure of Office Act, which all along he had regarded as unconstitutional, attempted to remove Stanton from office, but the Secretary of War in turn defied the President and kept possession.

Immensely pleased with so excellent an opening, the Radicals in the House of
Impeachment of Johnson Representatives, led by the now infirm but still indomitable Stevens, brought impeachment charges to the Senate. Nine of the charges

dealt with the President's violation of the Tenure of Office Act, the tenth charged the President with attacking Congress in his addresses, and the eleventh served as a kind of catch-all for all sorts of presidential misdeeds.

In March, 1868, the trial of the President began, with Chief Justice Chase presiding, and the Senate acting as jury. It was soon evident that the prosecution was out to "get" Johnson, regardless of the law, and that it thought that it had the necessary two-thirds vote for that purpose in sight. Johnson, however, was represented by an able panel of lawyers, who pointed out, among other things, that such a contingency as the removal of Stanton, an appointee of Lincoln's, had been considered when the law was passed, and that many prominent members of Congress had at that time assumed that the Tenure of Office Act would not be applicable to such a case. Moreover, inasmuch as the President believed the act to be unconstitutional, he was taking the only possible course, in dismissing Stanton, to get it before the courts for final decision — a procedure on his part that could hardly be regarded as a "high crime and misdemeanor."

Faced by these arguments, and fully aware of the purely political nature of the attack on the President, seven Republi- **Acquittal by one vote** can senators voted with twelve Democrats for acquittal, and by the narrow margin of one vote (35 to 19) the President was left in possession of his office. The seven Republicans who voted for the President were soon made to feel the full weight of party discipline, for not one of them was permitted to remain in politics, but the correctness of their position was attested years later when the Tenure of Office Act, in spite of certain congressional modifications, was held unconstitutional by the Supreme Court. Stanton, after the failure of the impeachment proceedings, retired from office, and General J. M. Schofield took his place.

Meanwhile the President, following as he

PHOTO OF ANDREW JOHNSON. Typical pose of the day, with hand in vest.

KING ANDY I. Graphic prophecy of Johnson as king with Liberty shackled at his feet. Thomas Nast in *Harper's Weekly*, 1866.

Andrew Johnson, Seventeenth President of the United States, was the third Vice-President to be elevated to the Presidency by the death of a President, and the only President to be tried on impeachment charges. His friendly attitude toward the defeated South might have served the nation far better than the vindictive attitude finally adopted.

TICKET TO THE IMPEACHMENT TRIAL.

TAKING THE VOTE. Senate chamber, May 16, 1868. Senator Ross of Kansas voting "Not guilty." From a sketch by James E. Taylor for *Leslie's Illustrated Newspaper.*

felt he must the recommendations of General

Radical reconstruction begins

Grant, had placed an army officer in charge of each of the five reconstruction districts of the South. The generals so chosen lacked nothing in authority, for the law set them above existing state governments, and empowered them to make arrests, to conduct military trials, and to carry on as they saw fit the ordinary processes of civil government. Specifically authorized by a "third reconstruction act," passed in the summer of 1867, to remove such state officials of the Johnson régimes as were in any way obstructing their efforts, they made various uses of their prerogatives. General Sheridan, in charge of Louisiana and Texas, gave proof of his radicalism by removing from office the governors of both states, the attorney-general of Louisiana, the mayor of New Orleans, and numerous other officials, all of whom he replaced with his own appointees. On the other hand, General Schofield, in charge of Virginia, made comparatively few removals and interfered as little as possible with the existing civil government of the state. Protests, both from the northern Radicals, who resented any appearance of softness on the part of the "brigadiers," and from the southern victims of their misrule, resulted in repeated and disconcerting changes in personnel. Sheridan, for example, was succeeded by General Winfield S. Hancock, whose honorable behavior led to his being superseded by General J. J. Reynolds, who in turn gave way to General R. C. Buchanan.

The main business of these military overlords was, of course, to organize new state

Registration of voters

governments according to the plan laid down in the Reconstruction Acts. The first step in the process was to register the voters, a task that presented many difficulties. Army officers, Freedmen's Bureau agents, and loyal citizens generally, among them many Negroes, were made members of the registration boards. Eligible whites, although admonished by many of the best-beloved southern leaders to roll up the largest possible majorities for their race, were reluctant to register, but the Negroes presented themselves gladly.

Immediately at the close of the war, many Southerners had had no very great fear of Negro suffrage, believing that

Southern opinion on Negro suffrage

the blacks could be persuaded to vote as their former masters directed. Indeed, one of the most telling of the arguments made against giving the freedmen the vote was based on precisely this premise. It was a well-known fact that the Negro population was concentrated in the best cotton-growing areas where before the war the great planters had held sway. Sometimes in these "black counties" the number of Negroes far exceeded the number of whites, although in the less favored "white counties" of the interior the exact reverse was true. And so it could be maintained that, in case the few favored whites of the "black counties" were aided by Negro votes, they could control the various state governments in complete disregard of the far larger number of whites in the back-country. Negro suffrage was thus feared, not so much for itself as for the danger it might involve of turning the South back to the rule of the old pre-war plantation aristocracy.

The northern Radicals, however, had taken great pains to wean the Negroes away from their natural allegiance to

The Union League

their former masters. Working mainly through the Union League, a private organization that during the war had existed to disseminate northern propaganda, but that after the war had turned its attention to the Negro problem, they taught the freedmen that their former masters were not to be trusted, and that in all political matters they must rely strictly upon Republican advisers. To make the League the more appealing to the blacks, it was converted into a kind of lodge, with an elaborate ritual and much ostentatious ceremony. Soon, with the aid of the northern soldiers stationed in the South and the agents of the Freedmen's Bureau, the League organizers had most of

Negro suffrage and *office-holding, thrust prematurely upon the freedmen, gave rise to an infinite amount of abuse. Influenced by northern carpetbaggers and southern scalawags, southern governments were shot through with corruption, and southern treasuries were looted. But it should not be forgotten that conditions in many northern cities, where corrupt machines held sway, were not much better.*

THE FIRST VOTE. Negroes going to the poll in their first state election. Drawing by A. R. Waud, 1867.

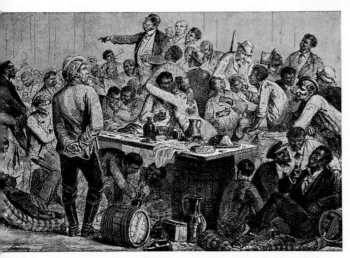

CARPETBAGGERS AND SCAL-AWAGS. One way to control Negro votes.

the Negroes under their control, so that when the time came for registering them as voters there was no question that they would both register and vote as the Radicals desired.

Slowly and painfully the reconstruction process worked itself out. When the eligible voters were duly registered, it **The new electorates** was found that in five of the ten states the number of Negro voters exceeded the number of whites, while in all the other states, with the possible exception of North Carolina, the white majorities were very slender indeed. Late in 1867 or early in 1868 these electors, or such of them as were permitted to vote, chose delegates to con-

stitutional conventions, which with a minimum of delay, began their deliberations. In every such convention there was a large block of Negro delegates and a considerable sprinkling of southern whites, mostly of the less-favored classes, but the leaders turned out to be Northerners rather than Southerners — men who had come South with the army or with the Freedmen's Bureau, or perhaps merely to fish in troubled waters.[1] These "carpetbaggers," as they were called,

[1] The number of Negroes in each of the southern conventions was approximately as follows: South Carolina, 76 (out of 124); Louisiana, 49 (out of 98); Georgia, 37; Virginia, 25; Alabama, 18; Florida, 18; Mississippi, 17; North Carolina, 13; Texas, 9; Arkansas, 8.

were thoroughgoing Radicals, almost to the last man, and they saw to it that such constitutions were adopted as the Radicals in Congress would favor. Those southern whites who were willing to follow the lead of the "carpetbaggers" were generally termed "scalawags."

The new constitutions, as a matter of fact, contained some admirable provisions. They New state looked forward to the establishconstitutions ment of far better public-school systems than the South had ever known before — an end eagerly sought by the Negroes, who regarded their lack of education as the most serious obstacle they confronted in their struggle for racial equality. These documents also copied the latest reforms in systems of taxation and finance, of local government, and of judicial organization that had found their way into northern state constitutions, but had not previously been current in the South. Such reforms, however, were small compensations to the dispossessed Southerners for the prospect of "carpetbag rule" that the suffrage provisions of every constitution seemed to make certain. Some of these provisions were even more drastic than those which Congress had prescribed. Nor could the various attempts to insure social as well as civil and political equality between the races be viewed with equanimity.

When the newly drawn constitutions were submitted for adoption or rejection at the Ratification polls, the tendency was for the whites of every class, whatever their previous political connections, to unite in opposition. Sometimes these opponents of adoption called themselves Conservatives; more and more frequently they came to be called Democrats, and to accept that designation. The Negroes, "carpetbaggers," and some of the "scalawags" remained steadfastly Republican, supported the new documents, and in most cases were able to command majorities for them. In Mississippi, however, the proposed constitution was rejected at the polls, while in Alabama ratification was defeated temporarily by a

ruse. The law required that for a constitution to be adopted the total vote cast in the election must constitute a majority of the whole number of registered voters. The whites, by systematically abstaining from voting, succeeded in keeping down the number of votes cast to a minority of the registered voters, and so in defeating the constitution in spite of the fact that a large majority of those who voted were for it. But their rejoicing was short-lived, for the Radicals in Congress promptly pushed through a "fourth reconstruction act" which asserted that a majority of the votes actually cast, regardless of the size of the total vote, would be sufficient for ratification. Furthermore, to stop real or fancied discriminations against itinerant Negroes, who tended to forget where they had registered and even the names they had adopted for the purpose, residence for ten days preceding an election was declared sufficient to entitle such a person to vote "upon presentation of his certificate of registration, his affidavit, or other satisfactory evidence."

Between June, 1868, when Congress consented to the readmission of Arkansas under its new constitution, and July, The 1870, when Georgia, after much Fifteenth tribulation, was finally rein- Amendment stated, each of the ten southern states, including Mississippi whose constitution after some amendment was accepted by the voters, completed the process of reconstruction that Congress had prescribed. All but three of these states were rushed through to admission in time to vote for Grant in the election of 1868. As a culminating act each newly elected legislature ratified the Fourteenth Amendment to the Constitution of the United States, which in July, 1868, was declared in force. For those states that had not been readmitted before 1869, when the Fifteenth or Negro Suffrage Amendment was submitted, that addition to the Constitution (in effect, February, 1870) had also to be approved. Senators and representatives from the readmitted states, most of whom were Republicans and many of whom were

Negroes, were at length permitted to take their seats in Congress, and reconstruction, technically speaking, was over. But the promise of withdrawal of northern troops was not always fulfilled, for throughout the South opposition to "carpetbag" rule mounted so rapidly that its continuance was everywhere recognized as wholly dependent upon military support.

In carrying through this program of reconstruction, Congress had consistently shown the finest disregard of constitutional niceties. It had not only ridden roughshod over the executive branch of the government; it had also defied the judiciary. In 1866 a decision of the Supreme Court, *Ex parte Milligan*, read by Justice David Davis, condemned as illegal the trial of civilians by military courts in regions where the civil courts were open for business. Although this case came up with reference to the action of a military tribunal in Indiana during the war, the decision seemed to cast serious doubt upon the legality of any such structure of military rule as that which Congress, notwithstanding, soon proceeded to establish in the South. Furthermore, if this decision held, numerous important verdicts of military commissions had been illegal, among them the one that had resulted in the execution of four persons, including the innocent Mrs. Surratt, for conspiring to bring about the death of Abraham Lincoln, and another that had cost Henry Wirz, a Confederate official at Andersonville Prison, his life.

After the Milligan decision Radical denunciation of the Supreme Court went to violent extremes, and leading Republicans in Congress took thought as to how they might most effectively destroy its power. In July, 1866, they pushed through a law reducing the number of judges from nine to seven.[1] By providing that the next two

The Supreme Court and reconstruction

vacancies among the associate justices should not be filled, they not only, in effect, reprimanded the court, but they also diminished the danger that President Johnson might appoint any liberals to sit upon it. Two years later another measure, providing that a two-thirds majority of the justices should be required to set aside a law of Congress, passed the House, but was not brought to a vote in the Senate. Although Thaddeus Stevens favored legislation to deny the Court any jurisdiction whatever over the enforcement of the Reconstruction Acts, Congress provided only that the Court might not hear appeals from the lower courts in cases involving the right of *habeas corpus*. Reeling under these blows, the Court took pains to avoid as completely as possible all decisions that might offend Congress, although in the case of *Texas vs. White* (1869) it went on record as favoring the Johnson theory that the southern states, in spite of their acts of secession, had never legally ceased to exist.

The first elections in the reconstructed states resulted in the choice of a dubious array of officials. The highest places went mainly to Northerners who had not become residents of the South until after the war, and who had frequently seen it for the first time as members of the Union army. Lesser offices were held almost exclusively by Negroes, scalawags, and carpetbaggers. One Negro became lieutenant-governor of Louisiana, another secretary of state in South Carolina. Negroes were numerous in every legislature, and in South Carolina they outnumbered the whites eighty-eight to sixty-seven. Most of the office-holders were men of little property. In Louisiana only ten members of the legislature were taxpayers; in South Carolina the total taxes paid by the members of both houses were less than seven hundred dollars; in Georgia, they were less than one hundred dollars. Most of the Negroes and many of the whites chosen to office, including even judicial positions, were utterly illiterate.

The inevitable result of entrusting the

Elections in the South

---

[1] By an Act of March 3, 1863, Congress had raised the number of Supreme Court justices to ten, but Johnson's nominee to fill a vacancy which occurred early in 1865 was not confirmed by the Senate.

powers of government to such persons was **"Carpet-bag rule"** an orgy of corruption. Private enterprises, such as railroad and canal companies, were expected to pay sizable bribes in order to secure charters, and, indeed, in order to carry on their legitimate business. If any enterprise happened to be thoroughly dubious, however, the chances were good that public money or public credit would be generously voted toward its support. Contracts were let to favorites at ridiculously high figures, and the public servants responsible took a cut of the profits. Public printing in Louisiana during a three-year period cost approximately a million and a half dollars a year, about seven hundred thousand of which was paid in two of these years to a newspaper belonging to the governor of the state, H. C. Warmoth, whose private fortune, incidentally, rose to a tidy sum before he left office. Worthless real estate, acquired for next to nothing, was sold by connivance to states or municipalities for prodigious figures. A single session of the carpetbag legislature in Louisiana cost nearly a million dollars, whereas before the war the cost of a session had never been more than one tenth that amount. What happened to this money was explained by a governor who had good reason to know the facts:

It was squandered in paying extra mileage and per diem of the members for services never rendered; for an enormous corps of useless clerks and pages, for publishing the journals of each house in fifteen obscure parish newspapers, some of which never existed, while some never did the work; in paying extra committees authorized to sit during the vacation and to travel throughout the state and into Texas; and in an elegant stationery bill which included ham, champagne, etc.

The rule of the carpetbaggers raised tax-rates to figures never known before, and piled up debts which most of the southern states felt obliged later on to repudiate; but it must not be forgotten that such political depravity was no monopoly of the South. In New York, for example, during this same period, the Tweed Ring reduced graft to a science that the carpetbaggers might well have envied, while the word "racketeering," with all its relevant connotations, was the product of a much later age. Of all those who participated in the work of Radical reconstruction the Negroes were the least to blame for its excesses. Only a few of them understood what was being done, and only a few of those who did were shrewd enough to line their pockets with plunder. For the most part they were but helpless victims of the conscienceless rogues who controlled them.

Strange as it may seem, there was a brighter side to the rule of the carpetbaggers. They and their allies represented, however crudely, the underprivileged classes in southern society, and they inaugurated many policies that were designed to better the lot of the ordinary man. Free public schools for the children of both races were generously supported, although with little regard for available taxation resources. The tax burden itself, unreasonable as it became, was distributed with better regard for ability to pay than formerly. Poor relief had never been less neglected, and the rebuilding of roads, bridges, and public buildings that had been damaged or destroyed during the war was carried forward with little regard for expense. Most of all, the taste of democracy that the lowly of both races obtained was not soon forgotten. The rights of the Negroes were soon curtailed, but the incentive remained, at least with some of them, to win back by merit privileges that they had lost because they had been given them too soon. As for the poorer whites, from whose ranks many of the "scalawags" had been recruited, they were never again quite so inarticulate as they had been in the days before their kind had sat in the seats of power.

Bibliography

Many of the books cited for the preceding chapter are also useful for this. On reconstruction leaders, R. N. Current, *Old Thad Stevens: A Story of Ambition* (1942), is objective and critical, and does much to rehabilitate Stevens' reputation, especially for his earlier years. Samuel W. McCall, *Thaddeus Stevens* (1899), set the original Stevens pattern, which has been much improved on since, not only by Current, but also by James A. Woodburn, *The Life of Thaddeus Stevens* (1913); and by T. F. Woodley, *The Great Leveller; The Life of Thaddeus Stevens* (1937), which is a revised version of the author's *Thaddeus Stevens* (1934). There are two fairly satisfactory biographies of Sumner: Moorfield Storey, *Charles Sumner* (1900); and G. H. Haynes, *Charles Sumner* (1909); but much more can be learned from *Memoir and Letters of Charles Sumner*, edited by E. L. Pierce (4 vols., 1877–93). Excellent short sketches of the leading participants in American history are to be found in the *Dictionary of American Biography*, Allen Johnson and Dumas Malone (20 vols., 1928–36).

Paul H. Buck, *The Road to Reunion, 1865–1900* (1937), traces with impartial hand the slow process of reconciliation between the victorious North and the defeated South. Carl Schurz, "Report on Conditions in the South," published in *Speeches, Correspondence and Political Papers of Carl Schurz*, edited by Frederic Bancroft (6 vols., 1913), I, 279–374, is also valuable here. Samples of the southern black codes are given in *Documents of American History*, edited by H. S. Commager (5th edition, 1949), items 246–47. This collection of sources is invaluable for handy reference.

On the subject of the adoption of the Fourteenth Amendment, B. B. Kendrick, *The Journal of the Joint Committee of Fifteen on Reconstruction* (1914), and H. E. Flack, *The Adoption of the Fourteenth Amendment* (1908), are very useful. On the constitutional aspects of reconstruction, see Charles Warren, *The Supreme Court in United States History* (2 vols., new edition, 1937). This work is valuable for the whole period of recent American History.

On the struggle between Johnson and Congress, see, in addition to the Johnson biographies already cited, C. E. Chadsey, *The Struggle between President Johnson and Congress over Reconstruction* (1896); D. M. Dewitt, *The Impeachment and Trial of Andrew Johnson* (1903); Frederic Bancroft, *The Life of William H. Seward* (2 vols., 1900); Horace White, *Lyman Trumbull* (1913); and the *Diary of Gideon Welles* (3 vols., 1911).

Of the many state histories of reconstruction, the least biased and the best is F. B. Simkins and R. H. Woody, *South Carolina during Reconstruction* (1932). Others of merit, most of them reflecting a more or less official "southern white man's" point of view, are J. W. Garner, *Reconstruction in Mississippi* (1901); J. G. deR. Hamilton, *Reconstruction in North Carolina* (1914); W. W. Davis, *The Civil War and Reconstruction in Florida* (1913); W. L. Fleming, *Civil War and Reconstruction in Alabama* (1905, new ed., 1949); E. M. Coulter, *Civil War and Readjustment in Kentucky* (1926); C. Mildred Thompson, *Reconstruction in Georgia, Economic, Social, Political, 1865–1872* (1915); C. W. Ramsdell, *Reconstruction in Texas* (1910); Ella Lonn, *Reconstruction in Louisiana after 1868* (1918). The state histories cited in the preceding chapter are also useful here.

James S. Pike, *The Prostrate State: South Carolina Under Negro Government* (1874, new ed., 1935), is a classic picture of "carpetbag rule." Another excellent contemporary account is Charles Nordhoff, *The Cotton States in the Spring and Summer of 1875* (1876). For later opinions, see W. F. Nowlin, *The Negro in American National Politics* (1931); Charles S. Johnson, *The Negro in American Civilization* (1930); A. A. Taylor, *The Negro in the Reconstruction of Virginia* (1926); John H. Franklin, *From Slavery to Freedom; A History of the American Negroes* (1947); and *A Documentary History of the Negro People in the United States*, edited by Herbert Aptheker (1951). For one of the brighter aspects of carpetbag rule, see E. W. Knight, *The Influence of Reconstruction on Education in the South* (1913). E. M. Coulter, *The South during Reconstruction, 1865–1877* (1947), restates the case against the carpetbaggers. F. B. Simkins, *The South Old and New: A History, 1820–1947* (1947), follows the main currents of southern history with admirable impartiality.

3

The Grant Régime

Election of 1868 — Grant and Colfax — The ambitions of Chase — Grant, the politician — Civil service reform — The "Ohio idea" — Legal-tender cases — Taxation reform — The Ku Klux Klan — The "Solid South" — Liberal Republicanism — Election of 1872 — The Grant scandals — Grant's foreign policy — Treaty of Washington

THE impeachment proceedings that ultimately failed by so narrow a margin to make **The Election** Andrew Johnson a private citi- **of 1868** zen were still in progress when the Republicans, no longer under the necessity of disguising themselves as Unionists, met in convention at Chicago to make General Grant their standard-bearer in the campaign of 1868. From the time the war ended it had been quite apparent that, when the next election year rolled around, Grant could have whichever nomination he wished, Democratic or Republican. The course of events had given him to the Republicans. Before the war, to be sure, he had been a Democrat if he had been anything, and he had never yet voted the Republican ticket. But his quarrel with Johnson had endeared him to the Radicals, who, on that account, according to Thaddeus Stevens, were ready to "let him into the Church." Also, as General of the Army he, rather than the President, had had command of military reconstruction, and his ready compliance with Radical desires had made for mutual trust and admiration. Most of all, the rank and file of the Republican Party, among whom could be counted an overwhelming majority of the men who had fought in the Union armies, were determined to have him; they were certain that they had the votes to elect him;

and their active insistence was more than one so unaccustomed to political pressure could be expected to resist. On the first ballot every one of the six hundred and fifty delegates to the Republican Convention voted for Grant.

The other business of the convention was also quickly done. For the Vice-Presidency, after a short but exciting con- **Grant and** test, it named Schuyler Colfax **Colfax** of Indiana, the amiable, albeit Radical, Speaker of the House, whom one observer had likened to "a good-tempered, chirping, warbling, real canary bird." It congratulated the country on the "assured success of the reconstruction policy of Congress"; defended Negro suffrage as a necessity in the South, although timidly conceding it to be a matter for each state to decide for itself in the North;[1] urged the payment of the national debt in the "spirit of the laws under which it was contracted," the reduction of taxation, the strictest economy in national administration, the most liberal encouragement to immigration; and finally, exhausted its vocabulary of vituperation upon Andrew Johnson, whose acquittal of the crimes

[1] The Fifteenth Amendment was not submitted until after the election. Then, in spite of this plank in the Republican platform, the Radical leaders maintained that the election of Grant amounted to a mandate to write Negro suffrage into the Constitution.

Salmon P. Chase of Ohio had won

public attention before the Civil War as an uncompromising opponent of slavery. He had been in turn a member of the Liberty, Free-Soil, and Republican Parties, and had reached the Senate as a Free-Soiler in time to participate in the debates on the Compromise of 1850. During the war he served with distinction in Lincoln's cab-

inet. His lifelong ambition for the Presidency continued even after he became Chief Justice, and was unconcealed during the impeachment proceedings against Johnson. "The Political Niagara," a Thomas Nast cartoon, derides the Democratic Party as "a drowning man grasping at a straw" when it considered nominating Chase for the Presidency in 1868.

---

charged against him was already clearly foreshadowed.

To Salmon P. Chase (1808–1873), Chief Justice of the United States Supreme Court,

The ambitions of Chase

the Republican determination to select Grant came as a bitter disappointment. Chase was a New Englander by birth and ancestry, and a graduate of Dartmouth College, who as a legal practitioner in Ohio had early commanded attention for his able arguments in defense of fugitive slaves. Always prominent in the anti-slavery crusade, he became United States Senator from Ohio in 1849, governor of Ohio in 1855, and Secretary of the Treasury under Lincoln in 1861. Handsome and impressive in appearance, scholarly and proud of his scholarship, he was not one to hide his light under a bushel. He cherished deeply the customary ambition to achieve the Presidency, and while still a member of Lincoln's cabinet did not hesitate to allow his name to be urged by Lincoln's opponents as one more fitting than the President for the Republican nomination in 1864. This lack of loyalty Lincoln over-

looked with his customary magnanimity. "If he becomes President," he told his private secretary, "all right. I hope we may never have a worse man." But when shortly after Lincoln's renomination, Chase, because of a fancied slight, presented his resignation, Lincoln accepted it. Nevertheless, a few months later, on the death of Chief Justice Taney, Lincoln unhesitatingly redeemed an outstanding promise to Charles Sumner to make Chase Chief Justice.

When Johnson became President, Chase, whom Lincoln had described as "a little insane" on the subject of the Presidency, soon had his eyes fixed on 1868. He made an extensive trip through the South in 1865, and from time to time sent back public reports on conditions as he saw them. When he maintained, with much argument as to the superior qualities of the freedmen, that Negro suffrage was a prime necessity, he won the hearty approval of the Radicals, whose candidate he hoped to be. Aided socially by his daughter, Kate Chase Sprague, the most charming hostess in Washington, he had good reason to believe

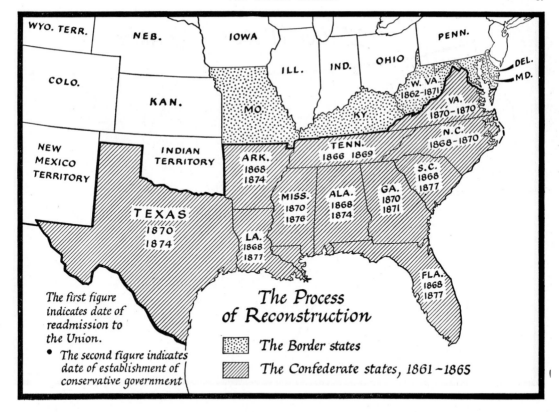

WYO. TERR.

NEB.

IOWA

PENN.

COLO.

KAN.

ILL.   IND.   OHIO

DEL.

MD.

W. VA.
1862-1871

VA.
1870-1870

NEW
MEXICO
TERRITORY

INDIAN
TERRITORY

MO.

KY.

N.C.
1868-1870

ARK.
1868
1874

TENN.
1866 1869

S.C.
1868
1877

TEXAS
1870
1874

MISS.
1870
1876

ALA.
1868
1874

GA.
1870
1871

LA.
1868
1877

FLA.
1868
1877

The first figure
indicates date of
readmission to
the Union.
• The second figure indicates
date of establishment of
conservative government

*The Process
of Reconstruction*

The Border states

The Confederate states, 1861–1865

that his dreams might come true. But the Johnson trial, over which he presided so impartially as to make the Radicals boil with rage, was his undoing. Indeed, the whole-hearted way in which his former friends deserted him for Grant commended him to the Democrats, who talked enough of naming him to arouse his hopes once more. That he earnestly desired the Democratic nomination and would have accepted it had it been tendered him, there can be no doubt.

Logically the Democrats should have nominated President Johnson, and this they **The Demo-** seriously considered. But John- **crats name** son's record of political inepti- **Seymour** tude, together with the fact that he had made no practical move to secure the nomination, told against him. The Democratic Convention, meeting in July at Tammany Hall in New York City, gave him sixty-five votes on the first ballot, and extravagant praise for "exercising the powers

of his high office in resisting the aggressions of Congress upon the constitutional rights of the States and the people"; but, after much fruitless balloting, the convention passed over both the President and the Chief Justice in order to give the nomination to Horatio Seymour, the Democratic war governor of New York, who as chairman of the convention had supposedly favored the nomination of Chase. Seymour's views on reconstruction were moderate, but for the Vice-Presidency the Democrats chose Francis P. Blair, Jr., of Missouri, perhaps the most violent critic of Radical reconstruction in the party.

The Democratic platform, by its scathing denunciation of the congressional plan of reconstruction, made opposition **Issues of the** to that policy the chief issue in **campaign** the campaign. Congress, it declared, instead of restoring the Union, had, "so far as in its power, dissolved it, and subjected ten states, in the time of profound peace, to military

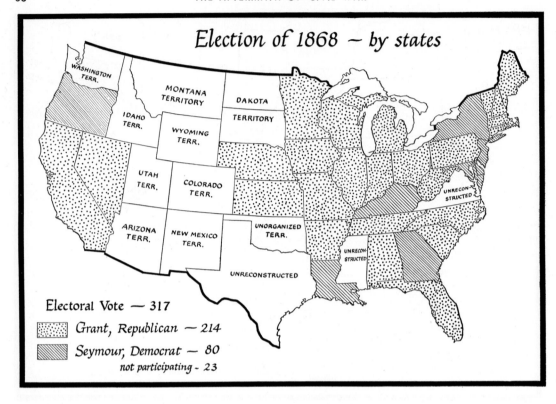

Election of 1868 — by states

Electoral Vote — 317

Grant, Republican — 214

Seymour, Democrat — 80

not participating - 23

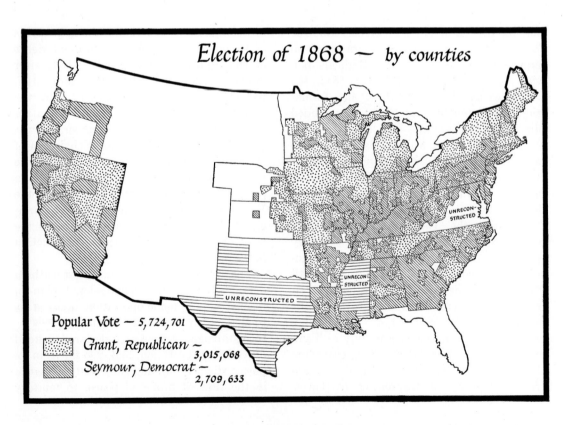

Election of 1868 — by counties

Popular Vote — 5,724,701

Grant, Republican — 3,015,068

Seymour, Democrat — 2,709,633

despotism and Negro supremacy." But there was a definite undercurrent of interest in the money question. So far, Republican policy had shown every disposition to befriend the holders of United States bonds, and in general to protect the interest of the creditor class. In protest against this, George H. Pendleton, a prominent Ohio Democrat, had some time before advanced the theory that the Civil War bond issues should be paid off in greenbacks, whenever the letter of the law would permit, instead of gold, as "hard-money" men were wont to advocate. Pendleton's "Ohio idea" was incorporated in the Democratic platform, but the nomination of Seymour, whose views on the money question were regarded as "sound," did much to eliminate this issue from the consideration it probably deserved.

The campaign was more vigorous than the one-sided result would seem to indicate. **A Republican victory** Radical reconstruction still excluded three southern states from voting, and made certain that several others would vote for Grant. A generous campaign chest, contributed by businessmen who were unwilling to take any chances on the Democratic "soft-money" platform, was also useful. Nor were voters allowed to forget the historic connection of the Democratic Party with secession and Copperheadism. Nevertheless, the outrageous character of the Radical usurpation of power, both in the national government and in the South, was so courageously exposed by Democratic campaigners that eight states, including New York and New Jersey, voted for Seymour, while in most of the twenty-six that voted for Grant the Democratic minorities were far too large for Republican comfort. In a total popular vote of nearly six millions, Grant's majority was only about three hundred thousand, and far more than that many Negroes had voted! Of the total white electorate, therefore, clearly Grant was a minority choice. The electoral returns gave Grant 214 votes to Seymour's 80. Both houses of Congress remained in the hands of the Radicals, but the death of

Ulysses S. Grant

EIGHTEENTH PRESIDENT of the United States Grant, like Washington, Jackson, and Harrison, won the attention of the public by military rather than by political achievements. "Let us have peace," he said, in accepting the Republican nomination for President. But in spite of his generous treatment of Lee's defeated army at Appomattox, and his favorable report to President Johnson on conditions in the South, he speedily fell into the hands of the northern Radicals, and supported the vindictive measures by which they long postponed the day of reconciliation.

Stevens, late in the summer of 1868, had deprived them of their most competent leader.

Some of the very qualities that had made Grant the soldier a success, made Grant the politician a sore trial to his **Grant the politician** colleagues and to his country. In the army most of the men he liked he trusted, and because the men he felt drawn to instinctively were generally good soldiers, they rarely betrayed his trust. In politics he met a different breed. Those he liked he trusted, but his instincts often played him false. In the army, Grant had learned to stand loyally behind his subordinates, regardless of popular criticism. In politics, this trait sometimes made him the last to recognize that one of his appointees was a rogue. In the army, when counsels were divided, he had often been compelled to think things out for himself, and to follow his own course. In politics, where his counsels were usually divided, his lack of expert knowledge sometimes made his independent judgments ridiculous. Years of political experience taught him something, and he left office a better politician than when he entered it; but not until after the Second World War were the people of the United States again willing to trust the Presidency to a professional soldier.

Grant's extraordinary capacity for political bungling was at once apparent when his **Grant's** nominations for cabinet positions **cabinet** were announced; some of those named he had not so much as consulted in advance. For Secretary of State he chose Elihu B. Washburne, the congressman from his home district in Illinois who, early in the Civil War, had urged Grant's appointment as brigadier general. For Secretary of War, he at first made no nomination, but presently chose his most trusted staff officer and personal friend, John A. Rawlins, also a neighbor from Illinois. For Secretary of the Treasury he chose a millionaire New York merchant named A. T. Stewart, who, according to law, was ineligible for the post because he was "concerned in trade or commerce." For Secretary of the Navy he further indulged his growing fondness for rich men by selecting a Philadelphia merchant, Adolph E. Borie, who had contributed generously to the Republican campaign chest, but had no desire to serve. The other appointments were not so unusual, but the whole cabinet had been constructed without regard to political consequences, and was no sooner made than the process of remaking had to be begun. According to a prearranged plan Washburne resigned after a week to become Minister to France, and Hamilton Fish of New York, an excellent choice, became Secretary of State. At the insistence of the politicians George S. Boutwell, one of the Radical impeachment managers at the trial of Johnson, became Secretary of the Treasury. Borie was replaced within a few months, and as

time went on numerous other changes were made.

Many people had acclaimed Grant's independent essay at cabinetmaking as the beginning of the end for the **Civil service** spoils system, but it turned out **reform** that, as soon as the President had taken care of his personal friends and indigent relatives, he fell easily into the hands of the Radical leaders, and followed their advice almost exclusively. Similarly, most of his cabinet, notably Boutwell, found the spoils system a satisfactory way of making appointments. His Attorney General, E. Rockwood Hoar, and his Secretary of the Interior, Jacob D. Cox, however, sometimes refused to do as the politicians bade, and mainly on this account Grant soon forced them out of office. All this led to a violent outcry from a small but influential group of civil service reformers. Led by such men as E. L. Godkin of the New York *Nation*, George William Curtis of *Harper's Weekly*, Thomas A. Jenckes, a representative from Rhode Island whose study of the English civil service had made him an ardent advocate of reform, and Carl Schurz, now United States Senator from Missouri, the agitation went to such lengths that Grant, in his second annual message to Congress, urged the passage of a law to govern "the manner of making appointments." In 1871 Congress, not unwilling to cultivate the reform vote on the eve of a presidential election, actually authorized the appointment of a commission to inquire into the matter. When George William Curtis was made head of the commission and promptly reported a set of rules to be followed in making appointments, the hopes of the reformers ran high, but after the election was over Congress failed to supply the funds necessary to keep the commission alive, and all its work came to nothing.

The "sound-money" men who hoped for help from the Grant administration fared far better than the civil service **The "Ohio** reformers. They claimed that **idea"** the election of 1868 constituted a mandate

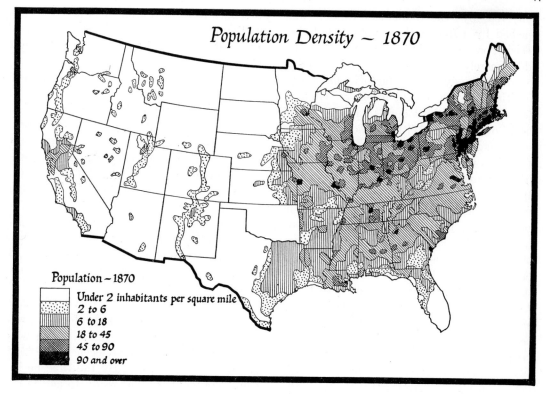

Population Density ~ 1870

Population ~ 1870

☐	Under 2 inhabitants per square mile
⣿	2 to 6
▦	6 to 18
▩	18 to 45
▨	45 to 90
■	90 and over

to save the country from the "Ohio idea," according to which billions of greenback dollars might conceivably be printed to pay off the national debt. One of the first measures to pass Congress, in March, 1869, pledged the United States to redeem its bonds "in coin or its equivalent," a phrase which Grant's and successive administrations interpreted to mean "in gold." Thus bonds that had been paid for in depreciated greenbacks were to be redeemed in dollars that were worth up to twice as much as the dollars originally lent the government. A refunding act, passed in July, 1870, provided for the systematic refinancing of the national debt on a long-term basis. Quite properly, in view of the friendly attitude the government had taken toward its creditors, the new bonds carried a much lower rate of interest.

What to do with the greenbacks that had been so freely issued during the Civil War, and that were still in circulation, was another serious problem. In Johnson's ad-

ministration the expedient of reducing them in quantity, in order ultimately to raise their value to a parity with gold, had been tried, but the outcry from the country when prices began to drop was so great that Congress in 1868 called a halt. At the time Grant became President the greenback circulation stood at $356,000,000, far more than the government had, or could easily get, the gold to redeem. For the moment it seemed inexpedient to work for the resumption of specie payments, but "sound-money" men looked forward anxiously to the time when a greenback dollar should be equal in value to a gold dollar.

In February, 1870, the Supreme Court became involved in the matter. In the case *Hepburn vs. Griswold*, it reached **The legal-** the unexpected conclusion that **tender cases** the "legal-tender" quality with which Congress had endowed the greenbacks was unconstitutional to the extent that it applied to debts contracted before the passage of the acts in question. The opinion of the Court, delivered by Chief Justice Chase, was reached by a four-to-three vote. Had this decision been allowed to stand, it would have added merely one more element of instability to the already unsatisfactory monetary situation, but a combination of circumstances enabled the Court to reverse itself the following year. With Johnson out of the way, Congress had again raised the number of justices to nine, and on the very day that the Hepburn case was decided, President Grant had sent to the Senate the names of two new justices, who, shortly after their confirmation, joined with the minority of the Hepburn decision to affirm by a five-to-four vote the constitutionality of the legal-tender clause. It has often been argued that the Court was deliberately packed to bring about this reversal, but the general consensus among historians seems to be that Grant had decided on his nominations without particular reference to the greenback decision. That the prestige of the Court suffered considerably from the proceedings, however, can hardly be denied.

In the campaign of 1868 the Republicans had definitely committed themselves to the **Reduction of taxes** reduction of taxation, a policy which, in fact, was already under way. Just before the end of the war, Congress had authorized the appointment of a special commission to study how new revenues might be obtained, but by the time the appointments were made the war was over. The commission, therefore, turned its attention to the problem of how the tax burden might best be reduced, and so impressed the Secretary of the Treasury with its diligence that when its term had expired he kept on its able chief, David A. Wells, as "special commissioner of the revenue." Both the commission and the special commissioner advised the gradual reduction of tariffs and excises, and on the latter subject Congress responded willingly. When Grant became President, however, many of the war taxes were still in force, so in July, 1870, an act was passed which eliminated most of the "nuisance" taxes, restricted the internal revenues to a small number of articles, such as liquor and tobacco, and greatly reduced the income tax, which, two years later, was abolished entirely.

For a long time efforts to lower the tariff met with successful opposition from those who profited from the high rates, **Tariff legislation** and during Johnson's term Congress was actually persuaded to raise the duties on raw wool, woolen goods, copper, and copper ore. Not until 1872 were the first real reductions made. At that time many non-protective duties, such as those on tea, coffee, spices, and various raw materials, were lowered or abolished, and a ten per cent cut was reluctantly conceded for a few carefully chosen duties on manufactured articles.

Grant at the end of the Civil War had shown his thorough sympathy for the prostrate South, and perhaps at **Grant and** that time he could have been **the Radicals** counted on to help it. By the time he became President, he was ready to act as the willing agent of the Radicals, and it was during his administration that the worst excesses of carpetbag rule occurred. With the co-operation of the army assured, detachments of soldiers were always available to put down revolts, real or fancied, and to sustain the carpetbaggers. States that showed signs of going over to the Democrats were apt to be subjected to a congressional investigation, and then dealt with most drastically. On several occasions, for example, military officers deliberately purged southern legislatures of undependable members. Some of the carpetbag governors also made use of Negro militia, whose chief duty, apparently, was to terrorize "disloyal" whites.

It was inevitable that violence of this sort would beget similar violence. As early as 1866 a group of young men who **The Ku** had lately been soldiers in the **Klux Klan** Confederate army organized, at Pulaski, Tennessee, a secret society, which, from the Greek word κύκλος, meaning circle, they called the Ku Klux Klan. The society at first spread slowly, and seemed as barren of any real reason for existence as most such societies; but the mysterious name, and the equally mysterious letters, K.K.K., that stood for it, were soon utilized to frighten the Negroes. Before long night riders in various disguises, such as ghostly gowns, false faces, and tails, were visiting the cabins of bothersome Negroes, breaking up meetings of the Union League, beating up Negro militiamen, frightening black Republicans away from the polls, and occasionally attacking both scalawags and carpetbaggers. As soon as the vigilante possibilities of the Klan were realized, it grew like wildfire, and was paralleled by numerous similar organizations such as the Knights of the White Camellia, the Constitutional Guards, the Pale Faces, and the Knights of the Rising Sun. By the year 1869 these various orders had covered the South with their activities, and had attracted to membership, or to imitation, which amounted to much the same thing, men who would stop at nothing. Murders now replaced whippings as a common proceeding, and the most fiendish acts of torture were by no means rare. Horrified at the turn events had taken, and certain that such an opportunity for reprisals would not long be neglected, the responsible heads of the various orders, as early as the spring of 1869, did everything they could to disband them. But the worst of the "midnight banditti" continued their activities unabated.

Congress replied to the Ku Klux challenge with a series of three drastic Enforcement

The Enforcement Acts

Acts. The first, passed in May 1870, laid down heavy penalties for all found guilty of using force, bribery, or intimidation to prevent citizens from voting. All such cases were to be tried in the federal courts, and the President was authorized, in case of necessity, to use the army and the navy to enforce court decisions. In spite of this law, the Democrats in the South won many substantial victories in the elections of 1870, so in February, 1871, Congress passed a second Enforcement Act along the same lines as the

first, but more drastic in its provisions.[1] The third Enforcement Act, passed in April, 1871, was aimed directly at the Klan, and was sometimes known as the Ku Klux Act. It listed as high crimes subject to severe penalties the various activities of the Klan, such as forming conspiracies, wearing disguises, resisting officers, and intimidating witnesses, and it authorized the President to suspend the writ of *habeas corpus* wherever he deemed such action necessary to suppress "armed combinations" in rebellion against the authority of the United States. Grant knew precisely how to enforce such a law, and did it thoroughly. He singled out for an example nine counties in South Carolina where the lawlessness had been most marked, suspended the writ of *habeas corpus* within their borders, and brought hundreds of law-breakers to trial. Federal troops stood by to see that the courts were left free to do their work, and in less than two years United States judges in South Carolina imposed heavy sentences upon eighty-two persons for violation of the act. The example proved effective, and in part on this account the number of outrages attributed to the Klan declined sharply from this time on.

Congress, at the time the Ku Klux Act was passed, had also appointed a committee to investigate "affairs in the late insurrectionary states." The committee began at once to take

The Ku Klux Klan Committee

testimony on the Klan, and sent subcommittees into the South to find out more definitely what the situation there was like. Reputable Southerners did not hesitate to denounce the Klan, and to reveal its atrocities, but they shrewdly took advantage of the opportunity to read into the record the incompetence of Negro voters, the excesses of the carpetbaggers, the misconduct of Federal soldiers, and the generally deplor-

[1] These laws, which gave the United States government control over state and congressional elections, were made use of, not only in the South, but also in the northern cities, to restrain the tendency of immigrants to vote the Democratic ticket. They were repealed in part during the Hayes administration and in full under Cleveland.

The Ku Klux Klan, which terrorized many Negro and carpetbag voters, tended to help the Democrats, and to threaten Republican control of the South. The organization itself was bad enough, but thanks to the anonymity it encouraged, many unauthorized crimes were committed in its name.

TERRORISM. Klan members stealing a victim's crop. Woodcut, 1880.

POLITICAL SIGNIFICANCE. Antidemocratic cartoon branding the ticket with KKK initials, appeared in *Harper's Weekly*, 1868.

MURDER. A common practice of the Klan. Wood engraving of the contemplated murder of John Campbell, 1871.

'TIS BUT A CHANGE OF BANNERS.

able conditions that Radical reconstruction had wrought. Their testimony, published in northern as well as southern newspapers, and ultimately set forth in twelve large volumes of congressional documents, brought home for the first time to many Northerners the disabilities under which the South was laboring. Southerners, likewise, were impressed with the sum total of Ku Klux violence, and realized the necessity of using less dubious methods if ever their efforts to rid themselves of alien rule were to succeed.

Ultimately the attempts of Grant and the Radicals to maintain Republican majorities in the South came to nought. Southerners, bent on the restoration of home rule in the South, learned to stop short of violence in their efforts to restrain the Negroes from the exercise of their newly acquired political rights, but they often found more peaceable means quite as potent. Also, the pressure of northern opinion for greater leniency toward the South forced Congress to pass an Amnesty Act, in May, 1872, that reduced the number of ex-Confederates excluded from the suffrage to about five hundred. Gradually, in state after state, Democratic majorities took over the administration of government, carpetbaggers were expelled, and great numbers of Negroes ceased to vote. The chief legacy of reconstruction, from the party point of view, was the emergence of the "Solid South." Thereafter a vast ma-

Emergence of the "Solid South"

jority of the southern whites, scalawags along with the rest, felt obliged, regardless of important political differences, to stand together as members of the Democratic, or "white man's," Party. Thus Radical reconstruction, instead of producing a solidly Republican South, as had been intended, produced instead a solidly Democratic South.

By the year 1872 the opponents of Radical reconstruction within the Republican Party **Liberal Republicanism** itself had come to be embarrassingly numerous, and to have a name. As "Liberals," or "Liberal Republicans," they stood ready to leave the party, if necessary, in order to prevent the further punishment of the South. This movement for reform started in Missouri, as an effort to get rid of some of the unreasonably vindictive provisions that a state constitution, adopted in 1865, had aimed at all citizens who had been southern sympathizers. Such persons were not only denied the right to vote and to hold office, but they might not so much as act as trustees, practice law, teach, preach, or solemnize marriages. By 1870 the animosities that the war had bred had died down to the point where amendments to remove these disabilities could be submitted for ratification, but the Radical ring that ruled the state, fearful that their adoption might drive it from power, determined on their defeat. This led to a split in the party, with the Liberals supporting the amendments and a ticket of their own, headed by B. Gratz Brown for governor. In the election, with the aid of such Democrats as were permitted to vote, the Liberal ticket won and the amendments were adopted. Schurz, an outstanding Liberal, was already a member of the United States Senate.

The spirit of revolt that had thus manifested itself in Missouri soon became national in scope, and swept into **Opposition to "Grantism"** its ranks many prominent citizens, among them Horace Greeley, who brought to the movement the powerful support of the *New York Tribune*.

Opposition to "Grantism" went much farther with some Liberals than mere denunciation of the southern policy. Grant's administration of the civil service, and the excesses of the spoils system generally, led to his denunciation by most of those who hoped for a day when appointments would be made on merit. Tariff reformers within the Republican Party, of whom there were many, particularly in the West, likewise found little consolation in the Grant régime. When the Radicals, in spite of this growing volume of criticism, made known their determination to bring about the President's renomination, a split in the party became inevitable. Finally the Missouri Liberals took matters into their own hands, and called a national convention of all who shared their views to meet in Cincinnati, May 1, 1872.

The Cincinnati Convention turned out to be a comedy of errors. It could, and did, condemn the administration **The Liberals nominate Greeley** heartily on every aspect of its southern policy, and it could even agree to the inclusion in its platform of a demand for civil service reform. But on the matter of the tariff, which so many Liberals wished to see lowered, the convention collided with the views of Horace Greeley, who threatened to desert the cause if a low tariff plank were adopted. The platform committee therefore determined upon an undignified evasion, and voted to refer the tariff question to the people in their congressional districts, and to Congress. This was bad enough, for the Liberals intended to seek Democratic support for their ticket, and the historic position of the Democratic Party favored a low tariff. But the crowning calamity came with the naming of a presidential candidate. The longest-headed of the Liberal leaders wished to nominate Charles Francis Adams, the distinguished son of one President and grandson of another, who had so ably represented his country as Minister to England during the war. But Adams suffered acutely from an oversupply of New England frigidity; Greeley wanted the place for himself; Justice

David Davis of the United States Supreme Court, already the candidate of a National Labor Reform Convention, was equally determined to have it; Chief Justice Chase, as ever, was ready and willing; and numerous minor candidates, such as Governor B. Gratz Brown of Missouri and Senator Lyman Trumbull of Illinois, had their adherents. In spite of the best efforts of Schurz, who presided over the convention, and to the dismay of most of the leaders, a "stampede" to Greeley gave the New York editor the nomination he so much craved. For second place on the ticket, B. Gratz Brown was chosen.

Could the Democratic Party support such a ticket? If not, the Liberals had no chance whatever to win. Greeley had been anti-slavery and anti-southern before the war, and had been an ardent Republican from the time the party was founded. After the war,

The South supports Greeley

however, he had endeared himself to Southerners by signing the bail-bond of Jefferson Davis when, in 1867, the Confederate ex-President was being held under an indictment for treason. Davis, it turned out, was never brought to trial, and Greeley's part in freeing him was not forgotten. This fact, together with the telling attacks of the *Tribune* on the Radical program, made the New York editor far more palatable to the South than might have been expected, and northern Democrats had little choice but to forgive and forget. When the Democratic Convention met, it accepted both the ticket and the platform.

In the campaign that followed the Liberal-Democratic coalition proved to be no match for the realistic Radicals. The latter saw to it that in the South the administration tightened up on its prosecutions of southern violators of the Ku Klux Act, so that on election day the intimidation of Negro voters could be held at a minimum. With the Union League hard at work to get out the full Republican vote, the Negroes came to the polls in sufficient numbers to carry for Grant all of the lately reconstructed states except Georgia and Texas. In the North appeals to party loyalty and to patriotism — "vote as you fought" — were ably reinforced by ridicule of the Liberal ticket and platform. Thomas Nast, the cartoonist, heaped insults upon the eccentric Greeley, whose moon-shaped, bespectacled face, surrounded by a ludicrous border of beard, made him a veritable cartoonist's delight. George William Curtis of *Harper's Weekly*, still suffering from the delusion that Grant meant business about civil service reform, not only printed Nast's cartoons, but also editorialized in similar vein. Greeley toured the country, an unusual procedure then for a presidential candidate, and did what he could to spread the gospel of better understanding between North and South. But he never had a chance. In addition to Georgia and Texas, Greeley carried four border states, Missouri, Tennessee, Maryland, and Kentucky, but Grant won all the

Election of 1872

"Emergence of the Solid South." Nast proclaims the Solid South is "here to stay" in *Harper's Weekly*, April 19, 1879.

Horace Greeley is shown here rejoicing in the news of his nomination by the Chicago Democratic Convention. "A Philosopher in Ecstasy. By George! I've got it!" Currier and Ives lithograph, 1872.

rest. Worn out by the strenuous campaign he had made, deeply disappointed at its result, and saddened by the death of his wife, Greeley fell ill and died three weeks after his defeat.

Most of the scandals that are associated with the Grant administration occurred **The "gold** during the second term, but an **conspiracy"** unsavory beginning was made in the first term. The infamous "gold conspiracy," engineered in 1869 by two speculators, Jay Gould and James Fisk, was actually accomplished with the effective, although unintended, assistance of the President himself. While gold did not then circulate as money, it was constantly in demand for such needs as the payment of customs duties and the adjustment of international trade balances. The government of the United States, although not on the gold standard, constantly received large quantities of gold into the Treasury, and from time to time the Secretary of the Treasury was accustomed to sell enough gold to satisfy the normal demands of trade. It occurred to Gould, who already controlled large stores of gold, that if the government would only stop its sales of gold

for a while he might "corner" the country's supply, drive the price to a fancy figure, and so make a huge profit. Gould therefore managed, through one of Grant's numerous brood of unsavory relatives, to meet the President from time to time, and even to win his confidence. On one such occasion he set forth at length a fine-spun theory to the effect that it would be a great help for western farm prices if the government should cease its sales of gold. Grant naïvely fell for this talk, and presently, even before the order had been given, Gould learned through his confederate, Grant's relative, that the President was about to stop the Treasury from selling gold. Immediately Gould began his activities, but, finding his own resources inadequate for the undertaking, he invited into the speculation his ally, Fisk, who not only bought heavily, but, in order to induce others to buy, spread the false story that the President himself and all his political friends were in on the deal. Between Monday, September 20, and "Black Friday," September 24, the price of gold rose from 140 to $163\frac{1}{2}$. Then the Secretary of the Treasury, under emergency orders from the President, announced the sale of

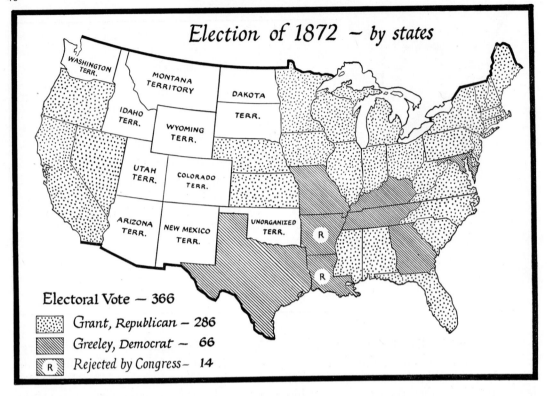

Election of 1872 — by states

WASHINGTON TERR.

MONTANA TERRITORY

IDAHO TERR.

DAKOTA TERR.

WYOMING TERR.

UTAH TERR.

COLORADO TERR.

ARIZONA TERR.

NEW MEXICO TERR.

UNORGANIZED TERR.

R

R

Electoral Vote — 366

Grant, Republican — 286

Greeley, Democrat — 66

R Rejected by Congress — 14

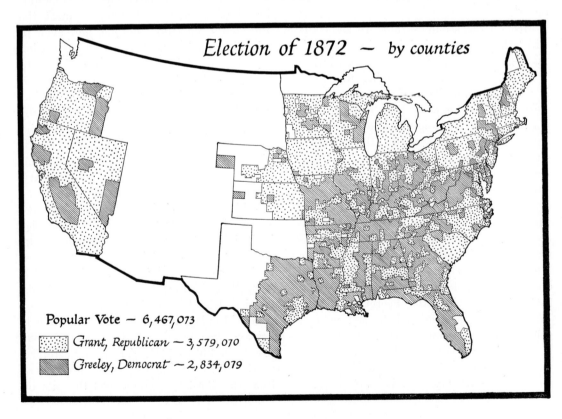

Election of 1872 — by counties

Popular Vote — 6,467,073

Grant, Republican — 3,579,070

Greeley, Democrat — 2,834,079

government gold, and the price came down. In the meantime, however, many legitimate businesses had been disastrously affected, and the stock exchange had experienced a violent panic. The investigation of the whole matter by Congress exonerated the President from any intentional wrongdoing, but his bad judgment was hard to explain away.

In 1872 came the revelation of another precious scandal which, while it had oc-

The Crédit Mobilier curred before Grant took office, nevertheless touched closely many of the men who were associated with his administration. The Crédit Mobilier was a joint-stock company, organized in Pennsylvania ostensibly for the purpose of assisting in the building of the Union Pacific Railroad. Its real purpose, however, was to enable a few of the Union Pacific stockholders, who were also stockholders in the Crédit Mobilier, to drain off huge profits from construction contracts. Inasmuch as the funds of the Union Pacific came in considerable part from a subsidy granted by Congress, it was deemed wise to forestall trouble from that quarter by offering blocks of Crédit Mobilier stock to members of Congress at a generous discount, and on the understanding that the purchase price need not be paid until earned by profits from the stocks. The agent of the Crédit Mobilier in this brazen attempt to buy good-will was Oakes Ames, a congressman from Massachusetts, who was able to induce such prominent politicians as Vice-President Schuyler Colfax, Senator James W. Patterson of New Hampshire, and Representative James Brooks of New York to accept the favors he offered. Many others were involved, some quite innocently, some not so clearly so. A congressional investigation got well toward the bottom of the matter, and a number of individuals, including all those mentioned, had their reputations badly smirched. In general, the frank admission of speculation in Crédit Mobilier stock was regarded by the public as far less reprehensible than any attempt at concealment.

During Grant's second administration one unpalatable revelation succeeded another with disheartening regularity. **The "Salary Grab" Act** The Forty-Second Congress, on the day before its final adjournment in March, 1873, voted to increase the salaries of Senators and Representatives from $5000 a year to $7500 a year, with back pay for two years. This "Salary Grab" Act was mainly the work of Benjamin F. Butler of Massachusetts, who aspired to fill the position of leadership in the House left vacant by the death of Stevens, and who in fact had far more influence than was good for Congress or the country. The measure drew such hearty public criticism that it was repealed by the next Congress, and many of those who accepted the back pay were speedily retired from public life by the voters.

In May, 1874, the House Ways and Means Committee brought to light a scandal in the Treasury Department. It ap- **The Sanborn contract** peared that one John D. Sanborn, under contract with the department, had collected some $427,000 of overdue revenue, and had received for his services a commission of fifty per cent. This fact in itself was bad enough, and was even of doubtful legality; but Sanborn, as everyone in politics knew, was only the political henchman of the notorious Ben Butler. When Sanborn swore that he paid most of his earnings to his assistants, the public was not slow to conclude that the money was really used to maintain Butler's political machine. William A. Richardson, Grant's second Secretary of the Treasury, resigned to escape the formal censure of Congress for allowing the contracts.

Before another year was up Grant's third Secretary of the Treasury, Benjamin H. Bristow, had uncovered a **The "Whiskey Ring"** composed of revenue officers and distillers who made a business of defrauding the government out of a part of its excise on liquor. Grant at first seemed sympathetic, and commanded, "Let no guilty man escape!"

The Grant scandals were the worst the national government had ever known. For them some blamed the inexperience of a non-political President, but others saw in Grant a man of integrity behind whom venal politicians tried to hide. Undoubtedly the spoils system bore much responsibility for the prevalence of corruption, but neither party took much interest in civil service reform.

THE NOMINATION. General John A. Logan nominates Grant at the National Union Republican Convention, Chicago, May 20, 1868. From a sketch by James E. Taylor for *Leslie's Illustrated Newspaper*, 1868.

SCANDAL. Cartoon of Grant scolding Belknap when graft in the Indian service was revealed. Engraving, 1876.

THE SCAPEGOAT. Nast depicts Grant as the scapegoat for his party's failure — Congressional blunders, hard times, fraud. From *Harper's Weekly*, 1876.

"OUR MODERN BELSHAZZAR." British criticism of political corruption in Grant's régime. Roscoe Conkling pouring. Cartoon by Matt Morgan, from *Leslie's Illustrated Newspaper*, 1872.

CIVIL SERVICE REFORM. Grant: "Both parties say they love it. But——." Thomas Nast's cartoon for *Harper's Weekly*, 1875, on success of reform efforts.

But when the scandal involved John Mc-Donald, a prominent Missouri Republican from whom Grant had received marked favors, and even Grant's private secretary, General Orville E. Babcock, the President's attitude underwent a change. He actually helped his guilty secretary to escape, rewarded him with another office, and seemed somehow to blame Bristow for stirring up so much trouble. Finally, in the summer of 1876, Bristow, in disgust, resigned, and the President paid him no compliments.

Already another major scandal had broken, this time out of the Indian country, **Graft in** where graft at the expense of **the Indian** the red men and the govern-**service** ment had become the rule rather than the exception. A House committee found that William W. Belknap, Grant's current Secretary of War, was deeply involved. Belknap in 1869 was an obscure collector of revenue out in Iowa, but because of a favor he had done for one of Grant's relatives the President, following the death that year of Secretary Rawlins, had brought him into the cabinet. It now developed that Belknap, as the price of keeping in office a post-trader at Fort Sill, in the Indian Territory, had since 1870 received annual payments, through his wife as intermediary, amounting in all to $24,450. The House by a unanimous vote promptly brought impeachment charges against him, and the Senate refused to convict only because Grant, in the meantime, had accepted Belknap's resignation, and by so doing, according to many senators, had placed the offender outside the jurisdiction of the Senate.

It is a relief, after this sordid recital, to turn to the foreign policy of the Grant **Grant's for-** administration, which, while in **eign policy** part misguided, was in the main highly creditable. The misguided part was almost wholly the fault of Grant himself, who became obsessed with the strange desire to add the republic of Santo Domingo to the United States. A few Americans, hoping to profit from speculative investments on the island, doubtless connived at this end, and the Dominican government, what there was of it, was ready to accept annexation as preferable to the revolution it might normally expect at any time. Ignoring his State Department, Grant sent his private secretary, General Babcock, to investigate conditions in Santo Domingo, and on receiving a favorable report authorized Babcock to negotiate a treaty of annexation. This was done, and Grant immediately began to exert every effort to secure its ratification. In spite of the President's pressure, the Senate refused to concur unless another investigation should be made, and after the second investigation it still refused. Charles Sumner, chairman since 1861 of the Senate Committee on Foreign Relations, led the fight against the treaty, and won the undying enmity of Grant, who succeeded in having Sumner's chairmanship taken away from him, but not in obtaining ratification of the treaty.

Probably the most creditable performance of the Grant administration was the settlement of all outstanding diplo- **The Fenian** matic differences between the **movement** United States and Great Britain. The most serious of these troubles came from the lax interpretation of neutral duties that, to the great grief of northern shipping interests, had characterized British policy during the Civil War. It soon became apparent that a similar laxity on the part of the United States could be equally unpleasant to the British. In 1866 the Fenian Brotherhood, an organization composed mainly of Irish-Americans who were interested in securing freedom for Ireland, planned as a part of its program an invasion of Canada from the soil of the United States. Recruiting went on openly and actively, and many veterans of the Civil War, including some who were not Irish but were enthusiastically anti-British, agreed to serve. Troops and supplies were concentrated along the Canadian border, and although American authorities seized most of the supplies, several hundred Fenian soldiers actually crossed into Canada, captured Fort

Erie, fought a battle with some Canadian volunteers, and retreated to the United States. Although Johnson acted somewhat belatedly, he properly denounced the whole scheme in a presidential proclamation, and sent General Meade, with a detachment of the United States Army, to prevent any further misconduct by the Fenians. When the British government raised the question of compensation by the United States for the damage the Fenian invaders had done, however, the American government was not impressed. Several years later President Grant nipped in the bud another Fenian project for the invasion of Canada.

Whether because of the Fenian incidents or not, the British government showed an **The Ala-** increasing disposition to accept **bama claims** responsibility for the depredations of the *Alabama*, and such other Confederate cruisers as had operated from British ports during the war. In 1869 Reverdy Johnson, Adams's successor as Minister to England, negotiated a "convention" with Lord Clarendon to submit the *Alabama* claims to arbitration, but early in Grant's administration the agreement was rejected by the United States Senate, 54 to 1. Charles Sumner, in opposing ratification, argued that the unneutral conduct of Great Britain had prolonged the war by two years, and that the United States was therefore entitled to damages amounting to half the cost of the war, or approximately two billion dollars. He even had the temerity to suggest that Great Britain, in lieu of cash, should turn over Canada to the United States. This ended, for the moment, all possibility of agreement, but Grant's Secretary of State, Hamilton Fish, worked tactfully toward a settlement, and representatives of the two countries at length affixed their signatures to the Treaty of Washington (1871), which provided the means for its achievement. In the treaty the British government definitely expressed its regret for the "escape" of the Confederate cruisers, accepted as binding a set of rules that amounted to a clear confession of unneutral action, and agreed to submit the matter of damages to an arbitration tribunal of five, one each to be chosen by the United States, Great Britain, Italy, Brazil, and Switzerland. Meeting at Geneva the *Alabama* Tribunal, as it was often called, awarded the United States damages of $15,500,000, a sum so large as to arouse indignant protests in England. Nevertheless, full payment was made, and the United States did the best it could to reimburse the individuals who had suffered the losses.

The Treaty of Washington arranged also for the settlement of several other disputes between the two coun- **Minor** tries. One had to do with the **disputes** claims of British subjects for damages they had suffered from the United States during the Civil War, such, for example, as the destruction of British-owned cotton, and the illegal detention or capture of British merchantmen. This subject also was referred to an arbitration commission, which assessed damages of nearly $2,000,000 against the United States. Another problem that claimed attention was the perennial disagreement over the North-Atlantic fisheries. A satisfactory *modus vivendi* was worked out, but the British negotiators held that the privileges granted Americans were more generous than those granted the subjects of Great Britain. To settle this matter another commission was created, which encountered many difficulties, but ultimately, in 1877, ordered the United States to pay Great Britain $5,500,000 in gold for the advantages its citizens enjoyed. Still another problem considered in the treaty had to do with the exact boundary between the United States and British Columbia in Puget Sound. The German Emperor, to whom this dispute was referred for settlement, decided in favor of the United States, and so cleared the American title to the island of San Juan and several lesser islands.

The numerous settlements reached under the terms of the Treaty of Washington emphasized once more to the two English-speaking nations, and for that matter to many others, the advantage of peaceful over warlike methods in adjusting international disputes. For the third time, once soon after the War of 1812, once in the forties under the leadership of Webster and Ashburton, and now once again during the seventies, Great Britain and the United States had made differences of far greater consequence than those which often resulted in war the subjects of successful negotiation. Such a succession of precedents, as subsequent events have proved, could not easily be broken.

Bibliography

The surface facts concerning the campaign of 1868 and subsequent presidential campaigns are set forth in Edward Stanwood, *A History of the Presidency* (2 vols., new edition, 1928); and with pictorial embellishments in Stefan Lorant, *The Presidency: A Pictorial History of Presidential Elections from Washington to Truman* (1951). See also, C. H. Coleman, *The Election of 1868* (1933). On the money question in this campaign, see M. S. Wildman, *Money Inflation in the United States* (1905); W. C. Mitchell, *History of the Greenbacks* (1903); and H. R. Ferleger, *David A. Wells and the American Revenue System, 1865–1870* (1942). A. B. Hart, *Salmon Portland Chase* (1899), is inadequate, but still the best biography of Chase available. See also Mary M. Phelps, *Kate Chase, Dominant Daughter; The Life Story of a Brilliant Woman and Her Famous Father* (1935), and Hugh McCulloch, *Men and Measures of a Half Century; Sketches and Comments* (1888).

W. B. Hesseltine, *Ulysses S. Grant, Politician* (1935), traces with a sure hand the progress of Grant's political career. L. A. Coolidge, *Ulysses S. Grant* (1917), and Helen Todd, *A Man Named Grant* (1940), are also useful; but W. E. Woodward, *Meet General Grant* (1928), is more interesting than important. Lloyd Lewis, *Captain Sam Grant* (1950), is an excellent study of Grant's earlier career. See also Bruce Catton, *U. S. Grant and the American Military Tradition* (1954).

On the Ku Klux Klan, see J. C. Lester and D. L. Wilson, *Ku Klux Klan, Its Origin, Growth and Disbandment* (new ed., 1905); Susan L. Davis, *Authentic History, Ku Klux Klan, 1865–1877* (1924); W. G. Brown, *The Lower South in American History* (1902); W. A. Sinclair, *The Aftermath of Slavery* (1905); S. F. Horn, *Invisible Empire; The Story of the Ku Klux Klan, 1866–1871* (1939).

The revolt against Grantism is competently traced in E. D. Ross, *The Liberal Republican Movement* (1919); and T. S. Barclay, *The Liberal Republican Movement in Missouri, 1865–1871* (1926). Greeley's part is told in Henry L. Stoddard, *Horace Greeley, Printer, Editor, Crusader* (1946), an interesting journalistic account. Horace Greeley, *Recollections of a Busy Life* (1868), is excellent as a basis for character evaluation. J. B. Crawford, *The Crédit Mobilier of America* (1880), is an early study of one of the worst of the Grant scandals.

On the subject of diplomacy during the Grant administration, Allan Nevins, *Hamilton Fish; The Inner History of the Grant Administration* (1936), is best. Sumner Welles, *Naboth's Vineyard* (2 vols., 1928), covers American diplomatic ambitions in Santo Domingo. The settlement of post-Civil War differences with Great Britain is best treated in E. D. Adams, *Great Britain and the American Civil War* (2 vols., 1925); but in this connection C. F. Adams, *Charles Francis Adams* (1900), is also useful. See also *The American Secretaries of State and Their Diplomacy*, edited by S. F. Bemis (10 vols., 1927–29), VII, 165 ff. The articles in this series are of unequal merit, but the work as a whole is the most complete study of American diplomacy yet undertaken. On all subjects connected with American diplomacy satisfactory accounts can be found in the two outstanding textbooks on the subject, S. F. Bemis, *A Diplomatic History of the United States* (3d ed., 1950); and T. A. Bailey, *A Diplomatic History of the American People* (4th ed., 1950).

4

The Last Frontier

The Far West — California prospectors — Mining booms — Colorado — Nevada — The Northwest — The Southwest — Staging and freighting — Evolution of law and order — The Indian wars — The new Indian policy — The killing of the buffalo — The "sod-house" frontier — The range cattle industry — The passing of the cattleman

THE exciting events of the Civil War and reconstruction served somewhat to obscure **The Far West** the importance of what was happening far out on the western frontier. Americans were accustomed to an advancing frontier — there had always been one; but this last American frontier differed markedly from all the rest. As Professor Webb so aptly points out, civilization east of the Mississippi proceeded comfortably into the West on three legs — land, water, and timber. But beyond the Mississippi on the Great Plains, two of these legs, water and timber, gave out, and thereafter civilization limped along as best it could on only one leg — land. This newest West was a frontier of miners and cattlemen as well as of farmers, a frontier where mounted Indians fought desperately and sometimes successfully to hold back the tide of white invasion. Moreover, it was all that was left of the area within the national boundaries for civilization to conquer. The end of the frontier process, which from the beginning had been a kind of common denominator of American history, was in sight.

Within a few years after the "forty-niners" had invaded California, they and **California prospectors** their successors had exhausted practically all of the free gold that that region had to offer. California mining then became a capitalistic enterprise;

expensive machinery was required to do the work that formerly anyone with a shovel and a "washpan" felt himself adequately equipped to do. As this situation unfolded, some of the adventurers turned to agriculture for a livelihood, others went back to the "States," and still others became "prospectors," men who searched the mountains for signs of gold, and sometimes made a "strike." These prospectors went everywhere, for gold had a way of appearing in the most unlikely places. Not content with having prospected every bleak plateau and every hidden valley of the Rocky Mountains, they found their way to such distant regions as South Africa and Australia, and there, too, they discovered gold. Only rarely did one of them acquire wealth, but thanks to their efforts the world's supply of gold was soon to be doubled.

The Pike's Peak gold rush, which occurred just a decade after the rush to California, laid the basis of Colorado. As **Colorado** compared with the forty-niners, the fifty-niners had an easy time of it. Those who came from the East had less than half as far to go, they had no mountains to cross, and the trail they followed was well supplied with ferries, merchants, and even stagecoaches. Denver arrived full-grown almost overnight, and within a matter of weeks other mining camps in the "hills," such as

Central City and Idaho Springs, achieved sizable proportions. Horace Greeley, of the *New York Tribune*, who went out merely to see what a gold rush was like, vividly described one of these early camps:

As yet the entire population of the valley sleeps in tents or under booths of pine boughs, cooking and eating in the open air. I doubt that there is ... a table or chair in these diggings, eating being done on a cloth spread on the ground, while each one sits or reclines on mother earth.

Far sooner than in California the free gold of Colorado gave out, and for a time it even seemed as if no permanent settlement might result. Covered wagons that had gone west displaying the hopeful legend, "Pike's Peak or Bust," returned east by the same route with the label changed to read, "Busted, by gosh." Some, however, stayed on, as in California, to farm; as early as the summer of 1859 radishes, lettuce, onions, and peas brought high prices on the Denver market. Native grasses were cut for hay; claims were staked out and claims clubs formed; irrigation, after the manner of the Mormons in Utah, was introduced. Soon capitalistic mining replaced the crude efforts of the first comers, and such "valley" towns as Golden, Colorado City, and Pueblo showed sure signs of permanence. Efforts to follow the example of California in making a new state without going through the customary territorial stage came to nought, although an unauthorized Territory of Jefferson existed for a few months. In 1861 Congress made Colorado a territory, and a few years later, in order to obtain more Unionist senators and representatives in Washington, would have admitted it as a state. This offer, however, was wisely declined, for as late as 1870 the population of Colorado was only 40,000. Admission as the "Centennial State" came finally in 1876. Shortly afterward the exploitation of silver mines around Leadville inaugurated an era of prosperity that the region had not known before.

While the rest of the country resounded

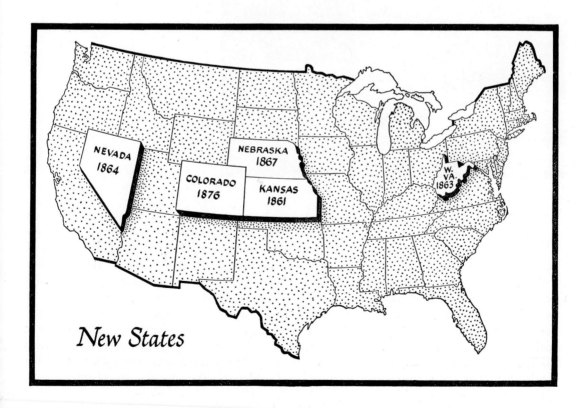

New States

CORDUROY ROAD. A hazardous mountain route to mines at Leadville, Colorado. Engraving by E. Jump, 1879.

The mining frontier contrasted markedly with the earlier agricultural frontiers. Absorbed in the acquisition of gold, it was largely indifferent to the amenities of civilization, had little place for women, and struggled with the most baffling problems of transportation.

A BILLIARD SALOON. "Two-bit" sleeping accommodations in the mining country. From a sketch by E. Jump.

GOLD MINING. Scene in a California mining camp. Currier & Ives lithograph, 1871.

Nevada to the din of Civil War, the mineral empire of the West expanded with unconcerned rapidity. Close on the heels of the Pike's Peak gold rush came a similar rush to the western part of what is now Nevada, where gold had been discovered along the main trail to California. The famous Comstock Lode, discovered in the spring of 1859, brought in no less than fifteen million dollars' worth of gold and silver in a single year. Located in the heart of a desert, a less auspicious place for the development of a new area of settlement could hardly have been imagined, but such was the richness of the mines that adventurers by the thousand flocked in from California and Oregon to the West, as well as from the settled regions of the East. Such towns as Carson City and Virginia City fantastically flaunted their wealth in the face of a desert where water was almost as dear as the other liquid refreshments the miners so liberally con-

BANKING HOUSES. Miners bringing gold dust for weighing to C. A. Cook & Co., bankers. Theodore R. Davis, for *Harper's Weekly.*

MARRIED MUM? NO SIR!

WOMEN ON THE FRONTIER. One of the scarcer and more highly prized imports from the East.

sumed. In 1861 Congress made Nevada a territory, and three years later, with a population probably greater than it possessed in later years, Nevada accepted the same hasty offer of statehood that Colorado rejected. Unlike most of the mining regions, the opportunities for agriculture in Nevada were negligible, and the prosperity of the new state was limited almost exclusively to the exploitation of its mineral resources.

After the opening of Nevada, mining booms came thick and fast. In the vicinity

Mining booms in the Northwest of Lewiston, Idaho, then a part of Washington Territory, gold was found in 1860, and next year the inevitable boom occurred. As news of new strikes came in, the miners rushed from place to place founding, as they went,

such permanent settlements as Florence and Boise City, but leaving often as suddenly as they had come. "The Idaho miners," said H. H. Bancroft, "were like quicksilver. A mass of them dropped in any locality, broke up into individual globules, and ran off after any atom of gold in their vicinity. They stayed nowhere longer than the gold attracted them." In 1863 the Territory of Idaho was created, but by that time the miners had crossed the Bitter Root Mountains to lay the foundations of Montana. Such mining centers as Bannack City, Virginia City, Deer Lodge, and Missoula not only drew population away from the farther western camps, but also attracted newcomers from the East, many of whom came up the Missouri River to Fort Benton, which in high water could be reached by steam-boats. Among those who came were a number of refugees from the guerrilla war-fare that raged along the Kansas-Missouri border during the Civil War, and others who preferred the hazards of the mines to the prospect of being drafted into the army. In 1864 Montana was separated from Idaho as an independent territory.

During this same period the Far South-west, too, had its mining booms. The min-**The Far Southwest** eral resources of New Mexico, twin territory with Utah, had long been known, but the Spanish-Mexican population, located mainly in the upper Rio Grande Valley, subsisted upon agriculture and ignored the mines. The Americans, however, reopened the ancient diggings near Tucson and Tubac, and found placer gold in considerable quantities in the valley of the lower Colorado. When in 1862 Colonel James H. Carleton attempted to lead a col-umn of eighteen hundred Californian vol-unteers to the aid of the Union forces in New Mexico, he was plagued by desertions to what he described as "one of the richest gold countries in the world." Thus another mining boom got under way, and in 1863 Congress, as usual, obliged by creating out of the western half of New Mexico the new Territory of Arizona.

The prosperity of these new mountain territories varied markedly in the years that followed the war. As long as the Comstock Lode continued to yield up its riches, Nevada fared best, but by 1880 this magnificent deposit had been worked out, and the desert cities faded as rapidly as they had bloomed. Stocks in Nevada mines valued at $393,000,-000 in 1875 could be bought five years later for $7,000,000. The fate of the mines in Colorado, where the quartz lodes could be reached and reduced only with the aid of heavy financial outlays, fluctuated according to the availability of capital and the intelli-gence with which it was utilized. In Idaho and Montana the fortune hunters of 1866 numbered probably thirty and forty thou-sand respectively, but the census of 1870 found that only half that many had seen fit to remain. A dozen years later, the opening of rich copper mines near Butte, Montana, ushered in an era of unprecedented pros-perity for that region which the exploitation of other base metals, such as lead and zinc, handsomely reinforced. Ultimately the world's largest copper smelters were to be located at Anaconda, Montana. In the Southwest the exhaustion of placer gold brought the Civil War boom to a quick con-clusion, and, in the years that followed, the warlike nature of the Apache Indians tended to discourage even the prospectors. Here, as in Montana, copper presently became a more important product than gold. None of the other mountain territories achieved the prosperity that came to Utah, where the Mormon leader, Brigham Young, urged the saints to eschew mining and devote them-selves to agriculture. Indeed, hard as was the lot of the farmer in these regions of in-adequate rainfall, Indian raids, and grass-hopper plagues, the prosperity of any ter-ritory could almost be measured by the number of its inhabitants who forsook the mines for the farms.

Social conditions on the mining frontier differed little from place to place. Most mining towns consisted of a **The mining** single long crooked street that **towns** followed, and occasionally crossed, a moun-tain stream. Horses hitched along the street testified to the almost universal de-pendence upon horseback means of com-munication, and no other criminal was so utterly despised or so certainly punished as the horse-thief. Most of the houses were hastily improvised, one-roomed, one-storied structures, the kind that frequently appear near city dump heaps. Invariably the most pretentious buildings were occupied by saloons and gambling-houses, to which the men turned for amusement after the hard and lonely labor of the mines. Few women reached the early mining camps, and those who came were usually of easy virtue. Drunkenness and debauchery were too common to attract much notice, and for a long time individual vengeance provided almost the only punishment that was meted out for crime. Medical help for the sick and injured was of the crudest sort, or, more likely, was altogether missing, and the death rate was high. The romance of the mines, so dear to the heart of the fictionist, was built on the slenderest possible basis of fact.

The business of supplying the mining camps with the necessities of life and of Staging and transporting to the East the freighting product of the mines soon reached formidable proportions. Stage-coaches and freight-wagons made their appearance on the western plains during the fifties, and by the time the Civil War ended there were few places too remote for them to reach. As early as 1857, when the United States government asked for bids to carry the mail to California, there was no dearth of plains express companies ready to do the work. The contract went to John Butterfield, whose "Overland Mail" operated until 1861 along the southern route, and thereafter by the central route. During the years 1860–61 the firm of Russell, Majors, and Waddell, without a government subsidy, relayed light mail by "pony express" from St. Joseph, Missouri, to Sacramento, California, in less than two weeks. The pony express and the company that backed it were put out of business by the completion of a telegraph line to the Pacific in 1861, but stage-coach connections, with the aid of generous mail contracts, continued to be multiplied so that by 1866 Ben Holladay, into whose monopolistic grasp most of the western routes had fallen, could claim a total of five thousand miles of stage-lines. That same year Holladay sold out to Wells, Fargo, and Company.

Travel by western stage was an experience not to be forgotten. The stage itself, with its high, heavy wheels, its wide, thick tires, and its sturdy leather thorough-braces instead of springs, was no western invention, but rather the product of centuries of experience. It was equipped with three inside seats for passengers, an outside front seat for the driver, and a rear container for baggage. Painted a bright red or green, and drawn by two or more teams of horses, it bowled along the prairies, forded bridgeless streams, ignored wind, sand, and dirt. Dangers abounded from the charges of angry buffaloes, from attacks by hostile Indians, from robberies in a region that long knew no law. Passage through these hazards from the Mississippi to the Pacific cost about two hundred dollars, with corresponding charges for shorter distances. One articulate traveler, a certain Demas Barnes, who took the stage to Denver in 1865, described his trip as follows:

It is not a *pleasant*, but it is an *interesting* trip. The conditions of one man's running stages to make money, while another seeks to ride in them for pleasure, are not in harmony to produce comfort. Coaches will be overloaded, it will rain, the dust will drive, baggage will be left to the storm, passengers will get sick, a gentleman of gallantry will hold the baby, children will cry, nature demands sleep, passengers will get angry, the drivers will swear, the sensitive will shrink, rations will give out, potatoes become worth a gold dollar each, and not to be had at that, the water brackish, the whiskey abominable, and the dirt almost unendurable. I have just finished six days and nights of this thing; and I am free to say, until I forget a great many things now visible to me, I shall not undertake it again.[1]

Freighting on the western plains was no less important than staging. Little of this went through to the Pacific coast, for water transportation served that purpose better, but the great interior region opened up by the mines was served, for the most part, by slow-moving freight-wagons, drawn by ox teams from such Missouri River towns as Independence, Leavenworth, Nebraska City, and Omaha. After the building of the Union Pacific the freight-wagons, and the stages also, took off into the interior from such railroad stations as lay nearest the desired destinations, but in any event huge freight

[1] D. E. Clark, *The West in American History* (1937), p. 517.

Western outlaws and gunmen such as Calamity Jane and Wild Bill Hickok were probably less numerous and less daring than legend portrays, but their activities, whether real or fancied, live on persistently in the movies.

charges had to be paid. According to a reliable estimate the total freight bill of the mountain towns for one year, 1866, was $31,000,000. High prices gave merchants a chance for long profits, and laid the basis for many pioneer fortunes, such, for example, as those amassed by the Creighton brothers of Omaha, and William A. Clark of Montana. Demas Barnes was much impressed with the freighting activities he witnessed:

The great feature of the Plains is the transportation trains, usually consisting of thirty to fifty wagons, five yoke each. . . . As they wind their slow course over the serpentine roads and undulating surface in the distance, a mile in extent (I saw one train five miles long), the effect is poetic, grand, beautiful. They select a high position for camping, draw the wagons in a circle, enclosing say a quarter, half, or full acre, the exterior serving as a fort, the inside as a camp, and a place wherein to drive the animals in case of danger, and to yoke or harness them for the next trip. One of these camps, seen at sundown, with night fires kindled, and from five hundred to a thousand head of animals feeding near by, is well worth a long visit to behold.

The traffic of the plains, particularly the cargoes of gold that the stage-coaches took out, led inevitably to many robberies. Gangs of "bad men," **Lawlessness** drawn together to live by their wits rather than by their labor, terrorized the stage-routes, and took a heavy toll, not only in gold but also in lives. The gang led by Henry Plummer of Montana during the sixties was guilty of over a hundred known murders and an untold number of robberies. In Montana, as in California, vigilantes, administering lynch law, finally put the disorderly elements of society out of business. One might note, indeed, four stages of development on any given mining frontier: (1) peaceful exploitation by the original prospectors; (2) the mining "boom," with its full quota of violence and crime; (3) the establishment of vigilance committees to punish the worst criminals and to introduce a reign of law; and (4) the creation of regular legal governments. In many instances, however, the third and fourth stages were reversed. Legal government in Montana, for example, preceded the work of the vigilantes; Plummer himself was a sheriff, and local government throughout the territory was in the hands of the "bad men" until the vigilantes broke their power.

In 1876, the last great mining boom of the West broke forth in the Black Hills region **The Black Hills** of southwestern Dakota Territory — a wild, barren region, long suspected of harboring gold. Deadwood, the principal city, lay in the heart of a wilderness, and depended for the necessities of life upon stage-coaches and freighters from Bismarck to the east and Cheyenne to the south. Bandits and Indians were plentiful, but Wells, Fargo, and Company carried out the gold in steel-lined, heavily guarded coaches that were not lightly attacked. In a single trip, July, 1877, $350,000 in gold was taken out, and before the stage-line surrendered its business to the railroad, the grand total of such shipments had reached $60,000,000.[1] Deadwood, as the chief supply station for the various mining camps near-by, built up a lively prosperity. Here, too, gathered a notable array of gamblers and outlaws, the backwash of all the mining booms; among them, "Wild Bill" Hickok, who shot from the hip and rarely missed his mark, and "Calamity Jane" Canary, a colossal sinner whose fame spread far and wide. Deadwood was more sophisticated than most of the early mining towns, and boasted, along with its gambling-houses and saloons, several theaters, particularly the *Gem*, which provided living quarters for its players, and produced numerous plays of merit. During one season, before street-carnivals, dance-halls, and bar-room singers put the theater out of business, the *Mikado* had a run of one hundred and thirty nights.

For all its seeming tumult, life in the mining camps was founded upon a sound **Evolution of law and order** substratum of common sense. Lawlessness eventually was curbed, and the normal in-

stitutions of government were evolved. Agriculture, even under the most adverse circumstances, was speedily introduced. Rule-of-thumb arrangements — such, for example, as those which enabled the discoverer of a mine to "stake out his claim," or the first farmer to use the waters of a given stream for irrigation purposes to have a "priority right" over all others — presently received the sanction of law. More women came in, and with them schools, churches, and the amenities of life. Frontier characteristics gradually gave way before the advance of civilization: the individualism of the early miners to the cooperative, capitalistic enterprises that were required to carry on their work; the actual democracy of the boom days to the astounding inequalities between those who "struck it rich," and those whose poverty endured; the radicalism of a new society to the conservatism of one that approached middle age. And yet, the social inheritance from the mining frontier could hardly be called negligible. Throughout the region first opened by the mines, the tendency to paint an overbright picture still reflects the chronic optimism of the prospector, and the ease with which the speculative spirit is fanned into a flame shows that the gambling instinct is not yet quite dead. Here, too, where unruly elements from all over the world broke the "cake of custom" most thoroughly, the old willingness to try anything new remains a hardy perennial. Widely separated from the rest of the country, and for a long time a law unto itself, the Far West retained for many decades a certain aloofness — it was a part of the United States, and yet at the same time apart from it. Californians long spoke, as the miners did before them, of going back to the "States."

Among the inevitable complications that resulted from the opening of the mining West was the necessity of developing a new Indian policy for **The Indians** the United States. The old policy of leaving the region west of the "bend of the Missouri" for the exclusive use of the Indians had broken down badly in the decade before the Civil War. Thousands of emigrants, crossing the plains to Oregon, to Santa Fe, to Utah, and to California, came into contact and often into conflict with the Indians. Demands for protection of the trails led to the establishment of army posts in the Indian country at such strategic centers as Fort Kearney and Fort Laramie, and to treaties between the United States and most of the Indian tribes, describing the tribal boundaries, and authorizing the government to build both roads and posts wherever it wished. While the Indians received annuities as compensation for the losses they sustained from the white intrusion, they found the new agreements far from satisfactory, and frequently forgot their promises not to molest the emigrants. The requirement of new cessions in Minnesota, in Iowa, in Kansas, and in Nebraska added still further to the unrest, both on the part of the tribes that had to find new homes, and on the part of those who had to make room for unwanted newcomers. Altogether, the time was ripe for trouble from the Indians when the Civil War broke out, while the combing of the mountains for gold that accompanied the conflict furnished still further cause for alarm.

In 1862 came the first uprising. The Sioux of Minnesota, reduced by land cessions **The Sioux** to a narrow and indefensible **outbreak in** reserve along the Minnesota **Minnesota** River, had long suffered from the dishonesty of traders and government agents. With the regular army garrisons withdrawn, and their places taken by unsuspecting volunteers, the Indians' temptation to seek revenge was great. Nevertheless, the trouble, when it came, was precipitated by the unauthorized action of a few irresponsible braves who on August 18, 1862, murdered five whites near New Ulm, Minnesota. The white population of the vicinity, sure that a general attack was impending, fled for their lives, while the Indians, no less frightened, divided into two groups, one of which made a hasty retreat to the west,

while the other under Little Crow, knowing that the whites would never forgive the murders, took the warpath, burning farmhouses and villages, and killing men, women, and children by the hundreds. In due time the Indians were met by overwhelming numbers of state militia, decisively defeated, and many of them captured. Of the captives some four hundred were tried by court-martial in St. Paul, and over three hundred were sentenced to death. All but thirty-eight of those sentenced were pardoned by President Lincoln, but these unfortunates paid the full penalty for their crime at a great hanging-bee, held at Mankato, Minnesota, the day after Christmas, 1862. Settlers came from far and near to witness the executions, which were made the more weird by the fact that the unhappy Indians during their imprisonment had been converted to Christianity, and had come to be known as the "praying Indians." In 1863 the remnants of the Sioux were harassed by an expedition into Minnesota and Dakota, and the entire Sioux holding in Minnesota was confiscated. Little Crow himself was killed in July, 1863, and his tanned scalp, his skull, and his wrist bones presently became prized exhibits of the Minnesota Historical Society.

The rigorous punishment meted out to the Minnesota Sioux failed to deter the plains Indians from following **The Arap-** their example. Among the tribes **aho and** most affected by the coming of **Cheyenne** the miners were the Arapaho and Cheyenne, who were persuaded in 1861 to make way for the white advance into Colorado by withdrawing into what was generally known as the Sand Creek Reserve, a barren and gameless tract in the southeastern part of the territory. Sullen and resentful, they began by the spring of 1864 to raid the trails along the South Platte, and to push on down into Nebraska. Companies engaged in staging and freighting were put out of business, settlers and travelers were killed, and the whole frontier as far east as the Blue River, was thrown into a panic. Promptly Governor John Evans called out the Colorado militia, but before ordering an attack he urged all peaceable Indians to concentrate in certain designated posts where they would be safe from harm. Not until fall, when the best fighting weather was over, did any considerable number of Indians choose to accept this invitation, but by that time about five hundred of them, including Black Kettle, their leading chief, had reported to Fort Lyon on Sand Creek, and were encamped nearby. As evidence of their peaceful intentions they flew both a white flag and the Stars and Stripes above their camp.

Meanwhile, however, Major-General Curtis of the United States Army, in command of the West, had telegraphed, "I want no peace till the Indians suffer more," and Colonel J. M. Chivington in command of the Colorado militia made ready to oblige him. Although there were bands of Indians still on the warpath, Chivington chose to ignore them, and instead to make a surprise attack upon the camp at Sand Creek. At the break of day, November 29, 1864, with about nine hundred men he fell upon the unsuspecting camp and murdered in cold blood about one hundred men, women, and children. Following the practice of the savages, the soldiers indulged in indescribable mutilations of the dead bodies, the mildest of which was scalping. Next year the government made a new treaty with the Arapaho and Cheyenne, pushing them farther to the southeast, but the Senate failed to confirm it, and the homeless Indians were sometimes guilty of attacks on settlers and travelers. Expeditions against them in 1867 and 1868 culminated in another massacre, this time on the Washita, near the Texas border, where Major-General George A. Custer with a detachment of regulars duplicated Chivington's unsavory exploit (November 27, 1868). Black Kettle himself was slain, and his people at length accepted lands assigned to them in the Indian Territory.

The western Sioux, who ranged north of the Platte and east of the mountains, were deeply disturbed, both by the **The western** fate that had overtaken the **Sioux** Arapaho and Cheyenne, and by the advent of mining activities in Montana. When, in 1865, the government decided to open a road along the Bozeman Trail, from Cheyenne northwestward to the mouth of the Rosebud in Montana, the Sioux determined to resist this invasion of their finest hunting-grounds with all their might. That year General P. E. Connor in command of sixteen hundred men, and guided by Jim Bridger, the noted plainsman, marched over part of the route, but was turned back by the Sioux; and in 1866 a second expedition under Colonel H. B. Carrington succeeded only with the greatest difficulty in building Fort Phil Kearny and Fort C. F. Smith to the east of the Big Horn Mountains. Red Cloud, the Indian leader, and his Sioux warriors risked no open fighting, but they continually harassed wood-trains sent out from the forts, and otherwise hampered the operations. On one occasion, a brash young officer, Captain W. J. Fetterman, was dispatched from Fort Phil Kearny to the aid of a wood-train with definite orders not to take the aggressive. New to western fighting and disdainful of Indians, he disobeyed orders, was ambushed, and in the resulting combat (December 21, 1866) every member of his party was slain. Two years later, when the government made peace with Red Cloud and his warriors, it was on condition that the "country north of the North Platte River and east of the summits of the Big Horn Mountains shall be held and considered to be unceded Indian Territory," and that the forts on the Bozeman Trail should be abandoned. This was one of the few instances in American history in which an Indian treaty registered a white retreat.

Meanwhile the government had taken steps toward the formation of a new Indian policy. A congressional Com- **The new** mittee on the Condition of the **Indian** Indian Tribes, created in 1865, **policy** visited the West, took full testimony on such

The plains Indians were skilled horsemen, and adept in the use of either bows and arrows or (when they could get them) guns. Well led, they put up a terrific battle against the white advance, and only in defeat accepted the humiliation of reservation life.

RED CLOUD. Leader of western Sioux, from Pine Ridge, South Dakota. Photo, circa 1877.

GERONIMO. Apache Indian chief. Photo by Ben Wittick, 1880.

SITTING BULL. Sioux medicine man and warrior. Photo by D. F. Barry, 1885.

INDIAN RESERVATION. Opening of Sherman, South Dakota, Sioux reservation.

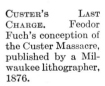

CUSTER'S LAST CHARGE. Feodor Fuch's conception of the Custer Massacre, published by a Milwaukee lithographer, 1876.

gruesome events as the Chivington massacre, and revealed how utterly untenable the status of the Indians had become. Its illuminating *Report on the Condition of the Indian Tribes*, made in 1867, led to the creation of an Indian Peace Commission, composed of three generals and four civilians, whose duty it was not only to stop the Indian wars, but also to work out a permanent solution of the Indian problem. The commission planned two great meetings, one for the southern tribes at Medicine Lodge Creek, near the southern border of Kansas, held in 1867, and one for the northern tribes at Fort Laramie, held in 1868. At these councils treaties were concluded that definitely foreshadowed the reservation system. Confiscation of the western half of the holdings of the Five Civilized Tribes in the Indian Territory, on the ground that the tribes had sided with the Confederacy during the Civil War, made possible the resettlement in that region of the Arapaho and Cheyenne and other plains Indians. In the North the Sioux were left in peaceable possession of southwestern Dakota, and such minor tribes as the Utes, Shoshonis, and Bannocks were concentrated within appropriate narrow limits. Subsidies in the form of annuities, payments for lands, and outright doles helped the dispossessed Indians to eke out a precarious existence, and unconsciously introduced pauperization as a means of insuring docility. A new Board of Indian Commissioners, composed of civilians, was created in 1869 to advise with the Bureau of Indian Affairs, which, since 1849, had been a part of the Department of the Interior. Believing that the Indians could eventually be made over into peaceful and contented farmers, the civilian commissions tried to break down tribal autonomy, and in 1871 they induced Congress to abolish the legal fiction of dealing with the tribes by treaty as if they were foreign nations. This was a definite improvement, but the road to civilization for the Indian was long and hard.

By this time most of the Indian fighting

was at an end, although occasional outbreaks occurred until as late as 1890. The worst of these was precipitated by the Black Hills gold rush, which brought thousands of whites into the heart of the region reserved for the Sioux. Even before the rush started, military maneuvers, designed merely to check up on the rumors of gold, and wholesale frauds, perpetrated systematically at the Red Cloud Indian Agency, had alarmed the Sioux, and many of them had left the reservation. Led by two able braves, Sitting Bull and Crazy Horse, the fugitives ignored all orders to return, and fought bravely when troops were sent to herd them in. During this campaign General George A. Custer and his command of over two hundred cavalrymen met the same fate that Custer had meted out to the Indians on the Washita eight years before. Lured into an ambush that he should have known enough to avoid, Custer and his entire command lost their lives.[1] The campaign, however, could have but one end, and within a short time General Nelson A. Miles had restored order. Crazy Horse was captured, and Sitting Bull fled to Canada. In 1877, a somewhat similar uprising among the Nez Percés of Idaho came to the same inexorable end. Chief Joseph, the Indian leader, gave a good account of himself, but at length surrendered. "I am tired of fighting," he told his chiefs. "My heart is sick and sad. From where the sun now stands I will fight no more forever." Down in New Mexico the Apaches repeatedly gave trouble, and the campaigns against them amounted almost to wars of extermination. Not until 1885, when Geronimo, their principal chief, was captured and exiled to Florida, was a lasting peace established. Trouble broke out again about 1889 with the Sioux in Dakota. A religious frenzy, based upon hope for an Indian Messiah, led to demonstrations by Indian "ghost dancers" that frightened the Indian agents into calling for troops. Fearful of soldiers' vengeance, many Indians left the reservation, only to be mas-

Later Indian uprisings

---

[1] The Custer Massacre occurred June 25, 1876.

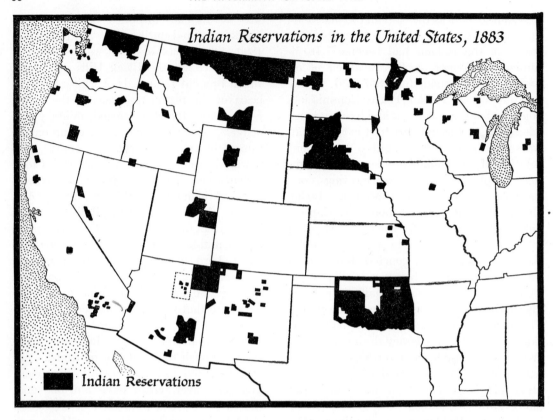

Indian Reservations in the United States, 1883

■ Indian Reservations

sacred at the so-called Battle of Wounded Knee (December 29, 1890). Two weeks before, Sitting Bull, who in 1881 had returned to the United States and had been allowed to live with his people, had lost his life while resisting, or seeming to resist, arrest.

The wars against the Indians, conducted after 1865 exclusively by regular army detachments, were far from popular with the American people, and protests against the inhuman treatment that the tribes received grew more and more insistent. The publication in 1881 of Helen Hunt Jackson's *A Century of Dishonor*, with its stinging indictment of the American Indian policy, brought public opinion strongly behind all efforts to alleviate the lot of the Indians. Their retention upon reservations, however, was an obvious necessity, and was long continued. In 1887 the Dawes Act paved the way for the gradual extinguishment of tribal ownership of lands,

Lands in severalty

and the substitution in its place of individual allotments of one hundred and sixty acres each to heads of families, eighty acres each to single adults or orphans, and forty acres each to dependent children. Only a "trust patent" to the land was given at first, and complete ownership was delayed for twenty-five years. In 1906 the Burke Act gave the Secretary of the Interior a discretionary right to lessen the probationary period, and corrected other defects in the original law. Compulsory education for Indian children was introduced in 1891, and full citizenship was conferred in 1924 upon all Indians in the United States. It cannot be said, however, that the government's policy, granted the best of intentions, was ever an unqualified success. Many of the Indians retained to a degree their tribal identity, and showed remarkable powers of resistance against the white man's way of living. And yet others, particularly in Oklahoma, eventually achieved that full equality with whites that was once only the dream of idealists.

The victory of the whites over the Indians was not won entirely by military means; **The killing of** buffalo hunters, by destroying **the buffalo** the principal food resource of the Indians, also did their rather considerable bit toward bringing Indian resistance to an end. Shortly after the Civil War the killing of the buffalo began. Organized hunting parties equipped with repeating rifles killed them by the tens of thousands to obtain "buffalo robes," soon regarded as almost a necessity in the average American home. Others were killed, by Indians and whites alike, for their meat, but often only the tongue and a few choice cuts would be taken, and the rest of the carcass left to rot. Hunters killed them just for the sport of it, although one English sportsman who came to America primarily to hunt buffalo refused to take part in a game that he described about as exciting as shooting cows in a pasture. The building of the Union Pacific Railroad [1] aided the hunters greatly, and divided the buffalo into two herds, one to the north and the other to the south. By 1870 from five to seven million buffalo still existed, but in the succeeding years the slaughter was terrific. The southern herd was gone by 1875, and in 1883 Sitting Bull and his braves destroyed the last sizable remnant of the northern herd. Probably not more than a thousand head were left alive. For years buffalo bones were gathered for shipment by the trainload to eastern factories, where they were turned into fertilizers, or into carbon for the use of sugar refineries.

The passing of the buffalo, unpleasant as it is to contemplate, was not an unmixed evil. The government purposely did nothing to prevent the tragedy, for as long as the herds remained intact the Indians had a sure food supply, and could the more easily defy governmental control. Some of the later Indian uprisings were caused in part by the Indians' concern at the threatened destruction of their herds, but once the buffalo were

[1] See p. 130.

gone the end of Indian resistance had been reached. Furthermore, the disappearance of the buffalo, together with the building of the western railroads and the pacification of the Indians, gave western agriculture the chance it needed to grow.

Directly to the west of the "bend of the Missouri" lay a broad belt of prairie land that invited the settlers in. Here the map-makers had **The "sod-** marked out the boundaries of **house frontier"** Dakota Territory to the north, Kansas and Nebraska in the middle, and the unorganized Indian Territory to the south. For the time being white settlers were in law, although not in fact, excluded from the Indian Territory, but from the southern boundary of Kansas to the Canadian border a new agricultural frontier pushed inexorably into the West. Since in general this area was treeless, pioneers found a substitute for the traditional log cabins in sod houses built from the heavy prairie sod turned up by their breaking plows; hence the term, "sodhouse frontier." The problem of water was not always so easily solved. In the eastern third of the region rainfall was usually adequate to produce crops, and the water-table for wells was not far below the surface. But the western third lay in the high, arid plains, while the middle third was intermediate, with "wet years" when there was no problem of rainfall and water supply, and dry years when the problem was acute.

Generous land legislation did its part to induce the restless farmer, the discontented artisan, the newly-arrived im- **Federal** migrant, and the former soldier **land policy** to make a try at the West. Not everyone who wished to seek a new home on the "sodhouse frontier" could raise the price of the trip, but for those who could do so the acquisition of a farm was made easy. The Homestead Act of 1862, for a few dollars in fees, made it possible for any American citizen, or any alien who had declared his intention of becoming a citizen, to obtain one hundred and sixty acres of unoccupied government land by living on it for five years.[1] Or, as cynics put it later, the government bet a man a one hundred and sixty acre farm that "he couldn't live on it for five years without starving to death." An Act of 1870 extended special privileges to soldiers who had fought in the Union army. Any such veteran might count his time of service toward the five-year period required for proving up on a homestead, and any widow of a soldier might count the full term of her dead husband's enlistment in the same way. Furthermore the Pre-emption Act of 1841, which remained on the statute books until 1891, allowed the settler to locate a claim of one hundred and sixty acres, and after six months' residence to buy it from the government at the minimum price, $1.25 an acre under ordinary circumstances.[2] The government even made an effort to adapt its land policy to the conditions of life in the farther West. The Timber Culture Act of 1873, for example, was designed to encourage the planting of trees. Under its terms the settler who would plant forty acres (later reduced to ten) in trees, and keep them in growing condition for ten years, could obtain title to a quarter section of land. These

[1] If the land lay within a railroad land grant, the homestead right was limited to eighty acres.
[2] In railroad land grants the price was $2.50 an acre on the theory that the coming of the railroad would double the value of the land.

laws permitted the enterprising settler to extend his holdings far beyond the traditional one hundred and sixty acres of land. They opened the way also to a veritable orgy of fraud and perjury, both on the part of legitimate settlers and on the part of conscienceless speculators. To cheat the government out of land, as long as plenty of it existed, was regarded on the frontier as a very minor offense, if an offense at all.

The hazards of the new western environment were far greater than most of the pioneers had foreseen. Some- *The hazards of pioneering* times in the fall when the high grass was dry prairie fires swept over the land destroying everything they touched. Lack of timber posed not only a serious problem in the matter of housing, but equally serious problems also in fuel and fencing. For fuel, settlers often resorted to such makeshifts as cow-dung, twisted prairie hay (called "cats"), sunflower stalks, and when they were available the far more satisfactory corncobs. Without fencing farming was practically impossible, but out on the prairies the rail fences of earlier frontiers were out of the question. There was much experimentation with hedges, particularly the osage-orange hedge, which was long used to good advantage, but a far better solution was soon supplied by the invention of

Buffalo hunters who sometimes killed for a purpose, but often only for the love of slaughter, were rampant in the seventies. "The Still Hunt" was painted by J. H. Moser in 1888.

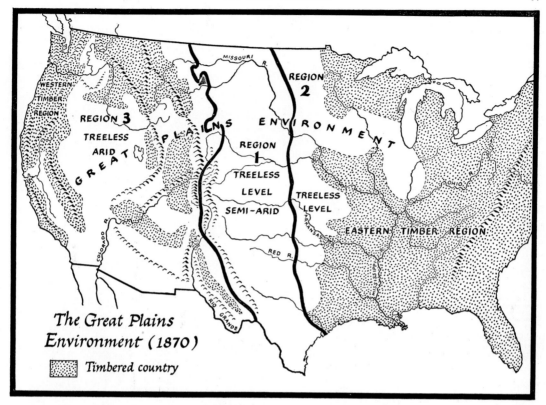

The Great Plains
Environment (1870)

Timbered country

barbed-wire. The trouble with this commodity was that it cost money, a great deterrent for most of the newcomers. There was, too, a great adjustment necessary to meet the weather conditions of the new region. Where the rainfall proved to be inadequate or undependable, windmills were often pressed into use, and, on the high plains, irrigation. Storms of great violence swept over the level terrain, "cyclones" by summer that did terrific damage, blizzards by winter that froze to death both livestock and unsheltered human beings. Most baffling of all were the grasshopper plagues which came every eight or ten years, sometimes oftener. In vast clouds that darkened the sun these insects invaded the prairies, consuming all vegetation, and leaving the farmers' crops a shambles.

They came like a driving snow in winter, filling the air, covering the earth, the buildings, the shocks of grain, and everything. According to one observer their alighting on the roofs and sides of the houses sounded like a continuous hailstorm. They alighted on trees in such great numbers that their weight broke off huge limbs. ... At times the insects were four to six inches deep on the ground and continued to alight for hours. Men were obliged to tie strings around their pants legs to keep the pests from crawling up their legs. In the cool of the evening the hoppers gathered so thick on the warm rails of the railroad that the Union Pacific trains were stopped. Section men were called out to shovel the grasshoppers off the track near the spot where Kearney, Nebraska, now stands, so that the trains could get through. The track was so oily and greasy that the wheels spun and would not pull the train.[1]

In spite of all these handicaps the settlers kept on coming, aided and abetted by the railroads along whose lines they settled, and for whom their presence meant the difference

Growth of the West

[1] Everett Dick, *The Sod-House Frontier, 1854–1890* (1937), pp. 203–4. Quoted by permission of Appleton-Century-Crofts, Inc., and the author.

Western emigrants, before the railroads came, traveled often in covered wagons, or "prairie schooners," grouped together in "wagon trains" for safety. Later on a select few made use of the stagecoach. Land seekers who eluded the speculators could buy at local land offices. Where timber was scarce, sod-houses were common.

WAGON TRAINS. Corral of wagons on a main street in Denver.

THE STAGE COACH. Before the railroads, stages provided the fastest overland travel.

LAND OFFICE. Land was plentiful and land offices numerous. Wood engraving by Frenzeny, circa 1874.

between solvency and bankruptcy. Veterans of the Civil War flocked to Kansas and Nebraska in such numbers as to give those states for a generation, or even longer, top-heavy Republican majorities. Substantial farmers throughout the North, but more especially those of the upper Mississippi Valley, sold their high-priced holdings to buy the cheaper lands of the West. Farm boys lately grown to manhood, small businessmen who had seen, or who hoped to see, better days, and not a few unemployed artisans joined the procession to the West.

Europeans, persuaded by railroad and steamship agents to leave their Old-World homes, were herded aboard ship, and having reached America were sent by special trains from the port of entry to some prearranged location on railroad lands. As a result of these outpourings the "sod-house frontier" did not last long. Within a single generation a region that had started as wilderness was settled up, and had achieved to a considerable degree the normal paraphernalia of civilization.

During the same years that the "sod-house

SOD-HOUSE. S. D. Butcher photo taken in Custer County, Nebraska, circa 1888.

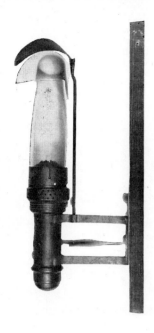

CANDLE LAMP. Type used on emigrant railway cars in the 70's.

frontier" was taking form, a cattlemen's frontier was also developing on the western plains. The various posts that dotted the western trails, some wholly private, and others centered about a garrisoned fort or an Indian agency, got an early start in cattle from the emigrants, who were frequently only too willing to exchange for urgent necessities any livestock they happened to have brought along. It was soon discovered that cattle could fend for themselves on the plains the whole year through, for the wiry "buffalo grass" cured on the ground and remained all winter long as nutritious as hay. There was no temptation, however, to increase these herds beyond immediate needs as long as the plains swarmed with Indians and buffalo, and outside markets were beyond reach.

The cow country

With the Indians curbed, the buffalo killed, and the transcontinental railroads pushing out upon the plains, the western cattle industry got the chance it needed to grow. But its real beginnings were Mexican rather than American, and dated back for centuries. Both the cattle themselves, and the horses without which the industry would have been vastly different (to say the least), were the descendants of European stock brought over

Beginnings of the cattle industry

by the Spaniards in the sixteenth century, and allowed to go wild. Survival of the fittest produced by the nineteenth-century cattle that were more noted for their speed and endurance than for tender cuts of beef, each blessed also with an incredible spread of horns. The horses, sprung no doubt from noble Arabian forebears, had developed into sure-footed, quick-witted, wiry broncos, well under a thousand pounds in weight, but ideally suited for riding. The technique of cattle-raising, to the last detail, was worked out in Mexico long before it was introduced into the United States, and was practiced for years in New Mexico, Texas, and California before it was known on the western plains. The cowboy's saddle, bridle, bit, lariat, and spurs were adaptations, for the most part, of equipment used by Spanish cavalrymen, while the "round-up" and the use of "brands" to indicate ownership were early invented to meet obvious needs. The unimportance of the cattle industry for so many years was not due to inability to produce cattle. Anyone in the Southwest with a little ambition could have all the cattle he wanted. What the industry needed was a market for its produce, and until that could be found it remained insignificant.

Attempts to drive Texas cattle to an out-

The cattle country got its start mainly from "Texas longhorns," driven northward along the cattle trails. From Texas and elsewhere, herds were collected at such railroad towns as Abilene, Kansas, for shipment eastward to the packing plants. Cowboys after one of these long drives sometimes compensated for the long weeks of loneliness by shooting up a town.

ROUNDUP TIME. Supper preparations in camp, Cheyenne. *Leslie's Illustrated Newspaper,* 1888. From a photo.

A KANSAS CORRAL. Cattle at rest after long journey from Texas. Woodcut by Frederick Remington, 1888.

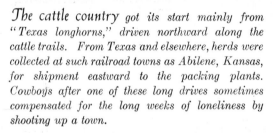

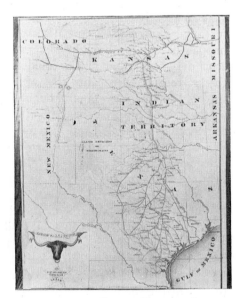

CATTLE TRAILS. Section of map published by Kansas-Pacific Railroad, 1875.

COWBOYS PLUNDERING A TOWN. A common incident in Southwestern life. Sketch by Frenzeny, circa 1880.

side market were made from the time of the
The long drive Mexican War on, but all such ventures amounted to little until the railroads began to push out across the western plains. Then the idea of the "long drive" from somewhere in Texas to a shipping point in Kansas or Nebraska immediately took hold. Abilene, Kansas, a station on the Kansas Pacific, became noted as early as 1867 as a "cow-town." Here untold numbers of Texas cattle, driven northward through the Indian Territory, or the "Nation," as cowboys called it, were purchased for the use of the newly-established packing-houses. Early each year drovers assembled herds for the "drive," or else individual ranchers rounded up their cattle and threw them upon the trail — a route generally known as the "Chisholm Trail," regardless of where it ran. Grazing the cattle as they went, cowboys moved them slowly northward in herds of two or three thousand head. Such a group required the services of sixteen or eighteen cowboys, a cook with a "chuck-wagon," and a "wrangler" with extra cow-ponies. Trials on the march included the danger of stampedes due to lightning, buffalo, or Indians.

On the "long drive" the cowboy developed those peculiar characteristics that made him, like the fur-trader, **The cowboy** the lumberjack, and the prospector, a unique specimen of the American frontier. He found the revolver indispensable to the protection of his herd, and of great advantage in the actual business of herding. Naturally he became a fair marksman. He sang to the cattle, whether to help him bear the loneliness, or to keep the cattle aware of his presence, or to prevent or promote a stampede. The verses he invented were colorful, they told of the life he led, and they became as authentic a part of the American folklore as the songs of slavery and freedom that the southern Negroes sang. In reality, just a "plain everyday bow-legged human," the cowboy's occasional excesses after periods of long riding and lack of sport caught the eye of the fictionist, and

were romanticized out of all proportion to the facts. A wanderer, an adventurer, and sometimes a refugee, the cowboy's actual exploits did make good stories, but most of his life was given over to hard and monotonous labor.[1]

The advance of the frontier into Kansas and Nebraska drove the "Chisholm Trail" farther and farther west, and determined the location of new cow-towns to take the place of those enclosed in settled areas. Dodge City, Kansas, for example, soon replaced Abilene as the leading shipping-point for Texas cattle. Settlement interfered with grazing; moreover, the Texas cattle brought with them the germs of the dreaded "Texas fever" to which they themselves had become immune, but which brought almost certain death to other cattle that caught it. Quarantine laws were passed that pushed the drive still farther into the west. Also, a new market was discovered when the northern plains had been cleared of buffalo. Northern ranchers, eager to expand their herds, paid good prices for the Texas longhorns, bred them up rapidly by the introduction of blooded cattle from the East, and laid the basis for a short, but spectacular, prosperity. Points on the Union Pacific such as Ogallala and Sidney, Nebraska, were visited by western as well as eastern buyers, and Cheyenne, Wyoming, which had once had no other excuse for existence than the railroad, now found itself the center of an exciting cattle industry. Texas cattle were driven northward as far as Dakota and Montana, and even westward into New Mexico, Arizona, Colorado, and Utah.

The profits of cattle-growing on a well-policed range, for the use of which the government made no charge, and to which,

---

[1] The following lines are inscribed on a tombstone in the Cemetery at Douglas, Wyoming:
"Underneath this stone in eternal rest
Sleeps the wildest one of the Wayward West.
He was gambler and sport and cowboy too,
And he led the pace in an outlaw crew.
He was sure on the trigger and staid to the end,
But he was never known to quit on a friend.
In the relations of death all mankind is alike,
But in life there was only one George W. Pike."

The range-cattle industry thanks to the railroads, markets were now easily accessible, did not fail to attract capital, not only from the American East, but also from Europe, particularly England. Ranchers, or "cattlemen," as they were called to distinguish them from their employees, the "cowboys," figured that an original investment of five thousand dollars should pay profits of from forty to fifty thousand dollars in four years' time. Ranching companies, some of them with capital investments well up into the millions, were formed to crowd more and more cattle upon the range. Access to water was, of course, essential, and each individual or company engaged in the cattle business took care to obtain title to some land so situated. Here the ranch house and other necessary buildings were located, and from this headquarters operations were carried on over a range bounded by the distance the cattle were willing to travel to water. Large "outfits," as the companies were called, sometimes had access to water at many different places, and companies existed that claimed the grazing rights to strips of land no less than a hundred miles long and fifty miles wide.

The law of the range, like the law of the mining camp, was to a great extent invented to meet the needs of the situation. Stock-growers' associations were formed, at first for mutual protection, but later to work out rules for users of the range that actually had the effect of law. Indeed, the Wyoming Stock-Growers' Association, formed in 1873, came to have more power than the territorial government of Wyoming, which, as a matter of fact, it controlled. The Association promoted community rather than individual round-ups, regulated the use of brands and recorded them, required that "mavericks" (unbranded calves that no longer followed their mothers) should be sold to the highest bidder and the proceeds paid into the Association treasury, discouraged overstocking of the range by refusing membership to outsiders, and made relentless warfare upon all who were suspected of "rustling" (stealing) cattle. Punishment for defiance of the Association might or might not await court action.

The day of the cattleman soon passed. Trouble with rustlers who branded mavericks and "worked" (altered) brands cost the ranchers heavy losses, both in cattle stolen and in fees paid to detectives and inspectors. **The passing of the cattleman** Trouble with "nesters" (farmers) whose fences interfered with the free access of cattle to water-holes not only caused heavy losses in property, but frequently resulted also in loss of life. Cowboys learned to carry wire-cutters as part of their equipment; and finally, in self-defense, the cattlemen themselves began to fence the land they used but did not own, only to have their fences branded as illegal by the United States government, and ordered down. But the greatest calamity that befell the cattlemen was the overstocking of the range. By the middle eighties so many millions of cattle had been turned loose to pick up a living from the plains that one severe winter was sure to bring disaster, and instead of one such winter most of the range country saw two, 1885–86, and 1886–87. The result was wholesale ruin and bankruptcy, and a complete change in the nature of the cattle industry. After this time, ranchers tended more and more to raise hay for winter feed, and in general to carry on farming as well as ranching activities. On many ranges sheep replaced cattle, although not without resort to actual warfare between sheepmen and cattlemen. The close-grazing sheep left the range stripped of grass, so when sheepmen came to stay cattlemen had to fight or leave. In some of these conflicts, sheep-herders were slain, the wagons that carried their supplies were burned, and the herds themselves were destroyed.

Short-lived as it was, the range-cattle industry left its mark upon the West and upon the country as a whole. It did its share to promote the growth of the meat-packing industry. It made clear the absurdity for the Far West of land legislation devised to meet the needs of the eastern half of the continent, and paved the way for important changes, such as the Desert Land Act of 1877, and the Timber and Stone Act of 1878.[1] It bequeathed to the residents of the plains a breezy, slangy language, cowboy costumes, "dude" ranches, and rodeos. It lived persistently in stories of the "Wild West" such as Owen Wister's *The Virginian*,

[1] The former permitted the acquisition in the arid states of 640 acres of land at $1.25 per acre on condition that the claimant would irrigate his holding; the latter made possible the purchase at $2.50 per acre of an additional quarter section valuable chiefly for timber and stone.

and the multitudinous works of Zane Grey; in the infinite number of scenarios derived from them for the use of the motion-picture industry; in the "Wild West" shows first popularized by "Buffalo Bill" Cody; in the solemn melodies and bungling rhymes of the cowboy songs.

Oh, beat the drum slowly and play the fife lowly;
  Play the dead march as you carry me along.
Take me to the green valley and lay the sod o'er
  me.
  I'm just a poor cowboy and I know I've done
  wrong.

Bibliography

For the western half of the continent the interpretation of Frederick Jackson Turner, *The Frontier in American History* (1921), is significantly supplemented by Walter P. Webb, *The Great Plains* (new ed., 1936), which emphasizes convincingly the contrasts between the Great Plains and the earlier frontiers. The advancing frontier is the theme of many excellent one-volume texts, among them Frederic L. Paxson, *History of the American Frontier, 1763–1893* (1924); Ray A. Billington, *Westward Expansion* (1943); D. E. Clark, *The West in American History* (1937); R. E. Riegel, *America Moves West* (new ed., 1947); and E. D. Branch, *Westward, The Romance of the American Frontier* (1930). Concentrating on the trans-Mississippi West are LeRoy R. Hafen and Carl Coke Rister, *Western America* (1941); F. L. Paxson, *The Last American Frontier* (1910); and Emerson Hough, *The Passing of the Frontier; A Chronicle of the Old West* (1918). Everett Dick, *Vanguards of the Frontier* (1941), is a social history of the traders, trappers, and others who preceded the settlers on the Great Plains. Two interesting collections on western subjects are *The Westward Movement: A Book of Readings on Our Changing Frontiers*, edited by Ina Faye Woestemeyer and J. Montgomery Gambrill (1939); and *America Is West: An Anthology of Middlewestern Life and Literature*, edited by J. T. Flanagan (1945).

There is a wealth of regional, state, and local history writing, among the best of which the following books may be listed: Oscar O. Winther, *The Great Northwest* (1947); LeRoy R. Hafen, *Colorado: The Story of a Western Commonwealth* (1933); P. S. Fritz, *Colorado, The Centennial State* (1941); H. H. Bancroft, *History of Nevada, Colorado, and Wyoming, 1540–1888* (1890); Effie M. Mack, *Nevada: A History of the State from Earliest Times through the Civil War* (1936); Merrill G. Burlingame, *The Montana Frontier* (1942); J. K. Howard, *Montana: High, Wide, and Handsome* (1943); and N. P. Langford, *Vigilante Days and Ways* (1912), a vivid, first-hand account of mining days in early Montana. Charles Lindsay, *The Big Horn Basin* (1932), tells the story of a typical mountain region in Wyoming which passed through every stage of the frontier process. William M. Stewart, *Reminiscences* (1908), is a more interesting than accurate account by a United States Senator from Nevada. Samuel L. Clemens (Mark Twain), *Roughing It* (1872), gives a classic picture of early days in the Far West. V. V. Masterson, *The Katy Railroad and the Last Frontier* (1952), deals with the Missouri-Kansas-Texas Railroad.

On mining development, W. J. Trimble, *The Mining Advance into the Inland Empire* (1914), is a work of dependable scholarship. C. H. Shinn, *The Story of the Mine* (1896); and C. B. Glasscock, *The Big Bonanza* (1931), describe vividly the exploitation of the Comstock Lode.

More general in their approach are G. C. Quiett, *Pay Dirt, A Panorama of American Gold Rushes* (1936); C. H. Shinn, *Mining Camps; A Study in American Frontier Government* (1885, new ed., 1948); and Rodman Paul, *California Gold; The Beginnings of Mining in the Far West* (1947).

Dorothy Gardiner, *West of the River* (1941), features trails and transportation west of the Mississippi; J. V. Frederick, *Ben Holladay, The Stagecoach King* (1940), concentrates on the period 1862–66. J. C. Alter, *James Bridger* (1925), tells the story of this typical plainsman. Useful also are two volumes by Stanley Vestal, *Mountain Men* (1937), and *Kit Carson* (1928).

On the Indian wars, W. W. Folwell, *A History of Minnesota* (4 vols., 1921–30); and T. C. Blegen, *Building Minnesota* (1938), both brilliantly written works of scholarship, present faithfully the story of the Sioux uprising in Minnesota. G. B. Grinnell, *The Fighting Cheyennes* (1915), is among the best of the books on the Indian wars of the plains. See also his more elaborate, *The Cheyenne Indians; Their History and Ways of Life* (2 vols., 1923). Among the best of the many popular books on the Indians are Flora W. Seymour, *The Story of the Red Man* (1929); F. E. Leupp, *The Indian and His Problem* (1910); Paul I. Wellman, *Death on Horseback: Seventy Years of War for the American West* (1947), which combines the author's two earlier volumes, *Death on the Prairie* (1934), and *Death in the Desert* (1935). Consult also N. A. Miles, *Serving the Republic* (1911); G. A. Custer, *My Life on the Plains* (1874); C. C. Rister, *Border Command, General Phil Sheridan in the West* (1944); P. E. Byrne, *Soldiers of the Plains* (1926); *General George Crook: His Autobiography*, edited by Martin F. Schmitt; E. E. Dale, *Cherokee Cavaliers, Forty Years of Cherokee History* (1939); and Ralph H. Ogle, *Federal Control of the Western Apaches, 1848–1886* (1940).

Two extremely colorful narratives of the farmers' frontier are Everett Dick, *The Sod-House Frontier, 1854–1890* (1937); and Harold E. Briggs, *Frontiers of the Northwest; A History of the Upper Missouri Valley* (1940). S. K. Humphrey, *Following the Prairie Frontier* (1931), recaptures much of the spirit of the headlong advance into Kansas and Nebraska. The trials of an immigrant group are recorded in C. H. Smith, *The Coming of the Russian Mennonites* (1927). The two best books on the public lands are B. H. Hibbard, *A History of the Public Land Policies* (new ed., 1939); and R. M. Robbins, *Our Landed Heritage* (1942); but see also appropriate sections in *Readings in the Economic History of American Agriculture*, edited by L. B. Schmitt and E. D. Ross (1925). Thomas Donaldson, *The Public Domain* (1884), contains large quantities of undigested material.

E. D. Branch, *The Hunting of the Buffalo* (1929), is an excellent literary, as well as historical, account of the brief period of the buffalo-hunters' frontier which helped give the livestock industry its chance to grow. P. A. Rollins, *The Cowboy* (1922), and J. H. Cook, *Fifty Years on the Old Frontier* (1923), give colorful accounts of the origins of the range cattle industry. Much valuable information is also contained in Emerson Hough, *The Story of the Cowboy* (1897); and in E. D. Branch, *The Cowboy and his Interpreters* (1926). Several collections of cowboy songs exist: *Cowboy Songs and Other Frontier Ballads*, compiled by John A. and Alan Lomax (1945); *Songs of the Cattle Trail and Cow Camp*, compiled by John A. Lomax (rev. ed., 1950); *Sun and Saddle Leather*, compiled by Badger Clark (1936). The best works on the cow country are E. S. Osgood, *The Day of the Cattleman* (1929); and E. E. Dale, *The Range Cattle Industry* (1930). But see also J. W. Thompson, *A History of Livestock Raising in the United States* (1942); Louis Pelzer, *The Cattleman's Frontier* (1936); Ora Brooks Peake, *The Colorado Range Cattle Industry* (1937); and W. P. Webb, *The Texas Rangers* (1935).

5

Post-War Society

The Panic of 1873 — American slums — The newly rich — Moral laxity — Business ethics — Political scandals — The Tweed ring — Godkin, Curtis, Schurz — High schools and universities — Philanthropy — Education for women — Negro education — American letters — Mark Twain — William Dean Howells — — Humanitarian reform — Woman suffrage — Practical Christianity — The Centennial Exposition

ON THURSDAY, September 18, 1873, the banking firm of Jay Cooke and Company **The Panic** closed its doors in New York, **of 1873** Philadelphia, and Washington. Cooke's fame had risen during the Civil War with his successful flotation of the bond issues by which the North financed its operations. After the war he turned his attention to railway securities, and again demonstrated his ability to win the confidence of investors. In attempting to back the Northern Pacific Railroad, however, he met with disaster. The huge sums needed for this undertaking could not be obtained without European assistance, and after the outbreak of the Franco-Prussian War in 1870 foreign capital became harder and harder to get. The result was that Cooke tied up so much of his firm's resources in advances to the railroad that his partners, without his knowledge or consent, finally took the drastic step of closing. Already a number of bankruptcies had made the business world nervous, and on the day before Cooke's failure there had been a ruinous decline in values on the New York Stock Exchange. But no one dreamed that the firm of Jay Cooke and Company, long regarded as the last word in financial solvency, was in danger. Hence, when the suspension was announced, the Exchange was immedi-

ately thrown into a panic so severe that, in comparison, the disturbance of the preceding day looked like nothing at all. The Panic of 1873 had begun. Two days later, with the price of stocks still going down, the Exchange was closed, and it remained closed for ten days. Bankruptcies followed thick and fast, factories shut down, business came to a standstill; a depression that was to last for nearly six years had begun. Thus dramatically did the "boom" that the Civil War unleashed come to its inexorable end.

Overinvestment in railroads, many of which, especially in the West, were built into unpopulated regions where for years operations could be **Causes of** carried on only at a loss, to- **the panic** gether with the wildest sort of speculation in railroad securities, had much to do with bringing on the panic of 1873. During these years the amount of capital invested in railroads alone had reached a billion dollars, while other huge sums had gone into the development of the new American industries. Capital from abroad amounting to over a billion and a half dollars had been borrowed to carry on the expansion, and interest charges of eighty million dollars annually had to be met. To pay these charges, and to remedy an adverse balance of trade, more gold had to be sent abroad each year than

The Chicago fire of 1871, one of the most devastating on record, swept through great sections of the lakeshore city. This view from the West Side was published by Gibson & Co.

the United States could well spare. The new national banks yielded to the temptation to overextend their loans, and in the five years preceding the panic let out many times as much money as they took in by way of new deposits. Insurance companies were hard hit by the Chicago Fire of 1871, which cost them $200,000,000, and the Boston Fire of 1872, which added another $73,000,000 to the bill they had to pay. Conditions in Europe were similarly gloomy, and a sharp panic on the Vienna Bourse in May, 1873, inaugurated a general European depression that could not long be kept from America. It was the unloading by European investors of their American holdings that so depressed the New York Stock Exchange during the summer of 1873, and prepared the way for the crash that the failure of Jay Cooke and Company precipitated. Then, following the panic, came the long period of hard times.

This sudden descent from post-war prosperity to post-panic adversity plunged the American people into an atmosphere of the deepest gloom. Critics of American society had not been lacking while times were good, but their comments, all too frequently, had fallen on deaf ears. Now, with each succeeding year a little harder than the one that had gone before, the apostles of pessimism reigned supreme. Long and earnestly they dwelt upon the sins of society, the wickedness of business, and the total depravity of the politicians. Could the United States hope to survive the moral collapse it had suffered?

There was reason for the gloom. America had long been regarded as the land of opportunity, but a trip through the slum district of any great American city seemed to show rather that it was the land of want. In New York City, out of a hundred thousand slum-dwellers, twenty thousand lived in cellars; in Boston, one fifth of the total population lived in flimsy, overcrowded tenements. Unemployment estimates for the country at large revealed that from two to three million people were out of work, and for most of these the long, expensive trip to the "free lands" of the West completely closed that "safety-valve." Wages dropped precipitately, woman and child labor were ruthlessly exploited, actual starvation was by no means unknown. Everywhere, but most of all in the crowded city centers where ignorance of the simplest sanitary precautions was rivaled only by indifference to those that were known, preventable diseases, such as smallpox, typhoid, and typhus, took a heavy toll. Always such suffering fell most heavily upon the poor. At any given time three fourths of the sickness and death in New

York City was furnished by the less-favored half of the population.

Hardly less distressing than the plight of the poor was the vulgar ostentation of a **The newly rich** small army of *parvenu* rich. War profiteers, successful speculators, oil men and miners who had "struck it rich" flocked to the cities to display their wealth. Few of them could approximate the extravagances of the notorious Jim Fisk, but many of them tried. Fisk, at the height of his glory, had sumptuous offices in "Castle Erie," a huge marble building on Eighth Avenue in New York that also housed his privately owned and operated Grand Opera House. From his theatrical stars and dancers, many of whom were imported, he recruited a harem that might well have been the envy of an Oriental potentate. The chief recipients of his favor lived in palaces, and fared forth in handsome carriages, drawn sometimes, when Fisk went along, by three teams of fine horses, whites to the left and blacks to the right. Among Fisk's other fancies were canary birds, hundreds of which, in gilded cages, adorned his rooms, and the well-appointed steamboats that he also owned and loved. On occasion he would dress himself up in the gold lace of an admiral's uniform, and once, when so arrayed, he contrived to receive President Grant. The colonelcy of the Ninth Regiment of the New York National Guard, a position he obtained by means of generous gifts, furnished him another opportunity to indulge his penchant for gaudy pageantry. During the summer of 1871 he took the entire regiment to Boston at his own expense to celebrate the anniversary of the battle of Bunker Hill. He died on January 7, 1872, from bullet wounds inflicted by one of his own kind, Edward S. Stokes, a "business and amatory rival." Stokes, for his crime, was sentenced to four years in the penitentiary at Sing Sing, but there he received many special privileges, such, for example, as being permitted to drive about at night with the span of horses he kept for the purpose at a local livery stable. On his re-lease he became the proprietor of the Hoffman House at Broadway and Twenty-Sixth Street, New York, a hotel chiefly noted for the daring paintings on its barroom walls.

While the loose living of a Jim Fisk could hardly be said to reflect against the character of the American people as a whole, there was an abundance **Moral laxity** of other evidence at hand for the use of alarmists who held that morality "to a fatal extent" had broken down. It was disheartening to have the name of the leading preacher of the time, Henry Ward Beecher, bandied about among the unregenerate because of an affair he was alleged to have carried on with a woman of his congregation. Beecher may have been innocent, but in any event the conspiracy to disgrace him and the long trial it involved were ugly enough. Conventional citizens were shocked, in a day when divorce had not yet become a national pastime, at the ease and frequency with which marriages were annulled under the lax laws of two offending states, Connecticut and Indiana. From West Virginia to Arkansas, the region over which the Civil War had been fought, bands of ruffians continued their wartime habits, and for years escaped arrest. Most noted of these outlaws was Jesse James, who in 1872 robbed the Kansas City Fair of ten thousand dollars, and until the time of his death a decade later kept the Kansas-Missouri border in a state of frightened expectancy. City gangs likewise defied the law, and committed depredations that would have taxed the talents of twentieth-century racketeers. Gambling, particularly in the cities and along the frontier, flourished covertly or openly as the taste of the community preferred. The State of Louisiana raised money by a lottery. Prostitution was railed at and preached against, but flaunted itself in every sizable town. Intemperance was the commonest vice of all, and since the Civil War had seemingly been definitely on the increase. During the war most of the state prohibition laws had been repealed, while the national government, by placing a tax on intoxicants,

SLUMS. The East Side of New York during a famous heat wave.

Social extremes in the United States during the late nineteenth century are well depicted in the accompanying illustrations. In any large American city the ease of life among the well-to-do contrasted sharply with the squalor of the tenements.

A FIVE O'CLOCK TEA. After a painting by J. L. Stewart, 1884.

had, in a sense, given the liquor traffic its blessing. Saloons, as the places where liquor was sold came universally to be called, were outfitted with clublike attractiveness and their popularity is attested by the fact that the total capital invested in the liquor business grew from $29,000,000 in 1860 to $193,000,000 in 1880. Most of the immigrant groups gave the liquor interests their enthusiastic support.

The sordidness of business during the post-war years was another subject that **Business ethics** aroused the anxiety of thoughtful critics. The well-nigh universal devotion of Americans to the pursuit of wealth was in itself a heavy curse, but the devious means that men used to gain their ends hit at the very foundations of society. In part this alarming laxity of conduct could be blamed upon the war itself, which, for literally millions of young Americans, had stood in lieu of a college education. As students of war they had been taught to deceive the enemy, to take his property, to destroy, and to kill; as graduates of such a course they sometimes failed to perceive that the virtues of war were not also the virtues of peace. Furthermore, with business expanding so rapidly, executive experience of any kind was in great demand. American capitalists had not often gone to war themselves, but when peace was restored they made good use of the war-trained heroes. Army officers were, after all, trained executives, and the high-ranking officer who was not promptly solicited to accept a "business opening" was rare indeed.

It would be a mistake, however, to blame the war for every evil practice of the business world. Far more important was the utter novelty of large-scale business operations. Before the Civil War most American businesses were relatively small, and their fields of activity were local. Standards of conduct existed which the prudent business man, to retain the good-will of his customers and the public, felt obliged to recognize. But for large-scale business no code of ethics had yet been evolved. With monopoly, or at least near-monopoly, as the goal, the struggle for survival among the competitors was intense, and as a rule only the ruthless had a chance to win. The law offered no restraint, for, since similar problems had never before been faced, laws to meet them had never been devised; furthermore, as business organizations grew in size and power they found that they could, when they chose, have a hand in both the making and the enforcement of laws. The situation was not unlike that on the high seas in the days when piracy and buccaneering, unchallenged by international law, amounted almost to legitimate occupations.

Corporation methods of finance offered an opportunity, never long neglected, for **Corporation** astounding frauds in the issu-**finance** ance and manipulation of stocks and bonds. "Wildcat" or "blue-sky" securities were easily sold to a public made gullible by the unprecedented number of fortunes that the "boom" times actually produced. Oil companies were organized that never drilled a well, mining companies that never sunk a shaft, railroad companies that never laid a rail, all for the sole purpose of separating careless investors from their savings. General Robert C. Schenck, an ex-congressman from Ohio whom Grant sent as Minister to England, gave his support to the promoters of a mining venture that sold fifty thousand dollars' worth of worthless stock to British investors.[1] General George B. McClellan, more innocently, backed a ten-million-dollar corporation that proposed to exploit a mythical diamond and ruby field in California.

Even the most substantial corporations were frequently led to "water" their stock and to incur bonded indebtedness altogether out of proportion to their assets. Daniel Drew, a pious old fraud who hoped to purchase pardon for his sins by making generous pledges, mostly never paid, to Drew Theological Seminary, wormed his way into the

directorate of the Erie Railway, became its treasurer, and for years manipulated the price of its stock in such a way as to enhance his private fortune. According to a current Wall Street saying: "Dan'l says up — Erie goes up. Dan'l says down — Erie goes down. Dan'l says wiggle-waggle — Erie bobs both ways." In 1868 Cornelius Vanderbilt, who already controlled the New York Central and the Hudson River Railroad, proposed to add the badly wrecked Erie to his domain. A battle royal followed in which Drew, supported by his apt "pupils," Jay Gould and Jim Fisk, finally won. To do so, however, Drew and his associates found it necessary to issue fifty thousand shares of fraudulent stock, to flee to New Jersey to escape arrest, and to bribe the New Jersey legislature to legalize their transaction. But Drew's luck did not last. His two "pupils" raised the price of Erie stock by sales abroad, thanklessly cornered their teacher, and trimmed him of a million and a half. The Panic of 1873 also hit him hard, and by 1876 he was bankrupt with liabilities of over a million dollars and no assets to speak of. Long a target of reproach, he died three years later with none to mourn his passing.

Not many types of sizable business enterprise came through the cycle of boom and depression with clean records. **Bank fail-** Three New York savings banks **ures** failed in 1872 under the most scandalous circumstances; while small investors suffered acutely, the former bank officials continued to live in luxury. During the first eight years of the seventies, twenty-eight New York life insurance companies either failed outright, or avoided failure by amalgamation with some stronger concern. Losses to policy-holders amounted to a nominal total of $159,000,000 insurance. Even the solvent companies unblushingly "froze out" aged and undesirable policy-holders, usually by increasing rates. "The whole chapter," said the *Commercial and Financial Chronicle*,[1] "is so dark a record of betrayal of corporate

---

[1] Schenck further distinguished himself by writing a treatise on poker-playing.

[1] April 19, 1879.

Eastern United States

The Tweed Ring, even more than the hapless carpetbag governments of the southern states, showed the depths to which political depravity in a democracy could fall. But these cartoons indicate also how public opinion could be aroused against the offenders. In the end the Ring had to go.

A PROPOSED MONUMENT. The cartoonist Grey-Parker's design for a fountain in the City Hall Park. *Harper's Weekly,* 1871.

POLITICAL BACTERIA. Reinhart's unique presentation of Tweed Ring figures as germs in a drop of water. *Harper's Weekly,* 1871.

THE TAMMANY TIGER LOOSE. Nast's portrayal of the mauling of the Republic is credited with defeating the Tweed Ring. *Harper's Weekly,* 1871.

trust — incapacity being so blended with dishonesty that it is impossible to separate them — that if we had the space and the data, we should not have the desire to expose its details."

Whatever the shortcomings of business may have been, they met their match in **Political scandals** politics. The Grant administration was known, even before it had ended, as the most corrupt that the Republic had yet experienced. Reconstruction, with its attempt to perpetuate the rule of the northern Radicals by forcing Negro rule upon the South, would have been a scandal even if honestly carried out, but the number of honest officials in the "carpetbag" South seems to have been negligible. And yet the scandals that rocked the country were as frequently associated with the North or the West as with the South. The Crédit Mobilier, the Whiskey Ring, the frauds in the Indian service, and the Salary Grab Act [1] had no southern or reconstruction connotation whatever. In the fields of state and local government political degradation reached its lowest depths. The spoils system, everywhere deeply entrenched, had produced an unsavory set of petty party "bosses," each presiding over his county or city or state because, by fair means or foul, he had gathered into his hands the disposal of the "patronage." Working together as a party "machine," the bosses could levy assessments, win elections, reward the faithful, punish the disobedient, and, if they chose, line their pockets with public money and exact a heavy toll from business.

As befitted its size and prominence, New York City furnished the country with the outstanding example of municipal corruption. There the Tammany Society, a political organization that dated back to the eighteenth century, controlled the local machinery of the Democratic Party, and regularly rolled up huge majorities for the Democratic ticket. Tammany Hall, as the society was usually called (after its meeting-place on Fourteenth Street), won the support of the masses by providing them with a kind of unofficial social insurance. Tammany leaders in each ward made it their business to find jobs for the unemployed, to relieve the needy, to care for the sick, to aid the newly arrived immigrants in their efforts to become adjusted. In return for all this, Tammany chiefs expected and obtained unquestioning political support. When extra votes were needed, wholesale frauds were easily possible, for the election machinery was in Tammany hands. In the election of 1868, for example, it was generally believed that the returns from New York City and Brooklyn were held back until the rest of the state could be heard from so that enough votes could be cast for John T. Hoffman, the Tammany candidate for governor, to insure his election.

When Grant became President of the United States the "Grand Sachem" of Tammany Hall was William M. **The Tweed Ring** Tweed, a thoroughgoing corruptionist who had worked his way up in politics from membership in a volunteer fire department. Tweed's opportunity for wholesale graft came after he and his associates by the most barefaced bribery had secured from the state legislature a city charter that was specifically designed to enable them to avoid responsibility for their crimes. The principals of the "Tweed Ring" were "Boss" Tweed himself, whose presidency of the board of supervisors of New York County (coterminous with New York City) had obvious possibilities; A. Oakey Hall, the mayor, an aspirant for social recognition whose fastidious appearance won him the sobriquet, "Elegant Oakey"; Peter B. Sweeny, treasurer of both city and county, useful not only because of his position, but also because of his unquestioned ability as a lawyer; and Richard B. Connolly, the controller, otherwise and appropriately known as "Slippery Dick." In 1869 this disgusting crew began a series of peculations that mounted year by year until at the height of their power they were dividing among themselves and their confederates eighty-five per

[1] See pp. 49–51.

cent of the total expenditures made by the city and county. Tweed received as his share twenty-four per cent of the "take," and the rest was apportioned out according to a prearranged plan. The actual cost of maintaining the city's armories, for example, totaled for a given period $250,000, but the amount paid out allegedly for that purpose was $3,200,000. A courthouse was built that cost about three million dollars, but the county's books showed expenditures for that purpose of about eleven millions. The plastering of this building alone cost the taxpayers $2,870,464.06, and its carpeting $350,000, "enough to cover the whole City Park three times." During a period of thirty months the city and county printing bill ran to over seven million dollars. Probably the total loot taken by the Tweed Ring reached a hundred million dollars.

At last, scathing editorials in the *New York Times*, and cartoons by Thomas Nast **The ring broken up** in *Harper's Weekly*, began to take effect, and the public was aroused. George Jones, the owner of the *Times*, was offered a million dollars to quiet his paper; Nast, a half million to go to Europe and cease his campaign of caricature. Long baffled for lack of direct evidence, the *Times* finally had the proofs it wanted put into its hands by an insider with a grievance. The exposure that followed was complete and devastating; the more so when the efforts of Tweed, Hall, and Sweeny to lay the entire blame on Connolly drove the latter to open his records to the reformers. Under the brilliant leadership of Samuel J. Tilden and Charles O'Conor, they were able by the end of 1872 to drive every member of the "ring" out of office. Tweed himself died in jail.

The national rejoicing that Tweed had at last been brought to bay was tempered by the reflection that his misconduct differed only in degree from what went on almost everywhere. James Russell Lowell well expressed the national sense of humiliation when he wrote, apropos of the opening of the Centennial Exposition at Philadelphia:

Columbia, puzzled what she should display
Of true home-make on her Centennial Day,
Asked Brother Jonathan; he scratched his head
Whittled awhile reflectively, and said,

. . . .

Show your State Legislatures; show your Rings;
And challenge Europe to produce such things
As high officials sitting half in sight
To share the plunder and to fix things right;
If that don't fetch her, why you only need
To show your latest style in martyrs — Tweed.
She'll find it hard to hide her spiteful tears
At such advance in one poor hundred years.

Lowell's bitter sarcasm well expressed the feeling of hopelessness that overcame so many Americans when they saw **A brighter** depression added to the length- **side** ening list of their nation's woes. Nevertheless, there was a brighter side to the picture, even if most men failed to see it. The United States could not have been wholly bad; if so it would have produced fewer Jeremiahs. There is an element of hope in the recognition of an existing evil, and the number of Americans who now sprang forward to denounce the shortcomings of their nation and their fellow citizens was so great as to constitute in itself good evidence that the times were not altogether out of joint. Three of these unconscious optimists, Edwin Lawrence Godkin, George William Curtis, and Carl Schurz, deserve particular mention. A nation that could list such men among its leaders of thought had no reason to despair. There was yet "balm in Gilead."

E. L. Godkin (1831–1902) was Irish-born but of English stock, the son of a distinguished Protestant clergyman **E. L. Godkin** and journalist. Educated for the law, young Godkin chose instead to make journalism his career, and after a brief connection with the London *Daily News* and the Belfast *Northern Whig*, he emigrated in 1856 to America. Here he at once made friends, and forged ahead so rapidly that in 1865, when he was not yet thirty-four years of age, forty interested stockholders subscribed one hundred thousand dollars with which he was to start a weekly newspaper, the *Nation*. Despite many early financial embarrassments, the venture succeeded beyond its founders' highest hopes, and the *Nation* came to exercise an influence upon American life second to none. According to James Bryce, it was "the best weekly not only in America but in the world." Its pronouncements were awaited eagerly by ministers, editors, and minor publicists who pushed the radius of its influence far beyond the number of its readers. Godkin fearlessly attacked every evil he saw, and aimed his most barbed shafts at the venal politicians whom the spoils system had foisted on the country. He stood steadfastly for a sound-money policy, but he denounced scornfully the business rascality that the age produced. He saw, far more clearly than if he had been a native American, the elemental flaws in American society, and bitingly headed an editorial on the Beecher trial "Chromo Civilization." Ruefully he pointed out what the witnesses revealed about American "ways of living, standards of right and wrong, traits of manners, codes of propriety, religious and social ideas." Floral tributes sent by Beecher's congregation to grace the trial he likened to "wreaths round the manhole of a sewer."

George William Curtis (1824–1892) was a New Englander by birth who had come to George William Curtis New York City as a boy. He maintained the best traditions of Puritan New England: read Emerson, lived for a while at Brook Farm, and before the Civil War wrote several books of travel and criticism. Stirred deeply by the war, he became in 1863 editor of the strongly pro-northern *Harper's Weekly*, which, in the ascendancy it soon gained over men's minds, was rivaled only by its more strictly intellectual contemporary, the *Nation*. Allotting generous space to pictorial representation of current events, frequently drawn on the spot, and featuring the cartoons of Thomas Nast, *Harper's Weekly* appealed to a far wider audience than the *Nation;* nor was it, out of deference possibly to the publishers' profits, so avowedly militant in its advocacy of reform. Curtis's influence, however, was exerted from the lecture platform almost as actively as from the editor's desk. Scores of audiences heard his lecture on "Political Infidelity," but he did not always deal exclusively with politics. Concerned because American materialism was deadening the moral sensibilities of the people, he once cried out:

Are we satisfied that America should have no other excuse for independent national existence than a superior facility of money-making? Why, if we are unfaithful as a nation, though our population were to double in a year, and the roar and rush of our vast machinery were to silence the music of the spheres, and our wealth were enough to buy all the world, our population could not bully history, nor all our riches bribe the eternal justice not to write upon us: "Ichabod, Ichabod, thy glory is departed."

Carl Schurz (1829–1906), like Godkin, was alien-born. His father, a small-town German schoolmaster, made every sacrifice in order to permit Carl Schurz young Carl to work for a doctor's degree in history at the University of Bonn. Here the boy was caught up, along with many other student liberals, in the revolutionary movements of 1848–49, joined the rebel forces, and escaped capture only by fleeing to France. Later he went to Switzerland, where many other German refugees had gathered, and where he might have remained but for his determination to rescue one of his Bonn professors, Gottfried Kinkel, who was under sentence of imprisonment for life at Spandau, near Berlin. The exciting story of Kinkel's rescue by Schurz, and of their joint flight to England, is not often paralleled except in fiction, but much of the rest of Schurz's life also reads like a romance. He tried living in France, only to be expelled as a dangerous radical, and at last sailed for America where, naturally, he joined the German colony in Wisconsin. Because of his intense interest in liberal democracy, he was soon drawn into politics, and his anti-slavery sentiments made him a Republican. A born orator, he spoke not

Three Reformers, George William Curtis of *Harper's Weekly*, E. L. Godkin of the *Nation*, and Carl Schurz, politician and publicist, played outstanding roles in developing a healthy public reaction against dishonesty in government business, and private life.

only in German, but had soon acquired such facility in the use of English that his assistance in campaigns was in great demand. He fought loyally in the Civil War, from which he emerged a major-general, and after the war made an official tour of the South at the behest of President Johnson. In 1867 he became part owner and editor of a German-language newspaper, published at St. Louis, and was soon in the thick of the fight for Liberal Republicanism. By the time he went to the United States Senate in 1869 his Americanization was thoroughgoing and complete. Like Lincoln, he was intensely interested in proving that democracy as a form of government was fit to survive, and the venality of the spoilsmen who stood ready to betray it for a price drove him to the highest invective. When he spoke in the Senate the galleries were packed, and when he took to the lecture platform, as he often did, great crowds came out to hear him.

In the business and political world the work of such men as Godkin, Curtis, and Schurz was not wholly without effect. Scandals were ruthlessly exposed, and sometimes, as in the case of Tweed, the guilty parties were punished. A governor in Nebraska and a state treasurer in Minnesota were impeached and removed from office. A member of the Kansas legislature laid on the speaker's desk seven thousand dollars that he had been paid to vote for the re-election of Samuel C. Pomeroy to the United States Senate, and Pomeroy was not re-elected. The Whiskey Ring was put out of business; thievery in the Indian service was restrained; wholesale attempts to bribe Congress, as in the Crédit Mobilier, were not again attempted; alien rule in the South and the corruption it bred were soon overthrown. Even more significant, the people, as the Granger movement abundantly attested,[1] were beginning to show a disposition to use the power of government to restrain corporation practices which they believed were interfering unjustly with the personal and property rights of individuals.

Even more noteworthy than all these efforts to purify politics and to regulate business were the spiritual strivings of a people, now acutely conscious of its shortcomings. The success of the American experiment in democracy depended in the last

[1] See pp. 135–137.

analysis upon the character of the individual citizens who made up the population. If the citizens were honest, capable, and intelligent, the future of the nation, however much it might be temporarily eclipsed by the depression, was bright; but if the citizens were unworthy, prosperity itself could not dispel the gloom. Out of such heart-searchings there came a significant educational renaissance, a renewed interest in literary activity, and a wholesome enthusiasm for humanitarian reform.

With respect to public elementary education, the Civil War, at least so far as the **Educational advances** North was concerned, merely interrupted a trend of development that had begun long before. After the war, as before, the "little red schoolhouse," or its equivalent, continued to be the chief citadel of rural education, and from its lowly rostrum young men and maidens, only a little older than the "scholars" they taught, dispensed knowledge of the "three R's" — reading, writing, and arithmetic. In the towns and villages, buildings of several "rooms" could be found, and the process of separating the various "grades" from one another, with a teacher for each, was an ideal more and more frequently attained. Most rapid progress, however, was made in the cities, where new ideas in education did not put so severe a strain upon taxable resources. In 1873, for example, St. Louis, following the lead of Mrs. Carl Schurz, whose efforts to introduce the European kindergarten idea into America antedated the Civil War, accepted the innovation, and so began a movement that was soon to spread to the whole country. The rapid multiplication of tax-supported normal schools (of which there were only twelve when Lincoln was inaugurated) served greatly to improve the quality of instruction: teachers who themselves had no opportunity to attend such schools learned the latest methods at summer "institutes," locally provided for the purpose. The spell cast by the Webster spellers and by the McGuffey readers had not yet been broken, but new

and better books were being written. Publishers did not long neglect this opportunity for profit, and the means they used to secure "adoptions" sometimes failed to square with the precepts so generously sprinkled through the books they sold. The fact that the several states, operating through local school districts set up by state law, had complete control of educational policy accounts for the wide variety of educational practice in the different parts of the country, but in 1867 the national government took a hand by creating the office of the United States Commissioner of Education, whose business it was "to collect statistics and facts concerning the conditions and progress of education in the several states and territories and to diffuse information respecting the organization and management of schools and school systems and methods of teaching."

Even more striking than the rapid development of the elementary schools was the movement for free public high **High schools** schools that swept the country during the post-war period, and persisted throughout the dark days of depression. Before the Civil War private academies had generally carried forward the education of such students as intended to enter college; indeed, when the war broke out, there were only about one hundred public high schools in the whole United States. The next few decades, however, witnessed the almost complete elimination of the old-fashioned academy and the substitution in its place of secondary instruction at state expense. By 1870 the country had about five hundred public high schools; by 1880 the number had risen to eight hundred; by the end of the century, to six thousand. With the state so thoroughly committed to expenditures for high schools, insistence upon better qualified teachers was inevitable, and systems of certification were devised for the purpose of weeding out the unfit. As the children of the masses pushed on into the high schools, revision of the curriculum to meet the needs of those who had no thought of entering college began to be made, although an undue emphasis upon mathematics and the classical languages long persisted. From shorter beginnings the high-school term generally lengthened out to four years, which, together with the eight years usually assigned to the elementary school, provided a total of twelve years' instruction. Eight or nine months of school per year was the customary goal toward which educators worked, but frequently, especially in the country districts, the school year was much shorter. Many of the northern states enacted compulsory education laws of varying terms and efficacy.

In these significant developments the South, necessarily, lagged far behind. What little **Education in** there was of free public educa**the South** tion in the South before the war had vanished during the conflict, and the freeing of the slaves now placed upon the limited financial resources of the reconstructed states a double burden, schools for the children of the freedmen, and schools for the children of the whites. As already noted, most of the carpetbag governments made generous legal provisions for education, although the distance between promise and performance was often very great. Nevertheless, to cite a single example, South Carolina by 1876 had a public-school population of fifty thousand whites and seventy thousand colored children as against a total of only twenty thousand in 1860.

Quite the most striking educational development of the times, however, appeared in the field of higher education. It would seem, almost, that from this source Americans expected to draw the inspiration and the information that would confound the critics of democracy and make of the United States a kind of Utopia. Even the uneducated masses showed a touching faith in the power of learning. Education, especially higher education, they tended to regard as an unfailing panacea for all of the ills that beset both the nation as a whole and the individuals that composed it.

The remarkable transformation that came over higher education in the United States during the generation that fol- **American** lowed the Civil War owed much **universities** to the statesmanship of a small group of university presidents. Chief among these, no doubt, was Charles W. Eliot, the brilliant young chemist, who in 1869, when only thirty-five years of age, took the helm at Harvard. Much older, but fully alive to the currents of the age and destined to serve for many years, was Frederick A. P. Barnard, the president after 1864 at Columbia. Almost equally noteworthy were such other newly chosen presidents as Andrew D. White of Cornell (1868), James McCosh of Princeton (1868), Noah Porter of Yale (1871), James B. Angell of Michigan (1871), John Bascom of Wisconsin (1874), and Daniel Coit Gilman of Johns Hopkins (1876). Six of these eight men were of New England birth, and all but one of them, McCosh, a Scot from the University of Edinburgh, were graduates of New England colleges. Most of them, according to the prevailing custom of American scholars, had traveled or studied abroad, and possessed a fair familiarity with European university methods. Their concern, however, was neither to preserve the traditional New England college nor to imitate what was being done in Europe. Rather, what they set out to do was to revise the American system of higher education in such a way as to make it fit the needs of a rapidly changing America.

The best efforts of educators would have been in vain but for the liberal financial resources they were able to tap. **Philan-** The profits of the new industrial **thropy** age were not all put back into business; millions of dollars were poured by philanthropists into education. Before the Civil War such a gift as that of Stephen Girard, who at his death in 1831 left two million dollars to found a school for boys in Philadelphia, was so rare as to brand its donor as an eccentric. After the war such gifts became increasingly common, in fact, they were both sought after and expected. In 1865,

Educational opportunities for Americans increased rapidly during the two decades that followed the Civil War. Kindergartens at the lowest level were balanced by increasing facilities for graduate work at the highest, particularly at Johns Hopkins and Harvard. Philanthropists gave generously to establish colleges for women, and land grants from the federal government greatly encouraged agricultural education.

KINDERGARTEN. North-end industrial home in Boston, Mass. From a sketch by Charles Upham for *Leslie's Illustrated Newspaper*, 1881.

DANIEL COIT GILMAN. First president of Johns Hopkins University. Engraving by J. K. Campbell.

VASSAR FEMALE COLLEGE. Lithograph by Mayer & Co. at time of founding, 1865.

Ezra Cornell, whose fortune had been made from the electric telegraph, gave a half-million dollars to found Cornell University in Ithaca, New York. In 1873, a similar gift from Cornelius Vanderbilt, the railroad magnate, made possible the establishment of Vanderbilt University in Nashville, Tennessee. Three years later, Johns Hopkins University opened its doors because a rich merchant, banker, and railroad director of Baltimore had endowed it with property worth four and one half million dollars, and his name. Supplemented presently by the outpourings of such philanthropists as John D. Rockefeller, Andrew Carnegie, and Edward Stephen Harkness the total endowment of colleges and universities in the United States ultimately reached enormous figures. The resources of Harvard, for example, amounted to only two and one half million dollars when Eliot became its president in 1869; two thirds of a century later this sum had grown to one hundred and thirty millions.

A powerful stimulus to higher education at public expense came from the generous gifts of land made by the federal government to the states under the terms of the Morrill Act of 1862. Each state, in return for a land subsidy of as many times thirty thousand acres as it had senators and representatives, was required within five years to establish at least one college which, "without excluding other scientific and classical studies," would "teach such branches of learning as are related to agriculture and the mechanic arts." The law provided also that whenever any of the land so given should be sold, the principal must be kept intact, and only the interest used; furthermore, depletions in the fund must be made good by legislative appropriation. Unfortunately the original law failed to

Federal land grants

CHARLES W. ELIOT.
President of Harvard
University, 1869–1909.

LAND GRANTS. Facsimile of scrip issued
to the State of New York.

specify a minimum price per acre below which lands might not be sold, and the correction made in 1889 that fixed a minimum of ten dollars per acre came too late to do much good. Nevertheless, the sums realized by the states were considerable, and in a few instances they were about all that could have been expected. Ezra Cornell, for example, so successfully located and sold the lands handed over by New York to the university that bore his name that he was able to pile up for it an endowment of five and one half million dollars.

Hardly less important than the financial aspect of the Morrill Act was the obligation it laid upon the states to support a greatly extended program of higher education. The intent of the law was clearly to place a college course within the reach of anyone who wanted it, and to make this privilege a charge on government. Nevertheless, state after state revised its educational system in order to meet the terms of the act. Many

State-supported universities

states used their grant to help along, or sometimes to found, a single state university; others showed a preference for separate colleges of agriculture and engineering; only a few attempted in any way to dodge the issue. Once a college or university was accepted as a financial responsibility of the state, it could almost certainly count upon annual legislative appropriations to keep it alive and growing. Many of the western state universities, notably Wisconsin, Illinois, Minnesota, and California, rose to prominence as a result of the Morrill Act, and ultimately not less than sixty-nine "land-grant colleges" profited from its terms.

But the changes that came over higher education during these years went far deeper than mere size and numbers; no less in the endowed than in the state institutions there came a determined break from the traditional idea of what a college course should be. The backbone of the old curriculum had been

Changes in the curriculum

the classical languages and mathematics, with somewhat less attention to such subjects as ethics and rhetoric. Courses in the modern languages and history were occasionally tolerated, and a little science, with the laboratory work confined to what experiments the professor could do in the presence of the class. Most of the teachers were all-around scholars who were as much at home with one subject as with another. Indeed the "chairs" that some of them occupied were veritable benches of learning; one heroic Columbia professor taught mental and moral philosophy, English literature, history, political economy, and logic. But the old curriculum bore scant resemblance to the new civilization that was growing up outside the college walls. Its drill on the classics and its moralistic, theological bent were designed at best only to fit the needs of the few — most of whom expected to enter some "learned" profession — rather than the many, most of whom in the new age were destined for decidedly materialistic careers. If higher education was to be opened to the masses, then its content must be such as would have meaning for them. There was, moreover, an infinite quantity of new data to be evaluated and assimilated into the scholar's store of knowledge. An economic revolution was in process that the colleges and universities had all but ignored, while every field of science cried out for further exploration and investigation.

Under the leadership of President Eliot, Harvard University began to emphasize the **The elective system** right of a student to have some voice in the selection of his course of study. In most colleges the studies were rigidly prescribed, but Harvard's experiments with "electives" during the sixties convinced Eliot that the elective principle was the correct one upon which to build a new curriculum. Year after year the number of "prescribed" courses was cut down and the number of "electives" was lengthened. This process served a double purpose. On the one hand, it permitted the student to escape from subjects for which he lacked interest or aptitude; on the other, it permitted the indefinite expansion of the number of "subjects" that a given institution might offer. Once more, as in the Middle Ages, the totality of knowledge became the university's goal, rather than merely the set pattern of disciplines that tradition had developed; and an infinite number of subjects that previously had been regarded as well beyond the pale of educational respectability — some of them frankly "bread-and-butter" courses — began to enter the curriculum. The elective idea spread like wildfire all over the country, and awakened both enthusiastic approval and fierce denunciation. President McCosh of Princeton was among the skeptics, and on one occasion he met President Eliot in a public debate on the topic. Critics of the new system complained, as Henry Cabot Lodge said later, that it permitted students "to escape without learning anything at all by a judicious selection of unrelated subjects taken up only because they were easy or because the burden imposed by those who taught them was light." But, for good or for ill, electives had come to stay, although most institutions ultimately insisted upon a central core of "required" subjects.

Quite as revolutionary as the elective system was the equally determined insistence upon technical and professional training. The Morrill Act gave a great stimulus to agricultural education, and as **Technical and professional schools** time went on more and more students who were primarily interested in the problems of farming began to put in their appearance. For a long time, however, the agricultural colleges were decidedly on the defensive because of their low enrollment. The University of Wisconsin, for example, had only one graduate in agriculture by 1880. Nevertheless, the building up of a staff of experts went on, and ultimately the public realized that the agricultural colleges reached a far wider field than the small number of students who attended them. Remarkable progress was made in the investigation of such subjects as the diseases of plants and animals, the proper treatment of soils, and the selection of seeds. All this information was passed along in one fashion or another to the farm population, and the schools themselves became headquarters not so much for the training of farmers as for the training of experts to advise the farmers. The Morrill Act did a similarly important service for engineering, particularly with respect to the more practical aspects of the subject. Courses in mechanical and civil engineering, mining and metallurgy, and architecture were established which presently produced sufficiently well-trained graduates that the business world was eager to obtain their services.

Perhaps the most astonishing development of all began in the medical schools, **Medical education** which before the Civil War had been nothing less, according to one authority, than a "social disgrace." Most of these early institutions existed to make what little money they could out of the students who patronized them, and the so-called "doctors" they turned out were quite definitely a liability to society. Even at Harvard, which possessed one of the best of the medical schools in the country, the student who took two lecture courses for a term less than four months in length was entitled to his degree if he could prove that his total medical experience ran to three years, and could pass a simple examination. Written examinations were said by the head of the school, as late as 1870, to be out of the question, because "a majority of the students cannot write well enough." President Eliot had much to do with the progress that Harvard made in medical education, and that was soon communicated to other colleges. Supported by Oliver Wendell Holmes, whose service to American medicine ranks parallel to his service to American literature, Eliot insisted upon actual attendance for the three-year period, together with laboratory and clinical training. Drawing freely upon the superior knowledge and techniques of European scientists, American medical scholarship was soon to be fully abreast of the times.

What was being done for the teaching of medicine was also being done for the law. Instead of a few months' cramming, law students were now introduced by Dean C. C. Langdell of the Harvard Law School to the "case method," by which they were required to dig out for themselves the rules of law that had grown out of judicial decisions. Here again, as with the colleges of arts and sciences when the elective system was introduced, there arose from conservative sources a great outcry of opposition, but the new method had come to stay, and in the course of time was adopted by practically every reputable law school in the country. As with medicine, the course was lengthened, standards were raised, and competent scholars were engaged to devote their full time to teaching.

Perhaps the best evidence that American scholarship was reaching maturity was supplied by the establishment of a **Graduate schools** considerable number of graduate schools. Prior to this time the determined devotee of learning had little recourse from the requirement of study abroad. American scholars were European made. Some obtained their training in England, but an apparent disdain on the part of English savants for Americans who pretended to scholarship led the latter to prefer the Continent, especially Germany, where they were more cordially received. When the time came for the establishment of American graduate schools, therefore, it was the German, not the English, model that was followed; and presently the Ph.D. (Doctor of Philosophy) degree, then virtually unknown in England, was to become in America, as in Germany, the heart's desire of every budding young scholar. The first Ph.D. ever conferred in America was given by Yale in 1861, but it was not until ten years later that the Yale graduate school was organized. By 1872 Harvard had established a graduate school, and in 1876 Johns Hopkins University sought to set a new precedent by making graduate work its main concern. Before long even the new state universities of the West were emphasizing the importance of research and the training of scholars, and the day had passed when the only possible place to do advanced work was in Europe. According to President Ira Remsen, Gilman's successor at Johns Hopkins, there had been in 1850 only eight graduate students in the whole United States; by 1875 this number had risen to 399; by the end of the century it was 5668.

The new emphasis on intellectual achievement was revealed also in the activities of a **Science and** small but able group of scholars. **philosophy** Major J. W. Powell, a war veteran who served for a time as a professor in Illinois Wesleyan University, established his reputation as a geologist by an exploration in 1869 of the Grand Canyon of the Colorado that led presently to its systematic survey under the auspices of the Smithsonian Institution. In 1879 Powell became director of the United States Bureau of Ethnology, and a year later of the United States Geological Survey. During the same period Lewis Henry Morgan, who had won fame even before the Civil War for his studies of the Iroquois Indians, brought out two notable works, *Consanguinity and Affinity* (1868) and *Ancient Society* (1877), which still rank among the most distinguished of the writings of American anthropologists. During these years also Othniel Charles Marsh, professor of paleontology at Yale after 1866, made a number of dangerous but fruitful expeditions into the Rocky Mountain region, and as vertebrate paleontologist for the United States Geological Survey discovered more than a thousand new fossil vertebrates. Other names of note were Simon Newcomb, the astronomer, Benjamin Peirce, the mathematician, and John Fiske, the philosopher. Fiske, as an ardent disciple of Herbert Spencer, did much to popularize in America the Darwinian views on which Spencer's *Synthetic Philosophy* was based; and when, years later, he turned to the writing of American history he treated that subject as a strictly evolutionary process. At best, however, the list of American scholars was not a long one. According to one authority, for every work of research published in the United States during this period not less than fifty appeared in Europe. What interested Americans more than research was the widening of educational opportunity so that everyone might have his chance at learning. The deepening process could wait.

Even the women shared in the new opportunity. Their right to equal treatment in elementary and secondary **Education** schools was fairly well acknowl- **for women** edged before the Civil War, but their chance of obtaining instruction on the college level remained slight. In 1865, however, Vassar opened its doors at Poughkeepsie, New York, as a strictly women's college, only to be followed a decade later by Wellesley, not far from Boston. Both institutions struggled along for years without adequate endowments and without adequately prepared students — "between the devil of bankruptcy and the deep sea of the young ladies' seminary." In 1875, Smith College, with a gift of $365,000 from Sophia Smith of Hatfield, Massachusetts, to found an institution that would provide educational opportunities for young women equal to those available for young men, opened at Northampton, Massachusetts, with only fourteen freshmen. Each year it admitted a new class, but continued to insist on adequate preparation, however small the numbers. When Bryn Mawr was established in the eighties, near Philadelphia, enough young women were being fitted for college work that the battle for high standards had no need to be fought over again. The beginnings of Radcliffe College go back to 1879 when the "Annex" at Harvard offered its first courses for women.

It was not through women's colleges, however, but through coeducation that most American women were to get **Co-** their chance at a college course. **education** The demand for coeducation antedated the

Civil War and was for a long time closely connected with the movement for women's rights. After the war it grew mainly as an economical and common-sense western idea. Reassured by the experiments of Oberlin, Antioch, and Iowa, all of which had admitted women along with men before the Civil War, the University of Wisconsin set up a special normal department for women in 1863, and was presently drawing no distinction between men and women students. Ohio State University admitted women from its beginning in 1870. Other western universities fell into line, and with them the small denominational colleges, not only in the West, but to a considerable extent also in the East and even in the South. While coeducation thus promptly became the rule in the West, the number of skeptics in the older sections of the country was great, and in the South separate state institutions for women were often established as a lesser evil.

Higher education for the Negro made progress in 1867 with the incorporation of **Negro education** Howard University in Washington, named after one of its most active promoters, General O. O. Howard of the Freedmen's Bureau; and in quick succession such other institutions as Fisk University in Nashville, Straight University in New Orleans, and Shaw University in Raleigh began to function. For these and similar schools northern philanthropy retained for a time a certain fondness, born of the abolitionist crusade.[1] The Peabody Fund, already mentioned, was administered mainly with a view to the improvement of common schools for Negroes, but the Peabody Normal College in Nashville, which it aided generously, also served notably the cause of education among the whites. Unfortunately the Negroes at first thought of education, particularly higher education, primarily as a means of escape from manual labor, and showed little interest in substituting for Latin and Greek the more "practical" subjects that were crowding into the cur-

[1] See p. 10.

riculums of the northern colleges and universities. Nevertheless, the Hampton Normal and Agricultural Institute, which opened at Hampton, Virginia, in 1870 with funds provided by the American Missionary Association, struck out along new and bold lines. Its purpose was to emphasize the dignity and importance of skill in labor with the hands, and to prepare its students as well as might be for the type of work that was actually available to them in the South. Means were provided at the Institute whereby the poorer students might "work their way through," and in 1872 Hampton's most distinguished student, Booker T. Washington, walking and begging rides to make a five-hundred-mile journey from his home in West Virginia, arrived with fifty cents in his pocket to take advantage of the opportunities that the Institute offered. Less than ten years later, Washington was chosen to head a school for Negroes at Tuskegee, Alabama, that under his leadership was soon to rival Hampton in its success with the same type of instruction. Critics of so much emphasis upon industrial education for the Negroes complained that such training was designed merely to keep the colored race in a permanently inferior status, but in the main the aims and efforts of Hampton, Tuskegee, and their imitators were applauded by both Negroes and whites. Probably the gradual easing of the tension between the two races owed much to the activities of these institutions.

The Civil War dealt harshly with American literary talent. The old generation of American writers — Emerson, **American** Longfellow, Lowell, Whittier, **letters** Bryant, Holmes — lived on and continued to write, but the roar and bustle of the new age had passed them by. The America they represented was dead and gone. This was not true of Walt Whitman, perhaps, whose *Leaves of Grass* was presently to become, according to one opinion, the "Bible of democracy," but the hiatus between the old generation and the new was nevertheless well marked. The period represented politi-

William Dean Howells, who

was born in 1837 and died in 1920, made rich contributions to American literature through no less than six decades, and was often called the "Dean of American letters." He not only knew well such great writers of the Middle Period as Longfellow, Lowell, and Hawthorne, but he outlived many of his contemporaries, including his friend Mark Twain, who said of him: "He seems to be always able to find that elusive and shifty grain of gold, the *right word*." Howells also admired the work of Mark Twain, particularly *Tom Sawyer* and *Huckleberry Finn*. In their first publications these books were replete with distinctive illustrations, such as this sketch of Huckleberry Finn by E. W. Kemble for the original edition, 1885.

---

cally by the Civil War and reconstruction was one of stalemate for American letters. Whether this was because too many men of potential literary genius perished on the battlefield, or because the martial spirit dulled the interest of Americans in bookish pursuits, will never be known. "For ten years," said a discouraged observer, "the new generation read nothing but newspapers."

That a new day was soon to dawn became evident when the literary world discovered **Mark Twain** that Samuel Langhorne Clemens (1835–1910), better known by his pen name, Mark Twain, had more to his credit than an irreverent, western sense of humor. Definitely out of line with the American literary tradition was Mark Twain's birthplace, the western town of Florida, Missouri. Quite as unorthodox was his education, which, to begin with, was derived less from the ungraded school which he attended than from the Mississippi River, which flowed by the town of Hannibal, Missouri, where he spent his boyhood. Always fascinated by the river, and curious about the unknown world from which its steamboats came and into which they went, young Clemens, after spending a few years as an itinerant printer, apprenticed himself to a river pilot, and learned the river "by heart" from St. Louis to New Orleans.

In that brief, sharp schooling [he wrote later] I got personally and familiarly acquainted with all the different types of human nature that are to be found in fiction, biography, or history. When I find a well-drawn character in fiction or biography, I generally take a warm personal interest in him, for the reason that I have known him before — met him on the river.

Clemens's career as a river pilot was cut short by the Civil War in which he fought for two full weeks as a Confederate bushwhacker. His heart was not in the fray, and his sympathies ultimately turned to the North. Before the summer of 1861 had ended, he was on his way to Nevada, and by the time the war was over, he had seen most of the mining West, making his way about by reporting for various newspapers. A visit to Hawaii in 1866 gave him the material for a story published in *Harper's Magazine* that same year, and set him to lecturing. Immensely successful with Pacific Coast audiences, he soon had the means to return by way of New York and Panama for a visit to his old home, to make a trip to Europe, and to establish himself in a new home at Hartford, Connecticut.

His writings, based upon his varied experiences and interpreted by the lore he had learned on the river, came thick and fast. *The Celebrated Jumping Frog of Calaveras County, and Other Sketches* (1867), was sheer hilarity; *Innocents Abroad* (1869) became immediately a best-seller because of the fun it poked at the tourist's Europe; *Roughing It* (1872) introduced Easterners to a Far West that was immensely interesting and vital, although in writing it Mark Twain undoubtedly followed the advice he later gave to Rudyard Kipling, "Young man, first get your facts; then distort them as you please"; *The Gilded Age* (1874), written in collaboration with Charles Dudley Warner, satirized skillfully the corrupt politics, ruthless fortune-chasing, and social bankruptcy of the reconstruction era; *Life on the Mississippi*, published first as a series of articles in the *Atlantic Monthly* for 1875, preserved for all time what Mark Twain knew so well about the fast-ebbing civilization that had centered about the river; *Tom Sawyer* (1876) recovered the scenes of the author's childhood in what William Dean Howells called "the best boy story ever written"; and for a generation longer the list continued to grow. Europeans sooner than Americans recognized that Mark Twain's books had literary merit as well as humor; that in a manner quite at variance with respectable tradition they set forth themes that were

equally new. Brahmin Boston, still the self-confessed literary capital of America, was slow to acknowledge that this upstart westerner was a man of parts, but on December 17, 1877, when the *Atlantic* gave a dinner in honor of Whittier's birthday, Mark Twain was invited to make one of the main addresses. Unfortunately, he resorted to a type of burlesque better suited to the west than to his hearers, who were definitely unamused. But the recognition he had at last received was not recalled.

Mark Twain was not so much the founder of a new school of American writers as he was the ablest representative of **Other western writers** a considerable group of westerners who exploited the frontier theme in literature well before Frederick Jackson Turner had introduced it to the historians. Far-famed also was Bret Harte, who, although a New Yorker by birth, grew up in California while the spirit of lawlessness was still strong in the mining camps, and with a vividness that has seldom been surpassed described that West in such stories as "The Luck of Roaring Camp" and "The Outcasts of Poker Flat," both of which were published in the *Overland Monthly* during 1868. Harte also stooped sometimes to the writing of charming doggerel, such as the tale of the "Heathen Chinee" whom two white men tried unsuccessfully to cheat at cards:

> Which is why I remark,
> And my language is plain,
> That for ways that are dark
> And for tricks that are vain,
> The Heathen Chinee is peculiar.

Joaquin Miller, born a Hoosier, was taken to Oregon as a child, saw life as a gold miner, soldier, journalist, lawyer, and judge, but won distinction mainly as a minor poet of the West.

The period of the seventies witnessed the rise of numerous "local-color" writers from other sections of the country also. **William Dean Howells** William Dean Howells, an Ohioan, went East instead of West, and from the time of the Civil War to the end of the century he was connected in an editorial capacity successively with the *Nation*, the *Atlantic*, and *Harper's*. While he wrote of the East, he never forgot the experiences of his youth, and he featured in his writings the problems of adjustment that confronted one who came from a primitive to a cultured environment. Howells's fame rests mainly upon a long and distinguished sequence of novels, beginning with *Their Wedding Journey* (1871), *A Chance Acquaintance* (1873), and *A Foregone Conclusion* (1875). Edward Eggleston, a Methodist "circuit-rider" who had experienced much of what he wrote, portrayed in his first and best novel, *The Hoosier Schoolmaster* (1871), the quaint country life of southern Indiana. Mention also should be made of George W. Cable of New Orleans, whose *Old Creole Days* appeared in 1879, and Sarah Orne Jewett of Maine, whose exquisite delineations of New England character were printed first as stories in the *Atlantic*, and were later collected into books, *Deephaven* (1877) and *Country Byways* (1881). In these years, too, Henry James, who "was born an American and died an Englishman," began with his *Roderick Hudson* (1875) and *The American* (1876) to write finely spun novels dealing with the contacts of Americans with European sophistication.

Paralleling the educational and literary achievements of the post-war period came **Humanita-** a definite upsurge of humani- **rian reform** tarian reform. To a great extent this can be accounted for on the ground that exactly such an interest had preceded the Civil War, and that with the war and the immediate problems it raised out of the way, the old desire to better the lot of the unfortunate reasserted iteslf. It should not be forgotten, however, that the work of such organizations as the United States Sanitary Commission and the United States Christian Commission had done much to keep alive the humanitarian spirit, even while the war was on; and that the crying needs of the freedmen had made for an awareness of the problems that confronted downtrodden humanity, whether white or black.

Among the many factors that contributed to the popular interest in humanitarianism doubtless the religious revival **Moody and** that swept through Protestant **Sankey** America during these years was one of the most important. Poured forth from thousands of pulpits, the doctrine that the depression was but a just judgment upon men for their sins produced a multitude of penitents. Rivalry with the Catholics and the Jews, whose numbers were being enormously increased by immigration, and rivalry among the various Protestant denominations themselves, spurred on religious workers to greater and greater activity. Leadership was furnished less by the great preachers of the day, such as Henry Ward Beecher and Phillips Brooks, than by the evangelists, among whom Dwight L. Moody, the exhorter, and Ira D. Sankey, the singer, were pre-eminent. In 1875 Moody and Sankey, just returned from a series of successful revivals in the British Isles, began a meeting in Philadelphia that lasted three months, and then went on to New York, Chicago, Boston, and other great cities; in Chicago for four months their "tabernacle" was crowded daily by an audience of from five to ten thousand persons. The narrow and traditional doctrines of these evangelists, and of the host of lesser lights who imitated them, had but little direct bearing upon the social problems of the current age, but they at least extolled the Christian virtues and filled "converts" with an earnest if unguided desire to better the lot of their fellowmen.

Far more conscious than the churches of the needs of the time were the Young Men's and Young Women's Christian **Practical** Associations, both of which **Christianity** dated back to the middle of the century, but began to be really effective only during the seventies. Religion, for them, meant wholesome recreation, study classes, and even musicales, far more than the inculcation of Christian theology. Immediately effective among the submerged classes was the Salvation Army, which invaded the United States from England in 1879, and soon extended its interest from saving the souls of the down-and-out to an extensive program of social activity. Quite at the other extreme of society was Christian Science, which took its tenets from *Science and Health with Key to the Scriptures*, a book published by Mrs. Mary Baker G. Eddy in 1875. Rejecting medicine, and claiming for the Divine mind a complete superiority over matter, the Christian Scientists preached a doctrine which, they claimed, wrought many healings of all types of disease and discord, and which, for a certainty, wrought notable cures among those whose nerves were unstrung by the increasing tempo of civilized life; its influence, also, reached over into other denominations and into medicine itself. While Christian Scientists were at pains not to ascribe their cures to the human will, the belief grew among those who made this assumption that a vigorous will had much to do with the attainment of happiness and health.

One shocking cause of unhappiness and ill-health was intemperance, a vice that the Civil War, as already noted, had **The** done much to promote. At the **W.C.T.U.** end of that struggle only two states, Maine and Massachusetts, remained true to their earlier stand for prohibition, and in 1868 Massachusetts voted in favor of the licensing system. Representatives of the old school of temperance reformers, such as John B. Gough, were still at work, but it was clear that their efforts alone would avail little against the effective organization that the liquor interests were able to achieve. In 1867, a National Brewers' Congress openly went on record against the election of any candidate to office, whatever his party, in case he showed himself favorable to the cause of total abstinence, and very generally the cause of one liquor dealer became the cause of all. Faced by this situation the evangelical churches, especially the Methodists, the Baptists, and the Presbyterians, presented a united front against the "Demon Rum,"

W.C.T.U. members singing hymns in front of bar rooms to aid in the temperance movement. Such scenes as these were by no means uncommon. Sketch by S. B. Morton for *Leslie's Illustrated Newspaper*, 1874.

and began to urge such measures as the raising of license fees to liquor dealers, local option for towns and counties, and the revival of state-wide prohibition. A few gave their votes to the Prohibition Party, which was founded in 1869, but by far the greater number stood steadfastly by their old party affiliations regardless of their interest in the temperance cause. Outside the churches, the most effective organization of temperance advocates was the Women's Christian Temperance Union, which, founded in 1874, campaigned energetically, with Frances E. Willard of Evanston, Illinois, as its leader, for temperance instruction in the schools and the better awakening of the public to the evils of intemperance. By the end of the seventies the temperance forces could point to only a few victories, but their confidence in the future was complete.

Because women seemed to be more easily aroused against intemperance than men, **Woman Suffrage** temperance advocates very generally favored the "emancipation of women," particularly with respect to conferring upon them the right to vote. The woman suffrage movement, like the temperance movement, had attracted attention long before the Civil War, but the attainment of suffrage by the illiterate freedmen of the South had spurred the women reformers on to renewed activity. Surely women were as fit to cast their ballot as ex-slaves. Led by such intrepid workers as Susan B. Anthony and Elizabeth Cady Stanton, and joined by a host of professional reformers who before the Civil War had centered their attack upon slavery, the suffragists made a little progress. A few states reluctantly conceded to women the right to vote in school elections, and far out in the West the two territories of Utah and Wyoming established complete political equality. Eventual victory for the suffragists was forecast by the increasing freedom with which women attended college, entered such professions as the ministry, the law, and medicine, and organized Women's Clubs.

That the zeal for reform, so characteristic of Americans during the generation preceding **Other reformers** the Civil War, had been eclipsed rather than destroyed by that struggle was apparent in a multitude of ways. Dorothea L. Dix, to mention a single name, laid down her war work only to resume her earlier efforts for the improvement of conditions among criminals, paupers, and the insane. In state after state boards of charities were set up to deal with the problem of relief. State schools for the deaf and the blind were established, and occasional efforts were made to deal separately with the problem of juvenile delinquency. In Massachusetts, for example, an industrial school for delinquent girls was opened during the seventies at Lancaster. Even the humane treatment of animals was demanded, and an American Society for the Prevention of Cruelty to Animals, founded in 1866 by Henry Bergh on the model of the British Royal Society for the same purpose, made rapid progress. Through its efforts American children by the million read the well-told tale, *Black Beauty* (1877), by Anna Sewell, an English writer; more important still, the Society interested itself in the well-being of children as well as animals, and did much to rescue the unfortunate from conditions that were sure to drag them down. All such efforts, however, were at best only piecemeal, and comparatively little thought was given to the underlying causes of insanity, poverty, and crime. Some light was shed on the subject by the work of R. L. Dugdale, *The Jukes: A Study in Crime, Pauperism, Heredity, and Disease* (1877), which traced the history of a feeble-minded and diseased family that had cost the state of New York a million dollars since 1800.

Probably only a few Americans were able to take comfort during the dismal years of depression from the fact that an **The Centennial Exposition** educational and literary renaissance seemed imminent, or that their humanitarian instincts were still alive, but a great many had their faith in their country restored by a visit to the Centennial Exposition, held in Philadelphia from May to October, 1876. Similar "world's fairs" had

Susan B. Anthony throughout

most of her long lifetime (she was born in 1820 and died in 1906) was outstanding in reform circles. A Quaker strain in her ancestry conditioned her early to the idea of equality for women and other radical ideas. Irritated by the insistence, even among reformers, that women were expected to "listen and learn," not to participate actively in any public movements, she soon made the pursuit of woman's rights her principal goal. From 1892 to 1900 she was president of the National American Woman Suffrage Association. "The Age of Brass," an early satire on the feminist movement, depicts the fancied results of the triumph of woman's rights. Currier and Ives lithograph, 1869.

recently been staged in Europe, notably at London, Paris, and Vienna, but the Philadelphia Exposition was the first ever to be undertaken in the United States. Preparations for it had been begun before 1873, and in spite of bad business conditions the project was not abandoned. Interested individuals gave heavily of their time and money, the city of Philadelphia contributed generously, and still further assistance was obtained from the various states and from the government of the United States. The railroads, famishing for lack of business, offered greatly reduced rates to Philadelphia, and from all over the country the people came. By the time the Exposition closed, more than nine million visitors had entered its gates, and on a single day as many as 275,000. With total receipts of $3,000,000 the fair was a brilliant financial success.

Compared with later exhibitions, the Philadelphia Centennial had little to offer. Its architecture was mediocre, and its art exhibits, while representative of the best that the United States could then supply, suffered from the unwillingness of foreign nations to send their treasures to America. England, however, was more generous than her Continental neighbors, and for the first time thousands of Americans were able to view the works of such masters as Gainsborough and Reynolds. English furniture and household decorations, German porcelain, French textiles, Japanese bronzes and lacquer wares, and Indian shawls and jewels were also freely displayed. These foreign exhibits greatly impressed the common run of visitors, whose provincialism had always made them slow to recognize that Americans in some ways might possibly be excelled by foreigners. Such exhibits also definitely stimulated interest in foreign lands, and more than ever before Americans began to find opportunity for travel abroad.

The greatest success of the fair was along materialistic rather than artistic lines. Its very size was impressive. The **Successes of** Main Building, covering twenty **the fair** acres of land, was reputed to be the largest building in the world. Numerous other buildings, four of them also of large dimensions, occupied an enclosure of two hundred and thirty-six acres in Fairmount Park, overlooking the Schuylkill River. Machinery Hall housed a magnificent Corliss engine and numerous other symbols of the triumphs of

American industry. When it came to commercial and industrial exhibits, European nations, eager to advance their trade in America, vied with the United States in the richness of their offerings, but Americans were able to feel pleasantly elated as they observed that in such matters as these their own country was more often than otherwise in the lead. The agricultural exhibit opened the eyes of farmer visitors to the possibilities of scientific agriculture; the educational exhibit forced the attention of educators to the progress that was being made in educational methods both at home and abroad; the Woman's Pavilion presented in a full acre the products of feminine industry; the mining and mineral exhibit revealed effectively the tremendous resources of the Far West.

Americans who visited the fair returned home with far more faith in the future than they had had before. After all, the depression could hardly be so dark as it seemed if so many persons could afford the trip to Philadelphia. Nor could an America that in a hundred years had made such marked advances be forever arrested in its progress by a single unfavorable turn of the business cycle. As for the mediocrity of American painting, sculpture, and architecture, most Americans were not aware of any shortcomings in what they saw and were surprised and pleased, rather, that so much was being done by their fellow countrymen along these lines. The years that followed 1876 saw a veritable rash of centennial celebrations, as one important anniversary after another recalled the times in which the foundations of the Republic had been laid. It might not be flattering to compare Grant, Blaine, and Ben Butler with Franklin, Jefferson, and Washington, but it was true, nevertheless, that since the time of the "founding fathers" the United States had conquered a continent, had exchanged economic dependence upon Europe for a remarkable degree of self-sufficiency, and had at least begun to create a civilization of its own. The cloud of depression was still dark, but the silver lining was in sight.

Bibliography

There are a number of excellent works on American social and intellectual history. Merle Curti, *The Growth of American Thought* (2nd edition, 1951), is an admirable textbook. Henry S. Commager, *The American Mind: An Interpretation of American Thought and Character since the 1880's* (1950); and Ralph H. Gabriel, *The Course of American Democratic Thought* (1940), are valuable contributions. See also Joseph Dorfman, *The Economic Mind in American Civilization* (3 vols., 1946–49), III; Harvey Wish, *Society and Thought in America* (2 vols., 1950–52), II; Oscar Cargill, *Intellectual America; Ideas on the March* (1941); and Richard Hofstadter, *Social Darwinism in American Thought, 1860–1915* (1944).

Allan Nevins, *The Emergence of Modern America, 1865–1878* (1927), furnishes a well-balanced account of the social adjustments made during the machine age. Thomas C. Cochran and William Miller, *The Age of Enterprise: A Social History of Industrial America* (1942), is a left wing view of the development of big business. Gustavus Myers, *History of the Great American Fortunes* (3 vols., 1910, new ed., 1936), shows little sympathy for its subject.

On the panic of 1873 see appropriate sections in William J. Shultz, *Financial Development of the United States* (1937); and D. R. Dewey, *Financial History of the United States* (new ed., 1936). See also E. P. Oberholtzer, *Jay Cooke, Financier of the Civil War* (2 vols., 1907); and the later but more limited study by Henrietta Larson, *Jay Cooke: Private Banker* (1936).

Don C. Seitz, *The Dreadful Decade, 1869–1879* (1926), makes no effort to avoid over-statement on the seamy side of the American social scene in the seventies. A picture of the newly rich of the period is found in R. H. Fuller, *Jubilee Jim; The Life of Colonel James Fisk, Jr.* (1928). See also Herbert Asbury, *The Gangs of New York; An Informal History of the Underworld* (1928); and Frank C. Sharp and Philip G. Fox, *Business Ethics: Studies in Fair Competition* (1937). Bouck White, *The Book of Daniel Drew* (1910, new ed., 1937); and A. D. H. Smith, *Commodore Vanderbilt* (1927), are true in picture if not in detail. On Tammany Hall and the Tweed Ring see Gustavus Myers, *The History of Tammany Hall* (rev. ed., 1917); and D. T. Lynch, *"Boss" Tweed; The Story of a Grim Generation* (1927). Albert B. Paine, *Thomas Nast, His Period and His Pictures* (1904), reproduces many of Nast's cartoons. On this general subject see also Oberholtzer, *A History of the United States since the Civil War*, II; and J. F. Rhodes, *History of the United States from the Compromise of 1850*, VII.

The literature on reform and reformers is fairly extensive. Two excellent general works are Eric Goldman, *Rendezvous with Destiny* (1952); and Thomas H. Greer, *American Social Reform Movements; Their Pattern since 1865* (1949). Other books of merit are Frank M. Stewart, *The National Civil Service Reform League* (1929); Clifford W. Patton, *The Battle for Municipal Reform: Mobilization and Attack, 1875–1900* (1940); Edward Cary, *George William Curtis* (1894); and *Life and Letters of Edwin Lawrence Godkin*, edited by Rollo Ogden (2 vols., 1907). C. V. Easum, *The Americanization of Carl Schurz* (1929), treats of Schurz's pre-civil war career; Joseph Schafer, *Carl Schurz, Militant Liberal* (1930), his whole life.

On woman suffrage and temperance see Elizabeth Cady Stanton and others, *History of Woman Suffrage* (6 vols., 1881–1922); Mary G. Peck, *Carrie Chapman Catt: A Biography* (1944); Ray Strachey, *Frances Willard: Her Life and Work* (1912); Mary Earhart, *Frances Willard: From Prayers to Politics* (1944); and Frances E. Willard, *Glimpses of Fifty Years* (1889).

Excellent manuals on the general subject of education are Ellwood P. Cubberly, *Public Education in the United States* (rev. ed., 1934); Edgar W. Knight, *Education in the United States* (3rd ed., 1951); and E. G. Dexter, *A History of Education in the United States* (1904). A comparison of Edward Eggleston, *The Hoosier Schoolmaster* (1871), with Herbert Quick, *One Man's Life* (1925), shows how rapidly conditions were changing. Special subjects are treated in Edgar W.

Knight, *Public Education in the South* (1922); and Charles H. Ambler, *A History of Education in West Virginia: From Colonial Times to 1949* (1951). *Letters of Noah Webster*, edited by Harry W. Warfel (1953), are interesting and informative. On higher education two works by C. F. Thwing, *A History of Higher Education in America* (1906); and *The American and the German University: One Hundred Years of History* (1928), are helpful. The latter shows the Teutonic influence upon American educational development. See also Thomas Woody, *History of Women's Education in the United States* (2 vols., 1929); and H. M. Bond, *The Education of the Negro in the American Social Order* (1934). Also revealing are Booker T. Washington, *Up from Slavery* (new ed., 1945), one of the most significant of Negro autobiographies; and Basil Mathews, *Booker T. Washington* (1948).

Fabian Franklin, *The Life of Daniel Coit Gilman* (1910), furnishes excellent insight into the way in which a great university was built; but on the same theme see also Charles W. Eliot, *A Late Harvest* (1924); and Ferris Greenslet, *The Lowells and their Seven Worlds* (1946). Many of the great universities have produced histories by their own historians, among them James Gray, *The University of Minnesota, 1851–1951* (1951); Merle Curti and Vernon Carstensen, *The University of Wisconsin: A History, 1848–1925* (2 vols., 1949); Jonas Viles, *The University of Missouri* (1939); Samuel E. Morison, *Three Centuries of Harvard, 1636–1936* (1936); Horace Coon, *Columbia, Colossus on the Hudson* (1947); Thomas W. Goodspeed, *The Story of the University of Chicago, 1890–1925* (1925); John T. Ellis, *The Formative Years of the Catholic University of America* (1946); Edward P. Cheyney, *History of the University of Pennsylvania, 1740–1940* (1940); S. Willis Rudy, *The College of the City of New York* (1949); James F. Hopkins, *The University of Kentucky: Origins and Early Years* (1951); John C. French, *A History of the University Founded by Johns Hopkins* (1946).

E. D. Ross, *Democracy's College: The Land-Grant Movement in the Formative Stage* (1942), describes the Morrill Act and its results. It is supplemented by John Ise, *The United States Forest Policy* (1920); Paul W. Gates, *The Wisconsin Pine Lands of Cornell University: A Study in Land Policy and Absentee Ownership* (1943); Carl L. Becker, *Cornell University: Founders and the Founding* (1943); and E. D. Ross, *A History of Iowa State College of Agriculture and Mechanic Arts* (1942).

A. C. Cole, *A Hundred Years of Mount Holyoke College* (1940); and James M. Taylor and Elizabeth H. Haight, *Vassar* (1915), are histories of two women's colleges. See also Marion L. Brittain, *The Story of Georgia Tech* (1948); Leon Richardson, *History of Dartmouth College* (2 vols., 1932); Nora C. Chaffin, *Trinity College, 1839–1892: The Beginnings of Duke University* (1950); and Edward Mims, *History of Vanderbilt University* (1946). David D. Wallace, *History of Wofford College, 1854–1949* (1951), is an account of a small denominational college.

No adequate history of American science exists, but see Bernard Jaffe, *Men of Science in America: The Role of Science in the Growth of our Country* (1944); James G. Crowther, *Famous American Men of Science* (1937); *A Century of Progress*, edited by Charles A. Beard (1933); Edward S. Dana and others, *A Century of Science in America* (1918); *A Popular History of American Invention*, edited by W. B. Kaempffert (2 vols., 1924); F. R. Packard, *History of Medicine in the United States* (2 vols., new ed., 1932); and William M. and M. S. C. Smallwood, *Natural History and the American Mind* (1941). For the life history of a Negro who became one of the nation's greatest scientists see Rackham Holt, *George Washington Carver: An American Biography* (1943). On the popularization of the evolutionary hypothesis, J. S. Clark, *The Life and Letters of John Fiske* (2 vols., 1917), is informative.

On the religious trends of the period consult Henry F. May, *Protestant Churches and Industrial America* (1949); Frank G. Beardsley, *A History of American Revivals* (rev. ed., 1912); and Gamaliel Bradford, *D. L. Moody, A Worker in Souls* (1927). On Christian Science, Sibyl Wilbur, *The Life of Mary Baker Eddy* (1938); Norman Beasley, *The Cross and the Crown* (1952); Lyman P. Powell, *Mary Baker Eddy* (1930, new ed., 1950); or the more critical E. F. Dakin, *Mrs. Eddy* (1929). On the Y.M.C.A., C. Howard Hopkins, *A History of the Y.M.C.A. in North America* (1951); and Sherwood Eddy, *A Century with Youth: A History of the Y.M.C.A. from 1844 to 1944* (1944).

On literary history there are many good books, among them *Literary History of the United States*, edited by Robert E. Spiller and others (3 vols., 1948), II; F. L. Pattee, *A History of American Literature since 1870* (1915); V. L. Parrington, *The Beginnings of Critical Realism in America, 1860–1920* (vol. 3 of *Main Currents of American Thought*, 1927–30); and James D. Hart, *The Popular Book: A History of America's Literary Taste* (1950). Van Wyck Brooks, *New England: Indian Summer, 1865–1915* (1940), pictures entertainingly the twilight of literary New England; and Franklin Walker, *San Francisco's Literary Frontier* (1939), is an account of the literary beginnings in the Far West. See also Dixon Wecter, *Sam Clemens of Hannibal* (1952); Bernard DeVoto, *Mark Twain's America* (1932); Albert B. Paine, *Mark Twain: A Biography* (new ed., 2 vols., 1935); Kenneth Andrews, *Nook Farm: Mark Twain's Hartford Circle* (1950); William Dean Howells, *Years of my Youth* (1916); George R. Stewart, *Bret Harte: Argonaut and Exile* (1931); and Irving McKee, *"Ben Hur" Wallace* (1947).

6

From Hayes to Harrison

Elections of 1874 and 1876 — The disputed returns — Hayes and home rule — Civil service reform — Resumption — Free silver — Bland-Allison Act — Election of 1880 — Garfield and Arthur — The Pendleton Act — The "Mongrel Tariff" — Blaine vs. Cleveland — The tariff — Election of 1888 — Benjamin Harrison — The Fifty-first Congress — Elections of 1890

THE ascendancy of the Republicans in the years that followed the Civil War, already shaken by the excesses of recon
Elections of 1874 struction and the scandals of the Grant régime, tottered almost to a fall with the advent of depression. For the customary two-thirds Republican majority in the national House of Representatives, the congressional elections of 1874 substituted a Democratic majority of more than seventy. The Senate remained Republican, although by a greatly reduced majority, and the signs of the times could be further read in the fact that among the minority members were many ex-Confederates, many former "Copperheads," and even the hated Andrew Johnson himself, who, until the time of his death, July 31, 1875, again represented the State of Tennessee. North as well as South, state after state had passed to the control of the Democrats, and Republican leaders were unable to disguise their presentiments that unless something drastic were done the Presidency would soon be in Democratic hands. To loyal Republicans, many of whom had marched in the Union armies, such a calamity must be prevented at whatever cost. What sensible person could wish to entrust the safety of the United States to a man who drew his support from one-time enemies and traitors?

As the election of 1876 approached, the nervousness of the Republicans was intense. To many of them the loss of the **Nominees** Presidency seemed almost the **in 1876** equivalent of having lost the war. Not daring under the circumstances to select anyone as a standard-bearer who was even slightly tainted with scandal, the Republican National Convention turned for its nominee to the spotless but relatively unknown Rutherford B. Hayes, an able volunteer officer in the Civil War, and three times governor of Ohio. Such a choice was the more necessary because the Democrats seemed certain to nominate, and did nominate, Samuel J. Tilden, whose part in the overthrow of the Tweed Ring had made him governor of New York. Tilden's name was thus indelibly connected with political reform, a strong attraction for the Liberal Republicans whose return to the fold was essential, if the Republicans were to win. More by accident than by conscious planning, both candidates for the Presidency proved to be conservative in their economic views, particularly on the money question. Defeated factions took some comfort, however, from the nominees for the Vice-Presidency, for the Republican candidate, William A. Wheeler of New York, had been a dependable Radical, while the Democratic candidate, Thomas A. Hendricks

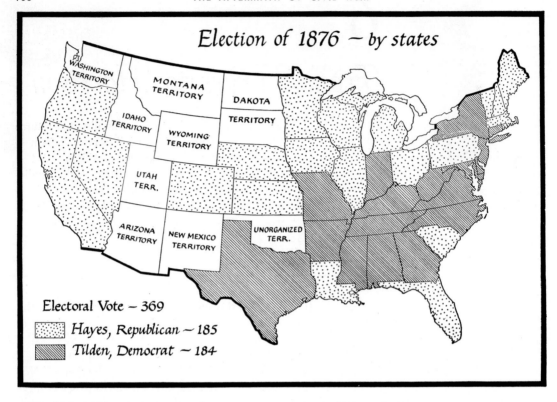

Election of 1876 — by states

Electoral Vote — 369

Hayes, Republican — 185

Tilden, Democrat — 184

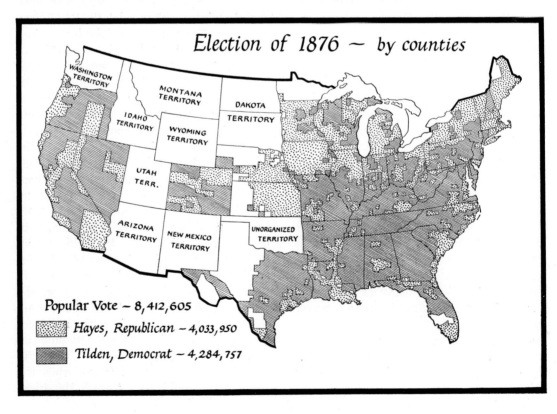

Election of 1876 — by counties

Popular Vote — 8,412,605

Hayes, Republican — 4,033,950

Tilden, Democrat — 4,284,757

of Indiana, was an ex-Copperhead of soft-money tendencies. Extremists on the money question gave their votes to a new Independent, or "Greenback," Party, which favored expansion of the currency by the issue of more paper money, and supported the candidacies of Peter Cooper of New York for President and Samuel F. Cary of Ohio for Vice-President. Most voters, however, even if they held soft-money views, were too enthralled by the main contest to take the Greenbackers seriously.

By the time the election was held, the supremacy of the carpetbaggers had been **The** overthrown in all but three of **disputed** the southern states, South Caro-**returns** lina, Louisiana, and Florida. It was known in advance that every other southern state would vote for Tilden, and on the evening of election day, November 7, it appeared that these three states, too, were safely in the Democratic column. Since New York and several other northern states had gone Democratic, the election of Tilden seemed assured. But the Republican leaders, confident that they could correct the conduct of the three carpetbag states, claimed that these states had in reality voted for Hayes and Wheeler, who would thus have 185 electoral votes to their opponents' 184. The electoral contest thus begun rocked the country, and for a time hope of a peaceful settlement seemed faint. Finally Congress decided to refer the double returns received from the carpetbag states to an Electoral Commission of fifteen, five each from the Senate, the House, and the Supreme Court. By a strict party vote, eight to seven, the Commission gave the election to the Republicans. While on the face of the returns it would seem that the election had been stolen, as the Democrats charged, no doubt many thousands of Negro voters in the South who had wished to vote for Hayes had not dared to vote at all. The real victory of the election rested less with either party than with the American people as a whole, who, in spite of the tenseness of the situation, kept their tempers, and accepted in good faith the decision that had been reached.

Rutherford B. Hayes

NINETEENTH PRESIDENT of the United States, Hayes had been brevetted major-general at the close of the Civil War, but his honesty as a politician, not his military record, was what won him the Republican nomination. It was ironic that the Presidency should have come to a man of such integrity by dubious means.

Rutherford B. Hayes (1822–1893), the new President, was Ohio born and educated. Like Tilden he was a lawyer, but he had never counted many of the **Rutherford** country's great corporations **B. Hayes** among his clients. Unlike Tilden, who had avoided as nearly as possible any stand on the Civil War, Hayes had served loyally, if without distinction, as a volunteer officer in the Union army, and at the close of the war had been brevetted major-general. As governor of Ohio he had made an excellent record: he took his duties seriously, his judgment was good, his word could be trusted, he made appointments for merit even to the extent of naming Democrats to office. During the campaign he astonished reformers by the earnestness with which he denounced the spoils system, and he irritated party regulars by the assertion that "he serves his party best who serves his country best." Utterly unable to bend to expediency, he confided to his diary during the campaign that "if elected, the firmest adherence to principle, against all opposition and temptations, is my purpose. I shall show a *grit* that will astonish those who predict weakness." As President, however, his good intentions frequently betrayed him into bad politics. His cabinet, for example, which was called by some the ablest since Washington's, contained four men who had voted for Greeley in 1872. One of them, the Postmaster-General, was an out-and-out Tilden Democrat from Tennessee, and Hayes had even considered naming General Joseph E. Johnston, the ex-Confederate, as Secretary of War. A man so unversed in political finesse could never become the successful leader of a party, however great his integrity. His wife, a strong temperance advocate, did her husband no good with the politicians and socialites by refusing to serve wine at White House functions.

The first concern of the Hayes administration was to end the scandal of reconstruction. **Restoration of home rule**   In Florida, although its vote was counted for Hayes, carpetbag rule came to an end with the inauguration of a Democratic governor on January 2, 1877. In the two other southern states that were counted for Hayes, South Carolina and Louisiana, Republican state administrations retained power only because they were supported in each instance by small detachments of federal troops. On all sides it was conceded that if these troops were withdrawn, the rival Democratic candidates, whom nearly every white voter had preferred, would promptly seize the reins of power. Should Hayes continue to support carpetbag rule in these two states by ordering the troops to remain, or should he withdraw the troops and permit the southern whites to have things their own way? Knowing full well that his course would greatly strengthen the case for those who claimed he had no right to the Presidency, and that he would assuredly be accused of having bargained with the Southerners to give them "home rule" in return for the necessary votes to put himself into the White House, Hayes ordered the removal of the troops. The reaction in Columbia and Baton Rouge was instantaneous; Democratic officials moved in as Republicans moved out. The

"solid South" had become a fact; military reconstruction had broken down. Six years later, when the Supreme Court of the United States ruled in the Civil Rights cases that the Fourteenth Amendment could not be used to restrain individuals from conduct designed to enforce social discriminations against the Negroes, civil reconstruction may be said to have broken down. Within another decade, as one southern state after another began to devise laws that made the Fifteenth Amendment a mockery, the last remnant of political reconstruction faded away.

Hayes's next move was in the direction of civil service reform, but to accomplish much along this line he needed a really **Civil service** effective civil service commis- **reform** sion, something Congress refused to give him. Nevertheless, Hayes did what he could, unaided by Congress and with comparatively little help from public opinion, to make good appointments. His record in this respect was the best of any President's since John Quincy Adams, but his occasional mistakes annoyed the reformers, who spoke slightingly of his "opportunities and failures," while his successes won him the undying hostility of the most powerful Republican leaders. Early in his administration he engaged in a battle with the Senate over the rule of "senatorial courtesy," according to which every senator of the dominant political party claimed the right to block confirmation of the appointment within his own state of any individual to whom he personally objected. In this fight he won a partial victory. His removal of Chester Alan Arthur, collector of the port of New York, gave great offense to Roscoe Conkling, senator from New York, who succeeded in preventing confirmation of the first man Hayes chose for the place. But with the help of Democratic votes Hayes's second nominee was confirmed. Hayes's unpopularity with the leaders of his party helps explain why he was the only man that the Republican Party ever nominated and elected to the Presidency, and then refused to accord the honor of renomination.

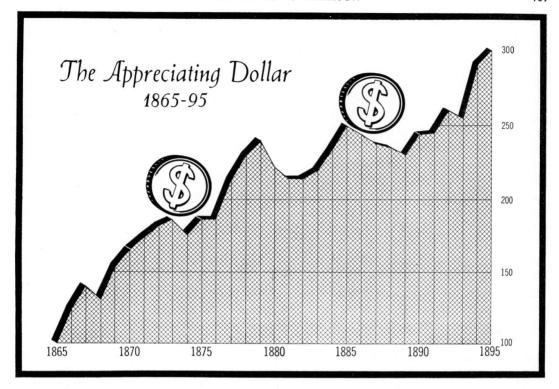

The Appreciating Dollar
1865-95

Hayes's tenacious adherence to hard-money views, even in the face of persistent **Resumption** depression, was in keeping with his character. On this issue he saw eye to eye with the leading men of his party, and he approved cordially the action taken by Congress during Grant's administration to bring about the resumption of specie payments. By a law passed early in 1875, before the Democrats took control of the House of Representatives, Congress had authorized the Secretary of the Treasury to prepare for resumption on the first of January, 1879, by building up a gold reserve. John Sherman was chiefly responsible for this measure, and as a member of Hayes's cabinet it fell to his lot to carry it into effect. Backed steadfastly by the President, he sold bonds for gold, and ultimately accumulated a gold reserve of $100,000,000. As this fund grew, confidence that the government would be able to exchange gold dollars for greenbacks on the appointed day grew with it, and the value of the greenback dollar, expressed in terms of gold, also grew. Worth only sixty-seven cents in 1865, the greenback dollars had risen to eighty-nine cents in 1875, to ninety-six cents in 1877, and well before January 1, 1879, to one hundred cents. In 1878 Congress decided that $346,681,016 in greenbacks should remain a permanent part of the national currency, but the existence of the gold reserve made every greenback dollar "as good as gold." Accustomed by long usage to a paper currency, no one cared to make the exchange, and the greenbacks continued to circulate.

The steadily appreciating value of the dollar insured comfortable profits to money lenders, particularly those who **Soft-money** made long-term loans. For bor- **ideas** rowers, however, the situation was far different. The farmer who mortgaged his farm as security for a five-year loan found to his sorrow when the time for payment came that the dollars he had borrowed were worth far less than the dollars with which he must repay. Dearer dollars meant lower prices for the wheat, or corn, or livestock he had to sell. He must therefore in effect pay back not only principal and interest, but enough more to cover the amount which the dollar had appreciated. When he borrowed, a thousand bushels of wheat might equal in value the amount of his loan; when he repaid, it took from twelve to fifteen hundred bushels of wheat to raise the money he needed, and more for interest. Protests against dearer dollars and lower prices came thick and fast as one depression year after another compounded the gloom, and in the West and the South, where debtors were numerous and creditors were few, soft-money ideas, such as Pendleton's "Ohio idea," found much favor. In general the Democratic Party was more hospitable to soft-money views than the Republican, but in both parties hard-money men, representing the point of view of eastern creditors rather than of southern or western debtors, were in the ascendancy. With resumption imminent, the Greenback Party, founded in 1876, won more and more adherents. In the elections of 1878, it polled a million votes, as against eighty thousand two years before, and elected fifteen members of Congress. Disappointed western Grangers in search of a new panacea accounted in considerable part for the increasing strength of the Greenbackers, and for the Republican loss of the Senate as well as the House.[1]

The success of resumption, and the return of prosperity in 1879, tended to discredit Greenbackism, and the high-water mark of 1878 was never **Free silver** attained again. In the meantime, however, a new soft-money panacea had been discovered in what was popularly known as "free silver." For ages the two precious metals used as money, gold and silver, had depended for their value, not upon the fiat of government, but upon commercial demand. By a curious and long-sustained coincidence the relative value of the two metals had been almost constant; and it took fifteen or sixteen times as much silver to equal in value a given unit of gold. In early times the slight fluctuation in the ratio of value between the two metals had been of small concern. Methods

[1] On the Granger Movement, see pp. 135–137.

of refinement and of measurement were too crude to make the variations noticeable, and governments themselves were not above deceiving the public all they could. With the progress of modern science, however, the exact amount of silver and of gold in a coin could be easily ascertained, and nations made an effort to establish coinage ratios that would harmonize with the existing commercial ratio. Always this was difficult, or even impossible, for the commercial ratio was inevitably a variable, while the coinage ratio established by law was a constant. Human nature being what it is, people who knew the difference hoarded the overvalued coins, and spent those undervalued; or, as the ancient Gresham Law expressed it, the cheap money drove the dear money out of circulation. Paper issues, being as a rule less valuable than either gold or silver, rarely had much difficulty in driving both out of circulation. Such had been the case in the United States during most of its history, while during and after the Civil War the rule of the greenbacks and the national bank notes had been supreme.

Hopeful that the time had come at last when a metallic currency could be provided for general use, the Secretary of **The "crime** the Treasury obtained from **of 1873"** Congress in February, 1873, a new coinage law. This measure took account of the theory, generally observed in European practice, that only one metal could be used as a standard. Accordingly it dropped the silver dollar, which at the old coinage ratio of sixteen to one contained too much silver to permit it to circulate anyway, from the coinage lists. This was the famous "crime of 1873," committed, according to a generation of silver orators, as the result of an "international conspiracy to demonetize silver." Actually, no one would have thought of branding this law as a crime had not the ratio of value between silver and gold begun suddenly to change. This was due, no doubt, primarily to the huge outpourings of silver from mines in the American West, although the diminished demand throughout the world for the use of silver as money may also have been a factor. Whatever the causes, the trend in the price of silver for the next twenty-five years was downward, a situation which led the despairing silver miners to demand the "free and unlimited coinage of silver at the ratio of sixteen to one" as a remedy. The silver miners were soon joined by the debtor farmers of the Middle West, and to a lesser extent by those of the South, neither of whom had any interest in a higher price for silver, but both of whom were convinced that "free coinage," or "free silver," as they termed the desired policy, would mean a cheaper dollar and higher prices for what they had to sell. Former Greenbackers altered their paper money arguments to fit this new demand. If the government would only take silver from all who offered it, as it still took gold, then coin the silver into silver dollars at the old ratio of sixteen to one and put the new silver dollars into circulation, the country would have more money and cheaper money, just as surely as if greenbacks had been issued. Free silver thus became the adopted child of the Greenbackers.

The silver issue continued as a constant factor in American politics for the rest of the **The Bland-Allison Act** nineteenth century, and during Hayes's administration the silver forces won what they mistook at first for a considerable victory. By the Bland-Allison Act, passed in 1878 over Hayes's veto, the Secretary of the Treasury was ordered to purchase each month from two to four million dollars' worth of silver at the market price, and to coin it into silver at the ratio of sixteen to one. This meant limited coinage, however, instead of unlimited coinage, and while the new silver dollars were made legal tender, Secretary Sherman and others saw clearly that if only they could be backed by gold, as was the case with the greenbacks, they would be "as good as gold." In practice not only Sherman, but his successors also, whether Republicans or Democrats, completely defeated the hopes of the silverites by standing ready at all times to redeem silver dollars, whatever their "intrinsic value," in gold.

As the time approached for the election of 1880, it became apparent that the Republicans could count upon that most **Election of 1880** valuable of all political allies, prosperity. Foreign trade had increased; the United States enjoyed in 1880, not only a greater volume of trade than had ever been recorded in any previous year, but also a favorable balance of trade. Farm prices, particularly wheat and cotton, were up, and manufacturers were reaping rich harvests from the markets provided by a steadily increasing population. A feeling of confidence replaced the feeling of gloom that had characterized the depression years. But could the Republican Party take advantage of the situation? As everyone knew, it was sadly torn by internal strife. At one extreme were the "Stalwarts," hard-boiled realists who believed in practical politics and scoffed at reform. They were led by Roscoe Conkling of New York, whose great ambition at the moment was to nominate for a third term ex-President Grant. Only a little less conservative were the "Half-Breeds," who regarded James G. Blaine, the "man from Maine," as their leader, and were determined to make him President. In addition to these factions there were many Independents, most of whom were more friendly to Blaine than to Conkling, but had little use for either. Finally there was the President himself, who had no wish or hope for renomination, and his insignificant number of friends. It was obvious that only a compromise could save the day, and that the National Convention, after many ballots and much heart-burning, produced. For President the Republicans chose a "dark horse," James A. Garfield of Ohio, a Blaine man who was satisfactory to the reformers, and for Vice-President, Chester Alan Arthur of New York, Conkling's trusted friend and subordinate. The ticket was as strong as compromise could make it.

The Democrats, quite as badly divided as the Republicans, were less successful in

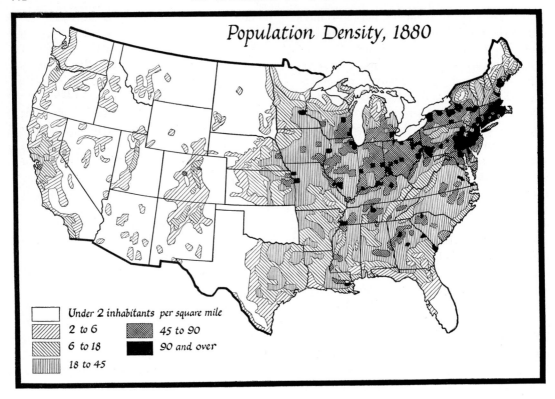

Population Density, 1880

Under 2 inhabitants per square mile
2 to 6
6 to 18
18 to 45
45 to 90
90 and over

achieving a united front. The northern wing of the party was extremely suspicious, and not a little ashamed, of the southern wing; and *vice versa*. Moreover, in both sections there was internal strife that dated at least as far back as the Civil War. Northern Democrats who had been loyal to the Union during the war had not yet forgiven the "Copperheads" whose desire for peace had almost led them to support the South. Southern Democrats whose devotion to the party stemmed from the leadership of Andrew Jackson had little use for the ex-Whigs and conservative "Bourbons," who now, under the necessity of maintaining white supremacy, called themselves Democrats and sought to monopolize party leadership. Native Americans generally, of whatever section, regretted the dire necessity of cultivating the immigrant vote, particularly the Irish vote, which in many American cities had become a factor to be reckoned with. So long out of power as to have lost its personality, bereft of intelligent leaders, tainted

with treason and with pacifism, the Democratic Party floundered helplessly through the campaign. Tilden was too old and too ill to be a candidate, and the nomination went, almost by default, to General Winfield S. Hancock of Pennsylvania, who had won distinction as a Union officer at Gettysburg, and had later pleased the South by the way he conducted himself as military commander of Louisiana during reconstruction. In politics, however, he was only, as one wag expressed it, "a good man, weighing two hundred and fifty pounds." For Vice-President the Democrats named William H. English of Indiana, a political anachronism whose last significant deed had been to promote the admission of Kansas as a slave state during the Buchanan administration. Such a ticket amounted almost to an open confession of political bankruptcy.

As a matter of fact, both parties were completely bankrupt. The issues that divided them were historical merely. **Lack of** The Republican Party had come **party issues** into existence because of the stand it had taken on slavery, and it had lived on because of its determination to free the slaves, to save the Union, and to punish the South. Its program was now finished and its excuse for existence had disappeared. The Democrats, likewise, had so long centered their attention upon the issues of slavery, the Civil War, and reconstruction that they failed to observe that the era in which these issues meant anything had rolled by. The platforms of the two parties in 1880 revealed few real differences of opinion as to policies and no real awareness of the problems that confronted the nation. Neither Democrats nor Republicans seemed to sense the significance of the vast transformation that was coming over business, nor the critical nature of the relationship between labor and capital, nor even the necessity of doing something definite about civil service reform, the money problem, and the tariff. The Republican Party existed to oppose the Democratic Party; the Democratic Party existed to oppose the Republican Party. Real issues cut across both parties, and even when recognized, which was rare, had to be evaded or ignored. When the Republican Convention prepared to adopt the customary meaningless platitudes about civil service reform, a delegate from Texas named Flanagan protested in plain language: "What are we up here for?" What, indeed, if not for the offices?

With issues lacking, the campaign turned on personalities. The Republicans, in rejecting the candidacy of General Grant, had freed themselves of the charge of "Bonapartism." Their nominee was, to be sure, a Union officer in the Civil War, but he had been, like Hayes, a volunteer officer, and had won distinction in politics rather than in the army. The Democrats, on the other hand, in their effort to shake off the charge of treason, had nominated a professional soldier. If anyone was prepared to play the rôle of "the man on horseback," it was Hancock, not Garfield. Efforts were made to prove that Hancock, whose exploits on the battlefield had won him the sobriquet, "the

James A. Garfield

TWENTIETH PRESIDENT of the United States, Garfield was born in a log cabin, lived the hard life of a pioneer farm boy, drove mules along an Ohio Canal towpath, worked his way through college, read law, preached for the Disciples Church, went into politics, and reached the Presidency, only to be cut down by an assassin's bullet.

Superb," was in reality a coward, and that Garfield, whose record was far cleaner than that of most politicians, had been deeply involved in the Crédit Mobilier and other scandals. Neither charge carried much weight. Garfield, as a matter of fact, was satisfactory enough to the reform element in the Republican Party and most Independents gave his candidacy their warm support. The Democratic platform, written by Colonel Henry Watterson of Kentucky, called for "a tariff for revenue only." When the Republicans showed a disposition to press this issue, Hancock declared that it was unimportant because the tariff was a "local affair." For this statement he was roundly ridiculed, but he spoke far more truly than he knew. Tariff rates must be levied by Congress, but they have generally been fixed, item by item, because of some local demand.

Fought with fury, and as if the result would really be important, the campaign settled nothing much except that Garfield, not Hancock, was to be **Election results** the next President of the United States. The Republican plurality, out of a total vote amounting to over nine million, was about

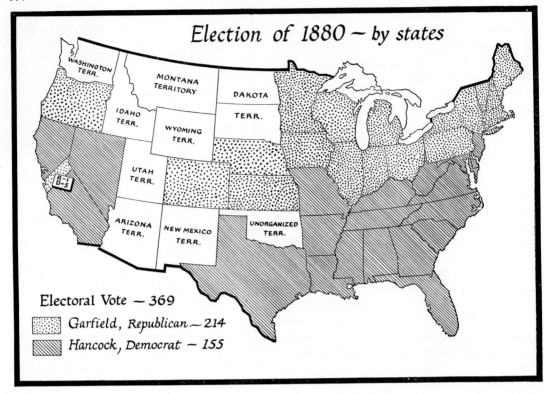

Election of 1880 — by states

Electoral Vote — 369

Garfield, Republican — 214

Hancock, Democrat — 155

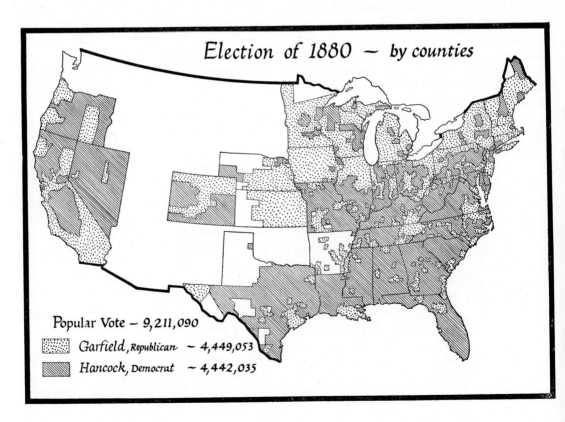

Election of 1880 — by counties

Popular Vote — 9,211,090

Garfield, Republican — 4,449,053

Hancock, Democrat — 4,442,035

nine thousand. Neither of the two leading candidates had a majority of all the votes cast, for James B. Weaver of Iowa, the Greenback candidate, polled over three hundred thousand votes. The Republicans, however, won enough local victories to enable them to recapture the Senate, and, although the membership of the House was so evenly divided as to leave its control in doubt until Congress actually met, the Republicans were finally able to organize it also. For the first time in six years the Presidency and both houses of Congress were under the control of a single party.

But as events proved, the Republicans failed signally to capitalize upon their vic-

James A. Garfield tory. Their first misfortune was the death of the promising new President they had elected. James A. Garfield (1831–1881), like Abraham Lincoln, was a typical product of the American frontier, but he had lived a generation later than Lincoln and had enjoyed advantages, particularly in education, that Lincoln never knew. He served for a time as a volunteer officer in the Civil War, but after 1863 represented an Ohio district in the lower house of Congress. Here he proved to be a finished debater, a tireless committeeman, and a dependable party regular. None could doubt that a brilliant future lay before him, and had he not achieved the Presidency when he did, the honor might well have been his later on. Four months after his inauguration as President he was shot by a disappointed office-seeker. For weeks he lingered between life and death, but finally on September 19, 1881, he died. It cannot be said that with his passing the country lost a great man, but it can perhaps be said that it lost one who was potentially great at a time when great men in politics were rare.

Garfield's death elevated to the Presidency Chester Alan Arthur (1830–1886), a New

Chester A. Arthur York politician whose record made him the despair of reformers. Early in life Arthur became an organization Republican, and his code of ethics, while calling for the strictest personal honesty, tolerated freely the time-honored custom of rewarding the faithful with the spoils of office. As collector of the port of New York he had, as a matter of course, overstaffed his force with party workers, and he never hesitated to call upon the men who held their positions through his favor to do their full political duty during campaigns and on election days. As President, however, he was scrupulously on guard against criticism. He bore himself with becoming dignity, refused to indulge in a wholesale proscription of Garfield's appointees, and took up the cudgels in favor of civil service reform, and even tariff revision, with wholly unexpected zeal.

Despite the President's best efforts, Congress showed little disposition to inaugurate any disturbing innovations until after the election of 1882. That year, however, the electorate seemed to register an emphatic rebuke for the ruling party by returning a decisive Democratic majority to the House of Representatives. Was this reverse the result of Republican failure to do something about civil service reform and the tariff? Fearing that this indeed was the case, the Republican leaders in Congress decided to pass laws on both subjects during the "lame-duck" session that began the month after the election and lasted until the fourth of March following. Such a "death-bed" repentance might not be very convincing, but it might in the long run be better than no repentance at all.

The need for civil service reform was given added emphasis by the exposure of a series of fraudulent contracts for the **Civil service** carrying of the mails on the **reform** western stage routes. These **again** scandals, called the "star-route" frauds because they concerned routes designated by stars on the post-office lists, were denounced by Arthur, and their perpetrators were prosecuted, although there were no convictions. Belatedly eager to demonstrate their opposition to the spoils system, which had made such frauds possible, the Republicans were now ready to establish a civil service com-

Chester A. Arthur

TWENTY-FIRST PRESIDENT of the United States, Arthur was the fourth Vice-President to become President because of his predecessor's death. His preparation for the Presidency was inadequate, but he made a far better President than his critics had expected. Unlike Grant, Hayes, and Garfield, he had seen no military service during the Civil War.

mission, but the Democrats were unwilling to permit their opponents to have full credit for such an undertaking. In fact, it was George H. Pendleton, Democratic Senator from Ohio, who introduced and gave his name to the reform measure which an overwhelming bipartisan majority enacted into law in January, 1883.

The Pendleton Act authorized the President to appoint three civil service commis-
The Pendleton Act sioners, not more than two of whom should belong to the same political party, whose duty it should be to provide "open competitive examinations for testing the fitness of applicants for the public service now classified, or to be classified." Only the lowest offices were at first classified, but the law provided that the President might extend the classified lists at will to include other executive appointees. President Arthur administered the law in complete good faith. He appointed as the first chairman of the commission Dorman B. Eaton, who as secretary of the Civil Service Reform Association had been an ardent advocate of reform. During the first year of its existence the commission was given jurisdiction over about fourteen thousand offices out of a total of one hundred and ten thousand, or about twelve and one half per cent. In contrast with the British system, which examines a candidate upon what fields he happens to know, the American system is based upon strictly practical tests.

Changes of national administration from Arthur's time on worked to the advantage of civil service reform. It happened that Arthur was succeeded by a Democrat, Cleveland; then Cleveland was succeeded by a Republican, Harrison; Harrison in turn was succeeded by a Democrat, Cleveland; and Cleveland, by a Republican, McKinley. Each President, as he was about to retire from office, tended to protect his own appointees by extending the classified lists. Men thus "blanketed" into the civil service were not required to take examinations, but when they died or resigned, their successors received appointments only on recommendation of the commission. By 1893 the number of civil servants under the merit system had reached forty-five thousand; by the turn of the century it was about one hundred thousand; by the time of the First World War nearly half a million — over sixty per cent.

Tariff reform was as long overdue as civil service reform, and in practice it proved to be much harder to accomplish.
The "Mongrel Tariff" The slight reductions in the Civil War rates obtained in 1872 were practically wiped out in 1875 on the pretext of the depression, and the duties on a few items, such as molasses and sugar, were actually increased. To the reform demands long voiced by David A. Wells, the nation's outstanding expert on the subject, were now added the arguments of such economists as William Graham Sumner of Yale, and Frank W. Taussig of Harvard; also, the public was becoming increasingly insistent. Finally, on the recommendation of President Arthur, Congress created in 1882 a nonpolitical tariff commission to study the subject, and, in spite of the fact that every one of its nine members was an avowed protec-

tionist, the commission speedily reported back that the existing duties should be cut by as much as twenty per cent. Acting this time without any considerable Democratic collaboration, the Republicans were able to hurry into law before the adjournment of Congress in March, 1883, what one writer has aptly called the "Mongrel Tariff." Partly because of the necessity for haste, partly because of the effective work of the lobbyists, and partly because of the log-rolling tendencies of congressmen themselves, the measure failed completely to accomplish the purpose for which it had been intended. As Senator Sherman admitted, it retained "nearly all the inequalities and incongruities of the old tariff and yielded to local demands and local interests to an extent that destroyed all symmetry and harmony."

The passage of the "Mongrel Tariff" was not without important political results. Since the Republicans were obliged to defend their handiwork, their party inescapably came to be identified more and more with the policy of protection, whereas the Democrats, who were in duty bound to oppose whatever they could in the Republican program, drifted gradually in the direction of an out-and-out low-tariff policy. When the Democrats in 1883 took control of the House of Representatives, they ignored the claims of Samuel J. Randall, a Pennsylvania protectionist who before 1881 had been three times elected Speaker, in order to place in that office a dependable low-tariff advocate, John G. Carlisle of Kentucky.

The campaign and election of 1884 turned less on the tariff, however, than on the personalities of the two outstand-
Blaine ing individuals who contested for the Presidency. The Republicans overlooked the claims of Arthur, who had offended the regulars by vetoing in 1882 an $18,000,000 rivers and harbors ("pork-barrel") bill, and had never been able to live down his past to the complete satisfaction of the liberals. Instead, they nominated their outstanding leader, James G. Blaine (1830–1893), whom Garfield had made Secretary of State, but

James G. Blaine was the outstanding Republican of his time, but failed to achieve the Presidency.

whose resignation from that office Arthur had not hesitated to accept. Blaine was born in Pennsylvania, but had entered politics in Maine. Unlike most politicians his background was journalism rather than the law; he had been connected with both the *Kennebec Journal* and the *Portland Advertiser*. He was deep in state politics before the Civil War, and after 1858 served three terms as a member of the state legislature. When war broke out, he did not join the army, but in 1863 entered the national House of Representatives, and remained there until 1876, when he went to the Senate. During Grant's administration he emerged as the outstanding leader of the Republican Party. A firm believer in the righteousness of Radical reconstruction, and a veritable incarnation of Republican prejudice, he appealed strongly to a party-loving age. Both on and off the platform he possessed great personal charm, a quality which he used, no less than Henry Clay, to excite the worshipful support of his followers. Both in 1876 and in 1880 far more sentiment had existed for Blaine than for the men the Republicans had nominated, but Blaine's record had offended the liberals, and lesser lights had won the prize.

Even now the "Mulligan Letters," which revealed that Blaine as congressman had helped obtain a land grant for an Arkansas railroad from which he hoped to make a financial profit, were flaunted as good reason to keep Blaine in retirement, but the "Blaine or bust" crowd was not to be denied.

The Democrats, as in 1876, nominated a reform governor of New York. Grover Cleveland (1837–1908) was born **Cleveland** in New Jersey, but had early removed to New York. After a hard struggle with poverty he had become by 1859 a practicing lawyer in Buffalo. During the Civil War, when other young men were joining the army, he borrowed money to hire a substitute because his meager earnings were needed for the support of his mother and sisters. In 1863 he received a welcome appointment as assistant district attorney, and in 1870 he was not above accepting a nomination as sheriff of Erie County. Elected, he revealed qualities of scrupulous honesty and unflinching courage that soon made him a marked man. He refused to hire a hangman when two murderers were to be executed, and sprang the trap himself. He made life consistently uncomfortable for local crooks and grafters. In 1881, nominated and elected mayor of Buffalo to placate the "better element," he reorganized the city administration, purged it of venal politicians, vetoed dubious measures, and in general endeared himself to reformers. The fame of the "veto mayor" spread, and when in 1882 the New York Democrats needed a candidate for governor with an unimpeachable record to oppose the Republican candidate, Secretary of State Folger, they turned to Cleveland and elected him by a majority of nearly 200,000 votes. As governor, he struggled irritably against a bewildering accumulation of governmental inefficiency or worse, made some progress and many enemies, particularly among the Tammany leaders of New York City. "We love him most for the enemies he has made," General E. S. Bragg told the Democratic Convention of 1884, mindful of Tammany's earnest desire to prevent Cleveland's nomination for the Presidency.

The nomination of Cleveland insured that a large number of Republican liberals, now called "Mugwumps," would swing their support to the Democratic ticket. Ordinarily this would have insured his election by a wide margin, but he happened to be a bachelor, and flaws were uncovered in his private life which in some minds offset his irreproachable conduct of his public responsibilities. The campaign reached an all-time low in mud-slinging, but the sober second thought of most Americans seemed to coincide with that of a philosophical Mugwump who held that "we should elect Mr. Cleveland to the public office he is so eminently qualified to fill and remand Mr. Blaine to the private life which he is so eminently fitted to adorn." For whatever might be said of Blaine's public record, his private life was blameless.

The decision in 1884 was almost as close as in 1880. Cleveland's plurality over Blaine in the country as a whole was **Election of** only 23,000, and the electoral **Cleveland** vote stood 219 to 182. Cleveland carried the solid South, Delaware, Indiana, Connecticut, New Jersey, and New York. All the rest of the states voted for Blaine. The Democrats won control of the House of Representatives by a comfortable margin, but the Republicans retained their majority in the Senate. Benjamin F. Butler, the Greenback candidate, received a total of 175,370 popular votes, and John P. St. John of Kansas, Prohibitionist, 150,369. The Prohibitionist vote in New York State alone ran to over 25,000, another factor in the defeat of Blaine. Had the temperance forces not had a candidate of their own, undoubtedly most of them would have voted for Blaine and against Cleveland, whose bibulous habits were well known.

Cleveland's efforts to inaugurate reforms met many obstacles. He protected the Civil Service Commission all he could, **Cleveland** and even extended the classified **and reform** lists, but in order to avoid an outright revolt within his party he was obliged to yield many non-classified offices to the spoilsmen. He had trouble with the veterans of the Civil War, now organized into a powerful society known as the Grand Army of the Republic, because he stood athwart their desires for more and larger pensions. Already the Arrears of Pensions Act of 1879 had permitted pensioners, whatever their service disability, to recover back payments for the period between the time of mustering out and the time a given pension was granted. The abuse of this privilege greatly angered the President, but he could do little about it; on the other hand, he could and did veto a "pauper" pension bill that would have given a pension to all who stood in need of it, regardless of disability. He also vetoed hundreds of the private pension bills that lenient congressmen delighted to push through for the benefit of favored constituents who had seen service, but according to the general law were not entitled to pensions. This attitude on the part of the President, together with his willingness to restore to the states from which they had come all captured Confederate battle-flags, won him the undying hatred of the "G.A.R.," sometimes appropriately called the "Grand Army of the Republican Party."

Cleveland's chief bid for reform came during the second half of his administration, **The tariff** when he forced both parties to take their stand on the tariff issue. In his annual message of December, 1887, he dealt exclusively with the tariff, presented a well-reasoned, hard-hitting argument against the existing high rates, and, pointing to the annual surplus of about $100,000,000 brought in each year by the Tariff of 1883, declared: "It is a *condition* which confronts us, not a theory." Thus briefed by the President, the Democratic majority in the House of Representatives, with only four dissenting votes, accepted the low-tariff bill presented by Roger Q. Mills of Texas, chairman of the House Ways and Means Committee. This measure called for reductions from an average level of about

Grover Cleveland

Twenty-second and Twenty-fourth President of the United States, was one of the many children of a small-town Presbyterian minister. His father's death kept him from going to college and to war. He practiced law, entered politics as a Democrat, reached the Presidency at the age of forty-eight, was known as a man of courage.

forty-seven per cent to an average level of about forty per cent, and placed such items as wool, flax, hemp, salt, lumber, and tin-plate on the free list. In response to this Democratic challenge, the Senate Committee on Finance, under the leadership of Senator Allison, presented a sample of what the Republicans would be glad to do if only they could win control of the government in the election of 1888. As passed by the Republican majority in the Senate, the Allison bill proposed to maintain a generally high level of duties, but it insured a smaller revenue by resort to prohibitive duties, by the lowering of excises, and by a cut in the duty on sugar. As anticipated, the House would not accept the Senate bill, and the Senate would not accept the House bill. But as Cleveland had foreseen, both parties had been committed to positions that they could not possibly abandon in the coming presidential campaign.

As was now inevitable, the Democrats renominated Cleveland, and made tariff reform their principal issue in **Election of** the campaign of 1888. The Re- **1888**

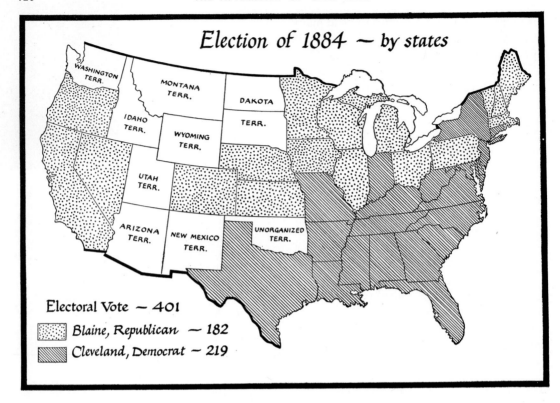

Election of 1884 — by states

Electoral Vote — 401

Blaine, Republican — 182

Cleveland, Democrat — 219

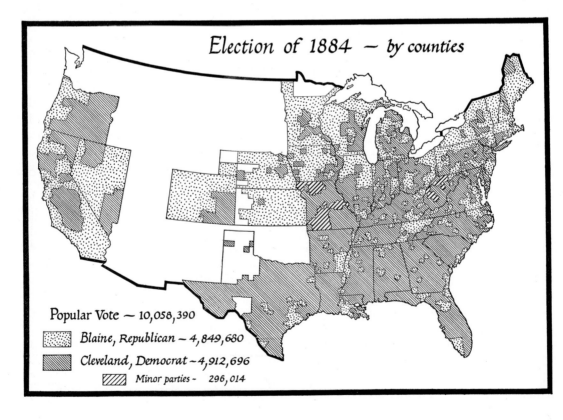

Election of 1884 — by counties

Popular Vote — 10,058,390

Blaine, Republican — 4,849,680

Cleveland, Democrat — 4,912,696

Minor parties — 296,014

publicans, having lost with Blaine in 1884, turned to one of their lesser lights, Benjamin Harrison of Indiana, who had the triple advantage of a presidential grandfather, residence in a close state, and a clean, if almost empty, political record. The campaign was a revelation to the Republicans, for they learned for the first time how advantageous an issue the tariff could be. Campaign contributions as insurance against Democratic tariff reductions poured into the Republican coffers in a flood. The funds thus collected were used both to carry on an extensive campaign of education, and to "get out the vote." For the former purpose Republican orators and publicists made much of maintaining the high wages of American labor, something that could not be done, they insisted, if the products of low-paid European labor were admitted freely to American markets. When it came to "getting out the vote," party-workers, particularly in the doubtful states, scrupled at nothing. The scandals of the election were so open and notorious as to give great impetus to the movement for the "Australian" system of secret voting, which down to this time had made little headway in the United States. Even so, Harrison won the election by only a slender margin. In the popular vote Cleveland led by more than 100,000, but Harrison carried the crucial states of New York and Indiana, and so amassed 233 electoral votes to Cleveland's 168.

Benjamin Harrison (1833–1901) was at the time of his nomination a successful

Harrison
lawyer of great party regularity who had served one term in the United States Senate. He was in no sense the leader of his party, and James G. Blaine, whom he made his Secretary of State, completely overshadowed him. Harrison was a good platform orator, but cold in his personal relationships. "Harrison can made a speech to ten thousand men," said one of his associates, "and every man of them will go away his friend. Let him meet the same ten thousand in private, and every one will go away his enemy." His honesty was probably as

Benjamin Harrison

TWENTY-THIRD PRESIDENT OF THE United States, Harrison was a grandson of the ninth President, and a great-grandson of Benjamin Harrison, signer of the Declaration of Independence. He served as a Colonel of Volunteers in the Civil War, and at its close was brevetted Brigadier-General. He was a conscientious Chief Executive, but lacked popular appeal.

unimpeachable as Cleveland's, but he lacked Cleveland's forceful nature. During Cleveland's administration the Democratic Party leaders, one by one, acknowledged the President's supremacy, whereas Harrison from the beginning of his administration to its end, had far less to do with charting his party's course than many another of lesser rank.

Harrison's record on civil service reform and pensions was by no means as courageous as Cleveland's. Like President Grant, he saw fit to allot many minor offices to his indigent friends and relatives. In making other appointments, he leaned on the advice of the politicians, and did what they wanted if he could. His chief contribution to civil service reform was his appointment of Theodore Roosevelt to membership on the Civil Service Commission, an appointment which Roosevelt earned as a reward for serving his party faithfully during the campaign of 1888. As civil service commissioner, however, Roosevelt made it his business to see that no such rewards as he had received were made through the agency of the commission. In the pursuit of this course, he soon fell

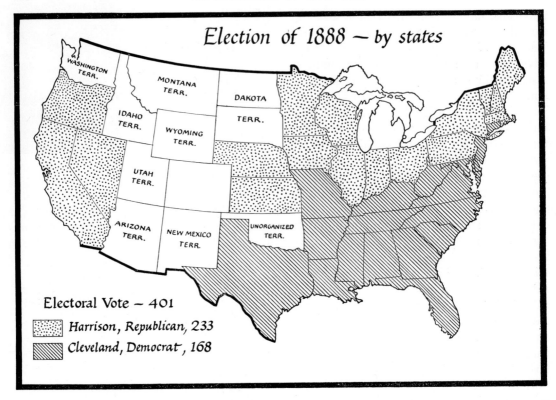

Election of 1888 — by states

Electoral Vote — 401

- Harrison, Republican, 233
- Cleveland, Democrat, 168

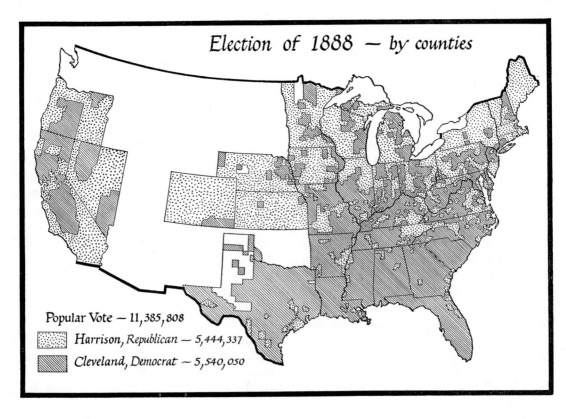

Election of 1888 — by counties

Popular Vote — 11,385,808

- Harrison, Republican — 5,444,337
- Cleveland, Democrat — 5,540,050

afoul of the President, whom he came to dislike, and of many of the President's friends, but Harrison retained the obstreperous commissioner in office and when in 1893 Cleveland became President again, he, too, retained Roosevelt. As for pensions, the G.A.R. got exactly what it wanted in the Dependents' Pension Act, which provided that all veterans of the Civil War who had served for as long as ninety days, and who had suffered from any serious mental or physical disability, should receive pensions of from six to twelve dollars a month, according to the degree of disability from which they suffered. Widows of veterans, if dependent upon their own labor for support, were awarded pensions of eight dollars a month, and minor children, two dollars a month. As a result of this law the number of pensioners rose from 489,725 in 1889 to 966,012 in 1893, and the amount of money appropriated for pensions in the same period from $89,-000,000 to $157,000,000. By 1911 the total expenditure of the United States for Civil War pensions had exceeded four billion dollars, a sum far in excess of the original cost of the war, and the end was not yet in sight.

The main business of the Fifty-First Congress was to pass a high protective-tariff bill, **The Fifty-First Congress** but to accomplish this strictly partisan end political strategy of a high order was required. The Republicans had a majority in each house of Congress, but particularly in the House of Representatives the majority depended upon too few votes for comfort. To expedite the business in hand, the Republican Speaker, Thomas B. Reed of Maine, broke traditional rules right and left. Members present, but not voting, were counted to make a quorum, and a powerful Committee on Rules, of which "Czar" Reed himself was chairman, brought in from time to time whatever special rules were needed to push the Republican program along. To bolster up the Republican majority, especially in the Senate, two new northwestern territories, Wyoming and Idaho, were added to the four,

North and South Dakota, Montana, and Washington, that the preceding Congress had authorized to take the steps necessary to become states. Since the voters of this region were predominantly Republican, the control of the Republican Party in Congress was greatly strengthened by their admission. Finally, as a sop to the silver Republicans of the West, who refused to vote for a high tariff until something should be done for silver, the Sherman Silver Purchase Act of 1890 was passed. This measure required the Treasury to buy 4,500,000 ounces of silver a month, the estimated output of all the silver mines in the United States. Not all the silver need be coined, but it was to be paid for in Treasury notes redeemable "in gold or silver coin," and so provided for a substantial addition to the amount of money actually in circulation. Efforts to enact a Federal Elections Bill, or "Force Bill," which would again give the national government control over elections in the South, as during reconstruction, failed; otherwise, the Republicans might have forged a weapon by means of which they could have controlled the national government almost indefinitely.

The McKinley Tariff Act, which became law on October 1, 1890, was the Republican answer to the prayers, and the **The McKinley Tariff** contributions, of the American industrialists. It provided first and foremost a set of duties on manufactured articles higher than the American government had ever levied before. Some of these duties turned out to be, as their authors had intended, actually prohibitive; others went to the length of offering protection to non-existent industries, provided only that responsible persons could demonstrate their intent to begin manufacture. The law also embodied an impressive list of agricultural duties, charged against such imports as eggs, butter, potatoes, wheat, and barley. These items were included primarily for their psychological effect upon the farmer vote. Duties levied upon commodities of which the United States had an excess for export, and the price of which was fixed on the world

WASH.
1889

MONTANA
1889

N. DAK.
1889

IDAHO
1890

WYOMING
1890

S. DAK.
1889

New States

nations that produced them failed to grant equivalent advantages to American exports.

Public reaction to the behavior of the Fifty-First Congress was far from cordial. Each of its measures made a generous quota of enemies, and the grand total of accumulated grievances grew with each succeeding month. To the effect of the McKinley Bill on the revenue, which was sure to be disastrous, was added the orgy of spending in which Congress permitted itself to indulge. Its lavish appropriations for pensions, river and harbor improvements, federal buildings, coast defenses, and other extravagances led the newspapers to refer to it as the "billion-dollar Congress," a description strikingly lacking in political appeal. Unfortunate as a Treasury surplus might have been, a deficit, even less desirable, appeared to be in sight. Consumers found that the higher rates of the McKinley Tariff meant higher prices for what they had to buy; when its rates were made known, John Wanamaker, the store-keeper Postmaster General, with more business than political acumen, openly urged his customers to "buy now, before prices go up." The Force Bill, based as it was upon an attempt to revive sectional antagonisms, was unpopular, North as well as South. As Elihu Root phrased it a little later, the whole country was ready to concede "the failure of the plan formulated at the close of the war to elevate the black man by conferring the suffrage upon him."

Held only a few weeks after the passage of the McKinley Bill, the congressional elections of 1890 showed how un-   **Elections of** popular that measure, and the   **1890** Congress that passed it, had become. Democratic campaigners did not fail to take full advantage of the opportunity to denounce "Bill McKinley and the McKinley Bill." Peddlers were sent through the country, so the Republicans claimed, to offer tin cups at twenty-five cents each and tin pails at a dollar apiece in order to show the rural voters how much the McKinley duties had increased the cost of living. Merchants and

market, amounted, as was well known, to little more than empty gestures.

The reduction of the revenue, deemed imperative by both Democrats and Republicans, was accomplished in part by the discouraging effect on importation of the high duties, but in greater part by placing raw sugar on the free list. This was in effect an aid to the manufacturers of refined sugar, whose product was still protected, but who could now buy raw sugar for less, but it was very disturbing to the sugar producers of Louisiana until the idea of a bounty of two cents a pound on all raw sugar of American origin was included. Thus the sugar schedule, figuratively speaking, succeeded in taking money out of the Treasury with both hands. To please the Secretary of State, James G. Blaine, a reciprocity clause was included in the McKinley Tariff, although its provisions were much more restricted than Blaine had hoped. The President was authorized to enforce a specified schedule of tariff rates on items listed as free in case the salesmen apologized for high prices, whatever the truth might be, on the ground that the new tariff law had made them necessary. The Republicans, with tea, coffee, and sugar on the free list, had hoped to make much of the "free breakfast table," but the fact that the sugar duties were retained for six months after the passage of the bill made this battle-cry seem decidedly premature. When the votes were counted, the Republicans discovered that they had received the most emphatic rebuke in the history of their party. In the Senate the Republican majority was narrowed to eight, and would have been wiped out altogether but for the hold-over senators from the newly admitted states of the Northwest. In the House the Democrats had 235 seats, and the Republicans 88, while nine Farmers' Alliance men, or Populists, refused to vote with either of the older parties. The appearance of this group of independents in Congress marked the beginning of an agrarian revolt in the Middle West and the South, which, with the assistance it received from the silver mining states of the Far West, threatened for a time to bring about a complete realignment of political parties in the United States.

Bibliography

An unrestrained popular account of the political life of this period is Matthew Josephson, *The Politicos, 1865–1896* (1938). Wilfred E. Binkley, *American Political Parties: Their Natural History* (1945), is an excellent textbook. The most thorough study of the election of 1876 is P. L. Haworth, *The Hayes-Tilden Disputed Presidential Election of 1876* (1906). A. C. Flick, *Samuel Jones Tilden* (1939), is a more objective work than the older John Bigelow, *The Life of Samuel J. Tilden* (2 vols., 1895). L. B. Richardson, *William E. Chandler, Republican* (1940), is useful on elections and politics from 1876 to the end of the century. Hayes has two excellent biographies, C. R. Williams, *The Life of Rutherford Burchard Hayes* (2 vols., 1914); and H. J. Eckenrode, *Rutherford B. Hayes, Statesman of Reunion* (1930). Two useful studies of Hayes' Secretary of State are C. L. Barrows, *William M. Evarts, Lawyer, Diplomat, Statesman* (1941); and Brainerd Dyer, *The Public Career of William M. Evarts* (1933). The active part taken by Sherman in many phases of American politics is told by himself, John Sherman, *Recollections of Forty Years* (2 vols., 1895).

On James A. Garfield see T. C. Smith, *Life and Letters of James Abram Garfield* (1925); R. G. Caldwell, *James A. Garfield* (1931); and W. W. Wasson, *James A. Garfield: His Religion and Education* (1952); and on Garfield's successor see G. F. Howe, *Chester A. Arthur* (1934). Harry

J. Sievers, *Benjamin Harrison, Hoosier Warrior, 1833–1865* (1953), traces the early career of the twenty-third President.

On the restoration of home rule in the South, two books by C. Vann Woodward, *Reunion and Reaction: The Compromise of 1877 and the End of Reconstruction* (1951); and *Origins of the New South, 1877–1913* (1951), are excellent. Helpful also are Allen J. Going, *Bourbon Democracy in Alabama, 1874–1890* (1951); Albert D. Kirwan, *Revolt of the Rednecks: Mississippi Politics, 1876–1925* (1951); W. B. Hesseltine, *Confederate Leaders in the New South* (1950); and G. W. McGinty, *Louisiana Redeemed: The Overthrow of Carpetbag Rule, 1876–1880* (1941).

A satisfactory account of the money question is contained in A. D. Noyes, *Forty Years of American Finance* (1909). F. E. Haynes, *Third Party Movements Since the Civil War, with Special Reference to Iowa* (1916), presents a good account of the Greenbackers. See also D. C. Barrett, *The Greenbacks and Resumption of Specie Payments* (1931). An excellent study of the rise of the silver issue is given in J. L. Laughlin, *History of Bimetallism in the United States* (1892). Jean Paul Hütter, *La Question de la Monnaie d'Argent aux États-Unis des Origines à 1900* (1938), shows the interest of at least one European historian in American affairs. On the same subject, consult also M. S. Wildman, *Money Inflation in the United States* (1905); and W. V. Byars, *An Amer-*

ican Commoner, The Life and Times of Richard Parks Bland (1900), which recounts the successive failures of "Silver Dick."

The standard work on civil service reform is Carl R. Fish, *The Civil Service and the Patronage* (1905). For the later period it is admirably supplemented by A. B. Sageser, *The First Two Decades of the Pendleton Act* (1935).

Ida M. Tarbell, *The Tariff in our Times* (1911), is popular and dependable. It may be supplemented by F. W. Taussig, *Tariff History of the United States* (8th ed., 1931), which adds a new chapter for each tariff bill; and by Edward Stanwood, *American Tariff Controversies in the Nineteenth Century* (2 vols., 1903), which shows strong sympathy for the protectionist point of view. See also Percy Ashley, *Modern Tariff History: Germany, United States, France* (3rd ed., 1926). W. D. Orcutt, *Burrows of Michigan and the Republican Party* (2 vols., 1917), reveals clearly the mind of a typical protectionist. C. S. Olcott, *The Life of William McKinley* (2 vols., 1916), is highly partisan, but contains much useful material on this subject.

One of the best biographies of a man of this period is J. A. Barnes, *John G. Carlisle* (1931). The best biography of Blaine is D. S. Muzzey, *James G. Blaine* (1934); but see also C. E. Russell, *Blaine of Maine: His Life and Times* (1931). The biographies written by Blaine's contemporaries are too prejudiced to be of value. Blaine's own autobiographic account, *Twenty Years of Congress* (2 vols., 1884–86), treats only of his earlier career. Every aspect of Blaine's efforts as a diplomat is treated admirably in Alice F. Tyler, *The Foreign Policy of James G. Blaine* (1927). Allan Nevins, *Grover Cleveland: A Study in Courage* (1932), is in reality a well-rounded history of the period; also useful is *Letters of Grover Cleveland, 1850–1908*, edited by Allan Nevins (1933). Together these works completely supplant the earlier biographies of Cleveland. D. S. Alexander, *Four Famous New Yorkers: The Political Careers of Cleveland, Platt, Hill, and Roosevelt* (1923), is an excellent and comprehensive study. S. P. Orth, *The Boss and the Machine* (1919); and H. J. Ford, *The Cleveland Era* (1919), are interesting and accurate, but somewhat superficial. On Cleveland's first Secretary of State, there are two admirable books by C. C. Tansill, *The Congressional Career of Thomas Francis Bayard, 1869–1885* (1946), and *The Foreign Policy of Thomas F. Bayard, 1885–1897* (1940). S. W. McCall, *Thomas B. Reed* (1914), gives a good picture of the Reed personality; but W. A. Robinson, *Thomas B. Reed, Parliamentarian* (1930), is the more scholarly.

On the significance of political parties in the United States, there is an admirable and brilliantly written book, Herbert Agar, *The Price of Union* (1950). Entertaining older accounts of the period, somewhat lacking in perspective, are H. T. Peck, *Twenty Years of the Republic, 1885–1905* (1907); and Elisha B. Andrews, *The United States in Our Own Time* (1903). There are two revealing monographs on Civil War military pensions: J. W. Oliver, *History of the Civil War Military Pensions* (1917); and W. H. Glasson, *Federal Military Pensions in the United States* (1918). Frank H. Heck, *The Civil War Veteran in Minnesota Life and Politics* (1941), throws much light on the political activities of the G.A.R. Henry L. Stoddard, *Presidential Sweepstakes: The Story of Political Conventions and Campaigns* (1948), features the more colorful contests beginning with 1832.

THE NEW NATION EMERGES

1865-1898

With the Civil War there began an era of change in the United States frequently called the economic revolution. Some historians, identifying the war itself with the changes that accompanied it, have called the Civil War the "Second American Revolution." But the war served only to accelerate changes that were already in progress; had there been no war undoubtedly they would have occurred anyway.

Basic in the new dispensation was the revolution in means of communication that centered on the railroads. The railroads were new; until the 1840's they were still in the experimental stage, and only in the 1850's were their full possibilities beginning to be realized. The Civil War, which was the first great railroad war in history, resolved all doubts about them, and after the war the expansion of the nation's railway system proceeded at a rapid rate, too rapid, as events proved, for the economy of the country to stand the strain. But when the depression of the seventies ended, the building was resumed, and by the 1890's the American railway network was virtually complete.

With a national transportation system in the making, American industry was also revolutionized. The domestic system was already on the way out well before the 1860's, and the necessities of the war finished it off. After the war, manufacturers found in the needs of civilians an adequate substitute for the needs of the military, and in the improving transportation facilities ample means for getting their produce to market. Business on a local scale gave way to business on a national scale; more and more, big business tended to drive little business out of business. Steel supplemented or replaced iron; oil for illumination made possible another great new enterprise; dozens of other opportunities opened the way for a host of entrepreneurs.

The new business world operated at first without the restraint of government; lawmakers could not foresee so vast a transformation, much less make laws to control it. But the great new corporations, although they undoubtedly supplied more jobs for more people, made the achievement of independence for the ordinary individual far more difficult than it had ever been before. Labor was increasingly at their mercy; even the farmer found himself obliged to buy and sell at the prices they set. Inevitably there was a demand for governmental action. As a result, the full freedom of railway corporations was limited somewhat by the Granger laws and the Interstate Commerce Act; that of other corporations, by state and national anti-trust legislation. Even so, the pre-eminence of business leadership in the United States was not seriously threatened during the nineteenth century. The business world exerted a far greater measure of control over government than the government over business.

The organization of labor was an inevitable accompaniment of the organization of business; "big business" and "big labor" go hand in hand. A labor movement had existed in the United States during the Jacksonian era, and trades' unions on the English model had been common before the Civil War. But now unions on a national scale replaced unions on a merely local scale. The Knights of Labor during the 1870's and early 1880's, and the American Federation of Labor thereafter, gave leadership to the cause of union labor, and achieved some results, both by championing legislation favorable to labor, and by strikes, when necessary. But in general the American public tended to be apathetic or hostile toward union activities, and labor violence, however great the provocation, aroused resentment and alarm. A problem of labor, and of the country at large, was the assimilation of the great numbers of immigrants who flocked to American shores, and who for the most part found employment as workers in industry.

The capture of the American nation by industrial enterprise placed the farmer at a marked disadvantage. Hitherto the nation's economy had depended principally on him; now the tables were beginning to turn. Flight to another frontier could no longer serve as a solvent for discontent; the frontier had virtually disappeared. Moreover, the economic revolution had tremendously altered the nature of farming. Subsistence agriculture had given way to specialized agriculture; the farmer raised to sell, not to consume, and whatever affected the rest of the business world also affected him. But whereas business could organize in larger and larger units, the farmers still had to operate as individuals. Out of this situation came the Populist revolt in the South and the West, and the search for a panacea in free silver.

By the 1890's American society had settled down to a well-defined pattern. Sectional differences were still marked, but there was a growing tendency toward uniformity that affected even the newly-arrived immigrant. Urban America was increasing in importance; rural America was beginning its relative decline. Educational influences brought the different sections closer together, and lessened the gap between city and country ways. In every activity — business, politics, literature, religion, sports — the American imprint was easy to discern. The United States by the end of the century had achieved a degree of homogeneity that accentuated its unity, and marked it out as a nation.

7

The Revolution in Communications

THE significance of means of communication in a country as large as the United States can hardly be overlooked. Indeed, the whole history of the nation could easily be written around this theme. The primitive methods of transportation available for land travel during early American history held settlement close to the Atlantic and, with relatively better transportation facilities available by sea, determined that for a long time the New World would remain dependent on the Old. Turnpikes, steamboats, and canals wrought a revolution that diverted the attention of the nation from the seaboard to the interior. The conquest of the continent now proceeded at a stepped-up tempo; without this acceleration the words "manifest destiny" could never have achieved their magic meaning.

The railroads Most phenomenal of all the change-producing agencies was the railroad. Not until the 1840's had this new means of transportation passed the experimental stage, but during the next two decades it came into its own.[1] These early railroads, judged by contemporary stand-

[1] For the earlier history of railroads, see John D. Hicks, *The Federal Union* (2d. ed., 1952), 505–509.

ards, were extremely crude affairs, with little wood-burning locomotives, unsightly, inefficient rolling stock, and light iron rails, shaped like an inverted letter "V". But they got places in a hurry, and they carried huge loads. The progress of civilization may be measured, in a sense, by how fast man can travel and how much baggage he can take with him. It is not too much to say that the common denominator for all the remarkable changes that took place in the last half of the nineteenth century was to be found in the rapidly expanding railroad system of the country. Manufacturers strained themselves to produce the almost unlimited supplies that the railroads required for their own use, then redoubled their efforts to meet the demands of the new markets that the railroads opened up. Agriculture was equally stimulated, and achieved an ever widening base of operations, for the railroads assured the annihilation of every remaining frontier. The immigrant tide rose with the increased number of jobs. Corporation methods, designed first to meet the needs of the railroads, were copied and modified by the rest of the business world.

Greatly overbuilt before the Civil War,

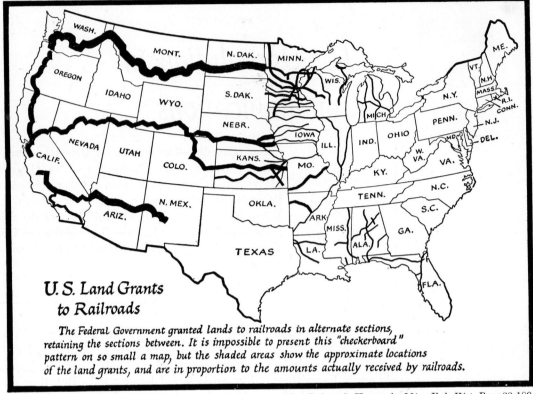

U.S. Land Grants to Railroads

*The Federal Government granted lands to railroads in alternate sections,
retaining the sections between. It is impossible to present this "checkerboard"
pattern on so small a map, but the shaded areas show the approximate locations
of the land grants, and are in proportion to the amounts actually received by railroads.*

After Robert S. Henry, in *Miss. Val. Hist. Rev.*, 22:180.

the railroads of the country enjoyed a tremendous prosperity while the war was on. Rates soared, except where the competition of the Great Lakes and the Erie Canal kept them down, and companies that had never made profits before now felt obliged to disguise their heavy earnings by issuing stock dividends. Railroad managers, as long as they could count on a wartime abundance of traffic, showed little interest either in new construction or the improvement of their equipment. Indeed, by 1865 the number of railroad accidents due to avoidable defects in roadbeds and rolling stock had reached the point where the public would no longer have tolerated such neglect except for the immunity to tragedy that accompanies war. With the return of peace the time was ripe for the renovation of the old roads and the building of new ones. Capital for the purpose was easily obtained by Jay Cooke and other promoters, who convinced investors, both at home and abroad, that railroad securities were among the safest and the most profitable to be found.

The government itself, particularly by its generous subsidies to the building of transcontinentals, did much to stimulate the railroad boom. This policy, contemplated for many years before the war broke out but postponed because of southern opposition, was inaugurated in 1862 when Congress chartered the Union and the Central Pacific Railroads. In addition to the original reasons for building a transcontinental road, proponents could now cite the necessity of connecting California closely enough to the Union to insure its loyalty for all time to come. The Union Pacific was to build westward from Omaha, Nebraska; the Central Pacific, eastward from Sacramento, California. Each company, after the completion of an initial forty miles of track, was eligible to receive from the government, for each mile of track laid, ten square miles of land in

The first transcontinental

alternate sections, checkerboard fashion, along the right of way; and also, for each mile of track laid, the loan of sixteen, thirty-two, or forty-eight thousand dollars (for plains, foothills, or mountain country, respectively) in government bonds. Generous as these offers seemed, they proved to be inadequate to attract the modest sums necessary to build the first essential divisions of forty miles each, so in 1864 Congress amended the original terms. The government now doubled the land grant, accepted a second mortgage for the loans it made, and permitted the companies to borrow private capital, up to the amount of the government loans, on first-mortgage bonds. The prospect of title to nearly twenty million acres of land and loans amounting to about sixty million dollars proved to be a sufficient inducement to moneylenders, and building soon began in earnest. At first it was stipulated that the eastern boundary of California should be the dividing line between the two roads, but ultimately they were permitted to race for distance, and in 1869, when they met near Ogden, Utah, the Union Pacific had laid 1086 miles of track and the Central Pacific 689.

To complete the road the two companies had had to solve problems that in some **Problems of construction** respects were quite similar, in others vastly different. Both operated at great distances from their source of supply. When the Union Pacific began construction at Omaha, the nearest railhead to the east was far away on the Iowa plains, and until late in 1867, when the Chicago and North Western reached the Missouri River, all supplies had to be brought overland by freight wagons, or up the river by steamboat from St. Joseph. The Central Pacific was little better off, for many of the materials it used had to be sent by sea, a ten months' voyage from Philadelphia or New York. On this account the first years of construction, before the builders were able to make accurate predictions of their needs, witnessed a succession of disappointments and delays. Much credit for the ultimate solution of these

vexatious problems belongs to Theodore D. Judah, the able engineer and original promoter of the Central Pacific. The Union Pacific, building out over the plains, met a minimum of construction difficulties, although the lack of timber and stone was keenly felt, and materials of this sort often had to be brought long distances. The Central Pacific had no lack of timber or stone, but it was confronted with the difficult engineering feat of crossing the Sierra Nevada. In a single stretch of sixty miles fifteen tunnels had to be bored. Neither road was built according to specifications that would be regarded as tolerable today, although in this respect the Central Pacific was far superior to the Union Pacific. Curves and grades were regularly taken with the greatest unconcern.

The labor problem was about as perplexing for one company as for the other. The builders of the Union Pacific solved it by employing, among others, thousands of Irish immigrants, many of them ex-soldiers, who, under the efficient direction of General Grenville M. Dodge, not only built the road, but on occasion fought off the attacks of hostile Indians besides. Terminal towns on the Union Pacific, which moved westward as the road advanced, often had a population of as many as ten or twelve thousand people, and a type of life by night or day that led the pungently accurate Samuel Bowles, editor of the *Springfield Republican*, to name the town he visited in 1868 "Hell on Wheels." The Central Pacific, after many initial difficulties, finally resorted to the use of some ten thousand Chinese coolies, who excelled the Irish in tractability, if not in versatility. On the matter of food, for example, the bulk of which both roads had to import, the Chinese were far more easily pacified than the Irish, although hunting parties from the Union Pacific insured the latter a fair supply of fresh meat.

Unfortunately the building of both roads was accompanied by the most shameless profiteering. In each case the **Profiteering** device of a construction com-

THE 9:45 ACCOMMODATION. Painting by E. W. Henry.

American railroads were basic to the transportation revolution that the United States experienced during the nineteenth century. The "trains" invaded nearly every populated center, crossed the Great Plains, climbed the Rocky Mountains, eventually connected the Atlantic and Pacific Oceans. As the network expanded, fortunes were made and lost in railroad securities.

FIRST TRANSCONTINENTAL. Ceremony at the driving of the Golden Spike, 1869.

THE GREAT WEST. Currier and Ives lithograph, 1870.

THE
UNION PACIFIC
RAIL ROAD CO.

Are now constructing a Railroad from
OMAHA, NEBRASKA,
westward toward the Pacific Ocean, making with its connections an unbroken line
ACROSS THE CONTINENT.
The Company now offer a limited amount of their
First Mortgage Bonds
having thirty years to run, and bearing annual interest, payable on the first day of January and July, in the City of New York, at the rate of
SIX PER CENT. IN GOLD,
AT
Ninety Cents on the Dollar.
This road was completed from Omaha, 305 miles west, on the 1st of January, 1867, and is fully equipped, and trains are regularly running over it. The Company has now on hand sufficient iron, ties, etc., to finish the remaining portion to the eastern base of the Rocky Mountains, 212 miles, which is under contract to be done September 1st of this year, and it is expected that the entire road will be in running order from Omaha to its western connection with the Central Pacific, now being rapidly built eastward from Sacramento, Cal., during 1870.

MORTGAGE BONDS. Union Pacific advertisement for bonds to finance the transcontinental. *Harper's Weekly*, 1867.

PALACE-CAR. Interior and sleeping accommodations. Woodcut.

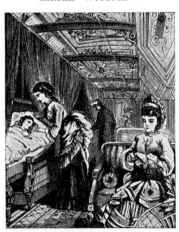

pany, controlled by the leading stockholders of the railroads concerned, was utilized to drain off through unreasonably high contracts all possible profit from the building of the road. The Crédit Mobilier of America[1] served this purpose so well for the Union Pacific that it received, according to a congressional committee, a total of $73,000,000 for construction that cost about $50,000,000. In one year, 1868, the favored holder of Crédit Mobilier stock took dividends amounting to 230 per cent in first-mortgage bonds, 515 per cent in Union Pacific stock, and 60 per cent in cash. The construction companies that did the work for the Central Pacific were two in number. At first the firm of Charles Crocker and Company received the contracts, but Crocker's close connection with the Central Pacific was so well known that in 1867 a new firm, the Contract and Finance Company, was formed. The two Central Pacific construction companies did even better for their stockholders than the Crédit Mobilier was able to do for its, for their profits on an investment of $121,000,000 amounted to $63,000,000. Most of this sum went to the four leading officials of the Central Pacific, Leland Stanford, Collis P. Huntington, Charles Crocker, and Mark Hopkins. Unlike the original owners of Union Pacific stock, most of whom sold out their holdings as soon as the road was built, the original Central Pacific group operated their road for many years, and took excellent profits from it. Each of the four mentioned left a fortune at his death of forty million dollars, or more.

When the Union Pacific engine "No. 119" touched noses with the Central Pacific's **Other railroad construction** "Jupiter," a celebration was staged, not only at the meeting-place, where speeches were made and gold and silver spikes were driven, but throughout the country. The excitement over the completion of the first transcontinental, however, was doubtless accentuated by the fact that railroad progress was by no means confined to this one project, but was

[1] See pp. 49, 84.

general. Everywhere new rails were being laid, new lines were being planned. The United States itself had chartered two other transcontinentals on terms almost as generous as it had given the Union and the Central Pacific, and was soon to charter a third. These roads received no subsidy in bonds, but they were allowed a double portion of land — twenty sections per mile in the states, and forty in the territories. The Northern Pacific (1864) was designed to connect the head of Lake Superior with Puget Sound; the Atlantic and Pacific (1866), to build southwestward from Springfield, Missouri; the Texas and Pacific (1871), to cross the continent still farther to the south through Texas, New Mexico, and Arizona.

National assistance to state-chartered railroads, after the pattern set by the Illinois Central grant of 1850, also continued unabated. The Chicago and North Western, the Chicago, Rock Island and Pacific, the Burlington and Missouri River, the Chicago, Milwaukee and St. Paul, the Missouri Pacific, the Atchison, Topeka and Santa Fe, the Kansas Pacific, and a host of minor western lines all profited, directly or indirectly, from government aid, and built feverishly. In the East and the South there was not only much new building, but, even more important, the consolidation of many lesser lines into systems that rivaled in their magnificent reaches the projected transcontinentals of the West. By 1873 Commodore Vanderbilt, the ruthless ruler of the New York Central, had extended his control from New York City to Chicago. J. Edgar Thomson, the associate of Andrew Carnegie, had done much the same thing for the Pennsylvania; and Jay Gould, for the Erie, had found a way through Cleveland and Cincinnati to St. Louis. In the South the Chesapeake and Ohio connected Norfolk with Cincinnati, and easy communication through Tennessee linked both Charleston and Norfolk with Memphis. Within five years after the Civil War the South had twenty-five hundred more miles of railroad than ever existed in the old Confederacy, while in the single year,

The Brooklyn Bridge, which connected western Long Island with lower Manhattan, was both an engineering and an artistic triumph. It was dedicated May 24, 1883. Photolithograph by Shugg Brothers the year it opened.

1873, new construction for this area reached a total of thirteen hundred miles. For the country as a whole, the eight years following the Civil War saw the laying of about thirty-five thousand miles of new track, an increase during the period of almost exactly one hundred per cent.

A great variety of improvements kept pace with the new construction. In 1864 George **Railroad improvements** M. Pullman built his first sleeping-car, the "Pioneer A," at a cost of twenty thousand dollars, and a few years later he was actively at work on separate dining-, drawing-room, and reclining-chair cars. In 1868 George Westinghouse demonstrated on a Pennsylvania passenger train his epoch-making airbrake, a device which by 1872 became an automatic appliance. During these years steel rails were introduced, although a heated debate continued for some time as to the relative merits of iron and steel for this purpose, and it was not until 1877 that the rapid replacement of iron by steel began. As the roadbeds were improved, heavier locomotives and rolling stock were built and a uniform gauge of four feet, eight and one half inches — the gauge

used by the Union Pacific — came into general use. Terminal facilities were greatly improved, union stations made easier the transfer of passengers, and extensive freight yards expedited the traffic in "through freight." Long bridges, after the beginning of work on the Brooklyn Bridge in 1867, became a sort of passion. In 1869 the Missouri River was bridged at Kansas City, and in 1872 at Omaha. Between 1867 and 1874 James B. Eads built the famous bridge that bears his name across the Mississippi at St. Louis. John A. Roebling, the man who planned the Brooklyn Bridge, had first spanned the Ohio River at Cincinnati. These great bridges, and numerous lesser ones, enormously enhanced the speed and ease of railroad transportation.

As already noted,[1] the burst of railroad expansion that had followed the Civil War ended with the panic of 1873. **The railroads and the public** Thereafter for a period of over five years business was at low ebb, and new construction almost non-existent. The railroads, however, had not only hard times to combat, but they were also,

[1] See p. 77.

even before the panic broke, under vigorous attack for their monopolistic tendencies. As a matter of fact, they were not particularly more reprehensible in their conduct than other big businesses, but their public nature made their behavior more easily observable; moreover, with the railroads, sooner than with most other enterprises, the breakdown of the competitive system was fully apparent. Among the first to protest against railroad extortions were the grain-growers of the upper Mississippi Valley, whose dependence upon the railroads was well-nigh complete. Only by means of the railroads could they ship their produce to market; only in the same fashion could they obtain from the outside world the manufactured articles they had to have. Inasmuch as the number of regions served by competitive lines was few indeed, the ordinary farmer had no choice but to use the road that ran nearest his farm. Competition was a myth; the railroads regularly charged "all the traffic would bear," and dictated at will the terms on which they chose to serve their patrons. Elevators and warehouses, often owned or controlled in turn by the railroads, did likewise; and middlemen, themselves compelled to pay a heavy toll in freight to the roads, were not far behind. Efforts to "get another railroad" so as to restore competition rarely availed; more frequently companies that had once been competitive joined forces and ceased to compete.

Ripe for an organized revolt, the farmers of the Northwest found in the Patrons of Husbandry, or the Grange, as it was more frequently called, the tool they needed. The founder of this order, Oliver Hudson Kelley, a government clerk at Washington, had intended it to be a farmers' lodge with an attractive secret ritual that might induce the farmer and the farmer's wife, who was also eligible to membership, to listen to expositions of the latest ideas on scientific farming. Founded in 1867, the order began to grow only in the early seventies when the northwestern farmers seized upon it as a means of

The Granger movement

attacking the railroads. Then Granger orators inflamed public opinion against the railroads, and the Granger organization cleared the way for action.

The Granger idea — that the state should regulate the railroads, if necessary to the point of fixing maximum rates — was older than the movement. Toyed with gingerly in Massachusetts, its real beginning was in Illinois, where during the late sixties laws were passed to restrain both the elevators and the railroads. These early measures proved unavailing, but a new state constitution, adopted in 1870, specifically stated:

Section 15. The General Assembly shall pass laws to correct abuses and to prevent unjust discrimination and extortion in the rates of freight and passenger traffics on the different railroads in this state, and enforce such laws by adequate penalties, to the extent, if necessary for that purpose, of forfeiture of their property and franchises.

With a similarly strong mandate to regulate warehouses, the Illinois legislature of 1871 promptly established maximum rates for the transportation of passengers, required that freight charges should be based entirely upon distance traversed, provided regulations for the storing and shipping of grain, and created a state board of railroad and warehouse commissioners charged with the duty of enforcing the laws. Against these measures the railroads made a determined, and at first a successful, fight, for on the first test case the Supreme Court of Illinois held the laws to be unconstitutional. But the Grangers, now thoroughly aroused, promptly voted out of office one of the judges who had held against them and replaced him with a judge who shared their views. The result was that in 1873 a new law, better drawn but designed to effect the same ends, was sustained.

Meantime the Grangers, bent on using the power of the state to curb the railroads, had gone into politics throughout the Northwest. Sometimes they were content merely to vote for Republicans or Democrats who shared their views, but

Granger legislation

The Granger movement grew out of an effort to provide better scientific information for the farmers through local lodge meetings, but the Grangers eventually turned their attention principally to the elimination of middlemen and the establishment of legal restraints on the railroads.

OBJECTIVES. Lithograph describing the organization, by Strobridge Company, 1873.

MAIL-ORDER BUSINESS. Montgomery-Ward met the needs of the Grangers and directed advertising to them. Cover of catalogue.

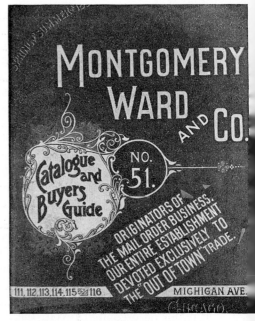

POLITICAL ACTIVITY. Grangers in Illinois enroute to a meeting. Sketch by Joseph Beale.

frequently they chose third-party candidates on separate "Anti-Monopoly" or "Independent" or "Reform" tickets. Independence Day, 1873, was long remembered as the "Farmers' Fourth of July," for on that day hundreds of Granger audiences gave their approval to a *Farmers' Declaration of Independence*, which repeated in well-worn phraseology the grievances from which farmers suffered, and announced in no uncertain way their determination to find relief. Presently Granger legislatures had enacted, not only in Illinois, but also in Wisconsin, Minnesota, and Iowa, measures of drastic regulation for railroads and warehouses. In each instance litigation followed, and the railroads, despairing of aid from the Granger-minded state courts, at length took their cases to the federal courts. The Granger laws, railroad attorneys claimed, were impairments of contracts that the states had already made in granting charters to the railroads, and they provided for the taking of private property without due process of law. But in the spring of 1877, the United States Supreme Court ruled against the railroads in a series of decisions, the most important of which were *Munn vs. Illinois* and *Peik vs. the Chicago and Northwestern Railroad.* Thus the "right of a state to regulate a business that is public in nature though privately owned and managed" won striking vindication, and a weapon was forged with which, it was hoped, not only the railroads but other monopolistic enterprises also could be attacked. Most of the early Granger laws were defective and had to be repealed, but the principle on which they were founded endured, and before long railroad and warehouse commissions were hard at work in nearly every state.

The Granger movement, although short-lived, left other important legacies besides **Granger** the point of law it had made. **contribution** Convinced that they were being robbed by manufacturers and middlemen, the Grangers made strenuous efforts to establish cooperative farm-implement factories, elevators, creameries, and general stores. They experimented with purchasing agencies, and tried out cooperative selling. Many of these ventures were unsuccessful, not so much because they were wrong in principle as because of the inexperience and mismanagement of the men who were placed in charge. These business failures, more than anything else, account for the sudden decline in Granger popularity about 1876, and the relegation of the Patrons of Husbandry once more to the inconspicuous rôle of a farmers' lodge. But the farmers who had participated in the movement did not soon forget the fright they had given the politicians by their independence, the victory they had won over the railroads, and the good times they had had at lodge meetings and picnics. Also, the occasional surviving cooperatives paved the way for an important development later on.

Neither the hard times nor the Grangers could hold back indefinitely the final con- **Railroad** quest of the Far West by the **building** railroads. Sure signs of revived business activity appeared as early as 1878 when the Northern Pacific, the misfortunes of which had plunged Jay Cooke and Company into bankruptcy, again prepared to build. Under the leadership of Frederick Billings, a conservative Vermont capitalist, investors were persuaded to put their money once more into Northern Pacific securities, and for three years the westward march of Billings's railroad builders went forward without incident. In 1881, however, Billings's plans came into conflict with those of Henry Villard, a hard-headed German-American whose Oregon Railroad and Navigation Company controlled the railroad and steamboat lines of the Pacific Northwest. Villard had long sought to induce Billings to agree to some traffic arrangement that would prevent competition between the two systems when the Northern Pacific should be finished, but Billings received all such overtures with cold refusals. Thereupon Villard induced his financial backers in New York to put money into a "blind pool" upon which, for an unrevealed purpose, he might draw at will. With this money he bought up enough stock to secure complete control of both the "N. P." and the "O.R. and N.," and organized a holding company, the Oregon and Transcontinental, through which to manage them. He then deposed Billings as president of the Northern Pacific, took the place for himself, and as president of all three corporations achieved the harmony he desired. On the completion of the Northern Pacific in 1883, by way of celebration he ran a "Golden Spike Special," filled with the most distinguished company of American notables that he could assemble, the entire length of the line.

By this time, however, the American public could no longer be thrilled by news that another transcontinental **The** railroad had been finished. In **Transcon-** addition to the Union Pacific, **tinentals** completed in 1869, the Southern Pacific was

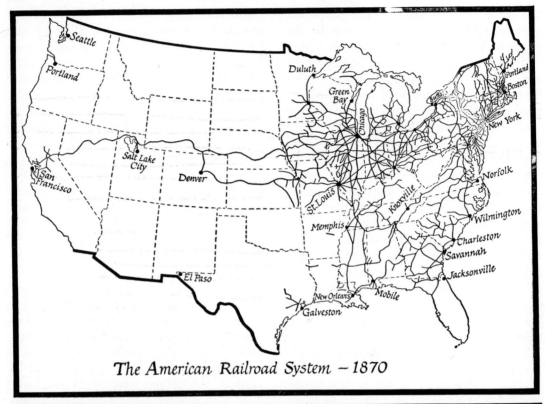

The American Railroad System – 1870

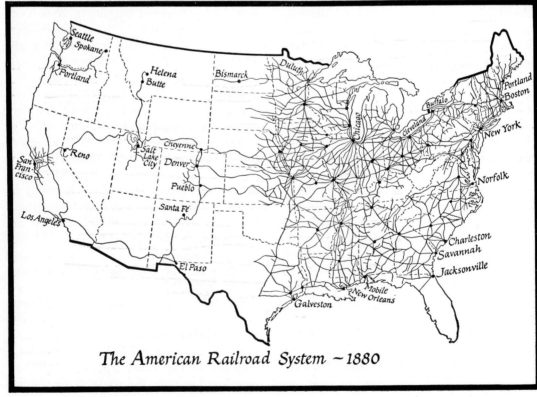

The American Railroad System – 1880

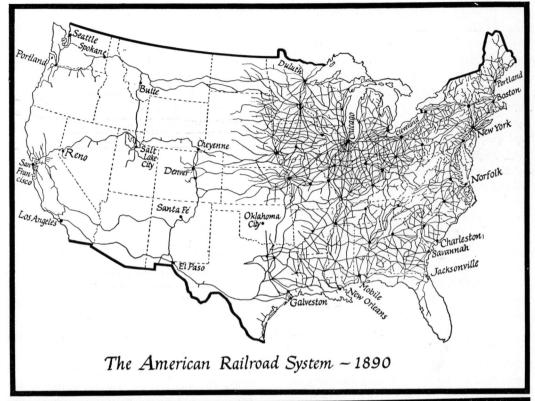

The American Railroad System – 1890

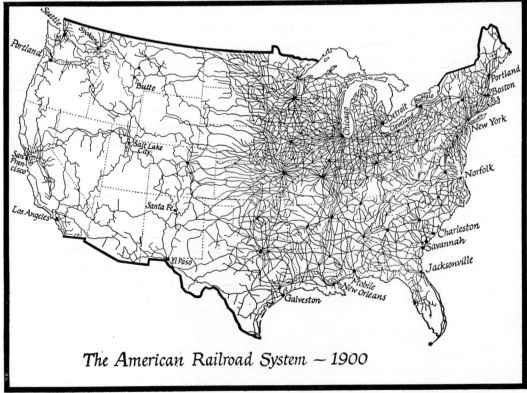

The American Railroad System – 1900

now running trains to the western coast. The Southern Pacific was a California corporation which had shrewdly acquired the right to build within the borders of that state to meet any eastern land-grant railroad. Owned and managed by the same able group that had built the Central Pacific, it had pushed its lines southward through the state, and was prepared to receive all newcomers at Fort Yuma and the Needles, the two points on the border of southern California where the canyon of the Colorado could be crossed. With the aid of territorial charters from Arizona and New Mexico and a state charter from Texas, the Southern Pacific built eastward from Fort Yuma to meet the old Texas Pacific, which it presently absorbed. By January, 1882, it had through trains running over this route from San Francisco to St. Louis, and by February of the next year it had opened up an alternative route through southern Texas to New Orleans. Alert to every opportunity, the Southern Pacific also connected at the Needles with the Atchison, Topeka, and Santa Fe, which had built westward through Kansas on a state land grant, and from Albuquerque to the Needles on the federal grant of the defunct Atlantic and Pacific. Trains were running the entire length of this route shortly after Villard's

"Golden Spike Special" made its much-advertised tour. In 1884 the owners of the Southern Pacific, who were now in a position to monopolize the railroad business of the Southwest, followed the example of Villard and created a holding company, the Southern Pacific of Kentucky, through which to administer their extensive properties. The Southern Pacific owned no railroads in Kentucky, but the laws of that state were friendly to its purposes, while incorporation in a state far removed from the scene of the road's activities seemed likely to reduce to a minimum the danger of investigation and regulation.

Other western railroads extended their lines during these years with the same feverish speed. The Burlington, the Rock Island, the North Western, and the Missouri Pacific competed with the transcontinentals and their branches for the exploitation of the Great Plains. The Denver and Rio Grande built heroically around the Colorado mountains, by way of the Royal Gorge of the Arkansas, to connect with the Union Pacific at Ogden. James J. Hill of Minnesota advanced the fortunes of the St. Paul, Minneapolis and Manitoba slowly but surely until by the time the next panic broke, in 1893, it had become, under a new name, the Great

Elevated trains to relieve city traffic congestion were increasingly common after 1870. Here is an artist's representation of the first such train on the Gilbert Elevated Railroad in New York City. *Leslie's Illustrated Newspaper*, 1878.

Northern, another transcontinental. North of the United States, in Canada, Donald A. Smith, later known as Lord Strathcona and Mount Royal, brought the Canadian Pacific to completion in 1885, while south of the United States, in Mexico, the Mexican Central, an affiliate of the Santa Fe, had reached Mexico City the year before.

While the most spectacular railroad activities of the period occurred in the trans-Mississippi West, the southern and eastern roads were by no means idle. In the South the Richmond and West Point Terminal Railway and Warehouse Company, a holding company formed in 1881, laid the foundations for what later became the Southern Railway system. In the East the great systems that had taken form before the Civil War — the New York Central, the Pennsylvania, the Erie, and the Baltimore and Ohio — built or acquired branch lines, consolidated their holdings, and, when well-managed, made money. Everywhere the substitution of steel for iron rails, together with an equally revolutionary improvement of rolling stock and equipment, called for enormous expenditures, funds for which, in spite of much cut-throat competition, the railroads somehow managed to find. Because of these expensive innovations, statistics on mileage fail to give a complete picture of the railroad development of the period. Nevertheless the statistics are impressive. From 52,000 miles of railroad in 1870 the total mileage in the United States had risen by 1880 to 93,000 and by 1890 to 163,000 — an increase of 70,000 miles in ten years. Construction more than kept pace with the expansion of population. In 1870 the United States had 1380 miles of railroad per million inhabitants; in 1880 it had 1858 miles, and in 1890 it had 2625 miles. By the last-mentioned date the main outlines of the American railroad map were complete; after that date the mileage continued to increase, but such new tracks as were laid served mainly as feeders for existing lines. The age of railroad pioneering was over.

Southern and eastern roads

James J. Hill, founder of the Great Northern, was typical of the American railroad pioneers.

Typical of the railroad builders was James J. Hill (1838–1916), the creator of the Great Northern. Hill was born in a log cabin near Rockwood, Ontario, the third child of a hard-working Scotch-Irish farm couple. His father died when James was only fourteen, and the boy quit school to go to work in a village store. Four years of this was enough, and at eighteen the lad made his way to St. Paul, Minnesota, then a town of only four or five thousand, to grow up with the new country. He was not slow to see that the future of the Northwest was intimately bound up with transportation, and the opening in the early sixties of a ten-mile stretch of railroad between St. Paul and Minneapolis fired his imagination. Successful, seemingly, at everything he undertook, he soon had a contract to supply the rapidly growing "St. Paul and Pacific" with the fuel for its wood-burning engines, and he took advantage of the opportunity to find out more about the affairs of the road than most of its officials ever knew. Overexpanded in its haste to acquire title to a land grant, and in chronic trouble with the stronger Northern Pacific, the St. Paul and Pacific went into bankruptcy when the panic

James J. Hill

broke in 1873. For years its later-built portions were described as "Two streaks of rust and a right of way," but in 1878 Hill and three associates, including Donald A. Smith, with borrowed money bought themselves into its control. Reorganized as the St. Paul, Minneapolis, and Manitoba, Hill soon had the road earning good profits out of the rich trade of the Red River Valley. Unlike some railroad builders, he was not interested primarily in acquiring a land grant or making money out of road construction. What he hoped to do was to build up the country as he advanced his lines so that the settlers would support the road through the business they made for it. Time proved that his faith in the future of the Northwest was justified. Within fifteen years after he assumed its management, his little local road had been transformed into the Great Northern system, with lines that really reached the Pacific, and an income that had made its builder rich.

The creation of these great railroad systems was not usually accomplished without the elimination of a multitude of lesser lines. Back in the pre-Civil War era more or less accidental connections had played a considerable part in railroad consolidation. In this way the work of Cornelius Vanderbilt in welding together the New York Central had been greatly facilitated. Panics and periods of depression had also done their bit. During the years following 1857, and even more after 1873, the weaker roads had gone into bankruptcy only to emerge as parts of some stronger, and usually much larger, system. During the depression years of the seventies no less than four hundred and fifty railroads, fully two fifths of the roads of the country, had suffered this experience. The holding company idea, well exemplified by the Oregon and Transcontinental in the Northwest, the Southern Pacific of Kentucky in the Southwest, and the Richmond Terminal Company in the South, also greatly facilitated consolidation. Great sectional systems were thus created that could monopolize the business of the region they covered. Within

Railway consolidations

these areas competition was stifled, and only the interposition of governmental authority could prevent railroad monopolies from charging for their services "all the traffic would bear."

Competing systems, however, could not always be united, and wherever competition existed it tended to become both ruthless and costly. Rebates were given to favored shippers, particularly to those who shipped large quantities of goods long distances. Regions or cities that were served by more than one railroad were granted cut rates, while those dependent upon the services of a single road were overcharged in an effort to make up the losses from the competing rates. More was charged for a short haul where there was no competition than for a longer haul over the same line when competition between the terminal points existed. Efforts on the part of the roads to eliminate competition usually came to nought. Sometimes competing roads, after a disastrous "rate war," made rate agreements, but the temptation to break such self-imposed promises when to do so meant good profits was always more than some managers could resist. Pools were tried through which a common treasurer collected all earnings and paid out profits according to a ratio agreed upon, but these, too, led mainly to wrangling and non-observance. From the railroad point of view consolidation into large non-competitive systems seemed the only ideal solution.

Public criticism of the railroads, common during Granger times, had diminished somewhat during the later seventies. For a time, perhaps, there was less to criticize. Railroad managers, remembering the effective protests of the Grangers, took care when they could do so not to revive them. Even more to the point, many of the worst of the railroad offenses were associated primarily with a period of expansion, whereas contraction, not expansion, had been the watchword of the depression. During the eighties, with an unprecedented amount of railroad building going on, most of the old abuses reappeared, and with them a new

Criticisms of the railroads

wave of protests. The way in which the railroads, as corporations, enjoyed privileges not accorded to the ordinary individual came in for heated denunciations. Their charters, obtained by fair means or foul, endowed the fortunate possessors with "eternal life," and yet gave them rights and privileges before the law designed originally for natural persons whose life-span was limited. By right of eminent domain a road might take whatever land it wanted, and pay a price for it that to the dispossessed owner seemed unfair and inadequate. Special privileges of taxation enabled the roads to be taxed only on their gross or net earnings, whereas the ordinary individual had to pay taxes on whatever property he possessed, whether it brought him an income or not. Railroads went into politics, determined who should and who should not be nominated to office, and by distributing free passes to legislators, governors, judges, and other office-holders put all those who had authority to restrain them in their debt.

Critics of the railroads could multiply their charges at will. Communities in dire need of a railroad connection were forced to subscribe heavy subsidies under threat of being left off a projected line. When the railroad came, the outraged citizens found themselves obliged to pay a double tribute — high taxes because of the subsidy they had voted, and high rates because the railroad now had them at its mercy. Western railroads, thanks to the land-grant policy of the United States government, were usually the owners of great tracts of land that otherwise might have been available for settlers to take as homesteads. Thus the charge of land monopoly could be hurled. Stock-watering and stock-manipulation were the rule rather than the exception, and most railroads, in addition to paying dividends on a capitalization far in excess of their value, were also bonded for all they were worth. High freight and passenger rates to keep such overcapitalized, debt-ridden structures from collapse could not be avoided. Graft and dishonesty in railroad administration were all too common. Printed

schedules of rates were deliberately kept out of shippers' hands so that rebates and other special favors might the more easily be granted favored shippers. Small stockholders were "frozen out" when large stockholders found such an operation to their advantage. Roads were built — often roads that were not needed — for the benefit of the contractors, who presently unloaded a bankrupt company upon unsuspecting stockholders and unappreciative communities.

The Granger movement had called attention to many such grievances, and had led to the creation in most of the **Railroad** states of governmental commis- **regulation** sions for the regulation of the railroads. These commissions, ill-informed as to the problems that confronted them, and often subservient to the corporations they were supposed to regulate, accomplished comparatively little. Knowledge, to be sure, came with the years, but it added nothing to the effectiveness of state regulation; by the time a railroad was large enough to need regulation, it was too large for a state commission to regulate it. Local intrastate roads that the commissions could handle were being quietly absorbed into powerful interstate systems that were beyond them. "The number of separate railroad companies operating distinct roads in Minnesota was as high as twenty, three years ago," wrote a perplexed Minnesota commissioner in 1881. "Now the number is reduced to substantially one third that number." Other state commissions reported the same trend toward consolidation, and the census of 1880 proclaimed it eloquently. While, according to the Granger decisions, the regulatory authority of a state did not necessarily stop at the state's borders, the fact of the matter was that increasingly it did. Finally, in 1886, the Supreme Court of the United States admitted the inadvisability of its earlier ruling, and in a case involving the Wabash Railroad and the State of Illinois held in effect that Congress alone had authority to regulate interstate commerce.

Meantime one investigating committee

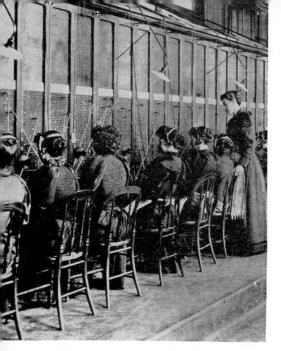

Telephones and cables, together with the earlier telegraph, greatly improved the communications system of the American nation. The first crude "Bell telephones" were in use during the late seventies, while Cyrus W. Field, with the help of the enormous Great Eastern, completed an enduring transatlantic cable in 1866.

ALEXANDER GRAHAM BELL. Scientific men observing telephone demonstration in Salem, Mass. *Leslie's Illustrated Newspaper,* 1877.

EARLY TELEPHONE. Magneto bell with two hand telephones — one for transmitting and one for receiving, 1878.

THE ATLANTIC CABLE. Completion of the cable at Newfoundland, July 27, 1866. From a lithograph by Kimmel and Forster.

after another had studied the railroad prob-

Investigations lem. As far back as Granger times a Senate committee, headed by William Windom of Minnesota, had urged that a federal bureau of commerce be created, and twice during the seventies the national House of Representatives had passed bills to that effect. Another of Windom's proposals, that trunk lines should be built by the government to compete with private lines, and so reduce rates, won less approval. In 1879 the Hepburn committee in New York State submitted a wealth of evidence on the misconduct of the railroads, and inferentially pointed to national regulation as the proper way out. In 1885, after both the House and the Senate had passed measures looking toward railroad regulation, but had failed to agree on details, the Senate appointed a new investigating committee with a larger range of powers than had been accorded the Windom committee. Headed by Shelby M. Cullom of Illinois, this committee traveled widely and investigated carefully the regulatory efforts of the state commissions. It reported in 1886 that three fourths of the railroad business of the country was interstate in character, hence, under the rule of law laid down in the Wabash decision, beyond the control of state regulation. Four possible methods of dealing with the situation were listed: (1) the continuance of private ownership and management, but with more effective governmental regulation; (2) government ownership and management; (3) government ownership and private management under public regulations; and (4) government ownership and management in competition with private companies. Noting the widespread opposition throughout the country to government ownership, the committee recommended regulation by the national government as the preferable alternative.

Congress was now ready to act, and in 1887 it established an Interstate Commerce Com-

The I.C.C. mission to consist of five members, of whom not more than three might belong to the same political party, to be appointed by the President for six-year terms. The law forbade most of the evil practices uncovered by the various investigating committees, and in a sense made national the current trends in state regulation. Rebates, pools, and discriminations were branded as illegal, and the rule that more could not be charged for a short haul than for a longer one over the same line was established. The commission was authorized to investigate complaints against the railroads, and to make decisions which, however, it could enforce only through court action. This provision for a judicial review of its rulings proved to be the undoing of the early commission. Although headed by an eminent ex-judge, Thomas M. Cooley of Michigan, it failed to obtain the judicial backing through which, alone, its decisions could be made effective. Delays and reversals permitted the railroads to operate about as they had operated before. Not until the Presidency of Theodore Roosevelt did the Interstate Commerce Commission become a really effective body.

While railroads undoubtedly played the principal role in revolutionizing the means of communication on which Amer-

Telegraph and cable icans depended, they were not alone in the field. When it came to the sending of news and information from place to place, they were far outclassed by the electric telegraph, used for years before the Civil War, but now extended to parallel every railroad right of way and to serve practically every hamlet in the nation. Cable service also steadily improved. The first transoceanic cable, laid in 1858, had soon been destroyed by the use of too strong electric currents, but by 1866, through the persistent efforts of Cyrus W. Field, a better one had been laid, and soon thereafter many others. American newsgatherers, diplomats, and businessmen were thus able to keep in as close touch with London as with New York, and to be far better informed on world affairs than had been possible before. Improvements in ocean-going steamships also helped, for they facilitated foreign travel for Americans, and brought numerous visitors to America from distant shores. Under these circumstances the extremes of provincialism, so common in the United States of an earlier period, began to disappear.

Of incalculable importance also was the telephone, the invention of Alexander Graham Bell, an American Scot **The telephone** who taught deaf mutes, and had interested himself in acoustics. At the Centennial Exposition of 1876 Bell exhibited his instruments, and made a deep impression on the American public. He was not the first to study the problem of transmitting human speech by electricity, nor the only one to find a solution, but he did develop the first practicable telephone. Even so, it was not easy to induce capital to invest in so fantastic an enterprise, and the successful launching of the telephone owed much to the organizing genius of Theodore N. Vail, later president of the American Telephone and Telegraph Company. During the eighties telephone systems were introduced into virtually every American city, and by the end of the decade no less than 440,000 instruments were in use. Well before the turn of the century successful long-distance connections had been generally established. Among its numerous contributions, the telephone provided at its switchboards a new occupation for women, and through its rural extensions an effective weapon against social isolation.

Meantime the United States Post Office, regardless of deficits, cheapened its rates and amplified its service. Railroad **Postal** extensions were followed every- **changes** where by postal extensions. Mail delivery at the door was inaugurated in a few American cities as early as 1871, and thereafter was rapidly bestowed upon smaller and smaller communities. Catalogues and printed circulars were accorded special rates to facilitate general distribution. The penny postal card, introduced into the United States from Europe in 1873, brought the cost of personal mail service to an irreducible minimum; but the two-cent letter rate, inaugurated in 1883, was not far behind. The result of all these changes was to bring the American people closer together than had ever been possible before. The sharper lines of sectionalism were blurred, and the triumph of nationalism was assured. Probably most significant of all, the way was paved for the organization of business along national rather than local or sectional lines. The revolution in means of communication provided a firm foundation for the new industrialism.

Bibliography

For the general history of railroads see E. R. Johnson, *American Railway Transportation* (1912); Slason Thompson, *A Short History of American Railways* (1925); and L. H. Haney, *A Congressional History of Railways in the United States* (2 vols., 1908–10). An immense amount of miscellaneous information is contained in the report of the Cullom committee, Forty-Ninth Congress, First Session, *Senate Report*, Number 46 (serial 2356). On the Interstate Commerce Commission there are two useful treatises by W. Z. Ripley, *Railroads: Rates and Regulation* (1912), and *Railroads: Finance and Organization* (1915). C. F. Adams, Jr., *Railroads: Their Origins and Problems* (rev. ed., 1887), is the work of an acute contemporary, and is still valuable. The Granger Movement is fully covered by Solon J. Buck, *The Granger Movement* (1913); and less extensively by the same author, *The Agrarian Crusade* (1921).

Among the best books on the railroad expansion of this period are John Moody, *The Railroad Builders* (1919); Robert E. Riegel, *The Story of the Western Railroads* (1926); and Glenn Chesney Quiett, *They Built the West* (1934). The building of the Union Pacific has attracted many historians, among them: G. M. Dodge, *How We Built the Union Pacific Railway* (1894); John P.

Davis, *The Union Pacific Railway* (1894); and E. L. Sabin, *Building the Pacific Railway* (1919). On the Central Pacific see the extremely lively and interesting Oscar Lewis, *The Big Four: The Story of Huntington, Stanford, Hopkins, and Crocker* (1938). The spectacular career of Henry Villard is best followed in his own *Memoirs of Henry Villard* (2 vols., 1904). Also useful are E. V. Smalley, *History of the Northern Pacific Railroad* (1883); J. B. Hedges, *Henry Villard and the Railways of the Northwest* (1930); and Stuart Daggett, *Chapters of the History of the Southern Pacific* (1922). An appreciative biography of the builder of the Great Northern is J. G. Pyle, *The Life of James J. Hill* (2 vols., 1917). Richard C. Overton, *Gulf to Rockies* (1953), deals with the history of the Fort Worth and Denver, and Colorado and Southern railways from 1861 to 1898. See also by the same author, *Burlington West: A Colonization History of the Burlington Railroad.* 1941.

On the significance of the telephone there are two useful books: H. N. Casson, *The History of the Telephone* (1910); and Catherine Mackenzie, *Alexander Graham Bell, The Man Who Contracted Space* (1928).

8

The New Industrialism

A PRECISE date for the beginning of the new industrialism that engulfed the United States during the decades following the Civil War would be difficult to cite, but the close connection between the war and the rising significance of industry is abundantly apparent. The Civil War is unique in that it was fought during a period of economic revolution; changes of a fundamental nature were taking place that could never have been prevented, war or no war. What the war did was to crowd into a few hurried years developments that might otherwise have taken decades to unfold. New and larger factories appeared in prodigious numbers; machine-made goods took the place of hand-made goods; the value of manufactured articles annually produced in the United States accelerated at a far more rapid pace than the value of agricultural commodities; the national income grew in every aspect, but its rate of growth in industry far surpassed its rate of growth in agriculture; population figures showed a steadily rising proportion of city dwellers over country dwellers. In short, a new era was being born. But this transformation only accompanied and followed the war; it was not caused by it.

Furthermore, such evidence as is sometimes adduced to prove that the Civil War was primarily the result of a conspiracy

Effects of the Civil War

of industrialists bent on obtaining larger profits is not convincing. The industrialists made much of the advantage that the war offered them, and after the war was over they enjoyed a tremendous prosperity; but there is no reason to suppose that the war was essential to their triumph, or that they thought of the struggle in any such light. As for the all-important steel and oil industries, it would be difficult indeed to maintain that the Civil War was in any direct way responsible for their development. In fact, the early growth of steel manufacturing in the United States was doubtless retarded because of the necessity of keeping up the flow of the standard iron products demanded by the war, and it is quite possible that the uses found for oil might have been greater had the nation been at peace. Wartime necessities, however, acted as a powerful stimulus to many other industries, such, for example, as meat-packing, flour-milling, and the manufacture of prepared foods, textiles, and leather goods. But it is impossible to believe that these developments would not have come, more slowly, to be sure, but quite as certainly, had there been no war.

New machines did their part, both during and after the war, toward pushing forward the new industrialism. The **The machine age** United States Patent Bureau (whose head had contemplated resigning in 1833 because there was nothing left for inventors to do) had granted only 36,000 patents before 1860, but during the three decades from 1860 to 1890 granted approximately 440,000. While by no means all of these inventions were of real significance, some of them were of far-reaching consequence. Americans also borrowed heavily from European ideas, and showed their customary skill in adapting them to American needs. There was plenty of work to do. With the population of the country growing at a prodigious rate, both from the increase in the native stock and from immigration, the needs of more and more people had to be met. Such newly formed industries as steel and oil had to expand and equip their vast establishments. The use of agricultural machinery, greatly expedited during the war, showed no signs of abatement, and new inventions brought more and more machines to the farmers' attention. Probably most significant of all, the extension and improvement of the railroads was being pressed with all possible speed. And, in opening up the farther west to miners, cattlemen, and farmers — all latter-day pioneers who were by no means self-sufficient — the railroads produced still more demands for machinery, equipment, and supplies.

Fortunately the capital needed to maintain this rapid economic growth was not difficult to find. War profits had been **Sources of capital** handsome, and graft at the expense of the government so common as scarcely to excite comment. About two billion dollars' worth of United States bonds were outstanding, and regardless of how cheap the money with which they had been purchased, both interest and principal were paid in gold. Capital so invested multiplied with startling rapidity. Gold and silver poured in from the western mines. European investors readily purchased large blocks of American securities. Banks, with credit so inflated, flourished as never before. Not until 1864 had the national banking system, created during the war, really begun to function, but by 1865 there were more than fifteen hundred national banks scattered throughout the country, with a bank-note circulation that was soon almost to equal that of the greenbacks. Furthermore, Secretary McCulloch's efforts to reduce the greenbacks in quantity, and so to raise their value, were unsuccessful, so that the cutting of prices and wages that would certainly have occurred had they been withdrawn was avoided.

Under these circumstances it is not surprising that manufacturing lost none of the momentum it had accumulated **Rise of big business** during the war. The United States, indeed, became a sort of paradise for industrialists. A dependably high tariff assured them of the right to exploit the steadily growing American market, while soldiers returning from the war and immigrants streaming in from Europe supplied a comfortable abundance of labor. One by one the high records of production set up during the war fell below the higher records that came with the first five years of peace. "More cotton spindles were set revolving, more iron furnaces were lighted, more steel was made, more coal and copper was mined, more lumber was sawed and hewed, more houses and shops were constructed and more manufactories of different kinds were established, than during any equal term in our earlier history." [1] The economic transformation of the United States that had begun with some deliberation before the war had thus reached the crescendo of revolution. Agricultural America had no chance to keep up the pace being set by industrial America; Jefferson's dream of a nation composed mainly of small free farmers had faded before the realities of the machine age. The America of the future was to be less rural than urban, more factory than farm. The black belt of the cotton kingdom was to recede in importance before a northern black belt, traced by the smoke of factory chimneys, a

[1] Allan Nevins, *The Emergence of Modern America, 1865–1878* (1927), p. 32. Quoted by permission of the Macmillan Company.

The first skyscraper to be erected anywhere in the world was the Home Insurance Building in Chicago, 1885, with William LeBaron Jenney as the architect. Buildings of far greater height and size were soon to appear in every large American city.

belt that ultimately was to extend far into the South itself.

Circumstances conspired to locate the preponderance of American factories in the Northeast, especially in New England and the North Atlantic states, but with important extensions along the Great Lakes and the Ohio River into the West, and down the Appalachians into the South. These regions provided some of the richest of the nation's resources in coal and iron and water-power; also, their abundant population, both native and immigrant, furnished a dependable source of labor supply. Here, too, were superior means of transportation, both by water and by rail, to facilitate the assembling of needed raw materials and the marketing of finished products.

The barometer of the new industrialism

was steel. Before the Civil War the high cost of steel confined its use to The romance the manufacture of such small of steel articles as tools and cutlery in which quality was demanded regardless of price. That anything so bulky as railroad rails, or the heavy locomotives that ran on the rails, should ever be made of steel rather than of iron seemed utterly fantastic. All this was changed as the result of a remarkable discovery made independently and at about the same time by an American, William Kelly, and an Englishman, Henry Bessemer. Kelly, a resident of Eddyville, Kentucky, who made wrought-iron sugar kettles for his neighbors, observed one day that the effect of an air-blast on molten iron was to make it white-hot. From this he readily deduced that the molten metal itself contained enough carbon to burn out its impurities, if only a strong blast of air could be directed against it. Plainly this "air-boiling" process, if only it could be made practicable, would tend to eliminate the expensive use of charcoal, and so greatly reduce the cost of refinement. In a series of experiments, carried on between 1851 and 1856, Kelly demonstrated the soundness of his idea, although his patrons obstinately insisted upon wrought-iron kettles made in the old-fashioned way.

In 1856 the Englishman, Bessemer, who had been carrying on similar experiments, announced the successful ap- The Besse- plication of a "fuel-less" process, mer process and obtained a United States patent upon it. Kelly, however, soon convinced the Patent Office that he was the original inventor, and it was some time before the conflicting interests could be reconciled. Before the Civil War ended, successful efforts were being made within the United States to make commercial use of the "Bessemer process," as it was generally called, and in 1866 one Alexander Lyman Holley, by obtaining the right to use both the Bessemer and the Kelly patents, paved the way for a phenomenal development. Within a few years the number of Bessemer steel works

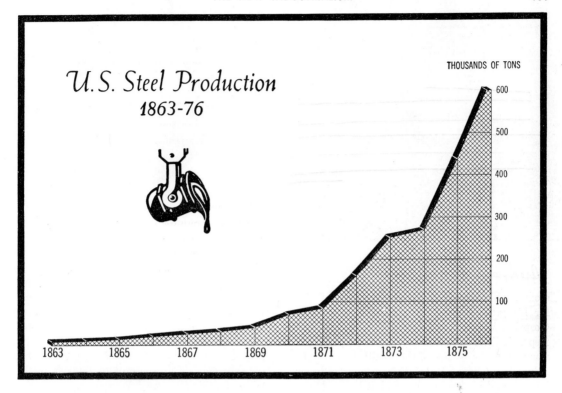

U. S. Steel Production
1863-76

THOUSANDS OF TONS

600

500

400

300

200

100

1863   1865   1867   1869   1871   1873   1875

in the country could be counted by the dozen, and the price of steel had dropped to a figure that made its use instead of iron entirely practicable. Another new method of producing steel, known as the "open-hearth" process, was introduced into the United States from Europe in 1868 by Abram S. Hewitt, who shared with his father-in-law, Peter Cooper, control of the New Jersey Steel and Iron Company at Trenton. Ultimately far more open-hearth than Bessemer steel was to be made, but until well toward the end of the century Bessemer steel cost less to produce, and so enjoyed a great advantage.

The steel industry was to produce many great names, but none more glamorous than that of Andrew Carnegie (1835–1919), the Scottish immigrant lad whose career became an almost perfect pattern for the typical American success story. The son of a humble, but by no means unintelligent, Dunfermline weaver, young Carnegie was brought to America in 1848 by his parents in the proverbial quest

of opportunity. He found it, first as a bobbin-boy at a dollar and twenty cents a week in a western Pennsylvania cotton factory, then as a messenger at two dollars and a half a week in a Pittsburgh telegraph office. Soon he was a telegraph operator, one of the first to learn to read "by sound" the messages that came over the wire, and a little later, as much because of his personal charm as because of his outstanding proficiency, the private secretary of Thomas A. Scott, a Pennsylvania Railroad official. From that position to railroading was an easy transition; and then from railroading to bridge-building, where he made a specialty of supplanting outmoded wooden construction with iron. Astoundingly versatile, he pursued many side lines, nearly all of which turned out well. He built bridges, made money out of oil, and sold railway bonds in Europe — all at the same time. On one of his trips to England he saw steel being made by the Bessemer process, and returned to the United States determined to put "all of his eggs in one basket," the manufacture

Andrew Carnegie

Andrew Carnegie won fame, not alone for his success as a business man, but also for his great interest in philanthropy. "The Gospel of Wealth," as he proclaimed it, involved responsibilities as well as privileges. A rich man was merely the trustee of the wealth that society helped him amass. He might care generously for his own and his family's needs, but he would die "disgraced" if he left great accumulations undistributed. Carnegie in his lifetime gave away over $350,000,000, some $60,000,000 of which went to public libraries, and most of the rest to promote peace, education, and the arts. The photograph of Carnegie is by Francis Johnson; the drawing of the Free Library of Allegheny City, Pennsylvania, a Carnegie gift of 1890, is by B. Dabbs, *Leslie's Illustrated Newspaper*.

of steel. By 1873, the date when he opened the J. Edgar Thomson Steel Mills — named after a powerful partner in the enterprise — his career as a steel magnate had begun.

The Pittsburgh area took an early lead in steel production, for in this vicinity lay enormous beds of coking coal, limestone, and iron ore, the three principal raw products necessary for the manufacture of steel. But the immense deposits of iron ore, discovered as early as 1844 near the western shore of Lake Superior, made inevitable the westward expansion of the industry. Thanks to the St. Mary's Ship Canal, which had been constructed by 1855 between Lake Superior and Lake Huron, the Great Lakes provided a natural waterway from the mines to the numerous manufacturing cities that lined their southern borders; it was easier to ship the ore to the plants than to build new plants adjacent to the mines. As a result, such cities as Cleveland, Detroit, Gary (Ind.), and Chicago became increasingly important centers for the manufacture of iron and steel. Here, too, were located a large proportion of the factories that used iron or steel products in the items they manufactured.

The depression years of the seventies called a halt to the rapid expansion of industry in the United States, but it was only a temporary halt. Indeed, businesses that escaped **Effects of the depression** annihilation were often the better off for the restraints that the depression imposed upon them. In flush times comfortable profits were too easily achieved; in hard times even small profits were won, more than likely, only as the reward of efficiency. In flush times American manufacturers had depended all too exclusively upon the American market; in hard times they sought to adapt their products to the needs of other lands, and began to sell abroad. Solvent organizations bettered their positions by absorbing their weaker rivals, and by devising trade agreements with their stronger rivals to forestall the menace of cut-throat competition. When, at last, the depression was over, business, particularly big business, was in position to begin another era of spectacular expansion.

Steel was no exception to the rule. Even during the depression years steel production had reached fantastic figures, and by the end of the 1870's American steel mills were turning out nearly a million tons of steel. In another decade production had shot up to over four million tons. With fantastic rapidity steel replaced iron in the making of numerous heavy items, such, for example, as locomotives, railway cars, and the rails on which they ran, or farm machinery, and the still more complicated machinery of the factories. Likewise steel proved its merit for an incredible number of new uses, structutal steel for the building of bridges and skyscrapers, steel wire for wire nails and wire fences, steel castings for wheels and axles, steel sheets or skelp for pipes and tubes, steel bars for machine tools, steel plates for battleships, and steel in many other forms to meet an infinite variety of needs. The demand for steel became almost insatiable, but American manufacturers were equal to the occasion. Before the end of the century the United States led the nations of the world in the production of steel, even exceeding the output of British steel mills almost twice over.

No less startlingly new than the steel industry, and almost as revolutionary in its

"Rock oil"   possibilities, was the production and refinement of oil. For centuries petroleum, by seeping to the surface in various parts of the earth, had advertised its existence to mankind, but, strangely enough, no one had seemed to realize that it was of any particular value; much less that, by sinking wells, great pools of it could be tapped. Years before the Civil War enterprising farmers in Venango County, Pennsylvania, were accustomed to skim the substance from Oil Creek, a branch of the Allegheny, and use it to grease their wagons.

Some even bottled it and sold it as a medicine "guaranteed," when externally applied, to cure rheumatism, and good for almost anything, if taken internally. A Pennsylvania manufacturer, Samuel M. Kier, whose wells persisted in pumping up petroleum as well as salt water, resolved this dilemma by putting "Kier's Rock Oil," a medicine for which he made the most extravagant claims, upon the market. The chief contribution of the salt producers to the oil industry, however, was to be the methods of boring deep wells and of pumping that they had worked out. These methods the early oil men were able to take over almost without modification.

The possibility that petroleum could be refined into a practical illuminant was not unrealized by the versatile Kier, **Oil for** who made some significant ex- **illumination** periments along that line, but the chief credit for this epochal discovery belongs to a graduate of Dartmouth College, named George H. Bissell, who remembered, curiously, some of the experiments with crude oil that one of his teachers had made. Convinced that ultimately he could supplant the old-fashioned tallow candles and whale-oil lamps with something far superior, Bissell leased some land in western Pennsylvania, and sent a sample of the oil it produced to Benjamin Silliman, Jr., professor of chemistry in Yale College, for analysis. In a memorable document, written in 1855, Silliman reported that an excellent illuminant could be made from petroleum, that the cost of refinement would be slight, and that from it a number of important by-products, such as naphtha and paraffin, could also be recovered. Bissell now turned promoter, won sufficient support from capitalists to begin operations, and sent Edwin Drake with the standard equipment for opening a salt-well out to Titusville, Pennsylvania, to drill for oil. In August, 1859, "Drake's folly," as the incredulous natives called this venture, was producing oil at the rate of twenty barrels a day.

What followed was hardly less tumultuous

FARM WELLS. Church Run near Titusville, Pennsylvania, 1870.

The oil industry grew in a few decades from humble and speculative beginnings to a position of eminence and stability in American economic life. By means far better known for their effectiveness than for their scrupulosity, John D. Rockefeller brought order to the industry and wealth to himself.

FILLING BARRELS FROM TANKS. Sketch by F. H. Schell in *Leslie's Illustrated Newspaper,* 1865.

JOHN D. ROCKEFELLER. As he looked in his middle years, and as he approached the age at which familiar photographs generally show him.

OIL CREEK RAILWAY. Depot at Titusville. Sketch by F. H. Schell in *Leslie's Illustrated Newspaper,* 1865.

TRUST CERTIFICATE. Standard Oil issued 35,000 shares when first trust was formed. Illustration from Charles Austin Whiteshot, *Oil Well Driller,* 1905.

than a gold rush. That fabulous sums were to be made from oil, few could deny, and the venturesome flocked to western Pennsylvania by the thousands. Farmers who had known only the extreme of poverty sold their land for fantastic prices, or, by good luck, sometimes became part owners in oil wells that speedily made them rich. Oil derricks dotted the landscape; crossroads became towns, and towns became cities, almost overnight. Pittsburgh, and other strategic centers, found a new source of wealth in the business of oil refining, while the whole country bought the new "coal-oil" lamps, and began to sit up nights. Inasmuch as almost anyone with a little capital could make a start in the oil business, competition for a while was utterly unrestrained. On this account, and also because of the unpredictable nature of both the supply and the demand, the prices of crude oil and of kerosene varied from year to year, from month to month, and even from day to day. Fortunes were lost as well as made. Nevertheless, by 1864 the oil fields around Titusville had expanded to four hundred square miles, and by 1872 not only western Pennsylvania, but parts of West Virginia and Ohio also, were included within the two thousand square miles in the United States devoted to the production of oil. With a total output to date of nearly forty million barrels, the petroleum industry had in a dozen years climbed to a place of high prominence in the nation's business. In a single year, 1871, foreign purchasers took over one hundred and fifty thousand gallons of American oil, making this commodity the fourth largest item among the country's exports.

The petroleum industry

Inextricably intertwined with the history of oil refining in the United States is the name of John D. Rockefeller (1839–1937), a native of Richford, New York, who had moved with his parents to Cleveland, Ohio, when he was thirteen years old. Young Rockefeller had only a common-school education, but he early exhibited extraordinary business talent.

John D. Rockefeller

Before he had reached his majority he had become a partner in a produce commission firm that took excellent profits, particularly after the outbreak of the Civil War. Shrewd, calculating, and thrifty, he made up his mind in 1862, while other young men of his age were patriotically going off to war, that the "coal-oil" business had a future worth sharing. With characteristic good judgment he first backed a refinery that the inventive genius of one Samuel Andrews had provided with a highly improved process; then, at the end of the war, when it was apparent that he had made no mistake, he gave up his commission business, formed a partnership with Andrews, and started out as an oil refiner on his own. By this time the two chief western centers for the refining of oil were Pittsburgh and Cleveland, but the advantage, as Rockefeller sensed, lay with Cleveland, which had easy access, both by water and rail, to the East no less than to the West, whereas Pittsburgh, for its eastern market, was wholly dependent upon the Pennsylvania Railroad. Five years later, reinforced by two new allies, H. M. Flagler and S. V. Harkness, Rockefeller had founded the Standard Oil Company of Ohio, which that year refined four per cent of the nation's total output. By 1872, with monopoly as his goal, he had acquired twenty out of the twenty-five refineries in Cleveland and was laying plans for further conquests that within a decade were to bring him control over ninety per cent of the oil refineries of the country.

Both the steel and the oil industries did their part toward widening the geographic basis of American industrialism by extension into the West, but there also came into existence in that area many industries designed to process the foodstuffs that it produced, or otherwise to serve its particular needs. Such, for example, were the meat-packing and the flour-milling industries.

Probably the meat-packers owed as much as any of the industrialists to the Civil War, and yet the causes of their phenomenal success are more closely **The meat-packers** associated with railroads and refrigeration than with war profits. Early Americans thought of the meat business as a strictly local affair. The "butcher" who supplied a village or a community bought his stock from near-by farmers, slaughtered it at night, and hurried its sale next day. His offerings, especially in the smaller communities, were apt to be monotonous and, particularly in the summer months, undependable. The advent of railroads made it possible to ship live animals considerable distances, and well before the Civil War large consignments of livestock from the Ohio and Mississippi valleys were being shipped regularly to eastern slaughter-houses. Such a system, however, was uneconomical, for freight had to be paid on the whole animal when only a part of it could be turned into meat; also, the losses from shrinkage and deterioriation were heavy. As a partial remedy for this situation, pork was often salted down, packed in barrels, and shipped long distances — an age-old process that gave the "packing industry" its now inappropriate name.

Cincinnati, as the first city to gain a reputation for its pork-packing, was often referred to as "Porkopolis," but other western cities, especially Milwaukee and Chicago, were quick to follow its example. Late in the Civil War, Philip Armour, of a Milwaukee firm, Plankinton, Armour, and Company, laid the basis for his subsequent great fortune by contracting for future deliveries of pork in New York at about forty dollars a barrel. Armour foresaw more clearly than most the speedy collapse of the Confederacy, and the consequent drop in prices that the cessation of war orders would insure. When the time came for him to make deliveries he was able to buy pork at about half the price he received for it. The result was a profit of about two million dollars for Armour, and ruin for many of the traders who bought from him. Shortly after the war, Armour began to concentrate his activities in Chicago, where in 1865 the Union Stockyards had been incorporated to furnish better facil-

ities to the shippers and buyers of livestock. Under the firm name of Armour and Company, he and his brothers soon made the Armour brand known all over the world. No less successful was another Chicago packer, Nelson Morris, who had made a good thing of supplying livestock to the Union army during the war, and was one of the first to experiment in the transporting of dressed beef from Chicago to the Atlantic seaboard. The earnings of Morris's company by 1873 had reached the startling total of eleven million dollars a year. Lively competition for the Armour and Morris firms was soon furnished by Gustavus F. Swift, an eastern buyer of western livestock, who finally located in Chicago. By perfecting the refrigerator car to a degree that would permit of warm-weather as well as cold-weather shipments, Swift contributed to the packing industry a development of incalculable significance.

Added impetus came when, shortly after the Civil War, the "long drive" of Texas cattle to the western railroads **Western** furnished a cheap source of **cattle** supply for livestock. This supply, soon heavily reinforced by the range-cattle industry of the Great Plains, led to the establishment of packing centers even farther west than Chicago, particularly at Kansas City, which became, next to Chicago, the greatest packing center in the country. Other towns along the bend of the Missouri, such as St. Joseph, Omaha, and Sioux City, also shared in this new source of prosperity. The time was not far distant when throughout the country meat from the local slaughterhouse was to be almost entirely supplanted by a standardized product shipped from one of the great packing centers.

Another notable group of industrialists, the flour-millers, like the packers, found it necessary, if they were to take **The flour-** full advantage of their oppor- **millers** tunities, to follow the producers into the West. During the eighteen-forties the center of the wheat belt crossed the Alleghenies, and before the outbreak of the Civil War more than sixty per cent of the flour that the nation consumed was made in the West. The work was still done, however, by thousands of gristmills scattered throughout the country, and the methods of manufacture were not materially different from those in use during the early years of the republic when Oliver Evans first perfected a strictly mechanized flour-milling process. Given an immense lift by the war, the milling industry showed unmistakable signs at its close of concentrating in the upper Mississippi Valley, where thousands of acres of new wheat land were being opened up each year. By 1870 Minnesota ranked fourth among the states of the Union in the manufacture of flour, and Minneapolis, located at the Falls of St. Anthony, had begun the forward march that was to make it within twenty years the leading flour-milling center in the country.

During the early eighteen-seventies those "revolutionary changes," so characteristic of the times, began to transform the manufacture of flour. Edmond N. La Croix, a Frenchman who had come to Minnesota by way of Canada, contributed the first startling innovation when he installed in the Minneapolis mill of George H. Christian a process newer to American than to French millers, whereby the hard spring wheat of the Northwest could be turned into as good a grade of flour as could be made from winter wheat. Soon not only Christian, but other Minneapolis millers also, notably Cadwallader C. Washburn and Charles A. Pillsbury, were making effective use of the "new process," and were seeking earnestly for other improvements. When a delegation sent abroad to investigate European methods reported favorably upon the Hungarian "high-milling" or gradual-roller process, all the millers who could afford to do so promptly installed the chilled-iron rollers it required, and began to produce at low cost a fine white "patent" flour of high gluten content. Other ingenious improvements, mostly of American invention,[1] made the changes that took place in the flour-milling industry during these few eventful years quite as significant as all the changes of the preceding two hundred years put together; while the wisdom of the northwestern millers in picking Minneapolis as the proper site for their activities was amply attested by the fact that within half a century the mills of Minnesota were producing each year more than twice as much flour as the mills of any other state in the Union. Other important milling centers tended to develop wherever grain was grown near-by in great quantity or the cost of shipping it in was not prohibitive. New York, Pennsylvania, Ohio, Illinois, and presently Kansas, all manufactured great quantities of flour. The small flour-mill did not at once disappear, but as time went on the local miller found himself fighting a losing battle against the same forces that were putting his neighbor, the "butcher," out of business.

Before the Civil War the South had made beginnings in manufacturing, but almost everywhere the complete supremacy of agriculture had gone unchallenged. How great a mistake this had been the results of the war seemed only too clearly to indicate. The industrial North had triumphed; the agricultural South had lost. Even before the war was over, with the southern armies paralyzed for lack of equipment that the northern armies possessed in abundance, this lesson had been brought home. The almost inevitable reaction, once the war was over, was that the South must imitate its conquerors. If the North had cities and factories and wealth, then the South, too, must find some way to have them. In response to this reasoning, it was not many years before the new industrialism was on the march in the South. Throughout the long tongue of piedmont and

The "new process"

The "New South"

[1] The original American inventor of the roller mill is generally conceded to be John Stevens of Neenah, Wisconsin, who made his invention about 1870, but did not receive a patent upon it until 1880.

mountain country, extending southward from the border of Pennsylvania throughout western Maryland, the Virginias and Kentucky, the Carolinas and Tennessee, into Georgia and Alabama, a "New South," filled with a startling devotion to industry, had developed. Much that it had to offer was not so new as enthusiasts stated, for the roots of the New South lay deep in the Old. But beyond a doubt times had changed.

It was a hard struggle. Impoverished by the war and handicapped by reconstruction, the builders of the New South had next to wait out the depression of the seventies. Outside capital was reluctant to come in, so Southerners who had "caught the vision" pooled their own meager resources and made the best start they could. They had a few important advantages. The world still needed southern cotton and the price it brought was high. As southern agriculture came back, its profits, slender as they were, could be tapped to expand the southern infant industries. Southern land was cheap and the cost of factory sites was negligible. The labor supply was inexhaustible, utterly unorganized, and willing to work at any price. Cotton mills, the chief industrial hope of the South, could be located so close to the cotton-fields as to hold at a minimum the cost of freight-handling. Water-power was abundant, if only it could be harnessed, and the mountains were known to harbor formidable quantities of coal. The politicians, once the "black and tan" governments of reconstruction times had been eliminated, were friendly and helpful. Indeed, the so-called "Bourbon" Democrats who succeeded the carpetbaggers in the rule of the South were little more than agents of the new industrialists. They kept the cost of government at a minimum, and sometimes even exempted new industries from taxation. They leased out convicts, most of whom were ex-slaves, at ridiculously low rates, to all who wished to use them, and gave the employers whatever disciplinary powers they needed. Eventually, as the southern manufacturers began to make

money, northern capital sensed the opportunity for profits and came to the southerners' aid.

By the eighties the industrial road to wealth had become almost a religion in the South. Henry W. Grady, able editor of the influential *Atlanta Constitution*, radiated enthusiasm for it in his editorials. "He did not tamely promote enterprise and encourage industry," wrote one of his contemporaries, "he vehemently fomented enterprise and provoked industry until they stalked through the land like armed conquerors." Others preached the same gospel, among them Benjamin H. Hill, senator from Georgia, who wrote, after one of the annual cotton expositions held in Atlanta during the eighties:

Factories are springing up in all directions. Our industries are being multiplied as never before. Thousands of the best men of the North have gone home from the exposition enthused with the brightening prospects of all business in the State. Our taxes were scarcely ever so low. Our credit was never so high. Capital and people and machinery are flowing in, and everybody is brushing away the tears of war, and laughing with a new hope in a new era!

The manufacture of cotton in the South before the Civil War had achieved more prominence than is generally supposed. By 1860 the South had one hundred and sixty cotton mills, with 300,000 spindles, and a total output valued at $8,000,000. During the war many of the mills were worn out and many others destroyed, so that in 1870 there were fewer southern mills in operation than in 1860. By 1880, however, the prewar level had been passed, and from that time forward progress was rapid. By 1890 there were about 1,750,000 spindles in the South, and every mill, seemingly, paid excellent profits. At the end of the century the South had nearly half the cotton mills of the country, and accounted for about the same proportion of the cotton goods manufactured. Most of the mills were located along the piedmont in North Carolina, South Carolina, Georgia, and Alabama, usually in small towns and villages, or adjacent to, rather than actually within, some of the larger cities. At first the southern mills produced mainly the coarser grades of cotton, such as denim, leaving to New England the manufacture of the finer grades, but as time went on the variety of southern-made textiles was steadily expanded. The allied knitting industry also made rapid headway, no less in Tennessee and Virginia than in the lower South.

Quite as natural as the development of the textile industry in the South was the **Cotton-seed products** utilization of cotton-seed, long regarded as little more than a nuisance. Before the Civil War, and for some time after, cotton-seed at best was rotted in barnyard manure to be used as fertilizer, and at worst was dumped into the streams along which, for power purposes, so many of the cotton-gins were located. A little cotton-seed was fed to livestock, great quantities of it were burned. Realization that the cotton-seeds were saturated with an oil which, when extracted, was both digestible and inoffensive in taste, opened the way to innumerable possibilities. With the help of the chemists cotton-seed oil was made available as a cheap substitute for such expensive items as olive oil, lard, and butter; it was used also for making soap, cosmetics, and numerous other oil products. The crushed seeds, after the oil was removed, were still rich in nitrogen and could be turned into fertilizer, or pressed into oilcake and fed to cattle. From the seeds, too, great quantities of "linters," or short, close-clinging cotton fibers, were recovered, to be used, again with the help of the chemists, in making celluloid, collodion, and a great variety of other commodities. Not every use to which cotton-seed products are now put was known in the nineteenth century, but the beginnings had been made in an industry that by the time of the First World War was adding annually over $200,000,000 to the income of the South.

Almost as significant as the cotton and cotton-seed industries of the New South were its mining industries. The **Coal and iron** existence of rich coal and iron deposits in the southern mountains was known long before the Civil War, but with comparatively little effort at exploitation. The coal-fields of West Virginia, Maryland, Kentucky, and Virginia, however, were in too easy reach of the great industrial cities of the North to be long ignored. Partly to satisfy the needs of northern industry the output of southern coal mines was speeded up from six million tons in 1880 to fifty million tons in 1900. Meanwhile, the iron mines of eastern Tennessee and northern Alabama began to attract attention. Located, as they were, adjacent to inexhaustible fields of bituminous coal, and in the Birmingham area close to limestone as well, they furnished an ideal setting for the development of the iron and steel industry. Birmingham, named after Birmingham, England, and soon called "the Pittsburgh of the South," was not incorporated as a city until 1871, but by 1900 it had 38,000 inhabitants, by 1910, 132,000, and by 1930, nearly 260,000. Its growth may be taken as a kind of barometer of southern iron and steel, although the city became an important center for nearly every type of industry represented in the South.

More and more the industrial diversification of the South approached that of the North. The manufacture of **Tobacco and lumber** tobacco was helped rather than hindered as a result of the war. Northern soldiers who had grown accustomed to southern makes of tobacco wrote back for more to the southern towns where they had been quartered, and such enterprising Southerners as the Dukes of North Carolina took advantage of the opportunity to expand their markets. Small tobacco factories grew into larger ones, or, as the inevitable concentration in industry proceeded, were eliminated; but the total output of tobacco manufactured in the South steadily increased. Lumbering opened another opportunity for wealth, and southern yellow pine was soon competing strongly with the white pine and hemlock of the Northwest. Southern hardwoods also proved to be easily adaptable for use in all sorts of woodwork, particularly furniture, and by the opening of the twentieth century, High Point, North Carolina, was becoming to the furniture industry of the South what Grand Rapids, Michigan, was to the furniture industry of the North. In the making of fertilizer the South took advantage of another natural opportunity. Rich phosphate deposits in the Southeast, together with the abundance of cotton-seed, gave the southern states a long lead in this industry over the states of any other section. Other types of industry that came to be well represented in the South were corn- and wheat-milling, meat-packing, the making of cement and cement products, brick, pottery, turpentine, and coal-tar derivatives.

It would be impossible even to list all of the industries, Northeast, West, or South, that in the years following the Civil War **Other industries** were caught up in the new industrialism. The manufacture of boots and shoes by machine rather than by hand labor became common during the war, and was expanded at its close until practically all the footwear of the country was factory made. The use of newly invented machinery, such, for example, as the McKay shoe-soling machine, greatly cheapened the price, and made for increased comfort as well. Lynn, Massachusetts, became the leading city of the country in the manufacture of shoes. Tanneries, with a new source of supply from the western cattle ranges, expanded to meet the new demands. Readymade clothing became as much a necessity as readymade shoes, and was as effectively supplied. In 1872 the installation of cloth-cutting machines by a Staten Island establishment registered the first significant advance in this industry since the invention of the sewing-machine. Meanwhile, the manufacture of textiles brought handsome profits to the industrialists of New England and the North Atlantic states. By 1870 the United States was making about one fifth of

the world's output of machine-spun cotton goods, and was using weaving machinery of unexcelled excellence. Woolens and silks, carpets, blankets, and flannels, knit goods and linens, of nearly every sort and kind, poured in increasing abundance from American factories. Among the numerous other businesses that developed along factory lines in the post-war period, mention should be made of refined sugar; prepared foods; intoxicating beverages, particularly whiskey and beer; pottery, glass, and enameled wares; clocks and watches; organs and pianos; stoves and hardware; farm machinery; and building materials. All these expanding activities widened the base of industrial operations to include the steel producers of Birmingham, the meat-packers of Kansas City, the millers of Minneapolis, the watchmakers of Elgin, Illinois, and the farm-implement manufacturers of Moline, in the same state. No longer could it be said, without ample qualification, that the South and the West were merely agricultural sections.

Labor for the new factories was recruited both at home and abroad. As the war ended, an occasional ill-starred **Labor supply** prophet arose to predict that the great armies of the North could never be peacefully disbanded; either they must remain in service to lay the basis of a military dictatorship, or they must dissolve into an army of the unemployed to spread disorder throughout the land. Both guesses were wrong. The soldiers, as fast as they could be mustered out, rejoiced to abandon military for civilian life. Many returned to the pursuits they had left when they went to war, many followed the frontier into the West, and many found work in some department of the rapidly expanding industrial life of the times. Employers could count also upon a steady influx of immigrants from Europe who were conditioned to a lower wage scale and lower standards of living than most native Americans were willing to tolerate. So economical was it to employ these immigrants that manufacturers sometimes

MEAT PACKING. Dressing beeves at Plankinton & Armours, Kansas City, Missouri. Illustration from McCoy's *Historic Sketches of the Cattle Trade in the Southwest*, 1874.

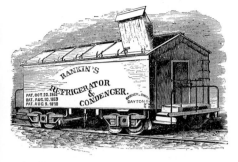

REFRIGERATION. Rankin's refrigerator and condenser car. Illustration from *Hearth and Home*, 1871.

American industry expanded into a great variety of fields during the years immediately following the Civil War. The Northeast was the principal center of manufacturing, but better means of transportation and refrigeration made possible the processing of agricultural products close to the source of supply.

IRON WORKS. View of the Jones & Laughlin plant at Pittsburgh. From *History of Allegheny County, Pennsylvania*, 1876.

MILK FACTORY. Interior of Borden Condensed Milk Company plant. *Leslie's Illustrated Newspaper*, 1879.

GLASS FOUNDRY. Theodore R. Davis sketch in window-glass factory from *Harper's Weekly*, 1884.

Thomas A. Edison, greatest of American inventors, seated beside one of his early phonographs. This picture shows him at about thirty years of age. At the right is one of his early electric light bulbs. During his lifetime Edison took out 1097 patents with the United States Patent Bureau.

combined to send agents abroad to recruit the supply.

As already noted, the railroad network that during these same years was extending **Significance** to all parts of the country was a **of railroads** basic factor in the new industrialism. The steel manufacturers found their greatest market in supplying steel rails and other new equipment for the railroads; the oil men at first depended upon the railroads for the transportation of the crude oil that they refined no less than for the refined oil that they sold; the packers owed their very existence to the facilities that the railroads provided them; industrialists of every kind saw their establishments grow in direct ratio as the railroads grew. Moreover, the railroads promoted in a great variety of ways the same tendency toward consolidation and monopoly that characterized their own operations. Nationwide markets were now available where formerly only local, or at most sectional, markets could be exploited. Plants well located for large expansion began to grow; plants geared only to limited markets began to disappear.

The trend toward consolidation was aided and abetted also by the use of other revolutionary means of communica- **The** tion, particularly the telegraph **telegraph** and the telephone, both of which **and the** proved to be aids of extraordi- **telephone** nary importance to business. Through them, for example, business executives were now able to keep in constant touch with a veritable army of subordinates, and to command activities hundreds or even thousands of miles away. Furthermore, both the telegraph and the telephone, as natural monopolies, furnished in their own tightly woven business organizations examples of national unity that other businesses strove earnestly to follow. For a time the American Bell Telephone Company and the Western Union Telegraph Company were competitors, but by the end of the century the American Telegraph and Telephone Company had brought together under one management the two related services they offered.

In addition to the telegraph and the telephone, electricity was being made to serve many other new uses. Wizard **Edison** of electrical inventors was Thomas A. Edison (1847–1931), an Ohioan by birth whose formal schooling had been limited to three months, but whose natural ingenuity has probably never been surpassed. At fifteen he had learned to send and receive telegraph messages, but his fondness for experimentation doomed him to frequent dismissals by irritated employers. In 1879 he made his first really revolutionary invention, a practicable incandescent light. Others had already devised the arc light, which served well enough for street-lighting, but was wholly unsatisfactory for indoor use. By January, 1880, Edison had taken out a patent on his light bulb, which before long he was able to manufacture, in quantities for commercial use, at a factory in Harrison, New Jersey. Improvements in generators followed, and soon business houses and even dwellings were depending for illumination on the new device. The next need was for central electric power stations, an opportunity for business expansion so fully appreciated that the number of such stations increased from eight in 1881 to 2774 in 1898. While Edison, with his numerous inventions, including among others the phonograph, motion pictures, automatic telegraphy, the stock ticker, and the microphone, ranks as the leading electrical engineer of his time, he was by no means the only one. Soon electric railway systems were banishing horse cars from the city streets, electric elevators were adding innumerable stories to the height of skyscrapers, and electric power was being used to turn a larger and larger proportion of the wheels of industry.

The typewriter met another business need. Its inventor was a Milwaukee printer, Christopher Latham Sholes, who as early as 1867 had devised a machine that would write with fair rapidity. **The typewriter** Fortunately, a letter written on one of Sholes's typewriters fell into the hands of James Densmore, a Pennsylvania businessman, and led him to come to the aid of the inventor with money and ideas. Within a decade the collaborators had sufficiently perfected their machine that it was finding its way into business offices, and within another decade it had become a business necessity. Sholes's machine, which was first manufactured commercially by the firm of E. Remington and Son, had many imitators, and by the end of the century nearly a hundred different models were on the market. Like the telephone, the typewriter provided a new gainful occupation for women. Women operators, it turned out, were not only quite as efficient as men, but they could also be hired for less. Soon it was generally assumed that the noun stenographer was feminine gender, and that it referred to any

The *dynamo room* of the first Edison electric lighting station in New York. Drawing from *Scientific American*, 1882. Edison's persistence laid the basis for modern systems of illumination.

member of the vast army of young women whose skill at shorthand and typewriting made their services indispensable to the smooth functioning of business offices.

Nationwide advertising also did its share toward the widening of business horizons.

Advertising Catalogues took on new meaning with the invention of the halftone process, through which the image recorded by the camera could be transferred to print paper. Improvements in photography served the same useful end. The cost of job printing was reduced by the invention of the linotype and the monotype.[1] And, as already mentioned,[2] better postal services and lower postal rates gave the advertiser entrance into practically every American home.

It is not difficult to see why business, with all these aids, became increasingly national

Tendencies toward monopoly rather than local in scope. With nationwide competition at work only the ablest, the most selfish, and the most unscrupulous of the competitors could survive. Great producers tended to become the cheapest producers, and little companies tended to disappear. Close observers of business trends during the eighties noted that the current formula of business evolution called for a greatly increased output from a steadily diminishing number of plants. In 1880, for example, the nation had 1990 woolen mills, in 1890, only 1311; in 1880 it had 1934 factories that made agricultural implements, in 1890, only 910. During the same decade the number of iron and steel mills decreased by one third, and the number of leather establishments by three fourths. In every case, however, the total capital investment and the total output of the industry had vastly increased, while ownership, or at least management, had been concentrated far more rapidly than even the reduced number of plants would indicate. What the nation was witnessing was the emergence of a large number of near-monopolies, each of which aspired to the complete control of some important national necessity.

Public awareness of the situation began with the appearance of an article, "The Story of a Great Monopoly," by Henry Demarest Lloyd, in the *Atlantic Monthly* for March, 1881. Lloyd's article was a scathing attack on the Standard Oil Company, and the deep impression it made was fully attested by the fact that that particular number of the *Atlantic* sold out seven editions. John D. Rockefeller, the guiding genius of Standard Oil, had planned monopoly from the start. The first important step toward this goal, control of the oil-refining business of Cleveland, Ohio, he had accomplished by the time the Panic of 1873 broke. This gave him perhaps one third of the oil-refining business of the country, and undismayed by the depression he set out to get the rest. Skillful at obtaining financial backing, and always equipped with a large cash balance of his own, he bought up whatever refineries would sell, induced others to join forces with him, and drove still others out of business. By the time the depression was over, the Rockefeller interests, with control over all the greatest refineries in New York, Philadelphia, Pittsburgh, Baltimore, and Titusville, had approximated the complete monopoly their leader had sought.

Rockefeller's ruthless methods left him a rich legacy of hatred. The railroads, hard-pressed for business during the **The Standard Oil Company** depression, had little choice but to give him the rebates he demanded. Shippers less favored either were ruined by the unfair competition or sold out to Standard Oil. When it came to the marketing of oil, Rockefeller gave no quarter. The United States was divided up into convenient sections, each with its agent and subagents, with every agent under instructions to "sell all the oil that is sold in your district." Agents who succeeded in this undertaking were rewarded with higher salaries and promotions; agents who failed were

---

[1] Ottmar Mergenthaler, a naturalized American of German birth, invented the linotype in 1885, and Talbot Lanston, a clerk in the Pension Office in Washington, D.C., invented the monotype in 1887.

[2] See p. 146.

THE TYPEWRITER. Young lady working at Sholes model. Woodcut, 1872.

WASHING MACHINE. Steam boiler doubled as grain and vegetable cooker. Engraving shows improved model of 1882.

American ingenuity made available many labor-saving devices such as the typewriter and the washing machine. It also substituted numerous manufactured items for the products of the shop or the home.

WE ALL USE THEM

Standard Screw Fastened Boots and Shoes.

FOOTWEAR. Trade card, about 1880.

Don't thee wed for money, friend;
For money hath a sting;
Don't thee wed a pretty face;
'Tis but a foolish thing;
Don't thee wed for place nor fame;
'Twill disappoint thy hope;
But when thee marries, choose a girl
Who uses Ivory Soap.

IT FLOATS.

SOAP. Proctor and Gamble advertisement in *Harper's Weekly*, 1890.

summarily dismissed. Railroad records were spied upon by Standard Oil men so that the business of competitive refineries could be stolen. Price-cutting was carried to any extreme necessary to put a competitor out of business, and as soon as his defeat was assured the price of oil was set again at a figure as high as or higher than before the price-war began. Pipeline companies that carried the crude oil to railway centers, and even hundreds of miles to the refineries, were gathered up by Standard Oil, one by one, usually at its own price. Determined to pay no man profits, Rockefeller built terminal warehouses of his own, established factories to make barrels and other necessary articles, and eliminated hundreds of wholesalers and middlemen. Finally, in order to facilitate centralized control and to insure against unintentional competition among the various Standard properties, the Standard Oil Trust was formed. This device, first adopted in 1879, but revised and more completely applied in 1882, consisted merely of a group of nine trustees to whom was surrendered all the stock of the Standard Oil Company and its various affiliates. Trust certificates were then issued to each Standard stockholder in the proportion of twenty trust certificates for each share of Standard stock. For several years the nine trustees, with John D. Rockefeller at their head, made the decisions for all of the stockholders and all of the companies that were dominated by Standard Oil.

"This is the original trust," declared a New York committee that in 1888 began the investigation of Standard Oil. "Its success has been the incentive to the formation of all other trusts or combinations. It is the type of a system which has spread like a disease through the commercial system of this country." What the committee charged was fully borne out by the facts. One after another "an incredible number of the necessaries and luxuries of life, from meat to tombstones," had fallen into the hands of some tightly organized little group that frequently only by the most unscrupulous and underhand methods had achieved control. Sugar, salt, whiskey, matches, crackers, lead, cottonseed oil, linseed oil, wire and nails, agricultural machinery, electrical supplies, and a host of other items could be obtained only by paying tribute to some such trust or combine. The exact pattern of the Standard Oil Trust was not always followed, but the results were generally about the same. Sometimes the possession of exclusive patent rights promoted the cause of monopoly, and thus made of the liberal patent laws of the United States a kind of subsidy to big business.

The evils of the "trusts," as the public without much discrimination described all big businesses, became increasingly apparent. Prices were fixed without benefit of competition, and sometimes at higher levels than before the trust was formed. Raw producers were compelled to take what the trust chose to pay, for there was no one else to whom to sell. Labor was forced into line by the closing of troublesome plants, and by the circulation of "blacklists" that made it difficult for agitators to obtain employment. Politicians were influenced by free passes from the railroads, by campaign contributions, and by outright bribes. Oliver H. Payne, treasurer of the Standard Oil Company, was reputed to have spent one hundred thousand dollars

to secure the election of his father, H. B. Payne, to the United States Senate in 1886. Powerful lobbies appeared in Washington and in the several state capitals charged with the duty of winning favors from lawmakers and law-enforcers. The Washington lobbyists were sometimes described as the "third house" of Congress. Plants that experience had shown to be well located were enlarged, and others less ideally situated were closed down, without regard to the inevitable unemployment involved or the municipal problems that arose from the concentration of vast numbers of people at whatever centers business leaders deemed strategic. Individual freedom suffered blow after blow as the owners of small establishments became the employees of larger ones, and as the chance to enter business independently grew less and less. Employees were pushed farther and farther from the sight and hearing of employers, and fewer occasions existed for emotions of the "heart" to influence the conduct of businessmen who prided themselves upon their "hardheadedness."

And yet the "trusts" were by no means without their good points. Much of the competition that they eliminated was sheer waste, and without it prices could be, and often were, reduced. Large-scale businesses were usually far more efficient than the small concerns they supplanted, and were able to make money out of by-products that the smaller operators were forced to throw away. The packers, for example, claimed that they paid more for a live steer than they received for the dressed meat it yielded. Their profits came from the use they made of horns, hoofs, and other materials that the local slaughterhouse wasted. Big business could afford to take heavy initial losses while waiting for ultimate profits. It could bear the cost of advertising and of the slow enlargement of markets. Usually, too, it was better managed, better located, better equipped. Small establishments could not so easily afford to scrap expensive machinery because new inventions made better equipment possible.

They could not compete with big businesses in paying salaries to the ablest managers. Even without the cutthroat competition to which they were subjected, many of them would have lost out anyway because of their inefficiency.

As public awareness of the trust problem grew, an insistent demand set in that something should be done about it. This meant, to most Americans, that the government should take action against the trusts, but unfortunately governmental action under the existing system was not easily attainable. The Constitution gave the central government only definitely specified powers, and left all others to the states. Since the "founding fathers" had never heard of a trust, the only power to control such organizations that they had lodged with the central government was whatever might be inferred from the right to control interstate commerce. Obviously, the extent to which any such implied power might be exercised would have to be determined by the courts after extensive litigation. The states, on the other hand, had ample power within their several jurisdictions, but their boundaries were too small, for the activities of any important trust extended through many states. Moreover, the requirement of the national Constitution that each state must give "full faith and credit . . . to the public acts, records, and judicial proceedings of every other state" had embarrassing possibilities. Under the terms of this clause special favors obtained in one state might easily be interpreted to mean special favors in every state. Another constitutional advantage enjoyed by corporations flowed from the Fourteenth Amendment which required that the states might not "deprive any person of life, liberty, or property, without due process of law." In 1886 the Supreme Court, reversing an earlier ruling, held that the use of the word person in this clause was meant to apply to corporations as well as to individuals.[1] Thus the states,

Legal status of the trusts

themselves the creators of the corporations, were restrained by the federal government from any measures of taxation or regulation that the courts chose to regard as depriving the corporations of property "without due process of law."

Attempts to restrain the trusts were made nevertheless. Just as the Grangers had invoked to good advantage the old rule of common law that a common carrier was subject to regulation because it was quasi-public in nature, so now the states fell back upon the common-law prohibition of conspiracy in restraint of trade. During the later eighties state after state passed statutes based on this principle. Finally, Congress also fell into line, and on July 2, 1890, the Sherman Anti-Trust Act received the President's signature. This measure, named after Senator Sherman, for no other reason, according to Senator Hoar, "except that Mr. Sherman had nothing to do with framing it whatever," lacked nothing in vigor of language. It branded as illegal "every contract, combination in the form of trust or otherwise, or conspiracy in restraint of trade or commerce among the several states, or with foreign nations." It defined as a misdemeanor any "attempt to monopolize, or combine or conspire with any other person or persons to monopolize, any part of the trade or commerce among the several states or with foreign nations." Penalties for persons held guilty of violating the act were set at a fine not to exceed five thousand dollars, and imprisonment not to exceed a year, one or both, as the court might prescribe. Furthermore, any person injured by means that the act declared unlawful might recover in court "threefold the damages by him sustained."

The Sherman Anti-Trust Act

Enforcement of these acts was quite another matter. A number of suits were lodged by the states, and a few decisions unfavorable to the corporations were obtained. In New York State, for example, the North River Sugar Refining Company, a part of the sugar trust,

Difficulties in enforcement

[1] *Santa Clara County vs. Southern Pacific Railroad,* 118 United States Reports, 396.

lost its charter; and in Ohio, the Standard Oil Company was held guilty of attempting "to establish a virtual monopoly." Since the technical trust was so clear-cut a violation of both the common law and the statutes, that type of organization was generally discontinued, but in its place new devices to accomplish the same end were speedily invented. Chief among these was the holding company, through which a controlling fraction of the stocks in a great number of enterprises was owned and voted by a single corporation, but many of the trusts chose instead to incorporate as a single great company in the most friendly state they could find. As for the Sherman Anti-Trust Act, for all its brave language, it proved to be un-

enforceable. Seven out of the first eight attempts to invoke its penalties went against the government, and in the Knight case (1895) the Supreme Court of the United States held that the mere purchase of property, even if it made for monopoly and the restraint of trade, was not in itself illegal; further, that manufacture and production (in this case the refining of sugar) were no part of interstate commerce. Confronted by this rebuff, the government made little further effort to enforce the Sherman Act, and lawyers felt free to advise their clients that the Supreme Court of the United States had conceded the legality of private monopoly.

Bibliography

There are many books on the development of the various big businesses. J. R. Smith, *The Story of Iron and Steel* (1908), gives the essential points on the rise of the steel industry. *Selected Writings of Abram S. Hewitt*, edited by Allan Nevins (1937), contains an illuminating report by Hewitt, as Commissioner to the Paris Exposition in 1867, on "The Production of Iron and Steel in Its Economic and Social Relations." See also Allan Nevins, *Abram S. Hewitt: With Some Account of Peter Cooper* (1935). The *Autobiography of Andrew Carnegie* (1920) presents the author's life story with few reservations. See also J. K. Winkler, *Incredible Carnegie* (1931).

Ida M. Tarbell, *The History of the Standard Oil Company* (new ed., 1937), is an early attempt at muckraking which was very critical of Rockefeller. More friendly, but less satisfactory, is G. H. Montague, *The Rise and Progress of the Standard Oil Company* (1903). Allan Nevins, *John D. Rockefeller* (2 vols., 1940); and Nevins' recent reevaluation, *Study in Power: John D. Rockefeller, Industrialist and Philanthropist* (2 vols., 1953), are both generally sympathetic to the great oil pioneer. J. T. Flynn, *God's Gold: The Story of Rockefeller and His Times* (1932), is exciting and colorful. The rise of the great industrialists is told in journalistic and thoroughly antagonistic

style by Matthew Josephson, *The Robber Barons* (1934). W. T. Hutchinson, *Cyrus Hall McCormick*, Vol. II, *Harvest, 1858–1884* (1935), is an admirable history of a developing "big business." For short general accounts, see Burton J. Hendrick, *The Age of Big Business* (1920); and John Moody, *The Masters of Capital* (1921).

Among the many industries that have attracted historians, the following may be cited: R. A. Clemen, *The American Livestock and Meat Industry* (1923); Institute of American Meat Packers, *The Packing Industry* (1924); C. B. Kuhlmann, *The Development of the Flour-Milling Industry in the United States* (1929); F. J. Allen, *The Shoe Industry* (1922); A. H. Cole, *The American Wool Manufacture* (2 vols., 1926); M. T. Copeland, *The Cotton Manufacturing Industry of the United States* (1912); Robert F. Fries, *Empire in Pine: The Story of Lumbering in Wisconsin* (1951); and W. B. Gates, Jr., *Michigan Copper and Boston Dollars* (1951).

On the New South, Holland Thompson, *The New South* (1919); and P. A. Bruce, *The Rise of the New South* (1905), are sympathetic studies. W. B. Hesseltine, *The South in American History* (1943), contains a valuable chapter on industrial developments in the South. An early enthusiastic account by a prominent southern editor is H. W.

Grady, *The New South* (1890). Other books of interest in this connection are Broadus Mitchell and G. S. Mitchell, *The Industrial Revolution in the South* (1930); Broadus Mitchell, *The Rise of Cotton Mills in the South* (1921); Holland Thompson, *From the Cotton Field to the Cotton Mill* (1906); Ethel Armes, *The Story of Coal and Iron in Alabama* (1910); B. W. Arnold, *History of the Tobacco Industry in Virginia from 1860 to 1894* (1897); W. K. Boyd, *The Story of Durham* (1925); J. W. Jenkins, *James B. Duke* (1927); and M. A. Potwin, *Cotton Mill People of the Piedmont* (1927).

The remarkable transformations wrought by inventors and inventions may be traced in F. L. Dyer and T. C. Martin, *Edison, His Life and Inventions* (2 vols., 1929); George Iles, *Leading American Inventors* (1912); Holland Thompson, *The Age of Invention* (1921); and Ida M. Tarbell, *The Nationalizing of Business, 1878–1898* (1936).

Some of the best works on the trusts are J. W. Jenks and W. E. Clark, *The Trust Problem* (1900, 5th ed., 1929); John Moody, *The Truth about the Trusts* (1904); W. Z. Ripley, *Trusts, Pools, and Corporations* (new ed., 1916); and Eliot Jones, *The Trust Problem in the United States* (1921). W. P. Webb, *Divided We Stand* (1937), vigorously attacks the extension to corporations of immunities that were intended, Webb believes, only for individuals.

9

The Organization of Labor

The status of labor — Trades unions — The "Molly Maguires" — Railway strikes of 1877 — Disorders in Pittsburgh — Unrest in California — The Knights of Labor — Strikes of 1886 — The Haymarket riot — The A. F. of L. — Samuel Gompers — Homestead and Pullman strikes — Use of the injunction — "Coxey's Army" — Southern mill workers

A DIRECT result of the new industrialism was an increased emphasis on labor organization; or, as a later generation might have put it, "big business" gave rise to "big labor." The transition from the domestic system of manufacture to the factory system, already far along when the Civil War had broken out, had progressed with great rapidity during and after that struggle. Many strikes occurred during the war, and at its close, with the ex-soldiers home in search of work and the immigrant tide beginning, the need of organization was more marked than ever before. As small factories gave way to large factories, and individual proprietors to "soulless" corporations, all of the ills from which the laborers had suffered tended to be compounded. Concentration gave the employer greater power to oppress, whether by way of low wages, long hours, or bad working conditions. Concentration meant also a diminishing number of employers, and a proportionately larger number of employees. Contacts between employers and employees grew ever more remote; machines took the places of skilled workmen; the competition of immigrants drove wages down. But the very fact that so many workers found themselves in identical predicaments tended to draw them together. Large factories, large corporations, large working-class sections in the cities, all

The status of labor

served to promote the idea of common action in the interest of the common good. Only by acting together might the workers hope to protect themselves from those who wished to exploit them. Skilled laborers, in a desperate effort to save their status from the encroachments of the machines on the one hand and the immigrants on the other, usually took the lead in labor organization, but there were significant efforts to unite all laborers, of whatever crafts, under one leadership.

Almost without exception the great new corporations, whether they were engaged in manufacturing, or in transportation, or in mining, or in any other field of enterprise, showed implacable hostility to the idea of labor organization; industrialists were known to circulate among themselves "blacklists" containing the names of agitators who tried to form labor unions. As a matter of fact, the American public, still wedded to the frontier ideal of individualism, had little sympathy for the unions, and believed that an employer might rightfully "hire and fire at will." The workers themselves were surprisingly lacking in class consciousness; for a long time the great masses remained relatively inert. Most of them had come from the farm, and many of them, immigrants included, expected to return to it. Others hoped to rise from the status of employee to

Working conditions in American industry during the late nineteenth century left much to be desired. The prevalence of low wages, the exploitation of women and children, and the employment of cheap foreign labor led to occasional acts of violence and insistent demands for reform.

MINER'S PAY DAY. Sketch by Frenzeny for *Harper's Weekly*, 1873.

"SLAVES OF THE SWEAT SHOPS." Drawing by W. A. Rogers for *Harper's Weekly*, 1890.

EIGHT-HOUR WORK DAY. Britton & Rey lithograph published in celebration of eight-hour law for government employees, 1868.

RACIAL PREJUDICE. Anti-Chinese riot in Denver, Colorado. From a sketch by N. B. Wilkins for *Leslie's Illustrated Newspaper*, 1880.

the status of employer, and frequently saw their dreams come true.

Local labor unions had existed in the United States since the early nineteenth
Trades unions century, and the Jacksonian period had witnessed the development of a well-defined labor movement; but the depression that began in 1837 had been disastrous for labor, and not until the time of the Civil War was any considerable part of the ground lost regained.[1] During the fifties and sixties a few national organizations, formed by such groups as the printers, the locomotive engineers, and the bricklayers, came into existence, but for a long time none of them succeeded in drawing into its ranks any large percentage of those eligible, while attempts at all-labor organizations were even less satisfactory. In August, 1866, a National Labor Union was formed at Baltimore by a group of seventy-seven delegates, representing a great variety of labor interests. It was built upon the federative principle, and included among its affiliates a motley array of organizations, some of which could hardly be regarded as labor unions. It held seven annual congresses, and advocated such important reforms as the eight-hour day, the use of arbitration in labor disputes, the establishment of profit-sharing cooperatives, and the improvement of factory laws. By 1868 it claimed to represent through its member unions a total of 640,000 workers. Numerous flirtations with reforms that were not directly the concern of labor brought the organization to an untimely end. Its leaders showed interest, at one time or another, in women's rights, civil service reform, money inflation, and even the repudiation of the national debt. Half converted to socialist doctrines and intent on separate political action, they backed an abortive Labor Reform Party of 1872, only to be thoroughly discredited by its dismal failure. What little was left of the National Labor Union crashed with the Panic of 1873, but, while it lasted, it had given the movement

[1] On this earlier labor movement, see John D. Hicks, *The Federal Union* (2d. ed., 1952), 438–441.

for an eight-hour day a good start, and had promoted in a variety of ways the study of labor problems. It furnished, also, an example of concerted action by labor that was not forgotten.

The labor troubles of the seventies came in spite of the fact that labor was imperfectly organized, and some of them **The "Molly** might actually have been averted **Maguires"** had the unions been strong enough to bargain successfully with employers. One of the worst outbreaks came in the anthracite coal mining region of Pennsylvania, where the "Molly Maguires," a secret society of terrorists, had for a decade carried on their depredations. Conditions in the mining towns were bad enough to justify the firmest protests, but the "Mollies" depended primarily upon murder for results. The name of the order, together with its methods of operation, were imported from Ireland, and membership was confined to Irish immigrants and their sons. By 1865 the "Mollies" were beginning to make their influence felt. "Bosses" who refused special privileges to a member were murdered. "Scabs" were notified in writing that they might have a week in which to go, but if they dared stay, "on next Saturday you will die." Superintendents who were carrying money to pay the miners were set upon and robbed, and sometimes murdered. Members of the society became policemen, and gave protection to their friends. Others went into politics, stuffed ballot-boxes, won local elections, and grafted generously. Finally, when the terror could no longer be tolerated, a former district attorney of Schuylkill County hired a Chicago detective named James McParlan to gather the evidence necessary to crush the "Mollies." McParlan worked his way into the order, and two years later emerged with the evidence he had been commissioned to obtain. In a series of spectacular trials nearly a dozen death sentences were obtained, and many long prison terms. The first executions occurred in June, 1877.

Less than a month later the country was

startled by the news that a series of strikes,

Railway strikes of 1877 accompanied by much violence and disorder, was sweeping over the eastern railroads. The railroad unions were not very strong, and a strike on the Philadelphia and Reading only a few weeks before had been easily defeated by the employment of non-union workers. But the strikes that broke out in July, 1877, were supported by non-union as well as union men. All employees felt keenly the injustice of a ten per cent cut in wages that four great systems had decreed, and in many of the railroad towns sentiment in support of the strikers was so intense that to the faint-hearted it looked as if the day of revolution had come. During the early years of the depression the four systems in question, the New York Central, the Erie, the Pennsylvania, and the Baltimore and Ohio, had competed ruthlessly for what little business there was, and on the long hauls from St. Louis or Chicago to the Atlantic seaboard had quoted ruinously low rates. At one time cattle were hauled from Chicago to New York for a dollar a carload, and the low passenger fares that the "rate wars" promoted had had much to do with the success of the Centennial Exposition at Philadelphia. After many unavailing efforts, the presidents of the competing roads finally reached an agreement in April, 1877, to call off the rate wars, and to recover by a ten per cent reduction in wages some of the losses they had suffered. The pay cuts were announced without warning, and without consultation with minor officials who might have foretold the result. They came, too, after a long period of depression during which few trainmen had had anything like full-time work. The punishment they inflicted was simply more than the men were able to take without protest.

The trouble began, July 16, at Martinsburg, West Virginia, on the Baltimore and Ohio, when railroad firemen, just apprised of the cuts, began to abandon their engines, and succeeded in persuading other workers to join them. Enthusiastically supported by

the unemployed and by many mere roisterers, the strikers stopped all trains, destroyed railroad property, and staged a general riot. The governor promptly called out the state militia, three companies strong, but the state troops were no match for the rioters, so on July 18 he appealed to President Hayes for help. The two hundred and fifty regulars that Hayes sent to the scene restored order, but it took several days to break the strike. Trains that went through Martinsburg were stopped elsewhere, and even with the promise of protection it was difficult to find men to handle them.

Meantime the excitement had spread to the neighboring state of Maryland. Disorder at Cumberland, far out in the western panhandle, led the governor, on July 20, to summon the Baltimore militia to strike duty. They never went, for an angry mob inter-

Certificate of membership in Brotherhood of Locomotive Firemen. Lithograph by Hammerstein Bros. & Co., 1878. Such elaborate certificates as these were common also among fraternal orders.

vened, and Baltimore itself became the scene of determined street fighting. Again the President had to be importuned for aid, and again detachments of United States regulars had to be sent to the rescue. Order was restored on July 22.

Three days earlier the strike had opened in Pittsburgh, where an order to run double-**Disorders in** headers over the mountains, and **Pittsburgh** so to cut down on the number of trainmen employed, was resented even more than the wage cut. Here the mayor and the police seemed to sympathize with the strikers, and the Pittsburgh militia fraternized freely with the mob. State troops from Philadelphia, however, opened fire on the rioters, an action that seemed to add fuel to the flames. For days the city was in the grip of terrorists. Railroad buildings and rolling stock were burned, freight cars were pillaged, stolen barrels of liquor were opened and drunk. When federal troops arrived on July 23 at least nineteen rioters and several militiamen had lost their lives. Not until July 29, after more than a week of confusion, was the first freight train permitted to leave the city, and either it or the next one after it was wrecked. But by the end of the month the strike was completely broken and the men were back at work.

Elsewhere, in New York, New Jersey, Ohio, Indiana, Michigan, and Illinois, similar incidents occurred. In every instance, the power of the state, reinforced by federal troops, was used to break the strike. For two weeks the whole country was in a fever of excitement. Even when the railroad strikes were ended, and the trainmen went back to work at the lowered wages, anxious citizens wondered if the danger was over. In Scranton, Pennsylvania, the rolling mill men of the Lackawanna Coal and Iron Company had struck for a thirty-five per cent increase in wages, and the miners for twenty-five per cent, both in a sense sympathetic strikes. Here, as in the railroad strikes, violence was the order of the day, and federal troops were required to stand guard for a month. Could the government really

govern, or would the next such outbreak mean revolution?

News that began to come through from California was far from reassuring. On July 23, 1877, a mass meeting of **Unrest in** workingmen in San Francisco, **California** called to express sympathy for the Pittsburgh strikers, got out of hand and turned into a prolonged riot. California was seemingly the ideal place in the United States for revolutionary sentiment to grow. Its people were descended, lineally or spiritually, from the "forty-niners," and Californians, ever since the days of the mining camps, had shown a tolerance of lawlessness and a resentment of constraint rarely met with elsewhere in like degree. Speculation, too, was in the very air that they breathed, and it seemed reasonable to suppose that individuals who were ready at all times to take a chance on mining stock might be willing also to take a chance on something different in government. Isolation from the rest of the United States added to the danger. Only one transcontinental railroad connected the Pacific coast with the East, and the conservative influence of the older states was too far away to have much effect. Added to all this was a unique and perplexing problem, the Chinese. Welcomed in the days when the whites were interested primarily in the mines, and used freely in building the Central Pacific Railroad, their popularity ebbed away when times grew hard and jobs were scarce. In 1870 California had about fifty thousand Chinese, and by the end of the seventies about seventy-five thousand. They constituted approximately nine per cent of the total population of the state, and, since practically all of them were men, at least twice as large a percentage of the total number of laborers. They worked for "coolie wages," on which a white man would starve, and their presence was held responsible for the large number of California's unemployed. They made no attempt to accept American ways, and the Chinese quarter of any city was sure to be a plague spot of vice and disease. This was particularly true of San

Francisco, the greatest center of Chinese concentration.

The full effects of the Panic of 1873 arrived late in California, for out on the coast the depression was scarcely felt until 1876. The year before that Californians, hypnotized by stories of some great new "bonanza" finds, had indulged in a veritable orgy of speculation. When the bubble broke, thousands had lost their savings. Agriculture, too, suffered acutely from the light snowfall during the winter of 1876–77. Streams essential for irrigation dried up, and crops were sure to be short. Distressed farmers, as in the Middle West, blamed the railroads as well as the weather for their calamities, and not without some reason. In California the Southern Pacific had monopolized the railroad opportunities of the state. It had received the customary rich land grants; it charged all the traffic would bear; it had gone deeply into politics to obtain taxation favors and other valuable privileges; its word was law with most of the state's officials. The farmers of the coast, still enthusiastic Grangers, demanded the greater taxation of wealth, control of the railroads by a really representative state government, and an end to the railroad monopoly on land. For good measure, they held that something must be done about the Chinese.

By the summer of 1877 San Francisco had become a city of job-hunters — miners, "Kearney-ism" farmhands, laborers of every kind, including the hated Chinese. Feeling was keen against the upper classes, particularly the newly rich, who lived ostentatiously on "Nob Hill," and were accused of employing Chinese in preference to whites. Self-appointed orators who addressed the meeting of July 23 did not confine themselves to expressions of sympathy for the Pittsburgh strikers, but took full advantage of the opportunity to denounce the capitalists and the Chinese in fervid language. More meetings followed, and because they were held on the vacant sand-lot opposite the city hall those who attended them were called "Sand-Lotters."

The idol of the crowd was Denis Kearney, an eloquent but ungrammatical Irishman, who had seen the seamy side of life as a sailor and a drayman, and now made it a practice to wind up each of his harangues with the words, "The Chinese must go!" Soon a Workingmen's Party had taken form, through which the Sand-Lotters hoped to "cinch" capital, and drive out the hated Chinese. Kearney sometimes threatened direct action. "A little judicious hanging right here and now," he told one meeting, "will be the best course to pursue with the capitalists and stock sharps who are all the time robbing us." Again, at a meeting held on Nob Hill itself, he told the railroad owners that they had but three months in which to discharge all Chinese laborers. "Remember Judge Lynch," he warned.

Curiously, however, it was to regular legal procedure rather than to lynch law that the Sand-Lotters appealed. By California chance a proposal for a state con- constitution stitutional convention had al- of 1879 ready been submitted to the people at the polls, and in September, 1877, the voters gave their consent to the project. Instead of going on with the idea of revolution, the Workingmen's Party now set out, with the assistance of the discontented Grangers, to capture a majority of the delegates to be elected in June, 1878. So successful were their efforts that when the votes were counted it was apparent that the farmers and laborers together had won a clear majority of the seats in the convention. Continuing their cooperation, the Workingmen and the Grangers wrote a new constitution for the state that embodied most of their radical ideas. The Chinese were forbidden to hold property and to engage in certain occupations; taxation was shifted to the "wealthy," with "bonds, notes, and evidence of indebtedness" called upon to bear a heavy burden; a railroad commission was set up with full authority to regulate the railroads; home rule, which meant rule by the Workingmen's Party, was granted to San Francisco in generous measure; and the state judicial system was radically reformed in order to enforce more effectively the new provisions. Conservative delegates, certain that some of the more fantastic provisions would insure the defeat of the document, made little effort to eliminate them. They realized their mistake, however, when in May, 1879, the constitution was adopted by a majority of about 10,000.

Nevertheless, the victory of the radicals was short-lived. Many of the new clauses, including the anti-Chinese provision, were held by the courts to be in conflict with the Constitution of the United States or treaties with a foreign power, and so became null and void. The railroads quickly captured the commission set up to regulate them. Prosperity returned, and both Grangers and Workingmen thought less about politics. Amendment after amendment was submitted and adopted until the difference between the California constitution of 1879 and other state constitutions was comparatively insignificant. In San Francisco the labor forces long ruled, but unfortunately not without permitting the same type of scandals that characterized city government elsewhere. Kearney went East to popularize the Workingmen's Party there, but failed to win support, and soon dropped back into the obscurity from which he had so suddenly emerged. And yet the movement was not without a certain deep significance. Revolution in the United States, even in so hospitable an environment as California, came hard. Peaceful and orderly means of protest were preferred, often by the most radical. Violent departures from long-established precedents failed to endure. Few could deny that the workingmen's movement in California and the strikes on the eastern railroads presaged an era of conflict between labor and capital, but the average American, reassured that his government could really govern, soon gave up worrying about the danger of revolution.

Nevertheless, the increasing concentration of capital that characterized the eighties had **The Knights** its counterpart in a steady **of Labor** growth of labor organization.

Attention for a time centered chiefly on the Noble Order of the Knights of Labor, which, like the National Labor Union that had preceded it, sought to organize labor along national lines. The Knights of Labor was founded in 1869 by Uriah S. Stephens, a Philadelphia garment-cutter, who provided it with a secret ritual, a password, and a grip. Since the name of the order was at first represented in public notices by five asterisks, it was long known to the uninitiated as "the five stars." Unlike its predecessor, the Knights of Labor built directly u₁ on the individual, rather than upon existing trade unions. "One big union," to which all workers, skilled or unskilled, should belong, was the ideal; indeed, practically anyone, regardless of race, color, or occupation, could become a "Knight." Under these circumstances members of the more exclusive trade unions, who took pride in their craft skills, tended to hold aloof, and for a decade the growth of the Knights was only moderate. After 1878, however, when Terence V. Powderly (1849–1924) of Scranton, Pennsylvania, became its "Grand Master Workman," the order took on new life. Powderly, as his name would indicate, was of Irish origin, but he was a native American, not an immigrant, born in Carbondale, Pennsylvania. At thirteen years of age he joined the ranks of labor as a switch-tender; later as a Scranton machinist he took so prominent a part in the work of the Machinists' and Blacksmiths' Union that he not only lost his job, but also won a place for his name on an employers' blacklist. This happened in 1873, after which he worked for a time in Ohio and western Pennsylvania, but on returning to Scranton won election as mayor of the city in 1878 on the Greenback-Labor ticket. When later a meeting was held at Reading, Pennsylvania, to reorganize the Knights, Powderly dominated the proceedings, and for the next fifteen years his name and the Knights of Labor were almost synonymous terms. Secrecy was done away with, the name of the order was publicly proclaimed, and Powderly, with only the

Compare to AFL.

barest apology of a salary, traveled at his own expense wherever he felt he could gain more recruits for the Knights. From a membership of only 28,000 in 1880 the organization shot forward to 52,000 in 1883, 104,000 in 1885, and perhaps as many as 700,000 by 1886.

The ideals of the Knights were by no means new. They believed, with Edmund Burke, that "When bad men combine, the good must associate, else they will fall, one by one, an unpitied sacrifice in a contemptible struggle." Like the National Labor Union they favored the eight-hour day, the "establishment of cooperative institutions productive and distributive," the use of arbitration as a substitute for strikes, and such legal innovations as were calculated to improve the status of labor. Powderly saw especial virtue in the cooperative idea, and under his urging not less than one hundred and thirty-five such ventures were undertaken, some of which for a time seemed destined to endure. But bad management, internal dissensions, insufficient funds, and cut-throat competition accounted for the undoing of most of them. Labor cooperatives proved to be no less difficult to inaugurate than farmer cooperatives.

In spite of their insistence upon arbitration the Knights became embroiled in a series of violent strikes. In 1884 a business recession set in, accompanied by the inevitable increase in unemployment and in labor unrest. Companies that took advantage of the opportunity to discharge union men, particularly Knights, were sometimes fought successfully by boycotts, but the chief weapon of labor proved to be the strike. By use of it, for example, the Missouri Pacific, early in 1885, was forced to restore a wage-cut made without warning and without even the excuse of declining earnings. Public sympathy was almost unanimously with the strikers, and the company in yielding felt obliged to grant its employees time and one half for overtime, something the strikers had not even asked. In many minor instances during the middle eighties the Knights helped to win such victories.

Terence V. Powderly, 1887. By this time the Knights of Labor, whose cause Powderly championed, were losing ground.

Sometimes, however, the outcome was far different. In March, 1886, when a foreman in the Texas and Pacific car **Strikes of** shops at Marshall, Texas, was **1886** dismissed apparently because he was a member of the Knights of Labor, another important strike occurred. Under the leadership of Martin Irons, some nine thousand shopmen employed on the Gould system (of which the Texas and Pacific was a part) quit work, and attempted by sabotage to make all freight-hauling locomotives unfit for duty. So successful were their efforts that along five thousand miles of railroad in the Southwest freight traffic was at a standstill; only passenger trains carrying United States mails were permitted to move. At first popular hatred for Jay Gould worked in favor of the strikers, but when food shortages began to be felt and factories had to close down for lack of coal, the public had had strike enough. Four state governors, strongly backed by public opinion, ordered the strikers to cease interfering with trains, and Powderly himself, hoping for arbitration, intervened to call a temporary halt. When Gould refused to arbitrate, the strike was resumed with renewed violence, but the public was now so definitely against the strikers that their cause was soon lost.

Excitement over the southwestern railroad strike had scarcely subsided when the **The Haymarket riot** May Day strikes of 1886 claimed the attention of the country. The purpose of these strikes, in which perhaps 340,000 men participated, was to promote the cause of the eight-hour day. Although the claim was made that half the strikers won a reduced work day, an episode that occurred in Chicago, the storm-center of the strike, gave organized labor the most severe set-back it had yet received. Chicago happened to be the headquarters of a small group of foreign-born anarchists who welcomed the opportunity to expound to the strikers, both orally and in print, their principal tenet, the abolition of the state. To promote this end they were ready to advocate, although far less ready to perform, deeds of violence and terror. On the afternoon of May 3, August Spies, anarchist editor of the *Arbeiter Zeitung*, was addressing a meeting of strikers and strike sympathizers on a vacant lot not far from the McCormick Harvester Works, when the police attempted to disperse the assembly. In the ensuing melée several strikers were killed, and about twenty were wounded. That night a circular, printed in English and German, called lustily for "Revenge! Revenge! Workmen to arms!" Next day many meetings of protest occurred, the most notable being set for the evening at Haymarket Square, where a crowd of fifteen hundred assembled to listen to speeches by three leading anarchists. Although the crowd was orderly, the police again appeared and attempted to disperse it. This time, however, the officers of the law were met with a bomb that exploded with terrific violence, killing one policeman and wounding many more. Hard fighting followed, and when the casualties were reckoned it was found that of the policemen seven had lost their lives and over sixty had been seriously wounded, while of the civilians, four were dead and about fifty wounded.

The feeling of blind rage with which the public reacted to the "Haymarket riot" demanded victims. Efforts to find the guilty culprits, however, proved singularly unavailing. "For days," wrote one observer, "the police stations were filled with suspected persons, rigorously examined in the method of the third degree; persons for the most part that had no knowledge of the bomb nor of the meeting, nor of anything connected with either, and could not have." At length, for lack of better scapegoats, eight well-known anarchists, including Spies, were marked for trial. Evidence that any one of the eight had had anything to do either with the making or the throwing of the bomb was never produced, but seven of the men were given death sentences, and the eighth, imprisonment for fifteen years. The convictions were made on the assumption that these men, by advocating violence, had influenced some unknown person to throw the bomb, but this was merely an assumption utterly unbuttressed by evidence. It was clear that the men were convicted because of the opinions they held. In general, the public applauded the sentences, and rejoiced when four of the convicted men were hanged. One of the others had managed to blow out his brains with a bomb, and two had had their sentences commuted to life imprisonment. A few hardy souls condemned the whole proceedings as a miscarriage of justice, and in 1893, Governor John P. Altgeld, by pardoning the two men who were serving life sentences, classed himself with this number, an act of courage that wrecked his political career.

It was the irony of fate that the public saw in the Haymarket riot occasion for further condemnation of the **Decline of** Knights of Labor. Actually the **the Knights** strike for the eight-hour day had been promoted mainly through local trade unions, and Powderly had counseled against it on the ground that the weapon of the strike should not be invoked until all other means of protest had been exhausted. Nevertheless, the Knights had already won a reputation for violence and they received the blame. Anarchists and other advocates of revolution had found it easy to obtain membership in the order and had used its forums to propagate their views. Powderly even charged that an attorney for one group of employers confessed that anarchists had been paid to become Knights so that "they might stir up the devil and bring discredit upon your whole movement." As the control of the central organization over the behavior of the locals disintegrated, strikes were often undertaken "against the advice of the General Executive Board." The result was that skilled workers, alienated by the ruthless way in which the unskilled precipitated conflicts, tended to withdraw from the Knights in order to build up their own trade unions. By 1888 the membership of the Knights of Labor had declined to less than 260,000, and by 1890 to about 100,000. Within a short time the order had disappeared entirely.

Meantime a rival organization, which discarded the "one big union" idea in favor of **The A.F. of L.** the older federative plan, had begun to make headway. The American Federation of Labor, which was founded in 1881 at Pittsburgh as the "Federation of Organized Trades and Labor Unions of the United States and Canada," shortened its name in 1886, and at about the same time began to lengthen its membership list. While individuals, as such, were excluded from membership, almost any kind of labor organization, whether national, state, or local, might belong. The intent of the new order was no less to protect skilled labor from competition by the unskilled than to protect labor as such from the oppression of capital. It had, in fact, no real quarrel with capitalism as an economic system. Its mission, rather, was to insure that labor should share generously in the profits of capitalistic enterprise. To this end it set for itself such definite goals as an eight-hour work day, a six-day work week, a high wage level, greater security of job tenure, and the elimination of child labor. It showed little interest in the establishment of labor cooper-

atives, and it convincingly resisted all efforts to make the Federation over into a separate political party. Instead of going directly into politics, it supported candidates and platforms, of whatever party, provided only that they were favorable to the program of the Federation. While it hoped to see labor win most of its victories peacefully, either by obtaining favorable legislation or by collective bargaining with employers, the Federation, like the Knights, was willing in case of necessity to rely on the strike and the boycott. Its organization lent itself admirably to the use of the sympathetic strike, by means of which workers in a related craft, although lacking a grievance of their own, might come to the aid of a striking union. A sizable "war chest," supported by a per capita tax levied on members, enabled the Federation's central board of control to aid unemployed strikers and to prolong any conflict it chose to support.

What Terence V. Powderly was to the Knights of Labor, Samuel Gompers (1850–1924) was to the American Federation. **Samuel Gompers** Gompers was born in London, the son of a cigarmaker. At ten years of age he began to learn the shoemakers' trade, but he soon gave that up in favor of his father's trade, because the latter was organized and the former was not. In 1863 he came with his parents to America, and a year later he joined the first cigarmakers' union ever organized in New York City. Always an enthusiastic member, when he grew to manhood he became first the union's secretary and later its president. The training that he thus received was of great significance, for in many ways this local New York cigarmakers' union was a model organization. It followed the British system of benefit payments in case of unemployment, sickness, or death; it tried to encourage skill and intelligence among its members; it gained many of its victories by collective bargaining, by arbitration, and by retaining the good-will and respect of employers. Gompers never forgot this early training, and much of the conservatism of

Samuel Gompers Memorial on Massachusetts Avenue, Washington, D.C., commemorates the contributions of the great American labor leader to the labor cause.

his later career may properly be attributed to it. He was one of the original group of delegates that founded the Federation in 1881, and was even more active in the reorganization of 1886. From 1885 to the time of his death, with the exception of a single year, 1895, he was regularly elected president of the Federation.

Under Gompers's devoted leadership, the Federation scored many successes. It backed the strike for the eight-hour day in 1886, and claimed substantial gains in spite of the unfavorable reaction to the Haymarket riot. It conducted another strike for the eight-hour day in 1890, this time in the carpenters' union, with fairly satisfactory results. It supported innumerable movements, both in the states and in the nation as a whole, that resulted in the enactment of laws favorable to labor. In part through its activities practically every state in the Union was soon equipped with a bureau of labor statistics, and in 1903 Congress went so far as to establish the Department of Commerce and Labor, with a seat in the cabinet. The Federation encouraged member unions to set up their own systems for sickness and unemployment

benefits, and could soon point to many instances in which its advice had been followed. Its assistance could be counted upon, also, in efforts to secure adoption by employers of the "closed shop," which meant that only union labor might be employed in a given plant, and to eliminate "yellow dog" contracts, by which workers were obliged to agree in advance of employment that they would not join labor unions.

The decade of the nineties, four full years of which saw American business in the depths of depression, witnessed a series **The Home-** of industrial conflicts almost, if **stead strike** not quite, as alarming as those of the eighties. Gompers, whose approach to labor problems was essentially conservative, even lost office for a year during this period, for the prevailing temper of labor was impatient with restraint. The Homestead strike of 1892 precipitated in the Pittsburgh area a scene of incredible violence, an omen of worse to come. This dispute involved on the one hand the Amalgamated Association of Iron and Steel Workers, a well-established labor organization that had been formed as early as 1876 by a merger of several smaller craft unions, and on the other hand the Carnegie Steel Company, perhaps the most powerful of the several American steel corporations. Carnegie himself was no labor-baiter, and three years before he had agreed to a satisfactory contract with the union, but at the time trouble broke out in 1892 he had gone to Europe, leaving the affairs of the company in the hands of Henry Clay Frick, a man whose detestation of organized labor was open and unconcealed. The chief point at issue between the company and the workers was a proposed reduction in the pay for piecework. The company argued that such a reduction was justified because more efficient machinery had been installed. The worker who made use of the new tools could turn out more pieces than formerly in a given time without any greater expenditure of energy. Thus, according to the employers, a reduction in the piecerate could be made without reducing the worker's daily or weekly earnings. The union, however, refused to be persuaded, and held that the real intent of the company was a wage-cut.

When on July 1 the union refused to accept the company's terms, Frick anticipated the strike by closing the Homestead works. Technically, therefore, what followed was the result of a "lockout" rather than a strike. The union at once began to picket the works, while Frick showed that he meant business by surrounding the company's property with a wire fence fifteen feet high and three miles long, and also by ordering three hundred guards from the Pinkerton Detective Agency. The boats which brought the "Pinkertons" to the scene of conflict, however, were immediately attacked by the strikers, and fighting that occurred on July 6, 1892, resulted in numerous deaths and injuries on both sides. The Pinkertons were no match for the enraged strikers, who captured and disarmed their entire force and, after holding them for a day as prisoners of war, ran them out of town. Frick then appealed to the state for protection, and the governor responded by sending enough militia to turn the little mill town of Homestead into an armed camp. The strikers held out for nearly five months, but at length public opinion turned against them and they resumed work on the company's terms. An important factor in alienating the public from the strikers, whose case at first had aroused considerable sympathy, was the mad attack, by Alexander Berkman, a young anarchist, on the life of Frick. Frick, although seriously injured, soon recovered, and Berkman for his crime spent fifteen years in prison.

Of all the many labor disturbances that punctuated the years of depression the Pullman strike of 1894 was by far **The Pullman** the most significant. In 1880 **strike** George Mortimer Pullman, the inventor and builder of the Pullman sleeping-car, had established for the benefit of his employees the "model town" of Pullman on the outskirts of Chicago. This project carried paternalism to an extraordinary extreme. Model dwellings were built by the company and rented to employees; company stores were opened at which Pullman employees were encouraged to buy; a company church, a company school, a company park, and a company theater ministered to the various social needs of the community. The entire village, indeed, was owned and operated by the Pullman Palace Car Company as a business investment — a kind of modern feudalism, so critics were accustomed to say. The situation was changed somewhat in 1889 when the village was annexed to Chicago, but for the most part the property rights of the Pullman Company remained undisturbed.

Pullman had no use for labor unions, but during the first year of the depression organizers of the American Railway Union made rapid headway with his men. This union was the brain-child of Eugene V. Debs (1855–1926), who was later to become the outstanding leader of the Socialist movement in the United States. Debs was born in Terre Haute, Indiana, of French-Alsatian ancestry, and at the time of the Pullman strike was still less than forty years of age, He had worked in the railway shops of his home town when he was a boy of only four-teen, and at sixteen he had become a locomotive fireman. A passionate defender of the underprivileged and devoted to the union idea, he held high office in the Brotherhood of Locomotive Firemen, and for a time edited *The Locomotive Fireman's Magazine*. He became increasingly impatient, however, with the unaggressive attitude of the railway brotherhoods and the American Federation of Labor, with which the brotherhoods cooperated, although they would not join it. Convinced that industrial unions were preferable to trades unions and that railroad men should all be members of one organization, in 1893 he founded the American Railway Union, and such was his persuasiveness that within a year the new union had enrolled one hundred and fifty thousand members.

The Pullman strike was precipitated in the spring of 1894 when the Pullman Com-

Railroad tie-ups pany, hard hit by the depression, laid off one third of its men and cut the wages of the rest from thirty to forty per cent. No reductions, however, were made in the rent charged for company houses nor in the price of goods at the company stores. In protest the men quit work, and with the demand for sleeping-cars at a standstill Pullman showed no disposition to call them back. With their credit withdrawn at the company stores, the strikers were on the verge of starvation when the American Railway Union came to the rescue with relief money and with the threat of a boycott against the hauling of Pullman cars. On June 26 Debs ordered the boycott to be applied on all the western railroads, and "A.R.U." men obeyed by cutting out Pullman cars from their trains and leaving them on side-tracks. When boycotters were discharged for such acts, the strike became general, and not Pullman cars alone but whole trains stood on side-tracks. From Cincinnati to San Francisco the effects of the strike were felt. Traffic between Chicago and the West was virtually paralyzed and hoodlums who joined the strikers stooped to every sort of violence, as the unemployed multitudes

poured their accumulated bitterness and resentment into the strife. Engines were crippled, freight-cars were overturned and looted, loyal employees were driven from their posts.

The railroad operators, faced by this dangerous situation, would normally have been willing to trust the governor **Federal** of Illinois — the state most **troops** seriously involved — to keep order, if necessary by calling out the militia to aid the civil authorities. But the governor of Illinois happened to be John P. Altgeld, already notorious among conservatives for his pardoning of the Haymarket anarchists. The operators, therefore, demanded that federal troops be brought in, and when Altgeld took no steps in that direction they appealed directly to the President for aid. Cleveland was in a quandary, for while the Constitution authorized the President to protect a state against domestic violence, it expressly stated that such action was to be taken "on application of the legislature, or of the executive (when the legislature cannot be convened)." The legislature of Illinois was not in session and the governor of the state had issued no call for help, but the President at length decided that he might intervene on the pretext that the Chicago disorders interfered with the free transport of United States mail. By the fourth of July two thousand regulars, including cavalry and field artillery, had moved into the troubled zone. Having arrived there, they exerted themselves not merely to see that the mails were carried, but also to break the strike. Altgeld protested vigorously that Cleveland's action was unconstitutional and demanded the immediate withdrawal of the federal troops, but Cleveland stood his ground. No doubt Altgeld, had he been given time to do so, would have restored order, but it is by no means certain that he would have tried to break the strike.

Governmental action against the strikers was not confined to the use of troops, for the federal courts soon took a **Use of the** hand. Debs, who had assumed **injunction**

THE PULLMAN STRIKE. First meat train leaving Chicago under escort of U.S. Cavalry. Drawing by G. W. Peters for *Harper's Weekly*, 1894.

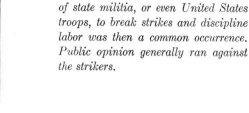

THE HAYMARKET RIOT. Climax of friction between police and strikers during eight-hour workday movement, 1886.

THE STEEL INDUSTRY. Militia behind a barricade inside Carnegie works during strike to gain recognition of the union. *Scribner's Monthly*, 1896.

THE COAL MINERS. Violence near Scranton, Pennsylvania. From a sketch by J. Becker in *Leslie's Illustrated Newspaper*, 1871.

direct supervision of the strike, and several other leaders were arrested by federal officers on the charge of conspiracy to obstruct the mails, and although released on bail were enjoined by Federal Judges Grosscup and Woods against doing anything to prolong the strike. In direct defiance of this order, Debs urged a group of labor leaders on July 12 to promote a general strike by all the labor organizations of the country. Thereupon he and six others were cited for contempt of court and sentenced to six months in jail. Thus summarily removed from the scene of conflict, Debs was left free to read and to think, and when he emerged from confinement he announced his conversion to socialism. His imprisonment served also to call attention to the fact that the courts were not averse to obtaining results by the use of the injunction that they could not so certainly have obtained had the normal procedure of a jury trial been followed. Criticism of "government by injunction" and of the use of the regular army to break strikes was freely expressed. To many the now familiar Populist charge that a corrupt alliance existed between business and government to suppress the liberties of the people seemed only too well substantiated.

That another view of the duty of government could be taken was shown by Governor Davis H. Waite of Colorado, whom the **"Bloody Bridles" Waite** Populists, with Democratic assistance, had elected in 1892. "It is better," he had said, "infinitely better, that blood should flow to the horses' bridles rather than our national liberties should be destroyed." Known thenceforth as "Bloody Bridles" Waite, he did not hesitate to help the striking miners during the so-called "Cripple Creek War" of 1894 instead of giving the customary aid and comfort to the employers. When an army of deputy sheriffs made ready to attack the strikers, Waite called out the entire state militia to preserve the peace, and marched his troops between the opposing forces. Waite was a man of no tact and little judgment, but his attitude, like Altgeld's, gave

courage to the forces of labor. Throughout the nineties in Colorado, Idaho, and Montana the Western Federation of Miners battled employers with a degree of violence that bordered on revolution. In May, 1897, the president of this organization urged every union in Colorado and Idaho to arm itself "so that in two years we can hear the inspiring music of the martial tread of 25,000 armed men in the ranks of labor."

Attempts to induce the government to help solve the problem of unemployment by means of work relief, while not **"Coxey's army"** entirely unknown, proceeded usually from the minds of men whom the public regarded as "crack-pots." Most famous of these was General Jacob S. Coxey of Massillon, Ohio, a Greenbacker and a Populist, who advocated that Congress should issue $500,000,000 in legal-tender notes to be expended at the rate of $20,000,000 a month on the building of good roads. Wages of one dollar and fifty cents per eight-hour day were to be paid to all who needed employment. Coxey also urged that municipalities desirous of making public improvements should be authorized to issue non-interest-bearing bonds equal to half their assessed valuation. These bonds might then be used as security with the Secretary of the Treasury to obtain loans of legal-tender notes to pay for the construction of schools, courthouses, paved streets, and other worthy projects. Both schemes, on the financial side, were highly inflationary in character, but they aimed at a type of governmental activity that in the next great depression became extremely familiar.

In seeking to promote his ideas Coxey hit upon the expedient of presenting, by means of a march of the unemployed on Washington, a "living petition" to Congress. Newspaper men, no less amused by the General's picturesque personality than by his fantastic notions, gave much-needed publicity, and by Easter Sunday, 1894, when the march was scheduled to begin, a motley array of recruits had converged on Massillon. Most of the unemployed walked, but General Coxey, his wife, and his infant son, Legal Tender Coxey, rode in carriages. At the beginning of the march "Coxey's army" consisted of not more than one hundred men, including newspaper reporters, but in spite of continuous desertions its number increased as the march progressed. Many of the men were able to demonstrate that they had had experience in living off the country, but Populists and labor organizations took up the cause of the crusaders and provided them plentifully with supplies. On the first of May, five hundred strong, the army entered Washington determined to lay its demands before a Congress, now thoroughly excited. At the end of Pennsylvania Avenue the marchers met a cordon of police under orders to halt their advance. Several of the leaders, including Coxey, were arrested for disobeying an ordinance to keep off the grass, the army was turned back to its camp, and the speech Coxey had prepared to deliver from the Capitol steps reached the public only through the newspapers. It was an effective document:

Up these steps the lobbyists of trusts and corporations have passed unchallenged on their way to the Committee rooms, access to which we, the representatives of the toiling wealth producers, have been denied. We stand here today in behalf of millions of toilers whose petitions have been buried in committee rooms, whose prayers have been unresponded to, and whose opportunities for honest, remunerative, productive labor have been taken away from them by unjust legislation, which protects idlers, speculators, and gamblers.

Coxey's army was not the only organization of its kind to march on Washington. Other labor An army of six hundred men marches under the command of General Lewis G. Fry had set out from Los Angeles six weeks before Coxey's followers reached Washington, and by the end of May at least two hundred of them had joined Coxey's camp on the outskirts of that city. Another detachment that had taken a different route arrived before the end of June. A San Francisco army under

General Charles T. Kelly "bummed" its way twelve hundred strong to Utah, captured a Union Pacific train of twenty-six boxcars, and arrived at Council Bluffs, Iowa, April 15. Traveling by foot, by river steamboat, and by rail the army held together as far as Ohio, where it was scattered by a succession of adversities, although Kelly and a handful of the more persistent reached Washington before the summer was over. Similar movements from the Far West, from the Middle West, even from New England, made news during the summer of 1894. But the concentration of so many unemployed in the Washington area overtaxed the charitable resources of the city and ended inevitably in starvation and distress. Finally the Commissioners of the District of Columbia found means to send most of the marchers home, while stragglers in Virginia and Maryland were rounded up and either driven across state boundaries or sent to workhouses.

The fact that violence went no further and did no worse during the turbulent nineties, labor and the nation owed in A. F. of L. considerable part to Samuel policy Gompers, President of the American Federation of Labor. Gompers anchored his policies on two fundamentals: (1) labor must not seek to set itself up as a substitute for capitalism, but must confine its activities primarily to seeking better wages and better working conditions for the laborer; and (2) labor must avoid like a plague all efforts to establish a separate labor party. Thus organized labor became, in a sense, an ally of the capitalists, especially those who were willing to bargain with it and deal with it generously, while it was at the same time no threat to the major political parties. These latter, Gompers firmly believed, were primarily coalitions of sectional leaders and bosses, men whose chief purpose in life was to achieve office rather than to serve principle. However this might be, labor by holding the balance of power between the two parties could, and did, extract dependable commitments from each.

Under Gompers the American Federation of Labor grew in membership from about one hundred and fifty thousand in 1886 to more than a million in 1900, to a million and a half by 1905, and to two millions by the outbreak of the First World War. The greatest weakness of the American Federation lay in the fact that it represented only a favored minority of labor. All unskilled workers were excluded from membership, together with all skilled workers who did not belong to a union. Moreover, a number of labor organizations, including the four great railway unions, refused to affiliate with the Federation on the ground that they were able to take care of themselves, and were not eager to accept responsibility for others. The railway unions, however, as already noted, ordinarily could be counted on to cooperate fully with the Federation.

Labor conditions in the South differed markedly from labor conditions in the North. **Southern mill workers** For one thing, until well after the beginning of the twentieth century the South failed to attract immigrant labor, or even the children of the immigrants. Whites from the poorer lands of the piedmont and from the mountains furnished the bulk of the labor supply for the textile mills and such others as required skilled operatives, while a preponderance of blacks did the harder work of the mines, the blast furnaces, and the lumber industry. Only in the rarest instances were the two races employed to work side by side at the same tasks; industries that used both whites and blacks took care that there was a division of labor that separated the races, with the inferior position being regularly assigned to the blacks. In the textile mills the employment of women and children was practically universal, although the extent to which small children were exploited has doubtless been exaggerated. Nevertheless, one of the chief attractions of the mills to the rural whites was the opportunity they furnished for the whole family to be gainfully employed. Wages were low, at first far lower than wages paid in the northern mills, but with the wife and children at work as well as the head of the house the total income realized was so much larger than could be wrested from a rundown southern farm that the temptation to leave the farm for the factory was well-nigh irresistible. It often turned out that women and children kept their jobs, while the men, less easily adaptable to the new type of work, lost theirs. Not every husband who stayed home while the rest of the family went to work did so of his own volition. Hours of labor were long, sometimes as much as seventy-two hours per week.

Most of the southern mills and factories developed along definitely paternalistic lines. Someone had to provide houses for the workers, and the "company" made it its business to provide them. The company likewise opened stores, and in many instances paid the workers in scrip, good at any time for payments to the company, but redeemable in cash only at infrequent intervals. The company also provided such schools and churches as it deemed desirable, and hired both the teachers and the preachers. To the country people who flocked to the mills these acts of forethought were accepted without suspicion. The houses of the mill villages were better than the houses of the farms, the company stores were easy of access, and charged little more, if any, than other stores; while the schools, the churches, and the factories themselves furnished such an opportunity for community life as the workers had never known before. At first labor unions were virtually unknown, and throughout the nineteenth century labor agitators were given little encouragement either by employers or by employees. In the twentieth century, however, unionism took strong hold in the South and worked many changes.

Bibliography

On the subject of labor, John R. Commons and associates, *History of Labour in the United States* (4 vols., 1918–35), is indispensable. Selig Perlman, *A History of Trade Unionism in the United States* (1922), is compact and reliable. There are good chapters on the subject in Thomas H. Greer, *American Social Reform Movements* (1949). Other books of merit on the labor theme include Mary R. Beard, *The American Labor Movement: A Short History* (1924); N. J. Ware, *The Labor Movement in the United States, 1860–95* (1929); S. P. Orth, *The Armies of Labor* (1919); F. R. Dulles, *Labor in America* (1949); and C. R. Daugherty, *Labor Problems in American Industry* (1933, rev. ed., 1948). On the subject of Negro labor, consult C. H. Wesley, *Negro Labor in the United States, 1850–1925* (1927).

Oberholtzer, IV, treats the subject of the Chinese in California in great detail, but see also Mary R. Coolidge, *Chinese Immigration* (1909). James Bryce, *The American Commonwealth* (2 vols., 1888, new ed., 1931–33), contains an illuminating account of the Kearney movement in California. Ira B. Cross, *History of the Labor Movement in California* (1935), is confined principally to the nineteenth century.

Terence V. Powderly, *Thirty Years of Labor* (1889), recounts somewhat subjectively the history of the Knights of Labor; see also *The Path I Trod: The Autobiography of Terence V. Powderly*, edited by H. J. Carman and others (1940). The most satisfactory history of the A. F. of L. is L. L. Lorwin, *The American Federation of Labor* (1933). Samuel Gompers, *Seventy Years of Life and Labor* (2 vols., 1925), is an excellent autobiography, which may be supplemented by R. H. Harvey, *Samuel Gompers, Champion of the Toiling Masses* (1935); and Charles A. Madison, *American Labor Leaders: Personalities and Forces in the Labor Movement* (1950), a left-wing view.

Samuel Yellen, *American Labor Struggles* (1936), covers all the important strikes after the Civil War, and Louis Adamic, *Dynamite* (1931, rev. ed., 1934), the more violent labor outbreaks. J. W. Coleman, *The Molly Maguire Riots* (1936), is the best study of this subject; Rhodes, VIII, and Oberholtzer, III, treat fully the subject of the railway strikes; Henry David, *The History of the Haymarket Affair: A Study in the American Social Revolutionary and Labor Movements* (1936), is excellent. George Harvey, *Henry Clay Frick* (1928), throws some light on the Homestead strike. Almont Lindsey, *The Pullman Strike* (1942), is the best available account of that labor disturbance. Ray Ginger, *The Bending Cross: A Biography of Eugene Victor Debs* (1949), is a valuable contribution to the history of American political and economic radicalism. McAlister Coleman, *Eugene V. Debs: A Man Unafraid* (1930); and Floy W. Painter, *That Man Debs and His Life Work* (1929), both review fully Debs' connection with the Pullman Strike. The case for the President in the Pullman strike is stated in Grover Cleveland, *The Government in the Chicago Strike of 1894* (1913); but this should be compared with Harry Barnard, *Eagle Forgotten, The Life of John Peter Altgeld* (1938); W. R. Browne, *Altgeld of Illinois* (1924); and Edward Berman, *Labor Disputes and the President of the United States* (1924). Benjamin Rastall, *The Labor History of the Cripple Creek District* (1908), is concerned with a particularly troubled area. Donald L. McMurry, *Coxey's Army* (1929), deals fully with the various labor "marches" of the period. On southern labor see Thomas Tippet, *When Southern Labor Stirs* (1931); and G. S. Mitchell, *Textile Unionism and the South* (1931).

10

The New Immigration

A nation of nations — The waves of immigration — The dominant strain — Why the immigrants came — "The uprooted" — Reception of the immigrants — Immigrants as farmers — City immigrants — Anti-foreigner sentiment — Tenements and slums — Religions of the immigrants — Labor and the immigrant — Non-European immigrants — Demands for restriction — New roots for old

THE significance of immigration in American history can hardly be overemphasized. In **A nation of nations** a sense all the people of the United States, except for a few of Indian blood, are either immigrants or the descendants of immigrants. It is therefore impossible to dissociate the history or the peopling of the continent from the history of immigration. Even assuming, however, that a distinction can be drawn between those who came earlier and those who came later, and that only the latter should be classed as immigrants, the tremendous importance of the late-comers in the making of the American nation is not to be denied. The American people, as a result of the immigrant tides, are compounded of many nationalities, not just a few; the United States is in truth a "nation of nations." To some extent the various peoples who have come to America have intermarried and amalgamated; for such the new environment has served as a "melting-pot." Others have maintained their separate identities, even through several generations; for such, the term "mixing-bowl" would be more appropriate. But for all who came to America the process of readjustment meant changes of a fundamental nature in their way of life; as Americans they soon differed in many respects from their relatives in the Old World. And, conversely, the impact of their coming changed America; with each new flood of immigration the United States tended in some degree to reflect the attitudes and characteristics of the newcomers.

Immigration to America has even had its effect on the Old World. Economically, it has served to reduce population pressures, and, because the immigrants so often sent back money to their relatives, to alleviate a little the grinding poverty from which the European lower classes suffered. Also, information about America trickled back to the old countries through letters written by immigrants, and through the return of many immigrants to their former homes. Thus American ways and ideas were communicated to Europe, just as through the original immigrants European ideas and ways were communicated to America.

The migration of peoples from the Old World to the New came in distinct waves; periods in which great numbers **The waves of immigration** of immigrants entered American ports have alternated with periods in which the numbers were small. The first great movement came during the seventeenth century, and was principally from England. But it is necessary to recall that other nationalities, particularly the Dutch along the Hudson and the Swedes along the

Delaware, participated in this early movement; even in the beginning the settlers were not all of one nationality. The next great influx came during the eighteenth century, when the Scotch-Irish and the Pennsylvania Germans, or Palatines, by the hundreds of thousands reached American shores. "One hundred per cent" Americans of the twentieth century could hardly have been more dismayed at the "new immigration" from southern and eastern Europe than the English colonials at the coming of the Scotch-Irish and the Palatines. The third immigrant wave came during the two or three decades that preceded the Civil War, and brought principally millions of Celtic Irish from the south of Ireland, and millions of Germans from western and southern Germany. These newcomers, also, were resented by those whose ancestors had reached America earlier; particularly did the fact that so many of them were Roman Catholics bring vigorous protests from many American Protestants. The fourth wave set in immediately following the American Civil War, and lasted on until the First World War. With it came many representatives from all the nationalities that had sent immigrants to America before, especially from the British Isles, the Scandinavian countries, and Germany; but as time went on an increasingly large number came also from southern and eastern Europe, people who in language and culture were far removed from the northern and western Europeans who had come to the United States before. This "new immigration," many thought, actually threatened the "native American" culture, and might serve even to cut the nation loose from its institutional moorings.

As a matter of fact the Anglo-American strain in the civilization of the United **The dominant strain** States remained dominant all the while. English settlers, because they were the first to come in numbers, had set the original pattern of American society; they had brought with them the English language and literature, English concepts of law and government, English religious practices, English institutions in general. All these they had modified as conditions in America seemed to warrant, and with the New World so far distant from the Old the modifications became more and more marked with each succeeding generation. With opportunity wide open in America, the English colonials had multiplied amazingly in numbers; the less numerous immigrants, when they came, had therefore to learn the English language and bow to Anglo-American customs. It was so with each succeeding wave of newcomers; no matter how numerous they were, they were at any given time far less numerous than the native Americans. The immigrants had an influence, a profound influence, upon the development of the American way of life. But their influence, like that of the American environment, was exerted to modify an existing culture, not to substitute another culture for the one they found. In one form or another, most of the old traditions lived on.

Opportunity in America had much to do with the coming of the immigrants. With the economic revolution in full **Why the** progress, the demand for cheap **immigrants** labor to man the new industries **came** far outran the domestic supply. Also, western lands existed for those who had the means to reach the West, and the relatively small sums of money needed to buy the land they coveted. During the first two years of the Civil War, immigration had fallen off precipitately, but by 1863 confidence in the future of America had revived, and the number of newcomers had swelled to a figure greater than had crossed the Atlantic in any one of the three years preceding the war. Official stimulation came from the American side, both by way of liberal bounties for those who would serve in the army, and by an immigration act, passed in 1864, which allowed the importation of laborers under contracts not particularly different in principle from the contracts that in colonial times had brought so many indentured servants to

ON TO AMERICA. A group of peasants begin the long journey.

Immigration to America was an ordeal for most who undertook it. Baggage was a problem, for they often started the journey afoot. In bundles and suitcases, or the wooden steamship trunks and wicker-baskets so typical of the period, they packed their meager possessions. The immigrants shown here appear to be from Central Europe and the Balkans.

ELLIS ISLAND. Immigrants lined up for examination.

THE LAND OF FREEDOM. Ocean steamer passing the Statue of Liberty. *Leslie's Illustrated Newspaper*, 1887.

THE LAST LAP. Humble baggage reloaded at Ellis Island for the unknown home ahead.

America. As further evidence of the current interest in promoting the flow of foreigners to the United States, both the federal government and many of the western states maintained immigration bureaus. Pamphlets distributed by some of the state agencies even rivaled the land offices of the western railroads in setting forth glowingly the advantages of life in the New World.[1]

The new steamship companies of the post-Civil War period also played a significant **Activities of** role in the fostering of immigra-**steamship** tion. Before the war immi-**companies** grants to the United States came as a rule in sailing ships; in 1856, for example, out of 131,000 entrants, only 5000 had come in steamships. But soon after the war steamships took over the bulk of the trans-Atlantic passenger traffic. The multiplication of steamships during the period came about in part as a result of the need many European nations felt for a strong merchant marine to supplement their navies in time of war. Steamship companies could thus count on heavy governmental subsidies to help them pay profits, but they were quick to see in the immigrant trade another lucrative source of income. Competition among the rival companies was keen, and the rates were correspondingly low. Often steamship companies and railroad companies collaborated in offering through transportation at a ridiculously low figure from a given point in Europe to a given point in the United States. At one time during the seventies it was possible to purchase a ticket from Stockholm to Chicago for only twenty-one dollars, while passage across the Atlantic, from port to port, fell to as low as twelve dollars, including meals. These prices were exceptionally low, but twenty-five dollars from somewhere in Europe to somewhere in the American Middle West was common enough. The existence of such favorable rates was advertised, not only by steamship and railroad companies, but also by numerous less responsible agencies who made it

their business to induce the restless and discontented everywhere to emigrate. These agencies, for a commission, sold the immigrants tickets to the New World, herded them westward to farms if they had the money with which to buy land, turned them over to labor contractors if they had not. By word of mouth, by brochures, by newspaper advertising, they painted a convincing picture of the easy road to wealth in the United States, and for thousands of hard-pressed Europeans the appeal was irresistible.

Within Europe itself powerful forces goaded many people into emigration. Of all these forces, no doubt popula- **Population** tion pressure headed the list. **pressure** For hundreds of years before the eighteenth century the population of Europe had not varied markedly from one generation to the next, but during that century the proportion of births over deaths began suddenly to rise. According to careful estimates there were not over 140,000,000 people living in Europe in 1750; one hundred years later this number had grown to 260,000,000, an increase of over eighty-five per cent. But this was only a start. By the time of the First World War, Europe had achieved a population of 400,-000,000, an increase of nearly fifty-four per cent since 1850, and this in spite of the heavy emigration that had taken place. Undoubtedly the opportunities presented by the industrial revolution had much to do with this phenomenon; the new machines provided jobs for new millions, so the millions appeared. The industrial revolution accounted also for the drift from the country to the city that characterized European society, no less than American, during these same years. England in particular became a great urban manufacturing center, dependent increasingly for its daily bread on food shipped in from the outside world. Even so, the country people in England and in every part of Europe found themselves desperately overcrowded. There was no more land than when the population had been less; even after the rush to the cities began there

[1] See p. 212. The federal bureau was discontinued in 1868, and not revived until 1891.

were always too many people for the amount of land. The peasants could not "make it stretch," there was not enough to go around. Still more of them must leave, either to search for jobs in their own cities, or to brave the unknown hazards of the New World.

Undoubtedly the economic urge was uppermost, but there were other important **Other** factors. Dislike of British rule **motives** continued as at least a secondary motivation among the Irish, after as well as before the American Civil War, while the steady descent into conservatism that followed the revolutions of 1848 in Germany and central Europe pointed the way to the New World for political non-conformists in that area. Here, too, minority groups were rarely well-treated, and were easily beguiled into emigration. Resentment against the requirement of military service, a situation common to most European countries, also sent its quotas. Even religious motives had by no means ceased to count. The Jews of Russia, which then included most of Poland, were subject to severe discriminations. They had to pay special taxes; they found it difficult or even impossible to own or rent land; they were forbidden to enter various occupations; their freedom of movement was circumscribed; they lived under the fear or the fact of bloody pogroms. To escape this kind of persecution they came to America in steadily increasing numbers, particularly after a series of bloody anti-Jewish outbreaks, beginning in 1881. Even among Christians there were reasons for religious unrest. - In most European nations established churches enjoyed special prerogatives that were deeply resented by the dissenting sects. In Sweden, for example, everyone according to law was born into the State Church, and could get out of it only after annoying formalities; also, everyone paid taxes to help support the Church. There were criticisms, too, of the indifference of the Church to the public welfare, and the worldliness of many of its clergy. Deeply religious dissenters, sometimes actually the converts of American missionaries, found excuses, if not reasons, in such charges for their move to America. In the United States, everyone knew, there was no established church, and there was complete religious freedom. Many, too, resented the caste system of the Old World, and listened with longing to the reports that in the New World there were no class distinctions, no counts, barons, or gentry, and that even a man who worked with his hands was not looked down upon as an inferior. In America, it was said, a man might by earnest endeavor actually rise in the world; he was not restricted in any way by the circumstances of his birth.

Oscar Handlin in a moving book, *The Uprooted*, tells in general terms the story of the emigrant who, after deep **"The** reflection, turned his back on **uprooted"** the dwindling resources of his native village, and his face toward what he assumed to be the boundless opportunities of America. In spite of the trend toward urbanization, most of the people who took this drastic step were country people, peasants; to some extent the movement toward America was thus only a part of the more general movement from country to city: some went to the cities of their own nation, others to the cities of the New World. The peasants of Europe, unlike farmers in America, tended to live together in villages from which they went out each morning to their fields, and to which they returned each evening. The habits and customs of the village were fixed by centuries of tradition; each person knew his status, felt that he belonged. The act of leaving thus involved a complete break with everything a given individual had ever known. From that time forward he was one of the "uprooted"; wherever he went, he would never again feel really at home. Poverty-stricken, frightened, and lonely, he made his way to the point of embarkation, and, far luckier than his predecessors who had crossed the Atlantic in sailing ships, took steerage passage on some westbound steamer. In the olden days the trip took weeks, now it could be done in from eight to twelve days. But the human cargo suffered nonetheless, from the jam-packed quarters, from the shameless trespass on their privacy, from the humiliation of language and custom barriers, from the utter strangeness of the whole proceedings. Then came the arduous tasks of getting ashore, passing inspection, keeping track of baggage, finding a place to live. Most of the entrants came to New York or Boston, but the immigrant tide touched nearly every port along the Atlantic seaboard, and as far around the Gulf of Mexico as New Orleans.

On Bedloe's Island in New York harbor the Statue of Liberty was unveiled on October 28, 1886. This huge work of art and engineering was a gift from the people of France to the people of the United States in commemoration of the alliance of 1778 between the two nations. On its base was inscribed these words:

Give me your tired, your poor,
Your huddled masses yearning to breathe free,
The wretched refuse of your teeming shore,
Send these, the homeless, tempest-tossed to me:
I lift my lamp beside the golden door.

But the immigrant who reached America found no such warming welcome as he had hoped. Certainly the government did almost literally nothing to help him. An inspector's report for 1871 had this to say: "If Europe were to present us with 300,000 cattle per year, ample agencies would be employed to secure their proper protection and distribution, but thus far the general government has done but little to diminish the numerous hardships of an emigrant's position. . . . All legislation having for its purpose the good of the poor and the lowly, will necessarily be opposed by those who make money off their ignorance and helplessness."[1]

Altogether too many people among those who met the immigrant, including even his

Reception of the immigrants own countrymen, were bent merely on doing him out of whatever small sums of cash he still

[1] Quoted in George M. Stephenson, *A History of Immigration, 1820–1924* (1926), 251.

retained. They acted as runners for hotels that swindled him, they made away with his baggage, they cheated him in turning his European currency into dollars, they sold him tickets to places that did not exist. After they were through with him, he walked the city streets in search of a job, only to find that every employer seemed eager to take advantage of his misery. Under the urging of self-appointed bosses, or padrones, as the Italians called them, he contracted to do the hard, unskilled, pick and shovel labor on some construction project, perhaps a building near at hand or perhaps a railroad far out in the West. He took whatever wages his boss could get for him, and handed over as a commission whatever part of his earnings his boss chose to demand. Operating in this way, many of the bosses and padrones got rich; the more enterprising among them even found it profitable to do some of their initial recruiting in Europe. With their assistance, or sometimes without it, the immigrants found their way to the nation's coal, lead, and copper mines, to its iron foundries and steel mills, to the harder and more menial tasks in all sorts of factories.

We Who Built America is the appropriate title that Carl Wittke gave to his history of the immigrants. Without the labor they furnished it is hard to see how the railroads, the factories, and the cities of the new America could ever have been built, or its rich mineral resources exploited. Members of nearly every immigrant group could be found practically everywhere that hard work had to be done, but there were some recognizable trends in the types of employment they obtained. The Italians, for example, took over in a general sort of way from the Irish the numerous jobs for unskilled labor in the cities; the various Slavic groups accepted stoically the arduous duties of the iron- and steel-works, the stockyards, and the mines; the Jews by the tens of thousands became city sweatshop workers. So each immigrant group in its own peculiar way contributed to the new industrialism.

The most favored of the immigrants got

Bandit's roost, a section of the New York tenement district, as photographed by Jacob Riis, about 1890. This was one of many short alleys in the neighborhood of the notorious Mulberry Bend.

back to the land. This was particularly true of the Scandinavians and the Germans, and to a lesser extent it was true also of the Finns, the Dutch, and the Czechs. On arrival at the eastern ports immigrants bound for western destinations were usually loaded at once into trains for Chicago, a trip that might take them as long as four days and nights. These "emigrant trains" were usually indifferently equipped, and sometimes the bewildered passengers were actually supplied only with box-cars. On their arrival in Chicago, they were met by new bands of runners and swindlers, all bent on taking something away from them. Land sharks, in particular, beset them on every hand, eager to sell them, if they could, worthless or even non-existent land. But by this time they had learned to be more wary, and some were always fortunate enough to find the kind of land they coveted, land that reproduced as nearly as possible the characteristics of the land they had known at home. Their selections were influenced, too,

Immigrants as farmers

by their desire to duplicate the old country climates, so the Scandinavians and Finns turned in great numbers to the Upper Mississippi Valley, particularly Minnesota and the Dakotas, the Germans centered on Wisconsin, the Dutch picked Michigan, the Czechs, Iowa and Nebraska. Earlier pioneers, immigrants who had come before the Civil War, had spotted these desirable regions, and had settled in them. Frequently they had also sent back "America letters" to their friends, relatives, and neighbors, letters that sang the praises of the new environment, whether to keep up the courage of the writer, or to induce some of his countrymen to join him, and so to lessen his loneliness, or merely to set forth in all honesty the opportunities that existed. Whatever the motives, the letters brought results, and the older immigrants helped locate the latecomers as close as possible to their own holdings. In general, the immigrants were reluctant to push to the farthest frontiers, and preferred to buy or rent land that had already been brought into production.

But at best all was strange and difficult. The soil was not like the soil they had known; it would not respond to the customary treatment. Crops, too, were different, and methods of farming required a dependence upon machinery that was baffling, for the machinery cost money that the immigrant rarely had. There was much more buying and selling than in the European villages; it was hard to live off the produce of the land as the peasants of Europe were wont to do. One had to buy so much, and to buy, one had to sell. And the villages themselves were absent. In America each farmer had a house for his family on his own land, miles distant, perhaps, from the nearest neighbor. There was nothing to take the place of the community life of the Old World village. The loneliness told heavily on the whole family, but especially on the women; it was all they could do to keep their sanity. There were discriminations, too. America might be the land of the free, where every man was as good as every other man, but many Americans did not act that way. Instead, they looked down on the foreigners, made fun of their ways, treated them with contempt. This seemed the more unreasonable to the immigrants as they noted the poor farming methods of the "Yankees," most of whom merely robbed the soil, and put back nothing in return for what they took from it. Indeed, the foreigners, once they had mastered the new environment, usually turned out to be better farmers than the natives. Strangely enough, this fact, instead of raising their status in the eyes of their neighbors, tended only to add to their unpopularity.

The immigrants who went to the farms, hard as their lot was, were the lucky ones;

City immigrants the great majority had no choice but to remain in the cities. Here they could rarely get ahead; when one job ended they could only seek another of the same kind at no better pay. At best the wages they earned barely kept soul and body together. They could afford only the cheapest housing, so they drifted inevitably into tenement districts and slums where the principal object of owners was to crowd a maximum number of people into a minimum amount of space. The buildings they lived in were sure to be located in the least desirable parts of the city; after the immigrants moved in, any place they lived was certain to be deemed undesirable anyway. Such cities as New York and Boston, where available land close in was scarce, had the worst slums, but in every large city conditions were bad enough. In New York the typical tenement might reach six stories in height, and would be so constructed as to use every available foot of space on a given lot, leaving only the streets and the alleys as places for the children to play. A typical tenement district block in New York would account for as many as four thousand people. Sanitary conditions were unspeakable, and the lack of privacy was almost as oppressive as in the steerage quarters of an Atlantic steamer.

But still the immigrants came. A quarter of a million of them landed on American shores in 1865, and three years later the annual total had reached 326,000, well above the average for the eighteen-fifties. By 1873, when more than 460,000 aliens entered the country, the immigrant tide had broken all preceding records. The census of 1870, which counted 38,558,371 people in the United States, described 2,314,000 of them as immigrants who had arrived during the sixties; while five years later the total number of foreign-born in the population was set at 7,500,000. The total for the decade of the seventies, in spite of the depression, was 2,812,191; while during the eighties all previous records were broken by an influx of 5,246,613, an average of more than half a million immigrants a year. By 1905 the million mark had been reached, and until the outbreak of the First World War in 1914 the avalanche continued.

Until the last decade of the nineteenth century, the great bulk of this immigration came, as before the Civil War, The "new from the British Isles and from immigration" Germany, but some notable new trends were in evidence. Immigration from Ireland, although still heavy, never again reached the startling totals of the forties and fifties, and was even exceeded during the seventies by the numbers coming from England. The Scandinavian migration, which had reached only slender proportions before the Civil War, also made spectacular gains; during the seventies the numbers coming from Norway, Sweden, and Denmark averaged about twenty-five thousand a year. The influx from Germany, which up to the middle eighties furnished about one-third of the total, began at that time to drop off, and by the end of the century it furnished not above one-seventh of the whole. Most significant of all was the really "new immigration" from southern and eastern Europe. From the middle eighties on the numbers coming from these areas rose as those coming from northern and western Europe fell. By the later nineties the former exceeded the latter in the proportion of three to two.

The descendants of colonial Americans

RUSSIAN MENNONITES. Interior of temporary communal home in Kansas. *Leslie's Illustrated Newspaper*, 1875.

Immigrant nationalities were even more numerous than the countries of Europe. Old World customs often aroused strong American "nativist" opposition, but even among themselves, the immigrants often had little in common.

LYNCHING THE ITALIANS IN NEW ORLEANS. A protest against the secret society, MAFIA. Illustration from *Scribner's Monthly*, 1896.

THE FIVE POINTS. A famous slum area occupied largely by Irish immigrants is shown on the lower half of Matthew H. Smith's title page, 1869.

SWEDISH IMMIGRANTS GOING WEST. Woodcut, circa 1860.

A GERMAN NEWSPAPER. Cover of first issue of *Keppler's Weekly*, 1869.

had long been familiar with immigrants from the British Isles and from Germany, and they found comparatively little difficulty in accustoming themselves to such other northwestern Europeans as the Scandinavians and the Dutch. All these peoples, despite their initial difficulties, took on American ways without undue resistance. But Italians and Poles, Russians and Rumanians, Magyars and Bulgars, Czechs and Croats, Slovaks and Slovenes, Jews and Greeks seemed somehow vastly different. Instead of welcoming amalgamation they seemed almost to set themselves against it. Immigrants of a given language group tended to settle together in the cities, and to retain tenaciously their Old World language and customs. In every sizable city there was likely to be an Italian quarter, a Jewish quarter, a Russian quarter, a Polish quarter, and so on. In each such section the principal language spoken was not English, but the language of the immigrants. Signs over the stores reflected this difference, newspapers published in America but written in the Old World language were for sale in the streets, cities within cities were as numerous as the nationalities represented in the total population. Under these circumstances, how could the traditional process of amalgamation be maintained? How could these foreigners resident in America become truly Americans?

There were also the shocking living conditions that characterized the immigrant sections. For these conditions certainly the immigrants were not wholly to blame. The men who built the tenements, refused to repair them, and charged all the traffic would bear were for the most part not immigrants, but native Americans. Nor can the city governments that tolerated such housing conditions be cleared of responsibility. The low rewards of employment in America, not the wishes of the individuals concerned, drove the immigrants into this sordid way of life. With very few exceptions they had not lived so

in the Old World, but native Americans rarely seemed to understand. The immigrants, to hear their critics talk, had deliberately reproduced in American cities the same ideal breeding grounds for disease that characterized European slums. In the immigrant sections life expectancy was low and infant mortality was phenomenally high. But it was not this that so much troubled the native Americans; what worried them more was that epidemics might, and sometimes did, start in the immigrant sections, then spread to other parts of the city, and even into the country. The immigrants were held responsible, also, for much disorder and violence. They were guilty, no doubt, of a certain amount of drinking and gambling, the inevitable outlets of frustration and despair. But many of the crimes laid to their door were not of their doing. Organized gangs, sometimes with police protection, often used the densely populated immigrant districts as hideouts from which to operate, and for the misdeeds of such miscreants the immigrants might be unjustly accused.

The religions of the immigrants also came in for criticism. Great numbers of them were devout Roman Catholics, and there were always Protestants to express alarm at any increase in the Catholic population. Good Catholics among the immigrants naturally sent their children, when they could afford to do so, to parochial schools instead of to the public schools, and for this they could be denounced. How could they ever expect to be digested into the American population if they neglected the Americanizing influence of the public schools? Out in the agricultural Middle West, where cities were deemed evil anyway and now even more evil because of the coming of the immigrants, the American Protective Association, a secret anti-Catholic order, was formed in 1887 to strengthen the bulwarks of nativism against the foreign invaders; to be a good A.P.A. one must swear not to employ Catholics and not to vote for Catholics. The order spread from the country to the cities in the 1890's, and claimed a million members by 1896. It was probably responsible for such wild tales as that Catholics meant to overthrow the American government, and were collecting arms for the purpose in the basements of Catholic churches. At least, some A.P.A. chapters gave this as an excuse for themselves collecting arms. In the face of the more exciting silver issue of the nineties, however, the A.P.A., like the pre-Civil War Know-Nothings when confronted by the anti-slavery crusade, soon lost ground and disappeared. But the temporary popularity of the order revealed a spirit of reckless intolerance that made the immigrant a little sceptical of American boasts of freedom of religion.

Catholic immigrants were usually extremely devoted to the doctrines of their **The Catholics** church, and in no way desirous of deviating from them. But they often resented their dependence on English-speaking priests, and they were deeply disturbed to find American church practices so different in many little ways from those they had known in their homelands. Understandably enough, they longed for priests of their own nationality, and for the right to maintain their nationalistic peculiarities. Such a course generally met with determined opposition, even from the Irish clergy, who in their time had waged a somewhat similar but spectacularly successful campaign for recognition by the American Church. Sometimes the disgruntled representatives of separate nationalistic groups went so far as to set up independent establishments, although such experiments were rare and usually short-lived. A group of Ruthenians, the Uniat Catholics, finally broke from the Roman Church altogether, and went over to the Orthodox faith, the rites of which more closely resembled their own. For the most part the efforts of the immigrants to hold tenaciously to the old ways only added to their troubles. However much they might try they could not reproduce in the New World what they had left behind in the

Old, and their attempts to do so only added to their unpopularity.

The Roman Catholics were not the only religious group among the immigrants to be made keenly conscious of their **Lutherans and Orthodox Catholics** religious affiliations. The Lutherans, both Scandinavian and German, tended to lean toward the most orthodox opinions of their homelands. This was but natural; everything else was so different in America that they would lean over backwards to keep religion just the same if they could. This meant, among other things, that each national group was likely to hold apart from other Lutherans; also, since in the New World the Lutheran clergy grew even more disputatious than in the Old, the number of separate "synods" was multiplied inordinately. The Lutherans aroused the suspicions of other Protestants by holding services in their native languages, by having images, just as the Catholics did, in their churches, and by sending their children, whenever possible, to their own parochial schools, schools which were often conducted in a foreign language. Then there were the Orthodox Catholics from eastern Europe and the Balkans, with practices that seemed particularly foreign to the Americans. The onion-shaped towers of their churches and the ornate robes of their bewhiskered clergy were a far cry from anything the native American sects had produced.

Most strikingly different of all were the Jews. There had been Jews in America from the very beginning, but **The Jews** never before in such numbers. The total Jewish population of the United States in 1840 had been about 15,000, but by 1880 it was no less than 250,000. At the latter date most American Jews had come from Germany, but thereafter the overwhelming majority came from Russia, or from the nations of eastern Europe adjacent to Russia; aided by this influx, the Jewish population of the country had increased by 1927 to about four millions. The earlier Jewish immigrants and their descendants tended in general to discard many of the old ways, and to participate in a reform movement that left them not far removed in belief and practice from the Unitarians; but those who came later were slower to compromise with the new environment and retained for a long time in their homes and synagogues the traditional Jewish rites and practices. In America, as in Europe, the Jews tended to be town- or city-dwellers and often tradesmen; as such, they were naturally objects of suspicion; they suffered from prejudices that were rife in the Old World and were easily communicated to the New. They spoke, or learned to speak, Yiddish; they published newspapers in that language; they lived apart from other immigrants in ghettos; they sent their children to the public schools, but after hours to their own schools to learn Hebrew; they ate different foods; they had a different look. Soon New York City alone had a million Jews, the largest Jewish city in the world. Actually, the Jews made the adjustment to New World conditions better than most immigrant groups, but they found to their sorrow that they had not left anti-Semitism behind. It pervaded every aspect of their lives in America hardly less, they sometimes thought, than in Europe.

Native Americans made a great to-do about the danger to the American system of **Critics of the immigrants** government from the untutored immigrants. It is true that the newcomers, desperately poor and in need of economic security, did indeed tend to fall in with the wishes of corrupt city machines. This happened in spite of the many mutual aid societies and associations through which they themselves tried hard to look out for each other during such unescapable emergencies as sickness and death; but the politicians could also help, and the immigrants were in no position to reject aid from any source. Jobs were an essential, however tedious and soul-searing the work, and the local party leader had some unexplained influence with contractors, especially those who were working on public projects of one kind or another. He could dispense other favors also. If a man found himself or a member of his family in trouble with the law, the party leader could fix it. If he had to have a little cash, the party leader might lend him the money. If Christmas gifts for the children were sparse, at least one could count on a basket from party headquarters. It followed naturally that one voted as the party leader said he should. The city machines might wax fat on the graft they collected in return, but to the immigrant the bargain seemed good. As for honesty in government, he had had little experience with that in the Old Country, and even when he suspected the truth about conditions in the New, he was not much shocked. To reformers this situation seemed unspeakably bad. The fault was not with the immigrant, but with those who exploited his needs, yet the immigrant got the blame.

It might be reasonable to suppose that all labor would stand together, and that the rights of the immigrant workers **Labor and** would be no less sacred to the **the** labor leaders than the rights of **immigrant** native Americans. But for a long time this was not the case. The trouble was that the coming of so many immigrants built up the labor supply to such an extent that employers could, and did, keep wages down. Strikes proved unavailing when the jobs of the strikers could readily be filled by immigrants; sometimes, indeed, immigrants were brought into the country with this very end in view. Unable to speak or read the English language, the strike-breakers were immune from labor propaganda, while wages that seemed low to the native workers seemed high enough to them. Labor unions, earnestly seeking to obtain higher wages, shorter hours, and better working conditions for their members saw in the great horde of immigrants their greatest menace. Skilled workmen among the immigrants, however, tended eventually to achieve membership in the unions, and in time the foreign element began to play an important part in the labor world. Rightly or wrongly, the foreigners were credited with encouraging the use of violence in labor dis-

The melting pot of America was well realized by the laboring man and well illustrated in John George Brown's oil painting, *The Longshoremen's Noon*, 1869.

putes, and with advocating such Old World doctrines as socialism or even anarchism. In general this charge was false, although a noisy few among the immigrants did hold radical views, and by advocating them persistently they gave all the immigrants a black eye.

Not all the immigrants who came were Europeans. Many Canadians crossed to the United States, but in the case **Non-European immigrants** of English-speaking Canadians their presence was hardly noted. With the French Canadians, it was different. They spoke a foreign language, they were Roman Catholic in religion, and they readily became skilled workers. During the last three decades of the nineteenth century they came in prodigious numbers to the mill-towns of New England, sometimes with the deliberate encouragement of the mill owners, who used them to break strikes and beat down wages. By 1900 there were 134,000 of them in Massachusetts alone, one-sixth the population of the state, and the proportions in the other New England states were not far behind. Even the Far West had its serious immigrant problem. The Mexican immigrant was primarily a phenomenon of the twentieth century, but the Chinese had entered Pacific ports during gold rush days, and had kept on coming for many years thereafter. At first

their labor was welcomed, particularly for the building of the western railroads, but by the depression years of the seventies, with thousands of whites out of work, it was a different story.[1] Even in the East there was occasion to fear the results of cheap Chinese labor. On at least two occasions, once at North Adams, Massachusetts, in 1870, and once at Beaver Falls, Pennsylvania, in 1877, Chinese coolies were used as strike-breakers.

The build-up in favor of immigration restriction grew with the immigrant tide, and by the end of the nineteenth century it had reached formid- **Demands for restriction** able proportions. The strangeness of the immigrants, their foreign accents, their religious idiosyncracies, their attitudes toward government, their competition in the labor market, all were held against them. Immigrants who had arrived earlier even deplored the coming of those who arrived later. Finley Peter Dunne's Mr. Dooley made this point crystal clear: "As a pilgrim father that missed th' first boats, I must raise me Claryon voice again' th' invasion iv this fair land be th' paupers an' arnychists iv effete Europe. Ye bet I must — because I'm here first." An initial, but not very important, step in the direction of restriction was taken in 1868, with the repeal of the

[1] See pp. 174–175.

law passed four years before to legalize the importation of labor under contract. But the first really significant triumph of the restrictionists came primarily in response to the insistent demand of the Pacific Coast for Chinese exclusion. In 1879 Congress sought to pass a law that would prohibit any ship from bringing to the United States on a single voyage more than fifteen Chinese passengers. This measure was obviously meant to stop the stream of Chinese migration across the Pacific, and was generally regarded as desirable. But unfortunately the United States had signed a treaty with China in 1868, the Burlingame Treaty, that gave the two powers mutual rights of immigration and emigration. While action by a single state would have no effect on such a treaty, and the efforts of California in this direction thus proved unavailing, a law of Congress, passed subsequent to its negotiation, would nullify it. Should the United States so insult a friendly power? President Hayes thought not, and votes enough to override his veto were not forthcoming. The remedy, he maintained, lay in negotiations with China, not in the passing of a law. Hayes's unpopularity on the Coast as a result of this veto was intense, although he promptly dispatched a commission to China to secure a change in the offensive treaty. Ultimately, the Chinese government agreed to give the United States the right to "regulate, limit or suspend but not absolutely prohibit" the immigration of Chinese laborers, and in 1882 a Chinese Exclusion Act, based on this principle, went into effect.

The demand for federal supervision of immigration, if not for outright restriction,

Legislation on immigration had by this time grown to such proportions that a general immigration law could be passed. An act of August 3, 1882, placed a tax of fifty cents per head[1] on immigrants brought into the United States by water transportation, the tax to be paid by the carrier, and to be used to defray the expenses of the immigra-

[1] This tax was raised to $1 in 1894, to $2 in 1903, to $4 in 1907, and to $8 in 1917.

tion service. This service was set up in the Treasury Department, the general catch-all for federal administrative agencies, but the Secretary of the Treasury was authorized to cooperate in the enforcement of the regulations with such state immigration boards and authorities as might exist. As a matter of fact, these state agencies, although handicapped by unfavorable judicial decisions, furnished prior to this time whatever immigrant service there was, and even after the passage of the law they still continued to do most of the work. Idiots, lunatics, persons who were likely to become public charges, and convicts, except those who were guilty only of political crimes, were specifically excluded. Steamship companies found guilty of bringing such immigrants to the United States were required to take them back again free of charge. More important still was a law of 1885 which specifically prohibited the importation of immigrants under contract. The law of 1864, which had authorized and even facilitated this practice, had been repealed in 1868, but it was well known that the practice had continued. The new law was specific enough, although the machinery for its enforcement was defective. An act of 1891, however, created at last the office of "superintendent of immigration," and made possible the establishment of a federal Bureau of Immigration through which the restrictive laws could be enforced. The new law added to the proscribed lists prostitutes, polygamists, and persons suffering from certain types of diseases; it also prohibited under penalty of fine those found guilty of recruiting foreign laborers by advertising or solicitation.

For the most part the restrictions that were provided for in these acts were reasonable, and ran equally against all **The literacy test** nationals. Demands that legislation be devised to discriminate against immigrants coming from southern and eastern Europe were sufficiently insistent, however, that during the 1890's Henry Cabot Lodge, first as a member of the national House of Representatives and later as a

United States Senator, took the lead in advocating a literacy test to be given to all prospective immigrants. According to a bill he introduced in 1896, only those who could read and write either their own or some other language might be admitted. The test, he stated frankly, would "bear most heavily upon the Italians, Russians, Poles, Hungarians, Greeks, and Asiatics, and very lightly, or not at all, upon English-speaking immigrants or Germans, Scandinavians and French." In his opinion, "the mental and moral qualities which make what we call our race" could be preserved only by excluding "the wholesale infusion of races whose traditions and inheritances, whose thoughts and beliefs are wholly alien to ours and with whom we have never assimilated or even been associated in the past." Lodge's measure won a majority in both houses of Congress, but was vetoed by President Cleveland two days before he left office. Cleveland argued cogently that the test proposed was not a test of ability, but only a test of opportunity; it might keep out many who were desirable, and admit many who were not. Similar measures were vetoed later by Presidents Taft and Wilson, but in 1917, during the excitement attendant upon the First World War, the literacy test became a law in spite of a second veto by Wilson. Then, shortly after the war ended, Congress adopted a policy of virtual exclusion.[1]

The process of assimilation Wanted or unwanted, most of the immigrants who came to America stayed on to adjust themselves as best they could to the new environment. Some did return, a few whose nostalgia for their homelands drew them back, others who came to America to earn a stake, and had planned all along to return. But of the fourteen million immigrants who entered American ports between 1860 and 1900 an overwhelmingly large proportion never again set eyes on their native lands. Some of them did very well, in spite of the pitfalls of the new environment. Country-dwellers did best, for they were used to work-

[1] See pp. 482–483.

ing with the soil; many of them eventually owned fine farms. City immigrants sometimes emerged as successful shop-keepers and small merchants, as bosses of construction gangs, as policemen and politicians, as labor leaders. Some moved to the outskirts of the city in which they dwelt, and as truck gardeners eked out a precarious existence on what vacant tracts they could find. Most of them worked hard at becoming Americans. The older immigrants could not always master the language of their adopted land, but the younger ones learned it, and the children who were born of immigrant parents in America usually spoke it with only the accent of their locale, not with the accent of their nationality. Most of the children attended the American schools, and they learned much from them, although in the cities they found little that rang true in the McGuffey-type readers and the other texts they studied. The authors of these books had known only a rural-minded America, and had paid no heed to city dwellers. But the children of the immigrants at least learned to read and write and figure a little. It was easier for them than for their parents to "get on" in the world. Some of them even went on through high school and college to enter the professions. As for the grandchildren of the immigrants, anything might happen. They might, as so often had been the case with their grandparents, be living at the lowest margin of subsistence, or they might have climbed well toward the top of the social and economic ladder, or they might be anywhere in between.

New roots for old One of the greatest problems of the immigrants and their descendants was to strike down new cultural roots to replace those so rudely pulled up by removal to America. The original immigrants held on to their Old World language because they could not help themselves, and taught it to their children. Naturally they tried to do the same with such Old World customs as they could transplant. But they found their children increasingly unwilling to do anything that might set them apart from other Americans; and their grandchildren even rebelled at learning the Old World language. In their haste to become Americans too many descendants of immigrants thus put aside their Old World culture before they were able really to replace it with a New World equivalent. This left them dangerously adrift from their moorings. As Carl Wittke so aptly has said: "The man with two cultural homes is much less to be feared than the man who has none at all." Fortunately, as time went on, each immigrant group tended to recover its interest in its natural origins, and to value its contribution as a nationality to American society. Filiopietistic historians often went too far in their claims, but their activities registered an important step in advance. The Old World connection was not something to be ashamed of; rather, it was something in which one could legitimately take great pride. It is perhaps still too early to evaluate with any great degree of accuracy what the new immigration has done for the United States, but it has undoubtedly left many permanent marks — on how Americans live and think, on their interest in music and the arts, on their agricultural, business, and manufacturing habits, on American literature, law, and politics. There would be few now to deny that the immigrants had the right to say:

> We came not empty-handed here
> But brought a rich inheritance.

Bibliography

The saga of the immigrant in America has attracted much attention, but the exploitation of this theme by historians is still far from complete. Oscar Handlin, *The Uprooted* (1951), an almost lyrical account of immigration written from the immigrant's point of view, is an illuminating study in its own right, but is no doubt a pre-view of more to come from Handlin's pen on the same subject. The most comprehensive volume on immigration is Carl Wittke, *We Who Built America* (1939), which follows through separately the experiences and contributions of each nationality. George M. Stephenson, *A History of American Immigration, 1820-1924* (1926), is also a convenient summary. Marcus Lee Hansen, *The Immigrant in American History* (1940), is more interpretative than factual, and points the way to further study of the subject. On earlier aspects of immigration, by the same author, *The Atlantic Migration, 1607-1860* (1940), is admirable, especially on the motives that led to emigration from the Old World. John R. Commons, *Races and Immigrants in America* (1907, rev. ed., 1920), is a pioneer work that has not been entirely superseded. The adjustment of the immigrant to American conditions is treated in J. W. Jenks and W. J. Lauck, *The Immigration Problem* (1912, new ed., 1926). S. P. Orth, *Our Foreigners* (1920), and William B. Seabrook, *These Foreigners* (1938), are more popular than scholarly. M. R. Davie, *World Immigration with Special Reference to the United States* (1936), contains an excellent bibliography and is otherwise useful. See also, Edith Abbott, *Historical Aspects of the Immigration Problem: Select Documents* (1926).

The various national groups have nearly all found their historians. Naturally, the peoples of northern and western Europe have attracted the most attention. The best work on the Irish, W. F. Adams, *Ireland and Irish Emigration to the New World from 1815 to the Famine* (1932), unfortunately does not cover later phases of the subject. Outdated and excessively filiopietistic is A. B. Faust, *The German Element in the United States* (2 vols., 1909; 1 vol., 1927). Much more modern and scholarly is T. C. Blegen, *Norwegian Migration to America* (2 vols., 1931–1940). Also of merit are C. C. Qualey, *Norwegian Settlement in the United States* (1938); Kendric C. Babcock, *The Scandinavian Element in the United States* (1914); John S. Lindberg, *The Background of Swedish Emigration to the United States* (1930); Florence E. Janson, *The Background of Swedish Immigration, 1840-1930* (1931).

On the immigrants from eastern Europe, Emily Greene Balch, *Our Slavic Fellow Citizens* (1910), covers, perhaps, a too extensive area, but may be supplemented by such books as Jerome Davis, *The Russian Immigrant* (1922); Thomas Capek, *The Czechs in America* (1920); D. A. Souders, *The Magyars in America* (1922); William I. Thomas and Florian Znaniecki, *The Polish Peasant in Europe and America* (5 vols., 1918–1920). There are a number of excellent studies of the Jewish immigrants, the best, perhaps, being Samuel Joseph, *Jewish Immigration to the United States from 1881 to 1910* (1914); but see also, *The Russian Jew in the United States*, edited by Charles S. Bernheimer (1905); Burton J. Hendrick, *The Jews in America* (1923); Beatrice C. Baskerville, *The Polish Jew* (1906); and Oscar and Mary W. Handlin, "A Century of Jewish Immigration to the United States," *American Jewish Yearbook*, 1948–49, pp. 1–85.

On the southern Europeans there are several competent studies: Robert F. Foerster, *The Italian Emigration of Our Times* (1919); Philip M. Rose, *The Italians in America* (1922); Henry P. Fairchild, *Greek Immigration to the United States* (1911); J. P. Xenides, *The Greeks in America* (1922).

The Chinese migration to the Pacific Coast furnishes a much more difficult subject for historical investigation. The best general studies are Coolidge, *Chinese Immigration*, already cited; and much older, but still useful, George F. Seward, *Chinese Immigration in Its Social and Economical Aspects* (1881). On the legal and economic status of the Chinese in America, E. G. Mears, *Resident Orientals on the American Pacific Coast* (1927), is essential.

Among the many useful special studies that have to do with immigration are the following: Darrell H. Smith and H. Guy Herring, *The Bureau of Immigration* (1924); Oscar Handlin, *Boston's Immigrants, 1790–1865* (1941); Marcus L. Hansen and J. B. Brebner, *The Mingling of the Canadian and American Peoples* (1940); G. M. Stephenson, *The Religious Aspects of Swedish Immigration* (1932); Isaac A. Hourwich, *Immigration and Labor* (1912); Herman Feldman, *Racial Factors in American Industry* (1931); Edward A. Steiner, *On the Trail of the Immigrant* (1906); Roy L. Garis, *Immigration Restriction* (1927); *Immigration and Americanization*, ed. by Philip Davis (1920); Humphrey J. Desmond, *The A. P. A. Movement* (1912); Lee J. Levinger, *The Causes of Anti-Semitism in the United States* (1925); Carey McWilliams, *A Mask for Privilege: Anti-Semitism in the United States* (1948); and Louis Adamic, *A Nation of Nations* (1945).

11

The Revolt of the Farmer

The revolution in agriculture — The agricultural South — Tenancy — Plight of the share-cropper — The New West — The railroads — The western boom — Drouth — "End of free land" — Common interests of West and South — The Farmers' Alliances — Third-party movements — Elections of 1890 — The People's Party — Election of 1892

AGRICULTURE, like industry, underwent a notable revolution during the middle decades **The revolution in agriculture** of the nineteenth century, and for closely analogous reasons. The railroads made possible the shipment of the farmers' produce far greater distances than ever before; the invention of new agricultural machinery tended to turn each farm from a self-sustaining unit into a kind of factory, the chief purpose of which was to produce a few staple products for an outside market; and the increase in the nation's population, particularly by the growth of urban centers, accelerated prodigiously the demand for what the farmer had to sell. In addition, the opening of the western half of the continent greatly widened the agricultural horizon. It is easy, especially for easterners, to overlook the fact that fully half the geographic area of the United States lies west of the bend of the Missouri, and that in the main the settlement of this region was a post-Civil War phenomenon. Not nearly all of the land of the farther West could be utilized for farming, for much of it was mountains or desert, but between better farming methods and the aid of irrigation a tremendous new acreage was opened up. Indeed, most of the great mineral empire of the Rockies produced more wealth from the products of the farm and ranch than from the products of the mine. Furthermore, the existence of a semi-tropical climate in the Southwest made possible the introduction of many new crops, such as citrus fruits, nuts, and vegetables for out-of-season sale.

The agricultural revolution began well before the Civil War, and like the changes in industry served the North during that struggle far better than it served the South.[1] Northern wheat, produced in the Middle West with the aid of the new machines, and shipped to eastern ports by rail for transport overseas, redressed the unfavorable balance of trade, and kept British sympathy for the South under control. After the war, the foreign demand continued, especially while the Bismarckian wars interfered with the normal productivity of western and central Europe; and the home demand also grew. During these years certain spheres of interest began to mark themselves out. The Upper Mississippi Valley produced wheat and other small grain in great quantity, but with a clearly discernible tendency for farmers in the newly opened areas to concentrate especially on wheat. South of the wheat-producing area, and extending into the west as far as rainfall would permit, lay the corn belt. Corn, being a heavy crop unsuitable for distant shipment, was fed to livestock on the better farms, and the livestock shipped to

[1] Hicks, *The Federal Union* (2d ed., 1952), 515–517, 596–598.

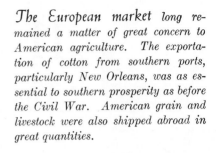

The European market long remained a matter of great concern to American agriculture. The exportation of cotton from southern ports, particularly New Orleans, was as essential to southern prosperity as before the Civil War. American grain and livestock were also shipped abroad in great quantities.

COTTON. Scene on the Levee, New Orleans. Currier & Ives lithograph, 1884.

GRAIN EXPORT. Elevator transferring grain from a canal-boat to a European steamer. *Leslie's Illustrated Newspaper,* 1874.

AMERICAN BEEF FOR ENGLISH MARKETS. Engraving after a drawing by I. Pranishnikoff, *Harper's Weekly,* 1879.

market; but there were corn farmers who did little else than grow corn for sale, year after year, on the same fertile land. Farm machines were powered almost exclusively during the nineteenth century by horses and mules, so pastures had to be provided, hay and oats grown and harvested, barns and stables maintained. In areas close enough to city markets dairy farming prospered, and the thrifty farm wife anywhere was likely to do a good side business with butter, eggs, and poultry. Eastern farmers found the competition of western agriculture hard to handle; whole great areas of eastern land, worn out by constant cropping, were abandoned altogether and allowed to grow up to "weed trees." Many eastern farmers joined the procession to the West to open up new farms; many left the farm for a job in the city; many took refuge in dairying and in keeping up with the insatiable demand of the cities for market gardening. Always the eastern farmer, however, if he had good land and could produce good crops, had the advantage of a nearby market, whereas the western farmer, as a rule, had to sell at a distance. The South, after as before the Civil War, was still dominantly agricultural, and devoted itself primarily to the production of two staple crops, cotton and tobacco.

Production for sale meant that farmers of the new era had to buy from outsiders many **Production for sale** of the items they formerly had obtained on their own farms through their own efforts. They no longer exchanged wheat for flour at the local mill, but sold their wheat for cash and purchased flour and groceries at some country or village store. They no longer thought of tanning leather and making their own boots or shoes; they could buy far more satisfactory foot gear from the stores. Farm women no longer devoted themselves to spinning and weaving and the fashioning of garments from home-made cloth; instead, they bought fabrics from the stores, and especially for the use of the men, even ready-made clothing. Farm machinery, fencing, windmills, sometimes even fuel were regular charges on the farmers' budgets. The farmer had thus become a capitalist and a businessman.

Except in certain parts of the South, he owned, or hoped to own, his farm, his livestock, and the machinery by means of which he produced the goods he must sell to live. His chronic complaint was that he set no prices. Those to whom he sold set the prices on what he had to sell; those from whom he bought set the prices on what he had to buy. Nevertheless, his way of life was far removed from that of his ancestors who had engaged in subsistence farming. As William Jennings Bryan put it, he was "as much a business man as the man who goes upon the Board of Trade and bets upon the price of grain."

For all the vast transformation wrought by industrialism in southern life, far more southerners were engaged in agriculture than in any other **The agricultural South** occupation, while most of the business and professional classes were dependent upon farm income for their support. The New South, like the Old, had few large cities, and its annual output of manufactured goods actually accounted for only about one eighth of the nation's total output. Southern cotton

Citrus fruit grew well in the semi-tropical climate of the southernmost parts of the United States. The illustration, a grove in Florida, is from sketches by C. Upham, *Leslie's Illustrated Newspaper*, 1883.

was still grown after much the same fashion, by nearly the same types of laborers, in approximately the same regions as before the war. The yield had steadily increased. By 1894 the production of cotton in the South exceeded ten million bales, nearly twice that of the pre-war years. Much the same could be said of tobacco, sugar-cane, cereals, and livestock, but if the total produce of the South had increased, so also had its population. For the great majority of the southern people, the industrial frenzy of the New South was of no direct or immediate consequence.

The southern farmer, whether white or black, had little of the restless energy that had characterized the pioneer farmer of the North. The climate was easy, survival after some fashion was reasonably well assured, and with farm prices ever falling the reward of ambition was slight. The rural South also suffered acutely from disease. The hookworm, an intestinal parasite common to most warm countries, was probably brought to the South by the Negroes, but it was far less disastrous in its effects upon them than upon the whites. Fortunately the disease it breeds yields easily to medical treatment, and in the twentieth century the Rockefeller Foundation, after a persistent and expensive campaign, succeeded in almost entirely eradicating it. In the nineteenth century, however, it was still sapping the vitality of a countless number of the lower classes; as was also the pellagra, a disease that resulted from their too restricted diet. The Negroes, especially after they had escaped from the care and supervision of their masters, showed themselves to be particularly susceptible to pulmonary diseases and tuberculosis. Physical unfitness was thus by no means least among the reasons for the backwardness of the rural South.

Seventy per cent of the farmers of the South, a generation after Appomattox, were tenants. The Negroes, starting as ex-slaves with nothing but their labor to sell, could hardly have been expected to do better; but they had made

Tenancy

almost as much progress toward individual ownership as the lower-class southern whites. For both races the tenant system, once it was well established, tended to become self-perpetuating. In general there were three types of tenants in the South: (1) the cash tenant, who paid rent in money or a specified number of bales of cotton, and was otherwise no different from a landowner; (2) the share tenant, who in lieu of rent paid for the use of his land from one fourth to one third of his crop, but furnished his own stock, tools, and foodstuffs; and (3) the share-cropper, who paid a larger proportion of his crop to his landlord, but furnished nothing whatever for himself. Some of the cash and share tenants, who were usually white, were fairly thrifty; the "croppers," on the other hand, among whom most of the country Negroes were numbered, were barely one degree removed from slavery.

One of the many unhappy results of the Civil War, and an important cause of southern tenancy, was the inadequate credit system from which the South long suffered. After the war the national banking system advanced so slowly into the impoverished South that by 1895 the ten cotton states had only four hundred and seventeen national banks among them, and of these more than one half were located in Texas. The dearth of local capital kept down likewise the number of state and private banking institutions; in Georgia, for example, more than a hundred counties lacked banking facilities altogether. Such money as was available for loans went in a disproportionate amount to industry rather than to agriculture; money to lend to farmers, even land-owners, was simply not available. Faced by these circumstances the South developed a unique institution, the country store. Such a store was not necessarily located in the country; it took its name from the fact that it catered to the country trade. The country storekeeper did not expect to sell for cash, for most of the country people had no cash. He sold on credit, and to insure himself against loss took a lien on

The crop-lien system

the farmer's crop and, if possible, a chattel mortgage also. If the farmer chanced to be a tenant, as might normally be expected, then the merchant's lien was taken only on the tenant's share of the crop. Landlords sometimes attempted to supervise these contracts, but the competition for tenants was so keen that independent crop liens to the storekeeper were generally the privilege of the humblest sharecropper. The storekeeper for his own credit needs was often compelled to rely in large part upon advances from cotton-buyers, whom he would pay off ultimately not in cash but in cotton.

While the landlord from whom the tenant rented his land and the storekeeper from whom he bought his goods were likely in the years immediately following the war to be two different persons, they tended as time went on to become one and the same person. Landlords themselves sometimes moved to town and went into the store business, not only for the profit involved, but also as a means of insuring that too much of their tenants' produce was not used up in trade. Merchants, at the same time, purchased land, or more likely took it over from unsuccessful landlords on mortgages. In general the merchant-landlord who lived in town and made only occasional tours of inspection into the country was preferred by the tenant over the landlord-neighbor, with his constantly exhibited interest in the tenants' industry. To the easy-going sharecropper of the South, absentee landlordism was regarded as a blessing rather than a curse.

Legal sanction for the crop-lien system was readily provided by the "Bourbon" legislators of the post-reconstruction South. To the merchant, in return for the promise of a year's supply of necessities in advance, the farmer was permitted to sign over title to as much of his future crop as might be necessary to settle his store bill. Furthermore, in case his purchases during the year exceeded the amount he was able to pay he was legally bound to trade the next year with the same merchant, or, as was so often the case, the

Plight of the share- cropper

same merchant-landlord, with whom he had contracted the previous year, and to whom he still owed money. Thus the way was opened for the establishment of a system of virtual peonage, for the number of farmers who could so plan their expenditures as to break even at the end of the year was few indeed. For many of them, the only means of escape from this new bondage was flight to a community so far distant that the law would not be likely to follow them.

The plight of the farmer who found himself ensnared by the crop-lien system was always hard. He might not purchase more goods than the merchant thought he needed; he must pay whatever prices the merchant asked, usually not less than double the prices asked of cash customers; he had little or no recourse against the merchant who chose to cheat him. Fully convinced of the hopelessness of his situation, the ordinary sharecropper rarely tried seriously to get cash ahead; if he raised more cotton than he needed to pay his store bill, he frequently picked only enough to discharge his obligation and left the rest unharvested. But the merchant, for all his long profits, had no sure road to wealth. A season of crop failures or low prices, when matched by the all too characteristic shiftlessness, illnesses, and jail sentences among his customers, might mean that the merchant would receive for his heavy outlays next to nothing in return. Storekeepers occasionally became rich, but they also more than occasionally went bankrupt.

In much of the lower South a tragic accompaniment of the crop-lien system was the one-crop evil, for merchants in the cotton-growing areas strongly preferred that their credit-customers plant cotton to the exclusion of other crops. Cotton could always be marketed at some price; it did not deteriorate with age; it could not, like corn, for example, be fed to livestock or consumed as "roasting-ears" by the farm family; its value in comparison to its bulk made it easy to handle. Furthermore, the farmer who raised cotton only was

The one- crop evil

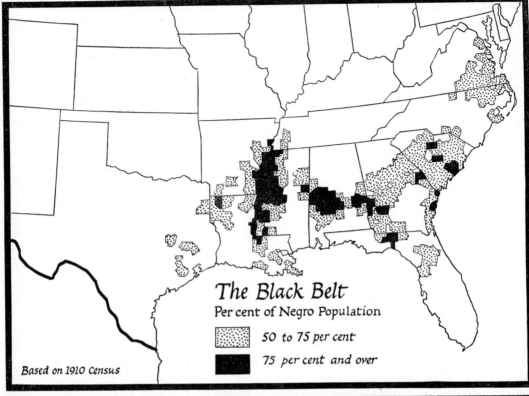

The Black Belt
Per cent of Negro Population

50 to 75 per cent

75 per cent and over

Based on 1910 Census

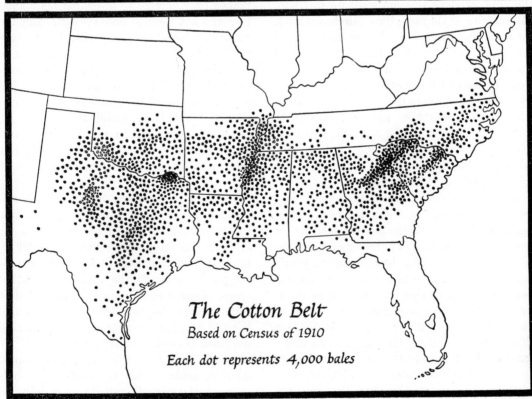

The Cotton Belt
Based on Census of 1910

Each dot represents 4,000 bales

a far better customer than the farmer who supplied his table and fed his mule from his own garden and fields; all such supplies he had to purchase at the store, together with such quantities of fertilizer as were necessary to produce cotton on his worn-out soil. Merchants rarely admitted that these were the reasons which led them to insist on cotton-growing. The Negro farmer, they said, and many of the whites also, knew how to grow cotton, and but little else; if permitted to try other crops, the returns were sure to be meager. Nor did the cotton-growers show much interest in emancipating themselves from the one-crop system. "Cotton-planting has been a mania," wrote one observer. "The neglected cornfield with all its consequences is a part of Southern history."

The one-party system which the reconstruction period had left as a legacy to the **The one-party system** South made it extremely difficult for the farmers of that section, whether black or white, to seek through political action the amelioration of their ills. The blacks were virtually disfranchised, and, because of the peculiar distribution of the white population, the power of the lower-class rural whites in politics was far less than their numbers would have justified. The best cotton lands lay along the river valleys and close to the sea, precisely the same lands that had grown the cotton of the prewar plantation South. Here the Negroes were concentrated, no longer as slaves but as tenants of a favored few of the whites. In these "black belts" the landlords and the merchants, supported by the votes of the townspeople, not only ruled supreme over a population predominantly Negro and non-voting, but exercised also a disproportionate influence in the politics of any given state. Since the assignment of membership in the legislature and of delegates in nominating conventions was according to population, the representatives of the "black counties" could practically always outvote the representatives of the "white counties." And, since white solidarity demanded unfailing support of whatever Democratic candi-

dates were nominated, the "Bourbons" of the "black belt," eager servants of the industrialists, the landlords, and the merchants, maintained their uninterrupted sway. Hardly less than before the Civil War the South remained in the hands of a favored ruling caste. Discontent with such a system, followed by an open revolt against it, was sure to come.

During the same period that the New South was emerging from the rigors of reconstruction, another New West **The New West** was also taking form. Its beginnings, with miners, cattlemen, and farmers contesting with the Indians and with each other for the advantages it offered, have already been traced.[1] Its oldest section, in point of settlement, was adjacent to the Pacific Coast, where California, Oregon, and Nevada had all achieved statehood before or during the Civil War, with Washington and Idaho lagging behind as territories. To the south lay New Mexico and Arizona, territories with a considerable Spanish-speaking population whose culture merged only slowly with that of the increasingly numerous Anglo-Americans. In the center the Mormon territory of Utah grew and prospered to the everlasting chagrin of its critics, who were outraged at the Mormon practice of polygamy and tried in vain to stop it by federal legislation. To the east, stretching from the bend of the Missouri to the Rockies, was a vast and largely arable plain, sometimes called the "Middle Border." It included Kansas, Nebraska, the Dakotas, and parts of Colorado, Wyoming, and Montana. Much of western Missouri, Iowa, and Minnesota was also newly settled, and belonged, at least in spirit, with the "Middle Border." The Indian Territory, from which whites were supposedly excluded, was nevertheless freely invaded by "Sooners," whose disregard of the law was more or less condoned. In 1889 the western end of the territory was officially opened to white settlement, and the next year, by act of Congress, it became a separate territory, Oklahoma.

[1] See p. 54 ff.

This great New West, with its infinite agricultural possibilities, was essentially the product of the railroads. Without them to bring in the population and to take out the produce, it could never have been. But the railroads were responsible for the development

The railroads and the West

Railroad advertisements, such as the one here reproduced, held out enticing terms to European emigrants. From the *Daily Champion*, 1867.

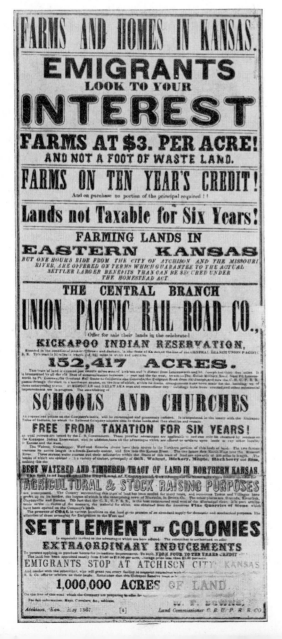

of this section in an even more literal sense, for they owned, advertised, and sold directly to settlers a good share of its lands. Only the great transcontinentals had received land grants directly from the United States, but many of the other roads had been recipients of state grants. Every land-grant railroad had at once set up a land department, and had begun an active campaign for settlers. Railroad agents, both in the United States and in Europe, distributed pamphlets which demolished the "myth" of the "Great American Desert," and proclaimed the boundless resources of the New West. Land was offered at prices as low as $2.50 per acre, and sometimes lower, with attractive credit features that stretched out almost indefinitely the period of payment. Land-seekers' excursion tickets were sold on the understanding that the price paid for the ticket might be counted as a down payment on any purchase of railroad land. Most railroads made little money out of the disposal of their lands. What they did, and what they meant to do, was to bring in the population and "build up" the country. Only by so doing could they hope for a volume of business adequate to maintain their lines; without people to pay freights and passenger fares a railroad could not long survive.

Indeed, the railroads did not much care whether the incoming settlers bought railroad land, or acquired lands from the government by purchase or homestead. In the numerous pamphlets that their land offices brought out they told settlers how to obtain land at minimum cost under the terms of the Homestead Act, the Pre-emption Act, and the Timber Culture Act.[1] For appropriate areas they set forth also how later land legislation had smoothed the way for settlers to acquire far more than the normal one hundred and sixty acre farm. Under the Desert Land Act of 1877, for example, which applied to eleven of the western states and territories, a person might buy an entire section of land — six hundred and forty acres — at the minimum price of $1.25 an acre, provided

[1] See p. 68.

WHEAT. Threshing by steam in the Red River Valley, Dakota Territory. Woodcut, 1878.

Western farming after the Civil War was increasingly mechanized and increasingly geared to a world market. The great wheat fields opened up along the frontier were made possible by new agricultural machinery and new transportation facilities. Most of what the farmer produced he expected to sell, not to consume. And the number of those who "farmed the farmers" increased amazingly.

THE LEAKY CONNECTION. Drains on profits benefited all but the farmers. Zimmerman in *Judge*, 1886.

GRAIN ELEVATORS. Duluth, Minnesota, the western tip of the Great Lakes, 1888.

that he would irrigate it within a period of three years after filing his claim. Only twenty-five cents an acre need be paid at the time of filing, and the rest when the proof of irrigation was submitted. Under the terms of this law many cattle and sheep ranchers got title to the land they needed for headquarters, and a few individuals, mostly speculators, opened up irrigation projects. Furthermore, under the Timber and Stone Act of 1878, an ambitious pioneer might purchase at not less than $2.50 an acre a quarter section of land valuable chiefly for timber and stone. As the railroad advertisers figured it, anyone with a little capital at his disposal could obtain in all two full sections of government land — 1280 acres — at an average cost per acre of $1.12½. Although the advertisers could not print such facts, it was also known to most Americans that the evasion of disagreeable requirements could easily be arranged.

The result of the railroad propaganda was such a wholesale migration of population as the nation had never known before. All the states and territories of the New West shared to some extent in the new growth, but the most amazing expansion occurred along the Middle Border where distances from older settled areas were least. Hard times in the East during the seventies led many of the discontented to try their luck in the West, but the good times of the eighties led even more to come.[1] The area of adequate rainfall seemed surely, if slowly, to be pushing farther and farther west. Grasshopper plagues, so destructive during the seventies, were not repeated in the eighties. With good crops western farmers prospered, or thought they prospered, even when the price of corn and wheat was low.

This rapid expansion of the western frontier would not have been possible, however, **Eastern credit to the West** without easy credit. The farmers who went into the new region rarely had enough capital to finance their venture, and many of them had almost nothing at all. The kind of farming

[1] See population table, Appendix, p. xvii.

that they wished to do, however, was expensive. They needed heavy breaking-plows to deal with the tough prairie sod, and high-priced oxen or horses to draw them. They needed planters, cultivators, mowing machines, reapers, and threshing machines. They needed houses and barns, cattle and hogs. For good or ill, the farmers of the western frontier, unlike the cotton growers of the South, could have what they wanted, or at least much that they wanted, on credit. Easterners with money to lend had a settled conviction that there was no security so safe as a western farm mortgage, and a long record of rising land values seemed to bear out their judgment. Interest rates were high. Farm mortgages brought from six to eight per cent, while loans secured by town property often brought even more. Chattel mortgages brought still higher interest rates, from ten to eighteen per cent and more. With plenty of eastern money to lend and plenty of western borrowers to borrow, the little banks of the West were unable to handle the traffic, and loan companies were organized to help them out. By 1890 Kansas statistics showed only 350 farms unmortgaged out of a total of 3107 that were tabulated, and the total mortgage indebtedness of the state was estimated at $146,563,000.

Western borrowing went much further than the mere outfitting of farmers. The new western communities made **The western boom** haste to reproduce as nearly as possible the conditions their citizens had been used to farther east. City dwellers went in for better homes and gardens. Counties needed and obtained courthouses and jails, roads and bridges. School districts put up school buildings, towns pledged their futures for city halls, waterworks, electric light plants, and, if they could find the slightest justification for it, streetcar systems as well. As the population increased, demands were voiced for more railroads, and companies to build them were promptly founded and financed. The newly settled region itself furnished for all this "development" next to nothing by way of capital, but the steady

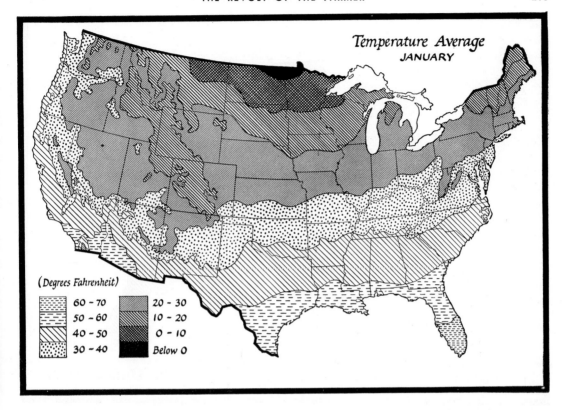

Temperature Average
JANUARY

(Degrees Fahrenheit)

60 – 70   20 – 30
50 – 60   10 – 20
40 – 50   0 – 10
30 – 40   Below 0

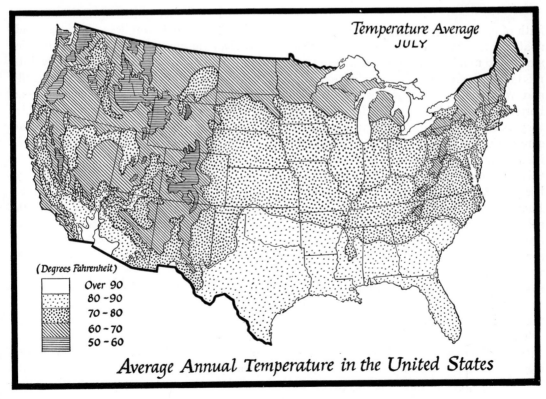

Temperature Average
JULY

(Degrees Fahrenheit)

Over 90
80 – 90
70 – 80
60 – 70
50 – 60

Average Annual Temperature in the United States

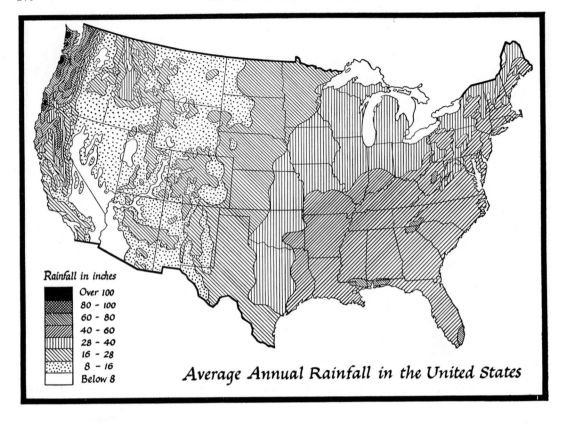

Rainfall in inches
Over 100
80 - 100
60 - 80
40 - 60
28 - 40
16 - 28
8 - 16
Below 8

Average Annual Rainfall in the United States

faith of eastern investors showed no signs of abatement. Western securities, railroad stocks and municipal bonds no less than farm mortgages, were regarded as "gilt-edged," and what the western pioneers wished to borrow they could have, provided only that they would promise high interest rates. So, sure of the future, they borrowed and promised. During the middle eighties, with all this easy credit, the whole Middle Border became the scene of a veritable "boom." Each sizable town was convinced that it was soon to become a metropolis. Around such strategic centers as Omaha, Yankton, Atchison, Topeka, and Kansas City new additions were plotted into lots that were sold, borrowed upon, and sold again, only to be returned in the end to the cornfields from which they had been taken.

The collapse of the western boom began with the summer of 1887, the first of a long **Collapse of** series of dry seasons. Time **the boom** proved that the myth of the

Great American Desert was no less groundless than the myth that the region of adequate rainfall was advancing steadily into the West. Settlers who had gone hopefully into western Dakota, Kansas, or Nebraska, and even out into eastern Montana or Colorado, learned to their sorrow that they had gone much too far.

Week after week [wrote one observer] the hot burning sun glared down from a cloudless steel-blue sky. The dread hot winds blew in from the south. Day after day they continued. All fodder, small grain and corn were cut short. Where farming had been carried on extensively rather than intensively the yield amounted to preciously near nothing. The careful expert got some returns for his work, though small.

The same covered wagons that had taken the settlers to the West were now turned toward the East, sometimes decorated with legends such as "Going home to the wife's folks," or "In God we trusted, in Kansas we busted," or

> Fifty miles to water,
> A hundred miles to wood,
> To hell with this damned country,
> I'm going home for good.

How many people left the drouth-stricken states during these hard years will never be known, but so many went that the census-takers of 1890 felt obliged to pad their records generously. It is not unlikely, however, that the New West had as many people in 1887 as the census claimed for 1890, and in some regions it probably had many more.

With the advent of the drouth, eastern moneylenders promptly changed their minds about the future of the West.

Drouth Not only was the flow of new money to the West abruptly stopped, but attempts to collect that which had already been lent became also more and more insistent. Foreclosures followed thick and fast. Hundreds of western bankers, unable to make collections, closed their doors. Loan companies disappeared overnight. As if to make the disaster doubly complete, farm prices showed a steadily declining curve, for the crop shortage of the New West, great as it was, failed to produce a similar shortage in the world market, or, for that matter, even in the United States. Moreover, the opportunity of flight to a new frontier, for generations the standard American formula for escape from economic distress, was no longer of much avail. The wholesale assault of railroads and individuals upon the lands of the West had all but used them up. The era of good cheap lands was coming to a close. Evidence of public alarm over this situation was not difficult to find. When, for example, a three million acre tract of former Indian land in what soon became Oklahoma was opened to homestead entry on April 22, 1889, the rush that ensued displayed all the violence of an explosion.

Whole outfits for towns, including portable houses, were shipped by rail, and individual families, in picturesque, primitive, white-covered

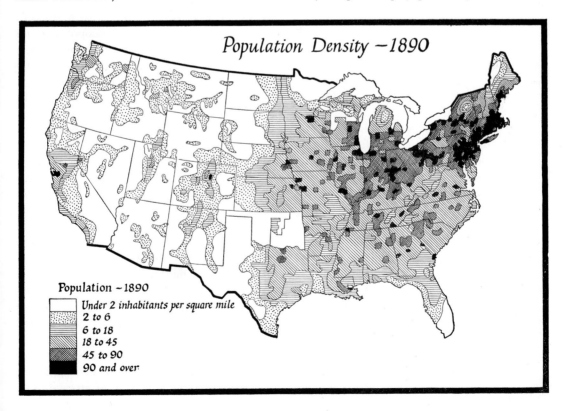

Population Density – 1890

Population – 1890
Under 2 inhabitants per square mile
2 to 6
6 to 18
18 to 45
45 to 90
90 and over

wagons, journeyed forward, stretching out for miles in an unbroken line.... The blast of a bugle at noon on a beautiful spring day was the signal for a wild rush across the borders. Men on horseback and on foot, in every conceivable vehicle, sought homes with the utmost speed, and before nightfall town sites were laid out for several thousand inhabitants each.

Fifty thousand people entered the region the first day, and the city of Guthrie achieved at one fell swoop a population of six thousand.

Commenting on the recklessness with which the government had squandered its resources in land, an indignant Nebraska editor complained:

Only a little while ago the people owned this princely domain. Now they are *starving for land* — starving for the right to create from the soil a subsistence for their wives and little children.... They would gladly buy land if they could. But the merciless contraction of money and fearful shrinkage of values and prices have put it out of their power to buy land, even though it may be offered at reduced prices. They want *free land* — the land that Congress squandered . . . the land that should have formed the patrimony of unborn generations.

The importance of the alienation of the national domain was not lost upon other and **The "end of** more sophisticated observers. **free land"** In 1887 Professor A. B. Hart of Harvard University published an article on "The Disposition of the Public Lands" in the first volume of the *Quarterly Journal of Economics,* and the year before Shosuke Sato, a Japanese student at Johns Hopkins University, had written a monograph on the *History of the Land Question in the United States.* The government, so these critics of its policy observed, had treated its lands as if the supply were inexhaustible, only to discover when it was too late that they were nearly gone. Of mountains and deserts and arid plains the government still possessed an abundance, but of lands suitable for the traditional types of agriculture perhaps less than two million acres remained. More philosophic than either Hart or Sato was Henry George, whose *Progress and Poverty* had ap-

peared in 1879. George's ideas, although actually published as early as 1871 in a forty-eight-page pamphlet, *Our Land and Land Policy,* and widely heralded abroad, were slow to attract attention in America. By the middle eighties, however, his writings were being extensively circulated on both sides of the Atlantic. "All who do not possess land," he argued, "are toiling for those who do, and this is the reason why progress and poverty go hand in hand." To remedy the situation there need be no redistribution of land. Instead, landowners should pay the equivalent of economic rent in taxation. From the proceeds of this "single tax" George believed that enough revenue would be realized to make possible the elimination of all other forms of taxation. Of particular interest to the agricultural classes was his assumption that growing crops, houses, and all other improvements upon the land should be exempted from taxation. With the abolition of customary taxes, because of which labor, capital, and enterprise alike were robbed, George held that economic laws would work with a smoothness never known before. Monopolies would disappear, wealth would be equitably shared, and the fear of recurring depressions would cease to be the nightmare of business.

Whether the reasoning of George was right or wrong, Americans of his generation felt that the "passing of free land" was an extremely serious matter. Probably they were wrong in their assumption that free land, up to their time, had been a perfect safety-valve for farmer and labor discontent. Only since the passage of the Homestead Act in 1862 had the government really given away land to settlers, and, as already noted, the policy of land sales had not even then been discontinued. As a matter of fact more free land was to be distributed in the twentieth century than in the nineteenth. It was not so much the high cost of land that hampered the pioneer as the high cost of farming with expensive machinery, the uncertainty of rainfall, and the low price of farm produce. Furthermore, the existence of free lands in

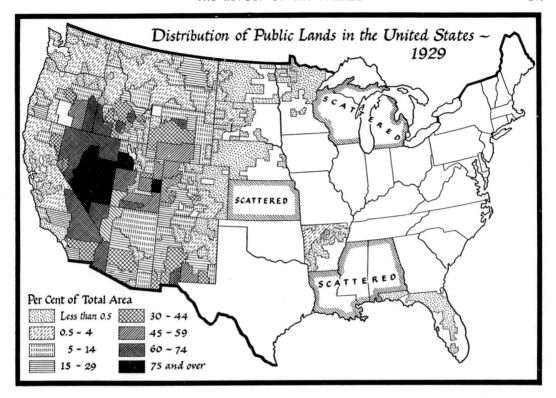

Distribution of Public Lands in the United States ~ 1929

SCATTERED

SCATTERED

SCATTERED

Per Cent of Total Area

Less than 0.5		30 ~ 44	
0.5 ~ 4		45 ~ 59	
5 ~ 14		60 ~ 74	
15 ~ 29		75 and over	

the West was always of uncertain benefit to laborers of the industrialized regions. Such lands might draw away farm families from regions adjacent to the factories, and so reduce the number of rural competitors for city jobs, but underpaid or unemployed laborers were rarely able to raise the funds necessary to transport themselves to the West to make a new start. The western settlements were mostly the work of men who had been farmers before, and of these the great majority came from near-by states. Nevertheless, the tradition persisted that the frontier should furnish a haven of refuge for all the distressed of the United States and of Europe, and information which tended to show that the West was no longer able to fulfill this rôle was received with deep apprehension. Someone was to blame. Denied the opportunity of flight to another frontier, and convinced that the ills from which they suffered were not of their own making, the farmers of the West and the farmers of the South were alike ripe for revolt.

In spite of their common problems, however, there were many obstacles in the way of the two sections working to- *Common* gether. The New West and the *interests of* New South had come into exis- *West and* tence while the rancors of recon- *South* struction were at their worst, and each had accepted as a matter of course the dominant sectional bias of the times. Many of the pioneers of the Middle Border had fought under Grant and Sherman; they were honored members of the Grand Army of the Republic; they had not yet forgiven the South for precipitating the Civil War. Likewise, the builders of the New South had marched with Lee and Johnston; they, too, had formed their military orders, only lately merged as the United Confederate Veterans; they held their tongues about the North, but thought what they had always thought. But even these historic political antagonisms could not prevent the development of a bond of sympathy between the impoverished farmers of the two sections. While industry flour-

ished, agriculture, whether western or southern, tended to languish. The downward
trend of cotton prices was matched only by
the downward trend of prices paid for wheat,
corn, and livestock. Railroads made money,
banks made money, factories made money;
but the farmers barely made a living, and
sometimes not even that. The suspicion
grew, in both the South and the West, that
some sinister force restrained agriculture,
while industry climbed steadily to the moun-
tain-tops of prosperity. Before the Civil
War the agricultural South and the agricultural West, to their own considerable advantage, had stood together and ruled the
country; now industry, with the forces of
agriculture divided and ignored, reigned supreme. Could the old agricultural alliance
be revived and the political advantages from
which industry had fattened be restrained?

Few people asked themselves that question
directly, but common grievances acted power-
fully to draw the farmers of the two sections
closer together. The western wheat-grower
who was convinced that, unless the price of
wheat was as much as a dollar a bushel, he
could not make money, talked the same language as the southern cotton-grower, who
held that any price less than ten cents a
pound for cotton meant disaster. The northern farm-owner who was chronically on the
verge of losing his property to the mortgage-
holder was only a trifle better off than the
southern tenant who each year turned over
his entire crop to the storekeeper, only to
learn, when the books were balanced, that he
was still in debt. The West had by far the
greater grievance against the railroads. The
railroads had built the West, but they had
built it for a price. Debts for lands purchased from them were hard to wipe out,
and the high cost of transporting bulky western crops to distant markets ate away an
alarming proportion of western farm receipts.
But the South, no less than the West, knew
how railroad companies watered their stock,
granted rebates, evaded taxation, bought
favors with free passes, and mixed business
with politics. Southern farmers, who sold

abroad and would have preferred to buy
cheap foreign manufactured goods in return,
could see more clearly the disadvantages of
the high-tariff system than the farmers of the
Northwest, but even the Westerners registered their objections to buying in a tariff-
protected market and selling against the
competition of the whole wide world. Both
sections recorded heated protests against the
tolls paid to trusts and middlemen, the high
taxes that for farmlands seemed inescapable,
and the steadily appreciating value of the
dollar. And, although the West knew it best,
both sections were seriously affected by the
fact that good cheap lands were rapidly disappearing. The prospect of a new alliance
between the dominantly agricultural sections
of the country was by no means an idle
dream.

Impressed with the occasional effectiveness
of labor unions and eager to win comparable
victories for agriculture, the **The Farmers'**
farmers of both sections began **Alliances**
to band themselves together into farm orders
of various names and natures. Most important of these organizations were two great
sectional "Alliances," the National Farmers'
Alliance representing the Northwest, and the
Farmers' Alliance and Industrial Union representing the South. Some of the smaller
orders, such as the Grange, which had lasted
on in spite of the collapse of the Granger
movement, the Farmers' Mutual Benefit
Association, and the Patrons of Industry,
continued to exist; others were absorbed into
one or the other of the two dominant organizations, which, commonly called the "Northern" or "Northwestern" Alliance and the
"Southern" Alliance, became the authorita-
tive spokesmen of agricultural discontent.

The Northern Alliance was founded in
1880 by Milton George, editor of the *Western
Rural*, a Chicago farm paper. George's paper
made a specialty of denouncing the railroads,
especially for the political favors they purchased by means of free passes, and the
"Farmers' Transportation Convention"
that George called together to launch the
Alliance, branded the order from its begin-

ning as an anti-railroad affair. Local alliances were multiplied throughout the Northwest, and, as soon as a state could count enough locals to warrant the step, a state alliance was formed. Each state alliance, as it gathered strength, tended to become autonomous, so that in the end the Northern Alliance turned out to be a loose confederation of state orders bound together by only the faintest of ties. The growth of the order was tremendously accelerated by the collapse of the western boom in 1887 and the hard times that followed. By 1890 it was fully organized in ten northwestern states, but the bulk of its strength lay in the wheat-raising sections of Kansas, Nebraska, the Dakotas, and Minnesota, where low prices, high freight-rates, oppressive mortgages, and, as a final crushing blow, the drouth had driven the long-suffering farmers to despair.

The origins of the Southern Alliance can be traced back to an organization that some frontier farmers in Lampasas County, Texas, formed in the middle seventies to catch horse-thieves, round up estrays, purchase supplies cooperatively, and defend their rights against land sharks and cattle kings. Armed with a pretentious secret ritual, the order expanded into a few neighboring counties, but mixed too freely in politics and died out. Revived at the close of the decade in Parker County, it kept clear of politics, and by 1885 it could claim fifty thousand members. Next year a new president, Doctor C. W. Macune, furnished the leadership necessary to make the Alliance a really important factor in the life of the South. Macune was a born promoter, and as president he dazzled his associates with the vision of transforming the Alliance into a money-saving business venture that every southern cotton-farmer would wish to join. Macune promptly established an Alliance Exchange through which the farmers of Texas were urged to buy and sell cooperatively, and, pointing to the temporary success of the Texas Exchange, he began to spread his gospel of business cooperation throughout the South. With amazing rapidity Macune's

organizers captured state after state. Sometimes they found local farm orders in operation and induced them to join forces with the Alliance; sometimes they had little to begin with but the presence of smouldering discontent. But invariably their doctrines won converts, and soon exchanges patterned after the Texas model appeared in nearly every southern state. Unlike the Northern Alliance, the Southern Alliance was a closely knit national organization in which the state alliances played definitely subordinate rôles. For Negro farmers a separate, but affiliated, Colored Alliance was established.

Circumstances conspired to drive both Alliances, contrary to their expressed intentions, into politics. The Northern Alliance, like the Southern Alliance, made numerous and sometimes successful ventures into cooperative buying and selling, and both orders earnestly stimulated among their members a wide variety of social and educational activities. But in spite of all such efforts farm prosperity failed to put in its appearance. More and more the conviction grew that the real trouble with agriculture lay in the unfair discriminations from which it suffered. Some sinister force restrained the farmers from the prosperity that their hard labor should have earned. The railroads, the bankers, the manufacturers, and the merchants were somehow robbing the farmers. Only through the power of government could these evil practices be brought to light and corrected, and to influence the government, whether in state or nation, political action was essential.

The Northern Alliance from its beginning had not hesitated to mix its business with politics. Northwestern Alliance men, on the assumption that what they did as individuals in no way involved the order to which they belonged, made it almost a point of honor to vote for farmers or farmer-minded politicians whenever opportunity offered. Through farmer-controlled legislatures they secured laws to insure the fair grading of grain, to impede the foreclosure of mortgages, and to

The Alliance in politics

Farmer leaders included Ignatius Donnelly of Minnesota, a notably gifted orator and literary light, and James B. Weaver of Iowa, a resourceful politician who had fought creditably in the Civil War. From steel engravings.

curb the unfair practices of railroads. Most of this legislation, however, failed of its purpose, whether because of the indifference of administrative officials, the hostility of the courts, or the inability of state laws to deal effectively with nation-wide problems. By the year 1890, with the pressure of hard times growing ever more acute, most western Alliance men were convinced that the only hope of the farmers lay in turning their organization into an out-and-out political party — a party which, at first in the states, and later in the nation, could drive both of the older parties from power. Accordingly, third-party tickets were nominated in every state where the Alliance was strong. As yet the name of the new party varied from state to state, but the Kansans, seeking to dramatize the battle between the people and the "plutocrats," called their organization the People's Party, a name that won increasing acclaim. "Populist" and "Populism" were natural derivatives.

Third-party movements are more nearly the rule than the exception in American **Third-party** political history. From the **movements** time when the "Quiddists" or "Quids," led by John Randolph of Roanoke, broke away from the leadership of Thomas Jefferson on the ground that the President had abandoned the original tenets of Jeffersonian democracy, such revolts have been common. Before the Civil War the Antimasons, the Abolitionists, the Free-Soilers, and the Know-Nothings aroused in turn the anxiety of all "right-thinking" citizens. After the war the Liberal Republicans, the Anti-monopolists or Grangers, the Greenbackers, and finally the Populists caused the same concern. Populism, like Grangerism and Greenbackism, was almost wholly the product of agricultural discontent.[1] In each movement the farmers sought to combat the disadvantages from which they suffered because of the rising tide of industrialism. Each built upon the foundations laid by its immediate predecessor; each failed to realize the fond hopes of its founders to create a major political party; but each succeeded in impressing the older parties with the necessity of making some concessions to the farmers' demands, and in this way justified its existence. The third party itself soon disappeared, but the principles for which it stood lived on, and in many instances were accepted.

[1] For the Granger movement, see pp. 135–136; for the Greenback movement, pp. 107, 109–110.

In the picturesque campaign that the northwestern Alliance men waged in 1890, a surprising number of really magnificent orators took up the farmers' cause. Ignatius Donnelly of Minnesota delighted hundreds of audiences with his inimitable wit and his biting sarcasm; James B. Weaver of Iowa hammered home his points with a degree of resourcefulness that suggested comparison with James G. Blaine; "Sockless" Jerry Simpson of Kansas combined the oddities of James Whitcomb Riley with the skill of the trained dialectician; Mrs. Mary Elizabeth Lease, also of Kansas, a hard-bitten pioneer mother who had experienced most of the tragedies of frontier life, discovered in herself a rare gift of words that thrilled her hearers to their fingertips. "What you farmers need to do," she is said to have told a Kansas audience, "is to raise less corn and more *Hell*."

Elections of 1890

But the professional politicians and the oratorical head-liners were not the only spokesmen of Populism:

It was a religious revival, a crusade, a pentecost of politics in which a tongue of flame sat upon every man, and each spake as the spirit gave him utterance. . . . The farmers, the country merchants, the cattle-herders, they of the long chin-whiskers, and they of the broad-brimmed hats and heavy boots, had also heard the word and could preach the gospel of Populism. . . . Women with skins tanned to parchment by the hot winds, with bony hands of toil and clad in faded calico, could talk in meeting, and could talk right straight to the point.[1]

They not only talked, they picnicked, they marched, they sang for their cause. One of their favorite songs, "Good-bye, My Party, Good-bye," which celebrated in forthright verse the break that so many of them had made with a beloved old party, certainly had much to do with the success of Populism in Kansas.

Meantime in the South events had taken a somewhat different course. Macune's

[1] Elizabeth S. Barr, "The Populist Uprising," in *A Standard History of Kansas and Kansans*, vol. II (1918), pp. 1148–9.

effort to solve the problem of the cotton-farmer by a policy of business cooperation received a fatal blow with the collapse of the Texas Exchange some eighteen months after it was founded. Discouraged with economic methods, Macune now turned to politics. Laws would have to be passed to improve the status of the southern farmer, the stranglehold of the "Bourbon aristocrats" on state government would have to be broken, a debt-paying system of finance would have to be evolved. Other Southerners, too, had similar ideas, among them Colonel L. L. Polk, editor of a North Carolina farm journal, Benjamin R. Tillman, a hard-hitting backcountry South Carolinian, and Thomas E. Watson, a picturesque lawyer-politician of Georgia whose hatred for the governing aristocracy knew no bounds. Under the leadership of such men as these the Southern Alliance, well before the election of 1890, had been transformed into a frankly political order, the chief business of which was to capture the machinery of the Democratic Party, in every southern state. Success in this undertaking, as the leaders well knew, would mean Alliance domination of the South, for there the one-party system insured that candidates once nominated were certain of election.

The enormous effectiveness of Alliance activities was mirrored in the election results. In at least four northwestern states, Kansas, Nebraska, South Dakota, and Minnesota, third-party candidates won the balance of power, although in no case did they obtain outright control. In the South, Alliance gains were even more spectacular. Alliance candidates for governor were nominated and elected in three states, South Carolina, North Carolina, and Georgia, while in no less than eight states Alliance-controlled legislatures were chosen. Even in Congress, the evidence of agrarian discontent was emphatically recorded. Two third-party senators, William A. Peffer of Kansas and James H. Kyle of South Dakota, were on hand for the opening session of the Fifty-Second Congress, while

Alliance successes

Thomas E. Watson, the stormy petrel of southern Populism, sought in vain to perpetuate the third party.

eight third-party representatives from the Northwest voted for Thomas E. Watson of Georgia for Speaker. Watson was the only southern Congressman to admit that he was now a third-party man, but among the southern delegations there sat perhaps thirty or forty Alliance members and many others who were drawn to the Alliance by bonds of sympathy. Indeed, the *Congressional Directory*, a volume which congressmen regularly compile about themselves, showed that during this period a remarkable number of senators and representatives, regardless of party or section, were at pains to confess their intimate connection with the farm and their deep devotion to farmer interests.

To the third-party men of the Northwest the logical next step was the formation of a new nation-wide party of the people, but to Southerners such a course seemed fraught with the greatest of peril. The Democratic Party of the South was primarily a symbol of white supremacy. Democratic rule meant white rule. If the white voters of the South were divided, Negro voting might become common, and the supremacy of the white race would be jeopardized. Perhaps even

the horrors of reconstruction might be repeated. Southern Alliance men preferred, therefore, to work within the framework of the Democratic Party, although there was one great objection to such a course. The southern wing of the party, however strong it might become, could hardly hope to dominate the party as a whole. Through an Alliance-controlled southern Democracy a certain amount of useful state legislation might be achieved, but reforms that depended upon nation-wide action would still be out of reach. The so-called "sub-Treasury plan," for example, to which the Southern Alliance was committed after 1889, could never be put into effect without a law of Congress. This plan, much ridiculed then, would seem less radical to a later generation. It called for national warehouses in which non-perishable farm produce might be stored and upon which the owners might borrow from the United States government as much as eighty per cent of the "local current value" of their deposits in Treasury notes, issued for the purpose by the United States government, and providing incidentally an unpredictable amount of money inflation.

Southern reluctance was insufficient to restrain the third-party ardor of northwestern Alliance men, and at Cincinnati, in May, 1891, a mass convention composed mostly of Westerners, but attended by a few Southerners, formally launched the People's Party as a national organization. The following February in St. Louis a delegate convention representing all the farm orders of the nation tried in vain to achieve organic union, but succeeded in adopting a common platform, the preamble of which, written and read by the versatile Donnelly, reflected with remarkable accuracy the spirit of the agrarian revolt:

The People's Party

We meet in the midst of a nation brought to the verge of moral, political and material ruin. Corruption dominates the ballot box, the legislatures, the Congress, and touches even the ermine of the bench. The people are demoralized. Many of the States have been compelled to isolate the voters at the polling places in order to prevent universal intimidation or bribery.[1] The newspapers are subsidized or muzzled; public opinion silenced; business prostrated, our homes covered with mortgages, labor impoverished, and the land concentrating in the hands of capitalists. . . . The fruits of the toil of millions are boldly stolen to build up colossal fortunes, unprecedented in the history of the world, while their possessors despise the republic and endanger liberty. From the same prolific womb of governmental injustice we breed two great classes — paupers and millionaires.

As these eloquent words attested, the Populists sought earnestly to interest labor in presenting a united front with the farmers against a common enemy. But in this effort they were doomed to failure. Only the old and weakened Knights of Labor, struggling valiantly to stave off the day of dissolution, signified any interest in cooperation. The American Federation of Labor, to which increasingly the labor world looked for leadership, adhered tenaciously to its policy of keeping the labor movement free from party politics. It was determined neither to become a political party nor to be absorbed in one. The disappointment of the Populists at the resultant failure of their new People's Party to become a genuine party of all the people was acute.

Four months later, at Omaha, Nebraska, the first national nominating convention of the People's Party came together. Amidst scenes of unprecedented enthusiasm the Populists adopted as their own most of the planks of the St. Louis platform, including a slightly revised version of Donnelly's rhetorical preamble. Land, transportation, and finance furnished the principal issues. Believing, as they did, that the value of the gold dollar had been artificially stimulated to the benefit of the creditor class and to the distress of the debtors, the Populists demanded first and foremost an extensive expansion of the currency — in other words, money inflation. The amount of the circulating medium, they contended, whether by direct paper-money

[1] This refers to the Australian system of secret voting, recently introduced into the United States, and strongly supported by the Populists.

issues or by the "free and unlimited coinage of silver at the ratio of sixteen to one," or by both, should "be speedily increased to not less than fifty dollars per capita." As for the transportation issue, they advocated that the government should own and operate the railroads, and also, for good measure, the telegraph and telephone systems of the country. On the subject of public lands they looked faintly in the direction of conservation by demanding the return to the government by "railroads and other corporations" of all lands received "in excess of their actual needs." Alien landownership the Populists also condemned, and among other reforms favorably mentioned in their platform were the sub-Treasury system, the Australian ballot, a graduated income tax, postal savings banks, shorter hours for labor, the initiative and referendum, election of United States senators by direct vote of the people, and a single term for the President and Vice-President. For their candidates the Populists chose James B. Weaver of Iowa who had fought for the North in the Civil War, to head the ticket, and James G. Field of

"That Wicked Little Farmer Boy." Cartoon depicting the rôle of the Populists in the election of 1890. From *Judge*, August 30, 1890.

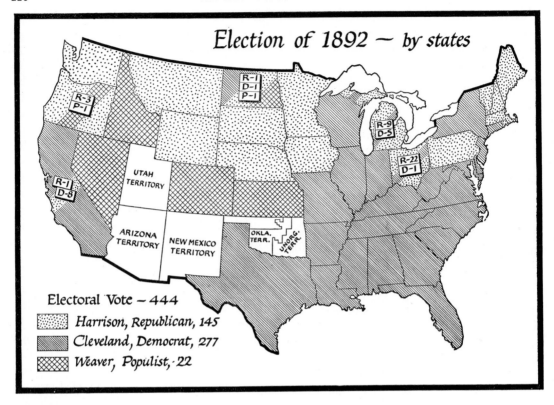

Election of 1892 — by states

Electoral Vote — 444

Harrison, Republican, 145
Cleveland, Democrat, 277
Weaver, Populist, 22

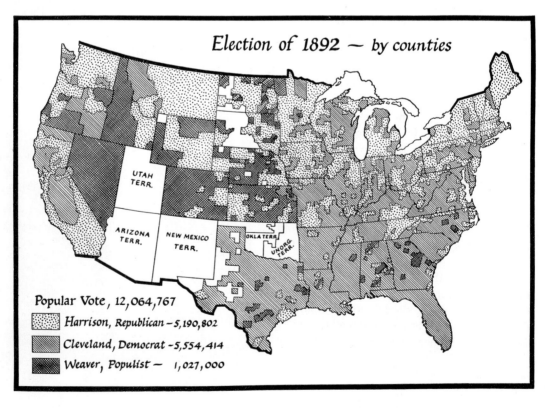

Election of 1892 — by counties

Popular Vote, 12,064,767

Harrison, Republican — 5,190,802
Cleveland, Democrat — 5,554,414
Weaver, Populist — 1,027,000

Virginia, an ex-Confederate, for second place.

The Populists, while predicting a victory of the "people" over the "plutocrats" in **Election of 1892** 1896, hoped only to make a good showing in 1892. Circumstances came ably to their assistance. The Republicans, in spite of the overwhelming rebuke they had received in 1890, had little choice but to renominate the unpopular Harrison and to defend the long list of dubious measures, including the McKinley Act, that were associated with his administration; while the Democrats, convinced that another battle must be fought over the tariff, turned for a third time to Cleveland. Signs of dissension in both old parties were apparent. Three days before the opening of the Republican Convention, Blaine had resigned as Secretary of State and had permitted his friends to work openly, if unavailingly, for his nomination. Cleveland, likewise, had met with formidable opposition. David B. Hill of New York had sought in every way to discredit the ex-President and to take the nomination away from him; moreover, among soft-money men of the West and the South Cleveland's hard-money views aroused the strongest antagonism.

The Populists went into the campaign as the one party willing to take a radical stand on the money question. Their free-silver plank was less a matter of conviction than of expediency, for the views of the original Populists were derived from the Greenbackers rather than from the Silverites. Nevertheless, "free silver" furnished the one really exciting issue of the campaign. On this issue, primarily, several states of the Rocky Mountain West broke from their Republican moorings and voted either for the Populists or, because of Populist secessions from the Republican Party, for the Democrats. Thanks in part to deliberate propaganda on the part of the silver interests, Populist campaigners in the Middle West and in the South found their audiences increasingly interested in the magic of free silver. The "sham battle" over the tariff went on to its logical conclu-sion, and, quite as the prophets predicted, Cleveland defeated Harrison. But, regardless of what might happen to the Populist Party, it was apparent that the silver issue had a future.

For the moment the triumph of the Democrats seemed complete. Cleveland's popular vote was 5,554,414 to Harrison's **A Democratic victory** 5,190,802 and Weaver's 1,027,000; the electoral vote stood: Cleveland, 277; Harrison, 145; and Weaver, 22. For the first time since the Civil War both houses of Congress as well as the Presidency were in Democratic hands. The Populists, for all their brave talk, had failed to make a dent in the "solid South," and the votes they had won in the West had been obtained in some instances only by cooperation with the Democrats. The country had again, as in 1890, voted its opposition to the McKinley Tariff; it had again rebuked the Republicans for their two-faced handling of the money question in the Sherman Silver Purchase Act; it had denounced anew the partisanship and extravagance of the Republican pension policy; it had condemned the inadequacy and ineffectiveness of the Sherman Anti-Trust Act; it had rebuked the President for his wavering attitude toward civil service reform; and it had shown its impatience with the effort to revive the nightmare of reconstruction by means of a "Force Bill." Significant and interesting was the fact that the six northwestern states admitted by the Republicans in 1889 and 1890 to insure Republican supremacy had actually contributed considerably to Republican defeat.

A casualty of the election was the Farmers' Alliance. In the Northwest it was absorbed into and replaced by the Populist Party. In the South it was torn violently asunder and destroyed by the third-party issue. The smaller faction, convinced that deliverance for the southern cotton-farmer was never to be found under the rule of the Democrats, dared the derision of neighbors and the loss of friends to join hands with the Populists. The larger faction, equally certain that white supremacy was still the one issue to which all others must bow, returned to the Democratic Party. Macune and a few of his adherents tried in vain to restore the Alliance to its former non-partisan status, but the scandals that pursued Macune's name undermined his influence, and the order he had done so much to create soon passed into oblivion.

Bibliography

R. B. Vance, *Human Geography of the South* (1932); and by the same author, *Human Factors in Cotton Culture* (1929), are unsurpassed as studies of the conditions of southern life. On the plight of the sharecropper E. M. Banks, *Economics of Land Tenure in Georgia* (1905), is excellent. C. H. Otken, *The Ills of the South* (1894), is an old but extremely revealing study. S. F. Raper and Ira DeA. Reid, *Sharecroppers All* (1941), is a more recent work on the same subject. See also Hammond, *The Cotton Industry*, already cited.

Books on the "New South" are increasingly plentiful. Woodward, *Origins of the New South*, already mentioned, is excellent. W. J. Cash, *The Mind of the South* (1941), shows the antebellum roots of southern society. R. B. Nixon, *Henry W. Grady, Spokesman of the New South* (1943), portrays well the part played by one of the prime movers in the southern economic revolution. Virginius Dabney, *Below the Potomac* (1942), is another book about the new South. Jonathan Daniels, *A Southerner Discovers the South* (1938), is illuminating on later developments. Thomas D. Clark, *Pills, Petticoats and Plows: The Southern Country Store* (1944), is as colorful as its title implies.

On the West much also has been written. For the theories of Henry George see G. R. Geiger, *The Philosophy of Henry George* (1933). Mark Sullivan, *Our Times*, I, *The Turn of the Century* (1926), chapter 8, discusses understandingly the problems of both West and South. The whole volume is useful as a social history of the nineties. John Carl Parish, *The Persistence of the Westward Movement and other Essays* (1943), is fertile in reinterpretations. Angie Debo, *Prairie City: The Story of an American Community* (1944), attempts a synthetic picture of the growth of a prairie town. James C. Olson, *J. Sterling Morton* (1942), is the biography of a prominent Nebraska pioneer and Democrat. James C. Malin, *Winter*

Wheat in the Gold Belt of Kansas: A Study in Adaptation to Sub-humid Geographical Environment (1944), is what its title implies. Earl S. Pomeroy, *The Territories and the United States, 1861–1890: Studies in Colonial Administration* (1947), throws light on the political growth of the West. Alfred N. Chandler, *Land Title Origins: A Tale of Force and Fraud* (1945), reveals the weaknesses of the land system. Glenn S. Dumke, *The Boom of the Eighties in Southern California* (1944), brings the farther West into the picture. J. D. Hicks, *The Constitutions of the Northwest States* (1923), deals with the six states admitted in 1889–90.

There are several good books on Oklahoma and the Southwest. Carl Coke Rister, *Land Hunger: David L. Payne and the Oklahoma Boomers* (1942), tells the story of white penetration of the Indian Country; by the same author, *No Man's Land* (1948), contains more material on the subject; and his *Southern Plainsmen* (1938), studies the folkways of the region. Angie Debo, *Tulsa: From Creek Town to Oil Capital* (1943), gives the life story of an Oklahoma boom town.

The changing point of view with respect to Populism may be noted by comparing F. L. McVey, *The Populist Movement* (1896), with John D. Hicks, *The Populist Revolt* (1931). The development of Populism in the South can best be traced through the several excellent state studies that have appeared: F. B. Simkins, *The Tillman Movement in South Carolina* (1926); J. B. Clark, *Populism in Alabama* (1927); A. M. Arnett, *The Populist Movement in Georgia* (1922); R. C. Martin, *The People's Party in Texas* (1933); and W. D. Sheldon, *Populism in the Old Dominion* (1935). A model biography of the leading southern Populist is C. V. Woodward, *Tom Watson, Agrarian Rebel* (1938). Stuart Noblin, *Leonidas LaFayette Polk: Agrarian Crusader* (1949), is also a valuable portrait. Francis Butler Simkins, *Pitchfork Ben Tillman, South Carolinian* (1944), gives a generally sympathetic picture of a leading southern agrarian. The Negro's part in Populism gets some attention in Helen G. Edmonds, *The Negro and Fusion Politics in North Carolina, 1894–1901* (1951).

Fewer northern than southern studies of Populism have achieved book publication. P. R. Fossum, *The Agrarian Movement in North Dakota* (1925), treats satisfactorily some aspects of the subject. Elizabeth S. Barr, "The Populist Uprising," in *A Standard History of Kansas and Kansans*, edited by W. E. Connelley, II (1918), is a delightful bit of historical rhetoric. Fred A. Shannon, *The Farmer's Last Frontier: Agriculture, 1860–1887* (1945), presents admirably the economic background of frontier Populism. Horace S. Merrill, *Bourbon Democracy of the Middle West, 1865–1896* (1953), concentrates on the conservative Democratic opposition to the agrarians. Chester McA. Destler, *American Radicalism, 1865–1901: Essays and Documents* (1946), contains many thoughtful observations on the nature of American radicalism. Russell B. Nye, *Midwestern Progressive Politics: A Historical Study of its Origins and Development, 1870–1950* (1951), follows in the main the unrest of the farmers.

Murray S. Stedman, Jr., and Susan Stedman, *Discontent at the Polls: A Study of Farmer and Labor Parties, 1827–1948* (1950), is also of some value. Henry Nash Smith, *Virgin Land; The American West as Symbol and Myth* (1950), is a searching reassessment.

On party problems in general consult M. I. Ostrogorski, *Democracy and the Organization of Political Parties* (2 vols., 1902). George H. Knoles, *The Presidential Campaign and Election of 1892* (1942), is an excellent monograph. Nathan L. Fine, *Labor and Farmer Parties in the United States, 1828–1928* (1928), is better on the labor than on the farmer aspects of his subject. The best biography of the Populist presidential candidate in 1892 is F. H. Haynes, *James Baird Weaver* (1919). Haynes, *Third Party Movements*, already mentioned, is also useful in this connection. Populist flirtations with Walter Q. Gresham, who became Cleveland's Secretary of State, are noted in Matilda Gresham, *Life of Walter Quintin Gresham* (2 vols., 1919). Anti-Populist sentiments appear in Horace S. Merrill, *William Freeman Vilas: Doctrinaire Democrat* (1954).

12

The Silver Crusade

The gold reserve — Condition of the Treasury — Panic of 1893 — Repeal of the Sherman Silver Purchase Act — Purchases of gold — Tariff legislation — Rise of the silver issue — Elections of 1894 — William Jennings Bryan — Plight of the Populists — Election of 1896 — The Dingley Tariff — International bimetallism — The return of prosperity

THERE is some reason to suppose that, even before his term of office ended, Harrison had occasion to rejoice in his defeat. **The gold reserve** A nightmare of his administration had been the condition of the "gold reserve." Authorized by the Resumption Act of 1875, and painstakingly assembled by John Sherman during Hayes's administration, this fund had originally amounted to only a little more than $100,000,000. With that sum the Treasury had successfully resumed specie payments in 1879, although the outstanding issues of greenbacks exceeded the gold reserve in the proportion of about three dollars to one. Businessmen assumed, however, that as long as there was $100,-000,000 in gold in the Treasury, the gold standard was secure. Each year the operation of the Bland-Allison Act of 1878 added somewhat to the burden borne by the gold reserve, for successive Secretaries of the Treasury invariably adopted the policy of backing the silver dollar, whatever its "intrinsic" value, with gold. But the plentiful revenues and the general prosperity of the eighties steadily increased the gold reserve, until by 1890 the Treasury was able to record that it possessed $190,000,000 in gold, nearly twice the essential minimum.

It was at this point that the financial measures of the Harrison administration began to take effect. In the first place, the McKinley Tariff, as its framers intended, had reduced the annual revenue by about $100,000,000 a year. Secondly, the lavish expenditures of the new administration, particularly for pensions, placed a new and heavy burden upon the Treasury. Thirdly, the Sherman Silver Purchase Act, which replaced the Bland-Allison Act of 1878, not only required the government to purchase nearly twice as much silver as before, but also provided for a new issue of Treasury notes, based on these silver purchases, that all sound-money men agreed must be redeemable in gold rather than in silver. Failure to maintain their parity with gold would mean that the silver standard would succeed the gold standard, and the purchasing power of the American dollar would decline to the commercial value of the silver dollar — a drop of nearly fifty per cent.

Well before the end of the Harrison administration the condition of the Treasury had begun to excite general alarm. **Condition of** By 1892, the Treasury surplus, **the Treasury** which recorded the excess of revenues over expenditures, had almost reached the vanishing point. Far more significant was the fact that the last two years had witnessed heavy withdrawals of gold. Faith that the government could redeem its greenbacks and Treasury notes in gold was obviously shaken, for gold flowed steadily out of the Treasury and paper flowed in. By January, 1893, the gold reserve had dwindled to only $108,000,000, and the Harrison administration, in order to stave off the inevitable crisis until after March 4, was driven to heroic measures. Late in January, Harrison's Secretary of the Treasury successfully implored the New York banks to exchange $6,000,000 in gold for paper, a sum that kept the gold reserve above the $100,000,000 mark until after Cleveland was inaugurated. But when the Democrats took over the Treasury, they found a gold reserve of only $100,982,410.

By April 21, 1893, within a matter of weeks after the change of government, the gold reserve dropped below the **Panic of 1893** $100,000,000 mark, and the Panic of 1893 was on. Before six months had passed no less than eight thousand business failures, involving liabilities of $285,000,000, were recorded. Four hundred banks, most of them in the West or in the South, closed their doors. Railroads followed each other into receivership in a procession that ended only after 156 companies, among them the Erie, the Union Pacific, and the Northern Pacific, had gone into bankruptcy. Panic conditions lasted throughout the summer, after which the country settled down to the long, hard process of waiting out a depression that was to last four full years.

While the condition of the Treasury, which gave rise to the fear that the government would be unable to maintain the gold standard, undoubtedly ushered in the Panic of 1893, there were other reasons in abundance that must be taken into account in explaining both the panic and the depression. Well to the front was the long-standing agricultural distress of the West and the South. For both sections the beginning of the depression might better have been set at 1887 than at 1893. The purchasing power of the stricken sections had steadily declined, and in consequence the earnings of all businesses that depended on farm markets or the handling of farm goods had suffered. The eighties, too, had been a period of overexpansion in

industry. The great transcontinental railroads, the huge industrial trusts, and the building of the larger cities and the new cities that they had made necessary had drained dry the investment resources of the nation. Furthermore, the depression, far from being a strictly American affair, was of world-wide dimensions. From 1889 on, and particularly after the so-called "Baring panic" of 1890 in England, all Europe had recorded subnormal business conditions; indeed, one reason for the depletion of the American gold reserve was the withdrawal of foreign capital from investment in America in order to bolster up the waning fortunes of European enterprise.

To twentieth-century Americans familiar with the economic activities of the Hoover and Roosevelt administrations, the refusal of Grover Cleveland to regard the problem of business recovery as a direct concern of the government may seem surprising. To Cleveland the depression was a business matter that lay quite outside the realm of politics. He regarded it as his duty, as President, to maintain the historic gold standard if he could, and to keep the government solvent; but beyond that neither he nor the majority he was able to command in Congress dreamed that the government had a duty to perform. Even the radicals of the time — the Populists and the Silverites — confined their demands almost entirely to money inflation of one sort or another. For this attitude Cleveland and his contemporaries are neither to be praised nor censured. They acted as nineteenth-century politicians had always acted. Van Buren, Buchanan, Grant, and Hayes had confronted major depressions during their terms of office, but neither they nor their advisers had conceived of it as the duty of the government to defeat depression and restore prosperity. The business cycle was a strictly business affair.

On the money question, however, Cleveland acted with vigor. Failure to maintain the gold standard would have **Repeal of** seemed to him a breach of public **the Silver** faith. Accordingly, he called **Purchase** Congress at once into special **Act** session and asked it to repeal the obnoxious Sherman Silver Purchase Act, which in his judgment had done so much to deplete the gold reserve. He could hardly have thought of a better way to alienate the West and the South, where silver orators were gaining converts every day. The debtor farmers, to whom the gold standard meant low prices and continued agricultural distress, had no desire whatever to save it; for them the fifty-cent dollar had no terrors. The silver interests of the Far West were even more violently opposed to repeal. What silver needed, they insisted, was a larger rather than a smaller subsidy; better still, "the free and unlimited coinage of silver at the ratio of sixteen to one." Congress at length supported Cleveland in his resolve, but only at the cost of a definite split in the Democratic Party. Enough eastern Republicans joined

The gold reserve became a kind of financial barometer during Cleveland's second administration, as is shown in this Keppler cartoon on the condition of the Treasury.

the eastern Democrats to repeal the Sherman Law, but the confidence of western and southern Democrats in the President they had chosen was sadly shaken.

Cleveland's next move alienated the soft-money men still further. In spite of the fact that silver purchases were discontinued, the drain on the gold reserve continued. By October the amount of gold in the Treasury was less than $82,000,000, and before the end of the year it was down to $68,000,000. Faced by this emergency the President, after some hesitation, authorized his Secretary of the Treasury, John G. Carlisle, to invoke the provisions of the still-unrepealed Resumption Act of 1875, and to buy enough gold to maintain the proper reserve. In January, 1894, an issue of $50,000,000 worth of five per cent bonds brought $58,000,000 in gold into the Treasury, but of this sum $24,000,000 was immediately withdrawn, and before the end of the year one more purchase of gold was necessary — an "endless chain," for in each case the gold was hardly in the Treasury until it was drawn out again.

By February, 1895, with the gold reserve down to $41,000,000 and currency depreciation once more seemingly in **Purchases** sight, the President saved the **of gold** situation by a deal with the Morgan and the Belmont banking firms, the latter representing the Rothschilds of Paris. According to the terms of this unusual agreement the favored firms were permitted to purchase a $62,000,000 issue of thirty-year four per cent bonds at 104½ instead of at their market value of about 111. Thus the bankers were insured an enormous profit. In return for this special consideration, however, the purchasers guaranteed two things, first, to procure half of the needed gold from abroad, and secondly, to use their influence to prevent further withdrawals of gold from the Treasury. This deal, while violently and perhaps justly criticized, did serve to restore confidence, and when some months later the government offered $100,000,000 in four per cent bonds to the highest bidder, the issue was promptly subscribed five times over. After this transaction all fear that the government could not maintain the gold standard speedily vanished. But to the strongly Populistic South and West the maintenance of the gold standard was more an evil than a good, and worse still, the President had attained this undesired end by "selling out" to Wall Street. The depths of Cleveland's unpopularity knew no bounds.

Part of the price that Cleveland paid for maintaining the gold standard was the defeat of his long-cherished plans for a genuine revision downward of the tariff. Of necessity, or so he thought, he had postponed the tariff battle until after the repeal of the Sherman Act. But when that end had been accomplished, his prestige with the silver wing of his party was so impaired that in that quarter his commands were no longer respected. Moreover, the alliance of eastern Democrats and eastern Republicans, originally called into existence against silver, soon found that it could also function effectively on the tariff. The result was a tariff measure, the Wilson-Gorman Act of 1894, so far removed from the party's pledges on the subject that Cleveland called it a "piece of party perfidy," and obstinately refused to sign the bill, although he did permit it to become a law without his signature.

When William L. Wilson of West Virginia, scholarly chairman of the House Ways and **Tariff** Means Committee, introduced **legislation** the tariff bill into the House, tariff reformers had good reason to congratulate themselves. The Wilson Bill, patterned after the Mills Bill of 1888, proposed to put raw materials, such as lumber, wool, and coal on the free list, in part as compensation to manufacturers for the reduced protection they were to receive, and in part as a means of lowering the prices that consumers would have to pay. Sugar, too, both raw and refined, was to be admitted free, and the expensive sugar bounty was to be abolished. On most factory-made items, such as cotton, woolen, and silken fabrics, crockery, and glassware, the duties were to be materially reduced, although their protective character was by no means destroyed. Fearful that the lowered duties might reduce the revenue below the needs of the government, the framers of the bill heeded the Populist demand for an income tax, and levied a flat two per cent against incomes over four thousand dollars.

As it passed the House, the Wilson Bill was an honest attempt at tariff reduction. In the Senate, however, two eastern Democrats, Brice and Gorman, aided and abetted by log-rolling Democrats from every section, and in particular by the "sugar senators" from Louisiana, joined with the Republicans to attach 633 amendments to the bill, wholly changing its character. The sugar bounty was not revived, but duties that were worth twenty million dollars annually to the Sugar Trust were placed on both raw and refined sugar. Throughout the revised measure the low-tariff principle was all but ignored. Reluctantly the House acquiesced in the wrecking of its work, and the President's attempts at intervention proved unavailing. In general the duties of the Wilson-Gorman Tariff were lower than those of the McKinley Tariff, and not far different from the duties set by the Tariff of 1883. The provision for an income tax, which actually reached the statute books, was declared unconstitutional by the Supreme Court in a five-to-four decision (1895). This was the more remarkable because of the fact that an income tax had been levied and collected during the Civil War without serious question as to its constitutionality. Populists were convinced that the action of the Court was just one more evidence of the unholy alliance between business and government that Donnelly had denounced in his famous preamble:

We have witnessed for more than a quarter of a century the struggles of the two great political parties for power and plunder, while grievous wrongs have been inflicted upon the suffering people. We charge that the controlling influences dominating both these parties have permitted the existing dreadful conditions to develop without serious effort to prevent or restrain them.

Neither do they now promise us any substantial reform. They have agreed together to ignore in the coming campaign every issue but one. They propose to drown the outcries of a plundered people with the uproar of a sham battle over the tariff, so that capitalists, corporations, national banks, rings, trusts, watered stock, the demonetization of silver, and the oppressions of the usurers may all be lost sight of. They propose to sacrifice our homes, lives and children on the altar of mammon; to destroy the multitude in order to secure corruption funds from the millionaires.

The acute labor unrest of 1894 drove fear into the hearts of the conservatives, and encouraged the Populists to hope that eventually farmers and laborers would learn to work together. If only such a union could be achieved, they believed that the people, not the plutocrats, would soon rule. But Populist strategy called for union through the agency of the Populist Party. First the Populists must capture the government, and then, as rapidly as possible, they must put into effect the numerous and complicated reforms of their cherished platforms. But the leaders of organized labor refused steadfastly to allow the movement they headed to become identified with any political party.

As events turned out, whatever union of the working classes was actually accom-

Rise of the silver issue plished came primarily on the issue of free silver, and more or less without regard for the wishes of party leaders. Propaganda from mine-owners in the silver states of the Far West flooded the country with denunciations of the "crime of 1873" and with innumerable arguments to prove that only "the free and unlimited coinage of silver at the ratio of sixteen to one" was required to restore prosperity. *Coin's Financial School*, a little book written by William H. Harvey and published in 1894, set forth in simple language, and seemingly with unanswerable logic, the doctrines of the silverites. "Professor Coin," as the author called himself, purported to run a school in Chicago for financiers, and the lectures he gave on the money question were recorded in the book. Illustrated with numerous car-

toons and diagrams, and sometimes reduced to the simplicity of a dialogue between the "Professor" and his students, the book appealed to an enormous audience. Silver orators, such as William Jennings Bryan, knew its arguments by heart and spread them far and wide. Soon countless thousands had come to believe that an international conspiracy to set gold above silver was at the root of the economic distress from which the nation suffered. The restoration of prosperity need not await the enactment of a long and complicated series of reforms. By the simple expedient of restoring silver to its historic status as money, all wrong would be righted.

It means work for the thousands who now tramp the streets . . . not knowing where their next meal is coming from. It means food and clothes for the thousands of hungry and ill-clad women and children. . . . It means the restoration of confidence in the business world. It means the re-opening of closed factories, the relighting of fires in darkened furnaces; it means hope instead of despair; comfort in place of suffering; life instead of death.

Unhappily for the plans of the Populists, the silver issue cut across party lines. Silver Republicans in the West and Silver Demo-

Cartoon Gold vs. Silver. "Will somebody show Uncle Sam how to see through the silver trouble?"

crats in both the West and South captured the old party organizations in state after state. Even the Populists themselves, caught up in the silver frenzy, were forced increasingly to ignore all the rest of their policies and to concentrate on "free silver," a panacea rather than a program.

> The dollar of our daddies,
> Of silver coinage free,
> Will make us rich and happy
> Will bring prosperity.

Elections of 1894 With the silver forces still divided among three parties, the state and congressional elections of 1894 turned upon hard times and the unpopularity of Cleveland. The Democrats were no more responsible for the depression than the Republicans, if as much so, but it was their misfortune to be in power when the panic broke, and the Republicans drove home the charge that Democratic supremacy and hard times went together. As a result the Republicans obtained a two to one majority in the national House of Representatives, greatly reduced the Democratic majority in the Senate, and captured nearly every state government outside the South. The behavior of the Populists during the campaign tended, if anything, to aid the Republicans. In the West the Populists, unable or unwilling to cooperate with the Democrats as fully as in 1892, tended to avoid fusion and to keep "in the middle of the road"; in the South, they unblushingly joined forces with the Republicans. The total Populist vote, however, was more than forty per cent larger in 1894 than in 1892, and enthusiastic Populists cited the rapid rise of Republicanism before 1860 as evidence of what their party could do by 1896. Leading Republicans held a different view of the situation; some of them boasted openly that in 1896 they could "nominate a rag baby and elect it President."

That the original Republican plan for 1896 did not contemplate a straight-out endorsement of the single gold standard was apparent from the record of the candidate slated for first place on the Republican ticket.

William McKinley (1843–1901), author of the McKinley Tariff Bill of 1890, and governor of Ohio from 1891 to 1895, was a tariff expert with no deep convictions on the money question. Indeed, in so far as he had committed himself, he seemed to have taken the silver side. In 1878 he had voted for the Bland-Allison Act, and in 1890, when the Sherman Silver Purchase Act was being formulated, he again advocated special favors for silver. As a compromise candidate, satisfactory to both the silver and the gold factions of the party, he seemed ideal, for his leanings toward silver were nicely balanced by the fact that he was a thoroughgoing party regular who could be trusted not to get out of step with the party leaders. His availability for the Republican nomination in 1896 was further emphasized by his creditable record as a Union officer in the Civil War, by his chivalrous devotion to his invalid wife, by his suave and genial manners, and by his abiding friendship with Marcus Alonzo Hanna, Cleveland industrialist and boss of the Republican Party in Ohio. Hanna had the normal attitude of his class toward tariff protection, but his regard for McKinley was personal no less than political. He early made up his mind that McKinley must be the Republican standard-bearer in 1896, and long before the convention met had rounded up the necessary votes.

The "battle of the standards" The steady drift of the electorate toward the free-silver "heresy" upset the Republican plan for a fence-sitting campaign on the money question. Southern Democrats, thoroughly frightened by the strength the Populists had shown in 1894, accepted free silver as a means of winning back the ground they had lost. Western Democrats, and frequently also western Republicans, made every effort to outdo the Populists in their devotion to silver. Thirty Democratic state conventions, all in the West or the South, emphatically endorsed "the free and unlimited coinage of silver at the ratio of sixteen to one." Shrewd observers could easily foretell that, in spite of the strenuous efforts of President Cleveland

and the gold-standard Democrats of the Northeast, the Democratic Party would be forced to include in its platform an uncompromising demand for free silver. Confronted by this situation, the Republican leaders, Hanna among them, finally determined to commit their party to the single gold standard. They could not hope by a straddling platform to compete with the unequivocal demands of the Democrats for free silver, and they might, by adhering steadfastly to gold, win over the dissident Democratic "gold-bugs" to the support of the Republican ticket. The tariff issue would have to stand aside. Republicans knew full well, when at St. Louis they nailed a "sound-money" plank into their platform, that the "battle of the standards" would dwarf all other party differences to insignificance.

We are unalterably opposed [this plank read] to every measure calculated to debase our currency or impair the credit of our country. We are, therefore, opposed to the free coinage of silver, except by international agreement with the leading commercial nations of the world, which we pledge ourselves to promote, and until such agreement can be obtained the existing gold standard must be preserved. All our silver and paper currency must be maintained at parity with gold, and we favor all measures designed to maintain inviolably the obligations of the United States and all our money, whether coin or paper, at the present standard, the standard of the most enlightened nations of the earth.

The complete conversion of the Republicans to the single gold standard was not accomplished without a party split. More than one hundred votes were cast for an amendment, introduced by Senator Henry M. Teller of Colorado, that favored the "independent coinage of gold and silver at our mints at the ratio of sixteen parts of silver to one of gold." When this amendment was rejected, thirty-four delegates, led by Teller, and including four United States senators and two representatives, left the hall in protest. That they would join the Democrats in case the latter came out for

silver seemed a foregone conclusion. But the Republicans adhered steadfastly to their program, nominated McKinley for President, with Garret A. Hobart of New Jersey for Vice-President, and adjourned in the hope that Marcus A. Hanna, their new campaign manager, could find the money and the means to restore their party to power.

The action of the Republicans left the Democrats, whose convention met a few weeks later at Chicago, no logical choice but to endorse free silver. The Democratic National Committee, however, was still in the hands of the men who had helped to nominate Cleveland in 1892, and they made a determined effort to halt the trend toward silver. But when their nominee for temporary chairman, David B. Hill of New York, a "gold-bug," was defeated by Senator John W. Daniel of Virginia, a silverite, 556 to 349, it was apparent that the radicals were in control. The platform they presented and adopted (628 to 301) on the money question bore no trace of compromise.

We demand the free and unlimited coinage of both silver and gold at the present legal ratio of sixteen to one without waiting for the aid or consent of any other nation. We demand that the standard silver dollar shall be a full legal tender, equally with gold, for all debts, public and private, and we favor such legislation as will prevent for the future the demonetization of any kind of legal tender money by private contract.

The Democrats had produced a platform; they were not long in finding a candidate. Before the convention met, the **William** leading aspirant among the sil- **Jennings** verites was Richard P. Bland, a **Bryan** congressman from Missouri. But Bland's candidacy had awakened little enthusiasm, and many delegates regretted the constitutional provision that alone would keep them from voting for the far more colorful John P. Altgeld of Illinois, a naturalized citizen of German birth. Among the numerous minor candidates was William Jennings Bryan (1860–1925) of Nebraska, a young man only thirty-six years of age whose reputation for

William Jennings Bryan

began his career as a lawyer, but found little satisfaction in legal practice, and soon gave up the law for politics. After his defeat for re-election to Congress in 1894, he turned to journalism, and rose rapidly to the editorship of the Omaha *World-Herald*. He indulged his remarkable talent as an orator by speaking constantly, especially before Chautauqua audiences, and was drawn irresistibly into the fight for free silver. Like many others, he believed in this panacea primarily as a means of lessening the ills from which underprivileged Americans suffered. He is portrayed here in the full vigor of youth; he expected, and almost always received, enthusiastic audience response.

persuasive oratory was already well known. Bryan had served two terms in Congress, 1891 to 1895, and had once attracted nation-wide attention by a powerful speech on the tariff. During the depression, without actually becoming a Populist, he had taken up with most of the Populist doctrines, particularly free silver. As Ignatius Donnelly, the most famous orator of Populism, complained, "We put him to school and he wound up by stealing the schoolbooks."

For months before the nominating convention met in 1896, Bryan had been speaking on free silver to western audiences, and had rehearsed many times the ringing phrases that were to bring him fame at Chicago. Fully conscious of his genius as an orator, he knew in his heart that if he could only find the occasion to make the speech he had learned so well the coveted prize would be his.

The opportunity came when he was asked to close the debate on a resolution that would have repudiated free silver and commended the Cleveland administration:

Serene and self-possessed, and with a smile upon his lips, he faced the roaring multitude with a splendid consciousness of power. Before a single word had been uttered by him, the pandemonium sank to an inarticulate murmur, and when he began to speak, even this was hushed to the profoundest silence. . . . He spoke with the utmost deliberation, so that every word was driven home to each hearer's consciousness, and yet with an ever-increasing force, which found fit expression in the wonderful harmony and power of his voice. His sentences rang out, now with an accent of superb disdain, and now with the stirring challenge of a bugle call. . . . The leaderless Democracy of the West was leaderless no more.

The scene enacted in the Convention, as Mr. Bryan finished speaking, was indescribable. Throughout the latter part of his address, a crash of applause had followed every sentence; but now the tumult was like that of a great sea thundering against the dykes. Twenty thousand men and women went mad with an irresistible enthusiasm. The orator had met their mood to the very full. He had found magic words for the feeling which they had been unable to express. And so he had played at will upon their very heartstrings, until the full tide of their emotion was let loose in one tempestuous roar of passion, which seemed to have no end.[1]

Bryan's speech was not a reasoned defense of the silver cause, and was not meant to be. Rather it was a leader's call to action. His closing words, "You shall not press down upon the brow of labor this crown of thorns, you shall not crucify mankind upon a cross of gold," summarized in a sentence all that had gone before. At that moment, had the convention been given the chance, it would doubtless have nominated Bryan by acclamation. When the proper time came, in spite of the fact that more than a hundred and fifty gold Democrats persistently abstained from voting, Bryan obtained the necessary two-thirds majority after only five ballots. For Vice-President the convention chose Arthur Sewall, a wealthy banker and shipbuilder from Maine.

Plight of the Populists The plight of the Populists when they learned what the Democrats had done was far from pleasant. The Democratic platform had not only appropriated the silver issue; it had denounced with Populistic fervor the "absorption of wealth by the few," and had called for a stricter control of trusts and railroads by the federal government. The Democratic candidate, Bryan, was a Populist in everything but name. The Populist leaders, confident that both the Republicans and the Democrats would be captured by the "gold-bugs," had set the date of the Populist Convention later than either of the old-party conventions, and had hoped to rally all free-silver men and all reformers to their standard. Now they were faced squarely with the problem of sacrificing their party by endorsing the Democratic nominee or aiding the Republicans by dividing the silver vote. In general western Populists were willing to accept Bryan and join the Democrats, but to southern Populists such a course, involving, as it did, full surrender to a hated enemy, was extremely painful to contemplate. After a heated battle the Populist Convention voted in favor of a compromise. It would name its vice-presidential candidate first on the assumption that a southern Populist would be chosen instead of the wholly unacceptable Sewall. Proponents of the plan argued that the convention might then nominate Bryan for President, if it chose, with the full expectation that the Democrats would withdraw Sewall, accept the Populist nominee for Vice-President, and so emphasize the separateness as well as the temporary fusion of the two parties.

The Populist ticket The Populist choice for Vice-President fell on Thomas E. Watson, the fiery Georgian, after which there was no further chance to stop Bryan for first place. Had the Democrats then substituted Watson for Sewall, the Populists could have held up their heads during the campaign. But the Democrats were satisfied that they had won what they wanted, and ignored Watson, who nevertheless remained in the race and campaigned vigorously. The anomaly of the situation led to endless confusion in the balloting, and many Populists voted the Democratic ticket in order to be sure that their ballots would count. The Populist Party, indeed, practically dissolved during the campaign. For the next three presidential elections it continued to put tickets in the field, but after 1896 it was never again a serious factor in American politics.

Campaign of 1896 By repudiating Cleveland[1] and absorbing Populism, the Democrats had placed their party in a position to challenge seriously the Republican expectation of an easy victory. Bryan as a campaigner was superb. "Probably no man in civil life," observed the New York *Nation*, "had succeeded in inspiring so much terror, without taking life, as Bryan." Between the time of his nomination and election day he

[1] Harry Thurston Peck, *Twenty Years of the Republic* (1907), pp. 498–502. The quoted sentences are interspersed between long excerpts from Bryan's speech.

[1] The gold wing of the Democratic Party subsequently held a convention and nominated John M. Palmer of Illinois for President and Simon B. Buckner of Kentucky for Vice-President. Cleveland supported this ticket, but like most of the "Gold Democrats" hoped for a Republican victory.

traveled eighteen thousand miles and spoke to hundreds of audiences. Inspired by the endless vitality of their leader, a host of lesser orators spread the gospel of free silver to every village and crossroads in the country. The Democratic campaign chest, however, was slender, for the only large contributions came from the hard-pressed silver interests of the Far West. It was at this point that the Republicans proved invulnerable. Conceding privately that "the Chicago Convention has changed everything" and that the campaign "will be work and hard work from the start," Hanna, the Republican campaign manager, began an earnest solicitation of funds from all the important business interests that had a financial stake in Republican success. Exactly how much money he and his subordinates collected will never be known, but Hanna later admitted receiving gifts of not less than $3,500,000, a huge sum for the times, and particularly for a lean year. With ample funds at his disposal and more always to be had for the asking, Hanna embarked upon a "campaign of education" well calculated to discredit the reasoning of the silverites. Hundreds of well-paid orators challenged the tenets of Bryan and his underfed volunteers, tons of shrewdly phrased pamphlets exploded the theories of "Professor Coin," batteries of skillful writers provided news and editorials for subsidized newspapers. By staking everything on so dubious an issue as free silver, the Democrats had laid themselves wide open to this kind of attack. No doubt the "bimetallists," as they called themselves, in contrast with the gold "monometallists," were sincere in their conviction that the need for free silver exceeded every other reform in importance, but they found few good economists who would agree with the arguments by which they defended it. Republican pamphleteers dwelt upon the absurdity of trying to maintain two different "yardsticks" with which to measure money, and featured the downright dishonesty involved in paying off valid debts with "fifty-cent" silver dollars. Among the reformers themselves there was much

Marcus Alonzo Hanna, whom most people knew as "Mark" Hanna, was the organizer of the McKinley victory.

dissent from the free-silver hypothesis and some genuine dismay at the overemphasis it received. Henry Demarest Lloyd, the author of *Wealth Against Commonwealth* (1894), a powerful indictment of the existing economic order, described free silver as a "fake" and called it the "cowbird of the reform movement. It waited until the nest had been built by the sacrifices and labors of others, and then laid its eggs in it, pushing out the others which lie smashed on the ground."

No doubt the Republican propaganda actually won over many free-silverites to Republican views, but not all that **Republican** Hanna's lieutenants did was **tactics** strictly educational. Every time-tested device for gathering in the votes was utilized — parades led by brass bands, torchlight processions, flaming posters, campaign caps and buttons. As the end drew near, threats were passed out freely. Workingmen were told that the election of McKinley would mean high wages and prosperity, but the election of Bryan, the loss of their jobs. Employers were known to reinforce this argument by telling their employees that if Bryan were elected they need not come back to work.

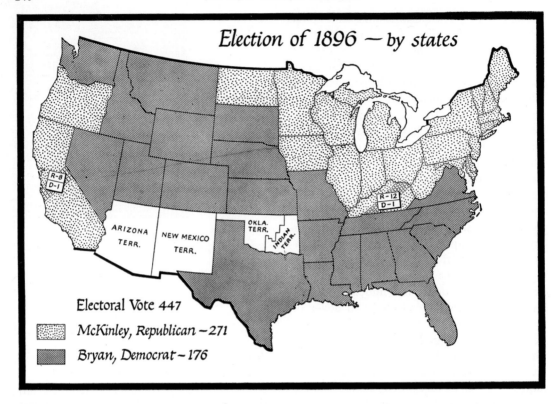

Election of 1896 — by states

Electoral Vote 447

McKinley, Republican — 271

Bryan, Democrat — 176

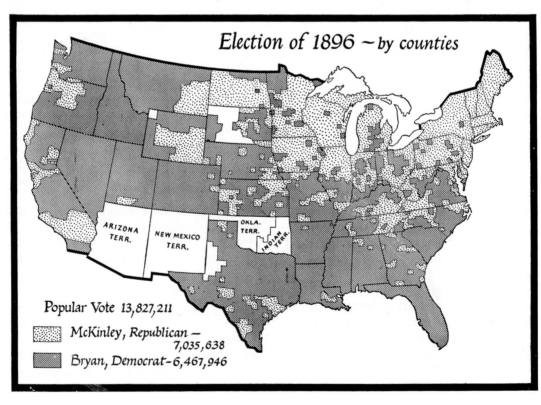

Election of 1896 — by counties

Popular Vote 13,827,211

McKinley, Republican —
7,035,638

Bryan, Democrat — 6,467,946

Farmers were informed that in case there was a Democratic victory their mortgages would not be renewed. Nor was there any lack of funds among the Republicans on election day to keep on duty a full quota of "workers at the polls." Not among the least of Hanna's shrewd moves was to keep McKinley discreetly in the background. Hanna well knew that in a rough-and-tumble campaign the Republican candidate would have been no match for Bryan. Small delegations were permitted to visit McKinley at his home in Canton, Ohio, and to be charmed by his personality, but they were given no fighting message. McKinley's famous "front-porch" speeches mainly recorded calm confidence; the others could do the fighting. Widely advertised as the "advance agent of Prosperity," he was never once really required to defend the title he had received.

It was a common statement that, if the election had been held in August instead of **Election results** November, Bryan would have been the victor. No one knows. Possibly a rise in the price of wheat due to a short crop abroad, whereas the American crop was abundant, seriously affected the results. However that may be, the Republicans undoubtedly picked up many votes as the campaign neared its close, and in the end they won an overwhelming victory. In general the agricultural South and West supported Bryan, while the industrial Northeast supported McKinley; but McKinley's Northeast extended as far west as Iowa, Minnesota, and North Dakota, while Bryan's solid South and West were broken by such notable Republican exceptions as Maryland, Delaware, West Virginia, Kentucky, California, and Oregon. McKinley received more than seven million popular votes to six and one half million for Bryan, while the electoral vote stood 271 to 176. The real meaning of the election was somewhat obscured by the unfortunate issue on which it had been fought. In actual fact Bryan represented the forces of agriculture, both in the South and in the West, and to a lesser

William McKinley

Twenty-fifth President of the United States, McKinley had served under Hayes during the Civil War, and emerged as a brevet-major. His many years in Congress and his experience as Governor of Ohio prepared him well for the duties of the Presidency. A shrewd and kindly regular, he became the conservatives' ideal President.

extent the forces of labor. McKinley, on the other hand, was the candidate of northeastern industry, which, ever since the Civil War, had been well-entrenched in the control of the national government and meant to hold its ground. The defeat of Bryan and the downfall of Populism freed the industrial leaders, temporarily at least, from the menace of popular interference with their monopolistic ambitions. Tom Johnson, the perennial mayor of Cleveland, Ohio, described the election as "the first great protest of the American people against monopoly — the first great struggle of the masses in our country against the privileged classes. It was not free silver that frightened the plutocrat leaders. What they feared, then, what they fear now, is free men." [1]

McKinley was inaugurated to the accompaniment of brightening economic skies and promptly took the necessary steps to identify Republican policies with the return of prosperity. Congress, being safely Republican in both houses, was called immediately into special session, not, as one might have supposed, to enact a gold-standard law, but

[1] Tom L. Johnson, *My Story* (1911), p. 109.

rather to revise the tariff along strictly protectionist lines. In the preceding session
the Republicans had already framed and
presented a tariff bill, so within record time
a measure introduced by Representative
Nelson Dingley, Jr., of Maine was enacted
into law. The rates it established quite
outdid all previous efforts at tariff protection.
Its purpose, as one inspired observer pointed
out, was not to produce revenue and incidentally to afford protection, but rather to
afford protection and incidentally to produce
revenue.

The Dingley rates were so high as to discourage importation. During the first year
The Dingley they were in force the total
Tariff revenue collected from tariffs
dropped twenty-five million dollars below
the returns for the preceding year under the
Wilson Act. Duties were reimposed on wool
and hides, which formerly had been on the
free list; an intricate sugar schedule was
devised to suit as precisely as possible the
desires of both the growers and the refiners
of sugar; and the high duties of 1890 on
woolens, cotton, linen, silk, crockery, and
steel products were either restored or increased. So ample was the duty of $7.84 a
ton on steel rails that American steel manufacturers were able to charge a higher price
for the rails they sold in the United States
than for those they shipped to London and
sold, presumably at a profit, in competition
with English rails.

The establishment of limited reciprocity,
as in 1890, was also provided for in the new
law. A few items such as tea and coffee
were put on the free list with the understanding that the President might proclaim specified duties in force if the nations that exported them failed to make similar concessions to American goods. Other items, such
as brandies, wines, and works of art, carried
duties that the President might reduce to
designated levels, also by proclamation, if
he could obtain adequate favors in return.
Finally, on all tariff-bearing articles, the
President might negotiate treaties with
foreign nations to scale down the American

rates as much as twenty per cent, but all
such treaties required ratification by the
Senate before they could become effective.
By presidential proclamation some minor
breaches were made in the high-tariff wall,
but the eleven reciprocity treaties negotiated
by the administration were all rejected by
the Senate.

McKinley's failure to ask Congress for a
rigid gold-standard law is not difficult to
explain. The Senate, while **Interna-**
safely Republican on the tariff, **tional bi-**
contained too many hold-over **metallism**
silver Senators to be regarded as trustworthy
on the money question. McKinley therefore
took advantage of the clause in the Republican platform that called for an international
conference on bimetallism to substitute diplomacy for legislative action. That he
would maintain the gold standard, with or
without the sanction of law, was apparent
from his choice of a conservative Chicago
banker, Lyman J. Gage, as his Secretary of
the Treasury. To give plausibility to the
negotiations on silver, which were almost
certain to fail, McKinley chose as his Secretary of State the aged John Sherman, whose
historic connection with American monetary
problems made his selection seem ideal.
Sherman's memory was known to be failing,
but this slight disqualification was more than
offset by the fact that his seat in the Senate
was coveted by McKinley's friend and pa-
tron, Marcus A. Hanna. On April 12, 1897,
McKinley named a commission of three
ardent bimetallists, headed by Edward O.
Wolcott of Colorado, to visit Europe in the
interest of international bimetallism. At
Paris the commission was received with some
show of cordiality, but at London it learned
that Great Britain positively would not open
her mints to silver on any terms satisfactory
to the Americans. The final failure of "international bimetallism," coupled with
heavy Republican gains in the election of
1898, enabled Congress at last to pass the
long-promised gold-standard law on March
14, 1900.

The close coincidence between the return

of prosperity and the return of the Republicans to power furnished a

The return of prosperity

valuable weapon to Republican campaigners for many years to come. It is possible, of course, that the prospect of Republican victory promoted business confidence and led to business expansion. Good times were on the way back, however, even before the election, and it seems reasonable to suppose that the course of events would not have been far different, even if Bryan had been elected. Undoubtedly one reason for the upward surge was an increase in the money supply. It is a curious fact that monetary inflation actually occurred in spite of all the Republicans had done to prevent it, and it occurred in a way they had least expected, by means of an increase in the world's supply of gold. For a quarter of a century before 1890 the amount of new gold mined each year was practically constant. Then a steady increase began which by the end of the nineties had reached spectacular proportions. In the year 1897, approximately twice as much gold was produced as in the year 1890; in 1898 nearly two and one half times as much. The cyanide process by which more gold was extracted from the ore mined, coupled with new discoveries of gold in Australia, South Africa, and the Klondike, accounted for the increase. Bryan was doubtless right when he first began to assert that the amount of gold in existence was inadequate to transact the world's business, but his arguments were less convincing with each succeeding year. Before Bryan became active in politics American business had to overcome the handicap of a steadily appreciating dollar, which meant also steadily diminishing price levels; by the time Bryan began to run for President, the value of the dollar had begun to diminish, and prices were on the rise. American agriculture no less than industry responded to the stimulus of gold inflation, while in the West the drouth at long last came to an end. Good harvests in America were matched by poor harvests abroad and the price of farm produce began to rise. Presently the Spanish-American War, the Philippine Insurrection, and the Boer-British War each added its quota to the boom that had already begun.

Bibliography

W. J. Lauck, *The Causes of the Panic of 1893* (1907), blames the panic mainly upon the currency situation; see also F. P. Weberg, *The Background of the Panic of 1893* (1929). Cleveland's stand on the money question can best be followed in Nevins, *Grover Cleveland*, already cited, and in Robert McElroy, *Grover Cleveland* (2 vols., 1923). Among the financial histories that treat fully of this subject are A. B. Hepburn, *A History of Currency in the United States* (1915); and Horace White, *Money and Banking* (6th ed., 1935).

Among the many contemporary studies that involve the silver question, the following may properly be listed: F. W. Taussig, *The Silver Situation in the United States* (1893); Horace White, *Coin's Financial Fool; or, the Artful Dodger Exposed* (1895); and Grover Cleveland, *Presidential Problems* (1904). Elmer Ellis, *Henry Moore Teller, Defender of the West* (1941), is an excellent biography of the most eminent silver Republican.

Herbert Croly, *Marcus Alonzo Hanna* (1912), is far superior to any biography of McKinley in its understanding of the forces that shaped McKinley's policies. Other useful studies include Thomas Beer, *Hanna* (1929); and Charles G. Dawes, *A Journal of the McKinley Years* edited by Bascom E. Timmons (1950). Unfortunately there is as yet no really good biography of Bryan. Probably the one most nearly satisfactory is M. R. Werner, *Bryan* (1929). Paxton Hibben, *The Peerless Leader, William Jennings Bryan* (1929); and J. C. Long, *Bryan, The Great Commoner* (1928), leave much to be desired, but are still superior to W. J. and Mary B. Bryan, *The Memoirs of William Jennings Bryan* (1925). W. J. Bryan, *The First Battle* (1897), was Bryan's report on his first campaign.

J. F. Rhodes, *The McKinley and Roosevelt Administrations, 1897–1909* (1922), is useful for its inside view of politics, but almost totally ignores economic and social history. H. H. Kohlsaat, *From McKinley to Harding* (1923), is a book of personal recollections by "one who knew." E. E. Robinson, *The Presidential Vote, 1896–1932* (1934), is a useful statistical compilation. Matthew Josephson, *The President Makers: The Culture of Politics and Leadership in an Age of Enlightenment, 1896–1919* (1940), is mainly biographic. A. W. Dunn, *From Harrison to Harding* (2 vols., 1922), is the report of a close observer. Frederick Lewis Allen, *The Great Pierpont Morgan* (1949), presents the bankers' point of view.

Many of the references for the preceding chapter will also be found useful here.

13

The Old American Way

BETWEEN 1876, the one-hundredth anniversary of the signing of the Declaration of Independence, and 1889, the one-hundredth anniversary of the inauguration of government under the Constitution, the United States became habituated to centennial celebrations. It was a foregone conclusion, therefore, that so available a date as the four-hundredth anniversary of the discovery of America by Columbus would not be overlooked. As early as 1890 an act was passed by Congress providing for an exhibition, to be held in 1892, that should commemorate the progress of the nation in art, industry, and agriculture. Rivalry for the honor and profit involved in staging the "Fair" was keen between New York, Washington, St. Louis, and Chicago, but Chicago, with a guaranty of ten million dollars, was the successful bidder.

Great were the preparations that were made for what its promoters were pleased to **The Chicago World's Fair** call the "World's Columbian Exposition." In its behalf the ablest of America's artists, under the general direction of Daniel Hudson Burnham, pooled their talents. Frederick Law Olmsted, the landscape architect who had laid out Central Park, New York; Stanford White, C. F. McKim, R. M. Hunt, and Louis Sullivan, architects; Augustus Saint-Gaudens, Daniel Chester French, Lorado Taft, and Frederick Macmonnies, sculptors; Kenyon Cox, Gari Melchers, and Edwin Blashfield, painters; all these and others contributed of their genius to produce an artistic setting of surpassing beauty for the exhibition. "Look here, old fellows," Saint-Gaudens once told these leaders as they pored together over their plans, "do you realize that this is the greatest meeting of artists since the fifteenth century?" For the site of the Fair ninety acres of Lake Front adjoining the business district of Chicago and six hundred acres in Jackson Park were dedicated. Here, at a cost of twenty-six million dollars, arose a "White City" so breath-takingly beautiful as to win the highest praise, not merely from the multitudes, but also from such professional skeptics and sophisticates as Henry Adams and Charles Eliot Norton. In full revolt against the grotesque architecture of the "General Grant" period, the planners of the White City adhered closely to classical designs — a confession, in a sense, that America had not yet produced a worth-while native architecture. But as a classical reproduction — "what the Romans would have wished to create" — it was superb.

The Fair was dedicated on Columbus Day, October 12, 1892, but it was not officially opened until the following spring. In spite of the depression, twelve million visitors entered its gates, and it was a financial success. Its exhibits well revealed the material and artistic achievements of America and the world, for nearly every foreign nation was represented. The Palace of Fine Arts satisfied Americans that they no longer had need to apologize for the work of their sculptors and painters. Buildings devoted in whole or in part to transportation, manufactures, machinery, electricity, mines and mining, agriculture, horticulture, floriculture, and the liberal arts mirrored the remarkable transformations of the age. The Midway Plaisance, with its exotic "villages," its exciting "Streets of Cairo," its enormous "Ferris Wheel," and its innumerable other amusement features, set the pattern for future American playgrounds. Less talked about than they deserved were the numerous "congresses" that accompanied the Fair. Their purpose was to present the most pressing scientific, literary, and religious problems of the times. A fitting climax to the series of religious congresses was a great "parliament of religions" in which Catholics, Protestants, and Jews rubbed shoulders and exchanged ideas with Buddhists, Confucianists, Mohammedans, and representatives of many other religious sects. Out of the Fair and the congresses Americans got a far better understanding of their country and its place in the world than they had ever had before. They went home to imitate its architecture, to seek for beauty in the replanning of their towns and cities, and to dream dreams, not wholly unrealized, of a more abundant life.

Among the World's Fair congresses the one on history attracted comparatively little **Frederick** attention, but at an evening **Jackson** session, on July 12, 1893, Fred- **Turner** erick Jackson Turner, a youthful professor from the University of Wisconsin, read a paper of great importance on "The Significance of the Frontier in American History." Pointing out that "the germ theory of politics" had been sufficiently emphasized, and that the evolution of institutions along the Atlantic coast was, after all, a fairly "familiar phenomenon," he urged

historians of the United States to study the West as well as the East.

American social development has been continually beginning over again on the frontier. This perennial rebirth, this fluidity of American life, this expansion westward with its new opportunities, its continuous touch with the simplicity of primitive society, furnish the forces dominating American character. The true point of view in the history of this nation is not the Atlantic coast, it is the Great West. . . . What the Mediterranean Sea was to the Greeks, breaking the bonds of custom, offering new experiences, calling out new institutions and activities, that and more, the ever retreating frontier has been to the United States directly, and to the nations of Europe more remotely.

Turner's words were heeded, and soon a veritable cult of the West had sprung up among the writers of American history. Sometimes the American Historical Association, founded in 1884 by scholars of unimpeachable eastern connections, was accurately, if facetiously, described as the "Turner-verein." Turner's disciples outdid their master in claiming significance for the frontier, and they often claimed too much. Nevertheless, it seems clear that the influence of a succession of frontiers had much to do with molding the character of American civilization. Years before, E. L. Godkin, editor of the *Nation*, had recognized this fact in an elaborate review of de Tocqueville's *Democracy in America*. The pioneering element, he wrote,

spread itself thinly over a vast area of soil, of such extraordinary fertility that a very slight amount of toil expended on it affords returns that might have satisfied even the dreams of Spanish avarice. The result has been very much what we might have concluded, *a priori*, that it would be. A society composed at the period of its formation mainly of young men, coming from all parts of the world in quest of fortune, released from the ordinary restraints of family, church, and public opinion, even of the civil law, naturally and inevitably acquires a certain contempt for authority and impatience of it, and individualism among them develops itself very rapidly. If you place this society, thus constituted, in the midst of a

Frederick Jackson Turner

made a deep imprint upon two generations of American historians, and for a long time his views went virtually unchallenged. By the time of his death in 1932, however, opponents of his theories had appeared who argued that he had underemphasized the importance of eastern and European sources of culture in the making of American society. The issue they raised was, in a sense, analogous to the arguments among biologists as to the relative importance of environment and heredity. Turner set great store by the differences that environment promoted, while his opponents stressed the importance of the social heritage. The illustration to the right shows the Court of Honor, World's Columbian Exposition, 1893, looking east over the main basin.

---

wilderness, where each member of it has to contend, tools in hand, with Nature herself for wealth, or even subsistence, the ties which bind him to his fellows will for a while at least be rarely anything stronger than that of simple contiguity; and the only mutual obligation which this relation suggests strongly is that of rendering assistance occasionally in overcoming material difficulties — in other words, the simplest bond which can unite human beings. Each person is from the necessity of the case so absorbed in his own struggle for existence, that he has seldom occasion or time for the consideration and cultivation of his social relations. He knows nothing of the antecedents of his neighbors, nor they of his. They are not drawn together, in all probability, by a single memory or association. They have drifted into the same locality, it is true, under the guidance of a common impulse, and this a selfish one. So that the settler gets into the habit of looking at himself as an individual, of contemplating himself and his career separate and apart from the social organization. We do not say that this breeds selfishness — far from that; but it breeds individualism.[1]

[1] E. L. Godkin, "Aristocratic Opinions of Democracy," in *North American Review*, C, 194–232 (January, 1865).

Whether Godkin was right or wrong in his explanation of its causes, few will deny the existence among early Americans of a strongly individualistic bent. If, as Godkin held and Turner preached, this emphasis upon individualism proceeded from "the frontier life," then it would seem to follow that the gradual extinction of the frontier would make a difference. Godkin may not have been fully aware of the fact, but by the time he wrote these words the kind of frontier he described was rapidly disappearing. A generation later, when Turner wrote, it was virtually gone. Enormous tracts of unsettled land still existed in the trans-Mississippi West, but most of this land was arid plains or rugged mountains, totally unfitted for the type of agriculture that earlier American pioneers had practiced. Radical changes in methods of farming made possible a long-sustained advance, but by the end of the century the law of diminishing returns had begun to operate. "Free land" still existed in quantities, and settlers who knew no better than to take it could still be found, but for

The frontier life

the ordinary farmer who pioneered in the twentieth century the returns were rarely such as might have satisfied "the dreams of Spanish avarice." Rather, they were such as to saddle upon the next generation a vexatious problem of resettlement and relief.

Undoubtedly the diminishing importance of the frontier life had its effect upon the character of American civilization. New forces were now at work that had little to do with the frontier life, except to stifle it. Coincident with the passing of the frontier an economic revolution had occurred that in its transforming influence had affected not only the United States but the whole world besides. Railroads permeated every part of the country, and at both coasts connected with steamship lines that crisscrossed every ocean. Telegraph, telephone, and cable service grew daily more complete. Cheap paper, cheap printing, and cheap postage greatly facilitated the circulation of newspapers, books, periodicals, and advertising literature. Inventions crowded forward in an exciting procession. Big business, equipped and re-equipped with new and then still newer tools, throve mightily, and in some instances approached monopoly. Labor and capital drew apart with an acute class-consciousness that the frontier life had never known. Before this barrage the individualism of log-cabin, covered-wagon days gave way. For the few it became an instrument with which to exploit the many; for the many it tended, more and more, to become merely a memory.

Whatever the forces that worked together to shape the pattern of American society in **Uniformity** the late nineteenth century, un-**in American** doubtedly the economic revolu-**society** tion, aided and abetted by the gradual disappearance of the frontier, played a principal part. Responding to the new impetus, an urbanized industrialized society swept rapidly from East to West. Labor, influenced no less by the influx of European ideas than by the influx of European immigrants, tended to subordinate the welfare of the individual to the welfare of the class.

Farmers, transformed by the machine age into petty business men who produced primarily to sell, forsook their individualistic traditions to battle cooperatively for their rights through Granges, Alliances, and even a third political party. With the whole nation open, almost equally, to the operation of the same forces, life in the United States became increasingly standardized. Sectional differences and local idiosyncrasies yielded slowly but surely before an insistent demand for uniformity.

Much has been written to show how the coming of the immigrants in the late nineteenth century brought diver- **Immigrant** sity rather than uniformity to **influences** the American people. It is possible that the immigrants, especially those who remained in the cities, may have acted, in a sense, as a counterweight for the frontier influence. If on the one hand the native Americans tended to be devotees of individual freedom, the immigrants on the other were apt to have a wholesome respect for group cooperation and no serious objection to paternalism in government. The native Americans might see in majority rule and the right of every man to vote a satisfactory guarantee of equality of opportunity, but the immigrants were under no such illusions; what a man really needed was a job and security in it. The native Americans, fortified by their frontier background, could think readily in nationalistic terms, but the city-dwelling immigrants were more likely to be particularistic; their primary interests lay in the welfare of their group, their sect, their party, their locality.

It must not be forgotten, however, that in spite of the rising immigrant tide, the native Americans continued to be overwhelmingly in the ascendancy. During the thirty years preceding 1900 the percentage of native-born inhabitants remained practically constant, varying through four sets of census figures less than one per cent from an average of eighty-six per cent. It is true, of course, that many native Americans — in 1900 about one fifth of the total population

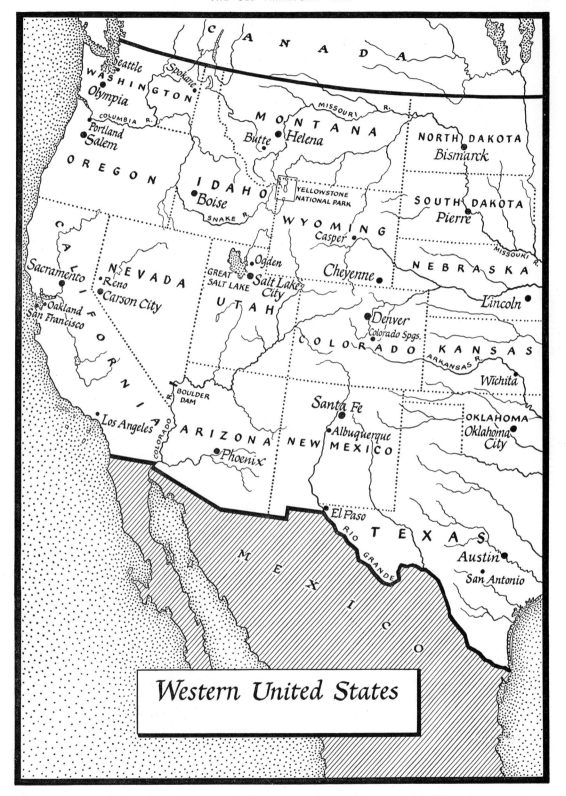

Western United States

Family group by Eastman Johnson, one of the ablest of nineteenth-century American portrait and genre painters, shows three generations, grandparents, parents, and eleven children, in the library of a sumptuous New York house.

— had at least one immigrant parent; but it is also true that until the last decade of the nineteenth century the immigrants, numerous as they were, came primarily from the British Isles and Canada, from Germany, and from the Scandinavian countries. In the seventies 82.8 per cent were so classified, in the eighties, 75.6; in the nineties, when the trend from southern and eastern Europe began in earnest, 41.8. During these three decades some 7,834,412 immigrants entered the United States from Canada or from northwestern Europe, as against only 2,953,714 from southern and eastern Europe. The former, as already noted, were quickly and easily assimilated into the American population; even the latter made all possible haste to imitate the American way of life. Against the winds of uniformity that were blowing, the nineteenth-century immigrants offered almost as little resistance as the descendants of the Puritans and the Cavaliers.

In a sense the frontier, while it lasted, had had much to do with the increasing homogeneity of the American people. Every part of the United States, at one time or another, had gone through the frontier process, and the experience had everywhere left its mark — more or less the same mark. Just as the child is father to the man, so the primitive society of frontier times bequeathed a number of its most distinctive characteristics to later generations. Such ideals as flowed from the frontier's love of conquest, of individual freedom, and of equality of opportunity lived on into a period when the actual conditions of life belied them. The frontier might have vanished, but the restless search for greener pastures that it had bred survived.

But if the frontier had promoted homogeneity, the passing of the frontier tended to promote it even more. It is not **Passing of** necessary to believe that while **the frontier** the West was young all of the more aggressive and energetic people went West, leaving to the East only a stagnant and unenterprising lot. Nevertheless, with the frontier at the vanishing point, with the railroads offering tempting rates, and with opportunity knocking more boldly in the eastern cities than on the western plains, there occurred in the late nineteenth century a remarkable return of the West upon the East. The enterprising Easterner going west was met by the enterprising Westerner going east. Western ideas got a hearing in the East, just as eastern ideas had all along got a hearing in the West. Western leaders in business, in politics, in the professions appeared in every eastern city.

Northerners, too, went south, and Southerners went north. The population was mixed up as never before, and the characteristics of one section became increasingly the characteristics of all.

This strikingly homogeneous nature of American society can perhaps be best appreciated when compared with European society during the same period. In Europe only a few hundred miles at most would bring the traveler to a region where the people saluted a different flag, spoke a different language, cherished a different culture. In America, for nearly three thousand miles east and west, and for half that many miles north and south, one met with the same flag, the same language, and essentially the same culture. Minor differences of course endured. New Englanders broadened their *a*'s, did curious things to their *r*'s, and sometimes forgot their final *g*'s. Southerners spoke with a soft and musical drawl that owed something, no doubt, to the influence of a large colored population; certain cities reflected the speech characteristics of a leading immigrant group — Jewish in New York, German in Milwaukee, Swedish in Minneapolis. Only by such trifles as these could the remnants of separate cultural heritages be observed. Far greater differences existed within the compass of the British Isles alone. Americans everywhere tended to talk alike, think alike, act alike.

"After all, business is the biggest thing in this country." So the editor of the Atlanta *Constitution* told his readers on January 8, 1890; and for good measure he added, "Politicians may talk, but businessmen will act, control, and dominate the destinies of this common-sense country." Embryo Populists, whether of the South or of the West, might not have approved the *Constitution's* cheerful acceptance of this situation, but few would have tried to deny the fact. Business, moreover, was not only the "biggest thing" in the country, it was also the greatest single agency of standardization. More and more the "princes of commerce and industry" thought and planned in national terms. With revolutionary improvements in means of communication at their disposal, they had expanded

Nation-wide business

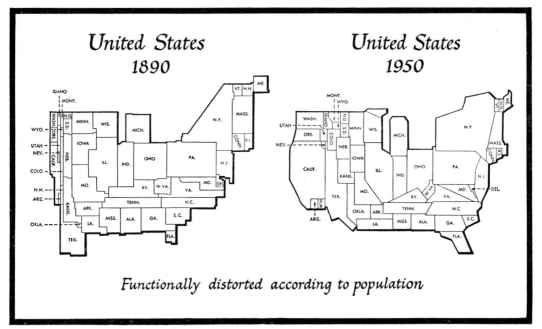

United States 1890

United States 1950

Functionally distorted according to population

From Baldwin, Recent American History
(American Book Company).

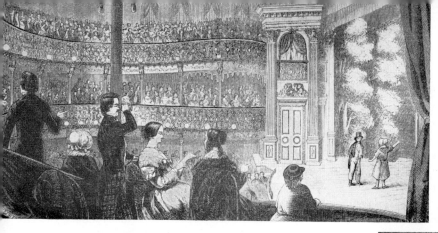

CULTURE. Before the days of movies, the theatre played an important part in city life.

DEPARTMENT STORE. Opening day at Lord & Taylor's. Illustration from McCabe, *Lights and Shadows of New York Life*, 1872.

DINNER PARTY. Entertaining during the early days of gaslight. Woodcut.

their interests to include the whole nation. No longer did the manufacturer seek mainly to reach a local market; he must now sell his product in every state and territory of the Union — beyond the national borders if he could. Local natural resources might determine that cotton factories should dominate in the South, iron- and steelworks in the Middle Atlantic states, and flour- and grist-mills in the new Northwest, but dependence upon a nation-wide market was universal. Merchants in every part of the country offered the same types of goods to their customers, and counted upon national campaigns of advertising, paid for by the manufacturers, to stimulate sales. Americans everywhere became accustomed to the same "makes" of washing-machines, farm implements, bicycles, wagons and buggies; wore the same styles of readymade clothes; painted their houses with nationally known brands of housepaint; purchased quantities of patent breakfast foods, patent toothpowder, and patent liniment ("good for man or beast"). Mail-order houses, selling commodities pictured in catalogues at cut-rate prices direct to the trustful purchaser, did a thriving business. Retail prices, in spite of widely divergent transportation costs, varied little from one section of the country to another, and even the methods of doing business became standardized.

Industrialism, of course, meant the growth of cities, but this was a development that spread itself with remarkable **Industrial-** uniformity the whole country **ization** over. While the Northeast led the way in urbanization, other sections of the country showed themselves excellent imitators. The South during and after reconstruction sought eagerly to crowd itself with factories and cities; as Henry Watterson put it, "The

252

City living in the later nineteenth century, particularly for the well-to-do, could be very gracious indeed. Men of wealth built massive, showy houses, entertained lavishly, sponsored in various ways the promotion of culture. Horse-drawn streetcars supplemented private means of transportation. Note the styles affected by ladies of fashion.

CITY MANSION. E. B. Crocker residence, San Francisco.

South, having had its bellyful of blood, has gotten a taste of money, and is too busy trying to make more to quarrel with anybody." The West, too, from the time of the Civil War on, tried hard to get rid of its overgreat dependence upon agriculture which made no one rich, and to embrace industry which made riches for at least a few. In 1871 the Milwaukee Chamber of Commerce lamented:

We are sending our hard lumber east to get it back as furniture and agricultural implements, we ship ores to St. Louis and New York, to pay the cost of bringing it back as shot, type, pipe, sheet lead, white lead, paint, etc., we ship away our wool crop and import cloth, carpets, blankets and other fabrics; we give rags for paper, and hides for boots and harness, and iron-ore for stoves — and our consumers all the while are paying the double costs of this unnecessary transportation.

What this chamber of commerce really wanted for Milwaukee was factories, of whatever kind, and Milwaukee soon got them.

So also did every other enterprising western city with good railroad or water connections. In 1870 only 20.9 per cent of the American population lived in places of eight thousand inhabitants or more, whereas in 1903 33.1 per cent were so situated. In the East the percentage of city dwellers ran well above this figure; in the South, the Middle West, and the Far West, well below it. But the trend toward urbanization was national, not sectional, and it affected every part of the country.

The new cities and the rejuvenated old ones showed remarkable similarities. According to James Bryce, "American cities with eight or nine exceptions differ from one another only herein, that some of them are built more with brick than with wood, and others more with wood than with brick." The checkerboard of "squares" in which William Penn had laid out Philadelphia became the favorite American pattern for city development, and each

American cities

new "addition" strove valiantly to be exactly like the rest. Pavements rarely kept up with expansion, and while asphalt and brick won increasing popularity, cobblestone, stone block, wood block, and macadam continued in general use. Telephone, telegraph, and electric light poles and wires, all rare or missing in the seventies, became chronic by the nineties, and competed with trees and fences for space at the sides of roads and railroads. Business districts at any given time were everywhere much alike, but each decade saw the height of downtown buildings increase. The first of the skyscrapers, made possible by the use of structural steel and iron, was the ten-storied Home Insurance Building of Chicago, completed in 1885. Thereafter, with one accord, city skylines rose, while traffic congestion increased in spite of the best efforts of horsecars, cable cars, elevated railways, and electric streetcars to keep pace with it. For those who could afford the time and cost of transportation to work, residence districts pushed farther and farther into the surrounding country; for those who could not, apartment houses, tenements, and slum districts were multiplied. Unknown to the cities of the nineteenth century were the long lines of automobiles, the garages, the filling stations, and the motion-picture "palaces" of today. Omnipresent then, but almost obsolete now, were horse-drawn vehicles, livery stables, blacksmith shops, and saloons with shuttered doors. But the uniformity of yesterday is matched only by the uniformity of today.

Behind these externals lay a pattern of life that varied little from city to city. The **Wages and hours** great majority of city-dwellers were employees of industry or trade, dependent upon wages for their daily bread. Wages, judged by present-day standards, were incredibly low; American workers, on an average, earned between $400 and $500 a year at a time when a dollar might be worth perhaps only three times what it is worth today. The unskilled worker might receive as much as $1.50 a day for his efforts,

but he was often unemployed; a total take of four or five dollars a week was not unusual. For such persons there were then no unemployment benefits; if one were out of work for long, he begged, borrowed, stole, or starved. The working day was ordinarily ten hours, and the six day week was taken for granted. Accidents among industrial employees were numerous, and all too lightly regarded by employers. The presence of women and children in industry tended to hold down wages, but was for many families an absolute necessity. While a few women in the upper strata of society grumbled that the opportunity for "careers" was still in large measure denied them, those on the lower levels suffered no such sorrows. The percentage of women gainfully employed rose from fifteen per cent in 1870 to twenty per cent in 1900. In Philadelphia, by the latter year, one third of the women (counting girls over ten years of age) worked for wages away from their homes. Wherever it could be used to advantage, child labor was ruthlessly exploited — in the cotton-mills of the South, in the sweatshops of the East, in the packing-plants of the West. According to one estimate, there were not less than ten million people in the United States living in abject poverty, people who, "though using their best efforts, are failing to obtain sufficient necessaries for maintaining physical efficiency."

Among the people who lived in cities, from eighty to ninety per cent rented the space in which they lived. Those who **Urban life** worked for low wages, whether immigrants or native Americans, lived under conditions that varied from bad to unspeakable. For all such, overcrowding was a necessity; families who rented a few shabby rooms added to the confusion by taking in roomers and boarders. In the tenement districts sanitary conditions could hardly have been worse. The alleys crawled with filth, the streets alternated clouds of dust with seas of mud. Water stood in the cellars, plumbing was chronically out of order, the odor of poverty enveloped the region like a cloud.

The middle classes lived farther out from the downtown section in flats or apartment houses, sometimes even in dwellings owned by the occupant. They depended upon regular incomes or salaries instead of wages, were for the most part native Americans who had come to the cities from the rural districts. Naturally, most of them retained in the cities the characteristics and customs of country-dwellers, so that American cities in their cultural aspects became, in a sense, merely overgrown country towns. A small fraction of the population enjoyed large incomes, and some of them, particularly the *nouveaux riches*, laid firm foundations for Thorstein Veblen's theory of conspicuous waste.

It would be a mistake, however, to assume that the United States was merely a nation **Rural** of cities. More than sixty per **America** cent of the people, as late as 1900, still lived in the country, or in towns of less than four thousand inhabitants. Practically all of these, and many more besides, depended directly or indirectly upon agriculture for their livelihood. Even the cities, in the last analysis, owed much to the farms, for throughout the nineteenth century an abundant farm demand, restricted from foreign purchases by a protective-tariff policy, absorbed the products of the city factories, and spared American manufacturers the necessity of finding in foreign markets an outlet for their goods. For agriculture, as for industry, these were revolutionary years. New tools had to be learned and used, new types of crops had to be raised to suit the city markets, experiments with diversification and standardization had to be carried through, a rising price for farmlands had to be faced. Less and less the American farmer farmed according to ritual; more and more he used his intelligence and the reports of scientific investigators to improve his profits. Caught securely in the meshes of the prevailing economic system, he made every effort to understand it and to bend it to his needs. The farmer movements of the period were not the work of wild-eyed radicals; the farm leaders and a host of well-informed

"The Children's Friend." A character sketch by W. H. Hyde at a crossing opposite young ladies school, 1877.

followers based their arguments upon reasoning as sound as that which guided the actions of the prudent industrialist. The interests of the farmers perhaps collided with those of the industrialists, but that did not necessarily make the farm policies radical.

Farm life tended gradually to merge with village life. On Saturdays farmers went to town to trade; on Sundays they went to town to church; on other days when work was not too pressing they went to town, with or without excuses. Retired farmers went to town to live and to be visited by their children, who in many cases were now their tenants. Farm boys and girls went to school in town, got jobs in town, and, when they could, set out with the town boys and girls for the city. Farmers and farm wives borrowed from the town the conveniences that the town had borrowed from the city. Steadily, the extreme isolation of farm life broke down — a process that the rural free delivery of mail, rural telephones, rural electrification, the automobile, and the radio were soon to accelerate immeasurably.

Country towns and villages enjoyed an

THE COUNTRY SCHOOL, 1871. Painting by Winslow Homer.

Country living in many ways contrasted markedly with city living. Educational opportunities were severely limited; much hard work still had to be done by hand. But farm life was brightened by home reading, holiday celebrations, and frequent visits by peddlers.

THANKSGIVING DAY. Shooting turkeys for the holiday.

Town life

importance during most of the nineteenth century that they have entirely lost today, and were beginning to lose at its close. As centers of trade for the surrounding countryside, they could count upon a certain amount of steady business. The stores might be strung along a single "Main Street," or they might surround a central block on which, in county-seats, the courthouse was certain to be located. Only in the business districts of the larger towns were the streets paved, and both horses and drivers took the mud, ruts, and dust philosophically. The dwellings, at least on one side of the inevitable railroad track, were quite commodious, and the yards even more so. Barns and outbuildings were numerous, for many townspeople kept a

horse or two, a cow, a pig to butcher in the fall, and some poultry. Room was usually found also for a few fruit trees and a sizable vegetable garden. The incomes of village-dwellers were not large, but they had no need to be.

All the town did deference to the railroad. Incoming passenger trains were met by as many of the inhabitants as were footloose, arrivals and departures were carefully noted, and the town paper was scanned each Wednesday or Thursday to see that no such news was omitted. The station agent was an individual of importance who often asserted his dignity by a superb indifference to the wants of customers. Over the railroad the crops from the surrounding country went to market, over it came the many necessities

CORN SHELLING. Painting by Eastman Johnson.

THE NEWSPAPER. Family enjoying *Hearth and Home*, an illustrated publication.

THE PEDDLER. Woodcut, 1868. His news and his wares were equally anticipated.

of life that the farmers and the villagers were unable to produce for themselves. By means of it, and the telegraph line that seemed somehow a part of it, contact with the rest of the world was maintained. Resentment against railroad extortions was rife, especially in the West, and demands for railroad regulation merged into demands for government ownership, but the awe-inspiring importance of the railroad was never forgotten. Not infrequently the railroad companies played leading roles in local as well as in state and national politics.

Before the automobile age annihilated distance, and while the city still seemed far away, the village had a lively and separate life of its own. At the center of this was the church, which gave excuse for and organization to the gregarious

Religion

instincts of the people. In the cities the immigrants and the children of immigrants had greatly increased the Catholic and Jewish population, but rural America stood steadfastly by the faith of its Protestant fathers. In every village on a Sunday morning the calm was shattered at regular intervals by the jangling bells of not less than three or four rival denominations. Church services went on all day, and attendance was good: Sunday School at ten o'clock, preaching at eleven o'clock, children's services in the afternoon, young people's meeting at seven o'clock, evening worship with liberal congregational singing at eight o'clock. Weekday services included prayer-meetings on Wednesday or Thursday evening, to which only a handful of the most devout repaired; better-attended meetings of ladies' aid societies,

Fire engine on "Main Street, New Jersey." Painting by E. Opper, 1880. The mad dash of the old-fashioned horse-drawn fire engine to put out a fire challenged the interest of Americans of all ages.

missionary societies, and guilds, all absorbed in money-raising efforts; choir-practice for the faithful, if somewhat storm-tossed, musical contingent; and "protracted meetings," or "revivals," held night after night for several weeks once or twice each year. For these long meetings evangelists who imitated the methods of Moody and Sankey were often called in to aid the local pastors, and with good luck hundreds might be induced to "make their profession of faith." The old emotionalism of the frontier was not quite dead. "Shouting" was not unusual, "conversion" was for many an intensely exciting experience, and preaching reached its climax of success when "not a dry eye was left in the house." A few country churches, each in its mournful setting of tombstones, still managed to survive, as the long rows of teams tied each Sunday to the church's hitch-racks well attested. Farm families, however, preferred increasingly to attend church in town and so the country congregations dwindled.

Theologically speaking, the great problem of the times was the attempt of religion to **Science vs.** digest the scientists' doctrine of **religion** evolution. For the older gen-

eration, of whatever denomination, this was asking a great deal. The idea of an infallible Church or an infallible Book had been too long and too steadfastly maintained to be surrendered without a struggle, and heresy charges drove many of the modernists from their pulpits. But the reasonableness of the evolutionary hypothesis could not be lost indefinitely on a world that owed so much to scientific discovery. Thomas Huxley, the English biologist, and Herbert Spencer, the English philosopher, both of whom visited America, greatly influenced American thinking toward the acceptance of the Darwinian concept, and John Fiske, the American historian, argued earnestly that, far from undermining religion, Darwinism made possible "a higher view of the workings of God and of the nature of Man than was ever attainable before." Prominent clerics, among them Henry Ward Beecher and Lyman Abbott, also attempted to reconcile science and religion, and the popular defense of evolution made by a Scot, Henry Drummond, in his book *Natural Law in the Spiritual World* (1884), profoundly impressed the American reading public.

For the most part American thinkers, in

the struggle over evolution and the literal interpretation of the Scriptures, merely followed the lead of Europeans; if there was an American contribution to the controversy, it was to the effect that, after all, conduct was far more important than belief. "Social Darwinists," who found in the law of the survival of the fittest an admirable defense for the "dog-eat-dog" rule of might in human relations, won far less response from most Americans than the more merciful interpreters of Darwin, who held that the evolutionary process was one in which all men, not just a powerful few, might hope to share. In line with this concept was what came to be called the "social gospel," which took pains to emphasize practical rather than theoretical Christianity. This point of view appealed strongly to the ordinary man, who was considerably befuddled anyway by the debate among the theologians. He cheerfully supported the temperance efforts of the Woman's Christian Temperance Union and the Anti-Saloon League; he supplied funds for the establishment of institutional churches that could minister to the spirit through the flesh; he applauded Jane Addams of Chicago and Lillian D. Wald of New York for their settlement work; and he held such agencies of "uplift" as lecture courses and Chautauqua programs to be laudable byproducts of Christianity. As already noted, Christian Science, the first new American religion since Mormonism, asserted the complete control of the Divine mind over matter. Thus might religion serve the practical purpose of keeping its devotees well.

What Americans wrote and read during the two concluding decades of the nineteenth century showed little improvement over the standards set
Literature
during the seventies. William Dean Howells continued to exploit American themes in such outstanding contributions as *A Modern Instance* (1882) and *The Rise of Silas Lapham* (1884); and Mark Twain continued to poke fun at sacred traditions in his *The Prince and the Pauper* (1881) and *A Connecticut Yankee*

in King Arthur's Court (1889). Much as these leaders were appreciated, however, the public taste was more completely met by Lew Wallace's *Ben Hur; A Tale of the Christ* (1880), in which the appeal of religion and romance were skilfully intertwined. *Ben Hur* sold a total of 300,000 copies in a period of ten years. To a generation that deferred to the G.A.R., Wallace's book lost nothing in interest from the fact that its author had been a general in the Civil War. The persistence of war memories no doubt accounted in part also for the success of Stephen Crane's *The Red Badge of Courage* (1895), a starkly realistic portrayal of the horrors of the battlefield. Because of this success, Crane's *Maggie, A Girl of the Streets* (1892), which had failed to attract attention when it had first appeared, was republished in 1896, and was widely read. Grimly realistic, it told a sordid tale of life in the city slums. Other writers on current themes also got a hearing, despite this same tendency to emphasize the less commendable aspects of American society. E. W. Howe's *The Story of a Country Town* (1884), and Hamlin Garland's *Main Travelled Roads* (1891), showed how full of wretchedness and "smoldering discontent" life on the much-idealized "Middle Border" could be. John Hay's *The Bread-Winners* (1883) attacked the excesses of radical labor leaders and sang the praises of economic individualism. H. H. Boyeson's *The Mammon of Unrighteousness* (1891) exposed the unscrupulous methods and the crudeness of the ultra-rich. Paul Leicester Ford's *The Honorable Peter Stirling* (1894) drew on Grover Cleveland's career to produce a revealing study of New York ward politics. Edward Bellamy's *Looking Backward* (1888), one of the most influential books of the time, contrasted the world the author knew with a socialistic utopia of the year 2000 in which all economic and political wrongs had been righted. But a little book by the Reverend C. M. Sheldon of Topeka, Kansas, *In His Steps* (1896), which also had a lesson to teach, outsold nearly everything except the Bible itself. Sheldon's book told the story of what had happened when a single congregation attempted to guide its conduct strictly by the motto: "What would Jesus do?" Sales estimates by 1925 ran to over eight million copies in the United States alone, with an additional twelve millions in the British Empire.

The lighter side was not unrepresented. Joel Chandler Harris's *Uncle Remus: His Songs and His Sayings* (1880) was the first of a long series of tales that delighted American children and their parents. Harris, an Atlanta journalist and a white man, recorded the speech-habits and folk-lore of the Negroes with rare fidelity. His "Uncle Remus" was an ancient Negro whose familiarity with the animal kingdom exhibited itself in priceless fables. Readers with a little perspicacity could see plainly enough in "Br'er Rabbit's" endless efforts to elude "Br'er Fox" and "Br'er Wolf" the story of the southern Negro's difficult relationship with his white overlords. James Whitcomb Riley's *The Old Swimmin' Hole and 'Leven More Poems* (1883) began another long series. Riley's rhymes were replete with Hoosierisms, and he was correctly termed the "Hoosier poet," but his verses were read and loved by Americans of every section. Eugene Field alternated unbridled humor with unrelieved sentimentality in his column "Sharps and Flats," which appeared for many years in the Chicago *Morning News* (later the *Record*). Reprinted and recited endlessly, and republished in such volumes as *A Little Book of Western Verse* (1889), Field's poems enjoyed a tremendous popularity. For the devotees of romance, there were the ceaseless outpourings of such writers as Mary J. Holmes, Bertha M. Clay, and Laura Jean Libbey; and, a cut above these in quality, novels by F. Marion Crawford and E. P. Roe. This, too, was the age of the dime novel, the blood and thunder story, the boy's books by Horatio Alger and by William T. Adams (Oliver Optic), and the *Elsie* books for girls, a "goody-goody" series by Martha F. Finley. It is not surprising that, with such books as these cap-

tivating the public, the greatest poet of her time, Emily Dickinson, was discovered only by a later generation.

Undoubtedly public education played an important part in the standardizing process so characteristic of the times. During these years the public **Public education** school system achieved the pattern that with only slight variations it has maintained ever since. In the rural districts the one-room country school, ungraded but designed to carry its pupils through the equivalent of eight grades in town, still endured. In the towns and villages an eight-grade elementary school, followed by a four-year high school, was the goal most often set and increasingly attained. State-supported normal schools for the training of teachers, a state-supported college of agriculture, and a state-supported university, which might or might not include the college of agriculture, completed the customary picture. Strangely, forty-five states and several territories, in spite of complete freedom to mold their educational systems as they chose, emerged with essentially the same system. Even the content of public education tended to become fixed. In the rural and elementary schools instruction in the "three R's" reigned supreme without much attention to "extras." High schools, in spite of some commendable efforts to prepare their graduates for life rather than for college, held steadfastly to a curriculum not far different from that of the old academies they supplanted.

Practically all of the colleges and universities took up with the elective system that Charles W. Eliot had intro- **Colleges and** duced at Harvard, but the **Universities** courses thus offered, cafeteria fashion, differed little from campus to campus. Most of the older generation of instructors had been trained in Germany; most of the younger generation at Harvard or Johns Hopkins, the two universities that had pioneered the way for graduate work in America. At the end of the century scarcely a college student anywhere was more than a single generation removed in his instruction from one or the other of these institutions. Students everywhere, thus exposed to about the same educational diet, tended to get about the same results from their college work and to emerge with strikingly similar points of view. Contacts in college with individuals from other parts of the country helped them to "rub off the rough corners," and still further promoted the cause of standardization. Private institutions, even those under religious leadership, shared almost equally, to the dismay of the orthodox, in the standardizing process. The earnest pursuit of truth for truth's sake, regardless of religious, political, or economic prejudices, met occasional setbacks, but the eloquent defense of academic freedom, made by the Regents of the University of Wisconsin in answer to an attack on Professor Richard T. Ely, the noted economist, raised a banner that institutions of higher learning the whole country over were increasingly willing to defend: "In all lines of academic investigation it is of the utmost importance that the investigator should be absolutely free to follow the indications of the truth wherever they may lead. Whatever may be the limitations which trammel inquiry elsewhere, we believe that the great State University of Wisconsin should ever encourage that continual and fearless sifting and winnowing by which alone the truth can be found." [1]

Other evidence of the rapid drift toward standardization in American life may be cited almost at will. Improved means of transportation led to the formation of a host of national organizations, each with its annual meeting attended by delegates from the whole country over. Subjected to the same influences, the delegates carried back home the same ideas. Better means of communication led to the astonishing expansion of the Associated Press and other news-gathering agencies, which furnished identical stories to the readers of hundreds of different newspapers and thus laid the basis for a common reaction. The day when an editor such as

[1] Richard T. Ely, *Ground Under Our Feet — An Autobiography* (1938), p. 232.

Booker T. Washington of Tuskegee Institute, Alabama, was one of the ablest of American Negro educators.

Horace Greeley of the New York *Tribune* or Charles A. Dana of the *Sun* expressed his personality through his newspaper had long since passed. Among the new editors Joseph Pulitzer of the New York *World*, and William Randolph Hearst of the San Francisco *Examiner*, did indeed introduce an exaggerated type of sensationalism, but their methods were quickly copied by all except a few of the most conservative journals. Newspapers imitated one another in format as well as in content; they not only read alike; they looked alike. Magazines, even of the popular variety, built up national circulations, and promoted whatever cause they served in a national way. Musical "hits" registered in New York were whistled a few days later by the newsboys in every other American city, and within weeks had reached the country towns. Plays that enjoyed a "run" in New York soon took to the road, and were produced also by the numerous stock companies that flourished in the pre-motion-picture age. Chautauqua circuits of popular lecturers and entertainers were formed to spin around like a top each season until the entire American map had been covered, and all who had ears to hear had heard.

LAWN TENNIS, 1887.
Aquarelle print by L.
Prang and Company.

Sports came to take an increasingly prominent part in the lives of most Americans. The first bicycles sometimes had front wheels five feet high and could travel twenty miles an hour. But the bicycle craze was far less permanent than football, baseball, and tennis. Note the costumes.

BICYCLING. First national meet at Newport, 1880. Illustration in *Leslie's Illustrated Newspaper*, from a sketch by Charles Upham.

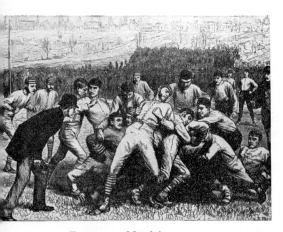

FOOTBALL. Match between Yale and Princeton, 1879. Drawing by A. B. Frost

PROFESSIONAL BASEBALL, 1887. Lithograph by the New York Lithograph Company.

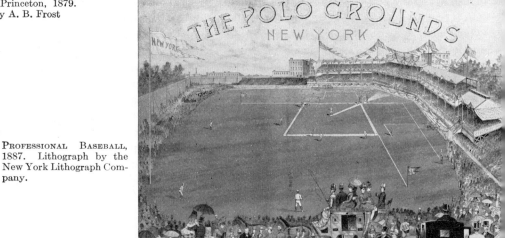

Even sports became nationalized. Base-ball had its origins in what the English called "rounders," a game which, after considerable modification, the Americans called "town ball." As early as 1845 the Knickerbocker Club of New York provided a rule book for the game, but its popularity really dates from the Civil War, during which it was played with enthusiasm by both the wearers of the Blue and the wearers of the Gray. After the war, its devotees carried it to every part of the nation, North and South alike. During the seventies and eighties it developed into the "great American game," with a complicated system of major and minor leagues that every boy and youth in America understood. Football, which was introduced into the United States during the seventies as an adaptation of English Rugby, had by the nineties conquered most of the American colleges and universities. Professional boxing approached the level of respectability when "Gentleman Jim" Corbett won the heavyweight championship in 1892. By this time, too, the bicycle had been tamed, and bicycling had become a fad that women and children as well as men could enjoy. For devotees of the less strenuous life there were such milder activities as lawn-tennis, roller-skating, and croquet. The poor no less than the rich, town- and country-dwellers no less

Sports

than city-dwellers, found in sports a satisfying refuge from the workaday world, which replaced, in a sense, the excitement once associated with a developing frontier. And, at least for masculine America, the doings recorded on the "sports page" furnished lively topics of conversation when all else failed.

It would, of course, be ridiculous not to concede that striking differences as well as striking similarities have always existed, and will always exist, in a nation as vast as the United States. In many ways, no doubt, the differences were more important than the similarities. But the fact remains that by the end of the nineteenth century, American civilization had achieved a distinct pattern, a pattern quite as unique as that possessed by any other nation. Bryce's *American Commonwealth*, which first appeared in 1888, revealed this pattern with all its faults to thinking Americans. Thereupon the book itself became a powerful agency of standardization. Seized upon as a college text and repeatedly reissued, it served for a generation as the mirror with which Americans viewed themselves. Some of the things they saw they liked and meant to keep; others they definitely did not like and meant to change. In part, at least, out of this new comprehension came the heavy rumblings of reform with which the twentieth century opened.

Bibliography

On the art achievements of the nation, particularly as revealed by the Chicago World's Fair of 1893, Charles Moore, *Daniel H. Burnham* (2 vols., 1921), will be found useful; also, William Walton, *World's Columbian Exposition, MDCCCXCIII; The Art and Architecture* (2 vols. in 3, 1893–95); and the appropriate section in Oliver W. Larkin, *Art and Life in America* (1949). An admirable pictorial history of the United States is Marshall B. Davidson, *Life in America* (2 vols., 1951).

Turner's essay, "The Significance of the Frontier in American History," together with other interesting information on the so-called "Turner hypothesis," appear in *The Early Writings of Frederick Jackson Turner* (1938). An illuminating interpretation of the role of the West in American history is contained in F. L. Paxson, *When the West Is Gone* (1930). Divergent views on the importance of the West are set forth in *Sources of Culture in the Middle West*, edited by Dixon Ryan Fox (1934). On the work of American historians in general, Michael Kraus, *The Writing of American History* (1953), omits few important names, but is less satisfactory from the point of view of interpretation than H. Hale Bellot, *American History and American Historians* (1952). *The Marcus W. Jernegan Essays in American Historiography*, edited by William T. Hutchinson (1937), is the work of many writers and of varying merit. Henry Adams, *The Education of Henry Adams, An Autobiography* (1918), tells the life story of a great historian. It may be supplemented by Robert A. Hume, *Runaway Star: An Appreciation of Henry Adams* (1951); and *Henry Adams and his Friends*, edited by H. D. Cater (1947).

The most satisfactory study of the transformation of American life wrought by the economic revolution is A. M. Schlesinger, *The Rise of the City, 1878–1898* (1933). Josiah Strong, *The Twentieth Century City* (1898), is a useful sociological study. Bayrd Still, *Milwaukee, The History of a City* (1948), is an admirable study of a single metropolis. *Historiography and Urbanization: Essays in American History in Honor of W. Stull Holt*, edited by Eric F. Goldman (1941), contains a number of suggestive essays. The growing influence of settlement work in Chicago and New York is set forth in Jane Addams, *Forty Years at Hull House* (1935); and in Lillian D. Wald, *The House on Henry Street* (1915). Robert Hunter, *Poverty* (new ed., 1912), describes urban poverty and pauperism as it existed around the turn of the century. Thomas Beer, *The Mauve Decade* (1926), is smart and cynical on all aspects of the society of the times. Thorstein Veblen, *The Theory of the Leisure Class* (1899), is a vigorous attack on orthodox theories with reference to capital and labor.

The social history of religion in the United States is attracting an increasing amount of attention. Among the best of the existing studies are H. K. Rowe, *The History of Religion in the United States* (1924); W. W. Sweet, *The Story of Religion in America* (1930); H. K. Carroll, *The Religious Forces of the United States* (rev. ed., 1912). Evangelistic trends and practices are treated in G. C. Loud, *Evangelized America* (1928); H. C. Weber, *Evangelism* (1929); and Beardsley, *A History of American Revivals*, al-ready mentioned. Effects of the new industrialism on religion are set forth in A. I. Abell, *The Urban Impact on American Protestantism, 1865–1900* (1943); and May, *Protestant Churches and Industrial America*, already cited.

There is a steadily lengthening list of books dealing with religious freedom and the conflict between science and religion. Among those most useful are Sidney Warren, *American Freethought, 1860–1914* (1943); Edward A. White, *Science and Religion in American Thought: The Impact of Naturalism* (1952); A. D. White, *A History of the Warfare of Science with Theology in Christendom* (new ed., 1910); Robert G. Ingersoll, *Letters*, edited by Eva Ingersoll Wakefield (1951); Anson P. Stokes, *Church and State in the United States: Historical Development and Contemporary Problems of Religious Freedom under the Constitution* (3 vols., 1950); Zechariah Chafee, Jr., *Free Speech in the United States* (1941); and R. Freeman Butts, *The American Tradition in Religion and Education* (1950). See also works listed in the bibliography for chapter 5.

On literary and educational trends during the period, the books mentioned on pp. 103–104 continue pertinent. In addition, D. C. Gilman, *The Launching of a University* (1906), tells the story for Johns Hopkins; while Henry James, *Charles W. Eliot* (2 vols., 1930), does a similar service for Harvard. On the part played by the University of Chicago in stimulating graduate study in the West, see T. W. Goodspeed, *William Rainey Harper, First President of the University of Chicago* (1928).

On the general subject of journalism, the best account is F. L. Mott, *American Journalism, A History* (1941). Philip Kinsley, *The Chicago Tribune: Its First Hundred Years* (3 vols., 1943–46), is written with considerable detachment. J. W. Barrett, *Joseph Pulitzer and His World* (1941), is an appreciative, uncritical biography.

There are a few good books on sports, among them F. R. Dulles, *America Learns to Play: A History of Popular Recreation* (1940); A. G. Spalding, *America's National Game* (1911); A. M. Weyand, *American Football* (1926); and Alexander Johnston, *Ten — and Out* (1927).

EXPANSION AND REFORM

1890 - 1917

The closing decade of the nineteenth century showed the United States reaching maturity as a nation. The national boundaries, long merely geographic lines, now marked also the extent of population expansion. The frontier line, long of interest to cartographers and more recently also to historians, could no longer be traced from north to south between territory that was already settled and territory that was yet to be settled. But the westward movement had been a constant factor all through American history; was the national habit of expansion so strong that it would continue even at the expense of new acquisitions?

Undoubtedly the United States was beginning by the 1890's to show an interest in distant lands, greater perhaps than it had ever known before; but it would be too simple an explanation to attribute this entirely to a persistence of the westward movement. The United States as a full-grown nation could not much longer avoid close contacts with all the rest of the world. Trade relationships were growing; Americans, especially since manufacturing had flowered, had more to sell than formerly, which to some observers suggested the need for colonies. The spirit of imperialism had affected other nations, and a mad scramble for empire was on, with Great Britain, France, Germany, and Russia leading the way. Nationalistic Americans, proud of their country's newly-achieved greatness, were not unaffected by what they saw. If other nations to flatter their self-esteem must have colonies, why not also the United States? Nor should the missionary impulse be overlooked. Americans were sure they had a way of life worth teaching to others; indeed, they were not sure but what they were under a deep moral obligation to share their blessings with peoples less favored. Politicians, possibly eager to divert attention from unpleasant domestic conditions, rang the changes on foreign affairs.

Some such motives as these lay back of the diplomacy of the 1890's. Harrison's Secretary of State, James G. Blaine, showed an interest in the Pacific, and sought a closer relationship with Latin America. Grover Cleveland belligerently invoked the Monroe Doctrine, even against Great Britain, whose navy in earlier years had been its chief defense. William McKinley, albeit somewhat reluctantly, intervened in Cuba to prevent Spain from suppressing a colonial insurrection, and emerged from the resulting war with the remnants of the Spanish empire, both in the Caribbean and in the Pacific, as American possessions. Then, in order to keep the Philippines, the United States had to suppress the same kind of insurrection that had faced the Spanish in Cuba. Under Theodore Roosevelt the new American Empire was consolidated, and the essential diplomatic and military measures taken for its defense.

But the American people, after the first taste of empire, found that they did not like it, and turned with far greater relish to the task of domestic reform. From the first years of the century to the time the United States was caught up in the First World War, the Progressive movement held the center of the stage. Its roots lay in part with Populism; many of its principal tenets had been expounded earnestly by Ignatius Donnelly and William Jennings Bryan. But they could be traced also in part to the ideas of European socialism, ideas that had caught on with a few earnest labor leaders, such as Eugene V. Debs. With the need for reform fully exposed by the muckrakers, many reform governors such as Robert M. LaFollette of Wisconsin, and two reform Presidents, Theodore Roosevelt and Woodrow Wilson, achieved notable results. The power of private monopoly over government was severely shaken, although by no means broken.

The course of the Progressive movement saw many political changes. The Republican Party under Roosevelt's leadership leaned toward reform, but under Taft's leadership made little progress. The result was a party split in 1912, with Roosevelt heading a new Progressive Party. But the Democrats, thanks to the divided opposition, won the election, and with Wilson as their leader put through much of the Progressive program. In so doing they branded the Democratic Party as the party of reform and tended to absorb the more aggressive membership of the Progressive Party, an organization which promptly died. For the Republicans there was little choice but to accept the mantle of Taft conservatism that had been thrown their way.

14

The End of Isolation

American isolation — Blaine's foreign policy — The Venezuelan controversy — The Cuban revolt — Spanish methods of warfare — The road to war — Admiral Mahan — The new navy — Theodore Roosevelt — The American army — Dewey at Manila — Admiral Cervera — Sampson's strategy — The Santiago campaign — An army of convalescents — Conquest of Puerto Rico

UNTIL well toward the end of the nineteenth century the foreign policy of the United States reflected primarily the interest of the American people in westward expansion. Washington's doctrine of isolation was designed to keep the new nation free from any European entanglements that might distract its attention from the main business in hand — the conquest of a continent. The Monroe Doctrine, by which European governments were warned to keep out of American affairs, was merely the converse of the same proposition. By it the United States hoped to end for all time the threat of outside interference with the workings of "manifest destiny." The War of 1812 and the war with Mexico were both expansionist wars, and the Civil War was fought, in considerable part at least, to decide whether the North or the South should have the advantage in the formation of new western states. During all these years the United States was busy at home. It cared little about the doings of other nations so long as they showed no desire to block the American policy of expansion. American political development was self-centered and introspective. American economic development was a frantic struggle to exploit the rich natural resources that the continent had divulged, and to satisfy, mainly by do-

American isolation

mestic production, the needs of a rapidly growing people. American diplomacy, especially during the quarter-century that followed the Civil War, was episodic and inconsequential.

By the last decade of the nineteenth century a change had set in. The era of continental expansion was over, the United States was full grown, the time-honored frontiering process was fading from the picture. Good free lands and good cheap lands were nearing exhaustion. Population penetration into the High Plains and the Rocky Mountain plateau all but eliminated from census maps the zone of uninhabited territory that until 1890 had stretched unbroken from the Canadian to the Mexican border. American industry was catching up on its assignment. Already, for many mines and factories, the time had come when the needs of the domestic market could be fully supplied, with a margin left over for sale abroad. American capital had been multiplied many times over, and considerable sums now sought foreign investment. The interest of the United States in itself alone began to give way to an active American interest in the whole wide world. Isolation had lost its charm; increasingly the American government felt called upon to play an important part in international affairs.

James G. Blaine, twice Secretary of State (1881, 1889–92), has often been spoken of as **Blaine's foreign policy** the "harbinger of the new era." This, no doubt, is an exaggeration, but Blaine did attempt to widen the sphere of American influence to include, in fact as well as in theory, all of the Americas. Toward European nations with an interest in the western hemisphere, but most particularly toward Great Britain, he adopted an uncompromising, almost belligerent, attitude. While serving under Garfield, for example, he made a blustering, but unavailing, demand that the British government give up its rights under the Clayton-Bulwer Treaty of 1850 to joint control of any interoceanic canal that should be built. Likewise, during his second term in office he tried to establish a kind of prescriptive right for the United States to the fur-seal fisheries of the Bering Sea, a contention that a joint Anglo-American arbitration commission was unable to approve. Most important of all, he sought consistently to promote the cause of "Pan-Americanism."

Blaine's fondest dream was to induce the Latin-American republics of North and **Pan-Americanism** South America to enter a kind of informal federation, with the United States as an interested and friendly "elder sister" at its head. Through such a union Blaine hoped to eliminate wars between the lesser American nations and to promote better commercial relationships between them and the United States. In pursuit of this goal, it fell to his lot to receive in Washington on October 2, 1890, the representatives of nineteen independent American republics. Nothing could be accomplished on so important a subject as arbitration, but the First Pan-American Congress, as this meeting came to be called,[1] made considerable progress in the discussion of such important problems as the standardization of sanitary regulations, the building of an intercontinental railroad, and the adoption of uniform weights and

[1] Name changed later to Inter-American Conferences.

measures, including a common silver coin. One permanent result of the Congress was the establishment of an International Bureau of American Republics, with headquarters in Washington. Another was the precedent set for the holding of such meetings; similar Congresses have been held from time to time ever since.

It is possible to discern in Blaine's foreign policy an effort to reserve the Pacific as a region for future American **Hawaii and** exploitation. Blaine cultivated **Samoa** good relations with Japan, and at the same time managed to keep friendly with China in spite of the deepening antagonism between the two great Oriental nations. Nor was Blaine displeased at the prospect of the speedy annexation to the United States of Hawaii, for generations the chief stopping-place in the mid-Pacific for vessels bound to Asia, and a center of steadily increasing importance for the production of sugar. These conditions, indeed, inspired the American State Department to negotiate a reciprocal trade treaty with Hawaii as early as 1875, which was renewed in 1884 and so amended (1887) as to give the United States an exclusive right to develop a fortified base at Pearl Harbor. When in 1893 Americans in Hawaii staged a revolution with annexation to the United States as their goal, Blaine offered no objections, and a treaty of annexation was actually signed shortly after he left office, but never ratified. Not until McKinley became President, in 1898, was annexation actually accomplished, but Blaine had favored it, and had hoped for it. Blaine also sought to retain for the United States a foot-hold in the Samoan Islands, first tentatively marked out as early as 1872. Both Germany and Great Britain had interests in the Samoans, however, and international rivalry for commercial privileges became acute. A conference of the three contending parties, called by Bismarck, met in Berlin in 1889, and decided on a tripartite protectorate, but this worked badly and was abandoned in 1899. The islands were then divided between the United States and Germany, while Great

Britain was indemnified for her withdrawal by title to the Gilbert and Solomon Islands, which had formerly belonged to Germany. These negotiations, from beginning to end, showed small regard for the traditional American doctrine of isolation.

While Blaine's policy in the Pacific was later to pay substantial dividends, his plans **Chile** for Pan-Americanism fell far short of the goals he had set. The United States minister to Chile, Patrick Egan, for whose appointment Blaine was responsible, openly took sides in a Chilean revolution, and even more unfortunately gave his support to the side that lost. While feeling against the United States was still high in Chile, American sailors on shore leave at Valparaiso became involved in street fighting that cost two of them their lives and others serious injuries. By threat of military reprisals, the United States collected an indemnity of $75,000 for this "outrage," and built up an amount of ill-will throughout all Latin-America that could not be measured. These incidents undid nearly everything Blaine had accomplished. Under the terms of the McKinley Act he negotiated a few useful trade treaties, and no doubt the Pan-American Congresses served a useful end, but for the most part Blaine's high hopes of international accord among the American nations were long to remain unrealized.

That the aggressive nature of American diplomacy was neither a personal policy of **The Ven-** Blaine's nor a party policy of **ezuelan** the Republicans was made evi- **controversy** dent shortly after Harrison left office by Cleveland's handling of the Venezuelan boundary dispute. The boundary line between Venezuela and British Guiana lay in a tropical wilderness and had never been properly delimited. Long a subject of desultory controversy, the subject became really interesting when the news came out that gold had been discovered in the disputed territory. To Cleveland the prospect of the British government enforcing its will upon Venezuela, as the American government had recently enforced its will upon

Chile, was extremely disquieting, for he had made up his mind that in case such action resulted in the taking of territory that properly belonged to an American nation the Monroe Doctrine would clearly have been violated. In his message to Congress of 1894, he therefore expressed his hope that the matter would be arbitrated, and Congress by resolution promptly echoed his sentiments. The British government, however, refused to submit the whole question to arbitration, although pointing out that it had long been willing to arbitrate within certain specified limits. This attitude satisfied neither Cleveland nor his aggressive Secretary of State, Richard Olney, who took the matter up with Lord Salisbury, the British Foreign Minister, in a dispatch of July 20, 1895. "Today," said Olney, "the United States is practically sovereign on this continent, and its fiat is law upon the subjects to which it confines its interposition." Any advance of the British boundary at the expense of Venezuela, Olney claimed, would "greatly embarrass the future relations between this country and Great Britain."

At first the British showed no signs of backing down, and Cleveland plainly threatened war. Eventually, however, a plan of arbitration satisfactory to the United States was accepted, and Americans talked loudly of their diplomatic triumph. Undoubtedly the British right-about-face was due to other circumstances than the American representations. The British people were in no mood to fight the United States; furthermore, a telegram of congratulations sent by Kaiser Wilhelm II of Germany to Paul Kruger, the anti-British Boer leader in South Africa who had successfully repulsed Jameson's raid of "outlanders" into Boer territory, emphasized the fact that the future enemy of Great Britain was to be Germany, rather than the United States. Indeed, friendship with the United States became from this time forward an earnest objective of British diplomacy. The strong stand that the United States had taken on behalf of a Latin-American republic should have made for better relations between the United States and her neighbors, also, but Olney's bombastic words robbed the American victory of its chance to bear such fruit. The "Colossus of the North" was still mistrusted.

Great Britain was not the only European power, however, whose concern with American affairs led to diplomatic difficulties with the United States. Spain still held a remnant of her once great American empire, notably the two islands of Cuba and Puerto Rico just south of the Atlantic seaboard of the United States. Cuba had long been a storm-center in Spanish-American relations. Before the Civil War southern expansionists had coveted the island; after the war Cuban insurrectionists had repeatedly sought to involve the United States in their struggles. For ten years, from 1868 to 1878, the island was in constant turmoil, and in 1895 another revolt broke out. This second insurrection came about in no small part as a result of American tariff legislation. The McKinley tariff of 1890, which admitted raw sugar free of duty and compensated American growers by a bounty, had enormously stimulated the Cuban sugar industry. Much new foreign capital was poured into Cuban plantations, and for a brief period the island enjoyed unusual prosperity. When, in 1894, the Wilson-Gorman Act again made raw sugar dutiable, Cuban sugar prices declined precipitately, and the era of prosperity vanished as rapidly as it had come. With the American market for other Cuban commodities, notably tobacco, also weakened by the depression, hard times and unemployment provided a convenient setting for insurrection. Even in prosperous times the ordinary Cuban, whose lot as a peon was only a little better than that of a serf, had abundant reason for discontent. Spanish policy discriminated not only in favor of the mother country, but also in favor of the small ruling caste of pure-blood Spaniards in Cuba. The Cuban "native," colored by a strong infusion of Negro blood, did most of the work, while the upper-class whites took most of the profits. Further-

more, the Spanish officials in Cuba were notably inefficient and corrupt.

It is an exaggeration to speak of the disorder in Cuba that broke out in 1895 as a revolution, although citizens of the United States tended to view it in that light. Maximo Gomez, the Cuban leader, was utterly unable to maintain a government, or even to keep an army in the field. What he promoted was insurrection rather than revolution, and his chief weapon was devastation. Small guerrilla bands, often operating by night rather than by day, destroyed sugar-mills and laid waste plantations belonging to Spanish loyalists. Carrying on at first almost without military equipment, the Cuban *insurrectos* were soon receiving aid from other Cubans who resided in the United States, and from American sympathizers, most of whom thought of Gomez and his guerrillas in terms that might better have been applied to George Washington and the patriot army of 1776. In New York a Cuban junta, which called itself the Cuban government, sold bonds, and with the proceeds bought and shipped arms to the insurrectionary forces.

Spanish methods of dealing with the insurrection were both brutal and effective. "Butcher" Weyler, the Spanish commander in Cuba, by using "corrals" of barbed wire and blockhouses to separate the more peaceful sections of the island from the more warlike, and by herding all suspects into *reconcentrado* camps, was well along with the task of restoring order when the Cuban situation began to make the headlines in American newspapers. Reporters told lurid tales of the bad conditions they saw, and Americans who resided in Cuba or who visited the island for the sights they could see corroborated the newspaper accounts. The American public, long unaccustomed to the horrors of war, began to feel that the government of the United States should take a hand in the situation, and do something to "reform" the war. Both Cleveland and McKinley tried hard to keep the peace, and the latter had only this object in mind when he made strong representations to the Spanish government "against the uncivilized and inhuman" conduct of Weyler's campaign. The Spanish government, conscious of the fact that the proximity of the United States to Cuba gave the Americans an immense military advantage, made every effort to comply with McKinley's requests, even ordering the abandonment of the *reconcentrado* policy, and the recall of Weyler. In fact, the American minister to Spain informed his government that the Spanish officials, if given a little time, would agree to whatever demands the United States cared to make.

Whatever chance there was of peaceful settlement evaporated as a result of two untoward incidents. The first was the publication of a private letter written by de Lôme, the Spanish minister in Washington, to a friend in Cuba. This letter, purloined from the mails and published in the newspapers, described McKinley as a "spineless politician." Inasmuch as the original one-hundred-per-cent American, Theodore Roosevelt, held that the President had "no more backbone than a chocolate éclair," de Lôme's statement may not have been altogether inaccurate, but it was one thing for an American citizen to speak his mind about the President, and quite another for a foreign minister to make such a statement. De Lôme's recall was immediately requested, and the offending minister resigned. The other unfortunate incident was the destruction of the battleship *Maine* in Havana Harbor, February 15, 1898, with heavy loss of life. That the Spanish government could have promoted such a catastrophe at a time when its officials were making every effort to keep on good terms with the United States seems incredible, but the American public jumped immediately to the conclusion that Spain was responsible. The battlecry, "Remember the *Maine*," rent the air, and the demands on Spain made by the American government became more and more peremptory.

It is possible that war might have been

The Maine saluting Spanish flagship *Alfonso XII* on arrival at Harbor of Havana. Illustration from *Harper's Weekly*, 1898.

averted had McKinley had the same sort of courage that John Adams exhibited in 1798, when he prevented hostilities between the United States and France from going the full length of declared war. Had the President decided to make a firm stand for peace, he would have received the cordial support of Marcus A. Hanna and many another leading capitalist who feared the economic unsettlement that war might bring. But McKinley knew that opposition to following the lead of the "plutocrats" on this, or on any other matter, was already rife among the young Republicans, and he believed that only by yielding to the popular clamor for war could he be certain of holding his party together. Finally, on April 9, the Spanish government, in response to a joint peace plea, delivered by the Great Powers of Europe to both Spain and the United States, ordered the cessation of hostilities in Cuba and gave in to the American contentions on every essential point. Nevertheless, the President on April 11 sent a war message to Congress. Six days later Congress by joint resolution demanded that Spain withdraw from Cuba, and authorized the President to use the military and naval

The road to war

forces of the United States to effect that end. Expressly disclaiming any intent to add Cuba to the United States, the resolution went on to assert that the people of the island were "and of right ought to be free and independent."

The outbreak of hostilities in this "needless war," as James Ford Rhodes, the historian, later described it, did not take place because of the failure of American diplomacy. War came in spite of the complete success of American diplomacy, and primarily because the American people wanted to have a war. The reasons for this strange state of mind, so hard for a later generation to understand, were complex. It is true enough that a few Americans had investments in Cuba, totaling perhaps fifty million dollars, and that these investors were eager for American intervention to protect their property. But the merely economic motive does not fully explain the Spanish-American War; Wall Street, indeed, threw its influence almost unanimously for peace. Undoubtedly the humanitarian motive helped arouse the crusading spirit, but it is hard to see why humanitarians should not have preferred to abate the Cuban nuisance by measures short of war. Probably the urge for empire affected some Americans; the great powers of the world had been busily engaged for a generation in carving up for themselves the pleasant and profitable places of the earth. Was it not about time that the United States should claim its share of colonial spoils? Nor can one overlook the lasting legacy of the Civil War, a struggle which for more than thirty years had colored almost every aspect of American thought and action. Veterans of the Civil War were held in honor because of their war record, and particularly in politics they tended to fare better than the men who had stayed at home. As the old soldiers grew older, they forgot the seamy side of war, and told tall tales of heroics and adventure. Young America, typified by Theodore Roosevelt, had grown to manhood on a steady diet of Civil War glorification. It envied the boys in blue or gray, and felt cheated that it had

had no chance to win distinction for itself in war.[1] Older Americans saw certain advantages in letting youth have its way. They took pride in the great new nation that they had seen emerge, but their faith was somehow tinctured with doubt. Could the United States really hold together; could it survive and grow as a nation? It had only lately suffered from a devastating depression; it had had a frightening amount of labor troubles; it had seen class arrayed against class in the bitter campaign and election of 1896. Perhaps it would serve to unite the country if everyone were to fight together in a common cause. Furthermore, if the United States could win a war against a European power, who then could deny the greatness of the American nation, or refuse to accord it great power status? Perhaps only by this baptism of blood could the country prove to itself and the rest of the world that it had arrived at full maturity.

As the American people entered the war, they were extremely conscious and proud of the new "white navy" by **Admiral** means of which they hoped to **Mahan** win it. The construction of steel ships had begun in the eighties, in part as a means of reducing the then vexatious surplus, and by the time the new navy was needed for war duty it ranked fifth among the navies of the world. Moreover, its *raison d'être*, not very clear when the first keels were laid, had been made plain by an American naval officer, Captain Alfred Thayer Mahan, whose book, *The Influence of Sea-Power on History, 1660–1783* (1890), had won international acclaim. Mahan argued persuasively that victory for a nation at war ordinarily depended upon its control of the seas. This was especially true in the case of imperialistic powers, with distant colonies and overseas commerce to protect; but it was also true of a nation such

[1] It is interesting to note that in England Winston Churchill and other ambitious young men were complaining also of the lack of a war, especially a war that would give them the chance to shoot at other white men! See Robert Lewis Taylor, *Winston Churchill: An Informal Study of Greatness* (1952), p. 90.

Admiral Mahan was graduated from the United States Naval Academy, class of 1859, with second honors. He served during the Civil War, mainly on blockade duty, and after the war saw much of the world on routine cruises. A bookish man from a bookish family, he first wrote a volume on Civil War history, but his development into a historian of note awaited his assignment in the middle eighties to the war college in Newport. Here he began to emphasize, both in his lectures and in a long series of books, the significance of sea-power in history, and to develop the theories associated with his name. The picture shown of the battleship *Oregon* is from an illustration in the Mariners' Museum.

as the United States, which had neither a colonial empire nor a large merchant marine. The United States, Mahan maintained, must be prepared in time of war to keep the sea-lanes open for foreign neutral shipping bound to and from American ports. This it could do only if it had strength enough to drive enemy blockaders away from its shores. For such a purpose "capital ships," that is, battleships, were needed, since the lighter vessels, of which before 1890 our navy mainly consisted, would be no match for the capital ships of foreign nations. The United States, to feel perfectly safe, must have a fleet of battleships large enough to deal successfully with any enemy force that any enemy nation might be able to send against it. This did not mean that the United States Navy should be as large or larger than any other navy; it need only be large enough to command the seas adjacent to the American coast.

Influenced undoubtedly by Mahan's ideas, some of which had gained currency even before his book was published, the **The new navy** building of capital ships proceeded rapidly during the early nineties.

American heavy industries were increasingly capable of supplying the necessary machinery, ordnance, and armor plate. The trend of American diplomacy seemed to indicate that the duties of the new navy would not long be confined to strictly national defense; there would be colonies also to consider. The national ego, moreover, demanded for the United States whatever trappings of greatness other nations possessed. If other nations, particularly Great Britain, the traditional enemy, had battleships, why should the United States lack them? In 1890 Congress authorized the construction of "three seagoing, coast-line battleships designed to carry the heaviest armor and most powerful ordnance," and before war broke out in 1898 the *Indiana*, *Massachusetts*, and *Oregon* had been built to these specifications. In 1892 Mahan published another book, *The Influence of Sea-Power upon the French Revolution and Empire, 1793–1812*, which provided further ammunition for the use of the strongnavy advocates, and in spite of the depression five more battleships were authorized before Cleveland left office. It seemed reasonably certain that their completion, together with the addition of numerous minor and auxiliary craft also authorized, would give to the United States Navy that supremacy in American waters that Mahan's theories demanded.

When President McKinley took office he appointed as Secretary of the Navy John D. **Theodore** Long, a prominent politician **Roosevelt** from Massachusetts of no known sympathy with the existing strong-navy policy. McKinley himself seems to have been both uninterested and uninformed on naval matters, but the deficiencies of the President and his naval chief were more than offset by the selection of Theodore Roosevelt to be Assistant Secretary of the Navy. Roosevelt had written a book on sea-power, *The Naval War of 1812* (1882), he was notorious for the lengths to which he carried his strong-navy views, and he was eager for the United States to embark upon a policy of extensive overseas expansion. In office he counteracted by every means in his power the lethargy of his superiors, and tried to make the nation ready for the war he was sure would come. He knew and liked the navy men, and with them, he later recounted,

I used to hold long consultations, during which we went over and over . . . everything necessary to do in order to put the navy in trim to strike quick and hard. . . . Sending an ample quantity of ammunition to the Asiatic squadron and providing it with coal; getting the battleships and the armored cruisers on the Atlantic into one squadron, both to train them in manoeuvering together, and to have them ready to sail against either the Cuban or the Spanish coasts; gathering the torpedo boats into a flotilla for practice; securing ample target exercise, so conducted as to raise the standards of our marksmanship; gathering in the small ships from European and South American waters; settling on the number and kind of craft needed as auxiliary cruisers — every one of these points was threshed over in conversations with officers who were present in Washington, or in correspondence with officers who, like Captain Mahan, were absent.[1]

[1]Theodore Roosevelt, *The Rough Riders* (new ed., 1919), pp. 2–3.

When war broke out at last, Roosevelt and the navy men were ready. In the afternoon of February 25, ten days after **Prepara-** the *Maine* went down, Roose- **tions for war** velt took advantage of Long's temporary absence from the Navy Office to put the entire navy on a war footing. The Assistant Secretary, so his superior complained, in one half-day's work had "come very near causing more of an explosion than happened to the *Maine*. . . . The very devil seemed to possess him." But Roosevelt was merely seeking to put the finishing touches on plans conceived long before and already in part carried out. As early as December, 1897, Commodore George Dewey, by Roosevelt's scheming, had been placed in command of the Asiatic Squadron and ordered to the Far East, there to make ready for a clash with the Spanish fleet in the Philippines the moment war should come. Early in 1898 the North Atlantic Squadron had been mobilized off Chesapeake Bay under the command of Captain (later Rear-Admiral) William T. Sampson, whose promotion over the heads of a long list of senior officers was as wholly merited as it was deeply resented. Later the bulk of Sampson's squadron was ordered to Key West, while the uneasy seaboard cities of the Atlantic, suffering from the illusion that a Spanish fleet was about to bombard them, were offered protection by a "North Patrol" under Commodore J. A. Howell off the coast of New England, and a "Flying Squadron" under Commodore W. S. Schley, stationed at Hampton Roads. The new battleship *Oregon*, uselessly located in the northern Pacific, was ordered to make ready at San Francisco for the long voyage around Cape Horn — a voyage that began on March 19 and for two months consumed the interest of the newspaper-reading public. The *Oregon*, after successfully steaming some fourteen thousand miles, finally joined Admiral Sampson's squadron, and participated in the Santiago campaign.

If the navy was well prepared for war, undoubtedly the army was not. The 2134 officers and 26,040 enlisted men of the regular army were distributed throughout the country at numerous army posts, the location of which bore no ascertainable relationship to the problem of mobilization. Some of these so-called "forts" had once been important when there was an Indian frontier; others had been selected mainly because powerful congressmen coveted the advantages of army building and trade for their constituents. There was no central army planning bureau such as the present general staff, and in the matter of promotions the rule of seniority was seldom broken. At the head of the army was its senior major-general, the sixty-year-old General Nelson A. Miles, whose experience in the Civil and Indian wars was of doubtful value in making ready for the war with Spain. Too many officers, with age rather than efficiency on their side, had grown accustomed to a life of easy routine, and while the soldiers were well drilled and well disciplined they were far better prepared for peace than for war. The Secretary of War, General Russell A. Alger, a match-manufacturer from Michigan with a dubious Civil War record, was no great help, and the politicians and bureaucrats who served under him were mostly handicaps. The second line of defense, the organized National Guard of the states, was of uncertain size and merit, but capable of great expansion in case of need. Everyone took it for granted, however, that if a really important war should develop, a volunteer army organized along the lines of the Union army in the Civil War would do the fighting. Unfortunately the army had had no such renaissance as had overtaken the navy during the eighties, nor had it had a Theodore Roosevelt.

The American army

Congress, for all its impatience to get on with the war, did little to make ready for the conflict before it came. On March 9, 1898, long after the strained relations between the United States and Spain made war a strong probability, Congress passed a bill appropriating fifty million dollars "for national defense and for each and every purpose connected there-

War legislation

Admiral Sampson, commander of the North Atlantic Squadron. From a photogravure in the Mariners' Museum.

with." But the President, to whom discretionary authority was given in the expenditure of this sum, spent it mainly on the navy and on coastal defense. When, later on, Alger's administration of the War Department was severely criticized, the Secretary complained that he had neither the funds nor the authority to prepare for war. Not until late in April, after the war resolutions had been passed, did Congress vote the increases in the army that the imminence of war would seem to have justified long before. It then authorized the increase of the regular army to 62,597 men, and the raising of a volunteer army of 125,000 men. As in the Civil War, each state was to be assigned its quota of troops, and the dual state and national character of the volunteer army was to be preserved.[1] A unique feature of the legislation, however, was the provision that the President might accept directly into the national service three regiments of volunteer cavalry. This provision was included primarily to enable Theodore Roosevelt, who now resigned as Assistant Secretary of the

[1] Cf. J. D. Hicks, *The Federal Union* (2d ed., 1952), pp. 565, 568).

Admiral Dewey the first hero of

the Spanish-American War, was soon to suffer from the fickleness of the American public. When his grateful admirers bought him a house in Washington, he deeply offended them by promptly deeding it to his second wife, whom he had just married. Next year irritation turned to ridicule when he naively offered himself for the Presidency with the comment that in his opinion that office would be "not such a very difficult one to fill." The likeness is from a detail of an engraving in the Mariners' Museum, done by E. S. King for the Society of Iconophiles, 1902. The Dewey Medal, awarded for participation in the Battle of Manila Bay, was designed by Daniel C. French.

Navy, to lead a regiment into battle. With the help of Captain Leonard Wood, an officer in the medical corps, Roosevelt brought together a motley array of ex-cowboys, college athletes, and adventurers to form the "First United States Volunteer Cavalry," or, as they were more generally called, the "Rough Riders." Since Roosevelt had had no military experience whatever, he modestly accepted only a lieutenant-colonelcy, while the command of the regiment went to Wood.

The first blow of the war was struck by Dewey at Manila Bay. A British proclama-

Dewey at Manila tion of neutrality, issued April 24, made it necessary for Dewey to leave Hong Kong, where he had been outfitting his fleet preparatory to the anticipated attack on the Spanish. On the twenty-fifth he left Hong Kong for the nearby Chinese port of Mirs Bay, where he would be under no compulsion to observe neutral regulations, and on the twenty-seventh he left Mirs Bay for the Philippines. His squadron consisted of the cruisers *Olympia, Balti-* *more, Raleigh,* and *Boston;* the gunboats *Concord* and *Petrel;* the revenue cutter *McCulloch;* and two colliers. Wisely disregarding mines that were possibly non-existent, and coast fortifications that were not available for use,[1] Dewey's fleet steamed through the wide entrance of Manila Bay before daybreak on the first of May. In leisurely fashion, with time out for breakfast, Dewey's ships proceeded methodically to the destruction of the Spanish ships, which their commander, Admiral Montojo, who knew full well what was in store for him, had thoughtfully stationed at some distance from the defenses of Manila so that the city might be spared the danger of shell-fire and in shallow water where as many as possible of his men might escape. The Spanish losses in this one-sided battle included three hundred and eighty-one killed, besides numerous wounded, while not an American was killed and only seven or eight were wounded.

It is hard to see what useful purpose was

[1] Mark Sullivan, *Our Times,* I, *The Turn of the Century* (1926), p. 316.

served by the sinking of this decrepit and unseaworthy Spanish squadron. If the war was being fought strictly for the liberation of Cuba, as was claimed, the Spanish ships in the Philippines might well have been ignored, for they could never under any circumstances have reached the Pacific coast of the United States, much less the Atlantic. While Roosevelt and the others responsible for Dewey's presence in the Far East may not have realized fully the weakness of the Spanish fleet in the Philippines, it is only reasonable to suppose that they were as much interested in colonial expansion as in setting Cuba free. The American public, without seriously considering the implications of Dewey's victory, rejoiced immoderately that a victory had been won. Dewey's name was on everyone's lips — at last the United States had a war hero. He was immediately raised to the rank of acting Rear Admiral, and as soon as Congress could pass the necessary legislation was made Admiral, a rank held before him by only two Americans, Farragut and Porter. His name and fame were even celebrated in hand-hewn verse:

Oh, dewy was the morning
Upon the first of May,
And Dewey was the Admiral
Down in Manila Bay,
And dewy were the Regent's eyes [1]
Them [sic] orbs of royal blue,
And dew we feel discouraged?
I dew not think we dew!

Conqueror that he was, Dewey's position in Manila Bay was by no means comfortable. The Spanish government, deeply disturbed at what had happened, prepared to send a superior fleet against him from Spain. Spanish forces held the city of Manila and Dewey had no troops under his command with which to dislodge them. Fortunately, or so Dewey thought, an insurrection against Spanish rule was in progress in the islands,

[1] Alfonso XIII, King of Spain, was at the time a minor and the Queen Mother was Regent.

and he attempted to cooperate with the insurrectionists, even bringing back their exiled leader, Emilio Aguinaldo. Naturally he lost no time in urging the American government to send an expeditionary force to aid him in the capture of Manila, but weeks or even months must elapse before American soldiers could reach the Philippines. In the meantime foreign warships began to drop anchor in Manila Bay, among them a British squadron and a German squadron, either of which could have disposed of Dewey's ships almost as easily as he had disposed of the Spanish. Under the circumstances the American admiral can be pardoned for the nervousness he exhibited, particularly toward the Germans, whom he and other Americans suspected of coveting the islands for their country. Dewey considered himself in control of the Bay and, some sharp exchanges occurred between him and Vice Admiral Otto von Diederichs, the German commander, who gave only hesitant obedience to the American orders. The good offices of the British commander, Captain Edward Chichester, were sufficient to straighten out the difficulties, but both Dewey and the American public tended to exaggerate the friction and to hold more against the Germans than the facts warranted.

Before the end of July, General Wesley Merritt had come to Dewey's rescue with a force of nearly eleven thousand men. By this time both the Spanish and the Americans were more afraid of the insurgents than they were of each other, and negotiations for the surrender of the city to the Americans, on condition that the insurgents should be kept out, were not difficult to arrange. On August 14, unmindful of the fact that the war had come to an end two days before, the Americans received the official capitulation of the city. Happily bloodshed had been kept at a minimum. American losses against the Spanish in the Philippines amounted altogether to eighteen killed and one hundred and nine wounded, and the Spanish casualty list was not much longer.

After the first stirring news of Dewey's

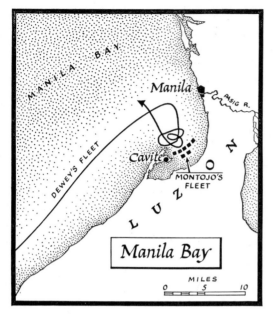

Manila Bay

Santiago de Cuba

victory at Manila Bay, American attention

Admiral Cervera turned quickly toward the coming conflict between the Spanish and American fleets in the Atlantic. It was common knowledge that a Spanish squadron under the command of Admiral Pascual Cervera had been collected at the Cape Verde Islands, and that on April 29 it had set sail for the west. Cervera's fleet was notably weak, consisting of only four armored cruisers, which together could not throw as much metal as the American battleship *Oregon*, and six torpedo boat destroyers, only three of which were seaworthy. Its crews were inadequately trained, and it lacked both ammunition and supplies. Conscious of the immense superiority of Sampson's squadron, Cervera was in despair when ordered to leave for the West Indies, and expressly refused to accept responsibility for what might result. Both he and the Spanish authorities knew full well that his ships were being ordered to their destruction, but the sacrifice was thought necessary as a sop to Spanish public opinion, which demanded that everything possible should be done to win the war.

The day before the battle of Manila Bay, American newspapers reported the sailing of Cervera's fleet. Presumably the voyage to

America would occupy about two weeks. Admiral Sampson, under orders to intercept and destroy the enemy before he could take refuge in a Spanish colonial port, made preparations to guard the approaches to Cervera's four most probable destinations — Havana, Cienfuegos, and Santiago in Cuba, and San Juan in Puerto Rico. Schley, in command of the Flying Squadron, was to patrol the southern coast of Cuba, while Sampson himself, with the rest of the fleet, was to remain north of the island with an eye out for Puerto Rico. The Atlantic seaboard cities, being thus abandoned, set up such loud cries of fright that the Navy Department, although it knew that an American harbor was the last place Cervera would wish to enter, felt obliged to detach some ships for coast-guard duty and to anchor a few obsolete gunboats in full sight of the excited populace.

Cervera proved himself an excellent seaman and succeeded in evading the blockaders. He appeared first on May 13, **The Spanish** off the island of Martinique in **fleet reaches** the Lesser Antilles, and next **America** day touched at the Dutch island of Curaçao near the coast of Venezuela. All this was reported to the Navy Department, which relayed the information at once to Sampson and Schley, but on May 19 the Spanish fleet slipped into the harbor of Santiago unobserved. Not until that same day did Schley leave Key West for his post to the south of Cuba, and Cervera had been at anchor a full week before the Flying Squadron reached the vicinity of Santiago. Even then Schley, although he had been apprised by Sampson of the probable location of the Spanish ships was sure that they were somewhere else. "The air," he said, "was very clear, and the high mountains back of Santiago could be seen, but nothing else." Accordingly, the Commodore decided to return to Key West for coal, and headed westward in spite of specific orders from the Navy Department to stand by at Santiago. His excuse for disobeying orders was that the heavy seas prevented him from taking on coal from the collier he had brought along. Finally better weather accomplished what his superiors had been unable to do, and, with his ships successfully recoaled at sea, he returned to Santiago. There on the morning of May 29 he beheld to his amazement the clear outlines of the *Cristobal Colón*, newest and best of Cervera's cruisers, anchored in full view from the mouth of the harbor. How his scouts could have failed to observe her three days before remains an unsolved mystery.

By the first of June, Admiral Sampson with the full Atlantic fleet, including the Sampson's *Oregon*, reached Santiago and strategy took command. Had the United States been willing to score a bloodless victory, Sampson need only have maintained his blockade of Cuba until the Spanish were ready to give up. Cervera was too wise and too humane to risk a battle if he could help it, and the Spanish forces in Cuba, cut off from supplies from the mother country, were helpless. Conscious of the fact that a fleet which could not leave its harbor was no better than a fleet sunk, and mildly concerned lest a tropical hurricane might disperse the American squadron, Sampson decided to block the narrow entrance of Santiago Harbor by sinking an old collier, the *Merrimac*, in the channel. This assignment

fell to Lieutenant Richmond Pearson Hobson, who with seven men succeeded in sinking the ship, although not in the proper spot, and the harbor remained open. By a miracle Hobson and his crew escaped unhurt and were taken prisoners by the Spanish. Overnight the youthful officer, although his exploit failed completely to accomplish its purpose, became in the eyes of the American public a hero second only to Dewey himself.

Hobson's failure left the escape of the Spanish fleet a theoretical possibility, and called for some other solution of Sampson's problem. Many people, not knowing that Manila Bay was a sizable body of water with an entrance several miles in width, wondered why Sampson could not do what Dewey had done. As a matter of fact Sampson was under instructions from the Navy Department to take no such risks with his ships. The channel into Santiago Harbor, it was supposed, was defended by mines and by effective batteries; hence any effort to make an entrance might easily end in disaster. But the Spanish ships showed no disposition to come out and fight, while the American public wanted to get on with the war. The best way through the dilemma seemed to be an expeditionary force that could operate in the rear of the Spanish fortifications, capture them, and thus either force the Spanish fleet to leave or enable the American fleet to enter. Sampson himself, confessing thereby that his squadron was unable to complete the task assigned it, asked for troops.

The War Department, meantime, had been struggling with the problem of how to prepare for war after the war had begun. Its first concern was to make Army ready the expedition to the activities Philippines under General Merritt. Troops for this purpose, both regulars and volunteers, were assembled from the western states at San Francisco, and before the end of June their transportation to the Philippines had begun. This venture alone was sufficient to tax the resources of the War Department to the limit, but in addition the possibility of an invasion of Cuba had to be faced. The Spanish garrisons in Cuba amounted, according to the newspapers, to no less than two hundred thousand men, and in actual fact to about eighty thousand men. If, therefore, the island should have to be conquered, foot by foot, a formidable army must be organized. After much preliminary indecision it was agreed that the bulk of the regular army should be concentrated at Tampa, Florida, while the volunteers, including such regiments of the National Guard as were accepted, were to encamp at the Chickamauga National Park, near Chattanooga, Tennessee. Roosevelt's Rough Riders assembled first at San Antonio, Texas, but at the insistence of their politically influential officers were soon transferred to Tampa.

The regular army, fully mobilized for the first time since the Civil War, found the experience mildly exhilarating, but the chaos that accompanied the encampment of the volunteers defied description. Army authorities had supposed that the military equipment previously issued to the National Guard would meet the most pressing needs of the civilian soldiers, but seemingly most of the equipment had evaporated. Whole regiments were turned over by the states to federal service, clad only in rags. Cooks went down in defeat before the rations and cooking equipment with which they were confronted, and occasionally unfortunate detachments had nothing to eat but hardtack. An ultra-democratic provision of the Enlistment Act made West Point graduates ineligible for appointment as officers in the volunteer army; hence, with a few exceptions, the officers were as unfamiliar with their duties as the privates with theirs. Out of the bedlam at Chickamauga an army might eventually emerge, but it would take a long time.

Meditating on this fact, and also on the report of his surgeon-general that from one third to one half of the American troops would surely die of yellow fever if landed on Cuban soil during the summer, General Nelson A. Miles had decided upon a deliberate plan of campaign.

Confusion at Tampa

He would first take Puerto Rico, which would be easy if not very significant, and would land a force of regulars at the eastern end of Cuba to organize the insurgents and assist them against the Spanish. Finally, when the American army was fully prepared, a frontal assault would be made on Havana. But Sampson's obvious need of army assistance led to an unexpected change of plans, and General William R. Shafter, in command at Tampa, was ordered to proceed instead, with the most effective force he could muster, to Santiago. This was far easier said than done, although General Miles rushed to Tampa in person to aid his unwieldy subordinate — General Shafter weighed three hundred pounds — in organizing the expedition. The selection of Tampa as a point of embarkation was absurd. Almost any Atlantic seaport would have been better. Tampa was not adequately served by railroads and lacked the docking facilities necessary to handle so great a rush of activity. "No word can paint the confusion," wrote Theodore Roosevelt, but the impatient politicians at Washington demanded immediate action.

On Tuesday, June 7, Shafter received word that "the President directs you to sail at once with what force you have ready." Powerless to effect an orderly embarkation, Shafter passed out the word that the expedition was to leave next day at daybreak, and that those who wanted to go would have to get aboard the best way they could. Thereupon individual initiative came to the rescue in a great variety of unorthodox ways, and next morning thousands of men, and some equipment, were aboard. Roosevelt's Rough Riders were naturally among the first to take possession of a transport, although it had long since been decided that they must leave their horses behind. The ships could not sail on Wednesday, as Shafter had threatened, but by nightfall the semblance of order had been restored. The general believed that he would soon be ready to go.

Then came a telegram from Washington that the expedition was not to sail after all. Rumors were about that some of the Spanish ships were elsewhere than in Santiago Harbor. Only after one of Sampson's officers, Lieutenant Victor Blue, reported that he had counted the Spanish ships from the hills above the harbor, would the navy permit Shafter's expedition to sail. So for a week the men stayed aboard ship at Tampa Bay, broiling in the tropical sun, and cursing their luck. At last, on June 14, the thirty-two transports carrying nearly seventeen thousand men put out to sea, and six days later they appeared off Santiago.

Now a new dilemma faced the expedition. What plan of campaign was it to follow?

The expedition to Santiago Where was the landing to be effected, and once the troops were ashore, what next were they to do? On this matter Sampson and Shafter conferred, and, as perhaps both thought, reached an agreement. But, if so, neither had understood the other. Sampson's interpretation of the agreement was that the army should land several miles to the east of the harbor and then proceed westward to attack the lofty *morro* that guarded its entrance. Shafter, however, had no such notion. He would land to the eastward, to be sure, but thereafter he proposed to encircle and capture the city of Santiago which lay some four or five miles inland at the back of the bay. To this plan he steadfastly adhered, whatever Sampson chose to think. With the help of lighters furnished by the fleet, the landing was effected without opposition, although the Spanish, had they chosen to make the effort, could have inflicted severe punishment upon the Americans, and might even have driven them off. By the evening of June 22, some six thousand American troops, including Theodore Roosevelt and the Rough Riders, were safely ashore, but it took until the twenty-fifth to land the entire force.

Shafter's plan of campaign was inaugurated with much impromptu modification on **Shafter's campaign** the part of his subordinates. "Fighting Joe" Wheeler, whose service with the Confederate army in the Civil War had won him a commission as major-general of volunteers, was determined that his troops, among whom were the Rough Riders, should be the first to see action. By forced marches, entirely contrary to orders, he managed to engage the Spanish on June 24 at Las Guasimas, an outpost which the enemy had planned to abandon without a fight. Here the Rough Riders had their first baptism of battle, and Roosevelt reported proudly that his regiment had "furnished over half the men and over half the loss." Then followed a week of inaction, while Shafter, himself and many of his command already handicapped by illness, prepared for the final assault on Santiago.

On the evening of June 30 the troops began to move again, and next morning a double attack opened, the lesser drive against a Spanish outpost at El Caney, well to the American right, and the major one against the Spanish entrenchments on San Juan Hill, as the series of high ridges before Santiago was called. It was supposed that the reduction of El Caney would occupy only a short time, and that the troops dispatched against it would be able also to participate in the action against Santiago. But the resistance at El Caney was more stubborn than had been anticipated, and the union of the two forces was delayed until the next day. Meantime the column intended for the assault on San Juan Hill moved forward slowly through a winding tropical road, its whereabouts carefully marked by an observation balloon which, until it was shot down, enabled the Spanish artillery to inflict heavy damage upon the invaders. The Americans, also, had a few batteries, but inasmuch as the American guns were still dependent on the use of black powder, they, too, provided, whenever they were fired, excellent targets for the Spanish artillerymen. Nevertheless, the Americans, with the Rough Riders in the thick of the fray, reached the hills they meant to attack, charged the Spanish entrenchments, and took them. But it was still a long way to Santiago; there were other and stronger entrenchments to be taken, and the attackers had suffered heavy losses. Next

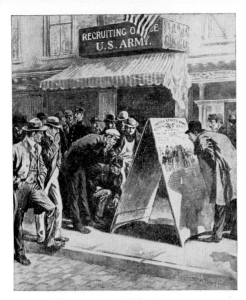

RECRUITING. U.S. Army recruiting office, 1898. Drawing by W. A. Rogers for *Harper's Weekly*.

MANILA BAY. Admiral Dewey commands the American fleet in the Philippines. Painting by Rufus F. Zogbaum.

The Spanish-American War provided the American people with much exciting news. Public attention focussed in turn on the calls for volunteers, the floating of war bonds, the victories by sea and land, the harrowing tales of sickness and death.

GOVERNMENT BONDS. Three per cent loan of 1898 issued to finance the war.

THE NIGHT AFTER SAN JUAN. Scene in a field hospital. Painted at the scene by William Glackens, 1898.

JUST BEFORE THE ENGAGEMENT. Painted at the scene by William Glackens, this depicts preparations at El Paso, 1898.

day Shafter began to consider the advisability of withdrawing from the positions he had occupied. Even Roosevelt, now in command of the Rough Riders, was worried. "We are within measurable distance of a terrible military disaster," he wrote to Lodge. "We must have help — thousands of men, batteries, and *food* and ammunition." He might well have added ambulances (of which the whole expedition possessed only three) and medical supplies.

But as events proved the Spanish were even more thoroughly disheartened than the **Naval battle** Americans. The army was short **of Santiago** of ammunition and the city was on the verge of famine. Nothing, it seemed, could halt the American advance. Ultimate surrender was inevitable. Foreseeing this situation, the Spanish authorities in Madrid and Havana had ordered Cervera to take the first opportunity to escape with his squadron from the harbor. In vain the admiral protested that "the absolutely certain result will be the ruin of each and all of the ships and the death of the greater part of the crews." He was told to "avoid comments," and to leave in case the city was about to fall, regardless of consequences. On the evening of July 2, Cervera despairingly ordered his ships to get up steam, and on the morning of July 3 he headed for the open seas, his ships turning sharply to the west one by one and proceeding at full speed along the coast. The moment was opportunely chosen, for Sampson on his flagship the *New York* had moved several miles to the east for a conference with Shafter, while the *Brooklyn*, with Commodore Schley aboard, stood farther out to sea than usual. But the fate of the Spanish ships was sealed. The American ships, after some unfortunate maneuvering by the *Brooklyn*, which forced the *Texas* to reverse her engines in order to avoid being rammed, drew alongside the enemy and began a running fight that ended only when the last Spanish ship was beached or sunk. The American gunfire, despite Roosevelt's efforts as Assistant Secretary of the Navy, was not particularly accurate, for no serious hits were registered on the hulls of the Spanish cruisers. But the decks of these ships were of wood, and the first shells to explode upon them set them afire. One of the Spanish ships, the *Cristobal Colón*, by virtue of her superior speed, would have escaped but for the fact that her supply of good coal gave out, and the coal she then had to use was so poor that she was unable to keep up steam. The Spanish casualties from the fight were nearly four hundred killed and wounded; the American casualties, one killed and one wounded.

For months the battle was fought over again and again by the American public to determine whether the credit for **Sampson or** the victory belonged to Samp- **Schley?** son, whose flagship reached the scene of action only as the last Spanish ship was beached, or Schley, who had been on hand all the while, but whose orders to the captains of the squadron had been mainly unnoticed or ignored. As a matter of fact, it was a captain's fight, but Sampson could claim that every captain had his orders from the Admiral before the fight began. Ultimately a court of inquiry investigated Schley's conduct both before and during the battle, and came to conclusions somewhat damaging to Schley's reputation; but Dewey, chairman of the inquiry, held that Schley had been in command at Santiago when the Spanish fleet was destroyed.

Sampson's (or was it Schley's?) Fourth-of-July present to the American public was nowhere more appreciated than in the American trenches before Santiago. Shafter, who before the naval victory had considered seriously the wisdom of withdrawing his troops, brightened up perceptibly. To be sure, early on the morning of the third he had dispatched a message to General Toral, the Spanish commander at Santiago, threatening bombardment of the city if it were not immediately surrendered. But Shafter knew full well that this message was only a bluff, and he feared that the Spanish knew it too. Not until Cervera's squadron had been destroyed did he think to inform his superiors in Washington of the demand he had made, and by this time the Spanish had turned it down. Shafter's next demand was on the navy. It was up to the navy, he told Sampson and the authorities back home, to effect an entrance into the harbor. If that were only done, the town would surrender, and further loss of life would be avoided. But Sampson had no notion of risking his precious ships against the Spanish mines and batteries (equipment later discovered to be all but harmless), and complained bitterly that the army was unwilling to "do the part which the proper conduct of war assigns to it." As a matter of fact, General Toral had every intention of surrendering, and merely wished to obtain the best possible terms by prolonging the negotiations. He finally struck a very good bargain, for Shafter agreed that the United States should provide free transportation back to Spain for all the troops under Toral's command. On July 16, the articles of capitulation were signed, and next day the American army took possession of the city. By an oversight not difficult to explain, the naval authorities were ignored during these proceedings as completely as possible.

The Spanish surrender came none too soon, for the tropical climate had begun to tell heavily on the American army. The troops had reached Cuba at the height of summer clad in woolen uniforms designed for winter wear on the Great Plains. Some of them had thrown away their blankets by day, to learn that they were desperately needed by night. Heavy tropical rains added to the discomfort and perplexity of the situation. Food supplies were uncertain, both as to quantity and quality; the expeditionary force got its first fresh meat on July 22, and the soldiers complained that the canned meat they were served — "embalmed beef," they called it — was an actual menace to health. Sanitary precautions were hopelessly inadequate, and dysentery, malaria, typhoid, and possibly even yellow fever began to strike. On July 27, the sick list totaled 4,122, three fourths of which were fever patients. The

An army of convalescents

army, having won its war, now demanded the privilege of returning home, but the Washington authorities were hesitant about ordering such a move because of their belief that to do so would spread disease. Finally Roosevelt wrote a letter, and some of the general officers signed a "round robin," both designed to reveal the situation to the American public through the newspapers. According to the "round robin,"

The army is disabled by malarial fever to such an extent that its efficiency is destroyed and it is in a condition to be practically entirely destroyed by the epidemic of yellow fever sure to come in the near future. . . . This army must be moved at once or it will perish. . . . Persons responsible for preventing such a move will be responsible for the unnecessary loss of many thousands of lives.

Roosevelt and his colleagues might well have saved themselves the pains, for orders to recall the expedition were issued a few hours before their protests appeared in print. On August 8 the withdrawal of the troops began, with the Rough Riders aboard the first transports to leave. Ultimately the entire force, which had been increased by the time of its departure to about twenty-five thousand men, was brought to Montauk Point, Long Island, and encamped. Four fifths of the returning soldiers were ill — "an army of convalescents." Five hundred and fourteen men had already died of disease — twice as many as were killed in battle — and two hundred and fifty-seven others died after reaching the United States. Roosevelt himself returned, feeling, as he admitted, "disgracefully well."

Meantime similar outbreaks of disease had almost demoralized the army camps in the United States. At Chickamauga heavy rains flooded the camp, and soon proved that its location, from the point of view of sanitation, was all that it should not be. Conditions were little better at Camp Alger, across the Potomac from Washington, or in Florida. Everywhere the usual diseases of filth, such

Disease in the army camps

as dysentery and typhoid, put in an early appearance; indeed, the germs that laid low the expeditionary force in Cuba seem to have been taken with the troops from the United States. Total deaths for the war amounted to about five thousand, but only three hundred and seventy-nine died in battle or of battle wounds — all the rest died from disease. All this made lively reading in the newspapers and reflected seriously on the efficiency of the War Department. Demands for the resignation of Alger multiplied, and at the harassed Secretary's request a commission was appointed to investigate the conduct of the department. The report of the commission, long delayed, was inconclusive in its findings, but Alger's political usefulness was at an end. Finally, a year after the war was over, the President found a pretext unrelated to the war upon which he could ask and obtain his unpopular Secretary's resignation. To succeed Alger, McKinley chose a man of really extraordinary ability, Elihu Root of New York.

In the final days of the war General Miles at last got off the expedition to Puerto Rico **Conquest of** with which he had planned to **Puerto Rico** start hostilities. Much had been learned from the mistakes of Shafter's expedition, and the transportation of troops to Puerto Rico was marked by far fewer blunders. Haste was required, however, for on July 18, three days before the Miles expedition sailed, the Spanish government had opened negotiations for peace. But Miles managed to reach his objective before an armistice could be signed, and thus, with somewhat better grace than if he had not sailed, the United States could lay claim to the island. The only sharply disappointing feature of the expedition was its almost total lack of opposition. Casualties of the entire operation amounted to three killed and about forty wounded.

And so the war came to an end. Considering the belligerent mood that enveloped the United States during the nineties, it was a matter of great good fortune that the nation had not been caught up in a far more serious struggle. Years later, a comment attributed to Theodore Roosevelt recaptured the atmosphere of 1898: "It wasn't much of a war, but it was the best war we had." It was war enough, fortunately, to cure completely the war fever that had preceded it. But it was war enough also to involve the United States deeply in world politics, and to end, in all but name, the tradition of isolation.

Bibliography

On the diplomacy of the late nineteenth century, appropriate sections in Bailey, *A Diplomatic History of the American People*, and Bemis, *A Diplomatic History of the United States*, are very satisfactory. J. H. Latané and David W. Wainhouse, *A History of American Foreign Policy* (2d rev. ed., 1940), is also a good guide to the diplomacy of the period. John Bassett Moore, *The Principles of American Diplomacy* (1918), writes with authority on certain special subjects. On Blaine's diplomacy, Tyler, *The Foreign Policy of James G. Blaine*, previously cited, continues valuable. Bemis, *American Secretaries of State*, VIII, contains a useful article on the subject by J. B. Lockey. S. B. Stanton, *The Behring Sea Controversy* (1892), is of some value. An excellent account of the movement that led to the annexation of Hawaii is contained in J. W. Pratt, *Expansionists of 1898* (1936), a book which is extremely useful for this whole period. Other books of merit dealing with the Pacific include: E. J. Carpenter, *America in Hawaii* (1899); G. H. Ryden, *The Foreign Policy of the United States in Relation to Samoa* (1933); F. R. Dulles, *America in the Pacific* (1938); H. W. Bradley, *The American Frontier in Hawaii: The Pioneers, 1789–1843* (1942). Ralph S. Kuykendall and A. Grove Day, *Hawaii: A History from Polynesian Kingdom to American Commonwealth* (1948). Herbert Millington, *American Diplomacy and the War of the Pacific* (1948), deals with the period, 1878–1883. Satisfactory accounts of Blaine's difficulties with Chile are contained in H. C. Evans, Jr., *Chile and Its Relations with the United States* (1927); and in W. R. Sherman, *The Diplomatic and Commercial Relations of the United States and Chile, 1820–1914* (1924).

On Cleveland's diplomacy, Henry James, *Richard Olney and his Public Service* (1923), is a good biography of Cleveland's aggressive Secretary of State. Good accounts of the Venezuelan affair are contained in A. L. P. Dennis, *Adventures in American Diplomacy, 1896–1906* (1928); Dexter Perkins, *The Monroe Doctrine, 1867–1907* (1937); and, by the same author, *Hands Off: A History of the Monroe Doctrine* (1941). On general relations with Great Britain, the most useful books are L. M. Gelber, *The Rise of Anglo-American Friendship* (1938); W. A. Dunning, *The British Empire and the United States* (1914); R. B. Mowat, *The Diplomatic Relations of Great Britain and the United States* (1925). G. R. Dulebohn, *Principles of Foreign Policy under the Cleveland Administration* (1941), is adequate for the period covered. R. H. Heindel, *The American Impact on Great Britain, 1898–1914* (1940), is a successful effort to show the influence abroad of American thought and action.

The rôle of American newspapers in promoting the war with Spain is well set forth in J. E. Wisan, *The Cuban Crisis as Reflected in the New York Press, 1895–1898* (1934); and M. M. Wilkerson, *Public Opinion and the Spanish-American War* (1932). Events leading up to the war are well chronicled in F. E. Chadwick, *The Relations of the United States and Spain: Diplomacy* (1909); but some new material is presented in Orestes Ferrara, *The Last Spanish War* (1937); and Bemis, *American Secretaries of State*, IX.

On the rise of American naval power, W. D. Puleston, *Mahan: The Life and Work of Captain Alfred Thayer Mahan, U.S.N.* (1939), is especially valuable. It is well supplemented, however, by another excellent study, Harold and Margaret Sprout, *The Rise of American Naval Power, 1776–1918* (1939). John D. Long, *The New American Navy* (2 vols., 1903), shows the evolution of interest in naval preparedness before the Spanish-American War. A. T. Mahan, *From Sail to Steam; Recollections of Naval Life* (1907), is the Admiral's own story. R. S. West, *Admirals of the American Empire* (1948), features Dewey, Sampson, and other Great White Fleet admirals. Roosevelt's contribution to the new navy is assessed in Gordon C. O'Gara, *Theodore Roosevelt and the Rise of the Modern Navy* (1943).

The most entertaining general account of the Spanish-American War is Walter Millis, *The Martial Spirit* (1931). The book is undocumented, but in the main shows careful use of source material. F. E. Chadwick, *The Relations of the United States and Spain: The Spanish-American War* (2 vols., 1911), is dependable but dull. J. H. Latané, *America as a World Power, 1897–1907* (1907), covers this period for the *American Nation* series. C. R. Fish, *The Path of Empire* (1919), performs the same service for the *Chronicles of America*. On the Battle of Manila Bay, see the *Autobiography of George Dewey* (1916). On Santiago, the work of Colonel H. H. Sargent, *The Campaign of Santiago de Cuba* (3 vols., 1907), provides sufficient military detail to satisfy the most demanding. Interesting personal accounts are Joseph Wheeler, *The Santiago Campaign* (1898); and John Bigelow, Jr., *Reminiscences of the Santiago Campaign* (1899). R. A. Alger, *The Spanish-American War* (1901), is an attempt at self-justification by McKinley's Secretary of War. W. S. Schley, *Forty-Five Years under the Flag* (1904), is written in much the same vein.

On Dewey's problems at Manila Bay, see Jeannette Keim, *Forty Years of German-American Political Relations* (1919); C. E. Schieber, *The Transformation of American Sentiment toward Germany, 1870–1914* (1923); Bertha A. Reuter, *Anglo-American Relations during the Spanish-American War* (1924).

15

The American Empire

THE destruction of Cervera's fleet and the surrender of the Spanish land forces at Santiago confirmed the fears felt all **Armistice terms** along by informed Spaniards that Spain had no slightest chance to win the war. The Spanish authorities, therefore, in order to escape further humiliation, asked the French government on July 18, 1898, to sound out the United States on terms of peace. Eight days later, Jules Cambon, the French ambassador in Washington, laid before McKinley a note containing the Spanish acknowledgment of defeat, and asking the conditions on which the United States would agree to end the war. McKinley's reply, delivered July 30, insisted that Spain must be prepared to withdraw altogether from the western hemisphere. Spanish sovereignty over Cuba must be relinquished, and all the rest of the Spanish West Indies, including Puerto Rico, must be ceded to the United States. On the other side of the world the American government demanded the cession of an island in the Ladrones (midway between Hawaii and the Philippines), and possession of the city, harbor, and bay of Manila, pending determination in the treaty of the "control, disposition, and government" of the Philippines. In view of these somewhat extraordinary territorial demands, the United States promised to waive for the time being "any demand for

pecuniary indemnity." On these terms an armistice was signed on August 12, and the war was over. In Cuba, as the Spanish garrisons withdrew, they were replaced by regiments of "immunes" under General Leonard Wood. Many of Wood's soldiers, it developed, were by no means as immune as they should have been, but a bright chapter in the history of American sanitation had begun.

On October 1, 1898, commissioners from the United States and Spain met at Paris to work out the details of the treaty of peace. Probably the thought never occurred to William McKinley that he himself might have a place at the peace table. Indeed, it was a well-established tradition, one which so conventional a President could have had no desire to break, that the President of the United States must not set foot on foreign soil. To head the American delegation, McKinley chose his Secretary of State, William R. Day, but even Day was required to resign his post as Secretary before he left the country. Mindful of the fact that a treaty must be ratified by the United States Senate, McKinley sent along three prominent senators, two Republicans and a Democrat — Cushman K. Davis of Minnesota, chairman of the Senate Committee on Foreign Relations, William P. Frye of Maine, president *pro tempore* of the Senate, and

George Gray of Delaware. None of them was expected to resign as senator, and none of them did so. The fifth place on the commission went to a newspaper man, Whitelaw Reid, Republican editor of the New York *Tribune*. McKinley's instructions gave the commissioners no option as to the expulsion of the Spanish Empire from America, but the Spanish delegation argued plausibly that, inasmuch as there was no Cuban government worthy of the name, the island should be ceded directly to the United States, who would thereby become responsible for the Cuban debt. The Americans refused this dubious proffer. They agreed that the United States should occupy the island temporarily, but they successfully insisted that Spain should assume the island's debt.

The most heated dispute between the Spanish and the American delegations was **Treaty of** over the Philippine Islands. The **Paris** Spaniards argued earnestly that the situation in the Orient should be considered as of August 12, when the armistice was signed, instead of August 14, when the city of Manila was officially surrendered to General Merritt. But the Americans refused to concede this point, and before the end of the month they were instructed by President McKinley to obtain the cession of the entire Philippine Archipelago. To the Spanish, and to many Americans, this demand seemed incredible. The total area of the Philippine Islands was seven thousand square miles greater than that of the British Isles, and the United States had actually occupied only the city of Manila. But McKinley had been watching American opinion closely, and had become convinced that the great majority of the American electorate favored annexation. That there would be trouble from the Filipinos he knew, and it worried him. One evening, after he had sought divine guidance in prayer, he made up his mind. "There is nothing left for us to do," he decided, "but to take all the islands and to educate the Filipinos, and uplift, civilize, and Christianize them and, by God's grace, do the very best we can for them as our fellow men,

for whom Christ also died." Already three members of the commission, Davis, Frye, and Reid, had made up their minds the same way, and Day, the chairman, was ready to take Luzon, the large island on which Manila was located. Senator Gray, however, held out for a time that to annex any single part of the islands was a "shameful stepping down from the high moral position" the United States had taken in entering the war.

The President's will prevailed, and the American commissioners told the Spanish delegation what had to be done. The protests were long-drawn-out, and in the end the Spanish won an extraordinary concession. Without exactly explaining why it was to be done, the United States agreed to "pay to Spain the sum of twenty million dollars within three months after the exchange of the ratifications of the present treaty." Ordinarily money payments were demanded of vanquished powers instead of being accorded to them, but, in view of the extensive territorial cessions the United States had obtained, a money indemnity could hardly have been required. The twenty million dollars was variously explained as representing the difference in value between what the United States had actually conquered and what it insisted on taking, or the investment the Spanish government had made in the Philippines, or what it was worth to the United States in satisfaction just to have a war and win it. On December 10, 1898, the treaty was finally signed, and early next month the President submitted it to the Senate for ratification.

For a time there was danger that the necessary two-thirds majority could not be obtained. Led by the resourceful **Ratification** William Jennings Bryan, "anti-imperialists" gave battle the whole country over against so wide a departure from American tradition as was involved in the acquisition of the Philippines. Not Democrats merely, but many prominent Republicans also, including Senator Hale of Maine and Senator Hoar of Massachusetts, objected strenuously to the terms of the treaty, and when the time came voted against ratification. Speaker Thomas B. Reed was "terribly bitter" in his opposition, and according to Senator Lodge was "saying all sorts of ugly things about the Administration and its policy." Ultimately Reed resigned his seat in the House and retired from politics rather than stand with his party on such an issue. Andrew Carnegie went to Washington and lobbied against the treaty. Strange as it may seem, the man who finally saved the treaty was Bryan. According to one point of view, the "Great Commoner" was convinced that free silver would not provide the Democrats with a winning issue in 1900, and saw in a battle over imperialism the best chance for a Democratic victory. But according to another point of view he was not seeking primarily to create an election issue; all he wanted to do was to insure that so important a question as Philippine independence should be decided separately from the rest of the treaty, and solely on its own merits. Whatever his motives may have been, he maintained that the proper policy was first to accept the treaty, and then to demand that the Philippines be set free.

Without the efforts of Bryan, who conferred in Washington with wavering Democrats and Populists, it seems certain that the administration would have lost. As it was, ten Democrats and eight Populists voted with thirty-nine Republicans to give the treaty one more than the two-thirds majority required for ratification.

By any standards of measurement, the United States emerged from the Spanish-American War a world power. It had defeated a European nation in war, and it had added to its possessions regions distant enough and different enough that none could deny the existence of an American Empire. Alaska, the Hawaiian Islands, the Philippines, Puerto Rico, Guam, all these and a number of minor islands, together with the temporary occupation of Cuba, satisfied for the moment the ambitions of the most rabid of expansionists. To some, however, it was only a beginning. Senator Albert J. Beveridge of Indiana, an orator worthy of comparison to William Jennings Bryan, scattered throughout one of his most popular addresses the refrain: "The march of the flag

The United States as a world power

United States Imperialism. Uncle Sam plants the American flag on the new possessions of the United States.

Imperialism meant that the United States must assume responsibility for Eskimos in Alaska, Polynesians and Orientals in Hawaii, and Filipinos in the Philippines. To many critics this type of colonialism was a complete contradiction of the American principle of self-government.

TYPICAL ESKIMO ADULT AND DWELLING. Man and house are covered with skins.

TWO HAWAIIAN WOMEN AND A GRASS HOUSE. The woman at the right is Queen Liliuokalani.

PHILIPPINE WOMAN WITH BAMBOO POLE. Native house is of bamboo and palm.

went on!" That anything could ever stop its further progress seemed to him incredible.[1]

Alaska the United States had owned since 1867, but only in the nineties had Americans begun to realize its value. In 1896 gold was discovered in the Klondike, a district in northern Canada adjacent to the Alaskan border that could be reached ordinarily only by crossing the Alaskan panhandle, or by ascending the Yukon River. For the next few years the search for gold in the frozen North produced scenes reminiscent of the gold rush to California. The prosperity and notoriety of the Klondike, short-lived though it proved to be, suggested the possibility of gold in Alaska, and new finds and new rushes came thick and fast. The remote village of Nome, Alaska, for example, swelled in population during the year 1899–1900 to twenty thousand, only to shrink again to insignificance. Here as elsewhere the amount of gold that could be obtained without expensive machinery was negligible, but during the next third of a century the gold taken from Alaskan mines exceeded fifty times over the price the United States had paid Russia for the territory. Other valuable mineral deposits, such as silver, copper, lead, and oil, soon proved that "Seward's Folly" was an extremely profitable investment. Governed at first by army, navy, and treasury officials, Alaska was accorded territorial status by an organic act passed in 1884, and revised in 1913.

Alaska

While the Spanish-American War was in progress, the United States acquired the Hawaiian Islands, with a population at the time of over one hundred and fifty thousand. The Hawaiian archipelago, lying some two thousand miles to the west of the California coast, consisted of eight large inhabited islands, and a dozen or so small ones virtually devoid of population. The total area of the islands was 6,412 square miles, two-thirds of which was accounted for by the largest island, Hawaii,

Hawaii

and all but six square miles, by the eight major units. The original inhabitants of Hawaii were primitive Polynesians, kindred in race and customs to the Samoans. The existence of the islands had perhaps been known to the Spanish during the sixteenth century, but for all practical purposes they were first discovered by Captain James Cook, an English explorer, in 1778. Thereafter they were visited repeatedly by sailing ships, mostly China traders or whalers, and began to acquire some white population. King Kamehameha I, an able warrior and statesman, united the islands under one rule early in the nineteenth century, and so put an end to the continual conflicts with which they had previously been afflicted. American Protestant missionaries, who first appeared about 1820, quickly and easily converted the natives to Christianity, and introduced the white man's manner of living. The Hawaiians, however, did not prosper under civilization. At one time they may have numbered as many as 300,000, but they soon began to die off. According to recent census reports, the number of Hawaiians and part-Hawaiians in the islands is not above 80,000 out of a total of over half a million. Other peoples, among them Chinese, Japanese, Koreans, Filipinos, and Puerto Ricans, as well as Caucasians, soon came in to replace the natives. The various races lived together with a minimum of friction, and often intermarried.

The fact that American imperialism antedated the Spanish-American War is apparent from the American record on Hawaii. Annexation to the United States was the object of a treaty signed in 1854, but the treaty went unratified. American sugar-planters and merchants, many of them the descendants of the missionaries, were eager to divest themselves of the annoyances they suffered from native rule, and had much to do with staging the revolution of 1893 which made Hawaii a republic.[1] The revolution had been intended only as a means to the end of annexation, but President Cleveland thwarted

[1] Claude G. Bowers, *Beveridge and the Progressive Era* (1932), p. 75.

[1] See also p. 268.

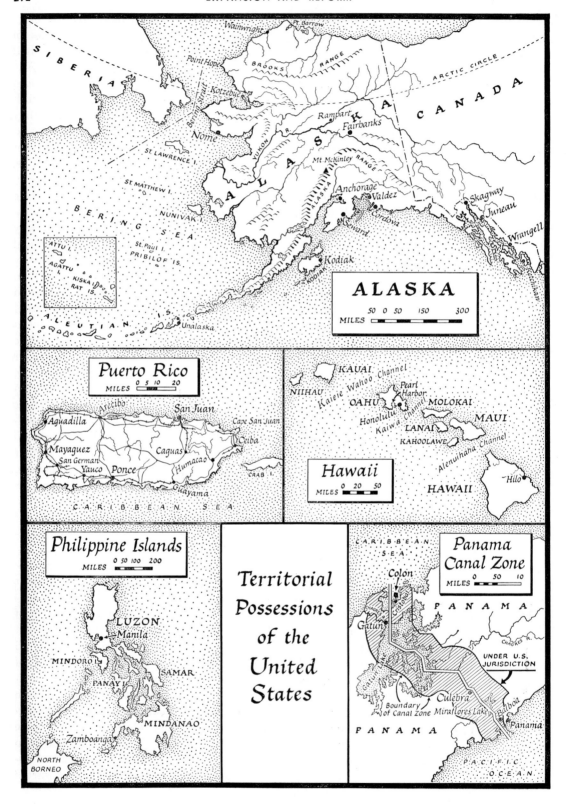

ALASKA

MILES 50 0 50 150 300

Puerto Rico

MILES 0 5 10 20

Hawaii

MILES 0 20 50

Philippine Islands

MILES 0 50 100 200

Territorial Possessions of the United States

Panama Canal Zone

MILES 0 50 10

UNDER U.S. JURISDICTION

the desires of the annexationists, although the new Hawaiian government was strong enough that he was soon obliged to recognize it. After McKinley became President, a new treaty of annexation was signed, June 16, 1897, but the chances of its ratification were so uncertain that Hawaii was eventually annexed by joint-resolution, a method which required a majority of both House and Senate, instead of a two-thirds majority of the Senate. The Japanese government, which claimed a population of 25,000 Japanese nationals in the islands, protested vigorously against the disturbance of the *status quo* in the Pacific that American annexation would involve. But with Dewey in command of Manila Bay, the need of the United States for a mid-Pacific base was easy to assert and defend. The Japanese, assured that their nationals would be well treated, were persuaded to withdraw their protest, and on July 7, 1898, McKinley signed the joint-resolution of annexation. On April 30, 1900, an Act of Congress accorded Hawaii full territorial status.

The acquisition of Hawaii seemed justified by the sugar the islands could produce, but **Acquisitions** the value of the former colonies **from Spain** of Spain had yet to be proved. Cuba, according to the resolution that Congress had adopted when the war with Spain broke out, must be set free, but just how this was to be brought about was not entirely clear. Here the United States faced, also, a baffling and expensive problem of sanitation, for the yellow fever and other tropical diseases were taking a heavy toll. Fortunately the Puerto Ricans accepted American sovereignty without visible signs of resentment, but for a long time the cost of American occupation was sure to exceed any possible profits. As for the Philippines, the United States had paid Spain twenty million dollars to get them, and had then added another hundred thousand dollars because the boundary zone outlined by the Treaty of Paris had left out a number of tiny islands that the American commissioners had meant to take. The prospect of returns on this invest-

ment seemed discouraging in the extreme, for the Filipinos, unlike the Puerto Ricans, had no notion of accepting American rule without a struggle.

The Philippines, probably unheard of by most Americans before the war, consisted of 7083 islands, of which 1668 were **The** large enough to be named, and **Philippines** 342 were populated. Together they had an area of 115,000 square miles, one fourth of which lay within the island of Luzon, which is approximately the size of Ohio. The Philippine population, which was a mixture of native races and immigrants from the Asiatic mainland, included about seven million Spanish-speaking and Roman Catholic Filipinos, besides perhaps two thirds of a million wild and uncivilized Igorrotes and Moros. Under Spanish rule the islanders had suffered from neglect, exploitation, and oppression, and, when the war between the United States and Spain broke out, Filipino insurgents were seriously challenging Spanish supremacy. The insurrection was immensely aided by Dewey's return of its exiled leader, Emilio Aguinaldo, whose forces, by the time the United States had acquired title to the islands, actually held the upper hand everywhere except in Luzon.

At first the Filipinos had assumed naïvely that the American promise of freedom for Cuba carried with it by implication the promise of freedom for the Philippines. Even the terms of the Treaty of Paris did not entirely disabuse their minds, for they knew that powerful opposition to annexation existed in the United States, and they hoped that something would happen to prevent it. But they were soon undeceived. On December 21, 1898, President McKinley asserted pointedly the determination of the United States to extend American sovereignty over the islands, and instructed the War Department to make this attitude clear to the Filipinos. General Elwell S. Otis, who had succeeded General Merritt as military governor of the islands, did not dare publish McKinley's message in its original form, although ordered to do so, but even when softened the

President's announcement had a very bad effect. As the debate over ratification proceeded, Aguinaldo and the Filipino leaders lost hope. If they were not merely to exchange Spanish rule for American rule, they must fight. On February 4, 1899, two days before the Senate ratified the treaty, an American outpost exchanged shots with some insurgents and the war in the Philippines was on.

The path of empire was to prove thorny indeed. Hard fighting soon drove the insur-

Revolt in the gents from their trenches around
Philippines Manila, but the natives took to the hills and inflicted severe punishment upon the troops sent against them. In the first two months of fighting the Americans admitted losses of nearly twelve hundred killed and wounded, and before the islanders were pacified these losses had been multiplied many times over. Most prominent of the American victims was General Henry W. Lawton, shot by a Filipino sharpshooter. The insurgent forces under Aguinaldo's command amounted in all to perhaps seventy thousand men, many of whom had seen service with the Spanish and were trained in western methods of warfare. Had their supply of arms been adequate they might have prolonged their resistance almost indefinitely, and even when reduced to the use of their native weapon, the bolo, a long, sharply pointed knife, they were formidable antagonists. Retreating from one tropical fastness to another, and from one island to the next, they kept busy an army of occupation as large as their own. The American officers and men, incensed at the constant losses, fought back with methods not much different from those of "Butcher" Weyler in Cuba. To William Howard Taft, of Ohio, benevolent head of a civilian commission sent to the Philippines in the summer of 1900, the Filipino was a "little brown brother," but to the soldiers who were doing the fighting:

He may be a brother of Big Bill Taft;
But he ain't no brother of mine.

In the end, of course, American might won, but not until Aguinaldo had been trapped in a most unchivalrous manner and brought back as a captive to Manila. On October 1, 1901, the complete suppression of the insurrection was formally announced, but the facts did not for many months justify such a statement.

Meantime the people of the United States had had a chance to express themselves at the polls on the issue of "impe- **Election** rialism." Republican successes **of 1900** in the elections of 1898 denoted little more than general satisfaction at the victories won by Americans in the war with Spain, but the presidential election of 1900 was a pitched battle, with the forces favoring annexation of the Philippines lined up solidly on one side, and those opposed on the other. The Republicans, with William McKinley once more their standard-bearer, and with Theodore Roosevelt, the hero of San Juan Hill, as their candidate for Vice-President, rejoiced in the "new and noble responsibility" that had come to the American people, and asserted that "no other course was possible" in the Philippines than the one that had been taken. The Democrats, still under the spell of Bryan's oratory, also renominated their leader of the preceding campaign, but for second place they had no war hero, only the time-worn Vice-President of Cleveland's second administration, Adlai E. Stevenson of Illinois. Bryan himself had been a colonel of Nebraska volunteers, but he had had no such luck with the War Department in obtaining a chance to fight as had the colonel on the Republican ticket. To Bryan, "imperialism" was the "paramount issue" of the campaign, and the Democratic platform recorded his sentiments:

We condemn and denounce the Philippine policy of the present Administration. It has embroiled the Republic in an unnecessary war, sacrificed the lives of many of its noblest sons, and placed the United States, previously known and applauded throughout the world as the champion of freedom, in the false and un-American position of crushing with military force the efforts of our former allies to achieve liberty and self-government.

The Filipinos cannot be citizens without endangering our civilization; they cannot be subjects without imperiling our form of government; and as we are not willing to surrender our civilization, or to convert the Republic into an empire, we favor an immediate declaration of the Nation's purpose to give to the Filipinos, first, a stable form of government; second, independence; and third, protection from outside interference such as has been given for nearly a century to the republics of Central and South America.

Throughout the campaign the debate on imperialism held the center of the stage. The arguments were not new; they had all been used while the Treaty of Paris was before the country. Nor was the decision ever in doubt. McKinley, as the cartoonists so graphically portrayed, always had his "ear to the ground," and he knew full well that he had read the public mind aright. Nevertheless, Democratic orators dwelt long upon the inconsistency of a democracy such as the United States fighting to suppress the ambitions of another people to be free. They cast William McKinley in the role of George III, and Aguinaldo in that of George Washington. They pointed out the practical difficulties involved. The United States was wholly without experience in the governing of colonies. How could it hope to solve the problems of a distant and alien race? A great navy and a great army would be necessary to protect the new possessions. Once the United States had depended upon the Atlantic Ocean and the Pacific Ocean for its defense. But with Asiatic possessions American military might must be expanded to reach far across the seas.

Republican orators had no difficulty in justifying all that had been done. The Philippines, they claimed, offered an inviting missionary field. The United States had at last an opportunity to extend the blessings of American civilization. The Filipinos were not yet capable of governing themselves; freedom would mean only anarchy and mis-

Imperialism the paramount issue

rule, or perhaps conquest by some predatory commercial nation, such as Germany or France. The United States had become a great power, and it must accept the responsibilities of greatness. Kipling's poem on "The White Man's Burden," published by *McClure's Magazine* in February, 1899, made "good sense":

> Take up the White Man's burden —
> Send forth the best ye breed —
> Go, bind your sons to exile
> To serve your captive's need;
>
> To wait in heavy harness
> On fluttered folk and wild —
> Your new-caught sullen peoples,
> Half devil and half child.

There would be profits, too, from imperialism. American trade in the Orient had grown

The Democratic nominee, Bryan, changing the 1896 issue to imperialism, the 1900 issue. Cartoon from *Harper's Weekly,* August 11, 1900.

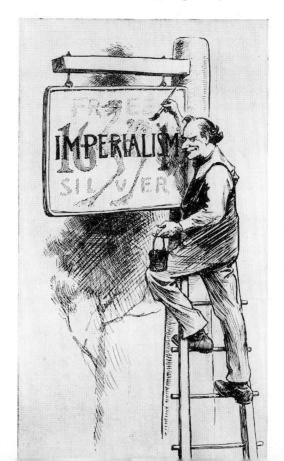

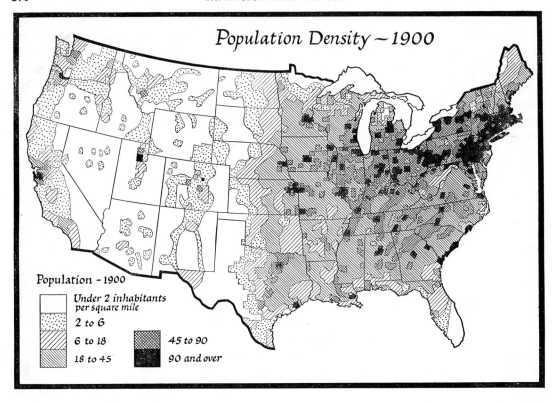

Population Density – 1900

Population - 1900

- Under 2 inhabitants per square mile
- 2 to 6
- 6 to 18
- 18 to 45
- 45 to 90
- 90 and over

of late, and with colonial possessions it would continue to grow. Even if the great powers of Europe partitioned China, as seemed likely to happen, the Philippines would more than compensate the United States for whatever losses it suffered in the China trade. "It is God's great purpose," said Senator Beveridge, "made manifest in the instincts of our race, whose present phase is our personal profit, but whose far-off end is the redemption of the world and the christianization of mankind." Besides, how could the United States be a really great nation if it had no colonies? Other great nations had colonies and were engaged in a mad scramble for more. Why should Americans deny themselves the right to boast with the British that the sun could never set on their national flag?

It would be a mistake to assume that imperialism was the only subject debated in

Other issues the campaign of 1900. The free-silver issue might be dead, as many Democrats privately conceded, but a

multitude of voters did not know it. Accordingly Bryan and the Democratic orators repeated the monetary demands of 1896, while the Republicans once more adhered firmly to the gold standard. The tariff, too, could not be entirely ignored, and here again both parties had historic positions to defend. This multiplicity of issues led to numerous complications. Strong advocates of imperialism, or "expansion," as the Republicans preferred to call it, might hold low-tariff or even free-silver views, while the bitterest enemies of an overseas empire might be convinced adherents of protection and the gold standard. Cartoonists made merry with the "hold-your-nose-and-vote" crowd. Some gold-standard men "held their noses" and voted for Bryan because they agreed with him on imperialism; some free-traders "held their noses" and voted for the obnoxious McKinley because they believed in expansion; in a variety of ways the old adage that "politics makes strange bedfellows" was proved to be true. Shrewdly, Republican campaigners turned attention away from these discordant issues all they could, and rang the changes on prosperity. By comparing the hard times of Cleveland's second administration with the good times of the McKinley era they were able to associate prosperity with Republican policies and to blame adversity on the Democrats. Slogans such as "The Full Dinner Pail," and "Let Well Enough Alone," pressed home the point.

In the end McKinley won a more overwhelming victory than in 1896. He had **Re-election of McKinley** again the advantage of a huge campaign fund, while Bryan's backers had even less to spend than four years before. Bryan carried only the "solid South," and four silver states, Colorado, Nevada, Idaho, and Montana, while McKinley carried all the rest, including Bryan's home state, Nebraska. The popular vote stood 7,219,525 to 6,358,737 and the electoral vote, 292 to 155. The election was notable for the large number of minor parties that had presidential tickets in the field. The regular Populist organization supported Bryan, but a dissident group, the "Middle-

of-the-Road" Populists, nominated Wharton Barker of Pennsylvania for President, and Ignatius Donnelly of Minnesota for Vice-President. Two Socialist tickets, one of them headed by Eugene V. Debs, and a Prohibition ticket, each polled appreciable numbers of votes, while several lesser parties won next to no support at all. In spite of his long list of opponents McKinley received a majority of the popular as well as of the electoral vote. Both houses of Congress were also assured to the Republicans by substantial majorities, and, except in the South, Republican candidates for state office were generally the victors. In so far as an election could decide anything, the country had given its approval to imperialism, the gold standard, and a high protective tariff.

Six months after his second inauguration William McKinley visited the Pan-American Exposition at Buffalo, New **Death of** York, and on September 5 made **McKinley** a speech in which he emphasized the importance of reciprocity as a means of promoting foreign trade. Next day, during a reception, he was shot by an anarchist who had no other motive for his crime, apparently, than

The slogans of the Republican campaign in 1900 were the "Full Dinner Pail" and "Let Well Enough Alone."

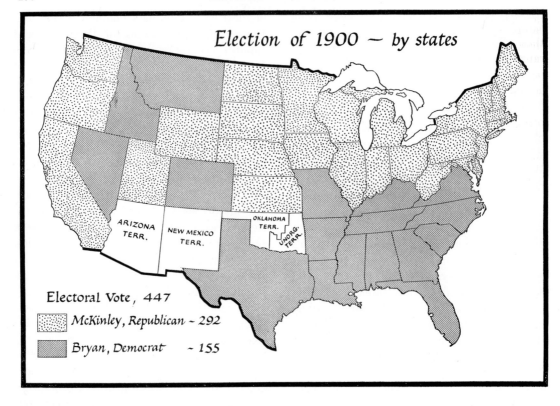

Election of 1900 — by states

ARIZONA
TERR.

NEW MEXICO
TERR.

OKLAHOMA
TERR.

UNORG.
TERR.

Electoral Vote, 447

McKinley, Republican ~ 292

Bryan, Democrat ~ 155

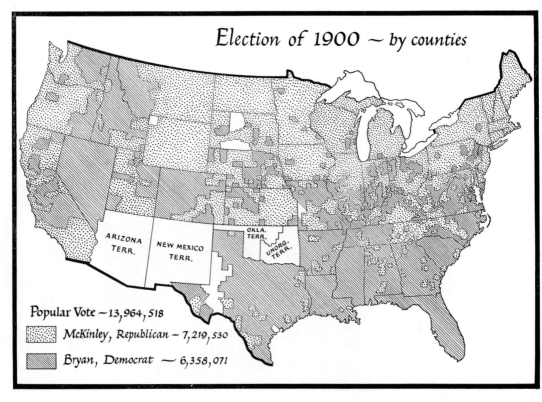

Election of 1900 — by counties

ARIZONA
TERR.

NEW MEXICO
TERR.

OKLA.
TERR.

UNORG.
TERR.

Popular Vote ~ 13,964,518

McKinley, Republican ~ 7,219,530

Bryan, Democrat — 6,358,071

his disbelief in government. For a few days the President lingered on, but on September 14 he died, and was succeeded by the youthful Vice-President, Theodore Roosevelt. In a sense it was altogether fitting that the problems of consolidating and administering the new American Empire should fall to Roosevelt, for he, far more than McKinley, was responsible for the adventure into imperialism that the nation had undertaken.

When Roosevelt took office the liberation of Cuba was not yet an accomplished fact, **Occupation** but much progress in that direc-**of Cuba** tion had been made. Almost the first concern of the American army of occupation was the sanitation of the island. Under the leadership of Major William Crawford Gorgas, an army physician, Havana, long a favorite breeding-place for tropical diseases, was scoured into a cleanliness it had never known before. When in spite of these measures a yellow fever epidemic broke out in 1900, a special commission headed by Doctor Walter Reed, went to Cuba to investigate. With the help of Doctor Carlos J. Finley, a Cuban whose "scientific clairvoyance" had enabled him to guess the correct solution, they proved that a mosquito, the stegomyia, was the guilty carrier. Two of the American investigators, Doctor Jesse W. Lazear and Doctor James Carroll, were infected in the course of their experiments, and both lost their lives as a result. Lazear died in a matter of days; Carroll recovered, but was so weakened that he died a few years later. The cause of the epidemic now ascertained, Gorgas went to work to eliminate the offending insect, with such success that before the year 1901 had ended Havana for the first time in "more than one hundred and forty years" was completely clear of yellow fever. General Wood, whose hearty cooperation as governor of Cuba had made possible the successes of Reed and Gorgas, extended American ideas of sanitation as rapidly as possible to the whole island. When the time came for American withdrawal, Cuba was almost as safe a place to live in as the United States itself.

Wood's administration also brought to the Cubans a higher degree of governmental efficiency than they had ever known before, and the promise of self-government. As early as June, 1900, municipal elections were ordered, and when critics of Republican imperialism asserted during the campaign of 1900 that McKinley never meant to set Cuba free, the President answered with orders for the election in September of a Cuban constitutional convention. The problem of the suffrage was somewhat perplexing, for a census taken by the Americans indicated that two thirds of the Cubans could neither read nor write, while none of them had ever had any experience with free elections. It was finally decided that voting should be restricted to those who could read and write, or who owned two hundred and fifty dollars in property, or who had served in the army of liberation. In November, 1900, thirty-one delegates were chosen, and by February, 1901, the convention had adopted a constitution closely patterned on the Constitution of the United States.

Quite significantly the Cuban Convention at first ignored the special relationship that the American government had **The Platt** assumed would exist between **Amendment** the United States and the republic it had created. On instructions from Washington, Governor Wood brought this oversight to the attention of the delegates, and indicated clearly the nature of the provisions the United States expected them to adopt. Even more emphatic was the action of Congress, which added to the Army Appropriation Bill of March 2, 1901, a series of eight clauses, known as the Platt Amendment, as follows:

1. That the government of Cuba should never by treaty with a foreign power impair its independence.

2. That it should keep its public debt within its capacity to pay from the ordinary revenues of the island.

3. That the United States should have

the right to intervene for the preservation of Cuban independence and the maintenance of a government adequate for the protection of life, property, and individual liberty.

4. That the acts of the American military government during the period of occupation should be validated.

5. That the plans for the sanitation of Cuba already begun should be carried out by the new government.

6. That the Isle of Pines should be omitted from the proposed constitutional boundaries of Cuba, and its title settled by treaty with the United States.

7. That Cuba should sell or lease to the United States lands necessary for coaling or naval stations.

8. That all these special provisions should be embodied in a permanent treaty with the United States.

Reluctantly, and under strong pressure from Washington, the Cuban Convention finally included the Platt Amendment as an appendix to the constitution it had drawn, and later on, when the new Cuban government had gone into operation, the treaty contemplated by the eighth clause was mutually ratified. Thus the Platt Amendment had the sanction of American statute law, Cuban constitutional provision, and treaty between the two nations. Obviously Cuba was not intended to be quite free; its status could be described more accurately as that of a protectorate of the United States.

On May 20, 1902, American authority was withdrawn from Cuba, and the government **Cuba as a** turned over to elected Cuban **protectorate** officials. That the Platt Amendment, particularly the third clause, which gave the United States the right of intervention, was not to become a dead letter was soon demonstrated. In August, 1906, an insurrection, aimed at the overthrow of the regularly elected government, broke out, and after a brief period of patience President Roosevelt sent his Secretary of War, William Howard Taft, to Cuba to "sit on the lid." Unable to effect a reconciliation between the contending factions, Taft, on September 26,

1906, assumed the full governmental authority of the island. For more than two years the American occupation continued, first under Taft and later under Governor Charles E. Magoon, and when finally the United States again withdrew it did so only with a warning to the Cubans from the President of the United States that "if elections become a farce and if the insurrectionary habit becomes confirmed . . . it is absolutely out of the question that the island should remain independent"; or, in effect, that if the United States had to intervene again in Cuba it would come to stay. Had Roosevelt remained President indefinitely, this threat might have been made good, but subsequent Presidents were more charitable. On several occasions the United States made use of its right of intervention in Cuba, but the island was not annexed. Under Franklin D. Roosevelt, indeed, the Platt Amendment itself was abrogated by agreement between the two nations, but by this time American investments in Cuba had made of the island an economic, if not a political, dependency of the United States.

The constitutional and governmental status of Cuba, which was merely administered by the United States while on its way to freedom, could be regarded as exceptional, but some more or less permanent *modus vivendi* had to be arranged for the other new acquisitions. According to the treaty of cession, "the civil rights and political status of the native inhabitants of the territory . . . ceded to the United States" were left to the determination of Congress. Did this mean that Congress could do as it pleased without extending the liberties guaranteed by the Constitution to its island possessions, or was the freedom of Congress in this respect as much subject to the Constitution in the new territory as in the old? In other words, as the public phrased the question, Does the Constitution follow the flag?

Congress soon revealed through the various acts by which it provided for the establishment of civil government in **Status of de-** the new possessions that it had **pendencies** no notion whatever of setting limits to its authority. In the Foraker Act of 1900, for example, which outlined a form of government for Puerto Rico, a tariff was levied against Puerto Rican imports into the United States equal to fifteen per cent of the regular Dingley rates. If Puerto Rico had become a part of the United States this provision was clearly contrary to the constitutional requirements that "all duties, imports, and excises shall be uniform throughout the United States." Obviously, therefore, Congress did not regard the island as a part of the United States in the constitutional sense of the term, nor did the President who signed the law. But what would be the attitude of the federal courts, which since the time of John Marshall had felt free to set aside laws of Congress that in their judgment did not harmonize with the Constitution?

In a series of five-to-four opinions on what came generally to be known as the "insular cases" the Supreme Court decided in 1901 not to interfere with the stand that Congress and the President had taken. The first of these cases, *De Lima vs. Bidwell*, was brought by an importer of Puerto Rican sugar against the collector of the port of New York who *before* the enactment of the Foraker Act, but *after* the acquisition of Puerto Rico by the United States, had charged the full Dingley duties. In this case the Court held that the money collected must be refunded, for Puerto Rico was no longer foreign territory. In another case, however, *Downes vs. Bidwell*, where the collections had been made *after* the passage of the Foraker Act and according to its terms, the Court held that a refund was unnecessary, for Puerto Rico was not exactly a part of the United States. To eight justices these decisions seemed utterly contradictory, for the result was achieved by Mr. Justice Brown changing sides, and voting in the second decision with the four justices who had constituted the minority in the first decision. The reasoning by which he justified this shift of opinion no one but himself seemed to understand. Mr. Justice Harlan, who, together

with three of his associates had voted in both cases that the Constitution must follow the flag, dissented from the *Downes vs. Bidwell* decision in vigorous terms:

I confess that I cannot grasp the thought that Congress, which lives and moves and has its being in the Constitution and is consequently the mere creature of that instrument, can, at its pleasure, legislate or exclude its creator from territories which were acquired only by authority of the Constitution.

Nevertheless Mr. Justice Brown's decision stood. Puerto Rico and the other dependencies, he maintained, were "territory appurtenant — but not a part — of the United States." Two other opinions, the "Fourteen Diamond Rings" case and *Hawaii vs. Mankichi*, applied the same principles to the Philippines and the Hawaiian Islands respectively. The Constitution followed the flag only when and in so far as Congress ordered.

"Mr. Dooley," a mythical Irish-American whose efforts to enlighten his slow-witted contemporary, "Mr. Hennessy," revealed through the newspapers the opinions of a shrewd commentator, Finley Peter Dunne, was much impressed by the decision of "Justice Brown — Fuller, C. J., Gray, J., Harlan, J., Shiras, J., McKenna, J., White, J., Brewer, J., and Peckham, J., dissenting fr'm me an' each other." The Constitution, Mr. Dooley concluded, had no business "to shadow the flag to all th' tough resorts on th' Passyfic Coast."

"Ye can't make me think th' constitution is goin' trapezin' around ivrywhere a young leftinant in th' ar'rmy takes it into his head to stick a flagpole. It's too old. It's a home-stayin' constitution with a blue coat and brass buttons on to it, an' it walks with a goold-headed cane. It's old an' it's feeble an' it prefers to set on the front stoop and amuse the childer. It wudden't last a minyit in thim thropical climes."

Then, reflecting on the victory of imperialism at the polls in the election of 1900, Mr. Dooley went on:

"Some say it laves the flag up in th' air an' some say that's where it laves the constitution.

*The **new empire** provided unexpected competition from overseas in such important items as tobacco, rice, and sugar. It also opened up new opportunities for trade, and in Alaska, long since acquired but still to be exploited, a full-fledged gold rush.*

TOBACCO. A product of the Philippines.

RICE. Cultivated in the Philippines.

NOME, ALASKA. A tent city in 1898, during the gold rush.

SUGAR. The principal crop of the Hawaiian Islands.

MANILA HARBOR. Chief port in the Philippines, 1898.

Annyhow, something's in the air. But there's wan thing I'm sure about."

"What's that?" asked Mr. Hennessy.

"That is," said Mr. Dooley, "no matter whether the constitution follows the flag or not, th' Supreme Court follows th' illiction returns."

The thoroughly conservative *Review of Reviews* put the matter much more prosaically. "The decision of the Supreme Court," it pontificated, "means that we are not to be hampered in our serious policies by the ingenious use of logic in the interpretation of an ancient document that was not intended to hamper posterity."

The beginnings of a Philippines policy had been made before the death of McKinley. In

Government of the Philippines 1899 a commission of five, headed by President Schurman of Cornell University, was sent to make a study of conditions in the islands, and to report back a plan whereby self-government might eventually be established. Impressed by the ignorance of the people and the variety of their races and languages, the commission urged delay in extending the American political system to the islands, but next year McKinley sent a second commission headed by William Howard Taft of Ohio, to make the start. Taft's commission, in spite of some friction with the military authorities, soon took over full legislative and administrative responsibility. It worked out a plan for extending self-government gradually to Philippine municipalities, and divided the islands into provinces, each with an appointive head. On July 1, 1901, under authority of an act of Congress passed the preceding March, Taft became civil governor of the Philippines (governor-general after 1905), while the commission, reinforced shortly afterward by the appointment of three Filipino members, continued to act as a legislature. A supreme court, appointed by the President of the United States, completed the familiar picture of three independent departments of government. In 1907 the Filipinos were allowed the privilege of electing an assembly, which became the lower house of the legislature, while the commission served as the upper house.

American rule accomplished much more than the mere pacification and governmental organization of the Philippines. An immediate major problem was the disposition of the so-called "friar lands," some four hundred thousand acres belonging to various Catholic religious orders. These lands had been coveted by the Filipinos, and during the abortive Philippine revolution many of them had been appropriated by rebellious tenants. The friars, however, insisted that their land titles should be defended by the United States. Perplexed by the conflict of religious and temporal rights, Roosevelt in 1902 sent Taft to Rome to negotiate through the Pope for a settlement, and for seven million dollars the friars agreed to relinquish their claims. Many American Protestants were outraged at this open recognition of papal power, but the government had exchanged a wholly alien problem for one with which it had considerable experience — the disposal of public lands. Probably no other act did so much to reconcile the Filipinos to American rule.

"Dominion over palm and pine" carried with it also certain familiar aspects of American culture. One of the most important transplantations was the American public-school system. In 1898 perhaps five thousand Filipino children were in school; by 1920, over a million. At first American teachers were placed in charge, but adequately trained Filipinos, many of them educated in the United States, were soon available to take over the work. By 1920 the number of American teachers had dwindled to three hundred, and the English language rivaled the Spanish as the most generally understood tongue in the islands. American notions of sanitation also reached the Philippines. Smallpox and cholera were stamped out, lepers were isolated in colonies and treated instead of being permitted to roam at will, and the infantile death rate was sharply reduced. Good roads, too, were built, and improved methods of transportation were introduced. Most significant of all, the modified tariff barriers that had at first restricted trade between the Philippines and the United States soon gave way to virtual free trade, thus opening the rich American markets to Philippine sugar, coconut oil, rice, tobacco, and hemp. The result of this favored economic status was a degree of prosperity such as the Philippines had never known before. Whatever their political differences, the economic ties that bound the islands to the United States became closer with each succeeding year. Rich resources in minerals and lumber that might also be sold to American customers were discovered, and plans for their exploitation were laid.

The net political effect of the new prosperity, however, was to make the Filipinos

The road to independence crave independence ever more and more. Both parties in the United States conceded that sometime this goal must be reached, and many of the Democrats insisted that it should have been reached long before. In 1916, while Woodrow Wilson was President and the Democrats controlled Congress, the Jones Act outlined a scheme of self-government for the Philippines that looked definitely in the direction of independence. Both houses of the Philippine legislature were made elective, and the prerogatives of the governor-general were materially reduced. Indeed, the new governor-general, Francis B. Harrison, practically turned over the reins of authority to a council of state dominated by Filipinos, and accepted more or less openly a rôle as perfunctory as that of a governor-general in one of the British Dominions. This steady drift toward independence was interrupted in 1921 when President Harding sent his former rival for the Republican nomination, General Leonard Wood, to be governor-general of the Philippines. No believer in independence, Wood asserted to the full his legal prerogatives, and until the time of his death in 1927 unrest accumulated in the islands at a rapid rate.

Wood's successors were more conciliatory, and by the time the Democrats returned to power in 1933 the movement for Philippine

independence was far advanced. Philippine agitators found new and extremely effective allies in the sugar, dairy, and tobacco interests of the United States, who objected to the competition of duty-free Philippine products, and saw in independence for the islands an opportunity to levy the customary high protective-tariff rates against them. Pacifists also threw their influence in favor of independence on the ground that Japanese expansion might sometime reach the Philippines, and thus bring on war between Japan and the United States. Since American investments in the islands had been comparatively slight, there was no effective protest against this point of view, and finally, on December 29, 1932, Congress provided in the Hawes-Cutting Act for a ten-year American protectorate over the islands to be followed by independence. Mindful of the chaotic economic and social conditions that would result from the loss of the American markets, President Hoover courageously vetoed the act, but Congress promptly repassed it over his veto. By this time, however, the Filipinos could see that independence was not without its disadvantages, and the Philippine legislature, by failing to call the constitutional convention prescribed by the act, deliberately allowed the measure to lapse. On March 24, 1934, with Franklin D. Roosevelt as President, a new measure, known as the Tydings-McDuffie Act, once more offered independence after ten years, and this time the offer was accepted. All American officials except a high commissioner were withdrawn from the islands, and the two governments were left with the problem of working out within the ten-year limit such plans as might be deemed necessary to prevent the collapse of the Philippine economic system when the special favors granted by the United States should be withdrawn. The future of Philippine foreign relations was also left open for negotiations, with no assurance given that the United States would feel obliged to aid the islands in maintaining the independence they were at last about to achieve.

The occupation of Puerto Rico[1] involved fewer perplexities than confronted American

Puerto Rico officials either in the Philippines or in Cuba. The population of the island was less than a million, nearly two thirds of whom were white, and the rest of Negro extraction. Virtually all of them were Spanish-speaking and Roman Catholic. There had been no revolution and no war damage of consequence. American rule was accepted without enthusiasm, but without protest. Even under the military régime rapid strides were made toward the better sanitation of the island, the building of roads, and the re-ordering of public finance. So smoothly was the transition accomplished that as early as April 12, 1900, Congress passed the Foraker Act establishing a civil government for Puerto Rico, the first to be accorded any of the new possessions. The pattern of government thus set for the dependencies was similar to that of the traditional American territory, but with a few conspicuous differences. Members of the upper house of the legislature, as well as the governor, were appointed by the President and confirmed by the Senate, while only the lower house — the House of Delegates — was elected directly by the people. Both the governor of Puerto Rico and the Congress of the United States had the right to veto any laws passed by the island legislature. Six administrative officers — secretary, attorney-general, treasurer, auditor, commissioner of interior, and commissioner of education — were endowed with ample powers, and were made responsible to the appropriate cabinet members in Washington rather than to the local governor. Residents of the island were not accorded full American citizenship, but were described as citizens of Puerto Rico. During Wilson's first administration most of these anomalies were ironed out. The Jones Act of 1917 made the island a territory of the United States, "organized but unincorporated," gave American citizen-

[1] By an act of Congress, signed May 17, 1932, the name Puerto Rico was officially substituted for Porto Rico.

ship to all Puerto Ricans who desired it, provided the customary territorial form of government with a popularly-elected senate and house of representatives, and a delegate to Congress who could speak but could not vote. During the Truman administration the Puerto Ricans were even given the privilege of electing their own governor. They were urged to consider, also, the alternatives of statehood and complete independence, but the majority of them seemed to prefer autonomous status.

Even more rapidly than in the case of the Philippines, tariff barriers between the United States and Puerto Rico were broken down. After the summer of 1901 complete freedom of trade existed, with the result that Puerto Rican shipments to the United States (consisting chiefly of coffee, sugar, rum, fruits, and tobacco) were soon multiplied many times over. As in the Philippines, American occupation meant better roads, better schools, better sanitation. The great problem of Puerto Rico was its ever-growing population. The area of the island was only 3,435 square miles, but its people increased in number from under a million at the time of annexation to over two million by the end of the Second World War. This meant, by 1947, a density of population of about 685 persons per square mile, the highest in any of the Caribbean Islands. The agricultural economy upon which the Puerto Ricans depended simply could not sustain so large a population, hence a steady stream of emigration to Hawaii and the United States set in, particularly of agricultural laborers, although of late many Puerto Ricans have crowded into New York City. But the numbers of those who left were not large enough to be missed, and with the general level of well-being in the island definitely below American standards, a certain amount of political unrest was inevitable.

Prideful Americans recounting the spoils of imperialism were aware also of certain minor possessions above which waved Other the Stars and Stripes. Besides possessions Alaska, Hawaii, the Philippines, and Puerto

Rico, American sovereignty now extended also to Tutuila and several other islands of the Samoan group in the South Pacific, to Guam, some fifteen hundred miles east of the Philippines, and to numerous uninhabited Pacific islets over which no other nation had chosen to raise its flag. With no form of government prescribed by Congress for these acquisitions, they remained under the absolute control of the President as commander-in-chief of the army and navy.[1] Two other tiny colonies came to the United States as a result of the decision to build a canal across the Isthmus of Panama. The Canal Zone, ten miles wide, obtained by treaty with Panama in 1903, came to be inhabited principally by government employees, and was eventually left to the government of Congress, the President, and the national courts. The Virgin Islands, acquired by purchase from Denmark in 1917, were deemed of value for the proper defense of the Canal. To govern the impoverished twenty-five thousand Negroes and mulattoes who inhabited them, the President was authorized to appoint a governor, subject to the approval of the Senate. The Danish code of laws, already in force, was retained. President Truman, in 1950, appointed the first Virgin Islander to the governorship.

The threat to American isolation involved in the acquisition of this great overseas empire was far more formidable than most Americans understood. Possession of the Philippines, in particular, made the United States, whether it so desired or not, an Asiatic power with a lively interest in whatever went on in Asia. But the great powers of Asia, with the exception of Japan, were also the great powers of Europe — Great Britain in India, France in

The open-door policy

[1] The United States Navy, aided in each case by a local advisory legislature, administered both American Samoa and Guam until well after the Second World War. By an order of July 1, 1951, however, President Truman transferred the administration of American Samoa from the Department of the Navy to the Department of the Interior; while by an act of Congress, approved August 1, 1950, Guam became an unincorporated territory of the United States, and its inhabitants, American citizens.

French Indo-China, Russia in Siberia, Germany in Shantung, the Netherlands in the East Indies. How could the United States play the part it must in Asiatic affairs, and at the same time avoid that entanglement in European affairs against which Washington and Jefferson had so pointedly warned?

This problem had reached an acute phase even before the Spanish-American War. China was in danger of dismemberment. During the last quarter of the nineteenth century the nations of Europe, in their mad scramble for colonies, had practically completed the partition of Africa. Now they had turned their attention to China as the last of the great "backward" nations as yet unappropriated. "Spheres of influence" were already marked out in which one nation or another had obtained "concessions" for the "development" of a specified region, and in many instances outright ownership was asserted. England, ever since the Opium War of 1842, had held Hong Kong; Japan, after a war with China in 1895, assumed control of Korea; Germany, in compensation for the murder in 1897 of two German missionaries, had obtained a ninety-nine-year lease on the port of Kiao-chau and the recognition of Germany's special rights in the whole of Shantung peninsula; France under the terms of a similar lease occupied Kwangchau Bay far down on the southwestern coast; Russia, besides enjoying special privileges in northern Manchuria, had forced from China a twenty-five-year lease on Port Arthur.

All this was a matter of grave concern to the American government, not only because of America's new proximity to China, but also because the new order in the East threatened to destroy lucrative trade that had long existed between China and the United States. In consequence Secretary Hay, on September 6, 1899, addressed identical notes to Great Britain, Germany, and Russia, asking them to accept the principle of the "open door" to world trade in China. Each power was invited (1) to respect the trading privileges and vested interests of other nations within its sphere of influence, (2) to allow the Chinese tariff to continue in force and to be collected by Chinese officials in all such spheres, and (3) to avoid discriminations against other foreigners in port dues and railroad rates. Similar notes were sent presently to France, Italy, and Japan. The only favorable reply came from Great Britain, to whom the open door was entirely satisfactory, since in free competition the British could easily hold their own against all newcomers. The other powers professed complete agreement with Hay's suggestions, but each avoided commitments on the ground that it must first know what the others intended to do. Thereupon, by a clever diplomatic stroke, Hay pointed out that, inasmuch as all the powers had agreed to the principles he had enunciated, the United States would now consider them "final and definitive."

Hay's verbal victory for the open door made little difference to the nations bent on **The Boxer uprising** exploiting China, and the outbreak among the Chinese in the spring of 1900 of a violent anti-foreigner movement seemed to play definitely into the exploiters' hands. Under the leadership of a Chinese athletic society known as the Boxers, foreigners in China, whether traders, missionaries, or government agents, were subjected to the grossest indignities, and many

of them killed. The Chinese government, which was dominated by a tradition-bound and utterly reactionary Empress Dowager, gave more or less open aid and sympathy to the Boxers, even designating the strongly pro-Boxer Prince Tuan as head of the Foreign Office. In Peking, the capital city, foreigners gathered at their embassies for protection, but there was good reason to fear that even the presence of several hundred legation guards might not suffice to hold the marauders in leash. On June 20, 1900, the German Minister ventured through the city streets to deliver an official protest, but was killed by a Chinese soldier in uniform. Thereupon the entire diplomatic corps took refuge in the British Embassy, and by converting it into a veritable fortress prepared to hold out until help should arrive. Military intervention now became a necessity, and informed observers generally took it for granted that the partition of China among the powers would be the inevitable result.

International negotiations in which the United States participated resulted in the sending of a joint expeditionary force of about twenty thousand men from Tientsin to Peking. During the second week of August, 1900, Japanese, Russian, British, American, and French detachments fought their

American troops in the Temple of Agriculture grounds, Peking, China, at the time of the Boxer uprising.

way together to the Chinese capital through a region thickly infested with hostile Boxers. The decision of the United States to take part in the expedition did considerable violence to the American tradition against entangling alliances, but McKinley and Hay believed that only by pursuing such a course could they hope to prevent the dismemberment of China. The arrival of the international army on August 16 brought deliverance to the beleaguered legations.

Meantime Secretary Hay had taken occasion to state the objects of the expedition in **Hay's diplomacy** terms that suited American policy. What the United States desired, he maintained, was not the partition of China, but a solution that would bring about permanent safety and peace in the Orient, while at the same time preserving Chinese national integrity and the open door for world trade. In this policy the British government expressed complete concurrence, and with its assistance Hay succeeded also in bringing Germany to his point of view. Finally an Anglo-German agreement not only endorsed Hay's principles, but also served notice on the other great powers that they might not take advantage of the existing situation to acquire Chinese territory or to establish new trade barriers. This announcement was received with some dismay by France and Russia, but they had no choice but to acquiesce. After extensive negotiations the powers agreed upon a set of twelve joint demands that required principally: (1) the punishment of the chief offenders, (2) the settlement of all foreign claims by a money indemnity instead of by land cessions or special privileges, and (3) the adoption of adequate measures for the safety of foreigners in China.

The indemnity required of China, $333,-000,000 to be paid in thirty-nine annual installments, was large, but it **The Boxer indemnity** would have been much larger had not the United States made every effort to keep it down. The portion awarded to the United States was $24,440,700, but later investigation showed that the original esti-

mates of American losses had been much too high. Accordingly Congress in 1908, on recommendation of President Roosevelt, reduced the obligation to approximately half its original size, and in 1924 remitted also an unpaid balance of $6,000,000. In appreciation of these friendly acts the Chinese government announced that it would devote the first remission to the education of Chinese students in the United States, and the second, to educational and scientific work in China. For many years Chinese students, supported by "Boxer indemnity" money, were a familiar sight on American campuses, and their absorption of western civilization seemed at the time to be influencing deeply the course of Chinese development. For a generation the Chinese, thanks to the handling of the indemnity matter, and to Hay's persistent efforts to preserve Chinese national integrity, tended to regard the United States as a kind of moral, if not political, ally.

The withdrawal of the expeditionary forces from China was set for the fall of 1901, and was carried out according to agreement by all the nations except Russia, which maintained a special concentration in Manchuria with a view to exacting further favors from China. It thus became apparent that if the open door were to be kept open, something more effective than moral suasion would have to be used. Had American public opinion been willing to tolerate the idea, which definitely it was not, an Anglo-Japanese-American alliance might then have been formed to preserve the integrity of China and to maintain the open door. At the moment the three nations seemed to possess a community of interests. Both English and American trade in China was well established, and in free competition would continue to prosper. Japan, recently westernized, and eager to exploit the rich mineral resources and the enormous markets of China, counted on proximity as a sufficient aid to enable her to compete on equal terms with the western powers. It is barely possible that had the three nations joined hands they might have brought enough pressure to bear upon Russia, short of war, to force her to live up to the agreements she had signed. But the United States had no stomach either for alliances or for war, and Hay could only make futile protests and receive empty promises.

Nevertheless, quite as the opponents of imperialism had predicted, the United States **Imperial** could not avoid the rapid expan- **defense** sion of its military might. If there was to be an American empire, that empire had to be defended. Under Elihu Root as Secretary of War the United States Army underwent a reorganization so thorough that the scandals of inefficiency that marred the prosecution of the war against Spain could not soon be repeated. In keeping with modern practice a general staff was created to take the place of the major-general in command of the army, and to lay plans for the proper defense of the United States and its possessions. By means of the Army War College, established in 1901, and other service schools, an attempt was made also to carry on the military education of officers after they had been commissioned. The size of the army was not greatly increased, but a new militia law, designed to make of the National Guard a more efficient second line of defense, was placed on the statute books in 1903. Even more striking than the reorganization of the army was the rapid expansion of the navy, to which one or two new battleships were added every year. In 1907 President Roosevelt spectacularly advertised the strength of the American Navy by sending a fleet of sixteen battleships, together with the necessary auxiliary craft, on a voyage around the world. Any power critical of American policies — and the President had Japan particularly in mind — might thus see what it would have to deal with should it provoke the United States to war.

Quite as striking a fact as the sudden acquisition of a colonial empire by the United **Decline of** States was the equally sudden **imperialism** subsidence of the imperialistic urge. To Senator Beveridge (unless perchance he too had changed his mind) the rapid loss of interest by Americans in expansion must have seemed disheartening indeed. The "march of the flag" would not go on. After the first excitement, interest in the newly acquired possessions diminished, and the public showed not the slightest appetite for more. When the United States entered the First World War in 1917, one of the certainties, unchallenged by any political party, was that the American nation would not emerge with more colonies. At the Paris Peace Conference the United States, almost alone among the victors, made no demands for territory, and all efforts to saddle the American government with disagreeable mandates came to nought. From the financial point of view colonial empire had proved to be almost a total loss; the Philippines in particular had cost the government huge sums, and had brought in next to nothing by way of profit. This, perhaps, need not have been so; other nations took a heavy toll from their possessions. But neither the American government nor the American people showed great aptitude along this line. Americans with a taste for foreign investments were not lacking, but they made as good profits, if not better, in lands that lay outside the American Empire. Discouraging, too, was the discovery that distant possessions meant involvement in world politics. American isolation was threatened and the danger of war was increased.

Perhaps a distinction might be drawn between possessions in the western hemisphere and elsewhere. Americans while somewhat indifferent toward territorial acquisitions made in the New World, showed little disposition to give them up. They even acquiesced while their government, under one pretext or another, made virtual protectorates for a time of nations bordering on the Caribbean Sea and adjacent to the Panama Canal. The Philippines, however, were a heavy load to carry, and without huge naval expenditures they were utterly indefensible. At this distant outpost the "march of the flag" seemed destined to stop, and from it a strategic retreat was soon under way.

Bibliography

On the general problems of empire, *The American Empire: A Study of the Outlying Territories of the United States*, edited by William H. Haas (1940), provides a satisfactory survey. W. F. Willoughby, *Territories and Dependencies of the United States* (1905), is useful on the legal and constitutional side. The expansionist position is well stated in *Selections from the Correspondence of Theodore Roosevelt and Henry Cabot Lodge, 1884–1918* (2 vols., 1925); and in Claude G. Bowers, *Beveridge and the Progressive Era* (1932). Bowers gives an excellent account of Beveridge's rôle as a leading imperialist, and reveals here little of the partisanship that characterizes much of his other writing. Appropriate sections in Olcott, *The Life of William McKinley*, previously cited, are also useful. The anti-imperialist argument is given in Merle E. Curti, *Bryan and World Peace* (1931); R. F. Pettigrew, *Imperial Washington* (1922); and M. A. DeW. Howe, *Portrait of an Independent, Moorfield Storey* (1932). On the Treaty of Paris, see W. S. Holt, *Treaties Defeated by the Senate* (1933); and Royal Cortissoz, *Life of Whitelaw Reid* (1921). J. F. Rippy, *America and the Strife of Europe* (1938), discusses the conditions that led to the acquisition of the Philippines. The report of an opponent of the treaty is given in G. F. Hoar, *Autobiography of Seventy Years* (1906).

A great deal has been written on the dependencies and protectorates of the United States. On Alaska see Jeannette P. Nichols, *Alaska* (1924); J. M. Callahan, *The Alaska Purchase and Americo-Canadian Relations* (1908); and Victor J. Farrar, *The Annexation of Russian America to the United States* (1937). On Cuba see R. H. Fitzgibbon, *Cuba and the United States, 1900–1935* (1935); D. A. Lockmiller, *Magoon in Cuba* (1938); and Carleton Beals, *The Crime of Cuba* (1933), which is very critical of American policy. Mark Sullivan, *Our Times*, I, contains an admirable chapter on the fight against the yellow fever in Cuba. Broader in scope are G. H. Stuart, *Cuba and Its International Relations* (1923); and Chester Lloyd Jones, *Caribbean Interests of the United States* (1916). On the Philippines see Grayson L. Kirk, *Philippine Independence* (1936), an excellent study of the relations between the Philippines and the United States from 1898 to the enactment of independence. The work of two governors in the Philippines may be followed in F. B. Harrison, *The Corner-Stone of Philippine Independence: A Narrative of Seven Years* (1922); and Hermann Hagedorn, *Leonard Wood* (2 vols., 1931). Criticism of American policy is voiced in Moorfield Storey and M. P. Lichauco, *The Conquest of the Philippines by the United States, 1898–1925* (1926); and A. S. Pier, *American Apostles to the Philippines* (1950). The Puerto Rican story is given in Knowlton Mixer, *Porto Rico* (1926); V. S. Clark and others, *Porto Rico and its Problems* (1930); and B. W. and J. W. Diffie, *Porto Rico: A Broken Pledge* (1931), which is very critical of the American occupation. On the Virgin Islands see Luther H. Evans, *The Virgin Islands: From Naval Base to New Deal* (1945); and J. Antonio Jarvis, *The Virgin Islands and Their People* (1944). On the United States in Guam there is an excellent book by Earl S. Pomeroy, *Pacific Outpost, American Strategy in Guam and Micronesia* (1951). On Hawaii, see references for the preceding chapter, p. 285; also Hilary Conroy, *The Japanese Frontier in Hawaii, 1868–1898* (1953).

A. T. Mahan, *Lessons of the War with Spain* (1899), emphasizes the defense problems of empire. Elmer Ellis, *Mr. Dooley's America: A Life of Finley Peter Dunne* (1941), is the biography of a political humorist who viewed the whole imperialistic venture with considerable misgivings.

John Hay's advocacy of the Open Door in China is well treated in Tyler Dennett, *John Hay* (1933); and somewhat less so in W. R. Thayer, *The Life and Letters of John Hay* (2 vols., 1915). Also useful in this connection are Tyler Dennett, *Americans in Eastern Asia* (1922, new ed., 1941); M. Pao, *The Open Door Policy in Relation to China* (1923); and P. H. Clements, *The Boxer Rebellion* (1915).

16
World Politics

THEODORE ROOSEVELT (1858–1919), twenty-sixth President of the United States, was the youngest man ever to have held the Presidency but in spite of his mere forty-three years he was by no means lacking in political experience. The descendant of a long line of well-to-do New York aristocrats, he was brought up in an atmosphere of culture and learning that contrasted sharply with the Lincolnian tradition, so dear to American hearts. He saw Europe as a child, was carefully prepared for college, attended Harvard, graduated with the class of 1880. His education began, he claimed later, "immediately after leaving college," and certainly he soon learned about politics. Unwilling to live the life of a rich man's son, he found occasion in 1881 to run for the legislature, and with the help of the local machine he was elected. For three terms of one year each he represented his district at Albany, and in spite of his youth he gave a good account of himself. In 1884 he attended the national nominating convention at Chicago as chairman of the New York delegation, and worked energetically, but in vain, to prevent the nomination of James G. Blaine. The sudden death of his young wife, together with his deep disappointment at Blaine's triumph, had much to do with Roosevelt's decision to engage in the cattle business far out

on the Dakota frontier. The new life was like a tonic; he loved it. "You would be amused to see me," he wrote to his good friend Henry Cabot Lodge, "in my broad sombrero hat, fringed and beaded buckskin shirt, horsehide chaparajos or riding trousers, and cowboy boots, with braided bridle and silver spurs." Roosevelt's western experience was brief, but it was also deep. He never quite got over it.

Roosevelt spent only a part of his time in the West, he soon remarried, and he was not long out of politics. "With the most genuine reluctance," or so he claimed, he accepted in 1886 the Republican nomination for mayor of New York, and ran third in a three-cornered race. Two years later he campaigned so energetically for Harrison that when the Republicans won he was rewarded by an appointment to the Civil Service Commission, a position that paid only thirty-five hundred dollars a year, and was accounted by the politicians of little consequence. But Roosevelt was not concerned about the salary, and in spite of the efforts of spoilsmen to cripple his work he soon made of civil service reform something more than an idealist's dream. In 1895, after six years with the commission, he accepted an even humbler office, the presidency of the New York police board, and again lifted the office to his own stature. For two years he warred with great earnestness, although with indifferent success, against vice and crime. Having seen with his own eyes how the "other half" lived, he emerged from the experience a convinced social reformer and the idol of such humanitarians as Jacob Riis. He emerged, too, with a habit of mind that was to remain strongly in evidence throughout his career. Both as civil service commissioner and as police commissioner, he had found that those who opposed his views were almost invariably insincere, or dishonest, or worse, while he himself was cast in the rôle of righteousness. Inevitably he became accustomed to thinking of himself as always right, and his opponents, whatever their views, as always wrong.

In spite of his activity in politics Roosevelt found time to make important contribu-

Roosevelt, the historian tions to the history of the United States. His *Naval War of 1812* (1882) was begun when he was a student in college, and was published two years after his graduation. He contributed two hastily written volumes to the American Statesmen Series, one of them on *Thomas Hart Benton* (1886), a work of considerable merit, and the other, on *Gouverneur Morris* (1888), not as highly esteemed. His best historical work was a four-volume series, *The Winning of the West* (1889-96), which traced from original sources the path of conquest by which the white man won the region from the Appalachians to the Mississippi. Roosevelt was less impressed with the significance of the frontier than with the tales of heroism and adventure in which it abounded, but it is noteworthy that even before Turner he had begun to write of the West. Possessed of an easy, flowing style, and an adept at story-telling, he might have ranked with Parkman and Prescott had he chosen history instead of politics as his vocation. Drawing heavily on his western experience he wrote, too, for popular consumption such books as his *Hunting Trips of a Ranchman* (1885), and *Ranch Life and the Hunting Trail* (1888).

Roosevelt again won for himself a place in national politics when he campaigned vigor-ously for McKinley in 1896; his appointment as Assistant Secretary of the Navy was offered and accepted as a fitting reward for service rendered. After his experience in Cuba he was immediately picked up by the Republican machine in New York to head the state ticket in what threatened, because of charges of corruption against the preceding administration, to be a Democratic year. Elected by a slender majority, he enjoyed hugely his work as governor, but was regarded with grave suspicion by Thomas Collier ("Me-Too") Platt, the "Easy Boss" of New York Republicanism. As a means of getting Roosevelt out of the state, Platt favored the nomination of Roosevelt for second place on the national ticket in 1900. Two other hard-boiled politicians, Matthew S. Quay and Boies Penrose, both of Pennsylvania, supported Platt's scheme for the anguish Roosevelt's nomination would give their upstart political rival, Mark Hanna. Soon an insistent national demand for Roosevelt had set in, and the combined protests of McKinley, Hanna, and Roosevelt himself were easily overruled. Roosevelt had stated publicly that "under no circumstances could I or would I accept the nomination for the Vice-Presidency," while Hanna had reminded some of the delegates to the Philadelphia nominating convention that there would be "only one life between this madman and the White House." Henry Cabot Lodge, who believed that Roosevelt should accept the Vice-Presidency if it were offered him, advised him not to go to the Republican nominating convention if he did not wish the nomination. But Roosevelt went, wearing his cowboy hat, and asserting noisily his unwillingness to run. There were those who quoted Shakespeare: He "doth protest too much, methinks." At any rate, he received the vote of every delegate to the convention, except his own, and he accepted the nomination.

Ever spoiling for a fight, he enjoyed the campaign, but with the election over he was prepared to be bored. "I would **Elected** rather be anything than Vice- **Vice-** President," he had once pro- **President** claimed, "say a Professor of History." He decided that he might as well while away his time by reading law, a study he had once begun and abandoned, and arranged to borrow the necessary books from Mr. Justice White. His labors on the law, which were to include a Saturday afternoon quiz by the same Justice, had not yet begun, however, when he found himself suddenly elevated to the office he had long before set as the goal of his ambition. For good or ill, he was never to take a lawyer's view of the Presidency.

The perfect good taste that characterized Roosevelt's every act in taking over the Presidency did much to allay the fears of those who had considered him only a brash young man. He at once announced that it would be his "aim to continue absolutely unbroken the policies of President McKinley for the peace, prosperity, and honor of our beloved country." Especially reassuring was the decision to retain McKinley's cabinet, for whatever his faults McKinley had proved himself to be an able judge of men. Two of the advisers on whom Roosevelt was to depend most, John Hay, Secretary of State, and Elihu Root, Secretary of War, were already in the cabinet, while a third, William Howard Taft, had been picked by McKinley for the difficult task of inaugurating civil government in the Philippines. Roosevelt even sought with some success to appease Mark Hanna, although, as both knew, the gulf between them on most matters of consequence was very wide. It was inevitable that eventually Roosevelt was to be his own President. For the most part McKinley had been content to follow public opinion, but aggressive leadership was an integral part of the Roosevelt personality. Fortunately the new President embodied to a remarkable degree the interests and prejudices of the average American. When he sought to lead there was no dearth of followers.

Better versed in world affairs than his predecessors, Roosevelt tackled with eager **Europe and America** enthusiasm the problems of diplomacy that came before his administration. He found European nations far less contemptuous of the United States than they had been before the Spanish-American War. To show that Germany had only the friendliest of sentiments toward the United States, the Kaiser conferred a medal on Roosevelt, sent his brother, Prince Henry, on a tour of America, invited Roosevelt's charming daughter, Alice, to christen a yacht he had ordered from an American shipyard, and presented a statue of his illustrious antecedent, Frederick the Great, to adorn the new Army War College on the lower Potomac. France, not wishing to be entirely outdone, founded some exchange professorships, and reminded forgetful Americans of the helpful part France had played in the American Revolution by forwarding to the United States a statue of Rochambeau. Great Britain, openly hopeful of an alliance with the United States, went much further than presents in demonstrating her friendship. How to take advantage of all this display of goodwill, and yet to escape commitments that might involve the United States in European affairs, taxed to the full the capacities of the new President and his able advisers.

Among the various problems that Roosevelt inherited from the preceding administration was a dispute with Canada **The Alaskan boundary** over the boundary of Alaska. **dispute** This came about as a result of Canadian irritation over the fact that the only two feasible routes to the gold of the Klondike lay through American territory, one by way of the Yukon River, and the other across the Alaskan panhandle. Canadian officials therefore began to examine old maps and treaties, and at length came out with a claim that the boundary line between Canada and the Alaskan panhandle had been incorrectly located, and should be shifted far to the west. The Treaty of 1825 between Great Britain and Russia, which originally fixed this boundary, provided that it was to follow the crest of the mountains parallel to the coast, but was never to be more than ten marine leagues from the shore-line, following its sinuosities. The Canadians claimed that the proper location of the shore-line was not, as had always been supposed, where sea-water left off, but rather along the farthest western reaches of the islands and promontories that skirted the coast. The boundary line could thus jump from peak to peak, giving Canada access to the Pacific at numerous points, particularly Dyea and Skagway, at the head of the trail to the Klondike. There was talk, even, of building a Canadian railroad to some far northern port.

The Canadian plan for a corridor across the Alaskan panhandle was fully presented by the British government, which at that time still represented Canada in foreign affairs. In 1898 an Anglo-American joint high commission sitting at Quebec failed to reach a decision, and the negotiations that followed were long and involved. Finally, in 1903, the United States agreed to a plan of settlement by which it stood no chance to lose. Three commissioners were to be appointed by each side, and decisions could be made only by a majority vote. In appointing the American commissioners, President Roosevelt took care that no one was chosen who might look with favor on the Canadian case, but the British government appointed only two members (both Canadians) whose

The Alaskan Boundary Dispute

.... Claimed by United States
———— Claimed by Great Britain
—·—· Boundary as fixed by arbitration, 1903

Columbia and Canada awaiting the decision of the Boundary Commission. Cartoon from *Review of Reviews*, 1903.

minds were already made up, and selected as the third representative Lord Alverstone, Chief Justice of England, who, to all intents and purposes, became sole arbiter. There is no reason to suppose that Lord Alverstone was instructed as to what course he should pursue, or that he needed to be so instructed. The Americans had the better case, and on every important point he so decided. The significant fact is that the British government, by appointing such a man as Alverstone, showed its willingness to see the United States win the decision, even at the cost of extreme resentment on the part of Canada.

Meanwhile the Hay-Pauncefote treaties had presented even stronger evidence of British good will. The long voyage of the *Oregon* around Cape Horn, coupled with the acquisition of **The Hay-Pauncefote treaties** new possessions in the Philippines, had piled up irresistible sentiment in the United States for the building of a strictly American interoceanic canal through some part of Central

America. Since the terms of the Clayton-Bulwer Treaty still stood in the way, the Senate as early as 1898 asked the President to obtain the desired changes from Great Britain. Contrary to earlier experience, when the matter was broached to the British government no difficulties were encountered, and in 1900 the first Hay-Pauncefote Treaty was signed. This agreement, however, failed to go as far as American sentiment demanded. It provided that the United States might build the canal as an exclusively American project, but it assumed that the canal would remain unfortified and that its neutrality would be internationally guaranteed. As a result the treaty was amended to death in the United States Senate, and a new treaty had to be negotiated.

In the second Hay-Pauncefote Treaty the British government virtually permitted the United States to write its own terms. The Clayton-Bulwer Treaty, which before had been merely revised, was now abrogated, and a new treaty was written to replace it. By its terms the United States was permitted to acquire territory in Central America and to police the canal — a provision that the American government interpreted to mean the right of fortification. Nevertheless, the canal, while strictly American, was to be "free and open to the vessels of commerce and of war of all nations . . . on terms of entire equality," nor were there to be any discriminations "in respect of the conditions or charges of traffic." What the United States appeared to have gained was the right to build a neutral canal and to guarantee its neutrality, but the new treaty satisfied the Senate, which ratified it, as Hay said, "with no opposition, except from the irreclaimable cranks. Seventy-two to six was near enough unanimity."

The significance of this treaty was deeper than most Americans realized. The British government, in granting to the United States a free hand in building the canal, meant to indicate its belief that the friendship between the two nations was permanent and could

Anglo-American accord

never be broken. Had the United States been ready to seal the pact by an outright alliance, Great Britain would have been all too willing; as it was she withdrew her fleets from Caribbean waters, and left to the United States the protection of British interests in that region, just as she had turned over some of her Asiatic interests to the protection of Japan after the Anglo-Japanese alliance. American observers felt certain that the United States had won a great diplomatic victory, but the assistance that Great Britain was able to obtain from America during the First and Second World Wars leaves in some doubt the question of which nation showed the greater diplomatic skill.

With the way cleared for the building of the canal, the next question to demand an answer was where to build it. Two apparently feasible routes existed, one through the narrowest portion of the Isthmus of Panama, the other farther to the north through the Republic of Nicaragua. Both routes had strong adherents in the United States, and the task of choosing between them was not an easy one.

The Panama route had been tried before. In the late seventies Ferdinand de Lesseps, the French builder of the Suez Canal, had organized a company for the purpose, and with his previous record of success as a talking point had induced European investors to stake large sums on the project. De Lesseps also hoped to sell stock in the United States, but the insistence of President Hayes that American policy called for a strictly American canal closed the American market to his blandishments. On faith and without sufficient funds he nevertheless went ahead, obtained a concession from the State of Colombia, bought the Panama Railroad, and in 1882 began operations. By 1889 his company was bankrupt and the work of excavation had ceased. Five years later the New Panama Canal Company was formed, ostensibly to finish the canal, but actually to sell out to the United States. The company claimed that the total capital invested in Panama had reached $260,000,000, but about the only thing of value it possessed was its franchise from Colombia, which would not expire until 1904.

The Nicaraguan route was longer, but because advantage could be taken of Lake

The Isthmian Canal Commission

Nicaragua and the river which connected it with the Atlantic, many believed that it was more practicable than the shorter, isthmian route. In 1890 an American company, in which Frederick Billings, builder of the Northern Pacific, was deeply involved, had begun work in Nicaragua, but after an expenditure of about six million dollars it, too, had gone bankrupt. The Nicaraguan route nevertheless strongly appealed to Americans, and the Isthmian Canal Commission, appointed by President McKinley in 1901 to assess the merits of the two routes, reported in its favor. Part of the reason for this decision was the price of one hundred million dollars that the New Panama Canal Company wanted for its property and rights. Forty million dollars, according to the committee, would have been enough. In accordance with the committee's recommendation, the House of Representatives passed a bill in 1902 which provided for the construction of the canal through Nicaragua.

Powerful forces were at work, however, in favor of the Panama route. They included President Roosevelt, who believed, quite mistakenly as it turned out, that a sea-level canal could be constructed through Panama, whereas locks would be a certainty through Nicaragua. They included also Marcus A. Hanna, who had obtained a contribution of sixty thousand dollars to the Republican campaign chest in 1900 from the New Panama Canal Company. Most important of all, they included a resourceful Frenchman, Philippe Bunau-Varilla, leading light in the New Panama Canal Company, who shuttled back and forth between Paris and Washington, and his New York lawyer, William Nelson Cromwell, who presently collected for his services a fee of eight hundred thousand dollars. Altogether this array of talent proved too formidable for the Nicaraguan

advocates, and on condition that the New Panama Canal Company should reduce its charges to forty million dollars the Senate was persuaded to substitute Panama for Nicaragua in the bill before it. Talk that some senators had hopefully invested along the Nicaraguan route, supplemented by the timely eruption of Mount Monotombo, Nicaragua's active volcano, played more or less important parts in the proceedings. Bunau-Varilla thoughtfully provided for each senator a Nicaraguan postage stamp on which the volcano was pictured in full eruption. Finally the House concurred in the Senate's decision, and the Panama route was officially adopted. Long before this the New Panama Canal Company had reconciled itself to forty million dollars as far better than nothing.

It was still necessary for the United States to negotiate a treaty with Colombia, for the American plan contemplated

Negotiations with Colombia

real or virtual landownership, not merely a permit to build. Secretary Hay, using the threat of the Nicaraguan alternative, drove a sharp bargain with Thomas Herran, the Colombian Representative at Washington. The United States would pay ten million dollars down and an annual quit-rent of two hundred and fifty thousand dollars for control over a strip of land six miles wide from Panama to Colón, but exclusive of those cities. That was all. Furthermore, it was specifically stated that Colombia might not negotiate with the New Panama Canal Company to obtain a portion of the forty million dollars it was to receive from the United States. The United States Senate promptly ratified the treaty, but the Colombian government, which resented both the terms and the manner in which they had been imposed, refused to ratify. No doubt the fact that the New Panama Canal Company's franchise had only a short time to run also entered the Colombian calculations. Once it lapsed, the Colombian government rather than the French stockholders, would be legally entitled to that payment also. As Roosevelt phrased it in a letter to Hay,

"They are mad to get hold of the forty million dollars of the Frenchmen."

Just why it should have been a matter of so great concern to Roosevelt whether some unidentified "Frenchmen" or Colombia got the money the United States stood ready to pay is not entirely clear. Perhaps the President's insistent desire for haste in getting the work under way was the controlling factor. At any rate he refused to bargain further with Colombia, and privately — but not too privately — admitted that he would "be delighted if Panama were an independent state; or if it made itself so at this moment." The secession of Panama, which had never been overloyal to Colombia and was naturally eager for the canal, had been in Bunau-Varilla's mind all along as a possible way out. Ably assisted by Cromwell, he now showed the liveliest interest in Panama's independence. A future President of Panama was found in the person of Doctor Manuel Amador, a physician employed by the Panama Railroad and Steamship Company, which was owned by the New Panama Canal Company. Amador came to the United States for a conference with Bunau-Varilla, and returned with a constitution for the Republic of Panama, a proclamation of independence, a message to be sent back to Bunau-Varilla asking him, although a French citizen, to become the first Minister from Panama to the United States, and one hundred thousand dollars in cash for preliminary expenses.

Meantime Roosevelt had discovered a treaty of 1846 between the United States **Secession** and New Granada (which be- **of Panama** came Colombia in 1863), by which the United States was bound to protect "the right of way or transit across the Isthmus of Panama." To make sure that revolutionary disturbances — should there be a revolution — would not interrupt transit across the isthmus, Roosevelt ordered American naval units to the vicinity of Panama, and instructed them to "prevent the landing of any armed force with hostile intent, either government or insurgent." Since the only possible route by which Colombia could bring

troops to Panama was by sea, and since Doctor Amador had bribed those who were already there, the revolution took place on November 3, 1903, without the usual accompaniment of violence and bloodshed. A Colombian gunboat that inconsiderately began next day to drop shells upon the city of Panama was ordered by the American naval commander to desist, and did so. On November 6, at 11.35 A.M. Roosevelt received official word to the effect that the revolution in Panama had been completely successful. On the same day, at 12.31 P.M., Secretary Hay accorded diplomatic recognition to the new republic. "I took Panama," Roosevelt is said to have boasted later, but this statement hardly gives full credit to Bunau-Varilla and Cromwell.

With Colombia out of the way and Bunau-Varilla representing Panama, a new treaty, the Hay-Bunau-Varilla Treaty, quickly cleared the way for the beginning of canal construction. The United States was permitted to acquire a zone five miles wide on each side of the canal "as if she were sovereign," and to fortify it at will. Panama was to receive an initial payment of ten million dollars, and two hundred and fifty thousand dollars per year, beginning nine years after date. The independence of Panama was guaranteed by the United States, but the principles of the Platt Amendment, including the right of intervention, were applied to the new republic. Between 1846 and 1903 Panama had been the scene of no less than fifty-three insurrectionary outbursts. Thereafter they ceased abruptly.

Colombia's deep resentment at the way it had been treated soon became a matter of real concern to the United **Colombian** States. Not only Colombia, **resentment** but other Latin-American nations, also, saw in Roosevelt's action a precedent that might be used for other imperialistic ventures at their expense. To alleviate the tension, Secretary Root proposed in 1909 a series of three treaties, between the United States and Panama, the United States and Colombia, and Panama and Colombia. By

Elihu Root, as Secretary of War and Secretary of State, was an outstanding organizer of the new American Empire.

European syndicates would be able to monopolize the rich oil resources of Colombia to the exclusion of American firms made the purchase of Colombian good-will a necessity.

The actual building of the canal was an engineering feat of extraordinary magnitude. The impracticability of a sea- **Building** level canal was soon discovered **the canal** and a lock canal, which would cost less to build both in time and in money, was decided upon. At first sanitation threatened to be an even greater problem than excavation, but the work of Colonel W. C. Gorgas in making the canal zone a fit place in which to live was so well done that trouble from that source was soon practically eliminated. Administrative difficulties arising from the fact that Congress insisted on delegating the control of operations to a commission instead of to an individual hampered work for a while, but Roosevelt at length made Major George W. Goethals, an army engineer, chairman of the commission, and extracted a promise from all other members of the commission never to disagree with the chairman. After that the work proceeded satisfactorily, and on August 15, 1914, the first ocean steamer passed through the canal. The cost of building it ran to $275,000,000, which the government raised by floating bonds, together with another $113,000,000 for fortifications; but receipts during the first fifteen years of operation brought in large enough net earnings to meet in full the interest on the bonds floated. Roosevelt always considered the building of the Panama Canal the greatest achievement of his administration.

In 1912 Congress, looking forward to the opening of the canal, passed a law exempting American coastwise shipping **The tolls** from the payment of tolls. This **controversy** law was signed by President Taft, who was certainly a good lawyer, but was immediately protested by Great Britain on the ground that the tolls exemption violated that clause of the Hay-Pauncefote Treaty which opened the canal to the vessels of "all nations" on terms of "entire equality." The British gov-

their terms the first ten installments of the two hundred and fifty thousand dollars quit-rent would have been assigned to Colombia. But Colombia would have nothing to do with the suggestion. While Taft was President another effort at appeasement was made. Would Colombia accept ten million dollars for a coaling station and any other canal route that might be available through her territory? Colombia would not. Even when the United States suggested informally that the sum might be raised to twenty-five million dollars, Colombia remained obdurate and asked for arbitration, something the United States dared not risk. During Wilson's administration Secretary Bryan negotiated a treaty with Colombia which expressed regrets for what the United States had done, and offered twenty-five million dollars by way of compensation. This proposal, which Colombia was ready to accept, was rejected by the United States Senate, in which sat many of Roosevelt's loyal friends. After Roosevelt's death, with Harding as President, a treaty very similar to the one Bryan had proposed, but with the "regrets" clause somewhat toned down, was ratified by both nations. By that time the fear that

CULEBRA CUT. View of bottom of Canal illustrates why the project was called "The Big Ditch."

The Panama Canal presented a challenge to American engineers that taxed their abilities to the full. The problem of sanitation was no less serious than the problem of excavation, and since a sea-level canal was not feasible great locks had to be built.

POSTAL COMMEMORATION. Stamp issued on the occasion of the 25th anniversary of the opening of the Canal.

GATUN LOCKS. Construction scene, 1910.

HEALTH CONDITIONS. Sanitation and disease presented problems as great as those of construction. View of Ancon Hill Hospital, *Harper's Weekly*, 1905.

ernment offered no objection to the United States returning tolls to American shippers as rebates or subsidies; what it did object to was the prospect that with the exemption in force the rates would be so set as to require foreign shipping to pay the entire cost and upkeep of the canal. American railroad interests, who foresaw the diversion of much transcontinental traffic from the railroads to the new sea route, also had legitimate grounds

for complaint, but Congress let the law stand until June, 1914, when President Wilson successfully insisted on its repeal. Although the President at the time stated no other reason for demanding repeal than that diplomatic negotiations of a very delicate nature were involved, it seems clear that he was primarily interested in obtaining the acquiescence of the British government in his Mexican policy.

Before he became President, and with his

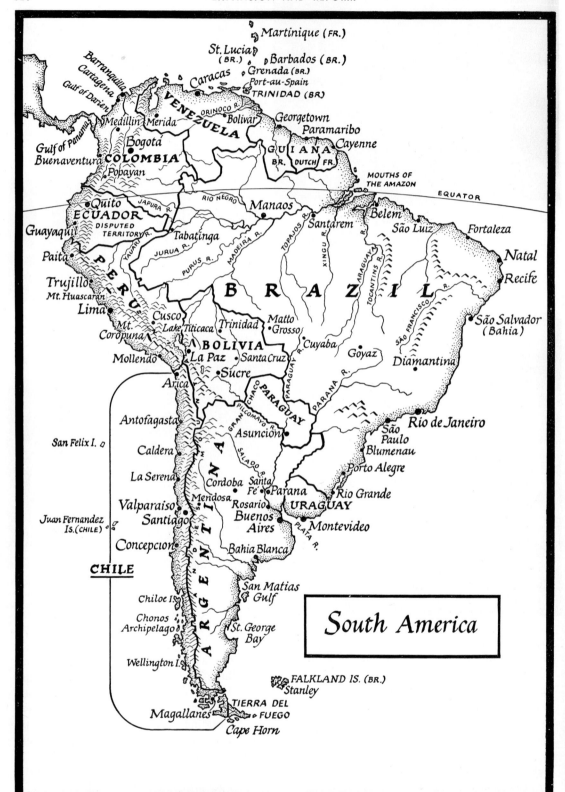

South America

thoughts on the New York Republican machine, Roosevelt had once quoted
an old adage: "Speak softly and
carry a big stick, and you will go
far." Later this statement was resurrected
and fittingly applied to his policy in Latin
America. Backed by the new American
navy, Roosevelt prepared to enforce the
Monroe Doctrine with aggressive determination; some said that he even intended to use
it as a cloak for further imperialistic ventures. Certainly he kept persistently in mind
the fact that the Panama Canal must be defended at all costs. Because of the canal
events in Latin America that in an earlier age
might have passed unnoticed now became
matters of grave concern.

The "Big Stick" policy

The Venezuelan incident of 1902 offered
the first occasion for the use of the "big
stick." The State of Venezuela, which bordered on the Carribbean Sea adjacent to the
proposed canal, was in trouble with Great
Britain, Germany, and other European nations because of the non-payment of debts
owing their citizens. There was a legitimate
difference of opinion as to the amounts due,
for in some cases no such sums had ever been
delivered as were claimed. But the Venezuelan dictator, Cipriano Castro, was an unsavory character who seemingly had no intention of paying anything if he could avoid
it. Finally Great Britain and Germany,
mildly supported by Italy, withdrew their
legations from Caracas, blockaded five Venezuelan ports, and even seized Venezuelan
gunboats. A British bombardment of
Puerto Cabello, in return for an alleged insult to the British flag, finally brought Castro
to his senses, and he agreed to arbitration,
something he had spurned when it had been
offered him by Germany the year before.
This offer was transmitted by the United
States "without comment" to London and
Berlin, and was accepted. The Hague
Tribunal finally settled the case, reducing
the claims of foreigners against the Venezuelan government from forty million to
eight million dollars.

Throughout these proceedings the United
States offered no official protest, and accepted
seemingly in good faith the assurances of
Great Britain and Germany that they meant
no violation of the Monroe Doctrine. Aside
from transmitting Castro's offer of arbitration, the American government had merely
expressed its hope that a peaceful solution
could be reached, and had recommended arbitration. It seems evident, however, that certain activities not recorded in the official
documents took place behind the scenes. No
doubt Roosevelt's version of these events,
written in 1916 when he had become an
ardent advocate of American entrance into
the First World War, was exaggerated and
inaccurate. He claimed then that Germany,
hoping to seize and fortify some Venezuelan
harbor, had declined to arbitrate. Only
when threatened with Admiral Dewey's fleet,
which was assembled near Puerto Rico for
maneuvers, was withdrawal and arbitration
accomplished. There is other evidence besides his own to prove that Roosevelt had
some dramatic interviews with the German Ambassador during this episode, and
that he warned Dewey to keep his fleet ready
for action. Exactly what happened may
never be known, but it is difficult to believe
that his version was wholly imagined.

Whatever the truth of this matter, Roosevelt soon reached the conclusion that the
United States must itself be prepared to intervene in Latin-
American affairs if it wished to be sure of
keeping other nations out. In 1902, while
the Venezuelan crisis was on, the Argentinian
Foreign Minister, Luis M. Drago, expressed
the opinion that "the public debt cannot
occasion armed intervention nor even the
actual occupation of the territory of American nations by a European power." [1] This
doctrine had never been maintained by the
United States, but its possibilities interested
Roosevelt, who soon went ahead to elaborate
it in a way Drago had certainly never intended. The Dominican Republic, which
occupied the eastern half of the island of

The Drago doctrine

[1] The Drago doctrine was later endorsed by the
second Hague Conference. See p. 329.

Santo Domingo closely adjacent to Cuba, was deeply in debt to European creditors, and was in a state of chronic revolution. Fearful that European intervention — probably by Germany, whose motives Roosevelt most mistrusted — might lead to occupation, and eventually, as with the British in Egypt, to virtual possession, Roosevelt as early as May 20, 1904, announced what came to be known as the "Roosevelt corollary" of the Monroe Doctrine. Restated to Congress in December of the same year, it left the world in no doubt whatever as to the meaning of the "big stick" policy:

If a nation shows that it knows how to act with reasonable efficiency and decency in social and political matters, if it keeps order and pays its obligations, it need fear no interference from the United States. Chronic wrongdoing, or an impotence which results in a general loosening of the ties of civilized society may in America, as elsewhere, ultimately require intervention by some civilized nation, and in the Western Hemisphere the adherence of the United States to the Monroe Doctrine may force the United States, however reluctantly, in flagrant cases of such wrongdoing or impotence, to the exercise of an international police power.

Roosevelt's interpretation of the Monroe Doctrine, as events proved, was applied with **Caribbean control** rigor only in the Caribbean zone, which guarded the eastern approaches to the Panama Canal. Here it supplemented and assisted the defense policy of the United States which maintained that the Caribbean Sea must become as strictly as possible an American lake. Property rights acquired by the United States on the borders of the Caribbean included: (1) Puerto Rico, annexed at the close of the Spanish-American War; (2) the Canal Zone, obtained on terms practically equivalent to annexation; (3) the Virgin Islands, purchased from Denmark in 1916 for twenty-five million dollars, a price utterly out of proportion to their economic value; (4) convenient sites for naval bases at Guantanamo in eastern Cuba, on the Corn Islands off Nicaragua, and elsewhere; and (5) a concession from Nicaragua giving the United States the sole right of constructing a canal through her territory. Cuba and Panama, thanks to the principles of the Platt Amendment, were virtual protectorates of the United States, while the application of the Roosevelt corollary eventually brought Santo Domingo, Haiti, and Nicaragua quite as completely within the American orbit. Other territory in the Caribbean Zone was either in the hands of friendly European nations who made no effort to match the strength of the United States in the region, or of independent Latin-American nations whose conduct was tempered by fear of the "big stick."

Affairs in the Dominican Republic, whose government had been appropriately described as "tyranny tempered **The Dominican Republic** by assassination," were in such a state by 1904 that Roosevelt deemed American intervention a necessity. The national debt of the little republic had reached $32,280,000, mostly owing to European creditors. Graft and inefficiency, together with the steady procession of insurrections, had paralyzed the collection of revenues. Pressure from European nations was mounting ominously. Finally the Dominican government, not without a certain amount of diplomatic preparation, asked the United States to take over the administration of its revenues. In 1905 a treaty was negotiated between the two nations, whereby the United States was to establish a kind of receivership for its bankrupt neighbor, to collect its revenues, and to supply fifty-five per cent of the receipts to the liquidation of outstanding obligations. Although American warships had already begun to patrol Dominican waters, and American marines had been landed in Santo Domingo, the United States Senate refused to accept the treaty. Roosevelt, undeterred by this rebuff, induced the Dominican authorities to accept his nominee for collector of customs, and to permit the deposit in a New York bank of all sums not actually needed to carry on the government. European creditors, pleased with the arrangement, agreed to reduce their claims to seventeen million dollars. Two years later the

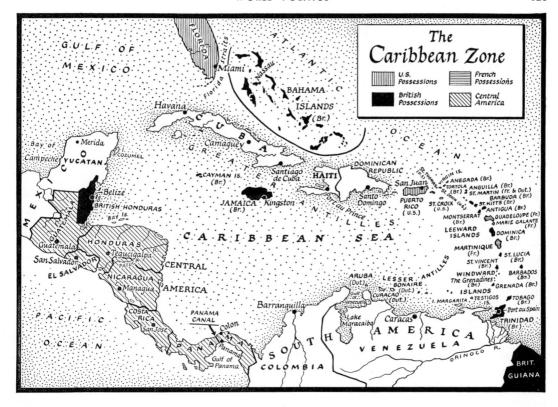

Senate, appeased by some minor modifications of the original treaty, approved the deal, and Roosevelt's extra-legal policy became official. By means of it Roosevelt claimed to have "put the affairs of the island on a better basis than they had been for a century."

Subsequent Presidents made even more complete use of the Roosevelt corollary than did Roosevelt himself. Wilson, although opposed to Roosevelt in politics, used it in 1916 when the Dominican Republic, again plagued by revolutions, threatened to ignore the Treaty of 1907. There could not then have been danger of European intervention, for the First World War was on, but there was such an abundance of "chronic wrongdoing" that Wilson suspended the Dominican government altogether, and turned over the administration of the republic's affairs to American naval officers, supported by the marines. The efficiency of the American occupation was attested by the building of good roads,

the improvement of sanitation, the promotion of education, the rehabilitation of government finances, and the ruthless suppression of all efforts of the Dominicans to regain their liberties. By 1924, however, this complete denial of the "right of self-determination" that Wilson had so strongly urged in Paris had aroused opposition both within the United States and throughout Latin America, the importance of whose goodwill the United States was at last beginning to appreciate. A local Dominican government was therefore established, and the American military occupation was brought to a close. The "financial protectorate," however, was not formally ended until 1941.

Haiti, the Negro Republic that occupied the western half of the island of Santo Domingo, had almost an identical experience with the United States. Overwhelmed by its debts, it was offered in 1914 the same type of financial receivership that Roosevelt had negotiated

Haiti

with the Dominican Republic nearly ten years before. This offer it chose to reject, but when serious rioting broke out in 1915, the United States landed marines at Port-au-Prince, restored order, and forced on the Haitian government the treaty it had previously refused. The treaty was to run for ten years, and for an additional ten years if the United States so desired. American officers, backed by American marines and a native constabulary, soon supplanted the Haitian authorities in the discharge of their duties; and from 1922 to 1930 the Haitian government was entirely suspended, with an American high commissioner in charge. The same forces that led to American withdrawal from the Dominican Republic operated also with reference to Haiti, and in 1930 President Hoover announced plans for the termination in 1936 of American intervention.

While Taft was President an abortive attempt was made to apply the Roosevelt corollary in two Central American republics, Honduras and Nicaragua. Agreements patterned on the Dominican model were negotiated, but failed of ratification. In Nicaragua, however, marines were landed in 1912 to keep order, and they stayed on until 1925. Without benefit of treaty, the United States policed the country, turned its financial affairs over to an American collector, and put its government on a dole. In 1914 the Bryan-Chamorro Treaty regularized what was going on, and for three million dollars the United States obtained an exclusive right to build an interoceanic canal across Nicaragua, together with appropriate leases for naval bases. In 1925 the American troops were ordered out, but a revolution the following year brought them back again. This time they stayed until 1932.

The charge has often been made that the purpose of American intervention in the "Dollar diplomacy" Caribbean Zone was primarily to promote the development of American financial interests in that area. It is demonstrable that a great increase in American investments and a somewhat more modest increase in American trade followed

in the wake of governmental policy, but it would be hard to believe that either Roosevelt or any of his successors were seeking merely to open new fields for American enterprise. Undoubtedly the objectives they had most in mind were the defense of the Panama Canal, the protection of American lives and property already in the troubled areas, and the abatement of governmental nuisances that threatened to become international scandals.

Meanwhile on the other side of the world equally momentous events had provided equally difficult problems for Japan's American diplomacy. When ambitions Russia, following the Boxer uprising, disregarded her promise to withdraw from Manchuria, Japan made every effort to throw her rival out. Whatever lip service Japan might have been willing to give to the open door policy, she was determined that if any nation was to obtain special favors in China it must be Japan, and not Russia. Japanese students of western civilization had reached the conclusion that the enormous and growing population of Japan could be supported only by the rapid expansion of manufacturing. But Japan lacked the two greatest essentials for a manufacturing nation, coal and iron, both of which China possessed in abundance. Access to these commodities, as well as to Chinese markets for Japanese goods, the Russian advance might eventually block. With the Japanese "life-line" thus endangered, Japanese statesmen made deliberate plans for the expulsion of Russia from Manchuria. On January 30, 1902, Japan signed a treaty of alliance with Great Britain, which recognized the independence of Korea and China, and applied the open-door policy to both. It was further agreed between the two contracting powers that if either should be attacked in defense of its legitimate interests by a single nation, then the other party to the alliance would remain neutral; but if either should be attacked by more than one nation, then the other ally must come to its aid. One advantage of this alliance from the British point of view was that it would permit the withdrawal of British naval units from the Far East for concentration in European waters where the naval might of Germany was on the rise. The fundamental consideration so far as Japan was concerned was that the Japanese army might now drive the Russians out of Manchuria without fear of attack from any other power.

The Russo-Japanese War that broke out in 1904 was soon over.[1] It was fought on Chinese soil, although China, **Russo-** strongly supported in this en-**Japanese** deavor by the United States, **War** succeeded in remaining neutral. Naturally American sympathy ran with Japan, for it was the Russians, rather than the Japanese, who had most openly flouted the "open door." Roosevelt even went so far as to send a private warning to France and Germany that if either of them entered the war on the side of Russia he would bring the United States to the aid of Japan. When revolution at home and Japanese victories in the Far East made peace a necessity for the Russians, and financial exhaustion made it equally imperative for the Japanese, Roosevelt sought and obtained assurance from both belligerents that his services as mediator would be well received. Thereupon he officially offered mediation, was accepted, and in the summer of 1905 received the envoys of the warring nations in the United States. On September 5, 1905, a treaty of peace was signed at Portsmouth, New Hampshire, according to which both parties agreed to evacuate Manchuria, and Russia transferred its leases of Chinese ports and territories to Japan. To the intense regret of the Japanese, who desperately needed the money, Russia was not required to pay the six hundred million dollars indemnity the Japanese had demanded, although Japan did obtain, partly by way of compensation, the southern half of the island of Sakhalin. For his services to the cause of peace Roosevelt re-

ceived the Nobel Peace Prize and the enthusiastic plaudits of his countrymen.

Once the war was over, the friendly relations between Japan and the United States came to an abrupt end. Roose- **Japan and** velt's failure to back Japan's de- **the United** mand for an indemnity was **States** deeply resented by the Japanese, who believed that with his support they might have collected a huge sum. Japanese immigration into the United States, beginning about 1900, was another source of friction. By 1906 the number of Japanese resident in the Pacific states had reached about seventy-five thousand and they had begun to give native Americans strenuous competition as day laborers and market gardeners. They even bought land, and by swarming all over it broke down the land values of neighboring tracts, and then bought still more. Racial antagonism was easily stirred, and in 1906 the San Francisco school board decided on separate schools for Japanese children, a discrimination that was deeply resented in sensitive Japan. Roosevelt also deprecated the San Francisco school order, and used his influence to secure its modification. More important still, he obtained from the Japanese government a "gentlemen's agreement" whereby Japan herself undertook to terminate the flow of Japanese laborers to the United States. Since these emigrants were also present in Hawaii, Mexico, Canada, and the Canal Zone, and at least among the Hawaiian sugar producers were still desired, the Japanese government retained the right to grant passports to those territories, but offered no objection to an American prohibition against the entrance of Japanese nationals from any of these regions into the United States. The "gentlemen's agreement" sounded far better than it worked, and anti-Japanese feeling on the Pacific coast failed to subside.

An even more serious menace to Japanese-American accord came from the policy Japan had adopted in the Far East. Left to fight alone on behalf of the open door, the Japanese now began to close the door in the face of

---

[1] The Japanese attack on the Russians at Port Arthur, February 5, 1904, preceded the declaration of war, a tactic repeated against the United States at Pearl Harbor, December 7, 1941.

The Russo-Japanese War opened with a decisive sea victory for Japan, and saw also many Japanese victories by land. The Russian government, beset also by difficulties at home, accepted Roosevelt's offer of mediation, and signed the Treaty of Portsmouth.

THE NAVY. Part of Russian fleet destroyed at the battle of Tsushima.

PEACE CONFERENCE. Japanese and Russian leaders at Portsmouth, New Hampshire, 1905.

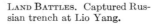
LAND BATTLES. Captured Russian trench at Lio Yang.

the rest of the world. What the Japanese desired, it soon became apparent, was the gradual subjection of China's resources to Japan's necessities. Korea, long under Japanese domination, was openly annexed. This need not have surprised Roosevelt, for in 1905, during the peace negotiations, he had privately agreed to it in return for a similar recognition by the Japanese prime minister of American sovereignty over the Philippines. But Manchuria, too, seemed marked for exclusive exploitation by Japan, and how far the new policy would lead none could tell. Japanese apologists began presently to talk of a Monroe Doctrine for Asia, in which Japan would play the same rôle in the Far East that the United States played in America. But the Japanese Monroe Doctrine obviously involved a kind of economic overlordship that the United States had never asserted in the New World. As the Japanese plans unfolded, there was much loose talk of the "yellow peril." Would Japan eventually seek to take the Philippines? Many people in the United States, probably Theodore Roosevelt among them, believed that war with Japan was imminent, and in 1907, with the intention of either heading it off or else bringing it to a head, the President sent the American battle-fleet around the world.

The Root-Takahira Agreement of 1908, which was embodied in an exchange of notes between the American Secretary of State and the Japanese Ambassador to the United States, was a face-saving device, designed primarily

Root-Takahira Agreement

to prevent a conflict that neither nation wanted. According to this document (1) the two nations asserted a common desire to develop their commerce on the Pacific freely and peacefully; (2) they agreed to maintain "the existing *status quo*" in the Far East, including the open door in China; (3) they stood together in support of the independence and integrity of China; and (4) they promised, in the event of any threat to existing conditions, to consult with each other as to what measures they should take. This polite exchange said all that the United States could ask, but it was utterly unenforceable on Japan, as both governments knew. The United States, without allies and unwilling to have them, was in reality powerless to defend either the open door or the integrity of China.

Nevertheless, the active participation of the United States in world affairs after the Spanish-American War led many thoughtful Americans to wonder if their nation in its new rôle could hope to escape involvements that would lead to war. With possessions as far away as the Philippines and with interests in every part of the globe, the very idea of American isolation seemed a contradiction. How then could peace be maintained? It did not require much logic to deduce that the surest way to keep the United States out of war was to keep war out of the world, and a strong movement for world peace set in.

When in 1899 the Tsar of Russia invited the nations having diplomatic representatives in St. Petersburg to participate in a conference on disarmament at The Hague, the United States sent an imposing delegation and took an active part in the proceedings. It soon appeared that nothing could be done on the subject for which the conference was called, but there was much discussion of methods for avoiding resort to war. Before adjourning, the conference recommended three means for settling disputes without resort to war: (1) through good offices and mediation, which, when offered by a third

The first Hague Conference

The flagship Connecticut leaving the Brooklyn Navy Yard to begin her 13,000-mile cruise as the leader of the battleship fleet. Illustration from *Harper's Weekly*, 1907.

party to powers at war or about to go to war, must not be considered an unfriendly act; (2) through international commissions of inquiry, for which so many precedents existed, particularly in the relations between Great Britain and the United States; and (3) through submission to a new court of arbitration to be established at The Hague. To this tribunal each member nation might name as many as four qualified judges, and from the list so obtained nations desiring to arbitrate a given case might pick as many or as few judges as they saw fit. They might define, too, the powers of the arbitrators, but they must consider themselves bound to submit in good faith to the award.

The recommendations of the Hague Conference were accepted by every participating power except Turkey, but in no nation with greater enthusiasm than in the United States.

Roosevelt promptly hunted up an old and somewhat unimportant controversy with Mexico, the Pious Fund Case, for submission to the Hague Tribunal — its first case. The finding of the Court was promptly accepted by both nations. The dispute that had led to the Venezuelan incident of 1902 was also settled by the Court, to the great satisfaction of Americans, particularly Roosevelt, who had recommended such a course. Roosevelt also made use of the newly proffered freedom to offer mediation in bringing the Russo-Japanese War to a close.

Keyed up to the idea that the United States must play an important rôle in the preservation of world peace, Roosevelt involved his country deeply in European affairs when he took a stronger part than his knowledge of the facts warranted in the settlement of the Moroccan crisis of 1905–06. He had a low opinion of the Moroccan government, based perhaps on the fact that Raisuli, a Moroccan brigand, had been able, on May 18, 1904, to kidnap an American citizen named Perdicaris in the outskirts of Tangier. A ringing message from the American State Department, "Perdicaris alive or Raisuli dead," got results that might have been achieved less dramatically had 1904 not been an election year. Perdicaris was promptly released. A month before this incident occurred, Great Britain and France had signed a notable agreement whereby Great Britain obtained a free hand in Egypt and France in Morocco. Secret articles, of which Roosevelt knew nothing, provided also for the eventual partition of Morocco between France and Spain, while Italy's consent to the bargain was purchased by granting the Italian government full freedom of action in Tripoli. The German Kaiser, convinced that a policy of "encirclement" was about to exclude Germany from another market, showed his displeasure by a visit to the Sultan in March, 1905, "to make it known that I am determined to do all in my power to safeguard efficaciously the interests of Germany in Morocco."

On the ground that another open door to world trade was about to be closed, the Kaiser asked Roosevelt to use his influence in favor of an international conference to settle the Moroccan question. Roosevelt, believing that "France was right on this issue," hesitated to interfere, but finally urged the French government to adopt a "course which would save the Emperor's self-esteem." At the instigation of the Sultan, who willingly did the Kaiser's bidding, a conference, to be held at Algeciras early in 1906, was arranged, and the United States agreed to send delegates. More important still, Roosevelt and his Secretary of State, Root, helped devise the formula for peace which the conference eventually adopted. According to its terms the nations were to respect Morocco's territorial integrity and to guarantee the open door for world trade within its borders. Moroccan finances were to be stabilized by the establishment of an international bank, and most significant of all, order was to be kept by a native police force *jointly supervised by France and Spain*. Heavy pressure was required to bring the Kaiser to accept these terms, and Roosevelt, although he knew full well that he was taking the United States far outside the isolationist rôle, did his share in applying it. It is possible that the President, mindful of the danger to the United States involved in Germany becoming an Atlantic power, helped prevent her from obtaining "compensations" in Northwest Africa that would have placed her in control of Casa Blanca on the African coast. Had anything of the kind happened, it almost certainly would have altered markedly the course of the Second World War.

The American delegates in signing the Algeciras Convention stated expressly that the United States assumed no responsibility for the enforcement of its provisions, while the United States Senate, which gave its approval only after prolonged debate, was even more cautious. The part played by the United States in the conference, so the Senate said, was merely for the protection of

The Algeciras Conference

American lives and property, and entirely "without purpose to depart from the traditional American foreign policy which forbids participation by the United States in the settlement of political questions which are entirely European in their scope." Had the Senate known how thoroughly the American President had violated this rule, it would hardly have ratified at all. Whether Roosevelt's diplomacy did his country any real service or not may well be questioned. He had helped to cement more closely the Anglo-French Entente, and by assisting Great Britain and France to score a victory over Germany he had done little to allay the Kaiser's fears. But undoubtedly his motive had been to preserve world peace.

At a second Hague Conference, held in 1907, the United States made strenuous efforts to commit the nations of **The second** the world even more completely **Hague** to the settlement of their dis- **Conference** putes by peaceful means. The American delegation, headed by Joseph H. Choate, was under instructions to work for the creation of an international court of justice, comparable to the United States Su-

preme Court, to which cases could be referred for a legal opinion rather than for arbitration. It was well understood that the Hague Tribunal, or any other court of arbitration, must decide cases before it more with a view to their acceptance than to the justice of the decision. The World Court proposed by the United States, however, was to be a permanent affair, consisting of fifteen judges who should be guided solely by the law and the precedents. This suggestion failed of adoption partly because only the American delegation had full instructions on the subject, but more because no agreement could be reached on the manner in which judges should be chosen. The great powers insisted that they should each have representatives in the Court at all times, and the lesser powers wanted the same privilege. This would have meant forty-four judges. The American suggestion that the problem might be solved by adopting the principle of rotation met with little favor, and the project was dropped.

The second Hague Conference spent much of its time in discussing the laws of war, and ultimately submitted its conclusions on many disputed points to the nations of the world

The Peace Palace at the Hague was built with funds given by Andrew Carnegie. Building and grounds cost $1,750,000.

Galloway

for ratification. Although the United States accepted the new regulations in full, other nations either failed to ratify altogether, or else made so many reservations that the Hague conventions could not be regarded as binding upon any power except by its express consent. A supplementary naval conference, held in London the following year, made a similar effort to codify the law of naval warfare. The Declaration of London, which it adopted, also failed of complete ratification. In Great Britain, the chief of the naval powers, and the one, therefore, whose approval was most essential, it was defeated by the House of Lords. These two attempts to agree upon what was lawful in time of war were not altogether barren of meaning. They registered in general the progress of world thought on the subject, and nations that observed the new rules had less to apologize for than those that did not.

The second Hague Conference made one really important contribution to the cause of world peace. It proposed a model arbitration treaty, known also as the mondel or world treaty, for all the nations of the world to follow in negotiating treaties with each other. According to this treaty, all disputes must be submitted to the Hague Tribunal for settlement unless they affected the vital interests, the independence, or the honor of the contracting nations.

By this time, as if in premonition of the desperate conflict soon to come, the United States was more engrossed than ever before with the idea of world peace. Andrew Carnegie, the ex-steel magnate turned philanthropist, provided an elaborate Peace Palace at The Hague for the use of the Hague Tribunal, and in 1911 established the Carnegie Endowment for International Peace, with ten million dollars to spend for the promotion of the cause. The year before, Edward Ginn, a Boston publisher,

The peace movement

had started off the World Peace Foundation on a similar mission with a million-dollar endowment. Successive American Secretaries of State, Hay, Root, Knox, and Bryan, strove earnestly to negotiate treaties of arbitration that would run the gantlet of the United States Senate, which in defense of its prerogatives furnished more opposition than came from outside nations. Under Hay and Root about twenty such treaties were negotiated, and finally ratified on condition that each special agreement made for the settlement of a dispute must also be submitted for the approval of the Senate. President Taft was earnestly devoted to the cause of world peace, and with his backing Secretary Knox negotiated two treaties, with Great Britain and France respectively, that provided for the arbitration of all "justiciable" questions — nearly universal arbitration; but the Senate amended them to death. Secretary Bryan, who had spoken to Chautauqua audiences all over the country on the subject of peace, believed that his appointment was a direct invitation to further the cause. More successful than any of his predecessors, he obtained the ratification of no less than thirty arbitration treaties, most of them based on what newspaper men called the "twenty minutes before you spank" principle. Bryan believed that war, if postponed until the period of acute tension had ended, could be averted. His treaties provided for the arbitration by international commissions of all disputes "of whatever character and nature." While the arbitration proceedings were in progress, the participating nations might neither increase their armament nor resort to war. It is worthy of note that by 1914 Bryan had obtained treaties of this nature with every one of the European nations allied against Germany in the First World War, while Germany, Austria, and Turkey had rejected his proposals.

Bibliography

The only adequately critical biography of Roosevelt is H. F. Pringle, *Theodore Roosevelt* (1931); but John M. Blum, *The Republican Roosevelt* (1954), provides an interesting reinterpretation. Most other writers on Roosevelt are content to expound or elaborate the "Roosevelt legend," so ably set forth in Theodore Roosevelt, *An Autobiography* (1913); and J. B. Bishop, *Theodore Roosevelt and His Time Shown in His Own Letters* (2 vols., 1930). Of this type are W. R. Thayer, *Theodore Roosevelt: An Intimate Biography* (1919); L. F. Abbott, *Impressions of Theodore Roosevelt* (1919); and W. D. Lewis, *The Life of Theodore Roosevelt* (1919). *Theodore Roosevelt Cyclopedia*, edited by A. B. Hart and H. R. Ferleger (1941), is also hagiographic, but handy for ready reference. Entertaining sidelights on the Roosevelt personality are contained in A. W. Butt, *The Letters of Archie Butt* (1924); and, by the same author, *Taft and Roosevelt: The Intimate Letters of Archie Butt* (1924). See also *The Letters of Theodore Roosevelt*, edited by E. E. Morison and others (8 vols., 1951–54).

On the Japanese-American problems of the time, A. W. Griswold, *The Far Eastern Policy of the United States* (1938), is excellent. It may be supplemented by Tyler Dennett, *Roosevelt and the Russo-Japanese War* (1925); P. J. Treat, *Diplomatic Relations between the United States and Japan, 1895–1905* (2 vols., new ed., 1938); and A. L. P. Dennis, *The Anglo-Japanese Alliance* (1923). T. A. Bailey, *Theodore Roosevelt and the Japanese-American Crises* (1934); and Rodman W. Paul, *The Abrogation of the Gentlemen's Agreement* (1936), are two useful special studies.

On Canada and the United States there are a number of good books, among them Charles C. Tansill, *Canadian-American Relations, 1875–1916* (1943); Lester B. Shippee, *Canadian-American Relations, 1849–1874* (1939); and P. E. Corbett, *The Settlement of Canadian-American Disputes* (1937). Allan Nevins, *Henry White; Thirty Years of American Diplomacy* (1930), sheds considerable light on the subject of the Alaskan boundary dispute.

On inter-American problems, J. Fred Rippy, *The Caribbean Danger Zone* (1940), is an excellent interpretation of American policy in this region; see also, W. H. Callcott, *The Caribbean Policy of the United States, 1890–1920* (1942). N. J. Padelford, *The Panama Canal in Peace and War* (1942), makes clear the importance of the Canal in American war strategy. On Canal diplomacy, Mary W. Williams, *Anglo-American Isthmian Diplomacy, 1815–1915* (1916), is excellent. J. H. Latané, *From Isolation to Leadership* (rev. ed., 1925), is an admirably reasoned statement of the fundamentals of American foreign policy. Other useful studies on the diplomacy of the period are H. C. Hill, *Roosevelt and the Caribbean* (1927); E. T. Parks, *Colombia and the United States, 1765–1934* (1935); J. F. Rippy, *The Capitalists and Colombia* (1931); and W. D. McCain, *The United States and the Republic of Panama* (1937). On the building of the Canal there are several good books: J. B. and Farnham Bishop, *Goethals, Genius of the Panama Canal* (1930); Marie D. Gorgas and B. J. Hendrick, *William Crawford Gorgas, His Life and Work* (1924); John M. Gibson, *Physician to the World; General William C. Gorgas* (1950); and M. P. DuVal, Jr., *And the Mountains Will Move* (1947). Later Caribbean policy can best be followed in three books by Chester Lloyd Jones, *Caribbean Interests of the United States* (1916); *The United States and the Caribbean* (1929); and *The Caribbean since 1900* (1936). See also J. Fred Rippy, *Latin America in World Politics* (new ed., 1938).

The Memoirs of Jeremiah Curtin, edited by Joseph Schafer (1940), provides an entertaining inside view of Tsarist Russia.

On the Algeciras Conference, Alfred Vagts, *Deutschland und die Vereinigten Staaten in der Weltpolitik* (2 vols., 1935), contains an excellent account, but Dennis, *Adventures in American Diplomacy*, and Nevins, *Henry White*, both previously mentioned, may also be consulted profitably. On the Hague Conferences, see W. I. Hull, *The Two Hague Conferences and their Contributions to International Law* (1908); and J. B. Scott, *The Hague Peace Conferences of 1899 and 1907* (2 vols., 1909).

17

"My Policies"

Roosevelt as President — Integration in industry —
— The trust problem — The "muckrakers" — Prose-
cutions of the trusts — Railroad regulation — The
Hepburn Act — Pure Food and Drug Act — The
"square deal" — Conservation — The Newlands Act
Roosevelt's popularity — Roosevelt and the Negro
problem — Election of 1904 — The Panic of 1907 —
Election of 1908

THE aggressive leadership that characterized
Roosevelt's handling of foreign affairs was
Roosevelt as President equally evident in the development of his domestic policies.
No lawyer, Roosevelt was unim-
pressed by the traditional allocation of separate powers to the executive, the legislature,
and the judiciary. The President, as the
head of the government, was in his judgment
meant to lead. If laws were needed to accomplish a purpose that the President deemed
useful, then it was his duty to see that the
laws were passed. If Congress proved refrac-
tory, then the President must use his power
and prestige to force it to act. If the courts
put obstacles in the way of presidential policies, then the President must have a care
to the appointment of more reasonable
judges. The Constitution, he later maintained, "must be interpreted, not as a
straight-jacket, not as laying the hand of
death upon our development, but as an instrument designed for the life and healthy
growth of the Nation." The length to which
the Constitution might be stretched, so far
as Roosevelt was concerned, was shown in
his contention that the President might do
anything not expressly forbidden by its
terms. Facetious critics even attributed to
him sympathy with the statement attributed

to a favor-seeker, "What's the Constitution
between friends?"

Economics was definitely not Roosevelt's
principal forte, but he would have been
blind indeed if he had not recognized in the
emergence of "big business" a problem of
fundamental importance to his administration. By the beginning of the twentieth century "rugged individualism" had run riot in
the United States. In one industry after
another great corporations, successfully
claiming the rights of persons before the law,
had grown to monopolistic proportions. The
total capital of million-dollar corporations
had increased from $170,000,000 in 1897 to
$5,000,000,000 in 1900, and to $20,500,-
000,000 in 1904. Railway mergers, such as
the one by which E. H. Harriman brought
the Union Pacific and the Southern Pacific
together in 1900, had become the order of the
day. Concentration in industry was effected
both by means of "horizontal" combination
through which several industries of the same
kind were united, and by means of "vertical"
combinations, through which businesses of
allied interests joined forces.

Typical of the "vertical" combinations, or
the "integrated" industries, as they were
also called, was the United **Integration in industry**
States Steel Corporation, which

J. Pierpont Morgan, long the outstanding American financial leader, achieved tremendous power through the successful role he played in reorganizing and refinancing the nation's railroads after the depression that began with the Panic of 1893. It was Morgan, also, who helped create the United States Steel Corporation and the International Harvester Corporation. He was not without rivals, as, for example, E. H. Harriman, but after Harriman's death in 1909 Morgan's supremacy in the field of finance was hardly open to question. Before the Pujo Committee of 1912, which investigated the "money trust," he confidently defended his activities. The illustration to the right shows the New York Stock Exchange, Trinity Church, and Wall Street.

the financial genius of J. P. Morgan helped knit together in 1901. This was the first of America's "billion-dollar" corporations; at the beginning of its second year, in April, 1902, its capital stock amounted to $1,384,-681,297. It included as a nucleus the Carnegie Steel Company, which in 1900 had alone made profits of $40,000,000, and in addition six or seven other leading steel producers. But the interests of the new corporation went far beyond the mere manufacture of steel. It came to own and operate the iron and coal mines which contributed its original sources of supply. It controlled the railroads that connected with its coal mines, and the steamers on the Great Lakes that brought the iron ore from the mines of northern Minnesota and Michigan. It had its own smelting furnaces to make pig iron, its blast furnaces for the production of steel, and its foundries and rolling mills for the manufacture of machinery, steel rails, armor plate, and other steel commodities. From mine to market every process was completed within the control of this one gigantic corporation.

What happened to steel happened in greater or less degree to tobacco, petroleum, sugar, copper, beef, starch, flour, whiskey, chewing gum, farm implements, and innumerable other commodities. These enormous industries, still called "trusts" in popular parlance, either achieved or closely approached monopoly, and because the public was determined to have what they produced, acquired virtually the privilege of private taxation. To their prosperity nearly every citizen must contribute. Sometimes, because of a high protective tariff, they were able to keep out foreign competition, and to increase correspondingly the toll that the American public had to pay. Among them a close community of interest existed, well symbolized by the interlocking nature of their boards of directors on which the same names appeared again and again. Since most of the great combinations were arranged by financiers, a few great banking firms, notably J. P. Morgan and Company, the National City Bank of New York, the First National Bank of New York, and Kuhn, Loeb and

Company, occupied a more commanding position than ever before in the nation's business structure.

Inevitably under such a system great fortunes became greater, and notable inequalities of wealth appeared. A writer in the *Arena* of August, 1901, claimed that one half the people owned nothing, that one eighth of them owned seven eighths of the wealth, that one per cent of the population owned fifty-four per cent of the wealth, that one family in every hundred could buy out the other ninety-nine with plenty of money to spare, that one two-hundredths of one per cent of the population — four thousand millionaires — had acquired twenty per cent of the nation's total wealth. The accuracies of all such computations could be easily assailed, but they at least drove home a general truth. America, once a land of opportunity, was rapidly becoming a land in which the best opportunities had been cornered for the benefit of the few. "The United States," according to one observer, "is like an enormously rich country overrun by a horde of robber barons, and very inadequately policed by the central government and by certain local vigilance societies."

The trust problem was not new to Roosevelt's day.[1] Industrial combinations much **The trust problem** smaller in size had aroused opposition during the seventies and eighties, both in states and in the nation. The Grangers had attempted to regulate the railroads by state authority, and the United States, under the terms of the Interstate Commerce Act of 1887, had made feeble beginnings at national regulation. The Sherman Anti-Trust Law of 1890, based also upon the right of Congress to regulate interstate commerce, was passed in response to the demands of an insistent public opinion, and the government made a few attempts to enforce it. The unfriendly attitude of the courts, however, soon made the law a dead letter. In the Knight Case of 1895 the United States Supreme Court held that the establishment

of a monopoly in manufactures, however reprehensible, could be dealt with only by the individual states. "Commerce," said the Court, "succeeds to manufacture, and is not a part of it." After that all effort to employ the power of the national government against the trusts was given up, while the states, although endowed with a plentitude of constitutional authority, had already been proved to be too small to cope with nation-wide corporations. During the depression of the nineties, with many of the trusts in trouble, the public was less critical of them than it had been before, and as good times returned the excitement of the Spanish-American War and the new adventure into imperialism kept in obscurity the remarkable transformations that were taking place in the business world. Not until the opening years of the twentieth century did public attention again focus on the trusts.

The new awakening was due in remarkable degree to the work of the "muckrakers," a group of energetic journalists **The "Muck-** who made it their chief concern **rakers"** to discover and exploit in popular articles the seamy side of business behavior. They owed their name to Roosevelt, who was by no means unsympathetic with their work, but who compared some of the most sensational of them to the character in *Pilgrim's Progress* "who could look no way but downward with the muckrake in his hands." A vehicle was available for the muckrakers in the popular magazines that the nineties had produced, *McClure's*, the *Cosmopolitan, Everybody's*, the *American, Pearson's, Munsey's*, the *Arena*, and a number of others. These magazines, most of them monthlies, sold for as little as ten or fifteen cents a copy, and aimed to please. When they found in the literature of exposure a sure road to public acceptance they embraced the opportunity with whole-hearted enthusiasm. S. S. McClure, probably the most able and energetic of the publishers, set a good example for the rest by encouraging his writers to do the most painstaking research before they burst into print. Often he kept writers on his payroll for

[1] See Chapter 8.

months, or even years, before they were ready to produce the articles he wanted.

Before they had finished, the muckrakers had given the public a very complete, if perhaps a one-sided, view of the methods by which big business operated. Lincoln Steffens, regarded by many as the ablest of them all, wrote a series of articles for *McClure's* on the "Shame of the Cities" that exposed the corrupt alliance between business and politics in nearly every American metropolis. Ida M. Tarbell, also for *McClure's*, wrote a "History of the Standard Oil Company" that left no doubt whatever as to the ruthlessness of the methods by which John D. Rockefeller had built up his monopoly. Thomas Lawson, an ex-stock manipulator, revealed for *Everybody's* a lurid, behind-the-scenes picture of the financial world that shot the magazine's circulation during the period his articles were being published from 197,000 to 735,000. The list of leading muckrakers is not a long one, but it contains some of the most distinguished names in American journalism, and the total output of each writer was remarkably large. Upton Sinclair, in a novel, *The Jungle*, set forth the loathsome conditions that existed in the meat-packing industry; Ray Stannard Baker wrote on a wide variety of subjects, including the railroads, and the exploitation of labor by the trusts; Burton J. Hendrick told the inside story of life insurance; David Graham Phillips denounced "The Treason of the Senate," which reflected, or so he claimed, primarily the wishes of the trusts; George Kibbe Turner exhibited at its worst the vice business of Chicago and New York; Charles Edward Russell wrote on the beef trust and numerous other matters; and Samuel Hopkins Adams, on patent medicines and fraud in advertising. Supplementing and often corroborating the findings of the muckrakers were the volumes of the census of 1900, which soon began to appear, and the compendious *Report of the Industrial Commission* (19 vols., 1900–02), an investigating committee set up by Congress in 1898. Unread by the public at large, but of notable perspicacity, were the philosophical treatises of

A section of F. Opper's "Alphabet of Joyous Trusts," published by the Democrats during the election campaign of 1904. Each verse attacked a different trust.

Thorstein Veblen, *The Theory of the Leisure Class* (1899), and *The Theory of Business Enterprise* (1904). Veblen's reasoning provided reformers of the next generation with some of their most cogent arguments against "predatory wealth."

In his first message to Congress, December, 1901, Roosevelt gave warning of his future attitude toward the trusts, but he was not quite ready to essay the rôle of "trust-buster" **Roosevelt and the trusts** in which later he so willingly allowed himself to be cast. Summarizing accurately the President's message, Mr. Dooley reported: "Th' trusts, says he, are heejous monsthers built up be th' enlightened intherprise iv th' men that have done so much to advance progress in our beloved country, he says. On wan hand I would stamp thim undher fut:

on th' other hand not so fast." By February, 1902, however, the President was ready to act, and on his orders the Attorney-General of the United States announced that he would bring suit under the terms of the Sherman Anti-Trust Act to dissolve the Northern Securities Company, through which the year before a merger of three northwestern railroads had been attempted. If the government could induce the United States Supreme Court to support it in this instance, Roosevelt believed that he might later make the Sherman Act a really effective weapon in arresting the trend toward monopoly that had set in.

The Northern Securities Company was a $400,000,000 New Jersey corporation, **The Northern Securities case** brought into existence November 13, 1901, primarily to take over controlling portions of the stock of three competing northwestern railroads, the Great Northern, the Northern Pacific, and the Chicago, Burlington and Quincy. By resorting to the device of a holding company James J. Hill, the guiding genius in the proceedings, hoped not merely to eliminate competition, but also to develop a well-articulated railroad system that could more effectively meet the transportation needs of the whole great region stretching from Lake Michigan to Puget Sound. Naturally he called in J. P. Morgan to work out the necessary financial arrangements, and both believed, on advice of highly competent counsel, that the scheme they had devised was perfectly legal. For the President's purposes, however, the Northern Securities Company made an admirable target. A local suit for its dissolution, brought in the state courts of Minnesota, had given the nature of the company excellent preliminary advertising, and the fact that the merger so clearly involved interstate commerce would effectively eliminate the argument on which the Supreme Court had based its decision in the Knight case.

The prosecution of the Northern Securities Company moved along slowly — too slowly to suit Roosevelt. The government won a lower-court decision in 1903, and an "Expedition Act," which Attorney General Knox obtained of Congress the same year, enabled the Supreme Court to give speedier attention to the case than otherwise would have been possible. The decision it announced in 1904, except for the five-to-four vote by which it was reached, was all that the President could ask. The Court held that the Northern Securities Company was a violation of free competition within the meaning of the Sherman Act, and must be dissolved. To the surprise of the President, Associate Justice Oliver Wendell Holmes, who had only recently been appointed to the Court, voted with the minority. Before appointing Holmes, Roosevelt had looked carefully into his record and had concluded that his vote could be depended on. But Holmes maintained that there was no more reason to hold the union of two railroads illegal than "a partnership between two stage-drivers who have been competitors in driving across a state line." Justice White, also dissenting, insisted that there was a complete parallel between the Knight case and the Northern Securities case and regretted the spectacle of the Supreme Court reversing itself. But Roosevelt was delighted that the "vicious doctrine" of the earlier decision was no longer "an obstacle to obstruct the pathway of justice." "This decision," he boasted in his *Autobiography*, "I caused to be annulled by the Court that had rendered it."

Acclaimed by the public as the "trust-buster," Roosevelt went ahead with other prosecutions. A total of twenty- **Other prosecutions** five indictments were brought by the Department of Justice during his administration, and in a few instances the government scored victories. Perhaps the most notable of them was the dissolution of the "beef trust," which counted among its sins an agreement whereby six tenths of the nation's dealers in fresh meat avoided bidding against one another in the purchase of livestock. Looking backward, both the wisdom of this policy and the interpretation of the law that made it possible, may well be

"Trust-busting." President Roosevelt revived the Sherman Anti-Trust Act and the Supreme Court supported him against the "railroad trust."

doubted. Efforts to dissolve the trusts were often likened to the unscrambling of eggs. Once a community of interest had been established, "gentlemen's agreements" could be used to serve much the same purpose as more formal organization. Effective regulation, as Roosevelt well knew, rather than a futile effort to restore competition, would have been far more to the point, but the President's best efforts to obtain legislation appropriate for this purpose met with the almost invariable hostility of Congress. Eventually Roosevelt came to distinguish between "good trusts," which showed a proper concern for the welfare of the consumer, and "bad trusts," which sought only selfish ends. The latter he prosecuted, the former he let alone. The Supreme Court, in the rule of reason it adopted in 1911, came to about the same conclusion. Only when the monopolistic actions of trusts "unreasonably" interfered with interstate commerce would the Court hold against them. By allowing itself this

wide latitude, the Court was free to ignore mere "bigness," while at the same time punishing the misuse of power that great size made possible.

Roosevelt's efforts to obtain regulatory laws from Congress most nearly approached success with reference to the **Railroad** railroads. The Interstate Com- **regulation** merce Act of 1887 had taken a step in this direction, but its primary purpose after all had been the maintenance of free competition. Even in that sphere the Interstate Commerce Commission, hampered repeatedly by court decisions, had been singularly ineffective, and without a new grant of powers it could never hope to cope with the great mergers that had taken place since its creation. A half-dozen regional systems, capitalized together at more than nine billion dollars, accounted for three fourths of the nation's mileage. They paid good dividends and attracted foreign as well as American investors. The automobile was yet in its in-

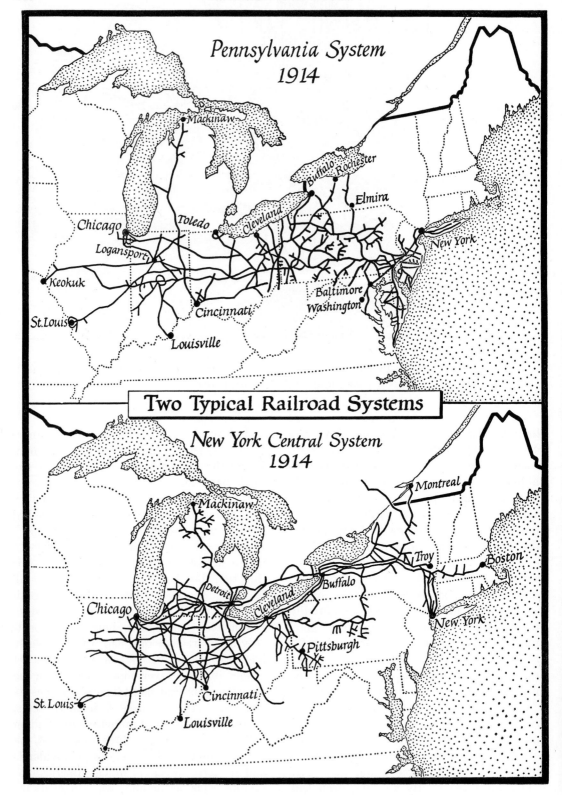

Pennsylvania System
1914

Two Typical Railroad Systems

New York Central System
1914

fancy, country highways were practically unknown, and in the realm of transportation the railroads reigned supreme. Upon their effectiveness the business of the country depended; without their cooperation the whole economic structure would fall. Conscious of their importance, the railroads were not without a trace of arrogance, and they resented bitterly all efforts of government to bring them to book. "It seems hard," wrote James J. Hill, a typical railroad magnate, "that we should be compelled to fight for our lives against the political adventurers who have never done anything but pose and draw a salary."

Backed by an aroused public opinion that believed more strongly every day that the people's pockets were being picked by the railroads, Roosevelt early in his administratiou sought regulatory legislation from Congress. The railroads offered no objection when in response to this summons Congress early in 1903 passed the Elkins Act in an effort to curb the rebate evil. The railroads themselves were weary of rebates and saw little to criticize in a statute that merely forbade variations from the published rates. They were more concerned when Roosevelt asked and obtained from Congress the establishment of a new Department of Commerce and Labor which was to include a fact-finding and possibly bothersome Bureau of Corporations. But the full force of their opposition was unleashed when in 1906, with the complete backing of the President, Representative Peter Hepburn of Iowa introduced into the House of Representatives a measure which, if passed, would grant the Interstate Commerce Commission full authority to regulate railroad rates.[1] The bill passed the House by a majority of 346 to 7, but the real test came in the Senate where the "vested interests" were more deeply entrenched. Eventually a compromise was

effected. The commission might regulate rates, but its decisions could be appealed to the courts. The contention of Senator La-Follette of Wisconsin, that the commission could not hope to set fair rates until the actual value of railroad property had been determined, fell on deaf ears. Roosevelt, LaFollette maintained, was ever ready to take the "half-loaf" if he could not easily get more.

Nevertheless, the Hepburn Act added immeasurably to the power and prestige of the Interstate Commerce Commission. No longer did it have to go to court to enforce an order; now the carrier had either to accept the rates set by the commission or go to court itself. Furthermore, the law also extended the jurisdiction of the commission to include other common carriers, such as express companies, pipe lines, sleeping-car companies, bridges, and ferries; it forbade the granting of free passes; it prohibited railroads from carrying commodities, except for their own use, that they had produced themselves — coal, for example; [1] and it empowered the commission to prescribe a uniform system of bookkeeping for all railroads, a provision of fundamental importance. Owing to the various methods of accounting in use among the railroads, it had been virtually impossible before to arrive at dependable comparative statistics. The new methods, worked out by Professor H. C. Adams, and installed during the next few years, gave the commission almost its first insight into what the railroads were really doing. In order the better to cope with its new duties, the membership of the commission was raised from five to seven. Within a few years, under the operation of the new law, it had not only effected drastic reductions in rates, but it had also won the respect of the public, the courts, and the carriers themselves, who increasingly tended to accept its decisions as final.

The Hepburn Act

---

[1] Roosevelt's original recommendations on the regulation of the railroads were set forth in his message to Congress of 1904. They were also embodied in the Townsend-Esch Bill, which passed the House in 1905 by the vote of 326 to 17, but was not brought to a vote in the Senate.

[1] This provision, it was hoped, would force the railroads to abandon other businesses than railroading, mining in particular. An exception was made in the case of timber.

The railroads were not the only trusts to feel the force of national regulation. The

Pure Food and Drug Act meat-packers, the food-processors, and the producers of drugs and patent medicines had much to explain when the muckrakers got through with them. Upton Sinclair's *The Jungle* made a deep impression on the public, and on Roosevelt himself. Muckraking articles in the *Ladies' Home Journal* and in *Collier's* proved conclusively that most of the popular nostrums depended for their effects upon such ingredients as opium or alcohol, that some of them were definitely habit-forming, and that nearly all of them were frauds. Doctor H. W. Wiley, chief chemist of the Department of Agriculture, and Doctor E. F. Ladd, food commissioner of the State of North Dakota, supplied scientific evidence too conclusive to ignore on the use of harmful preservatives and adulterants in the preparation of meats and other food products. Precedent was not altogether lacking in this field for federal regulation. Laws dating back to the eighties required inspection by the Bureau of Animal Industry of all meats destined for export. This legislation had been necessary to quiet the protests of Germany and other European countries whose people were incensed at having been sold American meat unfit for food; such, for example, as trichina-bearing pork. A law of 1906 extended federal inspection to all meats destined for interstate commerce, and a Pure Food and Drug Act, passed the same year, placed some restrictions, but not nearly enough, on the producers of prepared foods and patent medicines. An amendment to this act, passed in 1911, prohibited also the use of misleading labels, but events proved that the gullible public bought about as freely when the unpleasant truth was printed on the label as when it was not. The real root of the difficulty, fraudulent advertising, escaped unscathed. All such regulation, when undertaken by the federal government, depended for its validity upon the powers of Congress over interstate commerce, and the exact line of demarcation between state and national authority could be drawn only by the courts. Roosevelt, annoyed at the existence of this "twilight zone," strongly favored resolving all doubts in favor of the national government.

Always a happy phrase-maker, Roosevelt's insistence on a "square deal" for labor, capital, and the public gave him the **The "square** advantage of an attractive label **deal"** for his labor policy. Naturally the rapid development of industrial concentration aroused the fears of labor, and as the strength of organized capital grew, the strength of organized labor grew also. By 1905 the American Federation of Labor claimed for its affiliates a total membership of two millions, with perhaps six hundred thousand unaffiliated, but cooperating, union members. Under the circumstances a test of strength between labor and capital was almost inevitable.

The last serious strikes in the United States had centered about the Panic of 1893, but the turn of the century threatened to usher in a new and equally tumultuous period of strife. Labor conditions in the United States were probably at their worst in the coal mines of Pennsylvania, West Virginia, Ohio, and Illinois. Wages were low, employment was irregular, accidents were common, and workingmen's compensation was virtually unknown. The conditions of life in the squalid mining villages were depressing in the extreme. The mining companies owned everything. As Gompers said later, children were "brought into the world by the company doctor, lived in a company house or hut, were nurtured by the company store . . . laid away in the company graveyard." A steady stream of newly arrived immigrants, eager to work for any price, thronged to the mines, and slowed down the process of unionization. Nevertheless, in 1897, the United Mine Workers staged a successful strike in the central bituminous area, and under the leadership of the youthful John Mitchell they pushed the work of organization so rapidly in the anthracite districts of eastern Pennsylvania that within a few years they were ready to strike again. At Mitchell's call not less than one hundred thousand anthracite coal workers quit work in 1900, and in a legal, orderly way pressed home their demands. Mitchell's discipline over his men kept them sober and serious, and brought public good-will to his side. The real reason that the miners won, however, was that Mark Hanna, preparing to fight a campaign on the slogan, "the full dinner pail," persuaded the operators to concede some of the miners' demands rather than to embarrass him by such compelling evidence of labor unrest. And so the miners scored a partial victory.

After the election was over it was a different story. Hanna, and a good many other **The anthracite coal strike** capitalists, seemed genuinely to have hoped for an era of conciliation and compromise between capital and labor, but to some of the nation's industrialists the time seemed ripe for a "show-down." When in 1901 the Amalgamated Association of Iron and Steel Workers — the same that had lost the Homestead Strike of 1892 — struck for the recognition of their union, they were crushed within a month. Even the support of Samuel Gompers, head of the American Federation of Labor, was of no avail against United States Steel's ability to close mills affected by the strike and to produce everything it needed in non-union plants.

Next year the anthracite coal operators hoped to score an equally telling victory for the "open shop." When the coal miners, never fully satisfied with the agreement of 1900, asked for the recognition of their union, together with a wage increase of twenty per cent, and a nine-hour day, their request was spurned. Thereupon the miners struck, and from May 12 to October 23, at a total cost of perhaps one hundred million dollars to all concerned, they held their lines intact. According to Mark Hanna it looked as if there could be no agreement until "the miners are *starved* to it," but strike funds were collected from other miners, and the day of surrender postponed. Mitchell, as in 1900, kept his men from violence, and won much sympathy

for the strikers' cause. President George F. Baer of the Philadelphia and Reading Coal and Iron Company, who spoke for the operators, was far less skillful. In a letter that he carelessly allowed to fall into the hands of the press he revealed his true sentiments. "The rights and interests of the laboring man," he wrote a supposed sympathizer, "will be protected and cared for — not by the labor agitators, but by the Christian men to whom God in His infinite wisdom has given the control of the property interests of the country."

This bald-faced application of the divine-right theory to the holding of property won merited contempt from the public, and as cold weather set in the shortage of coal turned contempt to anger. In New York City the public schools had to be closed for lack of fuel, and the small stocks that dealers had on hand sold for as high as thirty to thirty-five dollars a ton. Roosevelt was outraged, and worried too about the political effect of a coal shortage on the party in power. "The big coal operators," he wrote later, "had banded together and positively refused to take any steps looking toward an accommodation. They knew that the suffering among the miners was great; they were confident that if order were kept, and nothing further done by the government, they would win; and they refused to consider that the public had any rights in the matter." Finally, when Roosevelt called the leaders of both sides to confer with him in Washington on a settlement, both sides attended, but the operators defied even the President of the United States. The attitude of one of them, probably Baer, so enraged Roosevelt, who was confined at the time to a wheel chair because of an injured leg, that he told a reporter: "If it wasn't for the high office I hold I would have taken him by the seat of the breeches and the nape of the neck and chucked him out of that window." The only man to keep his temper at the conference was John Mitchell.

But Roosevelt was not so easily balked. He sent Root to discuss with J. Pierpont

Morgan, as another interested observer, a **Presidential intervention** plan of settlement whereby five arbiters were to be appointed, "by the President or by you," to settle the strike; also, and more important, the means whereby the operators, who at the President's conference had already rejected this idea, were to be forced to accept it. The President's method was simplicity itself, although its constitutionality was far from demonstrable. The governor of Pennsylvania was to request federal troops to keep order. Roosevelt was then to send in a "first-rate general" under orders "to dispossess the operators and run the mines as a receiver." The public should have its coal, and the operators could think things over. This daring plan, which Roosevelt was absolutely determined to carry out if he had to, was kept a close secret from everyone, apparently, except the operators. As Roosevelt no doubt anticipated, it changed their minds quite perceptibly on the matter of arbitration; now they were all for such a settlement as the President had suggested, except that there must be no union man on the commission. A suitable board of arbiters, according to the operators, would be (1) an officer of the engineer corps, (2) a man of experience in mining, (3) a man of prominence, eminent as a sociologist, (4) the federal judge of the eastern district of Pennsylvania, and (5) a mining engineer. Roosevelt was puzzled, for he was convinced that a union man must sit on the board, but finally he saw a way out. A commission of seven, similar in personnel to the one desired by the operators, was arranged, but the "eminent sociologist" that Roosevelt appointed to it was E. E. Clark, head of the Brotherhood of Railway Conductors. Work was resumed at the mines, and in March, 1903, a decision that in the main favored the miners, although stopping short of union recognition, was accepted by both sides. Thus the President had obtained a "square deal" for labor.

Nor was this all. Repeatedly the President recommended to Congress legislation favorable to labor, such as the protection of women and children in industry, limitations on the use of injunctions in labor disputes, and employer's liability laws for workers on interstate railroads. Only the last-mentioned of these recommendations received the favorable action of Congress, and the first such law, passed in 1906, was annulled by the Supreme Court. A law of April, 1908, met the Court's objections. In general Roosevelt's thinking on the labor problem was not far in advance of his times, but it represented a distinct improvement over the positions taken by his predecessors.

Another policy dear to Roosevelt's heart was the conservation of the nation's natural resources. When he became **Conservation** President, the United States was "somewhat in the position of the man who had unexpectedly lost most of his fortune." Its greatest resource throughout its history, or so the people had always thought, had been its vast reservoir of public lands. Now the best of these had been used up; although at the turn of the century more than five hundred million acres still remained open to settlement, only a small fraction of this vast area could ever be farmed in the traditional American way. Moreover, even after the lands had passed into private or corporate hands the tendency had been to exploit them rather than to preserve their fertility. Millions of acres, particularly in the East and the South, had been returned, thoroughly despoiled, to nature, or could be farmed only by the constant use of fertilizer. What had happened to the lands had happened also in varying degrees to other natural resources. Four fifths of the nation's forests had been chopped down without thought as to their replacement, and many of those that remained had been acquired by a few large lumber companies bent on using them up. Mineral resources, too, whether of metals, coal, gas, or oil, had been exploited with the utmost wastefulness. Water-power sites, in return for next to nothing, had been allowed to pass into the hands of private companies who had developed their possibilities along profit-making lines, without regard for

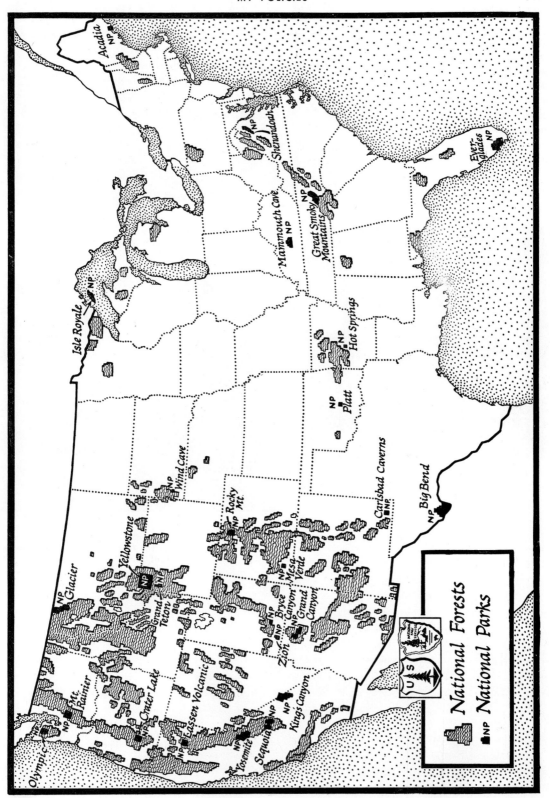

Acadia NP

Shenandoah NP

Everglades NP

Mammouth Cave NP

Great Smoky Mountains NP

Isle Royale NP

Hot Springs NP

Platt NP

Wind Cave

Carlsbad Caverns NP

Big Bend NP

Rocky Mt. NP

Yellowstone

Glacier NP

Grand Teton NP

Mesa Verde NP

Bryce Canyon NP

Zion NP

Grand Canyon NP

Olympic NP

Mt. Rainier NP

Crater Lake NP

Lassen Volcanic NP

Yosemite NP

Sequoia NP

King's Canyon NP

U S

■ National Forests
NP National Parks

Forest conservation as an essential duty of government received new recognition in 1901 when the Division of Forestry became a Bureau, and again in 1905 when the forest reserves were transferred from the Department of the Interior to Agriculture. Two years later, with the area set aside mounting rapidly, the term "national forests" replaced the term "national reserves."

FOREST FIRES. Effects of the great fire in Coeur d'Alene National Forest, Idaho, 1910.

TIMBER SURVEY PARTY making a valuation survey near Eckington, Virginia. Photo by A. Gaskell, 1904.

GIFFORD PINCHOT NATIONAL FOREST. Part of the vast acreage reserved by the federal government between 1901-1909.

FOREST RANGER. Locating distance to forest fire, Cabinet National Forest, Montana, 1907.

the destruction of beauty or prevention of floods. By the turn of the century, pessimists were beginning to foretell that the rich resources of the United States would soon be exhausted, and the poverty of the Old World would extend to the New.

Some earnest, but, as events proved, uninspired, prophets were convinced that the United States would not long be able to provide the food necessary for its teeming millions. This dire threat, reinforced by the demand of the West for a land policy more in accordance with the conditions of western life, led to a drastic revision of the federal land laws. Irrigation had long been regarded as the most likely means of making the western lands worth while, and in 1889, on authority of Congress, Major J. W. Powell of the Geological Survey had made a careful survey of irrigation sites throughout the country. Implicit in Powell's findings was the fact that the cost of irrigation ran so far beyond the means of individuals as to demand either cooperative or governmental action. The Carey Act of 1894, passed by Congress in an effort to encourage cooperative enterprise, authorized the gift of irrigable land to the western states on condition that they permit private companies to construct irrigation works upon it and to charge for water-rights. The land itself settlers could purchase from the state at fifty cents an acre, but inasmuch as water-rights in Carey-Act projects cost from thirty to forty dollars an acre plus maintenance, this privilege fell far short of free land. Nevertheless, in Wyoming, Idaho, Montana, Colorado, Arizona, California, New Mexico, and Utah the Carey Act was used to permit the opening of numerous new irrigation tracts. Each state was entitled, if it wished, to as much as a million acres for this purpose.

The Reclamation Act of 1902, sometimes called the Newlands Act in honor of its **The New-** sponsor, Senator Francis G. **lands Act** Newlands of Nevada, put the federal government itself into the business of building the dams, tunnels, flumes, and ditches necessary for irrigation projects. All revenue that came from the sales of public lands was set aside for investment in irrigation. As in the case of the Carey Act, the cost of construction, which amounted to from twenty to thirty dollars per acre, was assessed against the settlers, who were permitted to take twenty-, forty-, or eighty-acre tracts on condition of five years' residence and the cultivation of half their land. Their payments were put into a revolving fund, which was used to build still more irrigation works. Under the terms of this act several million acres of land were eventually made available for agriculture.

Irrigation dams proved to be useful also for the development of water-power, and pointed definitely toward government activity in that field. During Roosevelt's administration the Bureau of Corporations made a study of the water-power resources of the country, and discovered that they were adequate, if properly harnessed, to turn all the wheels of American industry. Hydroelectric corporations, however, such as the General Electric and Westinghouse, had already preempted some of the choicest sites, and were after more. In 1903 Roosevelt showed plainly where he stood on this subject by vetoing a law of Congress that would have permitted private construction of a dam and power-plant at Muscle Shoals, Alabama. The "ultimate effect of granting privileges of this kind," the President maintained, "should be considered in a comprehensive way," and a general policy adopted whereby "these valuable rights" would not be practically given away, but would be so disposed of as to "best substantiate the public interest." In many instances, however, the states, rather than the United States, had the disposal of these valuable concessions, and state officials all too frequently proved to be easy marks for the corporations.

The rapid destruction of the national forests had been noted occasionally for a quarter of a century before **Forest** Roosevelt's time, and in 1891 **reserves** Congress had passed a Forest Reserve Act under the terms of which the President could withdraw timber lands from entry. But neither the public nor the Presidents were much interested. Orders by Harrison, Cleveland, and McKinley set aside some 46,828,-449 acres, all told, that were not to be alienated, but no real halt was called in the process of exploitation. Gifford Pinchot, chief of the forestry service, was the man who more than any other was responsible for a change in this situation. Pinchot knew how other nations administered their forests, and he wished to adapt their methods to the forests of the United States. He knew, too, how intimately the destruction of the forests was bound up with other problems of waste, such as soil erosion, the clogging of river channels, and the promotion of floods. As a close friend of Roosevelt's, he was able to enlist the President's enthusiastic aid, and before Roosevelt left office the total amount of forest land withdrawn from entry had been raised to 172,230,233 acres.

Students of conservation were increasingly impressed by the unity of the problem that confronted them. Deforestation and the building of dams, whether for irrigation or for power purposes, might and sometimes did interfere with the navigability of streams, hence the preservation of internal waterways was involved. An Inland Waterways Commission, appointed by Roosevelt in 1907, not only made a survey of the nation's unused water routes, but studied also nearly every aspect of the conservation problem. The assumption that steamboat traffic might be revived to furnish competition for the railroads proved to be a fallacy, but out of the work of the commission came the plan for a national conference on conservation, to which representatives from all sections and from both parties should be invited. On May 13, 1908, at the White House Roosevelt met with an assembly of notables that included state governors, cabinet members, Supreme Court justices, members of Congress, businessmen, and a wide range of experts. For three days he kept the conference in session, and from it he obtained support for such important policies as the protection of the water supply of navigable streams, the control of forest fires, government regulation for the cutting of timber, the granting of surface titles to public lands separate from the right to exploit the minerals that lay below the surface, and the withdrawal from entry of lands bearing coal, oil, natural gas, and phosphate.

Following the work of the conference, Roosevelt, on his own initiative and without legislative authority, appointed a National Conservation Commission of forty-nine members to make a survey of the nation's resources in minerals, waters, forests, and soils. The members of the commission were unpaid, but the President directed that the executive department should give them all possible assistance. Congress, by no means pleased to see an investigating committee created solely by presidential prerogative, did what it could to hamper the work of the commission, but its first report, presented in January, 1909, filled three large volumes and provided much important information. Meantime forty-one state conservation commissions and many more private agencies had begun to supply the nation with more knowledge of its natural resources and how to deal with them than it had ever had before. On Roosevelt's order, the Secretary of the Interior added to the forest lands already withdrawn from entry some eighty million acres of coal lands, a million and a half acres of lands adjacent to water-power sites, and nearly five million acres of phosphate lands.

While the nation in general applauded Roosevelt's efforts to promote conservation, there were many dissident **Opposition** voices. Corporations engaged **to conserva-** in lumbering, mining, the pro- **tion** duction of hydroelectric power, and other exploitative activities were openly hostile. The representatives of western states, who saw little to admire about a policy that in some of its aspects could serve only to delay western development, asked pointedly, "What's posterity ever done for us?" In consequence, the President's interest in conservation far outran the willingness of Congress to legislate. He failed to obtain a law authorizing the permanent retention by the government of all lands bearing coal, oil, or natural gas, and not until 1920 was this reasonable policy adopted. In 1909, however, Congress did provide for the separate disposal of the agricultural, timber, and mineral resources of the public lands, while a year later it created the Bureau of Mines to discover and disseminate information on the mineral resources of the United States, and the best methods for their development. The Mondell Act of 1909, like the Reclamation Act of 1902, exhibited a side of conservation that pleased the West, for its effect was to promote rather than to retard development. In the interest of dry-farming, by means of which settlers with the aid of a little rain and some subsoil moisture stood a less than fifty-fifty chance to make a living, the Mondell Act permitted homesteaders to take up as much as three hundred and twenty acres of non-timbered, non-mineral, non-irrigable land. For proving up no residence term was required, only the evidence of successful cultivation.

By 1934 "overgrazed, wind-eroded expanses, interspersed with rocky peaks and barren slopes, were all that remained of the public domain." [1] In that year Franklin D. Roosevelt, whose ideas on conservation were not unlike those of Theodore Roosevelt, issued two orders withdrawing all remaining portions of the public domain from homestead entry. This he did in part under authority of the Taylor Grazing Act, which charged the Secretary of the Interior with the responsibility of creating grazing districts, classifying the land in these districts, and leasing lands suitable for grazing. In a sustained effort to prevent further depletion of the nation's landed resources, the Federal government also acquired title to much submarginal, badly-eroded, and worn-out land; also, it negotiated for the administration of similar state-owned lands. Despite some

[1] E. Louise Peffer, *The Closing of the Public Domain* (1951), p. 224. Quoted by permission of Stanford University Press.

confusion due to the overlapping interests of the Forestry Service in the Department of Agriculture and the Grazing Service in the Department of the Interior, the idea that the remaining public lands should not be alienated by the government, and that their various uses should be controlled in the interest of conservation, continued to grow. In 1946 the Grazing Service was merged with the General Land Office to create a new Bureau of Land Management.

There was a direct relationship between Roosevelt's policy of governmental interference in the affairs of business and his policy of conservation. In the former he brought businessmen face to face with the specter of effective governmental regulation, in the latter he served notice that in certain spheres, previously left open to private initiative, the government either would act itself or would permit individuals to act only on terms laid down by the government in advance. The day of rampant individualism was almost done. Perhaps the senior Robert M. La-Follette, never a very devoted admirer of Roosevelt, had these considerations in mind when he described conservation as Roosevelt's greatest work. According to the Wisconsin senator, Roosevelt deserved unstinted praise "for staying territorial waste" and for saving the things "on which alone a peaceful, progressive and happy race life can be founded."

Few other Presidents, if indeed any, have enjoyed the popularity while in office that came to Theodore Roosevelt. **Roosevelt's** To a phenomenal degree he ex- **popularity** hibited in his personality the traits that the average American most admired; the President was the ordinary citizen as he might have looked if seen under a microscope. The typical American loved sports, and the President was a disciple of the "strenuous life." He rode horseback, played tennis, boxed, and hunted. Tales of his prowess continually reached the public — a day's horseback ride over icy roads to prove to his "swivel-chair" generals that the thing could be done; the existence of a "tennis cabinet"; boxing matches in the White House (in one of them the President lost the sight of an eye); and a bear hunt in which the President refused to kill a planted bear — the original "Teddy bear." The typical American sometimes lost his temper and called people names, but none ever did it with greater artistry than the President, who took so many people to task for their truthlessness that the newspapermen gleefully described his victims as the "Ananias Club." Like most Americans, the President was a devoted family man, and stories of his cheerful unconcern when the Roosevelt children rode a pony into the White House elevator, or burst into a cabinet meeting to announce the birth of a new family of guinea-pigs, appealed strongly to every right-thinking American. All Americans liked entertaining, and the President was an indefatigable entertainer. Anyone who interested him was apt to be called to the White House for a luncheon or a dinner to exchange views with the President; only there was often not much of an exchange, for the President loved to talk and did most of the talking. Roosevelt's prominent teeth, his spectacles, his cowboy hat, and his general air of belligerency made him the cartoonist's delight, and his knack of clothing his every deed in an aura of righteousness did him no harm.

> T. R. is spanking a Senator,
> T. R. is chasing a bear,
> T. R. is busting an awful Trust,
> And dragging it from its lair.
> They're calling T. R. a lot of things —
> The men in the private car —
> But the day-coach likes exciting folks
> And the day-coach likes T. R.[1]

Not that the public always agreed with Roosevelt; sometimes it disagreed with him violently, and a few people hated him. When the President advocated uniform marriage and divorce laws for the states, he was generally applauded, but nothing much was done

[1] From Rosemary and Stephen Vincent Benét, *A Book of Americans* (1933). By permission of the publishers, Farrar and Rinehart, Inc.

about it. When he argued against "race suicide," and urged native Americans to have more children, he got no results whatever. When he denounced "nature fakers," whose books of highly imaginary animal lore delighted the youth of the land, the books continued to be written and read. When he joined the crusade for simplified spelling, he found adult America unwilling to sacrifice the spelling-book knowledge it had so painfully gained, and young America helpless before its elders. But these idiosyncrasies, for the most part, served only to endear the President to the public. He made friends with the newspapermen, furnished them good copy, and obtained valuable front-page publicity by making timely releases. Once the San Francisco earthquake and fire pushed an important presidential document far into the newspapers' insides, but accidents of that kind happened only rarely.

Roosevelt's relations with the public were at their worst in his handling of the Negro problem. Although his mother came from the South, he was a thoroughgoing northerner in his prejudices, and early in his administration he shocked southern whites by inviting Booker T. Washington, the great Negro educator, to have dinner with him at the White House. Southerners admired Washington, but they did not dine with him, or with any other Negro. "How should you address Washington?" ran one story, perhaps not apocryphal. "Well," said the southerner, "you can't call such a man 'Booker,' and I won't call any Negro 'Mister,' so I just call him 'Professor.'" It was a long time before the South could forgive Roosevelt's disregard of the color line. Nor did it like his determination not to distinguish between whites and blacks in appointments to office. Indianola, Mississippi, got a Negro postmistress, and Charleston, South Carolina, a Negro collector. He showed, too, the utmost contempt for the "lily-white" Republican organizations in the South which vied with the Democrats in their determination to keep Negroes out of politics. On the

Theodore Roosevelt, Twenty-sixth President of the United States, impressed the American people with his courage and vitality while serving as a volunteer officer in the Spanish-American War. He exhibited similar qualities as President, although he was a good politician, and knew how to compromise when he deemed compromise essential.

THE PRESIDENT.

THE COLONEL.

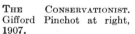
THE CONSERVATIONIST.
Gifford Pinchot at right, 1907.

THE ROUGH RIDER. Roosevelt on horseback leading capture of Block House at San Juan Hill.

Panorama of San Francisco after the earthquake and fire of 1906. Most of the destruction was caused by the fire, and by dynamiting to impede its progress.

other hand, he was as impetuous as any Southerner in his handling of the "Brownsville affair." Because a few Negro soldiers had been charged with shooting up the town of Brownsville, Texas, while absent from their barracks without leave, three companies of Negro troops were dishonorably discharged from the service. Subsequent investigations seemed to prove that the troops were much more sinned against than sinning, but Roosevelt left office without having admitted his mistake.

Roosevelt's popularity had much to do with the overwhelming victories scored by

Election of 1904 the Republicans in the four elections (1902, 1904, 1906, 1908) held during his administration, and his renomination and re-election in 1904 was a great personal triumph. Eager to be President in his own right, Roosevelt was unduly distressed at the tendency of ultra-conservative Republicans to rally around Mark Hanna for the nomination, but Hanna's death in February, 1904, left him a free field. As one observer remarked, he was nominated by acclamation and elected much the same way. Chosen to serve with him as Vice-President was Charles W. Fairbanks, an Indiana conservative. The Democrats, after two disastrous defeats under the leadership of the radical Bryan, chose as their standard-bearer Alton B. Parker, a "safe and sane" New York judge who accepted the nomination on condition that he be left free to support the gold standard. This attempt to commit the

party to a definite monetary policy, when all reference to the subject had been discreetly omitted from the platform, contrasted painfully with Bryan's declaration: "You may dispute whether I have fought a good fight, you may dispute whether I have finished my course, but you cannot deny that I have kept the faith." For a moment it seemed that the convention might replace Parker with Bryan, but it did not, and Bryan accorded the nominee his half-hearted support. For second place on the ticket the Democrats chose Henry Gassaway Davis, a rich octogenarian from West Virginia, who was expected to contribute heavily to the Democratic campaign chest, but proved to be a disappointment.

Parker ran a poorer race than Bryan ever had, receiving only 140 electoral votes to Roosevelt's 336. Roosevelt even broke into the border South by carrying Missouri, West Virginia, and one vote in Maryland. "Wall Street," to the disappointment of the Democrats, supported the Republican nominee, largely because businessmen regarded the Republican Party, in spite of Roosevelt, as more dependable than the Democratic. The Republican campaign chest was well filled with corporation contributions, and Parker won only a life membership in the Ananias Club for his charge that these donations were obtained as "blackmail" in return for the suppression of damaging evidence by the Bureau of Corporations, over which George B. Cortelyou, the Republican campaign man-

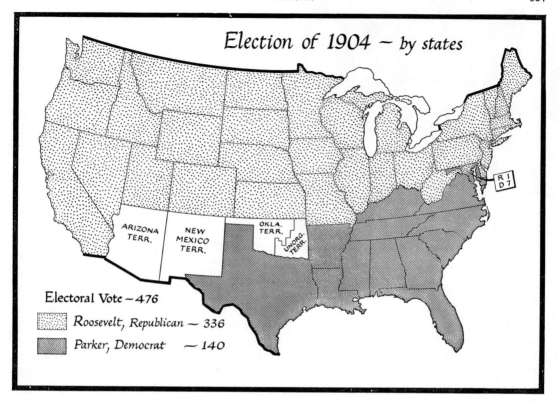

Election of 1904 — by states

ARIZONA TERR.

NEW MEXICO TERR.

OKLA. TERR.

UNORG. TERR.

R I D 7

Electoral Vote — 476

Roosevelt, Republican — 336

Parker, Democrat — 140

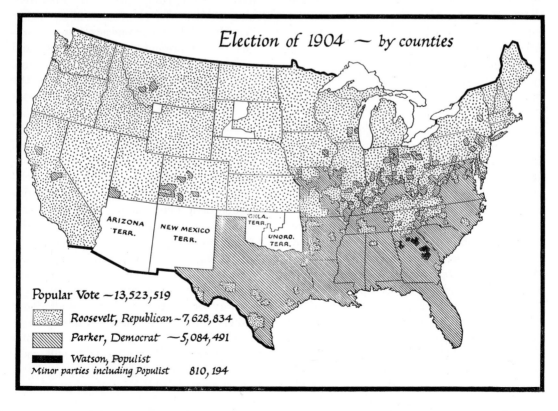

Election of 1904 — by counties

ARIZONA TERR.

NEW MEXICO TERR.

OKLA. TERR.

UNORG. TERR.

Popular Vote — 13,523,519

Roosevelt, Republican — 7,628,834

Parker, Democrat — 5,084,491

Watson, Populist

Minor parties including Populist   810,194

Panic of 1907. Scene outside Knickerbocker Bank. Illustration from *Harper's Weekly*, November 7, 1907.

ager, presided. Elated by the election returns, Roosevelt immediately issued a dramatic statement that he must have regretted later many times. "The wise custom which limits the President to two terms regards the substance and not the form, and under no circumstances will I be a candidate for or accept another nomination."

Roosevelt's second administration came nearest shipwreck in connection with the **The Panic** Panic of 1907, which was the **of 1907** result, so many claimed, of his unwarranted attacks on business. His prosecutions of the trusts and his attempts to regulate the railroads, hostile critics declared, endangered legitimate profits; the "square deal" encouraged labor to make unreasonable demands; and conservation called a halt to the lucrative exploitation of natural resources. Public confidence in business integrity was indeed somewhat shaken when in April, 1907, Judge Kenesaw Mountain Landis found the Standard Oil Company of New Jersey guilty on 1462 separate counts of obtaining illegal rebates from the Chicago and Alton Railroad, and assessed against it a fine of $29,240,000; nor was confidence wholly restored when a higher court reversed the sentence. Later in the same year the American Sugar Refining Company was proved to have tampered with the scales on which the sugar it imported was weighed, and the government by court action recovered over four million dollars. This, too, was a bit unsettling, both to the public and to business. Roosevelt was sensitive to the criticism that his policies were undermining confidence, but he claimed that the fault lay with business, and not with him. "If trouble comes from having the light turned on," he told a cabinet member, "remember it is not really due to the light, but to the misconduct which is exposed." He came, indeed, to believe that the Panic of 1907 was purely "psychological"; that it had been intentionally produced by "malefactors of great wealth," bent on discrediting his policies.

Undoubtedly an important factor in bringing on the Panic of 1907 was the wholesale multiplication of securities that had taken place in the early years of the century. United States Steel, for example, was capitalized at a sum far in excess of the total capital of the companies it incorporated. These securities were often sold at higher prices than the earning power of the corporations they represented would justify, and eventual disillusionment was sure to come. Another factor was the inelasticity of the currency and of credit. The United States government had no way of providing an extra supply of money to meet an emergency. The total amount of gold and silver, national bank notes, and Treasury notes that composed the money of the country was relatively fixed. If confidence lagged and money was hoarded, there was sure to be a shortage. Much the same thing was true of credit, which was limited primarily by the ability and willingness of a few great New York bankers to lend. Practically every financial institution in the country was connected in one way or another with the Wall Street bankers, and was amenable to discipline by them. They thus constituted a kind of a "money trust" that almost at will could grant or withhold the credit necessary to keep the nation's business moving.

Unmistakable signs of the gathering storm were apparent throughout the early weeks of

Roosevelt and the Panic October, 1907, and on October 22 a run began on the Knickerbocker Trust Company, the third largest in New York, which by noon of October 23 had exhausted its resources in cash. Runs on other New York banks eventually forced a dozen more to close their doors. On the stock exchange values plunged downward, and call money became practically unobtainable. To help meet the emergency, George B. Cortelyou, Secretary of the Treasury, deposited twenty-five million dollars of Treasury funds with the New York banks, while clearing-house certificates and payroll checks passed freely in lieu of money. The storm was soon over, but it left in its wake a train of wreckage that affected the whole country. Several railroads went into bankruptcy, factories were closed, and men were out of work. The situation was not as serious, however, as it seemed, and by January, 1908, recovery had set in. Roosevelt had done his part, as he thought, by promising the United States Steel Corporation immunity from prosecution so that it could absorb, and save from collapse, the Tennessee Coal and Iron Company. This, Morgan told the President, was necessary to stave off a really major disaster.

Convinced that the panic might have been averted, or at least that its worst effects might have been avoided, had the banking and currency system of the United States been on a sounder footing, Congress in 1908 passed the Aldrich-Vreeland Act which empowered the national banks of the country for a period of six years to issue emergency currency in times of financial stringency. This was but a mere stop-gap. The most important part of the act was to create a National Monetary Commission to investigate the currency systems of the world and to lay plans for a thoroughgoing reform in the American system. The commission reported in 1912, and on the basis of its findings the Federal Reserve Act of 1913 was adopted.

Meantime the end of Roosevelt's administration was fast approaching and the election of 1908 was at hand. In

Who should succeed Roosevelt? spite of Roosevelt's assertion of four years before, he was accused of wanting to run again, and certainly many of his admirers would have been delighted to see him have a third term. Nevertheless, Roosevelt had no intention of running again, and to head off the danger that his devotees might draft him, as they had once done for the Vice-Presidency, he decided to work actively for the nomination of another candidate as committed as himself to the Roosevelt policies. This was the more necessary because of the avowed determination of Republican conservatives to capture the nomination for one of their kind. Leading candidates from the "stand-pat" wing of the Republican Party were Joseph G. Cannon of Illinois, who as Speaker of the House of Representatives had again and again thwarted Roosevelt's plans; Joseph B. Foraker, who as Senator from Ohio had been equally antagonistic; and Charles Warren Fairbanks of Indiana, the Vice-President, whose correct behavior in office deceived no one as to his thoroughgoing dislike for the President's policies. There were rumors that a "slush-fund" was being collected to promote such "favorite son" candidacies and to insure that in the end a reliable conservative would be nominated.

If he were to choose his successor, three possibilities at once presented themselves to Roosevelt's mind. Next to the

Hughes President himself, Charles Evans Hughes (1862–1948) of New York was the reformers' delight. Before 1905 Hughes was only a brilliant New York lawyer, but his work as investigator of the New York insurance companies catapulted him at once into national fame. What amazed the insurance companies no less than it gratified the public was the way in which Hughes showed himself even more familiar with the intricacies of the insurance business than many of its high-salaried executives. But Hughes sought facts, not publicity. He demonstrated that the insurance companies had speculated freely with their clients' funds, that their methods had been both crooked and wasteful, and that they had never hesitated to mix politics with business. Had he permitted it, he might have been nominated for mayor of New York, but he chose rather to become the Republican candidate for governor in 1906, a prize that the machine dared not deny him. Elected, he became even more distasteful to the professional politicians than they had feared. He made appointments on merit, gave the most "pitiless publicity" to his conduct of official business, forced the legislature to adopt a direct primary law and to prohibit race-track gambling, and risked public disfavor by a judicious veto of a two-cent passenger-rate law that he claimed was unfair to the railroads. But Roosevelt did not like Hughes. He thought the New York governor too uncompromising, too utterly unwilling to play ball with the politicians. Besides, Hughes had never been associated with the Roosevelt policies; how could one be sure that he would maintain them? Might he not instead substitute policies of his own?

Roosevelt believed that of all his lieutenants Elihu Root (1845–1937), his Secretary of State, was the ablest. It was Root who as Secretary of War had welded the American Empire together. It was Root, too, who had carried forward undimmed the brilliant work of his predecessor, John Hay, in the State Department. Unfortunately, however, there was nothing about Root that appealed strongly to the public. As a lawyer he had served some of the very corporations that Roosevelt's administration had most opposed; nor had he always been scrupulous in his choice of clients. His first large fee came as a result of his work in defense of "Boss" Tweed. Roosevelt was confident that Root, as President, would serve the interests of the United States with the same single-minded devotion that he had shown as a cabinet member, but that was beside the point. Root was politically unavailable.

The third possibility was William Howard Taft (1857–1930), whose record was happily untarnished by a profitable law practice. The Taft family had long played a prominent rôle in the affairs of Cincinnati, Ohio, and Taft's father, Judge Alphonso Taft, had once been a member of Grant's cabinet. Taft's rise up the political ladder came principally by the appointive route. An honor graduate of Yale, he became successively a judge in the superior court of Ohio, solicitor-general in the federal Department of Justice, federal judge, commissioner to the Philippines and governor-general, and finally Secretary of War. A consistently able administrator and Roosevelt's favorite envoy abroad, he had had what seemed to be an almost ideal training for the Presidency. His personal inclinations lay toward the Supreme Court, but more than once he felt obliged to reject the appointment he craved in the interest of the unfinished business he had in hand. His family was more ambitious for him than he was for himself. His wife wanted him to be President, and so also did his wealthy brother, Charles P. Taft. He was a huge man weighing three hundred and fifty pounds, good-natured and affable, and blessed with an infectious chuckle. The people might like him. Roosevelt certainly did, and as early as 1907 let it be known that he would support Taft for the Republican nomination in 1908. Presidential support can be, and in this case it was, extraordinarily effective, and as a result Taft was nominated on the first ballot by a convention that would have preferred Roosevelt. Second place on the ticket went as a consolation prize to the conservatives, who counted the nominee, James S. Sherman of New York, as one of the most dependable of their number.

The Democrats, disastrously defeated four years before with the conservative Parker, renominated Bryan, who was still young, vigorous, and hopeful. For Vice-President they nominated John W. Kern of Indiana. Bryan as a favorite Chautauqua orator had probably been heard by more Americans than any other man in public life, and his adherents

The Democrats name Bryan

gave him the same unstinted devotion that Henry Clay and James G. Blaine had once commanded. In 1906 Bryan had made a trip around the world, had been well received, and had returned with his self-confidence restored. Ready at last to admit that free silver was a dead issue, he proposed in August, 1906, a new program for curbing the trusts. Corporations should be barred from contributing to campaign funds, interlocking directorates should be prohibited, and a federal license should be required of all engaged in interstate business. For the railroad problem he reverted to the Populist remedy, government ownership, "not as an immediate issue, but as an ultimate solution of the controversy." The trouble with Bryan's program was that it was so like Roosevelt's; indeed, well before election time Congress had passed and Roosevelt had signed a measure forbidding corporations to contribute toward the election of national officers, while Bryan had materially modified his views on the railroad question.

The real issue in the lackadaisical campaign of 1908 was whether Bryan or Taft **Election** could be the better trusted to **of 1908** carry out the Roosevelt policies. In the end Taft won by an electoral vote of 321 to 162. Besides the "solid South" Bryan carried only Nebraska, Colorado, and Nevada, but he at least surpassed Parker's record of four years before. Republican conservatives, looking carefully into Taft's record as a judge, concluded that they had little to fear from Roosevelt's political legatee. Later, not without a show of justice, Bryan complained that the Republicans had enjoyed an unfair advantage in the campaign. Taft the progressive carried the West, while Taft the conservative carried the East. Forty-six states participated in the election of 1908; for in 1907 the majority party in Congress had at last decided that Republican supremacy was well enough established to risk the admission of Oklahoma, an almost certainly Democratic state. A similar offer to admit New Mexico and Arizona as one state failed because of the opposition of Arizona to such a scheme.

William Howard Taft

TWENTY-SEVENTH PRESIDENT of the United States, Taft owed his office largely to the support of Theodore Roosevelt, whose policies he was expected to carry out. But he was by temperament more the judge than the executive. As President he lost the confidence of the public, but as ex-President and Chief Justice he was highly regarded.

The emphasis placed by both the older parties on reform called striking attention to the important rôle that minor parties, in spite of their inability to attract large numbers of voters to their standards, actually played in American politics. In the campaign of 1908 the Populist Party gasped its last, but many of its cherished principles had long since been espoused by Bryan Democracy and Roosevelt Republicanism. William Randolph Hearst's Independence League, formed primarily to advance the political ambitions of its author, furnished more effective opposition to the nomination of Parker by the Democrats in 1904 than came from any other source, and in 1908, as a third party with a ticket of Hearst's choosing, attempted to out-Bryan Bryan and to out-Roosevelt Roosevelt. Prohibition candidates in every election called emphatic attention to the liquor evil, and often induced the older parties, at least in local contests, to support their creed, while two warring factions, the Social Democratic (or Socialist), and the Socialist-Labor, persistently carried the torch for socialism.

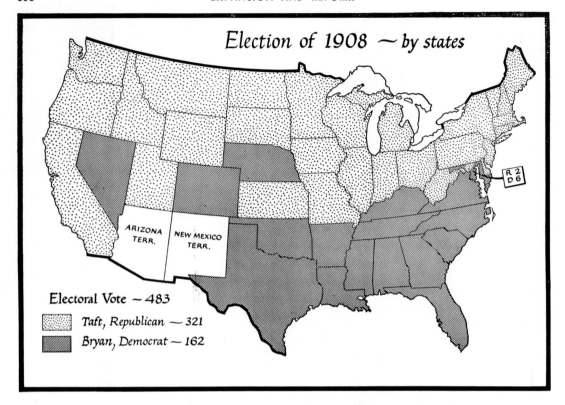

Election of 1908 — by states

ARIZONA
TERR.

NEW MEXICO
TERR.

R 2
D 6

Electoral Vote — 483

Taft, Republican — 321
Bryan, Democrat — 162

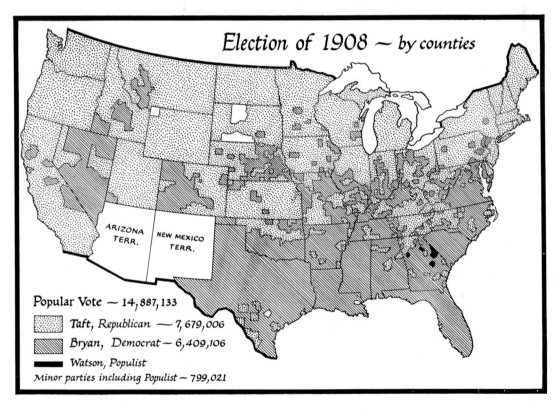

Election of 1908 — by counties

ARIZONA
TERR.

NEW MEXICO
TERR.

Popular Vote — 14,887,133

Taft, Republican — 7,679,006
Bryan, Democrat — 6,409,106
Watson, Populist
Minor parties including Populist — 799,021

Bibliography

The political history of this period is portrayed without embellishment in F. A. Ogg, *National Progress, 1907–1917* (1918); but with many embellishments in Sullivan, *Our Times*, II, *America Finding Herself* (1935); III, *Pre-War America* (1930); and IV, *The War Begins, 1909–1914* (1932). On Roosevelt's domestic policies, in addition to his *Autobiography*, and Pringle, *Theodore Roosevelt*, Harold Howland, *Theodore Roosevelt and His Times* (1921), is readable, but not very critical. P. C. Jessup, *Elihu Root* (2 vols., 1938), is admirably thorough, and useful for the entire period of Root's political activity. Roosevelt's administrations receive adequate treatment in several first-rate textbooks on the United States in the twentieth century: D. L. Dumond, *America in Our Time: 1896–1946* (1947); Harvey Wish, *Contemporary America: The National Scene since 1900* (1945); O. T. Barck, Jr., and N. M. Blake, *Since 1900* (new ed., 1952); F. R. Dulles, *Twentieth Century America* (1945); and L. M. Hacker and Helene S. Zahler, *The United States in the 20th Century* (1952).

The number of leading "muckrakers" was surprisingly small, and several of them have left important memoirs. Probably the best of these are Lincoln Steffens, *The Autobiography of Lincoln Steffens* (2 vols., 1931); F. C. Howe, *The Confessions of a Reformer* (1925); and Ray Stannard Baker, *American Chronicle: The Autobiography of Ray Stannard Baker* (1945). C. C. Regier, *The Era of the Muckrakers* (1932), is a book of careful scholarship, but not so well written as the wholly pessimistic John Chamberlain, *Farewell to Reform* (1932). On the large part played by the popular magazines, S. S. McClure, *My Autobiography* (1914), is very revealing. The whole period is admirably treated from the point of view of social reform in H. U. Faulkner, *The Quest for Social Justice, 1898–1914* (1931).

The first really cogent criticism by an American of the existing economic order came with the publication of H. D. Lloyd, *Wealth against Commonwealth* (1894, new ed., 1936). This is supplemented by a laudatory biography, Caro Lloyd, *Henry Demarest Lloyd* (2 vols., 1912). Further criticism was voiced by Thorstein Veblen, *The Theory of the Leisure Class* (1899); and *The Theory of Business Enterprise* (1904). Veblen's contribution is evaluated in Joseph Dorfman, *Thorstein Veblen and His America* (1934). On the other side, Ida M. Tarbell, *The Life of Elbert M. Gary: The Story of Steel* (1925), provides from the pen of a former "muckraker" a surprisingly friendly report on the activities of the United States Steel Corporation. Also useful on the world of business and finance are H. L. Wilgus, *A Study of the United States Steel Corporation in Its Industrial and Legal Aspects* (1901); Carl Hovey, *The Life Story of J. Pierpont Morgan* (1911); Lewis Corey, *The House of Morgan* (1930); and H. L. Satterlee, *J. Pierpont Morgan: An Intimate Portrait* (1939). On the relation between the government and the railroads, such biographies as Pyle, *James J. Hill*, already cited; and George Kennan, *E. H. Harriman: A Biography* (1922), are helpful. There are two early, but still useful, studies on the Northern Securities case: B. H. Meyer, *A History of the Northern Securities Case* (1906); and A. H. Walker, *History of the Sherman Law of the United States of America* (1910). On the labor side, Elsie Glück, *John Mitchell, Miner* (1929), gives an excellent account of the anthracite coal strike. See also John Lombardi, *Labor's Voice in the Cabinet* (1942).

An early and significant study of conservation is C. R. Van Hise, *The Conservation of Natural Resources in the United States* (1910). On the subject of irrigation, see F. H. Newell, *Irrigation in the United States* (1902); W. E. Smythe, *The Conquest of Arid America* (1905); and R. P. Teele, *Irrigation in the United States* (1915). On the general subject of federal land policies in the twentieth century, E. Louise Peffer, *The Closing of the Public Domain: Disposal and Reservation Policies, 1900–50* (1951), is a work of critical scholarship. C. C. Rister, *Oil! Titan of the Southwest* (1949), is descriptive and informative.

18

The Progressive Movement

The reform spirit — Socialism — Municipal reform — State reforms — LaFollette — Other crusaders — Labor legislation — Prohibition — Woman suffrage — Taft — Payne-Aldrich tariff — The Ballinger-Pinchot controversy — The fight on Cannonism — Roosevelt's return from Africa — Elections of 1910 — LaFollette's candidacy — Roosevelt's "hat in the ring" — Election of 1912

THE ROOSEVELT era saw the rise of a reform movement in the United States that affected **The reform spirit** every aspect of American life, state and local as well as national, social no less than political. Just as had been the case during the Jacksonian period, reform was in the air. Much of the momentum that the reform movement had attained came from the Populists, whose party had practically disappeared by the turn of the century, but whose principles had been espoused alike by Bryan Democracy and Roosevelt Republicanism. Paralleling the agrarian crusade, organized labor had called increasing attention to the inequalities visited upon the workers in the cities, and had emphasized the need for restraints upon the freedom of employers, particularly the great corporations, to deal with labor as if it were only a commodity. To this rising spirit of reform, the muckrakers, by providing new and exciting evidence for the use of all who had a cause to plead, contributed immeasurably. Of great significance, also, was the rise of socialism to a position of consequence in the American mind. Socialistic ideas had been brought to the United States, mainly by immigrants from Europe, far back in the nineteenth century, but only on the threshold of the twentieth century had American conditions become sufficiently comparable to those of Europe to make socialism seem plausible, even among the least favored of Americans. Before long, however, not only numbers of the underprivileged, but also many Americans of humanitarian bent whose personal lot was comfortable enough, were beginning to believe that the economic and political power enjoyed in the United States by a privileged few could not be reconciled with the American tradition of democracy, and boded no good for the future. Organized labor, in particular, although it consistently refused to encourage the formation of a strictly labor, or socialist, party, tended in many other matters to go along with the progress of socialist thought.

The first considerable growth of socialism in the United States began with the publication in 1888 of Bellamy's *Looking Backward*, which sold a million copies within a few years. Believers in Bellamy's theories **Socialism in the United States** formed themselves into "Nationalist Clubs" to promote socialism, but their views were mildness itself. "We advocate no sudden or ill-considered changes, we make no war upon individuals, we do not censure those who have accumulated fortunes," so the first Nationalist Club maintained. Far more aggressive was Daniel De Leon, an

Eugene V. Debs, five times an unsuccessful candidate for President on the Socialist ticket, had a far greater influence on American thought than his repeated defeats would seem to indicate. He was a forceful public speaker, and used the lecture platform, both during and between elections, to spread Socialist ideas. He also edited for a time the *Appeal to Reason*, a weekly paper through which much effective Socialist propaganda was disseminated. His greatest vote-getting achievements were in 1912 and 1920; in each case he polled over 900,000 votes. But the successes of Socialism came mainly through inducing the older parties to take up and put into effect Socialistic measures. To the right of the portrait, Debs is shown making a campaign address.

immigrant from the West Indies who believed that all compromise with capitalism served only to postpone the day of deliverance. De Leon revived the old Socialist-Labor Party that had been launched in the seventies, and beginning in 1892 it regularly nominated tickets in national campaigns. Toward the turn of the century De Leon's extreme radicalism led to a split in Socialist ranks, and in 1900 the Social Democratic or, as it was more commonly called, the Socialist Party, for the first time, but by no means the last, nominated Eugene V. Debs for the Presidency. Loyally supported by Morris Hillquit of New York, Victor L. Berger of Milwaukee, and other anti-Leonites, Debs polled 94,864 votes, nearly three times as many as his Socialist-Labor competitor. Four years later the Debs vote was 402,895, and in 1908 it was 420,890. Meantime the Socialist-Labor Party had lost ground rapidly.

The fundamental tenet of the Socialists was the abolition of the capitalist system in order to make way for the ownership by the public of all the means of production and distribution. This end they hoped ultimately to achieve by use of the ballot, rather than by revolution; nor did they "strive to substitute working-class rule for capitalist-class rule, but to free all humanity from class rule and to realize the international brotherhood of man." Pending more fundamental reforms, they were willing to support such halfway measures as public works for the relief of the unemployed, the collective ownership of the railroads, public utilities, and all existing national monopolies; the improvement of the industrial condition of the workers; the extension of inheritance taxes; a graduated income tax; woman suffrage; the initiative and the referendum; the abolition of the doctrine of judicial review; the election of judges by the people for short terms; and the enactment of further measures for general education and the conservation of health. Many so-called socialistic policies had an ancestry quite separate from the Socialist Party, but whatever their origin they had a way of seeping gradually over into the old-party platforms. The dying Populists conceded that Roosevelt had put more of their principles into effect than they could ever have believed possible without a Populist victory; the Socialists did not mean to die, but some of their views had received the earnest support of Roosevelt, and they hoped for similar favors from Taft.

It was in the local field rather than in national affairs, however, that the reform **Municipal** movement made its first sub-**reform** stantial gains. The evils of the Tammany machine in New York had been long in the limelight, and efforts to diminish its corrupt hold on the city's government reached back as far as the days of Samuel J. Tilden. But what went on in New York was no worse than could be found in almost every other large American city. Nearly everywhere crooked deals in the awarding of contracts and franchises, open or secret alliances with commercialized vice, and the protection of favored classes of criminals who paid well for their privileges were only the worst of the sins of the politicians in charge. As with Tammany Hall, the machine could count on the support of thousands of voters who received in return for their ballots a feeling of security. If a worker lost his job, got into trouble with the law, needed money to meet an emergency, or faced any personal crisis whatever, he went to his local leader for help, and got it. To make surer of success at the polls, however, ballot-boxes were stuffed, returns were falsified, and a thousand irregularities were condoned. Lincoln Steffens's articles made the "shame of the cities" better known than ever before, but reformers had already arisen. In Toledo Samuel M. Jones, better known as "Golden Rule" Jones, made successful war upon the private-contract system, and advocated the municipal ownership of public utilities. Elected to office in 1897, he was repeatedly re-elected, and in 1904 was succeeded by his friend and disciple, Brand Whitlock, who continued the good work. In Cleveland Thomas L. Johnson became mayor in 1901. A convinced "single-taxer," he secured among other reforms a long-overdue reassessment of property values, municipal control of the street-car system, and a three-cent fare. Under his régime Cleveland could claim to be the "best governed city in the United States," a claim that Milwaukee, under the Socialist leadership of Emil Seidel and Daniel W. Hoan, was soon to challenge.

To many thoughtful critics the reform of city government could best be promoted by a change in the system. City administration was primarily a business affair; why should it be hampered by a form of government patterned after that of the United States? Why should the Democrats and the Republicans run opposing tickets for city offices? What difference did it make whether a candidate for mayor or alderman believed in a high tariff or a low tariff, in imperialism or in isolation, in free silver or the single gold standard? In 1901 the city of Galveston, Texas, which the year before had been destroyed by a tidal wave and was in desperate need of efficiency in government, tried to obtain it by turning over the whole problem to a commission of five, each of whom would administer under rules laid down by a majority vote some department of city affairs. Soon many other cities were experimenting with the "commission form" of government, and out of it grew an even more reasonable scheme, the "city manager" plan. This system sought to duplicate the methods of the business corporation. The elected board or commission employed a manager, who ran the city with the same freedom of action that was normally accorded a business executive. Soon hundreds of American cities, large or small, were being administered, usually more efficiently than ever before, by commissions and city managers. Thousands, however, adhered to the old systems, and in all too many instances to the old ways.

Even more significant than the changes wrought in city government were those that in this same period revolution- **State** ized the government of the **reforms** states. State governors, each with a vision of reform, vied with Roosevelt during his Presidency for the limelight, and some of them had begun their efforts even earlier. They found the state governments almost completely in the control of whatever big business corporations happened to be most powerful in their particular part of the country. Well-oiled party machines in each state did the bidding of the state "boss," and the "boss" in turn did the bidding of the business interests that furnished the oil for his machine. Speaking before the New York Constitutional Convention of 1915, Elihu Root, an excellent authority, remarked:

Mr. Platt ruled the state; for nigh upon twenty years he ruled it. It was not the governor; it was not the legislature; it was Mr. Platt. And the capital was not here [at Albany]: it was at 49 Broadway. . . . The ruler of the state during the greater part of the forty years of my acquaintance with the state government has not been any man authorized by the constitution or by law. . . . The party leader is elected by no one, accountable to no one, bound by no oath of office, removable by no one. . . . I don't criticize the men of the invisible government. . . . But it is all wrong.

For a reformer to be elected to a governorship under such conditions was in itself a revolution; once in office his only chance of remaining there was to break the power of the machine.

Outstanding among the reform governors was Robert M. LaFollette (1855–1925) of **Robert M.** Wisconsin, a man whose influ- **LaFollette** ence upon the course of political events during his lifetime was more fundamental than that of many Presidents. "Fighting Bob," as he came to be called, had entered politics, without benefit of machine assistance, soon after his graduation from the University of Wisconsin in 1879. As county prosecutor of Dane County he made an excellent record, and in 1884 was nominated and elected for the first of three successive terms in the national House of Representatives. He was an indefatigable canvasser, delighted in controversy, and developed political speechmaking into a fine art. Like

many another Republican he was left at home by the election of 1890, and but for a controversy with the all-powerful Senator Philetus Sawyer, who was both a politician and a lumber baron, his ambitions for a career in state politics might easily have been gratified. When the Democrats took over the government of Wisconsin in 1891, they found that for years the Republican state treasurers had made a practice of depositing the state's funds, interest free, in certain favored banks. The new attorney-general promptly brought suit to recover this interest money for the state, and Sawyer, because he had acted as bondsman for the treasurers, came in for his share of the trouble. According to the LaFollette version of the story, Sawyer attempted through LaFollette to bribe the judge before whom the case was to be tried — a Democratic brother-in-law of LaFollette's. Deeply incensed, LaFollette made the whole matter public, and helped the state recover the funds of which it had been defrauded.

From that time on LaFollette was a crusader for reform. Determined to win the governorship, he was repeatedly denied the nomination in spite of a growing popular sentiment in his favor; not until 1900 was he able to line up a majority of the convention delegates. Elected, and twice re-elected, he forced through reluctant legislatures laws for the more effective taxation of the railroads and other corporations; for the establishment of direct primaries through which the people, not boss-ridden conventions, could select their own candidates for office; for the termination of the free-pass evil by prohibiting state officials from accepting them; and for the conservation of the natural resources of the state in forests and water-power. In his quest of good government he enlisted the aid of experts from the University of Wisconsin, whose new president, Charles R. Van Hise, was his close personal friend and his choice for the office. He was instrumental, also, in the creation of a Legislative Reference Bureau through which legislators might obtain expert advice on the drafting of bills.

Senator Robert M. LaFollette, Sr., in a characteristic pose, addressing a group gathered on a city sidewalk.

The "Wisconsin idea," which was fundamentally to free the state from business domination **Other crusaders** through venal party bosses and to turn over public administration to popularly chosen leaders willing to seek the advice of experts, exactly suited the temper of the times. Other governors in other states duplicated in varying degrees the LaFollette record in Wisconsin. In Missouri Joseph W. Folk won public attention as circuit attorney by successfully prosecuting the corrupt ring of St. Louis "boodlers" that for years had fattened on municipal graft. As governor for four years after 1905, he sought with moderate success to repeat in the state arena what he had done for his home city. In New York Charles Evans Hughes, as already noted, won deserved acclaim as counsel for a legislative investigating committee that examined into the methods of the New York life insurance companies. Hughes's sensational disclosures brought about a revolution in the insurance business and led to his election as governor in 1906. Out in California the star of Hiram Johnson began to rise. As early as 1902 he attracted attention as a member of the staff of prosecuting attorneys in charge of some San Francisco "boodling" cases. In 1908 he

secured the conviction of Abe Ruef, grafting municipal boss of San Francisco, after Francis J. Heney, the original prosecutor, had been shot in the line of duty. In 1910 Johnson was elected governor, determined above all else to end the domination of the state by the Southern Pacific Railroad.

The roll of reform governors was a long one, including, besides such prominent individuals as A. B. Cummins of Iowa and John A. Johnson of Minnesota, many lesser lights whose names never became nationally well known. Private individuals, such as William S. U'Ren of Oregon, crusader for "the Oregon system," also took a hand, while the public at large, fully aroused by the revelations of the muckrakers, demanded and obtained results.

The most fundamental of the political reforms effected during these years was the substitution of the direct primary **The direct** for the convention system of **primary** making nominations. Under the old system only a small fraction of the voters, certainly never more than fifteen per cent, attended the original caucuses or "primaries" by which convention delegates were chosen. A large proportion of those who attended were local office-holders and aspirants to office.

It was thus easy for the machine to secure a working majority of the delegates to almost every convention, and to put through the "slate" of nominees agreed upon by the leaders in advance. The direct primary, however, substituted voting at the polls by secret ballot for the caucus-convention system, and reduced immeasurably the chances of machine manipulation. Within a comparatively short time after the passage in 1903 of the Wisconsin primary law, similar laws had been enacted by nearly every state in the Union. The results were revolutionary. It would be idle to claim that the direct primaries completely eliminated either business domination of government or the power of venal party bosses. But the new laws greatly promoted the possibility of successful popular uprisings against corrupt machines, and because of them in state after state men were elected to office who under the old system would never have had a chance.

The initiative and referendum were twin measures of popular government that might

Initiative and referendum

be used as clubs over legislatures unresponsive to the popular will. By these devices laws could be initiated by petition, and voted on by ballot. The use of the referendum for constitutional provisions and for such local legislation as the flotation of bond issues was by no means new, but its application to ordinary law-making, coupled with the power of popular initiative, was decidedly an innovation. The initiative and referendum were first adopted in South Dakota, in 1898, but obtained their best test in Oregon, where from 1902 to 1910 no less than thirty-two measures were referred to the people for a vote. In Oregon, too, the recall, a measure by which faithless officials, on petition of a stipulated number or percentage of the voters, were required to stand for re-election at special elections, was given a thorough trial. Indeed, "the Oregon system" came to be the term most commonly used to describe the new adventures in popular government. Largely because of U'Ren's effective leadership, Oregon had adopted the Australian ballot in 1891, a

registration law in 1899, the initiative and referendum law in 1902, the direct primary in 1904, a sweeping corrupt practices act in 1908, and the recall in 1910. "In Oregon," so it was said, "the state government is divided into four departments — the executive, judicial, legislative, and U'Ren — and it is still an open question who exerts the more power." Within a decade nearly twenty states had the initiative and referendum, and nearly a dozen the recall. Acceptance of "the Oregon system" moved in general from west to east, and in the older states often met unyielding opposition.

That even the federal government might be affected by state reforms was proved when preferential primaries were in-

Direct election of senators

troduced whereby the voters might express their choices for United States senators. These laws assumed that in senatorial elections state legislatures would be guided solely by the popular mandate, and regardless of personal or party considerations would elect the primary winner to the senatorship. The movement for direct election of United States senators dated far back into the nineteenth century, and had won warm support not only from off-color politicians such as the Populists, but from many conservative citizens as well. Four times, in 1894, 1898, 1900, and 1902, the national House of Representatives had supported a constitutional amendment for the direct election of senators, but each time the Senate had refused to concur. Meantime the scandals involved in legislative elections became increasingly evident. At best state legislation tended to be treated as of secondary importance in years when a senator was to be chosen; at worst open bribery was resorted to by individuals and corporations bent on the success of a candidate friendly to their interests.

Undoubtedly the framers of the Constitution had intended that the upper chamber should represent not merely the individual states, but also the wealth of the nation. They had builded better than they knew. By the twentieth century the United States

TEMPERANCE SOCIETY. Parade of members during a demonstration, 1876.

PROHIBITION SYMBOL. Detail from a cartoon by Rollin Kirby, 1920.

ANTI-SALOON POSTER. Young boy being led by Guardian Angel, avoiding evil temptations. Drawing by P. Krafft.

Senate could be spoken of, not without a semblance of truth, as a "millionaire's club." Men of great wealth aspired to a seat in it as a crowning evidence of success. Corporations with privileges to protect made every effort to secure a senatorship for one of their directors, or at least for one of their attorneys. Party bosses themselves often sought and obtained election to the Senate. The general level of intelligence in the upper chamber therefore was high — has perhaps never been higher — but the senators, so critics insisted, represented the vested interests of the country rather than the people as a whole. Naturally the Senate refused, as long as it dared, to risk the results of popular election. But the preferential primaries, which eventually were adopted by more than half the states, brought about by indirection the change that the Senate had tried to avoid. Further, as popularly chosen senators took their seats, the opposition to direct election was broken down. By 1912 the Senate submitted to the inevitable and agreed to the Seventeenth Amendment, which a year later became a part of the Constitution.

The reforms of the Roosevelt era in state and city government greatly facilitated the efforts of those who wished to enlist the aid of the law in the improvement of social conditions. No longer so deferential to the rich

Prohibition advocates believed in the righteousness of their cause with an intensity of conviction reminiscent of the abolitionist crusade. When at last their goal had been achieved, and national prohibition became a fact, the discovery that liquor could still be illegally manufactured and sold in great quantity came as a real shock. In the end the failure of enforcement led to the recall of the Eighteenth Amendment by the Twenty-first.

SPEAK-EASIES. Signs such as this were numerous after passage of the Eighteenth Amendment

man's point of view, and unhampered by the constitutional limitations that so restricted the activities of the national government, the states crowded their statute books with laws that had rarely or never been obtainable before. A large part of the new legislation was designed to promote the "square deal" for labor, but other important subjects, particularly the prohibition of the liquor traffic, received careful consideration.

Most important of the new labor legislation, perhaps, was the series of employer's **Labor legislation** liability, or workmen's compensation, acts that followed Maryland's first feeble beginning in this direction in 1902. These laws were designed to reverse the old common-law rule that a work-man had to prove negligence on the part of his employer in order to obtain compensation for injuries, and that even this might be insufficient if he himself, or any "fellow-servant," had been guilty of contributory negligence. The new principle, which by 1921 had been accepted in all but six states, was that in hazardous occupations the employer was liable for all injuries that occurred to his employees while they were at work. As a result of the new laws millions of dollars were soon paid out each year in benefits to injured workmen or their families.

Efforts were made also to increase the protection given to women and children in industry. Most of the states eventually adopted laws forbidding in certain types of industry the employment of children under fourteen years of age, while laws for compulsory school attendance accomplished the same purpose in another way. Opposition from the southern textile industries caused some of the southern states to lag either in the enactment or in the enforcement of child-labor laws, and as early as 1906 a movement was begun to give Congress authority over child labor by a constitutional amendment. Such an amendment was actually submitted in 1924, but it failed of ratification. Laws limiting the number of hours per day that women and children might be employed, and fixing minimum-wage schedules that they must be paid, were also enacted by some of the states. Attempts to extend these same principles to employed men met with stronger opposition, but a few successes were recorded. In the whole field of labor legislation the United States lagged far behind European nations. Unemployment insurance and old-age pensions, for example, while common enough elsewhere, were hardly more than talked about in the United States.

Attempts by prohibitionists to do away with the liquor traffic date far back into the nineteenth century, but the era **Prohibition** of successful activity began with the formation of the Anti-Saloon League in 1893. This organization received the active support of all the evangelical denominations, and was maintained by the funds its agents were permitted to collect at regular church services. Its methods came to be quite as hard-boiled as those of the politicians with whom it had to deal. It knew one test, and only one test, for fitness to hold office. If a man favored the liquor traffic, the Anti-Saloon League was against him; if he opposed the liquor traffic, the Anti-Saloon League was for him. With a budget that by 1903 had reached four hundred thousand dollars a year, the League was in a position to hire hundreds of organizers and to maintain scores of offices. For a generation, under the leadership of Wayne B. Wheeler and William H. Anderson, it made the issue, "wet" or "dry," take precedence over nearly every other issue in state and local politics. As between low license and high license, the League favored high license. As between high license and "local option," whereby a town or county might vote to exclude saloons, it favored local option. As between local option and state-wide prohibition, it favored state-wide prohibition. And as between state-wide prohibition and national prohibition, it favored national prohibition. Never too squeamish about its methods or its political bedfellows, it took what it could get.

It got a great deal. The liquor business was open to attack for all the same reasons that other big businesses were vulnerable, and for many more besides. A veritable barrage of tracts, sermons, orations, and temperance journals set forth its shortcomings with a degree of passionate intolerance reminiscent of the abolitionists. The efforts of brewers, distillers, and wine-makers to obtain business favors from legislatures, county boards, and city councils were skillfully used to classify the liquor interests with the corruptionists. Local liquor dealers' associations were taunted as defenders of lawlessness and vice, and crooked politics was traced with an unerring eye to the door of the saloon. In the South the mistakes of the Negro were blamed upon liquor, and prohibition was demanded as a necessary preliminary to good relations between the races. While Roosevelt was President the successes of the Anti-Saloon League were mainly confined to the rural districts and were obtained by local option, but before he left office four southern states had voted dry, and within the next few years many others, northern as well as southern, were to follow. By the time the First World War broke out, nearly half the people of the United States lived in "dry" territory, while in three fourths of its total area the saloon had been outlawed. The ratification of the Eighteenth Amendment to the Constitution in 1919 merely completed a process that had been long under way.

Woman suffrage was a companion reform

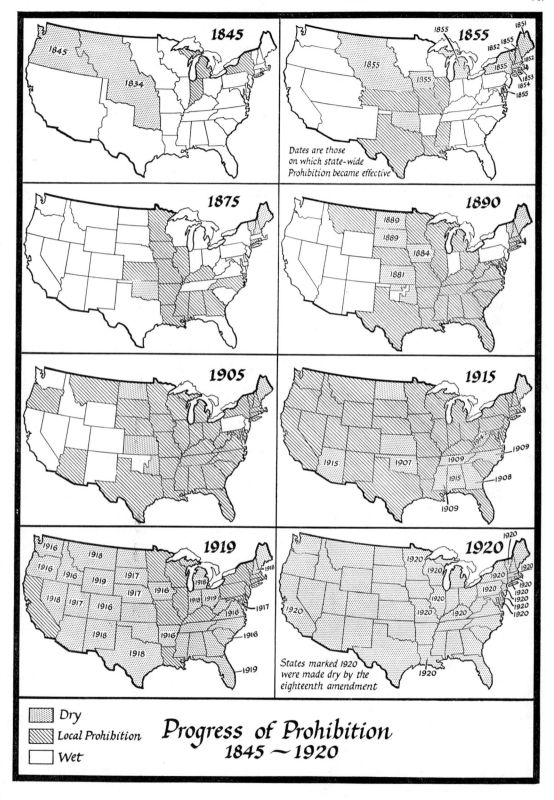

Progress of Prohibition
1845 — 1920

to prohibition. If women obtained the vote,

Woman suffrage so prohibitionists reasoned, they would with certainty aid the temperance cause. In 1869 the Territory of Wyoming had conferred the suffrage on women, and by 1911 six western states, Wyoming, Colorado, Utah, Idaho, Washington, and California, had accepted the innovation *in toto*, while many other states gave women the right to vote in certain elections. Like the prohibitionists the suffragists hoped to crown their efforts by obtaining an amendment to the Constitution that would end the denial of the suffrage to women, and, while adding state after state to their list of converts, they continued to work on Congress. An outbreak of "militancy," borrowed from Great Britain during the First World War, may have had something to do with bringing Congress to yield in 1919. The Nineteenth Amendment became a part of the Constitution in 1920.

The movements for prohibition and woman suffrage carried along in their wake a great variety of reforms designed to promote the public health and happiness. New building

"Congratulations." Symbolic cover of *Life* published October 28, 1920, when national women's suffrage became law.

codes were devised, and public parks and playgrounds were multiplied. Renewed efforts were made to wipe out gambling and prostitution. Special courts were established to deal with the problem of juvenile delinquency. Divorce laws were relaxed. Legal discriminations against women, aside from the suffrage, were brought near the vanishing point. Most of these laws, like prohibition and the labor codes, depended for their constitutionality upon the "police power"; that is, the right of the state to do whatever might be necessary to promote the health, happiness, and morality of its citizens. Such laws frequently interfered seriously with the full freedom of individuals, and led to an enormous amount of litigation. The courts, almost invariably hostile in the beginning, eventually relented, and in nearly every instance granted a grudging approval to the measures that the public desired.

When Taft took office as President in 1909, the reform spirit was at high pitch, and reformers confidently expected that the new administra-   **Taft takes office** tion would carry forward actively the program Roosevelt had begun. In his inaugural address Taft pledged himself to such a course, and in making up his cabinet he chose three of Roosevelt's chief advisers. Philander C. Knox, once Roosevelt's "trust-busting" Attorney-General, but now a Senator from Pennsylvania, became Secretary of State, while George von L. Meyer, Roosevelt's Postmaster-General, took over the Navy Department, and James Wilson stayed on as Secretary of Agriculture. "Never before in our time," said the New York *Tribune*, "has the entry of a new President into office marked so slight a break politically between the present and the past." In order the better to give his successor a free hand, Roosevelt took off immediately on a hunt for big game in Africa, and for a full year was lost to the civilized world. Persistent rumors of a rift between the outgoing and the incoming President were denied by their public behavior, and by a private letter from Taft to Roosevelt just before inauguration.

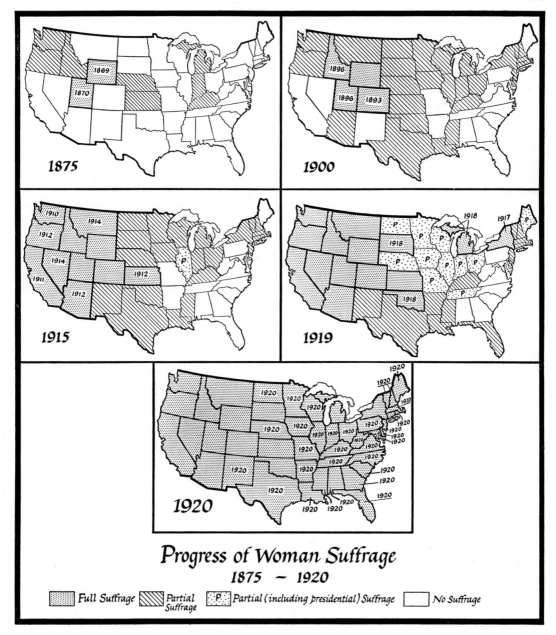

Progress of Woman Suffrage
1875 — 1920

Full Suffrage | Partial Suffrage | P. Partial (including presidential) Suffrage | No Suffrage

"You and I know that there has not been the slightest difference between us."

Tariff revision had certainly never been one of the Roosevelt policies. Roosevelt had occasionally toyed with the idea, but he had always found some excuse for avoiding an issue fraught with so many political perils. The chief demand for revision came from the middle-western agrarians who had discovered at last that high duties on manufactured articles not only increased the prices of the things they had to buy, but by limiting imports closed to agriculture many foreign markets. From about 1902 on the "Iowa idea," which called insistently for lower duties, had gained momentum. During the campaign there had been much talk of the tariff as the "mother of the trusts," and both parties had pledged themselves to do something about it. The Democratic pledge was

Nelson W. Aldrich, the outstanding Republican in the Senate, was generally regarded as the champion of the "moneyed interests."

provided for moderate reductions downward, but everyone knew that the Senate would rewrite the measure throughout. They knew, too, that the Senate was still far less responsive to the public will than the House. In the latter an increasingly large number of members owed their seats to the new direct primaries, but no such transformation had altered the character of the Senate. Only a few states had as yet adopted senatorial primaries, and in any event the six-year term for senators made the upper chamber, quite as the "founding fathers" had intended, extremely resistant to change. The chairman of the Senate Committee on Finance was Nelson W. Aldrich of Rhode Island, a man of brilliant intellect, but a multi-millionaire industrialist whose views on the tariff were the views of his class. Respected and feared by his colleagues, Aldrich was as nearly the political "boss" of the United States as any one man could be.

Aldrich's committee attached hundreds of amendments to the Payne Bill, very few of which reduced duties downward. Some of the new provisions were "jokers," which by changing specific duties to *ad valorem*, or *vice versa*, or in some other unapparent way, covered up cleverly a sharp revision upward. Regardless of intent to deceive, which was the exception rather than the rule, the bill was complicated and needed careful study to be understood; but Aldrich proposed to "railroad" it through the Senate by making it the sole order of business until passed. At this point a little group of middle-western Republican insurgents, led by Senator La-Follette of Wisconsin interrupted Aldrich's plans by a prolonged debate that revealed to the whole country exactly what was going on. LaFollette, ably assisted by Dolliver and Cummins of Iowa, Beveridge of Indiana, Bristow of Kansas, Clapp of Minnesota, and a few others, studied the bill by night and debated it by day. They were unable to prevent its passage, but ten of them joined with the Democrats in refusing to vote for it.

Taft, meantime, had at first encouraged

the more specific: "We favor immediate revision of the tariff by the reduction of import duties." The Republicans declared themselves "unequivocally for a revision of the tariff by a special session of Congress," but neglected entirely to be unequivocal as to whether they meant revision up or revision down. What they wanted, they said, was "the imposition of such duties as will equal the difference between the cost of production at home and abroad, together with a reasonable profit to American industry." This might, of course, mean anything or nothing just as Congress chose, and Taft was pressed to state whether the Republicans intended merely to revise the tariff or to revise it downward. Not so skilled in evasiveness as the platform-makers, he promised with complete candor that there would be revision downward.

Time was soon to prove that the promise was easier than the performance. Taft called **Payne-Aldrich Tariff** Congress into special session for March 15, and on April 9 the Payne Bill, already well formulated when Congress met, passed the House of Representatives by a strict party vote. Reformers were somewhat surprised that the bill, although frankly protectionist, really

the insurgents, thinking that they might ob-
Taft and tain a better bill, but finally, dis-
the tariff mayed at the prospect of a split
in his party, had joined forces with the conservative majority. The Payne-Aldrich Bill
that emerged from the joint House and
Senate conference committee was a complete
betrayal of Taft's campaign promises, but
he signed it nevertheless. It provided for
more decreases than increases in duties, but
the decreases were rarely on items of significance, and far more duties were left un-
touched than were changed. The average
rate on dutiable goods was about one per
cent higher under the new law than under
the Dingley Act of 1897. Taft's attitude
amazed and disappointed the public, which
during the preceding regime had become accustomed to presidential leadership, and had
expected him to bring enough pressure to
bear on Congress to get what he and the
country wanted. But Taft, as an able constitutional lawyer, had more respect for the
legislative independence of Congress than
Roosevelt had ever had; besides, he was
good-humored and peace-loving, whereas
Roosevelt was never happier than in the
midst of an "elegant row."

While Taft himself regarded some of the
bill, particularly the woolens schedule, as
indefensible, there were parts of it that were
legitimately entitled to praise. The European system of maximum-minimum rates,
which it incorporated, enabled the President
to apply a higher schedule of rates against
nations discriminating against American
trade. A bipartisan tariff board was also
established, the duty of which was to study
the relative costs of production at home and
abroad and to give Congress expert advice
as to the rates it should set. Furthermore, a
one per cent tax on the net income of corporations in excess of five thousand dollars opened
up new possibilities both for the production
of revenue and for the use of taxation as a
means of regulation.

Separately adopted, but related to the
tariff by its bearing on national finance, was
a resolution submitting to the states a constitutional amendment for the legalization
of a federal income tax. Submitted on
July 12, 1909, the Sixteenth Amendment was
fully ratified and declared in force on February 25, 1913, just before Taft left office.

Taft, painfully aware of his ebbing popularity, sought by a "swing around the circle"
to rehabilitate himself with his **Taft's**
western critics. In the fall of **Winona**
1909 he traveled sixteen thou- **address**
sand miles, and spoke repeatedly to large,
but unenthusiastic, audiences. At Winona,
Minnesota, he made the strategic blunder of
defending the Payne-Aldrich Tariff, insisting that it was the best tariff bill that the
Republican Party had ever passed. Had he
apologized for it as the best bill he could get,
he might have won the sympathy of the
West, but his outspoken support of the de-
tested measure convinced his hearers that
he was party to the betrayal of his own
promises. What chance had the Roosevelt
policies for survival under the leadership of
such a man?

Circumstances soon made it appear that
on the subject of conservation the new President was no more to be trusted than on the

"Tangled." Protest against the protectionist
Payne-Aldrich tariff act was vigorous but in-
effective. Cartoon by C. R. Macauley in the
New York World, April 5, 1909.

Richard A. Ballinger, Secretary of the Interior under Taft, became known, quite unfairly, as a foe of conservation.

tariff. Taft's Secretary of the Interior, R.

**The Bal-
linger-
Pinchot
controversy** A. Ballinger of Washington, was not unaware of the skepticism common to his section about the retardation of western development for the benefit of generations yet unborn. Nevertheless, his actions in reopening to private exploitation some water-power sites in Montana and Wyoming and in permitting the alienation of certain valuable coal lands in Alaska were undoubtedly due to legal scruple rather than to unconcern about conservation. As President, Roosevelt was accustomed to follow the dictates of his conscience, if no law stood in the way, whereas Ballinger and Taft both felt obliged to seek legal justification for their acts. Ballinger's behavior was vigorously protested during the summer and fall of 1909 by one of his subordinates, Louis R. Glavis, and by the chief of the forestry service, Gifford Pinchot, whose division lay within the Department of Agriculture. Taft, after careful investigation, decided that there was nothing against Ballinger, and dismissed both Glavis and Pinchot from office. In the case of Pinchot, he took action with great reluctance, for Pinchot, as everyone knew, was a close friend of Roosevelt's. Dismissal, however, was an administrative necessity, for Pinchot by writing Senator Dolliver in defense of Glavis had violated a rule prohibiting subordinates from corresponding directly with members of Congress. "There is only one thing for you to do," Senator Root had told the President, "and that you must do at once." But to the ever more hostile public Taft had lined up with the anti-conservationists. Even when Ballinger was frozen out of the cabinet a year later, it made little difference. Taft had been elected to carry out the Roosevelt policies, and he was carrying them out "on a stretcher."

Hard on the heels of the Pinchot-Ballinger controversy came an outburst of insurgency in the House of Representatives. **Insurgency in the House** When conservative Republicans in the House had tried to block an investigation of the Interior Department, a group of Republican insurgents had voted with the Democrats in favor of it, and had discovered that with Democratic cooperation they could control the House. This newly found power they now determined to use against the autocratic sway of the Speaker, Joseph G. Cannon of Illinois, an ultra-conservative who consistently and effectively stood in the way of all progressive legislation. From the early days of the republic the Speaker had been permitted to appoint all committees of the House, designating also the chairmen. This privilege gave him enormous power to punish the recalcitrant and to reward the faithful. Also, as dominant member of the Rules Committee, composed of only five members, he followed the precedents of "Czar" Reed in determining the course of legislation; without his consent it was all but impossible even to bring a measure to a vote. Discontent with "Cannonism" had been apparent in the first session after Taft's inauguration, when twelve Republican members voted against Cannon for the speakership, and a still larger number voted with the Democrats against the rules which gave him his power. The tariff battle and the uproar over conservation brought new recruits to the insurgents, and by March, 1910, they were ready for a new test of strength.

Ably led by Representative George W. Norris of Nebraska, they presented an amend-**Revision of** ment to the House rules de-**the House** signed to take the appointment **rules** of the Rules Committee out of the hands of the Speaker, and to make it elective by the House. With every parliamentary weapon in his power, Cannon and his conservative Republican supporters met the onslaught, and one session lasted continuously for twenty-six hours. But Norris proved to be quite as adroit as the Speaker, and the combination of Democrats and insurgent Republicans held together. On the final vote about forty Republicans joined the Democrats in voting to change the rules. Cannon, acknowledging defeat, offered his resignation as Speaker, but with his powers curtailed he was permitted to keep his post. When the next Congress met, the rules were still further amended. All committees were made elective, with the Ways and Means Committee acting as a committee on committees. The changes wrought were fundamental. No longer could it be said that the Speaker, next to the President, was the most powerful of American officials; moreover, the chief agency for maintaining party discipline in the House was destroyed. More and more members felt free to vote as their consciences or their constituents might direct, regardless of party pressure.

With insurgency rampant both in the Senate and the House, it was obvious that the party split which Taft had sought to avoid had come about. On the one hand were the conservatives led by Aldrich and Cannon, a faction with which the President, willy-nilly, had come to be allied. On the other hand were the insurgents, who stood for popular, not boss, control of the party, and believed that when the direct primary was established in every state their faction would be in the majority rather than in the minority. They stood also for real tariff revision, for genuine conservation, and for the expansion of governmental control over trusts and railroads. For leadership they looked beyond Norris and LaFollette to Africa:

Teddy, come home and blow your horn,
The sheep's in the meadow, the cow's in the corn.
The boy you left to 'tend the sheep
Is under the haystack fast asleep.[1]

On March 14, 1910, the Roosevelt hunting party disbanded at Khartum in the Anglo-Egyptian Sudan. Not without some assistance, Roosevelt had accounted for nine lions, five elephants, thirteen rhinoceroses, seven hippopotamuses, and no less than two hundred and sixty-two other specimens. In Egypt he observed the symptoms of mounting discontent, and two months later in London he told the British either to get out of there or else to stay in and do their duty. In Italy he missed an audience with the Pope because the Holy Father insisted on knowing in advance that Roosevelt would not visit the Methodist mission in Rome; for good measure the ex-President passed up the Methodists also, but he met the King and Queen. In Austria-Hungary he was banqueted by the Emperor; in Germany he helped the Kaiser review his army; in England, as the official representative of the United States at the funeral of Edward VII, he vied for attention with all the assembled royalty, dead and alive. He delivered carefully prepared addresses at the Sorbonne, at Christiania, at Berlin, and at Oxford. And between times he read letters and newspapers from home that featured the Taft betrayal. He had, too, more direct information; Gifford Pinchot had crossed the ocean to meet him on the *White Nile*.

Back in his country home at Oyster Bay, New York, Roosevelt maintained a discreet neutrality. "I shall make no **Roosevelt's** speeches or say anything for two **return** months," he wrote Taft in response to a letter of welcome, "but I shall keep my mind as

[1] *Life*, May 26, 1910, quoted in Mark Sullivan, *Our Times*, IV, 441.

open as I keep my mouth shut." LaFollette
called on the ex-President, and reported that
he was "very much pleased" with his visit.
Roosevelt saw other insurgents, also, but he
paid a friendly call on the President at his
summer home in Beverly, Massachusetts,
and he wrote in the *Outlook*, to which he had
become a contributing editor, that the Payne-
Aldrich Tariff was a definite improvement
over either the Dingley Act or the Wilson
Act. As for the dismissal of Pinchot, he had
written Lodge from Europe that he was "not
yet sure whether Taft could . . . have followed any course save the one he did."

Probably Roosevelt wished above all else
to heal the breach in the Republican Party,
for he knew full well that the alternative was
a Democratic victory, not only in the mid-
term elections of 1910, but also in 1912, and
he sincerely believed that the Democratic
Party was incapable of governing the country. It was with party success in view, not
the discomfiture of Taft, that in August,
1910, he took the temporary chairmanship of
the New York state nominating convention
away from Vice-President Sherman, whom
the conservatives had favored, and helped in
the nomination of a liberal candidate,
Henry L. Stimson, on a liberal platform for
governor. Only by such a course, he believed, could the Republicans hope to hold
the party together and maintain their control
of the state. He made two speech-making
tours, one through the West and another
through the South, as he thought in the interest of party harmony and Republican success at the polls. At Osawatomie, Kansas,
he gave a name, the New Nationalism, to the
principles for which he stood, and to which
he believed that he had committed the Republican Party. While the direction of his
sympathies was apparent, he made numerous
efforts to conciliate the conservatives. With
even-handed justice he endorsed Beveridge
the insurgent for re-election to the Senate
from Indiana, and Warren Gamaliel Harding, a consistent conservative, for the governorship of Ohio. In his address before the
New York Convention he praised the ac-

New States

complishments of the Taft administration in
the highest terms, and in September he again
called on the President.

All this was of no avail, for the country
was in a mood to rebuke the Republicans by
voting the Democratic ticket. **Elections**
Stimson, Beveridge, and Hard- **of 1910**
ing alike went down to defeat, and the House
of Representatives fell to the Democrats with
229 members to 161 for the Republicans and
one for the Socialists, Victor L. Berger of
Milwaukee. The Senate remained Republican by a vote of 51 to 41, but this majority
was so slender that the insurgents, of whom
there were a dozen or more, by voting with
the Democrats, could easily overturn it. The
conservative Republicans had thus lost control of both houses of Congress. In the states
the trend was equally pronounced. Not only
in New York and Ohio, but in such regularly
Republican centers as Massachusetts, Connecticut, and New Jersey, the Democrats
emerged triumphant.

There can be no doubt that the election
was intended as a rebuke to the Taft admin-

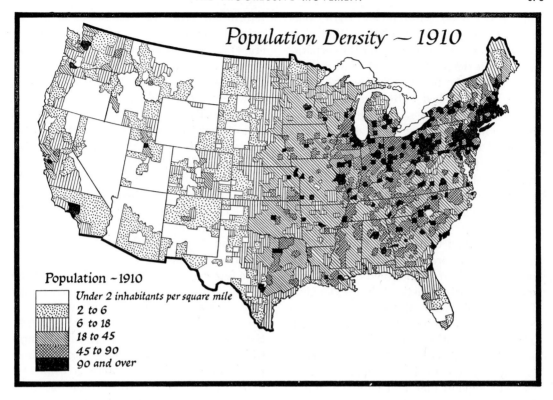

Population Density ~ 1910

Population ~1910

Under 2 inhabitants per square mile
2 to 6
6 to 18
18 to 45
45 to 90
90 and over

istration, but in many ways it was unde-served. In reality, Taft had carried out the Roosevelt policies with considerable success. He had secured a revision of the tariff, something that Roosevelt had not even dared to attempt. He had prosecuted the trusts with vigor and persistence; before his administration ended he had brought more than twice as many suits against them as were undertaken by Roosevelt. He had sponsored the Mann-Elkins Act of 1910, which gave the Interstate Commerce Commission jurisdiction over terminals and services of communication by telegraph, telephone, and cable. It also placed upon the carriers the burden of proving the justice of contemplated changes, for under its terms the commission might suspend new rates for ten months, pending investigation. It included, too, a plan that was essentially Taft's own, to create a special Commerce Court, composed of experts in the law of commerce, to which appeals from the decisions of the commission might be made. Taft's services to conservation were similarly

notable. He replaced Pinchot by the head of the Yale School of Forestry, who added to the national forests by the purchase of timbered tracts in the Appalachians. Taft also got authority from Congress that Roosevelt lacked to withdraw coal lands from entry, and he was the first President to withdraw oil lands. Other reform measures enacted during the Taft administration, but generally ignored by his critics, included the improvement of the public land laws; the requirement of safety appliances on railroads; the establishment of a Bureau of Mines charged among other things with the duty of studying the welfare of the miners; a postal savings law; a parcels post law; and the separation of the Department of Commerce and Labor into two departments.

Much of Taft's unpopularity may be attributed to his political ineptitude, and much of it merely to hard luck. He **Taft's** got little credit for the reforms **political** of the Mann-Elkins Act, for the **ineptitude** measure as finally passed was more radical than he had dared to recommend. His Commerce Court was well conceived, but it showed too great friendliness for the corporations to suit the public, and one of its judges, R. W. Archbald, had to be impeached. In 1913 it was abolished. He signed long overdue measures for the admission of Arizona and New Mexico, but when Arizona included the recall of judges in her constitution he refused to proclaim its admission until the obnoxious clause had been taken out. Once in the Union, Arizona ostentatiously readopted the clause it had been compelled to delete.

Taft even had trouble about his appointments to the Supreme Court. When Chief Justice Melville W. Fuller died in 1910, Taft promoted Associate Justice Edward Douglass White of Louisiana to fill the vacancy. This was a graceful compliment to a hard-working judge and a political opponent, but White, besides being a Democrat, was a Roman Catholic, an ex-Confederate, and a conservative. To appoint him Taft had to overlook the claims of Associate Justice J. M. Harlan of Kentucky, who was a Republican, a Protestant, a veteran of the Union army, and a liberal. Altogether President Taft appointed five new members to the Supreme Court, all able jurists; and his choices included liberals and conservatives, Democrats and Republicans. But even the appointment of Charles Evans Hughes in 1910 failed to win the applause it merited. Some said Hughes should have been made Chief Justice; others, that the appointment was designed merely to sidetrack a possible competitor for the Republican nomination in 1912.

Reciprocity with Canada was a favorite Taft policy, and seemingly quite in line with **Reciprocity** the views of the tariff reformers. **with Canada** At length, after persistent effort, he obtained an agreement in 1911 that noticeably lessened the trade barriers between the Dominion and the United States. The proposed schedules, however, reduced the tariff on agricultural imports into the United States from Canada, and offended the middle-western insurgents, whose interest in tariff

reform concerned industry more than agriculture. Only with the assistance of Democratic votes was the President able to obtain the endorsement of his program in Congress. But this, events proved, was not enough. Unwisely the President had said in defense of reciprocity that its ultimate result would be to "make Canada only an adjunct of the United States." Champ Clark, Democratic Speaker of the House and also a supporter of reciprocity, even looked forward to the time when Canada would become a part of the United States. All this was too much for the Canadians, who voted out of power the party that had negotiated the agreement and refused ratification.

In foreign affairs Taft was similarly unsuccessful. His Secretary of State, Knox, merely carried forward a well-worn **"Dollar** Roosevelt policy when he nego- **diplomacy"** tiated treaties with Nicaragua and Honduras to establish a kind of receivership for these two bankrupt Central American countries, with United States supervision of their customs service. The fact that this would provide security for United States bankers who lent money to the nations concerned, although equally true of the similar deals made during Roosevelt's time, now aroused sufficient apprehension in progressive circles to block their ratification by the United States Senate.[1] In the Far East, Knox sought to implement Hay's "open door" policy by promoting an international loan to the Chinese government which would enable it either to buy up railroads held by foreign interests in Chinese territory, or to construct competitive lines under neutral control. When this laudable plan failed, as he should have known it would, mainly because of opposition from Japan and Russia, Knox urged that American bankers be permitted to share in such international loans as might be made to China. With the foreign governments concerned he carried his point, and a "consortium" for the purpose with five other nations was arranged in 1910–12. Undoubtedly the American objective was still to do

[1] See pp. 322–324.

whatever was possible to maintain the open door, but the frank admission that profits for American investors were involved was sufficient to arouse the hostility of the reform element. Taft, indeed, provided his adversaries with excellent ammunition when he spoke of his efforts in Central America and in Asia as "dollar diplomacy." Not only were the Central American treaties defeated, but Taft's successor as President felt obliged to put an end to American participation in the consortium.

In the last half of the Taft administration, Congress, under the control of the Republican insurgents and the Democrats, did not hesitate to plague the President openly by passing piecemeal revisions of the tariff that he was certain to veto. A new woolens schedule to replace the unspeakable Schedule K, a farmers' free-list bill, and a cotton bill were sent to his desk in quick succession. Very properly the President took the stand that constant tariff tinkering was unsettling to business, and that if the tariff were to be revised at all, it must be revised as a whole, and not bit by bit. His opponents knew all this as well as he did, but they were interested primarily in forcing him to multiply vetoes that would add to his unpopularity.

The original program of the Republican insurgents was not the formation of a new party, but the capture of the **The La Follette candidacy** party to which they still belonged. This was made clear as early as January 23, 1911, when a group of them, meeting at Senator LaFollette's house in Washington, formed the National Progressive Republican League. Included in their program were the reforms designed to enable the people to defeat boss rule, such as the direct election of United States senators, direct primaries, the direct election of delegates to national nominating conventions, the initiative, the referendum, and the recall in the states, and a thoroughgoing corrupt practices act. The president of the League was Jonathan Bourne of Oregon, but before the year was over it had warmly endorsed the candidacy of Senator LaFollette for the Republican nomination. "LaFollette is the logical man," said Cummins of Iowa, and on the assumption that Roosevelt could not be persuaded to accept another nomination, the same sentiment was echoed by many another of the ex-President's admirers.

The motives that led Roosevelt, on February 24, 1912, to throw his "hat in the ring" are not easily explained. It is clear, however, that his personal friendship for Taft had cooled completely. The reasons for this were probably more intimate than the often-noted failure of Taft to keep all of Roosevelt's cabinet, as he may once have intended to do; or even his crediting his rich brother Charley no less than "dear Theodore" with having brought him into office. Roosevelt did not take all of his family to Africa, and some of those who stayed behind seem not to have got along any too well with the Tafts. With the personal relationship between the two men no longer what it once had been, Roosevelt listened with steadily increasing conviction to the charges dinned into his ears that Taft had betrayed his policies. One thing was especially hard to forgive. Roosevelt, during the Panic of 1907, had promised the United States Steel Corporation immunity for its absorption of the Tennessee Coal and Iron Company, but on October 24, 1911, Taft's Attorney-General, Wickersham, had brought suit for the dissolution of the corporation, citing against it the very deal that Roosevelt had approved. Worst of all, Taft had failed to hold the Republican Party together and had paved the way for a Democratic victory.

As for LaFollette, there was good reason to fear that he could not win the Republican nomination, or, having won it, **Roosevelt's "hat in the ring"** that he could not be elected. Roosevelt had studiously avoided committing himself to the LaFollette candidacy, and by the end of the year had made up his mind to try for the nomination himself. On February 2, 1912, LaFollette showed signs of nervous exhaustion at a dinner in Philadelphia, and on this flimsy pretext most of his followers incontinently deserted to

Roosevelt. The formal announcement of the ex-President's candidacy came three weeks later at the prearranged insistence of seven liberal-minded governors. LaFollette always believed that Roosevelt had used him as a stalking-horse to find out the trend of public opinion, and when it seemed favorable, had double-crossed him. This charge is impossible to substantiate, but LaFollette never forgave Roosevelt, and convinced himself that Roosevelt had cheated him out of a try at the Presidency. Certainly from the day of Roosevelt's entrance into the race the LaFollette candidacy was a lost cause.

It soon developed that Roosevelt had entered the campaign too late. The presidential machine had already lined up many of the submissive southern delegations, and it now made haste to gather in the rest. Elsewhere, in case the old convention system of choosing delegates was in force, the party regulars almost invariably controlled and obediently delivered their delegations to Taft. On the other hand,

Renomination of Taft

wherever the new system of preferential primaries existed, Roosevelt generally won; indeed, several states quickly adopted such laws in order to promote his chances. Roosevelt's greatest blunder during the campaign was his advocacy of the recall of judicial decisions, an idea that went too far to suit many of his liberal friends and caused the conservatives to harden their hearts against him. When the Republican Convention met in Chicago on June 18, it was apparent that the Roosevelt forces were approximately a hundred votes short of a majority. To make up this deficiency, they had brought contests involving about two hundred and fifty seats, some fairly reasonable and others merely for the "moral effect." But the national committee had already turned most of their contests down, and the convention did likewise. The Roosevelt men insisted that the convention, in making such decisions, should debar from voting all delegates whose seats were contested; such a rule would have enabled them to win. The convention decided, quite in accordance with precedent, to disqualify only the particular delegate or delegation that was being voted on, and to accept the ruling of the national committee on the others until it had been reversed. The application of this rule insured Taft's renomination on the first ballot, although 107 delegates voted for Roosevelt, and 344 sat silent in protest. For Vice-President the triumphant regulars renominated Sherman.

Roosevelt, who had come to Chicago to direct his forces, claimed that he was the victim of a "naked theft," but this was true only in the sense that the rank and file of the Republican voters would doubtless have preferred him to Taft. There was nothing irregular or unusual about what had been done. Precisely the same methods had been used with Roosevelt's approval to nominate Taft four years before. Nevertheless, it was obvious, even before the convention met, that Roosevelt was in no mood to accept defeat. If he lost the Republican nomination, he would run anyway. On June 22 he told a rump convention that met in Orchestra

"Listening." In 1912 the call did not come from the Republicans, and T. R. became the candidate for the Progressive or "Bull Moose" Party. Ketten in the *New York World*.

Hall, "If you wish me to make the fight, I will make it, even if only one state should support me."

In Democratic circles the contest between Taft and Roosevelt was viewed with ill-con-

The Democrats name Wilson cealed joy. It meant a certain Democratic triumph, and a large number of willing candidates for the presidential nomination were soon in evidence. Practically all of them were of the "favorite son" variety, for the long period of Republican rule had given few Democrats a chance to win national reputations. Champ Clark, the Speaker of the House, was the best known of the aspirants, but he represented primarily the claims of Missouri and the West to recognition. Friends of Oscar W. Underwood, a congressman from Alabama, insisted that the time had come when a candidate from the "deep South" should be chosen. Ohio and Indiana, both doubtful states, presented their newly elected governors, Judson Harmon and Thomas R. Marshall, respectively. New Jersey also introduced a new governor, but one with an unusual background — Woodrow Wilson, a professor of political science, turned university president and then politician. When the Democratic Convention met in Baltimore, July 25, 1912, it was evident that only by a long process of elimination could a nomination be achieved. After the tenth ballot it seemed certain that Champ Clark, who had obtained a majority of the votes, but not a two-thirds majority, would be the nominee. But William Jennings Bryan, still the most powerful man in the Democratic Party, switched from Clark to Wilson on the fourteenth ballot. The Tammany delegation from New York had voted for Clark since the tenth ballot, and Bryan's explanation of his conduct was that he could not support anyone who would owe his nomination to Tammany. Cynics insisted that Bryan was only trying to deadlock the convention so that it would again turn to him, but on the forty-sixth ballot it chose Woodrow Wilson. Second place went to Governor Marshall of Indiana.

All eyes now turned to Chicago, where on August 5 the new Progressive Party would meet to select Roosevelt as its **The new Progressive Party** standard-bearer. Already it had a symbol with which to match the Republican elephant and the Democratic donkey — the "bull moose." It was a favorite term with Roosevelt, one he had used as far back as 1900 when he had boasted to Hanna that he was "as strong as a Bull Moose." An enthusiastic audience of twenty thousand people heard the Progressive leader denounce both old parties as "husks, with no real soul within either, divided on artificial lines, boss-ridden and privilege-controlled, each a jumble of incongruous elements, and neither daring to speak out wisely and fearlessly what should be said on the vital issues of the day." For Vice-President the Progressives named Hiram Johnson of California.

On a great variety of issues the new party spoke out. Its trust policy recognized the corporation as "an essential part of modern business," but demanded effective regulation through "a strong federal administrative commission of high standing." It favored giving the Interstate Commerce Commission power to value the physical property of railroads. It urged the development of agricultural credit and cooperation. It advocated an amendment to the Constitution to bring "under effective national jurisdiction those problems which have expanded beyond reach of the individual states." It endorsed, too, all the current reforms such as the direct primary, woman suffrage, an easier way to amend the Constitution, tariff revision downward to reasonable protection, better working conditions in the factories, the prohibition of child labor, the better regulation of labor by women, minimum-wage standards, and an eight-hour day in continuous twenty-four-hour industries. Such pronouncements delighted social workers, such as Jane Addams, and gave the new party a crusading character that well became its leader. With a fervor reminiscent of Populism the Progressive Convention sang "Onward, Chris-

Jane Addams, who gave impetus to the "settlement house" movement, with a group of children at her Hull House in Chicago.

tian Soldiers," and quoted Roosevelt's challenge to the Taft forces at Chicago: "We stand at Armageddon and we battle for the Lord."

Roosevelt's decision to assist in the launching of a new political party made no sense whatever from the standpoint of personal ambition. Had he accepted his defeat by the Republican Convention, Taft would almost certainly have lost the election, and in 1916 Roosevelt could hardly have been denied the Republican nomination. A third-party candidacy, as Roosevelt in his thoughtful moments must have known, had not the slightest chance of success. With the Republican vote split, the Democrats were sure to win. But for the moment, at least, Roosevelt seems to have believed the words uttered to the Chicago Convention. The two old parties, in spite of the labored efforts of their platform makers, really stood for about the same things. The difference between them was principally that one "viewed with alarm," while the other "pointed with pride." Could not the present opportunity be utilized to form a genuine party of reform that would some day seize the reins of government? Under his leadership the thing might be done, and he meant to give it a try.

The campaign provided plenty of excitement and the public enjoyed it thoroughly. The presidential nominees spoke freely and with vigor. Roosevelt and Taft, throughout the primary contests and on into the election campaign, belabored each other as only two friends fallen out can do. Wilson proved to be an admirable public speaker, and those who bothered to follow what he said must have realized that his interpretation of the Democratic platform furnished a close approximation of what the Progressives believed they were fighting for. The high point of the campaign was the attempt of an anti-third-term fanatic to assassinate Roosevelt at Milwaukee on October 16. Ever the disciple of the strenuous life, the ex-Rough Rider delivered an address with a bullet in his right lung — probably as delighted to be able to carry on as he must have been uncomfortable. He had always hoped to die in battle; now at last he could claim to have been wounded in action. It was evident throughout the campaign that Progressive

The campaign of 1912

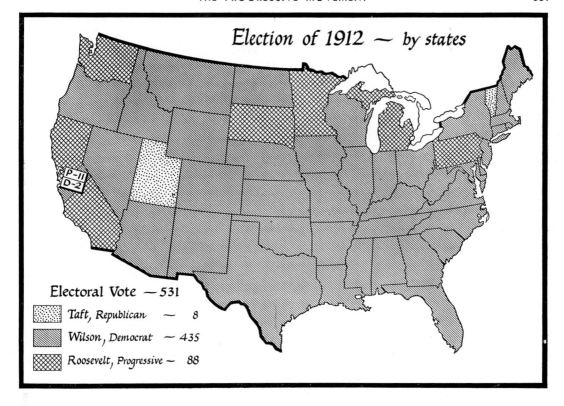

Election of 1912 — by states

P-11
D-2

Electoral Vote — 531

Taft, Republican	—	8
Wilson, Democrat	—	435
Roosevelt, Progressive	—	88

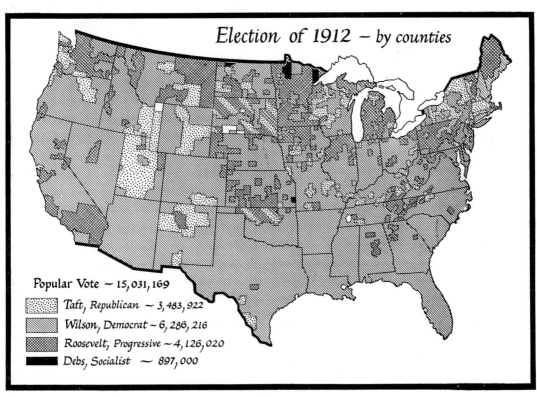

Election of 1912 — by counties

Popular Vote — 15,031,169

Taft, Republican	—	3,483,922
Wilson, Democrat	—	6,286,216
Roosevelt, Progressive	—	4,126,020
Debs, Socialist	—	897,000

strategy was in the hands of the practical politicians, and not the "lunatic fringe" that the movement had attracted. Wherever it could be done the Progressives ran state and local tickets, and they sought with the greatest earnestness to provide the whole intricate mechanism of party organization. Only in this way could a party be created that would endure.

The results of the election were what all astute observers were able to foresee. Wilson, with only 6,286,216 popular votes, fewer than Bryan had obtained in any of his three defeats, carried forty out of the forty-eight states, and amassed a total electoral vote of 435. Roosevelt was second with 4,126,020 popular votes, and eighty-eight electoral votes scattered through six states. Taft, with a popular vote of 3,483,922, obtained only the eight electoral votes of Utah and Vermont. With the Democrats equally victorious in the congressional and the sena-torial elections, Wilson was assured a comfortable working majority in both houses of Congress. In most of the state contests the Democrats also scored victories. Those who looked behind the more obvious results made two significant observations. One was that Eugene V. Debs, the hardy perennial of socialism, received 897,000 popular votes, more than twice as many as in 1908; to a large block of voters, it would seem neither Roosevelt nor Wilson went far enough in their liberalism. The other was that in the state and local contests the Progressives made almost no impression whatever. The Democrats and the Republicans had all the offices. This portent was not lost on Roosevelt. "The fight is over," he told a friend. "We are beaten. There is only one thing to do and that is to go back to the Republican Party. You can't hold a party like the Progressive Party together . . . there are no loaves and fishes."

Bibliography

An excellent chapter on reform within the states is contained in D. S. Muzzey, *The United States of America*, II, *From the Civil War* (1933). For the philosophical basis of the Progressive movement, the most understanding study is Herbert Croly, *The Promise of American Life* (1909), which was also an important motivating influence in itself. Useful also are W. E. Weyl, *The New Democracy* (1912); and C. E. Merriam, *American Political Ideas, 1865–1917* (1929). The best general study of the reform period is George E. Mowry, *Theodore Roosevelt and the Progressive Movement* (1946); but this should be supplemented by Nye, *Midwestern Progressive Politics;* Goldman, *Rendezvous with Destiny*, and Fine, *Labor and Farmer Parties*, all previously mentioned.

On LaFollette and the Wisconsin leadership in reform, there are several admirable books. LaFollette's life story is told with great completeness in his own *Autobiography* (1913); and in a biography written by his wife and daughter, Belle Case LaFollette and Fola LaFollette, *Robert M. LaFollette, 1855–1925* (2 vols., 1953). The forces LaFollette opposed are studied in a well-written biography by Richard N. Current, *Pine Logs and Politics; A Life of Philetus Sawyer, 1816–1900* (1950). Charles McCarthy, *The Wisconsin Idea* (1912), is the work of an enthusiastic LaFollette supporter, while McCarthy's own part is told in Edward A. Fitzpatrick, *McCarthy of Wisconsin* (1944).

There are many studies on other states also, among them George E. Mowry, *The California Progressives, 1900–1920* (1951); Winston Allen Flint, *The Progressive Movement in Vermont* (1941); H. L. Hurwitz, *Theodore Roosevelt and Labor in New York State, 1880–1900* (1943); Eric F. Goldman, *Charles J. Bonaparte, Patrician Reformer: His Earlier Career* (1943); and Louis G. Geiger, *Joseph W. Folk of Missouri* (1953). On the initiative and referendum, see A. H. Eaton, *The Oregon System* (1912); E. P. Oberholtzer, *The Referendum in America* (1911); and *Documents on the State-wide Initiative, Referendum and Recall*, edited by Charles A. Beard (1912). A. M.

Schlesinger, *New Viewpoints in American History* (new ed., 1937), contains an admirable chapter on the role of women. On prohibition, see J. A. Krout, *The Origins of Prohibition* (1925); E. H. Cherrington, *The Evolution of Prohibition in the United States of America* (1920); Justin Steuart, *Wayne Wheeler, Dry Boss* (1928); and Peter H. Odegard, *Pressure Politics: The Story of the Anti-Saloon League* (1928).

The battle for municipal reform may be followed in Lincoln Steffens, *The Shame of the Cities* (1904); Fremont Older, *My Own Story* (1925); C. H. Harrison, *Stormy Years* (1935); F. C. Howe, *The City, The Hope of Democracy* (1905); and Walton E. Bean, *Boss Ruef's San Francisco, The Story of the Union Labor Party, Big Business and the Graft Prosecutions* (1952), an entertaining and scholarly account.

On Taft's administration, H. F. Pringle, *The Life and Times of William Howard Taft* (2 vols., 1939), lacks some of the sparkle that makes Pringle's *Roosevelt* so readable, but is an even better study from the point of view of research. On Taft's earlier career, Mrs. W. H. Taft, *Recollections of Full Years* (1914), is interesting and informative. H. S. Duffy, *William Howard Taft* (1930), is less satisfactory than Pringle. The fight over the Payne-Aldrich tariff is best studied through Bowers' *Beveridge*, LaFollette's *Autobiography*; Claude G. Bowers, *Beveridge and the Progressive Era* (1932); and N. W. Stephenson, *Nelson W. Aldrich* (1930). On the Ballinger-Pinchot controversy, see Gifford Pinchot, *The Fight for Conservation* (1910); and Rose M. Stahl, *The Ballinger-Pinchot Controversy* (1926). On insurgency in the House, L. W. Busbey, *Uncle Joe Cannon* (1927), is of some value; but a more vivid

account is supplied by Blair Bolles, *Tyrant from Illinois: Uncle Joe Cannon's Experiment with Personal Power* (1951). On Taft's diplomatic record, see L. E. Ellis, *Reciprocity, 1911; A Study of Canadian-American Relations* (1939); Scott Nearing and Joseph Freeman, *Dollar Diplomacy* (1925); D. G. Munro, *The Five Republics of Central America* (1918); and J. G. Reid, *The Manchu Abdication and the Powers, 1908–1912* (1935).

Special accounts dealing with the election of 1912 are available in O. K. Davis, *Released for Publication* (1925); and B. P. DeWitt, *The Progressive Movement* (1915). The stand taken by the Republican National Committee in nominating Taft is explained and defended in Victor Rosewater, *Back Stage in 1912* (1932). Interesting commentaries on the Democratic convention are contained in Champ Clark, *My Quarter Century of American Politics* (2 vols., 1920); and W. J. Bryan, *A Tale of Two Conventions* (1912). There are interesting essays on Bryan, Roosevelt, and Wilson in Richard Hofstadter, *The American Political Tradition and the Men Who Made It* (1948). Also useful in this connection is Daniel Aaron, *Men of Good Hope: A Story of American Progressives* (1951); and a number of books on Socialism: I. Kipnis, *The American Socialist Movement, 1897–1912* (1952); A. E. Morgan, *Edward Bellamy* (1944); and Howard Quint, *The Forging of American Socialism: Origins of the Modern Movement* (1951), which ends with 1900, but is useful to that point. For the conservative point of view, see R. W. Leopold, *Elihu Root and the Conservative Tradition* (1954).

The economic history of the period is best covered in H. U. Faulkner, *The Decline of Laissez Faire, 1897–1917* (1951).

19

Woodrow Wilson

Woodrow Wilson — Underwood-Simmons Tariff — Banking and currency reform — The trust problem — Trust legislation — Administration of the Anti-Trust Acts — A "Magna Charta" for Labor — The Department of Labor — The I.W.W. — Mooney and Billings — Movement for immigration restriction — Rural credits — "Dollar-matching" — Federal Highways Act — Wilsonian vs. Jeffersonian democracy

WOODROW WILSON (1856–1924), was born at Staunton, Virginia, of Scotch and Scotch-Irish lineage. His father, a prominent southern clergyman, was for many years minister of the First Presbyterian Church in Wilmington, North Carolina. Throughout his life Wilson's religious training, with its strongly Calvinistic bent, never forsook him; it was no accident that the protocol of the League of Nations was called a "covenant." Young Wilson, as befitted his father's station in life, was carefully educated, first at Princeton, and then, after a brief bout with the law, at Johns Hopkins, where he took a Ph.D. in history and government. His doctoral dissertation on *Congressional Government* (1885) achieved and merited book publication. In it he made clear the extent to which the business of legislation was transacted through committees, a fact well known to the politicians, but little understood by the professors. He revealed, also, his conviction, elaborated later in another book, *Constitutional Government in the United States* (1908), that the President ought to be the real head of the government, no less in directing the course of legislation than in the enforcement of laws already passed.

Wilson's career led onward through minor positions at Bryn Mawr and Wesleyan to a professorship at Princeton in 1890, and to the presidency of the university in 1902. He wrote well, lectured well, and was even accused of oratorical ability. His books ranged through the fields of law, history, and politics, but only in politics can he be said to have made a contribution to scholarship. His studies in comparative government deeply impressed him with the vast powers wielded by the prime ministers in Great Britain and elsewhere, and convinced him that the principle of executive leadership must somehow be grafted into the American system. Roosevelt's expansion of the President's prerogatives was quite in line with Wilson's thinking. "The President," wrote the professor, "is at liberty, both in law and conscience, to be as big a man as he can. His capacity will set the limit."

Until he became president of Princeton, Wilson showed little evidence of the liberalism for which he later became famous. His views were not unlike those of the southern aristocrats who sat in his father's congregations. But the conspicuous lack of democracy that he noted at Princeton led him to insist as president on innovations that would have altered in marked degree the social life and instructional methods of the university. He met opposition, but that served only to bring out a trait in his character that all the world was soon to know; the more he was opposed, the more determined he became to put his principles into effect. The prosperity of Princeton, it developed, depended on the gifts of men who had no interest whatever in the Wilsonian reforms. If there came a difference of opinion between them and the president of the university, then the president must yield or get out. Wilson was not the man to retract his views and chart a different course. When, therefore, in 1910, James Smith, Democratic boss of New Jersey, offered him a nomination for the governorship of the state, he was happy to accept.

Smith had no interest whatever in reform, but reform was in the air, and with a candidate like Wilson to demonstrate that reform ideas had captured the Democratic Party, that party might capture the state. After the victory there need be no change. What chance would a mere professor have, whatever his views, in matching wits with political realists? Smith's word would still be law. It fell out for once that the boss had quite misjudged his man. Wilson was elected, but he then put into effect the doctrine of executive leadership he so long had taught. Why were there party bosses? Because the elected leaders failed to use the powers that were rightly theirs. The governor had power; Wilson used it. He could command the attention of the press; Wilson used that too. With the support of public opinion Wilson soon had the legislature doing the governor's bidding, not the party boss's. Smith told it to disregard the nominee of the senatorial primary, James Martine, and to elect James Smith to the United States Senate. But at Wilson's insistence the legislature chose Martine over Smith. On pressure from the governor's office it enacted, too, a number of laws that the Democratic platform had promised, laws to establish employers' liability, to punish corrupt practices, to control the public utilities, and to reform the ballot.

Wilson as governor

These victories in a state that had long been regarded as the "home of the trusts" made Wilson a marked man, but the honor of having first suggested his name for the

Woodrow Wilson

TWENTY-EIGHTH PRESIDENT of the United States, Wilson is remembered primarily as a war President, and a strong protagonist of the League of Nations. A university professor and university president in his earlier years, he owed much of his success to his long study of politics, and the effective way in which he could express his ideas.

Presidency probably goes to Colonel George Harvey, who had called the attention of the Democrats to him as far back as 1906. The list of "original Wilson men" soon grew immoderately, winning a particularly important recruit when another courtesy "Colonel," Edward M. House of Texas, rallied to the standard. House was an adept at backstage politics. In October, 1911, he brought Wilson to Texas for an address before the State Fair at Dallas, and thereafter his was the chief guiding hand in Wilson's campaign. As a candidate Wilson demonstrated conclusively that he had ideas, and could turn a neat phrase. With almost Rooseveltian pungency he charged that "the government of the United States is at present a foster-child of the special interests," and demanded a "new freedom" for the individual — a freedom that would insure economic no less than political liberty. Although Wilson obviously offered his views on the "New Freedom" as an alternative to Roosevelt's "New Nationalism," the similarities in the ideas of the rival reformers were more in evidence than the differences. Both recognized that by all odds the most important problem government had to face was its relationship with business, and both insisted that the power of government must be used to protect the rights of the ordinary citizen. But whereas Roosevelt placed his emphasis upon the expansion of national powers, Wilson placed his upon the protection of individual freedom.

Having achieved the Presidency, Wilson was determined to be the prime-minister type of President. With this **Wilson and** end in view he included in his **Bryan** cabinet as Secretary of State the man whose influence with the rank and file of the Democratic Party was still second to none, William Jennings Bryan. Wilson suffered from no illusions as to Bryan's fitness for the post assigned him, and once, years before, he had expressed the wish that Bryan might be "knocked into a cocked hat." But it was Bryan, more than Harvey or House or anyone else, who had made Wilson President, and Bryan, if left outside the Wilson *entourage*, had the power to cause the new administration endless trouble. Without Bryan's assistance Wilson could not hope to solidify his control over the Democratic majority in Congress, and no post save the highest would befit a man who had three times been a candidate for the Presidency.

The necessity of maintaining political cohesion shared about equally with the quest for administrative ability in determining Wilson's other cabinet selections. Aside from Bryan the cabinet contained no names familiar to the public at large. William Gibbs McAdoo of New York, Secretary of the Treasury, had helped Wilson win the nomination, and without being a banker he had an expert's knowledge of finance. Albert Sidney Burleson, a long-time congressman from Texas, brought to the office of Postmaster-General the understanding touch of the professional politician. For the Navy Department expediency directed the choice of a Bryan-like editor from North Carolina, Josephus Daniels, whose inexperience in naval matters was offset by the appointment as Assistant Secretary of Franklin Delano

Roosevelt, a young man from New York with a good name who knew about ships. More important than most of the cabinet members were Colonel House, whose rôle of unofficial adviser to the President gave him extraordinary power, and Joseph P. Tumulty, the President's faithful private secretary, a shrewd and practical politician upon whose natural talents Wilson relied in solving his patronage problems.

The President, Wilson once had said, "has no means of compelling Congress except through public opinion." That **Wilson's** he meant to use this power to **program** the full was apparent in his inaugural address in which he took pains to itemize, not so much for the benefit of Congress as for the benefit of the people, "the things that ought to be altered." Among them he listed:

A tariff which cuts us off from our proper part in the commerce of the world, violates the just principles of taxation, and makes the Government a facile instrument in the hands of private interests;

A banking and currency system based upon the necessity of the Government to sell its bonds fifty years ago and perfectly adapted to concentrating cash and restricting credits;

An industrial system which, take it on all sides, financial as well as administrative, holds capital in leading strings, restricts the liberties and limits the opportunities of labor, and exploits without renewing or conserving the natural resources of the country;

A body of agricultural activities never yet given the efficiency of great business undertakings or served as it should be through the instrumentality of science taken directly to the farm, or afforded the facilities of credit best suited to its practical needs;

Watercourses undeveloped, waste places unreclaimed, forests untended, fast disappearing without plan or prospect of renewal, unguarded waste heaps at every mine.

To make a beginning on the presidential program by passing a new tariff law, Congress was summoned into special session for April 7. Much to everyone's astonishment, the President opened the session in person, and for the first time since the administration of John Adams the two houses of Congress, sitting jointly, listened to a presidential message. It was a clever stroke of politics; according to an unconfirmed rumor Theodore Roosevelt was said to have remarked, "Why didn't I think of that?" The appearance of the President before Congress was an event. Senators and representatives, their families and friends, and all others who could crowd into the galleries were present. It was news, and all the newspapers played it up. Last, but by no means least, the message was short and to the point. Practically every newspaper in the country carried its entire text, and many of them found space for all of it on the front page. "We must abolish everything that bears even the semblance of privilege or of any kind of artificial advantage," the people read approvingly, and then awaited the action of Congress.

Wilson had other strings to his bow. If the Democratic *debâcle* of 1894 on the tariff **The Under-** were not to be repeated, some **wood-Sim-** means must be found for hold-**mons Tariff** ing wilful members to the party's promises. With the President's approval recourse was had to the party caucus, through which the majority of the majority settled all matters in dispute and achieved party unity. Frequently the President himself essayed the rôle of party whip; on occasion he even appeared at the Capitol to direct strategy and to reason with the recalcitrant. Nor did Wilson hesitate, whenever it seemed necessary, to appeal to the public over the heads of Congress. Lobbyists descended upon Washington as they always do when a tariff bill is being framed, and Wilson gave notice to the people through the press that "Washington has seldom seen so numerous, so industrious, or so insidious a lobby." Only by an aroused public opinion, he declared, could it be checked or destroyed. An aroused public opinion came promptly to the rescue. Soon the lobbyists, investigated by Congress and denounced by the press, were more embarrassed than embarrassing. There was also the patronage. Wilson kept himself as clear of such mundane matters as possible,

but evidence was quickly available to prove that senators and representatives who supported the administration had much less trouble getting offices for the "deserving Democrats" they favored than those whose votes were in doubt. Guided through the House by Representative Oscar W. Underwood of Alabama and through the Senate by Senator F. M. Simmons of North Carolina, the tariff measure took six months to frame, but at last, on October 3, it received the President's signature.

The Underwood-Simmons Tariff was neither a free-trade measure nor a low-tariff measure, and was not meant to be either. Its schedules of duties, however, were on the average about ten per cent lower than those of the Payne-Aldrich Tariff, and it placed a hundred new items, mostly raw materials or foodstuffs, on the free list. While a total of nine hundred and fifty-eight items were reduced, only eighty, mainly chemicals, carried increased duties, and only three hundred and seven were unchanged. More significant than their framers knew were the income-tax provisions which, thanks to the recent adoption of the Sixteenth Amendment, could be included in the act. One per cent was charged against all incomes in excess of $3000, or, in the case of married couples, $4000; while on incomes above $20,000 a surtax, beginning with an additional one per cent, was gradually stepped up to a maximum of six per cent on incomes above $500,000. At the time the Underwood-Simmons Bill became a law the possibilities of the income tax were only faintly realized, but within a few years it became the chief reliance of the federal government for revenue. As for the tariff schedules of the act, they were in force less than a year when their natural effect was nullified by the outbreak of war in Europe. What they might have done for business and for the revenue had times remained normal will never be known, but during the abnormal years they were in force they fell far short of providing the government with the revenue it needed. Indeed, the wartime demand for

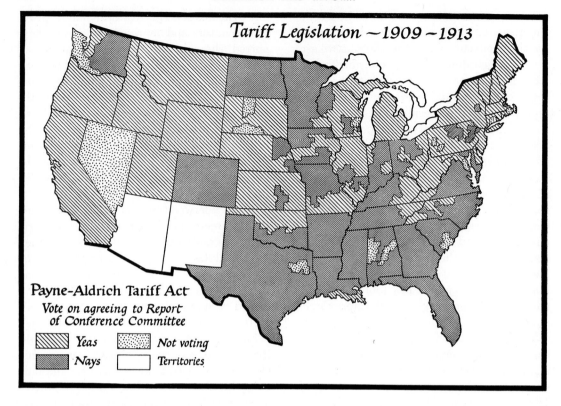

Tariff Legislation ~1909~1913

Payne-Aldrich Tariff Act

Vote on agreeing to Report of Conference Committee

	Yeas		Not voting
	Nays		Territories

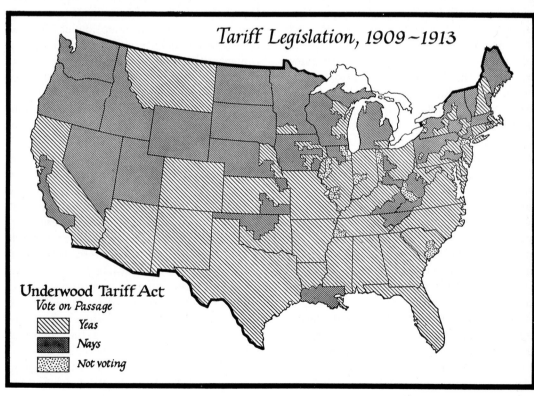

Tariff Legislation, 1909~1913

Underwood Tariff Act

Vote on Passage

Yeas

Nays

Not voting

American goods that set in proved to be a greater stimulus to American industry than the highest possible tariff rates could ever have provided.

Congress was not yet finished with its work on the tariff when Wilson, by means of

Banking and currency reform another short, strikingly phrased address, presented the second major item on his program of reform — a new banking and currency system. The need for legislation on this subject was universally recognized. From 1908 to 1912 the National Monetary Commission, chosen by the Republicans and headed by Senator Aldrich, one of the most conservative men in public life, studied minutely, with the aid of numerous experts, the banking and currency systems of the world, their history and operation. Forced to report in 1912 soon after the Democrats had captured the House, it revealed clearly the faults of the existing system, and recommended as a cure the establishment of what would have amounted to a third Bank of the United States. During the second half of the Taft administration the Democratic majority in the House of Representatives undertook a similar, although far less scholarly, investigation, with A. P. Pujo of Louisiana as head of the committee in charge. Among the many prominent financiers called before the Pujo Committee was J. Pierpont Morgan, whose arrogance was undisturbed by the questions he was asked, but whose answers failed to shake the conviction of the committee and the public that a "money trust," controlled by the whims of a few great bankers, actually existed. The Pujo Committee could not agree with the Aldrich Commission that there must be one great central bank. The ghosts of Andrew Jackson and the doctrine of states' rights prevented that. But it could agree that the situation demanded immediate attention.

The Federal Reserve System was the solution which the Democratic majority worked

The Federal Reserve System out, in close cooperation with the President, for the dilemma that it faced. Complete central-ization, however desirable from the economic point of view, was politically impossible, and a plan of organization that was both financially sound and at the same time would win the support of Bryan and the Populist wing of the Democratic Party had to be devised. To avoid the historic formula of a central bank with sectional branches, the framers of the new system hit upon the expedient of creating a series of sectional banks, held together only by a Federal Reserve Board. This board, which Wilson thought of as analogous to the Interstate Commerce Commission, was to consist of seven members, two of whom, the Secretary of the Treasury and the Comptroller of the Currency, were to be members *ex officio*, while the others (increased to six in 1922) were to be appointed by the President and confirmed by the Senate for ten-year terms. One of the non-political members was to be designated governor of the board. It took six months to work out the details of the Federal Reserve System and to obtain the support necessary for its adoption by both houses of Congress. In the House Carter Glass of Virginia bore the brunt of the battle, and in the Senate, Robert L. Owen of Oklahoma. More than once Congress was ready to postpone the task, and only pressure from the President prevented adjournment. Finally, on December 23, 1913, Wilson affixed his signature to the new law.

The Glass-Owen Federal Reserve Act provided for the division of the United States into not less than eight nor more than twelve districts, each of which would contain some natural metropolitan center in which a Federal Reserve Bank would be established.[1] In

---

[1] The drafting of this new financial map of the United States was wisely left by Congress to a special organizing committee that included the Secretary of the Treasury, the Secretary of Agriculture, and the Comptroller of the Currency. Twelve districts were created, and within them the banks were located as follows: First, Boston; Second, New York; Third, Philadelphia; Fourth, Cleveland; Fifth, Richmond; Sixth, Atlanta; Seventh, Chicago; Eighth, St. Louis; Ninth, Minneapolis; Tenth, Kansas City; Eleventh, Dallas; Twelfth, San Francisco. The assignment of two Federal Reserve Banks to the State of Missouri aroused considerable criticism, particularly from

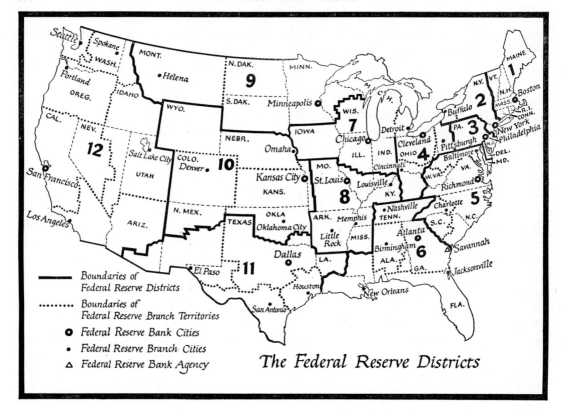

The Federal Reserve Districts

Boundaries of
Federal Reserve Districts
Boundaries of
Federal Reserve Branch Territories
Federal Reserve Bank Cities
Federal Reserve Branch Cities
Federal Reserve Bank Agency

each district a Federal Reserve Association was to be formed to which all national banks must belong and all other banks might belong. Each member bank was required to subscribe six per cent of its capital and surplus to the capital of the Federal Reserve Bank, whose governing board should consist of six members chosen by the member banks, and three by the Federal Reserve Board. The new banks were not to do business with individuals, but as strictly "bankers' banks" they received on deposit the reserves of member banks, rediscounted their commercial and agricultural paper, and granted them loans with governmental securities as collateral. The law also provided for a new type of currency, Federal Reserve notes, which the banks might issue upon their re-

residents of Denver, who felt that the Kansas City bank should have been theirs. There were those, too, who observed that a third Bank of the United States could hardly have done more violence to the doctrine of states' rights than the establishment of twelve regional banks rather than one for each state.

discounted paper, provided only that they must maintain a gold reserve of forty per cent. These notes were to constitute obligations on the United States and were to be redeemable in gold. Since they would vary in quantity according to the needs of business, it was believed that they would effectively overcome the inelasticity of the currency from which the country so long had suffered. The United States two per cent bonds upon which the old national bank currency had been issued were to be retired at the rate of $25,000,000 per year.

The Federal Reserve System was carefully devised to end the lack of cooperation between banks in time of crisis. In effect it pooled the credit resources of each district and provided a means whereby the strength of all the banks might be mobilized to sustain any one. Further, on order of the Federal Reserve Board the several regional banks were required to discount paper for each other, so that an abundance of credit available in any given part of the country could promptly be directed to whatever district or districts might be threatened with a shortage.

Other provisions of the act did away with the old Independent Treasury system, or the Sub-Treasury, in which since the forties the funds of the United States had been sequestered, and provided instead that the government might use the Federal Reserve Banks as depositories. These banks might also buy and sell gold and both foreign and domestic bills of exchange. A number of special restrictions were included to guard against the danger of speculative inflation.

When the Federal Reserve System was first proposed, the bankers of the country were extremely suspicious of it, and the fact that Bryan supported it, however necessary that may have been politically, was well calculated to exaggerate their fears. But before the measure reached final passage, the bankers had begun to see its advantages, and within a short time the best of them were enthusiastic in its praise. While it is a fact that at the time the Great Depression began only about one third of the banks of the country were members of the Federal Reserve, it is an even more striking fact that by that time the combined assets of the member banks accounted for more than four-fifths of the nation's banking resources.

When Wilson appeared before Congress on January 20, 1914, to direct attention to the **The trust problem** trust problem he found himself in a far more advantageous position than either Taft or Roosevelt had occupied when attempting to deal with the same subject. In Roosevelt's time the seriousness of the situation was barely being recognized, and an angry public could think of nothing better to do than to punish somebody. "Malefactors of great wealth" should land in jail, and fines such as Judge Landis had imposed against the Standard Oil Company should be made to stick. Roosevelt, seizing the Sherman Anti-Trust Act as the only weapon available, bludgeoned about with it, but did little good. Taft, loyal to

his campaign promises, carried out the Roosevelt policy even after the public had begun to realize its ineffectiveness. Hampered as he was by a rift within his party and lacking in political flair, he could have done little more had he tried. But by Wilson's time the nature of modern business had been better studied, and information was available that Wilson's predecessors had lacked. The Bureau of Corporations established in Roosevelt's time had begun to bear fruit. Economics had elbowed its way to the front in the colleges and universities as the most significant of the social studies. The Federal Reserve Act was possible only because of the elaborate research that had preceded it; but other businesses also had been studied and the time was ripe for the adoption of a policy based on an intelligent understanding of the conditions under which they must operate. Wilson had better control, too, of his party than either Roosevelt or Taft had ever had of theirs. He was a master strategist; besides, as a representative from Georgia blurted out, the Democratic majority had no choice but to "support the Administration or be turned into the wilderness for forty years more."

The platforms of the three major parties all pointed in much the same way on the trust problem. Only the Progressives openly admitted that **Party pledges on the trusts** the concentration of modern business in corporate hands was "both inevitable and necessary," and only the Democrats grew rhetorical in their denunciation of monopoly. All agreed that there were certain business practices which, as the Republican platform phrased it, were "abhorrent to the common sense of justice." Among these practices the Democrats listed the formation of holding companies, interlocking directorates, stock-watering, discrimination in price, and "the control by any one corporation of so large a proportion of any industry as to make it a menace to competitive conditions." The Progressives denounced the monopoly of natural resources, stock-watering, unfair competition and unfair privileges, and "sinister influences on the public agencies of state and nation." As a remedy for such practices the Democrats seemingly had little more to offer than the restoration of competitive conditions by the enactment of drastic anti-trust laws, but the Republicans suggested that the enforcement and administration of laws governing interstate enterprises be placed in the hands of a "federal trade commission," while the Progressives urged for the same purpose "the establishment of a strong administrative commission of high standing." With less ingenuity than is ordinarily required of platform-makers, the various trust planks in the three platforms could have been welded into one harmonious whole.

In his message to Congress on the subject Wilson pointed the way to some such synthesis. He was genuinely eager to prevent the formation of monopolies, but as a means to accomplish this and other worthy ends he particularly stressed the necessity of defining and prohibiting unfair practices. He had no desire to undermine business confidence, but he did insist that business methods be subject to governmental inspection. His Attorney-General, James C. McReynolds, whose reputation had been made as a "trust-busting" prosecutor, was already exhibiting a willingness to avoid anti-trust suits by showing the corporations how they could comply with the law; nor had he heeded the demand for criminal prosecutions, so insistently repeated in the Democratic platform. In addition to the cataloguing of unfair practices, Wilson also urged upon Congress the creation of a new commission with power to enforce the law.

Before the mid-term election of 1914, Congress, after much travail, had enacted two **Trust** significant measures, the Clay-**legislation** ton Anti-Trust Act and the Federal Trade Commission Act. On the latter there was the less disagreement, and it reached the statute books by September 26. The new commission was to consist of five members, appointed by the President for seven-year terms subject to confirmation by the Senate, and was to be bipartisan. It absorbed the duties, organization, and personnel of the Bureau of Corporations which it supplanted, but it had far greater powers. It might investigate the origin and management of corporations, and it might issue "cease and desist" orders enforceable through the courts against such "unfair methods of competition in commerce" as it might discover. On the understanding that the findings of the commission as to fact were final and conclusive, appeals from its orders were allowed to the Federal Court of Appeals, and thence to the United States Supreme Court. It was not due to an oversight that penalties for violations of the orders of the commission were omitted. The intent was first to establish what was fair and lawful. If in spite of the evidence produced by the commission disobedience should be persisted in, prosecutions could be undertaken for violation of the Sherman Act and its various amendments. To the list of dubious corporate practices already proscribed, the Clayton Act, which became a law on October 15, added the following: any discrimination in prices that tended to produce a monopoly; the acquisition by any corporation of the whole or a part of the stock of a competing concern; the existence of interlocking directorates among million-dollar corporations that were or had been competitors; and exclusive contracts that obligated a dealer not to handle the products of other manufacturers.

The Wilson administration may be credited with considerable success in its efforts to reach agreements with business **Administra-**as to what was fair and what **tion of the** was not. The Federal Trade **Anti-Trust** Commission issued hundreds of **Acts** "cease and desist" orders, and they were usually obeyed. The Department of Justice, continuing Attorney-General McReynolds's policy even after his elevation to the Supreme Court in 1914, brought fewer suits for dissolution than had been attempted under Roosevelt or Taft, and scored its greatest victories in inducing corporations to accept "consent decrees." In this fashion the government came to terms with the International Harvester Company, the Corn Products Refining Company, and the packers' trust. It continued the prosecution begun during the Taft administration against the United States Steel Corporation, but in 1920, with only seven justices participating, the Supreme Court by a four-to-three vote ruled against the government. The Steel Corporation, according to the Court, was not a monopoly; it had abandoned the practice of joining with competitors to fix prices; it was not engaged in any unfair practices; and it could not be punished for its size alone. As to the absorption of the Tennessee Coal and Iron Company, the Court called attention to the fact that the President of the United States had given his consent to the transaction.

Beyond a doubt Wilson's trust policy was adversely affected by the entrance of the United States into the First World War. While that struggle was on, there was little attempt to enforce the restrictions of the Clayton Act, and after the Republicans returned to power in 1921, there was little desire to enforce them.

The Clayton Act also incorporated, or so labor leaders optimistically contended, a

A "Magna Charta" for Labor "Magna Charta" for labor. The Act specifically stated that neither labor and agricultural organizations, nor their members, should "be held or construed to be illegal combinations or conspiracies in restraint of trade under the anti-trust laws." Further, it limited the use of the injunction in labor disputes, prescribed trials by jury in contempt cases, and legalized such labor weapons as strikes, picketing, peaceable assembly, boycotts, and the collection of strike benefits. The framers of the Sherman Anti-Trust Act had probably not meant to extend its provisions to labor unions, and a clause so stating had been considered for inclusion in it. Nevertheless, when in 1902 the Hatters' Union, seeking to force the firm of D. E. Loewe and Company of Danbury, Connecticut, to adopt the closed shop, instituted a nation-wide boycott against

Loewe products, the manufacturer brought suit for damages against the union under the terms of the Sherman Act. For years the case was in litigation, but in 1908 the Supreme Court ruled that a combination of labor unions attempting to boycott a dealer's goods was a combination in restraint of trade, and that the injured party might collect three times the eighty thousand dollars he was deemed to have been damaged. This amount, plus costs, the union actually had to pay, and until the passage of the Clayton Act interstate boycotting was too dangerous a weapon to be used. Judicial obstacles had been placed in the way of nearly every other labor practice also, and "government by in-

His Majesty the Toiler. Painting by Frank C. Kirk, A.N.A.

junction" had become a truism. The provisions of the Clayton Act were therefore hailed as a great boon to labor, and they were successfully enforced as long as Wilson was President. During the reactionary years of the twenties many of these guaranties were interpreted away by the courts.

Apart from the Clayton Act the record of the Wilson administration was also such as to inspire the confidence of labor.

The Department of Labor

The creation of the Department of Labor under a law signed by Taft just before he left office enabled Wilson to select the first Secretary of Labor. His choice fell upon William B. Wilson of Pennsylvania, a man who had risen from the ranks in the United Mine Workers and whose appointment was urged by the American Federation of Labor. Under the sympathetic guidance of the new Secretary the Children's Bureau, with Julia C. Lathrop at its head, sought to extend to the nation at least as good advice on the care of its youth as the Department of Agriculture had long made available to farmers in the case of livestock. In September, 1916, Congress, spurred on by the revelations of the Bureau, passed the Keating-Owen Child Labor Bill, which prohibited the labor of children under fourteen years of age in the production of goods intended for interstate commerce, but the Supreme Court held that the measure was unconstitutional. When an attempt to accomplish the same purpose by use of the taxing power met a similar fate, Congress sought, also in vain, to secure by an amendment to the Constitution the power it lacked. During the Wilson administration the Department of Labor made a persistent effort to deal more effectively with the problem of unemployment. It greatly expanded its employment service, and it proved to be particularly helpful in finding work for newly arrived immigrants.

The LaFollette Seamen's Act, while not directly sponsored by the Wilson administration, was passed by Congress in 1915, and signed by the President. The sinking in 1912 of the White Star steamship *Titanic*, the largest ocean liner in the world, had revealed the carelessness characteristic of the shipping interests, and had paved the way for the revolutionary legislation demanded by Andrew Furuseth, head of the Seamen's Union. The LaFollette Act bettered the physical conditions required for crews, and ended the tyrannical control over their men that sea captains had exercised since the days of Captain Bligh. Contrary to previous practice, a seaman might now demand half the wages due

The Titanic leaving Liverpool. On her maiden voyage she struck an iceberg and **sank** southeast of Cape Race. The disaster shook the world.

him when he wanted it, and he was no longer
at the mercy of the consular courts if he deserted at a foreign port. Maritime interests
claimed that the Act placed them at a serious
disadvantage in competition with foreign
shipping which had not been forced to make
such expensive reforms, but they found that
during the First World War there was an
abundance of business for all.

Such measures of appeasement as the
American Federation of Labor was able to
The I.W.W. offer and the Wilson administration to accept fell far short
of the goal set by a small but tempestuous
group of extreme radicals. A number of
these extremists, recruited largely from the
Western Federation of Miners, formed in
1905 an organization known as the Industrial
Workers of the World, and commonly called
the "I.W.W." or the "Wobblies." In a short
time the "Wobblies" became essentially a
union of the unskilled migratory laborers
who, when they chanced to be employed, did
the hard work of the western mines, the lumber camps, and the harvest fields. Under
existing conditions they saw no chance whatever for living wages and permanency of employment. Like the European syndicalists
they believed that the only effective remedy
for the ills from which they suffered was the
destruction of capitalism, and the methods
they used in pursuit of this aim amounted in
effect to war. Their outstanding leader was
William D. Haywood, whom public opinion
held responsible for the murder in 1905 of
ex-Governor Frank Steunenberg of Idaho,
although the best efforts of William E. Borah,
a rising young Boise lawyer, were insufficient
to procure conviction. After a long career of
violence in the West, the "Wobblies" came
East in 1912 to participate in the textile
strikes at Lawrence, Massachusetts, Pater-
son, New Jersey, and elsewhere. Their
frankly revolutionary objectives and their
warlike methods resulted in the passage of
criminal syndicalist laws by sixteen states
which seriously crippled their activities, and
in 1918 the United States government con-
pleted their destruction by bringing to trial

some one hundred and thirteen I.W.W.
leaders, including Haywood. Most of the
accused were convicted and given long jail
sentences. Haywood fled to Russia, which
was fast becoming the Mecca of radicals.

Other evidences of radicalism in the labor
movement were not difficult to find. When
Wilson became President the **Mooney and**
furor over the bombing in 1911 **Billings**
of the building which housed the Los Angeles
Times, a rabidly anti-union newspaper, had
barely died down. Two brothers named
McNamara were accused of the crime, and
in spite of generous labor contributions to
their defense, they ultimately confessed, and
were sentenced, while thirty-eight labor
leaders were later convicted as their accom-
plices. In 1916, during a San Francisco preparedness parade, a bomb exploded killing a
number of people. Thomas J. Mooney and
Warren K. Billings, two radical labor leaders,
were indicted for the crime, and were convicted on what was later proved to be per-
jured testimony. Exiles to the United States
from Russia who returned to participate in
the Communist Revolution carried the tale
of these convictions with them, and the incident thus obtained international prominence.
California courts, however, consistently refused to set aside the verdict by which the
accused men had been convicted, and while
the sentence was commuted from death to
life imprisonment, not until 1939 was a governor willing to take the political risk of
pardoning the prisoners.

The existence of extreme radicalism in the
labor movement was generally attributed to
the presence in the United States **Movement**
of foreign agitators whom the **for immigra-**
lax immigration laws had per- **tion restric-**
mitted to enter the country. **tion**
Partly on this account public opinion seemed
to demand that some means of restricting
immigration should be found. Data not previously available had been collected by an
Immigration Commission, created in 1907,
and the figures of the census of 1910 were also
revealing. In the first fourteen years of the
twentieth century about thirteen million im-

THE McNAMARA BROTH-
ERS. John (left) and James
(right) with labor leader
Samuel Gompers the day
before they pleaded guilty.

*Labor violence rose to an alarm-
ing height on October 1, 1911, when
nineteen persons lost their lives in
a fire following a bomb explosion
that wrecked the plant of the Los
Angeles Times. Organized labor
was blamed for the outrage, and
there was much wild talk on both
sides. Unexploded bombs were
also found under the houses of the
owner of the Times and the secretary of the Merchants' Association.*

LOS ANGELES TIMES BUILD-
ING. View of destruction.

migrants were admitted into the United
States, and of this number more than four
fifths were from southern and eastern Europe.
Perhaps half of the newcomers, after having
earned the stake they came for, went back
home, but the rest stayed on to swell what
threatened to become a permanently unassimilable element in the American population. To cut down on this influx a literacy test
had been proposed as far back as Cleveland's
administration, and had passed Congress
only to be vetoed by the President. Under
Taft the same thing happened, and twice
under Wilson. Passed by Congress in 1917
over Wilson's veto, the law provided that

"all aliens over sixteen years of age, physically capable of reading, who cannot read the
English language or some other language or
dialect" should be denied admission. The
real purpose of the law was not so much to
discriminate against the illiterate as to limit
the number of immigrants from southern and
eastern Europe, where illiteracy was common. Candidates for admission from the
northern and western countries of Europe
were expected to have little difficulty in passing the test. Wilson's veto message was
based upon the ground that the literacy test
proved nothing more than lack of opportunity, but the President, like his predecessors,

was no doubt influenced by the offense such a measure would give to many American voters of foreign extraction.

In his inaugural address Wilson had given prominent mention to the needs of agri-

Rural credits culture, and had particularly stressed the need of rural credits. Increasingly the methods of farming in the United States called for heavier investments, both in land and in machinery. The competition of free lands had ceased to keep down the price per acre of the farmer's investment, and the capital outlay required to enter the farming business in the new era had become almost prohibitive. Even for farmers who owned or inherited their land the cost of essential machinery and livestock led inevitably to a mortgage, and the rates charged by the local bankers and investment companies were by no means nominal. Taxes, too, mounted with the increasing valuation of land, and the toll paid for transportation and other handling charges left only the faintest margin between the cost of production and the farmer's receipts. The existence of unrest among the farmers, particularly in the Middle West, was revealed by the rapid growth of such farm orders as the American Society of Equity and the Farmers' Union, and the threat that the farmers might implement their grievances through political action was evident in the solid farmer support that the LaFollette organization obtained in Wisconsin, and the activity of the National Non-Partisan League after 1915 in North Dakota and adjacent states.

The Federal Reserve Act authorized short-term loans up to six months on farm mortgages, but the need for long-term loans, by means of which the purchase of farmlands could be financed, grew steadily more insistent. After two years' consideration of the problem Congress finally agreed to the Federal Farm Loan Act of 1916. The purpose of this measure, according to its enacting clause, was "to provide capital for agricultural development, to create standard forms of investment based upon farm mortgage, and to equalize rates of interest upon farm loans." The Federal Farm Loan System which the act set up was patterned closely upon the Federal Reserve System. A central board consisting of the Secretary of the Treasury and four appointive members was given general control over a dozen Federal Farm Land Banks operating in as many districts. Each of these banks was to be capitalized at not less than seven hundred and fifty thousand dollars, to which private individuals were invited to subscribe; but whatever sums less than the stipulated minimum were not raised in this way the government was obligated to supply. Farmers desiring to borrow money might then form themselves into cooperative farm loan associations in which each borrower took five dollars' worth of stock for each hundred dollars he wished to borrow. With their resources thus united, farm borrowers might obtain loans up to fifty per cent of the appraised value of their land, and an additional twenty per cent on its permanent improvements. Interest rates were kept at from five to six per cent, and provision was made for amortization over a period of thirty-three years. Out of deference to the wishes of private moneylenders, who objected to the government monopolizing the business of supplying rural credits, the law provided also for the establishment of joint-stock land banks, privately financed, except that their bonds were to be tax exempt. These banks might lend directly to individuals on farm mortgage security. The importance of the Federal Farm Loan Act is attested by the fact that by 1930 the two types of banks it established had together lent over two billion dollars to the American farmers.

Before the exigencies of war halted the course of domestic reform the Wilson administration inaugurated another **"Dollar-matching"** notable policy. Gifts from the federal government to aid the states in such matters as education and internal improvements were almost as old as the Constitution, but throughout the nineteenth century these gifts had been made primarily in the form of land or the receipts from land sales. By the

THE FIRST FORD, 1893.

GERMAN BENZ-PHAETON, 1896.

CADILLAC, 1903.

FORD MODEL "T," 1908.

FORD MODEL "T" COUPELET 1916.

The Automobile, denounced at first as a destroyer of good roads, became eventually the most important influence in stimulating the construction of an effective American highway system. The early progress from a "horseless carriage" to something resembling a modern motor car is shown in the illustrations. Assembly lines, such as those used by Henry Ford, made possible mass production and low prices, developments which soon put horse-drawn vehicles out of commission.

MUDDY ROADS. Such contretemps (1904) led to better roads and ultimately to the modern network of highways.

THE BLACKSMITH SHOP. Advent of the automobile soon made the blacksmith shop a thing of the past.

ASSEMBLY LINE, 1914. Large-scale automobile manufacturing is credited with being the father of modern mass production.

time Wilson became President this source of supply had so nearly approached exhaustion that some new form of subsidy had to be found. It was discovered in the form of the heavy receipts that came in, or could be made to come in, from the income tax. This revenue, it fell out, was collected from a comparatively small fraction of the total population, most of whom lived in the Northeast. But there was no gainsaying the fact that the earnings from which the income tax was paid were drawn from all over the nation. Coupled with the demand for better educational facilities and better transportation in the larger, poorer, and less densely populated states of the West and the South was the belief that in some fashion the government should attempt to redistribute among all the states the heavy earnings that were being piled up in the industrial areas of the Northeast. Southern and western votes on behalf of such a policy were easily accumulated, and the South and the West controlled the Democratic Party.

The new type of federal grants in aid of education began in 1914 with the passage of the Smith-Lever Act, which provided that the United States should match, dollar for dollar, the contributions of such states as chose to cooperate in a program of agricultural extension. The supervision of this work was left to the Department of Agriculture, working through the land-grant colleges. This measure was followed in 1917 by the Smith-Hughes Act, which appropriated funds, again on a dollar-matching basis, for education in commercial, industrial, and domestic-science subjects in schools of less than college grade. A board of vocational education, created by the act, was given the right to pass on the merits of the projects for which the various states proposed to use their allotments. The impetus which these acts gave to agricultural and vocational education, supplemented by the work of the Bureau of Education, the Children's Bureau, and other federal agencies, was felt in a steadily mounting number of the nation's high schools. Talk began in educational circles of the need

for a federal Department of Education with a seat in the cabinet, but opponents of the idea argued that federal control over the educational policies of the states must not be carried too far.

The Federal Highways Act of 1916 carried the dollar-matching principle into the field of road-building. The automobile, which was at first condemned because it tore up the roads, soon led to a demand for better roads that completely overtaxed the resources of the states. It was only natural in such an emergency to turn to the federal government for aid, and Democrats who could remember well Jackson's war on the Bank soon demonstrated that they had quite forgotten his Maysville veto. Aid was needed for a Lincoln Highway, just marked out from coast to coast, for a Dixie Highway from Lakes to Gulf, and for a half a hundred other projects. Yielding to the general pressure, Congress appropriated five million dollars the first year for distribution among the states. Size, population, and existing mail routes were all to be taken into consideration in determining the amounts allotted to each. Moreover, every dollar contributed by the federal government must be matched by a dollar from the state which received it, and federal control must be accepted in all such dollar-matching expenditures. When Congress made this first appropriation it knew little of the cost of road-building, but it soon found out a great deal. Nor could the process it had begun be ended until a complete set of federal highways, connecting every important center with every other, had been built.

Federal Highways Act

Viewing the manifold activities into which under Democratic auspices the national government had plunged, historically minded individuals could not fail to note the contrasts between Jeffersonian and Wilsonian democracy. The Jeffersonian ideal, so Jefferson himself had said, was "a wise and frugal government which shall restrain men from injuring one another, shall leave them

Wilsonian vs. Jeffersonian democracy

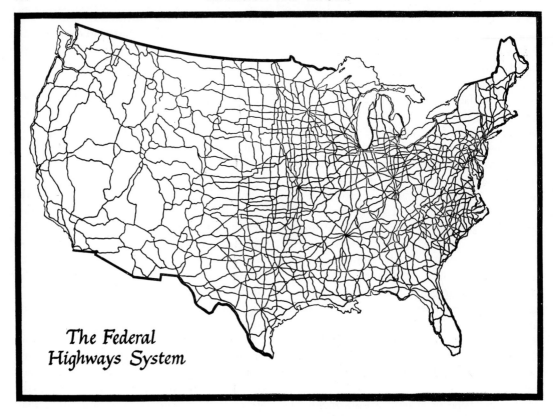

*The Federal
Highways System*

otherwise free to regulate their own pursuits
of industry and improvement, and shall not
take from labor the bread it has earned. This
is the sum of good government." However
the Wilsonian ideal might be described, it
could hardly be reconciled with the dictum,
"the less government the better." With
Hamiltonian thoroughness the professed disciples of Jefferson had devised a great national banking system that so far forgot
states' rights as to divide the United States
into twelve districts instead of forty-eight;
in their attempts to "restrain men from injuring one another," they had left industry
only a closely circumscribed area in which to
regulate its own pursuits; in protecting the
rights of labor they had limited the freedom
of individuals to a degree that Jefferson could
scarcely have imagined; and in taking thought
for the public welfare they had assumed for
government paternalistic privileges far more
sweeping than any he had fought. Fortunately historical consistency is often better
honored in the breach than in the observance.
It is no discredit to Wilson that in a new age
he reversed the tenets of the founder of his
party. States' rights and *laissez faire* in an
era of rapidly expanding national organization would have been anachronisms. Only
through a policy of enlightened nationalism
could the Democrats of Wilson's time hope
to find the "new freedom" which their leader
had promised.

Bibliography

Biographies of Woodrow Wilson are fairly numerous. R. S. Baker, *Woodrow Wilson, Life and Letters* (8 vols., 1927–1939), is extraordinarily detailed, and somewhat worshipful. Other biographies of consequence are Josephus Daniels, *Life of Woodrow Wilson* (1924); David Lawrence, *The True Story of Woodrow Wilson* (1924); W. A. White, *Woodrow Wilson* (1924); W. E. Dodd, *Woodrow Wilson and His Work* (1920); Eleanor Wilson McAdoo, *The Woodrow Wilsons* (1937); and Edith Bolling Wilson, *My Memoir* (1939). Special studies of merit on Wilson include William Diamond, *The Economic Thought of Woodrow Wilson* (1943); H. C. F. Bell, *Woodrow Wilson and the People* (1945); Arthur S. Link, *Wilson: The Road to the White House* (1947); and by the same author, *Woodrow Wilson and the Progressive Era, 1910–1917* (1954). McMillan Lewis, *Woodrow Wilson of Princeton* (1952), assesses Wilson's ability as a teacher and scholar.

Decidedly the best history of the Wilson administration is presented in Frederic L. Paxson, *American Democracy and the World War* (3 vols., 1936–48). The first volume of this series, *Pre-War Years, 1913–1917* (1936), deals principally with domestic phases of the first Wilson administration. Wilson's cabinet proved to be particularly fruitful in memoirs. In addition to Bryan's *Memoirs*, already mentioned, it produced W. G. McAdoo, *Crowded Years* (1931); D. F. Houston, *Eight Years with Wilson's Cabinet* (2 vols., 1926); W. C. Redfield, *With Congress and Cabinet* (1924); *The Letters of Franklin K. Lane, Personal and Political*, edited by A. W. Lane and L. H. Wall (1922); and Josephus Daniels, *The Wilson Era: Years of Peace, 1910–1917* (1944); and, by the same author, *Our Navy at War* (1922). John M.

Blum, *Joe Tumulty and the Wilson Era* (1951), is an interesting and informative biography.

Wilson's legislative program has also attracted the attention of many writers. On the establishment of the Federal Reserve System, for example, the literature is immense. Adequate guides through this maze for the student of history will be found in H. P. Willis, *The Federal Reserve* (1915); and P. M. Warburg, *The Federal Reserve System* (2 vols., 1930). Carter Glass, *An Adventure in Constructive Finance* (1927), throws light on the origin of the law. On Wilson's handling of the trust problem, O. W. Knauth, *The Policy of the United States towards Industrial Monopoly* (1914), is a good preliminary study, but for later developments see G. C. Henderson, *The Federal Trade Commission* (1924); and F. A. Fetter, *The Masquerade of Monopoly* (1931). On labor during Wilson's time, particularly for its more radical manifestations, see J. G. Brooks, *American Syndicalism; The I. W. W.* (1913); and P. F. Brissenden, *The I. W. W.; A Study in American Syndicalism* (1919). Other studies on significant subjects are J. G. H. Keith and W. C. Bagley, *The Nation and the Schools* (1920); and W. S. Holt, *The Bureau of Public Roads* (1923).

Wilsonian precepts found hearty support in the legal activities of Louis D. Brandeis, whom Wilson made an Associate Justice of the United States Supreme Court in 1916. On Brandeis's earlier career, see H. L. Staples and A. T. Mason, *The Fall of a Railroad Empire; Brandeis and the New Haven Merger Battle* (1947). Louis D. Brandeis, *Other People's Money* (1914), draws upon the findings of the Pujo Committee to set forth the facts about the existing system of finance.

WAR AND PEACE

1914 - 1929

The Wilson administration marks both the climax of an era of reform and the end of an era of relative peace. With the entrance of the United States into the First World War the progressive reforms that had seen their beginnings during the Presidency of Theodore Roosevelt came to an end; all else had to be sacrificed to the winning of the war. When the war was over, somehow, somewhere, the reform ardor of the earlier years of the century had vanished. For more than a decade the country was in the firm grip of conservatism.

The outbreak of general war in Europe made a far greater difference to Americans than most of them had foreseen. They were aware of the fact that the United States was full-grown as a nation, but they had not yet realized that the new status meant new responsibilities and new involvements. Wilson himself, when he undertook to defend the rights of a neutral nation, and incidentally the rights of all neutral nations, was not fully aware of the consequences that would follow his actions. The struggle to maintain neutrality was unavailing; the United States was caught up in the war whichever way it turned. By abandoning its neutral rights it would have helped the Central Powers to victory; by asserting them, it presently ceased to be a neutral, and ended up as a partner of the Allies. There was really no such thing as neutrality for a nation as large and powerful as the United States. Faced by that fact, the nation fought on the side from which it had little to fear, and against the side from which it had much to fear.

Wilson realized more fully than most of his countrymen that the only way to keep the United States out of war was to prevent the outbreak of war anywhere, at least war on a general scale, involving the great powers. His earnest fight for the League of Nations had this as its objective. It is by no means certain that the kind of League Wilson was able to have written into the Treaty of Versailles would have saved world peace, but it was the only comprehensive plan for world cooperation there was, and, looking backward, it is hard to see how giving it a try could have done any harm. The United States killed any chance that the League might prevent war when it refused adherence to the Covenant Wilson had drawn. This verdict at first was shot through with politics, but eventually it came to represent the will of the nation. Weary of war, unwilling to look its destiny in the face, the nation convinced itself that it could be a great power and at the same time enjoy the isolation it had known as a minor power. It turned its back on world leadership, and devoted itself to its own enrichment.

For a time this unrealistic retreat from the world seemed to bear pleasant fruit. American political leaders took the advice of American industrial leaders almost as completely as in the nineteenth century. In consequence, after a brief period of postwar readjustment, the nation — except for the farmers — enjoyed a period of lush prosperity. But before the decade of the twenties ended, it became apparent that the lush times were only the boom period of the old business cycle. With the year 1929 the crisis had come, and following it a depression as deep and dark as the preceding wave of prosperity had been high and handsome.

Nevertheless, a new American society had emerged that could never retreat to the old ways. It was geared to the automobile, the movies, and the radio; it was experimenting with the airplane and television; it had recorded notable gains in science, literature, and art; it made a fetish of mechanical gadgets and creature comforts; it sought to extend the blessings of education to every child; it experimented with prohibition, and struggled earnestly with the spirit of lawlessness, moral laxity, and crass materialism that had somehow infiltrated the fabric of prosperity. It had no inkling how hard the hard times that confronted it could be, but it was not without the latent abilities that would enable it to grapple effectively with whatever problems might come its way.

20

The Defense of Neutrality

Mexico — Fall of Huerta — Carranza — Constitution of 1917 — War in Europe — House's "Great Adventure" — Immediate causes of the war — American neutrality — International law and the war — Submarine warfare — The *Lusitania* — Election of 1916 — Wilson's bid for peace — The submarine again — Congress declares war — Why America fought

IT WAS apparent that Wilson in taking over the Presidency had little expectation of becoming a diplomat. His administration was organized with a view to domestic reform, a policy which extended even to his choice of Secretary of State, and neither in his inaugural address nor in his first message to Congress did he so much as mention foreign affairs. He was aware of impending difficulties between the United States and Mexico, but there is no evidence to show that this prospect caused him much concern. The imminence of a general war in Europe was as completely hidden from him as from other Americans.

Beginning in 1910, Mexico was in the throes of revolution. The old President,

Mexico

Porfirio Diaz, who for more than a third of a century had ruled as a military dictator, had at last been confronted with a revolt beyond his ability to suppress. From the point of view of outside investors Diaz had been a good ruler. By generous concessions he had encouraged foreign capital to develop the rich resources of his country, its railroads, mines, oil fields, public utilities, rubber and coffee plantations, and ranches. By 1912, so President Taft believed, American investments in Mexico had reached a total of not less than a billion dollars, while other huge sums came from European nations, particularly Great

Britain, Germany, and France. Naturally such heavy investments did not come unaccompanied, and the number of foreign agents resident in Mexico was very great — at least forty thousand from the United States alone. Under Diaz order was strictly kept, and foreigners had no more reason to be afraid than if they had remained at home.

Discontent with the Diaz régime was slow to develop, for the Mexican masses were ignorant and inarticulate, and Diaz had the guns. Diaz's policies, however, were as burdensome on Mexicans as they were helpful to foreigners. Political liberty was unknown in the republic, and active opposition to the President amounted to flirtation with sudden death. Nevertheless, as Diaz grew old his power began to wane, and some even of those who had long supported him joined forces with Francisco Madero, a sincere liberal, who in November, 1910, had raised the banner of revolt in northern Mexico. In less than six months Diaz was forced to resign and flee the country, whereupon Madero triumphantly assumed the Presidency. But Madero's devotion to constitutional principles annoyed those who wished merely for a younger Diaz, and in February, 1913, by a typically Latin-American *coup d'état*, Madero was arrested and murdered, and Victoriano Huerta, the man most responsible for the crime, took over the reins of authority.

Mexico

This was the situation that confronted Wilson when he took office. Deeply shocked **The fall of Huerta** by Huerta's behavior, the American President at once announced that he could show "no sympathy with those who seek to seize the power of government to advance their own personal interests or ambitions." Wilson's refusal to recognize Huerta as the President of Mexico left that country in an uproar, with counter-revolutionists active in nearly every section. When John Lind of Minnesota, whom Wilson sent on a special mission to treat with the various warring factions, failed to secure either the elimination of Huerta or the union of the forces opposing him, Wilson merely committed the American government to the policy of "watchful waiting," hoping that eventually Huerta would fall. Unfortunately, however, Huerta's régime was viewed with favor by most European nations, and with their encouragement and recognition it lasted on for many months.

"Watchful waiting" was easier to defend as an ideal than to practice. When on October 27, 1913, Wilson announced, **Vera Cruz** in an address at Mobile, Alabama, that the "United States will never again seek one additional foot of territory by conquest," strong detachments of the regular army were already mobilized along the Mexican border as if to strike, and impressive naval units were stationed in Mexican waters. These measures, the first of which was taken before Taft left office, were regarded as essential for the protection of American territory from Mexican marauders, and for the assistance of American citizens desirous of escaping from Mexico to the United States. Wilson's determination to be rid of Huerta led him also to lift the embargo on Huerta's opponents, while retaining it against Huerta. The danger of foreign intervention was lessened by American surrender to Great Britain on the Panama Canal tolls controversy [1] (supplemented presently by the outbreak of the First World War). Finally, on

[1] See p. 318.

the pretext that Huerta had failed to apologize properly for the arrest at Vera Cruz of a boatload of American sailors, Wilson asked and obtained of Congress permission to take such military measures as might be necessary to bring Huerta to terms. On April 22, 1914, American marines and bluejackets took Vera Cruz, occupied the customs house, and prevented the landing of munitions for Huerta from a German ship. Eighteen Americans and many more Mexicans were killed in the clash. Huerta promptly handed the American chargé d'affaires at Mexico City his passports, and the army and navy of the United States prepared for war.

The complete shipwreck of "watchful waiting" was prevented by the action of the

The Niagara Conference three leading Latin-American nations, the Argentine, Brazil, and Chile, who promptly offered mediation. This Wilson as promptly accepted, and instead of the war a conference was held at Niagara Falls, Canada, in which representatives of the United States and the two leading Mexican factions participated. The Niagara recommendations were of little consequence, but the conference at least afforded the United States an opportunity to welcome the assistance of other American nations in solving the Mexican problem, and, by postponing military action, it made possible the elimination of Huerta without resort to war. In July, Huerta resigned and left the country, and in August, Carranza, increasingly the favorite of the United States, entered the capital. In November of the same year the American occupation of Vera Cruz was terminated, but not until the summer of 1915, after a conference with what newspapermen called the "A B C" (Argentine, Brazil, Chile) and the "B U G" (Bolivia, Uruguay, Guatemala) powers, did the United States accord Carranza's government full recognition. Arms that Carranza was permitted to purchase in the United States helped the new President to restore order, much to the disgust of other revolutionary factions to whom American manufacturers were forbidden to sell. Carranza's chief opponent, Francisco Villa, vented his rage at the United States for this affront by twice crossing the international border in 1916, and murdering American citizens upon American soil. With the consent of Carranza an American military expedition under the command of General John J. Pershing advanced into Mexico in search of Villa, but it failed to catch him, and was presently withdrawn at Carranza's insistence.

With a semblance of order restored, Carranza proclaimed a new constitution in 1917 which was both anti-foreign and anti-clerical. It proposed to **Constitution of 1917** break up the great landed estates for distribution among the people and made many other provisions for the welfare of the working classes; it asserted that the nation had an imprescriptible title to the oil and mineral deposits within its borders; it limited landownership and concessionary rights to Mexicans; it ended the union of church and state, declared church edifices national property, and secularized the administration of all educational and benevolent institutions. From this time forward the relations between the United States and Mexico hinged upon the effectiveness with which the anti-foreign provisions of the Constitution of 1917 were enforced. Some Mexican Presidents, such as Obregon, who succeeded Carranza in 1920, treated American investors with considerable generosity, whereas others, such as Calles, whose ascendancy lasted for ten years beginning in 1926, were hard to handle. Wilson's policy toward Mexico was much criticized, but in spite of much insistence on military intervention, it at least stopped short of actual war, and it probably saved the Mexicans from another reactionary régime such as they had suffered from with Diaz.

Keeping out of war with Mexico became a matter of secondary importance for Americans after the outbreak of the **War in Europe** First World War in the late summer of 1914. To say that such a development was a shock to the American people is a gross understatement. They could hardly believe

Mexico during Wilson's administration was in the news north of the border to a degree unknown since the war of the 1840's between the two nations. Disorders within Mexico and along the border led to insistent demands that the United States intervene, but this was avoided, except for the Vera Cruz incident and the Pershing expedition.

PANCHO (FRANCISCO) VILLA. Revolutionary leader with his army on the march.

STREET SCENE. Violence and unconcern contrast strangely. City streets, midday.

the news they read. For years, in spite of the great earnestness with which they pursued the cause of world peace, they had taken it for granted that a general European war was impossible. The risks involved in such a conflict for all participants were too appalling. The international ramifications of capital formed too intricate a pattern; one great nation could not attack another without attacking itself. Little nations might fight each other, or a large nation might chastise a small one, but that the greatest and most enlightened nations of the world should fly at one another's throats seemed totally incredible.

Faced by the horrendous fact, the Ameri-can public, mainly through newspapers, went to school again and brushed up on its European history. Europe, it appeared, had depended for years on a "balance of power" to keep the peace. On the one side were Germany, Austria, and Italy, whose agreements as to military cooperation dated back to the days of Bismarck; on the other were Great Britain, France, and Russia, ancient enemies whom the rise of modern Germany had driven together. France and Russia had been allies since 1891, but the *entente* that bound Great Britain to France dated no further back than 1904, while the agreement between Great Britain and Russia came as

The balance-of-power system

THE MEXICAN ARMY. Troops assembled at Chihuahua.

MEXICAN BANDITS. Border towns were twice invaded by outlaws under Pancho Villa.

GENERAL PERSHING. Crossing the Rio Grande into Mexico.

late as 1907. Each set of partners made every effort to line up the lesser nations of Europe on its side. Some, like Switzerland, Belgium, the Netherlands, and the Scandinavian countries, maintained a rigid aloofness, but others more or less unofficially chose sides. The Triple Alliance, as the combination led by Germany was generally called, could count with some certainty on the support of Bulgaria and Turkey, while the Triple Entente, led by Great Britain, was on friendly terms with Spain and Portugal, and hoped for support from some of the Balkan nations.

Imperial rivalry, Americans learned, was another part of the picture. England, France, and Russia had old established empires to which they had added liberally in the last quarter of the nineteenth century. Germany, too, wanted a "place in the sun," but she had entered the competition too late to obtain the share of spoils to which she felt herself, as a great nation, entitled. She had a few colonies, but they were definitely second-rate. The Triple Entente, she believed, was created only to draw a "ring of iron" about her that would prevent the legitimate fulfillment of her de-

Imperial rivalry

sires. Imperial rivalry went further, however, than the mere acquisition of colonies. In the development of backward nations lay an equally inviting field. Rivalry for concessions in China, in Persia, in Morocco, in Turkey, in the Balkans, everywhere that money could be invested and profits taken, was acute, with sometimes one nation ahead and sometimes another.

In no region was the atmosphere more tense than in the Balkans and the Near East. **The Balkans** Here, in addition to the ever-present activities of the British and the Germans, the Austrians, the Italians, and the Russians all claimed special interests based on proximity, while the Russian government, as a cloak for its ambition to secure free access to the Mediterranean, essayed the additional rôle of protector to Greek Orthodox Christians wherever they might be found. In 1908 Austria had annexed Bosnia and Herzegovina, two Serbian provinces handed her for administration in 1878 after the Russo-Turkish War;[1] in 1911 Italy had fought a war with Turkey to justify her conquest of

[1] Russia had protested, but had been compelled to withdraw her objection when warned that an attack upon Austria-Hungary would lead to a war with Germany also. She promised Serbia, however, that she would not yield in such a fashion again.

Tripoli; and in 1912–13 two wars had been fought among the little Balkan countries themselves, as a result of which both Turkey and Bulgaria had lost much territory to Greece, Serbia, and Rumania. America did not know it, but for months before the war broke out the Balkan situation had European diplomats all on edge.

Another factor in the situation was the exaggerated nationalism that the nineteenth century had bequeathed to the twentieth. Anthropologists were **Nationalism** able to prove conclusively that most European nations, certainly all the great powers, were peopled by mongrel breeds, with no faintest title to racial purity, but nationalism owed more to a common language and history than to race. Each nation prided itself upon its cultural heritage, perverted its history to make its glories seem greater, and aroused the patriotism of its people to the highest possible pitch. It became, therefore, a matter of national pride to draw within the boundaries of any given nation all who spoke its language or shared its culture. France looked forward to the time when Alsace-Lorraine, taken from her by Germany in 1871, should be again a part of France; Italy dreamed of drawing *Italia*

News bulletins such as these posted outside the New York *Tribune* Building drew anxious crowds in 1914.

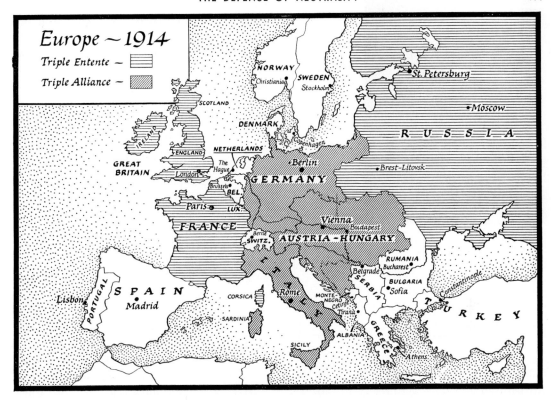

Europe ~ 1914
Triple Entente —
Triple Alliance —

irredenta within her borders; nearly every Balkan nation claimed a part of every other; subject nations like the Poles and the Czechs longed to be free. Austria-Hungary, a polyglot of nationalities, was every neighbor's envy.

All this was bad enough, but the dangers of the situation were compounded again and again by the rampant militarism and navalism that affected every European nation. Universal military training had long been a policy of all the great powers of Europe except Great Britain, and most of the lesser ones. Huge standing armies made every nation an armed camp, with preparedness a national watchword. The insular character of the British Isles saved Great Britain from the necessity of keeping pace in land armament with her rivals on the Continent, but she prided herself upon her navy, which she meant to keep overwhelmingly stronger than any other. Germany's challenge to British supremacy on the high seas — German naval officers toasted "the day" when they would

meet the British navy — not only aroused Great Britain to new building, but also led her to abandon her position of "splendid isolation," and to seek allies. On this account she had ended her ages-old rivalries with France and Russia, had made an alliance with Japan, and had sought with great earnestness to win the friendship of the United States.

In Europe the danger that war might break out at any moment was fully realized by the well-informed, and a few Americans understood the situation. Among them was Colonel House, the intimate adviser of the President, who in the spring of 1914 undertook what he called "the great adventure," a trip to Europe to promote the reduction of land and naval armament. House visited the Kaiser and talked with him for half an hour, established close connections with Sir Edward Grey and others in England, and had a try at Paris only to be frustrated there by the customary cabinet crisis. Everywhere he

House's "great adventure"

Colonel House, a non-military Texas colonel, was Wilson's close adviser at home and frequent representative abroad.

found "militarism run stark mad," but the British told him they were ready to talk reduction, and he so reported to the Kaiser. On June 28, 1914, shortly before he sailed for the United States, he learned that the heir to the Austrian throne, the Archduke Franz Ferdinand, and his wife had been assassinated at Sarajevo, in the province of Bosnia, but neither House nor his English hosts appeared to realize that this somewhat commonplace Balkan incident would lead to war. But war came nevertheless by the time House reached home. His "great adventure" was undertaken too late.

The incidents which led actually to the outbreak of war seemed trifling to Americans.

Immediate causes of the war The assassination of the Austrian heir-apparent, it appeared, was the work of some superpatriotic young Bosnian Serbs who disliked the Archduke's plan for making the "dual monarchy" of Austria and Hungary into a "triple monarchy" which would extend to the Slavs in the empire a right of participation comparable to that enjoyed by the Austrians and the Magyars. Should such a plan succeed, the creation of a greater Serbia might be long delayed, and it was with this thought in mind that the fatal shots were fired. Naturally the Austrian government took a serious view of the situation, the more so because it claimed, with some plausibility, that the Serbian government had guilty knowledge of the plot and had made no effort to prevent its execution. On the assumption that Serbian officials were in reality responsible for what had happened, the Austrian government decided upon punitive measures against its diminutive neighbor, and on July 5 obtained the German Kaiser's permission to go ahead. On July 23 an Austrian ultimatum was delivered to Serbia, which was purposely made so strong as to prevent complete acceptance, and when the Serbian reply proved "evasive" Austria began to mobilize for war.

The ramifications of the European network of alliances now came quickly into play. Russia, in her rôle of protector to all Greek-Orthodox nations, professed to fear that Austria's real intention was annexation rather than punishment, and supported Serbia's plea that the affair should be settled by the Hague Tribunal. Some such settlement was also strongly urged by Great Britain, France, and Italy, but Austria remained obdurate, while Germany, although bending every effort to localize the affair, refused to abandon her ally. On July 28, Austria declared war on Serbia, and on the following day Russia began mobilization. At this point the German Kaiser telegraphed frantically to his kinsman, the Tsar, to use his influence for peace, and the Tsar ordered that mobilization should be confined strictly to the Austrian frontier. But the Russian military leaders easily persuaded the Tsar to reverse himself, and on July 30 he gave the command for general mobilization. Thereupon the German government delivered an ultimatum to Russia, requiring the cessation of mobilization within twelve hours. When this demand fell on deaf ears, Germany on August 1 declared war.

France was the ally of Russia, and Germany now demanded to know in eighteen hours what France intended to do. Bound by her treaty with Russia, and ready to have a try at getting back Alsace-Lorraine, France replied that she would consult her own interests. Thereupon, on August 3, Germany declared war upon France and began at once to move troops toward the Belgian frontier. The German plan of campaign was to avoid the heavily fortified Franco-German frontier, demand passage through Belgium, and by speedy action outflank and destroy the French army before the anticipated Russian invasion of eastern Germany could do any vital damage — a plan that failed, for the Belgians resisted valiantly and the French re-formed their lines and eventually held the invaders at bay. Because the Belgians resisted, Germany, although bound by treaty to protect Belgian neutrality, declared war on Belgium. Great Britain, meantime, had been debating her obligations to France, which might mean less than aid in time of war, but the attack on Belgium, whose neutrality she, too, was pledged to defend, decided her. On August 5 she declared war on Germany.

The breath-taking speed with which Europe thus plunged into the abyss of war left **American neutrality** Americans aghast. The American course, however, was clear. Neutrality, since the days of George Washington, had become an American tradition. The only exception to the rule had been the War of 1812, an unconfessed blunder that no one expected to see repeated. On August 4 the President issued the first of a series of proclamations of neutrality by means of which the American State Department struggled to keep abreast of the rapidly spreading war. Two weeks later he urged the American public to be "neutral in fact as well as in name during these days that are to try men's souls. We must be impartial in thought as well as in action." Wilson's neutral course and the frenzied efforts of the government to bring stranded American tourists back from Europe met with universal approval. This was Europe's war, not America's, and with the help of a sizable army of war correspondents the American public pre-

pared to stand by and watch while the fire burned itself out.

But neutrality in thought and deed soon proved to be easier preached than practiced. Popular sympathy from the very **Sympathy for** outbreak of the war ran heavily **the Allies** in favor of the "Allies," as the nations opposed to Germany and Austria were called, and against the Central Powers. Austria and Germany had issued the first declarations of war; they were apparently the aggressors. Germany was the one nation which seemed wholly prepared for war. Her violation of her treaty with Belgium, called by one German diplomat a "scrap of paper," was hard to forgive. The ruthless progress of German troops through Belgium and northern France produced a deep feeling of sympathy for the under-dogs in the fight. Also, a certain amount of cultural solidarity between the English-speaking peoples came steadily to the fore. Not only Great Britain but the whole British Empire, including Canada, the near neighbor of the United States, was fighting with the Allies. Thus the war was in no small part a contest between the civilization that stemmed from England on the one side, and the German *Kultur* on the other.

American sympathy did not all run with the Allies. The large German element in the American population, ably led by **German-** the German-language press, sym- **Americans** pathized whole-heartedly with the Fatherland, and believed that the war was a British-led conspiracy to dismember and destroy Germany. Immigrants and the descendants of immigrants from the other Central Powers (eventually Turkey and Bulgaria joined Germany and Austria) tended also to be guided by sentiments imported from the Old World. The large American population of Irish descent was traditionally anti-British, and sometimes the hatred of Irish-Americans for England made them pro-German. In view of the strong minority sentiment these elements represented, neutrality seemed all the more essential as an American policy. Americans, it seemed, possessed a double loyalty;

they were loyal to the United States, but they were loyal also to the country from which they or their ancestors had come.

But there were problems of neutrality and a law of neutrality. Once, a century before, these problems and the American interpretation of the law which they involved had brought the United States into a European war; although most Americans thought of the War of 1812 as a mere continuation of the American Revolution, and were utterly unaware of the lessons it taught. Nevertheless, the similarities between the conditions that existed before 1812 and after 1914 were striking. In both cases the British navy commanded the high seas; in both cases the war meant an abnormal demand for American goods and American shipping; in both cases American neutral rights were frequently violated by both sides; and in both cases, as matters turned out, the United States was eventually drawn into the war.

International law was at least as old as Hugo Grotius, whose book, *De jure belli ac pacis*, was published in 1625. Its **International law and the war** rules had nothing more behind them than custom and the common consent of sovereign states. There was a law of peace that was rarely broken, and a law of war that was rarely kept. Invariably in time of war disputes broke out as to what the law really was, and how it should be construed. The rights of neutrals were particularly subject to debate. In general, Great Britain, who expected always to control the seas, was inclined to interpret neutral rights as narrowly as possible, whereas the United States, whose policy was permanent neutrality, and most other nations whose navies were inferior to the British, exaggerated the privileges of neutrals all they could. Attempts to obtain agreement on the meaning of the rules or to amend them met with no success. Neither the code of land warfare adopted by the Second Hague Conference, nor the Declaration of London with respect to naval warfare, was fully ratified. Promptly on the outbreak of the war Wilson asked the belligerents to adhere to the Declaration of

London, and the Central Powers agreed to do so if the Allies would bind themselves similarly. But the British feared the limitations on sea-power contained in the new rules and refused to accept them. The United States, therefore, in defending its neutrality had nothing better to depend upon than the jumbled mass of precedents and opinions that had accumulated from the time of Grotius on down. Many of these rules were utterly unrelated to the conditions of modern warfare, but obsolete as they were, they were the only rules that existed.

It was immediately apparent that the British had no notion of allowing the vast amount of American goods and shipping that soon took to the seas to proceed about its business as if there had been no war. This trade represented not merely, or mostly, the ordinary exports of the United States to Europe, but rather millions of dollars' worth of goods that were shipped purely in response to the wartime needs of the belligerents. The products of American farms and factories were earnestly coveted by both sides, and the United States, recovering from a business panic that the outbreak of war had precipitated, was eager to sell. All this was entirely satisfactory to the British, with the single important exception that they were determined to prevent anything of value to the Central Powers from reaching its destination. American goods might flow freely to the Allies, but not to their enemies. To accomplish their purpose the British had only to make use of their naval strength, but, unlike the Germans, they did what they could to reconcile wartime necessities with the existing rules of international law. For authority in dealing with neutral trade, they invoked three well-recognized belligerent rights: (1) the stoppage of trade in contraband goods, (2) the doctrine of continuous voyages, and (3) the blockade.

In each instance, however, British policy trod heavily on neutral toes. The British definition of contraband — that **Relations with Great Britain** is, goods that might be of direct (absolute contraband) or indirect (conditional contraband) use to the enemy — was so generous as to include every commodity that the Central Powers might wish to import. This, the American State Department claimed, was going too far. Further, British ships inspected trade between the United States and such neutrals as bordered on Germany, or on any of her partners, to make sure that none of it was ultimately intended for the enemy. If that was deemed to be the case, the trip was regarded as one continuous voyage which might be interrupted anywhere in its progress. This, too, was protested, although in the American Civil War the United States had done practically the same thing to prevent British commodities from reaching the South. Finally, a Ministry of Blockade was set up, which took good care that all shipping found anywhere on the high seas was carefully scrutinized to prevent the Central Powers obtaining anything that the British did not wish them to have. Such a blockade, the United States maintained, was illegal. It was enforced at long distance; it was applied against neutral as well as against belligerent coasts; and it was unenforceable against the countries that bordered on the Baltic Sea, because there the German navy, not the British, was supreme. But the British, while admitting that their methods might be somewhat unusual, argued that they were living up to the spirit, if not the letter, of the law.

The list of protests lodged by the United States against Great Britain included also vigorous denunciations of the British practice of taking neutral ships to Allied ports to be searched. The old rules contemplated search on the high seas, but with modern shipping such a practice was difficult, and after submarine warfare began, extremely dangerous. Sometimes American ships were held up for months at Allied ports. The British practice of searching American mail, both to and from Europe, also drew fire. The British held that American mail pouches, even when consigned to neutral countries, often contained things of value intended for the enemy, and they proposed also to know what information was going into and coming out of Germany. Exports from the Central Powers were given as scant courtesy as imports, and for long periods American industry was shut off from supplies obtainable only from Germany, such as dyestuffs, drugs, and sugar-beet seeds.

The American case against the British violations of neutrality was fully and conscientiously stated by the American State Department, but that was all. Probably the original intent was to collect damages after the war for proved violations, much as had been done after the Civil War. In private most American officials agreed that what the British were doing they must do to win, and that a British victory was to the best interests of the United States. Furthermore, American shippers soon grew accustomed to the British regulations, and by conforming to them escaped difficulty. Seized cargoes were usually paid for, but as time went on few cargoes were sent that were in any danger of being seized. Allied demands alone were sufficient to absorb all the surplus goods the United States could produce; indeed, war orders soon turned what might otherwise have been a depression into a boom. Other neutrals, such as Denmark and Holland, also acquiesced in the British regulations. Since the British rules occasioned no loss of life and practically no loss of property, and since for every market closed at least two new ones were opened, the American public had little heart to object.

The close community of interests that thus developed between the United States and the Allies was an object of great concern to the Germans, who were seriously handicapped by their inability to trade with America, and scarcely less to many German sympathizers in the United States itself. Some of the latter, including Senator William J. Stone of Missouri, chairman of the Senate Committee on Foreign Relations, favored a complete embargo on the sale outside the national borders of military supplies, particularly ammunition, but the State Department maintained with

Relations with Germany

GERMAN SUBMARINE U–10.

The submarine achieved great prominence in the eyes of the German militarists as a weapon to challenge British control of the seas. But its unrestricted use did not accord with American ideas of neutral rights, and helped bring the United States into the war.

THE LUSITANIA. Artist's impression of the catastrophe which figured prominently in ending United States neutrality.

THE ILLINOIS. U.S. Army tanker goes to its last berth. Photo taken by German U-boat that sank her, 1917.

unimpeachable logic that such trade was not a violation of neutrality. If Germany could not buy in the United States, it was the fault of the British navy, not of the American government. The German Foreign Office was frantic with rage. It not only lodged frequent and vehement protests against American acquiescence in British trade regulations, but it also encouraged the sabotage by German agents of such American industries as were aiding the Allies. For proved complicity in such plots the Austrian ambassador, Constantin Dumba, and several attachés of the German embassy, including Franz von Papen, were ordered to leave the United States.

Germany's most effective means of retaliation against the pressure of Allied sea-power **Submarine** proved to be the submarine, a **warfare** type of craft her engineers had brought to extraordinary efficiency. On February 4, 1915, in protest against the British stoppage of food shipments to Germany, the German government declared a "war zone" about the British Isles, and announced its intention to sink on sight every enemy merchantman within the area described. The United States was warned to keep American shipping out of the danger zone lest by mistake American ships and lives might be lost. Against this new type of warfare the American government lodged an immediate protest. Its illegality was obvious even to the German government, which defended it only on the ground of retaliation for allegedly illegal actions by the Allies, and the willingness of neutrals to acquiesce in them. The war-zone decree could not be defended as a blockade, for a blockade, to be binding on neutral nations, must effectively stop a major part of the shipping plying to and from the blockaded ports, whereas German submarines could not possibly hope to intercept more than an occasional ship. Visit and search by a submarine to ascertain the character of the ship and the nature of its cargo would be a virtual impossibility. Sinking on sight defied all the rules that required the attacking warship to provide for the safety of non-combatant passengers and crews. Reciting the evidence as to the illegality of the war-zone decree, Wilson's note of protest declared that the United States was "reluctant to believe" that the warfare contemplated would ever be carried into effect, and warned that in case American ships or lives were lost the German government would be held to a "strict accountability."

The threat to American neutrality posed by the submarine blockade led Wilson to **The** dispatch Colonel House to Eu- **Lusitania** rope on a "quest for peace." House cherished the chimerical hope that he might persuade the British to give up their blockade and the Germans their submarine attacks on merchantmen — the very weapons by which the two leading contenders hoped to win the war. Naturally his "quest" was fruitless, and on May 7, 1915, the British passenger liner, *Lusitania*, on which he had sailed to Europe a few weeks before, was torpedoed without warning and sunk off the Irish coast on her way to England. More than eleven hundred persons lost their lives, including one hundred and twenty-eight Americans. The sinking was a perfectly clear violation of neutral rights. Warning had not been given by a shot across the ship's bow, or in any other manner prescribed by sea usage. The fact that an advertisement in a New York paper had warned passengers of what might happen if they sailed on the *Lusitania* proved merely that the act was premeditated; no known rule of international law provided for a newspaper warning, and the advertisement was generally regarded as a hoax. The fact that the *Lusitania* carried ammunition designed for Allied use was equally irrelevant. The Germans had a perfect right to capture and confiscate the ship, even to sink it, but according to the existing rules they must first find out by a search what its cargo contained, and make satisfactory provision for the safety of non-combatants.[1]

American opinion on the *Lusitania* disaster was not entirely unanimous. The sinking was vigorously condemned, and frequently the old battle-cry, "Remember the *Maine*," was raised. Theodore Roosevelt, the most bitter of the anti-German leaders in the United States, described the attack on the *Lusitania* as an "act of piracy," and demanded immediate war. There were many who agreed with him, particularly along the Atlantic seaboard where the importance of keeping open the sea lanes to Europe was the

[1] The failure of the captain to zigzag his ship, as ordered, and to proceed at high speed through the submarine-infested zone, has led some persons to conclude that an unrevealed conspiracy existed to tempt the Germans to sink the *Lusitania*, so that the United States would be drawn into the war. There is no real evidence to support such a contention.

most keenly felt, but in the West and the South there was a tendency to ask why American citizens needed to venture into the danger zone. Should the American government not prevent such incidents in the future by prohibiting its nationals from sailing on belligerent merchant ships, or on ships carrying munitions? Bryan himself took this attitude, which Easterners called "provincial," and he would have been willing even to submit the *Lusitania* incident to arbitration. He signed the first note of protest that Wilson wrote, but the next one was too much for him, and he resigned from the cabinet rather than be party to a policy which in his judgment might easily lead to war. The same sentiment appeared in Congress, where only the vigorous intervention of the President prevented the passage of resolutions, sponsored in the House by McLemore of Texas and in the Senate by Gore of Oklahoma, forbidding American citizens to travel on belligerent merchantmen, except at their own peril.

The *Lusitania* incident led to a diplomatic correspondence between the United States **Germany** and Germany that lasted all **backs down** through the summer of 1915. Wilson's statement, made in a public address just before his first note was sent, "There is such a thing as a man being too proud to fight," seemed to betoken an attitude of weakness, but in three successive notes he argued the case with Germany, taking stronger ground each time. The submarine, he held, used as Germany was using it, was an illegal weapon, and any repetition of the *Lusitania* offense would be regarded as a "deliberately unfriendly" act. This was a threat of war, as the German ambassador to the United States, Count von Bernstorff, well knew, but the offense was repeated on August 10, when the *Arabic* was sunk with the loss of two American lives. Thereupon von Bernstorff, acting on his own initiative, promised the American State Department, in writing, that liners would not be sunk "without warning and without safety to the lives of noncombatants, provided that the

liners do not try to escape or offer resistance." Eventually the German government agreed to back up Bernstorff's words with deeds. Wilson had scored a signal diplomatic triumph, but he had won his victory only by the threat of war. When, either by accident or intent, a few more sinkings occurred, notably the *Sussex*, on March 24, 1916, Wilson in a spectacular appearance before Congress renewed his threat and forced from the German government a reiteration of its promises. German insistence that the United States should also force the Allies to give up their illegal practices, Wilson refused to consider as in any way pertinent to the problem. For nine months, whether because it feared the United States or because it had discovered a need for more and better submarines, the German government kept its promise.

In part, at least, to implement his threats, Wilson now put himself at the head of a strong demand for military **Prepared-** preparedness that, in spite of **ness** much "pacifist" protest, was sweeping the country. On the very day that he dispatched his third *Lusitania* note he authorized the Army and Navy Departments to draft plans for the strengthening of the national defenses, and in his annual message to Congress of December, 1915, he called emphatic attention to these proposals. Early in 1916 he toured the country to speak for preparedness, and on Flag Day, June 14, he led a preparedness parade down Pennsylvania Avenue. His determination to make the United States ready for war was strengthened by the failure of another House mission to Europe, this time in order to offer the Allies a "plan to compel peace." The idea was that Wilson, with Allied foreknowledge, should demand the cessation of hostilities and a conference of the belligerents to discuss peace terms. If the proposals of the Allies — to be agreed upon in consultation with the United States — were not accepted by Germany, then the United States would "probably" join the Allied war effort. Wilson's use of the word "probably," as an afterthought, no doubt wrecked the plan, and the war went on. It was Wilson's fear that if the war should continue the United States would be drawn into it that had led him to accept House's scheme in the first place; now with the failure of the plan the President was even more fearful of war and determined to be ready for it.

The battle of Jutland, fought May 31–June 1, 1916, gave Americans a rude jolt. In that engagement the German High-Seas Fleet boldly challenged the British Grand Fleet in the North Sea and inflicted such serious damage upon it as to serve warning that British command of the seas might soon be threatened. Already the Chicago *Tribune*, persistent champion of a foreign policy based on national self-interest, had warned its readers of the dire consequences to the United States in case the British fleet should be destroyed. "British naval supremacy," it pointed out editorially, "has been the stable factor in world diplomacy for so many years that all but diplomats are inclined to forget it." Americans were reminded that the Monroe Doctrine had been "largely built upon it" and that even the Oriental policies of the United States "had to look to it for sanction." If the British fleet were annihilated, every item of American foreign policy "would have to be scrutinized in the light of unknown conditions," and the nation's future might be gravely imperiled. To forestall such a calamity, many Americans, including apparently some of the makers of *Tribune* policy, were ready to form a definite alliance with Great Britain and enter the war.[1]

Opposition to preparedness in Congress now lost ground steadily, for even those who were unwilling to concede that the British navy was the first line of defense for the United States were not unaware of the dangers to America that might flow from German control of the seas. A National De-

fense Act which authorized the increase of the standing army to 175,000, and the National Guard to 450,000, became law early in June. Even more important was the Naval Appropriation Act, passed two months later, which provided for the immediate construction of four dreadnoughts and four battle cruisers. The total appropriation carried in this measure ran to $313,000,000, the largest sum Congress had ever voted at any one time for naval purposes. Three capital ships, the *Nevada*, the *Oklahoma*, and the *Pennysl-vania*, had just been completed. As two further means of promoting the national defense, Congress created (1) a Council of National Defense, to consist of six Cabinet officers and seven unpaid civilian experts, and (2) a United States Shipping Board, which might build, or otherwise acquire, and operate a fleet of merchantmen. The nation was preparing for war as it had never prepared for war before. And there were few who could ask seriously, "What war?"

The campaign and election of 1916 occurred during the months immediately following Wilson's diplomatic victory over Germany. That he would be a candidate to succeed himself in spite of the fact that the platform on which he was elected opposed a second term was universally taken for granted. Wilson was the leader of his party. Even the defection of Bryan gave the President no cause for alarm, for by the time Bryan quit the cabinet Wilson had wholly eclipsed him. The congressional elections of 1914 had found most of the Progressives back in the Republican fold, but the Democrats emerged triumphant in a straight-out two-party contest. The reason for this, everyone knew, was Woodrow Wilson. When the Democratic Convention met in St. Louis June 14, it had nothing to do but to renominate both Wilson and his running-mate of four years before, Thomas R. Marshall of Indiana, by acclamation, and to record in its platform complete approval of every action the administration had taken.

In a shrewd effort to unite all forces opposed to Wilson, the Republicans turned for

Election of 1916

---

[1] Chicago *Tribune*, March 14, 1916, and May 11, 1916. "Isolation, splendid or sordid, is not possible in our age. If the war has taught us nothing else, it has carried that lesson to the uttermost parts of the earth for those who will think." *Ibid.*, December 18, 1915.

their candidate to Associate Justice Charles Evans Hughes of the United States Supreme Court. With the discretion permitted to justices, Hughes had not openly taken sides for or against Germany, for or against intervention in Mexico, for or against preparedness. Nor had he been involved in any way in the disastrous split of four years before. His background as governor of New York was satisfying to the Progressive wing of the party, and his decisions as associate justice had caused the conservatives no alarm. Hughes's availabilty was so obvious that the Republicans, meeting at Chicago, June 7, named him on the first ballot, although he had done nothing to advance his candidacy and had not even said that he would accept the nomination. All fell out as planned. Roosevelt, by declining a Progressive nomination and supporting Hughes, dealt a death-blow to the party he had founded. Pro-Germans who thought Wilson had been unfair to Germany, anti-Germans who condemned his soft treatment of wanton aggressors, pacifists who were for peace with everybody at whatever price, war advocates who demanded, sometimes in the same breath, intervention in both Mexico and Europe, all rallied to the Republican standard. The day Hughes resigned from the Supreme Court to accept the proffered nomination he might have been elected, for then all factions could have claimed him as their own.

As the campaign progressed, the President's chances improved. His followers proclaimed truthfully that he had "kept us out of war," forgetting, perhaps, that he had a threat out that might draw the nation in. Many Progressives who had supported Roosevelt in 1912 were ready to change their allegiance to Wilson, for under his dynamic leadership a spectacular and comprehensive program of domestic reform had been achieved. Wilson got the "breaks" of the campaign. When a "hyphenate" American, Jeremiah A. O'Leary, whose object was to induce Irish-Americans and German-Americans to vote the Republican ticket, sent a long telegram to Wilson denouncing him for

unfairness to Germany, the President's reply was tart: "I would feel deeply mortified to have you or anybody like you vote for me. Since you have access to many disloyal Americans and I have not, I will ask you to convey this message to them."

Hughes, on the other hand, was obliged to conduct a campaign of carping criticism, while not being free to take **The Adamson Act** sides on anything. He had only one stroke of luck. The four great railway brotherhoods chose the Labor Day immediately preceding the election as a desirable time to strike for recognition of the basic eight-hour day and time and a half for overtime. Such a strike in an age when there was virtually no such thing as transportation by trucks would have throttled business and seriously hampered the President's efforts to speed up preparedness. Faced by this emergency, Wilson asked Congress to prevent the strike by enacting into law the demands of the brotherhoods. Congress obeyed with the passage of the Adamson Act, which became a law on September 1. Here Hughes had ample ground for criticism, and he made the most of it, but when he was asked if he would favor the repeal of the law, he could only reply, "You can't repeal a surrender."

The night of election day it appeared certain that Hughes had won. He had carried the East almost solidly, includ- **Wilson's narrow victory** ing the State of New York. He had carried also every state in the Old Northwest except Ohio. But the returns from the South and the farther West told a different story. The solid South was conceded to the Democrats, but nothing of the kind was expected from such dependable Republican centers as Kansas and California. Nevertheless Wilson carried every state west of the Mississippi except Minnesota, Iowa, South Dakota, and Oregon, which he lost by slender margins. In the electoral college the vote stood 277 to 254, the closest division since 1876, but the popular vote gave Wilson a lead of 9,129, 606 to 8,538,221. Again the Democrats captured both houses of Congress. Significantly the protest vote of nearly a million

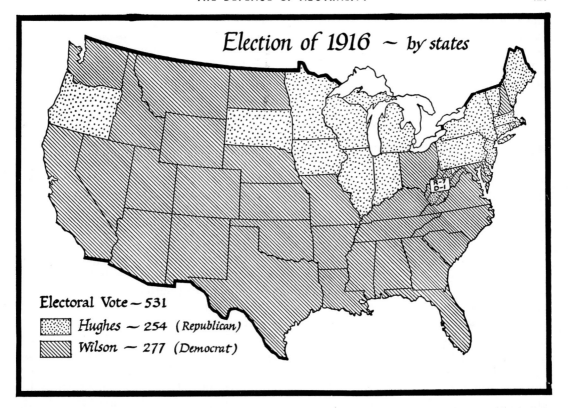

Election of 1916 ~ by states

Electoral Vote ~ 531

Hughes ~ 254 (Republican)

Wilson ~ 277 (Democrat)

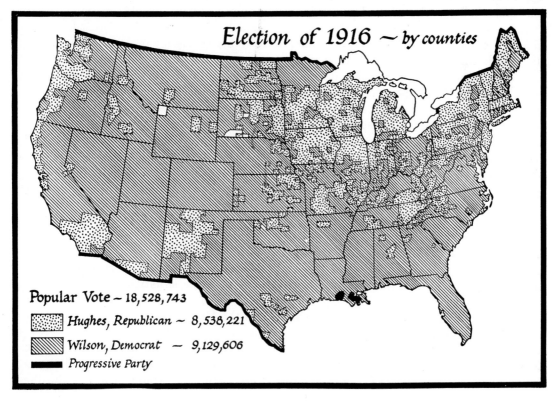

Election of 1916 ~ by counties

Popular Vote ~ 18,528,743

Hughes, Republican ~ 8,538,221

Wilson, Democrat ~ 9,129,606

Progressive Party

that had been cast for Eugene V. Debs, the Socialist candidate in 1912, dropped to 585,113 for Allen Benson, in 1916.

Deeply impressed by the popularity of the slogan, "He kept us out of war," Wilson **Wilson's bid** made another attempt shortly **for peace** after the election to bring the war to an end. In a note released December 20, 1916, he asked the fighting powers for "an avowal of their respective views" as to terms upon which the war might be concluded. Both sides, he observed, claimed to be fighting for "virtually the same" things, the rights of small nations and security for themselves. Perhaps if they would state their war aims more precisely, the differences between them would not be too great for statesmanship to bridge. Anticipating Wilson's offer, and with the military situation running strongly in their favor, the German authorities had already let it be known on December 12 that they were willing to enter a peace conference. They thus made Wilson's call for a statement of war aims appear to be a reinforcement of their offer. The Allies indignantly rejected the idea of treating with a victorious Germany, but, although deeply offended that Wilson should have made a move for peace at a time when Germany was winning, they replied at length to his inquiry. Peace, they said, must carry with it the restitution of conquered territories, full reparations for damages done, and guaranties that nothing of the kind would happen again. The Germans, however, refused in any way to divulge their peace aims, reserving for themselves full freedom of action at the council table.

Reading these replies, it seemed to Wilson that there could be no hope of a lasting peace if either side were permitted to have its way. On January 22, 1917, in an address before the Senate he began to argue the case for a "peace without victory," hoping that eventually the warring nations would heed the wisdom of his words. Such a peace as the victor might impose upon the vanquished, he said, "would be accepted in humiliation, under duress, at an intolerable sacrifice, and

would leave a sting, a resentment, a bitter memory upon which terms of peace would rest, not permanently, but only as upon quicksand. Only a peace between equals can last." He even outlined the terms of what he thought would constitute a just peace; equality of rights for small and great nations; universal recognition of the principle that governments derive their just powers from the consent of the governed; the right of every great people to have an outlet to the sea; the freedom of the seas "in law and in fact"; the limitation of armaments; and the avoidance by all nations of entangling alliances. Already he had made known his belief that there must be a league to enforce peace, and he told the Senate that if such a peace as he had outlined could be made the United States must do its part to maintain it.

These were brave words and true words, but before they were spoken the German government had already decided **The submarine** upon the policy which was to **rine again** rob them of their effect. Convinced by the German admiralty that unrestricted submarine warfare would speedily destroy enough shipping to isolate Great Britain and force her to sue for peace, the German government announced on January 31, 1917, that its submarines would sink on sight all ships found within specified war zones, whether neutral or belligerent. Its promise to the United States not to sink without warning and without making provision for the safety of non-combatants it withdrew on the ground that the United States had failed to stop the illegal practices of the Allies. Wilson had no choice now but to break off diplomatic relations with Germany, and this he promptly did.

For a time it seemed that the President was seeking a formula short of outright war to resolve the situation. Harking back to the undeclared naval war between France and the United States in 1798, he spoke of "armed neutrality," and asked Congress to grant him authority to provide American merchantmen with guns for their defense. A "little group of willful men," as the President called them, filibustered this measure to death, but the needed authority was found in an unrepealed law of 1797, and the merchantmen were armed. It was clear that if either the United States or Germany struck a blow there would be war. Wilson professed to believe that the Germans would never carry out their threats, but on March 18 German submarines sank three ships with loss of American lives. Thereupon Wilson called Congress into special session for April 2, and on the evening of that day read his call to arms. Everything else had been tried, he claimed, and now the only recourse was war. The President disclaimed any desire to fight against the German people, and distinguished between them and their government. That government, however, had challenged the security of democracy throughout the world. The United States was glad to fight it, he said,

for the ultimate peace of the world and for the liberation of its people, the German peoples included: for the rights of nations great and small and the privilege of men everywhere to choose their way of life and of obedience. The world must be made safe for democracy. Its peace must be planted upon the tested foundations of political liberty.

The response of Congress to the President's eloquent appeal was not unanimous, but it

Congress declares war

was overwhelming enough to be convincing. On April 4 the Senate passed the war resolution by a vote of 82 to 6, and on April 6 the House concurred by a vote of 373 to 50. Diplomatic relations with Austria-Hungary were promptly broken, but war was not declared until December 7. Against Germany's other allies, Turkey and Bulgaria, the United States issued no declarations of war. Claiming that the war against Germany was being fought on behalf of neutral rights generally, the United States urged other neutrals also to join in the crusade. As a result Cuba, Panama, Siam, Liberia, China, and Brazil entered the war on the Allied side, and several other nations broke off diplomatic relations. Long before, Japan

and Portugal had joined in order to fulfill their alliances with Great Britain, while Italy by generous promises and Greece by threats had also been brought into the Allied camp. Thus the war became in fact as well as in name a World War.

It is extremely difficult to catalogue all the factors that worked together to draw the United States into the war. Undoubtedly the diplomatic impasse over submarine warfare

Why America fought

did in fact precipitate hostilities, and he who says that the United States would have entered the war even if illegal sinkings had not been resumed says far more than he can

Declaration of War. Facsimile of President Wilson's proclamation, 1917.

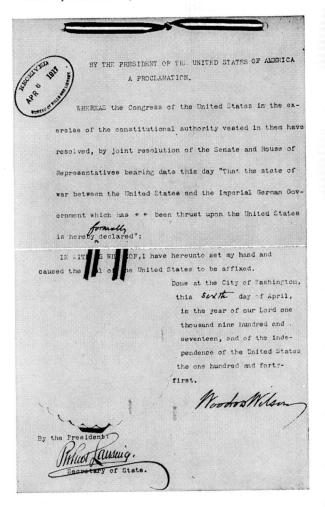

BY THE PRESIDENT OF THE UNITED STATES OF AMERICA
A PROCLAMATION.

WHEREAS the Congress of the United States in the exercise of the constitutional authority vested in them have resolved, by joint resolution of the Senate and House of Representatives bearing date this day "That the state of war between the United States and the Imperial German Government which has * * been thrust upon the United States is hereby *formally* declared";

IN WITNESS WHEREOF, I have hereunto set my hand and caused the seal of the United States to be affixed.

Done at the City of Washington, this *sixth* day of April, in the year of our Lord one thousand nine hundred and seventeen, and of the independence of the United States the one hundred and forty-first.

Woodrow Wilson

By the President:
Robert Lansing.
Secretary of State.

prove. But undoubtedly there were other considerations at work to influence the American people, such, for example, as British propaganda, which was skillful, and not always entirely honest. The stories of German atrocities in Belgium and northern France were exaggerated to the point of pure fiction. The German occupation was harsh and exacting, but the German troops, on the whole, were admirably disciplined, and behaved as ordered toward the civilian population. The British also took full advantage of their control of communications to cut off cable connections between the United States and the Central Powers, and to suppress in every way they could German arguments in defense of the actions their government had taken. But the German views got through in spite of British censorship, and were quite generally published in the American German language press, from which English language papers were free to copy at will. The fact of the matter was that British propaganda and British censorship were not necessary to convince the people of the United States that the Central Powers were the aggressors, and that the invasion of Belgium was a crime. The bulk of the American people took sides in August, 1914, and never wavered in their loyalties throughout the entire period of neutrality. But the British did present their case with skill, and they persuaded many Americans that a German victory would mean the beginning of the end for civilization.

There was also an economic side to the picture which it is difficult to state without **Economic factors** overemphasis. Most Americans were only faintly aware of it, but the facts were clear. The United States in the fall of 1914 escaped a depression only by virtue of war orders. These purchases were entirely legal, even when they were of contraband, and were so described by the American State Department. On loans to the Allies by American citizens to pay for war purchases, however, the State Department pursued a shifting course. At first it said that such loans were inconsistent with American neutrality, then it attempted to draw a distinction between loans and credits, but finally in August, 1915, it sanctioned both. By that time American prosperity was more closely bound up than ever with war orders, and without more loans there was the gravest danger that the orders would stop. With the spring of 1917 the Allies had too nearly exhausted their credit in the United States for comfort; already they owed American moneylenders over a billion dollars, and the limit for the sale of their securities had almost been reached. There was point to the argument of the American ambassador to Great Britain, Walter Hines Page, that direct loans from the United States were now necessary, both to avert a panic in the United States, and to save the Allied cause from collapse.

An indication of how completely American economy was geared to the war was given when the German submarine threat of January, 1917, precipitated a sudden stoppage of shipments from Atlantic ports. Thoroughly frightened by the German sinkings, neutral shipping refused to put to sea. Belligerent merchantmen continued to come and go, but they were utterly unable to handle the traffic that cluttered the docks and warehouses of the eastern seaboard, and tied up the railroads with unloaded freight as far west as Pittsburgh. Out of the transportation snarl a food and fuel shortage developed in some metropolitan areas; from the lower East Side in New York City, quite in the best revolutionary tradition, there was a march of angry women on the City Hall demanding food. Without American shipping to move American goods overseas, the United States faced economic collapse. And Great Britain faced the loss of the war.

In the spring of 1917 the Germans seemed closer to victory than Americans found comfortable. German offensives, particularly in the East, had been overwhelmingly successful; Allied offensives were invariably followed by "strategic retreats." Nearly all of Belgium and a large share of northern France lay in German hands. The Russians had lost most of Poland, while Rumania was no sooner in the war on the Allied side than her army was defeated and her territory occupied. Much of Serbia had long since been overrun. With Austria, Bulgaria, and Turkey completely subservient to the German will, the long-dreamed-of *Mitteleuropa* had become a fact. Germany had lost her colonies, and she was beginning to suffer from the Allied blockade, but with the assistance of the submarine she had good reason to believe that her road to victory was clear. From its inception unrestricted submarine warfare took a terrific toll. For weeks one ship out of every four that left British ports failed to return. Neutral shipping tended more and more to stay out of the war-zone. Even if the British navy remained afloat, Great Britain could be starved into submission.

That the United States was ready to rally to the Allied cause whenever such action should be necessary to prevent a German triumph seems far clearer today than it did at the time. Perhaps the Americans would have been willing to accept the "peace without victory" that Wilson advocated, provided that it left British sea-power in command of the eastern Atlantic. Whether they were ready to admit it to themselves or not, Americans knew that they dare not risk the exchange of a friendly power on the Atlantic for an unfriendly power. For a full century the American government had depended upon the friendly support of the British navy to guard the sealanes of the Atlantic. That navy alone had maintained the Monroe Doctrine when there was no American navy worthy of the name to assume the task. Anglo-American accord had made possible the location of part of the new American navy in the Pacific, where the threat of Japanese aggression was all too plain. Germany had long been restive under the restraints of the Monroe Doctrine, and had cast jealous eyes upon Latin-America as a field for colonial expansion. If she drove the British navy from the Atlantic, what would be her next move? As if to provide an unequivocal answer to this question, inter-

Fear of a German victory

cepted dispatches that the British secret service had turned over to the American government revealed on March 1, 1917, that Alfred Zimmermann, the German Foreign Minister, had offered Mexico the states of Texas, New Mexico, and Arizona, together with liberal financial aid, if Mexico would join Germany, in the event of war between Germany and the United States. Further, the President of Mexico was to urge Japan to shift to the side of the Central Powers, presumably in return for what spoils Japan might desire at the expense of the United States. After the news of the "Zimmermann plot" reached the public, a speedy declaration of war on Germany was inevitable.[1]

In explaining why war had to come, the Chicago *Tribune*, two days after Congress had acted, stated the case with admirable clarity:

So long as it seemed certain that Great Britain would retain control of the sea, the United States found merely an emotional interest in the war, regarding it as merely a question of European maps and European power. . . . The new naval weapon, the submarine, is effective. Great Britain's destiny is in doubt. . . . It is possible . . . that control of the seas would pass from the British. . . . It will comfort most Americans to know that the nation is doing what is needed for the guarding of the present and the guarantee of the future American republic.

In reality, the United States went to war in 1917 less because of German violations of international law, or Allied indebtedness to American producers, or the subtlety of British propaganda than because of the threat to American national interests that would have been implicit in German supremacy in the Atlantic. As a shrewd observer pointed out:

The United States took up arms in the last analysis because it seemed likely that without American intervention the scepter of the Atlantic would pass from the hands of English-speaking peoples

[1] The Zimmermann Note reached Mexico, January 19, 1917, and the British had decoded it well before they turned it over, on February 24, 1917, to the American authorities. Obviously its delivery was timed to obtain the maximum American reaction.

into those of a stranger. Of England the Americans had no genuine fears; the stranger might provoke them into a far more terrible war — with perhaps the Continent and a subdued Britain behind him — to settle the ascendancy of the Atlantic Ocean, and, beyond that, this Western Hemisphere.[1]

[1] Forrest Davis, *The Atlantic System* (1941), p. 245. Quoted by permission of Reynal and Hitchcock, Inc., publishers. Other similar comment is abundant. Secretary Lansing, as early as January, 1916, recorded his opinion that German absolutism threatened democracy everywhere, and hoped that the American people would soon realize that "it is safer and surer and wiser for us to be one of many enemies than to be in the future alone against a victorious Germany." Elihu Root, on September 14, 1917, said: "If we had stayed out of the war, and Germany had won, there would no longer have been a balance of power in Europe, or a British fleet to support the Monroe Doctrine and to protect America." Col. George Harvey, Harding's Ambassador to Great Britain, said at a dinner in London, with Department of State approval, May 19, 1921: "We sent them [our soldiers] solely to save the United States of America, and most reluctantly and laggardly at that. We were not too proud to fight, whatever that may mean. We were afraid not to fight. That is the real truth of the matter. And so we came along toward the end and helped you and your allies to shorten the war. That is all we did and all we claim to have done."

Wilson's argument that "we entered the war as the disinterested champions of right" was a rationalization. The United States entered the war because she dared not do otherwise. But Wilson touched a magic chord when he said, "The world must be made safe for democracy." With Russia in the throes of a democratic revolution a fair case could be made for the assertion that the war was a conflict between autocracies and democracies. With autocratic rulers free to build up military machines and to declare war at will, the peace-loving democracies were at a serious disadvantage. As long as autocracy was enthroned among the great nations of the world, a lasting peace could never be made. Thus the war became not only a war to make the world safe for democracy, but also a "war to end war." With these emotional overtones—afterthoughts though they may have been — ringing in their ears, the American people went to war in a mood of the highest idealism. They fought for the survival of democracy and for peace on earth.

The defense of the Atlantic

Bibliography

On the Mexican situation, Carleton Beals, *Porfirio Diaz, Dictator of Mexico* (1932), presents well the essential facts. Interesting sidelights are contained in Edith O'Shaughnessy, *Intimate Pages of Mexican History* (1920). Satisfactory discussions of American policy toward Mexico are given in J. F. Rippy, *The United States and Mexico* (new ed., 1931); and J. M. Callahan, *American Foreign Policy in Mexican Relations* (1932). See also G. M. Stephenson, *John Lind of Minnesota* (1935); and Harold Nicolson, *Dwight Morrow* (1935).

Two of the best works (not entirely in agreement) on the background of the European conflict are S. B. Fay, *The Origins of the World War* (2 vols., 1928); and B. E. Schmitt, *The Coming of the War* (2 vols., 1930). On American involvement, *The Intimate Papers of Colonel House*, edited by Charles Seymour (4 vols., 1926–28), provide a running commentary from the pen of an insider. See also the biographies of Wilson and his colleagues listed for the preceding chapter, p. 401, and the general treatises on American diplomacy listed on p. 285. F. L. Huidekoper, *The Military Unpreparedness of the United States* (1915), was among the books much quoted by preparedness advocates. Much information pertinent to an understanding of the period is in Mark Sullivan, *Our Times*, V, *Over Here, 1914–1918* (1933). The plight of German-Americans in the United States has been well studied in Carl Wittke, *German-Americans and the World War* (1936); and C. J. Child, *The German-Americans in Politics, 1914–1917* (1939).

On the problems of American neutrality, Charles Seymour, *American Diplomacy during the World War* (1934), takes the Wilson position, as does also the excellent study by Alice M. Morrissey, *The American Defense of Neutral Rights, 1914–1917* (1939); but see also Edwin Borchard and W. P. Lage, *Neutrality for the United States* (1937), which argues that the United States was not wholly neutral. An older but still useful study is J. W. Garner, *International Law and the World War* (1920). Wilson's foreign policy as a whole is well considered in Harley Notter, *The Origins of the Foreign Policy of Woodrow Wilson* (1937); and E. E. Robinson and V. J. West, *The Foreign Policy of Woodrow Wilson* (1917). B. J. Hendrick, *Life and Letters of Walter H. Page* (3 vols., 1922–25), reveals clearly the strongly pro-Ally bias of the American Ambassador to Great Britain; while Robert Lansing, *War Memoirs of Robert Lansing, Secretary of State* (1935), helps further to explain the steady drift from neutrality to war. For the side of the Central Powers, see Constantin Dumba, *Memoirs of a Diplomat* (1932); and J. H. von Bernstorff, *My Three Years in America* (1920). The experiences of the American Ambassador to Germany are recounted in J. W. Gerard, *My Four Years in Germany* (1917).

H. C. Peterson, *Propaganda for War* (1939), examines closely the effects of British propaganda in the United States. It should be compared with J. P. Jones and P. M. Hollister, *The German Secret Service in America* (1918); H. D. Lasswell,

Propaganda Technique in the World War (1927); and Armin Rappaport, *The British Press and Wilsonian Neutrality* (1951).

Most of the books specifically concerned with the entrance of the United States into the First World War are highly controversial. Newton D. Baker, *Why We Went to War* (1936); Charles Seymour, *American Neutrality, 1914–1917* (1935); and, by the same author, *Woodrow Wilson and the World War* (1921), all tend to blame the submarine primarily. Criticism of American neutrality was first effectively stated in C. H. Grattan, *Why We Fought* (1929). The case against American entrance into the war was carried further by Walter Millis, *Road to War: America, 1914–17* (1935); and C. C. Tansill, *America Goes to War* (1938). The curious attitude of the Chicago *Tribune* toward the war is stated in an unpublished University of Wisconsin Ph.D. thesis, Warren Jenkins, "The Foreign Policy of the Chicago *Tribune*, 1914–1917" (1942). The Second World War, with its indifference to neutral rights, seemed to indicate that the reasons for American entrance into the First World War lay much deeper than the earlier controversialists had believed. The need of Anglo-American solidarity, ignored by most of them, and its role in taking the United States into the war is stated forcefully in Forest Davis, *The Atlantic System: The Story of Anglo-American Control of the Seas* (1941).

21

The First World War

The American Army — Financing the war — The wartime government — The "home front" — The Navy in the war — The A.E.F. — The Russian Revolution — The American contribution to victory — The debate on war aims — Defeat of Germany — — Election of 1918 — The Paris Peace Conference — The Senate and the Treaty — Wilson's collapse — What the United States won by the war

BEFORE the entrance of the United States into the war most Americans had taken it for granted that geographic conditions would limit American participation primarily to naval and financial aid. A succession of missions to Washington from the Allied governments soon proved that the Allies needed everything — money, ships, supplies, men — if the Central Powers were ever to be defeated. Nor could they wait. The United States must act quickly, and avoid mistakes.

Most of all the Allies needed men, and the plans of the General Staff for raising an army **The Ameri-** in leisurely fashion were imme- **can army** diately speeded up. Convinced that the principle of volunteering, upon which both Great Britain and the United States had relied mainly in earlier wars, had been proved by England's recent experiences to be inadequate, the military leaders persuaded Congress to approve in May, 1917, a Selective Service Act. This measure required all men between the ages of twenty-one and thirty (later eighteen and forty-five) to register for military service. The registrants were then divided by local civilian boards into five classes, the first of which consisted of able-bodied, unmarried men, without dependents. The 2,810,296 men actually selected for service during the war came from this group alone. An elab-

orate lottery system determined the order in which they were called. Not all of the American army, however, was raised by the draft. The combined strength of the regular army and the National Guard stood at about 750,000 men when the Selective Service Act went into operation, and from this pool of trained and partially trained men the military leaders drew heavily in creating the various units that composed the new National Army. By the end of the war the continuous transfer of individuals and units from one division to another had broken down fairly completely distinctions as to origin. For the training of the men thirty-two camps and cantonments, mainly located in the South, were hastily constructed.

Almost as difficult as the problem of obtaining the men was the problem of supplying the army with competent **Officer** officers. For the higher ranks, **training** officers of the regular army and the National Guard were promoted, but for the lower grades the army depended upon the graduates of hastily organized officers' training camps from which "ninety-day wonders" were soon being turned out in profusion. At first only volunteers of excellent promise were accepted for officer training, but later candidates selected on merit from among the drafted men were also given a chance to earn commissions. Political appointments, such as had disgraced the formation of the Civil War armies, both North and South, were deliberately avoided. This decision was a great disappointment to Theodore Roosevelt, who had aspired to emulate his performance in the Spanish-American War, and lead a division of volunteers to France. The war, he complained, was a "very exclusive war," and his hatred for Wilson, already burning brightly, flamed up anew after his rejection.

The problem of financing the war would have been great had the United States had **Financing** only her own expenditures to **the war** consider, but she had also to finance her Allies in considerable part. Economists urged a "pay-as-you-go" system, with taxation of wartime profits and earnings furnishing most of the revenue, but such a system was a practical impossibility. For one thing, money was needed immediately, and newly devised taxes would take months, or even years, to produce the needed funds. Congress therefore resorted to loans, as well as taxes. The first loan act, which became law on April 24, authorized the borrowing of five billion dollars, and subsequent credits were voted as needed. Five huge bond issues were floated, the first four known as "Liberty Loans," and the last, which was offered after the fighting had ended, as the "Victory Loan." The total amounts so subscribed reached $21,448,120,300, and drew upon the savings of over sixty-five million individuals. Each loan was accompanied by a great "drive," in which every conceivable device was used to induce both those who had the means and those who had not to subscribe. The bonds were issued in denominations as low as fifty and one hundred dollars, and the purchase of such a bond, on the installment plan if need be, was made almost a test of loyalty. "Four-minute men" harangued theater, church, and school audiences on the iniquities of the Germans and the necessity of the war. Individuals who were suspected of being "pro-German" were compelled to prove their patriotism by particu-

larly generous contributions; if they did not, their houses might be decorated with yellow paint, or they might even be subjected to rough handling. Corporations with large payrolls put pressure upon their employees to subscribe. Thrift stamps and war-savings certificates were devised to tap even the savings of the children. Unfortunately the securities marketed by the government were negotiable, and because the government refused to buy them back ahead of dates set for maturity they depreciated materially in value. Speculators thus made excellent profits; worse still, the bonds, unlike the non-transferable bonds issued during the Second World War, served to promote rather than to restrict inflation. Prices rose rapidly, and without serious attempt on the part of the government to hold them down.

The income tax, with its surtax feature, offered an easy means of expanding the national revenue. The Revenue Act of 1916 had already doubled the normal income tax, but the War Revenue Act of 1917 doubled it again, bringing it to four per cent, and taxed incomes as low as a thousand dollars. The graduated surtax and the tax on corporation earnings were also raised, and a new graduated excess profits tax took from twenty to sixty per cent of such business earnings as exceeded the average for the years 1911–1913. The excise taxes on liquor and tobacco were steeply increased, and a host of "nuisance taxes" introduced — on railroad and sleeping-car tickets, on theater tickets and club dues, on telephone and telegraph messages, and on numerous other "luxuries." Postage rates went up, the ordinary letter rate from two to three cents. These were the beginning, and still higher taxes were written into the Revenue Acts of 1918 and 1919. Altogether the United States raised a total of $11,280,000,000 from taxation, nearly one third the amount spent or lent during the same period. The total expenditures from April, 1917, to October, 1919, aggregated $35,413,000,000 of which $9,406,000,000 was lent to the Allies.

The contribution of the American people

to the cost of the war included also millions
Private of dollars expended for private
benevolence benevolence. Probably the Red
Cross, with its emphasis on medical care and
hospitalization, was most appreciated by
soldiers and public alike. Its first drive for
funds, held immediately after the flotation of
the First Liberty Loan, netted over $100,-
000,000, and subsequent drives brought in
other huge sums. The Young Men's Christian Association, the Knights of Columbus,
the Jewish Welfare Board, and the Salvation
Army also solicited contributions for wartime activities, and spent lavishly in their
efforts to make life in the army camps and
overseas more bearable. Besides all this,
women's organizations knitted socks, prepared bandages, and provided numerous
other items of consequence to the soldier's
comfort. Undoubtedly the benevolent
agencies did much to substitute harmless
amusements for the traditional resort of the
soldier to intoxication and immorality, and
they sought also to bolster up army morale.
The "Y" suffered much criticism, partly because it accepted the task of vending such
supplies as candy and cigarettes, instead of
confining its efforts more exclusively to
straight-out gifts. Nearly all of the work
supported by benevolence had to be done;
if private agencies had not undertaken it, the
government itself would have been obliged
to do so. So valuable did this work seem
that the government encouraged all drives
for funds by benevolent societies while the
war was on. Gifts to churches, colleges, hospitals, and endowment funds, whether directly concerned in the war or not, at least
cultivated the important habit of giving.

In general the government itself took care
of the dependents of soldiers, and made what
War risk provision it could to prevent the
insurance men who fought the war from
becoming objects of charity in the future. By
rigorous examinations it kept out of the
service all those who might reasonably be
expected to break under the physical and
mental strain of war. Men who had families
dependent on them for support were given
deferred classification, which amounted in
effect to exemption from the draft. The
Bureau of War Risk Insurance, established
originally in 1914 to write marine insurance,
was enlarged in October, 1917, so as to permit it to assume for the military forces of
the United States the obligations ordinarily
associated with employers' liability. A soldier who had dependents was obliged to allot
a part of his pay to his family, and to this
sum the government, in accordance with a
prescribed schedule, added more. If a soldier
died in service, his widow received seventy-
five dollars a month until remarriage. If he
were disabled, he received compensation commensurate with the degree of his disability.
If he were maimed in such a way as to need
re-education, the government accepted the
responsibility for that also, and charged the
Federal Board for Vocational Education with
the duty of providing the necessary training.
And for all who would take it the government offered an insurance policy of from one
to ten thousand dollars, at cost, the premi-
ums to be deducted from the soldier's pay.
By 1919 over four and a half million such
policies had been written, representing an
aggregate of thirty-eight billion dollars. The
pay of the American private was thirty dollars a month, the highest in the world, and it
was supposed that the insurance system
adopted by the government would forestall
the customary drive for pensions at the end
of the war. This hope, as events proved, was
vain.

The raising of huge armies, the flotation of
unprecedentedly large loans, and the ruthless
expansion of taxation were tasks **Public**
that in a democracy would have **opinion on**
been impossible but for the sup- **the war**
port of a thoroughly aroused public opinion.
When war was declared in 1917, it is reasonable to suppose that the action was approved
by a majority of the people as well as by a
majority of Congress. But the popular majority was by no means so overwhelming as
the vote in Congress indicated; indeed, many
a congressman would have voted the other
way had he dared. Most of those who

doubted the wisdom of American entrance into the war were sympathetic with the Allied cause and ripe for conversion, but a small minority, composed of pro-Germans, Socialists, and pacifists, were bitterly opposed. Many of them were in complete agreement with Senator LaFollette, who in casting his vote against the war resolution maintained, "I say Germany has been patient with us," or with Morris Hillquit, the Socialist, who asserted, "The country has been violently, needlessly, and criminally involved in war." It was essential, if the sacrifices necessary to win the war were to be borne, that public opinion should support the government with virtual unanimity. Partly with this end in view the President, on April 14, 1917, designated the Secretaries of State, War, and Navy as a Committee on Public Information, charged with the duty of publishing the facts about the war. As the executive officer directly responsible for carrying on the work he named George Creel, a well-known and energetic journalist.

Creel's task was both to disseminate the news and to "sell" the war to the people. **The Creel Committee** He had no commission to act as censor; only in so far as military men and the Allies were able to exercise control of the news were the facts suppressed. But he could spread and interpret what news there was, and that he meant to do. Gathering about himself as able a group of journalists and historians as he could find, and adding artists, actors, photographers, and linguists as needed, he began to release a spectacular barrage of information and propaganda. Through the *Official Bulletin*, published daily beginning May 10, 1917, he told what was going on with little attempt to distort, and set an example in the treatment of war news that most of the newspapers of the country followed. But he never forgot that a part of his mission was to convince all Americans, and if he could the whole wide world besides, that the American case for war against Germany was unimpeachable. Through "Red, White, and Blue" books, compiled by its historians, the C.P.I. told

the public the things it needed to know: *How the War Came to America; The War Message and the Facts Behind It; The President's Flag Day Speech; German War Practices; Why Working Men Support the War; The War Cyclopedia; Conquest and Kultur; The German War Code; The Government of Germany.* Ready-made editorials were distributed by the million to overworked country editors, who ran them gratefully and believed what they said. Foreign-language newspapers were objects of special solicitude, and soon got the idea as to what they were expected to print. Speech-making material for the seventy-five thousand four-minute men and other orators was ladled out with a free hand; motion pictures taught similar lessons to those who lacked either the mind or the will to read; strikingly designed posters helped along the various "drives" by which the war was to be won. Unfortunately, talking pictures and the radio were not yet available; had they been the imagination palls at the thought of the uses the C.P.I. would have made of them.

The net effect of this propaganda was to convince Americans more deeply than ever that only by winning the war **Restrictions on civil liberties** could the "world be made safe for democracy"; only by a "war to end war" could a lasting peace be achieved. The war became a holy crusade, and those who dared oppose it were given short shrift. It was in response to this opinion rather than because there was any longer reason to fear the minority that the drastic Sedition Act of May 16, 1918, was added to the milder Espionage Act of June 15, 1917. Freedom of speech and of the press meant little in wartime, as the Supreme Court quickly explained. Said Mr. Justice Holmes, voicing a unanimous opinion: "When a nation is at war many things that might be said in time of peace are such a hindrance to its effort that their utterance will not be endured so long as men fight, and that no court could regard them as protected by any constitutional right." Long prison sentences were meted out to prominent critics of the war,

ENLISTMENT. James Montgomery Flagg poster, 1917. In the collection of the Museum of Modern Art.

SHIPPING. Poster by James H. Daugherty.

American artists contributed effectively to the winning of the war by the remarkable series of war posters and illustrations they produced. In this way they promoted the cause of enlistments, encouraged generosity in the purchase of war bonds, and helped magnificently to keep up the nation's crusading spirit.

VICTORY BONDS. Howard Chandler Christy poster, 1919.

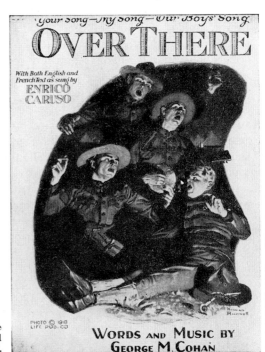

WAR SONGS. Cover of sheet music for the best known song from the First World War. Design by Norman Rockwell, 1918.

including Eugene V. Debs, four times the Socialist candidate for President, and Victor L. Berger, Socialist congressman from Milwaukee. Berger's newspaper, the Milwaukee *Leader*, and the even more outspoken New York *Masses*, a Socialist monthly, lost their second-class mailing privileges. Hundreds of conscientious objectors were sent to jail.

Neither the political nor the economic organization of the United States was fitted **Council of** to meet the emergencies of war, **National** and drastic changes had to be **Defense** effected in both. Fortunately the defense measures of 1916 had provided for a planning board known as the Council of National Defense. The six members of this council were cabinet officers with an abundance of other work to do, but they were expected to follow the recommendations of an Advisory Commission of seven civilians, also provided for in the law. Headed by Daniel Willard, president of the Baltimore and Ohio Railroad, and assisted by as many "dollar-a-year" volunteers as it could use, the Advisory Commission soon became what Professor Paxson has aptly called a "civilian general staff." Largely through the plans it devised, the government of the United States was reorganized for wartime efficiency, while industry, agriculture, labor, and every other form of American economic life were forced to operate with the single-minded purpose of winning the war. Temporarily the United States ceased to be a democracy, and the freedom of the individual was sacrificed to the larger necessity of a military victory. New and powerful administrative agencies, responsible only to the President, told the people of the nation what they might and might not do, and what they had to do.

Before the war was over, six great wartime agencies had taken over the chief respon-**The wartime** sibility for adjusting American **government** economic life to the necessities of the war. The oldest of these was the United States Shipping Board, which had been created the year before the war broke out. Through its Emergency Fleet Corporation it struggled valiantly, and with consid-

Bernard M. Baruch, American financier, began his long career of service to the government during the First World War.

erable success, to build ships faster than the submarines could sink them. A second agency, the Food Administration, had as its responsibility the supply of food, both for soldiers and for non-combatants, overseas. As Food Administrator, Herbert Hoover preached the "gospel of the clean plate," persuaded the American people to accept "wheatless" and "meatless" days, and encouraged all who could to plant "war-gardens." More important still, Hoover's Grain Corporation set high prices for wheat that led to a remarkable expansion of the nation's wheat acreage, with a corresponding increase in production. A Fuel Administration dealt similarly with the pressing coal and oil problem; a Railroad Administration took over all the railroads of the country and operated them as if they were a single system; a War Trade Board licensed foreign trade and took care that American commodities did not reach the enemy; and a War Industries Board, most powerful of all, took full command of American production. Under Bernard Baruch as chairman, the W.I.B. told manufacturers at will what materials they could use, and what materials they must save. It could order them to undertake totally new endeavors. It could determine priorities, and so give or withhold both the raw materials and the transportation upon which every manufacturer depended. It could standardize products, and with the President's approval it could, and did, fix prices. Of great assistance in working out the orders of the War Industries Board was the War Finance Corporation, which, operating with a half-billion dollar revolving fund granted by Congress and such other sums as it could borrow, lent to business that needed encouragement, while restraining vigorously all non-essential demands for capital.

Long before the war was won, the government of the United States was exercising powers that in ordinary times would have been deemed incompatible with democracy. The six great "war boards" — Shipping, Food, Fuel, Railroads, War Trade, and War Industries — owed responsibility for their acts to the President alone. Beginning in March, 1918, the heads of these boards met with him weekly as a kind of war cabinet. Such legislation as they required, Congress ordinarily felt obliged to supply. The most sweeping of these grants was contained in the Overman Act, signed May 20, 1918, by which the President, until six months after the war should end, was given free rein "to utilize, coordinate, or consolidate any executive or administrative commissions, bureaus, agencies, offices, or officers" at will; to create new agencies and abolish old ones, and to utilize funds voted for any purpose in whatever way he deemed that purpose best served. One critic of the bill suggested ironically an amendment: "If any power, constitutional or not, has been inadvertently omitted from this bill, it is hereby granted in full." Working closely together under the President, and assured of support by state councils of defense locally maintained, the war boards all but supplanted the ordinary civil authorities. The amount of grumbling that accompanied the resulting regimentation of American life was surprisingly small. The nation took pride in the fact that a democracy could make war efficiently, even if in the process it had to sacrifice many traditional liberties. The tyranny that existed, people well understood, was of their own creation, and could be destroyed when the war was over.

The support of organized labor for the war was greatly promoted by the earnest efforts of Samuel Gompers, one of the seven members of the Advisory Commission, whose insistence that the war must not be used to depreciate wages or labor standards became a governmental policy. Indeed, the draft, which took many men out of the labor market, and the cessation of immigration, which cut off an historic source of supply, led to a labor scarcity that drove wages to unprecedented heights. By 1918 the average worker was earning nearly twice as much as in 1914, and even allowing for the mounting costs of living he was fully twenty per cent better off than he had been when hostilities began. High wages and steady employment meant also prosperity for the labor unions, whose membership shot upward during the war by no less than thirty-seven per cent. To facilitate the mobility of labor the government greatly expanded the United States Employment Service of the Labor Department, and to fill labor shortages it encouraged the use of women in industry. Labor disputes were kept at a minimum. A War Labor Conference Board, created early in 1918, laid down the rules that should govern the relationship of capital and labor, and a National War Labor Board, under the co-chairmanship of William Howard Taft and Frank P. Walsh, acted as a court of last resort in the settlement of labor disputes. The formulation of labor policies in the new war industries was handed over to a War Labor Policies Board of which Felix Frankfurter became chairman.

Inevitably every American came to feel keenly the effects of the war. The Federal Reserve System stood up admirably under the unexpected burdens it had to shoulder, but the huge bond issues and expanding business they supported made for cheap money and currency inflation. In theory the gold

Labor and the war

standard was maintained, but gold did not circulate and dollars bought less and less. Salaried employees had greater difficulty than laborers in obtaining the wage increases necessary to meet the rising cost of living, and some of them suffered acutely. Women not only invaded industry, but they were also increasingly in evidence in business and the professions. For the most part the educational system of the country carried on as usual, although higher education was hard hit by enlistments, and, after the service age was lowered from twenty-one to eighteen, by the draft. In an effort to combine education and military training the Students' Army Training Corps was established in practically all the colleges during the fall of 1918. Young men of draft age were allowed to continue their studies in uniform and at the expense of the government, while learning the art of war from army officers. The compensation paid the colleges by the government for the use of their facilities saved many of them from financial collapse, but as an educational experiment the S.A.T.C. was a failure. With many of the nation's physicians mobilized for war, the influenza epidemic of 1918 became a serious plague. The "flu," indeed, baffled medical science, and took a heavy toll both in the cantonments and among civilians.

Undoubtedly the most unlovely feature of the "home front" was the ugly intolerance **The "home** bred by the war. Americans of **front"** foreign extraction suffered from it more acutely than any others, especially when they had been "pro-German" in the period of neutrality. Most of the acts of intolerance were not the acts of the government, but of the people. The German language, which before the war had been more widely taught in America than any other foreign language, was all but eliminated from the public schools, and suffered from drastic restrictions in the colleges. Printing, preaching, teaching, even talking in the German language were treated as if criminal offenses, and were sometimes made so. Musicians of German origin, such as Frederick Stock and Fritz Kreisler, were publicly humiliated.

Honorary degrees granted to Germans before the war were revoked by the universities that had granted them. All aliens and all citizens of recent alien origin were made to feel their inferiority to the so-called "native Americans." It was as Wilson himself had said on the eve of war: "Once lead this people into war and they'll forget there ever was such a thing as tolerance. To fight you must be brutal and ruthless, and the spirit of ruthless brutality will enter into every fiber of our national life, infecting Congress, the courts, the policemen on the beat." Conformity, as the President had foreseen, became the only true virtue, and the man who refused to conform had to pay a severe penalty. Perhaps the nation would never in any other mood have endured the sacrifices of war.

For actual combat duty the navy preceded the army to Europe by many months. Indeed, Rear-Admiral William S. **The navy** Sims, who was chosen for over- **in the war** seas command, was in London before the United States entered the war, and by May 4 the first detachment of American destroyers had crossed the Atlantic. Ultimately three hundred warships, large and small, and seventy-five thousand officers and men were serving in the overseas detachments of the American navy. Their activities extended from the vicinity of the British Isles to the Mediterranean. No doubt these reinforcements were partly responsible for the fact that the experiment of Jutland was not repeated. The American naval forces made no effort to operate separately, but became to all intents and purposes a part of the British Grand Fleet. American ships were used, among other things, to enforce the very rules of blockade against which the United States as a neutral had protested so vigorously.

The greatest single concern of the combined navies when the United States entered the war was the defeat of the submarine. This was eventually accomplished by a variety of means. American insistence had much to do with the laying of a mine barrage across the opening of the North Sea, between the Orkney Islands and the coast of Norway.

CONVOYS. Aerial view of convoy approaching French coast.

On the sea, American activities were less spectacular than during the Second World War. The American navy saw little actual fighting except against the submarine. But the success with which whole fleets of troop ships and cargo ships were convoyed across the Atlantic was one of the war's greatest victories.

DOCK SCENE. On-the-spot sketch of freight handling, St. Nazaire, France. By André Smith, 1918.

IRON, CANNED GOODS, AND HAY. Three of the many products destined for European consumption, 1918.

SMOKE SCREEN. Effective method of convoy defense. U.S. destroyer *Henderson*, 1918.

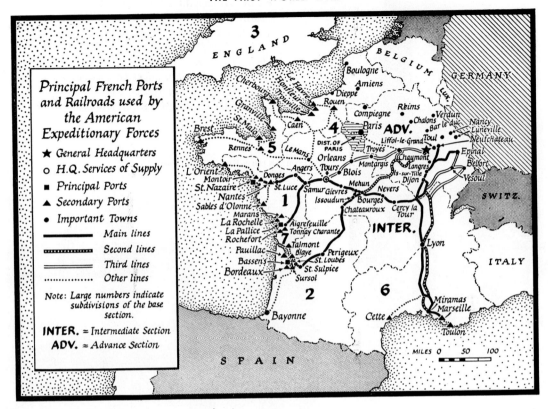

Principal French Ports and Railroads used by the American Expeditionary Forces

★ General Headquarters
o H.Q. Services of Supply
■ Principal Ports
▲ Secondary Ports
• Important Towns
——— Main lines
·········· Second lines
═══════ Third lines
············· Other lines

Note: Large numbers indicate subdivisions of the base section.

INTER. = Intermediate Section
ADV. = Advance Section

This, and a similar mine barrage across the Straits of Dover, seriously crippled submarine activities. Cruising destroyers, armed with improved means of detection, also hunted down the "U-boats," and sank them with depth-charges. By the end of the war about half the German submarine flotilla had been destroyed. American ships likewise played a leading rôle in convoying merchantmen and troop ships through the danger zone, thereby cheating the submarines of their prey.

The frantic pleas of the Allies for American troops in France led the General Staff to **The A.E.F.** revise its plans with respect to the training of the American army. It was decided that troops would have to be sent overseas only partly trained and partly equipped. The rest of the work could be done over there. Mainly as an earnest of good intentions General John J. Pershing was ordered to France in May, 1917, as head of the American Expeditionary Forces, and next month the first of the American detachments began to arrive. The American plan called for more than the mere transporting of troops. Already the facilities of France and her allies were being taxed to the limit to support their own armies, and the American contingent must be a help, not a burden. Ten thousand tons of wheat reached France in advance of the troops it was supposed to sustain, and, to make way for the coming of further detachments of the A.E.F., harbors had to be dredged, docks constructed, debarkation depots created, railroads made over, freight-yards laid out, telegraph and telephone lines erected, hospitals, barracks, and warehouses put together. All this was done by American labor on the American plan, and for the most part with American materials, although American sawmills sometimes condescended to turn European logs into lumber. Over five million tons of supplies were sent abroad by the United States before the armistice was signed. As to man-

OVER THERE. U.S. troops crossing Westminister Bridge. 1917

The American Army had to be transported thousands of miles to reach the fighting front, an experience new to most of the "doughboys," who had only recently ceased to be civilians. "Over there" they saw sights that as tourists they might have enjoyed, but that as soldiers they were only too eager to exchange for the crowded transports homeward bound.

WATCH ON THE RHINE. Rainbow Division sentries on the waterfront. Nieder-Breisig, Germany.

THE DOUGHBOY. Drawing by Capt. Harry Townsend, A.E.F.

power, the American records show that 2,079,880 men were transported overseas. Not all of these were fighting men, but from them Pershing netted forty-two combat divisions.

From the first General Pershing, who had himself written the orders under which he operated, insisted upon the creation of a separate American army. This did not please the Allies, who wished to use the American troops as replacements, to be brigaded with French or British units. But Pershing was convinced that three years of defensive fighting had unfitted the Allied armies for effective offensive tactics, and finally forced the Allied leaders to give in. The American army thus became a wholly independent unit, and in October, 1917, began to take over a quiet sector of the battle line. When in

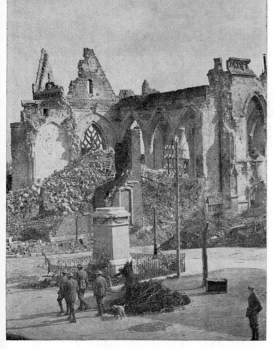

RUINS. Cathedral at Peronne.

THE RETURN. The *Mauretania* docking with the first boatload of soldiers.

March, 1918, however, Russia made a separate peace and the Germans began a great *Friedensturm*, designed to end the war in the West, Pershing did not hesitate to lend troops to the hard-pressed French. In the summer fighting before Paris, especially at Château-Thierry early in June, the Americans gave a good account of themselves. Surprised and pleased, Marshal Foch, now Allied commander-in-chief, saw the point to Pershing's insistence, and cooperated cheerfully in the creation of a separate American command. Pershing was never able to supply from American sources all the *matériel* of war necessary for the operations of a complete army. The ordnance, the tanks, and the airplanes he used were in considerable part of Allied manufacture. But the men were all Americans, and they did Pershing's bidding, subject only to the supreme command of Foch. Before the war ended, American troops held one fourth of the battle line, more even than the British.

Pershing's first action as an independent commander was the reduction of the Saint-Mihiel salient, where the German line protruded sharply across the Meuse River southeast of Verdun. With some French assistance, but following his own plans, he attacked both flanks of the salient and in two days' time had it completely straightened out. Half a million American troops participated in the battle; they suffered seven thousand casualties, and took sixteen thousand German prisoners. Had they been permitted to do so the Americans would gladly have pushed ahead toward Metz, across the German frontier, but no farther away than they had already come. Metz was a key city in the German defenses, and had it fallen the war might have ended in September rather than in November. Pershing was ready with his plans, but Haig, who headed the British forces, favored a different strategy, and Foch listened to Haig instead of

The Saint-Mihiel salient

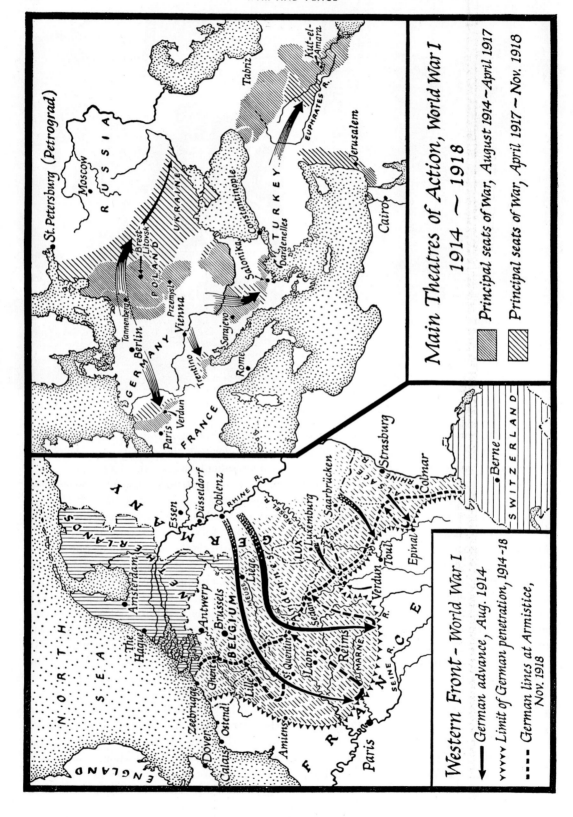

Main Theatres of Action, World War I
1914 ~ 1918

Principal seats of War, August 1914 ~ April 1917

Principal seats of War, April 1917 ~ Nov. 1918

Western Front ~ World War I

German advance, Aug. 1914

Limit of German penetration, 1914–18

German lines at Armistice, Nov. 1918

Pershing. The American army was shifted to the westward, and directed down the Meuse River and through the Argonne Forest toward Sedan. The war ended before Sedan was taken, but by November 11, Pershing explained later, the American troops "had cut the enemy's main line of communications, and nothing but surrender or an armistice could save his army from complete disaster."

The advance of the American army in the Meuse-Argonne was only a part of the larger **The Meuse-** campaign by which Foch **Argonne** smashed his way to victory through the supposedly impregnable Hindenburg Line, behind which the Germans had taken refuge. Three other major offensives, the Ypres-Lys, the Somme, and the Oise-Aisne, preceded and accompanied the American drive. With the Allied forces acting for once in complete coordination, an Allied drive was begun north of Saloniki against Bulgaria, another against the Turks in Palestine, and a third against the Austrians in Italy. Everywhere the Allied arms were successful. Before the end of September, Bulgaria was out of the war; Turkey quit in October; Austria surrendered early in November; on November 11 Germany, too, with her armies everywhere in full retreat, gave up the fight.

American participation in the war was not wholly confined to the fighting in France. In July, 1918, an American regiment was sent to Italy, and in October two American divisions were lent to the French for use in Belgium. More debatable was the part played by American troops in Allied maneuvers against Bolshevist Russia. Without authority of a declaration of war against Russia, five thousand Americans fought with the Allies in the Archangel-Murmansk campaign that lasted from September, 1918, to May, 1919; while ten thousand Americans joined an Allied expedition to Vladivostok and eastern Siberia that lasted until January, 1920.

The United States watched with tremendous interest the revolutionary experiment **The Russian** in Russia. As soon as possible **Revolution** after the overthrow of the Tsar in March, 1917, an American mission headed by Elihu Root, former Secretary of State, and Hugh L. Scott, chief of staff of the United States Army, was sent to Petrograd to help the new government to a good start, and to encourage it in the continued prosecution of the war against Germany. But the wheel of revolution in Russia turned rapidly to the left, and before the end of the year Nicolai Lenin and Leon Trotsky, leaders of the most extreme advocates of Communism, the Bolshevists, had climbed to power with the assistance of German gold, and on the promise to the Russian people of peace. Late in December, 1917, at Brest-Litovsk, they agreed to close out the war on German terms, convinced, no doubt, that when the time of world revolution came, it would make little difference what nation held what territory.[1] Finland had declared its independence in July, 1917, and when the Treaty of Brest-Litovsk was finally signed in March, 1918, Poland, Lithuania, and the Ukraine were also separated from Russia, preparatory to leisurely German assimilation. It was clear from this peace that Germany at the moment, whatever her original intent, was engaged in a war of conquest. Should the fighting on the western front end in a German victory, it seemed reasonable to suppose that similar terms would be imposed upon the rest of the Allies. The defection of Russia thus was a tremendous help to Germany, and the repudiation by the Bolshevists of their foreign debts by no means improved the feelings of the Allies. Naturally they wished to bring to power in Russia a government that would resume the war against Germany and agree to meet its financial obligations. The military activities on Russian soil, in which the United States participated, were parts of the ill-fated Allied projects for bringing about these results.

The military contribution that the United States made to the winning of the war was not inconsiderable. An army of **America's** 3,500,000 men was raised, of **contribution** whom 1,400,000 saw active serv- **to victory** ice overseas. Had the hostilities lasted over

[1] This was a preliminary agreement. The final treaty was signed three months later.

Women at war. Yeomanettes stationed at the Charleston Navy Yard.

into 1919, as the Allied plans anticipated, the American activities would have assumed a still more impressive character. As it was, the "Yanks" captured 44,000 prisoners, took 1400 guns, and brought down 755 enemy airplanes. The American contribution in the air was somewhat disappointing. In spite of the earnest activities of the Aircraft Production Board, and the creation of the new "Liberty engine," "the eyes of the army went aloft in foreign planes." But 11,000 aviators had been trained by the time of the armistice, and 4300 of them were in France. American casualties, considering the short period of time Pershing's troops were engaged, were heavy — heavier, probably, than in corresponding French and British units where the troops were better trained and the utmost effort was made to hold down losses in manpower. But the total number of deaths suffered by the American army from all causes was under 125,000 and of these less than half were battle deaths. Compared with the 1,700,000 battle deaths suffered by the Russians, the 1,600,000 by the Germans, the 1,385,000 by the French, the 900,000 by

the British, and the 800,000 by the Austrians, the American losses seemed inconsequential, but they were sustained during only about six months of actual fighting, while for the European belligerents the war lasted over four years. Excellent health precautions practically eliminated such filth diseases as dysentery and typhoid, from which so many American soldiers had died in previous wars, and skillful surgery and hospitalization returned five sixths of those wounded to their regiments. The worst scourge came from the influenza, which took as heavy a toll among civilians as among soldiers.

But it would be quite unfair to judge the part that the United States played in the war wholly from the military angle. **The will** The American troops came to **to win** Europe with a will to win, and their coming bolstered enormously the morale of the war-wearied Allies. Confidence in victory was standard equipment for all Americans, and it was systematically whipped up at every training camp, both in the United States and in Europe. It was a singing war, with tunes and verses inspired by cocksureness. The men went to camp, embarked and disembarked, marched and relaxed to "It's a long way to Tipperary," "Over There," and a dozen similar "hits." The American "dough-boy" refused even to be depressed by the petty vexations of army life. He made fun of them in the stories passed along by word of mouth, and in the *Stars and Stripes*, a newspaper that the soldiers of the A.E.F. themselves edited in a style that combined the best and the worst of the college daily and the American sports page. Punctilious officers saw themselves as privates saw them in cartoons and comic strips drawn by professionals. The unlimited assurance with which the American army tackled its task impressed even the Germans.

There was much more for which the United States could claim credit. Pershing was quick to point out that the Allies **Unity of** needed above all else a unified **command** command. "When one was at- **and supply** tacking, the other was usually standing still."

Allied Military Leaders. While the American, French, and British armies retained their separate identities under Pershing, Foch, and Haig (above), the establishment of a unified supreme command under Foch enabled them to coordinate their strategy more efficiently.

American insistence, together with the grave threat of German victory as a result of the *Friedensturm*, helped pave the way for the assumption of supreme command by Marshal Foch. The American genius for business organization led to another almost equally important reform — a unified system of supply. The American idea was that all resources — shipping, food, munitions, and other supplies — should be pooled, and drawn upon as needed. To accomplish this end much inertia had to be overcome, but before the war was over a remarkable transformation had been wrought. For this change much credit was due to General Charles G. Dawes, Pershing's purchasing agent. Last, but not at all least, came the ideal of a peace so even-handed in its justice toward all nations, great and small, victor and vanquished, that the causes of war would be forever abolished. Six thousand years of history proclaimed the illusiveness of such a hope, but the eloquent arguments of the American President made the hope itself a reality. Long before the entrance of the United States into the war, Wilson had been urging such a settlement,

and before its close his preachments had gained an almost miraculous ascendancy over world opinion. What he stated in general terms every nation translated into the specific terms its national aspirations demanded. A "peace of justice" meant something quite different to each people, but in every case it meant something worth fighting for. And if this war should be indeed the war that would end all war, the goal was doubly worth the effort. Wilson's idealism became a two-edged sword. On the one hand it provided the Allies with a unified purpose in the war; on the other it tended to break down enemy morale. Why fight against a peace of justice?

Wilson's interest in a peace of justice had been stated clearly in his "peace without victory" speech of January, **The debate** 1917. After the entrance of the **on war aims** United States into the war, he modified his stand only by insisting on a complete victory over the autocratic rulers of the Central Powers, but for the *people* of Germany and of her allies, as distinguished from their *governments*, he still adhered to generous terms. When Pope Benedict XV urged a negotiated

443

peace in August, 1917, Wilson in reply drew this distinction clearly. The United States, he said, wished neither punitive damages, nor the dismemberment of empires, nor the establishment of exclusive economic leagues after the war, but the autocratic rulers must go. That his ideas comported ill with the network of semi-secret treaties on the post-war world that the Allies had agreed to among themselves, the President must have known. These treaties planned a victor's peace rather than a peace of justice, but Wilson seemed to believe that the popularity of his views with the masses in all countries would bring the Allied governments eventually to his program. As a matter of fact, Lloyd George, the British Prime Minister, while fully aware of his country's commitments, echoed the President faithfully, although Clemenceau, the French Premier, admitted frankly, "My war aim is to conquer."

Wilson gave classic statement to his views in a speech delivered before Congress in January, 1918. If the world were to become "a fit and safe place to live in," the peace should embody these "Fourteen Points":

1. Open covenants of peace openly arrived at.
2. Freedom of navigation upon the seas, alike in peace and in war.
3. Equality of trade conditions among all nations consenting to the peace.
4. Guaranties that national armaments will be reduced.
5. The adjustment of colonial claims in the interests of the populations concerned.
6. The evacuation of all Russian territory.
7. Belgium must be evacuated and restored.
8. French territory should be freed and restored, and the wrong of Alsace-Lorraine should be righted.
9. Readjustment of Italian frontiers along clearly recognizable lines of nationality.
10. The peoples of Austria-Hungary should be accorded opportunity for autonomous development.
11. Rumania, Serbia, and Montenegro should be evacuated and restored, and Serbia secured an access to the sea.
12. The Turkish portions of the Ottoman Empire should be assured a secure sovereignty, but other nationalities under Turkish rule should have autonomy.
13. An independent Polish state with free and secure access to the sea.
14. A general association of nations for mutual guaranties of political independence and territorial integrity.

Wilson's program was not the product merely of his own thinking. In the main, it was suggested to him by the "Inquiry," a group of scholars drawn together by Colonel House to provide the American State Department with the specific data it would need at the peace conference. It was never formally accepted by the Allies as their own. Wilson spoke for himself and for the government he headed, but he could not speak officially for the nations he usually referred to as the "Associates" of the United States in the war.

The German government in repeated state papers showed that it had no interest whatever in the type of peace **German** Wilson sought. Its real answer **aspirations** to the Fourteen Points was the Treaty of Brest-Litovsk with Russia in March, 1918. This treaty sheared off from Russia over 300,000 square miles of territory, with a population of 56,000,000 people. It took away one third of Russia's railway mileage, seventy-three per cent of her total iron output, eighty-nine per cent of her coal production, five thousand factories, mills, distilleries, and refineries. By a supplementary agreement signed in August, 1918, Germany exacted also an indemnity of six billion marks. There is no reason to suppose that the terms of this treaty were unpopular with the people of Germany. Probably the people, no less than the government, were ready for a peace of violence, similar to the Treaty of Brest-Litovsk, against the western nations. Wilson's Fourteen Points were described by one German writer as a "real symphony of a will to no peace." It was only in defeat that either the German government or the German people began to show an interest in a "just peace."

The German defeat, when it came, was thoroughly and complete in a strictly military sense. Later on the German people were persuaded to believe that they had laid down their arms in the hope of a just peace when they might have fought on indefinitely. But they were badly beaten, and their commanding officers knew it. Their allies had been knocked out, one by one. Their supposedly impregnable Hindenburg Line had cracked. Their submarine campaign had failed. Their services of supply were breaking down. The morale of their troops, in full retreat, was declining. Revolution, born less of Wilson's promises than of military disaster, was in the air. Ludendorff and Hindenburg informed the German Emperor in September that all was lost, and that peace must be made at once. Ludendorff had a nervous breakdown. It was the hopelessness of the military situation and the certainty of Allied victory that led the German government, like a drowning man grasping at a straw, to ask Wilson for an armistice on the basis of the Fourteen Points. It was the impending collapse of the military front, and not merely unrest at home, that forced Germany to sue for peace.[1]

Defeat of Germany

The negotiations for an armistice were begun early in October, 1918, by a new German Chancellor, Prince Max of Baden, reputedly a liberal, who professed to Wilson that he spoke "in the name of the German government and the German people." Even so, the pre-armistice negotiations were long drawn out. Wilson's Fourteen Points were accepted by the Allied leaders only after elaborate interpretations and amendments, to all of which the Ger-

The armistice

mans were obliged, because of the military situation, to consent. Among other things, Wilson's second point, the "freedom of the seas," was ruled out altogether at the insistence of the British, while with reference to invaded territories, it was expressly stipulated that full compensation must be made for all damage done "by land, by sea, and from the air." When the German envoys signed the armistice they knew, therefore, that they were obtaining substantially less than the Fourteen Points, but they knew also that failure to sign meant only the substitution of unconditional surrender for what was left of the Wilson program. Even so, the armistice was not actually signed until the German fleet at Kiel had mutinied rather than put to sea for a final test of strength, the Kaiser himself had been forced to abdicate, and leaders who owed no allegiance to the former "autocratic rulers" were in complete control. With the signing of the armistice, November 11, 1918, the war came to an end.

The military terms of the armistice revealed still further the extremity of the German collapse. No nation with the faintest hope of victory could have accepted them. The German army must retire to the left bank of the Rhine, surrendering huge stores of military supplies and railroad equipment; the bridgeheads at Cologne, Coblenz, and Mainz must be occupied by Allied troops; Allied prisoners of war and deported inhabitants of occupied territory must be returned without reciprocity; the German submarines and battle fleet must be taken to a neutral or Allied port for internment (the Germans took their ships to Scapa Flow as required, but ultimately scuttled them); and the predatory treaties of Brest-Litovsk and Bucharest, with Russia and Rumania respectively, must be cancelled. The Allies on their part were at liberty to requisition such German property as their armies of occupation might need, and to maintain the blockade of Germany that they had set up during the war. All this the German leaders knew and agreed to when

Military terms of the armistice

---

[1] "The charge that Wilson purposely betrayed us over the Fourteen Points acquired greater prominence from the fact that a legend was fostered in Germany to the effect that we laid down our weapons in reliance on the Fourteen Points. This legend is a flat falsification of history, as everyone knows who then took any part in the negotiations. We had to lay down our arms because the Supreme Command insisted that we should do so in order to avoid a catastrophe, and then we invoked Wilson's help with an appeal to the Fourteen Points." *Memoirs of Count Bernstorff* (1936), p. 136.

they signed the armistice. Alone among the Allied commanders, General Pershing had opposed any armistice at all. He believed that only by a knockout blow delivered on German soil could the German people be made to realize the completeness of their defeat.

Wilson, meantime, had suffered a disastrous political setback at home. In the

Election of 1918 mid-term elections of 1918 the Republicans won the House of Representatives by a majority of twenty votes, and the Senate by a majority of two. Wilson himself had contributed to the Democratic defeat by an appeal on October 25 for a Democratic majority in Congress through which alone, he maintained, he could hope to carry on his policies. The Republicans skillfully turned this statement into a charge that they had not supported the war, and undoubtedly gained many votes as a result. But the Wilson administration had already accumulated about all the enmity it could hope to carry; every European nation that participated in the war had already had at least one change of government since it began. Wilson's propaganda for an early peace and a just peace had small appeal for the "bitter-enders," who with Theodore Roosevelt at their head blamed the President for his delay in getting into the war, and made fun of his note-writing and idealism. But the fact that he had led the country into the war at all was equally offensive to the pacifists and the German-Americans. To critics of his war policy were added those who disliked the liberal legislation of his first administration, his surrender to labor in the Adamson Act, and his attitude toward Mexico. Most important of all, the Republican politicians after six long years of separation from the spoils of office were alert to every opening that would facilitate their return to power, and directed their campaign with skill.

The logical place for the making of the treaty of peace, as had so often been the case after previous wars, proved to be Paris. Unwisely, perhaps, Wilson chose to represent the United States in person at the Conference, and to take along with him a delega-tion that would in no way interfere with his wishes.[1] So many experts, however, some of whom had been active in Colonel House's "Inquiry," accompanied the official delegates, that a large liner, the *George Washington*, was required to transport them all to Europe. The President's party reached France December 13, 1918, but the Paris Peace Conference did not actually convene until January 18, 1919. In the meantime Wilson paid official visits to Paris, London, and Rome, and inspected some of the battlefields of the war. Everywhere he was received with the most whole-hearted enthusiasm on the part of the people, and with every show of hospitality on the part of the heads of the Allied governments, although many of them regretted the necessity of having to deal with him personally.

The Paris Peace Conference was an extraordinary gathering. All the Allies were represented, including such non-participating belligerents as China and Brazil, but the Germans for good reason were denied any voice whatever in the proceedings. It was clear that the problem of reconciling conflicting Allied opinions would be a serious enough task without the presence of a German delegation ready to take every advantage of Allied disagreements. The Conference, of course, was too large to carry on the actual negotiations, and met only for plenary sessions to confirm what had already been agreed upon behind the scenes. All matters of consequence were settled by the "Big Four," Clemenceau of France, Lloyd George of England, Orlando of Italy, and Wilson of the United States. Of this group, Wilson was still committed in principle to the Fourteen Points, although some of his points had been seriously modified in the pre-armistice negotiations. But Clemenceau, Lloyd George, and Orlando considered themselves

[1] The other members of the American delegation were Robert Lansing, Secretary of State; Colonel House, the President's intimate friend; General Tasker H. Bliss, a military adviser; and Henry White, a Republican who had long since retired from active political life.

bound primarily by the secret treaties which the Allies had negotiated with each other early in the war. These treaties promised France Alsace-Lorraine, the Saar Basin, and an independent government for the rest of German territory west of the Rhine. Great Britain was to receive most of the German colonies, and a free hand in Egypt, Persia, and Mesopotamia. Italy was assured her *Italia Irredenta* — the Trentino, the southern Tyrol, and control of the Adriatic. Rumania had been assigned Transylvania and other territorial acquisitions. Japan was to succeed Germany in Shantung and in the islands of the northern Pacific. Russia, whose withdrawal from the war had forfeited her claims, was to have been given Constantinople and the Dardanelles. To the Allies these terms signified a just and lasting peace, and they proposed to obtain them as nearly as they might.

Wilson had hoped that the influence of an aroused world opinion would enable him **The Treaty** to persuade the Allies to forget **of Versailles** their harsh terms, and to accept more literally his Fourteen Points program. In the end he won only a compromise. Compared with the predatory Treaty of Brest-Litovsk that Germany had forced upon Russia only the year before, the Treaty of Versailles was extremely moderate; but compared with what Wilson had hoped to get, it left much to be desired. When delegates from the new German republic agreed to this treaty on June 28, they surrendered Alsace-Lorraine to France; gave generous blocks of territory including a corridor to the sea along the Vistula to Poland; and ceded border rectifications to Belgium and Denmark. The German colonies were all taken away, and handed over to the Allied countries, not for outright annexation, to be sure, but under a League of Nations mandate system that in practice amounted to nearly the same thing. The Saar Basin, Germany's richest coal-mining area, was turned over to French exploitation for a period of fifteen years, during which time it was to be under the political control of an international commission; at the end of the stipulated period the people of the Saar might decide by plebiscite whether the region should be returned to Germany, continued under international control, or ceded to France. Reparations for the damages done by the German armies had been agreed to in the pre-armistice terms, but the Conference was unable to fix upon the amount due, and left this to be decided by a Reparations Commission after peace was restored.[1] In some ways harder for the Germans to bear than the reparations bill (most of which was never paid anyway) was the assertion in the treaty that their country and her allies were responsible "for causing all the loss and damage to which the Allied and Associated governments have been subjected as a consequence of the war." This "war-guilt" clause, they maintained, quite indefensibly placed full blame upon the Central Powers for the outbreak of war in 1914.

The Treaty of Versailles also provided for the complete disarmament of Germany. Her standing army was reduced to one hundred thousand men and conscription was abolished; frontier fortifications not in Allied hands were to be razed; the manufacture, importation, or exportation of war materials was virtually prohibited; and the German navy was reduced to insignificance. The treaty promised, however, that the Allies would themselves soon take steps toward disarmament, a promise that was only in part fulfilled. Nor did Germany remain long unarmed.

Harsh as these terms were, they did not satisfy Clemenceau, who conceded even this much only on condition that **The League** there be a separate alliance be- **of Nations**

---

[1] In May, 1921, the Commission set the German bill for damages at about thirty-three billion dollars, well beyond the ability of Germany to pay. In 1922, on the ground that Germany had defaulted in her payments, the French seized the Ruhr Valley coal fields. Finally, after several fruitless efforts to solve the problem by international agreement, Germany under Hitler openly repudiated her obligations, and the Allies were unwilling to fight about it. France relinquished the Ruhr in 1925. Ten years later, the Saar voted by an overwhelming majority for reunion with Germany.

The Big Four. Lloyd George of England, Orlando of Italy, Clemenceau of France, and Wilson of the United States, as the political leaders of the major Allied belligerents, decided all important questions at the Paris Peace Conference.

tween Great Britain, the United States, and France to repel jointly any future attacks on France. Wilson consented to the alliance, but the Senate, as he should have foreseen, refused to accept so forthright a departure from the American tradition of non-intervention in European affairs. Wilson pinned his hope for future peace, however, less on the proposed alliance than upon the League of Nations, which by his persistent efforts the Allies were at length induced to include in the Treaty of Versailles. Through this organization, he hoped, many of the injustices of the treaty could be righted later on, when wartime fevers should have abated. The Covenant of the League described three principal agencies: (1) a permanent Secretariat with headquarters established at Geneva, Switzerland; (2) a Council of nine members (later enlarged), to consist of one representative from each of the great powers, France, Great Britain, Italy, Japan, and the United States, and four others to be chosen by the Assembly; (3) an Assembly in which every member nation was to have a representative and a vote. The members of the League agreed by the famous Article X "to respect

and preserve as against external aggression the territorial integrity and existing political independence" of all other members, and to recognize the right of every member nation to bring problems that might disturb the peace to the attention of the Assembly or the Council. Peace was to be achieved primarily by arbitration or adjudication, and the establishment of a permanent court of international justice was contemplated; but disputes not so adjusted must be submitted for settlement either to the Council or to the Assembly. Against nations making illegal war the Council might impose drastic economic sanctions, and in case it deemed military measures necessary to check aggressors it might make appropriate recommendations to members of the League.

The Treaty of Versailles was only one of many treaties that taken together may properly be called the Peace of Paris. **The Peace** Wilson's tenth point had ex- **of Paris** pressly stated that he wished to see the place of Austria-Hungary among nations "safeguarded and assured," but the disintegration of that unhappy power had been so complete that its resurrection as one nation was beyond the realm of possibility. Each of the many national groups that composed the old Empire was now determined to be free, except, possibly, German-Austria, which would have preferred union with Germany. But the Treaty of Saint-Germain, signed September 10, 1919, warned the new "Republic of Austria" to "abstain from any act which might directly or indirectly or by any means whatever compromise her independence." This action was taken partly in order to prevent Germany from being strengthened by the addition of so many Austrians, and partly to prevent the new state of Czechoslovakia from being nearly encircled by Germany. The Treaty of Trianon with Hungary was not signed until June 4, 1920. It cut down the domain of the old Magyar kingdom to an irreducible minimum. The Treaty of Neuilly with Bulgaria, signed November 27, 1919, trimmed off in similar fashion the borders of Germany's smallest ally, and the Treaty of Sèvres with Turkey, signed August 10, 1920, left little non-Turkish territory to the Turks.

Through these and numerous supplementary treaties the "Balkanization" of central Europe was completed. The states that had aided the Allies were rewarded by territorial gains; those that had supported the Central Powers were punished by territorial losses. Numerous new states appeared on the map of Europe: Finland, Estonia, Latvia, Lithuania, Poland, Czechoslovakia, Yugoslavia, Albania. Everywhere the problem of "minorities" threatened the permanence of peace, for boundary lines that would separate every nationality from every other simply could not be drawn. Even the victors were not wholly satisfied. During the Peace Conference Wilson had insisted that the Italians were not entitled to Fiume on the eastern coast of the Adriatic, and as a result the Italian delegation had left the Conference. Ultimately they came back, and by a *coup* Italy obtained the coveted port later on. But the Italians never forgave Wilson, although he consented to the inclusion within Italian borders of several hundred thousand Austrian Germans in the Trentino. This, like

Henry Cabot Lodge, Senator from Massachusetts, was a bitter opponent of President Wilson, and led the fight on the Treaty of Versailles.

many another such decision, was condoned on the ground that it was necessary to provide the nation concerned with a defensible frontier. By the time these treaties were written, Wilson must have realized that in much of Europe "clearly recognizable lines of nationality" simply did not exist. Even less attainable was the hope seemingly cherished by each of these little states of achieving economic self-sufficiency.

The seeds of future wars were thus strewed plentifully about, but Wilson hoped that through the League of Nations their growth might be prevented. Unfortunately, he was soon to **The Senate and the treaty** discover that for this innovation he was unable to win the support of his own government. All those forces that had worked to discredit him in the election of 1918 now made ready to destroy his latest handiwork, the Treaty of Versailles, and the League of Nations it established. The election had given the Senate to the Republicans by the narrowest possible margin, and Henry Cabot Lodge of Massachusetts, whose hatred for Wilson knew no bounds, had become chairman of the Senate Committee on Foreign Relations, to which the treaty must be referred. Once, when Wilson had returned to Washington during the Peace Conference, Lodge and his followers had made their attitude clear, but Wilson felt sure that he could carry the people with him. It was his theory of government that the people, if thoroughly aroused, would and could force their rulers to heed the popular will. The Senate might prefer not to ratify the treaty, but in the end it would have to give in.

But Wilson overlooked the lengths to which his opponents were willing to go in their determination to discredit him. He was probably right in his assumption that the American people were for the time being ready to accept the treaty, including the plan for world cooperation implicit in the League of Nations Covenant. Indeed, only a few "bitter-enders," such as LaFollette of Wisconsin, Reed of Missouri, and Johnson of California, were willing to go the whole length of outright rejection. The anti-Wilson forces pursued far shrewder tactics. Instead of voting to kill the treaty, they proposed to attach to it a series of reservations, or interpretations, most of which were directed against the League of Nations rather than the injustices of the treaty, and in reality meant comparatively little. But each reservation was well calculated to arouse the President's ire. If the opposition could make the reservations just strong enough to be sure that Wilson would reject them, and not so strong as to offend the public, they could not only insure the failure of the treaty, but could put the blame for its failure upon Wilson himself. The discrediting of the President and his following would thus be complete and devastating.

In the midst of the fight on the treaty, Wilson attempted to take his case to the **Wilson's** people on an extensive speaking **collapse** tour — had the radio then been available this hot summer trip, which completely sapped his vitality, would not have been necessary. Already badly shattered by an attack of influenza in Paris, and never robust, he broke down physically under the strain, and was obliged to return to Wash-

ington. There he suffered a paralytic stroke that for a time practically eliminated him as a factor in the government. The Senate did not hesitate to score a victory over its fallen foe. At first with fourteen reservations to match Wilson's Fourteen Points, but finally with fifteen, the majority stood ready to ratify, but the minority, staunchly loyal to Wilson, declined to accept the reservations, although it was well known that the leading European powers would have preferred ratification with the reservations to no ratification at all. Many votes were taken, and the treaty was twice before the Senate. On the final vote, March 20, 1920, the Senate was ready to accept the treaty by a vote of forty-nine to thirty-five, with the encumbering reservations attached. This was less than the necessary two thirds, but a change of seven votes would have meant ratification. Among those voting against the treaty were some of the President's closest adherents, Democratic regulars who were willing to accept the treaty precisely as it stood, but in no other form. Thus the treaty failed with an overwhelming majority of the Senate favoring its adoption, although some wanted it with reservations, and others only without reservations. Many observers believed that if Wilson had been well a compromise could have been reached, but others insisted that the reservations were designed to kill the treaty, and would have been made stronger had they been acceptable to the President. What would have transpired had Wilson followed the advice House gave him by letter to resign the Presidency and leave the battle to Vice-President Marshall may only be surmised. By this time the friendship between the President and his former intimate had cooled, and House's letter was never answered.

Himself a casualty of the war he had helped to make, Wilson could not yet understand the thoroughgoing nature of his defeat. From the news that filtered into his sick-room he continued to believe that the American people, who were now in reality drifting rapidly back into isolationism, were still with him. When Congress by joint resolution sought to declare the war with Germany at an end, he interposed his veto, charging that such a course would amount to an "ineffaceable stain upon the gallantry and honor of the United States." The election of 1920, he maintained, must be made a "solemn referendum" to decide whether the American people would accept or reject the obligations of the treaty and the League.

Looking backward from the vantage-point of a Second World War, it would seem that Significance the United States, by its half-of Wilson's hearted refusal to support the defeat League of Nations, destroyed whatever chance there was to prevent another general war. Had the American nation shown itself willing to accept the responsibilities of world leadership, it is possible that the return to international anarchy which marked the next two decades might have been forestalled. Conceivably, also, the mistakes and the injustices of the treaty, of which there were many, might have been ironed out through instrumentalities provided for in the League. But when the richest and most powerful of all the nations refused to cooperate in any effective way for the maintenance of peace, the possibility of another world war became a certainty. During the fight on the League, Wilson had recorded his conviction that, in case his efforts failed, the war would have to be fought all over again. What might have happened can never be known, but a generation later the war that Wilson predicted came to pass. It was this return of the United States to isolation which, according to Winston Churchill, made possible the Second World War:

It is my opinion that this war would have been prevented if the United States had been in the old League of Nations or, even if it had not, if a strong position had been taken by the leaders. Instead it was led by weak and feeble forces until the hostile forces seized control elsewhere and brought war down upon the world once more.

Failure to achieve in full Wilson's hopes led many Americans, after the war was over, to conclude that the entrance of the United States into the war had been a mistake, and that the war had been a failure. The Importance of victory over Germany world, for a certainty, had not been made safe for democracy, and the war to end war had seemingly led only to more war. Such critics overlooked the fact that by resort to war the United States had averted the very real danger of a complete German victory. What the consequences of that victory would have been, one may only surmise, but it is unlikely that they would have been pleasant. Had Germany won her submarine campaign against Great Britain, she would have emerged as the leading rival of the United States for the control of the Atlantic Ocean. She might have found it difficult to restrain her resentment of the Monroe Doctrine, which for so long had barred her from colonial expansion in Latin-America. And without the assistance of the British navy, the United States might have had great trouble in holding German imperialism at bay. Possibly the war that was fought "over there" might have had to be fought "over here." As early as 1906 Henry Adams had warned that the United States must "fortify the Atlantic System," meaning the tacit understanding for the protection of the Atlantic which the United States seemed to have with Great Britain. "For if Germany breaks down England," Adams continued, "she becomes the center of a military world and we are lost." Theodore Roosevelt, commenting in 1914, was more specific. As he viewed the matter, "If Germany were to subjugate England in this war, Germany would invade the United States in five years." Obviously, the United States did not achieve all that it hoped for from the defeat of Germany in the First World War, but at least it arrested for two full decades the German bid for world supremacy, an achievement of no inconsiderable importance.

Bibliography

The number of books that have been written on the First World War is simply incredible, and only a fraction of them can be cited here. Even the home front has attracted much attention. On the financing of the war, for example, there are at least three useful works: J. H. Hollander, *War Borrowing* (1919); E. L. Bogart, *Direct and Indirect Costs of the Great World War* (new ed., 1920); and J. M. Clark, *The Costs of the World War to the American People* (1931). On the contribution of benevolent agencies, Foster R. Dulles, *The American Red Cross: A History* (1950), is straightforward and competent; Katherine Mayo, *"That Damn Y"* (1920), has a cause to plead. On the mobilizing of public opinion in favor of the war, there are several useful books by George Creel, *The War, the World, and Wilson* (1920); *How We Advertised America* (1920); and *Rebel at Large: Recollections of Fifty Crowded Years* (1947). On the same subject, see J. R. Mock and Cedric Larson, *Words that Won the War* (1939); and G. F. Bruntz, *Allied Propaganda and the Collapse of the German Empire in 1918* (1938).

The mobilization of American resources to win the war is an unneglected subject. *How America Went to War*, edited by Benedict Crowell and R. F. Wilson (6 vols., 1921), is an account from official sources of the nation's various activities, and is admirably complete. W. F. Willoughby, *Government Organization in War Time and After* (1919), is a survey of the federal agencies created for the prosecution of the war. Other books of consequence in this connection include: B. M. Baruch, *American Industry in the War: A Report of the War Industries Board* (1921); W. L. White, *Bernard Baruch, Portrait of a Citizen* (1950); and Arthur Bullard, *Mobilising America* (1917). On the part played by American labor, see John Steuben, *Labor in Wartime* (1940); and Samuel Gompers, *American Labor and the War* (1919). On wartime education, see P. R. Kolbe, *The Colleges in War Time and After* (1919); and Lewis Paul Todd, *Wartime Relations of the Federal Government and the Public Schools, 1917–1918* (1945).

The best single volume on American participation in the war is F. L. Paxson, *American Democracy and the World War*, II, *America at War, 1917–1918* (1939). Useful also is Frederick Palmer, *Newton D. Baker: America at War* (2 vols., 1931). On the part of the Navy in the war, there are a number of excellent accounts, among them W. S. Sims and B. J. Kendrick, *The Victory at Sea* (1920); Louis Guichard, *The Naval Blockade, 1914–1918* (1930); Elting E. Morison, *Admiral Sims and the Modern American Navy* (1942); T. A. Bailey, *The Policy of the United States toward the Neutrals, 1917–1918* (1942); and T. G. Frothingham, *Naval History of the World War*, III, *The United States in the War, 1917–1918* (1926).

The work of the Army is told with greatest completeness in the *United States Army in the World War, 1917–1919* (17 vols., 1948), a work prepared by the Historical Division, Department of the Army. J. J. Pershing, *My Experiences in the World War* (2 vols., 1931), is an excellent memoir, although far less charitable toward the General's superiors than they were toward him. J. G. Harbord, *The American Army in France, 1917–1919* (1936), is another memoir written from the vantage point of a high-ranking participant. David Lloyd George, *War Memoirs* (6 vols., 1933–37), gives much attention to American participation; L. P. Ayres, *The War with Germany* (1919), is a valuable statistical study; T. G. Frothingham, *The American Reinforcement in the World War* (1927), is a clear and satisfactory account. J. B. McMaster, *The United States in the World War* (2 vols., 1918–20); and J. S. Bassett, *Our War with Germany* (1919), are full, but disappointingly dull. Other useful accounts are R. J. Beamish and F. A. March, *America's Part in the World War* (1919); Shipley Thomas, *The History of the A.E.F.* (1920); Frederick Palmer, *America in France* (1918); Hunter Liggett, *Commanding an American Army: Recollections of the World War* (1925); and R. L. Bullard, *Personalities and Reminiscences of the War* (1925). Frederick Palmer, *Our Greatest Battle* (1919), treats of the Meuse-Argonne. On the American adventures in Russia, see John Cudahy, *Archangel: The American War with Russia* (1924); W. S. Graves, *America's Siberian Venture, 1918–1920* (1931); L. I. Strakhovsky, *The Origins of*

American Intervention in North Russia, 1918 (1937).

On the Paris Peace Conference and the Treaty of Versailles, *What Really Happened at Paris*, edited by E. M. House and Charles Seymour (1921), presents the official American point of view. R. S. Baker, *Woodrow Wilson and World Settlement* (3 vols., 1922), is also friendly to Wilson, but provides an invaluable inside picture of what went on. It may profitably be compared with David Lloyd George, *Memoirs of the Peace Conference* (2 vols., 1939). Robert Lansing, *The Big Four and Others of the Peace Conference* (1921), contains good personality studies by a favored observer. Frederick Palmer, *Bliss, Peacemaker: The Life and Letters of General Tasker Howard Bliss* (1934), is of considerable value. Other books of merit on the Conference include *A History of the Peace Conference of Paris*, edited by H. W. V. Temperley (1924); C. H. Haskins and R. H. Lord, *Some Problems of the Peace Conference* (1920); B. M. Baruch, *The Making of the Reparation and Economic Sections of the Treaty* (1920); J. M. Keynes, *The Economic Consequences of the Peace* (1919); J. T. Shotwell, *At the Paris Peace Conference* (1937); and D. H. Miller, *The Drafting of the Covenant* (2 vols., 1928).

On the League of Nations, D. F. Fleming, *The United States and the League of Nations, 1918–1920* (1932), provides a comprehensive treatment. H. C. Lodge, *The Senate and the League of Nations* (1925), is bitterly hostile to the League and to Wilson personally. Karl Schriftgiesser, *The Gentleman from Massachusetts: Henry Cabot Lodge* (1944), is equally hostile to Lodge. John A. Garraty, *Henry Cabot Lodge* (1953), is reasonably objective, but generous to Lodge. T. A. Bailey, *Woodrow Wilson and the Lost Peace* (1944), and *Woodrow Wilson and the Great Betrayal* (1945), are both brilliantly written, but they place an undue share of the blame for the defects of the peace and the failure of the treaty on Wilson; they were reissued as one volume, *Wilson and the Peacemakers* (1947). R. J. Bartlett, *The League to Enforce Peace* (1944), follows the organization from its beginnings to its end. See also Josephus Daniels, *The Wilson Era: Years of War and After, 1917–1923* (1946); and A. M. Arnett, *Claude Kitchin and the Wilson War Policies* (1937).

The essential background for an understanding of the Russian revolution is provided in Max M. Laserson, *The American Impact on Russia, Diplomatic and Ideological, 1784–1917* (1950).

22

The Great Demobilization

Governmental impotence — Temporary unemployment — Post-war prosperity — The real estate boom — Strikes of 1919 — The "Red scare" — The Ku Klux Klan — A business decline — The depression in agriculture — Farmer organizations — Railway legislation — The merchant marine — Election of 1920 — Harding — The Washington Conference — The World Court

THE government of the United States has rarely, if ever, been less effective than it was

Governmental impotence

during the last eighteen months of the Wilson administration. After the President's collapse in September, 1919, he was never the same man again. Many responsibilities that would normally have been his devolved for a time upon his second wife, Mrs. Edith Bolling Wilson, whom he had married in December, 1915, after the death of the first Mrs. Wilson in August, 1914. His Secretary of State, Robert Lansing, in an effort to hold the administration together, called weekly cabinet meetings, but when this finally came to the President's attention, he angrily dismissed Lansing for his presumption, and named a new Secretary of State, Bainbridge Colby. Under the Constitution, in case of the inability of the President to discharge his powers and duties, they were to devolve upon the Vice-President, but Congress, unfortunately, had never seen fit to define by law how the "inability" of a President was to be determined. Wilson therefore stayed on in office, and eventually was able to discharge his duties after a fashion, although never again with the capability he had shown before his illness. The fact that the President was a Democrat while both houses of Congress were Republican also made for inefficiency.

Not only with reference to the Treaty of Versailles, but in many other matters also, the executive and legislative branches were in continuous conflict.

This alarming situation was by no means wholly responsible for the disorder that accompanied the transition from war to peace. The end of hostilities had come suddenly, far

Temporary unemployment

sooner than the public had been led to expect. As a result, neither the government nor the people were prepared for peace. For four years the American economy had been geared primarily to production for war; now it had to face the complications of a return to peace. To this subject, apparently, neither the Wilson administration, nor Congress, nor the industrial and labor leaders of the country had given much thought. There was complete agreement on the necessity of "bringing the boys home," and demobilization was pushed forward with the utmost speed, although the homesick American soldiers remained in Europe long enough to change the words incorrectly attributed to Pershing, "Lafayette, we are here," to "Lafayette, we are still here." Four and one-half million men were discharged within a year, and with no "G. I. Bill," as after the Second World War, to break the fall. The problem of reconversion of industry was handled with equal unconcern. As soon as the fighting ended, war contracts were cancelled ruthlessly and without regard to the effect on contractors, many of whom sustained unwarranted and unfair losses in consequence. Congress made haste, also, to abolish most of the war agencies it had so recently created, and to get the government as completely out of business as possible. Inevitably there was much temporary unemployment, from released servicemen, from business dislocation due to the termination of war contracts, from the discharge of federal employees. By the spring of 1919 the problem of unemployment became so acute that President Wilson convened in Washington a Conference of Governors and Mayors to discuss means of handling it, but Calvin Coolidge, Governor of Massachusetts, probably reflected well the sentiment of the Conference when he asserted that ninety per cent of the "boys" would be able to take care of themselves. The President, however, although expressing great confidence in "our spirited businessmen and self-reliant" workers, asked Congress to help out with a public works and reclamation program. But Congress did nothing. No doubt Senator Warren G. Harding of Ohio spoke its mind when in May, 1920, he told a Boston audience that "America's present need is not heroics but healing, not nostrums but normalcy."

And yet, in spite of some temporary distress, the inflated prosperity that the First **Post-war** World War had brought to the **prosperity** United States lasted on until the summer of 1920. To a very great extent this condition was due to an orgy of buying on the part of the American public. During the war the people had "hooverized," not only upon supplies needed for the armies at the front, but to some extent also upon nearly every other type of consumer goods. With the war ended, savings need no longer be invested in Liberty bonds; they could be spent, and they were spent. Indeed, many who during the war had followed the advice of the government not to dispose of their

bonds regarded the return of peace as an invitation to exchange them for coveted luxuries. Soldiers mustered out of service usually spent their discharge bonuses and back pay before settling down to work. Manufacturers found that to continue their high wartime profits they need turn only to the production of goods for civilians instead of for soldiers. The extraordinary demand for civilian goods led, indeed, to a disastrous inflation. Even during the war prices had been held down only on materials needed for the war effort, and there had been no really effective system of price controls on consumer goods. After the war, with the demand great and the supply limited, prices skyrocketed. Not only from within the nation, but also from abroad came an insistent demand for the products of American factories and farms. The war-ravaged countries of Europe needed American materials for the work of rehabilitation and American foodstuffs to feed their peoples. They bought freely also of South America, China, and Japan, and thus indirectly stimulated purchases from these quarters in the United States. American exports during 1919 were about a billion dollars higher than in any previous year of American history.

To their ultimate undoing, American farmers were convinced that the market for American foodstuffs in Europe **The real** had become permanent, and that **estate boom** their prosperity was guaranteed for all time. Their optimism, whipped up systematically by the real estate men and the country bankers who stood to make heavy profits every time a farm changed hands, developed throughout most of the Middle West into a thoroughgoing speculative boom. The price of wheat, guaranteed by the government for an eighteen-month period after September 2, 1918, at $2.26 a bushel, rose by the spring of 1920 to more than three dollars. At the same time corn sold for over two dollars a bushel, with other farm prices equally inflated. Naturally land prices went up, but sales were soon being made less because of the earning power of the land than because

of the profits that were to be made by selling
it at abnormally high figures. The land
buom reached its climax in Iowa, where land
worth from eighty to a hundred dollars an
acre before the war sold during 1919 and
early 1920 for from two hundred to four
hundred dollars an acre. During the year
that ended in March, 1920, the sale price of
Iowa farms increased on an average sixty-
three dollars per acre, or about thirty-two
per cent. Most purchases were made possible only by heavy mortgages, but money
for the purpose was available seemingly in an
unending stream at the country banks, whose
swollen deposits reflected the prosperity of
their customers. Farm purchases included
also electrical equipment, agricultural machinery, motor cars, and blooded livestock,
all bought on the installment plan in the hope
of future profits. Farmhouses were increasingly modernized, and for the first time in
American history a large class of country
dwellers lived under conditions that closely
approximated the advantages of the city.

The prosperity of farm and factory extended also in varying degrees to the workers, but tended if anything to
promote rather than to restrain
industrial conflict. Organized labor had
been greatly strengthened by the war, which
raised wages to unprecedented heights,
steadied employment, and added to the
unions many new, if somewhat undisci-
plined, members. The restraints imposed
upon labor by the patriotic desire of all
classes to win the war were removed by the
return of peace, and the mounting cost of
living gave rise to the charge that wages,
high as they were, had not risen correspondingly. Furthermore, the long period of prosperity had unfitted labor psychologically to
accept such readjustments as the restoration
of peacetime conditions made inevitable.
The year 1919 proved to be one of the worst
with respect to labor relations in the whole
history of the United States. During this
period the strikes that occurred were numbered in the thousands, and the number of
workers affected in the millions. Some-

Strikes of 1919

times labor won, as for example with the
clothing workers of New York and the textile
workers of New England, but in general
public opinion tended to be against the
strikes, and many of them failed. Especially important in determining public opinion was the Seattle general strike, which
started in the shipyards, but was joined by
practically all the unions in the city for five
days during early February. To many
people, including Mayor Ole Hanson of
Seattle, such tactics were only a prelude to
revolution and must be halted. The Boston
police strike later in the year, which left the
city at the mercy of the lawless until the
state militia could take over, tended to confirm this opinion. More important than
either, however, were the strikes that occurred in the coal and steel industries. The
United Mine Workers, led by John L. Lewis,
had been bound by a wage truce for the duration of the war, but, on the assumption that
the war was over in fact even if a treaty of
peace had not yet been signed, they demanded a sixty-per-cent increase in wages, a
thirty-hour week, and time and one-half for
overtime. This demand the operators rejected, unless they could also raise prices,
something the still-existing Fuel Administration refused to countenance. A strike
followed which President Wilson called "a
great moral and legal wrong," and which
Attorney-General Palmer halted by injunctions obtained under authority of wartime
legislation. A strike in the steel industry,
led by William Z. Foster, sought among
other goals collective bargaining and an end
to the seventy-two hour work week, but the
employers were better able to stand the strain
than the workers, and the strike failed. A
report made later by the Interchurch World
Movement, revealing the actual state of
affairs in the steel mills, so affected public
opinion, however, that in 1923 the steel industry itself abolished the twelve-hour day.

The strikes that occurred in American industries, although usually explainable on
other grounds, were often attributed to the presence of radi-

The "Red scare"

cals in the labor movement who were in sympathy with the aims and methods of the bolshevists in Russia. That the Communist rulers in Russia had in mind a world uprising of the proletariat was not open to doubt, and there was some evidence to indicate that they were making progress. For several months Hungary was under a Communist government, while alarming Communist outbreaks had occurred in Germany, Italy, and elsewhere. A series of bomb outrages in the United States gave color to the charge that the "Reds" were also on the move here. An unexploded bomb was found in the mail of Mayor Ole Hanson of Seattle, whose anti-Communist sentiments were well known. Another, intended for Senator Hardwick of Georgia, blew off the hands of a colored maid. Sixteen bombs, addressed to prominent individuals, were discovered before delivery in the New York City post office. A bomb wrecked the Washington residence of Attorney-General Palmer, and another, which exploded in Wall Street, September 16, 1920, took the lives of thirty-eight persons, caused injury to many others, and did damage estimated at two million dollars.

Under the circumstances it is not surprising that the country was gripped by an hysterical outburst against the Reds. The Department of Justice, both under Attorney-General Palmer and his successor, Harry M. Daugherty, waged vigorous war against the radicals. With the assistance of the Department of Labor, which had authority to arrest and deport dangerous aliens, Palmer's agents raided radical meetings, sought out suspects in their residences, and accounted eventually for some 556 deportations, about half of whom sailed for Russia in the *Buford*, sometimes called the "Soviet Ark," in December, 1919. With the blood-lust of wartime not yet fully abated, state and local governments sometimes acted with even less restraint. Following an attack on a 1919 Armistice Day parade in Centralia, Washington, remnants of the I.W.W. throughout the Northwest were arrested by the hundreds, brought to trial, convicted, and given long sentences. At least one of the alleged perpetrators of the Centralia outrage was lynched. The two most notable victims of the red rage, however, had a legal trial. They were Nicola Sacco and Bartolomeo Vanzetti, two Italian workmen who were convicted of a double murder that occurred in South Braintree, Massachusetts, on April 15, 1920. Many competent investigators believed that these convictions were obtained less because of the evidence, which was wholly circumstantial, than because of the records of the two men as radicals, but a prolonged nation-wide effort failed to save them from execution.

An equally unlovely aspect of the post-war hysteria was the rise of the Ku Klux Klan, a modern imitation of the secret **The Ku** order that according to tradition **Klux Klan** had played so important a part in saving the South from the excesses of the carpetbaggers. Founded by William J. Simmons of Atlanta, Georgia, the new order sought to enlist under its banner every type of "one-hundred-per-cent American" prejudice, and thanks in considerable part to the hatreds engendered by the First World War its agents soon began to meet with success. The Klan was ardently fundamentalist in religion and politics, denounced everything savoring of radicalism, and prided itself upon being at one and the same time anti-Negro, anti-Semite, anti-foreigner, and anti-Catholic. The Negro, according to many southern whites, had been spoiled by the high wages he had been permitted to earn during the war, and by the stories of racial equality that colored veterans had brought back from France. He needed to be "put in his place." Sometimes these sentiments were echoed by the white residents of the northern towns and cities that had imported colored labor from the South during the war. The Jews were denounced as un-American radicals, as conscienceless profiteers, and just as Jews. Recent immigrants and the children of immigrants, particularly in case they chanced not to be of "Nordic" blood, were accused of a

THE ACCUSED. Nicola Sacco and Bartolomeo Vanzetti in Charlestown Prison, awaiting trial.

The Sacco-Vanzetti case aroused intense interest in Europe and Latin-America as well as in the United States. Thousands of persons voiced their protests against the death sentence being carried out. But Governor A. T. Fuller of Massachusetts, on the advice of a commission headed by President Lowell of Harvard University, refused the pardon sought.

SYMPATHIZERS. Public protests occurred throughout the civilized world. This group stood near the State House in Boston.

desire to undermine and destroy American institutions. Besides, this was not their country, and why should they be here? Catholics were baited as half-hearted Americans who set their religion above their patriotism, and owed allegiance to a foreign potentate, the Pope. By 1920 Klan lodges were attracting attention throughout the South and the West; Klan members marched in white hoods and shrouds through village streets, burned "fiery crosses" on conspicuous hillsides, at best made themselves thoroughly ridiculous, and at worst committed insufferable crimes. In extreme cases individuals who had drawn the wrath of the order were beaten, tarred and feathered, or even killed. Membership in the Klan was a closely guarded secret, as well became an order that sometimes took the law into its own hands. The fading of prosperity served only to add new fuel to the fire, and for several years the Klan continued to increase in numbers. An exposé of the moral and financial irregularities of the Klan leaders, made by the New York *World* in the fall of 1921 and followed by a still more damaging congressional investigation, failed to check the growth of the Klan, which got a new "Imperial Wizard," and by the middle of the decade counted perhaps four million members. In due time, however, the conviction of the Klan leader of Indiana for murder, and

THE TRIAL. Throngs gathered outside the courthouse at Dedham, Mass, to glimpse the principals and follow the progress of the trial.

PROTEST. This armband, one of many, bears the date on which the defendants were executed.

THE VERDICT. Newsmen waiting outside the courthouse to relay the news to anxious waiters everywhere.

the revelation of serious corruption among the Klan-controlled officials of the same state, greatly damaged the prestige of the Klan, and speeded its decline. Respectable citizens soon saw that its practices constituted a complete denial of the American principles it was ostensibly created to promote.

A business decline

A premonition that the post-war prosperity might not last appeared as early as October, 1919, when the stock market broke badly, but there was little real distress until the summer of 1920. Undoubtedly the most important cause of the decline which then set in was the failure of Europe to continue its generous purchases of American goods. This was due in part to the unexpectedly rapid recovery of European agriculture, but there were other factors also. For months after the signing of the armistice the government of the United States continued the policy of lending to its associates in the war, but by 1920, confessing its inability to "assume the burdens of all the earth," it was making no new loans. Foreign exchange, influenced by the enormous debts owing the United States, dropped precipitately; in February, 1920, the English pound was worth only about three dollars, the French and Belgian francs only seven or

The Ku Klux Klan, *a secret nativist order patterned after the post-Civil War Klan, was founded at Stone Mountain, Georgia, in 1915. Its activities were directed against minority groups, both racial and religious, and against unorthodox social and political ideas. In the middle twenties its membership may have reached five million, but by 1930 estimates were down to 9000.*

PARADE. Klan members marching through the streets of Washington, 1926.

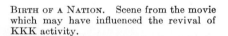

BIRTH OF A NATION. Scene from the movie which may have influenced the revival of KKK activity.

eight cents each, and the German mark only two or three cents. European purchasers found it practically impossible to pay the prices demanded for American goods, the more so because of the high American tariff, raised still higher in 1921, which interfered seriously with their desire to exchange what they could produce for what they needed to buy. The American public itself added to the general distress by indulging in a "buyers' strike" against the abnormally high retail prices that were being charged. Aimed mainly at luxuries, the "strike" fell with particular force upon silk, which within a seven-month period fell from $18.40 a pound to $5.81. The resulting prostration of the silk industry in Japan lessened, in turn, the ability of the Japanese to buy American cotton.

The years 1920 and 1921 saw a general slackening in nearly every field of business. Retailers and wholesalers who had bought at high prices found their shelves stocked with goods that no one wished to buy. Manufacturers who had made heavy purchases of high-priced raw materials were confronted by wholesale cancellations of orders. Railroad

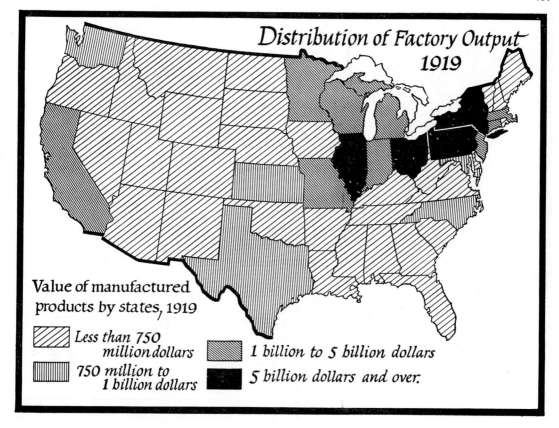

Distribution of Factory Output 1919

Value of manufactured products by states, 1919

Less than 750 million dollars

750 million to 1 billion dollars

1 billion to 5 billion dollars

5 billion dollars and over.

earnings went down, and banks were forced to contract their loans. Stocks and bonds slumped disastrously, and speculators were particularly hard hit. A total of 8881 business failures, with liabilities of $295,121,805, occurred in 1920, and 19,652, involving $755,-777,685, in 1921. With nearly three and a half million men out of work the country faced for the first time in many years a serious problem of unemployment.

The suffering in agriculture was even more acute than in industry. The European mar-

The depression in agriculture

ket upon which American farm prosperity had come to depend seemed irretrievably lost. European purchasers had not merely cut down on their buying; they had turned to other sources of supply. During the war half the British imports of fresh beef, for example, had come from the United States, but by 1923 this proportion had declined to only five per cent. Meat and wheat from the

Argentine, from Canada, from Australia, and from Russia supplied the European market, leaving the American farmer high and dry. When at the end of May, 1920, the government guaranty on the price of wheat was removed, a steady fall in all farm prices began that within a year had brought wheat down to a dollar a bushel, and corn to the lowest figure in twenty-five years. Cotton-growers fared quite as badly as the growers of food crops. By 1919 the price of cotton had risen to thirty-eight cents, and the extraordinary wartime demands had led to the opening of vast quantities of new cotton land in the Southwest. But by 1920 the price of cotton was only eighteen cents, and it kept on going down until before the end of the decade it sold for as little as seven cents. Cotton from Egypt and India had begun to wrest from the American South the world supremacy in its greatest crop that it had held unchallenged for a hundred years.

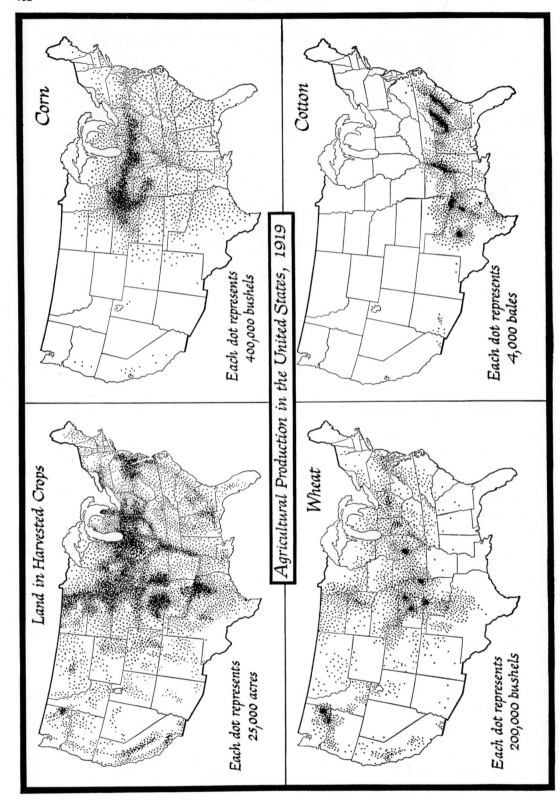

Corn

Each dot represents
400,000 bushels

Cotton

Each dot represents
4,000 bales

Land in Harvested Crops

Each dot represents
25,000 acres

Wheat

Each dot represents
200,000 bushels

Agricultural Production in the United States, 1919

Even the American market failed the farmers. The war had done much to change the food habits of Americans, and while the "wheatless" and "meatless" requirements of the Food Administration were soon gladly forgotten, less wheat and less meat were consumed in proportion to other foods. Health preachments took another toll; Americans generally, and American women in particular, were cutting down on their surplus weight. In the first quarter of the twentieth century the per capita consumption of wheat flour declined twenty per cent, of corn meal and rye flour sixty per cent, of barley — no longer in demand for the manufacture of beer — ninety per cent. Excepting only pork and dairy products, the American per capita consumption of animal foods showed also a sharp decline. Moreover, lands devoted to growing crops had increased during the war decade by nearly fifty million acres, while better machinery and better methods of farming had tended to increase the yield per acre. But the rate of increase in the American population was slowing down; immigration was restricted by law to a small fraction of those who wished to come; and the size of American families showed a marked tendency to decline. To add to the confusion in agriculture, mechanized farming, together with the use of trucks and automobiles in towns and cities, had cut down heavily upon the production of horses and mules, and upon the food crops, such as oats, used to maintain them. Thus still more acres were freed for the production of still more human food for a market that did not exist.

The American farmer soon realized that with his mortgage payments wholly out of **Bank failures** proportion to his income, with taxes boosted sky-high to correspond with the new land values, and with the cost of labor, machinery, and transportation still approximating wartime levels, his day of prosperity was done. He tried to borrow at the country banks whose easy lending policy had played so large a part in his undoing, only to find that the banks themselves were in trouble. Not content to lend from their own resources alone, they had borrowed heavily from the Federal Reserve Banks, which until 1920 had made little effort to check credit expansion. But in that year the Federal Reserve Board decided to take such measures as might be necessary to bring credit under more effective control. The discount rate was raised, and banks that had overreached themselves struggled frantically to collect enough loans to meet their obligations. Failures among the western country banks became increasingly common, some of them the fault of farmers who were determined to hold their crops until prices should rise, whether they could meet their debts to the banks or not. Farm mortgages were frequently foreclosed, but there was comparatively little retreat from the land. Farmers who had lost their property rights stayed on as tenants, and mortgage-holders often preferred the postponement of payments to foreclosure. Thus, in spite of the low prices farm yield tended to increase. During the three years that followed the disastrous break of 1920, production levels in nine basic field crops maintained or surpassed the levels of the preceding three years.

As in previous periods of agricultural distress, the farmers most seriously affected by the hard times showed a strong **Farmer organizations** disposition to work through farmer organizations for the redress of grievances. The old Grange, although more active in the Northeast than in the states of the Middle West where its fame had once been greatest, showed renewed vitality. The American Society of Equity, founded in Indiana in 1902, and its subsidiary, the Equity Co-operative Exchange, enjoyed the support of numerous grain-growers all the way from Wisconsin to Montana. In the same region the Farmers' Union, also dating back to 1902, but of Texas origin, developed its greatest strength. More national in scope was the American Farm Bureau Federation, an unforeseen by-product of the Smith-Lever Act of 1914. The purpose of this measure was to encourage agricultural education among farmers, a

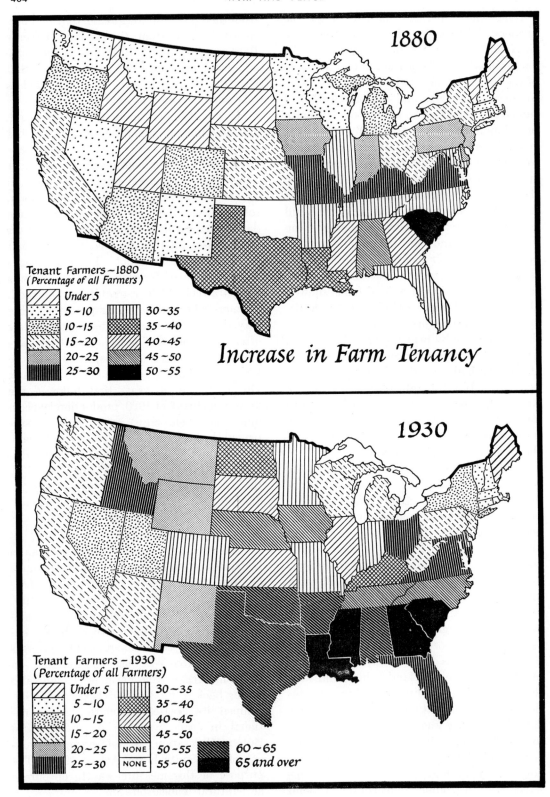

Increase in Farm Tenancy

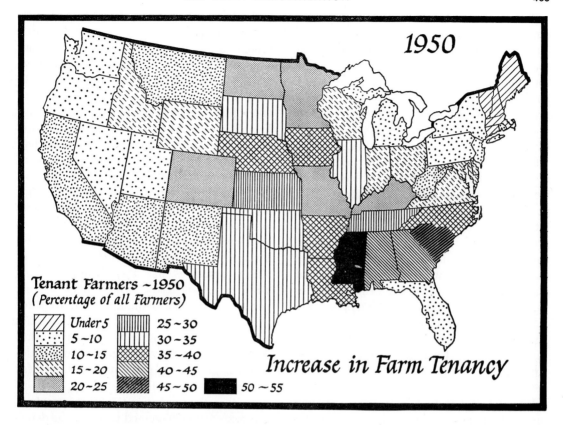

1950

Tenant Farmers ~1950
(Percentage of all Farmers)

	Under 5		25~30
	5~10		30~35
	10~15		35~40
	15~20		40~45
	20~25		45~50	50~55

Increase in Farm Tenancy

work that came to be carried on in large part through county farm bureaus, each of which was provided with a county agent. Naturally the local bureaus soon joined together in state organizations, and by 1920 the American Farm Bureau Federation provided a national capstone for the edifice. By September 1, 1921, with forty-six states participating, the Federation claimed a membership of nearly a million farmers. Derided by the less favored farm orders because of its close connection with the government, it was nonetheless capable of expressing with vigor the farmers' point of view.

Quite in a class by itself was the National Non-Partisan League, which spread from **The Non-Partisan League** North Dakota as a center into a dozen northwestern states. Although the American Society of Equity had done much to prepare the way for the League, the organization that took form in 1915 was essentially the brain-child of one man, Arthur C. Townley, a gifted pro-

moter only thirty-five years of age. Townley had been a member of the Socialist Party, and the experiment upon which he wished to embark was essentially one in state socialism. First he proposed to weld the farmers of the state together into a powerful dues-paying organization, and then through their votes to seize control of the state government and through it to accomplish his reforms. Most of the League program was as old as Populism, but it still had an irresistible appeal for the North Dakota wheat farmer: (1) the state ownership of terminal elevators, flour-mills, packing-houses, and cold-storage plants; (2) state inspection of grain and grain dockage; (3) the exemption of farm improvements from taxation; (4) state hail insurance on the acreage tax basis; and (5) rural credit banks operated at cost. The object of these reforms was primarily to eliminate the profits of the middlemen, and thus to save for the farmer a greater proportion of the wealth that he produced.

Townley's experiment opened auspiciously, for the harvests of 1915 were good, and the farmers were able to pay the high dues that the League exacted. A weekly newspaper, the *Non-Partisan Leader*, kept up a constant barrage of League propaganda, and high-pressure organizers traveled all over the state in automobiles recruiting members. When little more than a year old, the League went into the Republican primaries, nominated most of its candidates for state office, including the governorship, and elected them. Two years later it won majorities in the state legislature, and began to pass the laws it had promised. Before its ascendancy came to an end, it had provided for a state-owned elevator and a state-owned flour-mill, and had made a beginning on the rest of its program. But it encountered the unflinching opposition of capital, both from within and from without the state, and it had constant trouble with the courts. By 1921, when the League-dominated governor, Lynn J. Frazier, was defeated in a recall election, it was on the defensive. Meantime League organizers had spread their gospel across the state border into Minnesota. Unable to capture the Republican machinery, they made common cause with organized labor, and set up a Farmer-Labor Party, which in 1920 won strong support, although it failed to elect its ticket. From this time forward, both in North Dakota and Minnesota, and to a lesser extent in many other northwestern states also, the League furnished a convenient rallying center for the forces of agrarian discontent.

With the exception of the Non-Partisan League, the farmer organizations generally **Cooperative** emphasized cooperative market-**marketing** ing as the best means of solving the problem of low prices. Through their influence many selling associations were formed, some of which succeeded remarkably well, but many of which failed. Most influential among the promoters of cooperative selling was Aaron Sapiro, a shrewd California lawyer who before he became general counsel for the American Farm Bureau Federation in 1923 had already helped organize cooperatives among the producers of tobacco, wheat, broom-corn, milk, potatoes, and many other commodities. The success of a cooperative depended in large part upon its ability to enforce among its members an ironclad contract for the prevention of private sales. Enabling legislation was therefore required of the states, and although a few states had satisfactory laws on the subject, in most instances they had yet to be obtained. Sapiro's ideas were finally incorporated into a standard Cooperative Marketing Act, which was adopted by Kentucky in 1922 and thereafter, with sundry variations, in nearly every state. Probably the most consistently successful of the cooperatives was the California Fruit Growers' Association, which over a long period was able to dominate the market for western citrus fruits, and to set substantially what prices it chose. Cooperatives that dealt in such widely produced commodities as wheat, livestock, and cotton obtained far less satisfactory results.

Neither the boom nor the crisis aspects of the years 1919–20 seemed to affect the determination of the Republican Congress to avoid as much as possible any extension of governmental authority into the realm of private enterprise. The impossibility of turning the clock back to prewar days, however, was well illustrated by the problem of the railroads. The experience with a centralized railroad administration had demonstrated the folly of unrestrained competition, and the railroad unions, which had prospered under government operation, even wished to see the wartime system made permanent. Realizing that the country was in no mood for such a settlement, the unions, with considerable public support, turned instead to the so-called "Plumb plan," which contemplated government purchase of the railroads, but their operation as a unit by a board of directors on which representatives of the public, the operating officials, and the workmen should sit. But all such socialistic schemes fell before the conservative reaction that gripped the nation at the close of the war.

The Esch-Cummins Transportation Act of 1920, which Congress finally adopted, made **Railway legislation** no such compromise with socialism as the unions desired, but it did break much new ground. Some of its terms turned out to be quite unworkable, but others were of lasting importance. Consolidation ceased to be a crime, and was definitely promoted by a clause which instructed the Interstate Commerce Commission to lay plans for reducing the number of railroad systems in operation, even at the cost, if need be, of ignoring the various anti-trust laws. Under this grant of power the commission presently proposed to consolidate all the railroads of the country into nineteen systems, but objections from the railroads themselves defeated the plan, and only a few such combinations were effected. The act sought also to resolve all conflicts between state and national regulatory authorities in favor of the national government. The Interstate Commerce Commission was given a free hand in dealing with such discriminations against interstate commerce as arose from intrastate regulations, a grant of power that ultimately reduced almost to insignificance the authority of the states over the railroads. "Commerce is a unit and does not regard state lines," said Chief Justice Taft, in holding that the law was not an improper invasion of state prerogatives. Other useful provisions of the act gave the commission authority to rule on what new securities the roads might issue, and how the money so obtained should be spent; also, it permitted the consolidation of the four great express companies of the nation into one American Railway Express Company.

Certain well-advertised features of the law proved to be less important than had been anticipated. In response to a long-continued demand the commission was authorized to proceed with the evaluation of railroad property, and to set such rates as would be fair to patrons and would bring the stockholders a reasonable return on their investment. Much difficulty was encountered in determining the rules by which evaluation should proceed.

The commission sought to base its estimates upon reproduction costs as of 1914, believing that these figures would furnish a close approximation of "actual original costs," but the Supreme Court in the O'Fallon decision of 1929 held that the evaluation should be based upon current reproduction costs — a much higher figure. Another provision that led to trouble was the so-called "recapture clause," according to which the better-paying systems were required to pay half their profits in excess of six per cent into a reserve fund for their own use, and the other half into a contingent fund from which the commission might make loans to the weaker roads. By implication this clause set six per cent as "a fair return," but neither the roads nor the public were satisfied with the arrangement. Eventually the "recapture clause" was repealed, and the impounded funds returned to the roads that had earned them. The act also contained elaborate provisions for the establishment of a Railroad Labor Board of nine members, three representing labor; three, the employers; and three, the public. Through this body, it was hoped, all labor disputes might be amicably adjusted. The board permitted generous pay increases in 1921 and the commission allowed the railroads to meet the increased cost of operation by charging higher rates. But the board failed to stop a shopmen's strike in 1922, and in 1926 it was replaced by a Federal Board of Mediation which had no authority to act except on invitation of one or the other of the parties to a dispute.

The railroads, events proved, would have had a new world to face even if there had been no war. For three quarters of a century they had held an easy supremacy in transportation, but they were now compelled increasingly to compete for business with motor trucks, passenger buses, and automobiles, to say nothing of airplanes, pipe lines, and water transportation, particularly coastwise traffic by way of the Panama Canal. It cannot be said that in meeting the new conditions the railroads showed either forethought or resourcefulness. They tended rather to complain bitterly about the "unfair competition" they were compelled to face and to run to the government for help. For them times had greatly changed since the days of the Grangers when all they had asked was to be let alone.

Another post-war legacy almost as perplexing as the railroads was the disposal of

The merchant marine the great fleet of merchantmen that the government had acquired during the war. In this instance there was no prospect of returning the property to former owners, for the American merchant marine of prewar days had been relatively inconsequential. The government itself had built or otherwise acquired its ships for special wartime service. It might operate them, to be sure, in time of peace the same as in time of war, but the prejudice against government ownership was strong, and growing stronger. An important complication was the realization that shipping was an absolute essential in time of war; should war come again to America it ought not to be found so short of ships.

The Jones Merchant Marine Act of 1920 was the first effort of Congress to deal with the shipping problem. By the terms of this act the Shipping Board and its subsidiary, now called the Merchant Fleet Corporation, were continued, with authority to operate the ships as long as necessary, to lay out new shipping lanes for American commerce, and to turn over the ships and the routes to private companies as fast as American purchasers could be found. To induce private capital to invest in shipping, the Merchant Fleet Corporation was provided with a revolving fund of twenty-five million dollars from which it could make liberal loans to private operators. The ships themselves were offered for sale at bargain rates. Two hundred wooden ships, for example, brought little more than the building of a single vessel had cost the government. Special favors to American shipping interests included preferential tariffs on goods imported in American bottoms, a monopoly on all trade with the American colonies, and liberal contracts for carrying the mails. All this was insufficient to tempt many American investors into the shipping business, and hundreds of ships rotted or rusted at their docks.

Eventually, by the Jones-White Act of 1928 Congress offered new and still more generous inducements, with somewhat better results. Shipbuilders could borrow three fourths of the costs of construction from the government, and by way of subsidy operators could obtain mail contracts that ran for long periods and bore no important relationship to the cost of carrying the mails. Even so, the Fleet Corporation failed to extract itself completely from the shipping business, and throughout the Great Depression, with foreign trade languishing, the American merchant marine fell far short of the goals that had been set for it.

The various problems posed by the necessity of demobilizing the nation from its unusual wartime activities gave **Election of 1920** abundant opportunity for the display of partisan politics. In general the Republicans showed themselves better able than the Democrats to take advantage of the situation. During the last half of Wilson's second administration, the Republican Congress elected in 1918 had gone far toward taking the government out of the President's hands. It had crippled his peace program almost beyond repair, and it had written Republican views on domestic policy into legislation, particularly on the railroads and the merchant marine. But the party needed a Republican President as well as a Republican Congress in Washington to carry out more effectively the conservative principles to which its leaders were committed. It was important, of course, that the right man should be nominated for the Presidency, but most Republicans were ready to predict that, regardless of whom the Convention might choose, the election would be a resounding Republican victory. If anything further were needed to make the Republican triumph a certainty, the economic decline that set in during the summer of 1920 would assuredly provide it. Hard times could always be

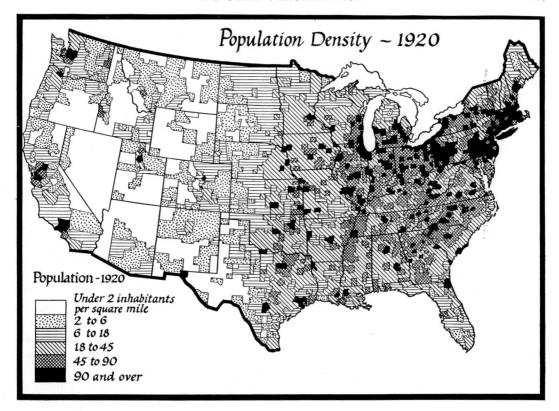

Population Density ~ 1920

Population - 1920

Under 2 inhabitants per square mile
2 to 6
6 to 18
18 to 45
45 to 90
90 and over

blamed on the party in power, which in the public mind meant the party that held the Presidency.

The death of Theodore Roosevelt in 1919 removed the logical Republican candidate **Wood's candidacy** from the scene, but the Roosevelt following found in General Leonard Wood an admirable successor to the Roosevelt tradition. Wood had been on intimate terms with Roosevelt from the days of the Rough Riders, and had, like Roosevelt, been left at home during the First World War. Wood's military ability was not open to question, and he did admirable duty in training troops for overseas service, but Wilson regarded him as troublesome and insubordinate while Pershing was definitely determined not to have him around. Wood's nomination was opposed by the politicians, who looked upon him as an interloper, and by many others who, mindful of the unhappy experience with General Grant, objected to the elevation of a regular army officer to the

Presidency. To treat that high office as a consolation prize seemed also inappropriate. Wood nevertheless obtained an early lead over all other aspirants, and for a time it looked as if his nomination could not be prevented.

Others who were willing to answer the call of duty if it came included Senator Hiram Johnson of California, Roosevelt's running-mate in the Progressive campaign of 1912, and an irreconcilable during the fight on the Treaty of Versailles; Governor Frank O. Lowden of Illinois, the successful businessman in politics; Senator Warren G. Harding of Ohio, an amiable Senate regular who had been permanent chairman of the Republican nominating convention in 1916; and Herbert Hoover, Wilson's Food Administrator during the war. Of all these men Hoover was by far the ablest, and was generally so recognized, but before the war he had spent much time outside the United States, and he was out of touch with American politics. Closely identified with the Wilson administration and a supporter of the League of Nations, he even seemed uncertain as to whether he wished to be considered for the Republican or the Democratic nomination; and as long as that uncertainty existed his candidacy could not be disregarded by either party. When he finally announced that he was a Republican, his chance of obtaining a nomination vanished. The Democrats could not name him, and since that was so the Republicans need not. His chief support came from the women he had taught to "hooverize," from the college professors, and from the *Saturday Evening Post*. Altogether they netted him a maximum of only thirteen votes in the balloting.

The presidential primaries that had figured so conspicuously in the Taft-Roosevelt **Nomination** contest of 1912 were brought **of Harding** again into prominence in 1920. Wood's friends included many men of wealth who spent generously to promote his candidacy, and the relationship between these

Harding's platform, typified by its ambiguity, is derided by John Knott in the *Dallas News,* October 2, 1920.

ON THE SAME PLATFORM

HARDING WILL SCRAP THE LEAGUE OF NATIONS !

HARDING WILL GIVE US A LEAGUE OF NATIONS

ENEMIES OF LEAGUE

HIRAM JOHNSON

TAFT

FRIENDS OF LEAGUE

GERMAN AMERICANS

HARDING'S PLATFORM

heavy expenditures and the large number of delegates pledged to Wood received much unpleasant publicity. Lowden also had means at his disposal, and the number of votes he could count upon was next to Wood's. Johnson attached a considerable block of liberals and isolationists, but Harding's candidacy had failed to arouse enthusiasm outside his own state, and very little even there. Nevertheless, the Republican Convention, which met in Chicago on June 8, nominated Harding on the tenth ballot. Party leaders were convinced that any Republican could win, and were weary of "supermen" in the White House. They wanted, and obtained, an ordinary politician whom they could control. Harding was personally likable, looked the part of a President, and was untroubled by any deep-seated convictions. For Vice-President the convention would gladly have chosen Johnson, but he refused to be considered. The party leaders then decided on Lenroot of Wisconsin, but the delegates got out of hand and nominated the almost forgotten favorite son of Massachusetts, Calvin Coolidge. The Republican platform, on the all-important issue of the League of Nations, was intentionally obscure. It pledged the party to "such agreement with other nations of the world as shall meet the full duty of America to civilization and humanity," but this, as was intended, could mean everything or nothing. On domestic matters it was somewhat more forthright. It objected to "price fixing" in aid of agriculture, urged voluntary tribunals for the settlement of industrial disputes, mentioned but neglected to approve collective bargaining, hinted at further limitations on immigration, favored high protective ta.iffs, lower direct taxes, and national economy.

The Democratic Convention met at San Francisco on June 28. There is some reason to believe that Wilson himself, **Cox and** although not a candidate, wished **Roosevelt** the opportunity to decline a complimentary nomination, but the convention contented itself with approving his administration and

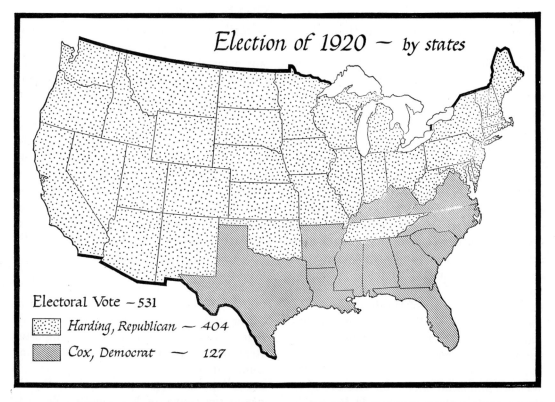

Election of 1920 — by states

Electoral Vote — 531

Harding, Republican — 404

Cox, Democrat — 127

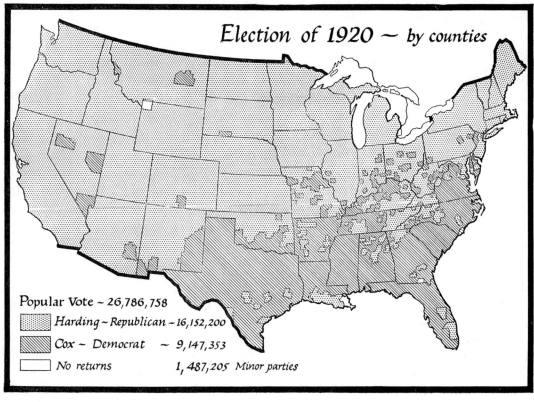

Election of 1920 — by counties

Popular Vote ~ 26,786,758

Harding ~ Republican ~ 16,152,200

Cox ~ Democrat ~ 9,147,353

No returns   1,487,205 Minor parties

advocating unqualified ratification for the Treaty and the League. With Hoover out of the picture, a three-cornered contest developed between William G. McAdoo, the President's son-in-law, A. Mitchell Palmer, the Attorney-General, and James M. Cox, Governor of Ohio. McAdoo made no effort to secure the nomination, perhaps because he could foresee nothing better than defeat and held hopes for 1924. Branded as the "crown prince," his position at best was difficult. Palmer as Alien Property Custodian had been involved in many unpleasant dealings with foreigners in the United States, and as Attorney-General his intemperate attitude toward labor and political agitators cost him much liberal support. Cox was finally nominated on the forty-fourth ballot, mainly, as in the case of Harding, because he was satisfactory to the professional politicians, particularly the city machines. His nomination was regarded as a defeat for Wilson, since he was in no way connected with the Wilson administration, but for Vice-President the convention chose Franklin D. Roosevelt, Wilson's Assistant Secretary of the Navy.

There is no evidence to support the opinion, long held, that Cox and Roosevelt, un-
The "solemn til they met with the President,
referendum" were ready to ignore his plea for a "solemn referendum" on the League of Nations, and to wage their campaign on issues that had a wider popular appeal. From the outset they stood steadfastly by Wilson's record. Harding had been a reservationist in the Senate, but during the campaign he hedged so successfully that such League advocates as Hughes, Root, and Taft came earnestly to his support, while the Johnson-Borah irreconcilables thought he shared their views. His naturally befuddled mind, and his unusual command of obscure English, provided an excellent concealment for his views, if, indeed, he had any. The "league to elect Harding" was united on little else, for it contained pro-League and anti-League Republicans, anti-Wilson Democrats, "hyphenates" who hated Wilson for all he had done or had failed to do for the nations they

had left, liberals who denounced the "white terror" under Palmer, and millions who had suffered from what they had begun to suspect was a needless war. Cox bore the Democratic label and stood on the Wilson record. On that account he was defeated. The American people held no brief for Harding, but he was the only alternative, and they elected him, as one journalist observed, "by disgust." His popular majority was nearly seven millions, and in the electoral college he received 404 votes to Cox's 127. He was assured, also, of a Congress that would be overwhelmingly Republican in both houses.

Warren Gamaliel Harding (1865–1923) was a prominent citizen of Marion, Ohio, a typical middle-western town of **Harding** some thirty thousand inhabitants. Most of his education he obtained as editor and proprietor of the Marion *Daily Star*. From his youth up he had supported Republican principles through thick and thin, and he presently became recognized as one of the small group of leaders who directed the course of Republican policies in Ohio. He made the nominating speech for Taft against Roosevelt in the convention of 1912, and in 1914 he won both nomination and election to the United States Senate. He was a genial good fellow, well liked by his neighbors, and thoroughly imbued with the common man's vanities and prejudices. He knew that he was no intellectual giant, but prided himself on his ability to "get along with" people, and took comfort in the thought that as President he could command the judgment of the "best minds" in the party. His most devoted political friend was Harry M. Daugherty, another Ohio machine politician, whose knowledge of the seamy side of politics was unexcelled. Daugherty's greatest ambition was realized when, as Harding's campaign manager, he piloted his candidate to victory at the Chicago Convention.

In forming his cabinet Harding hit upon some of the best minds in the party, and some of the worst. He was per-   **The "best** suaded to forego his desire to ap-   **minds"** point Senator Albert B. Fall of New Mexico as Secretary of State, for Fall was an insistent advocate of intervention in Mexico, and chose instead the distinguished ex-jurist Charles Evans Hughes, Republican nominee in 1916. But Fall was a crony whom Harding liked, and into the cabinet he went as Secretary of the Interior, although he happened to be also a rabid anti-conservationist. For Secretary of the Treasury Harding finally decided upon Andrew W. Mellon of Pittsburgh, one of the two or three richest men in the United States; and by a stroke of luck he was able to persuade Hoover to become Secretary of Commerce. The rest of the cabinet was mediocre or worse. Daugherty, who had won no laurels as a lawyer, was made Attorney-General, and Edwin Denby of Michigan, a man whose chief qualification for the position seems to have been that he had once been a member of the marines, was made Secretary of the Navy.

In his other appointments Harding showed the same inability to distinguish between good and bad. He made ex-President Taft Chief Justice of the Supreme Court when opportunity offered, a graceful and deserved compliment, but he turned over the newly organized Veterans' Bureau to a rogue named Charles R. Forbes who eventually landed in a federal prison. In general, the new President regarded political offices as the lawful spoils of victory, and to members of the unsavory "Ohio gang" that followed him to Washington went many choice plums.

Whatever he might have meant by the ambiguities he uttered during the campaign, **Separate peace with Germany** Harding interpreted his election as a mandate against American participation in the League of Nations. The Treaty of Versailles, therefore, which embodied the Covenant, could not be ratified. Following the resolution of July 2, 1921, by which Congress declared the war at an end, negotiations with Germany led to a treaty signed August 25, 1921, whereby the United States obtained all the advantages of the Treaty of Versailles, and none of the responsibilities.

Warren G. Harding

TWENTY-NINTH PRESIDENT of the United States, Harding was an amiable party regular far below the level of ability that had characterized his immediate predecessors. And yet the proportion of the popular vote by which he was elected was greater than that received by any other President in recent times. The likeness is from an oil painting by Henry R. Rittenberg.

Well before this time the Harding administration had taken occasion to show its goodwill toward one of the greatest American industries, oil. American business interests had long complained that the failure of the United States to back them up in their efforts to promote overseas expansion had put them at a severe disadvantage in competition with the corporations of other nations whose governments were not so scrupulous. The oil interests, in particular, were convinced that they were entitled to the strongest possible diplomatic assistance. Oil had become a war necessity, for by this time the navies of all the great powers depended on it for as high as ninety per cent of the fuel they used; worse still, experts then believed that the oil resources of the world were nearing exhaustion. The British government, acutely conscious of the fact that the British Isles produced no oil, gave British oil interests the most vigorous support, not only in the British Empire, but also in the British mandates obtained under the League of Nations, and in every other area where unexploited oil deposits were known to exist. In general, American policy favored the "open door" everywhere, that is, equality of opportunity for all nations, but the rivalry was intense, and the temptation to work for exclusive privileges was great. In the Americas, the Monroe Doctrine, properly interpreted, might promote this end. Should not the United States at least seek to obtain for its corporations preferential treatment in the western hemisphere?

Without precisely answering this question in the affirmative, the Harding administra-

A treaty with Colombia tion promptly went on record in favor of ending the long dispute with Colombia over the means by which Theodore Roosevelt had promoted the Panama Revolution. Colombia had rich oil resources, and the resentment Colombians still felt for the action taken by the United States played into the hands of the ever-present British oil interests. The Harding administration was only four days old when the new President informed his cabinet and the press that the Thompson-Urrutia treaty with Colombia, which proposed the payment of $25,000,000 to Colombia for whatever damage she might have suffered, would be re-submitted in its latest form, with the "sincere regret" clause stricken out. This treaty had been negotiated early in the Wilson administration, but had failed of ratification by the Senate, both before and after the death of Theodore Roosevelt. Advocates of ratification frankly admitted that the object of the treaty was to help along the American oil interests that were seeking concessions in Colombia. Senator Lodge, the close friend of Theodore Roosevelt, who had at first been violently opposed to anything that might look like the appeasement of Colombia, now led the fight for the treaty, pointing out that "the question of oil is one that is vital to every great maritime nation," and urging that the United States should stand behind its overseas investors. On the other side, Senator Watson of Georgia complained that the payment to Colombia amounted only to "an indirect subsidy to the oil interests." But the treaty was ratified, April 20, 1921, by a vote of 69 to 19. In Colombia there was still opposition to any settlement with the United States that failed to include an outright apology, but the money payment in itself could be so construed, and at length the treaty was accepted. It was proclaimed in force March 1, 1922, and worked as had been intended to the considerable advantage of American oil interests.

The let-down from Wilsonian idealism with which the Harding administration took office was broken somewhat by the International Conference on Limitation of Armaments that the new President called to meet in Washington on Armistice Day, November 11, 1921. The program of naval expansion begun by the United States, Great Britain, and Japan during the war, had developed at its close into an unhealthy and expensive rivalry that threatened to continue indefinitely. Senator Borah was most prominent among the advocates of limitation, and Harding's invitation was issued in no small part as the result of Borah's insistence. Every possible device was employed to build up the Conference as the Republican counterpart of the Wilsonian program. It was persistently spoken of as the "Peace Conference," although it was nothing of the kind, and a great to-do was made over its opening. At eleven o'clock on the appointed day the whole nation paused in commemoration of the restoration of peace, while at the Arlington National Cemetery the body of an unknown American soldier was ceremoniously interred.

Next day, after the formal welcome by President Harding was over, Secretary Hughes presented a program of **The Washington Conference** naval reduction so drastic as to startle the Conference. Exhibiting a knowledge of detail that was in itself amazing, he advocated that the naval strength of the great powers should be fixed at stipulated ratios, that naval tonnage in excess of specified maxima should be scrapped, and that no new ships should be constructed for a period of ten years. In the end five powers, the United States, the British Empire, Japan, France, and Italy, agreed to limit their strength in capital ships to total tonnages that bore to each other roughly the ratios of 5 : 5 : 3 : 1.7 : 1.7, respectively. Unfortunately this agreement left unsolved the important problem of lesser craft. Some critics said that the elimination of capital ships was inconsequential, since the battle of Jutland had proved that they were no longer of value. But the limitations adopted at least resulted in tremendous budgetary savings for the nations concerned, and naval experts generally refused to concede that dreadnoughts and battle-cruisers were obsolete. In 1927, at the suggestion of President Coolidge, a conference met at Geneva to discuss the limitation of auxiliary ships, but failed to reach an agreement. In 1930 at London, a conference called by President Hoover fared somewhat better. Some limitations were imposed on the building of lesser craft, Japan was appeased by a more generous quota for all the nations involved, and the naval holiday in capital ships was extended to 1936.

An unforeseen, and perhaps unforeseeable, result of the disarmament program was to leave Japan relatively stronger in the Far East, and the United States and Great Britain relatively weaker. The Washington agreement actually referred only to capital ships, and placed no limitations on the building of auxiliary craft of any kind, but the United States for a period of three years following the conference failed to lay down a single keel, and for three years more did little building of consequence. Only after Japan, followed by some of the other powers, had begun to build cruisers again did the United States in 1928 re-enter the rivalry. Even after the agreement of 1930, the United States, and to a lesser extent, Great Britain, failed to build up to their treaty limitations. Japan, on the other hand, built to the very limit of her quotas, and in 1934, when she began to feel cramped by them, denounced the agreement that bound her until 1936. After that date the race for naval supremacy was resumed in earnest, but Japan started it in a far stronger position, relatively, than she had been in before the negotiations on limitation of armaments had begun. It is possible that the Washington Conference and the agreements that flowed from it, instead of promoting peace by disarmament as the western powers intended, may actually have furnished Japan the necessary incentive to start her on the road to Pearl Harbor.

The Washington Conference resulted in the drafting of two other noteworthy treaties, one signed by four powers, and **The Four-** the other by nine. The Four- **Power Pact** Power Pact, agreed to by the United States, the British Empire, France, and Japan, paved the way for the abrogation of the Anglo-Japanese Alliance, which had become distasteful to both Great Britain and the United States. The new pact proposed to preserve the peace in the Pacific by pledging the contracting powers mutually to respect one another's rights "in relation to their insular possessions and insular dominions in the region," and to refer to a joint conference such disputes as might cause trouble. The four powers also bound themselves to "communicate with one another fully and frankly" on the action to be taken in case their rights were "threatened by the aggressive action of any other power." Had the pact ever been taken seriously, as it was not, it might have constituted almost as decisive a departure from the American doctrine of isolation as if the United States had entered the League of Nations. Closely connected with it was Article XIX of the Treaty on Naval Limitation which bound the United States, the British Empire, and Japan to maintain the *status quo* with respect to "fortifications and naval bases in the Pacific."

The Nine-Power Treaty related to "principles and policies to be followed in matters concerning China," and was **The Nine-** signed by the United States, **Power Pact** Belgium, the British Empire, China, France, Italy, Japan, the Netherlands, and Portugal.

CONFERENCE TABLE. This view gives a feeling of the size and importance of the conference.

U.S. DELEGATES. Left to right: Elihu Root, Oscar Underwood, Charles Evans Hughes, Henry Cabot Lodge, and Basil Miles.

The Washington Conference not only set limits to the building of new capital ships, but also scrapped many ships already built or under construction. French opposition prevented similar action on cruisers, destroyers, and submarines, and blocked all efforts to put land armaments on the agenda. The Conference also dealt with Far Eastern affairs, and the nine treaties that came out of it were all ratified.

The situation in the Far East had changed materially as a result of the First World War. In 1915 Japan had in effect repudiated the doctrine of the open door by presenting to China twenty-one notorious demands for special privileges, many of which China was forced to concede. In 1917, by the Lansing-Ishii Agreement, Japan once more gave lip-service to the open door, but won from the United States recognition "that territorial propinquity creates special relations between countries." At the Paris Peace Conference, Japan insisted on being awarded the German concessions in Shantung, although the Japanese delegates promised Wilson that Japan would eventually withdraw from the peninsula, which, at least in a military sense, she did. The purpose of the Nine-Power Pact was to reconcile this situation, as nearly as possible, with the open door for world trade in China and the integrity of the Chinese Republic. In words the new treaty seemed to administer a strong rebuff to Japanese policy, for it pledged the signatory powers to respect Chinese sovereignty, to aid China in maintaining an effective government, to use their influence in favor of "equal opportunity for the commerce and industry of all nations" in China, and to "refrain from taking advantage of conditions in China to seek special rights." But Japan by the decade of the thirties was violating all these pledges with impunity, and the treaty provided no means whereby an offending power could be restrained.

Certain minor agreements were not written into the Nine-Power Treaty. A separate **Minor agreements** treaty provided for the return of Shantung to China on condition that China should buy from Japan the former German railway line serving the peninsula, and should also honor numerous private contracts obtained by the Japanese during the occupation. The United States had objected also to the status of the island of Yap, which the League of Nations had handed over to Japan as a mandate, together with numerous other Pacific islands north of the equator that Japan had seized from Germany during the war.[1] Yap, because of its importance as a cable station, should have been internationalized, according to the American contention. The result was a separate treaty between the United States and Japan, signed during the Conference, that gave the United States the cable privileges it desired on the island. Resolutions of little binding force called also for the removal of foreign post offices and radio stations from China, the acknowledgment of her right to tariff autonomy, and a study of extra-territoriality.

Harding's formula of peace by disarmament proved to be a poor substitute for Wilson's formula of peace by international cooperation. But it satisfied the growing isolationist spirit of the times. While the First World War was in progress, and for some time afterward, there was good reason to believe that a majority of the American people favored the Wilson approach. But as the years wore on, public opinion veered

[1] Although Japan withdrew from the League of Nations in 1933 (effective 1935), she retained her mandates in the Pacific islands, and fortified them well, as many "G.I.'s" who fought in the Second World War can testify.

around to a demand for what Harding called "normalcy." For over a century before the First World War the United States had held aloof from world affairs; it should return to its traditional policy and let the nations of Europe and Asia go their own way. With adequate naval disarmament, Harding's apologists reasoned, the United States need not fear an aggressor, and it never meant to be one. Pleased with this easy approach to perpetual peace, they overlooked the inadequacy of the disarmament actually achieved, and failed to observe the even more important fact that a great and powerful nation in an increasingly interdependent world had no chance to escape outside responsibilities.

The Washington Conference was not the only Republican effort, however, to promote world peace. The idea of a per- **The World** manent court of international **Court** justice had been advocated by the American delegation to the Second Hague Conference in 1907, and was far more closely identified with Republican than with Democratic policy. When, therefore, under Article XIV of the League of Nations Covenant, plans were drawn in 1920 for such a court, there seemed no good reason why a Republican administration should not give the new institution its blessing. Indeed, Elihu Root, respected elder statesman of the Republican Party, had assisted in drafting the World Court protocol, and John Bassett Moore, America's foremost authority on international law, was slated for a place on its bench of eleven (later fifteen) judges. The only difficulty in the way of American participation seemed to lie in the fact that the judges were to be chosen by the Council and Assembly of the League of Nations, but it was proposed that for this purpose only, the United States might have a voice in the proceedings. Certain that public opinion was "overwhelmingly in favor of participation," President Harding urged American adherence to the Court, only to be rebuffed by the Senate, in which the irreconcilables were able to prevent any action whatever. Extreme isolationists professed to fear that adherence to the Court would be only the entering wedge to further involvement in world affairs, and the still-embittered critics of "Wilsonism" would have nothing to do with anything even remotely connected with the League. Harding was not the last American President to advocate the adherence of the United States to the World Court. Cool-idge, Hoover, and Roosevelt all urged the Senate to ratify its protocol, but they all failed to get results. In spite of non-participation by the United States, an American judge always sat on the court. Moore was succeeded by Charles Evans Hughes in 1928; Hughes, by Frank B. Kellogg in 1930; Kellogg, by Manley O. Hudson in 1936.

Bibliography

Most of the textbooks in American economic history give satisfactory accounts of the business conditions that followed the war. Among the best of them are F. A. Shannon, *America's Economic Growth* (3d ed., 1951); H. U. Faulkner, *American Economic History* (6th ed., 1949); E. L. Bogart and D. L. Kemmerer, *Economic History of the American People* (2d ed., 1947); E. C. Kirtland, *A History of American Economic Life* (3d ed., 1951); and James A. Barnes, *Wealth of the American People* (1949). A flood of detail is available in the report of the Conference on Unemployment, *Recent Economic Changes in the United States* (2 vols., 1929).

For labor problems, Selig Perlman and Philip Taft, *History of Labor in the United States, 1896–1932* (Commons, *History of Labour in the United States*, IV, *Labor Movements*), is indispensable. The publication of a thorough investigation into the Steel Strike, Interchurch World Movement, *Report on the Steel Strike of 1919* (1920), had much to do with the shaping of public opinion on the rights of labor. See also V. W. Lanfear, *Business Fluctuations and the Labor Movement, 1915–1922* (1924). The story of the red scare and its consequences may be gleaned from Jane P. Carey, *Deportation of Aliens from the United States to Europe* (1931); Felix Frankfurter, *The Case of Sacco and Vanzetti* (1927); and G. Louis Joughin and Edmund M. Morgan, *The Legacy of Sacco and Vanzetti* (1948).

On Negro problems Gunnar Myrdal, *An American Dilemma: The Negro Problem and Modern Democracy* (2 vols., 1944), is a work of unusual excellence and objectivity. On the related constitutional problems, Bernard H. Nelson, *The Fourteenth Amendment and the Negro since 1920* (1946), is helpful. J. M. Mecklin, *The Ku Klux Klan* (1924), is a good contemporary study.

The problems of agriculture for the country as a whole are dealt with in Edward Wiest, *Agricultural Organization in the United States* (1923). On the critical problem of marketing, E. G. Nourse, *American Agriculture and the European Market* (1924); and B. H. Hibbard, *Marketing Agricultural Products* (1921), are scholarly and illuminating. Theodore Saloutos and J. D. Hicks, *Agricultural Discontent in the Middle West, 1900–1939* (1951), traces the history of the principal farm orders from their formation, and shows their effect on the political life of states and nation. The Nonpartisan League has attracted the attention of many writers, among them Andrew A. Bruce, *Non-Partisan League* (1921), which is hostile to the League; and C. E. Russell, *The Story of the Nonpartisan League* (1920), which is somewhat friendly. See also H. E. Gaston, *The Nonpartisan League* (1920); A. S. Tostlebe, *The Bank of North Dakota* (1924); H. H. Bakken and M. A. Schaars, *The Economics of Co-operative Marketing* (1937); and C. C. Taylor, *The Farmers' Movement, 1620–1920* (1953).

On transportation, Rogers MacVeagh, *The Transportation Act, 1920: Its Sources, History, and Text* (1923), presents basic data on the return of the railroads to private operation, but see also D. P. Locklin, *Economics of Transportation* (1935); and H. G. Moulton and associates, *The American Transportation Problem* (1933). On the merchant marine and its problems there are several good books: E. W. Zimmermann, *Zimmermann on Ocean Shipping* (1921); National Industrial Conference Board, *The American Merchant Marine Problem* (1929); D. H. Smith and P. V. Betters, *The United States Shipping Board* (1931); and P. M. Zeis, *American Shipping Policy* (1938).

On the politics of the twenties there are two useful guides, J. C. Malin, *The United States after the World War* (1930); and L. M. Hacker, *American Problems of Today* (1938). The question of the succession to the Presidency during Wilson's illness is covered in C. M. Thomas, *Thomas Riley Marshall* (1939). The most complete study of the nomination of Harding is in Mark Sullivan, *Our Times*, VI, *The Twenties* (1935); but for a colorful picture of the whole Harding administration, see Samuel H. Adams, *Incredible Era: The Life and Times of Warren Gamaliel Harding* (1939). Certain aspects of the return to peace are covered in the first essay in F. L. Paxson, *The Great Demobilization and Other Essays* (1941); and more fully, by the same author, in *American Democracy and the World War*, III, *Post-War Years, 1918–1923* (1948).

The atmosphere of the Washington Conference is well captured in Mark Sullivan, *The Great Adventure at Washington* (1922). Some behind-the-scenes activities, not often written about, appear in H. O. Yardley, *The American Black Chamber* (1931), an exciting story of the work of the cryptographic bureau. Useful accounts of the Conference are given in R. L. Buell, *The Washington Conference* (1922); and Yamato Ichihashi, *The Washington Conference and After* (1928); and Harold and Margaret Sprout, *Toward a New Order of Sea Power* (1940).

On the Far Eastern situation, consult Eleanor Tupper and G. E. McReynolds, *Japan in American Public Opinion* (1937); F. R. Dulles, *Forty Years of American-Japanese Relations* (1937); H. M. Vinacke, *A History of the Far East in Modern Times* (5th ed., 1950); and Dorothy Borg, *American Policy and the Chinese Revolution, 1925–1928* (1947).

On the League and the Court, see D. F. Fleming, *The United States and World Organization, 1920–1933* (1938); M. O. Hudson, *The Permanent Court of International Justice and the Question of American Participation* (1925); D. F. Fleming, *The United States and the World Court* (1945); Allan Nevins, *The United States in a Chaotic World: A Chronicle of International Affairs, 1918–1933* (1950); and F. P. Walters, *A History of the League of Nations* (1952).

23

The Road to Prosperity

The veterans' bonus — Budget reform — The tariff — Restrictions on immigration — The Farm Bloc — The Harding scandals — Death of Harding — Calvin Coolidge — The recovery program — Economy — — Reduction of taxes — Governmental withdrawal from business — Restraints on regulation — Government aids to business — The disciplining of labor — Business recovery — Farmer and labor discontent — The C.P.P.A. — Election of 1924 — The Coolidge landslide

"THE war will last a hundred years," ran a soldier saying, "five years of fighting and ninety-five of winding up the barbed wire." While Secretary Hughes was engaged in his none-too-successful effort to adjust the United States to the new world order, Congress was busily at work trying to roll up some of the barbed wire at home. An anticipated result of any war is the problem of the returned soldier. For those who might sustain injuries from the war the government had made generous provision in 1917 through the Bureau of War Risk Insurance, and when the war was over these provisions were still further liberalized. In 1921 all problems pertaining to service men were turned over to a Veterans' Bureau, which built and administered hospitals, supervised rehabilitation activities, and ruled on claims for compensation. Its work cost the government on an average a half billion dollars a year.

But the demand for aid did not end with the men who had sustained injuries or illnesses traceable to the war. Veterans who had suffered no disability found frequently that the jobs they had once held had been given to others, while the task of getting and holding new jobs was by no means easy. They observed, too, that

The veterans' bonus

the men of their age who had stayed at home had made a good start in the world, while the returned soldier found himself two years behind in the competition. Furthermore, the high wartime wages and salaries earned by civilians contrasted sharply with the dollar a day paid to the soldiers. To tide them over the period of unemployment following their return to civil life, the government had paid a small discharge bonus to the soldiers, and to this a number of the states added small sums. But many veterans soon convinced themselves that the United States still owed them something by way of "adjusted compensation." This plea the American Legion, which was founded in 1919 and soon emerged as the leading organization of veterans, pushed earnestly upon Congress, and in 1922 a bill that would have granted fifty dollars for each month of service to every veteran of the war failed of enactment only because of a presidential veto. But the Legion continued its pressure and in 1924 succeeded in marshaling a large enough majority in Congress to override the President's opposition. As passed the law took the form of a grant of paid-up insurance to fall due twenty years later. The amount owing each soldier was computed on the basis of a dollar and a quarter for each day overseas, and a dollar for each day in service at home. On an average the policies ran to more than one thousand dollars each, and against his policy each veteran was permitted to borrow up to 22.5 per cent of its face value. Altogether this "bonus bill," as its opponents insisted on calling it, added about three and one half billion dollars to the total cost of the war.

The colossal expenditures of the war called striking attention to one of the anomalies of **Budget reform** the American system of government. Since the founding of the republic, Congress had been content to make such appropriations and to levy such taxes as it saw fit, hoping, but not consciously planning, that expenditures and receipts would somehow cancel each other. Government bureaus asked largely of Congress and sometimes duplicated activities. In both houses numerous committees had authority to recommend expenditures, and each was free to act without reference to what any other committee was doing. The need for a planned national budget had long been apparent. As far back as 1911 President Taft had appointed a Commission on Economy and Efficiency that had recommended the adoption of a budget system. President Taft was unable to induce Congress to accept such an innovation, but at the end of the war the demand for economy at last moved Congress to act. Before the end of the Wilson administration a bill providing that a national budget should be drafted each year under the supervision of the President had passed both the House and the Senate, only to be vetoed by Wilson. Wilson had no objection to the budget system; on the contrary he believed in it. But he resented a clause in the proposed law which made it impossible for the President to remove the comptroller, an officer charged with the responsibility of auditing all expenditures to see if they were being made in harmony with the law, and to be appointed for a fifteen-year term. Provision for such an arrangement, Wilson believed, was unconstitutional, and might well produce — did indeed pro-

Charles G. Dawes was the first director of the Bureau of the Budget, and Vice-President under Coolidge.

duce under the second Roosevelt — a situation in which the President and the comptroller could not agree.

If President Harding was worried by the prospect of a difference of opinion between himself and his comptroller, he failed to show it. In June, 1921, the Budget Act became a law, although the provision to which Wilson had objected was retained. As director of the budget, the President named Charles G. Dawes, a Chicago banker whose talents had been proved by his work as agent for the A.E.F. in France. All regular expenditures came within the scrutiny of the director, who made every effort to eliminate duplications and to pare down requests to reasonable dimensions. Estimates so obtained were then submitted to Congress, where in each house a single Committee on Appropriations determined the final recommendations. That the work of Dawes and his successors resulted in considerable savings there could be little doubt.

Another problem of immediate concern was to deal with wartime taxation. With the war at an end an insistent **Financial legislation** outcry had been raised against the high taxes being collected to support it.

In spite of the fact that the public debt had mounted to over twenty-four billion dollars, Secretary Mellon believed that the revenues were excessive and ought to be reduced, and the Revenue Act of 1921 followed his recommendations in part. The act repealed the excess-profits tax, but in reducing the surtax rates cut the maximum rates only from sixty-five to fifty per cent, whereas Mellon had urged an initial cut to forty per cent, and an ultimate cut to thirty-three per cent. Other adjustments he found even less satisfactory. The tax on corporation incomes, for example, was raised from ten per cent to twelve and one half per cent. Urged on by representatives from the western farmers, who pointed to the distress that post-war deflation had brought to agriculture, the special session enacted also an Emergency Tariff Act. The new law was designed merely as a stopgap to last until a more permanent revision could be made. It raised the tariff on wheat in order to protect northwestern farmers against Canadian importation, and gave added protection to such other farm products as meat, wool, and sugar. The dumping of foreign goods in the United States was also strictly prohibited, and an embargo was laid on German dyestuffs.

The thoroughgoing tariff revision upward historically associated with a Republican triumph was effected by the Ford-ney-McCumber Act, signed September 21, 1922. The new law raised tariff rates to the highest levels yet known. Not content with approximating the heavily protective schedules of the Payne-Aldrich Tariff, it retained with only slight alterations the agricultural tariffs of the Emergency Act of 1921; placed practically prohibitive duties on dyestuffs and chemicals; raised to fantastic levels the rates on many cheap articles imported from Japan; and virtually excluded all but the finest foreign woolens. In acceptance of the principle that tariff rates should merely equalize the cost of production at home and abroad, the act empowered the Tariff Commission (established in 1916) to suggest such changes to the President as its

The tariff

investigations might warrant, and authorized the President to shift the rates as much as fifty per cent up or down. This provision for flexibility proved to be more important in theory than in fact. Neither President Harding nor President Coolidge felt obliged to follow the recommendations of the commission, and in a six-year period only five reductions were ordered, on mill feed, bobwhite quail, paint-brush handles, phenol, and cresylic acid. Thirty-two changes upward were recorded, including certain dairy products, chemicals, and pig iron. Among the recommendations of the commission that were pigeonholed was one advocating a reduction in the rates on sugar.

Further efforts to adjust the United States to the conditions of the post-war world led to the shattering of one of America's oldest and most cherished traditions — a hearty welcome to immigrants. In a sense, however, this was only another aspect of the isolationism that was in the air. Premonitions of the coming change were apparent in May, 1917, when Congress passed over Wilson's veto the same provision for a literacy test that he had defeated two years before. But the cessation of hostilities soon proved conclusively that something more drastic than a literacy test would be necessary if the distressed multitudes of Europe were to be prevented from seeking refuge in America. In the year ending June 30, 1921, over eight hundred thousand immigrants came to the United States, and in spite of the attempted restriction nearly two thirds of them came from the countries of southern and eastern Europe. Confronted by this situation, Congress in 1921 passed an Emergency Immigration Act that assigned to each nation an immigrant quota consisting of not more than three per cent of the number of its nationals resident in the United States according to the census of 1910. Immigrants from other American nations were exempted from the quota system, but in 1922 an amendment required that all aliens resident in an American country must have lived there not less than five

Restrictions on immigration

years before being freed from the quota restrictions.

The law of 1921 was meant merely as a temporary stopgap while the details of the new immigration policy were being worked out, and in 1924 Congress passed another immigration act. This time the quota was set at two per cent of the nationals resident in the United States in 1890, thereby reducing still further the numbers eligible for admission, particularly from southern and eastern Europe. The law also provided that after July 1, 1927, the number of quota immigrants was to be limited to one hundred and fifty thousand, while quotas were to be based upon "national origins," the same to be determined from a study of the census of 1920. The difficulty in determining the national origins of the American people completely baffled the committee of cabinet members (the Secretaries of State, Commerce, and Labor) charged with that duty, and not until 1929 were its half-hearted recommendations put into effect. Whatever their imperfections, the new quotas insured that an overwhelming proportion of the thin trickle of immigrants permitted to enter the United States originated in those countries that had first contributed to its settlement. Great Britain and northern Ireland, for example, were permitted to send 65,721 immigrants annually, while the Italian quota was only 5802. A peculiarly unfortunate aspect of the Act of 1924 was the exclusion of all aliens ineligible to citizenship, a provision aimed specifically at the Japanese, who deeply resented the discrimination. Since under the regular quota system the number of Japanese immigrants would have been insignificant anyway, the affront thus given a proud and sensitive people was as unnecessary as it was unwise. Undoubtedly it was one of the factors that led to the growing anti-American sentiment in Japan that culminated in Pearl Harbor.

The special favors shown to nations of the western hemisphere led at first to a heavy immigration from Mexico, but immigration officials tried to put a stop to this by refusing entrance to Mexican laborers on the ground that they were likely to become public charges. Ways of defeating the immigration regulations, however, were not hard to find, and whenever the demand for migratory agricultural workers was strong enough Mexican immigrants by the thousands crossed the border into California and the Southwest. These "wetbacks," as they were sometimes called, were frequently rounded up in large numbers and returned to Mexico, only to evade the immigration authorities again at the next convenient opportunity.

Nevertheless, the Census of 1930 revealed that the proportion of aliens resident in the United States had indeed begun to decline. The significance of this change did not go entirely unnoticed. Recent immigrants and their children, particularly those whose homelands lay in the areas discriminated against, could not but feel that they had been branded as unwanted, second-class citizens who were regarded as suspect solely because of their ancestry. They were ripe politically for protest, and ready to give their allegiance to whichever party might the more generously extend them the promise of equality. But the end of immigration had even more important connotations. It meant, no doubt, that northern European domination of American culture had been preserved; the infiltration of southern and eastern Europeans, with their different political, religious, and social concepts, was virtually brought to a close. But it meant also that American farms and factories, long dependent upon immigration for a steady supply of cheap labor and for a growing volume of domestic consumption, had thoughtlessly sacrificed both. The competition for labor would be stiffer; the demands of the immigrants for foodstuffs and manufactured articles would be missed. The embargo of the United States on immigration even had its international aspects. Where was the surplus population of Europe to go? Some of it was drained off to Latin-America and to the overseas nations of the British Commonwealth. But there were plenty of would-be immigrants left at home to feed the

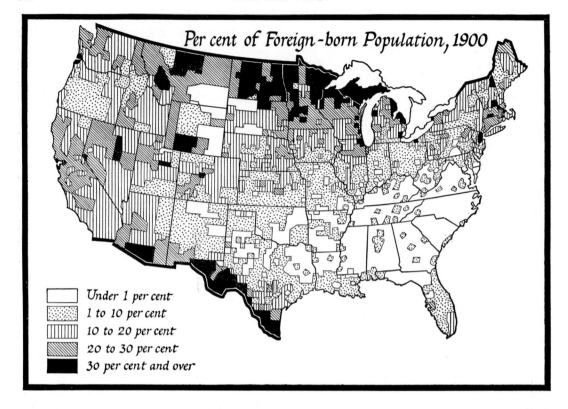

Per cent of Foreign-born Population, 1900

Under 1 per cent
1 to 10 per cent
10 to 20 per cent
20 to 30 per cent
30 per cent and over

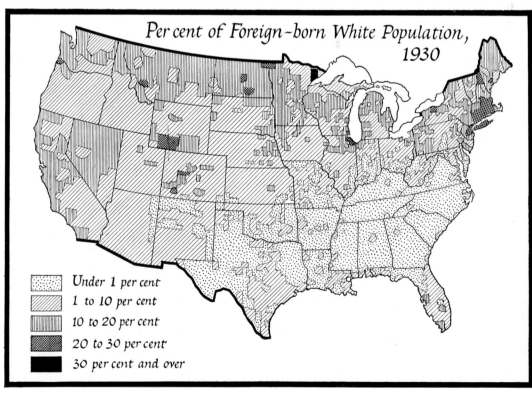

Per cent of Foreign-born White Population, 1930

Under 1 per cent
1 to 10 per cent
10 to 20 per cent
20 to 30 per cent
30 per cent and over

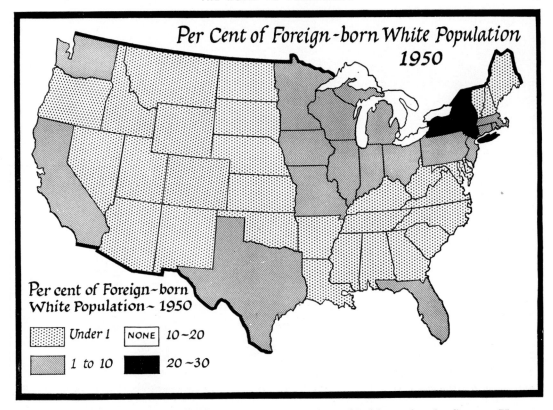

Per Cent of Foreign-born White Population 1950

Per cent of Foreign-born White Population ~ 1950

Under 1   NONE 10~20

1 to 10   20~30

fires of discontent, and to encourage the ambitions of demagogues. Germany's search for *Lebensraum*, Italy's demand for colonies, and Zionist ambitions for a Jewish homeland in Palestine were not altogether unconnected with the reversal of the American policy of welcoming all who sought refuge on American soil.

While dealing thus drastically with the problem of immigration, Congress found **The Farm Bloc in Congress** itself also called upon to chart an almost equally novel course with reference to agriculture. American farm leaders, seeking methods to deal with the dislocations that had followed in the wake of war, naturally did not overlook the possibility of aid from the federal government. In May, 1921, on the suggestion of Grey Silver, head of the American Farm Bureau Federation, the creation of a "Farm Bloc" in both houses of Congress was undertaken. In the Senate the Bloc came to consist of fourteen Republicans and twelve Democrats, all from the West or the South, and led for a time by Senator Kenyon of Iowa, then by Senator Capper of Kansas. In the House the membership of the Bloc was less clearly defined, but its existence was nonetheless real. For three or four years the Farm Bloc held together, and during this period it exerted a powerful influence upon the course of legislation.

Most of the measures promoted by the Bloc had as their purpose either the easement of rural credits or the promotion of cooperative marketing. A bill sponsored by Senator Norris of Nebraska would have created a gigantic government-owned corporation, with power to build warehouses, and to buy, sell, and export farm products with a view to the stabilization of prices. But the administration regarded this measure as sheer socialism, and persuaded the Farm Bloc to accept instead an extension of life of the War Finance Corporation, which was given a hundred million dollars to lend to the producers, sellers, and exporters of farm products. Of greater permanent importance was the Inter-

Teapot Dome. Oil reserves located in Wyoming.

"The Furst Good Laugh They've Had in Years." Satire on the exhilaration of the Democrats over the expose. Ding in the *New York Herald Tribune*, May 14, 1937.

mediate Credits Act of 1923, which the Farm Bloc successfully pushed through Congress. Twelve intermediate credit banks were to be established in the same cities and under the same control as the Federal Land Banks, but as distinct corporations. Each bank was to have a capital of five million dollars, and was empowered to discount agricultural paper from commercial firms for terms not less than six months nor more than three years. This measure met the needs of such farmers as the growers of livestock, for example, whose business required credit for a longer period than the Federal Reserve Banks were permitted to give, but not for the long terms available under the Federal Farm Loan Act of 1916. The Intermediate Banks were also authorized to lend to cooperatives, and to the exporters of agricultural produce. Still another measure designed to have a salutary effect upon rural credits added a "dirt farmer" to

the membership of the Federal Reserve Board.

Pressure from the Farm Bloc brought the enactment of a number of laws which farm leaders hoped would promote the more profitable marketing of farm produce. After a hot fight in which opponents of the bill insisted that an attempt was being made to raise the price of cattle by legislation, Congress prohibited packing-houses from discriminating among those from whom they purchased, and from seeking to control or manipulate the prices they paid. Enforcement of these regulations was vested in the office of the Secretary of Agriculture, whose authority extended to the examination of the packer's books. Even more significant was the Capper-Volstead Act of 1922, known frequently as the "Magna Charta of Cooperative Marketing." Mindful of the many protests against the jailing of cooperative

Oil scandals of the Harding administration involved the Teapot Dome reserve in Wyoming and the Elk Hills reserve in California. Secretary Fall secretly leased the former to oilman Harry F. Sinclair and the latter to oilman Edward L. Doheny. Investigations by a Senate committee headed by Thomas J. Walsh of Montana brought the facts to light. Fall was convicted of the acceptance of bribes, but Sinclair and Doheny were acquitted.

EDWARD L. DOHENY. Acquitted.

ALBERT B. FALL. Guilty.

HARRY F. SINCLAIR. Acquitted.

members for combination in restraint of trade, Congress now exempted cooperative associations from the restrictions of the antitrust laws, and set forth the conditions under which they might engage in interstate commerce. By another act an attempt was made to prevent gambling in futures. As originally passed, this law rested upon the taxing power of Congress, and was invalidated by the Supreme Court. Repassed as an exercise of the interstate commerce power, it was sustained.

While Congress under conservative domination was thus trying to keep abreast of the times, a host of political termites had invaded the executive branch of the government. Their presence was in no small part due to the foolish search for mediocrity that had obsessed the Republican leaders when they looked about for an accommodating nominee in 1920. They wanted a man in the White House who could be managed, one who could be trusted not to exhibit any of the distressing qualities of independence that had characterized Theodore Roosevelt and Woodrow Wilson. What they failed to foresee was that a man weak enough to have no troublesome ideas of his own might turn out to be putty in the hands of others than the self-appointed leaders of the party. Harding's cronies, many of them Ohio friends of earlier days, came with him to Washington. They were still his friends, and he still trusted them. Perhaps the President was inspired by his office to adopt a higher code of political ethics than he had ever recognized before, but his associates had experienced no such change of heart. To them victory meant spoils in a very literal sense, and the greater the victory the greater the spoils.

The Harding scandals

Harry M. Daugherty, the Attorney-General, was Harding's closest political adviser; **Daugherty and Miller** between his office and the White House there was a private wire that was used many times each day. Equally close to Daugherty on the other side was Jess Smith, a member of the "Ohio gang" whose influence professional lobbyists and fixers soon knew to be for sale. Smith's abilities were better suited to the atmosphere of a courthouse ring than to the fast company he was keeping in Washington, and he soon became frightened by his involvements. Told by Daugherty that Harding wished him to leave Washington, and fearful of the consequences whether he left or stayed, he committed suicide. Ultimately it came out that in a single case he had taken fifty thousand dollars to arrange a favorable settlement before the Alien Property Custodian, Thomas W. Miller, another of Daugherty's friends. Miller was also a crook, and had to be dismissed from office; in 1927 he was jailed on conviction of having taken a bribe. Daugherty was cleverer and far more circumspect than his henchmen, but his close association with dubious characters made him suspect, and his resignation was required the year after Coolidge became President. When brought to trial for having conspired to "defraud the United States," he was not convicted because the jury disagreed. During the trial he refused to answer questions on the ground that the testimony he would be obliged to give might tend to incriminate him. He also left room for the inference that, if he were compelled to testify, what he would have to say might reflect seriously upon Harding, although no financial wrongdoing was ever traced directly to the President.

Another set of scandals involved the work of the Veterans' Bureau, at the head of which Harding had placed Charles R. Forbes, a chance acquaintance whom he had met on a trip to Honolulu. Forbes was soon making deals with contractors in the building of hospitals and the purchase and sale of supplies that meant great personal gains for himself, but heavy losses for the government. Daugh-

erty was not responsible for the Forbes appointment, and reported the rumor of irregularities to Harding, who arranged that Forbes should go abroad, and then resign. But a Senate investigating committee was soon hot on Forbes's trail, and the suicide of his closest adviser, Charles F. Cramer, heightened suspicions. In 1925 Forbes was convicted of defrauding the goverment, and sentenced to a term in a federal prison.

But the worst scandals of the Harding administration involved another member of the cabinet, Albert B. Fall, Secretary of the Interior, who ac- **Fall and the oil men** cepted generous bribes for facilitating the transfer of the naval oil reserves at Teapot Dome, Wyoming, and Elk Hills, California, to the Sinclair and Doheny oil interests, respectively. These reserves were under the control of the Secretary of the Navy, Edwin Denby, but Fall easily persuaded that amiable and incompetent individual to consent to their transfer to the Interior Department. Wholly unsuspecting, Harding signed the transfer, while Theodore Roosevelt, Jr., Assistant Secretary of the Navy, missed the opportunity of a lifetime by failing to discover and denounce the fraud that was being perpetrated. Once Fall had the coveted reserves in his hands, he signed contracts permitting the favored oil interests to exploit them. On the assumption that borderline borings were draining the government's oil away, he made a reasonable case that the navy was better off to accept a percentage of the oil taken out than to leave its fields unopened, but he found difficulty later in explaining why competitive bids were avoided and why the whole affair was kept secret as long as possible. Again a senatorial investigation, demanded in a resolution introduced by Senator LaFollette and conducted by Senator Thomas J. Walsh of Montana, brought out the facts. Fall's attitude had evidently been affected by a "loan" of one hundred thousand dollars from Doheny and several times that amount from Sinclair. Several years later civil suits in the federal courts resulted in the cancellation of the

Doheny lease because of "fraud and corruption," and the Sinclair lease because of "collusion and conspiracy." Criminal prosecutions were less successful. Fall was finally tried and convicted in 1929 of taking a bribe, was fined one hundred thousand dollars, and was sentenced to a year in jail, but the adage, "You can't convict a million dollars," seemed fully demonstrated when the two multi-millionaires, Harry F. Sinclair and Edward L. Doheny, won acquittals. Sinclair, however, was compelled to serve two short jail sentences for contempt, one for having refused to answer questions put to him by a Senate investigating committee, and the other for having employed detectives to shadow jurors during the course of one of his trials.

Harding never knew the whole truth about the scandals that were to label his administration as the most corrupt since General Grant's, but he knew enough by the summer of 1923 to feel sick at heart. In search of rest and solace he decided on a trip to Alaska, but the speech-making and traveling tired him out physically and failed to ease his mind. When he spoke at Seattle on the return trip, July 27,

Death of Harding

he was ill; six days later in San Francisco, on August 2, he was dead. Shocked by the suddenness of his passing, and not yet fully aware of his shortcomings, the country made a fine pageant of his funeral, but there was little real grief. He had failed completely during his brief term of office to capture the public imagination, and the yearnings for normalcy which he shared with the people had been only faintly realized. Even among those responsible for his nomination in 1920 there was a feeling that his death was perhaps a blessing, for shrewd prognosticators believed that the Republican Party, with Harding as its nominee, would have had little chance for success in the campaign of 1924.

Quite apart from the scandals in which it became involved, the Harding administration showed in every legitimate way its interest in promoting the welfare of the business world. In this respect the policies of Harding and his successor, Calvin Coolidge (1872–1933) were identical. In a much-quoted phrase, "The business of America is business," Coolidge well expressed the sentiments of both executives. Nomi-

Calvin Coolidge

Harding's death shocked the nation. His body lay in state in the East Room of the White House.

Calvin Coolidge

THIRTIETH PRESIDENT of the United States, Coolidge was the sixth Vice-President to succeed to the Presidency because of the death of his predecessor. Quite as conservative as Harding, but of irreproachable honesty, he was described by one biographer as "A Puritan in Babylon." He was the darling of the business interests, who approved his opposition to McNary-Haugenism and his untarnished isolationism. In 1928 he maintained that the country could "anticipate the future with optimism."

nating conventions often choose their presidential candidate to represent one wing of his party, and the Vice-President another; this, indeed, was the intention of the manipulators who awarded the Republican nomination to Harding. But the nomination of Coolidge was a political accident that threw the Vice-Presidency to a man whose economic prejudices corresponded precisely with those of his predecessor. A Vermonter by birth, Coolidge attended Amherst College, studied law, and began to practice in 1897 at Northampton, Massachusetts. Always a dependable regular, he climbed aboard the political escalator in 1899 when he became a councilman; by 1901 he was city solicitor; by 1904 clerk of courts; by 1907 a member of the legislature; by 1910 mayor of Northampton; by 1912 a member of the state senate; by 1916 lieutenant-governor; and by 1919 governor.

Throughout his long career of office-holding Coolidge had done little to excite either opposition or approval. He was conscientious in the discharge of his duties, abstemious of spoken words, utterly uninterested in trouble-making reforms. His most publicized act came in 1919 during the Boston police strike, when he somewhat belatedly called out the state militia to keep order. His telegram on this occasion to President Gompers of the American Federation of Labor well illustrated his gift for making commonplace statements sound significant: "There is no right to strike against the public safety by anybody, anywhere, anytime." Woodrow Wilson was one of the many to congratulate Coolidge upon his stand, thus contributing to the volume of publicity that was soon to transform him from an obscure governor of Massachusetts into the Republican nominee for the Vice-Presidency. After the inauguration Harding broke a precedent by inviting Coolidge to sit in on cabinet meetings, but the Vice-President interpreted his rôle as that of the silent observer merely, and took little part in the proceedings. As presiding officer of the Senate he had no chance to distinguish himself, but some articles he found time to write for the *Delineator* on "Enemies of the Republic" featured the dangers that American college women were encountering from "red" propaganda, and made him faintly ridiculous.

Coolidge as President accepted the Harding cabinet, making changes reluctantly and only under heavy pressure, and carried forward the work of the Harding administration without any perceptible change in direction. Fortunately he brought with him to his high office no faintest trace of corruption, and he had never been the kind of person who attracted to himself a "gang." Gradually the corruptionists who had saddled themselves upon Harding were eliminated, and the Republican leaders began to congratulate themselves on having escaped so successfully from the consequences of the Harding scandals. If Coolidge could be "built up" to presidential proportions, perhaps the defeat they had foreseen in 1924 could be avoided. Unimpressive in appearance and given to long lapses into silence, the new President was conspicuously lacking in glamor, but his unalloyed conservatism made him friends in influential circles, and before many months in spite of his handicaps he had become one of the most popular of American Presidents.

A major concern of the Republicans was to deal effectively with the depression that had **The recovery program — economy** extended from agriculture to business during the months immediately preceding their return to power.[1] The economic difficulties with which the Harding and Coolidge administrations had to deal were not nearly as serious as those which confronted Hoover and Roosevelt during the Great Depression, but there was trouble enough. The Harding-Coolidge formula for business recovery was never precisely stated in a political document, but it soon became fully apparent. First of all came economy in federal expenditures, a policy that under Harding was tolerated as a political necessity, but under Coolidge accurately reflected the presidential state of mind. Budget directors took their duties seriously, and the normal peace-time disbursements of the national government, if not actually reduced, were given little opportunity to expand. Considerable saving was accomplished by cutting down on the naval and military appropriations, but all such gains were seriously discounted by the mounting bill for pensions and veterans' relief. Nevertheless, whereas expenditures due to war had absorbed ninety-four per cent of the national budget in 1920, they accounted for only eighty-six per cent in 1924. It is worth noting in this connection that throughout the early twenties state and local expenditures mounted even more rapidly than federal spending declined. It is difficult to believe, therefore, that there was the direct relationship between "Coolidge economy" and the return of prosperity that Republican politicians were wont to claim. After 1925 even federal expenditures began to mount again.

[1] See p. 459.

A second item in the recovery program was the reduction of taxes, particularly those that "penalized success" by **Reduction of taxes** robbing business of its "legitimate profits." Not content with the repeal of the excess-profits tax and the surtax reductions contained in the Revenue Law of 1921, Mellon pressed Congress at every opportunity for further reductions:

High rates [he maintained] tend to destroy individual initiative and seriously impede the development of productive business. Taxpayers subject to the higher rates cannot afford for example to invest in American railroads or industries or embark on new enterprises in the face of taxes taking away 50 per cent or more of any return that may be realized. These taxpayers are withdrawing their capital from productive business and investing it instead in tax exempt securities and adopting other lawful methods of avoiding the realization of taxable income. The result is to stop business transactions that would normally go through and to discourage men of wealth from taking the risks incidental to developing and opening new businesses. Ways will always be found to avoid taxes so destructive in their nature and the only way to save the situation is to put taxes on a reasonable basis.

Mellon was unable to persuade Congress to reduce the maximum surtax as rapidly as he had hoped, but in the Revenue Act of 1924 the rate was brought down from fifty to forty per cent, and two years later to twenty per cent. Other reductions did away with most of the wartime excise taxes, radically reduced the normal income tax rates, modified the estate tax, and abolished the gift tax. In 1921 a man with a million-dollar income paid a federal tax of $663,000; by 1926, with the Mellon reductions in force, he paid less than $200,000. Unhappily a considerable proportion of the funds thus released for private use seems to have gone into highly speculative investments. Had the tax rates been permitted to remain at the wartime levels, it seems reasonable to suppose that the liquidation of the national debt might have proceeded even more rapidly than it did, and that the speculative craze of the later twenties

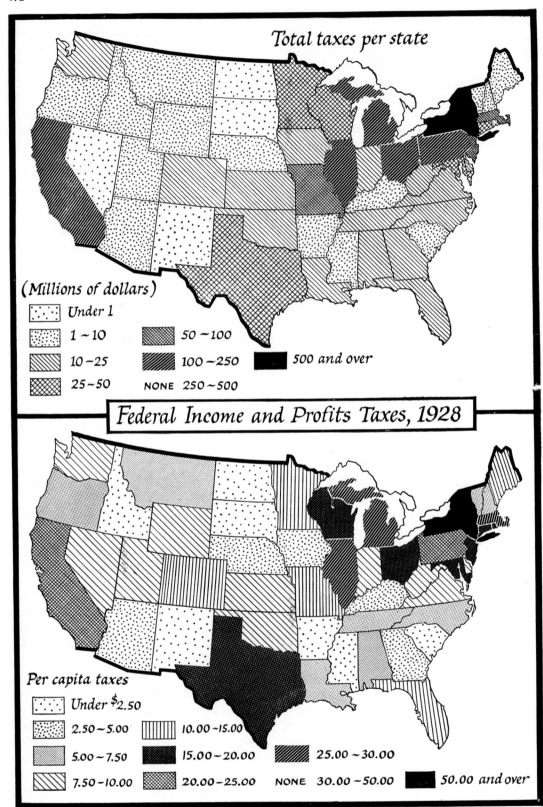

Total taxes per state

(Millions of dollars)
Under 1
1 ~ 10
10 – 25
25 ~ 50
50 – 100
100 – 250
NONE 250 ~ 500
500 and over

Federal Income and Profits Taxes, 1928

Per capita taxes
Under $2.50
2.50 – 5.00
5.00 – 7.50
7.50 – 10.00
10.00 – 15.00
15.00 – 20.00
20.00 – 25.00
25.00 ~ 30.00
NONE 30.00 ~ 50.00
50.00 and over

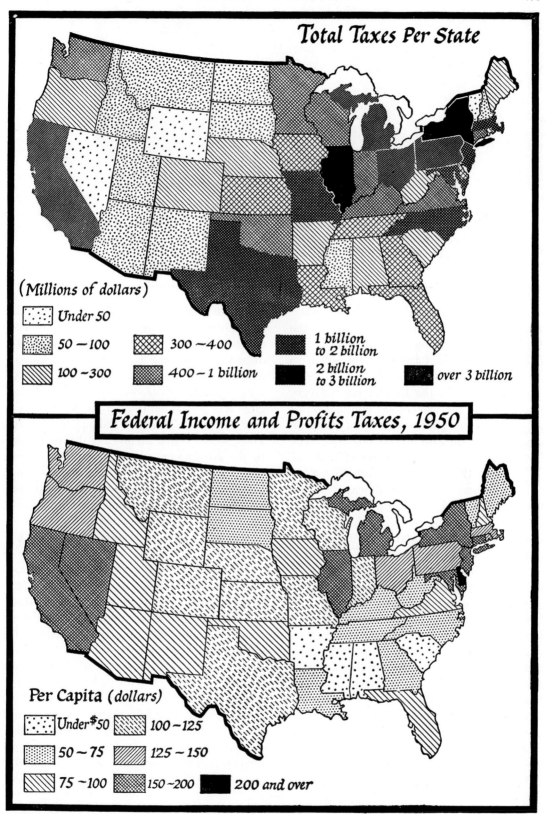

Total Taxes Per State

(Millions of dollars)

- Under 50
- 50 – 100
- 300 ~ 400
- 400 – 1 billion
- 100 ~ 300
- 1 billion to 2 billion
- 2 billion to 3 billion
- over 3 billion

Federal Income and Profits Taxes, 1950

Per Capita (dollars)

- Under $50
- 100 – 125
- 50 ~ 75
- 125 ~ 150
- 75 ~ 100
- 150 ~ 200
- 200 and over

The National Gallery of Art in Washington and a $35,000,000 art collection were gifts of Andrew W. Mellon, Secretary of the Treasury under three Presidents, and one of the nation's richest citizens.

might have been avoided. As it was, Mellon was able to lower the obligations of the United States during the decade of the twenties from about twenty-four billion to about sixteen billion dollars.

A third item in the Republican recovery program was the systematic elimination of

Government withdrawal from business

the government from competition with private business. The Transportation Act of 1920, although passed before Wilson left office, was essentially a Republican measure, and in full accord with the policies adopted during the Harding-Coolidge régime. The same may be said of the frantic efforts of the Shipping Board to dispose of government owned ships. But the most striking case in point was the refusal of the administration to countenance any plan for the effective governmental operation of the Muscle Shoals power development in Alabama, begun during the First World War to aid in the production of nitrates. In a single stretch of thirty-seven miles the Tennessee River falls one hundred and thirty-four feet. To make use of this power the government planned a series of dams and two nitrate plants. One of the nitrate plants was in operation by 1918, but the great Wilson Dam was not completed until 1925, when the wartime need for ni-

trates had long passed. To Senator Norris of Nebraska and others who were undismayed by the prospect of a government-owned business, the Muscle Shoals development seemed to offer an ideal opportunity for the production of cheap power, but Congress was persuaded to offer the whole property for sale. The only bidder was Henry Ford, whose terms involved so heavy a loss to the government that they could not be accepted. A small trickle of power was leased to the Alabama Power Company for distribution in the surrounding territory, but for the most part the potentialities of this development remained unexploited until the time of the New Deal.

The distaste of the administration for governmental interference in business went far beyond these efforts to avoid **Restraints on** competition with private enter- **regulation** prise, and called also for a drastic reduction in the amount of federal regulation. Legislation to accomplish this end would have been difficult to obtain, but the same purpose was achieved by indirect means. One by one the great regulatory bodies created by preceding administrations were packed with the friends of the very businesses they were supposed to regulate. The Interstate Commerce Commission was in effect handed over to the railroads, the Federal Trade Commission to the trusts, and the Federal Reserve Board to the bankers. For good measure the Tariff Commission was delivered into the custody of the protectionists. In criticism of a series of such Coolidge appointments, Senator Norris had this to say:

The effect of these appointments is to set the country back more than twenty-five years. It is an indirect but positive repeal of Congressional enactments, which no Administration, however powerful, would dare to bring about by any direct means. It is the nullification of federal law by a process of boring from within. If trusts, combinations, and big business are to run the government, why not permit them to do it directly rather than through this expensive machinery which was originally honestly established for the protection of the people of the country against monopoly and control?

Not content merely with removing in so far as possible all discouraging checks to private enterprise, the administration in a great variety of ways gave business direct and substantial aid. For the shipping business and the new aircraft industry it provided generous subsidies. For all businesses that might stand a chance to profit from tariff protection, it kept the tariffs high. For those with a taste for foreign investment, the State Department promised to lend a hand by denouncing bad foreign securities, and whether because of this, or in spite of it, American capital sped abroad in a seemingly endless stream. For the better promotion of foreign trade the Department of Commerce extensively and expensively reorganized its foreign service. For the benefit of domestic producers the Bureau of Standards offered elaborate facilities for testing, and recommended standard types in all sorts of manufactured articles from building-bricks to automobile tires. Secretary Hoover, as head of a commission to study waste in industry, brought in numerous suggestions bearing upon business efficiency. His work as head of the Department of Commerce was generally credited with having "elevated a relatively

Government aids to business

George W. Norris of Nebraska was the leading advocate of federal ownership and operation of hydroelectric power.

unimportant cabinet position to one of major rank." The *Detroit News* enthusiastically credited his activities with having ended the "threat to our prosperity."

Finally, the return of the Republicans to power was accompanied by a drastic change in the attitude of the national government toward labor. Appointments to the federal courts, whose decisions on the legality of many labor policies remained of fundamental importance, went with but rare exception to dependable conservatives. To Harding in his brief term of office fell the selection of four members of the United States Supreme Court, and the men he chose, Taft, Sutherland, Butler, and Sanford, were all traditionalists of the old school. Less apparent, but hardly less important, was the careful attention given by Daugherty as Attorney-General to the records of all proposed appointees to the lower courts and to subordinate positions in the Department of Justice. Before he left office in 1924 he was thus able to make an indelible imprint upon the administration of justice in the United States. Characteristic of the stiffening attitude of the courts toward labor was the sweeping injunction he

The disciplining of labor

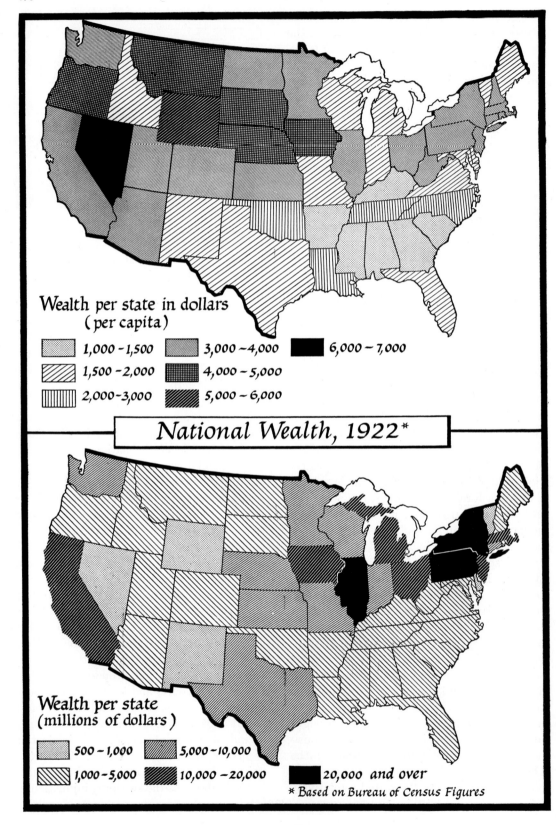

Wealth per state in dollars
(per capita)

1,000 – 1,500	3,000 – 4,000	6,000 – 7,000
1,500 – 2,000	4,000 – 5,000	
2,000 – 3,000	5,000 – 6,000	

National Wealth, 1922*

Wealth per state
(millions of dollars)

500 – 1,000	5,000 – 10,000	
1,000 – 5,000	10,000 – 20,000	20,000 and over

*Based on Bureau of Census Figures

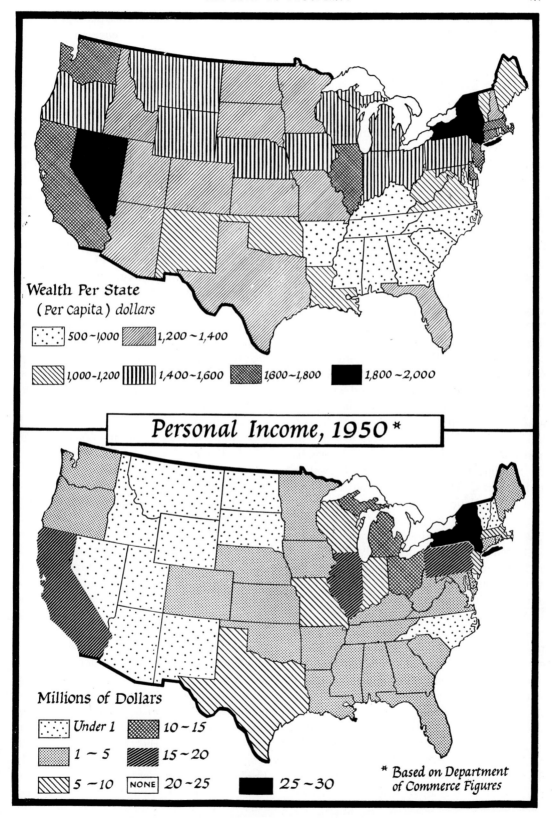

Wealth Per State
(Per Capita) dollars

⋯ 500~1,000	▨ 1,200~1,400	
▨ 1,000-1,200	▥ 1,400~1,600	▨ 1,600~1,800	■ 1,800~2,000

Personal Income, 1950 *

Millions of Dollars

⋯ Under 1	▨ 10~15
1~5	▧ 15~20
▨ 5~10	NONE 20~25	■ 25~30

* Based on Department
of Commerce Figures

obtained when a strike of the railroad shopmen seriously disrupted interstate commerce. From Federal Judge J. H. Wilkerson
of Chicago, a Harding appointee, Daugherty
obtained a temporary injunction that forbade every conceivable type of strike activity. "Not merely violence but picketing of
all sorts, strike meetings, statements to the
public, the use of union funds to carry on the
strike, and the use of any means of communication by the leaders to direct it," all fell
under the ban of the court. The fact that
this injunction was sustained on appeal demonstrated the hollowness of the hope that the
Clayton Anti-Trust Act had furnished an
enduring "Magna Charta for Labor."

Whether because of the administration's
policies, as their defenders claimed, or in spite
Business   of them, as a few critics con-
recovery   tended, the recovery of business
from the depression that had gripped the
country when Harding was inaugurated was
phenomenal. By the time Coolidge became
President the tide had turned, and when the
campaign of 1924 had to be faced the Republicans could count on prosperity as their best
talking point. Steady gains were reported in
iron and steel, in the automobile industry, in
the building trades, and among wholesalers
and retailers. Dividends that had vanished
during the depression were resumed by a
large number of corporations in 1923 and
1924, while occasional stock dividends demonstrated still more conclusively that times
had changed. Even the railroads began to
increase their earnings, and all signs pointed
to brightening economic skies.

Of fundamental consequence in the new
business vitality was the rapid rise of the
The automo-   automobile industry, which was
bile industry   still in its infancy before the war,
but during the twenties multiplied its output
again and again. Between 1920 and 1925
the annual production of motor vehicles in
the United States doubled, while the number
of automobiles in actual use almost quad-
rupled. The growth of the automobile industry meant a corresponding prosperity for
the manufacturers upon whom it depended

for iron and steel, for fabrics, plate-glass, and
tires; it brought into existence an unending
number of new establishments for "sales
and service"; it was the making of the oil
industry, from oil well to filling station; it
provided the wages and profits to promote a
building boom that extended all the way
from the humble dwelling-houses of the
workers to the magnificent skyscrapers where
the industrial leaders had their offices. The
success of the automobile industry was made
possible largely by the mass-production
methods popularized by Henry Ford, and
generally adopted. Ingenious machines fash-
ioned standard parts and assembled them
into cars with a maximum of speed and a
minimum of human labor. The completed
product was then offered to the public at a
low price, on easy installments, with profits
for manufacturer and dealer dependent primarily upon a large volume of business. Even
the foreign market could sometimes be
tapped, for the efficiency of mass production
in American factories offset the lower wages
paid abroad.

But automobiles were not the only products of the factory to be manufactured and
sold in the Ford way. Phono-   **Installment**
graphs and radios, household   **buying**
and office equipment, furnaces and plumbing, electrical supplies, and a thousand miscellaneous items were similarly made available for the multitudes. American purchasers found themselves able to buy for a
small payment down and for many similar
payments in the months or years to come a
host of luxuries that in an earlier age the
ordinary citizen could never have hoped to
own. Money was even left over for amusements, and "motion-picture palaces" provided low-priced theatricals not for just a
few Americans but for all of them. Naturally this more abundant life came to be
closely associated with Republican policies,
for the Republicans were in power when it
arrived, and they cheerfully admitted their
responsibility for bringing it to pass. In
Coolidge, the accidental occupant of the
White House, the public came to recognize a

kind of personification of the new prosperity, and in spite of his conspicuous lack of charm his popularity rose to unbelievable heights. Long before the time set for the Republican nominating convention of 1924 it was a foregone conclusion that he would be the nominee.

Discontent with the blessings of Coolidge prosperity was nevertheless rife among two **Farmer and labor discontent** powerful elements of American society, the farmers and laborers. With the farmers the hard times that had begun in 1920 continued, to the complete discomfiture of those theorists who held that without agricultural recovery there could be no business recovery. With the laborers the return of good times meant prosperity also for the unions, and a determination to share more fully in the long profits that industry was beginning to take. The example of Russia, where a workers' commonwealth seemed well on the way to success, was not without its psychological effect. Imperfections in the American industrial system, such, for example, as technological unemployment, were not difficult to detect. The research bureaus that every enlightened employer maintained, aided and abetted by the research activities of the government and the universities, produced new machines and new processes that threw thousands out of work. Often those who lost their jobs found new types of employment, but often also they did not. In spite of the unparalleled prosperity there were literally millions of men out of work all the time. Might there not be a hope of improvement in direct political action along class lines? Why should the discontented farmers and the discontented laborers remain apart? Why not a new political party to represent particularly their needs?

The beginnings of a third-party movement along national lines could be traced back to **The "left wing"** the months and years that immediately succeeded the war. A few extremists went the whole length of Communism, and in 1919 organized at Chicago as the American section of the "Third International." Their purpose was revolution after the Russian pattern, and their willingness to take orders from the Bolshevist leaders was, and remained, apparent. Under the ban of the government as long as the special wartime legislation lasted, the Communists operated covertly for several years, but by 1924, known as the Workers' Party, they were openly and actively at work. Their membership was insignificant in number, and they in no sense represented the point of view of labor in general. The Socialists differed from the Communists less in the ends they hoped to see achieved than in the means by which they would achieve them. They, too, were deeply interested in the Russian experiment, but they were content to work along evolutionary rather than revolutionary lines. In the election of 1920, with Debs as their candidate for the fifth time, they polled nearly a million votes. Debs was in federal prison at the time, under sentence for violation of the Espionage Act. He was later pardoned by President Harding. But the prospect for a really effective third party lay with neither the Communists nor the Socialists, whose close connection with Old World radicalism deeply offended the average American, but with a new Farmer-Labor Party, which in 1920 at a Chicago convention sought with some success to fuse into one organization a National Labor Party organized the year before, Townley's National Non-Partisan League, and a handful of old-fashioned 1912 Progressives represented by a self-appointed Committee of Forty-Eight. The Progressives wanted Robert M. LaFollette of Wisconsin as the Farmer-Labor nominee for President, but the Labor Party leaders refused to accept him, and the nomination went instead to Parley P. Christensen of Utah, an unknown western lawyer whose total vote in the election amounted to little more than a quarter of a million.

Nevertheless, the work of building a new party that could hope for something more than merely a protest vote went steadily on. In 1922 a Conference for Progressive Political Action was sponsored by the **Conference for Progressive Political Action**

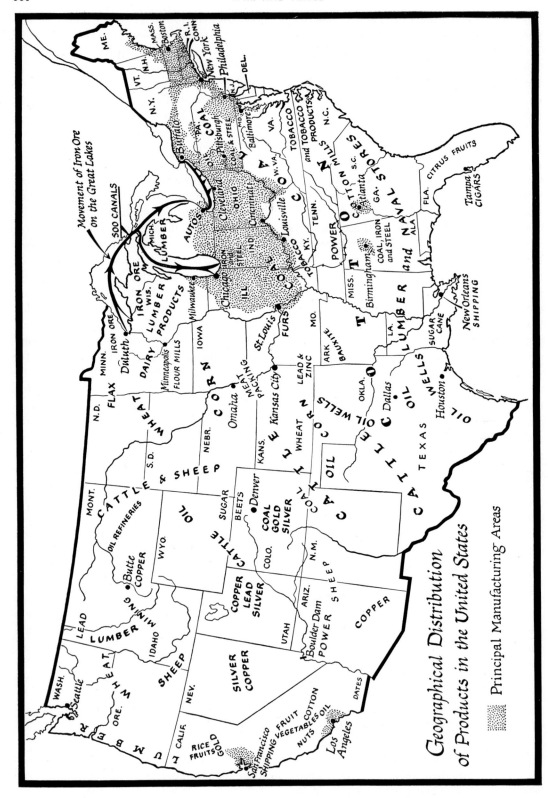

Geographical Distribution of Products in the United States

Principal Manufacturing Areas

railroad unions, whose members could not forget the advantages they had enjoyed under governmental operation, and saw little prospect of change under either Republican or Democratic leadership. The C.P.P.A. sought support not only from the groups that had formed the Farmer-Labor Party of 1920, but also from the Socialist Party, and from organized labor in general. It established a Committee of Fifteen which took an active part in the congressional campaign of 1922, claimed some credit for the rebuke which the election returns administered to Republican policies, and rejoiced in the re-election of LaFollette to the Senate, together with the astounding victories of such other liberals as Henrik Shipstead of Minnesota, Lynn Frazier of North Dakota, Smith W. Brookhart of Iowa, Burton K. Wheeler of Montana, and R. B. Howell of Nebraska. Numbers of congressmen who had voted for the Esch-Cummins Act were defeated, while most of those who had opposed it survived. According to *Labor*, a railroad union journal, the election

wasn't a "Democratic landslide," but it was a Progressive triumph, such a victory as the Progressives have not won in this country in many a day. It was gloriously non-partisan. Party lines were smashed and labor displayed its political strength in a manner unparalleled in the history of the country. . . . LaFollette was the outstanding winner and Washington is already talking of him as a most formidable presidential possibility in 1924.

Activities of the C.P.P.A. following the elections of 1922 led directly toward the nomination of an independent ticket, although until 1924 the cloak of non-partisanship was maintained. That LaFollette would be the third-party standard-bearer if he would accept the nomination was increasingly apparent, and when the C.P.P.A. Convention met in Cleveland, July 4, 1924, he was not only nominated, but was allowed to write his own platform and to name his own running mate. For Vice-President his choice fell upon Burton K. Wheeler, Democratic senator from Montana, and for a platform he

suggested a program only a little more socialistic than the Progressive platform of 1912.

Eager "to break the power of the private monopoly system over the economic and political life of the American people," LaFollette demanded such standard reforms as the public ownership of the railroads and certain natural resources including water-power, coal, oil, ores, and timber lands; the reduction of taxes on small incomes, with high surtaxes, inheritance taxes, and excess-profits taxes for the rich; a constitutional amendment to limit the right of the Supreme Court to set aside the laws of Congress; restrictions on the use of injunctions by the courts; and a series of relief measures for the farmers. A few days after the meeting of the C.P.P.A., the Socialist Convention, by a vote of 106 to 17, decided to support LaFollette, and a little later the American Federation of Labor also gave him its blessing. When the Farmer-Labor Party virtually eliminated itself from the political scene, a "united front" of all the left-wing forces was obtained, except for the Communists, whose offer of support LaFollette rejected in no uncertain terms.

The La- Follette candidacy

The Communists have admittedly entered into this political movement not for the purpose of curing, by means of the ballot, the evils which afflict the American people, but only to divide and confuse the progressive movement and create a condition of chaos favorable to their ultimate aims. . . . [They] stand for the substitution of the soviet form of government for the one we now have and propose to accomplish this change through a revolution with a class dictatorship as their ultimate aim instead of a democracy. To pretend that the Communists can work with the progressives who believe in democracy is deliberately to deceive the public. The communists are antagonistic to the progressive cause and their only purpose in joining such a movement is to disrupt it.

It is possible that the Democrats, by nominating a liberal candidate and adopting a liberal program, might have forestalled the appearance of a third-

Democratic dissensions

party ticket. The Harding scandals were theirs to capitalize upon as well as the unrest in farm and labor circles, but unfortunately they found themselves rent asunder by a factional fight over the Ku Klux Klan. This order, like its predecessors the Know-Nothing Party and the A.P.A., had carried its program of racial and religious discrimination into politics, and in the rural states of the South and the West where the native-born Protestant population was dominant had scored telling victories. In Oklahoma an anti-Klan governor was impeached and removed from office; in most of the states of the Southwest, particularly Texas, Louisiana, and Arkansas, the Klan held the balance of power; in Indiana, Ohio, Kansas, Missouri, Colorado, and elsewhere it was too strong to be ignored. The Klan was no respecter of parties and counted Republicans as well as Democrats among its members, but it proved to be a far greater menace to the Democrats than to the Republicans. To win the election the Democratic Party required not only the support of rural voters in the South and the West, but full cooperation from the Democratic city machines, many of which, like Tammany in New York, were dominated by Catholics of recent immigrant origin. The bonds that held these two widely separated elements together were weak at best. Country Democrats, not always without reason, suspected city Democrats of every kind of iniquity; city Democrats were as contemptuous as they were ignorant of the problems of rural life. The two factions were diametrically opposed on the prohibition issue; the city Democracy was aggressively wet, while the country Democracy was fanatically dry. There were other confusing cross-currents. In the South, for example, the Democratic leaders were usually conservative on problems involving industry and finance, while in the West the legacy of Bryanism was still strong. "A Democrat would rather fight another Democrat than a Republican any day," ran a familiar saying, in which there was more than a modicum of truth.

When the Democratic nominating convention met in Madison Square Garden, New York, on June 24, a large block of delegates from the eastern city-dominated states were determined to draw blood. In Alfred E. Smith, brilliant Roman Catholic governor of New York, who had worked his way up from the "sidewalks of New York" through the Tammany organization, they had a candidate for the nomination of whom they could justly be proud. They had also a plank, that expressly denounced the Klan, ready for insertion in the platform. When the platform committee discreetly refused to tempt defeat by openly insulting the Klan, the anti-Klan delegates carried the fight to the floor of the convention, only to see their resolution lost by a majority of four and one half votes. In the balloting for nominations the Klan forces threw their support to William G. McAdoo, who by no means shared their views, but was neither a Catholic nor in any intimate way identified with city machines. But McAdoo was vulnerable on the score that he had accepted substantial legal retainers from one of the oil magnates who had been involved in the Harding scandals. With the two-thirds rule still in effect neither Smith nor McAdoo could be nominated, and on the one hundred and third ballot the convention turned to John W. Davis of West Virginia and New York, a brilliant but conservative lawyer whose connection with the firm of J. P. Morgan and Company completely disqualified him in the eyes of labor and the western liberals. To offset this blunder the convention made another. For Vice-President it chose Governor Charles W. Bryan of Nebraska, brother of William Jennings Bryan, a man who had nothing but his name to recommend him for the post, but whose name alone was sufficient to alienate the eastern conservatives. With such a ticket, nominated after such a fight, the Democrats had no slightest chance of winning the election. They had done everything necessary "to snatch defeat from the very jaws of victory."

Meantime the Republicans, meeting at

Davis and Bryan

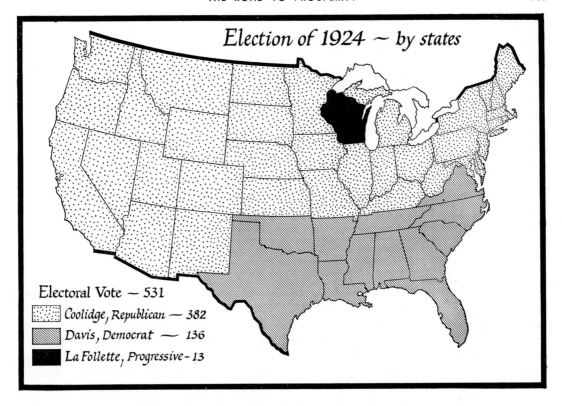

Election of 1924 ~ by states

Electoral Vote — 531

Coolidge, Republican — 382
Davis, Democrat — 136
La Follette, Progressive - 13

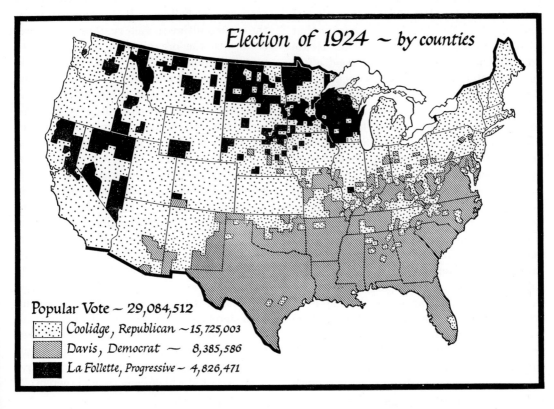

Election of 1924 ~ by counties

Popular Vote ~ 29,084,512

Coolidge, Republican ~ 15,725,003
Davis, Democrat — 8,385,586
La Follette, Progressive ~ 4,826,471

Cleveland on June 10, had completed their **Coolidge and Dawes** ticket by nominating Charles G. Dawes for Vice-President, and by adopting a platform highly complimentary to the policies which they claimed were responsible for the return of prosperity. They were able to succeed, where the Democrats had failed, in keeping the Klan issue in abeyance, and they gave becoming lip-service to the enforcement of prohibition. During the campaign Republican speakers more or less ignored the Democrats, whose candidate for the Presidency would have better graced the Republican ticket than the far less able Coolidge, and centered their fire upon the Progressives, who had laid themselves open to attack along two lines. A few inadequately informed third-party men had claimed that LaFollette might win enough electoral votes to throw the election into the House, where the even division between the parties might enable the Progressives to determine the choice. A little study of political history would have demonstrated the extreme improbability of such a result, but Republican campaigners made much of the threat to prosperity that a long-drawn-out contest in the House would involve, and urged with good effect that the voters must choose between "Coolidge or chaos." LaFollette's attack on the courts, particularly his insistence that the power of the Supreme Court to invalidate congressional legislation should be limited, provided another good talking point. With the independence of the judiciary threatened, the principal safeguard of constitutional government would be removed, or so Republican orators claimed, leaving racial and religious minorities at the mercy of the majority. LaFollette's war record, the threat of socialism, and the supposed un-Americanism of a three-party system all came in for denunciation at the hands of both old parties. But the chief advantage enjoyed by the Republicans over their adversaries was the abundant prosperity which engulfed the country. Agriculture, to be sure, was not yet able to share equally with industry in the profits that were being taken, but even the price of wheat and corn rose obligingly during election year.

The election was a Coolidge landslide. In the popular vote the Republican ticket won a plurality of more than **The Coolidge landslide** seven million, and a majority of about two and a half million. The electoral college gave Coolidge 382 votes, Davis 136, and LaFollette 13. All of the Davis vote came from the South and LaFollette carried only his own state, Wisconsin. Congress was safely Republican in both houses, and by much wider margins than after the elections of 1922.

The defeat was a crushing blow to Progressive hopes, although in reality the third-party ticket had done extremely well. LaFollette polled a total of nearly five million votes and ran ahead of Davis in eleven western states. Seven far western and three southern border states gave the Progressive and Democratic tickets together more votes than went to Coolidge and Dawes. But the forces that had combined to support LaFollette had looked upon his candidacy as a kind of trial balloon. If it seemed to point the way to ultimate victory, they would proceed with the organization of a new third party all along the line; if not, they would drop the project altogether. There had been no attempt during the campaign to set up state and local third-party tickets; Progressives were encouraged merely to vote for the men on other tickets whose views best represented their own. After the overwhelming triumph of Coolidge, further effort seemed futile and was not undertaken. LaFollette himself, full of years and worn out by the strenuous campaign he had made, died a few months later. His son, Robert M. LaFollette, Jr., elected to his father's seat in the Senate, took office as a Republican. Surveying the wreck of their hopes, the discouraged reformers could only lament with Jeremiah: "A wonderful and horrible thing is committed in the land; the prophets prophesy falsely, and the priests bear rule by their means; and my people love to have it so: and what will ye do in the end thereof?" [1]

[1] Jeremiah, v, 30, 31.

Bibliography

The record of the Harding administration in legislative and administrative matters may be followed in Adams, *Incredible Era*, and other books cited for the preceding chapter; also, in H. M. Robinson, *Fantastic Interim* (1943), an entertaining but highly-colored account; and in Harold U. Faulkner, *From Versailles to the New Deal; A Chronicle of the Harding-Coolidge Era* (1950), which is less opinionated. There are three good books on budget reform by W. F. Willoughby, *The Problem of a National Budget* (1918); *The National Budget System* (1927); and *Financial Condition and Operations of the National Government, 1921–30* (1931). Mellon's policies as Secretary of the Treasury are critically examined in Harvey O'Connor, *Mellon's Millions* (1933), an extremely unfriendly biography. The best book on the post-war handling of the immigration problem is Garis, *Immigration Restriction*, but see also other books cited on this subject for chapter 10, p. 203. On the influx from Mexico, the best study is Manuel Gamio, *Mexican Immigration to the United States* (1930); but see also P. S. Taylor, *Mexican Labor in the United States* (2 vols., 1928–34). Satisfactory accounts of the Harding scandals are contained in Mark Sullivan, *Our Times*, VI; and in F. L. Allen, *Only Yesterday* (1931), a delightful satire on American foibles. The policy of the government toward oil may be traced in M. E. Ravage, *The Story of Teapot Dome* (1924); M. R. Werner, *Privileged Characters* (1935); and John Ise, *The United States Oil Policy* (1926).

The Coolidge era in American politics can perhaps be best approached through biographic and autobiographic studies. *The Autobiography of Calvin Coolidge* (1929) is a reasonable self-estimate, but far less informative than three books by William Allen White, *Calvin Coolidge: The Man Who Is President* (1925); *Masks in a Pageant* (1928); and *A Puritan in Babylon: The Story of Calvin Coolidge* (1938). C. M. Fuess, *Calvin Coolidge, The Man from Vermont* (1940), is also an excellent biography. *The Autobiography of William Allen White* (1946) has some material in it on the 1920's, but covers the author's whole lifetime. *Fighting Liberal: The Autobiography of George W. Norris*, edited by James E. Lawrence (1945), is disappointing, for Norris was a far greater man than his memoirs make him out to be. The obligations of the government toward World War I veterans are discussed in Katherine Mayo, *Soldiers, What Next!* (1934); Roger Burlingame, *Peace Veterans* (1932); and the National Industrial Conference Board, *The World War Veterans and the Federal Treasury* (1932). André Siegfried, *America Comes of Age* (1927), provides a brilliant analysis of the contradictory forces at work within American political parties, and sheds much light on other unique aspects of American life. On the Progressive movement of the 1920's, the best books are F. E. Haynes, *Social Politics in the United States* (1924); and K. C. MacKay, *The Progressive Movement of 1924* (1947).

On the industrial trends of the times, there are several interesting contemporary accounts, among them: T. N. Carver, *The Present Economic Revolution in the United States* (1925); R. G. Tugwell, *Industry's Coming of Age* (1927); Stuart Chase, *The Tragedy of Waste* (1925); *Men and Machines* (1929); and *Prosperity; Fact or Myth* (1929). On labor, see Felix Frankfurter and Nathan Greene, *The Labor Injunction* (1930); E. E. Witte, *The Government in Labor Disputes* (1932); and A. T. Mason, *Organized Labor and the Law* (1925).

On the problems of agriculture, see Arthur Capper, *The Agricultural Bloc* (1922); Clara Eliot, *The Farmers' Campaign for Credit* (1927); J. D. Black, *Agricultural Reform in the United States* (1929); Wilson Gee, *The Place of Agriculture in American Life* (1930); B. H. Hibbard, *Effects of the Great War upon Agriculture in the United States and Great Britain* (1919); Grant McConnell, *The Decline of Agrarian Democracy* (1953); E. R. A. Seligman, *The Economics of Farm Relief* (1929); Bernard Ostrolenk, *The Surplus Farmer* (1932); E. F. Dummeier and R. B. Heflebower, *Economics with Applications to Agriculture* (1934); and E. G. Nourse and associates, *America's Capacity to Produce* (1934).

24

The Road to Depression

America and the world — Reparations — The Kellogg-Briand Pact — The McNary-Haugen Bill — The export debenture plan — Election of 1928 — Hoover's victory — The Federal Farm Board — Stabilization activities — The Hawley-Smoot Tariff — Background of the Great Depression — Stock speculation — Panic of 1929 — Causes of the depression

IN SPITE of the continuing devotion of most Americans to the doctrine of isolation, evidence that the United States **America and the world** must play a leading rôle in international affairs accumulated rapidly during the twenties. As a result of the war, the American nation had enormously expanded its industrial plant; it had discovered unsuspected possibilities by way of agricultural production; it had accumulated out of its profits huge sums for new investment. Moreover, if the high speed to which its economic machine had been geared were to be maintained, the country must import many materials which it could not produce, such as rubber, silk, nickel, and tin, and many others which it could produce only in limited quantities, such as sugar, wool, hides, and nitrates. What the United States really needed was a peaceful and friendly world generally committed to the open door. That American statesmen of the twenties failed to achieve this goal should have occasioned no surprise. They were faced at home by a sentimental regard for political isolation and a deep-rooted belief in the protective-tariff system; they were faced abroad by the jealousies and hatreds engendered by the war and the peace, feelings compounded so far as they concerned the United States by the conviction that the American people had escaped

most of the war's ravages, but had taken most of its profits.

Among the most perplexing of the problems before the American government during the twenties was the collection of the loans by which the United States had so largely financed the Allied cause after 1917, and the work of reconstruction after the war was over. To the American people these intergovernmental loans seemed no different from the loans of one individual to another, and their repayment was regarded as a matter of simple honesty. Europeans took a somewhat different view of the situation. The war, they argued, was a common endeavor, in which each nation had given all that it had to give. The United States had entered the conflict late, and its casualty list was short; why should it begrudge the dollars it had spent? Why should it not forgive its debtors, especially since American prosperity so far outstripped anything European nations could boast? Moreover, most of the money lent had been expended in the United States, and goods rather than gold had been sent abroad. Was it fair to ask European nations to pay back gold that they had never seen; indeed, half the world's supply of gold was already in the United States. Nor could European nations hope to build up large balances in America by the shipment of goods; the high American tariff forestalled that. To the war-heated imaginations of European critics "Uncle Sam" became "Uncle Shylock," and hostile feeling ran high.

Nevertheless, in 1922 Congress created a World War Foreign Debt Commission which opened negotiations with the various Allied nations, and ultimately succeeded in reaching refunding agreements with fifteen of them. American policy called for settlements in accordance with ability to pay; hence the interest charges ranged from as low as four tenths of one per cent in the case of Italy to the normal three and three tenths per cent required of Great Britain and the more solvent states. The British settlement was effected as early as June, 1923, and the others during the next few years. Opposition to repayment reached its maximum in France, where the costly work of reparation threatened to bankrupt the government, but an agreement was signed in April, 1926, which set the interest rate at one and six tenths per cent, and allowed a period of sixty-two years for payment. The grand total of all the funded debts was fixed at more than eleven and one half billion dollars, with ninety per cent of the amount owing by Great Britain (4.6 billions), France (4.02 billions), and Italy (2.04 billions). Repayments by December 31, 1930, amounted to about two and one half billion dollars, of which more than seventy per cent came from Great Britain. Next year, following the Hoover moratorium, a few nations met their obligations, but thereafter payments from all nations except Finland virtually ceased.

Russia alone among the European nations that had borrowed from the United States refused to consider the funding of her debt. The Soviets, in keeping with their views on capitalism, repudiated all financial obligations incurred by preceding Russian governments, and denied the claims for indemnification lodged by foreigners whose property had been confiscated or destroyed during the revolutions of 1917. On this account, and also because of the persistent Communist propaganda carried on by Russian agents in the United States, the American government long refused to accord recognition to the Soviet government. No attempt was made, however, to prevent American firms from trading with Russia at their own risk. This remained the official attitude of the United States toward Soviet Russia until November, 1933, when the Franklin D. Roosevelt administration, after receiving solemn pledges that the Soviets would no longer countenance or promote propaganda against the American government, agreed to an exchange of diplomatic representatives.

Inevitably the problem of war debts became closely intertwined with the problem of German reparations. If Germany could meet her obliga- **Reparations** tions to the Allies, then the Allies could make their payments to the United States. Any connection between these two problems was vigorously denied by the American government, but its existence in fact if not in theory was abundantly clear. The difficulties experienced by Germany in paying the extortionate sums required by the Reparations Commission in 1921 were only in part responsible for the disastrous currency inflation that overwhelmed that unhappy land. But Germany's troubles led to two efforts at reparations readjustment, one in 1924, and another in 1929. It was significant that in each case the commission of experts entrusted with the negotiations was headed by an American, in the first instance by Charles G. Dawes, and in the second by Owen D. Young. The Dawes Plan reduced the sums required from Germany each year, arranged for a foreign loan to support the German monetary system, and required French withdrawal from the Ruhr. For four years, in large part by borrowing in the United States, Germany was able to meet the new payments, but by 1928 she was again in trouble. The Young Plan proposed another set of annuities to run for a period of fifty-nine years, the capitalized value of which would amount to only about ten billion dollars, approximately the sum due from the Allies to the United States. Further, it stipulated that additional reductions might be made proportional to any readjustments in the inter-Allied war debts; in other words, if the United States would reduce its demands, the Allies would also reduce theirs. But the Young Plan, although possibly sound economically, exceeded the willingness of Germany to pay, and after 1931 all reparation payments were discontinued. As a matter of fact, German payments were always closely geared to what Germany could borrow from abroad, particularly from American investors who regarded German securities as a good risk. Some of the borrowed funds the German government used to make permanent improvements, such as good roads, which might help to revive the German economy. But much of what was borrowed, directly or indirectly, went into reparations. Before the end of Hoover's administration American investors had ceased altogether to lend to Germany, while the attempt of Germany to set up a customs union with Austria had frightened off French money-lenders. Altogether Germany paid the Allies about four and one half billion dollars, more than half of which she had borrowed from American investors. Since the funds so borrowed were never repaid, the reparations collected from the German government could not have hurt Germany very much.

The search for a means to insure world peace went on insistently throughout the **The quest** period of Coolidge prosperity. **for peace** Unfortunately the organizations most actively concerned with the problems were in complete disagreement as to the best means to promote the cause they held so dear. Peace-lovers of the Wilson school kept up the fight for American entrance into the League as the surest way to prevent the outbreak of war. They rejoiced when the representatives of the United States, at first unofficially, but later on terms of entire equality, sat in on the non-political discussions of League committees, such, for example, as the conference on the opium traffic. Ultimately, they asserted, the United

States could no longer ignore the obligations of membership. Others who still saw in the League nothing more than a convenient instrument for enforcement of an unjust peace urged that the United States should give its full support to the World Court. Still others, perhaps with greater faith than wisdom, believed that the peace could best be maintained by a simple declaration on the part of every nation that it would not resort to war. Chief leader of the third group, whose panacea was labeled the "outlawry of war," was Senator William E. Borah of Idaho. Most American politicians, including the President, were inclined to regard the "outlawry" scheme as impractical, and possibly contrary to the Constitution of the United States which specifically gave Congress the right to declare war, but a pact signed by seven European nations at Locarno in 1925 seemed to indicate a certain willingness on their part to flirt with the idea. By that document Germany, Belgium, France, Great Britain, and Italy undertook mutually to guarantee the peace of western Europe, and Germany agreed to arbitrate her disputes with France, Belgium, Poland, and Czechoslovakia. Further, the signatory powers agreed not to attack each other, not to invade each other's territory, and not to resort to war against each other, except for purposes of defense or in response to their obligations under the League of Nations, to which, it was decided, Germany must be admitted.

Hailed as at least a partial renunciation of the "right to make war," the Pact of Locarno stimulated the "outlawry" advocates in the United States to renewed endeavors. The United States, they pointed out, stood now almost alone in its resistance to every plan for world peace. They were soon aided by Aristide Briand, French foreign minister, who on April 6, 1927 — tenth anniversary of the entrance of the United States into the First World War — urged a treaty between France and the United States similar to those agreed upon by the European nations at Locarno. What Briand really had in mind was to replace the Root Arbitration Treaty of 1908, which was due to expire in 1928, with a stronger one, but "outlawry" enthusiasts were quick to seize the opportunity he had given them. They persuaded the Secretary of State, Frank B. Kellogg of Minnesota, who had succeeded Hughes in 1925, to expand the scope of the negotiations. Replying to Briand, Kellogg said:

It has occurred to me that the two governments, instead of contenting themselves with a bilateral declaration of the nature suggested by M. Briand, might make a more signal contribution to world peace by joining in an effort to obtain the adherence of all the principal Powers of the world to a declaration renouncing war as an instrument of national policy.

Kellogg's proposal resulted in prolonged negotiations which led finally to the signing **The Kellogg-** at Paris, on August 27, 1928, of **Briand Pact** a general treaty along the lines he had proposed. The representatives of fifteen nations, including Japan, Italy, and Germany, affixed their signatures to a document which contained the following clauses:

I. The High Contracting Parties solemnly declare in the names of their respective peoples that they condemn recourse to war for the solution of international controversies, and renounce it as an instrument of national policy in their relations with one another.
II. The High Contracting Parties agree that the settlement or solution of all disputes or conflicts of whatever nature or of whatever origin they may be, which may arise among them, shall never be sought except by pacific means.

Ultimately sixty-two nations gave their adherence to the Kellogg Pact; but the futility of all such declarations, unless buttressed by a firm desire to live up to them, was soon demonstrated by the attacks of Japan on China, Italy on Ethiopia, and Germany on Poland, Denmark, Norway, the Netherlands, Belgium, and Luxemburg. The pact may, indeed, have lulled into a sense of security nations that might otherwise have been better prepared for the assaults of their predatory neighbors. Nevertheless, European

William E. Borah, United States Senator from Idaho, favored the limitation of naval armaments and the outlawry of war.

statesmen saw significance in the willingness of the United States to cooperate at last, however faintly, in the effort to maintain world peace, but the customary Senate reservations revealed the microscopic nature of the involvement. Although the Senate ratified the treaty with only one dissenting vote, it insisted that there could be no curtailment of America's right of self-defense, that no obligations had been assumed which were incompatible with the Monroe Doctrine, and that the United States was not bound to take action against states that broke the treaty. Kellogg did the best he could to make the pact to which he had given his name a success. He negotiated supplementary treaties of arbitration with such nations as would consent to them, and took particular pains to make arbitration compulsory between the United States and other American nations.

The contradiction that existed between the American doctrine of isolation and economic realities was well illus- **American** trated by the agricultural prob- **agriculture** lem that confronted the United States throughout the decade of the twenties. The Republican formula for recovery worked well for a while in industry, but it failed to achieve resu ts for the farmer pr marily be-

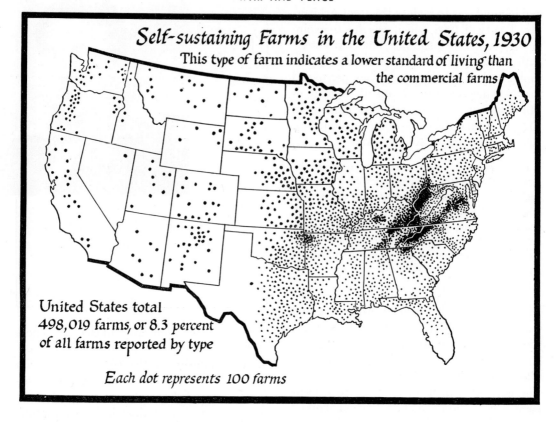

Self-sustaining Farms in the United States, 1930
This type of farm indicates a lower standard of living than the commercial farms

United States total
498,019 farms, or 8.3 percent
of all farms reported by type

Each dot represents 100 farms

cause the price of his principal products depended upon world-wide conditions of supply and demand. The United States produced far more wheat, for example, than it could possibly consume at home, and must sell its surplus abroad in competition with all the other wheat-producing nations. Thus the price of wheat in the United States depended upon the price of wheat on the world market; American prices differed from world prices only in the cost of transportation to a given foreign port. Manufacturers when confronted by a similar situation either reduced their output, or sometimes, with the help of the protective tariff, sold their excess product abroad at a loss, while keeping the American price high. But the farmer was able neither to control his surplus nor to take advantage of the tariff. As an individualist, each farmer raised what crops he chose, and sold to whomever he wished, while his wisest calculations might be completely upset by the weather. Nor could he without nation-wide

organization maintain a two-price system, such as monopolistic industries found easily possible. With but few exceptions the high tariff rates on farm products did him no good. The price brought by the exportable surplus, and not the duties on mythical imports, set the price for whatever he had to sell. (As the map above shows, there were still large numbers of low-standard farms in the United States.[1])

With the experts in the United States Department of Agriculture, the economists in the agricultural colleges, and the businessmen whose prosperity depended upon farm sales all pointing to the exportable surplus as the chief cause of the farmers' woes, it is not surprising that plans for its more advantageous disposal were soon forthcoming. Of these the most publicized was embodied in the McNary-Haugen Bill, which was intro-

The Mc-Nary-Haugen Bill

[1] See also p. 205.

duced into Congress as early as 1924. Its authorship could be traced directly to George N. Peek, president of the Moline Plow Company, and Hugh S. Johnson, his assistant and general counsel, who had both discovered that for their organization, at least, there could be no prosperity until the farmer was able to buy. What their measure was designed to do was to make the agricultural tariff effective by establishing a two-price system for American farm produce, one a tariff-protected price for the American market, and the other, the world price for the foreign market. A government agency should be established which during emergencies would buy up any given surplus at a price based upon prewar averages, thus setting a higher price in the United States than existed abroad. The surplus might then be held for disposal until a lean year, or it might be sold to foreign buyers for whatever it would bring. In the latter case, the loss sustained was to be charged back against American producers by an equalization fee, but their net returns, it was believed, would be far higher than under existing conditions. "If it is a wise policy to protect industry in the East," they argued, "it must be equally wise to protect agriculture in the West."

The McNary-Haugen Bill, in one form or another, was repeatedly before Congress during the Coolidge administration. It won the ardent support of nearly all the farm organizations, and of the Secretary of Agriculture, Henry C. Wallace, whose death in 1924, however, enabled the President to replace him with a man of less pronounced views. Twice, in 1924 and in 1926, the bill was voted down, largely because it failed to recognize the needs of the southern farmer, but in 1927, with the list of commodities to which it applied including cotton and tobacco along with wheat and corn, it passed the Senate by a vote of 51 to 43, and the House by a vote of 214 to 178. The opposition to "McNary-Haugenism" of President Coolidge and his cabinet, particularly the Secretary of Commerce, Herbert Hoover, had long been known, so that the veto message

by which the measure was defeated occasioned little surprise. Next year the farmers again mobilized their strength, and pushed the bill through Congress by still more substantial majorities. But they met another veto, and they fell short of the two-thirds majority necessary to enact the measure without the President's consent. Opponents of the bill argued throughout the debates that the plan was "economically unsound." If it were adopted, the whole population would have to pay higher prices for food, while the farmer's certainty of good returns would invite ever larger and larger crops until the system itself would in time break down. They pointed, too, to the difficulties that would have been encountered in "dumping" the American surplus abroad at a time when many foreign nations were making every effort to build up their economic self-sufficiency.

As an alternative to the McNary-Haugen idea the Grange offered the export debenture plan, a somewhat simpler system for raising the price level of American farm products. Export bounties equal to one half the existing tariff rates on specified agricultural commodities — wheat, corn, rice, cotton, tobacco, swine, and cattle — were to be paid by the United States in the form of "debentures," which, in turn, would be receivable for customs. On the presumption that these debentures would be purchased at a discount by importers, proponents of the plan argued that the bounty to the farmers would come directly out of the protective tariff. No less than the McNary-Haugen Bill, the export debenture plan would serve to "get the farmers up on stilts" along with the manufacturers, whose high prices the tariff guaranteed. To forestall overexpansion it was proposed that a federal farm board be created with power to reduce or even to abolish the debentures in proportion as crop yields went up. But "sound economists" were as much opposed to the debenture as to the McNary-Haugen plan, while the farmers were less certain that it would work.

The export debenture plan

Several times it was brought before Congress, but invariably it was voted down.

With farm prices believed to be well below the cost of production, the demand for farm relief threatened to become a principal issue in the presidential campaign of 1928. Would the President, in spite of the third-term tradition, seek re-election? Judging from the comfortable Republican majorities returned to both houses of Congress by the mid-term elections of 1926, the chances of Republican victory seemed good. But although Coolidge was still the idol of the world of industry and finance, his popularity seemed definitely on the wane in the Middle West; the flattery he received elsewhere for his "courage" in vetoing the McNary-Haugen Bill of 1927 was not echoed by farmers who compared the low prices they received for what they had to sell with the high tariff-protected prices they must pay for the things they had to buy. Perhaps to regain western support the President that same year spent the summer vacation on a fishing trip in South Dakota. "He who, until last year, never threw a line into a stream — unless it was the muddy pool of politics. He who, posing as a farmer, has never been out of political office since maturity." It was difficult to see in this move anything other than a bid for renomination and re-election, but on August 2, 1927, Coolidge announced cryptically, "I do not choose to run for President in 1928." Whether he feared the opposition of the farmers, or wished merely to be drafted, may never be known. But he was taken at his word, and other aspirants for the Republican nomination immediately made their candidacies known.

By the time the Republicans met in convention at Kansas City, June 12, 1928, it **Nomination of Hoover** was evident that their candidate for President would be Herbert Hoover. This was a great disappointment to the middle-western farmers who would have preferred Lowden of Illinois, a firm believer in the McNary-Haugen idea. But efforts to display their strength by means of "processions of Fords" to Kansas City failed to secure either the nomination of Lowden or the endorsement of the agricultural program for which he stood. When the convention went on record against McNary-Haugenism by a vote of 817 to 267, Lowden withdrew his candidacy, leaving Hoover virtually a clear field. Hoover had learned a great deal about politics since 1920 when his friends had mustered only thirteen votes for him in the nominating convention. He was not beloved by the politicians, for he was not one of them, and they questioned their ability to control him, but he had built up a strong personal following that the politicians dared not ignore. Hoover, more than any other man except Coolidge, was identified in the public mind with the exuberant prosperity that the country as a whole — the farmers excepted — had come to enjoy. He was popular with the masses precisely because he was not a politician. He was the best vote-getter in sight, and on that account the politicians dared not repeat the slight of 1920. On the eve of the convention Vare of Pennsylvania, a political boss of the old school, came out for Hoover, and Mellon, the Secretary of the Treasury, echoed the same sentiments. After these declarations the battle was over, and Hoover was nominated on the first ballot. For his running-mate, as a gesture of good-will toward the unhappy middle-western farmers, the convention chose Senator Charles Curtis of Kansas.

The Republican platform said little of the future, but it recited with gusto the accomplishments of the Coolidge administration, and credited it with the prosperity which the country enjoyed. Economy had been "raised to the dignity of a principle of government"; debt reduction and tax reduction had both been achieved; the protective tariff, "as vital to American agriculture as it is to American manufacturing," had been maintained; foreign debts had been adjusted and foreign trade promoted and expanded; the outlawry of war had been accomplished; the prohibition amendment had been loyally supported. As a substitute for the McNary-Haugen plan the platform offered a program known to have the support of the Republican nominee, a federal farm board which through stabilization corporations should attempt to push farm prices to higher levels. On the subject of labor, its declarations were somewhat hazy, although it admitted that the over-free use of injunctions in labor disputes presented "a serious question for legislation."

The Democratic nomination had also been decided in advance. Of the two leading contenders for the honor in 1924, **Smith and Robinson** McAdoo had been completely eliminated by the now well-publicized stories of the large fees he had received from the oil interests, a reflection upon his judgment rather than upon his honesty. Furthermore, leaders of the conservative South and the radical West had resigned themselves to the necessity of allowing the city machines for once to name their candidate, and to find out by bitter experience that he could not win. Meeting in a southern city — Houston, Texas — for the first time since the Civil War, the southern and western delegates swallowed their misgivings and permitted the nomination of Smith on the first ballot, knowing full well that, as a Catholic, a wet, and a Tammany man, he was sure to have an uphill fight. For Vice-President the Democrats presented Senator Joseph T. Robinson of Arkansas, a Protestant and a dry from a state that had no large cities within its borders. But no one was deceived. The ticket of Smith and Robinson, despite its "one-hundred-per-cent American" names represented primarily the descendants of recent immigrants who made up the bulk of the voting population in all the great cities of the East.

In view of their nomination of Smith, the Democrats had little need for a platform, for it was a certainty that their candidate would be their platform. They took occasion, however, to denounce the Republican record of corruption under Harding, to pledge a reform in banking that would prevent speculation, and to promise for agriculture equality with other industries. Perhaps in part because of the close relationship between tariff protec-

tion and the various plans of farm relief before the country, the Democrats retreated from their historic low-tariff position, and in language that might well have been borrowed from the Republicans urged tariff rates to equal the "actual differences between the cost of production at home and abroad." Toward labor they showed the greatest friendliness, denouncing the injunction evil, urging the construction of public works during times of unemployment, and emphasizing the protection of women and children in industry. On the Eighteenth Amendment, they declared for enforcement, but, as they had clearly foreseen, their candidate came out flatly for repeal. He also went beyond the commitments of the platform to give his whole-hearted endorsement to the McNary-Haugen plan for farm relief, including the equalization fee.

The two candidates for the Presidency afforded an unusual contrast. Herbert Hoover (1874–   ) was born at **Hoover** West Branch, Iowa, the son of Quaker parents. Left an orphan at an early age, he worked his way through college, and ultimately graduated in mining engineering at Leland Stanford University. In pursuit of his specialty he saw much of the world — Mexico, Canada, Australia, India, China and Russia — and as a promoter he amassed a modest fortune. Living in England at the outbreak of the First World War, he was a natural choice to head overseas relief work, and served as chairman, first of the American Relief Commission, and later of the Commission for the Relief of Belgium. In these offices, as Food Administrator during American participation in the war, and as Secretary of Commerce he had demonstrated repeatedly his extraordinary ability as an administrator. His life-history was the typical American success story; with variations it could be made to fit the hopes of every normal American youth.

Alfred Emanuel Smith (1873–1944) had a background more unusual in a presidential candidate. He was born in an **Smith** East-Side New York tenement,

Herbert Hoover

THIRTY-FIRST PRESIDENT of the United States, Hoover, like Cleveland and Van Buren, was a "depression" President. A traditional economist, he hoped that economic forces would revive business and restore prosperity, but when his hopes were not realized he anticipated the New Deal by using the power of government against the depression. He was renominated but not re-elected.

the son of humble working-class parents of Irish descent. He was perhaps no poorer than Hoover, but quite out of keeping with the American tradition he rose from the city sidewalks rather than from the country cornfields. He attended parochial school, but never went to college. Thrust into politics as a birthright, he accepted without hesitation the rule of Tammany, and as an organization Democrat played the political game honestly according to the established rules. Once he was rewarded for faithful service by being made sheriff of New York County, a position that carried with it many lucrative fees, but most of the offices he held were not very remunerative. His career was crowned by his election for four terms as governor of New York. Liberal-minded, and devoted to the interests of the working classes from which he sprang, he displayed a rare genius for political administration and achieved noteworthy results in spite of constant opposition from a Republican-controlled legislature.

The development of the radio placed a new burden upon presidential candidates. No longer could they escape the limelight by a "front-porch" campaign. The public wanted to hear them and if possible also to see them. Smith yielded to the new technique, and toured the country extensively, speaking at various points before nationwide hook-ups. With radio broadcasting still in its infancy, he failed to make a good impression. He spoke from notes rather than from manuscript, and, while fascinating enough to the audience before him, he was often inaudible or inarticulate to the listeners-in. Moreover, his New York accent and his occasional mispronunciations caused much unfavorable comment. Hoover, on the other hand, although a far less effective public speaker, poured what he had to say directly into the microphone, and it came out better than it went in. His pronunciation was no better than Smith's, but it was the kind that most Americans were themselves accustomed to use, and so gave little offense.

Ignoring his opponent, and scarcely admitting that he was conducting a campaign, Hoover gave a new dignity to the doctrines in which Republicans had long believed, but had not quite known how to defend. Convinced that in the American system of capitalism, with its constantly turning factory wheels, its high wage scales, and its widespread ownership, lay the key to permanent prosperity, he was vehemently opposed to anything savoring of socialism. Equality of opportunity was a priceless heritage that must be maintained at all costs, and strictly by traditional means. Individual enterprise, unhampered by governmental interference, had built the American nation, and through the same effective leadership the problems of the future could best be solved.

We in America today are nearer to the final triumph over poverty than ever before in the history of any land. The poorhouse is vanishing from among us. We have not reached the goal, but given a chance to go forward with the policies of the last eight years, we shall soon with the help of God be in sight of the day when poverty will be banished from this nation.

Hoover's triumphant victory at the polls in November was due primarily to four factors: **Hoover's victory** (1) the belief which he assiduously cultivated that the continuance of Republican rule meant the continuance of prosperity; (2) the prejudice of rural America against the Tammany background of a corrupt machine based on immigrant votes from which Smith had risen; (3) the deep-seated opposition of many American Protestants to the elevation of a Catholic to the Presidency; and (4) the determination of the evangelical churches to retain prohibition, which Smith denounced, but Hoover called a "noble experiment." "Hoover Democrats," voting the Republican ticket in large numbers, shattered the solid South; for the first time since reconstruction the Republicans carried Virginia, North Carolina, Tennessee, Florida, and Texas. Smith also lost his own state, New York, and every western and border state. The electoral vote stood 444 to 87, and the popular vote 21,392,190 to 15,016,443. Naturally the Hoover landslide carried with it overwhelming Republican majorities in Congress and in some of the states. The heavy protest vote that had been cast for LaFollette four years before had dwindled to a mere quarter of a million votes for Norman Thomas, the Socialist candidate.

The Hoover administration was certain to encounter difficulties even if it had been blessed with good times. The new President was fundamentally a business executive rather than a politician, and showed little skill in appeasing the leaders of his party, many of whom were disgruntled at his success in "muscling in." His cabinet, headed by Henry L. Stimson, formerly governor-general of the Philippines, was undistinguished, and added little to his political strength. Mellon was kept on as Secretary of the Treasury less because Hoover wanted him, or so many believed, than because of the esteem in which he was held by the business interests of the country; all the others, including the Secretary of State, were virtually unknown to the general public. The

insurgent bloc in the Senate, while reduced in numbers as a result of the campaign, was still strong and troublesome. Prohibition was sure to be a nightmare, and farm relief a perpetual despair. Furthermore, tariff revision, the political reef upon which many preceding administrations had been wrecked, was imminent. During the campaign Hoover in a weak moment had promised the farmers an increase in agricultural duties. He hoped to escape a general tariff revision, but a more experienced politician would have foreseen that once tariff tampering had begun, there would be little chance of limiting its scope.

The new Congress that met in special session April 15, 1929, was willing to go along with Hoover on the subject of **The Federal** farm relief, and in two months **Farm Board** time had embodied his recommendations in a comprehensive Agricultural Marketing Act. The price-fixing and subsidy features of the McNary-Haugen and export debenture plans were now discarded in favor of an effort to

Al Smith, wearing his famous brown derby, is shown making one of his equally well remembered "raddio" addresses in Times Square.

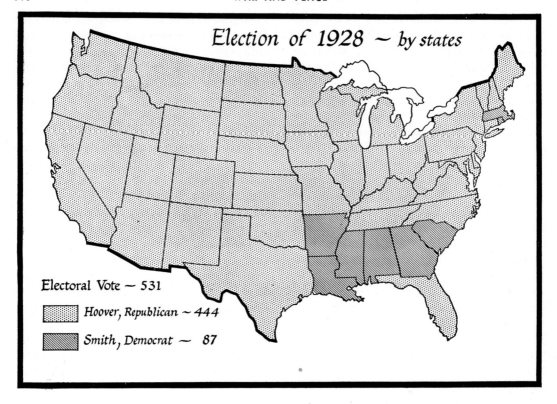

Election of 1928 ~ by states

Electoral Vote ~ 531

Hoover, Republican ~ 444

Smith, Democrat ~ 87

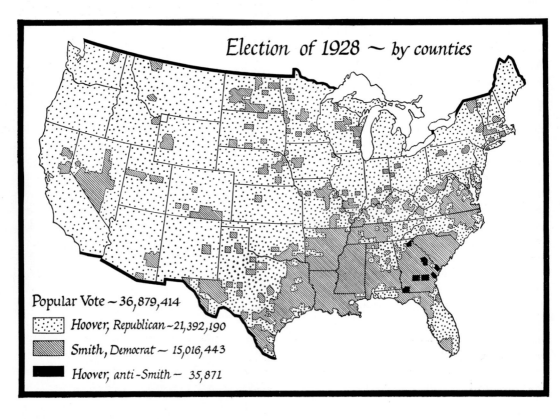

Election of 1928 ~ by counties

Popular Vote ~ 36,879,414

Hoover, Republican ~ 21,392,190

Smith, Democrat ~ 15,016,443

Hoover, anti-Smith ~ 35,871

stimulate voluntary cooperation. Proponents of the measure believed that agriculture, with appropriate federal encouragement, would be able to save itself. Working together through cooperatives, the farmers could apply to their business the same principles of orderly production and distribution that governed the activities of a prudent manufacturer. They could thus find means to curtail production whenever necessary, to shift to different crops as demands changed, and to eliminate wasteful and expensive methods of marketing. The act created a Federal Farm Board of eight members, and provided it with a half-billion-dollar revolving fund from which it could lend to cooperatives, and to such stabilization corporations as it might set up for the purpose of buying, storing, and selling surpluses.

The Federal Farm Board began operations at once, with Alexander Legge of the International Harvester Company as its chairman. In its efforts to stimulate the formation of cooperatives it was entirely successful, and loans for this purpose during the first year of its operation amounted to over $165,000,-000. There is no reason to doubt that these activities contributed significantly to the orderly marketing of nearly every type of crop produced in the United States. Much sound advice was also distributed as to the curtailment of production in crops where the market was glutted, although other governmental agencies, particularly the Department of Agriculture and the agricultural colleges, considerably confused the situation by explaining to the farmers how more and more of the same commodities might be grown on fewer acres but better soil.

With respect to wheat and cotton it soon became apparent that something far more **Stabilization** drastic than cooperative mar-**activities** keting was necessary if the rapid downward trend of prices was to be stopped. Accordingly, in 1930, a Grain Stabilization Corporation and a Cotton Stabilization Corporation were set up, each with authority to buy in the open market in order to raise prices. As long as governmental purchases continued, the effect on the price of wheat and cotton was good, but after a year or two the Stabilization Corporations found themselves in possession of vast stores of produce that they were unable to market. In June, 1931, the Grain Corporation, with an unmarketed and seemingly unmarketable supply of 257,000,000 bushels of wheat on its hands, ceased its purchases, and the next month the price of wheat dropped to fifty-seven cents. Meantime, the Cotton Corporation, after purchasing the carry-over from two successive seasons, had accumulated three and a quarter million bales of cotton in its warehouses, and was also forced to acknowledge defeat. In 1932 the price of cotton dropped to as low as five cents a pound. The following year the Federal Farm Board ended its brief career with total losses set at about $184,000,000.

Meantime, Congress had plunged eagerly into the revision of the tariff that Hoover had promised. For months before **The Hawley-** the special session of Congress **Smoot** convened, the House Ways and **Tariff** Means Committee had been holding hearings, and on May 7, 1929, its chairman, Willis C. Hawley of Oregon, introduced a bill that did not far exceed the limited recommendations of the President. But a log-rolling generosity at once developed which resulted in the amendment of the original bill to suit the demands of practically every congressman with a constituency to conciliate. As it passed the House later in the month, the Hawley Bill was already a general revision of the tariff with a scale of duties far higher than those of the record-breaking Fordney-McCumber Act of 1922. The Senate Finance Committee, headed by Reed Smoot of Utah, altered the bill in detail, but not greatly in principle. When the Senate debate opened, insurgency developed, and for a time it seemed that a coalition of Democrats and independent Republicans might bring about some important readjustments. Unfortunately a succession of deals with individual members of the coalition weakened the opposition and made possible the retention of the extremely high rates. Some of the supposedly most intransigeant insurgents were induced to vote for increases that they would otherwise have opposed in order to obtain in return increases that pressure groups among their constituents earnestly desired. Such insurgents as could not be bought off tried to improve the measure by including within it the export debenture plan for the relief of agriculture, and a flexible schedule clause which would have given Congress rather than the President authority to act on changes recommended by the Tariff Commission; but ultimately, largely because of pressure from the President, both provisions were stricken out. The Hawley-Smoot Tariff, as it came from the conference committee, accepted in the main the higher rates proposed by either house, and raised the general level of protection by about seven per cent. In the Senate the final vote was 44 to 42. Five Democrats, from Louisiana (sugar), Florida (fruit), and Wyoming (wool), voted with the majority, while eleven Republicans and one Farmer-Laborite voted against it.

In spite of a rising volume of criticism directed against the measure, Hoover gave it his signature. It was not what he had wished, and he did not disguise his disappointment; but neither did he heed the petition of more than a thousand American economists who explained cogently the pressing need for a presidential veto. According to this "round robin," which was signed by practically all the leading economists of the country, the Hawley-Smoot Tariff was certain (1) to raise prices for the American consumer; (2) to encourage wasteful and unnecessary concerns to remain in business; (3) to limit the exportation of American products, both from farm and factory, by restricting imports, (4) to yield no benefits to the farmers whose prices were fixed by what the exportable surplus would bring; and (5) to insure reprisals from foreign countries whose trade would be adversely affected. Probably all of these predictions came true, but on the last there was no room for doubt. While the bill was under consideration, pro-

tests against its passage were registered by trade associations in nearly every European country, and immediately after its passage reprisals set in. One of the first came from Canada, which promptly increased the rates on most of its important imports from the United States, and others came thick and fast. In 1932 Great Britain, whose devotion to free trade had long been slipping, veered completely over to the protective tariff policy. For the establishment of these higher trade barriers in the face of world-wide depression the United States bore a leading responsibility.

Long before the passage of the Hawley-Smoot Tariff the Great Depression had begun. It was preceded, quite in the fashion of many previous depressions, by a prolonged period of speculation, this time mainly in the stocks and bonds of business corporations. The prosperity of the twenties was to a remarkable extent corporation prosperity. Few individuals owned great businesses; Henry Ford was an outstanding exception. Most "big businesses" were jointly owned by hundreds or thousands of stockholders, whose investments might vary from a hundred-dollar share to values running far into the millions. Throughout the prosperous twenties the multiplication of stocks went on with ever-increasing tempo, and into such investments multitudes of individuals placed their savings, great and small. The fact that American business was actually owned by millions of investors was regarded with satisfaction by President Hoover and others as proof of its essential democracy, but any careful examination of corporation statistics was apt to prove that a comparatively small number of investors owned the greater part of the stock. Moreover, the direction of a given industry lay inevitably with the few insiders represented on boards of directors. In a sense the control of business was less democratic than ever before. With investments so widely diffused, the individual with a three per cent holding might be as powerful as the majority stockholder of an earlier age.

Background of the Great Depression

While many of those who purchased stocks were genuinely interested in obtaining sound investments, many others operated only as speculators, buying when prices were low, and selling when they rose. Most small purchasers bought "on margin," depositing only enough money with their brokers to cover the probable range of fluctuation. They were sure to encounter difficulties if their guesses went wrong. This speculative demand for stocks was to a great extent responsible for the generally high price-level to which securities rose during the later twenties. More frequently than not the actual earning power of a given stock was far too low to justify the prices at which it sold; valuations equal to twenty-five times the interest returns were by no means uncommon. Optimists refused to be alarmed at the situation, and insisted that the high prices paid for American securities were merely an evidence of the healthy condition of American enterprise. Investors had faith, and were willing to back it with their dollars, in the soundness of American business. Even the Federal Reserve Board, at least indirectly, supported the speculation, for it allowed loans to corporations ostensibly interested in programs of expansion, only to see the funds so obtained quickly passed along to the speculators. Between September, 1927, and September, 1929, borrowings for speculation on the New York Stock Exchange rose from three and one third to eight and one half billion dollars. Prices of stocks, in the language of one misguided observer, soared upward to "what looks like a permanently high plateau." An issue never known to pay a dividend climbed steadily from forty dollars to four hundred and fifty dollars a share.

In the midst of all this madness a few warning voices pointed out that the business cycle might not be as obsolete as many seemed to believe, and that a crisis was probably close at hand. Too much of the country's credit was being diverted into stock-exchange loans, and industry as a result of the easy money was being tempted to over-expand. Who was to buy all the goods that producers could make and sell? Already the building boom that had characterized the earlier twenties was on the decline, automobile sales were off, and oil production far exceeded the demand. But these wise protests were brushed aside by optimists in high places who counseled against selling America short, and assured investors that all was well. Two days before the market crashed, Charles E. Mitchell, president of the National City Bank of New York, asserted unequivocally: "I know of nothing fundamentally wrong with the stock market or with the underlying business and credit structures."

The stock-market collapse came in October, 1929, when English interest rates were raised to six and one half per cent in order to bring home needed capital that had been attracted to the United States by the high speculative profits. As a result many European holdings were thrown on the market, and prices began to sag. Frightened at the prospect, and no longer able to borrow at will, American speculators also began to unload. On Thursday, October 24, 1929, 12,800,000 shares changed hands, and until October 29, when the sales reached 16,410,030 shares, the frantic selling continued. During the month of October the value of stocks listed on the New York Stock Exchange declined from eighty-seven billion to fifty-five billion dollars, or about thirty-seven per cent. And this, it developed was only the beginning. In spite of repeated assurances from high authorities, both in government and in finance, that prosperity lay "just around the corner," no less than nine similar declines to "new low levels" were recorded within the next three years. By the first of March, 1933, the value of all stocks listed on the New York Stock Exchange was set at only nineteen billion dollars, less than one fifth the inflated figures of October 1, 1929.

In spite of optimistic efforts to maintain that the stock-market collapse was purely a paper loss which would not seriously undermine the fundamental soundness of American

Stock speculation

Panic of 1929

The Panic of '29 created scenes like this on Wall Street. Investors rushed, unbelieving, to verify the news of the crash.

business, it was soon evident that a period of unparalleled depression had begun. Prices dropped sharply; foreign trade fell off; factories curtailed production, or in many cases closed their doors never to reopen them; real estate values (but not mortgages) declined; new construction, except on governmental works, practically ceased; banks went under; worst of all, wages were cut drastically and unemployment figures began to mount. By the end of 1930 about six or seven million workers were out of jobs; two years later the number had doubled. Nor was the United States alone in its distress. No longer able to secure American loans, foreign nations fell likewise into the abyss of depression; indeed, many of them, like Germany, had not far to fall. Once again the isolationist-minded people of the United States were to learn by experience that whatever seriously affected one great nation was bound to affect all.

Efforts to account for the plunge from prosperity to adversity soon demonstrated conclusively that no one factor alone, but only a great number of factors working together, could have produced such startling results. Economists were also able to reach substantial agreement as to the principal causes of the depression, although they were by no means in harmony as to the degree of responsibility to be assigned to each cause. Among other disturbing influences they cited the following:

Causes of the depression

1. Agricultural overexpansion, both in the United States and elsewhere. American farmers produced more wheat, cotton, corn, livestock, and other commodities than they could sell at satisfactory prices, and to some extent the same condition existed in much of the rest of the world. Agricultural surpluses piled up at home and abroad with devastating effect on the price of each new crop. Farm purchases steadily declined, for the farmers had less and less with which to buy. Payments on the heavy mortgage burden assumed in more prosperous times still further curtailed the farmers' buying power, and drove many of them to tenancy.

Agricultural overexpansion

2. Industrial overexpansion. The American industrial plant had been overbuilt during the period of the boom, and could not be operated at maximum capacity. There were too many factories, and too much machinery. American industry was geared to produce far more than it could sell. Automobiles, for example, had been turned out in steadily increasing numbers during the twenties to supply a new market. But the time came when every American family that could afford to own an automobile (and many who could not) had one or sometimes more than one. With twenty-six and one half million

Industrial overexpansion

motor cars in operation by 1929, the market for automobiles was confined largely to replacements. The same condition existed in the housing industry. Rapid building during the twenties had overexpanded the lumber industry and others concerned with the production of building materials. But the time came when all the people who could afford to build new houses had built them, and plants that had once flourished stood idle.

3. The increasing effectiveness of machines. Ingenious labor-saving devices **Labor-saving** made possible greater produc- **machines** tion with comparatively less labor. Fewer and fewer men produced more and more goods. "Technological unemployment" might not be permanent, but at least the men who were thrown out of work by the new machines had to seek other jobs, and they sometimes failed to find them. Thus the buying power of labor was diminished. The new machines might make more goods, but whose wages were to pay for them? Introduction of these labor-saving devices might well have been paralleled by increased wages, a shortening of the labor day and the labor week, and a diminishing use of women and children in industry. But only occasionally were such accompaniments recorded.

4. Capital surpluses were too high; as a prominent banker, Frank A. Vanderlip, ex- **Capital** pressed it, "Capital kept too **surpluses** much and labor did not have enough to buy its share of things." This was the more easily possible because of the monopolistic nature of much American business, which so greatly facilitated the control of prices. Throughout the boom years the tendency of business was to take too long profits, and to reinvest the capital thus accumulated in order to produce still more goods, which in return might produce still more profits. A wider distribution of earnings, particularly if paid out in the form of higher wages, might well have stimulated purchasing power and diminished the danger of ultimate collapse.

5. The overexpansion of credit, both for productive and consumptive purposes. Money was plentiful and cheap **Over-** throughout the twenties, and **expansion** the policy of the Federal Re- **of credit** serve Board was definitely to keep it so. It was too easy to borrow, whether for business expansion, for speculation, or for the satisfaction of personal desires. There was too much installment buying, and too much of the national income was diverted into interest payments. In keeping with the speculative spirit of the time, purchasers cheerfully mortgaged their futures to obtain goods that would often be consumed before they could be paid for.

6. International trade was out of balance. European nations, with their economies badly shattered by the war, had **Decline of** depended mainly on funds bor- **international** rowed from American investors **trade** to pay for imports and to stabilize foreign exchange. The only way they might have repaid these obligations was by shipping goods to the United States. But the Fordney-McCumber Act of 1922, followed by the Hawley-Smoot Act of 1930, definitely forestalled any such possibility. The debtor nations of Europe in self-defense were obliged to adopt high-tariff policies, and by various other expedients to stimulate whatever industries were necessary to cut down their reliance on foreign goods. During the years of 1922–27 the production of British-made automobiles, for example, was increased from forty-nine per cent of the domestic supply to eighty-six per cent. Thus the United States, blindly committed to the protective principles of an earlier age, stood to lose both its export business and a good share of the money by which this business had been sustained. Many manufacturers understood the situation, and did their best to prevent the adoption of tariffs that in the long run were certain to bring disaster, but most Americans were slow to recognize that international trade was a "two-way street," and were quite unprepared for the collapse that followed the withdrawal of American credits.

7. Political unrest throughout the world,

particularly in Europe, Asia, and South
Political America, added to the difficul-
unrest ties in the way of a sustained
prosperity. The intergovernmental debts,
whether funded or not, constituted a continuing threat both to trade and to international good feelings. The reparations problem remained unsettled. Most countries
were overburdened with governmental debts,

and few national budgets were in balance.
Agitation for independence was chronic in
India, the designs of Japan toward China
were abundantly clear, and warfare soon
broke out between Bolivia and Paraguay
over the Chaco. Altogether the international skies seemed dark, and the prospects
of a return to "normalcy" as far away as
ever.

Bibliography

The diplomatic activities of the Coolidge ad-
ministration centered mainly on the war debts
problem and the Kellogg-Briand Peace Pact.
On the former, a brief statement is available in
B. H. Williams, *Economic Foreign Policy of the
United States* (1929). For fuller accounts, con-
sult National Industrial Conference Board, *The
Inter-Ally Debts and the United States* (1925);
Karl Bergmann, *History of Reparations* (1927);
H. N. Moulton and Leo Pasvolsky, *World War
Debt Settlement* (1926); and, by the same authors,
War Debts and World Prosperity (1932). On the
Kellogg-Briand Peace Pact, see D. H. Miller,
The Peace Pact of Paris (1928); J. T. Shotwell,
War as an Instrument of National Policy (1929);
David Bryn-Jones, *Frank B. Kellogg* (1932); and
John E. Stoner, *S. O. Levinson and the Pact of
Paris: A Study in the Techniques of Influence*
(1942).

On farm problems see references on p. 505;
also, James E. Boyle, *Farm Relief: A Brief on
the McNary-Haugen Plan* (1928); G. N. Peek
and Samuel Crowther, *Why Quit Our Own* (1936);
and G. C. Fite, *George N. Peek and the Fight
for Farm Parity* (1954).

The election of 1928 furnished the inspiration
for an unusually large number of books on politics. R. V. Peel and T. C. Donnelly, *The 1928
Campaign* (1931), is valuable on the election in
general. On the Smith side, a pre-campaign
biography of merit is H. F. Pringle, *Alfred E.
Smith: A Critical Study* (1927). Smith's own
story appears in A. E. Smith, *Up to Now: An
Autobiography* (1929). Less friendly to the Democratic candidate are W. H. Allen, *Al Smith's
Tammany Hall* (1928); and M. R. Werner, *Tammany Hall* (1928). Frank Graham, *Al Smith,
American: An Informal Biography* (1945), is

a good re-evaluation. Hoover's well-reasoned
statement of the Republican creed is available in
two widely-distributed books, Herbert Hoover,
American Individualism (1922); and *The New
Day* (1928). The last-mentioned consists of his
campaign addresses in 1928. The same philosophy, oriented with reference to the New Deal, is
the theme of two later books by Hoover, *The
Challenge to Liberty* (1934); and *Addresses upon
the American Road, 1933–1938* (1938). Hoover
has also published three volumes of *Memoirs* (3
vols., 1951–1952), the second of which, *The Cabinet and the Presidency, 1920–1933* (1952), is pertinent here. David Hinshaw, *Herbert Hoover:
American Quaker* (1950), is less a biography
than an interpretation of Hoover's career in the
light of his Quaker principles.

The activities of the Hoover administration are
also covered intimately and defended in two diffi-
cult books, W. S. Myers and W. H. Newton, *The
Hoover Administration: A Documented Narrative*
(1936); and R. L. Wilbur and A. M. Hyde, *The
Hoover Policies* (1937). On various aspects of
the Hoover administration, see R. G. Tugwell,
Mr. Hoover's Economic Policy (1932); W. S.
Myers, *The Foreign Policies of Herbert Hoover,
1929–1933* (1940); Alexander De Conde, *Herbert
Hoover's Latin American Policy* (1951); and J.
M. Jones, *Tariff Retaliation* (1934).

The best economic history of the period is
George Soule, *Prosperity Decade* (1947). A good
analysis of the causes of the Panic of 1929 is
given in the Brookings Institution, *The Recovery
Problem in the United States* (1936). See also
W. Z. Ripley, *Main Street and Wall Street* (1927);
W. B. Donham, *Business Adrift* (1931); and Gilbert V. Seldes, *The Years of the Locust: America,
1929–1932* (1933).

25

The New American Way

The automobile — Henry Ford — The "movies" — Talking pictures — Radio — The airplane — A mechanized age — Prohibition — Problems of enforcement — The bootleggers — The Wickersham Commission — Racketeering — Educational trends — Scientific achievements — American literature — Music — Painting — Sculpture — Architecture — Century of Progress Exposition — World's Fairs of 1939

IT SEEMS probable that the automobile effected a greater change in the American way of life than ever proceeded from any other single cause. The civilization of the nineteenth century remained to the end a "horse-and-buggy" affair; the civilization of the twentieth century was soon geared to the automobile. Starting from insignificance during the later nineties, the automobile industry by the time of the Great Depression outranked all others in importance, even steel. The new system of mass production at low cost which it introduced put motor transportation within the financial reach of nearly every American family; by 1929 twenty-six and one half million motor cars of one kind or another were registered in the United States, by 1950 the number had reached fifty million, five sixths of the world's total. The requirements of automobile travelers stimulated a movement for good roads, one significant result of which was to bring the city closer to the country, and the country to the city. With good roads available family vacations could be taken far from home, and every summer huge armies of tourists took to the road. Because the owner of an automobile might live a considerable distance from his work, suburban developments expanded as never before. Buses and trucks took over

The automobile

the short-haul traffic of streetcars and railroads. Hazards to life and health increased as traffic speeded up, and automobile accidents soon provided one of the commonest causes of death or injury. By the year 1953 automobile accidents had claimed the lives of as many Americans as all the wars in which the United States had ever participated. Crime was made easy, for the automobile assured law-breakers of a ready means of escape. Thousands of pleasure-bent children and youths at large on the roads increased the worries of parents, and drove the chaperon out of business. As a visiting senator from Hawaii complained, there were always "too many people in too many cars in too much of a hurry going in too many different directions to nowhere for nothing."

"The saga of the motor car" was intimately connected with the life-history of Henry Ford, whose dream of a good low-cost car was realized in an incredibly short time. Beginning at Detroit as early as 1893, Ford was making a fairly dependable car by the turn of the century, and by 1914 had produced a half-million of his famous "Model T." It was an unsightly car, designed for service and not for beauty, but it would run and it was cheap. Ford's methods of production were

Henry Ford

Henry Ford produced in 1909 the first Model T motor car, commonly known to its appreciative public as the "flivver."

even more important than the car he built, for he used standardized, interchangeable parts, and by means of a "production line," along which each workman did his one assigned task and no other, he brought the process of manufacturing to a new level of efficiency. Other producers gave him competition, particularly the General Motors Corporation, which was established by William C. Durant as early as 1908. But for a long time Ford held the upper hand in the small-car field, and not until 1927 would he retool his plants in order to produce a better-looking car, the "Model A." Meantime, cars of every size and price had found their market, although three great companies, the Ford, the General Motors, and the Chrysler-Dodge companies controlled all together about four fifths of the motor-car industry. Almost alone among manufacturers Ford continued to own and operate his own company, and consistently refused to impair his complete control by selling stock to outsiders. He paid high wages, but had little use for labor unions, and demanded the complete loyalty of his employees.

Second only to the automobile in their revolutionary results were the "movies," or as they were more properly **The "movies"** called, motion pictures. This new form of amusement was the gift of America's greatest inventor, Thomas A. Edison, who with the help of European ideas had worked out most of the essential principles of the process before 1900. But the earliest movies were of interest merely because of their scientific novelty, and not because they presented pictures worth seeing. Prizefights, parades, street crowds, and news events provided the material for the first reels, which were shown sometimes in connection with vaudeville performances, and sometimes as independent "nickel shows" in abandoned store buildings, Chautauqua tents, or other improvised quarters. But improvements were gradually introduced, and producers soon learned to unfold a story on the screen that the public would like to watch. After a period in which they imitated too closely the legitimate theater, they learned at last to suit the action to the techniques they were able to employ. The showing in 1915 of the *Birth of a Nation* marked the beginning of a new era in which the "silent drama" carried everything before it. This picture, based upon Thomas Dixon's *The Clansman,* set forth effectively the agonies endured by the South during reconstruction. It was cheered by packed houses in North and South alike, and revealed clearly the profit possibilities of the new industry. With interest assured, elaborate motion-picture theaters appeared in every town and city, the price of admission was raised, and in southern California, where the sun shone dependably a good share of the year, the making of motion pictures became a major occupation. Film artists, such as Charlie Chaplin, Douglas Fairbanks, and Mary Pickford, were soon better known than politicians, and magazines devoted exclusively to the doings of the movie colony began to appear on most of the newsstands.

The movies had just succeeded in outgrowing their early crudities **Talking pictures** when the invention of talking

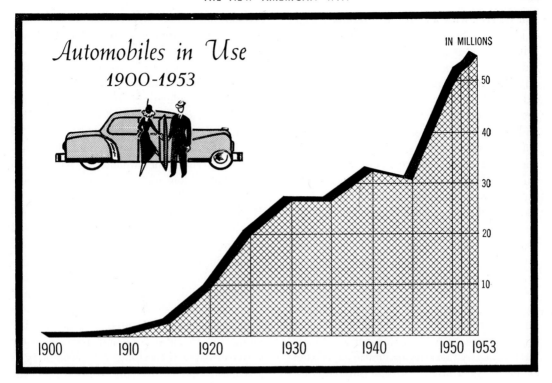

Automobiles in Use
1900-1953

IN MILLIONS

50

40

30

20

10

1900   1910   1920   1930   1940   1950 1953

pictures forced them to start all over again. In October, 1927, Al Jolson's success in *The Jazz Singer* proved that sound effects had come to stay, and within two years' time the movies had everywhere been converted into "talkies." The change eliminated scores of actors whose voices were unsuited to sound transmission, but it also served to open the profession to artists of the legitimate stage who had formerly regarded the screen performances with unconcealed contempt. Many competent artists passed back and forth freely from one medium to another, while successful plays on the legitimate stage were often reproduced in the movies. One of the best received of these was *The Barretts of Wimpole Street*, by Rudolph Bezier, in which the screen star, Norma Shearer, imitated closely the admirable acting of Katherine Cornell, America's greatest actress, on the legitimate stage. While many inferior pictures were made, the public tended more and more to become conscious of good acting, and to demand it as a matter of course. With the increasing perfection of sound instru-

ments, musical plays grew rapidly in favor, paving the way for the successes of such singing artists as Jeanette MacDonald and Deanna Durbin. Walt Disney's *Silly Symphonies* introduced a new technique, the animated cartoon, which won many a well-earned laugh, and graduated eventually into the wholly admirable *Snow White and the Seven Dwarfs*. The invention of technicolor gave great vitality to the films that employed it, but was surprisingly slow to achieve general use. It attained a high degree of perfection in Margaret Mitchell's *Gone with the Wind*, starring Clark Gable and Vivien Leigh, which was produced in 1939.

As the motion picture industry assumed big business proportions, it inevitably reflected big business attitudes. **The picture** A few large Los Angeles, or in **industry** popular parlance, "Hollywood," companies accounted for most of the films and competed with each other for the control of the market. By the year 1937 there were in the United States ninety-two motion picture companies, representing an investment of about two billion dollars, with a combined annual budget of about $135,000,000. The salaries of executives, directors, and "stars" in "pictures" matched the highest paid in any industry anywhere. Naturally box-office receipts became the chief criterion of excellence, and producers catered to the public taste, good or bad. As a result art often suffered; with the major pictures costing millions of dollars, and the average feature about $350,000, a single failure could be ruinous. American pictures were in great demand not only in the United States, where there were in 1937 nearly 90,000 motion picture theaters, but also throughout the world. Unfortunately they often gave a most mistaken impression abroad as to the nature of American society. "Grade B" westerns featuring cowboys, Indians, and hold-ups, gangster films full of sound and fury, and "Joe College" pictures of campus absurdities were all too frequently taken as authentic expositions of life in the United States. But American pictures, in spite of their popularity, by no means monopolized the market, either at home or abroad. The competition of British producers was particularly keen, as the popularity of such films as *The Private Life of Henry VIII*, in which Charles Laughton played the title rôle, abundantly attested. Actually, American production accounted for only about forty per cent of the world's total output of motion pictures, although the value of the American product was proportionately much higher. The competition of television, which set in after the Second World War, gave the moving picture producers some hard times. Gross box office receipts, estimated at $1,750,000,000 in 1946, were down to $1,166,000,000 in 1951, after which they began to rise again slowly.

The significance of the movies in American life was difficult to assess, but hard to over-emphasize. Practically every-**Influence of** one, of high or low degree, at-**the movies** tended the motion picture shows with more or less regularity, and for the rising generation the lessons they taught were doubtless far more effective than the precepts of the schoolroom. The suggestions of the screen as to styles, manners, taste in furniture and art, and even morals, did not go unnoticed. It seems reasonable to suppose, for example, that there was some causal relationship between the popularity of the *Birth of a Nation* and the subsequent revival of the Ku Klux Klan. Pictures featuring the careers of criminals may also have accounted for numerous juvenile delinquencies, while such feminine fashions as the universal use of cosmetics probably owed at least as much to Hollywood as to Paris. Since the same movies were shown everywhere, they tended to emphasize strongly the national tendency toward uniformity. Probably the well-modulated voices and correct speaking of the film artists did far more than the high-school teachers of English to make young Americans talk better and talk alike. Whether the morals of movie actors and actresses were above or below the average for the country as a whole would be difficult to prove, but the interest of stage stars in publicity, whatever the cost, made their doings generally known, and they may have had imitators. Censorship of pictures, sometimes effective but often of little consequence, was established in nearly every state, but producers learned mainly by trial and error what would be well received and what would not. As a kind of supreme arbiter in all matters of public relations, the picture industry chose Will H. Hays, who resigned as Postmaster-General under Harding to accept the assignment.

Another new influence upon American life was furnished by the radio. Wireless telegraphy and telephony were **Radio** known before the outbreak of the First World War, but during that struggle they proved to be of such tremendous military value that revolutionary improvements were made within a few years' time. After the war radio "fans," whose interest was primarily that of amateur scientists, bought millions of dollars' worth of equipment, and counted with joy the number of distant stations they could hear. By 1920 the manufacturers of radio supplies were beginning to furnish programs as a means of promoting the use of what they had to sell, and from this practice the institution of radio broadcasting developed. The pioneer station in this endeavor was KDKA of Pittsburgh, which among other things successfully broadcast the returns of the election of 1920. Soon many broadcasting stations, generously supported by advertisers, were competing for control of the air, and to prevent complete chaos Secretary Hoover maintained an informal system of licensing in the Commerce Department. When in 1926 the Attorney-General ruled that the Secretary of Commerce was exceeding his legal authority, the resulting confusion led Congress to establish next year a Federal Radio Commission of five members with the right to license broadcasting stations, and to determine the power, wave lengths, and hours of operation to be allotted to each. Presently chains of stations, linked together at first as "stunts" but later because of the advantages observed, formed nationwide networks over which the same program could be trans-

mitted to every receiving set in the country. Steady improvements by what speedily became one of America's biggest businesses soon enabled listeners also to hear and enjoy broadcasts by short wave from abroad.

The influence of the radio on American society is as difficult to assess as the influence of motion pictures. It furnished a new weapon for the use of advertisers, who found that through broadcasting they could reach an audience that was hardly touched by the billboards, the newspapers, and the periodicals. Experts were soon able to chart with accuracy the effects of a new program or a change of hour upon the sales volume of those who paid for time on the air. It introduced a new form of dramatic art which must appeal only to the ear, as the first movies had appealed only to the eye. Such comedians as Amos 'n' Andy, whose black-face make-up had to be imagined, and Charlie McCarthy, a ventriloquist's creation, became fireside favorites. It stimulated interest in music, including good music, and made millions of ordinary citizens familiar with the works of

Growing pains in radio included such agonies over sound effects as those indicated in the illustration. The crew shown here helped with a production of *Rip Van Winkle*.

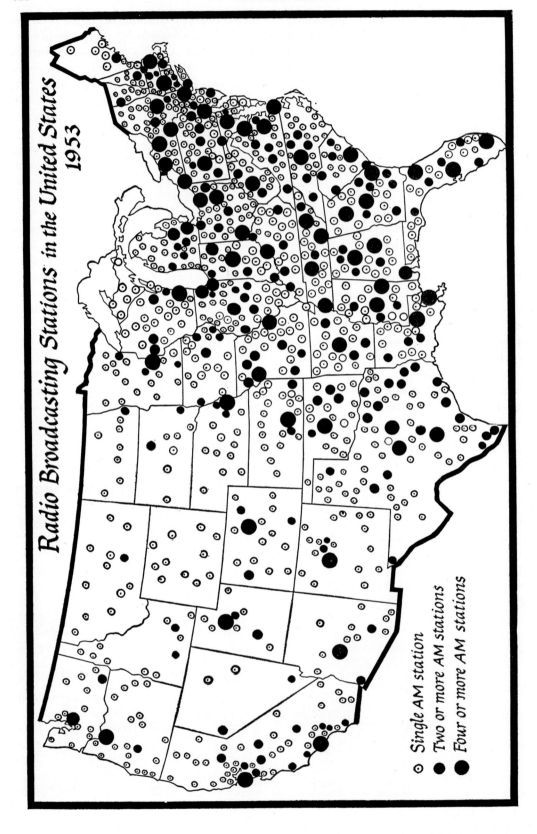

Radio Broadcasting Stations in the United States 1953

o Single AM station
● Two or more AM stations
⬤ Four or more AM stations

the great composers. It provided also a powerful means for swaying public opinion. During election years candidates for President could argue their cases with the whole nation as an audience; radio orators such as Father Coughlin could build up nationwide followings; and promoters of almost any cause, good or bad, could get a hearing for a price. News bulletins acquainted the listener with what was going on in the world, and a host of able commentators interpreted the news. Crises in diplomacy, such as those that preceded the outbreak of the Second World War, were followed by the whole American people with an intensity of interest that newsprint seemed powerless to evoke.

Fraught also with great potentialities was the airplane. As early as 1903 Orville and **The airplane** Wilbur Wright had made successful flights with power-driven planes at Kitty Hawk, North Carolina, and an incredulous world was soon convinced that the thing could be done. When war broke out in 1914, aviation was still in its infancy, but the importance of aircraft, at first for scouting purposes and later for use in actual combat, led to revolutionary improvements in design and construction. Among other things American inventors pooled their knowledge to produce the new "Liberty motor," an admirable engine, but the war was over before it could be turned out in large enough numbers to have had any important effect on the result. After the war "gypsy" fliers, who made a precarious living by taking passengers up in the air for the thrill they would get, kept the public conscious of the airplane, and prepared the way for its use in commercial transportation. "Stunt-fliers" also revealed its possibilities, particularly for long-distance flights. The Atlantic was crossed by way of the Azores as early as May, 1919; from Newfoundland to Ireland in June of the same year; and from Great Britain to New York by a British dirigible the following July. But the achievement that most caught the country's fancy was the solo flight of Charles A. Lindbergh, a youthful aviator who took off from Roosevelt Field, Long Island, on May 20, 1927, and thirty-three hours later landed successfully in the vicinity of Paris. By order of President Coolidge, Lindbergh was brought home on a warship, and rose immediately to the status of the nation's greatest hero. The fact that he was not the first to fly the Atlantic, and that other Americans, Clarence D. Chamberlain and C. A. Levine, flying from the same field on July 4 for Berlin, got within a hundred miles of their destination, in no wise diminished Lindbergh's fame. Later in the month Commander Richard E. Byrd at the head of a party of four also flew to Europe, and two army aviators reached Honolulu from California, while in June, 1931, Wiley Post flew around the world in less than eight days' time.

The development of commerical aviation in the United States did not begin in earnest until several years after the sign- **Air mail** ing of the armistice, although the government early gave its assistance by air-mail contracts. By 1924 a regular mail service had been established between New York and San Francisco, and four years later there were as many as forty-eight airways in the United States, covering twenty thousand miles, and serving three hundred and fifty-five cities. Most of these lines depended upon government mail contracts for their profits, and regarded the incidental carrying of passengers or freight as somewhat of a nuisance. When Hoover became President in 1929 his Postmaster-General, Walter Folger Brown, resolved to remedy this situation. The government subsidies were paid, he believed, not merely for carrying the mail, but also to encourage the development of a new and useful means of transportation which might incidentally serve the country well in time of war. Brown wrote new contracts, which, by abandoning the "per pound" basis for carrying the mail in favor of the "space-mile" principle, placed a premium on the building of larger planes. He also used his discretionary power in the awarding of contracts in such a way as to eliminate the small operators, whose ability

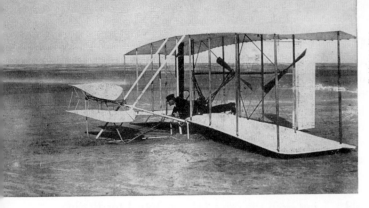

FIRST FLIGHT. The Wright Brothers' famous plane at Kitty Hawk, North Carolina, in 1903, the year of their first successful flight.

ATLANTIC CROSSING. Charles A. Lindbergh's flight in 1926 rocketed him to fame and opened the way to trans-Atlantic flying.

Aviation, so commonplace a part of life today, is a strictly twentieth-century development. The experiments of the Wright brothers at Kitty Hawk paved the way for innovations that were startlingly exploited during the First World War and after.

GROWTH OF AIRLINES. By 1941, when this picture was taken, commercial airlines were well established and the age of flight was on regular schedule.

to develop the industry was obviously less than that of the well-established and adequately financed lines.

As a result of Brown's policy American aviation was able to survive the blows it suffered from the Depression. Many "little fellows" went under, but great systems developed which brought transportation by air into common use. Passenger comfort became a matter of first importance, and sufficient private business was obtained by the air lines to make possible the gradual reduction of governmental subsidies. It was inevitable, however, that the success of the large, government-aided operators should arouse the jealousy of their less favored competitors, and bitter complaints were poured into the receptive ears of James Farley, who became Postmaster-General after the election of 1932. Convinced that collusion had existed between his predecessor and the various successful bidders, Farley cancelled all domestic air-mail contracts by an order of February 19, 1934, and for two weeks the country was without any air-mail service whatever. Then the President ordered the army air corps to take over the task of carrying the mails, but the army pilots were unaccustomed to the highly specialized type of flying required, and in quick succession a dozen of them lost their lives. As speedily as possible, new air-mail legislation was rushed through Congress, and new contracts were let to commercial companies, but the government's change of policy resulted, to say the least, in much temporary confusion. By the Mead-McKellar Air-Mail Act of 1935 the Interstate Commerce Commission was given power to raise or lower rates of payment under existing mail contracts, an innovation that served somewhat to emancipate the air lines from the complete control of the Post-Office Department.

Passenger travel by airplane Regardless of its difficulties with the government the aviation industry was soon expanding with great rapidity. A six-cents letter rate, introduced June 1, 1934, greatly increased the volume of mail carried by air, and helped the companies recover much of the loss suffered from the cancellation of contracts. Steady improvements in airplane design and in safety and cheapness of service made the public more "air-minded" with each succeeding year. By the end of 1939 the nation's scheduled air lines reported that they had carried 1,900,000 passengers during the year; but for 1952 this figure had grown to 27,800,000. By the latter year, American air transport had become a billion dollar industry, with its planes carrying more passengers than railway pullmans, as well as immense quantities of mail, express, and freight. The volume of air traffic, together with the introduction of air tourist service, made possible considerable reductions in rates. World transport services, also extensively organized before the Second World War, grew to prodigious proportions at its close, with the United States accounting for about one third of the world's total commercial aviation, and Great Britain the next largest fraction. British experiments with jet-propelled passenger aircraft opened up new possibilities for the annihilation of distance that American airlines made preparation to exploit. The growth of the aircraft industry in other countries, as well as in the United States, was greatly accelerated by the governmental subsidies paid, through mail contracts, or otherwise. In time of war, civilian planes could become war planes, and civilian pilots, war pilots. The Second World War, with its extraordinary emphasis upon the airplane as a weapon of war, introduced a new era in military aviation, and led to a period of more intense activity among the airplane builders of the United States than they had ever known before.

A mechanized age The automobile, the movies, the radio, and the airplane were but the more visible symbols of a highly mechanized age. The gadgets of science had invaded every phase of American life. The farmer no longer followed a plow, but drove a tractor. The most humble of physicians must surround himself with thousands of dollars' worth of expensive equipment. Alert industrialists expected to retool their plants at frequent intervals. School buildings must be elaborately provided with the machines necessary for vocational training. Ordinary citizens took a thousand things for granted that their ancestors would have regarded as miracles; central heating, running water, sanitary plumbing, gas for cooking, electric energy for lighting and a dozen other household purposes; direct telephone connections with the outside world. Thoughtful observers sometimes wondered about the effect of all these "improvements" upon the people who depended upon them. Was the resourcefulness of the individual being undermined? Was overreliance upon machines

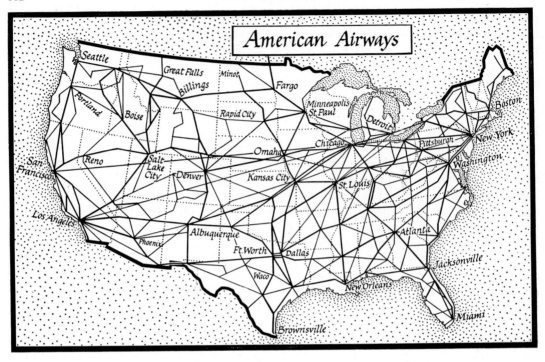

softening the fabric of American character? Whatever the answers, there were few to advocate that the new machines be scrapped, and the older and harder ways revived.

To inheritors of the Puritan tradition there was much about the changing American scene that was alarming. Among most of the Protestant denominations church-going had declined precipitately. A few popular city preachers held their congregations, but in the country towns the competition of the automobile, the movies, the radio, and the golf links had proved impossible to meet. The younger generation made open sport of the old morality; styles in feminine apparel left little to the imagination; and flippancy in speech and manners became almost a national obsession. Fundamentalism was in full retreat. The action of several southern legislatures during the twenties in prohibiting the teaching of evolution was more in the nature of a confession of defeat than a call to action. William Jennings Bryan, by aiding the prosecution at Dayton, Tennessee, of a young man who had disobeyed the law, was generally thought to have made himself

and his cause ridiculous. But the greatest blow that the evangelical churches suffered was the failure of prohibition. Effectively organized through the Anti-Saloon League, the church people had won state after state to the temperance cause, and when the Eighteenth Amendment was adopted in January, 1920, they had rejoiced almost as immoderately as over the signing of the armistice. Less than fourteen years later they looked on with despair while the Twenty-First Amendment recalled the Eighteenth, and the "noble experiment" came to an end.

The rock on which prohibition foundered was enforcement. It was one thing to outlaw the existing liquor traffic, **Prohibition** but quite another to prevent its replacement by illicit vendors of liquor who profited from breaking the law. The Eighteenth Amendment made no great change in the national appetite for strong drink, and a large minority of the population felt outraged that any such attack on personal liberty had been made. This was particularly true of the city populations in which the immigrant element constituted so important a part. Others who had never drunk before were impelled out of sheer perversity to do what the law forbade. Americans from colonial times on down had never felt obliged to obey a law that they did not like; indeed, many argued that the only way to defeat an obnoxious law was to prove that it could not be enforced. Thus a market for liquor still existed, and to supply it a whole new industry came into being. The ways of the "moonshiners," who since the days of the Whiskey Rebellion had hidden their stills in the mountains to avoid the payment of revenue, were extensively imitated; "rum-runners" brought a steady stream of cargoes from abroad to unpatrolled sections of the American coast; heavily laden smugglers crossed the border from Mexico and from Canada; chemical formulae, sometimes dependable and sometimes not, were used to "renovate" industrial liquor by the removal of denaturants; private citizens set up toy stills, manufactured "home-brew" and

"bathtub gin," turned the pure unfermented juice of the grape into more or less palatable wine.

The Volstead Act, by which Congress (over Wilson's veto) defined intoxicating beverages as those containing **Problems of** as much as one half of one per **enforcement** cent alcohol and created the machinery for enforcement, imposed upon federal officials an almost impossible task. "Bootleggers" had already gained valuable experience in the states where prohibition had preceded the Eighteenth Amendment. They knew how easily the problem of distribution could be solved by automobiles and trucks, and they were past-masters of the art of bribery and deception. Against these experts the Prohibition Bureau, which until 1927 was outside the civil service, mobilized a miscellaneous army of petty politicians and their friends. Furthermore, the entrance of the national government into the field of enforcement led the states to relax their efforts; wet states in many instances repealed the

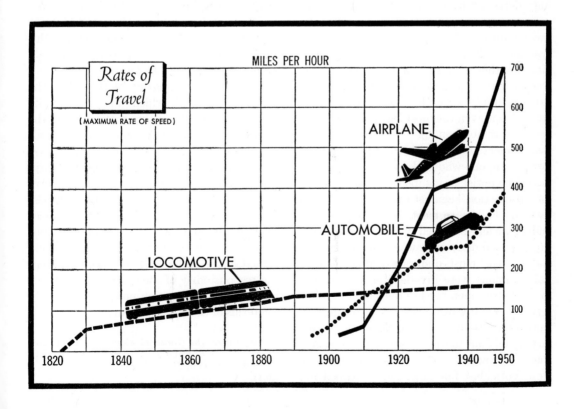

limitations they had once placed on liquor dealers, while dry states cheerfully resigned to federal agents the task of matching wits with the bootleggers. The United States Department of Justice found itself suddenly swamped with a type of business it had never known before, and prohibition cases clogged the federal courts. Thirty-five hundred civil cases and sixty-five thousand criminal cases were brought within a period of less than two years.

Soon the illicit liquor business was one of the nation's biggest and most profitable. **The bootleggers** Since it operated wholly outside the law, all restraints were eliminated, and competitors traded bloody blows. Backed by dependable gangs of thugs, the "big shots" fought furiously for the enormous profits of monopoly, and in each large city a well-recognized king of the underworld emerged, to whom, while his reign lasted, the whole business paid tribute. Deaths among the gangsters were numerous, but trials for these murders were rare and convictions still rarer. The gang leaders, successfully defended by highly paid criminal lawyers known as "mouthpieces," not only sneered openly at the prohibition agents, but systematically instituted one new "racket" after another. Gambling, prostitution, the trade in narcotics, and other illegal activities came naturally within the orbit of the "racketeers," but even the most legitimate of businesses were not immune. Restaurant keepers, cleaners and dyers, laundrymen, garage owners, anyone who took in cash might at a moment's notice be compelled to pay heavily for "protection" against these selfsame protectors. Failure to meet the racketeers' demands meant smashed windows, flattened tires, burned delivery trucks, bombed stores, and for the most obdurate sudden death. Labor unions were invaded for the chance to graft from membership dues, and in altogether too many instances city governments paid more attention to the demands of the racketeers than to the welfare of the citizens. Racketeering was at its worst in Chicago and New York, but few large cities escaped its ravages, and the whole nation paid tribute, directly or indirectly, to the gangsters.

With conditions fast becoming unbearable, a Law Enforcement Commission of eleven members was appointed by President Hoover in 1929 to conduct **The Wickersham Commission** an investigation. Headed by George W. Wickersham, formerly Attorney-General under Taft, the commission took its duties seriously, but when it reported in 1931 it was still undecided. Its findings of fact seemed to recognize the hopelessness of adequate enforcement, but a majority of the commissioners recommended that the prohibition experiment be continued.[1] In the summer of 1932 President Hoover, in spite of the impending campaign, admitted that some changes in the existing system would have to be made, while the Democratic platform went the whole length of demanding repeal. Following the triumphant Democratic victory at the polls, Congress acted even before the new administration could take office. In February, 1933, the repeal amendment was submitted, and by the end of the year it was a part of the Constitution.

The end of prohibition, however, did not mean the end of racketeering, for by this time the gangsters were deeply **Racketeering** entrenched in all sorts of rackets. One of the most amazing of these was the "snatch racket," which in May, 1932, claimed its most famous victim when the infant son of Charles A. Lindbergh was kidnaped for ransom by a lone operator, and killed. As the profits of bootlegging disappeared, criminals turned instead to kidnaping, bank burglaries, and other bold crimes, and in an alarming number of instances easily made good their escape. Finally Congress, by a series of "crime control" acts passed in the spring of 1934, faced squarely the responsibility of the federal government in bringing the situation under control. By the terms of these laws criminals who crossed

[1] Report of the National Commission on Law Observance and Enforcement, Seventy-first Congress, third session, *House Document* No. 722 (serial 9361).

state lines during the course of their exploits were made liable to drastic penalties (for kidnapers, death), and the Investigation Division of the Federal Department of Justice, headed by J. Edgar Hoover and known later as the Federal Bureau of Investigation, was given great freedom of action in enforcement. At the end of the year Hoover's agents had accounted by death for a dozen of the country's most notorious criminals, and had brought many others to justice. State officers, forced to compare results with the effective "G-men," also began to take their duties seriously. Early in 1935 the kidnaper of the Lindbergh baby was convicted and sentenced in New Jersey. That same year Thomas E. Dewey was made special prosecutor to conduct a drive against organized crime in New York, and achieved such conspicuous success that in 1937 he was given a popular mandate to continue the work as district attorney of New York County. When other evidence failed, racketeers were sometimes convicted for federal income-tax evasion. This had happened to "Scarface Al" Capone, the underworld ruler of Chicago, as far back as 1931, and his long imprisonment at Alcatraz, the escape-proof federal penitentiary located on an island in San Francisco Bay, served as a continual warning to would-be imitators. Toward the close of the decade there was reason to hope that at last the era of unrestrained lawlessness had approached its end.

If young America embraced lawlessness, it was not because its education had been **Educational** neglected. Compulsory school **trends** attendance up to sixteen or even eighteen years of age was required by law in most states, and was well enforced by public opinion. School buildings were elaborately equipped, not only with teaching paraphernalia, but also with auditoriums, gymnasiums, swimming pools, and such other facilities as might contribute to well-rounded lives on the part of the pupils. Bus service made possible the elimination of the weaker country schools, and the establishment, especially for the higher grades, of well-ap-

J. Edgar Hoover brought to a high degree of efficiency the work of the Federal Bureau of Investigation.

pointed consolidated systems. New principles of education, emanating chiefly from Teachers College, Columbia, revolutionized the methods of teaching, and emphasized the need of "education for life." The influence of John Dewey, who insisted that the chief end and aim of schooling should be the development of socially useful adults, permeated nearly every classroom. Preparation for college played a diminishing rôle in high-school curriculums, where a host of young people who had no interest in nor aptitude for a college course must be kept occupied. Vocational education and manual training flourished as never before. For the most part primary and secondary education in the United States meant public education, although many private schools existed, particularly in the East. Toward the end of the twenties the annual bill for education in the United States approached three billion dollars.

Higher education flourished in spite of the indifference toward it exhibited in many of the lower schools. During that **Colleges and** part of the twentieth century **Universities** which preceded the outbreak of the First World War the number of students enrolled

John Dewey, Columbia University philosopher and educator, was the chief protagonist of progressive education.

in colleges and universities increased from about 114,000 to nearly a quarter of a million. The years of American participation in the war diminished somewhat the rate of acceleration, but after the war was over, the rise began again, and until 1929 continued at about the rate of an additional quarter of a million every five years. Junior colleges were provided in many states so that the first two years of a college course could be obtained by great numbers of students without the necessity of leaving home. State teachers' colleges, designed to provide the proper "teacher training" for those whose duty it would be to put the new principles of education into effect, also multiplied amazingly. Graduate schools, with courses leading to the master's or the doctor's degree, appeared in all the larger universities, and the Ph.D. degree became almost as essential for the aspirant to a college instructorship as the teacher's certificate to the beginner in the public schools.

In spite of their steady flow of customers the institutions of higher education in the United States were subjected to endless criticism. The elective system by which students were permitted to collect a hodgepodge of relatively unrelated courses toward a baccalaureate degree was denounced as warmly as in the days of President Eliot. To some observers the dominance of sports and society on college campuses constituted the principal shortcoming of higher education; others were disagreeably impressed by the ages-old tendency of youth to flirt with radical ideas. Probably most college students expected as a result of their educational endeavors to get a better job than would otherwise have been open to them. Many "bread-and-butter" courses aided them in this ambition, but wise employers recognized that a four years' residence in a stimulating environment was in itself a valuable experience. The advent of the depression at first cut down materially on college and university enrollments, but not many institutions actually went under, and the students soon returned. It should be noted that college faculties were for the most part concerned not merely with instruction, but also with research. A large proportion of the discoveries in pure science, and a still larger proportion of the exploratory ventures in other fields, were the contributions of university professors. To a considerable extent on this account, most of the great foundations for philanthropy, such, for example, as those established by Rockefeller, Carnegie, and Ford, continued their interest in higher education.

Perhaps the most successful of the achievements that stemmed from the educational world lay in the realm of science Scientific and health. The diagnosis of achievements deep-seated disease, and sometimes the cure also, received an enormous impetus from the steady improvement in x-ray technique; the discoveries of bacteriologists sent such dread diseases as diphtheria into the discard along with typhoid and malaria, and tremendously reduced the toll taken by most of the contagions from which children suffered; the significance of vitamins in food was carefully explored and the results made available to the public; the employment of blood transfusions was greatly facilitated by the proper attention to blood-matching; and the use

Literature. *Following the First World War such novelists as Fitzgerald and Lewis shared with other intellectuals the spirit of disillusionment that pervaded the times, but the excellence of their craftsmanship belied their pessimism. Frost was four times the recipient of the Pulitzer Prize for poetry, and Lewis was the first American to receive the Nobel Prize in Literature.*

SCOTT FITZGERALD. Reflecting the glitter of the twenties, his writing was perhaps the best literary mirror of the time. John Held, Jr., was a popular cartoonist of the jazz age.

SINCLAIR LEWIS. His broad satire and photographic realism made him an influential critic of American foibles. One of his best-known novels was *Main Street*.

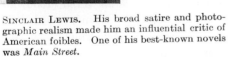

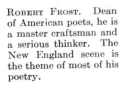

ROBERT FROST. Dean of American poets, he is a master craftsman and a serious thinker. The New England scene is the theme of most of his poetry.

of sulfa drugs and penicillin greatly diminished the danger of death from infections. In making these and a thousand other advances, the scientific world worked together without regard for international barriers, but to the sum total of advancement American investigators contributed an honorable part, while in the United States more than in most nations the results of medical knowledge were made immediately available to the masses. Hospital facilities were provided for those who could pay for them, and in most instances also for those who could not. Rising standards in medical education meant better physicians, and the attention to health given in the schools bore significant results. Americans lived longer. Between 1901 and 1927 the average life expectancy in the United States rose from forty-nine to fifty-nine years; by 1935 it had risen to sixty years, and by 1950 to sixty-eight. The increasing number of deaths from such diseases as cancer and heart ailments proved merely that more people were living long enough to die from the afflictions of old age.

American literature The First World War served in a general way to mark the beginning of a new era in American literature. Mark Twain died in 1910 and William Dean Howells in 1920. With their passing the generation of writers that dated from the period of the Civil War and Reconstruction had practically disappeared. The new generation was deeply influenced by the social conflicts that developed out of the machine age, conflicts that the world's descent into war served so greatly to accentuate. In the novel they found their best medium of expression, and in their desire to be true to reality they sometimes overshot the mark. Some of them, like Frank Norris, in *The Octopus* (1901), and Winston Churchill in *Coniston* (1906), both of whom were impressed by the overweening power of the railroads, wrote with the muckraker's hope of reform. Others, like Jack London, in *The War of the Classes* (1905) and *The Iron Heel* (1910), saw no hope for society except in revolution. Still others were content to set forth what they saw, and to present no solution. The plight of the underdog particularly fascinated Theodore Dreiser, whose hapless characters in *An American Tragedy* (1925) might well have been copied from the crime columns of the daily newspapers, and probably were.

The passion for reality led to many re-examinations of the American past, none more fruitful than those pertaining to the frontier. Hamlin Garland's autobiographic *A Son of the Middle Border* (1917) recaptured much of the harshness of the pioneer environment, but only as an old man recounts experiences from which he emerged as a great success. Willa Cather in *O Pioneers* (1913) and *My Ántonia* (1918) strove also to strip away the glamor that had attached itself to the frontier, and in accomplishing her task displayed literary craftsmanship of a high order. James Boyd in *Drums* (1925) and *Long Hunt* (1930) did a similar, but less notably excellent, service for an earlier age. O. E. Rölvaag's *Giants in the Earth* (1927) told with stark realism the bitter struggle of the immigrant farmer against the bleak Northwest, while Mari Sandoz's *Old Jules* (1935) varied the scene to fit the conflict fought by another immigrant, the author's father, against the semi-arid, treeless plains. Ellen Glasgow, writing of the post-Civil-War South instead of the frontier, portrayed in a long series of volumes from the *Battle Ground* (1902) to *Vein of Iron* (1935) the decay of the old southern society, while Margaret Mitchell, exploiting in *Gone with the Wind* (1936) another phase of the same theme, revealed the soul-searing methods by which the New South was built.

Most American writers, however, preferred the theme of the present, although they found little in it to praise **Sinclair Lewis** and much to condemn. In rugged, forthright prose F. Scott Fitzgerald in *The Great Gatsby* (1925), John Dos Passos in *Manhattan Transfer* (1925), and Ernest Hemingway in *The Sun Also Rises* (1926) belabored the "lost generation" of which they were a part. In dealing harshly with the American scene, however, none showed greater proficiency than Sinclair Lewis. Thoroughly out of patience with the selfish commercialism that was exhibited in every phase of American life, Lewis satirized the rundown country town in *Main Street* (1920), the growing city and its prosperous "realtors" in *Babbitt* (1922), the medical profession in *Arrowsmith* (1925), the evangelical clergy in *Elmer Gantry* (1927), and the opulent American abroad in *Dodsworth* (1929). What Sinclair Lewis sought to do through fiction, Henry L. Mencken attempted in the field of criticism, first as a writer for the *Baltimore Sun*, but after 1924 as editor of an ultra-smart magazine *The American Mercury*, which for several years was the favorite diet of all who sought to appear sophisticated. Mencken's particular delight was to bait the prohibitionists, whose cant and sophistry he found it easy to expose. The prevailing literary mood of the prosperous 1920's lasted over into the depressed 1930's, with such writers as Thomas Wolfe, William Faulkner, James Farrell, and John Steinbeck adding new fuel to the flames.

American verse of merit, for the first time since the days of Bryant and Whitman, was **Poetry** again being written. Most of it, too, was deeply critical of society. Edgar Lee Masters in his *Spoon River Anthology* (1915) recited with telling irony the aimless life-histories of the people whose gravestones might be seen in any village cemetery. Vachel Lindsay in *The Congo and Other Poems* (1919) at once startled the literary world with his unusual verse forms and turned attention toward the American Negro as a theme for exploitation. Robert Frost in *North of Boston* (1914) and *New Hampshire* (1923) dealt sympathetically, but in utter realism, with the peculiarities of rural New Englanders. John G. Neihardt in *The Song of Hugh Glass* (1915), *The Song of Three Friends* (1919), and *The Song of the Indian Wars* (1925) attempted with considerable success an epic of the frontier. Stephen Vincent Benét in *John Brown's Body* (1928)

and (with Rosemary Benét) *A Book of Americans* (1933) wrote good history in vivid verse. Carl Sandburg in *The People Yes* (1936) described in homespun language the drab daily deeds of ordinary men, and dripped "corrosive sublimate" upon "formalities, conventionalities, 'stuffed shirtfronts,' the high proprieties of the high." Far out on the Pacific Coast, Robinson Jeffers couched his bitter disillusionment in allegorical verse of great power and beauty.

The United States produced also a few good playwrights. Foremost among them was Eugene O'Neill, whose long **Plays and** series of dramatic successes in- **playwrights** cluded *The Emperor Jones* (1921), *Desire Under the Elms* (1924), *Marco Millions* (1924), *The Great God Brown* (1925), *Strange Interlude* (1927), *Mourning Becomes Electra* (1931), *Ah, Wilderness!* (1932), and *Days Without End* (1933). O'Neill's plays exploited complex psychological themes, and sometimes dwelt almost morbidly upon the problems of sex. Of the many other less gifted but extremely able American playwrights perhaps Maxwell Anderson and Elmer Rice are most worthy of mention. Anderson in *What Price Glory* (1924) brought home with tremendous effectiveness the grim realities of war, including the artistic nature of military profanity, and in *Both Your Houses* (1933) skillfully satirized the national capital in the throes of the New Deal. Rice, in such plays as *On Trial* (1914), *For the Defense* (1919), and *Counsellor-at-Law* (1931), dealt understandingly with legal complications, but rose to new heights in his *Judgment Day* (1934) which courageously faced the conflicting ideologies of the international scene. In spite of strenuous competition from the movies the legitimate stage maintained its hold upon New York and Chicago audiences, while many of the more popular plays took to the road and were shown all over the country. Stock companies generally succumbed, but amateur theatricals, particularly those sponsored by the schools and colleges, flourished as never before.

American music, which for the most part

Theater. Eugene O'Neill, America's outstanding dramatist, won the Pulitzer prize in 1920 for his Broadway production, Beyond the Horizon, *and the Nobel prize in literature in 1936. His plays, which touched in turn nearly every new development in the theater, included an unusual combination of Greek tragedy and Freudian psychology.*

EUGENE O'NEILL.

SETTING FOR 'DYNAMO.' This modern stage set suggests the theme of the play — the crushing, inhuman power of the machine.

EXPERIMENT. Cover of the original program for *The Emperor Jones*, produced at Yale.

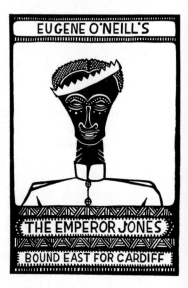

EUGENE O'NEILL'S

THE EMPEROR JONES

BOUND EAST FOR CARDIFF

Music

had been derivative throughout the nineteenth century, began during the twentieth to show encouraging signs of originality. The absorption into the American population of numerous European immigrants with musical talent, the growing availability of good music through the phonograph, the radio, and television, and the constant teaching of music, both privately and in the public schools, accustomed the American people to music of merit, and even prepared a great many of them to appreciate the efforts of innovators. Symphony orchestras, supported by only a few great cities at the turn of the century, multiplied in number until by 1951 there were no less than 659 "symphonic groups" in the country, with at least fifteen hundred different concert series in as many American towns and cities.[1] Most of the eminent conductors, however, and many of the musicians were of European extraction, while the number of works by American composers that merited production was comparatively few. Grand opera flourished where the financial strain could be borne, but its offerings were generally restricted to the great European classics. The Metropolitan Opera House in New York City, nevertheless, produced *The King's Henchman* by Deems Taylor (1885–   ) in 1927, and his *Peter Ibbetson* in 1931. These and other works by Taylor were essentially traditional in nature, but a number of Ameri-

[1] F. L. Allen, *The Big Change* (1952), p. 274.

can composers sought with determination to break with the past. Among the most successful of the innovators were Roy Harris (1898–   ), who produced four symphonies during the 1930's, Aaron Copland (1900–   ), whose numerous orchestral compositions included a notable *Third Symphony* (1946), and Roger Sessions (1896–   ), with two symphonies, a violin concerto, and much chamber music to his credit. American-born vocalists of superior talent included John Charles Thomas, Lawrence Tibbett, Rosa Ponselle, Marion Talley, Marian Anderson, Dorothy Maynor, Grace Moore, and Gladys Swarthout.

Music in lighter vein won the approval of far greater numbers of Americans, and in this the United States had much to contribute. Victor Herbert (1859–1924) wove his marvelous melodies into no less than forty much-loved operettas; John Philip Sousa (1854–1932) quickened the steps of millions of Americans with his marches, particularly *The Stars and Stripes Forever*, justly famed the whole world over; Irving Berlin (1888–   ), wrote an incredible number of popular songs, some of which, like *Alexander's Ragtime Band* (1912), won far more than temporary fame. Musical shows in an endless procession delighted American audiences. Jerome Kern (1885–1945) in *Show Boat*, with its unforgettable *Old Man River;* George and Ira Gershwin in *Of Thee I Sing* (1931); and Richard Rodgers (1902–   ) in *I'd Rather Be Right* (1937), *Oklahoma* (1943), and *South Pacific* (1949), all gauged accurately the musical taste of the public. American folk music, particularly the melodies and rhythms of the Negroes, greatly influenced the development of popular music, as it wended its way through the various stages known as ragtime, jazz, blues, swing, boogie-woogie, and be-bop. Not only the dance orchestras, which improvised elaborately on every score, but serious composers also took the new forms to heart. George Gershwin (1898–1937), after the success of his *Rhapsody in Blue*, performed by Paul Whiteman in 1924, became the outstanding exponent of the new

school. His *Porgy and Bess* (1935), a folk opera of Negro life, was increasingly recognized as an achievement of the highest merit. It was produced originally by an all-Negro cast.

American art was at last beginning to show signs of emancipation from its long apprenticeship to Europe. It is true that several American

Painting

painters of the later nineteenth century tended to be more European than American, and that some of the best of them, notably James McNeill Whistler (1834–1903), Mary Cassatt (1855–1926), and John Singer Sargent (1856–1925), preferred even to live abroad. But at home such men as Winslow Homer (1836–1910) with his water colors and scenes of the sea, John La Farge (1835–1910) with his murals, and Thomas Eakins (1844–1916) with his figures and portraits emphasized American themes and made genuine contributions, although none of them, unless possibly Eakins, broke very seriously with the past. With the coming of the twentieth century, however, the well-established revolt of European artists against traditional subject matter and techniques began to manifest itself in America in two primary movements: (1) an intense and unsentimental realism in dealing with the American scene, and (2) a reaction against naturalism which, while based on European techniques, was uncompromisingly American in content. These two movements, while working simultaneously, alternated with each other in national prominence with wave-like regularity. The first to appear was the new realism, promptly denounced by the traditionalists as the "Ash-can School," but most of its members and followers, including Robert Henri (1865–1929), John Sloan (1871–1951), and George Wesley Bellows (1882–1925), lived on to see their work regarded with admiration. The second movement came into prominence during the 1920's, notably with John Marin (1872–1953), sometimes characterized as the most distinguished American artist since Whistler, who sought to "paint not things but the experience of things, not

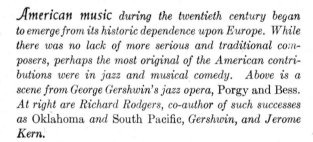

PORGY AND BESS. Scene from the original production of the jazz opera by George Gershwin which went far toward establishing a new musical form.

American music during the twentieth century began to emerge from its historic dependence upon Europe. While there was no lack of more serious and traditional composers, perhaps the most original of the American contributions were in jazz and musical comedy. Above is a scene from George Gershwin's jazz opera, Porgy and Bess. *At right are Richard Rodgers, co-author of such successes as* Oklahoma *and* South Pacific, *Gershwin, and Jerome Kern.*

the structure of the Elevated but its speed and clatter, not the height of a building but its will to outreach."[1] The 1930's saw a return to realism, headed by the "Regionalist" painters, Thomas Hart Benton (1889–) of Missouri, Grant Wood (1892–1942) of Iowa, and John Steuart Curry (1897–1946) of Kansas, who exploited Middle

[1] Oliver W. Larkin, *Art and Life in America* (1949), p. 358. By permission of Rinehart and Company, Inc.

Western themes and did much to decentralize the study of painting from eastern locations. In their wake a host of younger artists, who tended to be more interested than their European contemporaries in the social problems of the time, and who often used their talents to convey a message or to promote a cause, gave American painting an even more distinctive flavor. During the Great Depression they received unexpected encouragement and support from the Federal Art Project, which recognized the value of art to the nation and the wisdom of keeping promising artists at work. This realist movement, in its turn, was succeeded after the Second World War by a renewed interest in technical experimentation, abstraction, and expressionist distortion.

American sculpture was also coming of age. Augustus Saint-Gaudens (1849–1907),

Sculpture famous for his *Adams Monument* in Washington, his equestrian *Sherman* in New York, and his standing *Lincoln* in Chicago, had not only shown great originality in his own productions, but had also influenced deeply the development of his contemporaries and successors. Ablest of these, no doubt, was Daniel Chester French (1850–1931), who also won pre-eminence for monuments and memorials, most notably his *Minute Man* in Concord, Massachusetts, a product of his earlier years, and his *Lincoln* in the Lincoln Memorial at Washington, completed in 1920. Lorado Taft (1860–1936) not only attained distinction as a sculptor, but in two books, *Modern Tendencies in Sculpture* (1920), and *The History of American Sculpture* (1924), did much to promote a better understanding by the public of the sculptor's contribution to society. George Gray Barnard (1863–1938) did many statues of heroic proportions, among them thirty-one figures for the state capitol at Harrisburg, Pennsylvania, and a bronze *Lincoln* for Lytle Park, Cincinnati, that won both fulsome praise and bitter criticism. Gutzon Borglum (1871–1941) was best known for his colossal figures, a head of Lincoln in Washington, and the gigantic heads of Washington, Lincoln, Jefferson, and Theodore Roosevelt, carved out of "living rock" at Mount Rushmore, South Dakota. Later American sculptors, such as William Zorach, Gaston Lachaise, and Alexander Calder, broke with the academic tradition, which considered sculpture primarily in terms of public monuments and memorials, and, in line with the prevailing rejection of literalism, developed more personal and idiosyncratic styles.

The growing interest in art was reflected in the multiplication of art museums and art galleries throughout the nation. To the older, well-established museums, such as the Metropolitan Museum of Art (1870) in New York City, the Philadelphia Museum of Art (1875), the Boston Museum of Fine Arts (1870), and the Art Institute of Chicago (1879), the twentieth century added many others of consequence, among them the Cleveland Museum of Art (1913), the Baltimore Museum of Art (1914), the Detroit Institute of Art (1919), the Fine Arts Gallery (1925) in San Diego, California, and the Frick Collection (1935) in New York City. Altogether the nation could count no less than one hundred and seventy museums devoted to art. Educational institutions, from the public schools on up, accepted the fine arts into their curriculums, and often provided art galleries and art libraries for student, faculty, and public use. Private citizens of wealth invested huge sums on art collections that sooner or later were usually opened to the public. American collections naturally could not compete with the historic museums of Europe, but many Old World works of art found their way to the New, and the New World itself had much to contribute.

No doubt the greatest achievement of American art lay in the field of architecture. It was Louis Sullivan (1856– **Architecture** 1924) who more than anyone else led the way in abandoning outworn modes, and in creating new ones more in keeping with the times. In the newly conceived skyscraper he found an ideal opportunity to relate form and function. Sullivan was not the first to design a skyscraper — that honor went to William LeB. Jenney for the Home Insurance Building (1885) in Chicago, but Sullivan's Wainright Building in St. Louis, built in 1890, provided an important example both in structure and design for the guidance of other architects who attempted tall buildings. The full possibilities of the skyscraper were not realized until designers gave up the attempt to embroider

REGIONALISM. Thomas Hart Benton's *Homestead.*

IMPRESSIONISM. John Marin's water colors represent the finest of American modern. This is *Lower Manhattan.*

REALISM. George Bellows depicts a New York street, *Under the Elevated.*

their buildings with irrelevant decorations, and began to emphasize vertical lines and related masses. In 1916 New York City furnished an unexpected boon to builders when it legislated the "set-back" into existence in order to insure that some daylight should reach the city streets. This furnished an opportunity to introduce variety into architectural designs that led to notable improvements, but the skyscraper was still not without its limitations. This became abundantly apparent when William F. Lamb (1883–   ), with his Empire State Building, raised the New York skyline, perhaps for the last time, to a new altitude, 1,245 feet. The physical difficulties involved in getting so many people into and out of so large a building, and back and forth from their homes to their work, indicated clearly the desirability of smaller buildings more widely dispersed. Public buildings offered another opportunity for significant architectural innovations. Outstanding among these was the state capitol at Lincoln, Nebraska, designed by Bertram Goodhue (1869–1924), which broke the monotony of the Nebraska prairie with an imposing shaft, and provided at the same time an abundance of well-lighted office space. Its decorations, generous with color and bold in design, told in well-thought-out symbolism the history of western civilization and its impact upon the

American sculpture, while perhaps less strikingly original than American painting, was not without certain tendencies toward innovation. At one extreme Gutzon Borglum, with gigantic heads of Washington, Jefferson, Theodore Roosevelt, and Lincoln, did his "sculpture with dynamite"; at the other, Alexander Calder discarded size and weight to produce light and airy mobiles.

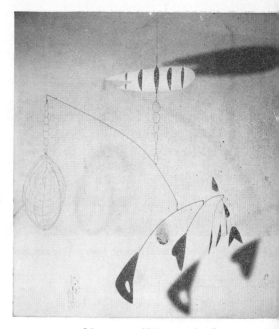

MOBILE. Abstract, fragile, and whimsical, this prototype, called *Lobster Trap and Fish Tail*, is by Alexander Calder, creator of the form. In the collection of the Museum of Modern Art.

MONUMENT. The heads of four patriots were carved in the stone side of Mt. Rushmore, South Dakota, by Gutzon Borglum.

Indian culture of the plains. In domestic architecture many influences were at work, and much mere experimentation was in evidence. At once novel and practical were the designs by one of Sullivan's pupils Frank Lloyd Wright (1869–   ), whose house on the Wisconsin River, Taliesin, was extensively copied by himself and many imitators. Wright's first principle was that a building must harmonize with its natural surroundings, and "be made to grow easily from its site."

Of tremendous interest in revealing the trend away from traditionalism in architecture toward the new ideal of "functionalism" was the Century of Progress Exposition which opened in Chicago during the spring of 1933, just forty years after Chicago's earlier world's fair had first startled the na-

Century of Progress Exposition

tion. From an architectural point of view the two expositions could hardly have stood in greater contrast. Visitors of 1893 saw a dream of classical beauty done in the purest white; visitors of 1933 saw huge, strangely shaped structures, painted with the boldest colors, and suggestive of nothing they had ever seen before. Only after nightfall, when the floodlights were loosed, could the ordinary observer appreciate the setting. But the buildings, windowless and curiously shaped as they were, served well the purposes for which they were built, a lesson that was by no means lost on the millions who saw them. Soon "modernistic" structures appeared all over the nation as architects vied with one another in the effort to make an honest adjustment of their materials to the needs they were meant to serve. The location of the Exposition also taught a lesson.

A TYPICAL FRANK LLOYD WRIGHT HOUSE.

American architecture during the twentieth century was in full revolt against the heavy and over-ornamented buildings of the "General Grant" and "Benjamin Harrison" periods. The new designers turned skyscrapers into graceful "cathedrals of commerce," broke away from the traditional dome and portico for public buildings, and constructed low-lying, functional dwelling-houses that brought indoors and outdoors together. Frank Lloyd Wright, by adapting materials, planes, and spaces to setting, helped create a new concept of domestic architecture.

NEBRASKA STATE CAPITOL. Design by Bertram Goodhue.

The land on which it stood was all "made land," dredged up from the bottom of Lake Michigan to provide a wide approach to the waterfront. After the fair was over the area was made into a city park, and still more dredged-up land was used to facilitate the construction of an elaborate system of automobile highways bordering upon the lake. City planning had made much progress since 1893, and the example of Chicago in taking better advantage of its natural setting was followed by many other cities. The Fair, in spite of the hard times, was no less successful financially than its predecessor of forty years before, and was held over for the following year.

Six years later two other American cities, San Francisco and New York, held fairs.

World's Fairs of 1939 The setting for the Golden Gate Exposition was a four-hundred-acre man-made island in San Francisco Bay, and its purpose was to show

how completely civilized western America and the Pacific Basin had become. The buildings essayed a blend of Mayan, Incan, Malayan, and other Pacific forms. In New York the "World of Tomorrow" was the principal theme of the most elaborate fair ever staged in America. The exposition grounds occupied nearly two square miles of territory in Flushing Meadows, at the very heart of Greater New York, and the project involved an expenditure of over one hundred and fifty million dollars. The buildings showed that the search for architectural innovations had by no means ceased, but the garish colors and angular lines of the Century of Progress were much toned down. Both the Golden Gate Exposition and the World of Tomorrow were reopened the succeeding year, but in spite of large attendances neither was able to duplicate the financial success of the Century of Progress.

These three world's fairs, quite apart from

the revolt they registered against architectural traditions, made significant contributions to American life. The millions who visited them came away with a better understanding of the intricate processes by which the scientific advancement of their age had been attained, and with a conviction that the wonders of the future would far surpass anything they had yet seen. They learned much, too, about the rest of the world that schoolroom lessons in geography could never have taught them, and in consequence were better prepared for the era of international change so soon to burst upon them. And whether they traveled to the East or to the West or to both, by automobile or by streamlined train or by airplane, they could hardly fail to observe the limitless resources with which their country was blessed, and the anachronism of poverty and unemployment in a land so rich.

Bibliography

An excellent general study of American society during the twenties is P. W. Slosson, *The Great Crusade and After, 1914–1928* (1930). C. A. and Mary R. Beard, *America in Midpassage* (1939), which also features social history, begins in the 1920's, where the *Rise of American Civilization* leaves off. Much useful material is presented in the President's Research Committee on Social Trends, *Recent Social Trends in the United States* (2 vols., 1933). F. L. Allen, *Since Yesterday* (1940), which opens with the Panic of 1929, is a worthy successor to *Only Yesterday*. It may be supplemented by Lawrence Greene, *The Era of Wonderful Nonsense* (1939). D. W. Brogan, *The American Character* (1944); and Graham Hutton, *Midwest at Noon* (1946), are the observations of highly intelligent British travelers. Simeon Strunsky, *The Living Tradition: Change and America* (1939), features the social aspects of American history. John Gunther, *Inside U.S.A.* (1947), is an interesting journalistic travelogue. Stimulating essays on a variety of subjects are contained in A. M. Schlesinger, *Paths to the Present* (1949); Dixon Wecter, *Changing Patterns in American Civilization* (1949); Howard Mumford Jones, *Ideas in America* (1944); and E. E. Robinson, *The New United States* (1946). On recent religious developments, see H. W. Schneider, *Religion in Twentieth Century America* (1952).

On the automobile, see Henry Ford, *My Life and Work* (1922); H. L. Barber, *Story of the Automobile* (1917); Keith Sward, *The Legend of Henry Ford* (1948); S. T. Bushnell, *The Truth about Henry Ford* (1922); and David L. Cohn, *Combustion on Wheels, An Informal History of the Automobile Age* (1944).

On the movies and the theater, Alice M. Mitchell, *Children and Movies* (1929); H. B. Franklin, *Sound Motion Pictures* (1929); W. M. Seabury, *The Public and the Motion Picture Industry* (1926); Lewis Jacobs, *The Rise of the American Film* (1939); J. W. Krutch, *The American Drama since 1918* (1939); Glenn Hughes, *A History of the American Theatre, 1700–1950* (1951); and A. H. Quinn, *A History of the American Drama from the Civil War to the Present Day* (2 vols., 1927, new ed., 1 vol., 1936).

On the radio, Paul Schubert, *The Electric Word: The Rise of the Radio* (1928); and Federal Council of the Churches of Christ in America, *Broadcasting and the Public* (1938).

On the development of the airplane, *Miracle at Kitty Hawk: The Letters of Wilbur and Orville Wright*, edited by Fred C. Kelly (1951); Jeremiah Milbank, Jr., *The First Century of Flight in America: An Introductory Survey* (1943); Fred C. Kelly, *The Wright Brothers* (1943); and Henry Ladd Smith, *Airways: The History of Commercial Aviation in the United States* (1942), which shows the similarity between early railroad and early aviation organization. The relatively slow progress of aviation in the United States, in comparison with Europe, is evident from W. J. Davis, *The World's Wings* (1927). Charles A. Lindbergh, *"We"* (1927), is the story of the author's non-stop flight across the Atlantic; his *The Spirit of St. Louis* (1953), is a much more finished account, with autobiographical flashbacks.

The literature of pessimism as applied to this period is painfully voluminous. Samples worth citing are J. T. Adams, *Our Business Civilization* (1929); Walter Lippmann, *A Preface to Morals* (1929); F. R. Kent, *Political Behavior* (1928); *Civilization in the United States: An Inquiry by Thirty Americans*, edited by H. E. Stearns (1922);

and M. A. Hallgren, *Seeds of Revolt* (1933). The nearest approach to a scientific study of the social scene is presented in R. S. and H. M. Lynd, *Middletown* (1929); and, by the same authors, *Middletown in Transition* (1937).

On prohibition, an excellent study is the Federal Council of the Churches of Christ in America, *The Prohibition Situation* (1925). Two popular accounts are Charles Merz, *The Dry Decade* (1931); and Herbert Asbury, *The Great Illusion: An Informal History of Prohibition* (1950). For the report of the Wickersham Committee, see Report of the National Commission on Law Observance and Enforcement, Seventy-first Congress, Third Session, *House Document* No. 722 (serial 9361).

On racketeering, M. A. Kavanaugh, *The Criminal and His Allies* (1928); and R. W. Child, *Battling the Criminal* (1925), are somewhat sensational in character. R. B. Fosdick, *American Police Systems* (1920); and A. A. Bruce, *The Administration of Criminal Justice in Illinois* (1929), are more dependable. Of particular interest because of its author's position is J. Edgar Hoover, *Persons in Hiding* (1938).

On education, the general works mentioned on p. 103 continue useful here. In addition to these, John Dewey, *The School and Society* (1899); and *Democracy and Education* (1916), present the author's thesis that social utility should be the principal aim of education. See also E. H. Wilkins, *The Changing College* (1927); R. L. Kelly, *Tendencies in College Administration* (1925); J. E. Kirkpatrick, *The American College and Its Rulers* (1926); R. C. Angell, *The Campus* (1928); and Raymond B. Fosdick, *The Story of the Rockefeller Foundation* (1952). Howard K. Beale, *A History of Freedom of Teaching in American Schools* (1941); and *Are American Teachers Free?* (1936), are unduly pessimistic.

Books on scientific subjects include R. T. Young, *Biology in America* (1922); *Chemistry in Medicine*, edited by Julius Stieglitz and others (1928); and L. I. Dublin, *Health and Wealth* (1928). R. H. Shryock, *American Medical Research, Past and Present* (1947); and Helen Clapesattle, *The Doctors Mayo* (1941), give good pictures of the rise of modern medicine. See also Williams Haynes, *Men, Money and Molecules* (1936).

On American literature, see for the novel A. H. Quinn, *American Fiction* (1936); F. L. Pattee, *The New American Literature, 1890–1930* (1930); J. W. Beach, *American Fiction, 1920–1940* (1941);

Percy Boynton, *America in Contemporary Fiction* (1940); Maxwell D. Geismar, *Writers in Crisis* (1942); and Harry Hartwick, *The Foreground of American Fiction* (1934). Granville Hicks, *The Great Tradition* (1933), is a left-wing view. On literature in general, see *The Cambridge History of American Literature*, edited by W. P. Trent and others (3 vols., 1936); and A. P. Hackett, *Fifty Years of Best Sellers, 1895–1945* (1945). Sterling A. Brown, A. P. Davis, and Ulysses Lee, *Negro Caravan* (1941), gives a sampling of the work of Negro writers. On American poetry, see Amy Lowell, *Tendencies in Modern American Poetry* (1917); and J. L. Lowes, *Convention and Revolt in Poetry* (1919)

On music, a valuable treatise is John T. Howard, *Our Contemporary Composers: American Music in the Twentieth Century* (3d ed., 1946). Other useful books on this subject include David Ewen, *American Composers Today* (1949); Aaron Copland, *Our New Music* (1941); Isaac Goldberg, *Tin Pan Alley* (1930); S. W. Finkelstein, *Jazz, A People's Music* (1948); and W. Sargeant, *Jazz, Hot and Hybrid* (1939).

On recent development in art John I. H. Baur, *Revolution and Tradition in Modern American Art* (1951), is outstanding. Other books of merit include *Art in America: A Complete Survey*, edited by Holger Cahill and Alfred H. Barr, Jr. (1934); Martha Cheney, *Modern Art in America* (1939); Oliver H. Larkin, *Art and Life in America* (1949); and Darrell Garwood, *Artist in Iowa: A Life of Grant Wood* (1944). On sculpture, Joseph Hudnut, *Modern Sculpture* (1929); Lorado Taft, *The History of American Sculpture* (new ed., 1930); A.V. Adams, *The Spirit of American Sculpture* (1923); and Jacques Schnier, *Sculpture in Modern America* (1948). The rôle of the government in subsidizing the arts during the depression is discussed in Grace Overmyer, *Government and the Arts* (1939); and Robert C. Binkley, *The Cultural Program of the W.P.A.* (1939). Holger Cahill, *New Horizons in American Art* (1936), shows the best work done under W.P.A. sponsorship.

On architecture, Frank Lloyd Wright, *An Autobiography* (1932); and Louis H. Sullivan, *The Autobiography of an Idea* (1924), are personal accounts by the ablest of American architects. See also T. S. Tallmadge, *The Story of Architecture in America* (1927); Frank Lloyd Wright, *Modern Architecture* (1931); Carl W. Condit, *The Rise of the Skyscraper* (1952); and *Built in U.S.A., 1932–1944*, ed. Elizabeth Mock (1944).

DEPRESSION AND WAR

1929 - 1945

The depression that began during the first years of the Hoover administration lasted on in varying degrees of intensity until the outbreak of the Second World War. Hoover as President bent every effort to restore normal times, a radical departure from the behavior of most earlier Presidents, to whom a downward turn of the business cycle was a matter for business itself to handle, rather than the government. But Hoover soon realized that without governmental intervention the whole economic structure of the nation would collapse. For the banks, the railroads, the insurance companies, and a vast number of other great business corporations to be forced into bankruptcy was a greater calamity than the government could sit idly by and permit. Furthermore, as the needs of the unemployed outran the resources of state and local authorities, the national government had to assume an increasing responsibility for the problem of relief.

The measures taken by the Hoover administration thus served as a kind of springboard for the New Deal. Under Franklin D. Roosevelt the government went much further than Hoover had contemplated in its efforts to cure the depression, but the methods of the two administrations differed more in degree than in kind. The New Deal was not nearly as revolutionary as radical theorists wished it to be, or as thoroughgoing conservatives have portrayed it. It sought to preserve, not to destroy, the capitalist system, but to achieve this end it was ready to make startling innovations. Roosevelt himself was less the theorist than the man of action, willing to try almost anything once that seemed to give promise of help, and totally unembarrassed by contradictions and inconsistencies. He hoped by economic planning and the use of governmental authority to put an end to the business cycle, to maintain full employment, and to better the lot of the underprivileged, but it was principally reform that he had in mind, not revolution. By the end of his second administration, he had achieved a great deal, but at a cost in governmental indebtedness that then seemed colossal.

The international background of the New Deal was the breakdown of world peace. While the United States had turned aside from the main currents of world affairs to enjoy the prosperity of the 1920's and to struggle against the adversity of the 1930's, the makers of national policy both in Europe and in Asia had pursued courses that could lead only to war. Russian Communism, Italian Fascism, German Naziism, and Japanese stateism all had their predatory sides; each planned to expand its system and interests at the expense of its neighbors. Against these movements the League of Nations could make only futile gestures, while in the United States the number of those who were willing to risk anything by way of collective action against the potential aggressors was small indeed. The isolationists were in the saddle; the rest of the world could have its war if it wished, but the United States would keep out.

It was apparent that Roosevelt leaned toward the side of collective security, but he was not able to secure a substantial following until war in Europe had actually broken out; then, as far as keeping the peace was concerned, it was too late. But it was not too late to show a united front toward the aggressors, and the danger to the United States involved in a complete Axis victory brought many belated conversions. With the defeat of France, the control of the Atlantic was imperiled, while in Asia Japanese conquests at the expense of China, and the will for other conquests elsewhere, made Americans realize the danger to their Pacific outposts. No doubt Roosevelt saw well in advance of most Americans the inevitability of American participation in the war, and he did what he could to prepare his countrymen for it. With the attack on Pearl Harbor, "measures short of war" gave way to war measures on a more prodigious scale than the nation had ever known before.

The war was fought through to a complete victory, both in Europe and in Asia. In the Pacific theater the United States had the chief responsibility, but chose to fight a holding war until the defeat of the Axis powers in Europe. In Europe, the United States furnished the bulk of the troops and equipment required for the invasion of North Africa and Italy, and for the cross-channel attack from England that led to Germany's defeat. For all Allied participants American supplies were of fundamental importance. To carry on these vast undertakings, the American economic machine, lagging during the depression, went at last into high gear.

26

The New Deal Begins

IN A sense Herbert Hoover rather than Franklin D. Roosevelt inaugurated the New

Hoover be-
gins the
New Deal

Deal. While the Hoover policies in some respects contrasted markedly with the Roosevelt policies, it was not Roosevelt, but Hoover, who first accepted as a governmental responsibility the task of defeating the depression. Hoover was not the only American President to face such a crisis; many of his predecessors, notably Van Buren, Grant, and Cleveland, had been depression Presidents. But none of these had regarded the elimination of hard times as a problem of government. The government merely took care of itself the best it could while the lean years lasted, and left to business the task of fighting its own way back to recovery. Whenever bankruptcies and reorganizations had reduced the debt totals to a point where business could again carry on profitably, the upward turn began. Had this normal course of liquidation been permitted after 1929, it is possible that the railroads, the life insurance companies, the building and loan associations, the savings banks, and nearly every other important type of American business might have gone down in the crash. The whole capitalistic system of economy was endangered. Fully aware of the gravity of the situation, Hoover set himself resolutely against so ruthless a

collapse and took personal charge of the fight to prevent it.

For a time the President directed his efforts mainly toward obtaining the voluntary cooperation of business and labor leaders in measures of self-help. At a series of conferences in Washington he talked against the curtailment of buying power that must inevitably follow the reduction of payrolls, and urged that "the first shock" of the depression "must fall on profits and not on wages." He insisted that wage scales ought not for the moment to be lowered at all, and that when reductions became unavoidable they should be made only in proportion as the cost of living went down. He hoped that expenditures for construction would not be curtailed, and succeeded in committing many industries to a policy of expansion in spite of the unsettled economic conditions. But "business as usual" soon proved to be a difficult formula for executives to maintain in the face of declining receipts and mounting inventories. Sometimes efforts were made to "spread the work" by lessening the number of hours per week permitted each individual, but in spite of good intentions wages did go down and unemployment figures began to mount.

Hoover was quite as much interested as Roosevelt later became in providing public

works to take up the slack of depression
Public   unemployment. As early as Jan-
works   uary, 1930, he was asking Congress to increase by huge sums its appropriations for public buildings, for the improvement of rivers and harbors, and for public
roads. He was also deeply interested in a
long-standing project for the building of a
great dam across the Colorado River below
the Grand Canyon. By this means water
could be stored up for irrigation and power
purposes, the Imperial Valley of California
could be protected from danger of overflow,
and the city of Los Angeles could be assured
an adequate water supply. Called at first
the Hoover Dam, the project was renamed
the Boulder Dam during the next administration, but the actual work of construction
began while Hoover was President, and with
his full consent and cooperation. When
finished it raised the water level of the Colorado River by nearly six hundred feet, and
was regarded as one of the greatest engineering achievements of all time.[1] Actual expenditures for public works during Hoover's
four years in office reached a total of more
than two and a quarter billion dollars, and
had much to do with unbalancing the national budget, a condition which Roosevelt
at first criticized, but later adopted as one
of the primary essentials to recovery.
Hoover was distressed that so many different
governmental agencies were carrying on
building operations, and recommended in his
annual message to Congress of December 8,
1931, that all such operations should "be
consolidated into an independent establishment under the President to be known as the
Public Works Administration directed by
a public works administrator." But the
actual establishment of the "PWA" awaited
the legislative enactments of the Roosevelt
régime.

While thus in complete sympathy with indirect aid for the unemployed, Hoover was
Relief   convinced that the responsibility
policies   for direct relief must be left as

[1] Completed in 1936, the name Hoover Dam was
restored, May 1, 1947.

fully as possible in the hands of states, municipalities, and voluntary agencies. He
feared that federal appropriations might rob
local authorities of the incentive to do what
they could, and he was convinced that the
appropriation of the huge sums it would
necessitate would not only serve further to
unbalance the budget, but would also stimulate unfortunately the "pork-barrel" instincts of Congress. Under the urging of a
voluntary "President's Emergency Relief
Organization," every locality in the country
made a desperate effort to "take care of its
own," but an abundance of evidence soon
accumulated that national aid could not be
avoided indefinitely. Some states were far
harder hit than others, and correspondingly
less able to shoulder the heavy burdens of
relief. In the mining districts of West Virginia, for example, the economic props
dropped almost completely from under many
communities, while in the ordinarily prosperous states of the lower Mississippi Valley a
drouth of unprecedented severity during the
summer of 1930 produced near-famine conditions. It was apparent that only the national government had the resources in taxes
and credit with which to meet these emergencies. By the spring of 1932 the President,
with the help of the Red Cross and local committees set up by his Emergency Relief Organization, was using the wheat and cotton
surpluses of the Federal Farm Board for
relief; when that means proved inadequate
he secured from Congress an appropriation
of three hundred million dollars to be lent
to such states as were no longer able to
finance their relief expenditures. Throughout
his administration the distribution of all relief grants remained in the hands of local
nonpartisan committees on a strictly decentralized basis. The fact that this work was
done without building up a "paid bureaucracy" of federal employees seemed to
Hoover a matter of great importance, but
before he left office the demand for precisely
the type of organization he deplored had
reached impressive proportions.

Loans to the state for relief and loans for

a great variety of other purposes were made through the instrumentality of a Reconstruction Finance Corporation, established by Congress early in 1932 at President Hoover's suggestion. The necessity of direct governmental loans to prevent the further collapse of business became apparent when a National Credit Corporation, also sponsored by Hoover, failed to mobilize resources sufficient to meet existing needs. The RFC, with Charles G. Dawes of Chicago as its first president, lent freely to banks, agricultural credit corporations, life insurance companies, and other financial organizations, and also to the hard-pressed railroads. Many bankruptcies were thus forestalled or delayed, and the President was able only with difficulty to restrain Congress from permitting RFC loans "for any conceivable purpose on any conceivable security for anybody who wants money." With his approval Congress extended the scope of the corporation to include loans to states for relief, to public and private agencies for construction work, and to prospective purchasers of agricultural commodities, both at home and abroad. Unfortunately, Congress did much to defeat the purpose of RFC loans

The RFC

to financial institutions by insisting on full publicity for all such transactions. Many banks thus lost face with their depositors, and were subjected to runs that in some cases caused them to close their doors. A large loan to the Chicago bank in which Dawes was interested convinced many critics that favoritism played an important part in obtaining RFC credits, but the loan was made after Dawes had severed his connections with the RFC, and over his protest. Loans actually disbursed before Hoover left office amounted to nearly two billion dollars.

New Dealers complained later that the chief trouble with the RFC during Hoover's administration was that it poured money into the financial structure "at the top instead of at the bottom." Businesses to which it lent were able to meet the most pressing of their obligations, but their earning power was not materially improved. Some of them, because of their unsound management and overcapitalization, might better have been permitted to fail. What was really needed, these critics maintained, was a restoration of the purchasing power of needy individuals. However this may have been, it seems evident that the lending policy of

The Hoover Dam reflects in Lake Mead the original purpose of its construction. Electrical power from its turbines is transmitted as far away as the West Coast. It set the pattern for many New Deal constructions.

the Hoover régime was the direct lineal ancestor of the pump-priming activities that so notably characterized Roosevelt's efforts to deal with the depression.

Another Hoover policy with a definitely New-Dealish flavor was embodied in the **The Home** Home Loan Bank Act of July 22, **Loan Banks** 1932. Under its terms a series of Home Loan Banks were established to discount home mortgages, and thus to provide home-owners with a service similar to that rendered by the Federal Reserve Banks in the commercial field. Building and loan associations, savings banks, insurance companies, and other dealers in home mortgages were eligible for membership in the system. Unfortunately the Home Loan Banks were not established until after thousands of home-owners had already lost their property, but when at last the banks began to operate they were able to cut down materially on foreclosures and to promote some new building. After Roosevelt became President they were permitted to continue in operation, and by 1937 they counted over four thousand mortgage-holding organizations, with loans of over a billion dollars, among their members.

While Hoover was willing to ease the credit situation of the country in a great variety of ways, he was deter- **The Bonus** mined to maintain the gold **Bill** standard and opposed with vigor a mounting demand for money inflation. This inflationary idea reached Congress by way of a plan for veterans' relief. Early in 1931 Congress voted over the President's veto to permit veterans to borrow from the government as much as fifty per cent of the face value of their bonus certificates, instead of the twenty-two and one half per cent originally authorized. This imposed upon the Treasury a cash outlay of between one and two billion dollars at a time when the government was already facing a deficit, and in spite of the fact that not more than one fifth of the veterans were in real need. But agitators soon began to insist that the veterans had been only half paid, and that if the government could not afford to pay them in any other way it should authorize an issue of fiat money. This proposal was embodied in the Patman Bonus Bill, which passed the House on July 15, 1932, under pressure of a "Bonus Expeditionary Force" of about eleven thousand men, mostly unemployed veterans, who had assembled in and near Washington to

Bonus Marchers descended upon Washington in the summer of 1932, and some lingered on until they were dispersed by the United States Army. Eventually the veterans obtained most of the benefits the "BEF" sought.

collect what they insisted was due them. Ultimately the Senate rejected the Patman Bill, but the BEF stayed on ominously. Congress then provided the President with funds to pay the way home for legitimate veterans, and by this means about half the number were induced to leave. The rest were driven from their camps and ejected from the District by the United States Army. Hoover claimed that in this action the military authorities exceeded their orders, but the incident was widely exploited as evidence of his heartlessness. By 1932, however, annual expenditures on behalf of veterans of the First World War had mounted to $860,000,000.

The attempts of Hoover's Federal Farm Board to deal with the depressed condition **Relief for** of agriculture have already been **agriculture** recounted. In addition to its activities, credits were extended through the RFC to the banks upon which the farmers depended, and to drouth-stricken sections for the purchase of such necessities as feed for livestock and seed. Hoover also negotiated a treaty with Canada for the building of a Great Lakes–St. Lawrence seaway which, when and if completed, would presumably reduce the cost of transporting middle-western crops to foreign markets.[1] Had he remained in office he was ready to organize a "land-use" program, which would aim to divert lands from unprofitable to profitable use, and to end "the cultivation of lands the chief return of which is the poverty and misery of those who live upon them." But all his plans and efforts paled into insignificance before the hard fact that farm prices refused to rise, and in many instances sank to lower figures than had been known for decades. In Iowa a Farmers' Holiday Association under the leadership of Milo Reno attempted to use the technique of the strike against production at a loss. Farmer picket-lines intercepted milk trucks on their way to market and dumped their contents into ditches. Sometimes, also,

grim groups of farmers prevented foreclosure sales by force, or excluded from them all legitimate purchasers so that they themselves might bid in the mortgaged property at nominal sums and return it to its owner.

Not all of the actions taken by the Hoover administration in its efforts to deal with the depression were concerned with internal affairs. When in March, 1931, France refused to permit Germany and Austria to unite in a customs union, a train of events was set in motion which led to the almost complete collapse of European finance. Until that time the depression had remained primarily an American affair, but from then on its world-wide character was abundantly apparent. The finances of central Europe sank first, but eventually every European nation was affected, including Great Britain, which in September, 1931, was forced to abandon the gold standard. American investors in foreign securities, particularly those of Germany, were hard hit, and American trade with Europe was more drastically curtailed than ever before.

Believing that the huge burden of intergovernmental debts constituted one of the chief impediments to world **Hoover's** trade, and therefore to world **moratorium** recovery, Hoover in June, 1931, advocated a moratorium for one year on both the principal and interest of all such obligations. This action was deeply resented by France, who wished to continue her collections from Germany, and it was far from popular in the United States; but in due time it was accepted by the fifteen governments involved and went into effect. At the Lausanne Conference of 1932 the European powers attempted to solve the debt riddle for all time by granting Germany a three-year moratorium on reparations, and by establishing a new low figure, $714,000,000, as the amount to be paid. All this, however, was contingent upon the willingness of the United States to cancel its war debts. Many American businessmen, believing that private debts from abroad could be more readily collected if the public debt were out of the

[1] This treaty remained unratified until 1954, during the Eisenhower administration.

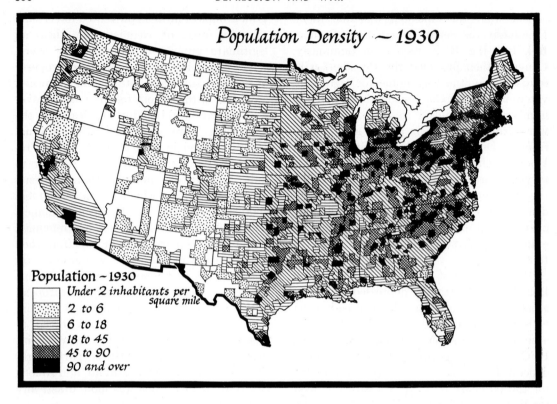

Population Density ~ 1930

Population ~ 1930
- Under 2 inhabitants per square mile
- 2 to 6
- 6 to 18
- 18 to 45
- 45 to 90
- 90 and over

way, favored cancellation, but neither Hoover nor his successor, Roosevelt, conceded this point. Reparation payments were never resumed by Germany, and when the moratorium ended in 1932 only six governments, Great Britain, Czechoslovakia, Italy, Finland, Latvia, and Lithuania, met their obligations to the United States. The next year all these nations, except Finland, made only small token payments, and after that no payments at all. The attitude of Finland, which paid in full every year, even after its territory was invaded by Russia in the winter of 1939–40, won much acclaim in the United States, but the sums involved were small. In 1934 Congress passed the Johnson Act, which prohibited Americans from purchasing the securities of any nation in default on its debt to the United States. By this time the debts in fact, if not in law, had ceased to be, and their restraining influence upon the course of international trade could not have been great.

The effect of the depression upon the polit-ical fortunes of Herbert Hoover and the party he represented was bound **Elections** to be disastrous. More and **of 1930** more the tendency grew to hold the President personally responsible for the economic difficulties from which the country suffered. His efforts to restrain the government from embarking upon a program of direct relief were cited as evidence to prove that he cared little about the sufferings of the unemployed, but much about the tax burden on the well-to-do. His nomination of Charles Evans Hughes to succeed Taft as Chief Justice was criticized as a move to strengthen the conservative majority on the Supreme Court, and was opposed by twenty-six senators, many of them Republicans. His nomination of John J. Parker of North Carolina as Associate Justice was defeated on the same ground. The mid-term elections of 1930, although held before there was any real comprehension of the seriousness of the economic situation, indicated clearly that the administration had lost the confidence of the country. The new Senate was almost evenly divided between Democrats and Republicans, but among the latter there were perhaps a dozen insurgents whose denunciations of Hoover often exceeded the fiercest outbursts of the Democrats. In the House an overwhelming Republican majority was turned into a minority, and a Democratic Speaker, John N. Garner of Texas, was chosen. In spite of frequent protestations that they had no intention of hampering the President in his efforts to deal with the depression, the Democrats, both in and out of Congress, were not unmindful of their opportunity to return to power, and gave the administration only the most temperate cooperation.

When the time came for the presidential campaign of 1932, the Republicans had no **Presidential** choice but to stand on their **nominations** record. Meeting at Chicago on **of 1932** June 14, they renominated both Hoover and Curtis, and gave unstinted praise to the policies that had guided the country through the past four years. By this time the breakdown of prohibition was generally conceded, and the Republican platform promised to submit a repeal amendment, although leaving individual members of the party free to decide for themselves whether to support it or not. Interest centered on the Democratic Convention, which met later in the month, also in Chicago. Its nominee most careful observers believed to be certain of victory. Among the more prominent aspirants for the honor were Speaker Garner, to whom William Randolph Hearst had given his blessing; Alfred E. Smith, the unsuccessful nominee of four years before; Newton D. Baker, Secretary of War under Wilson; Governor Albert Ritchie of Maryland; and Governor Franklin D. Roosevelt of New York. It soon developed that the active pre-convention work of James A. Farley, Roosevelt's campaign manager, had given the New York governor a commanding lead over all the rest, and after the third ballot a deal with the Garner forces resulted in the ticket of Roosevelt

and Garner. The Democratic platform denounced the Republicans for their policy of "economic isolation," accused them of favoritism to monopolies, and held their administration of the government strictly responsible for "a state of financial distress unprecedented in peace times." By way of remedy the Democrats promised among other things a competitive tariff for revenue, reciprocal trading agreements, more adequate relief for the unemployed, effective assistance to agriculture, the regulation of stock exchanges, the repeal of prohibition, the reform of the banking system, and "an immediate and drastic reduction of governmental expenditures."

In Franklin D. Roosevelt (1882–1945), the Democrats had a candidate whose picturesque career rivaled that of **Franklin** his distant relative, Theodore **D. Roosevelt** Roosevelt. Born to a comfortable fortune, as the other Roosevelt had been also, he was a graduate of Groton and Harvard, had been frequently abroad, spoke French almost as fluently as English, and had acquired at least an elementary knowledge of the law. In 1905 he had married his sixth cousin, Eleanor Roosevelt, a favorite niece of the President's; and, like the other Roosevelts, they became the parents of a large and versatile family. Young Roosevelt, although a Democrat by birthright, never disguised his admiration for the President whose name he bore, and tended consciously or unconsciously to pattern after him. In 1910 he was a member of the New York legislature, and won the undying enmity of the Tammany machine by his fight against its candidate for the United States Senate, William F. Sheehan. Partly because his name was Roosevelt, and partly because he knew about ships, he became Assistant Secretary of the Navy under Woodrow Wilson, a post of great responsibility which he filled with ability during the First World War. In 1920 he was the unsuccessful Democratic candidate for Vice-President, and after the campaign made preparations for a business career.

The transformation of Roosevelt from a defeated minor politician to a dynamic leader of men was promoted rather than retarded when he was laid low in August, 1921, by an attack of infantile paralysis that left him hopelessly crippled in both legs. By an unsurpassed exhibition of will power he fought his way back to health and even learned to walk again, although not without need of firm support. Utterly unconquered in spirit, he read widely, corresponded with the leaders of the Democratic Party, and dedicated himself to its rebuilding along liberal lines. In 1928, although he was not sure that his recovery was sufficiently complete to warrant it, he consented to run for governor of New York, largely because Alfred E. Smith, his close personal and political friend, believed that Roosevelt's name on the Democratic ticket would help his own chances of carrying the state. To the surprise of all concerned, except possibly Roosevelt himself, Roosevelt ran far better than Smith and survived the Hoover landslide. As governor for only four years, and that in the midst of the depression, he inaugurated few policies of note, but his ability to deal adroitly with all matters affecting human nature, his unfailing good humor, and his consuming interest in new ideas made him a marked man. He alone of all the candidates for the Democratic nomination afforded any real contrast to Hoover. Just what he might do as President no one, perhaps not even he himself, could be quite sure. But the fear that he would use his remarkable powers of leadership to promote untried and unorthodox policies led conservative Democrats to oppose his nomination with every weapon at their command. To their dismay he had the votes. Alfred E. Smith, although once Roosevelt's friend, stood out to the end against him, and after the nomination gave him only the most grudging support.

At the outset of the campaign Hoover really seemed to think that he had a chance **The** to win. He even turned over **campaign** the work of campaigning to sub-ordinates, and refused for weeks at a time to be drawn away from his desk in Washington. But Roosevelt, although convinced that only the gravest misstep could prevent a Democratic victory, launched a slashing attack. Unwilling to await the normal formalities of notification, he flew to Chicago in order to accept the nomination in person before the Democratic Convention adjourned. It was here that he first promised the country a "New Deal," and throughout the campaign he made the need for new men and new measures his central theme. He drew about himself a "brain trust" of "bright young men," including Raymond Moley, Rexford G. Tugwell, and Adolph A. Berle, Jr., who helped him formulate his plans and work up his addresses. He made campaign speeches the country over, traveling in all some twenty-five thousand miles before the day of election. He excoriated the Hoover administration with telling effect:

I sum up the history of the present administration in four sentences: First, it encouraged speculation through its false economic policies; second, it attempted to minimize the crash and misled people as to its gravity; third, it erroneously charged the cause to other nations of the world; and finally, it refused to recognize and correct the evils at home which had brought it forth: it delayed relief, it forgot reform.

Read in retrospect, Roosevelt's speeches did far more to outline a program of action than many who heard them realized. They were in fact, as one observer noted, "almost without parallel for their comprehensiveness." They amplified the very specific demands of the Democratic platform, and presented the case for such innovations as governmental operation of Muscle Shoals. They also sought to elaborate a New Deal philosophy to set over against Hoover's somewhat discredited "rugged individualism." But what Roosevelt had in mind was not some new and revolutionary system, but rather a modified capitalism. By more careful economic planning he believed that the booms and crises from which earlier generations had suffered could be averted; furthermore, the government, if need be, must use its power to prevent the predatory few from taking away all chance of prosperity from the less successful many. To attain these ends what was needed was to adapt "existing economic organizations to the service of the people."

Every man has a right to life, and this means he has a right to make a comfortable living. He may by sloth or crime decline to exercise that right; but it may not be denied him.

Every man has a right to his own property; which means the right to be assured, to the fullest extent attainable, in the safety of his savings. By no other means can men carry the burdens of those parts of life which, in the nature of things, afford no chance of labor; childhood, sickness, old age. In all thought of property, this right is paramount; all other property rights must yield to it.

Driven to defend himself by the Roosevelt onslaught, and at last fully aware of his diminishing chances, Hoover also took the stump. If the Democrats should win, he told the country, "the grass will grow in the streets of a hundred cities, a thousand towns." But under Republican rule, he claimed, the depression was already beginning to lift. He pointed with considerable pride to the various measures his administration had taken to speed the return of prosperity. To deal with the international aspects of the situation he promised American participation in a World Economic Congress, already called, through which the stabilization of currencies was to be achieved and the way paved for a recovery in world trade. During the early months of the campaign there were some indications that the tide had turned, and that prosperity really was "just around the corner," as the President seemed to think. But before election day the downward trend began anew, and with this development the Republicans saw their last faint hope disappear. The audiences that Hoover faced during the closing days of the campaign saw before them a broken and defeated man, and his voice over the radio

sounded tired and weak. Roosevelt, on the other hand, impressed the public everywhere with his confidence and charm, and as a radio speaker his technique was unsurpassed.

There was really only one issue in the election — the depression. For year after year the number of persons out of work had mounted, until by 1932 many who had scarcely dreamed that want could come to them were face to face with the stark reality. For those at the bottom of the economic ladder who were already accustomed to frequent unemployment, the experience was not altogether unnatural; even during the prosperous 1920's the average annual number of unemployed was estimated at about two and one half millions. But as the depression deepened, people who had never known unemployment before lost their jobs, used up their savings or lost them when banks folded up, cashed in their life insurance, gave up their partly-paid-for homes and farms because they could not continue the payments. Far up into the ranks of the middle classes the dread calamity struck. When a man lost his job, he could not, as formerly, go out and find another. For months he would try, then finally, broken in spirit, would likely give up and stay home, if he had a home. Tramps abounded, panhandlers plied the streets, transients slept on the steps of public buildings, on park benches or lawns, along the highways. Once prosperous factories were closed, their windows broken out or boarded up; mines were no longer worked, or were worked only part time; steel mills, iron foundries, every variety of indusrial plant put out only a fraction of the goods they were geared to produce; trains ran with only a handful of passengers or with a pitiful quantity of freight; automobiles degenerated to jallopies; stores lacked customers and many of them closed their doors; ships stayed in port; hospitals were half-empty, not because their facilities were unneeded, but because people could not afford them; hotels and restaurants, along with every kind of luxury business, went bankrupt. Under these circumstances the party in power had no faintest chance to win. Whether the Republicans were responsible for the existing conditions, or not, mattered little. People wanted a change. Nothing they could think of could be worse than what they had.

The certainty of a Roosevelt landslide was recognized well before the election. Be-

The Democratic landslide sides the solid South that any Democratic candidate could normally expect to carry, there appeared to be in the making an equally solid West. Such insurgent Republicans as Norris of Nebraska, LaFollette of Wisconsin, Johnson of California, and Cutting of New Mexico came out openly for Roosevelt, and millions of ordinary voters prepared to cast a Democratic ballot for the first time in their lives. In the industrial centers of the East the forces of discontent also played into Roosevelt's hands. When the vote was counted, it was apparent that Hoover had been as badly defeated by Roosevelt as four years before Smith had been defeated by Hoover. The electoral vote stood 472 to 59, and the popular vote, 22,809,638 to 15,758,-901. Hoover carried only six states, Maine, New Hampshire, Vermont, Connecticut, Delaware, and Pennsylvania. Both houses of Congress were as overwhelmingly Democratic as they had been Republican four years before, and in the states the Democratic landslide carried into office many candidates who had regarded their names on the party ticket as either a courtesy or a joke. In general, the dissatisfied elements of society supported Roosevelt, but the existence of a small more radical minority was revealed by the vote of 884,781 for Norman Thomas, the Socialist candidate, and 102,991 for William Z. Foster, the Communist.

According to the Republican version, it was the prospect of Roosevelt's election, cli-

The "lame-duck" amendment maxed by the election itself, which gave the final blow to business confidence, and caused the very bottom to drop out of the depression. Worst of all, the discredited Hoover administration, together with the Congress that had been elected in 1930, must remain in office for nearly four months; until March 4, 1933, the New Deal that the election had demanded could not be dealt. Foreseeing just such a situation, Senator George W. Norris of Nebraska had for years been pressing upon Congress an amendment to the Constitution which would do away with the "lame-duck" session of Congress after the election, and would permit the newly chosen President, Vice-President, and members of Congress to take office in January instead of in March. Finally in March, 1932, the Norris proposal was submitted to the states for adoption, and on February 6, 1933, it was proclaimed in effect as the Twentieth Amendment to the Constitution. But its adoption came too late to save Hoover and the "lame-duck" Congress that assembled in December, 1932, from the embarrassment of having to deal with a crisis after they had been discredited by a vote of no confidence.

How to meet the pressing problems before him under such a handicap gave Hoover much concern. He might have **Hoover and** followed the course that Presi- **Roosevelt** dent Wilson was said to have had in mind should Hughes have won the election of 1916. The President could have appointed the President-elect Secretary of State, after which both the President and the Vice-President could have resigned. According to the law the Presidency would then have devolved upon the newly chosen head of the cabinet.[1] Probably a procedure so out of keeping with American tradition was possible only in theory, and it was certainly given little, if any, consideration. But Hoover did hope to secure the cooperation of the President-elect in deciding important matters of state. First, he invited Roosevelt to confer with him at the White House on the war debts question, which Great Britain and most of the other nations concerned were determined to reopen at once. Roosevelt accepted the President's invitation, but he refused to commit his ad-

[1] The law has since been changed to provide that in such a case the succession would fall to the Speaker of the House rather than the Secretary of State.

UNEMPLOYMENT.
Unable to earn even
the bare necessities,
thousands stood in
line for free but
meager meals.

APPLE-SELLERS. Unemployed
were given a quota of apples to
sell in the streets to the more
fortunate.

The depression brought *humiliating
want to hundreds of thousands of Americans who had never before known what it
meant not to be able to earn their own
livings. Breadlines, apple-sellers, and
panhandlers appeared in every American
city. Literally millions of people were on
relief.*

RELIEF. In the depth of the
depression, local and federal relief
was extended to numbers never
equalled in this country before or
since.

ministration in advance to anything more
specific than a willingness to discuss war
debts and other economic problems with a
British representative soon after March 4.
Hoover tried also to induce Roosevelt to join
with him in an effort to check the spread of
bank failures during February, 1933, a condition which privately the President attributed to "the breakdown of public confidence
in the new administration now coming in."
What Hoover really wanted was a statement
from Roosevelt that he would not countenance money inflation, an unbalanced budget,

or the flotation of loans so heavy as to impair
the credit of the government. In view of the
later policies of the Roosevelt administration
it is not surprising that the President-elect
side-stepped this suggestion. As Hoover
himself admitted, it would have meant the
"abandonment of ninety per cent of the
so-called New Deal." Congress, too, now
more responsive to the wishes of Roosevelt
than to the pleas of the President, turned
down the latter's recommendations for reduced expenditures and new taxes to balance
the budget, for a complete reorganization of

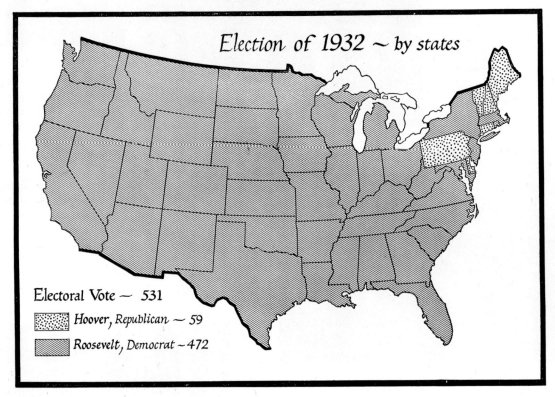

Election of 1932 ~ by states

Electoral Vote — 531

Hoover, Republican — 59

Roosevelt, Democrat ~ 472

the executive departments, and for such reforms in the nation's financial system as, he believed, would put an end to bank failures.

Whether it was fair or not to blame the banking crisis that had developed upon an **The banking** administration that had not yet **crisis** taken office, there could be no doubt as to the gravity of the situation. Unemployment was at its worst during the winter of 1932–33, with the number of men out of work estimated at anywhere from thirteen million to seventeen million. Production in one great industry after another dropped to almost negligible proportions. Fear that the financial structure of the country was endangered showed in the mounting totals of gold exported and of gold and currency hoarded; by the middle of February each item had grown to about fifteen million dollars a day. In Detroit, where the drastic curtailment of automobile production had created a peculiarly difficult situation, the banks held on grimly, but by Lincoln's Birthday they were near the breaking point.

Loaded down with frozen assets and drained of their deposits by frightened customers, they escaped collapse only when the governor of the state on his own authority extended the holiday period by eight days, and then obtained from the legislature the right to prolong it if need be still further. With the Michigan banks suspended, the panic spread to one state after another, and nearly every state executive declared a long bank holiday. Meantime, President Hoover, unable to secure any cooperation from the President-elect, watched helplessly while the financial machinery of the nation came virtually to a standstill. When Roosevelt took office the zero hour had seemingly been reached.

Whatever unwillingness he might have shown to accept responsibility before he took office, the new President showed **Roosevelt's** no such hesitation after March 4, **cabinet** 1933. His cabinet included none of the great names — Owen D. Young, Newton D. Baker, John W. Davis, Alfred E. Smith, and the like — pressed upon him by those who doubted his ability, and showed his evident determination to be his own master. Cordell Hull of Tennessee, the Secretary of State, was a dependable party wheel-horse devoted to the now almost forgotten low-tariff views of the party. William H. Woodin, the Secretary of the Treasury, was a New York banker who had always been regarded as a Republican; because of ill-health he was soon replaced by a personal friend of the President's, Henry Morgenthau, Jr., also of New York. Two other ex-Republicans were included, Harold L. Ickes of Illinois, the Secretary of the Interior, and Henry A. Wallace of Iowa, the Secretary of Agriculture. Both were previously unknown to national politics, although Wallace succeeded to the post his father had held in the Harding administration. James A. Farley, now national chairman of the Democratic Party, became Postmaster-General and chief dispenser of the patronage. For the first time a woman, Frances Perkins (Mrs. Paul Wilson), the new Secretary of Labor, received a cabinet assignment, to the considerable distaste of organized labor, which had tried in vain to dictate a different choice. The one really outstanding figure that the President had meant to include in his official family, Thomas J. Walsh of Montana, who had been slated for the attorney-generalship, died a few days before inauguration. All observers agreed that the President's private "brain trust" would have much more to do with the shaping of his policies than the somewhat nondescript cabinet he had constructed.

But there was no lack of presidential leadership. In his inaugural address the President alluded to the possibility that the "need for undelayed action" might call for a "temporary departure" from the "normal balance of executive and legislative authority." He was ready, if need be, to ask Congress for "the one remaining instrument to meet the crisis — broad executive power to wage a war against the emergency as great as the power that would be given me if we were in fact invaded by a foreign foe." The next day after

The Emergency Banking Act

James A. Farley was Roosevelt's campaign manager, patronage broker, and Postmaster-General, but opposed the third term.

the inauguration the President closed every bank in the country, and by the time he had assembled Congress in special session on March 9 he had ready for instant passage an Emergency Banking Act. Breaking all known records, the law received the President's signature before the day was over. This measure authorized the Secretary of the Treasury to call in all gold, whether in the shape of coin, bullion, or gold certificates; it provided for the examination and reopening of all banks deemed sound, and for a system of "conservators" to take charge of all others; and it authorized an extensive issue of emergency currency to be used if necessary in halting runs. By March 13, such banks as federal examiners found solvent began to reopen, and the government's guaranty of their stability proved sufficient to restore public confidence. Only fifteen million dollars' worth of the new emergency currency had to be used, and millions of dollars that the banks had paid out during the crisis to anxious depositors began to flow back. Some three thousand banks, scattered throughout the country, were either reopened under conservators or were not reopened at all, but there was no longer any reason to doubt the essential soundness of the banking structure, and business proceeded as usual.

Before the end of March the President had pressed three other emergency measures **The Economy Act** through Congress. The first of these was an Economy Act by which he hoped to accomplish the "immediate and drastic reduction of government expenditures," promised by the Democratic platform, and repeatedly described by Roosevelt during his campaign as a fundamental necessity to recovery. The national debt had mounted rapidly during the Hoover administration, from $17,343,850,202 when he took office to $20,937,350,964, when he retired. This meant an increase of $3,593,-500,762 during the four years, nearly three fourths of which was due to expenditures undertaken during Hoover's last year to promote recovery and to provide relief. Whatever he might have thought during the campaign, the President now recognized the necessity of stupendous expenditures for relief, but he advocated a double-entry system of accounting by which emergency expenditures should be separated from ordinary expenditures, and budget-balancing confined strictly to the latter. The Economy Act, signed on March 20, authorized the President to cut salaries as much as fifteen per cent, to reduce payments to veterans, especially for non-service-connected disabilities; and to reorganize administrative agencies with economy in mind. Under its terms Roosevelt saved $125,000,000 on salaries and $300,000,000 on pensions in spite of the violent outcries of office-holders and ex-soldiers. Never before in the history of the country had pension payments been reduced, and as events were soon to prove they were not now reduced for long. Naturally many critics found fault with Roosevelt's plan for maintaining both a balanced and an unbalanced budget, but the public as a whole accepted his theory that the depression, like a war, must be fought to a finish, regardless of the emergency expenditures involved.

The Beer Act, passed on March 22, was heralded as a revenue measure, although in reality its chief purpose was to **The Beer Act** break down as far as was constitutionally possible the effectiveness of the Prohibition Amendment. The rigid one half of one per cent alcoholic content by which an intoxicating beverage had been previously defined was changed to three and two tenths by weight, and appropriate taxes were levied on the manufacture of beer and wine in such states as might permit it. The revenues derived from this measure were inconsequential, but the process of repeal went on with the greatest of speed. For this purpose the "lame-duck" session of Congress that had just ended had submitted a Twenty-first Amendment to the Constitution, with the proviso that it should be ratified by special state conventions, instead of in the customary way by the action of state legislatures. Thus each state was able to vote directly on the question of repeal. It was soon apparent what the verdict would be, but not until December 6, 1933, did the Twenty-first Amendment become a part of the Constitution.

The third of these emergency measures, signed March 31, 1933, was a pet project of the President's, to which he had **The CCC** alluded early in his campaign. It created a Civilian Conservation Corps, the purpose of which was to establish reforestation camps in every part of the country to provide work for unmarried young men between the ages of eighteen and twenty-five who were without employment. The CCC soon had more than a quarter of a million youths at work under army officers, clearing forests, planting trees, improving roads, preventing floods, and performing other equally useful tasks. Enlistments were for one year. The men received a dollar a day each in addition to medical care and maintenance, but were required to allot twenty-five dollars a month to dependents or relatives. Some observers saw in the move a surreptitious effort to strengthen the United States Army, but in general the CCC more than justified the President's hopes. Thousands of young men who had roamed the city streets searching in vain for jobs, or with too frequent success for trouble, thus found something worthwhile to do. Most of them were immensely improved in health and morale as a result of their experience, and there was no dearth of volunteers. By 1935 the original enrollment had been doubled, and the country had come to regard the CCC less as an emergency measure of relief than as a permanent American institution. But on June 30, 1942, with the youth of the land caught up in the Second World War, the agency was allowed to die for lack of a congressional appropriation.

During the few weeks necessary to push these measures to enactment, the President **Presidential leadership** had demonstrated ably his capacity for leadership. Relying as he must on the support of public opinion, he showed an unerring sense of the dramatic. Whether in a radio appeal to the nation or in a personally delivered message to Congress, he never failed to time his pronouncements exactly and irresistibly right. He held frequent conferences with the representatives of the press, took them freely into his confidence, made them like him, and obtained through them a steady stream of favorable publicity. Like Theodore Roosevelt and Woodrow Wilson before him, he had no scruples as to the constitutional right of the Executive to direct the course of legislation. His energetic "brain-trusters," sometimes without much help from congressional committees, drafted the laws that Congress was called upon to pass. Whenever he could he used the same tactics on legislators that he used on newspapermen, but he was entirely capable of sterner measures. Farley, his patronage broker, kept books on every congressman, and it was an open secret that those who voted with the President could hope to have their recommendations for appointments honored, while those who voted against him could not. The President knew, too, that the best time to get his program through was while the country still regarded the steps taken as essential to meet an emergency, and while congressmen, with their hunger for patronage unappeased, were unwilling to interrupt the "honeymoon" period with which each new administration begins. To forestall long debates over bothersome details he frequently induced Congress to delegate much discretionary authority to the President himself, or to some executive officer. Thus many of the New Deal measures were passed in more or less skeleton form, with the details to be filled in later by the President and his advisers. Operating in this hasty fashion the special session of Congress enacted into law within a hundred days the principal policies of the New Deal.

The Emergency Banking Act foretold at the very outset the direction in which the New Deal was to go. With the **Direction of** whole financial system in a state **the New** of collapse, the President might **Deal** have turned toward the left, with social revolution somewhat after the Russian pattern as his goal. Had he directed Congress to nationalize the banking system, a long step toward the state ownership and administration of all industry and finance would have been taken. He might also have turned to the right, toward what, in contrast with com-

The Civilian Conservation Corps afforded employment to many young men and performed valuable service to the country as a whole.

Franklin D. Roosevelt

THIRTY-SECOND PRESIDENT of the United States, Roosevelt was the first President to break the third-term tradition. The outbreak of the Second World War accounted mainly for his third nomination and election, and the involvement of the United States in the war for his fourth. Few other American Presidents have been so deeply loved or so roundly hated. He succeeded to a remarkable degree in capturing the confidence of the underprivileged, and in inspiring the intense dislike of those who defended the rights of property.

munism, was currently called fascism, and drew its inspiration from the exploits of Mussolini in Italy. His goal then would have been to preserve the private profit system at the expense, if need be, of democracy. But neither communism nor fascism had any deep rooting in America, and one seemed as likely as the other to develop into an irresponsible dictatorship. There is no evidence that Roosevelt considered either. What he proposed was a middle course, more in line with American precedents. The business of the nation should be left in private hands, but controls should be set up by the government to prevent the ever-recurring booms and crises from which capitalism had suffered so long. Extreme individualism had already been limited by extensive governmental regulation; what Roosevelt had in mind was to extend regulation to the point

where it would result in a planned economy. The powers of government would be amplified, but the rights of the individual would not be destroyed. In addition to this interest in permanent reform, the President was determined also to make more adequate provision for the relief of the unemployed, and to promote by every means at his disposal the restoration of a normal business prosperity.

Very early in his administration the President was called upon to decide whether he could achieve these objectives **The London** and at the same time carry on a **Economic** program of international coop- **Conference** eration. Apparently he at first thought that the two were not incompatible. He accepted, seemingly without reservation, the commitments of his predecessor with respect to American participation in the World Economic Conference to be held in London during the summer of 1933. He received cordially the British Prime Minister, J. Ramsay MacDonald, who visited Washington in April to discuss plans for the conference, and a little later he gave equally friendly audiences to the special emissaries of France, Italy, Germany, and Japan. He even showed some disposition to extend the scope of the conference to include the revision of war debts, and he appointed as head of the American delegation the Secretary of State, Cordell Hull, whose devotion to tariff reduction and the reopening of world trade amounted almost to a religion. The conference opened auspiciously on June 12, and in spite of much jockeying for position on the part of participants, its sessions seemed by no means destined to futility. Roosevelt proclaimed publicly his belief that its duty was to "establish order in place of the present chaos by a stabilization of currencies, by freeing the flow of world trade, and by international action to raise price-levels."

But for reasons not entirely clear Roosevelt turned away from the international approach to war on the depression, and decided that the United States must work its way back to prosperity alone. Perhaps his change of mind was due to his decision to devalue the dollar, a measure that was sure to upset currency exchange and irritate foreign governments. Perhaps also he was disgusted with the way in which some nations, in response to his suggestion of a tariff truce to precede the Conference, first raised their tariff rates, then accepted his proposal. Whatever the explanation, early in July he cut the ground completely from under Secretary Hull by renouncing any considerable interest in the stabilization of currencies, and by asserting his determination to seek recovery in America through the establishment of a "sound internal economic system." Whatever the motives that led the President to this decision, it was a fact that the program of legislation he had pushed through Congress was based on the assumption that the United States must "go it alone." For the moment international cooperation was to be side-tracked and economic isolation given a trial. Since American assistance was fundamental in the development of any world program, there was nothing left for the London Conference to do but to wind up its affairs and go home. To the surprise of most observers Secretary Hull resisted the temptation to resign from the cabinet, while Raymond Moley, the "brain-truster" who was credited with bringing about Roosevelt's change of front, soon lost favor with the President and returned to private life.

Bibliography

References for the preceding chapter apply also to those aspects of the Hoover administration treated in this chapter. A useful documentary record of the Hoover administration is provided in *The State Papers and Other Public Writings of Herbert Hoover* (2 vols., 1934). Hoover's political career was the subject of a number of ephemeral biographies, for example: T. G. Joslin, *Hoover, Off the Record* (1934); W. W. Liggett, *The Rise of Herbert Hoover* (1932); Clement Wood, *Herbert Clarke Hoover: An American Tragedy* (1932); Herbert Corey, *The Truth about Hoover* (1932); and Eugene Lyons, *Our Unknown Ex-President* (1948). On Hoover's problems with the veterans, see W. W. Waters, *B.E.F.: The Whole Story of the Bonus Army* (1933). A useful handbook on the campaign of 1932 is R. V. Peel and T. C. Donnelly, *The 1932 Campaign* (1935). E. E. Robinson, *They Voted for Roosevelt: The Presidential Vote, 1932–1944* (1947), provides dependable election statistics.

The active part played by the President himself during the Roosevelt administrations is apparent from *The Public Papers and Addresses of Franklin D. Roosevelt* (13 vols., 1938–1950). L. M. Hacker, *A Short History of the New Deal* (1934), furnishes an excellent summary of governmental activities during Roosevelt's first year. Basil Rauch, *A History of the New Deal, 1933–1938* (1944), is still the best work on the subject. Dixon Wecter, *The Age of the Great Depression, 1929–1941* (1948), treats of the social aspects of the New Deal; Denis W. Brogan, *The Era of Franklin D. Roosevelt: A Chronicle of the New Deal and Global War* (1950), is more concerned with politics and economics. Broadus Mitchell, *Depression Decade: From New Era to New Deal, 1929–1941* (1947), is excellent economic history.

A satisfactory analysis of the Roosevelt personality has not yet appeared. Frank Freidel, *Franklin D. Roosevelt, The Apprenticeship* (1952), and *The Ordeal* (1954), open a valuable scholarly work. Robert E. Sherwood, *Roosevelt and Hopkins: An Intimate History* (1948), is by all odds the best book on Roosevelt to date, but it is warmly pro-Roosevelt and pro-Hopkins. *F. D. R.: His Personal Letters, 1905–1945*, edited by Elliott Roosevelt (4 vols., 1947–50), provide much inside information. Books about Roosevelt, none of them notably good, are legion, for example: Emil Ludwig, *Roosevelt: A Study in Fortune and Power* (1941); Alden Hatch, *Franklin D. Roosevelt, An Informal Biography* (1947); E. K. Lindley, *Franklin D. Roosevelt: A Career in*

Progressive Democracy (rev. ed., 1934); G. W. Johnson, *Roosevelt: Dictator or Democrat?* (1941); and John Gunther, *Roosevelt in Retrospect* (1950).

Those associated in any way with Roosevelt could rarely resist the temptation to write a book about their experiences. Among the many volumes of this kind, perhaps the following best deserve mention: James A. Farley, *Jim Farley's Story: The Roosevelt Years* (1948); Harold L. Ickes, *The Autobiography of a Curmudgeon* (1943), which stops at 1932, but is continued in "Twelve Years with FDR," *Saturday Evening Post*, June 5–July 24, 1948; and in *The Secret Diary of Harold L. Ickes* (2 vols., 1953–54); Edward J. Flynn, *You're the Boss* (1947); Samuel I. Rosenman, *Working with Roosevelt* (1952); Raymond L. Moley, *After Seven Years* (1939); Frances Perkins, *The Roosevelt I Knew* (1946); Eleanor Roosevelt, *This Is My Story* (1937); and, by the same author, *This I Remember* (1949). Bascom N. Timmons, *Garner of Texas* (1948), is a useful biography of Roosevelt's first Vice-President.

From its very inception the New Deal produced a host of interpreters and critics whose writings for the most part are best forgotten. Samples representing various points of view are as follows: C. A. Beard and G. H. E. Smith, *The Future Comes* (1933); E. K. Lindley, *The Roosevelt Revolution: First Phase* (1933); H. A. Wallace, *America Must Choose* (1934); William McDonald, *The Menace of Recovery* (1934); Walter Lippmann, *The Method of Freedom* (1934); Norman Thomas, *After the New Deal, What?* (1936). There are a few useful special studies of importance for this chapter, among them Marcus Nadler and J. I. Bogen, *The Banking Crisis* (1933); A. G. Mezerik, *The Revolt of the South and West* (1946); and P. L. Kleinsorge, *The Boulder Canyon Project* (1941).

The Changing Indian, edited by Oliver La Farge (1942) shows the effect of the Indian Reorganization Act of 1934.

Dwight Macdonald, *Henry Wallace: The Man and the Myth* (1948); and Russell Lord, *The Wallaces of Iowa* (1947), are useful biographies of Roosevelt's Secretary of Agriculture.

27

The New Deal in Operation

The three R's — Relief, recovery, and reform —
Relief agencies — Recovery agencies — The NRA —
The labor split — The C.I.O. — The "sit-down" strikes
— The AAA — Wheat and cotton controls — Social
changes in the South — Reform efforts— The cur-
rency — The SEC — Railroad coordination — The
merchant marine — The housing problem — National
Housing Act of 1937

IT WAS soon apparent that the New Deal had set itself the triple task of relief, recov-
The three R's ery, and reform. The legislation of the "hundred days," hastily conceived as it was, all pointed toward one or more of these objectives. Inconsistencies were frequent; relief sometimes got in the way of recovery, and recovery in the way of reform. But occasionally, also, reform meas-ures promoted recovery, and recovery al-most always helped solve the problem of relief. Whatever their contradictions and interactions, the three goals remained con-stant, and they were never long forgotten. From time to time changes based on expe-rience, or even on political expediency, ap-peared, but they were invariably defended as merely a better way of accomplishing what the New Deal had set out to do.

In the matter of relief the New Deal am-plified and extended what the Hoover ad-
Relief — FERA ministration had already begun. Through a Federal Emergency Relief Administration, created May 22, 1933, unreturnable contributions instead of RFC loans were made available to the states for relief purposes. Out of an appropriation of half a billion dollars fifty per cent was to be allotted on the basis of one dollar of federal funds for every three dollars of local money, while the remainder was to be used for direct grants to states whose relief needs exceeded their financial resources. In actual fact only three states were able to meet as much as half the cost of their relief load, and many contributed less than ten per cent. The law permitted local authorities to provide either work relief or an outright dole, but since in practice the dole was far more economical than "made work," it was used unsparingly. In February, 1934, Congress appropriated $950,000,000 more for the use of the FERA, and by the end of the year about one sixth of the population of the country was on relief. Of this number fully ninety per cent were dependent on the dole. Additional aid to the needy was given through the Federal Surplus Commodities Commission of the Department of Agriculture, created in Octo-ber, 1933, which spent thirty million dollars during the first year of its existence in buying surplus farm products for distribution through local relief organizations. One of the most difficult of the relief problems was the army of transients which roamed the country. Since these men possessed no legal residence,

Harry L. Hopkins, a professional social worker, was Roosevelt's chief adviser on relief problems and many others.

local authorities were hesitant to accept responsibility for them, but transient camps were established which took care of many of them, while others were induced to join the CCC. Of some assistance also was the United States Employment Service, established during the "hundred days" by the Wagner Act to coordinate all local, state, and national employment agencies into one comprehensive system. Before long the amount of "panhandling" on the city streets was materially reduced.

At the head of the FERA was Harry L. Hopkins, a professional social worker who had been in charge of relief activities in New York while Roosevelt was governor. For psychological reasons, Hopkins believed emphatically in work relief as preferable to the dole. What most people wanted was neither charity nor public support. Provided with a dole a man tended to become a pauper; but provided with a job he retained his self-respect and might become again a useful member of society. With this principle in mind the President established the Civil Works Administration in October, 1933, as a branch of the FERA, to provide emergency jobs for workers who might otherwise have to spend the

The CWA

winter on relief. The CWA actually gave the first employment they had had for years to millions of men, but the work provided was of indifferent merit, and the haste with which the organization was set up led to an unknown amount of graft and favoritism. Meant merely as a temporary expedient, the CWA was discontinued the following spring. It had demonstrated, however, that the unemployed were eager for work; also, that whatever money was paid out in this fashion was quickly spent, and tended to stimulate business recovery all along the line. Altogether the CWA cost the government about $845,000,000.

In one respect the relief activities of the government proved to be enormously disappointing. The relief rolls somehow failed to shorten, and for the most part tended even to lengthen. People who had savings to rely upon in the earlier years of the depression saw their savings dwindle and disappear until they had no recourse except to seek relief. Private charities broke down in the face of burdens too stupendous. Young men came of age and sought for jobs that were not to be found. Newly devised machinery threw more men out of work. Year after year there seemed to be no really significant falling-off in the relief rolls, while there were at any time other millions of unemployed men who had not yet exhausted their savings or who were helped out by solvent friends or relatives.

Federal relief workers thus became convinced that the situation they faced could hardly be deemed a mere emergency; or, if so called, that the emergency would not be short-lived. In harmony with these views, the new Relief Act of April 8, 1935, called upon the government not only to provide relief, but also to provide "work relief, and to increase employment by providing useful projects." For this purpose a total of nearly five billion dollars was appropriated on the understanding that federal relief officials would help devise work projects, would prescribe rules for the selection of workers, and would regu-

Work relief — WPA

late the conditions of labor. The relief program met immediate opposition from two sources: chamber of commerce groups who for reasons of economy to the taxpayer preferred the dole to the far more expensive work projects, and the labor leaders, who feared the adoption of low wage schedules that might break down the prevailing rates of pay on private work. Nevertheless, the new program was put into effect during the summer of 1935. The FERA handed over to a new Works Progress Administration, established in July under the direction of the energetic Hopkins, the task of providing work for all employables. It was hoped that all unemployables, such as the aged, the blind, dependent children, and the like, could be returned to the care of the states, with such federal assistance as the new Social Security Act would make available.[1]

The trifling projects sometimes sponsored by the FERA, the CWA, and in its earlier months the WPA, gave rise to the derisive epithet, "boondoggling," a term often used indiscriminately to describe all made work. As time went on, the nature of the projects undertaken was much improved. The ideal which the WPA set for itself but never fully attained was to provide the unemployed with the kind of work they were best fitted to do. For the unskilled laborers, who constituted the great majority of the relief workers, jobs were found in connection with such projects as the construction of country roads and city streets, the improvement of parks and playgrounds, and the building of flood-control or irrigation dams. Carpenters, plasterers, masons, plumbers, and other skilled laborers were used to erect or repair schoolhouses, libraries, city halls, courthouses, and other public buildings. Even the "white-collar" classes were not neglected, and projects were devised to aid artists, writers, actors, musicians, architects, and many others possessed of more or less professional abilities. Among the projects undertaken were several of great interest to historians, such as the surveys of historical records, and of national, state, and

[1] See pp. 597–598.

local archives. There were indeed few aspects of American life that were not in some way affected by the activities of the WPA. Supplementary to its program was the work of the National Youth Administration through which needy high-school and college students were enabled to earn small sums for non-instructional assistance to their teachers, while equally needy young people who were not in school were provided with useful part-time jobs. NYA workers earned on an average more than fifteen dollars each per month.

The sums spent on work relief during the first two Roosevelt administrations ran far into the billions, and the number of workers aided far into the millions. Efforts were made to cut down on WPA activities whenever an upward trend in business was indicated, but all such reductions met the violent protests of discharged workers, most of whom found it impossible to obtain other employment. WPA wage scales were adjusted as nearly as possible to fit local circumstances. Unskilled laborers earned on an average fifty dollars a month, and white-collar workers considerably more. The hours of work required per week likewise varied, but they were never excessive. Labor unions, armed with the same formidable lists of rights and grievances with which they confronted private employers, soon put in their appearance, and professional radicals found in the WPA a happy hunting ground. In 1939 the federal theater project, although it was almost able to pay its own way, had to be discontinued because of persistent accusations that it was being used to spread radical propaganda.

Undoubtedly the substitution of work relief through the WPA for the dole system that might have been developed **WPA** by the FERA was an extremely **results** expensive proposition, but the nation got something for its investment. Scarcely a community could be found that had not benefited by repaired or even newly constructed public buildings, improved streets and highways, new or renovated parks and

AIR CORPS BARRACKS. Southeast headquarters, Maxwell Field, Alabama.

STATE PARKS. Reconstruction of Fort Recovery, Columbus, Ohio.

FLOOD CONTROL. Workmen constructing emergency levee along the Potomac River.

playgrounds, together with dozens of other more or less permanent contributions to the convenience and comfort of the public. WPA artists decorated public buildings with murals that revealed much hitherto hidden talent, writers devised guidebooks that served well the needs of the states and localities whose places of interest they charted, while other white-collar workers indexed newspapers, located historical documents, classified and rearranged archives, and did a countless number of other useful chores.

Undoubtedly the original intent of the New Deal was to bring about a degree of business recovery that would provide normal employment for all who were capable of earning a living. To this end the RFC, which had been established during Hoover's administration, was continued, with the added function of lending to private industry as well as to financial institutions, railroads, and public agencies. All such loans were to be made on a strictly business basis, with the expectation of repayment. The easement of credit that the RFC provided was eagerly accepted by the

Recovery — RFC loans

HOLLYWOOD BOWL. Constructed under the Music Project.

PUBLIC BUILDINGS. State Highway Department Building, Montgomery, Alabama.

business world, and its loans soon totaled many billions of dollars. Money lent to financial corporations, such as banks, building and loan associations, insurance and mortgage companies, was almost invariably soon repaid, but loans to railroads, industrial enterprises, and public agencies came back slowly. Nevertheless, of the seven and one half billion dollars lent by the RFC to December 31, 1939, over seventy-seven per cent had been repaid.

To supplement its lending policy the government proposed to stimulate industry still **Public** further by a program of direct **works —** spending. This was to be ac- **PWA** complished mainly through a Public Works Administration, for the use of which the hundred days' session of Congress appropriated $3,300,000,000. It was supposed that the erection of public buildings and other such construction projects would provide much new business for the heavy industries in particular, and less directly for business in general. This, rather than work relief, was the main purpose of the PWA, although the reduction of unemployment was anticipated as an important by-product of its activities. Contractors, however, were not required to select their employees from relief rolls. At the head of the PWA the President placed his Secretary of the Interior, Harold L. Ickes, whose determination to

Social projects sponsored by New Deal agencies attempted to do for the intellectual and professional worker the equivalent of what was being done for skilled and unskilled labor. Projects were devised to meet the needs of writers, artists, teachers, actors, and other similar groups. Inevitably there was much criticism of government spending for such purposes, and charges of extravagance, inefficiency, graft, and waste flew thick and fast.

ART. WPA artists designing works destined for public buildings.

VOCATIONAL SCHOOLS. Facilities and instructors were supported from WPA funds.

LITERATURE. Federal Writer's Project display at the New York *Times* Book Fair.

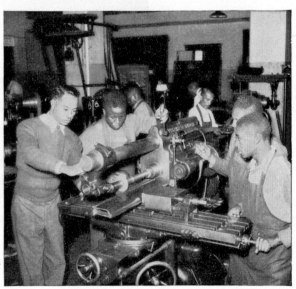

get value received for all the assignments he made considerably slowed down the pump-priming aspects of his organization. The Administrator ruled out all boondoggling activities, and required detailed plans before the spending process could begin. Since architects' drawings for large buildings took many months to complete, after which contracts still had to be let and materials assembled, Ickes's policy inevitably resulted in interminable delays. Furthermore, a large proportion of the projects were undertaken in collaboration with state or local governments which were required to contribute the major part of the cost of construction in the form of bonds delivered to the PWA. In many instances this meant difficulty and delay because of constitutional limits on indebtedness and referendum requirements on the issuing of bonds.

The PWA found no difficulty in obtaining an abundance of acceptable projects upon which to expend its funds, but the program was too slow in developing to give business

TECHNOLOGY. Adult classes were offered in many fields.

THEATER PROJECT. A short-lived WPA function, but useful in a time of need. This scene is from *Pinocchio*.

THE HANDICAPPED. WPA projects included programs for the handicapped. This group is transcribing Braille.

the "shot in the arm" that had been expected. On this account some of the PWA funds were diverted to CWA and other spending agencies, while new appropriations for public works went mainly to WPA. The business recession of 1937–38 served, however, to revive the PWA, and with plans by this time available in abundance it was able to give much immediate aid to industry. By the end of 1939 it had sponsored projects in all but three counties within the United States at an estimated cost of only a little less than six billion dollars. Federal PWA expenditures centered chiefly upon the improvement of waterways and harbors (including dams for flood control and irrigation purposes), the construction of federal-aid highways, and the building of post-offices,

Harold L. Ickes, able New Deal administrator, because of his honesty and irascibility, won the soubriquet, the "Old Curmudgeon."

courthouses, warehouses, and such other structures as were needed for federal purposes. Large sums were also used for the building of naval and coast-guard vessels, and for the improvement of army camps, aviation fields, and national parks. Non-federal expenditures made possible hundreds of new municipal waterworks, sewerage, and electric light systems, innumerable public office buildings and hospitals, and schoolhouses of every description from kindergarten to university. While these improvements were constantly criticized as "spending money that we haven't got for buildings that we can't afford," the PWA investments undoubtedly did much to keep the wheels of industry turning and to make jobs for men who otherwise might have been unemployed. Also, with but few exceptions, the structures erected served a useful social purpose.

Quite the most ambitious of the New Deal efforts to restore prosperity was the National

The NRA Recovery Administration, authorized June 16, 1933, under the terms of the National Industrial Recovery Act. The NRA was the principal New

Deal answer to those who demanded a planned economy. Its purpose was to facilitate the cooperation of all American employers in a gigantic effort to shorten working hours, raise wages, and increase employment. Whatever anti-trust legislation barred the way to reasonable group understandings was swept aside. Just as the War Industries Board had promoted the smooth functioning of American business during the First World War, so now the NRA was to enable industry to pull together in a joint battle against the depression.

Roosevelt's appointment of Brigadier-General Hugh S. Johnson (retired) as chief administrator of the NRA served still further to emphasize the kinship of the new policy with the regimentation of industry that had been accomplished during the First World War. Johnson had been closely associated with Baruch in the work of the War Industries Board, and his activities as head of the NRA strongly reflected his earlier experience. He revived the methods of popular appeal that had proved effective during the war, and sought to instill in the public mind the conviction that support of the NRA was a patriotic duty. He furnished a handsome emblem, the Blue Eagle, to be displayed by all business houses that agreed to follow NRA regulations and by all householders who pledged themselves to buy only from Blue Eagle firms. And he used his limitless energy to induce manufacturers, mine operators, common carriers, utility corporations, merchants, and every other type of business men in the country to devise "codes of fair competition" by which, group by group, they agreed to standardize their behavior. The existence of numerous trade associations greatly furthered this type of activity.

At first Johnson's efforts were crowned with conspicuous success. His vigorous and colorful personality won for him **NRA codes** a degree of popularity that for a time rivaled even the President's; next to the President he was certainly the most conspicuous figure in American life. Within a matter of months he was able to secure from the representatives of perhaps ninety-five per cent of the business interests of the country the adoption of satisfactory codes, which, when approved by the President, were invested with the full force of law. For all businesses not organized under their own code authorities the President issued a "blanket" code, which abolished child labor, fixed a thirty-five-hour week for ordinary labor and a forty-hour week in white-collar jobs, and established minimum-wage scales of forty cents an hour for the former and from twelve to fifteen dollars a week for the latter. The privately negotiated codes varied considerably, depending upon the type of industry they were designed to fit, but in addition to the prohibition of child labor and the establishment of maximum hours and minimum wages, they usually made elaborate provision for the control of prices and sales practices, and the limitation of production.

The NRA assumed that the best way to revive business was to increase purchasing power, and that this could best be accomplished by means of higher wages and re-employment. But inasmuch as employers very generally felt obliged to balance their increased labor costs with increased prices the net effect was somewhat disappointing. Furthermore, difficulties in enforcement soon began to appear that made the problems of prohibition pale into insignificance. "Chiselers" who displayed the Blue Eagle, but ignored the rules, put the honestly intentioned dealer at a serious disadvantage. War-time methods of compulsion were lacking, and the hope that the code authorities set up by each business group could secure the obedience of all members proved illusive. A few important establishments refused entirely to cooperate. Henry Ford increased wages, but subscribed to no code. Montgomery Ward and Company neglected to pay the dues required of retailers to cover the cost of code administration. Furthermore, the Federal Department of Justice soon found that it could not depend with certainty upon the support of the courts.

But the most discouraging problems of the NRA flowed from the labor provisions included in Section 7(a) of the National Industrial Recovery Act, which stated:

(1) That employees shall have the right to organize and bargain collectively through representatives of their own choosing, and shall be free

The NRA eagle (left) flew over many business establishments until the Supreme Court declared the Act unconstitutional on May 27, 1935, as symbolized by the cartoon at the right.

from the interference, restraint, or coercion of employers of labor, or their agents, in the designation of such representatives or in self-organization or in other concerted activities for the purpose of collective bargaining or other mutual aid or protection;

(2) That no employee and no one seeking employment shall be required as a condition of employment to join any company union or to refrain from joining, organizing, or assisting a labor organization of his own choosing; and

(3) That employers shall comply with the maximum hours of labor, minimum rates of pay, and other conditions of employment approved or prescribed by the President.

These provisions were hailed with delight by labor leaders, who recruited their depression-torn ranks with great rapidity, and stood guard militantly against every tendency on the part of employers to turn the codes to the disadvantage of the workers. To aid in the settlement of such disputes as might crop up, the President established a National Labor Board, headed by Senator Robert F. Wagner of New York, which successfully mediated thousands of grievances, but was compelled to rely mainly upon moral authority to enforce its decisions. Particularly vexing was the failure of the National Industrial Recovery Act to specify whether company unions might participate in collective bargaining, and whether a union that represented a majority of the workers in a given industry might be construed to represent the minority as well. In the summer of 1934 Congress replaced the NLB with a more powerful National Labor Relations Board, which strongly supported the most extreme contentions of labor. By this time industry was in full revolt against the NRA in general and Section 7(a) in particular, and the real or fancied grievances it furnished led to one violent strike after another. A strike of longshoremen that began in the ports of the Pacific coast early in May developed into a general strike throughout the San Francisco area. It was broken in July only after a corps of vigilantes had raided the strikers' offices and had seized their leaders. In September a strike in the textile industries kept half a million men out of work for nearly a month, but ended in an almost complete victory for the employers. These, together with many less extensive outbreaks, marked the year as one of the most disturbed in the whole history of American industrial relations. Johnson held labor mainly responsible for the turn events had taken, and in a speech delivered in New York, September 14, 1934, openly denounced the textile workers for having broken faith with him. Ten days later he resigned.

Bereft of Johnson's dynamic leadership, and no longer able to count on the full support of either industry or labor, **End of** the NRA played a steadily di- **NRA** minishing rôle in American economic life. By law the organization was due to expire after two years unless given a longer lease of life by Congress. It lasted on in reorganized form under the guidance of Donald R. Richberg until May, 1935, when a decision of the United States Supreme Court gave it the *coup de grâce*. In the so-called Schechter case the Court held that Congress had overstepped constitutional limits both in delegating "legislative authority to the President to exercise an unfettered discretion," and in presuming that the interstate commerce clause applied to "all enterprises and transactions which could be said to have an indirect effect upon interstate commerce." As for the contention that exceptional powers were necessary to meet a pressing emergency, the Court held that the Constitution had been designed no less for emergencies than for ordinary conditions. The President was deeply incensed at the stand the Court had taken, but he bowed to its authority and the whole NRA organization was rapidly dismantled.

Efforts to salvage some of the gains attributed to the NRA were not entirely lacking. At the insistence of the administration the Guffey-Snyder Act was passed in August, 1935, to promote the stabilization of conditions in the bituminous coal industry. This measure seemed to the President so important that he told the House Ways and Means

Committee: "I hope your committee will not permit doubts as to the constitutionality, however reasonable, to block the suggested legislation." But a five-to-four decision of the Supreme Court in May, 1936, invalidated the law, and returned the soft-coal business to its customary chaos. Another measure, the Wagner-Connery Labor Relations Act, was designed to soften the blow sustained by labor in the loss of Section 7(a). The new act stated that the policy of the United States was to protect the rights of laborers to organize and to bargain collectively with employers through representatives of their own choosing. A new National Labor Relations Board, also of three members, which replaced the NLRB of the year before, was authorized to halt unfair practices on the part of employers and to seek enforcement for its orders through the federal courts. The new NLRB successfully ran the gantlet of the Supreme Court, although the board's right to interfere where the process of manufacture was strictly local in character was sustained by a bare majority.

One result of the labor turmoil that characterized these years of change and experi-**The labor** ment was the division of organ-**split — C.I.O.** ized labor itself into two competing camps. The American Federation of Labor, led since 1924 by William Green, adhered consistently to the Gompers policy of cooperating with capital as long as wages and working conditions remained satisfactory. With the capitalistic system as such it refused to quarrel, provided only that labor obtained a reasonable reward for the work it was called upon to do. Furthermore, the A.F. of L. still set much store by the crafts union type of organization, and opposed with vigor all attempts to organize into one union all the workers in a given industry, regardless of their skills or their lack of skills. The Federation, so its critics complained, had thus lost touch with the problems of the ordinary worker. After the destruction of the NRA in 1935, John L. Lewis, militant head of the United Mine Workers, took the lead in the formation of a Committee for In-

dustrial Organization, the purpose of which was to promote the unionization of industries as units, and not in accordance with specified trades or skills. In this endeavor he was officially opposed by the A.F. of L., but, with the support of his own and several other powerful unions, he sent organizers into many of the great mass-production industries, such as automobiles, steel, textiles, rubber, aluminum, plate-glass, and furniture. Unmindful of LaFollette's warning as to the hazards of Communist infiltration,[1] Lewis, to make haste, accepted the assistance of numerous Communist sympathizers. The effectiveness of their work was immediately apparent, but the presence of Communists and "fellow-travelers" in high places was to plague the C.I.O for many years to come. In most instances the C.I.O plan of organization seemed to meet a long-felt need; old unions took on new life, and new unions were founded as needed. For cooperating with Lewis in this work ten unions were suspended in 1936 by the A.F. of L., and as a result the

[1] See p. 501.

Organized labor, split between the A.F. of L. and the C.I.O., competed vigorously for membership. The leaders, William L. Green and John L. Lewis, are depicted as "Rival Builders" by Pease in the Newark *Evening News.*

C.I.O. assumed a permanent character that its prime movers had not at first intended. Claiming to represent a membership of nearly four million workers as against the five million of the A.F. of L., the C.I.O. changed its name in November, 1938, to the Congress of Industrial Organizations, adopted a constitution after the A.F. of L. model, and elected Lewis as its first president.

The methods by which the C.I.O. had risen to such great importance involved **"Sit-down" strikes** among other things the use of a weapon new to American labor history, the "sit-down" strike. Workers instead of first leaving the factories, and then picketing them to prevent the employment of "scabs," simply retained in idleness the posts they ordinarily held, and forcibly resisted removal. This technique was successfully employed in C.I.O. strikes against two great automobile companies, General Motors and the Chrysler Corporation. In both instances, with the assistance of Governor Frank Murphy of Michigan, agreements were finally reached to vacate the plants on condition that the C.I.O. union should be recognized as the bargaining agent for its members, while later negotiations won other concessions. The United States Steel Cor-

poration, long the despair of labor leaders, did not await the coming conflict, but in March, 1937, accorded the C.I.O. Steel Workers' Organizing Committee full bargaining authority for all its membership. Most of the other so-called "Big Steel" companies also capitulated, but "Little Steel," led by T. M. Girdler of the Republic Steel Corporation, fought back. Strikes that began in May, 1937, spread rapidly through Pennsylvania, Ohio, and Illinois, and were accompanied by much disorder. But the timely action of employers prevented "sit-down" strikes, and without this weapon the strikers lost. Moreover, the public had become thoroughly weary of labor conflict, and was disposed to blame the violence that accompanied C.I.O. strikes on Communist agitators. William Green, the A.F. of L. leader, complained bitterly that the C.I.O. methods were discrediting the whole labor movement. Even when the police brutally shot down a number of picketers at the Republic Steel Works in South Chicago, there was little effective protest.

This succession of labor troubles undoubtedly influenced Congress to take action toward the re-establishment of **Wages and Hours Act** controls over wages and hours

The 'sit-down' strike was effectively employed in the thirties. These strikers sat **it out** in the Fisher Body Plant, Flint, Michigan, in 1937.

that the invalidation of the NRA had removed. The Fair Labor Standards Act of June, 1938, was designed to put "a ceiling over hours and a floor under wages" that would make possible "minimum standards of living necessary for health, efficiency, and well being of workers." The bill, although sponsored by Senator Black of Alabama, met violent opposition from many southern Democrats who believed that only by low wages could the South continue to compete with the North in industry, but eventually it won a majority in both houses of Congress. It applied only to employees who were engaged in interstate commerce, or who were producing goods for interstate commerce, and it specifically excluded such important groups as agricultural laborers, domestic servants, and seamen; but for such workers as the law did cover it set a twenty-five cents an hour minimum rate of pay, to be increased gradually to forty cents by 1945, and fixed the work week at forty-four hours, to be reduced by stages to an eventual forty hours in 1940. Time and one half pay was required for overtime, and the employment of children under sixteen, or in hazardous occupations under eighteen, was forbidden. The exact numbers of those affected by the law were hard to estimate, but its passage undoubtedly resulted in the raising of wages for hundreds of thousands of workers, and the shortening of hours for many more. President Roosevelt characterized the Act as "the most far-reaching, far-sighted program for the benefit of workers ever adopted in this or any other country." More important, the Supreme Court, reversing an earlier stand on the same subject, upheld the law as constitutional.

Parallel to the New Deal program for industry and labor was an equally comprehensive plan for the rehabilitation of agriculture. Striking out along what the President himself called "a new and untrod path," the Agricultural Adjustment Act of May 12, 1933, sought a remedy for the chronic overproduction that had for so long kept American farm prices

The AAA

down. Frankly recognizing that the foreign market could not be depended upon, the framers of the act proposed to restrict the American output, if need be, to what the United States alone could consume. By careful supervision of production, prices were to be brought back to the average levels of the five years preceding the First World War. To accomplish these ends an Agricultural Adjustment Administration was set up with authority to buy and hold surpluses, and to contract with the producers of specified basic commodities for whatever cooperation might be needed to insure crop control. Since the farmers were to be paid generously for their cooperation, agriculture stood to receive a double subsidy, one by way of direct money payments on the basis of the contracts signed, and the other through higher prices for crops harvested. The cost involved in the crop-restriction program was to be met by a tax levied against the processors of farm produce, who in turn would pass the burden along to the consumers. The farmer, if this elaborate scheme of economic planning worked, would find himself at last on a parity with other economic groups. Basic commodities at first brought within the scope of the act were cotton, wheat, corn, hogs, rice, tobacco, and milk, but a year later the list was greatly lengthened.

The AAA was organized within the Department of Agriculture, and operated under the watchful and sympathetic supervision of Secretary Wallace. It experimented first with cotton, and in the summer of 1933 succeeded in persuading about three fourths of the cotton-growers of the country to sign contracts reducing their cotton acreage by about one third. Since the planting had already been done, this meant that much growing cotton had to be plowed under. Cash payments for obedience to the government's orders amounted to from seven to twenty dollars per acre. To offset this expense a tax of four cents a pound was levied on cotton processed by manufacturers. The results from the farm-

Cotton control

ers' point of view were good, for benefit payments amounted to about two hundred million dollars, while the price of cotton climbed from five and one half to nine and one half cents a pound. It was clear, however, that the amount of cotton produced had not declined in proper proportion to the acreage taken out of cultivation. Farmers generally plowed under their poorest stands, and generously fertilized the rest. Accordingly, a Cotton Control Act was passed April 21, 1934, which enabled the AAA to assign definite quotas for states, counties, and individual farmers throughout the cotton-growing area. For those who produced beyond their quotas a penalty tax of five cents a pound or more was collected at the gins. By these means the cotton crops of 1934 and 1935 were held down to approximately ten million bales instead of the fourteen million average of the preceding five years. Much the same plan was carried out, with equally noteworthy effect, among tobacco-growers.

The AAA made no effort during its first season to reduce the plantings of wheat and

Wheat, corn, and hogs corn, but bad weather conditions kept down production of both commodities to subnormal

levels, and prices were better than usual. In 1934 an attempt was made to reduce wheat acreage by fifteen per cent, corn acreage by twenty per cent, and hog production by twenty-five per cent. Benefit payments for the estimated reductions were to be made at the rate of twenty-eight cents per bushel for wheat, thirty cents per bushel for corn, and five dollars per head for hogs. The processing taxes assessed to meet these expenditures were fixed at thirty cents per bushel on wheat, five cents per bushel on corn, and $2.25 per hundredweight on hogs. A devastating drouth that extended over almost all the grain-growing states during the summer of 1934 gave more aid than was desired to the crop-reduction program, and obliged the AAA to join with other governmental agencies in providing direct drouth relief. So complete was the drouth in some of the western states that many farmers had nothing to live on except the money they received from the government under their crop-reduction contracts; furthermore, the windstorms that swept ceaselessly through the western "dust bowl" threatened to render much land permanently useless. Nevertheless, the AAA continued its crop-reduction program in

John L. Lewis presented the case of labor at the coal parley in New York, 1939. Frances Perkins at left.

1935, and claimed for its activities an important influence in striking a better balance between supply and demand. Other farm products to which the program was extended included sugar, rice, rye, cattle, and dairy products.

Caustic criticism of so vast an undertaking was inevitable. Crop reductions, at a time when drouth conditions threatened the country with actual shortages, were difficult to defend, and in many instances had to be modified. But some actions had been taken, such as the purchase and slaughter of thousands of young pigs and sows, that could not be reconsidered. Farmers whose lifelong habits had been based upon growing more and more found it difficult to adjust themselves to an economy of growing less and less. They signed the contracts and accepted the benefit payments because they needed the money, but they resented the system. Processors complained bitterly at the heavy taxation forced upon them, and found themselves seriously handicapped in competing for markets outside the United States. Consumers paid steeply increased prices for nearly everything that came from the farm.

In spite of these criticisms the country was hardly prepared for the drastic action of the **The AAA** United States Supreme Court **invalidated** which announced January 6, 1936, in a six-to-three decision, that the Agricultural Adjustment Act was unconstitutional. In an opinion read by Justice Roberts the Court held that there was nothing in the Constitution to justify federal control of agricultural production, and that, in attempting to deal with the strictly local business of farming, Congress had invaded a right reserved to the states. Since the processing taxes and benefit payments existed only as means to an illegal end, the Court held that they, too, were invalid. The implications of this decision worried the minority of the Court, which in a dissenting opinion read by Justice Stone warned the majority that "courts are not the only agency of government that must be assumed to have capacity to govern." Nor could agricultural economists quite understand how farming could be classified as a strictly local business when most farm prices, if unregulated, would depend upon nation-wide and even upon world-wide conditions.

In wrecking the AAA the Supreme Court did not destroy the entire New Deal structure for dealing with agriculture. **Rural credits** Since not less than two out of **— FCA** every five American farms were mortgaged, many of them, as matters stood, for far more than they were worth, the importance of rural credits was obvious. In June, 1933, President Roosevelt, acting on authority of Congress, sought to eliminate unnecessary duplication of effort by consolidating under the control of a new Farm Credit Administration every federal agency in the United States that had anything to do with agricultural credits. Included in the reorganization was the Federal Farm Loan Board, which governed the banks that dealt in long and intermediate term credits to farmers, the Federal Farm Board established during Hoover's administration, and certain rural credits functions that had previously been connected with the Reconstruction Finance Corporation and the Department of Agriculture. With the help of such supplementary legislation as experience proved to be desirable, the FCA by 1934 was lending at the rate, on an average, of five million dollars a day. Much of this credit was used to refinance mortgages that might otherwise have been foreclosed, but loans for production and for marketing were also supplied. Frequently the new government loans were for less than the face of the old mortgage, but creditors gladly accepted the loss involved rather than take over the mortgaged property. Some loans were made also to buy back property that had been lost through foreclosure proceedings.

As a further check on the trend toward tenancy the Frazier-Lemke Bankruptcy Act of June, 1934, prohibited creditors from holding foreclosure sales for a period of five years, provided that the farmers concerned could

Erosion, drouth, and dust waged a constant and often victorious battle against the efforts of middlewestern and southwestern farmers. Drifting topsoil such as this in Cimarron County, Oklahoma, impoverished thousands and stripped hundreds of acres.

pay what government officials regarded as a reasonable rental on their property. This law was too much for the Supreme Court, which invalidated it as a taking of private property without due process of law, but a new measure, the Frazier-Lemke Moratorium Act of August, 1935, which accomplished much the same purpose, was sustained. This second act delayed foreclosure proceedings for a three-year period, provided a court of law would give its approval, both to the propriety of the delay and to the adequacy of the rental to be paid.

Spurred on by the acute agricultural distress that accompanied drouth conditions, **The RA and FSA** the New Deal in April, 1935, added to its rapidly lengthening list of alphabetical agencies still another, the Resettlement Administration. Headed at first by Rexford G. Tugwell, a college professor with a strong belief in the necessity of economic planning, the RA took over and greatly expanded the work of rural rehabilitation already begun by the FERA and other governmental agencies. Outright grants for subsistence needs and loans secured by crop

liens for the purchase of seed, tools, fertilizer, and other essentials were made to hard-pressed farmers; millions of acres of marginal and submarginal land that ought never to have been cultivated were bought by the government for reforestation, conversion into grazing land, or other conservational use; the resettlement in "healthy rural communities" of dispossessed farmers who were unable to find adequate opportunities for themselves was attempted; and work on a few "greenbelt" suburban communities, designed "to provide low-rental houses for low-income groups," was begun. The RA found much difficulty in inducing farmers to leave their lands, however undesirable they might be, and its resettlement activities soon turned out to be of minor importance. In view of this fact, in 1937 it was renamed the Farm Security Administration, and turned its attention chiefly to making loans to competent farm tenants, share-croppers, and farm laborers to enable them to become farm owners. It experimented, also, with the establishment of rural village communities from which as centers cooperative farming might be carried on; but so alien a system found little response among American farmers.

The hostility of the Supreme Court was sufficient to put an end to the NRA, which had begun to break down anyway, but the critical condition of agriculture required that some substitute be found immediately for the AAA. As a stopgap measure, designed mainly to save the situation until something better could be devised, Congress enacted in February, 1936, the Soil Conservation and Domestic Allotment Act. Instead of the control of production at which the AAA had aimed, the primary objective of the new act was to be soil conservation. The all-important payments to farmers were to be continued, but henceforth they were to be made in return for cooperation with the government in an elaborate program for the promotion of soil fertility, the prevention of erosion, and the more economic use of farm land. By placing restrictions on the planting of soil-depleting crops, some effort was made to hold down the production of such basic commodities as cotton, wheat, and corn, but by 1937 the cotton yield reached the startlingly high figure of 18,945,028 bales, while most other crops showed a wide margin over the nation's ability to consume. Furthermore, there was no longer a processing tax to meet the cost of the benefit payments, and the money had to come directly out of the Treasury. Mindful of the tender susceptibilities of the Supreme Court, Congress provided that state agencies should eventually be given a conspicuous part in carrying on the new program.

Finally in 1938 Congress enacted a new Agricultural Adjustment Act as "the Nation's well-matured answer" to **The new** the needs of the American **AAA** farmer. It retained the soil-conservation and benefit-payment features of the preceding program; it made provision in five key crops, wheat, cotton, corn, tobacco, and rice, for the limitation of acreage allotments in accordance with probable needs; it authorized the making of storage loans as a means of holding agricultural surpluses off the market; and it sanctioned resort to marketing quotas in emergencies, provided that two thirds of the growers of the commodity concerned recorded their approval in a referendum vote. All this was a part of an elaborate effort to raise the income of farmers to "parity," that is, to the same ratio with the incomes of other groups that had existed in the five years prior to 1914; to make doubly sure of this goal the sum of $212,000,000 was appropriated in 1939 for "parity payments" to help bridge the gap between current prices and "parity prices." For the benefit of wheat-growers, a Federal Crop Insurance Corporation was established in the Department of Agriculture from which guaranties could be obtained to the amount of fifty or seventy-five per cent of normal yields. Payments of losses and premiums were to be made either in wheat or in its cash equivalent.

Although participation in the AAA program was kept on a purely voluntary basis, the generous subsidies offered were hard for farmers to resist. About five and a quarter million agricultural producers, working through three thousand county conservation associations and many more subordinate committees, took part in the 1939 program. Nearly three fourths of the crop land of the nation was involved. In accordance with the wishes of Secretary Wallace, an "ever normal granary" was promoted by loans on warehoused surpluses which amounted approximately to nine cents per pound on cotton, sixty cents per bushel on wheat, and fifty-seven cents per bushel on corn. By this device it was hoped that both producer and consumer would be protected against shortages and price fluctuations. The marketing quota provisions of the act were also promptly invoked to protect the prices of cotton and of several types of tobacco, while nearly one hundred and seventy thousand wheat-growers, some of them in drouth-threatened areas where there was little prospect of a crop, took out federal crop insurance. The cost of all this to the government exceeded half a billion dollars a year.

While the New Deal measures served undoubtedly to increase farm incomes, they **Wheat surpluses** left many of the fundamental problems of American agriculture still unsolved. Wheat surpluses threatened to remain permanent in spite of every effort to turn the activities of wheat farmers into other lines. Against a normal domestic consumption of 650,000,000 bushels of wheat, American farmers produced 932,000,000 bushels in 1938 and 755,000,000 in 1939. The lower figure for 1939 was due less to the activities of the AAA than to drouth conditions on the western plains, and since the average wheat production during the ten-year period that ended in 1937 was about 753,000,000 bushels, it was evident that not much progress had been made toward crop control. Meantime the world supply of wheat had mounted to the highest figure on record, and the struggle to find export outlets became correspondingly strenuous. Hopes that the outbreak of war in Europe might greatly stimulate the demand for American wheat were unrealized as late as the spring of 1940, when the successes of the German arms in Flanders led to a drop of thirty cents in July futures on the Chicago market. And what was true of wheat was true in greater or less degree of most basic American food crops.

The plight of cotton was even more distressing, for American cotton-growers needed **The plight of cotton** to dispose of a full half of their normal crop abroad. Cotton had long since ceased to be an American monopoly, but during the thirties the speed with which the rest of the world had begun to achieve its independence of the American product took on a tremendous acceleration. This was due in part to the trend of the times toward national self-sufficiency, but the American habit of reducing cotton acreage after each low-price season led British importers to encourage the development of new sources of supply in Latin America, Egypt, and India. When the AAA first began to operate, about forty-five per cent of the cotton used abroad was American cot-

ton; five years later the proportion had dropped to twenty-three per cent. During the cotton year ending July 31, 1939, American cotton exports amounted to only 3,362,000 bales, the smallest figure since 1882. Meantime, in spite of frantic efforts on the part of the AAA to cut production, the 1939 cotton carry-over had mounted to more than thirteen million bales, an increase since the year before of over eleven per cent, and an all-time high. Moreover, the greater part of this excess cotton was stored in government warehouses as collateral for loans, and could not be disposed of except with the consent of the owners. The amount of American cotton actually available for immediate sale was thus small enough to insure a maximum amount of foreign competition. The outbreak of hostilities in Europe led to some heartening export activity during the late summer and fall of 1939, but the next spring the threat of a speedy German victory served, as in the case of wheat, to undermine confidence. The panic that hit the American markets in May, 1940, lowered the price of July futures by about ten per cent.

The effect of the New Deal measures upon the social organization of the deep South was far more revolutionary than **Social changes in the South** had been foreseen. Reductions in the cotton acreage meant that thousands of share-croppers were left without land to work, while AAA benefit payments enabled landlords to purchase the machinery necessary to throw still other thousands off the land. Former share-croppers dropped to the status of agricultural day laborers, with at best only seasonal employment, and with frequent to constant dependence on relief. These conditions, greatly augmented in the southwestern dust bowl by the persistent drouths, raised up an army of wanderers who roamed the West in "jalopies," searching endlessly for employment. Far out into the Southwest, through New Mexico and Arizona to California, the blight of cotton-growing extended, and wherever it went the poverty-stricken cotton hand went with it. All over the South the need for diversified farming was as apparent as it was difficult to promote, while with "normalcy" forever fading into the future, the gains that industry was able to make over agriculture were slight.

In many of the New Deal measures the reform motive stood out clearly. This was **Reform —** certainly true of the monetary **the currency** policy, which, as the President told the World Economic Conference of 1933, was designed to provide "the kind of dollar which, a generation hence, will have the same purchasing and debt-paying power as the dollar value we hope to attain in the near future." In other words, while the President was ready to cheapen the dollar as a means of promoting recovery and facilitating the payment of debts, he set as his ultimate goal the old Populistic ideal of a dollar that could be depended upon not to fluctuate in value. To the dismay of many conservative economists, he promptly took the United States off the gold standard, secured from Congress a Gold Repeal Resolution which invalidated the gold clauses employed in so many public and private contracts, and prepared to experiment with a managed currency. Gold exports were forbidden; gold coin, gold bullion, and gold certificates were taken out of circulation; and a price fixed by the government was paid for all gold newly mined in the United States or offered for sale from abroad. Finally, under authority of the Gold Reserve Act of January 30, 1934, the amount of gold in the standard dollar was reduced to 59.06 per cent of its former content.

While the President's program for raising prices by cheapening the dollar met at first with some success, the net results proved to be far less significant than he had hoped or his critics had feared. The new dollars, regardless of their theoretical value as expressed in terms of gold, bought almost as much as the old dollars, and the President, although permitted by law to reduce the former gold content by as much as fifty per cent, made no further move toward devaluation. Under the terms of a new Silver Purchase Act, signed June 19, 1934, he did, however, begin the purchase of silver, ostensibly to increase the supply of silver in the national monetary stocks until it had reached a value equal to one fourth the total amount. But this policy in practice turned out to be little more than a generous bounty to the silver producers of the country, who were thereby assured a market for their output at a figure far in excess of the current world price. Unhappily, none of these measures provided any reasonable assurance that the purchasing power of the dollar would or could be stabilized.

That the President had no intention of risking any extensive currency inflation was evident from his failure to issue **Roosevelt** the three billion dollars of fiat **opposes** money authorized by the so- **inflation** called Thomas Amendment to the Agricultural Adjustment Act of 1933; also, from his veto of the Soldiers' Bonus Bill of 1935, which proposed to pay off in the same type of currency all outstanding adjusted compensation certificates. The next year a similar Bonus Bill was passed over the President's veto, but without the inflationary feature. Some economists believed that the huge sums of gold and silver acquired by the government under its new monetary policy constituted in themselves a potential threat of inflation. By January 1, 1940, the United States had in its possession over seventeen billion dollars' worth of gold and about two billion dollars' worth of silver as against a total amount of currency in circulation of less than eight billions (a sum well above the Populist goal of fifty dollars per capita). But the government's riches were tightly guarded, and played no greater part in determining currency values than the Federal Reserve authorities chose to permit. After 1936 about one third of the gold supply was transferred to Fort Knox, a newly constructed depository in the hills of Kentucky.

In order to prevent the recurrence of such an epidemic of bank failures as had ushered in the Roosevelt administration, **The Glass-** Congress made repeated changes **Steagall Act** in the national banking system. The Glass-Steagall Act of 1933 responded to a strong popular demand by creating a Federal Deposit Insurance Corporation through which deposits up to $2500 might be immediately guaranteed, and still larger sums after six months' time. Further, the act provided for divorcement of commercial and investment banking, permitted national banks to establish branch banks in states that accorded that privilege to state banks, gave the Federal Reserve Board the right to place severe restrictions upon banks that lent too freely for speculative purposes, forbade loans from their own banks to the executive officers of Federal Reserve Banks, and expanded the Federal Reserve System to include industrial and savings banks. Two years later another banking act greatly strengthened the control of the national government over the whole Federal Reserve System. The old Federal Reserve Board was replaced by a board of governors of seven members, all to be appointed directly by the President for terms of fourteen years each. The powers of the new board included a veto over selections for chief executive officers made by the various Federal Reserve Banks, practically complete control over the expansion and contraction of bank credits, and the right to raise the reserve requirements of member banks.

Also included within the list of the Roosevelt reforms was an attempt to deal with the problems of speculative investments. **The SEC** A Federal Securities Act, signed on May 27, 1933, insisted that the vendors of securities must be made to tell the public the truth about what they had to sell, and imposed heavy penalties for the interstate circulation of fraudulent advertising, through the mails or otherwise. The next year another act established the Securities and Exchange Commission to take over from the Federal Trade Commission the administration of these regulations. While it was beyond the power of the SEC to guarantee the purchasers of securities against loss, it could and did compel the disclosure of such information as might enable investors

to form intelligent opinions of their own. The SEC was authorized also to license stock exchanges, and to regulate their practices in such a way as to stimulate legitimate trading and to discourage mere gambling.

Under the terms of the Public Utilities Act of 1935 the SEC obtained a special grant of power with respect to the activities of public utility holding companies. During the prosperous twenties the holding company device had been carried to unreasonable extremes, partly to enable favored financial groups to exercise monopolistic control over a given area, and partly to multiply securities for sale to a gullible public. Holding companies were pyramided one upon another in topheavy edifices that at best were likely to siphon off the profits of operating companies into the pockets of a few insiders, and at worst were ready to topple over of their own weight the moment anything went wrong. Of the latter type was the utility empire of Samuel Insull, which collapsed in 1932 leaving thousands of investors ruined. There were many who favored a "death sentence" for all utility holding companies, but Congress was content merely to bring them under the regulatory authority of the SEC, and to limit their operations "to a single integrated public-utility system." Much litigation followed the attempt of the SEC to set up its controls in the utility field, but as time went on recognition of its powers tended to grow.

Partly to promote recovery, but partly also with a view to reform, the New Deal instituted drastic changes in the **Railroad co-** control of transportation. The **ordination** railroads in particular required attention, for the competition of automobiles, trucks, and pipe lines, with such inevitable loss of business as accompanied the depression, had brought them to the very brink of ruin. Railroad equipment was run down or worn out, roadbeds needed reworking, and the cost of operation all too frequently exceeded the passenger fares and freight charges taken in. Hampering regulations required maintenance of service that was no longer necessary, and habits of competition prevented long-overdue retrenchments. To meet this situation two extreme measures were commonly discussed. One was for the government itself to take over and administer the railroads as it had done during the war, perhaps even purchasing them outright; the other was to put the railroads through the "wringer" of ruthless bankruptcy proceedings, and thus to reduce their indebtedness to a point commensurate with their earning capacity.

The New Deal was unwilling to seize either horn of this dilemma. On the one hand, it was a matter of common knowledge that government operation of the railroads had been tolerated by the public during the war merely as an emergency measure, and that government ownership could be attained only by the purchase of railroad property at a highly fictitious valuation. On the other hand, it was also known that railroad securities in large amounts were held by insurance companies, savings banks, and other institutional investors whose collapse would serve only to extend the scope of the depression and deepen the general gloom. As a kind of compromise Congress passed, and on June 16, 1933, the President approved, an Emergency Railroad Transportation Act, which provided for a federal coordinator of transportation whose duty was to eliminate wasteful competition, to coordinate train service, and to effect needed economies.

As federal coordinator the President appointed Joseph B. Eastman, a believer in government ownership who nevertheless exerted himself to the utmost to make the existing system work. At his suggestion the western lines cut their passenger fares to two cents a mile, with such satisfactory results to their incomes that in 1936 the Interstate Commerce Commission made the rate change general. In 1938, however, an increase was allowed to two and one half cents, but early in 1940 the ICC restored the two-cent rate. RFC loans were used freely to buy new railroad equipment, and to permit improvements in service. It was in this way

that many of the roads obtained the funds to experiment with streamlined, air-conditioned trains, drawn by Diesel-electric or steam-electric locomotives. Thanks to the comforts so provided, a fair proportion of the traveling public was won back from automobile to railroad transportation, at least for long distances, and the profits to the railroads were good. Motor buses and trucks engaged in interstate traffic were brought under the control of the ICC by an act of August, 1935, and with business in general, except during the recession of 1937–38, on the upgrade, the financial condition of the railroads slowly improved. By 1939 the net operating income of all Class I railroads in the United States was $588,800,000 as against only $334,325,000 in 1932. After the entrance of the United States into the Second World War two years later, the railroads had all the business they could handle.

With respect to ocean-going means of transportation the New Deal frankly accepted the theory that a strong **The merchant** merchant marine was an essen- **marine** tial part of the national defense program. The Merchant Marine Act of 1936 declared: (1) that the United States should have shipping adequate to maintain its normal flow of water-borne commerce "at all times"; (2) that this shipping should be "capable of serving as a naval and military auxiliary in time of war"; (3) that it should be owned so far as possible by American citizens and operated under the American flag; (4) that it should be "composed of the best-equipped, safest, and most suitable types of vessels." The act supplanted the old Shipping Board and its subsidiary Merchant Fleet Corporation with a new Maritime Commission, one duty of which was to determine the ocean lanes in which American ships should ply, and another, to work out, in full cooperation with the Navy Department, a "long-range program for replacements and additions to the American merchant marine." The old system of subsidies by means of mail contracts now gave way to a new system whereby government assistance was so computed as to equalize the cost of construction and operation under foreign and American auspices, with further payments, if necessary, to offset foreign subsidies by an American equivalent. Also, the commission itself, provided the President approved, might build and operate ships. When private building, in spite of the subsidies offered, failed to achieve adequate results, the commission availed itself of this privilege, and in 1938 began a program of construction designed to provide fifty new ships each year for a period of ten years. During the recession of 1937–38 it bought many ships from private companies that had come to grief, and in 1939 it instituted with the consent of Congress a "turn-in and build" program which enabled American shipowners to receive a generous allowance toward new ships by turning over to the commission ships not less than seventeen years old. The result of these various measures was to make the year 1939 the busiest in the annals of American shipbuilding since the First World War. Altogether the year witnessed the construction of over 471,000 gross tons of shipping, and as it closed fifty-nine new ships were being built. When the Second World War broke out, the total American tonnage was two thirds as great as the British, and far in excess of any other. It was also vastly improved in serviceability.

Social workers who knew well the faulty housing conditions from which many under-**The housing** privileged Americans suffered **problem** were quick to urge governmental assistance for home-building as one of the best means of promoting both recovery and reform. Coupled with this problem, also, was the need of saving large numbers of home-owners from losing their property through mortgage foreclosures. To meet these needs government credit was for a time extended through the Home Owners' Loan Corporation, the purpose of which was to refinance home mortgages, and through Federal Savings and Loan Associations, locally established, which provided funds for new building. By June, 1936, when its lending ceased, the HOLC had acquired mortgages totaling three billion dollars and had

helped at least a million home-owners. Another agency, the Federal Housing Administration, established in 1934, undertook to insure home mortgages of which it approved up to eighty (later ninety) per cent of the appraised value of the property involved. This left to private capital the business of providing the money, but the FHA took most of the risk.

Far more revolutionary in character was the National Housing Act of 1937 under which a United States Housing **National** Authority was established to **Housing** aid local communities in remedy- **Act of 1937** ing their "shortage of decent, safe, and sanitary dwellings for families of low income." For this purpose an initial appropriation of eight hundred million dollars was made. That the program aimed specifically at slum clearance was evident from the stipulation that for each new building made possible by federal money there must be an equivalent destruction or improvement of inadequate housing. As a result of USHA activities, nineteen low-rent apartment houses had been constructed by the end of 1939 in thirteen different cities, and loans of more than a half-billion dollars for the use of 155 communities had been approved. USHA buildings cost on an average less than $3000 per family unit, with monthly rentals varying from $11.45 in the South to $15.80 in the North. The program looked forward to the ultimate removal of 640,000 persons from "substandard living conditions to new low-rent homes." Private builders, however, looked with great concern upon the housing activities of the government, and in 1939 their influence was sufficient to prevent the passage of a bill designed to expand the program. During the Second World War, because of the higher priority of the war effort, the USHA was discontinued, although government funds were used generously in providing temporary housing for war workers. After the war, with millions of returned veterans in search of homes, the need for housing was never greater, and taxed to the limit the combined efforts of private, federal, state, and local authorities.

Bibliography

Most of the writing provoked by the New Deal is both controversial and ephemeral. In matters of opinion it is seldom entirely trustworthy. With respect to unemployment and relief, the following books may be of service: Harry L. Hopkins, *Spending to Save; The Complete Story of Relief* (1936); Nels Anderson, *The Right to Work* (1938); and Grace Adams, *Workers on Relief* (1939). J. G. Frederick, *The New Deal: A People's Capitalism* (1944), is primarily campaign literature. Betty and E. K. Lindley, *A New Deal for Youth* (1938), tells the story of the NYA; other aspects of the New Deal youth program are discussed in Kenneth Holland and F. E. Hill, *Youth in the CCC* (1942); and L. L. Lorwin, *Youth Work Programs* (1941). Willson Whitman, *Bread and Circuses* (1937), is an account of the WPA theater project. On the PWA: H. L. Ickes, *Back to Work: The Story of PWA* (1935); A. D. Gayer, *Public Works in Prosperity and Depression* (1935); and J. F. Isakoff, *The Public Works Administration* (1938). On the NRA: H. S. Johnson, *The Blue Eagle from Egg to Earth* (1935); L. S. Lyon and others, *The National Recovery Administration* (1935); C. L. Dearing and others, *ABC of the NRA* (1934); C. R. Daugherty, *Labor under the NRA* (1934); and C. F. Roos, *N.R.A. Economic Planning* (1937).

On the subject of labor during the New Deal, Herbert Harris, *Labor's Civil War* (1940), treats of the break between the A.F. of L. and the C.I.O. Other books on labor include J. R. Walsh, *C.I.O. Industrial Unionism in Action* (1937); Benjamin Stolberg, *The Story of the CIO* (1938); and Edward Levinson, *Labor on the March* (1938).

On agriculture and the AAA: E. G. Nourse and others, *Three Years of the Agricultural Adjustment Administration* (1937); E. G. Nourse, *Marketing Agreements under the AAA* (1935); and Arthur Moore, *The Farmer and the Rest of Us* (1945). J. S. Davis, *Our Agricultural Policy, 1926–1938* (1939), is severely critical of the New Deal; Henry A. Wallace, *New Frontiers* (1934), defends the policies its author inaugurated. Cotton controls are discussed in H. I. Richards, *Cotton and the AAA* (1936); and C. S. Johnson and others, *The Collapse of Cotton Tenancy* (1935).

On the financial policy of the New Deal, Joseph E. Reeve, *Monetary Reform Movements: A Survey of Recent Plans and Panaceas* (1943), is critical and informative. Sidney Ratner, *American Taxation: Its History as a Social Force in Democracy* (1942), is mainly concerned with the income tax. William J. Shultz, *Financial Development of the United States* (1937), is useful on all aspects of the subject. R. L. Weismann, *The New Wall Street* (1939), tells of the changes wrought by the SEC; see also, by the same author, *The New Federal Reserve System* (1936). Marriner S. Eccles, *Beckoning Frontiers* (1951), is the autobiography of a longtime member of the Federal Reserve Board, and contains much valuable information. Other books worth mentioning on the subject of finance are E. A. Goldenweiser, *American Monetary Policy* (1951); A. W. Crawford, *Monetary Management under the New Deal* (1940); Charles C. Chapman, *Development of American Business and Banking Thought, 1913–36* (1936); H. G. Moulton, *Financial Organization and the Economic System* (1938); W. R. Burgess, *Reserve Banks and the Money Market* (1936); and *The Lessons of Monetary Experience*, edited by A. D. Gayer (1937).

On railroad coordination, the best account is J. B. Eastman, *Federal Coordination of Transportation*, in Seventy-Third Congress, Second Session, *Senate Document* no. 152 (serial 9790); and Seventy-Fourth Congress, First Session, *House Document* no. 89 (serial 9920). More general in scope is Claude M. Fuess, *Joseph B. Eastman, Servant of the People* (1952), the biography of a Wilson appointee to the I.C.C. who was reappointed by Harding, Hoover, and Roosevelt, and became Railroad Coordinator. Useful in a special way is Herbert Spero, *Reconstruction Finance Corporation Loans to the Railroads, 1932–37* (1939). On the merchant marine see titles mentioned on p. 478.

On housing, L. W. Post, *The Challenge of Housing* (1938); M. W. Straus and Talbott Wegg, *Housing Comes of Age* (1938); William Ebenstein, *The Law of Public Housing* (1940); T. R. Carskadden, *Houses for Tomorrow* (rev. ed., 1945); and Nathan Straus, *Seven Myths of Housing* (1944).

28

The Roosevelt Revolution

The "Roosevelt Revolution" — The TVA — Varieties
of TVA endeavor — Social security — Unemployment
compensation — Old-age insurance — The national
debt — Roosevelt haters — Elections of 1934 and 1936
— The new political division — The Supreme Court
controversy — Recession of 1937 — Elections of 1938
— The Hull trade pacts — The "good neighbor"
policy — Canada — Philippine independence

To SOME observers the term "Roosevelt Revolution" seemed a reasonable equivalent

The "Roosevelt Revolution." for what was more generally called the New Deal. Certainly the President himself was actively at the center of all the governmental changes that went on. On one occasion he likened himself to the quarterback on a football team whose business it was to choose the plays and call the signals. That his endless vitality accounted for the persistent drive of his administration and that he personally made most of the decisions on policy were matters of general knowledge. The New Deal without Roosevelt would not have been the New Deal at all. Also, there was much that was revolutionary about what had been done. Dozens of new agencies were at work that had virtually no precedents for their existence in the history of American government. By means of them the nation carried the regulation of business to lengths never before attempted in time of peace; it made an effort to tell the farmers what they might and what they might not raise; it sought with energy and persistence to better the lot of labor; it lent money where the bankers refused to lend; it even went directly into business itself. But the Roosevelt Revolution, if so it may be called, was after all a very temperate affair. Like the

Jefferson Revolution of 1800, and the Jackson Revolution of 1828, it left more unchanged than it changed. Compared with the Bolshevik Revolution which turned Russia upside down, or the Nazi Revolution which transformed Germany from a half-hearted republic into a totalitarian state, it was hardly a revolution at all. Private enterprise was retained and encouraged; personal liberty was in no wise endangered; and elections were still held.

Nevertheless, certain aspects of the New Deal program had a somewhat revolutionary tinge. The establishment of the **The TVA** Tennessee Valley Authority, for example, definitely put the government into business on a large scale; it amounted, in a way, to an experiment with socialism. The demand for the conservation of hydroelectric power, and its use in the interest of the people as a whole rather than for the benefit of privately owned utility companies, was not especially new, but it was taken up with great enthusiasm by the Roosevelt administration. Ever since the presidency of Theodore Roosevelt efforts had been made to prevent the unrestrained private exploitation of the nation's resources in water-power. Water-power sites had been freely withdrawn from entry, and in 1920 a Federal Water-Power Commission, consisting of the

Secretaries of War, Interior, and Agriculture, had been given the right to license and regulate all water-power projects that could be reached by federal authority. The duties of the commission soon proved to be too heavy for the three busy Secretaries, and in 1930 a Federal Power Commission of five appointive members was created with responsibilities analogous to those of the Interstate Commerce Commission. The New Deal, however, wished to go much farther than mere regulation, and to experiment with actual ownership and operation by the government. Effectively guided in all that concerned this subject by Senator George W. Norris of Nebraska, it singled out the Tennessee Valley for its first great project. This region, ramifying into seven different states — Tennessee, Kentucky, Alabama, Mississippi, Virginia, North Carolina, and Georgia — and embracing within its boundaries some forty thousand square miles, seemed to offer an ideal testing ground for the various New Deal theories on social and economic planning. It counted among its residents a high proportion of the underprivileged classes whose status cheap power was expected to benefit; and it possessed vast natural resources, most of which were either inadequately exploited or were being allowed to degenerate. Since the government had already spent huge sums upon the Muscle Shoals development, it was believed that here, if anywhere, results might speedily be obtained.

In May, 1933, Congress authorized the President to appoint a board of three directors, known as the Tennessee Valley Authority, into whose hands control of the mighty project was to be placed. The TVA was authorized to construct dams for the improvement of navigation and the control of floods; to develop new forms of fertilizer and to promote their use; to build and operate hydroelectric plants and to distribute the power they generated; and to take such other steps as it might see fit to promote the agri-

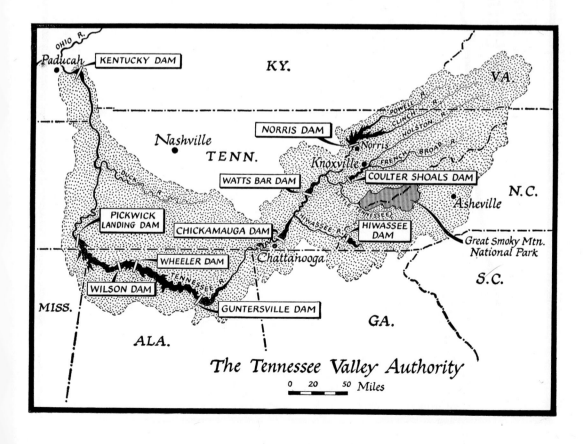

The Tennessee Valley Authority
0   20   50 Miles

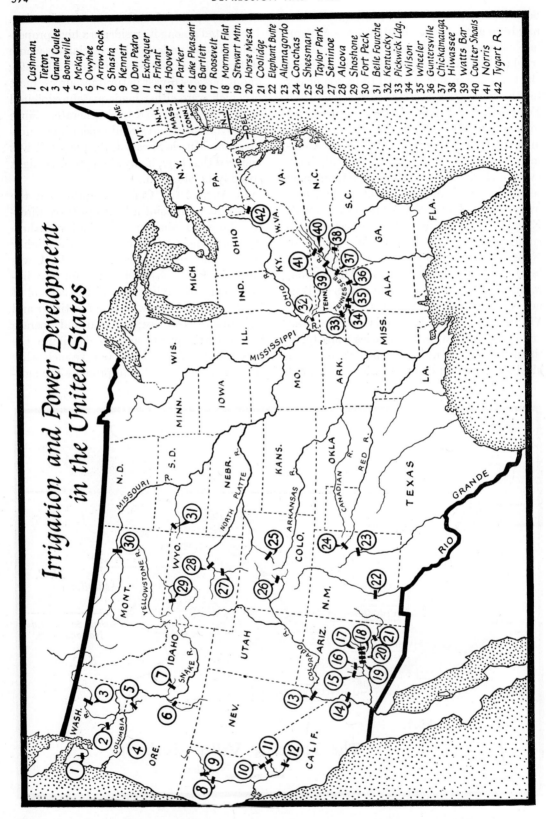

Irrigation and Power Development in the United States

1 Cushman
2 Tieton
3 Grand Coulee
4 Booneville
5 McKay
6 Owyhee
7 Arrow Rock
8 Shasta
9 Kennett
10 Don Pedro
11 Exchequer
12 Friant
13 Hoover
14 Parker
15 Lake Pleasant
16 Bartlett
17 Roosevelt
18 Mormon Flat
19 Stewart Mtn.
20 Horse Mesa
21 Coolidge
22 Elephant Butte
23 Alamagordo
24 Conchas
25 Sheesman
26 Taylor Park
27 Seminoe
28 Alcova
29 Shoshone
30 Fort Peck
31 Belle Fourche
32 Kentucky
33 Pickwick Ldg.
34 Wilson
35 Wheeler
36 Guntersville
37 Chickamauga
38 Hiwassee
39 Watts Bar
40 Coulter Shoals
41 Norris
42 Tygart R.

The TVA built nine main-river dams between the years 1933 and 1944, and many others of a subsidiary nature. Among its services, it supplied essential power during the Second World War for the production of aluminum and munitions, and for the great atomic energy plant at Oak Ridge, Tennessee.

KENTUCKY DAM. This striking example of modern industrial construction, by regulating the flow of the Tennessee River, can lower floods on the Ohio and Mississippi by as much as four feet.

NORRIS DAM. Named for the senator who ably guided the TVA, this dam helps to provide cheap hydroelectric power for an area of 40,000 square miles in seven states.

SOCIAL DEVELOPMENTS. The Kentucky Dam State Park illustrates another of TVA's social purposes.

cultural and industrial development of the region involved. The TVA was quickly organized, and with the Muscle Shoals plant as a starting-point was soon able to supply cheap electric power to a limited area. With the help of PWA funds it pushed rapidly the construction of six new dams; the greatest of which, the Norris Dam, was completed in 1936. By 1940 TVA power was being generated at four dams, and was being used both to carry forward new construction and to provide cheap power for residential and commercial consumers. By June, 1939, according to TVA estimates, the Authority was serving about 180,000 customers, either directly or indirectly, and its acquisition later in the year of facilities belonging to the Tennessee Electric Power Company added perhaps 150,000 more.

Because the TVA was a government-owned enterprise operating in direct competition with private business, it met with the most determined opposition. TVA rates were supposedly based upon the cost of production, but TVA officials, by charging off a large part of their costs to flood and navigation control, were able to devise a "yardstick" for measuring rates that to private companies seemed impossibly low. With this point of view the TVA chairman, Arthur E. Morgan, was disposed to agree, and for months he fought a losing battle with the other two members of the board, who were able as the majority to determine its policies. Eventually, after Morgan had refused a request from the President to substantiate his charges, he was removed from office, and the policy favored by his colleagues was continued. Opponents of the TVA also hoped in vain for aid from the courts. Did Congress have the right to permit the TVA to build transmission lines and distribute power under the guise of flood and navigation control? Were the TVA dams so built as to facilitate flood control, or was that a mere subterfuge, with their real purpose being the generation of power? In February, 1936, the Supreme Court upheld the sale of power from the Wilson Dam,

Opposition to TVA

built long before the TVA took charge, and three years later it refused to approve an injunction sought by private companies to prevent TVA from distributing power in competition with them. Neither decision ruled finally on the constitutionality of TVA activities as a whole, but the friendly support of the Court seemed assured.

The work undertaken by the TVA spread as time went on into a great variety of fields. It carried on an elaborate program for the control of water on the land, and the consequent checking of erosion; it produced great quantities of fertilizer, and tested its effectiveness in most of the states of the Union; it experimented with low-cost housing for the benefit of its employees; it promoted actively the use of the Tennessee River for commercial navigation; it extended the advantages of electricity to many farmers through a program of rural electrification; and it cooperated generously with local authorities in providing public health services, particularly with a view to checking the ravages of malaria and tuberculosis. These contributions to the general welfare were not invariably appreciated by the people they were meant to help, but the evidence seemed conclusive that the conditions of life in the Tennessee Valley had been enormously improved by the work of the TVA. Other hydroelectric developments under the New Deal, such as the Grand Coulee and Bonneville Dams on the Columbia, Boulder Dam on the Colorado, and Fort Peck Dam on the upper Missouri, were not accompanied by the extensive program of social betterment promoted by the TVA, but they were all intended to provide whatever benefits to society might accrue from the existence of an unlimited flow of cheap power.

Varieties of TVA endeavor

Probably the most revolutionary of all the New Deal undertakings lay in the field of social security. By an act passed August 14, 1935, Congress established a Social Security Board, the business of which was to provide for or promote old-age annuities, unemployment in-

Social security

surance, and more adequate care for the needy, the dependent, and the disabled. The necessity of some such legislation seemed abundantly apparent. Medical efficiency and a better understanding of health requirements had promoted longevity, while employers tended more and more to keep down the average age of the men on their payrolls. Technological unemployment and business readjustments were certain, even in the best of times, to throw many people out of work, and all the frantic efforts of the New Deal had failed utterly to provide complete re-employment. The aged, confronted by what looked to be a hopeless situation, listened with respect to such fantastic demands as those of Doctor F. E. Townsend of California, who urged a two per cent transaction tax to provide pensions up to two hundred dollars per month for everyone over sixty who would quit work and spend the money as fast as it came in. The unemployed looked with equal favor upon the program urged by Congressman Ernest Lundeen of Minnesota, who advocated payments of not less than ten dollars per week to all jobless persons over eighteen years of age. The discontented generally were ready to be impressed by the blandishments of Huey P. Long, a political trickster who, first as governor of Louisiana and later as United States Senator, promoted the organization of a "Share-the-Wealth Society," which set as its goal an income of not less than five thousand dollars a year for every American family. With so many political quacks making headway, it seemed essential that the government should take immediate steps to provide a workable system of social security.

The Social Security Act was said to be "the most complex measure ever considered by Congress." (1) By the familiar dollar-matching device it enabled the federal government to assist the states in the care of "unemployables." It particularly encouraged state provision for old-age pensions, for the care of dependent children, and for aid to the needy blind. (2) Further, it authorized grants to promote through state agencies the rehabilitation of the physically disabled, the care of mothers and children, and the improvement of the public health. Its most notable provisions, however, set up (3) an elaborate federal-state system of unemployment compensation, and (4) a strictly federal system of old-age insurance.

The plan for unemployment compensation required each state desirous of cooperating with the federal government to establish for the purpose an appropriate administrative agency. Unemployment compensation Because of the widely divergent conditions that existed in different parts of the nation, the states were permitted a considerable amount of latitude in suiting their regulations to local requirements. Funds for the support of the program were provided by a federal tax on payrolls. For the year 1936 the employers of eight or more persons were required to pay into the federal Treasury the equivalent of one per cent of the wages paid to all employees on their payrolls as long as twenty weeks; the second year the tax was to be two per cent; thereafter, three per cent. Toward this tax, however, employers were permitted to credit all payments up to ninety per cent of the federal tax made toward the support of a federally approved state unemployment system. The cost of authorized state administration was met by federal grants, but all state unemployment funds had to be deposited in the United States Treasury for investment in federal obligations.

By the summer of 1937 every state in the Union, together with the District of Columbia, Alaska, and Hawaii, had complied with the requirements of the Social Security Act, and the next year the payment of benefits began. Although the law excluded from its operation all government employees, farm laborers, domestic servants, casual workers, and the employees of charitable organizations, probably half the working population of the country came under its protection. Administration of the Act was vested in a new federal agency, the Social Security Board (later Social Security Administration) which in 1939 took over the United States Employment Service, and thereafter attempted to coordinate job insurance with job placement. Anyone thrown out of work was required to register at his local employment office, which must try to help him find another job. If, after a specified waiting period, he remained unemployed, benefit payments were authorized, which lasted on until the worker had either exhausted all his wage credits, or had reached the maximum period permitted by law, usually three or four months; provided, of course, that in the meantime he had failed to find another job.

The plan for old-age insurance included in the Social Security Act looked forward to the **Old-age insurance** payment of monthly benefits to qualified workers in industry and commerce who retired from employment at the age of sixty-five. The same groups were excepted from its operation as were denied the advantages of unemployment compensation. Payments of from fifteen to eighty dollars a month, depending upon the total amount of wages earned by the beneficiary after 1936, were to begin on January 1, 1942, and were to continue until the time of death, with lump-sum settlements payable to the estates of those who died before reaching the age of sixty-five. Funds for carrying out the program were to be obtained by an income tax on employees, deducted from their wages by employers, and an excise tax on payrolls. Equal sums were required of employers and employees, at first amounting in each case to one per cent of the worker's income. Amendments to the Act made in 1939 changed the date of first benefit payments to January 1, 1940, and provided for continuing allowances to the surviving dependents of deceased workers. All payments were to be made from a Trust Fund, established in the Treasury, and it was expected that over a period of years the receipts and disbursements would about balance. If the fund should become unduly large or small, however, the problem of adjustment would be passed along to Congress. By the time the

payments began, about 27,500,000 persons were eligible to receive unemployment insurance and about 25,500,000, retirement benefits.

Experience with the Social Security program led Congress during the next decade to devise repeated amendments to the original legislation, and to **Act of 1950** pass in 1950 a new Social Security Act which greatly increased the number of persons covered and the benefits obtainable. The new law extended coverage to the self-employed (except farmers and some professional classes), to regularly employed farm laborers and domestic servants, and under specified circumstances to federal, state, and local governmental employees not included in some other retirement system. A tax contribution of one and one half per cent was required from both employer and employee on the latter's earnings up to a maximum of $3,600, with a progressively rising assessment after 1953 to reach three and one half per cent by 1970. Retired workers over sixty-five years of age who qualified under the system and eligible survivors received per month on the average, as of December 31, 1951, for a single man, $43.20; for a married man and his aged wife, $70.20; for an aged widow, $36; and for a widowed mother with one minor child, $77.30. Non-contributory benefits, determined on the basis of need and made possible by federal contributions to state programs, provided additional assistance to the aged, and substantial help for dependent children, the blind, and the totally disabled.

The state-federal system of unemployment insurance, although not entirely uniform throughout the nation, provided by this time extensive benefits for unemployed workers. The average number of persons drawing unemployment insurance each week during July, 1952, a period of relatively full employment, was 870,000, and the total amount of benefits paid during the month was $88,612,000. For railroad workers there was a special retirement and unemployment program, administered entirely by federal

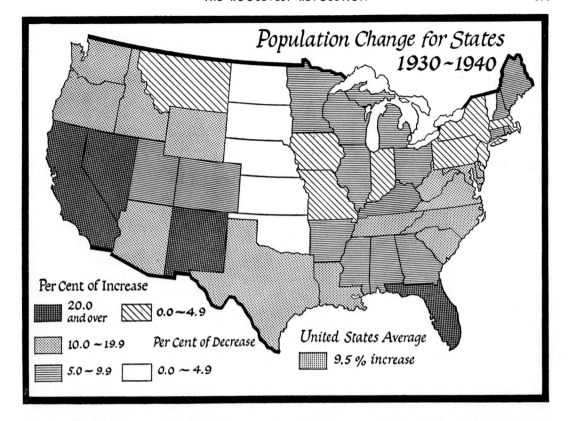

Population Change for States 1930~1940

Per Cent of Increase

20.0 and over

10.0 ~ 19.9

5.0 ~ 9.9

0.0 ~ 4.9

Per Cent of Decrease

0.0 ~ 4.9

United States Average

9.5 % increase

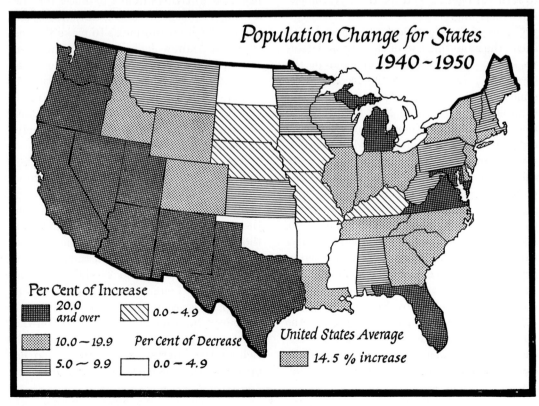

Population Change for States 1940~1950

Per Cent of Increase

20.0 and over

10.0 — 19.9

5.0 ~ 9.9

0.0 ~ 4.9

Per Cent of Decrease

0.0 ~ 4.9

United States Average

14.5 % increase

authorities, that furnished such persons and their families exceptionally complete coverage.

The initiation of so vast a social security program placed an extremely onerous tax burden upon employers, and increased greatly the distaste of the business world for the Roosevelt administration. Whether the New Deal because of its far-reaching innovations should properly be described as a revolution, a large number of Americans were perfectly certain that they did not like it. Business managers complained that private enterprise was being stifled by governmental regimentation and that individual liberty, at least for the business corporation, was being seriously curtailed. Labor too, they said, was being spoiled, both by the easygoing methods of such public agencies as the WPA and by the persistent governmental favoritism shown to organized labor. Since private capital could not readily be induced to take risks under existing conditions, the activities of the government would inevitably tend to increase; in time private business might have to retire altogether and let the government run everything.

Critics of the New Deal also viewed with alarm the mounting size of the national debt. **The national debt** The economies effected in the early days of the Roosevelt régime did not last long, and taxation sufficient to meet the rising tide of New Deal expenditures was politically inexpedient. The government therefore resorted to wholesale borrowing, and with investors uncertain as to the future of private enterprise, the appetite of the public for government bonds seemed insatiable. But how long could the nation thus continue to live on its fat? On June 30, 1933, the national debt was about twenty-two and one half billion dollars. On January 1, 1940, it was over forty-two billion, and was fast approaching the forty-five-billion-dollar debt limit set by Section 21 of the Second Liberty Bond Act, a sum which the public had become accustomed to regard as the highest reasonable maximum. But the ease with which the German armies overran

their western opponents in the spring of 1940 led to an expensive preparedness program, and the debt limit had to be raised again, an action that was to be repeated many times during the Second World War and after.

The most unsavory of the anti-Roosevelt epithets were saved for the President himself and the bureaucracy he headed. **Roosevelt haters** Roosevelt was undoubtedly one of the most popular of American Presidents, but he was also one of the most cordially hated. Himself a man of means, he was denounced bitterly as a "traitor to his class," who, in order to curry favor with the masses, stood ready to destroy his own kind. He was accused, too, of building up a powerful federal bureaucracy, the business of which was not only to man the various governmental agencies, but also to keep the Democratic Party in power. One of the reasons why Congress had been so easily persuaded to pass the laws that the President wanted was that in most instances new appointees were to be exempted from the usual requirements of civil service examinations. Such a policy meant an amazing number of offices for "deserving Democrats," and a nationwide machine of such magnitude as to make the best efforts of Andrew Jackson and his intimates seem petty indeed. Eventually the President extended the civil service regulations to include a large proportion of the newly created offices, but thousands of dependable partisans were at the same time "blanketed in" to permanent positions.

Not all of those who opposed Roosevelt were opponents of a revolutionary program. To many radicals the Roosevelt Revolution had not gone nearly far enough. Among these could be counted the eccentric and thoroughly corrupt Huey P. Long of Louisiana, who aspired to extend the borders of the dictatorship he had established in his home state. Long was ready, judging from his performance in Louisiana, to outspend Roosevelt, and he gave the impression that he was also more than willing to despoil the rich in the interest of the poor. No less openly hostile was Father Coughlin, a Roman

Catholic priest of Detroit with unorthodox views on the money question and a penchant for Jew-baiting. Father Coughlin established a National Union for Social Justice in the name of which he propagated his views every week by radio. Many Socialists and Communists, while convinced that Roosevelt's program was far too moderate, thought of it as an entering wedge for their doctrines, and for a time showed more friendliness for the New Deal than most of its other supporters wished. The Communists in particular, with the "party line" favoring a "popular front" of all liberals, gave Roosevelt their open support. This attitude ended abruptly, however, when Hitler and Stalin made common cause in 1939. Since Roosevelt was known to be an ardent protagonist of the western democracies, the Communists, whose duty it was to continue their obedience to Stalin at all costs, had no choice but to substitute denunciations for their former commendations.

Elections of 1934 By 1934, when the state and congressional elections gave the country its first opportunity to return a verdict on the New Deal, the Republicans had not sufficiently recovered from their rout of two years before to furnish much opposition. The Democrats again won by a landslide. Two years later, however, with a modicum of recovery seemingly assured, the Republicans took heart and prepared to fight. Such improvement in business conditions as had come to pass, they maintained, was due less to the New Deal than to the courageous conservatism of the Supreme Court, which had stricken down both the NRA and the AAA, and in numerous other decisions had revealed its opposition to the Roosevelt policies. The downward trend of business during the winter of 1932–33, culminating in the bank panic of 1933, they explained as only the natural result of fear on the part of business, fear as to what Roosevelt intended to do. The Hoover administration, according to this version of events, had already almost defeated the depression, and had Hoover been re-elected, normal times would

long since have returned. Aided by the American Liberty League, founded in 1934 by leading Republican industrialists, and openly supported by Alfred E. Smith and many other conservative Democrats, the opponents of Roosevelt entered the campaign of 1936 with high hopes of success.

Campaign of 1936 The Democrats, now more completely under the domination of an outstanding leader than at any time since the ascendancy of William Jennings Bryan, met in convention at Philadelphia, June 23, to renominate Roosevelt and Garner, and to endorse the New Deal. Annoyance with the attitude of the Supreme Court was apparent, but the Democratic leaders showed little desire to make the Court the principal issue of the campaign. The Republicans, however, were determined to force the fighting along this line. Meeting in Cleveland, June 9, they pointedly denounced the President for his usurpation of congressional authority, his indifference to the rights of the states, and his willingness to ride rough-shod over the Constitution as interpreted by the Supreme Court. The great dilemma of the Republicans was their lack of "presidential timber." The two New Deal landslides had carried down practically every outstanding Republican to defeat. Of those who survived, the three best known were United States Senator Arthur H. Vandenberg of Michigan, Senator William E. Borah of Idaho, and Governor Alfred M. Landon of Kansas. Since Borah's sporadic radicalism made him an impossible leader for a strictly conservative cause, and since Vandenberg was only passively interested, the choice of the convention fell, almost by default, upon Landon. The Vice-Presidential nomination went to Colonel Frank Knox, owner and publisher of the Chicago *Daily News.*

Three minor parties also entered candidates: the Socialists, Norman Thomas; the Communists, Earl Browder; and a new Union Party, William Lemke, Republican congressman from North Dakota. Thomas fought a valiant and honorable campaign, in which he criticized the New Deal for its halfway measures, and the Republicans for their devotion to reaction; Browder, on the other hand, made little effort to conceal his hope for a New Deal victory. Lemke tried to wear the mantle of the LaFollette Progressives who had gone down to defeat in 1924, but he won little support. In general the left-wing forces, including many normally Socialist or Communist voters, were solidly united behind Roosevelt. John L. Lewis, leader of the C.I.O., earnestly supported the President, and the C.I.O. contributed heavily to his campaign chest.

While Landon, for a Republican, was in reality outstandingly liberal, and while the

The new political division Republican platform by no means called for the complete rejection of all the New Deal

policies, the campaign inevitably impressed the voters as a contest between the forces of reaction, who wished to return to the ways of bygone years, and the forces of liberalism, who were willing to experiment in an effort to find a better way. It was evident that the "vertical" line of cleavage between the parties, so characteristic of nineteenth-century American politics, had given way to a "horizontal" division, which placed the more-favored economic groups in the Republican column and the less-favored elements in the Democratic. This was revealed with some clarity by the campaign contributions, which for the Republicans amounted to about nine million dollars, and for the Democrats to about five and one half million dollars. The great trouble with such a contest, from the Republican point of view, was that the lower classes had the votes. Thousands of citizens whose only means of support had been the relief payments or the made work of New Deal agencies saw little reason to exchange such small favors for the more rugged individualism promised by Republican campaign orators. Farmers whose antecedents were Republican were conscious of the fact that the benefit payments they received were quite as definitely Democratic. The country might be heading for disaster, as the Republicans claimed, but the personal

prospects of a great host of voters seemed to hinge on Democratic success. All this, according to the Republican version, amounted to little less than wholesale bribery by the use of public funds. Under these circumstances the only possible result of the contest was another Democratic landslide.

The situation was not helped by the nature of Landon's campaign. As a radio orator he was extremely inept, and in com-

Straw votes parison with the President's

finely modulated periods his utterances sounded schoolboyish. He offended the labor leaders by his rash attacks, and lost far more votes than he gained by coming out boldly against the Social Security Act. His audiences proved to be lukewarm or even hostile, while the President received an ovation everywhere he spoke. Straw ballots taken to discover the trend of public opinion predicted, with one notable exception, an easy Democratic victory. The *Literary Digest*, which had successfully foretold the result in every presidential campaign since 1916, depended upon the distribution of millions of postcard ballots to voters whose names appeared in telephone books and in similar lists. From its returns Landon appeared far in the lead except in the South, but the fact that a majority of those who voted in the poll had favored Hoover in 1932 caused many observers to discount its findings. What it really proved was that more Republicans than Democrats got their names in print, or at least took the trouble to fill out and return the postcard ballots. Thereafter forecasters tended to follow the "sampling" methods, used, for example, in the Gallup poll, which sought to ascertain the sentiments of a reasonable cross-section of the nation's voters.

The Democratic landslide of 1936 exceeded the expectations of all the most seasoned observers, with the excep-

Election results tion of James A. Farley, the

Democratic campaign manager, who accurately predicted that the Republicans would carry only two states, Maine and Vermont. The electoral vote stood 523 for

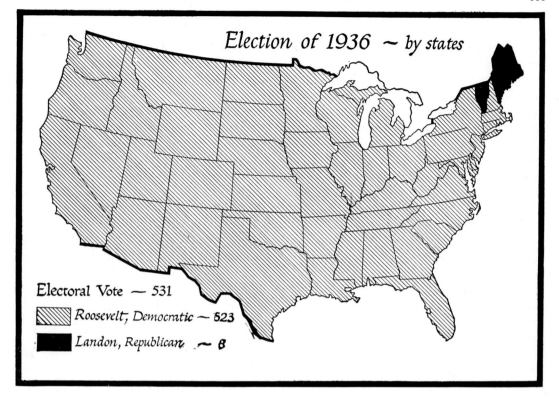

Election of 1936 ~ by states

Electoral Vote — 531
Roosevelt, Democratic — 523
Landon, Republican ~ 8

Roosevelt to 8 for Landon, and the popular vote 27,750,000 to 16,680,000. Not since James Monroe was re-elected in 1820 with but a single opposing electoral vote had an American election been so one-sided. Another significant aspect of the voting was the waning strength of the left-wing minor parties. The new Union Party polled only 892,000 votes, the Socialists 187,000, and the Communists 80,000. Undoubtedly much of this falling-off was due to the satisfaction felt by radicals with the direction the New Deal had taken. In both houses of Congress the Democratic majorities became so large as to threaten dissension. In the House the Democrats won 328 seats out of 435, and in the Senate 77 out of 96.

This overwhelming victory no doubt furnished in part the explanation for an attack on the Supreme Court that the President launched shortly after his second inauguration. Before the election he had not hesitated to express his irritation with decisions that were based upon precedents set in

"horse-and-buggy days," but he had studiously refrained from attacking the Court during the campaign. Now, with sixty per cent of the nation's voters behind him, what might have been hazardous before seemed safe enough. That the Court majority was bitterly hostile to the New Deal seemed obvious. Out of nine important decisions involving New Deal measures, only twice did the government score victories, and in one of these, the law invalidating gold clauses in contracts, the majority was only five to four. Not a single member of the Court had been appointed by Roosevelt; only Andrew Johnson of all the Presidents since the Civil War had served so long without being privileged to choose at least one justice. Of the nine members of the Court, six were more than seventy years of age, and of these six, five were fairly consistently conservative. That some of these veterans were determined to retain their seats until Roosevelt was out of office seemed at least a reasonable inference. With a "second New Deal" in the making to replace the measures voided by the Supreme Court, the President decided on a course of action which, he believed, would prevent any similar disaster in the future.

There were two ways in which reform of the Court could be effected: (1) by an amend-**Roosevelt** ment to the Constitution, which **attacks the** might either require retirement **Court** at a given age or set limits to the doctrine of judicial review; (2) by a law of Congress to provide for an increase in the number of justices, thus permitting the President to "pack" the Supreme Court with new appointees of less conservative views. The President chose the latter alternative, probably because it seemed to permit of speedier action, but he coupled with it an ingenious provision for calling attention to the advanced age of some of the justices. The measure he urged on Congress would have set the age of seventy for the voluntary retirement of Supreme Court justices, and for each member of the Court who reached that age and failed to retire the President might appoint an additional justice until a maximum Court of fifteen members had been reached. The measure also provided for an extensive reorganization of the lower federal courts with a view to expediting business and increasing efficiency.

Probably the President was quite unprepared for the furor that his "court-packing" bill evoked. Many Democrats, both in and out of Congress, professed to believe with the Republicans that the last safeguard of American liberty was endangered, and that what the President aspired to create was a dictatorship, pure and simple. In the Senate, where the administration forces chose to stage the initial contest, Burton K. Wheeler of Montana, an ardent New Dealer in every other respect, led the opposition with infinite resourcefulness. Wheeler held no brief for the Court as constituted, but whatever change was to be made, he held, should be made by constitutional amendment. In the end the President for the first time on a matter of major importance failed to carry Congress with him. Astutely led by Chief Justice Hughes, the Court itself took a major part in the proceedings; by a series of decisions favorable to the New Deal, it reminded older citizens of Mr. Dooley's famous observation, "The Supreme Court follows the illiction returns," and materially weakened the President's case. Possibly also at Hughes's suggestion, Justice Willis Van Devanter, senior member of the Court in point of service and a pronounced conservative, announced his determination to take speedy advantage of the act which Congress passed March 1, 1937, granting full pay to retiring justices over seventy years of age. Finally, the sudden death of Senator Joseph Robinson, administration floor leader in charge of the Court bill, put an end to the President's hopes. Congress passed a bill which instituted some of the reforms Roosevelt had called for in the lower courts, but it left the Supreme Court intact.

Nevertheless the President soon got what he wanted most, a court less conservative in character, which would no **The new** longer stand in the way of New **Supreme** Deal objectives. Had he been **Court** less impatient, he might have obtained the same result with far less bitterness and party dissension. The fight well illustrated two outstanding features of the American constitutional system: (1) the difficulties involved whenever one department of the government attempts to dominate another; and (2) the inability of any department, including even the Supreme Court, to resist indefinitely the popular will. When Justice Van Devanter resigned, the President chose as his successor Senator Hugo L. Black of Alabama, a man less learned in the law than he was loyal to the principles of the New Deal. When, after the appointment had been confirmed by the Senate, the country learned that the new justice had once been a member of the Ku Klux Klan, a loud demand for his resignation broke forth. But Black refused to resign, publicly admitted his membership in the Klan as a youthful indiscretion, and settled down under excellent tutelage to acquaint himself more intimately with the law. Before

Charles Evans Hughes, as Associate Justice from 1910 to 1916 and as Chief Justice from 1930 to 1941, exerted a tremendous influence upon the development of American constitutional law. During the New Deal period he took a middle position between the traditionalists and the liberals among his colleagues. With some assistance from Associate Justice Roberts, he sought to limit the judicial power of administrative agencies and at the same time to protect civil liberties and the freedom of the press. He was strongly opposed to Roosevelt's court-packing plan, and probably had as much to do as anyone with defeating it. The likeness here shown is from a steel engraving; to the right is the new Supreme Court Building.

the end of his second term Roosevelt made four more appointments to the Supreme Court: Stanley F. Reed of Kentucky, his able Solicitor-General; Felix Frankfurter, of the Harvard Law School; William O. Douglas, recently of the Yale Law School; and Frank Murphy, formerly Governor of Michigan and for a short time Attorney-General in the Roosevelt cabinet. Each of these men was adequately learned in the law, but judges of the lower federal courts and of the state courts were quick to note that the Supreme Court could no longer count within its membership a single man who had risen to the position he held by virtue of judicial experience. Partly on this account, and partly because the new court was evidently determined not to thwart the New Deal, they bemoaned the fact that a hard-working judge might follow consistently opinions handed down by the Supreme Court itself, and still see his judgments reversed.

The Supreme Court fight was barely ended when a downward trend in business, called by Democrats a recession and by Republicans a new depression, pro- **The recession of 1937** vided the administration with another major problem. The slump came unheralded, and caught New Dealers along with everyone else unawares. It was caused in no small part by the attempt of the national government beginning in 1937 to curtail expenditures, a fact which supported the argument of Roosevelt's opponents that there had been no real recovery all along, but only a continuous process of pump-priming. New Dealers, on the other hand, charged that capital itself had gone on strike, and that business contraction in the interest of maintaining high price-levels was a principal cause of the trouble. Whatever the merit of these contentions, the administration moved rapidly to halt the decline. The Board of Governors of the Federal Reserve System promptly reversed the deflationary policy it had been pursuing since the summer of 1936, and the "second New Deal," at which Congress had balked while the Court battle went on, was promptly instituted. This included much additional pump-priming, particularly through the WPA, the PWA, the RFC, and the USHA; the creation of a new AAA, already described, for the revival of agriculture; and somewhat belatedly (1939) a wide grant of power to the President to reorganize the federal departments of government in the interest of greater efficiency. The conviction that methods of price control had been devised in monopolistic industries led also to an attempt to enforce the moribund anti-trust laws. Since the days of the ill-starred NRA these regulations had been more or less in abatement, but the President now chose Thurman W. Arnold of the Yale Law School to be Assistant Attorney-General, and charged him with the duty of making them live again. Arnold was well but most unfavorably known to the business world for the caustic cricitisms contained in his book, *The Folklore of Capitalism* (1937). Important results were expected also from a National Economic Committee (better known as the Monopoly Investigation), authorized by Congress in June, 1938, and headed by Senator Joseph O'Mahoney of Wyoming. The Investigation disclosed that economic competition had indeed declined, and that a few great corporations had amassed tremendous power. As a result of Arnold's prosecutions, many corporations were obliged to accept "consent decrees" designed to restrain their monopolistic practices.

Well before the time for the mid-term elections of 1938, the recession seemed to be at an end and business was again on the upgrade. But the electorate was left in a far more critical mood toward the New Deal than it had ever exhibited before. With considerable logic the Republicans could argue that the country after over five years of spending was still on the relief basis, and that whatever prosperity existed was dependent on the continued outpouring of public funds. Once more the battle-cry was raised that business must be freed if any real recovery was to be expected. The

Elections of 1938

fight on the Supreme Court had also injured the Democratic chances, partly because so many voters of both parties had opposed the President's course, and partly because of the internal dissensions that the Court fight had engendered. This situation was **greatly** intensified by the President's attempt to "purge" the party of a selected group of senators and representatives who had frequently opposed his policies. Among those so proscribed were Senators W. F. George of Georgia, Millard E. Tydings of Maryland, and E. D. ("Cotton Ed") Smith of South Carolina, and Representative John J. O'Connor of New York, all of whom, except the last mentioned, were triumphantly renominated and re-elected. Republican gains were also spectacular, and included seventy-nine seats in the House and eight in the Senate. Many states that had abandoned the Republican column in recent elections also returned to their former allegiance, electing Republican governors, or legislatures, or both. Noteworthy among these changes were Pennsylvania, Massachusetts, and Connecticut in the East, and Michigan, Wisconsin, and Minnesota in the West.

Particularly surprising was the blow dealt what had seemed to be a promising third-party movement in the Northwest. For eight years the Farmer-Labor Party in Minnesota, ably led by Governor Floyd B. Olson until his death in 1936, and after that by Governor Elmer A. Benson, had dominated the government of the state, while in Wisconsin the Progressives, equally well captained by Governor Philip F. LaFollette, a son of "old Bob" and a brother of "young Bob," had won handily in the elections of 1934 and 1936. Plans were under way for a union of forces, and Governor LaFollette had already launched a movement for the transformation of his local state party into a nationwide organization. If, as at times seemed likely, the Democratic Party should turn conservative or split, the Progressive Party might function as a welcome home to the New Deal radicals. But in Minnesota a little known and extremely youthful

Third-party misfortunes

Republican named Harold E. Stassen defeated Benson, while in Wisconsin a Milwaukee industrialist, Julius P. Heil, defeated LaFollette. In both states the Democratic organization was all but extinct, and the third parties continued as the chief opponents of the Republicans; but the prospect that they would ever unite to become the nucleus of a new nationwide left-wing party seemed remote indeed.

By this time foreign affairs had come to play a much more significant rôle in American policy than had been anticipated when the New Deal first was instituted. After the collapse of the London Economic Conference of 1933, the United States had shown an evident determination to "go it alone," regardless of what might happen to the rest of the world, but Secretary Hull worked quietly, and as events proved effectively, in the opposite direction. Hull was convinced that the surest road to recovery, both for the United States and for the rest of the world, lay in the revival of international trade, something that could never happen as long as high tariff barriers blocked the way. He believed, too, that the free movement of goods throughout the world was an essential preliminary to the establishment of anything bordering upon permanent peace. To reduce the high tariffs, which so effectively excluded American goods from foreign markets, he advocated the negotiation of a series of reciprocal trade agreements. By this means the nations with which the United States wished to trade might be induced to lower their tariff barriers in return for equivalent American reductions. Furthermore, the "most favored nation" clause that had been written into so many treaties between the United States and foreign powers would operate to extend indefinitely the scope of any changes effected. This system had certain definite advantages over the old-fashioned general tariff revision. In the first place, bargains could be struck with foreign nations by which the United States might hope to gain as well as to give; secondly, the log-rolling proclivities of Con-

The Hull trade pacts

Cordell Hull, a conservative southern Democrat, served for twelve years as Roosevelt's Secretary of State.

gress, which had defeated so many efforts to lower the tariff, might be avoided.

Not until June, 1934, did Congress get around to the passage of the Trade Agreements Act necessary to enable Secretary Hull to carry his program into effect. That measure delegated to the President the right for a three-year period to negotiate agreements with other countries for the mutual lowering of tariff rates. Without so much as referring the matter back to Congress for its consent, he might lower American duties by as much as fifty per cent, provided only that the American free list be not disturbed, one way or the other. Under this grant of authority, which was renewed in 1937 and again in 1940, Secretary Hull went promptly to work, and in five years' time had concluded more than twenty agreements, among which those with Canada and Great Britain were particularly sweeping. Perhaps three fifths of the exports and imports of the United States were affected by these pacts. A large number of agreements were negotiated with Latin-American countries, whose good-will toward the United States was thereby considerably increased. American farmers, particularly those of the Middle

West, quite generally opposed the agreements on the ground that American agricultural interests were being sacrificed for the benefit of industry. It was true that some of the pacts did facilitate the importation of foreign foodstuffs, but Secretary Hull and the Trade Agreements Committee of specialists, upon whom he relied for technical advice, were convinced that whatever stimulated American industry increased the buying power of American labor, and so aided the farmer indirectly, probably far more than the limited importations of foreign farm products harmed him.

The deep-seated interest in securing the friendship of Latin-America that had long
The "good neighbor" policy
characterized American foreign policy was continued and intensified under Roosevelt. Hoover as President-elect had made a "good-will tour" of eleven Latin-American republics, and as President had worked steadily toward the withdrawal of American troops from occupied areas. During his administration, also, the Department of State had published the "Clark Memorandum on the Monroe Doctrine," which denied the validity of the Theodore Roosevelt Corollary, and asserted that the United States no longer felt obligated to supervise the behavior toward foreign nations of the Latin-American republics.[1] Roosevelt speedily let it be known that his policy toward Latin America was likewise to be that of the "good neighbor." He sent Secretary Hull to the seventh Pan-American Conference, held in Montevideo, and cordially approved the doctrine on which the Conference agreed, that "no state has the right to intervene in the internal or external affairs of another." Presently, in 1936, he journeyed seven thousand miles by sea to Buenos Aires in order to open a special Inter-American Conference for Peace, and told delegates that non-American states seeking "to commit acts of aggression against

[1] This memorandum was the work of J. Reuben Clark, Jr., Undersecretary of State in Coolidge's administration. It was dated December 17, 1928, but not officially published until 1930.

us will find a Hemisphere wholly prepared to consult together for our mutual safety and our mutual good."

A practical demonstration of how the "good neighbor policy" might be expected to operate was given in the case
Cuba
of Cuba, which dared at last to attempt the overthrow by revolution of its current dictator, Gerardo Machado. The depression which began in 1929 became particularly acute in Cuba after the passage in 1930 of the Hawley-Smoot Tariff, which increased the rates on sugar imported into the United States. Machado, a thoroughgoing tyrant who had maintained himself in office since 1924, should normally have been one of the first casualties of the depression and well deserved the honor. But American investors in Cuban securities liked him, for he consistently made the interest payments due on the huge sums that the Cuban government had borrowed in the United States. Out of deference to their wishes the Hoover administration had so strongly supported Machado that the Cubans, fearing American intervention even more than they feared Machado's tyranny, dared not revolt. When Roosevelt became President, he let it be known that Machado could expect no further backing from the American government, and as a result the dictator was promptly driven from office. Unhappily, however, the government which succeeded him lasted only three weeks, when another revolution occurred. Undoubtedly American pressure was applied from this time forward to insure the establishment of an orderly and competent government in the island, but no American troops were landed, and American interests were watched over exclusively by recognized diplomatic agents. For the first time since the Spanish-American war a serious revolutionary outbreak in Cuba came to an end without the customary military intervention by the United States. Furthermore, on May 29, 1934, a treaty between the United States and Cuba formally released the latter from the terms of the Platt Amendment, which for a generation had rankled in

The Commonwealth of the Philippines was officially launched November 15, 1935. The photograph shows Secretary of War George W. Dern reading President Roosevelt's proclamation at Manila.

Cuban breasts. That same year a reciprocal trade treaty materially reduced the tariff on Cuban exports to the United States and checked the decline of Cuban-American trade.

Other evidence that the "big stick" policy was really at an end accumulated rapidly. By an agreement reached in August, 1934, the financial receivership which the United States maintained in Haiti was greatly liberalized, and the last detachment of American marines was ordered to leave the republic. About the same time negotiations were begun with Panama to abolish the special privileges that that nation had been forced to accord the United States, and after a long delay this, too, was accomplished. Even the drastic action taken by Mexico in 1936, which ordered the expropriation of all foreign-owned oil property within Mexican borders, led only to relatively mild expostulations from Secretary Hull, who, after all efforts to settle the controversy through diplomatic channels had failed, requested merely that it be submitted to arbitration.

The Roosevelt administration also made a systematic effort to draw Canada more

Canada closely into the fraternity of American nations. This was somewhat facilitated by the greater independence which Canada enjoyed, after the First World War, within the British Empire, particularly by the fact that the United States and Canada had exchanged ministers since 1927 and were able to carry on their diplomatic relations directly instead of by way of London. Roosevelt was no more successful than Hoover in obtaining Senate ratification for the St. Lawrence Waterway Treaty, negotiated in 1932 to make possible a deep-sea channel from the Gulf of St. Lawrence to the Great Lakes, but on a visit to Canada in 1938 he reminded his hearers that the Monroe Doctrine applied as much to the territory north of the United States as to the territory south of it. "I give you assurance," he said, "that the people of the United States will not stand idly by if the domination of Canadian soil is threatened by any other empire."

The decline of "Yankee imperialism" in the Americas was paralleled across the Pacific by the progress of the Philippine **The Philip-** Islands toward complete inde- **pines** pendence. In accordance with the Tydings-McDuffie Act of 1934 the Islands had become an autonomous Commonwealth, with a President of their own choosing, Manuel Quezon, and an elective National Assembly. Except for control over foreign relations and a few other specified restrictions, the Philippine nationalists had thus obtained practically all the liberty they had ever sought, but they were still far from happy. They knew full well that the economic prosperity of the Islands had been built upon freedom of trade with the United States, a privilege that was now to be gradually withdrawn. They knew also that independence would carry with it the obligation of self-defense. Fully alive to this need, President Quezon in 1935 asked and obtained from President Roosevelt the services of General Douglas MacArthur, Chief-of-Staff of the United States Army. First as military adviser to the Philippine government, and then as Field Marshal of the Philippine army, MacArthur made it his aim to create a native constabulary strong enough to hold any foreign invader at bay, pending the anticipated assistance of the United States Navy. The date set for full independence was July 4, 1946, and the date was met. But in the meantime the tumultuous events of the Second World War had come and gone.

Bibliography

Many of the books cited for the preceding chapter continue useful for this. Perhaps the best contemporary evaluation of the progress of the New Deal during Roosevelt's first administration is *The New Deal: An Analysis and Appraisal*, by the editors of the London *Economist* (1937). Among the books on Roosevelt, not previously cited, the following are of some pertinence here: E. K. Lindley, *Half Way with Roosevelt* (1936); Earle Looker, *The American Way, Franklin Roosevelt in Action* (1933); *Social Change and the New Deal*, edited by W. F. Ogburn (1934); Stanley High, *Roosevelt — and Then?* (1937); John T. Flynn, *Country Squire in the White House* (1940); and, by the same author, *The Roosevelt Myth* (1948). For certain aspects of the later New Deal, Joseph Alsop and Robert Kintner, *Men Around the President* (1939), is informative.

Books of varying merit and points of view abound on the Tennessee Valley Authority, among them J. F. Carter, *The Future Is Ours* (1939); D. E. Lilienthal, *TVA: Democracy on the March* (1944); Louis B. Wehle, *Hidden Threads of History; Wilson through Roosevelt* (1953); Twentieth Century Fund, *The Power Industry and the Public Interest* (1944); C. H. Pritchett, *The Tennessee Valley Authority: A Study in Public Administration* (1943); Philip Selznik, *TVA and the Grass Roots* (1949); and Julian Huxley, *TVA: Adventure in Planning* (1943).

The subject of social security has also attracted much attention. Paul H. Douglas, *Social Security in the United States* (rev. ed., 1939), contains the text of the Social Security Act. Other books worth mentioning include Abraham Epstein, *Insecurity: A Challenge to America* (new ed., 1938); I. M. Rubinow, *The Quest for Security* (1934); Eveline M. Burns, *Toward Social Security* (1936); Lewis Merriam, *Relief and Social Security* (1946); and James Parker, *Social Security Reserves* (1942).

On the national debt, see H. L. Lutz, *Public Finance* (1947); and two books by the Twentieth Century Fund, *Facing the Tax Problem* (1937); and *Debts and Recovery, 1928–37* (1938).

Among the many vigorous assaults on Roosevelt two of the most telling were J. P. Warburg, *Hell Bent for Election* (1935); and *Still Hell Bent* (1936). But Warburg finally supported Roosevelt for re-election. On the other side, see J. P. Kennedy, *I'm for Roosevelt* (1936). Campaign biographies are of little significance, but they appear regularly every four years. Frederick Palmer, *This Man Landon* (1936), sets forth the virtues of the Republican candidate in 1936. It may be supplemented by W. A. White, *What It's All About* (1936); and A. M. Landon, *America at the Crossroads* (1936). E. E. Robinson, *The Presidential Vote, 1936* (1940), is a supplement to the author's earlier volume.

The controversy over the Supreme Court produced a vast amount of writing. Among the many books worthy of note are Charles Warren,

Congress, Constitution, and the Supreme Court (1935); E. S. Corwin, *The Twilight of the Supreme Court* (1934); and, by the same author, *Court over Constitution* (1938); Morris L. Ernst, *The Ultimate Power* (1937); Irving Brant, *Storm over the Constitution* (1936); Walter Lippmann, *The Supreme Court, Independent or Controlled* (1937); and Owen J. Roberts, *The Court and the Constitution* (1951). R. H. Jackson, *The Struggle for Judicial Supremacy* (1941), gives the background for Roosevelt's attack on the Court. Joseph Alsop and Turner Catledge, *The 168 Days* (1938), is a full account of the Court fight. C. Herman Pritchett, *The Roosevelt Court: A Study in Judicial Politics and Values, 1937–1947* (1948), carries over into the results of the fight on the Court. There are a number of useful biographies of justices, among them Merlo J. Pusey, *Charles Evans Hughes* (2 vols., 1951); Samuel Hendel, *Charles Evans Hughes and the Supreme Court* (1951); Joel F. Paschal, *Mr. Justice Sutherland* (1951); John P. Frank, *Mr. Justice Black: The Man and His Opinions* (1949); S. J. Konefsky, *Chief Justice Stone and the Supreme Court* (1945); and A. T. Mason, *Brandeis, A Free Man's Life* (1946).

The New Deal within the individual states is beginning to receive the attention it deserves. The California picture is admirably portrayed in Robert E. Burke, *Olson's New Deal for California* (1953) and on a particular phase in Clarke A. Chambers, *California Farm Organizations, 1929–1941* (1952). It also receives some attention in John W. Caughey, *California* (2d ed., 1953). Upton Sinclair, *I, Candidate for Governor and How I Got Licked* (1935), tells the story of the famous EPIC campaign. W. F. Raney, *Wisconsin, A Story of Progress* (1940), is an excellent state history which covers the New Deal period. Two biographies of Minnesota's Farmer-Labor governor are available: J. S. McGrath and J. J. Delmont, *Floyd Björnsterne Olson* (1937); and George H. Mayer, *The Political Career of Floyd B. Olson* (1951). J. M. Holzworth, *The Fighting Governor: The Story of William Langer and the State of North Dakota* (1938), is journalistic and undocumented, but useful. On the New Deal South, see Harnett Kane, *Louisiana Hayride* (1941); Carleton Beals, *The Story of Huey P. Long* (1935); and V. O. Key, *Southern Politics in State and Nation* (1949).

The New Deal tariff program has been much written about, usually in favorable terms. The following books are worthy of citation: H. J. Tasch, *The Reciprocal Trade Policy of the United States* (1938); Carl Kreider, *The Anglo-American Trade Agreement: A Study of British and American Commercial Policies* (1943); J. M. Callahan, *American Foreign Policy in Canadian Relations* (1937); Alonzo E. Taylor, *The New Deal and Foreign Trade* (1935); Francis B. Sayre, *The Way Forward: The American Trade Agreements Program* (1939); J. M. Letiche, *Reciprocal Trade Agreements in the World Economy* (1948); and Edward O. Guerrant, *Roosevelt's Good Neighbor Policy* (1950).

There are also numerous area studies of consequence. Nathaniel and Sylvia Weyl, *The Reconquest of Mexico: The Years of Lázaro Cárdenas* (1939), is wholly sympathetic with the Cárdenas program. Rexford G. Tugwell, *The Stricken Land* (1947), is a report on conditions in Puerto Rico by a former governor. H. F. Guggenheim, *The United States and Cuba* (1934), concerns American diplomatic activities in the island republic. On the diplomacy of the New Deal in general, see *The Memoirs of Cordell Hull* (2 vols., 1948); and H. B. Hinton, *Cordell Hull: A Biography* (1942).

29

The Disintegration of Peace

The Russian Revolution — Mussolini in Italy —
Hitler's Germany — Fascism in Japan — Manchukuo
— The Chinese "incident" — Ethiopia — The Spanish
Civil War — Appeasement — Rome-Berlin Axis —
Russian-German accord — War begins — "Collective
security" — Quarantine of aggressors — Naval expansion — Neutrality legislation — "Continental solidarity" — Act of Havana — The Far East

DURING the two decades that followed the First World War Americans who had enthusiastically supported that struggle in order "to make the world safe for democracy" suffered many disappointments. The failure of the United States to accept responsibility for anything that happened outside its borders was in itself disillusioning, and perhaps to some extent also a cause of the world's rapid descent into international discord. But quite as distressing was the discovery, as the years wore on, that democracy, both in Europe and in Asia, was on the wane; that dictatorships of such magnitude as modern times had never known before were being born; that the arbitrary will of autocrats to war, against which Wilson had hoped the League of Nations would insure the world, was present in an increasingly aggravated form. The League of Nations, in spite of American failure to participate in its counsels, was duly organized, but its weakness in the face of the appalling problems that confronted it soon became painfully apparent. What the League might have been had the United States chosen to be its leading member, the world can never know. But the strength it was able to muster, without American assistance, was insufficient to stem the tide that led to war.

The first of the great European nations to undergo drastic revolutionary change was Russia. The Tsar had abdicated in March, 1917, and had transferred his powers to a provisional government of liberal democrats, headed by Alexander Kerensky. But the real revolution began only in October, 1917, when the "Bolshevists," or extreme Communists, under the leadership of Nikolai Lenin and Leon Trotsky, undertook to establish their long-envisioned dictatorship of the proletariat. They made peace with Germany at the price of the infamous Treaty of Brest-Litovsk,[1] and then fought off with incredible success numerous uprisings against their authority, both from within and without. By the end of 1922, they had formed a large portion of the territory left to Russia into a Union of Soviet Socialist Republics, with the expectation that eventually non-Russian as well as Russian countries would wish to join up.

The Russian Revolution

The official guide of Bolshevist conduct was the *Communist Manifesto*, published in 1848 by Karl Marx and Friedrich Engels. In harmony with the Marxian ideal, the Bolshevist leaders sought to establish a classless society. The land and all large-scale indus-

---

[1] See p. 441. The Tsar, Nicholas II, and his entire family were brutally murdered, July 16, 1918, after the Bolshevists took over.

try was nationalized; only personal property was left in the hands of individuals. Such agencies of production as mines and factories were taken over by the state, and the government gradually assumed responsibility for the distribution of goods. Ideally there was only one employer, the government; and, while most labor was free, on occasion armies of "forced labor" were recruited for work in the forests or on the roads and railroads. Labor became the duty of every citizen; the "parasitic" classes of capitalist society who lived from past earnings or the earnings of others were to be no more. As the new order was set up, the old order was destroyed. The old bureaucracy, the professional classes, landowners, property-minded members of the upper and middle classes, whether great or small, were driven into exile or mercilessly liquidated. Slowly, but with inexorable certainty, the revolution penetrated even to the most remote country districts. "Collectivist" farms tended increasingly to replace the old peasant holdings, and well-to-do "kulaks" who resisted disappeared. The Russia that grew up was thus composed in large part of those who could be benefited by the new régime; the favored few who had prospered during the old régime had been eliminated.

In theory the Soviet system was extremely democratic, but practice and theory were notably unrelated. From the **The Soviet system** first, thousands of local "soviets," or committees each composed of workers or peasants, participated in governmental affairs, even selecting by indirect means a Congress of Soviets, supreme over all. Ultimately, under the Constitution of 1936, citizens of the "USSR" chose members to a Soviet of the Union according to electoral areas, on the basis of one deputy for each 300,000 of the population. But, since only the Communist Party was tolerated, an inner circle of party leaders managed somehow to win practically all the higher offices. Party membership was rigorously restricted; in 1939 party members numbered only about a million and a half, all true and tested be-

lievers in the Marxian dogma, as interpreted by the leader of the Communist Party, originally Lenin, and some years after his death in 1924, Josef Stalin. The Soviet Union was thus ruled in fact, if not in name, by a small group of Communists, often called the "Politburo," of whom Stalin was the chief. Whoever or whatever the state officials, all real authority was vested in the man, or the group, who could control the Communist Party.

The original Communist policy was that national revolution was only the prelude to world revolution. With this goal in mind, an organization known as the Third International,[1] or Comintern, was founded in 1919 by Lenin, with headquarters in Moscow. Theoretically, at least, the Comintern was not a part of the Russian government, but was wholly separate from it, a kind of supreme authority for Communists throughout the world. From this central agency revolutionary propaganda was dispensed, and to it professional revolutionaries operating outside Russia looked for guidance and support. But as time went on the Russian government showed far more concern for internal national interests than for overthrowing the capitalist system elsewhere. Particularly was this true after the accession of Stalin to power. Trotsky, a believer in immediate world revolution, was exiled, while three successive "five-year plans" were undertaken to make Russia self-sustaining, and able to defend herself in case of war. The Comintern continued to exist, but since the Russian Communist Party had the largest number of dues-paying members, it reflected accurately the policies of the Russian government. Finally, in June, 1943, presumably on orders from Stalin, the Comintern was abolished altogether, or so the world was told.

Foreign as the Russian system was to the

---

[1] The First International was the work of Karl Marx and lasted from 1864 to 1876; the Second International was a Socialist organization that began in 1889, and was opposed by the Third International. A Fourth International was formed by the followers of Trotsky after his break with Stalin in 1929.

The Russian Revolution was fraught with far greater significance than contemporaries realized. It not only helped Germany and hurt the Allies by taking Russia out of the war, but it also provided a safe center from which Communist doctrines could be spread.

INTERNAL VIOLENCE. Revolution and counter-revolution left in their wake scenes of destruction and ruin.

RELIGIOUS SUPPRESSION. Despite the prohibition of religious observance, peasants maintain the rites and traditions of their faith.

"American way of life," it was no more difficult for Americans to comprehend than the "Fascist" dictatorship in Italy that Benito Mussolini had set up in the years following 1922. Parliamentary government had never worked especially well in Italy, and in the face of the bewildering problems of the post-war era it threatened to break down altogether. Fear that in this event a Bolshevist revolution such as had overcome Russia might take place in Italy gave Mussolini his chance. His party, the Fascisti, although originally shot through with socialistic doctrines, had become "rightist" in character, and longed now for the opportunity to give Italy a strong government that could restrain the

Mussolini's rise in Italy

radicals and maintain order. Born to command, and with a personality almost irresistible to the Italian temperament, Mussolini had gathered into his following the sons of property-holders whose fear of socialism was only too well grounded, ex-veterans of the First World War who resented the aspersions cast on Italy's war record, and patriotic young bloods generally to whom his program of direct action against radicals strongly appealed. Organized Fascist bands, or "squadrists," called also "Black Shirts" from the garb they affected, paraded the streets in force, beat up the "reds," wrecked workers' clubs, and broke up strikes. By the summer of 1922 their strength was estimated at three hundred thousand.

IL DUCE.

Italy under Mussolini provided an example of how unsafe for democracy the world was becoming. Il Duce brought to an abrupt end the efforts of the Italian nation to achieve a democratic system of government, and turned the minds of his people toward the old Roman goals of military might and conquest.

THE BLACK SHIRTS. A detachment of the famous Fascist militia under inspection by Mussolini.

It was well known that Mussolini was now prepared to seize authority, and late in October, 1922, his adherents began their famous "march on Rome." But to avert violence, the King made Mussolini Premier, and the Black Shirts went home without the bloody fighting they had expected. Thereafter parliamentary government in any normal sense did not last long. Non-Fascist members of the Cabinet were dropped, opposition parties were disbanded, and the whole government down to the most minor offices was thoroughly "fascistized." Personal liberty disappeared, the press was rigidly controlled, courts ruled as they knew they must. A Fascist militia, composed of the most dependable elements of the Black Shirts, gave the color of legality to "squadrist" attacks on individuals known to be critical of "Il Duce." Thus Fascism in Italy, like Communism in Russia, became a weapon through which the will of the dictator became supreme. The young Fascist who revised Descartes' *cogito, ergo sum*, to read, "I never think, therefore I am," had the spirit of Fascism in a nutshell.

Fascist ideology set great store by the grandeur of ancient Rome. The party designation was derived from the word *fasces*, Latin designation **Fascism** for the bundle of rods surrounding a battle-axe that lictors once carried as symbols of authority before kings, consuls, praetors, and emperors. What ancient Rome was, united and powerful, feared and respected, Fascist Italy aspired to become. Nationalism was exalted and stimulated by pride in the old Roman past. The Roman salute of the uplifted arm was revived, and every aspect of the Roman legend held in veneration. Fascism also idealized physical energy and force. It glorified all the warlike attributes, es-

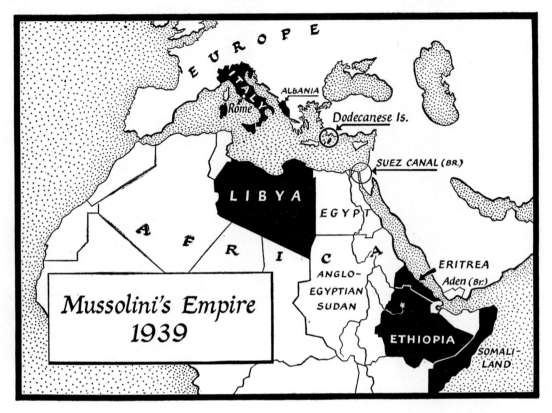

Mussolini's Empire 1939

teemed virility and efficiency, called for discipline and the will to conquer. Like ancient Rome, modern Italy must have the strength to expand its borders, and the right to boast of empire. Thickly spread over all Fascist activities was a heavy layer of theatricals and pageantry; Fascist pomposity and pretense always approached the very verge of the ridiculous. In political organization, Fascism experimented with the teachings of the national syndicalists, and in the "corporative state" claimed to have achieved a new governmental principle. Representation was based no longer upon political or geographic units, but upon organized economic interests, syndicates of employers as well as of employees. For the Fascists had no quarrel with capitalism; they meant to protect it, not to destroy it. And yet, the state must always be regarded as supreme; "nothing for the individual, all for Italy," was the motto of every believer. Only in this spirit could

"the moral and material greatness of the Italian people" be achieved.

Whatever may be said of its contradictory philosophic concepts, Fascism as personified in Mussolini did provide Italy with a government strong enough to govern. The Fascists despised democracy as outmoded, and too soft to confront the rigors of the twentieth century. Italian democracy had invited this criticism, but Mussolini's government was effective. The Duce soon had the national budget in balance, he launched public works that not only appealed to the national pride but helped also with the problem of unemployment, he stimulated both agricultural and industrial development, he put an end to labor strife, encouraged education, promoted foreign trade, developed natural resources, built up the army and navy, stimulated "air-mindedness," and to the everlasting joy of tourists "made the railroads run on time."

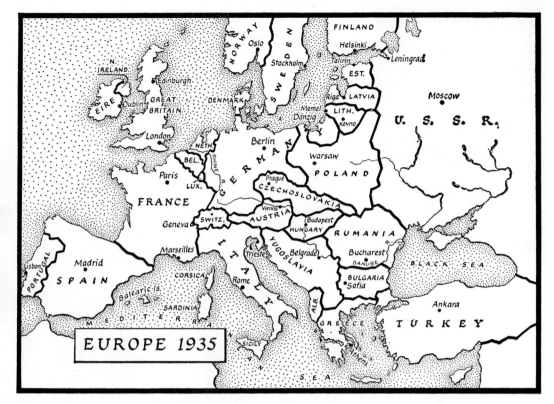

EUROPE 1935

The third great dictatorship to make its appearance in Europe came in Germany.

Hitler's rise in Germany

There the roots of democracy had never driven deep, and the Weimar Republic, established at the close of the First World War, had the additional disadvantages to overcome of having agreed to the hated Treaty of Versailles, and of having permitted the nation to descend into a catastrophic currency inflation. Disgust with the new régime was evident in the elections of 1925, when the voters selected as President one of the outstanding heroes of the old Germany, Field Marshal Paul von Hindenburg. By this time the land was filled with revolutionaries, some of whom wished to follow the example of Communist Russia, while others favored rather the precepts of Fascist Italy. Noisiest among the latter was Adolf Hitler, an Austrian-born German with a talent for soapbox oratory who was a member of the German Workers' Party, later renamed National Socialist. The

"Nazis," as these agitators were called, adopted the Fascist salute, chose the swastika as their emblem, organized a blackshirted bodyguard for the Nazi leaders, sent forth brown-shirted Storm Troopers to break up Communist meetings, made ready with small pretense at concealment to overthrow the existing democratic régime. A premature effort at revolution was made in 1923 at Munich. Its chief significance was the fact that it landed Hitler in jail, where he found time to write his dreams of a Nazi-dominated world into a book, *Mein Kampf*, thereafter the law and the gospel for all his followers.

Quite as hostile as the Nazis toward the democratic experiment in Germany was the army, organized after the war as the *Reichswehr* under General Hans von Seekt. This force, according to the Treaty of Versailles, was supposed to number only a hundred thousand men, but in actual fact it was probably much larger. Led by the ablest and most conservative elements in the old im-

DER FÜHRER.

Germany under Hitler followed the example of Italy in abandoning even the forms of democracy, and substituting instead a ruthless dictatorship. Hitler as Führer fed his people a steady diet of German racial superiority and military invincibility. Disregarding the restrictions of the Treaty of Versailles against rearmament, he pursued policies that led directly to the Second World War.

MILITARISM. Like most dictatorships, the Nazi régime was maintained by military might.

perial army, the *Reichswehr* was quickly welded into a center of reactionary sentiment, where Social Democrats were unwelcome, even in the ranks, and where longing for the good old authoritarian days was outspokenly apparent. That the *Reichswehr* was intended as merely a nucleus around which to build a much larger army as soon as possible became clearer with each passing year. Its leaders tolerated, and perhaps even connived at, the training of numerous bands of irregular soldiery, "free corps" adventurers such as Hitler's, which in time of stress could be absorbed into the national military forces. As a result of this policy, Germany, far from being disarmed, as the Treaty of Versailles contemplated, had probably as many as two million men under arms by 1930, a formidable beginning for complete remilitarization. Army officers were sent to Russia for training in the new military techniques, airplane and submarine factories were located outside Germany's borders, and industrial plants designed to be transformed overnight into war plants were operated within Germany itself. To restore German faith in military leadership, the public was fed on the "stab-in-the-back" legend, according to which Germany had never really suffered military defeat, but had been forced to make peace because of disloyalty on the home front, disloyalty that was ascribed mainly to Social Democrats, Communists, and Jews.

The ends sought by the Nazis and the army thus came to have much in common, and military leaders were able to view the rise of Hitler with considerable equanimity. To his support the Nazi spellbinder drew nearly all of the discontented elements of society for whom Communism had slight appeal — the white-collar workers, hard hit by the chronic hard times; small shopkeepers whose businesses were threatened by chain stores and trusts; discouraged peasants fearful of a Communist revolution; members of the professional classes who blamed Jewish competition for all their own shortcomings; unemployed intellectuals, particularly in and from the universities, for whom the existing economic system held little of promise; youth in search of adventure and a future; women intoxicated by the highly charged emotionalism of Hitler's appeal. All these, however, would hardly have been sufficient to install Hitler in power; it was the financial support of the great industrialists, who thought of the Nazis as a means of heading off the Communists, that insured the success of the movement.

As long as the Republic lasted, the Nazis were unable to command a majority of the Reichstag, but their growing strength was recognized by President Hindenburg in February, 1933, when he made Hitler his Chancellor. Within a few months the last vestige of democracy was wiped out, and the Nazification of the state was complete. Henceforth Hitler was the only "Führer," and a powerful secret police suppressed the slightest show of criticism. Germany, like Russia and Italy, had become a dictatorship. Just as Communism was what Stalin said it was, and Fascism was what Mussolini said it was, so now Naziism was what Hitler said it was. All three governments were totalitarian; in every instance the individual existed for the state, not the state for the individual.

The Nazi ideology, like the Fascist, was less noted for common sense and consistency

Naziism than for its wholesale appeal to the prejudices that Hitler found about him. The Nazis adopted in full the army theory that Germany had been betrayed in 1918, not defeated, and demanded the complete overthrow of the Versailles settlement. This was held to be Germany's due, not merely because of injustices in the treaty, but because Germans, as members of the master race, had superior rights. Race-

ism, more than anything else, was basic in the Nazi philosophy. The "Nordic," or "Aryan," races, among whom the Germans were held to be the only really pure strain, were born to command; all other races, Latin, Slav, Semite, Negro, Oriental, were born merely to take orders. Racial purity was supremely important, mixtures with "impure" blood an intolerable affront to the race. The Jewish race, of all races, was the most reprehensible. It was both parasitic and unassimilable, the source of most of the woes of the world. Acting on these principles, the most fiendish persecutions of the Jews were ordered by the Nazis on the slightest pretexts.

Blood-brother of raceism was German nationalism, for through the activities of the German nation the German race found expression. As nationalism was good, internationalism was the quintessence of evil. All organizations of an international nature were therefore suspect; Communism, which looked forward to world revolution, was the worst of all, but such international institutions as the Roman Catholic Church, the Masonic order, and the League of Nations came likewise under the ban. Furthermore, the German nation must have room to grow — *Lebensraum*. To fulfill its mission it must expand its borders to include the "heartland" of the European continent. Nazi-infected pseudo-scientists, calling their work geopolitics, drew ample boundaries for the greater, self-sufficient Germany that must come. To fill out these boundaries, and so accomplish the mission of the race, Hitler demanded an increase in the German birth rate — there should be two hundred and fifty million Germans instead of only eighty million. The German colonies, too, must be returned, and German mastery recognized throughout the world.

While the safety of democracy in Europe and America was being thus imperiled, news of alarming developments came **The rise of** also out of Asia. Although the **Fascism** government of Japan had been **in Japan** changed late in the nineteenth century to harmonize somewhat with Occidental practices, the theory of popular sovereignty had always been effectively excluded. The state was in a sense a theocracy, for the Emperor was worshipped as the Son of Heaven, and such privileges of government as were extended to the people were held to be merely gifts emanating from the divine will. In actual practice the Emperor was at the mercy of a small group of "elder statesmen" and privy councilors, whose advice he dared not reject. Following the form, if not the spirit, of the British constitution, a two-house Diet existed, the House of Peers and the House of Representatives, but the Cabinet was responsible to the Emperor rather than to the Diet, and a peculiarly independent status was assigned to the ministers of War and Navy. Invariably these men were selected from among the highest-ranking active officers of the branches concerned, and they were responsible for their acts neither to the Diet nor to the Cabinet, but only to the Emperor himself.

During the First World War, Japan had enjoyed an unusual prosperity. Her military contribution to the defeat of the Central Powers had been comparatively slight, but she had profited greatly from the sale of war goods to the Allies, and from the use they made of her excellent fleet of merchantmen. After the war, American purchases of Japanese silk long staved off economic disaster, but the Great Depression cut down American buying power and seriously imperiled Japanese prosperity. This situation played directly into the hands of the nation's powerful military leaders, who had long maintained that Japan need only essay the rôle of conqueror to get whatever she needed. In taking such a stand, they had the support of a carefully nurtured mythology, according to which the Japanese people were a superior race, destined to rule the world. War would bring plunder, and was thus an end in itself, but the military leaders had much civilian support for the theory that Japanese expansion was an economic necessity.

First on the calling list of the Japanese war lords was Manchuria. This region, it was argued, if fully exploited by Japan, would provide the nation with the raw resources and the manufacturing outlet that it needed. Japanese bankers and industrialists were already entrenched in Manchuria, and they were eager for the security that conquest would bring them. After Manchuria there were other worlds to conquer — as much of the rest of China as might be needed to keep that still unformed nation subject to the Japanese will, and, if the times broke aright, the white man's dominions in all eastern Asia and the Indies. Various terms were used to cloak the Japanese designs. For a time emphasis was laid on the similarity between Japanese ambitions in the Far East and the ambitions of the United States in the Americas. Japan wanted merely a "Monroe Doctrine for Asia." But the "New Order," or the "Co-Prosperity Sphere," that Japanese spokesmen soon began to talk about for eastern Asia exceeded the wildest dreams of American imperialists. What the Japanese leaders really wanted was to make their neighbors their slaves.

The Manchurian "incident" of 1931 was the beginning of a procession of events that led directly toward the Second World War. On the faintest pretexts, Japanese troops occupied large sections of Manchuria, organized it into the satellite state of Manchukuo, and set a puppet Emperor, Henry Pu-yi, on its throne. Because this act of aggression constituted a direct violation of the Kellogg-Briand Peace Pact, the United States, through Secretary of State Henry L. Stimson, refused to recognize Manchukuo's government, but the Stimson policy had no effect on Japanese expansionists. When the British-dominated League of Nations voiced mild disapproval, Japan gave notice of her intent to withdraw from the League (March 27, 1933). Only the Chinese did anything really effective about the matter. Through a nation-wide boycott on Japanese goods, the Chinese people inflicted notable punishment upon Japanese industry. China, next to the

United States, had been Japan's best customer, but in the months following the occupation of Manchuria sales of Japanese goods to China fell off by as much as two thirds. Wholesale discriminations against Japanese business interests in China became also the order of the day.

Another result of the Japanese aggressions was to unite the faction-torn Chinese for **The Chinese** self-defense. Even the deeply **"incident"** antagonistic Nationalists under Chiang Kai-shek and the Communists under Chang Hsueh-liang found ways of cooperating, with Chiang Kai-shek as Generalissimo. When, therefore, the Japanese decided in 1937 to prosecute an undeclared war against China, their troops were confronted by organized opposition. But the Chinese were no match for the well-trained and well-supplied Japanese armies, who took territory almost at will, and eventually had under their control most of the Chinese seacoast and much of the adjacent interior. While the Japanese refused to admit that the China "incident" was a war, the League of Nations seemed to regard it as such, and after much delay recommended that the various member nations extend what aid they could to China. Over the Burma Road, which by 1938 American-trained engineers had completed with the use of Chinese coolie labor, China was able to import some useful war materials, and eventually both the British and the American governments extended credits to China. At all times the Japanese invaders were at pains to visit their wrath upon British and American residents and business interests in the military area. An incident of the war was the destruction on December 12, 1937, by Japanese bombers, of an American gunboat, the *Panay*. The act was deliberate and intended but the American public was apathetic and the apologies of the Japanese goverment were accepted.

Meantime, the "robber" nations of Europe were also on the march. In 1935, **Ethiopia** Mussolini began a war of conquest against Ethiopia, with the avowed intent of adding that backward African kingdom to his empire. This venture was so fraught with peril for the peace of Europe that for a time it seemed as if the League of Nations might employ effective economic "sanctions" to prevent it. If Italy could be kept from obtaining oil, it appeared that the war could not go on. But the League finally backed down. It applied sanctions, but not the oil sanctions that alone were well calculated to achieve results. Perhaps the reason for this weak attitude lay in the fact that the British navy, upon which the main brunt of enforcing the sanctions would have fallen, was inadequately prepared for war. Whatever the reasons, the League of Nations as a means of keeping the peace of the world became a farce from this time forward. Mussolini went ahead, practically unimpeded, with his plan of conquest, drove the Ethiopian monarch, Haile Selassie, into exile, and on May 9, 1936, announced that the Italian King had also assumed the title of Emperor.

Inflated with one victory, Mussolini soon sought another. When in 1936 a revolt broke out in Spain against the **The Spanish** democratic government of the **Civil War** Spanish Republic, Mussolini sent his "legions" to the aid of the revolutionary leader, General Francisco Franco, whose Fascist tendencies were unmistakable. Aid for Franco came also from Germany, and a little help for the "Loyalists," as the government forces were called, came from Russia. The civil war in Spain was widely recognized as a dress rehearsal for the coming world war, but the democratic nations were unwilling to do anything effective for the hard-pressed Loyalists, who, after a bitter and bloody struggle, lost out. In General Franco, the new dictator of Spain, both Hitler and Mussolini recognized a kindred spirit and a potential ally.

Only those who wished to be deceived could believe that Hitler's rise to power in Germany would not still further **Appease-** unsettle the peace of Europe. **ment** The same year that Hitler became Chancellor — 1933 — Germany gave notice of her withdrawal from the League of Nations; two years later, after the plebiscite required by the Treaty of Versailles, she took back the Saar Basin; next year, in 1936, German troops reoccupied and remilitarized the Rhineland; two years after that, early in 1938, they occupied Austria, and added that formerly independent state to Hitler's "Third Reich." The portion of German *Lebensraum* next coveted by Hitler was Czechoslovakia, which Germany now almost completely surrounded, but the Führer chose at first to demand only the Sudetenland, a strip along the Czecho-German border mainly inhabited by Germans. To retain this region, which was essential to her defense, Czechoslovakia was ready to fight, but she was held back by nations she had thought were her friends, France and England. Among the people of the western democracies pacifism had become a passion; they simply would not have another war. Probably, therefore, their governments were quite in accord with public opinion

"All He Wants Is Elbow Room." Vaughn Shoemaker in the Chicago *Daily News*, February 1, 1939.

when they proposed to keep Germany at peace by a policy of "appeasement." After extensive preliminary threats by Hitler and concessions by the western democracies, Prime Minister Chamberlain of Great Britain and Premier Daladier of France met with Hitler and Mussolini at Munich in September, 1938, to find a solution short of war. They found it by demanding that Czechoslovakia yield to Hitler's demands, and as a result German troops marched into the Sudetenland. Then in March, 1939, Czechoslovakia itself, as the sadly mangled state was renamed, was occupied by Hitler, and most of its territory added to the Reich. Not to be outdone, Mussolini the very next month transported an army across the Adriatic and took possession of Albania. To diminutive Victor Emmanuel III went another title, King of Albania.

By this time a bond of friendship had been formed between Hitler and Mussolini, a bond that quite clearly was meant   **Rome-Berlin** also to include Japan. The ob-   **Axis** jection of all three nations to the spread of Communism found expression in the Anti-Comintern Pact signed between Germany and Japan in 1936, and adhered to by Italy in 1937. Then in May, 1939, immediately following the Czechoslovakian and Albanian incidents, Germany and Italy concluded also a ten-year military alliance — the "Rome-Berlin Axis." The agreement pledged that if either of the two powers should become involved in war, the other would come to its aid "with all its military forces, on land, sea, and in the air." Rumor had it that the next expansionist effort of the Axis Powers would be to acquire Tunisia for Italy.

What Mussolini had done in the Balkans, Great Britain and France were prepared to discount, but Hitler's extinction   **End of ap-** of Czechoslovakia, in complete   **peasement** disregard of his promise that the Sudetenland would be his final conquest, brought appeasement to an end. "If it is so easy to discover good reasons for ignoring assurances so solemnly and repeatedly given," said Chamberlain, "what reliance can be placed upon any other assurances that come from the same source?" That Hitler intended to press on with his program of expansion was clear to all. From Lithuania he demanded, and received, Memel. From Poland he demanded under threat of war consent to the restoration of the free city of Danzig to the Reich, and to the building of a strictly German highway and railroad across the Polish Corridor. Only a few years before, Hitler had signed a non-aggression pact with Poland, but by this time evidence of the worthlessness of his pledges was so overwhelming that these new demands occasioned little surprise. With British and French opinion now unwilling to support further appeasement, Prime Minister Chamberlain, with the full support of the French government as well as his own, promised the Polish government all possible aid in case the independence of Poland should be threatened. Similar guarantees were soon given Greece and Rumania, and an Anglo-Turkish pact provided for mutual assistance "in the event of aggression leading to war in the Mediterranean area." France, also, began to patch up her differences with Turkey over Syria, and even the United States showed concern. President Roosevelt, in a message of April 16, 1939, to the Axis dictators, asked them for assurance that they would not invade thirty named states. The recipients of the message treated it with ridicule, but they were unable to prove conclusively that their neighbors were not afraid of them.

Throughout these proceedings the great enigma had been Russia. That the signers **The Russian-** of the Anti-Comintern Pact had **German** anything but contempt for the **accord** Soviet system could hardly be doubted; they made it plain on every possible occasion that they intended to destroy it. But the western democracies had also had their suspicions of Russia; was not the Comintern as much dedicated to their destruction as to that of the Axis Powers? During the negotiations that preceded Munich, Russia had been deliberately slighted. In that conference, which decided the fate of Czechoslovakia, one of Russia's near neighbors, no Russian had been permitted a voice. Talk was rife that the western democracies were deliberately building up Nazi Germany as a counterweight to Soviet Russia, and that a war to the death between Germany and Russia was the real objective of British and French diplomacy. However this may have been, both Great Britain and France were by March, 1939, extremely eager for Russian collaboration, and a special British envoy was sent to Russia to negotiate an Anglo-Soviet pact. Throughout the summer of 1939, while Hitler breathed out more and more threats against Poland, these negotiations continued, but without results. Certain that nothing could drive such bitter enemies as Hitler and Stalin together, editorial writers and news commentators believed that the delay was over Russian insistence on a free hand in dealing with the Baltic countries, and speculated on just how much of what he wanted Stalin would be able to obtain. Then, to the amazement of most of the world, including the American Communists, who had not been briefed on the impending change in the party line, came the announcement that Russia and Germany had agreed late in August, first, to a commercial pact according to which German manufactured goods were to be exchanged for Russian raw materials, and then to a non-aggression pact which declared that each nation would respect the territory and sovereignty of the other. Thus reinforced, Hitler in a three weeks' blitzkrieg conquered two thirds of Poland, leaving the rest of that unhappy country to Russia, whose troops marched in from the East as German troops marched in from the West.

In response to the frantic demands of Poland, Great Britain and France, on September 5, declared war on Germany, but they were able to do **War begins** nothing whatever to restrain the Nazi drive. Both nations mobilized fully; the British reestablished the blockade they had found so effective in the First World War, and the French manned their much-touted Maginot

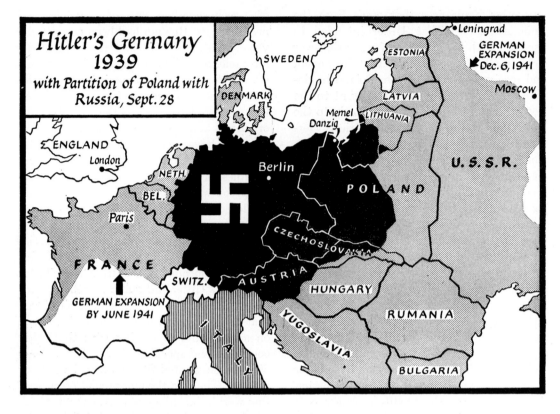

Hitler's Germany 1939 with Partition of Poland with Russia, Sept. 28

Line. But for more than half a year there was little real fighting, and the situation could be described with some propriety as a "phony war." During most of this period the spotlight was upon Russia rather than Germany, for Stalin took quick advantage of the opportunity presented him to seek a restoration of the old Russian frontiers along the Baltic. With only the slightest diplomatic preparation, his troops took over Latvia, Lithuania, and Estonia. His efforts to overrun Finland, however, were met with stiff resistance, for the Finns were determined to retain their independence at all costs. From December, 1939, to March, 1940, the Russo-Finnish War went on, and the tenacity with which the Finns defended their borders against the vastly superior foe excited the amazement and admiration of the whole free world. For her act of aggression Russia was expelled from the League of Nations, to which she had been admitted five years before, and war materials both from the Allied nations and from the Scandinavian countries were rushed in great quantity to the Finnish armies. Plans were even laid for the sending of an Allied expeditionary force to help the Finns, but before this could be done the Russians had begun to win, and the Finnish government made peace. By the terms agreed upon, the Finnish boundaries were "rectified," but the independence of Finland was left intact.

In April, 1940, the "phony war" in the West came to a sudden end. That month Hitler's armies overran Denmark and Norway, the former without resistance, and the latter in spite of all the help that Allied ships and Allied troops could give. In May the Nazi blitzkrieg struck Belgium and Holland with devastating fury, and by the end of June it had brought, not them alone, but France also, to surrender. Two weeks before France confessed defeat, Mussolini forced an unwilling Italy into the war on Hitler's side, while such of the lesser nations of Europe as had not yet been conquered made every effort to curry

The fall of France

France after Versailles built massive defenses along the German border that her people believed to be impregnable. This *Maginot-line mentality* was France's undoing in 1940, when the Germans with new weapons and new tactics quickly destroyed not only the fortifications, but also the army that manned them.

FRANCE. Behind the Maginot Line nearly everyone was anxious about Germany's intentions.

AFTER THE "PHONY WAR." The Germans in 1940 swiftly flanked the French defenses and occupied Paris.

favor with the victorious Third Reich. To most observers the invasion of England appeared imminent. The army that the British had landed on the Continent was able, almost by a miracle, to withdraw at Dunkirk, but it had lost practically all its equipment, and appeared to be easy prey for the conquering foe. Only the royal air and naval forces blocked the way. Fully mindful of this fact, the British navy took prompt action to keep as many French warships as possible out of Hitler's hands. The French squadron at Oran in North Africa was attacked by British units on July 3 and in large part destroyed, while a similar squadron at Alexandria was persuaded to remain immobilized.

In desperate but still defiant mood, the British nation and empire battened down to carry on the war alone. "I have nothing to offer," said the new Prime Minister, Winston Churchill, "but blood, toil, tears, and sweat." As if to help redeem this pledge the German *Luftwaffe* began an aerial bombardment of Britain in August, 1940, that destroyed large sections of London as well as many other British cities, and lasted on through the entire fall and winter. From fallen France, now ready to concede a German victory, there came few brave words or deeds. After the surrender to Germany, a government more subject to Hitler than to the will of the French people was set up at Vichy, with southeastern France and the overseas empire, theoretically at least, under its control. The Chief-of-State, aged Marshal Pétain, struggled with only

England

slight success to maintain the fiction of French independence. As for the other conquered countries, most of them established exile governments in London, where also a faction of "Free French," under the leadership of General Charles de Gaulle, refused to recognize that the Vichy government really represented France.

The steady disintegration of peace in Europe during the first six years of the Roosevelt administration had forced the American people, much against their wishes, to think seriously about what course their government should pursue in case another great war should break out. Many Americans, after reflecting on the results of the "war to end war" which they had entered in 1917, were convinced that the proper course of conduct for the United States was to maintain its neutrality, come what might. Undoubtedly this sentiment was greatly strengthened by the findings of a Senate committee, headed by Senator Gerald P. Nye of North Dakota, which in 1934 began to examine into the unsavory record of the munitions industries during and after the last war. Extreme isolationists began to demand insistently that Congress enact neutrality laws so strict as to preclude all possibility of American involvement in case war again broke out in Europe. Opposed to this point of view were the be-

lievers in "collective security" who argued that the world had become too small for any nation so large and **"Collective security"** influential as the United States to remain aloof from what was going on. If war came it might easily engulf the United States, regardless of any laws Congress might pass, or of the will of the American people for peace. Even if the United States failed to take part in a general war, it would still be intimately affected. Normal lines of trade would be broken up; the basis for a new world depression more calamitous than any ever known before would be laid; disease germs as destructive as those which in 1918 spread the influenza to every nation, neutral or belligerent, might be unleashed; and in a thousand other ways the United States would feel the impact of hostilities. The proper course, therefore, was to prevent war. Let the United States join with peace-loving nations to curb aggressors and to compel peace. Mere negative neutrality was not enough. War must be prevented.

As early as 1933, when Hitler rose to power in Germany and began his program of rearmament, Roosevelt made it clear that, whatever other Americans might think, the President of the United States leaned strongly in the direction of collective security. In an address to the nations of the world issued

The Evacuation of Dunkirk saved thousands of British soldiers, but vast stores of equipment had to be abandoned. The determination with which Great Britain faced the future after this disaster has been called her "finest hour."

MESSERSCHMIDT –109. This famous fighter plane was a powerful weapon of the German air force.

Great Britain suffered terrific bombardments from Nazi aircraft, especially during the earlier part of the war when British defenses were weak. Eventually, with American aid, British bombers visited far greater destruction on German cities than British cities had received. This aspect of "total war" left both victors and vanquished heavy losers.

THE BLITZ. In 1939 and 1940 Germany ruthlessly bombed British cities. This is the booksellers' quarter in London.

May 16, 1933, the day before Hitler was to make what was expected to be a warlike statement to the Reichstag, Roosevelt urged the adoption of the MacDonald plan for the elimination of weapons designed primarily for aggressive warfare. "Modern weapons of offense," he pointed out with admirable prescience, "are vastly stronger than modern weapons of defense. Frontier forts, trenches, wire entanglements, coast defenses — in a word, fixed fortifications — are no longer impregnable to the attack of war planes, heavy mobile artillery, land battleships called tanks, and poison gas." If the nations would agree not to possess or use these weapons, then the "frontiers and independence of every nation" would become secure. A few days later Norman H. Davis, American representative at the fruitless Geneva conference on disarmament, told the delegates that, pro-

vided only a satisfactory treaty could be arranged, the United States would be willing to consult with the other nations in case of a threat to peace. Further, should any disciplinary measures be undertaken against an aggressor nation, the United States "would refrain from any action tending to defeat such collective effort," that is, from insisting on its rights as a neutral. A good definition of an aggressor nation, Davis suggested, was one "whose troops are found on alien soil in violation of treaties." [1]

The disarmament conference died a lingering death, and many Americans were relieved that Roosevelt was not obliged to live up

[1] The subsequent fate of such nations as Austria, Czechoslovakia, Poland, Finland, Norway, Denmark, Belgium, and Holland led one observer to amend this definition as follows: "An aggressor nation is a little nation that has something that a big nation wants."

to the pledges he had made. The President
A quaran- nevertheless showed repeat-
tine of edly that he had not changed his
aggressors? mind. His classic utterance on
the subject, aimed apparently at Japan and
Italy for their operations respectively in
China and Ethiopia, came on October 5,
1937, during an address delivered in Chicago:

It seems to be unfortunately true that the epidemic of world lawlessness is spreading. When
an epidemic of physical disease starts to spread,
the community approves and joins in a quarantine of the patients in order to protect the health
of the community against the spread of the disease.... War is a contagion, whether it be declared or undeclared. It can engulf states and
peoples remote from the original scene of hostilities. We are determined to keep out of war, yet
we cannot insure ourselves against the disastrous
effects of war and the dangers of involvement....
There must be positive endeavors to preserve
peace. America hates war. America hopes for
peace. Therefore, America actively engages in
the search for peace.

The American search for peace did not
stand in the way of active naval expansion,
Naval particularly after the break-
expansion down of all plans for disarmament seemed assured. In January, 1938, the
President asked Congress to appropriate a
billion dollars for naval defense, and after
some delay and debate Congress acquiesced.
From the point of view of those who believed
in collective security the navy was necessary
if the United States was to have any influence
in restraining "warmongers," while from the
point of view of the isolationists it was necessary to defend American borders against a
warmongering world.

Probably the advocates of collective security were only a small minority in the
Neutrality United States, and Roosevelt
legislation found it expedient from time to
time to tone down or disavow the sentiments
he undoubtedly felt. In this instance Congress, rather than the President, represented
the dominant public opinion. By a series of
neutrality laws it attempted to legislate into
oblivion all possible opportunities for the

United States to be drawn into a non-American conflict. The first of these acts, passed
in 1935 during the Italian attack on Ethiopia,
required the President to impose an embargo
upon the shipment of arms to belligerent nations, and authorized him to prohibit Americans from traveling upon the ships of belligerents. The second act, passed the following
year, maintained these provisions, and added
a prohibition against the flotation of loans in
the United States by any non-American belligerent. The third act, more comprehensive
than the rest, became law in May, 1937. It,
too, included the preceding legislation on
neutrality and imposed additional restrictions. American merchant ships might not
carry munitions to belligerents nor arm themselves against attack. Certain discretionary
powers were also bestowed upon the President. He might forbid American ships to
transport commodities of any kind to a belligerent nation; he might require all shipments
to be made on a strictly "cash-and-carry"
basis; and he might exclude enemy warships,
submarines, and armed merchantmen from
the use of American ports. These acts went
far toward eliminating all the alleged causes
of conflict that had led the United States to
enter the First World War in 1917. By them
notice was pointedly served upon European
nations that the American people were no
longer willing to defend the principles of
neutrality for which they once had fought.

While the President found these laws somewhat unpalatable, he showed considerable
facility in adapting them to his **Roosevelt**
views on foreign policy. He rec- **urges changes**
ognized the existence of a state of war between Italy and Ethiopia, and declared the
embargo on arms in force. This was advantageous to Ethiopia, which could not have
purchased arms in America in any event,
and an intended handicap to Italy, which
might have done so. But since Japan had
not declared war against China, he refused to
recognize the hostilities in the Orient as war,
presumably in order to enable the Chinese to
continue their purchases of American munitions. In the case of Spain, where civil war

existed, but with the Italians and Germans helping the insurgents and the Russians helping the loyalists, he applied the embargo, much to the discomfiture of the loyalists, who had the money with which to buy. Finally, impressed by the near-certainty of a general war, the President asked Congress early in 1939 to modify the Neutrality Act of 1937 by removing the mandatory feature of the embargo on arms and armaments. It was his idea that the American government should be left free to follow traditional practice on this subject. But Congress was recalcitrant, and the President's efforts to amend the Act resulted only in a promise that neutrality legislation would be the first order of business at the next session of Congress.

Meanwhile the darkening war-clouds in Europe led Roosevelt to renewed emphasis **"Conti-** upon "continental solidarity" **nental** and "hemispheric defense." **solidarity"** When the eighth Pan-American Conference met in Lima, December 10, 1938, the United States was acutely conscious of the inroads being made by German and Italian propaganda in Latin-American states, and sought to unite the twenty-one republics of the New World in a common defense against "aggressor nations." The agreement which Secretary Hull was able to obtain was not nearly as binding as the American government had hoped, but it affirmed that the peoples of America still had faith in "absolute adherence to the principles of international law," and that they would work together to defend the peace of the continent. When war actually broke out, delegates from the various American republics met at Panama, October 1, 1939, to consider a common policy of neutrality. After several days' deliberation they issued a declaration which asserted that the "waters adjacent to the American continent" must be "free from the commission of any hostile act by any non-American belligerent nation." Two months later an engagement between German and British naval units off the mouth of the River Plate demonstrated conclusively that something stronger than words would be required

to keep the war far removed from American shores. In the spring of 1940 the assistance which Hitler's armies received from Nazi sympathizers in Norway, the Netherlands, Belgium, and France led to a new wave of excitement throughout the Americas. Was there a "fifth column"[1] in each American nation ready to betray it to some European invader? Fear that some such situation might exist led many Latin-American governments to affirm more earnestly than ever before their desire to cooperate fully with the United States.

The occupation of the Dutch West Indies by the Allies after the defeat of the Netherlands brought no protest from the United States, but when France was compelled to sue for peace notice was promptly served on Germany that the United States under the terms of the Monroe Doctrine could permit no transfer of American colonies from one European nation to another. This contention was scornfully rejected by Germany, which insisted that the United States had no right to advance such an argument unless willing on its part to keep entirely aloof from European affairs. The surliness of the Nazi reply, coupled with the fact that after the French surrender British and French warships seemed to be on the verge of a clash in American waters, led the President to advocate that the Pan-American Conference scheduled to meet in Havana on July 20 should adopt a new rule for territorial readjustments in the American hemisphere. On behalf of the United States he formally renounced all territorial aspirations, and he urged that the twenty-one American republics should act together, each having equal voice, in determining what post-war rearrangements would be permitted in the New World. He suggested further that the system he favored for the Americas might well be applied in other continents also. Instead of Asia for the Japanese and Europe for the

[1] This term was first used by General Mola, the commander of the Spanish insurgents, in his campaign against Madrid. Four columns, he announced, were marching on the city, and they would be joined by a secret "fifth column" from within the city itself.

Germans, let each of the nations of Asia have an equal voice in Asiatic affairs, and each of the nations of Europe an equal voice in European affairs.

Neither Europe nor Asia was in position to heed the President's advice, but at the **Act of Havana** Havana Conference the patient diplomacy of Secretary Hull bore significant fruit. An Act of Havana was adopted which forbade the transfer of any European colony to another non-American power, and stated that if any such transfer were attempted the colony in question would pass immediately under the joint control of the American states. To provide for the government of the colony a committee of twenty-one, to consist of one member for each American nation, might be summoned at will by any of the participating nations, and as an assurance against impotence this committee was to be considered ful'y constituted "from the date of the appointment of two thirds of its members." Furthermore, actions might be taken with the approval of two thirds of the members present, while a special emergency declaration gave any American nation, but presumably the United States, authority to take independent action:

If the necessity for emergency action be deemed so urgent as to make it impossible to await action of the committee, any of the American republics, individually or jointly with others, shall have the right to act in a manner required for its defense or the defense of the continent.

In spite of these apparent successes, it was obvious that many obstacles blocked the way toward any real union of the Americas. Culturally the English-speaking peoples of North America were infinitely farther removed from the Latin-Americans than the latter were from the peoples of southwestern Europe. Economic interests tended a'so to bind Latin America to Europe rather than to the United States, for Europe could provide a market for Latin-American goods, whereas the United States already had too much of what the other Latin-American nations wished to sell. In respect to government, too, the same pattern persisted. Dictatorships were the rule rather than the exception in Latin America, and democracy was only a thin veneer. Even in the matter of geography "hemispheric solidarity" was far less significant than it sounded, for South America lay entirely to the east of North America, and much of it was closer to the Old World than to the United States. The one important bond of union that Roosevelt could count on was fear.

Roosevelt's idea of American solidarity included Canada no less than Latin America. Fortunately his efforts to bring the two great English-speaking nations of North America together had the advantage of many ties, both in blood and history, that were lacking in dealing with the other Americas. By 1940 Roosevelt and the Canadian Prime Minister Mackenzie King were in close conference at Ogdenburg, New York, on how to promote measures of joint defense. In spite of the fact that the United States was a neutral, while Canada was a belligerent, the heads of the two governments solemnly agreed that a Permanent Board on Defense should be set up, to consist of four or five members from each country, the business of which would be to "commence immediate studies relating to sea, land, and air . . . defense of the north half of the Western Hemisphere." As head of the United States delegation, the President appointed Mayor Fiorello H. La Guardia of New York, a former Congressman who had distinguished himself as a member of the United States air service during the First World War. On both sides of the border this declaration was hailed as the practical equivalent of a military alliance.

In the Far East, while the United States seemed by no means unwilling to escape from the defense of the Philip- **The** pines, the American Secretary **Far East** of State, Cordell Hull, repeatedly made it clear that his nation had no intention of recognizing any new order imposed on China by force of arms; and on July 26, 1939, he startled the Japanese government by abrogating the commercial treaty between Japan and the United States that had existed since 1911. This move was generally believed to anticipate an embargo on American munitions shipments to Japan, but no such action was taken, and the conquest of China went on. In the summer of 1940, however, the United States forbade the export to any foreign country without license of essential war materials such as heavy scrap-iron and petroleum, and on September 27 it followed this announcement with a complete embargo on the shipment of iron and steel scrap, except to Great Britain and the nations of the western hemisphere. Within a few hours this blow was countered by the revelation that a joint "economic, political, and military" alliance, aimed primarily at the United States, had been formed by Germany, Italy, and Japan. Predictions were rife that the next move in the diplomatic chess game would be an agreement between the United States and Great Britain whereby the American battle fleet might be assured the right to use the great British naval base at Singapore, but in actual fact events took a very different turn.

It was the European scene, however, far more than the Asiatic, which cast a fateful spell over the American people. The sudden fall of France and the desperate peril of Britain aroused their deepest fears. American thinking, as before intervention in the First World War, had been predicated upon the assumption that the British navy was unbeatable, and that whatever happened in Europe the Atlantic Ocean would remain in friendly hands. But now the danger of a complete German victory had again to be faced. Suppose Hitler succeeded in sinking the British navy, or worse still, in capturing it? Would he then be content to rule in Europe and let America alone? What would be his attitude toward Latin America? Heretofore British economic interests and American national policy had coincided in relation to the Americas. The Monroe Doctrine had been possible no more because American sea-power stood back of it than because the British, too, gave it tacit support. Would the United States eventually have to fight Hitler alone? And whether the war came to the New World or not, what would international relations be like with the democracy-hating dictatorships supreme in Europe, Asia, and Africa?

American fears (margin note)

Hemisphere defense was the concern of Canadian Prime Minister Mackenzie King and President Roosevelt during their meeting in New York in 1940. They are shown reviewing First Army maneuvers.

Bibliography

The history of events in Europe leading up to the Second World War is well told in a number of textbooks, among the best of which are W. C. Langsam, *The World since 1914* (6th ed., 1948); F. P. Chambers, C. P. Harris, and C. C. Bagley, *This Age of Conflict* (rev. ed., 1950); Chester V. Easum, *Half-Century of Conflict* (1952); and Cyril E. Black and E. C. Helmreich, *Twentieth Century Europe* (1950). Hajo Holborn, *The Political Collapse of Europe* (1951), emphasizes the break-up that followed the First World War, and the failure of the United States to understand its significance. On the rise of Soviet Russia there are many books, few of them without an obvious bias. Worth citing are George Vernadsky, *The Russian Revolution, 1917–1931* (1932); James Mavor, *The Russian Revolution* (1928); M. T. Florinsky, *Toward an Understanding of the U.S.S.R.* (1939); I. Deutscher, *Stalin: A Political Biography* (1949); and John Somerville, *Soviet Philosophy* (1946). Serviceable accounts of fascism include H. W. Schneider, *Making the Fascist State* (1928); and Herman Finer, *Mussolini's Italy* (1935). On Germany, Department of State, *Documents on German Foreign Policy, 1918–1945* (2 vols., 1949), provides an extended record taken from the captured German documents. Alan Bullock, *Hitler* (1952), makes admirable use of this and other new material to present a far more complete picture of Naziism than was available before. Other useful accounts are F. L. Schuman, *The Nazi Dictatorship* (1935); William L. Shirer, *Berlin Diary* (1941); and *Ambassador Dodd's Diary, 1933–1938*, edited by William E. Dodd, Jr., and Martha Dodd (1941). On German rearmament, the best works are Hans Ernest Fried, *The Guilt of the German Army* (1942); Walter Goerlitz, *History of the German General Staff* (1953); and B. H. Liddell-Hart, *The German Generals Talk* (1948). See also Department of State, *Nazi-Soviet Relations, 1939–41* (1948). John F. Kennedy, *Why England Slept* (1940), is based on the observations of the American Ambassador to Great Britain. J. W. Wheeler-Bennett, *The Pipe-Dream of Peace; The Story of the Collapse of Disarmament* (1935); and *Munich: Prologue to Tragedy* (1948), are scholarly and perspicacious. For fascist penetration of Spain, see Herbert Feis, *The Spanish Story* (1948).

On Japan and the Far East before the war H. S. Quigley and G. H. Blakeslee, *The Far East: An International Survey* (1939), provides a good background. Joseph C. Grew, *Turbulent Era: A Diplomatic Record of Forty Years, 1904–1945* (1952); *Report from Tokyo* (1942); and *Ten Years in Japan* (1944), are from the pen of a veteran diplomat. See also Vinacke, *A History of the Far East in Modern Times*, previously cited; Güchi Tanaka, *Japan's Dream of World Empire, The Tanaka Memorial*, edited by Carl Crow (1942); Sara R. Smith, *The Manchurian Crisis, 1931–1932* (1948); Owen Lattimore, *Manchuria, Cradle of Conflict* (1935); and Claude A. Buss, *War and Diplomacy in Eastern Asia* (1941).

The part played by the United States in the years that immediately preceded the war has attracted the attention of many writers. Samuel Flagg Bemis, *The United States as a World Power* (1950), covers the first half of the twentieth century, and is adapted from his *Diplomatic History*. George F. Kennan, *American Diplomacy, 1900–1950* (1951), is a challenging interpretation by a State Department expert. The best accounts of American foreign policy during the pre-war years are W. L. Langer and S. E. Gleason, *The Challenge to Isolation, 1937–1940* (1952); and, by the same authors, *The Undeclared War, 1940–1941* (1953). Basil Rauch, *Roosevelt; From Munich to Pearl Harbor; A Study in the Creation of a Foreign Policy* (1950); and Allan Nevins, *The New Deal and World Affairs* (1950), are friendly to the course pursued by the United States. Bitterly antagonistic are Charles C. Tansill, *Backdoor to War: The Roosevelt Foreign Policy, 1933–41* (1952); and Charles A. Beard, *President Roosevelt and the Coming of the War, 1941: A Study in Appearances and Realities* (1948). On the American record in the Far East, Griswold, *The Far Eastern Policy of the United States*, previously cited, is excellent. H. L. Stimson, *The Far Eastern Crisis: Recollections and Observations* (1936), draws upon the knowledge and experience of a former Secretary of State. See also T. A. Bisson, *American Policy in the Far East, 1931–1941* (rev. ed., 1941); and John King Fairbank, *The United States and China* (1948).

30

The Second World War

Amendments to the Neutrality Act — Isolationists *vs.* interventionists — Preparedness — Measures "short of war" — The election of 1940 — Lend-Lease — Hitler attacks Russia — The Atlantic Charter — Pearl Harbor — North Africa — Tunisia — Italy — The second front — Conquest of Germany — VE Day — The Pacific — MacArthur's return — Asia — The atomic bomb — VJ Day

Amendments to the Neutrality Act FROM the very beginning of the war in Europe, President Roosevelt had used his influence to further the cause of the Allies. Immediately following the German attack on Poland, he convened Congress in special session on September 21, and asked for a revised Neutrality Act that would permit the United States to sell arms, ammunition, and implements of war to such nations as were able to pay for them in cash and to carry them away in foreign-registered ships. American public opinion was overwhelmingly with the Allies, and the President made no effort to conceal his hope that the control of the seas enjoyed by England and France would enable them to buy freely from across the Atlantic. Early in November, Congress acceded to the President's request, but in ending the embargo on munitions it made every effort to insure the United States against outright participation in the war. The prohibition on loans to belligerents was continued, American ships were barred from carrying passengers or materials to belligerent shores; and travel by American citizens on the vessels of belligerents was specifically forbidden. One result of the failure of the United States to defend its traditional rights as a neutral was that the minor neutral nations were left without a champion and helpless before the superior might of their predatory neighbors. Hundreds of neutral ships went down as German submarine warfare assumed at once the unrestricted character that it had attained in the preceding war only after more than two years of fighting, and at the cost of American participation on the Allied side.

Even after the fall of France and the British withdrawal from the Continent, a surprisingly large number of Americans **Isolationists vs. interventionists** were ready to take their chances on a Hitlerian victory. To them the consideration of chief importance was that, come what might in Europe, the United States must keep out of the war. Since there was no danger whatever of American involvement on the German side, they concentrated their attacks on those who wished to show in any tangible way the partiality that most Americans felt for the beleaguered British. Chief among the advocates of an adamant "isolationism" were Senator Burton K. Wheeler, of Montana, who had broken with the Roosevelt administration over the Supreme Court issue; Colonel Charles A. Lindbergh, the aviator, whose father had suffered much persecution as an opponent of the First World War; William Randolph Hearst and his editorial writers for the Hearst newspapers; Colonel Robert R. McCormick, of the Chicago *Tribune;* the two LaFollette brothers, of Wisconsin; Representative Hamilton Fish, of New York; and Senator Gerald P. Nye, of North Dakota. They were aided by a powerful and well-financed organization, attractively named the "America First Committee," which left no stone unturned to discredit all would-be "interventionists." Actually, very few Americans were prepared to advocate outright military intervention, but among those who were unable to look with complacency upon the final triumph of Hitler, all possible aid for the Allies "short of war" became an increasingly popular slogan. A "Committee to Defend America by Aiding the Allies" was headed for a time by the venerable William Allen White, of Kansas, but in general the "interventionists" lacked both the leaders and the funds to make their propaganda fully effective. They took comfort, however, in the fact that they had on their side the President of the United States. It was he who had persuaded Congress to permit the shipment of American-made munitions to the enemies of Germany and Italy; furthermore, he had deliberately turned back to the manufacturers as supposedly outmoded such military items as airplanes, knowing full well that they would promptly be shipped to the Allies.

It is not surprising, considering the unparalleled situation they faced, that the American people began to look with a critical eye at their defenses. **Preparedness** Naval preparedness, they well knew, had long been regarded with considerable favor, but no attempt had been made to build up separate Atlantic and Pacific squadrons. The United States possessed a fleet approximately equal to the British navy, and still, or so the American public fondly believed, somewhat superior to the Japanese. But American strategists had never faced the possibility of an attack in the Atlantic and Pacific at the same time. They had assumed always that the Panama Canal would enable American ships to shuttle back and forth as needed from one ocean to another. Now, with Japan determined to push its "new order" to unpredictable lengths in the Pacific, and with the plainly visible threat of

The America First Committee represented a large proportion of American isolationist thinking. Some of the leaders of this committee shown at a rally in Madison Square Garden are, left to right: Burton K. Wheeler, Charles A. Lindbergh, Kathleen Norris, and Norman Thomas.

German domination in the Atlantic, the country awoke with a start from its pleasant dream of security. Even the Panama Canal was vulnerable, if only an enemy nation could obtain a near-by American base for aircraft operation.

The success of the German methods of land warfare had also to be taken into account. While the rest of the world had struggled ineffectively with the problems of peace, the German nation had prepared for war. Under the complete domination of the Nazi hierarchy its people had been disciplined and trained, both physically and psychologically, for the supreme effort that lay before them. Autocratic rulers had demanded and obtained perfect coordination of military might, on land, by sea, and in the air, regardless of all hamstringing traditions. German scientists had turned their remarkable talents to the improvement of the weapons of warfare found most useful in the last war, and had conducted a ceaseless search for new ways to strengthen the nation's fighting power. While other nations had failed miserably to solve their problems of unemployment, Germany had devoted herself so intensely to the quantity production of war machines as to produce a chronic labor shortage.

The various battles by which the Nazi victories were won proved the potency of the **Lessons from the Nazi victories** new weapons, and the hopeless inadequacy of the old. The United States was particularly lacking in the equipment necessary for mechanized warfare. If British and American sea-power should be overcome, the military invasion of North America was no more an impossibility than it had been during the American Revolution or the War of 1812. Indeed, Canada, the northern neighbor of the United States, was already at war, and Winston Churchill, the fighting British Prime Minister who had succeeded Chamberlain after the British *débacle* in Norway, had promised, in case the British Isles were overcome, to move the British government to the "Empire beyond the seas," and from there to "carry on the struggle until, in God's

good time, the New World, with all its power and might, steps forth to the rescue and liberation of the Old." Should Germany attempt to invade Canada, the Monroe Doctrine would automatically bring the United States into the war, and should a German invasion prove successful, the undefended border between the United States and its northern neighbor might not be the boon it had always seemed. To meet even a minor mechanized invasion, existing methods and weapons would be well-nigh helpless.

Under these circumstances it seemed clear to most Americans, "isolationists" and "interventionists" alike, that the **The defense** least the United States could do **program** was to arm to the teeth with all possible speed. But even this minimum necessity met vigorous opposition. Professional pacifists, among whom the most prominent were Socialists, Communists, and members of the liberal Protestant clergy, joined forces with other extreme advocates of neutrality to denounce preparedness as merely a prelude to war. Nevertheless, Congress early in June, 1940, appropriated by decisive majorities more than three billion dollars for the national defense, and made clear its intention of adding whatever other sums might be regarded as necessary. By the end of September, total appropriations for defense purposes had reached the astounding figure of thirteen billion dollars. To facilitate further large-scale borrowing, the national debt limit was raised to forty-nine billion dollars, the first, but not the last, war increase. Additional income and excise taxes were also voted, in defiance of the tradition that new taxes were not to be thought of in an election year.

Appropriating the money, however, was quite a different thing from actual rearmament. At best, according to the *Army and Navy Journal*, the United States would still be "a year and a half hence, far behind the fighting forces of the European nations." Plans had yet to be formulated for adjusting the nation's productive plant to the manufacture of the necessary tanks and other mechanized equipment, and for raising and training the essential manpower. To furnish political supervision over the activities of Army and Navy, the President broke precedents right and left by making Henry L. Stimson, formerly Secretary of State under Herbert Hoover, his Secretary of War, and Frank Knox, Republican Vice-Presidential candidate in 1936, his Secretary of the Navy. To put the nation on a war footing, so far as industry was concerned, he set up a National Defense Advisory Commission of seven members, headed by William S. Knudsen, president of the General Motors Corporation, and Edward R. Stettinius, Jr., chairman of the board of the United States Steel Corporation. When production bottlenecks and labor difficulties proved too difficult for the commission to handle, the President tried again, creating this time an Office of Production Management, with Knudsen as director-

The draft, at the beginning, was in truth a lottery, the numbers being drawn from the historic "goldfish bowl" pictured below.

general, and Sidney Hillman as a representative of labor, associate director-general. Continuing complications were attributed by most critics to the President's unwillingness to place the whole problem of production under one-man control.

Unwilling to risk the delay involved in raising an army by volunteering, the President urged Congress to adopt a Selective Service Act comparable to the conscription measure of 1917. This plan met with the most determined opposition, but by the middle of September, 1940, preparedness leaders in Congress were able to score a complete victory. The new measure required all men between the ages of twenty-one and thirty-five inclusive to register for a year of military training, and on October 16 approximately seventeen million citizens presented themselves for the draft. From this number the Army planned to call into service during the first year about eight hundred thousand men, and to replace them with a similar number each succeeding year. Each class, at the end of its period of training, was to remain subject to recall for emergency service during a ten-year period. Congress might also at any time declare the nation in peril, and hold the men in training under arms indefinitely. As the nation's peril increased, the terms of the draft law were stiffened. The first class called had not yet completed its year of training when, on August 18, 1941, Congress authorized the President to hold all draftees in service for as much as eighteen months beyond the period for which they had been called originally. Four months later the requirement of registration was extended to include all men from eighteen to sixty-four years of age, with service liability limited to those from twenty to forty-five. The National Guard, as the nation's second line of defense, had long since been called into service.

While the United States was still at peace, it seemed to many Americans that the best possible insurance against the troubles that a Nazi victory was sure to bring would be more

Measures "short of war"

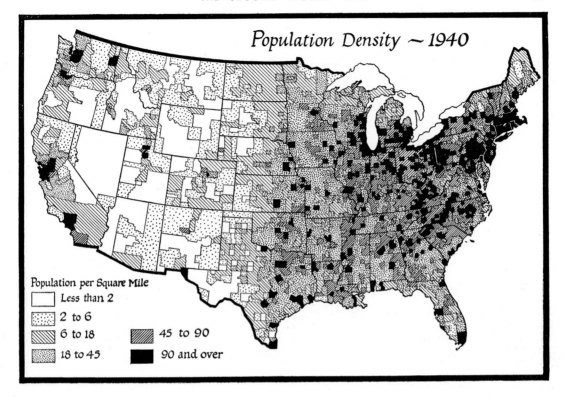

Population Density ~ 1940

Population per Square Mile
Less than 2
2 to 6
6 to 18
18 to 45
45 to 90
90 and over

effective measures "short of war" to help along the British war-effort. When it became known that the British navy was perilously short of destroyers, whereas the United States was not, a strong demand set in for selling outmoded American destroyers to the British, just as previously military airplanes had been sold to the Allies. Although specific legislation seemed to bar the way to any such action, the President was advised by Attorney-General Jackson that his powers as Commander-in-Chief of the Army and Navy would permit him to exchange obsolete destroyers for such naval bases as he might deem essential to the defense of the United States. Accordingly, the President announced early in September that the United States had leased from the British government for a period of ninety-nine years eight bases, one each in Newfoundland, Bermuda, the Bahamas, Jamaica, St. Lucia, Trinidad, Antigua, and British Guiana.[1]

[1] As finally worked out the bases in Newfoundland and Bermuda amounted practically to outright gifts.

When these advanced positions were fully equipped, it was supposed that the Atlantic coast line of the United States, as well as the Panama Canal, would be completely safeguarded against attack from the east. In return for this "dismemberment of the British Empire," as the Axis Powers chose to term the deal, fifty American destroyers were soon turned over to British crews. That the hard-pressed British, now fighting gamely against incessant attacks from the air as well as the constant threat of invasion by sea, could count on further aid from the United States when the need arose seemed evident.

With foreign relations at so critical a stage, and with the necessity of speeding up the national defense program so obvious, many observers regarded the necessity of holding a presidential election in 1940 as almost a calamity. In nations such as Great Britain, where the parliamentary system of government was in operation, an election could be postponed, but in the United States the Constitution

The presidential campaign

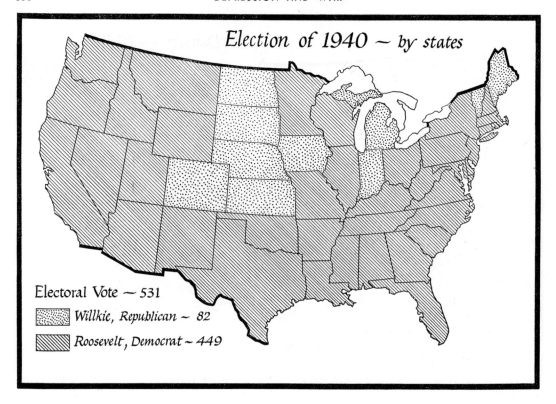

Election of 1940 — by states

Electoral Vote — 531

Willkie, Republican — 82

Roosevelt, Democrat — 449

was inexorable on this point; the election had to be held.

But, as events proved, this was no ordinary election. Shattering all precedents, the Democrats renominated Roosevelt for a third term, and chose Henry A. Wallace of Iowa, Secretary of Agriculture, as his runningmate. The Republicans, convinced that the leading contenders for their nomination lacked the popular appeal necessary to defeat the President, turned to an ex-Democrat and a businessman, Wendell L. Willkie of Indiana, with Senator Charles L. McNary of Oregon as vice-presidential candidate. Both conventions adopted platforms, the Democrats praising and the Republicans castigating the New Deal. But the platforms, as everyone knew, meant only what the candidates chose to make them mean. Roosevelt's record was not to be concealed, but where did Willkie stand on the issues of the day? Already he had made it clear that on many matters he saw eye to eye with the President, and as the campaign developed, it became evident that

almost the only question at issue was whether Roosevelt or Willkie, limited, of course, by the parties they represented, would be the better fitted to carry on the New Deal policies, both foreign and domestic. Willkie made a splendid campaign, stressing that in a democracy no one man should be considered indispensable, but the voters preferred in the crisis to stand by the President.

Among Roosevelt's most caustic critics in the campaign was John L. Lewis, who had supported the Democratic ticket in 1936 but now went over to the Republicans. Lewis even threatened to resign as president of the C.I.O. if Roosevelt should win, but his stand seemed to have little influence on the result.[1]

About fifty million voters went to the polls, the largest number in American history. Of these nearly fifty-five per cent voted for

[1] Lewis was as good as his word, and resigned his office, but he also took his union, the United Mine Workers of America, out of the C.I.O. After the war was over, in January, 1946, he returned with his union to the A.F. of L., but in December, 1947, he once more "disaffiliated."

Roosevelt, who carried 38 states with 449 electoral votes, while Willkie carried only 10 states with 82 electoral votes. Both houses of Congress and a majority of the state governments remained safely Democratic.

The most obvious conclusion to be drawn from the election, one that foreign powers were quick to point out, was that Roosevelt's policy with reference to the European war had received the emphatic endorsement of the American people. Thus fortified, the President reasserted his determination to give all possible aid to Britain, and set "four freedoms" as the American goal for the post-war world — freedom of speech, freedom of religion, freedom from want, freedom from fear. He also submitted to Congress a plan whereby the government of the United States should lend, lease, or otherwise transfer to the nations resisting aggressors such military equipment as American factories were able to produce and the American government to acquire. This measure, which amounted almost to a declaration of partial war, was fought for weeks by the isolationists in and out of Congress, but it ultimately passed both houses by decisive, nonpartisan majorities, and on March 13, 1941, received the President's signature. Among other Republicans to give the Lend-Lease Act hearty support was Wendell Willkie, whose relations with the President had become almost cordial. When Willkie decided to pay a visit to England, he conferred first with Roosevelt, and took a letter from him to be delivered in person to Prime Minister Churchill.

Other actions that left no doubt as to exactly where the United States stood on the war were soon coming thick and fast. Huge appropriations were rushed through Congress for the purchase of lend-lease materials needed by the British. Axis, Danish, and French ships in American ports were seized, and crews deemed guilty of sabotaging their ships were arrested. An executive agreement, reached April 10, 1941, between Secretary of State Hull and the Danish minister to Washington (who had refused to cooperate with his Nazi-dominated government), gave the United States permission to make military use of the island of Greenland. Amidst steadily mounting tension, the President during the next few weeks turned over fifty sorely needed tankers to the British government, closed the Axis consulates in the United States and deported their personnel, and, following the sinking in the South Atlantic of an American merchantman, the *Robin Moor*, proclaimed a state of "unlimited national emergency." The last pretense of American neutrality had all but evaporated.

Meantime Hitler, after a winter of diplomatic preparation, made ready in the spring of 1941 to march his armies southward into the Balkans. Acting under irresistible pressure, Hungary, Rumania, and Bulgaria agreed to receive his troops and cooperate with his régime. The government of Yugoslavia was like-minded, but the Yugoslav army revolted at the orders it was given, and staged a plucky but hopeless struggle against the invaders. Next the Greeks, whom Mussolini had been seeking in vain to conquer since the fall of 1940, were overwhelmed, and the little British army sent to their aid from Egypt was expelled in tattered fragments. For a time the British held Crete, but by the first of June an airborne Nazi invasion had forced them back on Africa. There the British commander, General Sir Archibald Wavell, had recently pushed the Italians far to the westward along the coast of Libya, but whatever chance he might have had to expel them from Africa altogether he lost with the collapse of the ill-fated Greek venture. The hold of the British on the eastern Mediterranean seemed tenuous indeed. To anticipate a possible Nazi thrust through Turkey or Palestine toward the oil fields of Iraq and Iran, British and "Free French" forces, early in June, occupied Syria, but their chances of resisting a Nazi attack in force seemed slender indeed.

Then, in a surprising reversal of policy, Hitler on June 22, 1941, with Hungary, Rumania, and Finland as allies, attacked

The Lend-Lease Act

Russia. He took this action, he claimed, because Russia was about to attack him, but there is little or no evidence to support such a theory. Indeed, the Soviet government was bending every effort to avert an attack by Hitler on Russia. Its deliveries of food and raw materials to Germany under an agreement of January, 1941, were faithfully maintained during the weeks immediately preceding the attack, while Communists all over the world, fully indoctrinated with the policy of friendship for Germany, denounced Hitler's enemies as warmongers, and harassed their war efforts in every possible way. Hitler knew, however, that the Soviets were rapidly building up their military strength and were keeping their army mobilized; his mistrust of them was measured only by their mistrust of him. He knew, too, that they regarded with suspicion his activities in the Balkans, and he feared that they might not restrain themselves indefinitely while he consolidated his gains in that direction. But his primary motive in embarking on the new war was his desire for expansion at Russia's expense. He had always claimed for Germany *Lebensraum* to the East, and this seemed the auspicious time to achieve his goal. He believed that his attacks on Great Britain by bomber and submarine had rendered her helpless, even if she would not capitulate. Once he had expanded his empire to the Urals, even the British would have to recognize his supremacy on the continent. He was certain that his army was invincible; why wait longer to seize the prize he coveted most?

Few private citizens anywhere in the world were aware of Hitler's intentions, least of all the American Communists, who were hard put to it to explain the new reversal in the party line. But both the British and the American governments had advance information on what was about to happen, and had so informed the Soviet government. They were prepared, also, to receive the new adherent to the anti-Nazi cause with every show of cordiality. From Churchill came the prompt announcement: "Any man or state who fights against Naziism will have our aid.

Lend-lease from the United States provided much-needed aid for the Allies and spelled the approaching end of American neutrality. Total lend-lease aid by the end of the war exceeded in value fifty billion dollars.

Any man or state who marches with Hitler is our foe." And from Roosevelt came the assurance that supplies would soon be flowing from the United States to Russia under the terms of the Lend-Lease Act. To the surprise of most experts, the Russians offered sustained military resistance to the invading armies. The Germans and their allies took much territory, but the collapse that they had expected failed to materialize. In the winter of 1941–42, the Russian armies for several months even held the offensive, and regained some of the ground they had lost.

With Russia, a totalitarian nation, fighting on the Allied side, the question of "war aims," so much discussed during the First World War, attracted increasing attention, particularly in the United States. In part to answer this question, and in part to give dramatic emphasis to the solidarity of Anglo-American opinion, President Roosevelt and Prime Minister Churchill met at an undisclosed point in the Atlantic, and on August 14, 1941, issued over their joint signatures the so-called "Atlantic Charter." This document disclaimed for Great Britain and the United States any desire for territorial, or other, aggrandizement, or for any territorial changes not in accord with the wishes of the people concerned. It asserted the right of all peoples to choose the form of government under which they wished to live, and promised to promote equal access for all states, "great or small, victor or vanquished," to the raw materials of the world. Other objectives named were improved labor standards, economic advancement, and social security, freedom from fear and want, the unhindered use of the high seas, and the disarmament of aggressor nations as a step toward the abandonment of the use of force in international relations. In many ways the Atlantic Charter was reminiscent of Wilson's Fourteen Points, as it was no doubt meant to be, but it was couched in general terms, and lacked the specific statements of war aims that characterized the earlier document.

By this time the increasing tempo of sub-

The Atlantic Charter

marine attacks had brought the "Battle of the Atlantic" to a crisis. Since a substantial number of the freighters being sunk carried lend-lease materials, many Americans demanded that the United States join with Great Britain in convoying merchant fleets overseas. A step in this direction had seemingly been taken when on July 7 the President had announced that units of the United States Navy had arrived in Iceland to supplement, and ultimately to replace, the British forces already there. But Roosevelt, although he believed that the United States should come to the aid of Great Britain as soon as possible, was reluctant because of the attitude of Congress and public opinion to start a "shooting war." He therefore ordered merely that American ships and aircraft should "patrol" the western Atlantic in order to advise the British as to the whereabouts of Axis craft. The effectiveness of these patrols brought speedy Axis retaliation. Eight American freighters had already been sunk when, on September 4, 1941, the American destroyer *Greer* was attacked, but not hit, while trailing a German submarine. Thereupon the President ordered destroyers to shoot submarines "on sight." In mid-October another destroyer, the *Kearny*, was hit, and eleven of her crew were killed. That same month, the *Reuben James* was torpedoed and sunk, with the loss of seventy-six of her crew. After these attacks, Congress, by a measure signed November 17, authorized the arming of American merchant ships, and freed them from the remaining restrictions of the neutrality laws, which thus far had kept them outside "combat zones." Complete participation by the United States in the war seemed close at hand.

The final dénouement, however, came from an unexpected quarter. The collapse of France had given Japan another opportunity to press on toward her goal of military and economic domination of all eastern Asia. From the subject French government, set up at Vichy after the surrender to Germany with the aged Marshal Pétain as Chief-of-State, the Japanese had obtained the right

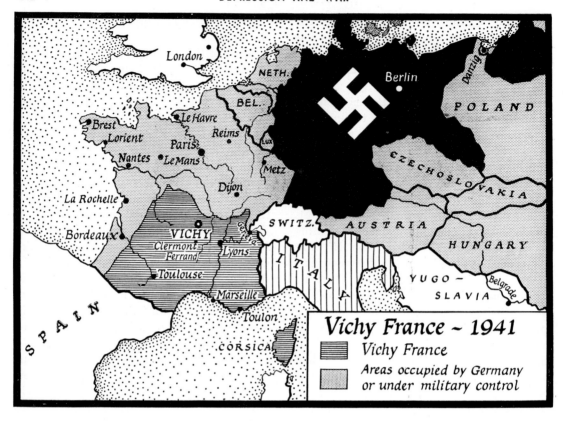

Vichy France ~ 1941

▤ Vichy France

▦ Areas occupied by Germany or under military control

in 1940 to occupy the northern part of French Indo-China, and on July 23, 1941, they were given permission to take over the rest of the former French dependency. Japanese troops pouring into this area posed a grave threat, not only to the Philippine Islands, but also to the British and Dutch possessions in the Far East. In protest, therefore, the American government on July 26 froze all Japanese assets in the United States, an action which the Dutch and British governments quickly paralleled. During the protracted discussions which followed, the United States proposed a settlement based on the following principles: (1) respect for the territorial integrity and sovereignty of all nations; (2) non-interference in the internal affairs of other countries; (3) equality of commercial and other opportunities; and (4) non-disturbance of the *status quo* in the Pacific except by peaceful means. Finally, when these principles were spurned, the United States demanded assurance from the Japa-

nese government that it intended to withdraw its troops from China and French Indo-China. A few weeks later, on November 15, a Japanese envoy, Saburo Kurusu, arrived ostentatiously by airplane in the United States with what purported to be new Japanese proposals. "We must all pull together for peace," Kurusu told American reporters.

But the Kurusu mission was only a blind, for the course Japan meant to follow had already been decided. On the **Pearl** early morning of December 7 **Harbor** while the peace conversations at Washington were still in progress, a Japanese carrier-borne air force of one hundred and five airplanes attacked the great American naval base at Pearl Harbor, in Hawaii. So complete was the surprise that most American aircraft were destroyed on the ground, leaving the American battle fleet at the mercy of the treacherous foe. Nineteen of the eighty-six American ships in the harbor were seriously hit, five great capital ships were

Pearl Harbor

a fact at last. As in the First World War, many other American nations were soon involved in the conflict. Some of them, notably Mexico and Brazil, went the whole length of declaring war, while others were content to show their "good neighborliness" by measures "short of war." Eventually every American power severed diplomatic relations with the Axis. Even the Argentine declared war in 1945.

For many months the war in the Pacific went badly for the United Nations, as the Allies now began to call them- **Allied** selves. The attack on Pearl **reverses** Harbor was followed immediately by attacks on the Philippine Islands, Wake Island, Guam, Hong Kong, British Malaya, and Thailand. The Thai government offered practically no resistance, Guam fell on December 11, Wake Island, December 26, and Hong Kong on Christmas Day. In the Philippines General MacArthur, whose forces during the last phases of the dispute with Japan had been somewhat augmented by troops from the United States, made a valiant stand on the Bataan peninsula and the island of Corregidor. But the assistance from the United States Navy on which his campaign was predicated was not forthcoming, and in the end the Japanese won by sheer force of numbers. Bataan capitulated in April, and Corregidor in May. Well before the end came, General MacArthur, in response to an insistent demand from both the United States and Australia, left the Philippines by stealth to take command of the United Nations forces in Australia. Meantime Japanese troops overran Malaya, captured the great British base at Singapore, conquered Burma, and except for a few precarious footholds forced the United Nations completely out of the East Indies. With the Burma Road closed, aid to China decreased to next to nothing, and the Allies fell back upon India and Australia as bases of operation.

either sunk or otherwise put out of action, and casualties to personnel reached 4575 killed, wounded, or missing. So complete was the catastrophe that the American government delayed an entire year before making public the full details. Had the Japanese brought with them troops to effect a landing, they might with ease have taken the whole of the Hawaiian Islands.

The day after Pearl Harbor was attacked, Congress, with only one dissenting vote, recognized the existence of a state of war between the United States and Japan, while Japan issued its overdue declaration of war against the United States and the British Empire. When a few days later Germany and Italy, in conformity with their commitments to Japan, declared war against the United States, Congress, by a unanimous vote in both houses, responded with similar declarations against the Axis powers in Europe. Thus the total war that most Americans had hoped so earnestly to avoid became

Outside the Pacific theater matters were almost equally desperate. German submarines, operating off the Atlantic coastline

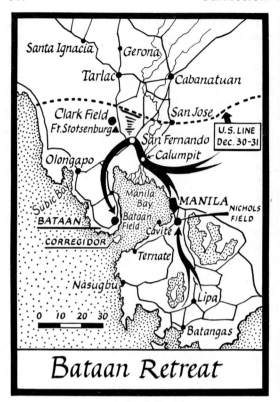

Bataan Retreat

nitely to have passed from the Japanese to the Allies on August 7, when the marines took Tulagi harbor and the airfield on Guadalcanal Island. Heartening news came also from Russia, where the German drive had stalled at Stalingrad, and from Egypt, where the Axis forces, defeated at El Alamein, were driven back westward again in precipitate retreat. Still disappointed in the progress made, the American people gave the Roosevelt administration a stinging rebuke on election day, November 3, by reducing substantially the Democratic majorities in both House and Senate, and by overthrowing Democratic control in many of the states.

Four days later, but on November 8, North African time, came the news that a huge Anglo-American armada had landed troops in French Morocco and Algeria, with the avowed intention of occupying the entire North African seacoast of the French Empire, both Mediterranean and Atlantic. This daring operation had been planned during a meeting of Churchill and Roosevelt in Washington the preceding June, but the secret was well kept, and the Axis Powers were seemingly taken completely by surprise. Thanks to the fact that an Allied "fifth column" had carefully prepared the way for the attack, General Dwight D. Eisenhower, in supreme command of operations on land, got his troops ashore with a minimum of opposition. Although Marshal Pétain's Vichy government, to which North Africa professed to be loyal politically, ordered resistance, there was little serious fighting except at Casablanca and Oran.

Invasion of North Africa

The Allies had planned to use General Henri Honoré Giraud, who had escaped from German imprisonment, as head of the French government in North Africa, but by chance Admiral Jean François Darlan, Vichyite commander of the French Navy, happened to be in Algeria at the time the invasion occurred. When Darlan's authority was found to be great and his cooperation available, he was assigned the rôle intended for Giraud, only to be removed from the scene by assas-

and in the Caribbean Sea, sank hundreds of American freighters, and produced an acute gasoline and fuel-oil shortage along the Atlantic seaboard. In northern Africa, by the end of June, an army of Germans and Italians under General Erwin Rommel had advanced along the coast to within sixty-five miles of Alexandria, and seemingly had the Suez Canal within its grasp. In Russia, the German drive for Moscow had been stopped at the time of Pearl Harbor, but by the summer of 1942 a new German thrust had penetrated as far to the southeast as Stalingrad, and still another, with the oil fields of the Caspian area as its goal, was in the edge of the Caucasus.

But with the increasing effectiveness of the American war effort, the tide of battle soon began to turn. In the Pacific the forces of the United Nations chalked up a series of costly but important naval victories — in the Coral Sea, off Midway, and in the Solomon Islands. The initiative seemed defi-

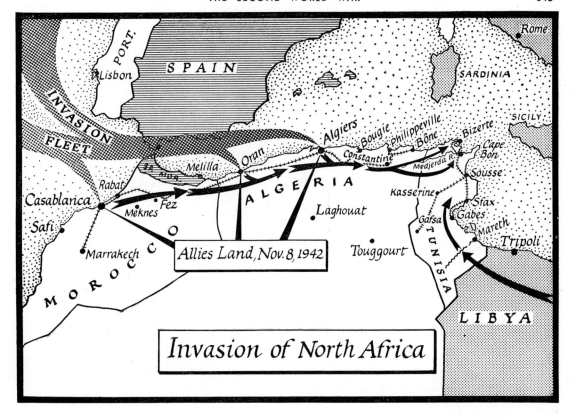

Invasion of North Africa

sination, December 24, 1942. Thereupon Giraud took over, in accordance with the original Allied plan, but his leadership, as well as Darlan's before him, was strongly contested by General Charles de Gaulle, head of the "Free French" government in London. At a meeting held in January, 1943, at Casablanca, Churchill and Roosevelt brought Giraud and de Gaulle together, and for a time both French leaders had seats on a governing council. Unfortunately this scheme worked badly, and in the end the Allied governments were obliged to permit the elimination of Giraud. As for the Vichy government in France, it became progressively more and more subject to German control. The southeastern half of France, which up to the time of the North African invasion had not been occupied by German troops, was quickly taken over, and the remnant of the French fleet at Toulon was obliged to scuttle itself to escape capture by German land forces.

Obviously the Allied governments had hoped that their African conquests would extend to Tunisia before that colony could be occupied by the Axis, but in this they were disappointed because of bad weather, long lines of communication, and prompt anticipation of their action by the Axis authorities. The final struggle did not come until May, 1943, when the British Eighth Army under General Sir Bernard Law Montgomery closed in from the east, and British, French, and American troops from the west. All of Tunisia, including the cities of Tunis and Bizerte, was quickly occupied by the victorious Allied troops, who, during the final phases of the struggle, took well over two hundred thousand prisoners. Before the collapse, General Erwin Rommel, famed commander of the Africa Corps, had escaped to Europe, but practically all the troops he left behind were either killed or captured.

The next great goal of Allied endeavor was

OPERATION "UPPERCUT." USAAF troop-carrier division fills the sky with men and supplies over the coast of southern France.

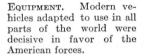

EQUIPMENT. Modern vehicles adapted to use in all parts of the world were decisive in favor of the American forces.

FIELD RATIONS. Self-contained units were frequently the only source of food on the fighting fronts.

Italy

Sicily, which Eisenhower's forces invaded on July 10, 1943, and conquered in less than six weeks. Before this task was completed, King Victor Emmanuel, assisted by elements in the Fascist grand council, forced Mussolini out of power, and set up a new government under Marshal Pietro Badoglio as premier. Badoglio's aim was peace, but the Italian peninsula was invaded before he accepted Eisenhower's terms of unconditional surrender and turned over the entire Italian navy to the Allies.

NATURAL PERILS. Not all wartime dangers were man-made. The U.S. Coast Guard performed an operation called the "Iceberg Census" to protect convoys on the North Atlantic.

PRISONER OF WAR CAMPS are the inevitable accompaniment of war. These POW's are in a German camp.

Stiff German resistance held the Allies back many months in Italy, but at length, on June 4, 1944, Rome was taken. Thereupon the King, although keeping his title, turned over his duties to his son, Humbert, and a new cabinet headed by a non-Fascist, Ivanoe Bonomi, replaced the Badoglio government. The chief strategic purpose of the North African and Italian campaign was to clear the Mediterranean of enemy seapower, and this end was fully accomplished. By the fall of 1944, with Italy recognized as a "cobelligerent," Allied arms had reached the valley of the Po.

The long-awaited "second front" was launched from England across the channel to the coast of Normandy, June 6, 1944. To conduct this campaign

The second front

Eisenhower and Montgomery were transferred from Italy. Despite great weather difficulties and the lack of a harbor, the invasion was completely successful, and the reconquest of France began. On August 24–25, Paris was occupied by Allied troops amidst riotous demonstrations of joy by its inhabitants. To reinforce the Channel invaders, another expedition landed August 15 on the Mediterranean coast of France, and worked its way northward with extraordinary rapidity. By November, 1944, nearly all of France and Belgium had been freed, part of the Netherlands had been cleared of enemy troops, and Allied armies were fighting on German soil. Somewhat tardily, the British and American governments recognized de Gaulle's "Free French" committee as the provisional government of France. For Belgium and the Netherlands, governments-in-exile, long since functioning in England, had only to be transferred to the Continent.

In the air and on the seas the German situation grew steadily more desperate. The **On the sea and in the air** attempt of the *Luftwaffe* to bomb the British into submission had not only failed completely, it had brought devastating retaliation. While the Germans were able to make only "nuisance" raids over England, British bombers and American flying fortresses attacked German, German-held, and Italian cities by night and day. Harbor installations, airfields, war factories, railway yards, power plants, bridges, and dams — every conceivable type of construction that might aid the Axis war effort was subjected to the most merciless bombing. After the Allied landings on the French coast had been effected, a German secret weapon, the robot bomb, did considerable execution among the civilian population of southern England, but it failed completely to halt the invasion. On the high seas, where German submarines had taken a discouragingly high toll, new devices for detecting and destroying them diminished drastically their sinkings and all but eliminated them as a factor in the war. Lend-lease supplies flowed in a steady stream

to Russia, while communications with the British Isles and the Mediterranean approached peacetime conditions.

Meantime on the eastern front the Germans had suffered equally devastating reverses. Completely defeated **The eastern** at Stalingrad, they lost the **front** offensive to the Russians, who in one overwhelming display of strength after another drove the invaders from their soil. By the fall of 1944 they had freed also three German satellite states, Bulgaria, Rumania, and Finland, each of which, like Italy, joined the Allies in the war against Germany. Much of Poland had also been occupied, and Russian troops had invaded Hungary, Yugoslavia, Czechoslovakia, and East Prussia. By the end of the year, British troops were far along with the re-conquest of Greece, and "Partisan" forces under Marshal Tito in Yugoslavia were giving great aid in the liberation of their country. The utter hopelessness of the German situation seemed plain to all except the Nazi leaders.

Many optimists, including even General Eisenhower, had dreamed of victory in 1944, but as winter set in, the Allied **The German** campaigns, both eastern and **counter-** western, slowed down to a halt. **attack** To make matters worse, the Germans, under General Karl von Rundstedt, launched on December 17 a terrific and utterly unanticipated counterattack in the Belgium-Luxembourg sector. So spectacular were the initial German gains that for a time it looked as if the important harbor of Antwerp, recently opened to Allied shipping, would be cut off. But as the old year ended and the new year began, the Allied command, mainly through the efforts of General George S. Patton's Third American Army, brought the German drive to a standstill, and regained the initiative. Before January was over, all the ground lost by the Allies had been retaken, and the battle of Germany had begun in earnest.

The time had now come for the careful synchronization of Allied activities on the eastern and the western fronts. In the east-

ern theater, the Russians delayed their cus-
Conquest of tomary winter offensive until
Germany January 12, 1945. Then they
struck out so forcefully with five huge armies
that the German defenses were smashed all
the way from the Baltic to the Carpathians.
By the end of February, Russian troops,
after clearing the Germans from most of
Poland, and from much of Hungary and
Czechoslovakia as well, stood on German soil
only thirty-one miles from Berlin. In the
west, Eisenhower had planned the destruction of the German armies facing him before
they could retreat across the Rhine, and to a
remarkable extent he was able to accomplish
this feat. His principal attack was somewhat delayed by the von Rundstedt offensive, but the month of February saw him in
full action, with his American, British, Canadian, and French troops fighting in admirable coordination. Before March was many
days old, Allied troops had penetrated into
nearly every stronghold of the famed West-
wall, doing untold military damage, and taking prisoners by the hundreds of thousands.
Many Germans succeeded in withdrawing
across the Rhine, but on March 7, owing to
the failure of the retreating forces to destroy
a bridge at Remagen, they were followed by
American soldiers in considerable numbers.
The Remagen bridge soon collapsed, but
from newly established bridgeheads Allied
forces in great strength pushed forward
through the very heart of the Reich. The
"scorched-earth" policy that the Nazi
leaders had ordered, together with the persistent bombing of German cities and the
wholesale devastation incidental to military
operations, left Germany a scene of incredible
ruin.

By the last week of April the eastern and
western invaders of Germany had met on the
VE Day banks of the Elbe, and the end
was in sight. Victorious Russian
armies occupied Rumania, Bulgaria, Austria,
and Hungary. The German armies that had
long stalled the Allied advance in northern
Italy began to crumble, then surrendered.
Italian "partisans" caught and executed the

hapless Mussolini, leaving his body and that
of his mistress to the studied insults of a
Milanese mob. The Russians fought their
way street by street through the rubble of
Berlin, and took possession of what was left
of the stricken city. Hitler himself committed suicide, following a weird marriage
ceremony in which he made his mistress his
wife. Shortly after, Admiral Karl Doenitz,
upon whom Hitler had directed that his
mantle should fall, notified the Allies that
Germany was ready to surrender, and on
May 8, 1945, the Allied victory in Europe,
VE Day, was officially proclaimed.

By this time Allied might had also made
itself dominant in the Pacific. There, in
mid-November, 1942, the Japa- **The Pacific**
nese tried to oust the Americans
from Guadalcanal, but failed, in large part
because of naval defeats administered by
American squadrons operating under the
command of Admiral William F. Halsey.
Japanese efforts to push across New Guinea
to Port Moresby in order to strike at Australia were also frustrated. After that, the
bitter fighting necessary to clear the way
back to the Philippines could begin. By this
time the American Navy had recovered from
the losses sustained at Pearl Harbor, and
with each succeeding month its strength increased enormously. Up in the cold and fog
of the Aleutians, where since June, 1942, the
Japanese had held two American islands,
Kiska and Attu, the Americans struck at
Attu, May 11, 1943, and before the end of
the month had conquered the island. When
Americans and Canadians landed on Kiska
in August, they found that the Japanese had
already departed. The next great effort of
the American Navy was to drive the Japanese from the islands of the mid-Pacific. In
November, 1943, marine and army forces
successfully invaded several atolls in the
Gilberts, among them Tarawa, where the
fighting was particularly bloody. Kwaja-
lein in the Marshalls was taken early in 1944.

It was now plain that the strategy of Admiral Chester W. Nimitz, commander-in-
chief of the Pacific fleet, called for a direct

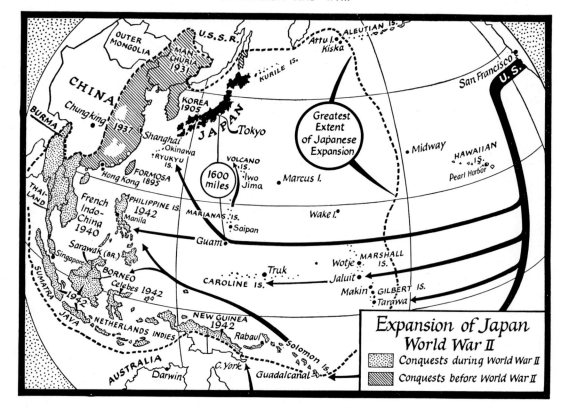

Expansion of Japan
World War II
Conquests during World War II
Conquests before World War II

advance across the Pacific to Asiatic waters. No effort was made to clear every island occupied by the Japanese, but important bases, together with airfields that could dominate wide stretches of ocean, were taken and strongly held. By June, 1944, the advance had reached Saipan in the Marianas, fifteen hundred miles from Tokyo and sixteen hundred miles from Manila. Frightened by the approaching danger, the Japanese sent carrier-based planes to attack the American ships off Saipan, but the attackers suffered heavily, while American planes in turn sought out the fleet from which the enemy planes had come and inflicted heavy damage upon it. The bloody but successful conquest of Saipan was followed in the next month by the occupation of Guam and Tinian, the former an American island held by the Japanese since the beginning of the war. Bomber attacks could now be made from these bases, as well as from China, upon Formosa and the Japanese homeland, and

the exploit of the *Hornet*, which had sent its planes in April, 1942, to attack Tokyo, was repeated by land-based planes from Saipan, November 23, 1944. From this time on, the destruction of Japanese cities and industrial targets proceeded mercilessly.

In order to shorten the bombing range to Japan, two more islands were assaulted and taken by American land and naval forces early in 1945. The **Iwo Jima** first, Iwo Jima, a tiny islet in the volcano group midway between Guam and Tokyo, was only five miles long by three wide, but it provided the Japanese with three airfields and a radar station. Enemy intelligence was thus able to detect flights of Tokyo-bound American planes and to flash the news to the homeland of their approach. So great was the nuisance value of this island that on February 19, after weeks of preparatory bombing, two divisions of marines, supported by a prodigious show of naval force, undertook its conquest. The fighting was terrific, for

Admirals William F. Halsey, Jr. (left) and *Chester W. Nimitz*
(right) played major rôles in the Battle of the Pacific. Admiral Nimitz took command of
Pacific operations ten days after Pearl Harbor.

the Japanese had expected the attack, and had crowded the island with a maximum of men and armor. For a full month the battle lasted, and American casualties mounted to twenty thousand, but the coveted terrain was won.

The last major amphibious operation in the advance on Japan began on Easter Sunday, April 1, when Okinawa, **Okinawa** largest island in the Ryukyus, situated only three hundred and seventy miles from Japan proper, was invaded. Fourteen hundred ships and upwards of one hundred thousand American soldiers and marines participated in the action. At first, resistance was light, and the Americans got ashore easily, but in southern Okinawa, toward which the Japanese retreated, the enemy staged a desperate and unexpectedly prolonged resistance. While the land engagement was in progress, a Japanese naval squadron sent perhaps five hundred planes to attack the American ships standing offshore, but most of the attackers were intercepted and shot down, while the Japanese naval units from which they operated were soon discovered and put out of action. During this engagement Japanese *Kamikaze*, specially trained pilots who deliberately

sought to smash their bomb-laden planes into the American ships, first made their appearance in large numbers. Enough of them succeeded in their suicidal missions to inflict serious losses, both in ships and in personnel, upon the American fleet; but, despite this setback and persistent *Kamikaze* harassment thereafter, the battle of Okinawa went on to its inexorable end. By the middle of June, the Americans were in complete control of the island, and the doom of Japan was sealed. American bombers, operating, not only from convenient airfields, but also from the decks of a host of task-force carriers, now burned and blasted the Japanese islands at will.

Meantime, the campaign of MacArthur, who had promised to return from Australia to the Philippines, had made **MacArthur's** similarly notable strides. Mac- **return to the** Arthur's strategy, depending al- **Philippines** ways on the careful coordination of land, sea, and air forces, was to bomb furiously and by-pass the principal Japanese bases, and by "leapfrog" tactics to land at unexpected, and sometimes undefended, points along the route he must clear. By January, 1944, he had begun to advance in this fashion along the northern shores of New Guinea, and well

The Pacific war began with American sea-power disastrously depleted at Pearl Harbor. But the Navy staged an effective come-back, and within two years the Japanese were on the defensive. Even before Hiroshima, their defeat was assured.

PEARL HARBOR. The U.S.S. West Virginia, one of the many ships completely crippled by the attack, is burning in the foreground.

TASK FORCE. The strength of the U.S. Navy in evidence at the rendezvous preceding the Marshall Island invasion.

before the end of the year he was ready to make the last long jump to the Philippines. On October 20, he landed in person with a large army of invasion on the island of Leyte, and began the reconquest he had promised. To defend MacArthur's movements, a heavy naval concentration under Admiral Halsey was obliged to fight one of the greatest sea-actions of history, for the Japanese at last decided that they must risk a major portion of their fleet. In the waters adjacent to Leyte, beginning on October 25, the Americans fought off the Japanese in a series of complicated and extensive actions so costly to the enemy as to reduce the Japanese Navy, the Americans claimed, to "fifth-rate" status.

After the battle of Leyte Gulf, organized resistance on Leyte and on the neighboring island of Samar disintegrated slowly but surely. By the end of the year, MacArthur had also landed troops on Mindoro Island, preparatory to his main attack, which he had reserved for Luzon. In January, 1945, with the aid of planes operating from Mindoro airfields, he put ashore a formidable force at Lingayen Gulf, and began the fateful march to Manila. Japanese resistance was light at first, but the approaches to the capi-

RELIGION. Chaplains of all denominations traveled with military forces everywhere to conduct religious services.

THE ATOMIC BOMB. Aerial photos taken over Hiroshima following the atomic explosion show devastation.

KAMIKAZE PLANE. One of the most effective and inhuman of the weapons used by the Japanese.

tal were stubbornly defended, and not until February 3 were American troops able to enter it. After that, the Japanese staged within the city a gruesomely effective last-ditch fight that lasted for weeks. Bitter fighting also continued elsewhere on Luzon, and the American reconquest of the island was hardly complete at the end of June, when it was officially announced by General MacArthur. Meantime Mindanao, the next largest of the Philippine Archipelago, as well as certain lesser islands, had been successfully invaded, and Japanese hopes were waning fast. Fighting still continued, however, in many of the islands until the end of the war.

While the war in the Pacific was thus being planned and fought, Allied forces were doing what little they could to hold the Japanese from further conquests on the mainland of Asia. The task could hardly have been more difficult. With India as a base, some Allied aid to the Chinese was soon being flown in over the Himalayas, but it was never enough. Bad relations between the government of Chiang Kai-shek and the armed Communist bands that controlled much of North China added

The Asiatic mainland

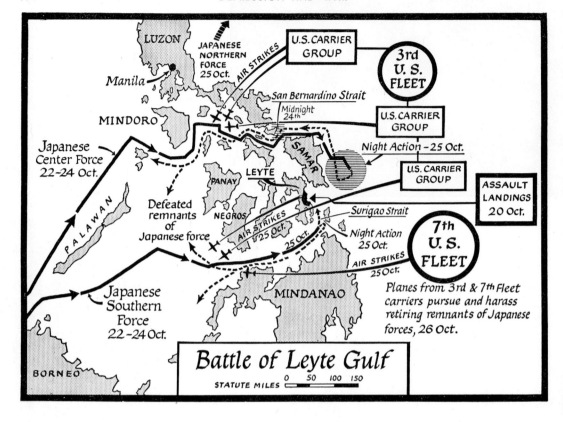

to the turmoil from which that unhappy nation suffered. Meager American air forces, operating under General Joseph W. Stilwell, gave great aid to Chiang's armies, but in spite of their best efforts Japanese troops were able to penetrate into Chinese territory about as far as they cared to go.

Perhaps Stilwell scored his principal triumph in clearing the Japanese from northern Burma so that a new route from India to China, the Ledo Road, could be opened. Using American-trained Chinese troops, he was nearing the completion of this task when, in the fall of 1944, he was relieved of his command and recalled to the United States. Personal differences with Chiang Kai-shek over the training and disposition of Chinese troops were said to account for this strange action. Under Stilwell's successor, General David I. Sultan, American engineers went on with the construction of the road, and in January, 1945, the first motor caravan crossed

it all the way from India to China. Allied successes farther to the south in Burma, under the leadership of Lord Louis Mountbatten, were also heartening, but in spite of the achievements in Burma the war ended with the Japanese still in control of their principal gains on the mainland of Asia.

Nevertheless, the Japanese will to continue the war had not much longer to go. Far-cruising American submarines, joining their successes to **The atomic bomb** those of American surface forces, helped to drive the Japanese Navy and merchant marine almost completely from the seas. In consequence, connections between the home islands and the overexpanded "Co-Prosperity Sphere" broke down. On occasion American task forces maneuvered close to the Japanese shore, and lobbed their shells into coastal installations. *Kamikaze* attacks became more numerous and daring, and they took a heavy toll of American lives and ship-

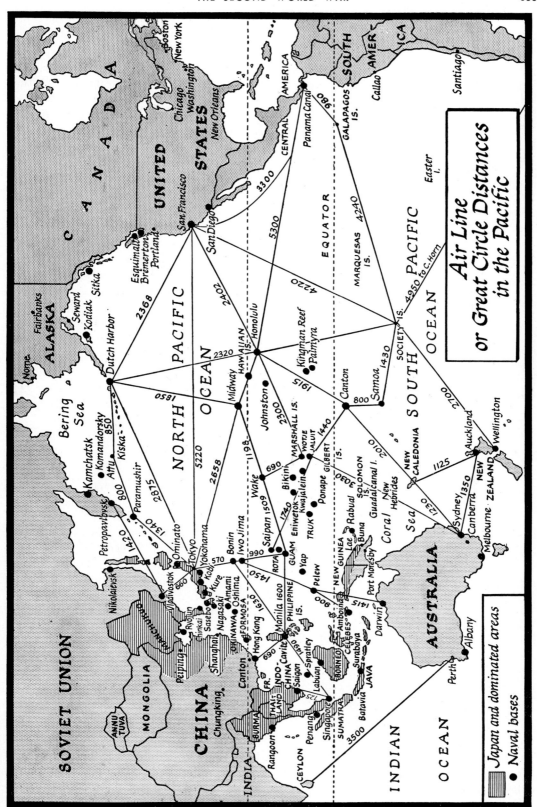

Air Line
or Great Circle Distances
in the Pacific

Japan and dominated areas
• Naval bases

INSTRUMENT OF SURRENDER

We, acting by command of and in behalf of the Emperor of Japan, the Japanese Government and the Japanese Imperial General Headquarters, hereby accept the provisions set forth in the declaration issued by the heads of the Governments of the United States, China and Great Britain on 26 July 1945, at Potsdam, and subsequently adhered to by the Union of Soviet Socialist Republics, which four powers are hereafter referred to as the Allied Powers.

We hereby proclaim the unconditional surrender to the Allied Powers of the Japanese Imperial General Headquarters and of all Japanese armed forces and all armed forces under Japanese control wherever situated.

Signed at TOKYO BAY, JAPAN at 09 04 I
on the SECOND day of SEPTEMBER , 1945.

By Command and in behalf of the Emperor of Japan and the Japanese Government.

By Command and in behalf of the Japanese Imperial General Headquarters.

Accepted at TOKYO BAY, JAPAN at 0908 I
on the SECOND day of SEPTEMBER , 1945,
for the United States, Republic of China, United Kingdom and the Union of Soviet Socialist Republics, and in the interests of the other United Nations at war with Japan.

Supreme Commander for the Allied Powers.

United States Representative

Republic of China Representative

United Kingdom Representative

Union of Soviet Socialist Republics Representative

Commonwealth of Australia Representative

Dominion of Canada Representative

Provisional Government of the French Republic Representative

Kingdom of the Netherlands Representative

Dominion of New Zealand Representative

The surrender of Japan, otherwise final and unconditional, left the Emperor as symbolic head of the Japanese state.

ping, but the "softening-up process" preliminary to invasion went on. Early in August, the climax was reached with the dropping of an atomic bomb on Hiroshima, a military point of some importance that until then had escaped the activities of American airmen. Shortly thereafter, a similar bomb was dropped on Nagasaki. The results obtained were cataclysmic — a single bomb was as devastating to an enemy city as the concentrated action of a thousand ordinary bombers equipped with full loads of ordinary explosives. The development of the atomic bomb was the result of cooperative efforts by numerous American, British, and Canadian scientists, who, with the full backing of their governments, had pooled their talents in a successful effort to split the atom. The cost of their experiments to the American people alone probably reached two billion dollars, but the bomb that the scientists produced undoubtedly served to shorten the war materially. It served also to make the peoples of the world realize, fully perhaps for the first time, how totally catastrophic another World War would be.

For some months it had been known to the British and American chiefs of state that Russia intended eventually to enter the war against Japan. **VJ Day** With the end so nearly in sight, the Russian government found it inexpedient to delay longer, and on August 9, following a formal declaration of war, issued the day before, Russian troops began to advance against light opposition into Manchuria. Faced by this new threat, and assured by the President of the United States that only surrender could save Japanese civilization from total annihilation by the further use of atomic bombs, the Japanese gave up. As early as August 10, the Japanese news agency, Domei, broadcast that Japan was willing to accept the terms of unconditional surrender, as defined by the Allies at Potsdam, Germany, the preceding month, provided only that Emperor Hirohito's sovereignty would not be questioned. The President of the United States, replying for the Allies, stated the willingness of the nations at war with Japan to retain the Emperor for the time being, on condition that he take orders from an Allied Supreme Commander, to be resident in Japan. This offer the Japanese government accepted, and by August 14 the world knew for sure that the war was over. Not for several days, however, did a Japanese delegation appear, as required, in Manila to arrange for the formal surrender, and not until September 1, when delegates from the principal Allies, with General MacArthur representing the United Nations, received a delegation of Japanese officials aboard the battleship *Missouri* in Tokyo Bay, were the documents of surrender actually signed. Thereafter the occupation of Japan by American forces proceeded rapidly, and the American commander, General MacArthur, began to give orders to the Emperor of Japan. September 2, 1945, was officially designated VJ Day by the President, but by this time the chief celebrations were over.

Bibliography

On the involvement of the United States in the Second World War many of the references cited for the preceding chapter are pertinent, particularly the two books by Langer and Gleason. Good general surveys are available in *The United States and Its Place in World Affairs, 1918–43*, edited by Allan Nevins and L. M. Hacker (1943); and Dexter Perkins, *America and Two Wars* (1944). The official presentation of the American case appears in Department of State, *Peace and War, United States Foreign Policy, 1931–1941* (1943). More informal, but semi-official, is Forrest Davis and E. K. Lindley, *How War Came* (1942). Walter Johnson, *The Battle against Isolation* (1944); and, by the same author, *William Allen White's America* (1947), deal with the movement for American aid to the Allies; while Wayne S. Cole, *America First; The Battle against Intervention, 1940–1941* (1953), presents the opposite view. Herbert Feis, *The Road to Pearl Harbor: The Coming of the War between the United States and Japan* (1950), is clear and convincing. George Morgenstern, *Pearl Harbor, The Story of the Secret War* (1947), places all the blame for the Japanese attack on the Roosevelt administration. Rear Admiral Robert A. Theobald, *The Final Secret of Pearl Harbor* (1954), is well calculated to "delight the most rabid Roosevelt hater," but will satisfy few others. Walter Millis, *This is Pearl!* (1947), is more satisfactory. Caustic but by no means convincing criticism of Roosevelt's Secretary of War is voiced in Richard N. Current, *Secretary Stimson, A Study in Statecraft* (1954).

On the 1940 election, see for the Republican side Mary E. Dillon, *Wendell Willkie, 1892–1944* (1952); and for the Democratic side, Farley, *Jim Farley's Story: The Roosevelt Years*, previously mentioned, which gives much attention to Roosevelt's third nomination. C. A. M. Ewing, *Presidential Elections from Abraham Lincoln to Franklin D. Roosevelt* (1940), is a useful statistical study. C. W. Stein, *The Third Term Tradition* (1943), ends with the election of 1940.

On the war as a whole, Winston Churchill, *The Second World War* (6 vols., 1948–53), is a brilliant interpretation by a leading participant. Efforts to put the story together in a single volume include Francis T. Miller, *History of World War II* (1945); W. P. Hall, *Iron out of Calvary: An Interpretative History of the Second World War* (1946); Roger W. Shugg and H. A. DeWeerd, *World War II: A Concise History* (1946); H. C. O'Neill, *A Short History of the Second World War* (1950); and Fletcher Pratt, *War for the World* (1950). A good running account of the American war effort is in George C. Marshall, *Biennial Report of the Chief of Staff of the United States Army* (1941–1943–1945). Books by military participants are increasingly numerous, among the most useful being Dwight D. Eisenhower, *Crusade in Europe* (1948); Omar N. Bradley, *A Soldier's Story* (1951); Mark W. Clark, *Calculated Risk* (1951); Lewis Hyde Brereton, *The Brereton Diaries: The War in the Air in the Pacific, Middle East, and Europe* (1946); Ernest J. King and W. M. Whitehill, *Fleet Admiral King; A Naval Record* (1952); Joseph W. Stilwell, *The Stilwell Papers*, edited by

Theodore H. White (1948); and Henry H. Arnold, *Global Mission* (1949).

The official American history of the Army's part in the war, based upon all available records, is in preparation by the Historical Division, Department of the Army, *The United States Army in World War II* (21 vols., 1947–54), with many more volumes projected. The maps and illustrations that accompany this series are no less important than the actual texts, which are excellent throughout. In progress also is *The Army Air Forces in World War II* (5 vols., 1948–53), edited by Wesley F. Craven and James L. Cate; a series of U.S. Marine Corps, *Monographs* (14 vols., 1947–54), and Samuel E. Morison, *History of Naval Operations in World War II* (9 vols., 1947–54). Other books of merit on combat operations are Walter D. Edmonds, *They Fought with What They Had: The Story of the Army Air Forces in the Southwest Pacific, 1941–1942* (1951); Jeter A. Iseley and Philip A. Crowl, *The Marines and Amphibious War; Its Theory, and Its Practice in the Pacific* (1951); D. S. Ballantine, *U. S. Naval Logistics in the Second World War* (1947); Walter Karig and Welbourn Kelley, *Battle Report, I, Pearl Harbor to Coral Sea* (1944); W. D. Puleston, *The Influence of Sea Power in World War II* (1947); Robert Sherrod, *History of Marine Corps Aviation in World War II* (1952); and Hanson W. Baldwin, *Great Mistakes of the War* (1950).

The presentation of the Axis side is less effective, but some useful volumes have appeared in English. On the naval side Anthony Martiensen, *Hitler and His Admirals* (1948), is helpful. Joseph Goebbels, *The Goebbels Diaries, 1942–1943* (1948); and Galeazzo Ciano, *The Ciano Diaries* (1946), present much inside information. Desmond Young, *Rommel, The Desert Fox* (1950), tells admiringly the story of one of the war's most colorful characters. Milton Shulman, *Defeat in the West* (1947), recounts the circumstances that led to the collapse of Hitler's Germany. The book is written by a Canadian, but is based on top secret German military documents, and interviews with leading German officers. H. R. Trevor-Roper, *The Last Days of Hitler* (1947), carefully sifts the evidence on what finally happened to Hitler. On this subject see also Alan Bullock, *Hitler* (1952). E. M. Zacharias, *Secret Missions: The Story of an Intelligence Officer* (1946), sheds light on the disintegration of the Japanese will to fight. James A. Field, Jr., *The Japanese at Leyte Gulf* (1947), attempts to explain what the Japanese were trying to do in this greatest sea-battle of all time.

On the diplomacy of the war *The Memoirs of Cordell Hull*, and Sherwood, *Roosevelt and Hopkins*, are indispensable. See also, for entertaining background material, Robert Lewis Taylor, *Winston Churchill* (1952). Thomas A. Bailey, *The Man in the Street* (1948), studies the impact of American public opinion on foreign policy. For relations with France and Spain during the war, see William L. Langer, *Our Vichy Gamble* (1947); and Carlton J. H. Hayes, *Wartime Mission to Spain, 1942–1945* (1945).

31

The Home Front

American production — Restraints on free enterprise
— Labor— The military effort — Public opinion on the
war — The Japanese in Hawaii and California — Cost
of the war — Election of 1944 — Death of Roosevelt
— Truman — Demobilization — "G. I." benefits — The
Peacetime Draft — Reconversion — Labor troubles —
Elections of 1946 — The Eightieth Congress

IN A sense the Second World War was primarily a contest between the abilities of the **American production** opposing forces to produce the *matériel* of war. The entrance of the United States on the side of the Allies brought to them an enormous potential in natural resources, but these resources had to be exploited in order to be made effective. Stung to desperation by the unbroken procession of Allied defeats, the government and people of the United States settled down with determination to create a war machine adequate to cope with the task they confronted. Defense efforts that had lagged before Pearl Harbor began suddenly to accelerate — it was one thing to prepare for a war that had not yet come, but quite another to provide the essentials for a war that literally threatened the life of the nation. Under the authority of a War Powers Act of December 18, 1941, the President gave the country the one-man economic leadership it needed by setting up a War Productions Board, with Donald M. Nelson, formerly an executive of Sears, Roebuck and Company, at its head. Nelson's authority thereafter was analogous to that exercised by Bernard Baruch in the First World War. He was responsible only to the President, and the subordinates he placed in charge of such vital matters as purchases, materials,

labor, and civilian supply were responsible only to him. Unhampered by the restraints of anti-trust laws, and with the cost-plus system substituted for competition, the whole American industrial machine was soon geared to the war effort. Existing factories were required to turn from the making of goods for civilian use to the making of goods for military use, often at the expense of extensive re-tooling. The manufacture of automobiles, for example, together with the sale of new cars, came to an abrupt end in January, 1942, and thereafter the automobile industry was obliged to devote all its facilities to war production. Whole new factories also were constructed, mainly at government expense, to meet such new needs as military airplanes in prodigious numbers, and synthetic rubber to replace the lost natural resources of Malaya and the East Indies. New shipyards, and old shipyards with greatly expanded facilities, operating whenever possible on the assembly-line principle, eventually more than made good the losses sustained by both battle and merchant fleets. The twenty-four hour day, composed of three eight-hour shifts, became general in nearly every industry that was engaged in the production of war goods. The results of all this activity were startling. By 1944 the United States alone was turning out twice

American production *went into high gear after the entrance of the United States into the Second World War. Defense plants in every part of the country soon began to turn out a volume of production never before equaled. Ships and aircraft were built with incredible speed on assembly-line principles.*

DEFENSE WORKERS. Both men and women kept plants operating twenty-four hours a day.

INDUSTRIAL STRENGTH. Dramatic scenes like this symbolized the might of American production.

SHIPS. Giant warships came down the ways in record-breaking time. This is the aircraft carrier *Wasp.*

AIRCRAFT. Airpower became more important than ever before and airplane and automobile manufacturers met the challenge of supply.

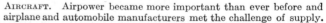

as great a volume of war supplies as all the Axis powers lumped together. Since 1941, according to Nelson,

Plane production, in dollar value, was multiplied nearly by ten, tanks by five, naval shipping by more than five, cargo shipping by more than ten. In 1939 our total output of fabricated metal had been 13 billion dollars' worth, and in 1944 it was 70 billions; while in the same period the machine tool industry alone expanded production by more than seven times.

This miracle of war production was not achieved without certain drastic changes in the American way of life. WPB regulations rationed the three most important metals, steel, copper, and aluminum, in such a way as to do the most good for the war effort; civilian production involving these items was rigidly controlled or brought to a complete standstill. "Priorities" became a life and death matter to businesses as one essential commodity after another was withdrawn from general use, and allocated to whatever war production demands were currently uppermost. In a thousand ways the ordinary individual found his freedom curtailed. He was obliged to observe low speed limits for automobile traffic, as well as the most rigid rationing of fuel-oil, gasoline, and tires. At every turn he met regulations laid down by

Restraints on free enterprise

the Office of Price Administration (OPA). If he chanced to be a landlord, he could not raise rents, despite the ever-increasing demand for housing in industrial centers. If he were a merchant, he was confronted with price freezes that held most commodities at approximately the price levels reached during the early months of the war. If he were a farmer, he might seek in vain to buy agricultural machinery, or adequate feed for his dairy cows, or enough fertilizer for his fields, but he must sell his produce at government-set ceiling prices. If anyone wished to buy such items as sugar, butter, meat, coffee, or canned goods, he could do so only with the use of rationing stamps, doled out in barely adequate quantities by serious-minded local rationing boards. By these drastic means existing supplies were conserved, new civilian goods were distributed more fairly, and inflation was curtailed. And, thanks to the intense interest of the public in the winning of the war, the amount of grumbling that went on was comparatively slight. Americans also learned to save. Drives for such items as scrap-iron and waste-paper yielded substantial results.

The record of labor throughout the war was phenomenally good; without its loyal support the economic effort of the nation could never have suc-

Labor

Housing of any description was at a premium, and temporary housing for defense workers in areas ill-prepared for the sudden influx was a common sight. This trailer camp was located in Erie, Pennsylvania.

Women at war. The WAC and the WAVES provided non-combat duties for women who volunteered for service in the army and the navy. Together with comparable units in the other services, they took over many activities which otherwise would have constituted a serious drain on the nation's man-power.

THE WAC.

MILITARY DUTIES. The training of the WAC extended even to rifle practice.

RECRUIT TRAINING. Many of the nation's colleges were used to train military personnel. This group of WAVES were trained at Hunter College.

ceeded so well. Immediately after Pearl Harbor a labor-management conference, called by the President, agreed to settle all labor disputes for the duration of the war without resort to strikes or lockouts, and to accept the decisions of a National War Labor Board in difficult cases. The NWLB, as constituted by the President in January, 1942, consisted of twelve members, divided equally between labor, management, and the public. It had plenty of work to do, for the efforts of OPA to hold down prices were not immediately effective, and many strikes for higher wages did occur. Also, there were jurisdictional disputes that frequently resulted in strikes. But settlements as a rule were quickly reached, and the loss of time involved was rarely large. A strike in "Little Steel" led to a fifteen per cent wage increase that provided a precedent for the settlement of many other wage disputes. The most serious strike of the war, which occurred during 1943 in the coal industry with John L. Lewis in command, was settled only by exceeding the "Little Steel" formula, but fortunately there were few other departures. Congress was alarmed, however, and over the President's veto passed the

Smith-Connally War Labor Disputes Act to deal with any such situation in the future. This measure increased the powers of the NWLB, required that union officials give thirty days notice before asking members for a strike vote, authorized the President to take over any war industries whose operation was imperiled by a labor dispute, and forbade unions to contribute to political campaign funds. But, as the President seemed to think, the war record of labor hardly justified action so drastic. The amount of overtime the workers put in no doubt far exceeded the amount of time they lost by strikes.

Meantime civilian draft boards drew upon the nation's manpower to supply the men **The military effort** needed to expand the armed services. The decision to induct eighteen- and nineteen-year-old boys was reached reluctantly in November, 1942, after the United States had been at war for nearly a year. Thereafter volunteering, which had been encouraged before, was virtually stopped, and not only the Army but the Navy and Marine Corps as well were obliged to depend upon the draft for additional manpower. The armed services encouraged women, however, to enlist for such specialized duties as they were able to perform. Early in the war Congress created a Women's Army Corps (WAC), a women's reserve of the Navy (WAVES), and a women's reserve of the United States Marine Corps (Marines), which together furnished the opportunity for service to more than 200,000 women. The total number of men and women mobilized reached approximately 14,000,000, of whom about half served with the Army Ground Forces, about 3,000,000 with the Navy, and 500,000 with the Marine Corps and Coast Guard. Civilian defense programs enabled still other millions to take a more limited part in the war effort. Beginning early in 1942 American troops poured overseas, to England and Northern Ireland, to Australia and New Zealand, to East Africa and Egypt, to every other theater as the war progressed. A new highway was built through Canada to Alaska, the military importance of which was beginning to be realized. Nor should it be forgotten that through the operations of Lend-Lease billions of dollars worth of American supplies

The Alcan Highway provided swift overland transportation from the United States to Alaska. Eventually it may be linked to roads south to Central America. This aerial view shows a section in the Yukon.

reached the overseas Allies of the United States, providing among other things aid to the Russians in the defense of Stalingrad, and to the British in the defeat of Rommel at El Alamein. Altogether the American industrial plants furnished to the Allies in this manner some 37.5 billion dollars worth of goods, including 21 billions in munitions and ships.

The solidarity of public opinion on the "home front" during the years of American participation in the Second World War was virtually unbroken. The Japanese attack on Pearl Harbor, followed as it was by declarations of war against the United States by both Germany and Italy, left little room for opposition to the war, and even the isolationists accepted hostilities as a necessary evil. There was some smoldering gossip to the effect that Roosevelt had deliberately connived at the Pearl Harbor attack, but only the most bitter of the "Roosevelt-haters" gave credence to such talk. Few Americans of German descent had ever had much to say in favor of Hitler, and those few took the stand they did mainly because of pathological quirks of character rather than because they were German. A small but sometimes noisy collection of these "Bundists" existed in nearly every large population center before American involvement in the war, but after hostilities started they were rarely heard from. Many Americans of Italian descent had been proud of Mussolini in his earlier days, but they had viewed with misgivings his Ethiopian adventure, and had regarded his subservience to Hitler with deep chagrin. They believed, probably quite correctly, that the great majority of Italians in Italy had no stomach for the war, and wished themselves out of it. The Japanese of the Pacific Coast and in Hawaii, as an identifiable racial group, were regarded with much suspicion, although throughout the war not one of them was ever found guilty of an act of sabotage or espionage.

Dissident political groups also caused little trouble. Anti-war sentiment among Com-

Public opinion on the war

munists during the period of neutrality was violent and outspoken until after the German declaration of war on Russia. Thereupon the Communists became ardent supporters of the Allied cause, although they had once branded it as wholly imperialistic and unworthy. When the United States entered the war, American Communists gave their government consistent support. This was especially important on the labor front, for during the three and one half years of American participation in the war strikes in unions where Communists or "fellow-travelers" were in control all but disappeared. Socialists quite generally followed the lead of Norman Thomas in denouncing the war, but they were few in number, and what they said made little difference. There was the usual sprinkling of conscientious objectors, particularly among the minor evangelical sects, but their influence, likewise, was slight, and was for the most part ignored.

Undoubtedly the worst outbreak of intolerance during the war had as its victims the members of the Japanese race in Hawaii and on the Pacific Coast. "Americans of Japanese Ancestry" (AJA's) were divided into two main groups, the first generation, or *Issei*, who were born in Japan and were therefore ineligible to citizenship, and the second generation, or *Nisei*, who were American born, and by virtue of the Fourteenth Amendment, American citizens. In addition there were a few of the third generation, or *Sansei*. In the Hawaiian Islands the number of AJA's amounted to approximately one third of the total population, and grave fear was expressed as to what they would do in case of a Japanese invasion. There was talk that they should all be interned, and perhaps even be sent to the mainland, but since any such action would have totally disrupted the sugar-pineapple plantation economy upon which the economic life of the Islands depended, the Hawaiian Japanese were allowed to remain in their homes. But the political rights of Hawaiian citizens, regardless of race or color, were almost totally obliter-

The Japanese in Hawaii

ated. After Pearl Harbor martial law was declared in the Islands, and for the duration of the war the normal procedures of democratic civilian government were suspended. Army officers assumed the duties of civilian officials, including judges and police magistrates, and enforced the most stringent military regulations upon the entire population. The complete docility of the Hawaiian Japanese became apparent at once; they stayed loyally at their work, and in every type of defense activity they outdid themselves to prove their patriotism. After the Battle of Midway, with the war moving ever farther and farther away, civilian government might have been restored with safety, but military rule continued until the very end. Regulations that might have been necessary with the war near at hand were enforced with ruthless military efficiency long after the reasons for their adoption had disappeared. Only with the greatest of difficulty did the Hawaiians obtain the restoration of their normal rights of self-government at the end of the war. This unhappy experience with military rule led the residents of the Islands to voice an insistent demand for statehood when the war was over. With statehood,

they reasoned, the extinction of civilian rights and civilian government would be more difficult, should there be another war. But they were destined to long disappointment. As late as 1954 their aspirations were still being blocked in Congress on one pretext or another.

In California the situation was different due to the fact that the Japanese constituted only a small fraction of the population, by all estimates well under two per cent. But a great outcry was raised that acts of espionage and sabotage could be prevented only by removing all the Japanese, aliens and citizens alike, from the immediate vicinity of the Pacific Coast. Finally, under military orders, the Japanese were herded together in "relocation camps," located at a considerable distance into the interior. The camps themselves were hastily thrown together, and conditions in them were far from satisfactory. Nevertheless, only a few minor outbreaks occurred, and on the whole the Japanese "evacuees" conducted themselves well. As early as December, 1944, it became evident that the Courts would soon free the Japanese if the Army did not, so as soon as the fighting was

The Japanese in California

Relocation centers for Americans of Japanese descent were communities in themselves. Looking backward, the relocation policy appears to have been unnecessary and unwise.

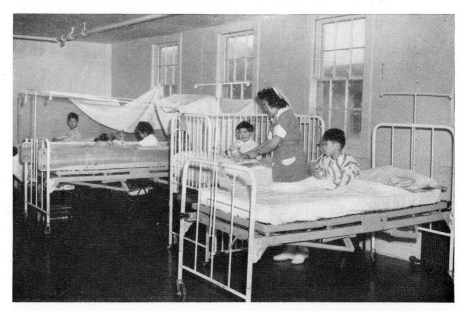

over they were allowed to return to their homes. Unfortunately, in many instances they had no homes to go to, and had lost their businesses and property. Some of them scattered throughout the country rather than to try to resume life along the Pacific Coast, but the majority preferred their pre-war environment, and in spite of sporadic cases of violence against them, were soon absorbed into the post-war economic boom that overtook the Pacific states. The superb record of the AJA's who fought in the American army during the war left most of those who had had any part in the persecution of the Japanese considerably shame-faced.

Except for the mistreatment of the Japanese, there were fewer evidences of intolerance during the Second than during the First World War. Occasional arrests and imprisonments were made, usually as a result of the activities of J. Edgar Hoover's Federal Bureau of Investigation (FBI); a few inconsequential newspapers were barred from the mails; some would-be saboteurs were brought to book; between three and four thousand enemy aliens were interned. But an attempted mass-trial of twenty-eight individuals accused of sympathy with the Nazis became somewhat farcical, and ended in a mistrial, with most of the accused escaping further difficulty. The so-called Dies Committee, created by the House of Representatives to investigate un-American activities, was less important than its name would seem to indicate. Actually, it took little interest in either pro-Nazis or pro-fascists, but concentrated primarily upon the exposure of "subversive" left-wing activities. The ardor with which Communists and fellow-travelers supported the war, however, left the Committee with little of importance to do. Its principal efforts were seemingly directed toward trying to confuse political liberals and labor leaders with Communists.

Perhaps the American people inherited a somewhat lighter burden of intolerance from the Second than from the First World War but the cost in dollars, lives, and social dislocations was very much heavier. Expend-

itures by the United States on the Second World War reached about three hundred billion dollars, more than eight times the amount spent on the First World War. The list of casualties exceeded a million and a quarter men, and the cost in lives was nearly 300,000, almost three times as many as in the First World War, although fewer in proportion to the amount of fighting done. Better training before battle action helped keep down the casualty lists, and greater medical efficiency not only prevented any such calamity as came from the "flu" in the First World War, but also returned to service a surprisingly large proportion of the nearly 700,000 wounded. The demand for war-workers drew great numbers of civilians from the small towns and country to factory cities, and especially to the seaboard, where ship-building on the assembly-line principle reached an amazingly high level of productivity. Many of the labor migrants, as in the First World War, were Negroes who left the South with little expectation of returning. The Pacific Coast, especially the state of California, gained rapidly in population from all sources; at the end of the war California, with nearly ten million people instead of its pre-war seven, had replaced Illinois as third most populous state in the Union, and was threatening the position of Pennsylvania as second. Cities everywhere, but particularly on the Pacific Coast, suffered from acute shortages in housing, water-supply, electric power, telephone service, and other similar necessities.

The cost of the war, as was more or less inevitable, had to be met in large part by borrowing. As a result the na- **Cost of** tional debt mounted during the **the war** war to about two hundred and sixty billion dollars, more than five times as much as it had been at the time of Pearl Harbor. Experience with war loans during the First World War and with deficit financing during the New Deal had built up a body of practice that made the flotation of loans a relatively easy matter. Bonds of every size and nature were devised to appeal to every variety of purchaser. The public was urged to invest in them at all times, and not merely during "drives," as in the First World War. Payroll deductions to aid in the acquisition of bonds were given every encouragement, and found many takers. Nevertheless, to speed up sales, there were no less than eight special "drives," each with a tremendous fanfare of advertising appeal. An earnest effort was made to tap the savings of the small investor, and the total sale of "E" bonds, a large proportion of which were in denominations as low as $25, reached about forty billion dollars. Unlike the bonds of the First World War, which were transferable and were frequently sold at a discount by hard-pressed investors, the new series were non-transferable, and were redeemable by the government on demand; thus purchasers who had over-bought, or who found that for any reason they could not hold their bonds, were guaranteed against the heavy losses that in the previous war had overtaken buyers of "Liberty Bonds."

Congress wisely did what it could to insure that a maximum amount of the war expenditures should come from taxation rather than from borrowing. As a result, approximately forty per cent of the cost of the war was paid for out of tax collections, a substantially larger proportion than came from tax sources during the First World War. The income tax, which was so designed as to take something from nearly everyone, and nearly everything from some who were in the higher brackets, was the principal source of revenue. Single persons with incomes above $500, and married persons with incomes of above $1200, paid a basic six per cent, with an additional thirteen per cent on the first two thousand dollars of taxable income, and steeply rising rates on each additional two thousand dollars. The rate on income in excess of $200,000 reached eighty-two per cent. To make sure that small incomes did not escape, the taxes were collected after July 1, 1943, as income was earned, instead of at the end of each year, while employers were required to withhold and pay the gov-

ernment at regular intervals the assessments against their employees. Corporation taxes, excess profits taxes, and all sorts of excise, or "nuisance," taxes on luxury and near-luxury items added greatly to the revenue. A Tax Simplification Act, passed in May, 1944, made the calculation of income taxes somewhat less difficult for many in the lower brackets, but it was not intended to reduce the rates. Furthermore, every citizen knew full well that the war would leave an enduring legacy of high taxation, one that might well plague many generations to come.

Nearly a year before the end of the war, the people of the United States were obliged to hold a presidential election. **Election** To many Americans the neces- **of 1944** sity of observing this constitutional requirement seemed even more unfortunate in 1944 than in 1940. The war was going well, and its successful prosecution had in most minds a long priority over domestic politics. But the Constitution still being what it was, the election had to be held, the first wartime election in the United States since 1864. Except for the existence of war, there is little reason to suppose that Roosevelt would, or could, have run for a fourth term, but the need of his continued leadership during the crisis was, for those who trusted him, a sufficient reason for retaining him as the Democratic candidate. He was nominated with little opposition by the Democratic convention, but the Democratic city bosses joined forces with the southern conservatives to oust Henry A. Wallace, the idealistic New-Dealer, as Vice-Presidential candidate in favor of Senator Harry S. Truman, of Missouri, an inconspicuous regular whose chief service to his country had been made as head of a Senate Committee on the investigation of the national defense program. The Republicans had expected a hard-fought campaign for the nomination between Governor Dewey, of New York, and Wendell Willkie, with some third candidate, possibly Governor John W. Bricker, of Ohio, the probable nominee. But when, early in the campaign, Willkie was decisively defeated in the Wisconsin primary, he withdrew, and the nomination went to Dewey on the first ballot, with only one opposing vote. Before election time, Willkie died of a heart attack. For Vice-President the Convention turned enthusiastically to Bricker.

The campaign which followed, like the campaign which preceded it, was notable for the wide range of agreement between the two candidates. Both of them endorsed, in the main, the social legislation of the New Deal. Both urged some kind of international organization after the war for the maintenance of peace. Dewey even went so far as to approve the findings of the Dumbarton Oaks Conference at Washington, in which just before the campaign the leading Allies had drawn tentative plans for an organization to preserve peace — plans strongly reminiscent of Wilson's League of Nations. What the campaign lacked in issues, it made up in personalities. In a series of well-delivered speeches Dewey charged the President with failing to prepare the country for war, claimed that the administration was composed of tired, corrupt, and quarrelsome old men, pointed with concern at the support the Communists were giving Roosevelt, and

urged insistently that it was time for a change. Roosevelt, in turn, capitalized on the willingness of the Republicans to accept so much of the New Deal program, noted the successes in the war that had been won under his leadership, questioned the devotion to international cooperation of the many pre-Pearl Harbor isolationists who supported Dewey, and implied that it was no time for a change.

For the fourth time Roosevelt won a decisive victory. The President led in thirty-six states with 432 electoral votes, while Dewey led in twelve states with only 99 electoral votes. The Democrats also retained their majority in the Senate, greatly improved it in the House, and won a majority of the governorships. The voting was closer, however, than these figures indicate. Roosevelt's popular majority, a little more than three million votes, was the slenderest given any successful candidate for the Presidency since Wilson's second election in 1916. Aside from registering the confidence of the majority in Roosevelt's military leadership, the election demonstrated clearly that the American people were far more ready than they had been twenty-five years earlier to accept for

War bond drives raised immense sums to help finance the war effort. Public figures donated their time and talents to boost sales as this array of movie stars shows.

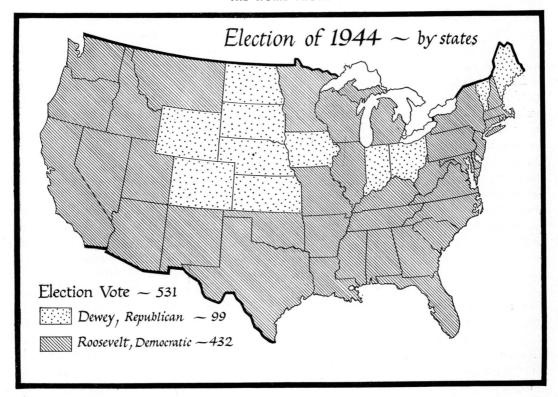

Election of 1944 — by states

Election Vote — 531
Dewey, Republican — 99
Roosevelt, Democratic — 432

the United States an important rôle in international affairs. Isolationism might rise again, but for the moment that historic American policy seemed dead indeed. The discriminating defeat of numerous outstanding isolationists and ex-isolationists, such, for example, as Representative Fish, of New York, and Senator Nye, of North Dakota, made certain that the new Congress would be receptive to any plan of post-war cooperation that seemed to offer a reasonable hope of world peace.

During the campaign of 1944, the health of President Roosevelt had become a matter **Death of** of considerable concern to the **Roosevelt** American public. From photographs and moving pictures it was apparent that the cares of office had greatly aged the President. The lines on his face had deepened, he had lost weight, and he was noticeably less willing to exert himself to stand or walk. He suffered much from colds and bronchial infections, and was frequently

obliged to take extended rests. So much was said on the subject that his personal physician publicly denied, almost too insistently, that the President was ill, while Roosevelt himself, in spite of an earlier promise not to "campaign in the usual partisan sense," took to the stump during the month of October, and gave a half-dozen full-length political speeches. He even braved a heavy downpour of rain to ride in an open car throughout a long campaign parade in New York City, and emerged seemingly none the worse for his experience. Apparently the country was convinced that he was capable of carrying on, or so the election returns seemed to show, but on April 12, 1945, he died suddenly at his winter home in Warm Springs, Georgia, of what his physicians called a massive cerebral hemorrhage.

Roosevelt was succeeded, of course, by Vice-President Harry S. Truman (1884–), whom the Democratic **Truman** convention of 1944 had preferred to the far more prominent Wallace. As Roosevelt was the perfect embodiment of the extraordinary American, so Truman, to an almost uncanny degree, was the typical ordinary American. He was a small-town product from Missouri, utterly undistinguished in appearance. He spoke with an unmistakable Middle-Western accent, played the piano a little, belonged to the Lions' Club and the Baptist Church. He had never attended college, but had served acceptably as a National Guard officer in the First World War. He had worked on a farm in his youth, lost money keeping store, gone into politics because he needed a job. As a regular organization Democrat, he was not above accepting a county judgeship at the hands of "Boss" Pendergast, an unblushing corruptionist who controlled the destinies of the Democratic Party in Kansas City, and aspired to control the State. In Missouri a county judge is an administrative officer, comparable to a county commissioner in many other states; Truman was neither a lawyer nor a "judge" in the usual sense. But he had under his control the expenditure of huge sums of money, particularly in the construction of highways and public buildings, and no faintest suspicion of dishonesty ever attached to any of his acts. At Pendergast's suggestion, he was nominated for the Senate in 1934, won as any other Democrat might have won that year, and in 1940 was renominated and re-elected. His emergence as a fearless and non-partisan senatorial investigator, one who was willing on occasion even to point out the shortcomings of the President, gave him much favorable publicity, but it was generally assumed that he had reached the zenith of his career. But when Wallace was passed by, Truman, partly because he was almost the only Middle-Westerner available, won the unexpected and unsolicited nomination that a few months later was to make him President.

As even the most casual student of American history might have predicted, the first **Demobilization** concern of the American people after the fighting of the Second World War had come to an end was to "bring the boys home." It had been so after every war in which the United States had ever fought. To most members of the armed forces the surrender of Germany and Japan meant not only that the war had come to an end, it meant also that the time of their deliverance was near, a subject upon which they began to speak their minds freely. At home, their wives and mothers, their fathers and children, vied with one another in putting pressure on Congress to implement the common desire. It had been a long war, and many of the American participants had been in uniform four or five years, some even longer. With the victory won, why should they not be released?

Speedy demobilization was not without its hazards, as thoughtful observers, both within and without the government, well knew. The United States would need large numbers of troops for occupation duty in the conquered countries; furthermore, the existence of a well-trained army and a powerful navy would undoubtedly give the nation great diplomatic strength during the impending sparring among the Allies for a peace settlement. But neither the civilian nor the military leaders were able to stand out against the insistence of the public. Shortly after VE Day a plan was announced whereby all service personnel would be discharged in accordance with an elaborate point system, based on such factors as length of service, length of time overseas, battle stars and decorations, and family responsibilities. As long as the war with Japan lasted, reason could be found for holding down the pace of demobilization, but with the arrival of VJ Day discharges were stepped up to the full limit of transportation capacity. In response to a determined demand "to get the boys home for Christmas," service discharges during the single month of December, 1945, reached a total of over a million and a half.

Under the so-called "G.I. Bill of Rights," signed June 22, 1944, discharged veterans were entitled to unemployment **"G.I."** compensation at the rate of $20 **benefits**

The death of Roosevelt stunned the entire nation to silence. The photo shows the funeral procession moving down Constitution Avenue in Washington, D.C.

per week for a period of one year, with certain compensatory allowances for veterans who obtained employment, but at less than $100 a month. Veterans might also obtain government-guaranteed loans of as much as $2000 for the purpose of buying homes or starting up in business. Also, veterans who wished to continue their college education or to obtain "job-training" might receive for as long a period as four years up to $500 a year for books and tuition, and $50 a month for living expenses, or, if married, $75 a month. As inflationary prices began to prevail, these allowances were raised, first to $65 and $90 respectively, and then to $75 and $105, with an additional allowance of $15 for married veterans with two or more dependents. While many veterans joined the "52-20 Club," and drew their unemployment benefits for a full year, the great majority either found employment, or went back to school. College enrolments, as a result, soon rose to startling figures.

This rapid disintegration of the armed forces, while politically expedient, was quite **The peace-** out of keeping with the naval **time draft** and military requirements of the nation. The Navy could not safely permit

crews to abandon ship the minute an American port was reached, nor could the Army withdraw every soldier immediately from its far-flung overseas bases. Besides, the obligations of occupation in Germany, Austria, Italy, and Japan had to be considered. Nevertheless, the announcement in January, 1946, of a less liberal policy of discharges was greeted by near-riots on the part of homesick servicemen all over the world and by a deluge of protests from the home front. There was much opposition to the idea of a peacetime draft, but it was soon evident that the only way to meet the situation was by substituting new draftees for the men who had fought the war. In consequence, Congress reluctantly extended, first for forty-five days and then for a full year, the life of the Selective Service Law, which by the terms of its enactment had been scheduled to expire on May 15, 1946. Changes in the law exempted from the draft eighteen-year olds fathers, and veterans who had served for six months in the United States or for any length of time overseas. The law also provided that the Army might retain only 1,550,000 men until July 1, 1947, and after that only 1,070,-000 men, while the Navy personnel, includ-

Surplus goods provided a post-war problem for every branch of the service. Some of the excess went to the Allies of the United States, but much valuable equipment had either to be abandoned or destroyed. In the Pacific theater, the outbreak of war in Korea led to the recovery and reconditioning of much such material.

STOCKPILES. Surplus goods were stockpiled, awaiting disposition.

MILITARY EQUIPMENT. Disposal of excess goods presented a problem sometimes solved only by wholesale destruction.

ing the Marine Corps, might not exceed 664,000 men. In actual practice an increase in voluntary enlistments, due mainly to higher rates of pay prescribed by Congress, led to the discontinuance of the draft in September, 1946. By the end of the year the strength of United States military personnel had dropped to 670,000 men for the Army, 395,000 for the Navy, and 83,700 for the Marine Corps.

Next in importance to demobilization, as the public saw it, was "reconversion," meaning the restoration of the nation's business to its normal peacetime behavior. The American people had submitted to many restraints during the war. Through such agencies as the War

Reconversion

Production Board (WPB) and the Office of Price Administration (OPA), the national government had made the most drastic conversion to a war economy. At the end of the war all this had to be reconsidered in the light of peacetime necessities. With this in view Congress voted in 1944 to change the Office of War Mobilization into an Office of War Mobilization and Reconversion, and to center in this agency national leadership of the return to normal conditions. Operating successively under such able directors as James F. Byrnes, later Secretary of State, Fred M. Vinson, later Chief Justice of the United States, John W. Snyder, later Secretary of the Treasury, and John Roy Steelman, special assistant to the President, the

OWMR discharged its obligations with fair effectiveness. The production of civilian goods started to climb, returning veterans and dislocated war workers found new jobs, and profits, both in business and agriculture, continued good.

But there were breakers ahead, particularly in the bad relations that developed between labor and management.

Labor troubles Strikes multiplied alarmingly. Workers demanded compensation in hourly rates for the loss of wages they had suffered when extra pay for overtime, dependably present throughout the war, was no longer available. Management, struggling with the problem of wholesale cancellation of government contracts and the expense of re-tooling and reconditioning war plants, was unwilling to settle on terms satisfactory to the unions. A strike in General Motors that affected 180,000 workers began in November, 1945, and lasted on until March, 1946. Two hundred thousand electrical workers and 750,000 steel workers quit their jobs in January, 1946. By the end of that month it was estimated that throughout the nation not less than 1,650,000 workers were on strike, while one set of strikes was no sooner settled than others appeared. In April, 400,000 United Mine Workers, led by John L. Lewis, went on strike. Worse still, on May 23 two of the great railroad brotherhoods, disregarding the fact that the government had seized the lines a few days before, tied up the entire railroad system of the nation. Faced by this emergency, the President asked Congress for drastic legislation, and announced by radio that he would use the army, if necessary, to operate the roads unless the strikers were back on the job the next day. With public opinion strongly on his side, the President's ultimatum worked, and the railroad strike was called off. As a result of the various strikes, new wage schedules, involving increases of about 18.5 cents per hour, or between seventeen and eighteen per cent, were worked out for most major industries. Before the end of 1948 a second and a third round of similar wage increases had occurred.

Higher wages, whether justifiably or otherwise, resulted in higher prices, and pushed along the pronounced trend toward inflation that had set in

Inflation

immediately after the war came to an end. Price controls had been accepted as necessary evils as long as the war lasted, but with the fighting finished the public echoed the impatience of business men for a return to "business as usual." Yielding a little to this mood, President Truman ended gasoline rationing short y after VJ Day. On articles that were still rationed or carried price ceilings, the public, no longer restrained by the necessity of winning the war, began to patronize the black markets in an ever increasing volume. The need of continued price controls was well stated by Chester Bowles, head of the OPA, but the people were in no mood to listen. According to Bowles's argument, shared by most economists, the great back-log of purchasing power built up during the war, if turned loose in free competition for the limited amount of goods available, would produce a violent inflation of prices. Such a development, Bowles warned, might lead to another boom comparable to the overexpansion of the 1920's, and another collapse, as in 1929. But the National Association of Manufacturers argued just the other way around. The removal of price controls, according to its elaborate propaganda, was the best way to fight inflation. With price controls off prices might rise temporarily, said the NAM, but the higher prices would lead to the production of a greater volume of goods, and when the supply caught up with the demand prices would come down again.

Whatever the merits of the argument, the people were tired of government restraint on their everyday living, and the end of controls drew near. In June, 1946, just three days before OPA was to expire by statute limitation, Congress passed a bill extending its life, but with such hampering modifications that President Truman, in angry frustration, vetoed the measure. For three weeks all controls were off, and the price ceiling soared upward nearly twenty-five per cent, as

The "G.J. Bill" afforded thousands of servicemen and women an opportunity to study. The result was an educational boom. The veterans shown above elected to study at Oxford.

against a rise of only a little more than thirteen per cent in the three years preceding. Then Congress passed, and the President signed, a bill not unlike the one just vetoed. Its hollowness was soon apparent. The law was not meant to be effective on most articles, and the attempt to enforce rigid limitations failed utterly. Meats, for example, all but disappeared from legitimate markets. Finally the harassed President, weary of trying to hold the line against such odds, announced by radio on October 14 that all price ceilings, except on rents, would have to go. The results seemed to bear out Bowles' predictions. By the end of the year the consumers' price index was 55.5 per cent higher than in August, 1939, and 31.7 per cent higher than in December, 1945. And prices had only just begun to rise, for with each round of wage increases there came inevitably a round of price increases.

Undoubtedly President Truman had had an eye to the mid-term elections to be held in November, 1946, when he **Elections** gave up his efforts to hold down **of 1946** inflation. But his gesture was one of despair, and it did him no good. Regardless of the merits of the case, the Democratic party had to bear the blame for all the post-war ills from which the people suffered. The Democratic Congress and the Democratic President had been at cross purposes in their efforts to head off inflation, and inflation had come. They had been no less at odds on how to handle the labor problem, for the President had vetoed the Case Federal Mediation Bill, in which Congress, in response, it had supposed, to the President's demands, had proposed stern measures for dealing with strikes. Administration efforts to deal with the housing shortage, which returning veterans found so acute, failed also to produce satisfactory results. Taxes remained high and the budget went unbalanced. Capitalizing on the dissensions of the Democrats and the discontent of the public, the Republicans won the Congressional elections by a landslide, 241 Republicans to 188 Democrats in the House, and 51 Republicans to 45 Democrats in the Senate. State and local elections showed a similarly strong Republican trend, and the Republicans looked forward confidently to a complete sweep in 1948.

If a Democratic Congress and a Democratic President could not get along together, there was even less to hope from **The Eightieth** a Democratic President and a **Congress** Republican Congress. The rift between the two became apparent soon after the Eightieth Congress convened, in January, 1947. Determined to reduce taxes and to make a record for economy, the Republican majority promptly attacked President Truman's recommendations for continued expenditures after the New Deal fashion, and for the retention of taxes at the high wartime levels. Not without some misgivings Congress stood ready to make substantial cuts, both on expenditures and on taxation, but the President fought back. He could not restore appropriations that Congress had lopped off, but he could, and did, veto the tax reduction bill that Congress passed. According to the President, the lower tax rates would have added more fuel to the fires of inflation and at the same time would have failed to give relief where relief was most needed. The House sustained the veto by the slender margin of two votes. The high tax rates were anything but popular, but at the end of the year the President had the consolation of being able to show a balanced budget.

An even worse breach between the legislative and executive branches of the government came with the passage of **The Taft-Hartley Act** the Taft-Hartley Labor-Management Relations Act, which made substantial amendments to the Wagner-Connery Act of 1935. In an effort to force labor unions to accept full responsibility for their acts, as management claimed that it was required to do, the new law permitted employers to sue unions for breach of contract and for damages due to jurisdictional strikes. The law also prohibited the closed shop, which forbade the hiring of any but union men, and permitted the union shop, in which all employees must join the union after being hired, only under specified conditions. Strikes and lockouts had to await a sixty-day "cooling off" period; unions might not make contributions to political campaign funds and must account publicly for their financial expenditures; they might no longer claim from management the "check-off" of union dues without the consent of the individuals concerned; and their officers, in order to seek the assistance of the National Labor Relations Board, must swear that they were not Communists. The Taft-Hartley Act was exceedingly distasteful to labor spokesmen, and was denounced by President Truman in a veto message of unparalleled severity. But the bill repassed both houses of Congress by overwhelming majorities, and late in June, 1947, it became law over the President's veto.

Bibliography

The internal aspects of the war effort have been somewhat less written about than the external, but a number of useful books exist. Records of some of the more important war boards and agencies are available as follows: Donald M. Nelson, *Arsenal of Democracy: The Story of American War Production* (1946); E. R. Stettinius, Jr., *Lend-Lease, Weapon for Victory* (1944); Herman Miles Somers, *Presidential Agency: OWMR, The Office of War Mobilization and Reconversion* (1950); and Frederic C. Lane and others, *Ships for Victory: A History of Shipbuilding under the U.S. Maritime Commission in World War II* (1951). Memoirs of more than ordinary importance are Henry L. Stimson and McGeorge Bundy, *On Active Service in War and Peace* (1947); and William D. Leahy, *I Was There: The Personal Story of the Chief of Staff to Presidents Roosevelt and Truman* (1950). Jesse Jones, *Fifty Billion Dollars: My Thirteen Years with the R.F.C.* (1951), reaches over into the war period. Eliot Janeway, *The Struggle for Survival: A Chronicle of Economic Mobilization in World War II* (1951), is an excellent summary. Some of the volumes published by the Historical Division, Department of the Army, *United States Army in World War II*, touch on domestic activities, among them Kent Roberts Greenfield, Robert R. Palmer, and Bell I. Wiley, *The Army Ground Forces: The Organization of Ground Combat Troops* (1947); and Robert R. Palmer, Bell I. Wiley, and William R. Keast, *The Army Ground Forces: The Procurement and Training of Ground Combat Troops* (1947). Useful also are the experiences recounted by the Under-Secretary of the Navy, James Forrestal, *Diaries*, edited by Walter Millis and Edward Duffield (1951). Dulles, *The American Red Cross: A History*, deals with an important civilian contribution to the war.

On the problem of Americans of Japanese ancestry, there are several excellent books. Dorothy S. Thomas and others, *Japanese-American Evacuation and Resettlement* (2 vols., 1946–52), tells the painful story of Japanese internment on the Pacific Coast. This is the principal theme, also, of two other books, Carey McWilliams, *Prejudice: The Japanese Americans* (1944); and Morton Grodzins, *Americans Betrayed* (1949). Four interesting books deal effectively with the situation in Hawaii: S. D. Porteus, *And Blow Not the Trumpet, A Prelude to Peril* (1947); T. B. Clark, *Hawaii, The 49th State* (1947); Gwenfread Allen, *Hawaii's War Years, 1941–1945* (1950); and A. W. Lind, *Hawaii's Japanese* (1946). W. S. Tsuchida, *Wear It Proudly* (1947), recounts the wartime experiences of an American Japanese.

The death of President Roosevelt touched off a barrage of biographies, most of which have already been mentioned, p. 567. Others of consequence include Grace Tully, *F.D.R., My Boss* (1949), a view of the President as seen by his secretary; Harold F. Gosnell, *Champion Campaigner, Franklin D. Roosevelt* (1952), which examines the Roosevelt technique for winning elections; and Stefan Lorant, *FDR; A Pictorial Biography* (1950).

On events subsequent to the death of Roosevelt, there are a few books worth mentioning. Harry S. Truman, *Mr. President*, edited by William Hillman (1952), is disarmingly candid. Maurice M. Milligan, *Missouri Waltz* (1948), tells the "inside story" of the smashing of the Pendergast machine in Kansas City. Harry A.

Millis and Emily Clark Brown, *From the Wagner Act to Taft-Hartley* (1950), is a useful study of national labor policy. Other books dealing with labor are Charles O. Gregory, *Labor and the Law* (1946); Harold Metz, *Labor Policy of the Federal Government* (1945); Institute of Labor Studies, *War Labor Policies* (1945); and *Labor in Post-War America* (1949), both edited by C. E. Warne and others.

On the return to peacetime conditions there are many useful studies. Ralph G. Martin, *The Best Is None Too Good* (1948), centers on the problems of the veterans. Economic reconversion is the theme in J. M. Clark, *Demobilization of Wartime Economic Controls* (1944); A. D. H. Kaplan, *Liquidation of War Production* (1944); and *Economic Reconstruction*, edited by S. E. Harris (1945). B. M. Baruch and J. M. Hancock, *War and Postwar Adjustment Policies* (1944), is an official statement. See also U. S. Office of Contract Settlement, *A History of War Contract Terminations and Settlements* (1947); and John D. Small, *From War to Peace: Civilian Production Achievements in Transition* (1946). On educational changes, see Richard D. Hofstadter and C. DeWitt Hardy, *The Development and Scope of Higher Education in the United States* (1952). On the gradual acceptance by Americans of responsibilities by the United States beyond its own borders, there is an excellent series of lectures in Malbone W. Graham, *American Diplomacy in the International Community* (1948).

SECTION SIX

THE POST-WAR WORLD

1945 - 1954

The people of the United States after the Second World War understood far better than after the First the need of American participation in world affairs. Most of the isolationists were silenced, if not wholly convinced, when Senator Arthur H. Vandenberg of Michigan, long their outstanding political leader, went over whole-heartedly to the internationalists, and became a member of the American delegation to the San Francisco Conference that launched the United Nations. Those who believed in world-cooperation as the only means of averting another World War hoped that Soviet Russia would abandon her interest in making all the world Communist, and would join with the United States and other free nations in a program of conciliation and peace. There seemed at first to be good reason for this hope. The Soviets helped create the United Nations, and ratified its charter. They drove hard bargains at Yalta and Potsdam, but for a time, even in the administration of occupied Germany, they seemed to be trying to get along with their former Allies.

The establishment of the Communist Information Bureau — the Cominform — in September, 1947, registered the long-foreshadowed abandonment by Russia and her satellites of whatever tendency they had previously shown to make terms with the rest of the world. Some time before this it became apparent that, although Soviet policy still called for One World, what it had in mind was one Communist World, with every other form of government marked for destruction. Soviet obstructionism took the place of whatever little cooperation the Russians had given the United Nations before, and destroyed every effort to promote the political and economic unity of Germany. Soviet assistance pushed the Communists on to victory in China, organized North Korea for an assault on non-Communist South Korea, and maintained in every free nation a hard core of Communist agents whose ultimate objective was the overthrow of the local government. This attitude on the part of the Soviets may have been inevitable, but it was greatly encouraged by the precipitate way in which the

United States, after the fighting in the Second World War was over, demobilized its army, inactivated its navy and air force, and weakened its defenses. Only in the sphere of atomic warfare did the Americans maintain a clear supremacy, and even in that the Russians were hard on their heels. The Soviet leaders, with their own military strength held at wartime levels, had little to fear from the Americans and acted accordingly.

With the Russian program of aggression too clear to be ignored, the United States was obliged to act. In accordance with the Truman Doctrine, Greece and Turkey received sufficient aid to enable them to ward off the blows that the Soviets and their satellites had prepared against them. The European Recovery Plan, first announced by Secretary of State Marshall, made available to European countries the funds they needed to work their way back to economic health. If only they could recover their normal prosperity, American leaders reasoned, they would not so readily yield to Communist propaganda. By the North Atlantic Treaty, the free nations of the western world allied themselves, under American leadership, to resist aggression. And, when the Soviets tried to take over all Berlin, a British-American air-lift defeated their plans.

But in Asia the efforts to block Communist aggression did not fare so well. China fell to the Reds, and in June, 1950, North Korea attacked South Korea. The United Nations, because for the time being the Russian delegation was boycotting sessions of the Security Council, was able to brand the North Korean action as an aggression, and to ask member nations to cooperate in resisting it. The result was the long-drawn-out Korean War, in which Communist China intervened to prevent a United Nations victory. The efforts of the United Nations to unify Korea were thwarted, but at least the aggressor also failed of his objective.

The death of Stalin early in 1953 led many people to hope that under Malenkov, his successor, there would be a reversion to the earlier Soviet policy of cooperation with the United Nations. The achievement of a truce in Korea may have stemmed from this cause; also, some softening of the rigors of Soviet rule in eastern Germany. But a popular uprising of the East Germans, who wanted far more freedom than they were being granted, was suppressed with great ruthlessness, and the Communist negotiators over Korea, backed firmly by Russia, made difficult the task of restoring peace.

Beset by war and by international complications of unprecedented magnitude, the American people hardly realized "the big change" that had come over their nation internally during the twentieth century. They had grown and prospered as a people; they had made material gains that to earlier generations would have seemed utopian. The Great Depression of the thirties was not only over; it was almost forgotten. But thoughtful observers were not unaware of the twin enemies from which the free world had suffered, war and depression. If either came again in full vigor, it would almost for a certainty undo the great gains the nation had achieved.

32

Post-War Problems

Allied unity — Yalta — Dumbarton Oaks — The San Francisco Conference — Potsdam — The pursuit of peace — Soviet policy — Minor peace treaties — Germany and Austria — Trials of war criminals — Russian intransigence — China — Korea — Japan — The Philippines — India, Burma, Malaya — Indo-China — Indonesia — Iran — Latin America

THE unity of effort that the Allies, commonly called the United Nations, achieved during the war was truly re-markable. No longer could it be said, as during the First World War, that when one Ally advanced, the others were sure to be standing still. Close coordination of policy, both in military and in diplomatic activities, was apparent on every hand. This fortunate development was due in consider-able part to the frequent conferences held by heads of states, their foreign ministers, and their military advisers. As early as August, 1942, Prime Minister Churchill visited Stalin in Moscow, with the American Ambassador to Russia representing the United States. Stalin was then pressing hard for a second front in France, something he long failed to obtain, but this conference was only the be-ginning of a series. After the invasion of North Africa, Churchill and Roosevelt, as already noted, met at Casablanca, North Africa, in January, 1943, to lay further plans. They conferred with de Gaulle and Giraud, and they had hoped that Stalin and Chiang Kai-shek would join them, but each of the latter two claimed that it was impossible for him to leave his own country at that time. Out of this conference came much undis-closed planning, and the announcement that only by "unconditional surrender" could the Axis nations obtain peace. At a conference

Allied unity

of foreign ministers, held in Moscow during October, 1943, definite plans were laid for the second front in France, and for some kind of world organization to follow the war. Next came a conference of Churchill, Roosevelt, and Chiang Kai-shek in Cairo during mid-November, 1943, and immediately thereafter the first meeting of both Churchill and Roose-velt with Stalin, at Teheran. So complete were the plans worked out at the Cairo and Teheran meetings that more than a year elapsed before the conferees got together again. Then, early in February, 1945, the "Big Three," Churchill, Roosevelt, and Stalin, accompanied by large retinues of "top-drawer" military and governmental advisers, met at Yalta in the Crimea. The Yalta Conference not only reached agree-ments on the "timing, scope, and coordina-tion of new and even more powerful blows" against Germany, but authorized also the call that brought the Conference of the United Nations to San Francisco the follow-ing April.

Undoubtedly the decisions of the Yalta Conference must go down in history as among the most significant ever to have been made by heads of state in modern times. The key to the future, as all the world knew, lay mainly in the hands of the Russian leaders. Would they in time of peace continue the cooperative attitude they

The Yalta decisions

QUEBEC. War strategy was the purpose of this meeting of British, American, and Canadian leaders in 1943.

Cooperation, first for the winning of the war, then for the winning of the peace, replaced the old American policy of isolation. President Roosevelt met repeatedly with the other Allied leaders to plan the strategy of the war and the program for peace at its close, and President Truman represented the United States at Potsdam. American plans, unfortunately, assumed good faith on the part of Soviet Russia, a mistake, as events proved, for at the war's end Soviet-inspired red imperialism soon succeeded German imperialism as the greatest threat to world peace.

YALTA. The Big Three met in the Crimea, February, 1945. President Roosevelt shows the strain of the war years.

had shown in time of war, or would they return to the original Bolshevik program, and make their goal the ultimate destruction, by whatever means they could employ, of every government that refused to follow the Communist party line? President Roosevelt, like Wilson before him, believed that the only pathway to world peace was through the establishment of a world organization of friendly states, and, again like Wilson, he was willing to concede a great deal to achieve what appeared to be an absolutely essential objective. He was deeply concerned by the fact that the Soviet leaders were obviously intent on welding all eastern Europe into a Russian sphere of influence, but he could think of no better way to deal with the problems this would present than through an effective world organization, of which Russia must be a member.

It was in this mood that Roosevelt gave in

during the Yalta Conference to Stalin's demand for what amounted to **Concessions** three Russian votes in the pro- **by Roosevelt** posed United Nations organization. On the pretext that Russia had given to the various Soviet republics control over their military establishments and foreign relations, Stalin insisted that Byelorussia (White Russia) and the Ukraine, as well as the Soviet Union itself, should be regarded as separate members of the United Nations. Probably at the time the President made this concession he had in mind asking for a similar voting advantage for the United States, but he found no support for the idea at home, and he soon abandoned it. As a further gesture of conciliation to Russia, Roosevelt agreed to the principle of a great-power veto on all important acts of the Security Council, a provision which he believed would also promote ratification of the United Nations charter by the United

States Senate. But the concessions to Russia went much further than this. Stalin was determined to extend the Russian frontiers, both in Europe and in Asia, and on these points also the President gave in. As to the European boundary settlements, Roosevelt conceded to Russia the right to annex all of eastern Poland, and to Poland the right to make compensatory annexations at the expense of Germany. With reference to the Far East, in direct contradiction of pledges he had once made Chiang Kai-shek, he agreed to provisions that would make Russia dominant in Manchuria at the close of the war, and, in addition, he promised the Soviets the right to annex the southern half of Sakhalin and the Kurile Islands.

In return for all this Roosevelt believed that he had obtained important pledges from **Concessions** Stalin. As to Poland, Russia **by Stalin** agreed that the "provisional government which is now functioning in Poland should be reorganized on a broader democratic basis with the inclusion of democratic leaders from Poland itself and from Poles abroad." A similar agreement was reached, and for similar reasons, with regard to Yugoslavia. Undoubtedly both the British and the American negotiators hoped that these agreements would result in Polish and Yugoslavian governments entirely free from Russian domination; they could hardly have foreseen the complete lack of good faith with which the Russians would treat their promises. Furthermore, they thought they had won full assurance of Russian cooperation in the creation and maintenance of a peacetime United Nations. As for the Far East, Stalin promised again — he had said much the same thing to Cordell Hull in 1943 — that "in two or three months after Germany has surrendered and the war in Europe has terminated the Soviet Union shall enter the war against Japan."

In the light of subsequent events, much criticism has been leveled at Roosevelt for

Military considerations his part in the Yalta decisions. It is well to remember, however, that these criticisms developed long after the event, in an atmosphere of victory achieved; whereas the actual agreements were made several months before the war was fully won, and at a time when the Russians were seemingly in a far stronger military position than were their western allies. When the Yalta Conference convened, Russian troops were already far into Germany, with their advance units on the Oder River, fifty miles from Berlin, whereas on the western front, the ground lost by the disastrous and frightening "Battle of the Bulge" had just been recovered, and Allied troops were only beginning to enter Germany. At this same time Russian occupation forces held eastern Czechoslovakia and most of Hungary in their grasp, and Tito's Russophile Partisans were driving the Germans out of Yugoslavia, whereas the Anglo-American invasion of Italy seemed hopelessly stalled in the Apennines. In the Far East, the war against Japan was by no means won, and Roosevelt's military advisers were deeply pessimistic. The atomic bomb had not yet been tested, and its possible usefulness as a military weapon had to be discounted completely. According to the American Secretary of War, Henry L. Stimson, the best military opinion was that to defeat Japan the invaders "would be faced with the enormous task of destroying five million men and five thousand suicide aircraft." It was still believed that the Japanese homeland would have to be attacked directly, and that the cost of victory would be not less than "a million casualties to American forces alone," while "the major fighting would not end until the latter part of 1946 at the earliest." Furthermore, many of the troops that would be needed for this campaign were still fighting in Europe, and would not be released until the final defeat of Germany.

Roosevelt's concessions to Russia at Yalta should be measured against this background. His military advisers wanted the fullest Russian cooperation, both in the East and in the West, and they had little concern for the political results of such concessions as might be necessary to obtain their objectives. It seemed merely realistic to give the Russians what they would be able to take in Europe anyway, whether the concessions were made or not. As for what was promised the Russians in Asia, the military planners were not thinking in terms of the post-war world, but in terms of how to achieve victory. In conceding what he did Roosevelt was merely yielding, as a civilian commander, to the insistent demands of his military experts.

The Yalta Conference also ratified a plan which had been in process of development ever since Teheran for the even- **Dismemberment of Germany** tual dismemberment of Germany into four zones of military occupation, one each for the British, American, Russian, and French forces. Berlin, the capital, although located deep in the Russian zone, was to be an international area under joint four-power control. There is no reliable evidence to support the frequently-made assertion that Roosevelt, either at the time of Yalta, or at any other time, conceded to Russian troops the honor of occupying Berlin in advance of the troops of other nations. The American advance was indeed halted when it might easily have reached Berlin far ahead of the Russians, but General Eisenhower took full responsibility for this decision, and justified it on military grounds. Military rather than political considerations seem also to account for the fact that American armies, which might have captured Prague, the Czechoslovakian capital, were stopped in their tracks, thus giving the Russians both the honor and the advantage of taking another capital city.

Meantime plans for the San Francisco Conference had long since been laid. Knowing full well that any plan of world **Dumbarton Oaks** cooperation, in order to succeed, must have the support of the four most powerful Allies — Great Britain, the United States, Russia, and China — representatives of those powers met at Dumbarton Oaks in Washington during the fall of 1944, and issued a set of tentative proposals. The Dumbarton Oaks plan foreshadowed a United Nations Charter, which would be similar in many respects to the Covenant of the League of Nations, but with conspicuous differences. The new plan contained nothing comparable to the famous "Article X" that had done so much to defeat the League of Nations for ratification by the United States Senate; it gave greater authority to the smaller Security Council (representing five great powers and six selected others) and less to the larger Assembly, thereby eliminating a principal cause for delay and indecisiveness in the actions of the League; it made more feasible the use of force against would-be aggressors, and put less trust in disarmament; it proposed as an integral part of the plan a Permanent Court of International Justice; and it presumed that the Charter, unlike the Covenant, would be entirely separate from any treaty of peace.

The first great concern of President Truman, after he took office, was to carry through to a successful conclusion the United Nations Conference on International Organization, already called by the United States, Great Britain, Russia, and China to meet in San Francisco, April 25, 1945. Roosevelt had earnestly promoted the holding of this conference before the war came to an end, and had promised to open it in person. Obviously, his hope was to utilize the habit of cooperation that had developed among the Allies in time of war as a foundation upon which to build a permanent world organization, designed to keep the peace in the future. He was eager, also, to avoid the complications that had embarrassed the similar efforts of Woodrow Wilson, when that President had sought in his day to create a League of Nations and to write a treaty of peace at the same time.

Invited to the Conference at San Fran-

cisco were all of the nations, now numbering upwards of fifty, that had joined **The San** in the hostilities against the **Francisco** Axis powers. At the Confer- **Conference** ence the smaller nations took an active and important part in the proceedings, and greatly influenced the results, although none of the fundamentals of the Dumbarton Oaks proposals was altered. Least palatable to the small nations was the insistence by Russia, agreed to by Churchill and Roosevelt at Yalta, that all of the five great powers (including France) must concur in important decisions of the Security Council. This left each of the nations so favored free from any effective restraint on its military or diplomatic activities. Optimists could only hope that the rule of self-restraint would be stronger than the rule of law. Whatever the faults and virtues of the Charter, it was widely ratified, and in the United States Senate met only negligible opposition.

In line with the general spirit of world cooperation exhibited at Dumbarton Oaks and San Francisco was a series **Other** of important international agree- **conferences** ments already reached on a wide variety of subjects. At Bretton Woods n New Hampshire, a conference held in July, 1944, proposed an International Bank for Reconstruction and Development, and a parallel organization to maintain stability in the exchange values of national currencies. Somewhat earlier, a United Nations Relief and Rehabilitation Administration (UNRRA), a Food and Agriculture Organization of the United Nations, and a Provisional International Civil Aviation Organization had been set up. Much still remained to be done before these efforts could become truly effective, but at least in the United States the hope was strong that the United Nations would be able to act effectively in time of peace no less than in time of war. If the three great Allies were ready to show the restraint necessary to keep the peace among themselves, it was evident that by acting together they could keep other nations at peace. Many observers professed to believe, also, that the lesser nations, as

time went on, would achieve a steadily growing recognition in the councils of the United
Nations.

Some of the more immediate problems of
peace were settled by the "Big Three" in a
The Potsdam meeting held at Potsdam near
Conference Berlin during the month of July,
1945. On this occasion President Truman
represented the United States, with his new
Secretary of State, James F. Byrnes, of South
Carolina, taking an important part in the
proceedings.[1] The British delegation was at
first headed, as usual, by Churchill, but before the conference ended, the results of
Britain's first general election since 1935 became known, and Churchill's place was taken
by a new Prime Minister, Clement R. Attlee,
leader of the Labor Party. Thus, when the
Potsdam Conference ended, Stalin was the
only member of the old wartime triumvirate
to remain in power. The new "Big Three"
laid down at Potsdam the political and economic principles that were to govern the
treatment of Germany in the initial period of
control. Supreme power was vested in an
Allied Control Council, composed of American, British, Russian, and French generals.
In accordance with the Teheran and Yalta
decisions, the conquered Reich was to be
divided into four zones of military occupation, one for each of the four nations mentioned, and Berlin, the capital, was to be
similarly partitioned. From this conference
came also the ultimatum to Japan, in conformity with which that nation surrendered.

It was all too soon apparent that the spirit
of cooperation built up among the Allies dur-
The pursuit ing the war was not to last over
of peace into the pursuit of peace. By
common consent the burden of peace-making
was not to be saddled upon the new United
Nations organization, but was to be undertaken directly by the nations that had participated in the fighting. In accordance with
a decision of the Potsdam Conference, peace

[1] Cordell Hull had retired on account of illness in
November, 1944, and had been succeeded by Edward
R. Stettinius, Jr., who as Secretary of State had
headed the American delegation during the San
Francisco Conference.

treaties with Italy, Finland, Hungary, Bulgaria, and Rumania were to precede any final
agreements on Germany and Austria. But
the best efforts of the United States, Great
Britain, and France to draft these treaties
continually ran afoul of endless bickering
on the part of the Russian negotiators. To
begin with, the task of negotiating treaties
with the five minor powers was turned over
to a Council of Foreign Ministers representing not only the "Big Three," but China and
France as well. At the first meeting of this
Council, held in London during September,
1945, it was decided that the actual work of
treaty drafting was to be done by the ministers of the nations that had signed the appropriate armistices. Thus the representatives of four nations, the United States,
Great Britain, the Soviet Union, and France,
were to draft the treaty with Italy; three nations, the United States, Great Britain, and
the Soviet Union, the treaties with Rumania, Bulgaria, and Hungary; and two nations, Great Britain and the Soviet Union,
the treaty with Finland. But the meeting
finally broke up over Russian insistence that
the participation of China and France in the
discussions should be more rigorously limited.
Objections came also from the minor Allies,
who resented the high-handed assumption of
all authority by the Great Powers. Finally
at a conference of the "Big Three," Byrnes,
representing the United States, Bevin, the
United Kingdom, and Molotov, the Soviet
Union, held in Moscow, December, 1945, it
was agreed that China should withdraw altogether from participation in the Council's
debates, while French participation should
be limited strictly to Italian matters. Also,
largely on Byrnes' insistence, a general peace
conference was scheduled to meet May 1,
1946, in Paris, which was to include, besides
the members of the Council, representatives
from all the European Allies, from the British Commonwealths and India, from Brazil,
Ethiopia, the Ukraine, and Byelorussia —
twenty-one nations in all. The Conference
might discuss the draft treaties, and might
suggest changes, but the right to make

amendments was reserved to the Council of Foreign Ministers.

By this time most American observers had come to the conclusion that the Soviet government had returned to its original policy of world revolution, and that in the peace negotiations its delegates had this goal constantly in view. The Russians, it seemed evident, far preferred the continuation of political and economic chaos in the countries concerned to any peace terms that might embarrass them in their plans for the expansion of Communism. Every month of delay in the establishment of normal governments compounded the chaos and played into the hands of the Russian propagandists. In each of the former German satellites, local Communist groups, acting on orders from Moscow, were busily preparing the way for the establishment of Communist control whenever peace should be concluded. The longer the delay and the greater the disorder, the better were their chances of success. Hence, the Russian delegates, both in the Council of Foreign Ministers and at the Paris Peace Conference, exhausted every pretext for prolonging the deliberations. Sensing finally that Roosevelt's policy of conciliation had failed, Byrnes and his colleagues, with strong British and French backing, stood their ground with such firmness against the Russian bickering that they were accused by Russian sympathizers of shifting to a "get-tough-with Russia" attitude. Chief among their critics in the United States was Henry Wallace, who had become Secretary of Commerce in President Roosevelt's cabinet after the election of 1944, and had been retained by President Truman. In a speech delivered in New York, September 12, 1946, which Wallace claimed the President himself had read in advance and had endorsed, the Secretary urged that the United States return to the Roosevelt policy of giving Russia a free hand in eastern Europe, and abandon its newly adopted attitude of "toughness." But President Truman, after some hesitation, dismissed Wallace from his cabinet, and gave the Byrnes policy his full support.

Soviet policy (margin note)

The ordeal of negotiation finally shifted from Paris to New York, where the Council of Foreign Ministers met from November 4 to December 12, 1946; then back again to Paris, where the five treaties were officially signed, February 10, 1947.[1] The war-making potential of all the five defeated nations was reduced to insignificance, heavy reparations were assessed against them, and all except Bulgaria were obliged to make extensive territorial readjustments. Italy, once Germany's closest associate, ceded land to France, Greece, Albania, and Yugoslavia, and turned over the administration of her colonies to the four principal Allies. Even before the end of the war she had been forced to give back their freedom to her two conquered provinces, Ethiopia and Albania. In the final negotiations, the city of Trieste, long a stumbling block to agreement, became also a free territory, with a governor to be chosen and paid by the Security Council of the United Nations. Among the Allied powers the principal gainer from these treaties was Yugoslavia, a nation in which the Communists under Marshal Tito had already achieved complete control. Yugoslavia's territorial holdings were greatly enhanced, her reparations bill topped the Allied list, and her right to arm remained unrestricted. Undoubtedly the Soviet negotiators intended that in this powerful Russian satellite they would have a strategic springboard for their expected jump to full control of the Mediterranean.

Minor peace treaties (margin note)

The restoration of peaceful relations with the minor enemy states had proved to be difficult, but with Germany and "liberated" Austria the task remained for years a total impossibility. In the first place, no steps could be taken toward a final settlement until the long-drawn-out negotiations with the minor powers had come to an end. And, secondly, the plans devised for temporary government, particularly in Germany, were so unworkable as to insure a maximum of ill-feeling and disagreement

Germany and Austria (margin note)

[1] With Italy, Finland, Rumania, Bulgaria, and Hungary.

Occupied Zones in Germany and Austria

Zones of Occupation: Germany, Austria, Berlin

among the occupying powers. The government of Germany as a whole was to rest in the hands of an Allied Control Council composed of the four high commanding officers of the four zones of occupation, while the subdivided city of Berlin was to be ruled by a *Kommandatura,* consisting of the four local commandants, aided by their technical staffs. All decisions, whether for the nation as a whole or for the capital city only, required the unanimous consent of the representatives of all four occupying powers. It was decreed further that Germany should be administered as "a single economic unit," with uniformity of treatment to all Germans everywhere in Germany, regardless of the zone in which they happened to live. As if to make sure that this incredible plan could never be made to work, the western democracies neither asked nor received from Russia guarantees of uninterrupted access by land to Berlin, although the only way they could reach the city was through the Russian zone.

The system designed for the occupation of Austria was hardly less complicated, but unlike Germany, where the national government had totally disappeared, Austria had a government of her own through which the occupying forces could operate. This government had been established with full Russian cognizance, just before the end of hostilities, but it was a multi-party, not a merely Communist affair, and it eventually won recognition from the three great western democracies as well as from Russia. The occupying forces adopted the same cumbersome division into four zones both for the nation as a whole and for Vienna, the capital city, that they had devised for use in Germany. When it became apparent that the Austrian government had no intention of surrendering to Communist domination, the Russians showed their irritation in many ways, most particularly by refusing to cooperate with the other Allies in the making of a treaty of peace; but no such friction developed between the western Allies and Russia in Austria as was soon to mar all efforts to

restore normal conditions in Germany. Unlike the trustful western powers who had depended on Russian good-will to insure their access to Berlin, the Russians had obtained formal consent from the other powers to their maintenance of "communication lines" with Austria through both Hungary and Rumania. This gave the Russian government the opportunity to keep military forces, not only in Austria, but in the two neighboring states also, even after a treaty of peace with them had been signed and ratified.

The occupation of Germany presented an interminable procession of virtually insoluble problems. The defeated nation had to be fully disarmed, and its **Occupation of Germany** military potential destroyed; "denazified" local governments had to be instituted; a reliable German police force had to be created; the rubble of war had to be cleaned up, and new housing provided; education had to be revamped in such a way as to eliminate the last vestige of Nazi propaganda; hundreds of thousands of "displaced persons" had to be cared for, the shattered remnants of the nation's economic life had to be collected together, and made the basis for a genuine recovery. All this, moreover, had to be done principally through the instrumentality of a joint military occupation, and by unanimous consent of the representatives of four mutually suspicious Allies. Perhaps the greatest miracle of all was that the Allied Control Council actually reached agreement on about fifty major measures, and as many minor directives, during its first sixteen months of existence.

Not among the least of the problems that confronted the Allies was the necessity of delivering on a promise they had **Trials of war criminals** reiterated, time and again during the period of hostilities, to bring to trial those Germans who were principally responsible for the war, and for the inhumanities practiced during it. They could not reach Hitler, Himmler, Goebbels, and Ley, for these four had committed suicide rather than face Allied retribution. But more than a score of other leading Nazis, including Gö-

The war crime trials were held before the International Military Tribunal at Nuremberg. The major German defendants are shown in the dock.

ring, were brought to trial before an international military tribunal at Nuremberg, November 20, 1945. Serving as one of the judges was a former Attorney-General of the United States, Francis Biddle, and as one of the leading prosecutors, a Justice of the United States Supreme Court, Robert H. Jackson. The proceedings dragged on interminably, but thanks in no small part to the patience and persistence of Justice Jackson, the whole sordid record of the Nazi leaders was fully revealed. Many critics of the trial denied that the heads of a conquered enemy state could be legally held accountable for their acts by an international tribunal. But Justice Jackson argued that Germany had been party to the Kellogg-Briand Peace Pact of 1928, which formally renounced war as an instrument of national policy, and had in other international agreements gone on record in opposition to what its Nazi leaders had done. He held further that the trial and conviction of the German war criminals by an international tribunal would set a valuable precedent, one which future heads of state would not regard lightly when tempted to

resort to war. After ten months of hearings, the court held all but three of the defendants guilty as charged, sentenced eleven of them to be hanged, and eight others to serve long prison terms. Göring managed to commit suicide before his sentence could be carried out, but on October 16, 1946, the other ten who had been condemned to die were executed. Later on many less notable criminals were also brought to trial, usually for incredible war atrocities, and a large number of death sentences were carried out. In these proceedings "denazified" German courts eventually took a considerable part.

The trial of the Nazi criminals was about the last evidence of full cooperation between Russia and the western democ- **Russian intransigence** racies over Germany. At the Paris meeting of the Council of Foreign Ministers during April and May of 1946 the United States had urged the making of a treaty of peace with Germany, but the Russians refused, insisting that they needed more time to study the situation. Nor would the Russians sign a treaty with other members of the Big Four, proposed by the

United States, guaranteeing for a twenty-five-year period the demilitarization and disarmament of Germany. Equally futile, as far as Russia was concerned, was the effort of the United States, at the close of the same meeting, to induce the four nations occupying Germany to maintain economic unity in administration. Only Great Britain showed an interest in this proposition, a fact of considerable importance, since in December, 1946, the United States and Great Britain agreed to the gradual economic unificat on of their zones — the beginning of "Bizonia."

It soon became evident that in the months following the Potsdam agreement Russian policy had shifted. At the time of the Potsdam conference all the great powers, Russia included, had wished to keep Germany decentralized, as the best available means of preventing the revival of the nation's military might. All had agreed to the removal of such industrial plants from Germany as might serve a military end, and many such plants had been removed, particularly for shipment to Russia. But the Russians soon found that they were unable to use their booty effectively — sometimes they could not even put the dismantled plants together again. They therefore made up their minds that the best thing for them to do was to turn Germany into "a high-powered industrial state," with the capacity for production that the Russians themselves lacked, but with a political system that would insure German subordination to Russia. In short, what the Russians wanted was a centralized Germany under Communist control, able and willing to pay Russian reparations, and they would settle for nothing less. Meantime, the Russians continued to rob their zone of occupation of everything of value, including the agricultural commodities that had once been used to supply the more industrialized sections of western Germany.

Struggling against odds to keep their sections together economically, the British and American "Bizonia" was soon turned into a British, American, and French "Trizonia," with the consequent division of Germany into two separate states becoming each day more clearly defined. The break between East and West approached finality in March, 1948, when the Russians refused all further participation in the work of the Allied Control Council, and thus destroyed almost the last vestige of unity among the occupying powers.

On the other side of the world, in eastern Asia, the road to peace was quite as long and tortuous as in Europe. China had gained much "face" during the war. She had become one of the five principal Allies, with great-power status in the Security Council of the United Nations, and the same privilege of vetoing unacceptable measures that had been accorded to the other four. Also, the United States and Great Britain, as early as 1943, had relinquished their claims to extraterritorial rights and privileges in China, special favors that had long been regarded by the Chinese government as humiliating in the extreme. Further, the Chinese record of resistance to Japan, both before and after Pearl Harbor, had won not only the admiration of the entire Allied world, but also a succession of loans and other aids from the United States. Nevertheless, the end of the war, instead of bringing peace to China, brought only the beginning of a war to the death between the Nationalist government of Chiang Kai-shek and an increasingly powerful Communist faction under Mao Tse-tung which, with the covert backing of the Russian government, operated with great effectiveness throughout northern China. Viewed in broad perspective, the contest in China appeared to be only another manifestation of the Russian program for spreading Communism, and with it Russian domination, throughout the entire world.

In an effort to restore peace in China the government of the United States, in December, 1945, sent General George C. Marshall, Chief of Staff of the United States Army throughout the war, on a special mission to China, under orders to bring the warring factions

China's President and Madame Chiang Kai-shek receiving a group of American publishers and editors at National Government headquarters in 1947.

together into one government. But Chiang Kai-shek, much as he desired to please the United States, was utterly unwilling to take any Communists into his government. Marshall did arrange an armistice, however, in January, 1946, but it was of use primarily to the Communists. Russia had agreed to withdraw her forces from Manchuria, but she had no intention of allowing the prize she had seized to fall into the hands of the Nationalist government. Instead, Russian policy called for turning Manchuria over to the Chinese Communists as fast as they were able to occupy it, and for arming them with captured Japanese munitions. Thus, when the armistice was broken a few months later, the Chinese Communists were stronger than they had ever been before. Marshall struggled on for nearly a year in search of a formula that would satisfy both parties, and bring peace, but he was obliged eventually to confess his failure and return to the United States. He held no brief for the Communists, but he was dismayed by the almost hopeless corruption and inefficiency of the Nationalist government, and by the unbridled inflation it had promoted. It showed itself impotent to enact the agrarian reforms so insistently demanded by the Chinese people and urged by the United States; it allowed war goods supplied by the American government to fall into the hands of the Communists; it was powerless, even, to prevent the post-war bounty dispensed by the United Nations from being sold on the black market. On Marshall's recommendation, the United States finally adopted a "plague-on-both-your-houses" attitude toward the Nationalists and Communists, withdrew its troops from China, and gave up all further efforts at mediation.

As the war continued, the Communists gained ground steadily. Because of their success in getting hold of American supplies, American aid to **"Red China"** Nationalist China, which from 1945 to 1949 amounted all told to no less than three billion dollars, had to be cut off for a time. Whole regiments of Chiang's troops, indeed, deserted with their American equipment to the Communists. Finally the Nationalist government, after being driven from one capital to another with bewildering rapidity, fled to Formosa; by the end of 1949 the Communists controlled the entire mainland of China, with the exception of Tibet, which they took later. Under these circumstances, the British government, mindful especially of its interests in Hong Kong, accorded Mao's government diplomatic recognition, and obviously hoped that the United States would follow its lead. But the Washington authorities, responding to the growing intensity of anti-Communist opinion in the United States, showed no disposition to follow such a course. The United States not only refused to recognize "Red China," but took the lead in opposing the demands of Russia and her satellites that Mao's representatives should displace Chiang's in the Security Council and Assembly of the United Nations. And, as Chiang consolidated his position on Formosa, the United States showed an unmistakable tendency to help him all it could.

In Korea, as in China, the pathway to peace encountered almost insuperable obsta-

Korea
cles. At the Cairo Conference of 1943, Roosevelt, Churchill, and Chiang Kai-shek had pledged themselves to establish an independent Korea, but at the end of the war the United States and Russia divided that unhappy nation between them at the thirty-eighth parallel for purposes of military occupation, the Russians taking the northern half of the country, and the Americans the southern half. During the Moscow Conference of December, 1945, the American and Russian representatives agreed to the establishment of a native Korean government under a four-power trusteeship of the United States, Great Britain, the Soviet Union, and China, but the mutual distrust of each other's motives on the part of the two occupying powers prevented the implementation of this agreement. Russian interpretation of the Moscow pact would have assured the establishment of a Soviet Republic in Korea; American interpretation, the exact reverse. With each passing month, the economic separation of the country became more rigid, and, in spite of a very earnest Korean spirit of nationalism, the hope of eventual unity, more remote. Finally, during the summer of 1948, two Korean governments appeared, one for each section, each claiming to be the rightful government of all Korea. In the Russian zone a Korean Peoples' Republic, modeled on the Soviet pattern, depended for its existence on the backing of Russia and a Russian trained Korean "red army" of about 125,000 men. In the American zone, a Republic of Korea, based on a Constitution drawn up by a Korean Assembly, had the support of the United States, and a small American-trained Korean constabulary of perhaps 26,000 men. Here, as elsewhere in the world, the tension between the United States and the Soviet Union was great, with an unstable peace at the mercy of the slightest incident. And it was here that the peace was broken on June 25, 1950, when the North Koreans crossed the thirty-eighth parallel and attacked South Korea.

With conditions on the Asiatic mainland so far from satisfactory Americans congratulated themselves that develop-

Japan
ments in Japan had turned out somewhat better than expected. The decision to retain the Emperor, and for that matter most of the essential features of the Japanese government, had proved to be a master stroke. Pleased with this concession, the people of Japan accepted the American occupation as at least a necessary evil, cooperated willingly with the American authorities, and strove in every way to regain the good-will of their former enemies. Furthermore, since the victory over Japan had been so completely won by the United States, it was only natural that military occupation should be primarily in American hands, and under American command. Thus Japan escaped the complications that arose in Germany from the partition of the nation among a number of conquerors, all of whom were determined to play a prominent part in governmental affairs. Compared with Germany, the situation in Japan, at least during the first months of American occupation, was simplicity itself. MacArthur gave the orders, and the Japanese government carried them out.

It was not long, however, before protests from such nations as Great Britain and Australia, no less than from Russia, led the United States to concede to the other Allies a voice in the disposal of Japanese affairs. At the Moscow Conference of December, 1945, it was agreed that a Far Eastern Commission should be created, to be composed of one representative from each of the eleven Pacific powers that had fought against Japan — the United States, the United Kingdom, the Soviet Union, China, France, the Netherlands, Canada, Australia, New Zealand, India, and the new Philippine Republic. Of these powers, the first four might exercise the right of veto. The Commission was to

China, Japan and Eastern Asia

meet in Washington, under the chairmanship of the American member, in order to formulate policies for the carrying out of the Japanese terms of surrender, and to review such directives as might be issued for the guidance of the Supreme Commander, or by him. In addition to the Far Eastern Commission in Washington there was to be also an Allied Council in Tokyo with four members, one each from the United States, the British Commonwealth (United Kingdom, Australia, New Zealand, India), the Soviet Union, and China. The Allied Council had little more than advisory authority, although on some matters of first importance the opposition of one of its members could force the Supreme Commander to refer an impending order to the Far Eastern Commission for approval. To emphasize the international character of the occupation, the American forces in Japan were now joined by a small number of troops from the British Commonwealth. China, also, was to have sent a contingent, but the Chiang government was never able to spare any of its fighting forces for occupation duty. Russia, too, was invited to send troops to Japan, but pointedly refused to do so.

In spite of all this display of international cooperation, the Japanese occupation still **Japanese war trials** remained primarily an American affair. Under MacArthur's efficient leadership every effort was made to demilitarize Japan and to destroy the ruling clique which had led the nation into war. Before the Americans took over, many of the wartime Japanese leaders had committed suicide, but in due time ex-Premier Hideki Tojo, and some twenty-seven others, were brought to trial under conditions analogous to those which ruled at Nuremberg, in Germany. Eventually, Tojo and six others were given death sentences and executed, while long terms of imprisonment were meted out to most of the remaining defendants.

Efforts were made, also, to revive and extend whatever democratic institutions Japan **Reforms in Japan** had known before the war. A representative diet, elected in April, 1946, under the observation of the occupation authorities, drew up a new constitution which renounced war as an instrument of national policy, denied the divinity of the Emperor, stripped his office of all real power, adopted a western-style bill of rights, and instituted responsible government with the legislative authority vested in a bicameral parliament, the lower house of which could, if necessary, override the opposition of the upper house. In the economic sphere, efforts were made to break up large landed estates in the interest of a wider distribution of holdings, to dissolve the large industrial and banking corporations that had lent their support to the war, to develop labor organizations after the western pattern, and to institute extensive educational reforms. But all these measures failed dismally to restore normal economic conditions in Japan. The cost of living soared to wildly inflationary heights; housing, clothing, and food shortages were disastrously apparent; and all efforts to revive international trade proved unavailing. Indeed, far down into 1949 the very survival of the nation seemed to depend upon the steady importation of unpaid-for supplies from the United States. The outbreak of the Korean War in June, 1950, did much, however, to alleviate these conditions. The use of Japan as a base of operations for United Nations forces created a new demand for Japanese labor, and extensive war orders placed by the United States produced for a time boom conditions in Japanese industry. American aid, except in this indirect fashion, could therefore be withdrawn, but the coming of peace in Korea was certain to involve many new economic perils.

In the summer of 1947 the United States urged that the eleven powers represented on the Far Eastern Commission **The Japanese peace treaty** should make a start toward the drafting of a treaty of peace with Japan. According to the American plan, decisions should be reached by a two-thirds majority of the powers, and the treaty thus drafted should be submitted to a general peace conference, in which all the states at

SHIGERU YOSHIDA. Japanese Prime Minister reads formal acceptance of the peace treaty from scroll in San Francisco, September, 1951.

Japan, in defeat, won the admiration of her conquerors by her whole-hearted efforts to cooperate with them. This was due in part to the retention of a Japanese government which could, and did, carry out the orders given by the Supreme Allied Commander, General MacArthur. The Japanese people, like their government, adapted themselves readily to the new situation.

OCCUPATION. American military policeman in the streets of Tokyo with native police.

FRATERNIZATION. Soldiers interviewing Japanese movie stars. Many American troops found wives and sweethearts in Japan.

GENERAL DOUGLAS MACARTHUR. As Supreme Commander he directed the occupation and demilitarization of Japan.

war with Japan should participate. But the American peace plan failed, primarily because of opposition from Russia and China, both of whom insisted that the unanimous consent of the Big Four should be required for every decision. Finally the American government undertook the task of achieving the desired treaty without the cooperation of either Russia or China. As the agent of the United States in this undertaking, President Truman chose a Republican, John Foster Dulles, who, as ambassador-at-large, visited Japan, the Philippines, Australia, New Zealand, Great Britain, and France. Dulles's efforts were notably successful, and the treaty he formulated was accepted by a peace conference of fifty-two powers held in San Francisco, California, on September 8, 1951, with only the Soviet Union, Czechoslovakia, and Poland dissenting. Neither of the two governments that claimed the right to speak for China was invited to the conference, but Japan was left free to conclude separate treaties with them on the same general terms as those laid down at San Francisco. Japan was stripped of her claims to Korea, Formosa, the Kurile Islands, southern Sakhalin, and the Pacific islands over which she held mandates, but was otherwise treated with great consideration. She was, for example, freed from the burden of reparations and indemnities that victors customarily imposed upon the vanquished. Her frank acceptance of defeat, and her earnest effort to achieve a democratic government, had made an excellent impression on all the free world. With her help badly needed in the struggle against Communism, punitive clauses seemed somehow out of order.

As for military clauses, the treaty provided that within ninety days after it went into effect all occupation forces should be withdrawn from Japan, but a separate agreement between the United States and Japan permitted American troops to remain until Japan should be able to take over adequately her problem of defense. In contrast with the Japanese constitution, so recently adopted, the treaty placed no restrictions on the right of Japan to maintain a military establishment. The emergence of Communist China and the events of the Korean War had made disarmament as a Japanese national policy difficult, if not impossible, to justify, although New Zealand, Australia, and the Philippines were deeply concerned at the prospect of reproducing a militarized Japan. The United States had met this problem in part, however, by concluding defense agreements with each of the three powers.

In the Philippine Islands the United States undertook to deliver on its long-standing promise, under the Tydings- **The** McDuffie Act, of independence **Philippines** on July 4, 1946. This was the more difficult because of the enormous destruction that the war had wrought, not only in Manila, which was at least fifty per cent destroyed, but to an equal or less extent throughout the Islands. In spite of all the obstacles to be overcome, however, General MacArthur, in February, 1945, turned over to President Sergio Osmeña full responsibility for Philippine civil administration. Osmeña had been the Philippine Vice-President, but had succeeded to the presidency on the death of Manuel Quezon in August, 1944, only to be supplanted in turn by Manuel Roxas as a result of the presidential elections of April, 1946.[1] It was obvious to most observers that independence, much as it was prized by the Filipinos, might become a hazard to the United States, as well as to the Islanders themselves, without adequate means of defense. The American Congress therefore passed a Philippines Military Assistance Act, the purpose of which was to create and maintain an effective Philippine army. At American insistence sites in the Philippines were also turned over to the United States for military and naval bases. Further, the American government could not ignore the responsibility that it had incurred by reason of the close economic ties that had so long bound the Philip-

[1] President Roxas died April 15, 1948, and was succeeded by the Vice-President, Elpidio Quirino, who was elected for a full term in 1949, but was defeated for re-election in 1953 by Ramón Magsaysay.

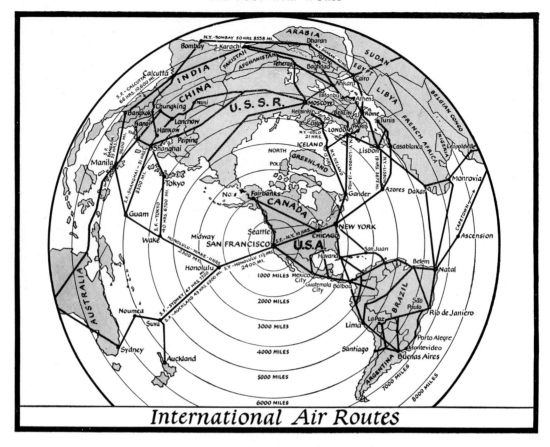

International Air Routes

pines to the United States. Would it be reasonable or right to cut the Islands loose from the connections in America upon which their prosperity had so long depended? After much debate, Congress in 1946 finally passed a Philippine Trade Act which provided for an eight-year period of free trade on a quota basis, to be followed by the gradual imposition of tariff duties over a twenty-year period, with an additional five per cent of the regular duties to be charged each year until the full amount should be reached.

It was clear, too, that the United States was under moral obligation to aid the Philippine government in the heroic task of rebuilding its ruined cities and restoring its shattered economy. To these ends Congress paralleled the Trade Act with a Philippine Rehabilitation Act, which appropriated a total of $720,000,000 to compensate the Philippine government and the owners of private property in the Islands for the damages they had suffered. And, as a final gesture of good-will, a Filipino Naturalization Act established for the Philippine Islands a quota similar to that permitted to other nationals entering the United States.

The internal problems of the Philippine Republic were by no means settled with independence and the various **The** agreements with the United **Hukbalahap** States. The old sugar-coconut-tobacco economy of the pre-war period, which had profited the landlord-merchant class a great deal, but the ordinary peasant very little, had been shattered by the war. Many of the peasants were loath to go back to it, and insisted on radical agrarian reforms. A left-wing organization of extremists known as the Hukbalahap played heavily on this spirit of discontent, and under the leadership of Luis Taruc broke forth into open revolt. Evidence that the Hukbalahap were not averse to revolution after the Communist pattern strengthened the government in its opposition to the movement, but the prospect of a durable peace seemingly depended upon the willingness of the Philippine authorities to undertake the reforms that the peasants desired. The success of Ramón Magsaysay, Secretary of Defense after 1950, in his campaign against the "Huks" led to his election to the Philippine presidency in 1953.

Although events in the rest of the Asiatic theater were apparently of less consequence to the United States, the American people had begun to understand that anything which happened anywhere in the world might concern them eventually. They therefore viewed with more than passing interest postwar developments in the Asiatic empires of European nations. It was apparent that most of the colonial peoples had no intention whatever of going back to the old system of subservience to white domination. They had seen the white man defeated and humiliated, and although they had little use for their Japanese conquerors, they had lost their awe and fear of the Europeans. What they wanted when the Japanese were driven out was self-rule such as the United States unhesitatingly granted to the Philippines.

In recognizing this new spirit among colonial peoples, Great Britain was not far behind the United States. American criticism of British colonial policy had always been extremely vocal, but it was considerably allayed by the decision of the British Labor Government to grant both India and Burma whatever degree of independence they might choose. In India, the task was far less how to get the British to leave than how to get the Hindus and Moslems in India to agree on a plan of self-government. At length a divided India was agreed upon, with a Dominion of India dominated by the Hindus, and a Dominion of Pakistan dominated by the Moslems. For Hindu India, an Englishman, Earl Mountbatten of Burma became governor-general, but for Pakistan, the outstanding Moslem

India, Burma, Malaya

Nehru and Gandhi, Indian leaders, as they appeared at the All-Indian Congress of 1946, during which Nehru became President of the Congress.

leader, Mohammed Ali Jinnah, was named at his own insistence. Independence day for India was set for August 15, 1947, at which time all British power was relinquished, and native responsibility began. Eventually, on January 26, 1950, India declared itself a sovereign democratic republic and cut loose from the British crown, although retaining a shadowy connection with the British Commonwealth of Nations. In Burma there was less internal friction than in India, but the Burmese leaders insisted upon, and obtained, complete independence, rather than dominion status, and the transfer of power to them came early in 1948. The new native government showed little ability to keep order, and the country was soon in the throes of a protracted Civil War, chiefly of Communist making. In Malaya post-war political reorganization was less drastic, but two new governmental units were set up, the Malayan Union, which brought together into a federation states that had previously been **governed** separately, and the colony of Singapore. Considerable progress was made toward the establishment of a common Malayan citizenship. The greatest problem of Malaya for the next few years was the large number of Communist terrorists who operated from the jungles and villages in an effort to disrupt normal economic life. In spite of the best efforts of the British to police the country, casualties were counted by the hundreds each year.

Unfortunately, the willingness of the United States and Great Britain to grant **Indo-China** home rule to their dependencies was not fully shared by other European nations who had possessions in the Orient. In Indo-China French policy was far from consistent, and concessions were made at first only grudgingly. By 1950, however, the French, without removing their resident advisers and commissioners, had recognized the three autonomous Indo-Chinese states of Viet Nam, Cambodia, and Laos as independent members of the French Union, but with foreign policy and military defense to remain in French hands until the end of the existing Civil War. This conflict, which had broken out in Viet Nam late in 1946 with Ho Chi Minh, a thoroughgoing Communist, in charge of the rebel, or as they called themselves, the Viet Minh forces, increased greatly in magnitude after the fighting ended in Korea, for from that time forward the rebels could count on maximum aid from Red China. The Viet Minh made the most of the native distaste for colonialism, and sought with much success to turn what might otherwise have been merely a struggle for independence into a part of the Communist effort to rule the world. The most outstanding Viet Minh victory came in May, 1954, when the French fortress of Dienbienphu fell to the Reds, giving them a valuable air-base from which to continue operations. By this time the people and government of France were tired of the long-drawn-out conflict, and eager to make peace on almost any face-saving terms. But the United States, which had long since begun to supply a steady stream of funds and military equipment for the French and Vietnamese

forces, made every possible effort to bolster up the French morale, and to insure against the further spread of Communism into southeastern Asia.

In the populous Dutch East Indies, the returning European overlords confronted an equally determined independence movement. At first the **Indonesia** Dutch authorities were reluctant to make extensive concessions to the revolutionists, but sharp and effective fighting on the part of the revolting Javanese brought a change of heart. Eventually a United States of Indonesia was agreed upon, to take over all local government in 1949. But before the agreement could be implemented, fighting broke out again between the Dutch and the natives. For a time intervention by the Security Council of the United Nations brought hostilities to an end. By January, 1948, the principles of a new agreement had been worked out, with the United States of Indonesia accepting equal status with the Netherlands under the Dutch crown in a Netherlands-Indonesian Union. But late in that same year the conflict was resumed, and lasted on for several weeks. Finally, after persistent efforts on the part of United Nations authorities, the Netherlands, on December 27, 1949, transferred all sovereignty over its former East Indies possessions (except New Guinea) to the new Republic of the United States of Indonesia. But when independence failed to bring about all the improvements that the revolutionists had expected, the new native government was beset by many troubles, some of them, as was inevitable, of Communist manufacture. When the federal principle failed in practice to provide local governments strong enough to cope with the situation, the various states abdicated their powers to the central government, and the Republic of the United States of Indonesia became the Republic of Indonesia.

Another trouble spot in the Asiatic world was the Kingdom of Iran, known before 1935 as Persia. Two circumstances **Iran** made Iran important. First, it

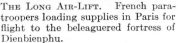

THE LONG AIR-LIFT. French para-
troopers loading supplies in Paris for
flight to the beleaguered fortress of
Dienbienphu.

*Indo-China, formerly a French colony, was
conquered by the Japanese during the Second
World War. After the war the French government, ignoring the demand for independence, sought instead to restore French authority, and so paved the way for a notable
Communist victory.*

VIET MINH PRISONERS. French troops
guarding captives. Many were found
carrying grenades in rice baskets.

was bounded on the north by the Soviet
Union; secondly, its rich resources in oil were
being exploited by the Anglo-Iranian Oil
Company, a corporation in which the British
government held stock. In 1941, after the
German invasion of Russia, Soviet troops
moved into Azerbaijan, the northernmost
portion of the Kingdom, and British troops
into the south. These operations were undertaken primarily with a view to protecting the
route to Russia from the Persian Gulf, but
the actual task of keeping the route open was
assumed in part by troops of the United
States. By a tripartite treaty between Iran,
Great Britain, and the Soviet Union, the
latter two powers guaranteed the territorial
integrity and sovereignty of Iran, and promised the withdrawal of their armed forces
six months after the end of the war. Soon
after the war was over, the American and
British troops departed, but the Russians
not only stayed on ominously, but also attempted to set up for Azerbaijan an independent Communist government. Appeals
to the United Nations apparently induced
the Soviets to withdraw their troops, after
which Iranian governmental authority was

re-established over the disturbed area. Nevertheless, the threat Russian might had
posed could not easily be forgotten.

Somewhat later a dispute broke out with
Great Britain over the royalties payable to
Iran from the Anglo-Iranian Oil Company.
Under the leadership of Mohammed Mossadegh, a strong nationalist, the Iranian government finally refused in 1951 to negotiate
further on the subject, took over all the
property of the Anglo-Iranian Oil Company,
and expelled its British agents from the
country. The resulting paralysis of the oil
industry in Iran gave great comfort to the
Communists, both inside and outside Iran,
and virtually bankrupted the nation, but
Mossadegh, who had become premier, held
grimly to his course despite every effort on
the part of the British, backed by the American government, to obtain an agreement.
Finally, in 1953, after the American President
had bluntly announced that the United
States would discontinue the financial aid it
had been giving to the government of Iran
unless the dispute were settled, the Shah replaced Mossadegh as premier with Fazlollah
Zahedi, an army officer, who after consider-

able turmoil established himself in authority, and with the encouragement of a promise of $45,000,000 aid from the United States made overtures toward a diplomatic settlement with Great Britain.

The great significance that citizens of the United States had learned during the war to Latin attach to events in Europe and America Asia served in a way to detract from their interest in the other Americas. Before the war the "good neighbor" policy had seemed to be a matter of fundamental importance in international relations; the end of the war left it no less important, perhaps, but far less in the news. Just before the meeting at San Francisco which resulted in the formation of the United Nations, an Inter-American Conference on Problems of War and Peace had met in Mexico City, and had adopted the Act of Chapultepec, a kind of substitute for the Monroe Doctrine. The Act declared that anything calculated to disturb the peace in the Americas was a matter of common concern to every American nation and a cause for consultation; further, the Act also asserted that aggression by a non-American power against any American nation was to be regarded by all as an attack on all. In other words, instead of the United States, unilaterally, pledging itself to defend the Americas, as under the Monroe Doctrine, now all of the various American nations agreed among themselves to accept joint responsibility for their common defense. This same determination to act collectively against aggressors was written into the Treaty of Rio de Janeiro, ratified by the United States Senate in December, 1947.

The one nation with which the United States found it most difficult to be good-neighborly was the Argentine. The Friction between the two coun- Argentine tries was of long-standing, and proceeded in no small part from the desire of the Argentine to exert the same kind of leadership in South America that the United States exercised for the Americas as a whole. Economically the two nations were rivals, each with practically the same agricultural exports to sell. Furthermore, businessmen from the United States after the First World War had given their nation a bad reputation with the Argentine people, a reputation which the inept diplomatic representatives sent out from Wash-

Anglo-Iranian refineries in oil-rich Iran (long coveted by Soviet Russia) produced great quantities of petroleum products until nationalized by the Iranian government some years after the Second World War. Then the British operators were expelled and the plants stood idle.

EAGER CROWDS. Scene at May Square awaiting address of Perón reflects the almost hypnotic grip which he holds over his people.

Perón, President of the Argentine, won the support of the masses in his country by his championship of the welfare of the common people. His fascist methods and attitudes greatly troubled United States Department of State officials.

PRESIDENT JUAN DOMINGO PERÓN.

ington did little to redeem. To make matters worse, the policy of the United States toward the Argentine seemed built on shifting sands. When, during the closing years of the war, the wheel of revolution turned up an army colonel, Juan Domingo Perón, as the strong man behind the Argentine government, the United States criticized his pro-fascist tendencies with the greatest of bluntness; then with great inconsistency championed successfully the admission of the Argentine to the United Nations; then as a means of preventing the election of Perón to the Argentine presidency, issued a "Blue Book" describing his pro-Axis record; then, when he was elected in spite of, or perhaps in part because of, this propaganda, switched again to trying to get along with him.

Whatever the inconsistencies of Washington diplomacy, it became clear as time went **Truman to** on that the principal objective **Mexico** of United States policy in the Western Hemisphere was to unite all the American nations against Communism, rather than against Fascism, as during the war. By an Inter-American Military Cooperation Act, passed in May, 1946, the President of the

United States was permitted to extend military aid and advice to the other American nations, and in a sense to try to organize them for defense. As a gesture of good-will President Truman, in March, 1947, visited Mexico City as the guest of the Mexican government, the first President of the United States to make such a trip. His visit was well received, and was followed by a similar visit by the Mexican President, Miguel Alemán, to Washington. Continuing Truman's policy, Secretary of State Dulles at the Tenth Inter-American Conference held in Caracas, Venezuela, during the spring of 1954, persuaded the nations represented to adopt with only one dissenting vote and two abstentions a resolution branding international Communist intervention as a "special and immediate threat to the national institutions and the peace and security of the American states." The resolution also called on the American republics to aid each other by the disclosure and exchange of information dealing with Communist activities.[1]

[1] This was a conference of the Organization of American States (OAM), the new name for the Pan-American Union.

Unfortunately the United States made little effort to revive the economic life of Latin America, which the dislocations of the war had left badly shattered. Inflation was the rule, and the avid demand for manufactured goods from the United States tended to increase rather than diminish the diffi- culties, for the Latin-American nations had not the goods to send to the United States in payment for what they wished to buy. Inevitably they blamed the "Colossus of the North" for many of the ills from which they suffered.

Bibliography

Among the numerous books that undoubtedly helped shape American thinking on foreign policy during the war were Walter Lippmann, *U.S. Foreign Policy* (1943), and *U.S. War Aims* (1944); Sumner Welles, *The Time for Decision* (1944); Wendell Willkie, *One World* (1943); and Carl Becker, *How New Will the Better World Be?* (1944). C. A. Beard, *American Foreign Policy in the Making, 1932–1940* (1946), comes to the defense of the isolationist attitude. Sumner Welles, *Seven Decisions that Shaped History* (1951), is strongly pro-Roosevelt throughout.

What happened behind the scenes at Yalta, and what interpretation should be given to these events, remain matters of heated dispute. James F. Byrnes, *Speaking Frankly* (1947), contains the report of an inside observer who later became Secretary of State. Even more revealing is Edward R. Stettinius, Jr., *Roosevelt and the Russians: The Yalta Conference*, edited by Walter Johnson (1949). There is an excellent chapter on the subject in Sherwood, *Roosevelt and Hopkins*, already cited. An anti-Roosevelt version by William O. Bullitt, "How We Won the War and Lost the Peace," in *Life*, XXV, 83–97 (August 30, 1948), 88–103 (September 6, 1948), received wide attention, but is less convincing than the account by Rear Admiral Ellis M. Zacharias, "The Inside Story of Yalta," *United Nations World*, III, 12–18 (January, 1949). See also Philip E. Moseley, "The Berlin Deadlock," *American Perspective*, II, 331–339 (December, 1948); and Rudolph A. Winnacker, "Yalta — Another Munich?" *Virginia Quarterly Review*, XXIV, 521–537 (Autumn, 1948). The text of the Yalta Agreement and many other documents appear in *War and Peace Aims of the United Nations, 1939–1945*, edited by Louise W. Holborn (2 vols., 1943–48).

On the situation in Germany, there are two admirable reports from the commander of the American occupation forces, Lucius D. Clay, *Decision in Germany* (1950), and *Germany and the Fight for Freedom* (1950); also, Hajo Holborn, *American Military Government; Its Organization and Policies* (1947); and Wolfgang Friedman, *The Allied Military Government of Germany* (1947). The Nuremberg trials are covered in R. H. Jackson, *The Nürnberg Case* (1947); and by the same author *The Case against the Nazi War Criminals* (1946). On this subject, see also Sheldon Glueck, *The Nuremberg Trial and Aggressive War* (1946).

On recent Asiatic affairs there are several useful general studies, among them Harold M. Vinacke, *The United States and the Far East, 1945–51* (1952); Richard W. Van Alstyne, *American Crisis Diplomacy: The Quest for Collective Security, 1918–1952* (1952); Kenneth Scott Latourette, *The American Record in the Far East, 1945–1951* (1952); and Maurice Zinkin, *Asia and the West* (1951). There are several helpful accounts on Japan: Nobutaka Ike, *The Beginnings of Political Democracy in Japan* (1950); Edwin O. Reischauer, *The United States and Japan* (1950); Evelyn S. Colbert, *The Left Wing in Japanese Politics* (1952); and Rodger Swearingen and Paul Langer, *Red Flag in Japan: International Communism in Action, 1919–1951* (1952). On China since the Second World War, perhaps the best general account is Herbert Feis, *The China Tangle* (1953), but there is much to be learned from Benjamin I. Schwartz, *Chinese Communism and the Rise of Mao* (1951); and the American Academy of Political and Social Science, *Annals*, "Report on China," edited by H. Arthur Steiner (September, 1951). H. Maclear Bate, *Report from Formosa* (1952), is based on careful observation. Garel A. Grunder and William E. Livezey, *The Philippines and the United States* (1951), is a serious study of recent relationships. George M. McCune, *Korea Today* (1950), provides an excellent backdrop for the Korean War.

The Foreign Policy Association, *Headline Series*, contains many interesting articles on recent world affairs.

33

One World — or Two?

The United Nations — Organization — Iran, Indonesia — Greece — Spain, Trieste — Palestine — Israel — The control of atomic energy — The Cominform — The "iron curtain" — The Truman Doctrine — The bipartisan foreign policy — The Marshall Plan — The North Atlantic Treaty — Russian aggressions — The Air-Lift — Election of 1948 — Truman's victory — The "Fair Deal"

FOR most Americans the chief hope of holding the world together lay in the United Nations. The process of putting the San Francisco Charter into effect began at London, January 10, 1946, when the General Assembly, widely heralded as the "town-meeting of the world," began its first session. Although each member nation was entitled to only one vote in the Assembly, it might have as many as five delegates, so the United States sent five of its most distinguished citizens as its first representatives — Secretary of State James F. Byrnes, Former Secretary of State Edward R. Stettinius, Jr., United States Senators Tom Connally and Arthur H. Vandenberg, and Mrs. Anna Eleanor Roosevelt, the widow of Franklin D. Roosevelt. For its first President the Assembly chose Paul-Henri Spaak of Belgium. Then, as the Charter required, it proceeded with the election of the six non-permanent members of the Security Council. Aside from this and certain other elective functions, the Assembly was supposed to be primarily a deliberative body, less important because of the power it exercised than because of the forum it provided for the discussion of world problems. Its sessions were ordinarily to occur only annually for short periods of time each, but in 1946 it met for a second time at Flush-

The United Nations

ing Meadows, Long Island, and chose New York City as the permanent headquarters of the United Nations. A gift of $8,500,000 by John D. Rockefeller, Jr., for the purchase of a six-block tract along the East River in Manhattan, made possible the building for the United Nations of a skyscraper capital in the heart of the great American metropolis.

Unlike the Assembly, the Security Council, with its five permanent members (the United States, the Soviet Union, the United Kingdom, France, and China) and its six members elected by the Assembly, was supposed to remain in continuous session. For the first non-permanent members of the Council, the Assembly chose Egypt, Mexico, the Netherlands, Australia, Brazil, and Poland. The first three of these six had terms of one year only; thereafter three new members were to be chosen each year for two-year terms, and were to be ineligible for immediate re-election. The presidency of the Council rotated among member nations, each serving for a month at a time. The Security Council held its first meeting in London, January 18. On its recommendation the Assembly chose Trygve Halfdan Lie, a Norwegian Labor Party leader, as the first Secretary-General of the United Nations.[1]

Organization

[1] Lie was succeeded in 1953 by Dag Hammarskjöld, a Swedish financial and trade expert.

UNITED NATIONS HEADQUARTERS.

United Nations permanent head-quarters on the East River in New York is an architecturally inspiring sight. Many nations contributed to the internal appointments. Overuse of the veto power by Soviet Russia tended to diminish the importance of the Security Council, and to build up the General Assembly, a glimpse of which is here shown.

THE GENERAL ASSEMBLY. Photo shows U.S.S.R. delegation conferring.

TRYGVE LIE, of Norway, first Secretary-General of the UN.

After the initial sessions in London, the Council held most of its meetings in New York, first at Hunter College, then later at Lake Success, Long Island; and finally in the new United Nations building.

It soon became apparent that the Security Council, under existing regulations, could **The Security Council** never become the effective instrument that at least some of the framers of the United Nations Charter had hoped. The chief difficulty lay in the provision which permitted each great power to veto any important action that might be proposed. According to the Charter, decisions by the Council could be taken only with the concurrence of seven members, and even this vote would be insufficient unless every one of the five great powers voted with the majority. But few of those who accepted this provision could have foreseen the ruthlessness with which one nation, Russia, would exercise the veto power. During the first three years of the life of the United Nations the Russian veto was interposed no less than thirty times. In practice Russian use of the veto power made the United Nations almost as ineffective after the Second World War as the failure of the United States to ratify the Treaty of Versailles made the League of Nations after the First World War.

In each instance the international organization continued in existence, but in each instance, also, its usefulness was almost fatally impaired.

In spite of the discouraging effect of the constant Russian vetoes, the United Nations completed most of the machinery for world cooperation that had been authorized by the San Francisco Charter, and accomplished what it could. Events of the Korean War, which broke out in 1950, put it to its most severe test. Because the continuing Russian vetoes rendered the Security Council impotent, the Assembly, under United States leadership, finally assumed authority to make recommendations for peace whenever the Security Council failed to act. If not in session at the time of such an emergency, the Assembly held that it could be convened within twenty-four hours, either at the request of the Security Council or of a majority of the members of the United Nations; and that it might, if it deemed such a course advisable, even authorize the use of armed force. This expansion of the Assembly's powers constituted, in effect, an amendment to the United Nations charter, and its legality was questioned heatedly by the Communist bloc.

1. The Economic and Social Council, composed of eighteen members to be chosen by the General Assembly, six each **Economic** year for three-year terms, was **and Social** duly constituted, and met per- **Council** sistently following its first session in London, January 23, 1946. The Council set up a wide variety of commissions to advise it, and through which to operate, some of them, such as the Commission on Narcotic Drugs, designed to take over the work formerly done by comparable bodies of the now defunct League of Nations. Especially commendatory was the work of a Sub-Commission on Reconstruction of Devastated Areas, which made a comprehensive report on eight war-torn nations, and suggested appropriate international action. The Economic and Security Council did not originate the United Nations Educational, Scientific, and Cultural

Organization but it reached an agreement with it, which gave UNESCO, as it was generally called, the blessing of United Nations sponsorship.

2. In addition to the Economic and Social Council, the United Nations also set up a Trusteeship Council of twelve **The Trustee-** members, six of whom repre- **ship Council** sented nations actually in charge of "trust territories," and six of whom represented other nations. The Trusteeship Council had somewhat shadowy supervisory authority over existing mandates, and over territory detached from a defeated nation, except that "strategic areas" were to be directly under the Security Council. In the latter category came the former Japanese mandates in the Marshall, Mariana, and Caroline islands, which were handed over to the United States for administration.

3. The Security Council also selected, in conjunction with the Assembly, the fifteen judges of the International Court of Justice. This Court **International** received its first case in 1947, **Court of** when the British government **Justice** referred a charge to it that illegally-sown mines had damaged two British destroyers, with heavy loss of life, in Albanian waters. Although Albania was not a member of the United Nations, its representatives appeared before the Court, and the Corfu Channel case, as it was generally called, dragged along for two years. Ultimately the Court decided, April 9, 1949, that Albania was responsible for the explosions, and for the consequent loss in lives and property, but that the British by sending their mine-sweepers into Albanian waters some weeks later had violated Albanian sovereignty. Other cases from time to time came before the Court, notably the Anglo-Iranian dispute over oil holdings in Iran, but the Court, although willing enough to make decisions, lacked the power to enforce them. Its advice was frequently sought with regard to interpretations of the United Nations charter and the rules of international law.

4. A Military Staff Committee, to be com-

posed of the chiefs of staff of the five great

Military Staff Committee powers, or their representatives, was supposed to advise the Security Council on the means by which armed force might be used to carry out United Nations decisions, but the chronic failure of this Committee to reach agreements robbed the Security Council completely of military weapons. When the Council took action on Korea, for example, it could only ask the support of member nations.

5. The constant inability of the Security Council to reach decisions, due to the impasse between the United States and Russia, threw more and more responsibility upon the General Assembly, which could at least debate matters freely. For this purpose its short, supposedly annual, sessions proved inadequate, so on motion of the United States an Interim Committee, sometimes called the "Little Assembly," was created. This consisted of one representative from each member nation, and its decisions, although in no way binding on anyone, could be reached by a two-thirds vote. It was promptly boycotted by Russia and her satellites, but its usefulness as a reflector of world opinion was so great that it seemed likely to become a permanent institution.

The "Little Assembly"

The United Nations, in spite of its seeming impotence, had some significant accomplishments to its credit. The government of Iran, in January, 1946, protested against the continued occupation of Iranian territory by Russian troops, and charged the Soviet government with interference in Iranian internal affairs. The charge was heatedly denied by the Russian representative on the Security Council, and for a time he withdrew from its sessions. The quarrel ended, without United Nations action, when the Russian government recalled its troops from Iran, but the evidence that the overwhelming majority of the Council sympathized with Iran may have had some influence in modifying the Russian attitude. The Ukraine, one of the three Russian Soviet

Iran, Indonesia

Republics given separate representation in the United Nations, next charged that Japanese troops were being used to suppress a native revolt in Indonesia, and moved that the United Nations institute an investigation. This motion was voted down, but the continued disorders in Indonesia soon had that subject before the Council again, and in August, 1947, the Council voted to send a "Good Offices Committee" of three to Indonesia to arrange a settlement. Undoubtedly United Nations intervention had much to do with the settlement of the Dutch-Indonesian dispute.[1]

United Nations efforts at mediation were often far less successful. In the dispute between Greece and her neighbors, the UN failed completely to achieve a settlement. The Ukraine first brought the problem of Greece before the Council in January, 1946, charging that the continued presence of British troops in Greece constituted a threat to the peace of the Balkans. This the Greeks not only denied, but they also hurled back a countercharge to the effect that Albania, Bulgaria, and Yugoslavia were directly supporting the Communist guerrillas along the Greek border who were trying to overthrow the Greek government. The Security Council then voted to send a United Nations Commission to Greece on another mission of investigation. The majority of this Commission came to the conclusion that the Greek charges were true, but the minority, consisting of the Russian and Polish representatives, held the exact opposite. When the Commission reported its findings to the Security Council in the summer of 1947 Russia used the veto to prevent action being taken in accordance with the wishes of the majority. The Council then helplessly turned the Balkan situation over to the Assembly for further investigation.

Greece

The Security Council was equally ineffective in taking action with respect to the Franco régime in Spain, which the Polish representative declared to be a threat to world peace. A ma-

Spain, Trieste

[1] See p. 698.

jority opinion admitted the potential threat
of Spanish fascism, but noted the absence of
any aggressive act, and recommended only
that if the Spanish government did not
change its spots in due time, the members of
the United Nations should withdraw their
representatives from Madrid.   This mild
action ran afoul of the usual Russian veto.
Russian intransigence also prevented the Security Council from appointing a governor
for Trieste, as called for under the terms of
the Italian treaty.   The net result was that
Trieste remained under Anglo-American
control until October, 1954, when a *de facto*
settlement, concurred in by the Western
powers, divided the Free Territory for administrative purposes between Italy and
Yugoslavia.

Infinitely perplexing likewise was the
Arab-Jewish contest for the control of Pales-

Palestine tine, which by the year 1947
reached the United Nations.
The Zionist movement for the creation in
Palestine of a Jewish national state received
a tremendous impetus after the war by the
arrival of thousands of Jewish refugees from
the European war zones.   Arab opposition

to Zionism, plus the problem of accepting
such large numbers of "displaced persons,"
posed a serious problem for the British government, which held a mandate over Palestine dating back to the year 1922.   The
United States was also involved, not only
because of the sentimental interest of many
American Jews in Zionism, but also because
of the possession by such neighboring Arab
states as Iraq and Saudi Arabia of great
oil resources which American companies
were either exploiting or hoped soon to exploit.   It was hazardous politically to offend
Jewish voters in the United States, and it
might be hazardous economically to run the
risk of offending the intensely anti-Jewish
Arab Kings.   An Anglo-American Committee of Inquiry, appointed in 1945, reported in April, 1946, that the British should
admit into Palestine 100,000 of the refugee
Jews from Central Europe who had suffered
at the hands of the Nazis, but that instead of
setting up an independent Palestinian state,
either Jewish or Arab, the British mandate
should be continued until a United Nations
trusteeship could be devised.   This report
pleased neither Arabs, Jews, nor British,
although President Truman approved it for
the United States.

With violence between Arabs and Jews on
the increase, the British government requested that the General Assembly of the
United Nations study the problem further.
As a result, the Assembly appointed a Special
Committee on Palestine in May, 1947, which,
three months later, brought in an elaborate
report.   In this document the majority proposed the partition of Palestine into three
states, one dominantly Arab and one dominantly Jewish, but with the City of Jeru-
salem independent of both, and all three
bound together in a single economic union.
This report, after prolonged debate, was
adopted, strangely enough with the United
States and the Soviet Union both supporting
it, but it served only to feed the flames of
conflict in Palestine, and its intense unpopularity with the Arabs led the United States
virtually to go back on the stand it had
taken.   The British, however, had resolved to

Trieste

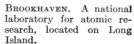

BROOKHAVEN. A national laboratory for atomic research, located on Long Island.

SAFETY PRECAUTIONS. **Ion** chambers and film meter are standard equipment. Small meters are optional.

REMOTE-CONTROL ENGINEERING. The Master-Slave Manipulator, designed to enable study of radiation without danger to personnel.

Atomic research, under the sponsorship of the Atomic Energy Commission, became a principal concern of American scientists. The vast expenditures required for the development of essential plants were borne necessarily by the national government. Major attention was at first given to such war-instruments as the "A-bomb," and the "H-bomb," but peaceful uses were also contemplated.

withdraw from Palestine, and in May, 1948, the British High Commissioner actually took his departure. Thereupon the Jews proclaimed the independent State of Israel, as of midnight, May 14–15, 1948. The new state received immediate recognition by the United States and the Soviet Union, but its Arab neighbors promptly attacked it with what little military might they could muster. In the fighting that followed, the Jews, in spite of their inferiority in numbers, showed remarkable ability to defend themselves, and it seemed evident that the Arabs could not

The new State of Israel

destroy the new "Israel." Obviously this war in the Holy Land was one that the United Nations could not overlook, but instead of taking any direct action to end the fighting the General Assembly merely authorized the five great powers to send a mediator to Palestine. For this task the powers chose Count Bernadotte of Sweden, who quickly achieved a truce, only to be assassinated by Jewish extremists who opposed partition, and wished the war to continue until the Jewish state should include all of Palestine. Despite this untoward incident, and much irregular fighting, a workable

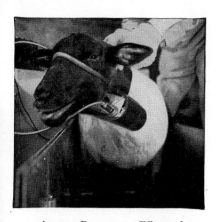

ANIMAL REACTION. Effects of radioactive iodine on sheep are tested at the Hanford Works, Richland, Washington. The iodine is a by-product of separating plutonium from fissionable materials.

GROWTH EFFECTS. Proximity to the source of radiated gamma rays inhibits growth in plants. Signs on the rows of corn indicate number of meters from the source.

ATOMIC POWER. Model of first U.S. atomic-powered submarine, the *Nautilus*.

settlement of the problem was eventually arranged, largely through the efforts of Count Bernadotte's American successor, Dr. Ralph Bunche. An uneasy tension continued, however, between Israel and the neighboring Arab states, and the danger that some untoward incident might provoke an outbreak of hostilities was great. As time went on, it became clear that in the broader sphere of world politics Israel's sympathies lay with the western democracies rather than with the Soviets, but in spite of this fact the Communists were unable to make durable friendships with any of Israel's neighbors.

By this time it was apparent that throughout the world the Soviet Union and the United States stood in deadly antagonism to each other. This was shown in a variety of ways, **The control of atomic energy** but perhaps most conclusively in the divergent attitudes of the two nations with reference to the control of atomic energy. Tests undertaken in July, 1946, by the United States Navy at Bikini Island demonstrated beyond a shadow of a doubt that the new atomic bomb was not merely another piece of ordnance, it was a cataclysm. A small number of bombs, strategically placed, could destroy a whole metropolitan area, and make it uninhabitable for years to come. A considerable number of bombs could paralyze an entire nation. A third World War, with atomic weapons in use by both sides, might mean the end of civilization.

Even before the Bikini tests, the General Assembly of the United Nations had established in January, 1946, an Atomic Energy Commission to investigate the entire problem, and to make recommendations for the control of atomic energy by international means, but a seemingly incurable difference of opinion developed between the Russian and the American points of view. The American plan, framed by a commission headed by Bernard M. Baruch, called for the creation of an International Atomic Development Authority with full power to control the use of atomic energy everywhere in the world, particularly with a view to preventing it from being turned to warlike ends. This Agency was to have unrestricted privileges of inspection in all nations, and its actions were not to be subject to the usual veto power of the United Nations. Over against the American plan, the Russians proposed merely an international agreement to abandon atomic warfare, with each nation free to enforce the agreement for itself. Furthermore, the veto power was to remain inviolate. As a part of the American plan, the United States offered to surrender its stockpile of atomic bombs whenever international control should be set up, but the Russians called for the destruction of the American bombs as a prelude to any agreement. Ultimately the Russians grudgingly conceded the necessity of international control and inspection, but they were unyielding in their insistence on the other items of their program, and nothing was accomplished. The United States, with its long lead in the development of atomic energy, could hardly give up its advantages without full assurance that some effective means had been devised to restrict the atomic activities of a potential enemy.

Within the United States, Congress,

meantime, had set up a five-man commission with exclusive authority over the development of atomic energy, and under civilian rather than army or navy control. As chairman of the commission, President Truman appointed David E. Lilienthal, for many years the efficient head of TVA, then, following Lilienthal's resignation (effective, February, 1950), Gordon Dean, a distinguished lawyer.[1] Under their leadership, American scientists earnestly pushed forward research into the secrets of nuclear energy, seeking to make their findings of use for peaceful as well as for warlike purposes. But President Truman's announcement in September, 1949, that an "atomic explosion" had occurred in Russia, together with the outbreak of the Korean War the following June, speeded up greatly the military phases of the program. If there should be a third World War, the United States could not afford to be behind in the atomic race. Repeated tests, both on and near Pacific atolls and in the Nevada desert, measured the progress of American research, which produced eventually not only a variety of atomic bombs, but also tactical weapons and a hydrogen bomb, a weapon the Russians had also achieved. During 1952 Prime Minister Churchill announced that the British government had detonated its first atomic bomb in the Monte Bello Islands. Efforts on the part of the United Nations to find a means of ending the atomic race continued to bring no results, although the Russians no longer insisted that all atomic weapons should be destroyed as a prelude to the discussion of a plan of control.

With the increasingly tense situation between Russia and the United States, the idea of "One World," which had **The** seemed so sure of achievement **Cominform** during the war, became each succeeding month a dimmer hope. When in May, 1943, the Comintern had been dissolved "as the directing center of the international working-class movement," the Soviet-inspired announcement had strongly advocated a

[1] In June, 1953, President Eisenhower chose Rear Admiral Lewis L. Strauss to succeed Gordon Dean.

"working-class movement of each separate country, working within the framework of its own country." This statement had been widely hailed as the end of the old Communist plan to promote world revolution, and the beginning of a new policy based on the principle of "live, and let live," the principle on which the new United Nations was to be built. But in September, 1947, Communist representatives from Russia and her satellites, augmented by a few others from France and Italy, met in Warsaw to establish a Communist Information Bureau, or Cominform, the purpose of which was to "coordinate the activity of Communist parties on foundations of mutual agreement," that is, to provide one leadership for Communist propaganda everywhere in the world. It was clear that the old policy of world revolution had been resumed, and that the Russian leaders were bent on creating "One World," to be sure, but one Communist world.

Both before and after the Warsaw Manifesto was issued, its words were matched with **The "iron** deeds. Wherever the Red Army **curtain"** controlled, either by direct occupation or by the heavy shadow it cast across an international border, free governments disappeared. By one means or another Communist minorities, backed by Moscow, took over the governments of Poland, Yugoslavia, Bulgaria, Rumania, Hungary, and finally even Czechoslovakia. Intercourse between these countries and the outside world became ever more difficult. The Russian zones in Germany and Austria were separated by heavy Red Army patrols from other zones of occupation, and under the guise of reparations were stripped of their resources. In Russian-occupied Austria, everything that the Nazis had stolen was defined as German property, and was taken over by the Russians. Much else went on of which only rumors got through to the West. From the Baltic to the Adriatic an "iron curtain" had descended, back of which the Soviet leaders could in safety and in secrecy consolidate their gains, and lay their plans for others.

The immediate objectives of the plotters were not long disguised. In Italy and France, Communist minorities were galvanized into action, with the control of the Italian and French governments, by fair means or foul, as their objectives. The government of Turkey was told that it must either cede territory to Russia, and permit the Russian government to establish military bases that would command the Dardanelles, or else take a consistently pro-Russian line such as its neighbors to the North had done. Most revealing of all, Greek Communist guerrillas were given every aid and comfort by neighboring Communist states in their effort to overthrow the existing non-Communist Greek government. If Russia could only draw Greece within her orbit, she could outflank the Dardanelles and Suez, and challenge the Anglo-American line of communications with the Far East, much as Germany had done before her.

It was this Greek situation that finally led the United States to take a positive stand against the Russian program of **The Truman** aggression. When the British **Doctrine** government, in line with its general policy of retrenchment, announced that it could no longer afford to maintain a garrison in Greece, and would withdraw its troops from that nation, the United States had a momentous decision to make. Either it must somehow take the place the British were vacating, or it must stand idly by while Russian-backed Communists went through the now familiar process of destroying the liberties of one more "liberated" country. The government of Greece had little to recommend it, but it was anti-Communist, and at least subject to improvement. If the Communists came in, then down would come the iron curtain, and the rule of force for an indefinite period would completely take the place of the rule of law and reason. Faced by this situation the President of the United States sent a message to Congress, March 12, 1947, calling for American aid both to Greece and to Turkey. His message, marking as it did a milestone in the history of American foreign

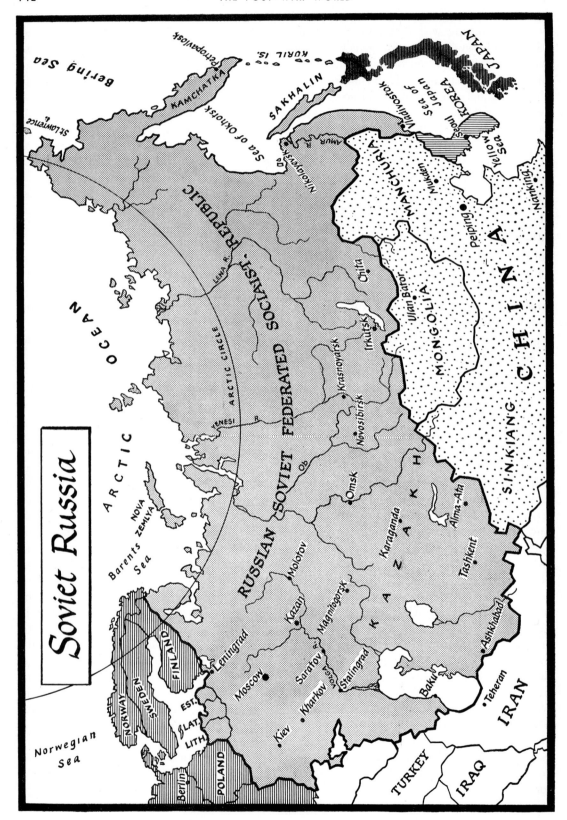

policy, was promptly called the Truman Doctrine. The world was confronted with two ways of life, the President pointed out, one based on majority rule, with generous guarantees for the freedom of the individual, and the other "based upon the will of a minority forcibly imposed upon the majority."

I believe that it must be the policy of the United States to support free peoples who are resisting attempted subjugation by armed minorities or by outside pressure.

I believe that we must assist free peoples to work out their own destinies in their own way.

I believe that our help should be primarily through economic and financial aid which is essential to economic stability and orderly political processes.

To give strength to his words, the President recommended that Congress appropriate $300,000,000 for aid to Greece and $100,-000,000 for aid to Turkey.

The Truman Doctrine aroused much discussion in the United States, and a small minority, headed by Henry Wallace, denounced it unsparingly. Others regretted that the United States had acted unilaterally instead of through the United Nations. To reassure this faction, Senator Vandenberg introduced, and both houses of Congress accepted, an amendment requiring the President to discontinue American aid in the event that the Security Council of the United Nations should at any time hold it to be unnecessary or unwise. On this issue the United States would waive its veto privilege. So amended the appropriation passed, and with the funds thus made available the United States began at once to ship military and economic supplies to the nations concerned. To administer the American expenditures in Greece, the President chose a Republican, ex-Governor Dwight Griswold of Nebraska.

The objectives of the American program in Greece and Turkey were achieved slowly but surely. As far as Greece was concerned, they were greatly assisted by the break between the Soviet Union and Yugoslavia that occurred in 1948, after which the two nations

were soon openly at odds. While Yugoslavia, under Marshal Tito as its prime minister, remained a Communist state, it ceased to be a Russian satellite and closed its frontier to the Russian-inspired guerrillas whose depredations had been such a sore trial to Greece. Greatly strengthened by financial aid from the United States and by the advice of American military experts, the Greeks soon brought their army to a high degree of efficiency, and restored order. In Turkey, the American grant was used to strengthen the Turkish army so effectively that the danger of a Russian attack all but disappeared. Indeed, by 1953, the Soviet government let it be known that it would no longer insist upon its earlier demands.

For a number of years American foreign policy exhibited a refreshingly bipartisan nature. The American dele- **The bipartisan foreign policy** gates to the United Nations contained members of both parties, with Senator Vandenberg, a Republican, quite as important a representative of the United States as any Democrat. The American member of the Security Council was another Republican, ex-Senator Warren R. Austin of Vermont,[1] who had succeeded former Secretary of State Stettinius to that important United Nations post in January, 1947. That same month, after the resignation of Secretary Byrnes allegedly for reasons of health, but actually because of differences with the President, Truman chose as Byrnes's successor former Chief-of-Staff George C. Marshall, who had never been in politics and never expected to be. Possibly Marshall was technically a Democrat, but he was as nearly a non-party man as the President could have chosen. One of Secretary Marshall's principal advisers, almost certain to be present in all overseas conferences, was John Foster Dulles, a Republican who was very close to Governor Thomas E. Dewey of New York, and was generally thought to be

[1] Austin was succeeded in 1953 by Henry Cabot Lodge, Jr., of Massachusetts, grandson of the Henry Cabot Lodge who had defeated Wilson's efforts to take the United States into the League of Nations.

THE FISHING INDUSTRY. Marshall Plan aid benefited the fishermen, shipyards, canneries, and distributors.

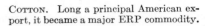

COTTON. Long a principal American export, it became a major ERP commodity.

The Marshall Plan, or *European Recovery Program (ERP), instigated by Secretary of State Marshall, brought needed aid to the war-shattered European economies, and helped ward off Communist expansion. "Foreign aid" soon became a principal weapon of American diplomacy. For his part in this program Marshall received the Nobel Peace Prize.*

GENERAL GEORGE C. MARSHALL. Formerly Chief of Staff, and Secretary of State under President Truman.

Dewey's choice for Secretary of State. With the Russian menace looming ever larger, it thus appeared that the Truman Administration had discarded party politics in foreign affairs, and that party leaders generally had decided that partisanship must stop at the water's edge.

The Truman Doctrine was quickly supplemented by what was sometimes called the Marshall Plan, and sometimes the European Recovery Plan. It seemed clear that the United States could not hope to achieve

The Marshall Plan — ERP

much success in the "containment of Communism" if it reserved its aid until a given nation was just about ready to go down, or if it helped only one or two of the weakest nations at a time. Europe as a whole needed to be put on its feet economically. If that could be done, perhaps the Communist drive could be stopped in its tracks. It was with some such thoughts as these in mind that Secretary Marshall, in an address delivered at Harvard University, June 5, 1947, called upon European nations first to get together on what they could do to help themselves, and then to state in concrete terms what additional aid they would need from the United States. If they could demonstrate a determination to cooperate for their own good, and would give assurance that the aid they received would be used for the economic benefit of Europe as a whole, the United States would help as it could. The Marshall Plan was enthusiastically received throughout all western Europe, but Russia and her satellites, to whom it was also open, held aloof.

As a matter of fact, the European Recovery Plan (ERP) was by no means the first **Background** contribution of the United States **of ERP** toward the rehabilitation of the war-torn world. Lend-lease activities, which began in March, 1941, and lasted on until terminated by President Truman in August, 1945, had funnelled some $48,500,000,000 worth of American assistance into the economies of the various Allied nations in return for reverse lend-lease valued at only $7,800,-000,000. In the post-war settlements, adoption of the principle that goods used up in the war effort should not be paid for reduced to millions rather than billions the obligation of the Allies to the United States; also, provisions for the repayment of these sums were made exceptionally generous, avoiding as completely as possible all actual transfers of cash. Except for a few minor nations, practically all the recipients of lend-lease aid, outside of the Russian orbit, had arranged settlements by the end of 1946, but the Soviet Union, in spite of an agreement in the spring of 1947 to negotiate, steadily refused to come to terms. The extent to which lend-lease aided the Allies in meeting their post-war problems cannot be measured, but it must have been considerable. As for Great Britain, her economy had been so closely geared to lend-lease that Congress, after lengthy consideration of the problem, voted late in 1945 to lend the British government $3,750,-000,000 over a five-year period, and an additional $650,000,000 to cover the British obligation to the United States under the lend-lease agreement. The interest charged on the British loan was to be only two per cent,

less than it cost the United States to borrow the money from its own people, and even this interest was to be waived when too detrimental to British exchange. Repayments of the principal were to be made in fifty equal installments, beginning in 1951.

American aid to recovery had also included substantial contributions to the United Nations Relief and **UNRRA** Rehabilitation Administration (UNRRA), the purpose of which was to bring relief to the victims of war in any area under control of the United Nations. The creation of this organization was the result primarily of American promotion, and dated back to an Allied conference held in Washington as early as 1943. The policies of UNRRA were set by a Council in which each member state was represented, but a central committee of nine — the five great powers and four others — was empowered to make emergency decisions. Administration was in the hands of a director-general and staff, the latter numbering by 1946 approximately 12,000 persons. During its lifetime UNRRA had successively three directors-general, all Americans: Governor Herbert H. Lehman of New York, Mayor Fiorello La Guardia of New York City, and Major-General Lowell W. Rooks of the United States Army. It obtained its funds from its more than forty member nations, each of which agreed on two occasions, first in March, 1944, and again in December, 1945, to contribute one per cent of its national income to the UNRRA treasury. Collections, however, were sometimes difficult, or even impossible. It was obvious from the start that the major contributions toward UNRRA would come from the United States; in actual fact 72 per cent of its funds came from this source, while 90 per cent of the food and other supplies it distributed came from American firms and factories.

During the summer and fall of 1945 UNRRA gave substantial aid to millions of starvation-threatened people in **Dissatisfac-** Greece, Yugoslavia, Czechoslo- **tion with** vakia, Poland, Italy, Austria, **UNRRA**

China, and the Philippines. It also undertook to look out for the needs of the hundreds of thousands of displaced persons in the western zones of Germany and Austria, and in Italy. By 1946 other nations such as Albania, Byelorussia, the Ukraine, Finland, Hungary, and Ethiopia were sharing the benefits of UNRRA. Undoubtedly its operations were of tremendous assistance to the nations it touched, but many Americans, including high officials of the State Department, soon became acutely dissatisfied with UNRRA operations. They charged that in many instances UNRRA supplies were used by governments that received them "to feed their political supporters and starve their political enemies." In Yugoslavia, for example, there could be no doubt that Tito, the Communist dictator, had so distributed these contributions as to strengthen the hold of his régime upon his people. There were also charges of graft and maladministration, notably with respect to China, where the Chiang government seemed unable to keep UNRRA supplies out of the hands of black market operators. Further, the question was constantly raised, were countries that received aid doing all they could do to help themselves? Or were they counting on a permanent dole, mainly to be contributed by the United States? By the end of 1946 UNRRA had lost the support of the American government, and was doomed. The policy of the American State Department called for more self-help on the part of the nations concerned, and strictly American, rather than international, control of any aid given. "It is our position," said Secretary Byrnes, "that whatever the United States does in the way of relief should be done by the United States unilaterally. We want to give aid as the United States and not as a member of an international organization."

Thus, in a sense, the Marshall Plan grew out of American experience with post-war **Russia rejects ERP** relief. The problem that confronted the United States was not how to avoid giving American aid, but rather how to avoid having American money and supplies used to build up hostility to the nation that provided them. The United States was not even averse to aid for Russia and her satellites. All of them were definitely within the scope of the American offer. But the American idea was that the various nations of Europe should plan and work together for joint recovery, and it was primarily because of this condition that the Russians withdrew. If all Europe, acting as one economic unit, or any substantial part of it outside Russian domination, should begin to prosper, the chance for the spread of the Russian system would go. Communism needed despair and hopelessness as the soil from which to grow. The Marshall Plan offered the prospect of recovery instead. So, when the customary three-power conference of foreign ministers, Ernest Bevin of Great Britain, Georges Bidault of France, and V. M. Molotov of Russia, met at Paris late in June, 1947, to consider the American offer, Molotov claimed that it would infringe on the sovereignty of the lesser states, and refused to have anything to do with it. Bevin and Bidault then called a conference of twenty-two European states to discuss the subject, excluding Russia and Spain, but not excluding the Russian satellites. All but the Russian-dominated nations of eastern Europe accepted the invitation, and of these Czechoslovakia at first accepted, then, on direct orders from Moscow, cancelled its acceptance.

Meeting at Paris in July, the sixteen nations that wished to take advantage of Marshall's offer appointed a Committee of European Economic Cooperation, consisting of one **Congress supports ERP** member from each nation, to draw up the necessary program. Two months later this Committee reported various ways and means by which the member-nations could help themselves, but estimated that to meet unavoidable deficits they would have to have from the United States within a four-year period the gigantic sum of $19,330,000,000. Scaled down by American scrutiny to $17,000,000,000 the sum was still so huge as to confront the Truman Administration with a tremendous task in obtaining from Congress the necessary appropriations. But public sentiment rallied to the support of "ERP," and at a special session held in November, 1947, "interim" aid of over half a billion dollars was voted to France, Italy, and Austria, with an additional $18,000,000 for China. Then the following April Congress voted $5,300,000,000 to carry the program through the coming year. The President's request for a pledge of $17,000,000,000 over a four-year period was modified to an annual appropriation, with further grants to be dependent upon the success of the program, but the evident intent of the bipartisan majority that pushed the plan through Congress was to continue the appropriations if only conditions in Europe would justify such action. To administer ERP Congress set up an Economic Cooperation Administration (ECA), at the head of which the President appointed Paul G. Hoffman, a Republican business executive from Indiana. Armed with ample funds, and backed by the goodwill of the overwhelming majority of the American people, ERP went rapidly to work on the "containment" of the Russian system behind the Russian-imposed iron curtain. The hope was that in due time the sixteen cooperating nations would be sufficiently prosperous to have no further need of outside aid, and no further fear of a Communist revolution.

Evidence that ERP had made a deep impression on European minds was not long in **European reaction** coming. In their eagerness to obtain American aid the governments of France and Italy had made bold to eliminate a l Communists from their cabinets, actions which led to prolonged strikes and violence on the part of the Communist-dominated unions. But the non-Communist governments stood their ground, and in both countries eventually got the upper hand. The Italian elections of April 18–19 were particularly significant. Italian Communists made the mistake of thinking that they could win in a free election, only to discover when the election was over that they had been voted down by overwhelming majorities, about 70 per cent of the electorate against them to only about 30 per cent for their "Popular Front." In France strikes and repeated cabinet crises at first crippled the efforts of the government to promote recovery, but in a political way strengthened the rightist movement headed by General de Gaulle rather than the Communists. But by the spring of 1949, the effect of American aid had so improved the economic life of both Italy and France that something akin to normal conditions seemed in sight, while progress toward economic unity in the low countries, Belgium, the Netherlands, and Luxembourg (Benelux), was heartening. Marshall's resignation as Secretary of State, which came in January, 1949, because of failing health, brought in a new Secretary, Dean Acheson, but no change of policy on the part of the United States.

As American aid began to give visible proof that it was really promoting recovery, the North Atlantic nations that **The North** felt themselves in peril from **Atlantic** Russian aggression began also **Treaty** to draw together in a military way. First Great Britain and France joined with the Benelux countries to create a regional system of collective defense, a course of action authorized by the United Nations charter. When the United States indicated its willingness to enter such an organization, negotiations began which ended on March 15, 1949, with the signing of the North Atlantic Treaty by twelve nations — Belgium, Canada, Denmark, France, Great Britain, Iceland, Italy, Luxembourg, the Netherlands, Norway, Portugal, and the United States.[1] According to this pact, "armed attack against one or more" of the member nations was to "be considered an attack against them all." Further, the clear implication was that the United States would help its overseas partners to re-arm.

[1] The treaty was ratified by the United States Senate, July 21, 1949. Later, Greece and Turkey were admitted to membership.

But the Russians were by no means idle. The establishment of the Cominform in September, 1947, was apparently

Russian ag-
gressions meant, at least in part, as an offset to the Truman Doctrine and the Marshall Plan. Then in February, 1948, with complete Russ'an support and connivance, the Communists seized power in Czechoslovakia, where until that time a middle-of-the-road multi-party government had been permitted to exist. Efforts were also made to discipline the Communist dictator of Yugoslavia, Marshal Tito, whom the Comintern in June, 1948, accused of dev'ation from the party line. But Tito, although fully cognizant of the hazards of his course, stood his ground, and refused to be erased. Just what this internal dissension meant the western world was unable to fathom, but it was evident that the solidarity of the eastern bloc of nations in opposition to the West had not yet been broken. This was registered clearly when an international conference on the control of the Danube River met in Belgrade, July 30, 1948. At every opportunity the seven Communist states of eastern Europe, including Yugoslavia, voted solidly against the three western powers, the United States, Great Britain, and France, to exclude all non-Danubian powers from a voice in the control of the river, and thus in effect to make Russia its mistress.

But the outstanding action taken by Russia to show her displeasure with the western world was with reference to Germany. When in the summer of 1948, despairing of ever reaching any further agreements on German affairs with the Russian authorities, the western occupation powers announced their intention of establishing a native German government for Trizonia, the intense displeasure of the Soviets was at once apparent. Russian policy called for a united Communist Germany, nothing less, with Berlin as its capital, and Russian promotion of discord and inefficiency in the four-power government had clearly been designed with that end in view. The three occupation authorities, as a step toward the union they contemplated, also issued a new currency to be used in common throughout western Germany, and in the western-occupied portion of Berlin. On the pretext that this currency reform would "place Berlin's economy and her working population in an untenable situation which only can be solved by Berlin's close connection with the eastern part of Germany," the Soviet authorities laid down a blockade against the movement of supplies from the West into Berlin, whether by rail, highway, or canal. Since there were some two millions of people in the western-occupied section of the city whose lives might depend on the continued importation of food from the West, it seemed clear that the Soviet intent was to force the western powers out of Berlin by the threat of wholesale starvation. With the western powers eliminated, nothing further would stand in the way of the Russians taking over the entire capital city — an important step toward their goal of a united Communist Germany under Russian control.

The answer of the western powers to this new Soviet approach could hardly have been anticipated by the Russians. **The Air-Lift** The air lanes to Berlin were still open, and the western powers at once undertook to fly in the supplies necessary to feed the beleaguered Germans. Both British and American planes were used on the "airlift," which within a matter of days developed an amazing efficiency. New airfields were opened up, and soon coal to keep the people warm and even to keep the factories going was reaching Berlin by air. Hundreds of airplanes were brought from the United States to participate in the operation, and both British and American military pilots got a superb training that the Russians could hardly have overlooked. Even dense fogs and winter weather failed to stop the steady movement across the Russian zone of the all-essential cargoes. General Lucius D. Clay, the United States Military Governor in Germany, stated clearly the American position with reference to Berlin when he said, "They can't drive us out by any action short

The Berlin air-lift carried food and supplies to the otherwise blockaded western sector of Berlin. White lines result from moving planes and vehicles at Berlin's Templehof Airport.

of war." The Russians, however, did everything else they could think of. They withdrew their representative from the *Kommandatura*, set up a separate police in their section of Berlin, excluded the personnel of the lawful city government from the City Hall, which was within their area, and installed a German Communist of their own choosing as mayor. But in spite of all this, month after month, in good weather or bad, the airlift continued. Eventually it was bringing to Berlin more tons of freight per day than the railroads had brought in during their normal operation. Furthermore, the Allies, in retaliation against the blockade of Berlin, established a counter-blockade on goods from Trizonia to the Russian zone of Germany, a devastating blow to the Eastern German economy.

One of the most notable results of the airlift was the change in attitude on the part **Divided** of the Germans toward the west- **Berlin** ern occupational authorities. Armies of occupation are rarely popular, nor do they often deserve to be, and dislike of their conquerors by the Germans, whether in the East or in the West, was intense. But the air-lift did much to make friends among the Germans for all who participated in it, part cularly for the Americans, who bore so

large a proportion of the expense, and furnished so many of the p'anes. With this assurance that they were not to be abandoned, the German leaders went promptly to work on the development of a constitution for the 45,000,000 Germans living in the western occupat:onal zones. The only requirements laid on them were (1) that the new constitution be democratic, (2) that it be based on the federal principle, and (3) that civil liberties be fully guaranteed. Nor need the new constitution be regarded as merely designed for that portion of Germany under western control. If and when the Russians should permit, there would be no bar on the states in eastern Germany joining the new government. In Berlin itself, although the failure of the air-lift wou'd mean dire retribution for all who had supported the western powers, the people in the city's western zones rallied strongly to the support of their deliverers. Eventually a divided city with two separate governments emerged. In the Russian sector, as already noted, the Communists took over, but in the western zones, at a free election held late in the year, which the Russians had urged the people to boycott, well over 80 per cent of the voters came out to register their support of anti-Communist candidates.

Meantime the western powers had exerted themselves in every possible way to induce **Efforts to compromise** the Russian government to accept a compromise settlement. In August, 1948, their ministers in Moscow opened direct negotiations on the subject, and seemingly reached an agreement that in return for western concession of an exclusively Russian-controlled currency in Berlin, the embargo should be lifted. But in Berlin, due to the obduracy of the Russian member of the *Kommandatura*, the implementation of this agreement broke down completely. Finally, in September, the western powers referred the whole matter to the Security Council of the United Nations, charging that it amounted to a threat to world peace. But here, too, every effort at agreement failed. During these proceedings, which were held in Paris, President Truman conceived the idea of sending a special mission to Moscow, headed by Chief Justice Frederic M. Vinson, but Secretary Marshall held that any such action would be an unwarranted snub for the Security Council, and the plan was abandoned. It was generally believed that the Russians no less than the western powers would have been glad to find some face-saving way out of the situation, but the trade barriers were maintained for nearly a year.

Finally, in the spring of 1949, the Russian leaders changed their tactics. Negotiations **End of the Air-Lift** at Lake Success, New York, between a member of the Russian delegation, Jacob Malik, and a representative of the United States Department of State, Philip Jessup, showed that the Russians were now willing to lift their blockade, if at the same time the western powers would end their counter-blockade and agree to a meeting of the Council of Foreign Ministers to discuss the whole German question. Since the western powers had been willing to accept such a settlement all along, the deal was quickly closed. All blockades were lifted May 12, 1949, and the meeting of the Council of Foreign Ministers began on May 23, a meeting that accomplished little.

Meantime, the West German constitu-tional convention had finished its work, and had submitted for approval of **Divided** the eleven West German states **Germany** its plan for a "Federal Republic of Germany." That the Russians had meant to forestall the actual establishment of such a republic was evident, but their hopes were doomed to disappointment. Before the end of the year the "Bonn Constitution," as it was generally called, had been adopted and West Germany had achieved a government of its own, with Konrad Adenauer, a Christian Democrat, as its first Chancellor. To offset this development, the Russians set up in the Soviet zone a so-called German Democratic Republic, with the now familiar Communist-type satellite government. Each of the two German governments claimed to represent all Germany, but for all practical purposes Germany had become two separate nations, with wholly incompatible and antagonistic governments. In eastern Germany, the Soviet leaders also established a German People's Army, ostensibly to relieve the Russian troops of their occupation and defense duties; but when a widespread and violent protest against Communist rule gripped the Soviet zone in June, 1953, the native German troops proved to be wholly undependable, and Russian forces had to be used to quell the riots. In western Germany, by an agreement effective in 1952, Allied troops stayed on, no longer as occupation forces, but as the first line of defense for western Europe against any further Soviet aggression.

Tension over the German situation and the air-lift was heightened by the fact that 1948 was an election year in the **Election** United States. Would the two **of 1948** political parties split on the foreign issue? Could Russia count on dissension in the United States as her ally in the program of expansion she had cut out for herself? It was apparent from the beginning of the campaign that most of the leaders on both sides, Republicans no less than Democrats, were determined that the bipartisan foreign policy to which they had subscribed must not be

Whistle-stop speeches, country-wide in scope, were an important part of President Truman's re-election campaign in 1948 and undoubtedly contributed to his victory.

abandoned. So evident was this that Henry Wallace early announced that he would head a third-party movement in opposition to the "get-tough-with-Russia" program, which, he claimed, would eventually lead the two nations to war. In Wallace's opinion, the old Roosevelt policy of generously conceding to Russia practically everything she wanted was still the only correct policy, and he denounced the Truman administration roundly for abandoning it. He held, further, that on domestic affairs Truman had yielded to the conservatives, and he called for a revival of the New Deal philosophy of the first two Roosevelt administrations. He persuaded Senator Glen H. Taylor of Idaho to join his ticket as Vice-Presidential candidate, and with the enthusiastic cooperation of Communist and "fellow-traveler" leaders a so-called Progressive convention, held in Philadelphia late in the summer, ratified these two self-nominations. Russian sympathy for the Wallace movement was warmly and officially expressed, and the Russian leaders seemed to think that Wallace's candidacy would strike a responsive chord in American hearts.

Both Republicans and Democrats held their conventions in Philadelphia, also, the

Conventions and candidates

Republicans in June and the Democrats in July. The Republicans felt certain of victory, for they had won the mid-term elections of 1946, and they were sure that the Wallace candidacy would cut in heavily on the Democratic vote. For a time it looked as if a strong public demand might force the Republicans to nominate General Dwight D. Eisenhower, but the popular war leader, who might have accepted an unsolicited nomination, was unwilling to fight for it, and accepted instead the presidency of Columbia University. This left Governor Thomas E. Dewey of New York, Senator Robert A. Taft of Ohio, and ex-Governor Harold E. Stassen of Minnesota as the principal candidates. Taft appealed strongly to the old-line conservatives, and Stassen to the younger, more liberal-minded element in the party. But Dewey took pains not to offend either side unduly, and lined up the votes. He was nominated on the second ballot, and at his suggestion the convention chose Governor Earl Warren of California as his running mate. The Republican platform, while by no means ready to abandon all the social gains made during the Roosevelt era, urged that greater responsibility should be given to the states in such matters as housing, conservation, public health, and security for the aged. It favored also "minimum" governmental controls over business, and lauded the American free enterprise system as the "mainspring of material well-being and political freedom." On the moot labor problem, it pledged the party to protect "both workers and employers against coercion and exploitation." The conservatism of these pronouncements was thinly veiled, and reflected well the point of view of the Republican majority in the Eightieth Congress.

The Democrats had little hope of victory. Some of them were so certain of Truman's **Democratic discouragement** defeat that they imitated the Republicans in trying to induce Eisenhower to accept their nomination, with precisely the same result. The more disgruntled then tried to rally around Justice William O. Douglas of the Supreme Court, but they could not induce him to help them. President Truman was thus practically unopposed when the convention met, and was nominated without serious opposition. The Convention experienced some difficulty in finding anyone of prominence willing to accept second place on a ticket that seemed certain of defeat, but at length it chose Senator Alben Barkley of Kentucky, the venerable leader of the Democratic minority in the Senate. The chief excitement in the Democratic convention came from a successful effort, led by Mayor Hubert Humphrey of Minneapolis, to write into the platform a plank calling on Congress to support the President "in guaranteeing these basic and fundamental rights: (1) The right of full and equal political participation, (2) the right of equal opportunity of employment, (3) the right of security of person, and (4) the right of equal treatment in the services and defense of our nation." This action was resented deeply by many southern delegates whose states used the poll-tax and other devices, some legal and some extra-legal, to discriminate against the Negroes, but the platform as finally adopted carried the drastic civil rights plank. It also denounced unsparingly the record of the Eightieth Congress, called for the repeal of the Taft-Hartley Act, advocated an extension of social security benefits and an increase in the minimum wage from 40 cents an hour to 75 cents, urged more adequate federal legislation on housing, and promised strong federal support of farm prices.

On foreign policy the two platforms were in fundamental agreement. Both supported the United Nations warmly, **The truce on foreign policy** while condemning the intemperate use of the veto by Russia. Both stood loyally by the foreign aid program, although the Republicans wished to be more generous to China than the Democrats had been. Both favored full recognition of the new Jewish state of Israel. Both accepted the policy of reciprocal trade agreements as a means of regulating the tariff. When Candidate Dewey criticized the Democratic platform for claiming that the Democrats had originated the bipartisan foreign policy, President Truman countered by appointing Dewey's intimate friend and adviser, John Foster Dulles, as one of the United States representatives to the third session of the United Nations General Assembly, which was to open on September 24 in Paris.

As the campaign got under way all signs pointed to the certainty of Republican victory. Republican chances were **The Dixiecrats** increased when the extreme states-rights faction of the Democratic Party, which had taken such offense at the Civil Rights plank in their party's platform, held a rump convention at Birmingham, Alabama, and nominated a separate States' Rights Democrat or "Dixiecrat" ticket, consisting of Governor J. Strom Thurmond of South Carolina for President and Governor Fielding Wright of Mississippi for Vice-President. It was apparent that this ticket would carry at least three or four states in the Lower South. All of the various public opinion polls predicted with extreme confidence the election of Dewey. Sixty-five per cent of the newspapers of the country supported the Republican candidates. Dewey himself campaigned as if he were a sure winner, avoiding controversial issues, and scarcely recognizing the existence of an opposition.

Truman, on the other hand, conducted a vigorous campaign, almost unaided. He called a special session of the Republican-dominated Eightieth Congress to **Truman** meet in September, right after the nominations, and asked it to put through legislation to halt rising prices, to meet the housing crisis, to protect civil rights, and to take various other steps called for by both platforms. When it adjourned without acting on his suggestions, he toured the country condemning it for its failure to deliver on promises in the Republican platform, and branded it as the worst Congress the nation had ever had. As the campaign wore on, it became apparent that the crowds were coming to hear the President, but were not coming to hear Dewey. Wallace also lost ground as the President hammered home the gains that labor had won and might still expect to win from the Democrats, and pointed out the losses it had suffered, and would continue to suffer, if the Republicans won. But most observers discounted the results of the Truman campaign. People came out just to see a President, they said, and to hear his intemperate remarks. The Wallace vote might not be as heavy as expected, but it would be heavy enough to insure Dewey's victory.

The election results were probably the greatest political upset in all American history. With 49,363,798 voters coming to the polls, more than in any other election except 1940, the Republicans went down to a resounding defeat. Truman failed to capture a majority of all votes cast for President, but his share amounted to 49.5 per cent of the total to Dewey's 45.1 per cent, and 5.4 per cent for all others. The Wallace vote, due in considerable part to the consistency with which Wallace's speeches during the campaign followed the Communist party line, reached only a little over a million, less than 2.5 per cent. In the electoral college, the vote stood Truman 303, Dewey 189, Thurmond 39, Wallace 0. One elector in Tennessee, although chosen on the Truman ticket, voted for Thurmond, otherwise Truman's vote would have been one more, and Thurmond's one less. In the Congressional and State elections the Democratic victory was even more decisive: indeed, 683,382 more voters cast their ballots for state, county, and local can-

Another Democratic landslide

Harry S. Truman

THIRTY-THIRD PRESIDENT of the United States, Truman was the seventh President to achieve office through the death of his predecessor. Like Theodore Roosevelt and Calvin Coolidge, he later won election in his own right. Almost overwhelmed at first by his feeling of inadequacy, he ultimately discharged his duties with pride and confidence. Few Presidents have initiated more important policies.

didates than cast their votes for President. Since, in these elections, well over fifty per cent of the total number of voters cast Democratic rather than Republican ballots, both houses of Congress were overwhelmingly Democratic, and Democratic governors were chosen in most of the states.

Looking backward, it was easier to explain why Truman won than it had been to foresee his victory. The forces of labor had rallied to his standard, and had quietly, but efficiently, got out the labor vote. Middle-western farmers in historically Republican states such as Iowa and Minnesota had voted Democratic because they feared that price supports for agricultural commodities might disappear under Republican rule. The housewives of the nation, harassed by inflationary prices on every purchase they made, remembered Truman's unsuccessful struggle to maintain price ceilings, and the assurances of conservative Republicans that if price ceilings were removed self-regulation would eventually bring prices down. Furthermore, many local Democratic candidates greatly

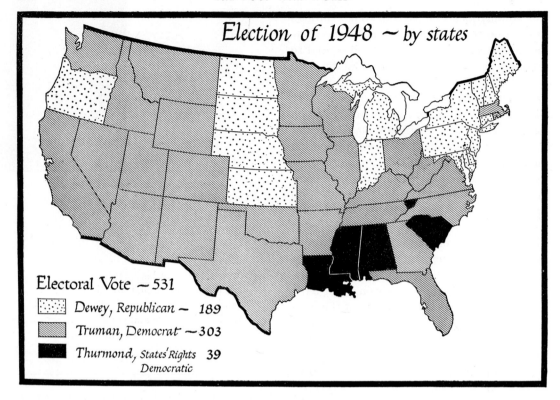

Election of 1948 ~ by states

Electoral Vote ~ 531
Dewey, Republican ~ 189
Truman, Democrat ~ 303
Thurmond, States' Rights 39
Democratic

appealed to the voters, and helped the national ticket along. In Minnesota, for example, the young and popular Mayor Humphrey easily defeated his Republican opponent in the race for senator. In Illinois, Paul Douglas and Adlai E. Stevenson, candidates for senator and governor, respectively, and both dependable Democratic liberals, quite overwhelmed their old-guard Republican opponents. So it was to a great extent throughout the nation. As for the two presidential candidates, Dewey's best efforts failed to convince the voters that he was not cold and calculating, while Truman, for all his lack of dignity, at least proved himself to be thoroughly human and in touch with the common man. Most of all, the election showed that the American people were not yet ready to turn their backs on the New Deal. As Truman so effectively pointed out, that was exactly what the Eightieth Congress had tried to do, and what might be expected from the Republicans, if they succeeded in winning both the executive and

the legislative branches of the government. In a sense, as many observers pointed out, the election of 1948 was the fifth straight victory for Franklin D. Roosevelt.

In spite of the spectacular Democratic triumph, the "Fair Deal" program that Truman submitted to the Eighty- **The "Fair** first Congress failed of complete **Deal"** acceptance. The President's efforts to establish equality of civil rights in the South by means of federal anti-poll tax and anti-lynching laws, and provisions to insure equal job rights for all, met death at the hands of a southern Democratic filibuster. The Republicans, aided by conservative Democrats, saved the Taft-Hartley Act from repeal. The President's ambitious and expensive plans for social security expansion, which included federal aid to schools, a public welfare department in the cabinet, and compulsory national health insurance, lost out.[1]

[1] In its second session, however, Congress extended social security coverage to include about ten million additional persons.

So also did his recommendation that means be found to raise four billion dollars in additional revenue in order to balance the budget, a proposition that the Republican minority insisted would, if carried out, seriously imperil the business life of the nation. The opponents of the President made much of the trend toward "stateism" and the "welfare state," that they professed to see in the "Fair Deal," and predicted the direst results if it should succeed.

Nevertheless the President found it possible to praise the Eighty-first Congress on its adjournment in October, 1949, for its "rather remarkable record of achievement." It had continued rent control to July, 1950, and had voted $2,734,000,000 for slum clearance and low-rent housing. It had balked at a new method of aiding agriculture by direct subsidies, submitted by Secretary of Agriculture Charles F. Brannan, but had agreed to maintain high farm price supports and to provide adequate storage facilities for surplus crops. It had also followed the President's recommendation that minimum wages be raised from 40 to 75 cents per hour.

But it was in the field of foreign affairs that it had given Truman his greatest victories. In his inaugural address the President had summarized in four points the policy he recommended for the United States in combatting the world-wide threat of Communism. The first three points emphasized such familiar ideas as continued support of the United Nations, adequate appropriations for the European Recovery Program, and the speedy conclusion of the North Atlantic Treaty. But "Point Four," which stressed the need of "a bold new program for making the benefits of our scientific advances and industrial progress available for the improvement and growth of underdeveloped areas," proposed a kind of "Fair Deal" for all the world. Congress went a long way toward endorsing the whole Truman foreign policy. It discharged its obligations toward the United Nations; voted $5.8 billion for economic aid under the Marshall Plan; accepted the North Atlantic Treaty; appropriated over $15 billion for national defense, and $1.3 billion for military assistance to the new Allies of the United States; and continued the authority of the State Department to make reciprocal trade agreements. As for "Point Four," Congress felt the need of more specific recommendations before appropriating the $45 million for which the President had asked, but it made $10 million available with which to initiate the program. Had not the Korean War intervened, with the huge expenditures it involved, it is possible that Truman's interest in "underdeveloped areas" might have awakened far greater response. That the free nations must somehow exert themselves to prevent these areas from falling an easy prey to Communism seemed all too apparent.

Bibliography

On the United Nations and its efforts to keep the peace of the world there is an ever-growing list of books. Vera Micheles Dean, *The Four Cornerstones of Peace* (1946), recounts the story of the formation of the United Nations. L. M. Goodrich and E. Hambro, *Charter of the United Nations: Commentary and Documents* (1949); and J. E. Harley, *Documentary Textbook on the United Nations* (1950), are serviceable reference works. *The Record of American Diplomacy: Documents and Readings*, edited by Ruhl J. Bartlett (1947), contains a concluding chapter on the United Nations. Of considerable value also are William G. Carr, *One World in the Making: The United Nations* (2nd ed., 1947); and Louis Dolivet, *The United Nations* (1946). On two of the more important United Nations agencies, see Herman Finer, *The United Nations Economic and Social Council* (1946); and Theodore Besterman, *UNESCO: Peace in the Minds of Men* (1951).

The problems raised by the release of atomic energy have likewise attracted many writers. The story of what happened at Hiroshima is graphically told in John Hersey, *Hiroshima* (1946). David Bradley, *No Place to Hide* (1948), gives the results of the Bikini tests. James R. Newman and B. S. Miller, *The Control of Atomic Energy* (1948), explores the possibilities of international restrictions. On the economic side, see S. H. Schurr and Jacob Marshak, *Economic Aspects of Atomic Power* (1951).

On the post-war foreign policy of the United States, an official view is given in Department of State, Publication No. 3972, *Our Foreign Policy* (1950). Dexter Perkins, *The American Approach to Foreign Policy* (1952), is based on the author's lifelong study of American diplomacy. Vera Micheles Dean, *Europe and the United States* (1950), assesses the existing situation intelligently. Floyd A. Cave and associates, *The Origins and Consequences of World War II* (1948), has excellent chapters on the post-war period. John C. Campbell and others, *The United States in World Affairs, 1948–1949* (1949), concentrates on a short but significant period. Conditions in France and Italy that helped determine American policy are set forth in G. Wright, *The Reshaping of French Democracy* (1948); and M. Grindrod, *The New Italy* (1947).

Relations with Russia would be better understood if penetration of the iron curtain were easier. Walter Lippmann, *The Cold War: A Study in U.S. Foreign Policy* (1947), states the opinions of an experienced publicist. Frederick Barghoorn, *The Soviet Image of the United States; A Study in Distortion* (1950), shows one of the great obstacles to a peaceful settlement. Thomas A. Bailey, *America Faces Russia; Russian-American Relations from Early Times to Our Day* (1950); and W. A. Williams, *American Russian Relations: 1781–1947* (1952), present fully the background

out of which present relationships with Russia have grown. Walter B. Smith, *My Three Years in Moscow* (1950), is an American Ambassador's memoir. Hugh Seton-Watson, *The East European Revolution* (1951), describes the sovietization of Eastern Europe. Other books worth mentioning in this connection are Albert Z. Carr, *Truman, Stalin and Peace* (1950); Vera Micheles Dean, *The United States and Russia* (1948); and E. M. Zacharias, *Behind Closed Doors: The Secret History of the Cold War* (1950).

On Truman's record, Jonathan Daniels, *The Man of Independence* (1950), is laudatory. Pertinent documents are available in Harry S. Truman, *The Truman Program: Addresses and Messages of the President* (1949); and Department of State, *Strengthening the Forces of Freedom: Selected Speeches and Statements of Secretary of State Acheson, February, 1949–April, 1950* (1950). On post-war assistance to war-damaged nations, see *UNRRA: The History of the United Nations Relief and Rehabilitation Administration*, edited by George Woodbridge (3 vols., 1951), an official history; H. S. Ellis, *The Economics of Freedom: The Progress and Future of Aid to Europe* (1950); and Paul G. Hoffman, *Peace Can Be Won* (1951). W. B. Hesseltine, *The Rise and Fall of Third Parties from Anti-Masonry to Wallace* (1948), contains interesting observations on the election of 1948. See also Stanley Walker, *Dewey: An American of this Century* (1944), a campaign biography that served during both the 1944 and 1948 elections. On Truman's much-discussed "Point Four" program, see J. B. Condliffe, "Point Four and the World Economy," in Foreign Policy Association, *Headline Series*, January–February, 1950. Halford L. Hoskins, *The Atlantic Pact* (1949), is clear and to the point.

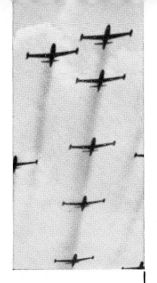

34

The Price of Leadership

The defense problem — Budgetary reductions —
South Korea invaded — UN reaction — The 38th parallel
— Chinese intervention — Military expenditures —
The loyalty issue — McCarthy and McCarran —
Elections of 1950 — The "Great Debate" — Troops
to Europe — The NATO army — Removal of
MacArthur — Stalemate in Korea — Scandals at home
— The 82nd Congress — Election of 1952

SINCE the United States was engaged in a "cold" war with Russia that at any time **The defense** might turn "hot," the American **problem** government could not long be unmindful of the problem of national defense. A National Security Act of July 26, 1947, attempted to capitalize on the experience of the Second World War by uniting under one command all the armed forces of the nation — land, sea, and air. The act created a new Department of Defense to be headed by a Secretary with cabinet rank. Under him, but not of cabinet status, were three other secretaries, one each for the Army, the Navy, and the Air Force. For the first Secretary of Defense President Truman chose his able Secretary of the Navy, James Forrestal, who devoted himself with such intensity to the task of unification as to undermine his health, and to lead to his resignation and untimely death two years later. For the better coordination of command the National Security Act set up a Joint Board of Chiefs of Staff, usually called the Joint Chiefs of Staff, consisting, as presently amended, of an overall chairman and one representative from each of the three services. The act also created several boards with specialized duties: a National Security Council, a National Security Resources Board, a Munitions Board, and a Research and Development Board.

How to get men enough to maintain even the peacetime needs of the American armed forces posed a perplexing problem. It soon became apparent that the volunteering principle, so dear to American tradition, could not be relied upon completely. Occupation duties, especially in Germany and Japan, demanded a steady flow of replacements for the men whose terms expired, and the danger of war with Russia forbade any serious weakening of the nation's fighting power. Army leaders, supported by many civilians, argued earnestly that the fairest way to obtain the needed manpower was through universal military training, and twice the President himself, in 1947 and again in 1948, recommended such a course to Congress. The President's plan called for six months' training for all young men at some time between the ages of eighteen and twenty, after which they might continue in training for another six months, or spend a like period taking some specialized course in college, or enlist in a branch of the armed services, active or reserve. Taking no chances, however, the President also recommended the revival of the selective service system that had served so well during the war. Congress, more mindful of public opposition than the President, refused to go along with him on universal military training, but did pass a new Selective Service Act, which became law on June 24, 1948. This measure provided for the registration of all men between the ages of 18 and 26, but specified that enrollees were not to be drafted until they had reached the age of 19. The term of service was set at twenty-one months; most veterans of the Second World War were exempted; and local boards were permitted to grant yearly deferments to high school and college students who were doing satisfactory work. Although the Selective Service Act of 1948 was designed to be only a temporary measure, its life was subsequently extended, while amendments raised the term of service to two years, permitted the drafting of men eighteen and one-half years old, and authorized also the drafting of such physicians, dentists, and veterinarians as the armed forces might require. Before the outbreak of the Korean War draft quotas could be kept small, or even non-existent, for volunteering was continued and re-enlistments were encouraged. But the Act made available, as its sponsors intended, a manpower pool upon which the armed services could draw whenever the necessity should arise. Meantime the National Guard had been reorganized and revitalized and Reserve Officers Training Corps in the universities maintained.

The gigantic post-war expenditures which the United States felt obliged to undertake **Budgetary** kept federal taxes almost at war **reductions** levels, and made difficult the task of balancing the national budget. Naturally there arose a strong popular demand for economy, a demand to which the Truman administration became increasingly sensitive. Since the outlays for defense accounted for so large a proportion of the national budget, the armed services were inevitably called upon to prepare for substantial reductions. Upon Louis A. Johnson, who succeeded Forrestal as Secretary of Defense, fell the difficult task of cutting expenses while at the same time seeking better coordination between army, navy, and air force activities. Johnson's plans spread the cuts as equitably as possible among the three services, but the navy was particularly aggrieved. With a great portion of the fleet, including all but one battleship, the *Missouri*, already relegated to a state of preservation ("in moth balls"), he stopped construction on a new super-carrier, the *United States*, the keel of which had already been laid. This decision was influenced, no doubt, by the claim of the air force that its gigantic new bomber, the B–36, could carry the atomic bomb from land bases to any part of the world. With the public eager to believe that in case of hostilities strategic bombing could be counted on to win an easy victory, there was much loose talk about "push-button" warfare, and much insistence that the air force should be favored at the expense of the two traditional services. In general, Americans assumed that if war should come it would be fought mainly in Europe, with Russia the principal antagonist of the United States.

Events in Korea soon produced a totally different war from the kind the United States had anticipated, and dem-   **South Korea** onstrated the fallacy of too com-   **invaded** plete reliance on the atomic bomb. Late in 1948 Russia claimed to have withdrawn all its troops from northern Korea, although United Nations inspection to ascertain the truth of this claim was not permitted. During the first six months of 1949, the United States similarly evacuated South Korea, with the exception of some five hundred army officers left to continue the training of the native constabulary. The intent of the American authorities was to make the South Koreans strong enough to defend themselves, but not strong enough to attack across the thirty-eighth parallel, which separated the territory held by the Republic of Korea from the Communist People's Republic. The intent of the Russians, however, seems to have been quite otherwise, for the régime they left in control of North Korea, using Soviet-made tanks and military aircraft, launched on June 25, 1950, a full-scale attack against the American-sponsored Republic of Korea. The planning of this action, which depended so much on Soviet armor and support, could hardly have taken place without Soviet foreknowledge and approval. Furthermore, it was completely in line with the teachings of Lenin, who had written:

The existence of the Soviet Republic side by side with imperialistic states for a long time is unthinkable. One or the other must triumph in the end. And before that end supervenes a series of frightful collisions between the Soviet Republic and the bourgeois states is inevitable.

Unwittingly the American Secretary of State, Dean Acheson, might have promoted this aggression by a public statement he had made in January, 1950, to the effect that the United States did not consider Korea vital to the national security. For this statement he thought he had the backing of responsible military authorities, and by it he could hardly have meant that the United States would be unwilling to defend the Republic of Korea in case it should be attacked. But the Russians and the North Koreans, convinced that they had the power to overwhelm the weak South Korean forces, may have decided that Acheson's words amounted, in effect, to assurance that an invading force would have nothing to fear from the United States. Here was an opportunity to gain an easy victory, and to advance a long step toward the goal of world Communism. For with Korea in Communist hands, Japan would be a natural next target; or, supposing that the United States and its allies intervened in force, their position in Europe might be so weakened as to make possible a Russian attack there. Whatever the line of reasoning that lay back of this move, the North Korean infantry, preceded by powerful tank columns, forced its way into Seoul, the South Korean capital, within three days' time, and drove back the inadequately armed South Koreans all along the border.

On the same day that the North Korean invasion began, the Security Council of the

UN reaction United Nations met at the request of the United States to

Korea

consider the Korean situation. At this meeting, as for some time past, Soviet Russia, in protest against the continued participation in Council activities of Nationalist China, was not represented; hence, it was possible for the Council to adopt a resolution presented by the United States which branded the North Korean action as a breach of the peace, and which demanded that the invaders withdraw to their side of the thirty-eighth parallel. Two days later, the Council also urged members of the United Nations to furnish such assistance as they could to help the South Koreans repel the attack. It is worth noting that neither of these votes could have passed had the Russian delegate been present to interpose a veto; and also, that the Soviets, on the ground that Russia had not been represented, held both votes to be illegal. Before the second vote was taken, President Truman had ordered American forces to assist the South Koreans by sea and air, and on the last day of the month American ground forces landed in Korea to participate in what the President called a "police action, not a war."

Truman was much criticized in some quarters for sending in troops without first obtaining a declaration of war by Congress. No doubt he was motivated mainly by the fact that to wait until such a declaration could be made would be to give the game away; unless speedy action could be taken, the North Koreans would win. But he asserted that the United States, by accepting the charter of the United Nations, had given him power, as commander-in-chief of the armed forces, to counter the attack that had taken place. By way of emphasizing the limited nature of the hostilities he had authorized, Truman also ordered the United States Seventh Fleet to prevent Communist China from attacking Nationalist Formosa, and vice versa, since any such action might threaten the position of the United States in the Far East. The determination of the future of Formosa, he maintained, must "await the restoration of security in the Pacific." On July 7, the Security Council authorized a unified command under the United Nations flag for all United Nations forces in Korea, and requested the United States to designate the commanding officer. To implement this action President Truman on July 9 named General MacArthur supreme commander of United Nations forces in Korea. For the first time in its history the new world organization was now prepared to use force in an effort to ward off aggression. For the first time, too, it was attempting to act without the support of one of the great powers, Russia. Unwilling to be left out of the deliberations of the Security Council any longer, the Russian representative returned on August 1, but he was unable to undo the action that had been taken in his absence.

Support of the stand taken by the United States and approved by the Security Council **World opinion on Korea** was general among those members of the United Nations not held in thralldom behind the iron curtain. The brunt of the fighting in Korea fell at first to the armed forces of the United States, and American participants at all times far exceeded in numbers all others put together, except for the South Koreans. Nevertheless, naval forces from Great Britain, Australia, Canada, New Zealand, France, and the Netherlands were soon operating with American warships in Korean waters, while in due time the total number of land, sea, and air participants on the United Nations side had reached sixteen. Throughout the free world, there was the greatest enthusiasm for the task that had been undertaken and complete belief in the righteousness of the common cause. Reports from a United Nations committee in Korea supplied conclusive evidence that the North Korean attack had been a deliberate breach of the peace, and that the South Koreans had done nothing to provoke it. The North Koreans, however, echoed by Soviet Russia and Communist China, held that the South Koreans had been first to cross the thirty-eighth parallel and had started the war. Since the North Koreans had from the beginning a great preponderance of troops, and a tremendous advantage in heavy armor and aircraft, the contention that they were not the attackers carried little weight.

For a time it seemed that the intervention of the United Nations might not serve to stem the invasion tide. As **The War in Korea** Syngman Rhee, the South Korean President, complained bitterly, it was the same old story of "too little and too late." American forces hurriedly landed from Japan cooperated as fully as possible with the South Koreans, and the navy maintained a tight blockade, but within six weeks the whole of South Korea, with the exception of a small triangle in the southeast adjacent to the port of Pusan, had been overrun. To add to the gloom, Major-General William F. Dean, commander of the United States Twenty-fourth Division, was taken prisoner late in July. The United Nations troops were heartened, however, by the success of their aircraft in attacking North Korean supply lines, by the excellent use they were making of a new bazooka in attacks on the Soviet-made tanks they encountered, and by the news of a landing in mid-September on the western coast of Korea at Inchon.

The Inchon landing was a difficult amphibious undertaking the success of which was by no means assured in advance. All went well, however, thanks in large part to the careful planning and the heavy shelling and bombing that preceded the attack. The Inchon invaders, consisting of both American and South Korean troops, soon drove a deep wedge into Communist-held territory, took back Seoul, and forced a general withdrawal of the North Koreans to the vicinity of the thirty-eighth parallel. Here the fighting might have been stabilized, but such a course would have left Korea divided, with the South Koreans in constant danger of further attacks from their predatory northern neighbors. So great was the confusion of the North Korean forces after the Inchon landing that, from a military point of view, the complete conquest of all the territory held by the People's Democratic Republic appeared to be easily possible.

Any such action, however, involved a political as well as a military decision, one **The thirty-eighth parallel** which the United Nations was obliged to make. With Russia again represented in the Security Council it was obvious that a Russian veto would prevent any action by that body, so a bloc of eight nations led by the United States turned instead for support to the General Assembly. The resolution they offered, adopted October 7, sanctioned the taking of such appropriate steps as might be necessary to stabilize conditions throughout all Korea, including the establishment for the war-torn nation of a unified democratic government. This action gave MacArthur full, if only tacit, authority to advance north of the thirty-eighth parallel, and aroused the fears of all who believed that Communist China, if pressed too far, might take a hand in the fighting. As early as October 1, the prime minister of Red China, Chou En-lai, had announced pointedly that the Chinese people would "not stand aside should the imperialists wantonly invade the territory of their neighbors," and a few days later Sir Benegal Rau, representing India, urged strongly that the resolution be modified. Nevertheless, the Assembly ignored these warnings, and not only authorized by implication the occupation of all North Korea, but also hinted strongly that United Nations forces would be left in charge until the ultimate goal of a free, democratic, and united Korea could be achieved.

Armed now with the authority he needed, MacArthur first called on the North Korean command to surrender, then, **Conquest of North Korea** when it ignored his summons, launched an all-out attack with the occupation of all North Korea as his goal. The Communist capital, Pyongyang, was soon taken, and United Nations troops moved up the peninsula as rapidly as the difficult terrain and the bitterly cold weather would permit. The uneasiness of United Nations authorities over the reaction of Red China to the invasion revealed itself in their persistent efforts to assure the Chinese Communists that United Nations troops would stop at the Manchurian border. In order the better to assess the situation, President Truman even took the extraordinary step of flying to Wake Island in the Pacific for a conference, held October 15, with General MacArthur. Apparently MacArthur convinced the President that there was no danger of Chinese intervention, but the General also warned United Nations flyers to regard as a buffer zone a forty-mile strip south of the Manchurian frontier, and to avoid bombing the huge hydroelectric power plants on the southern bank of the Yalu River, upon which Manchurian as well as North Korean industries depended so heavily.

Despite all these gestures of good-will, it soon became apparent that the closer the United Nations forces came to **Chinese intervention** the Manchurian border the stiffer the resistance they met, a change easily traced to the appearance among the

THE NATURAL ENEMY. The rugged Korean terrain made military operations hazardous.

BLOODY COMBAT. Hilly country kept the fighting at close range and advances were frequently measured from hill to hill.

The Korean War, fought to halt Communist aggression in Asia, became intensely unpopular with the American people, and with the men who fought it. Without this display of force, however, the Communists would have achieved an easy approach to Japan, which might well have become their next victim.

North Korean troops of Chinese "volunteers." That these "volunteers" were present in large numbers was known after November 1, when Chinese units ambushed and disastrously defeated an American regiment near Unsan. The same day United Nations flyers, long accustomed to easy control of the skies, met numerous Communist aircraft, including the first jet planes they had encountered in Korea. General MacArthur, in reporting the rapidly changing situation, charged the Chinese Reds with "one of the most offensive acts of international lawlessness of historic record," but he still thought that he could win, and ordered an all-out attack that was designed, he said, to get the men out of the trenches by Christmas. Unfortunately MacArthur's attack was met on November 26 by a Chinese counter-attack in such force and with such persistence as to leave the greatly outnumbered United Na-

tions troops no alternative but to retreat. This they did in good order, although units on the right flank, which in some instances had reached the Manchurian border, were unable to escape by land, and fell back hurriedly to the port of Hungnam for a notable rescue by sea. Late in December Lieutenant-General Walton H. Walker, commander of the United States Eighth Army and of all the United Nations ground forces, was killed in an automobile accident. To succeed him, Lieutenant-General Matthew B. Ridgway was chosen. The initial Chinese attack was followed by another early in January, 1951, which drove United Nations forces out of Seoul, and by still others which rapidly pushed them back to new defensive positions approximately fifty miles to the south of the thirty-eighth parallel. Later that same month, however, the United Nations troops, regrouped and reinforced, began to move

SEOUL-PYONGYANG DEATH MARCH. This photograph of the forced march of American prisoners, responsible for many fatalities, was identified by a survivor.

TRUCE NEGOTIATIONS. UN delegate, Gen. William Harrison, and Communist delegate, Gen. Nam Il, signing armistice document at Panmunjom after many months of negotiating.

forward, and by early April were astride the famous parallel, a position they were to occupy without appreciable change for a period of over two years.

From the first day of the North Korean attack, in June, 1950, the American people had followed events in Korea with excited interest. In general they had approved the decisions of the American President and the United Nations to strike back at the aggressor; even Henry Wallace came out in support of Truman's course, an act which ended his usefulness to the Communist-dominated Progressive party he had led in 1948. But there were also criticisms. Some were inclined to blame the Truman administration for not foreseeing the North Korean attack, and for acting on the assumption, as Secretary Acheson had said, that Korea was not essential to national security. Wise after

American opinion on Korea

the event, they could point out that it might have been better to have found some way to leave American troops a little longer in Korea. Most Americans believed that the Soviet leaders had inspired the attack and that the real enemy behind the scenes was Russia. But they were annoyed at the success of the Russian strategy. The United States, instead of being able to demonstrate its superiority in atomic warfare, was required to fight in a manner for which it was by no means well prepared. With its army at minimum strength, and its navy mostly de-commissioned, it stood in sore need of both. Even the air force had been obliged to cut down on its program for expansion, and air protection for the United Nations troops in Korea was an obvious necessity. Politically speaking, the situation demanded a scapegoat, and one was quickly found in the person of the Secretary of Defense, Louis A.

Generals James Van Fleet and Matthew B. Ridgway
shared the problems of command in the Korean War. Political rather than military
considerations barred their way to a complete victory, but the restraints imposed on
them were designed to avert a third World War.

Johnson, who had implemented the economy drive. To succeed Johnson, President Truman called on his former Secretary of State, General Marshall, whose health had recovered sufficiently to enable him to accept the post.

Congress, meantime, had reversed the economy trend in which it had once taken **Military ex-** such pride, and had begun to **penditures** vote huge sums for national defense. Eventually it supplemented its original figure of $13 billion for this purpose in the 1950 budget by an additional $27 billion. Before the end of the year 200,000 men had been inducted into service, and four national guard divisions had been called up, bringing the total ground forces of the United States to about a million men. For all three branches — army, navy, and air force — President Truman announced an ultimate goal of three million men. In working out the new defense program, not only the needs of the American forces in Korea had to be considered, but also the American contribution to the defense of Europe. In

September, 1950, the Council of the North Atlantic Treaty Organization (NATO) announced its determination to form "an integrated military force" adequate to defend "the freedom of Europe." It was understood, of course, that the United States would have to furnish much of the money needed for this purpose, but whatever reluctance Congress might once have felt about assuming such a burden was greatly modified by the fact that Russia, according to President Truman's announcement of September 23, 1949, now had the atomic bomb. The people of the United States had known all along that the defenses of Europe were paper thin, but they had counted on the exclusive possession by the United States of the atomic bomb as an important deterrent to Russian attack. Now that the Russians were, or would soon be, in a position to wage atomic warfare, the overwhelming preponderance of Russian might in Europe took on a new significance. The Mutual Defense Assistance Act of 1949, passed on the heels of Truman's announcement, together with

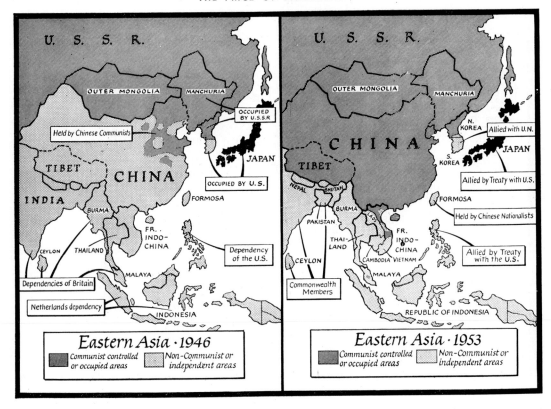

Eastern Asia · 1946
Communist controlled or occupied areas | Non-Communist or independent areas

Eastern Asia · 1953
Communist controlled or occupied areas | Non-Communist or independent areas

an amendment passed in the summer of 1950, made over three and one-half billion dollars available for military aid to foreign nations, principally to those of the NATO group.

Necessary as these huge expenditures seemed to be, many prominent Americans were alarmed at the economic risk involved in making them. Substantial increases in taxation were unavoidable, and Congress in two measures, the first passed in September, 1950, and the second in January, 1951, raised corporate, income, and excise taxes to the high levels endurable only in war time. The excess profits tax levied by the January act added a 77 per cent tax, retroactive to July, 1950, on all corporate earnings above the 1946–49 level, while at the same time increasing the regular corporate rates from 45 per cent to 47 per cent. Even so an unbalanced budget became a certainty. To combat the danger of inflation, a Defense

The economic front

Production Act, signed September 8, 1950, gave the President authority to seek voluntary cooperation from labor and business leaders in keeping wages and prices from soaring, but authorized him to use more forceful measures if necessary. The President added still further to his powers on December 16, 1950, by declaring a national emergency. Soon a variety of alphabetical agencies, reminiscent of the Second World War, were beginning to function, including an Office of Price Stabilization (OPS), a Wage Stabilization Board (WSB), and possibly most important of all, an Office of Defense Mobilization (ODM), the last-mentioned under the able direction of Charles E. Wilson, formerly president of the General Electric Company. The ability of the nation to produce for war was again put to the test and was again found equal to the task. But the emergency was not so great as to justify in the eyes of the public the restraints that had been cheerfully accepted during the

Income Taxes, 1950

NET INCOME BEFORE EXEMPTIONS	SINGLE PERSON NO DEPENDENTS		MARRIED COUPLE NO DEPENDENTS		MARRIED COUPLE 2 DEPENDENTS	
	FORMER TAX	NEW TAX	FORMER TAX	NEW TAX	FORMER TAX	NEW TAX
$ 800	$ 40	$ 44.60	$	$	$	$ ....
1,000	80	89.20	....	....	......	....
1,500	....	....	60	66.90	......	....
2,000	280	312.20	160	178.40	......	....
3,000	488	544.40	360	401.40	120	133.80
4,000	708	790.40	560	624.40	320	356.80
5,000	944	1,054.00	760	847.40	520	579.80
8,000	1,780	1,994.00	1,416	1,580.80	1,152	1,285.60
10,000	2,436	2,730.00	1,888	2,108.00	1,592	1,777.60
15,000	4,448	4,970.00	3,260	3,648.00	2,900	3,240.00
20,000	6,942	7,764.00	4,872	5,460.00	4,464	5,004.00
25,000	9,796	10,942.00	6,724	7,512.00	6,268	7,008.00
50,000	26,388	28,468.00	19,592	21,884.00	18,884	21,092.00
100,000	66,798	69,690.00	52,776	56,936.00	51,912	56,036.00
300,000	247,274	252,166.00	222,572	229,356.00	221,504	228,276.00
500,000	429,274	436,166.00	403,548	412,332.00	402,456	411,228.00
1,000,000	870,000	880,000.00	858,548	872,332.00	857,456	871,228.00

Second World War. Civilian goods continued to flow from American factories, although in diminished quantities, while purchasing power, thanks to the stepped-up defense spending, grew by leaps and bounds. The result was another series of price rises and wage increases that added materially to the cost of living for the ordinary individual. In industries where wage increases lagged, strikes or the threat of strikes brought results. Only by the direct intervention of the President, first in August, 1950, and again in February, 1951, were crippling strikes by railroad workers avoided. In the latter instance railroad switchmen, on the pretense of illness, deserted their posts, and returned only when the President ordered them to do so or be discharged.

The unsettled conditions in the country, coupled with actual warfare against Communist forces in Korea, led to **The loyalty issue** much agitation over the issue of loyalty. That the purpose of Communist party leadership was to overthrow the government of the United States by force and violence was the verdict of a federal jury in New York, which in the fall of 1949 convicted eleven outstanding Communists on this charge. Critics of the labor unions maintained that Communists had won actual control of many unions, and were deliberately fomenting labor unrest. Deeply concerned by these accusations, conservative labor leaders, such as Philip Murray, President of the C.I.O., made every effort to root out Communist office-holders from the unions under their control. Similar charges against college and university faculties led to some dismissals, and to an increasing tendency to require special loyalty oaths of teachers. There were charges, too, that Communists had worked their way into the federal government, particularly into the State Department. The outstanding case in this connection was that of Alger Hiss, who had held a position in the State Department from 1936 to 1947, had attended the Yalta meeting of the Big Three, and had been secretary-general of the San Francisco Conference which had drawn up the United Nations Charter. Hiss, on the basis of revelations made by Whittaker Chambers, a confessed ex-Communist, was convicted of perjury in January, 1950, and was sentenced to five years in prison for having sworn that he was not a Communist. The very next month Dr. Klaus Fuchs, a naturalized British citizen who had worked with both the British and the American teams on atomic research, confessed to British authorities that he had turned over to Russian agents vitally important secrets relating to the atomic bomb. He was promptly tried, convicted, and sentenced. Others convicted of helping reveal atomic secrets to Russia included Julius Rosenberg, an engineer, and his wife Ethel; Morton Sobell, an electronics expert; David Greenglass, Mrs. Rosenberg's brother; and Henry Gold, a biochemist. The Rosenbergs were convicted of treason, and after a long delay were executed in June, 1953; all the others drew long prison terms. It is probable that the secrets so obtained by the Russians did enable them to hasten the work of constructing an atomic bomb. It should not be forgotten, however, that Russian scientists, aided by numerous captured German scientists, were already hot on the trail, and were practically certain of eventual success.

Inevitably the anti-Communist issue found its way into politics. Senator Joseph R. McCarthy, a Republican from Wisconsin, charged that there were large numbers of Communist sympathizers and bad security risks in the State Department, and spearheaded an attack upon the Secretary of State. Acheson, McCarthy claimed, had failed to screen his subordinates properly and had been far too tender toward Communist interests in the Far East. Many of the charges made by McCarthy and his sympathizers lacked supporting evidence, but those who were interested in discrediting the Truman Administration demanded little by way of proof, and raised the battle-cry, "Acheson

McCarthy and McCarran

must go!" Responding to the anti-Communist furor, Congress in September, 1950, passed the McCarran Internal Security Act, which required all Communist and Communist-front organizations to register with the Attorney General, forbade aliens who had ever been Communists to enter the country, discriminated in naturalization proceedings against Communists who had already entered, and empowered the government to hold Communists and their kind in detention camps during time of war. The bill was vetoed by the President, who expressed particular concern with the way in which "Communist-front" organizations could be defined to interfere with the civil rights of individuals. But Congress was not to be denied, and passed the bill over the President's veto.

The mid-term Congressional elections of 1950 registered a general attitude of uneasiness and irritation on the part of the American people. The elections came before Chinese intervention had become a serious factor in Korea, and while it was supposed that victory for the United Nations forces was in sight. But the Korean War, win or lose, was intensely unpopular with a certain number of voters, and there were many who believed that it had come to pass because of blunders made by the Truman administration. The reappearance of excessively high taxes, an unbalanced budget, and inflation also found little favor with the electorate, while the party in power was held responsible, justly or unjustly, for permitting occasional Communists and Communist-sympathizers to worm their way into government service. The number of Communist party members in the country was relatively insignificant, and their power for evil could not have been as great as charged, but the McCarthy allegations, constantly reiterated, definitely hurt the Democrats and helped the Republicans. When the voting was over, the Senate remained Democratic, but only by a majority of 49 to 47, while in the House the Democratic lead was cut from about sixty to about thirty seats. Senator

Elections of 1950

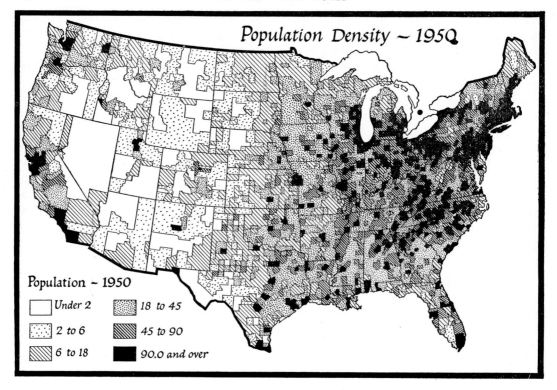

Population Density ~ 1950

Population ~ 1950

☐ Under 2	▦ 18 to 45
▦ 2 to 6	▨ 45 to 90
▨ 6 to 18	■ 90.0 and over

Taft of Ohio was triumphantly re-elected, in spite of strong opposition from labor and administration leaders, while Senator Tydings of Maryland, a Democrat who had defended the State Department against McCarthy's charges, was defeated, although only by the use of highly questionable tactics on the part of his opponents.

Hard on the heels of the election there followed an acrimonious debate over American **The "Great** foreign policy. The "Great **Debate"** Debate," as it was sometimes called, began on December 20, 1950, with a radio-television address by Herbert Hoover. The venerable ex-President urged that the threat of Communism could best be met by strengthening the defenses of the Western Hemisphere, particularly with reference to sea- and air-power. He cautioned the nation against sending its armies on vain missions to police the various threatened areas of the world. European nations, he asserted, were not doing enough to protect themselves, and

were relying altogether too much on American aid. Until they, themselves, had "organized and equipped combat divisions of such huge numbers as would erect a sure dam against the red flood," the United States should refuse to "land another man or another dollar on their shores." As for the Far East, Japan should be encouraged to re-arm in its own defense, and the non-Communist nations should not commit their "sparse ground forces" in a hopeless test of strength with Red China. Far better for the United States, with the aid of Great Britain and the British Commonwealth, to "hold the Atlantic and Pacific Oceans, with one frontier on Britain (if she wishes to cooperate); the other, on Japan, Formosa, and the Philippines." Hoover's thinly veiled isolationism was promptly attacked by Secretary Acheson, who likened it to "sitting quivering in a storm cellar waiting for whatever fate others may wish to prepare for us." The United States, he insisted, "must remain true to standing by its friends." John Foster Dulles, although a Republican, was equally outspoken. He saw no need to "crawl back into our own hole in a vain hope of defending ourselves against all the rest of the world," and pointed out that "solitary defense is never impregnable." And from Thomas E. Dewey came a call to "make united and mighty the forces of the free world, and swiftly, or we shall soon be isolated and left to die." Hoover countered with another speech in February, 1951, and as time went on new champions on both sides entered the fray, repeating all the familiar arguments for and against full participation by the United States in world affairs.

In Congress the debate centered on the intention of the administration to send more **Troops to** troops from the United States to **Europe** Europe. The appointment late in 1950 of General Dwight D. Eisenhower to head the NATO forces in western Europe, followed by the establishment of a Supreme Headquarters of the Allied Powers in Europe (SHAPE) at Rocquencourt near Paris, made it essential for the United States to reach a decision on this vital issue. Senator Taft agreed with ex-President Hoover that sea- and air-power were the primary essentials for the protection of the United States, and doubted the constitutional right of the President "to send troops to fight in Europe" under the authority of the North Atlantic Treaty. Senator Wherry, a Republican from Nebraska, went so far as to introduce into the Senate a resolution stating that no more troops should be sent to Europe until Congress had adopted a policy on the subject. Finally, however, when General Eisenhower, a potential Republican candidate for the Presidency, testified before the Senate Foreign Relations Committee that four United States divisions in addition to the two already in Europe were needed to insure the success of the NATO army, the Senate gave in, although it adopted a qualifying resolution that "no ground troops in addition to such four divisions" should be sent to Europe without Congressional approval. Since this resolution had not the force of law, the administration still adhered to the view that the President, as Commander-in-Chief, might send troops anywhere he chose, but it could not be unmindful of the fact that Congress held the purse-strings.

The process of achieving Western European unity in the cause of mutual defense proved to be long and arduous. **The NATO** Contributions from outside Eu- **army** rope to the NATO forces included, besides the six divisions from the United States, three armored divisions from Great Britain, and a brigade from Canada. That the nations of western Europe should furnish the bulk of NATO manpower was taken for granted, but difficulties arose because of American insistence that the new Federal Republic of West Germany must do its part. France, having felt the might of a German army in three disastrous invasions, had no desire to see a revival of German militarism, and refused for a long time her consent to German rearmament. Many West Germans, repelled by the very thought of war, were equally reluctant to allow their nation to re-arm. They, and some other Europeans, found it convenient, instead, to embrace the somewhat untenable doctrine of "neutralism," according to which their various countries would remain neutral in any conflict that might arise between the United States and Russia. Finally, in an effort to avoid the creation of an independent German army, the French proposed that there be set up a unified European Defense Community, consisting of France, Italy, West Germany, Belgium, the Netherlands, and Luxembourg. These nations, by pooling all their military resources under a single command, with a joint defense fund, a uniform system of procurement and supply, and an integrated general staff, could effectively, it was hoped, avoid all risk of conflict among themselves, while at the same time presenting a solid front against the common enemy. A total of forty-three such divisions was planned, fourteen from France, twelve from West Germany, twelve from Italy, and five

The NATO Army. Trainees from seven Treaty nations receiving instruction at Fort Benning, Georgia.

NATO Flag. Venetian Lion of San Marco, for centuries the symbol of the West's defense against the East, over command headquarters on Posilippo, Italy.

NATO, the North Atlantic Treaty Organization, was created to integrate the defenses of the Atlantic community. Contributions to the international forces were expected from all member nations. After much debate, Congress authorized the sending of four U.S. divisions for NATO duty in Europe.

Canadian Jets. Final inspection of fighter wing before leaving for NATO base.

from the Benelux countries, comprising altogether 1,290,000 men. During the latter half of the year 1951, plans for the adoption of this scheme went forward rapidly, although with considerable misgivings on the part of the United States because of the delay it might involve in the organization of German divisions.

As time went on, however, the enthusiasm of the American government for the European Defense Community (EDC) grew, while the French began to repent their willingness to permit German rearmament, and persistently postponed ratification. One reason for the change in the French attitude was the growing strength of NATO, which by 1953 had enough troops and material under the command of SHAPE to diminish materially the danger of a Russian attack. Another was the remarkable resurgence of western Germany, which, after the adoption of a new currency system and the institution of the new government at Bonn, went to work with a will, and prospered as no other European country prospered. With the French obliged to meet the heavy military demands of the war in Indo-China and to garrison their troubled holdings in North Africa, how could they prevent Germany from dominating EDC, and assuming the leadership of western Europe? Finally, in August, 1954, the French Parliament definitely turned its back on EDC, leaving the problem of German rearmament unsolved.

Inevitably the program of American aid to Europe for rearmament tended to replace to a considerable degree the program of Marshall Plan aid for economic recovery. For European nations the shift in emphasis was very significant. Under the Marshall Plan they had used American money to rebuild their railroads, to re-tool their factories, to facilitate the greater production of civilian goods, to make living conditions for Europeans more comfortable. But military aid was designed to stimulate the production of war materials; furthermore, European nations were now expected to divert additional funds from their already overburdened budgets for rearmament. These added sums strained to the limit the economies of the nations concerned. Countries that, with the assistance of Marshall aid, had just begun to regain their economic health found that the new heavy expenditures for defense tended to involve them again in the familiar cycle of higher prices, wage increases, and inflation. Under such circumstances a rising tide of "neutralism" and anti-Americanism was all too plainly perceptible.

Despite this discouraging situation, the nations of western Europe had charted a path toward union that, given the will to follow it, might eventually lead to a remarkable transformation.

European union

A Council of Europe, created in 1949, had by the end of 1951 come to embrace every nation west of the "iron curtain," excepting only Austria, Yugoslavia, Spain, Portugal, and Switzerland. The Council functioned through two bodies, a Committee of Ministers and a Consultative Assembly, but it lacked any real authority to bind member nations. Its discussions, however, kept alive the idea of European union, and gave support to other and more effective efforts. Fraught with far greater significance was the adoption by France, West Germany, Italy, and the Benelux countries of a plan sponsored by Robert Schuman,[1] at the time the French minister of foreign affairs, for the creation of the European Coal and Steel Community (ECSC), a kind of superstate. The purpose of ECSC was to bring into existence a single "High Authority" which could break down the economic barriers that each nation, in seeking to protect its own coal and steel industries, had built up against every other. As constituted, the High Authority was composed of nine members who were responsible only to an Assembly chosen by the participating governments. To this High Authority each government renounced its right of regulation and control over the industries concerned; in all six nations the rules laid down by the High Authority had the force of law. With headquarters at Luxembourg, the new economic superstate was soon making a promising beginning at cutting down tariffs, eliminating quotas, and altering discriminatory freight rates. Moreover, the money to keep it going came, not from the governments of the various nations that by control of the purse strings might have starved it to death, but from dues paid willingly to the Authority by the industries it controlled. Optimists hoped that successful cooperation in the limited sphere of coal and steel would spread to other areas until eventually most of western Europe

[1] The idea should be credited to another Frenchman, Jean Monnet, who eventually presided over the High Authority.

would enjoy something approximating the freedom of trade that existed within and among the United States of America.

The need for an effective political union back of the economic union represented by ECSC and the proposed military union of EDC was too obvious to be overlooked. Accordingly, representatives of the six co-operating nations in the spring of 1953 devised and submitted a plan for a supra-national authority with a two-house Parliament, the upper chamber to be chosen by the governments of the nations concerned and the lower by the people directly. There would be also an executive, with the premier responsible to the Parliament, and a court of justice through which the powers of the new organization could be determined. These powers, it was well understood, were to be limited strictly to matters pertaining to ECSE and EDC. Progress toward the implementation of this program, however, seemed hopelessly checked when France rejected EDC. As for the various plans proposed for the extending of the principle of union to all the nations of western Europe, the obstacles were formidable indeed. Great Britain, in particular, while friendly enough to the idea of intergovernmental cooperation, was totally unwilling to consider bowing to any supranational authority.

Beset with their own problems, and fearful of what Soviet Russia might be planning to **European** do to them, the nations of west-**opinion on** ern Europe showed little enthu-**Korea** siasm for prolonging the war in Korea. With obvious reluctance, the Assembly of the United Nations on February 1, 1951, adopted a resolution, sponsored by the United States, which branded Communist China as an aggressor, and called upon member nations to continue the fight. This action constituted in fact a considerable expansion of the Assembly's powers, but with the Security Council tied down by the inevitable Russian veto, the American delegation saw no alternative course short of complete frustration. But it was one thing to call Red China an aggressor, and quite another to try

to drive her forces out of North Korea. The European powers held, almost unanimously, that it would be far better to make peace on the basis of restoring the thirty-eighth parallel as a dividing line between North and South Korea than by an all-out attack to run the risk of bringing Russia to the defense of Red China, and so starting a third World War. Nations that had maintained a studious neutrality, such as India, also counseled restraint. Would it not be better to convince Red China of the futility of further fighting, and make peace as soon as possible? President Truman and his advisers tended more and more to accept this point of view. In spite of the fact that the United States was supplying about 90 per cent of the non-Korean manpower to fight the war, the American nation was hardly in a position to fly in the face of world opinion. If the United States wished to have friends and allies, it must have some respect for the views they maintained.

With this new line of reasoning General MacArthur was in profound disagreement. At the time the intervention of **Removal of** Red China assured his defeat at **MacArthur** the Yalu River, he had expressed the opinion that the United Nations was up against an "entirely new war." As he saw it, the rules that had applied while the North Koreans were doing their own fighting should now be discarded. He found particularly exasperating the restriction imposed on him against bombing enemy air bases in Manchuria, from which Communist planes took off freely, and to which they returned in complete security. He held, also, that the destruction of the Manchurian supply lines upon which the Chinese depended for their Korean activities was equally essential. Further, he favored a blockade of the Chinese coast to prevent the importation of war goods by Red China, and to cripple the economic life of the aggressor nation. He believed, too, that the closest possible relationship should be established with Chiang Kai-shek on Formosa, and that Chiang should be encouraged to invade the mainland of China if he could. Nor did he think that any or all of these measures would result in bringing Russia into the war. Not content with registering his opinions through regular channels in Washington, General MacArthur found frequent opportunity to make his views public. As early as July 31, 1950, he had taken occasion to visit Chiang Kai-shek in Formosa, in order to confer with the Chinese Nationalist leader on the defenses of the island. In February, 1951, after the United Nations forces in Korea had regained the initiative from the Chinese, he asserted on a trip to the front that any thought of advancing beyond the thirty-eighth parallel was "purely academic" as long as the Communists were allowed to operate unhampered from their "sanctuary" in Manchuria. Finally, on March 24, 1951, he offered to "confer in the field with the commander-in-chief of the enemy forces" with regard to terms of peace, but hinted broadly that, if the Reds would not listen to reason, the United Nations might depart from its "tolerant" attitude, and attack the "coastal areas and interior bases" of Red China. Whether or not MacArthur, in taking the stand he did, was guilty of insubordination will be long debated, but President Truman and the Joint Chiefs of Staff, who had no intention of pursuing any such course, were outraged, and decided on his recall. In a public statement, released April 11, 1951, the President expressed his "deep regret" that because General Douglas MacArthur was "unable to give his wholehearted support to the policies of the United States Government and of the United Nations in matters pertaining to his official duties" he would have to go. To replace him, both in Japan and in Korea, the President and the Joint Chiefs chose General Ridgway, and to replace Ridgway, General James A. Van Fleet.[1]

The dismissal of General MacArthur gave

Americans who were at odds with Truman's policy in the Far East an opportunity to vent their feelings anew. When the General returned to the United States he was given a series of magnificent ovations, culminating in his appearance before a joint session of the House and Senate in Washington, April 19, 1951. MacArthur at this time and later continued his attack on the weakness of the administration's Korean policy. He gave little comfort to those who decried the very existence of the war and blamed Truman for it, since he held that the decision to counter North Korean aggression was correct. What he advised was more rigorous prosecution of the war, not less, and the more drastic punishment of Red China for her intervention. MacArthur's comments revived "the great debate" over American foreign policy. The whole course of American action, not only in the Far East but elsewhere, came again under review. There were some now who even argued that the Asiatic interests of the United States were paramount, and had been woefully neglected in favor of European interests that were far less important. These "Asialationists," as they were sometimes called, were sure that Truman and his advisers were incompetents who had fallen for the blandishments of designing European diplomats. But after all the talk the situation remained about as it had been before. The President did not recede from his determination to avoid spreading the war beyond Korean borders, and the people of the nation showed no real desire to overrule his decision.

The stalemate in Korea was emphasized shortly after MacArthur's recall by the failure of an offensive undertaken by the Chinese. United Nations lines bent, but did not break; the Chinese effort to recapture Seoul failed, and later United Nations troops regained the territory they had lost. If, as MacArthur argued, the Allied forces could not hope to win a victory under existing circumstances, the same seemed to be true of the Chinese. Advocates of an armistice were heartened on

MacArthur's return to the U.S.

Stalemate in Korea

---

[1] In May, 1952, General Mark W. Clark succeeded General Ridgway, who was sent to Europe to replace General Eisenhower in command of SHAPE. See p. 747). A little later, Van Fleet was retired, and his command given to General Maxwell D. Taylor.

June 23, just two days less than a year from the time the fighting began, when Jacob Malik, then head of the Soviet delegation to the United Nations, put out a "peace feeler." As a result, negotiations looking toward an armistice soon began near the battle-front, first at Kaesong, then at Panmunjon. The talks were not accompanied by a cease-fire agreement except for the immediate vicinity of the negotiations, but hostilities died down mainly to patrol actions and aerial activity, with neither side gaining or losing much ground. In the air, the United Nations maintained a decisive superiority, although the number of Soviet jet fighters, or "Migs," that the American "Sabrejets" had continually to drive back to their Manchurian "sanctuary" was discouragingly large. In this fighting the "Sabrejets" shot down far more "Migs" than the "Migs" shot down "Sabrejets," and maintained control of the air for the United Nations forces. But well-directed ground fire from North Korean centers made air operations extremely hazardous, both for the "Sabrejets" and for the United Nations bombers that searched out Communist targets. Ultimately even the great power plants south of the Yalu were bombed, but United Nations planes were still restrained from flying over Manchuria, even in "hot pursuit." The genius of the Communists for sheer obstructionism was never better shown than in the Korean negotiations. Nearly two years after the talks began they were still going on.

Meantime, with the election of 1952 in prospect, the American people were turning their attention more and more to domestic politics. From the elections of 1950 on, the Truman administration had declined steadily in popularity. In addition to the charges voiced by the opposition in the campaigning of that year, the discovery of shadowy deals, or even downright corruption, in certain governmental departments raised a new and important issue. No one seriously doubted the President's personal honesty, but his previous association with the notorious Pendergast ma-

Scandals at home

chine in Kansas City could always be cited as evidence of his tolerance toward unethical political conduct. It was embarrassing to the administration when Senator Fulbright, Democratic chairman of a Senate subcommittee, reported after a long investigation that certain political personages were using their influence with the Reconstruction Finance Corporation to obtain loans for their friends or clients. It was equally embarrassing when Senator Kefauver, also a Democrat, conducted a series of spectacular televised hearings as Chairman of a special Senate Committee to Investigate Crime in Interstate Commerce, an investigation that demonstrated the venal nature of some of the Democratic city machines that had supported Truman. The name of Mayor William O'Dwyer of New York, for example, was connected with those of prominent leaders of the New York underworld, a situation that administration critics insisted might have had something to do with O'Dwyer's resignation as Mayor before his term was up and his appointment by Truman to be Ambassador to Mexico. A Subcommittee of the House Ways and Means Committee also brought to light irregularities in the Internal Revenue Bureau and its "prosecuting arm," the Tax Division of the Justice Department. Such crimes as bribery and extortion, the use of political influence to fix cases, and connivance at the falsification or concealment of tax returns, if not often provable, seemed to have been matters of all too frequent occurrence. In January, 1952, the Judiciary Committee of the House of Representatives ordered a complete investigation of the Justice Department. To facilitate this inquiry the President chose as chief investigator Newbold Morris, a New York Republican, but Morris and the Attorney General, James Howard McGrath, disagreed on matters of procedure, whereupon McGrath dismissed Morris, and the President dismissed McGrath. Truman's new Attorney General, Judge James P. McGranery, showed little enthusiasm for the investigation and allowed it to die.

The President had difficulties, too, with other aspects of domestic affairs. Actual **The 82nd** control of the Eighty-second **Congress** Congress, elected in 1950, lay with the Republicans and the conservative southern Democrats, who in the session of 1951 cheerfully side-tracked the civil rights and public health programs desired by the administration, did nothing to promote its plans for the St. Lawrence waterway and the Missouri valley authority, failed to act on statehood for Hawaii and Alaska, and passed, over the President's veto, measures for veterans' aid that he deemed unnecessary and unwise. The session of 1952, with charges and countercharges of communism filling the air, and with the uproar over Communist infiltration of the government undiminished, found time to pass the McCarran-Walter Immigration and Nationality Act, which continued the quota system of the Immigration Act of 1924, introduced new and stronger provisions for the exclusion and deportation of politically dangerous aliens, and gave special status to prospective immigrants of superior education and skills. The new act allowed small quotas to Asiatic peoples (a total of 2000) and removed the ban on their naturalization, but it held down the number annually admissible from all countries to 154,658 persons, only 308 more than permitted by earlier legislation. Although the President recognized certain "improvements" in the bill, he vetoed it. He feared that some of its provisions might be used to jeopardize civil rights, and he objected to the retention of what he called the "outdated national origins quota system." But his veto was not sustained, and the bill became law without his signature. Even more discouraging was the rebuff he received in his efforts to prevent a walkout that would tie up the steel industry, so vital to the defense program and the Korean war effort. Acutely eager to avoid another round of price rises, the Wage Stabilization Board, backed by the President, urged the steel representatives to absorb without increasing the price of steel a wage rise high enough to be acceptable to the United Steelworkers. When the steel representatives refused to go along with this program, the President, on April 8, 1952, ordered government seizure of the steel mills to prevent a strike. Then, two months later, the Supreme Court overruled the President's action as unconstitutional, and ordered the government to return the mills to their owners. As soon as this was done the strike began, and not until late in July were the leaders of labor and management able to get together on terms that were mutually acceptable. These terms, in spite of the stand the President had once taken, included increases in both wages and prices.

By this time the presidential campaign of 1952 was getting well under way. Governor Dewey, with two defeats against **Campaign** him, early made it known that **of 1952** he would not be a candidate for the Republican nomination, but his opponents for that honor in 1948, Taft, Stassen, and Warren, were still hopeful. Of these three, however, only Senator Taft, who well represented that wing of the party least interested in world cooperation, had a really strong national following. Taft's record on foreign affairs was notably consistent. He was a pre-Pearl Harbor isolationist who, after the war, had opposed the Truman Doctrine, the Marshall Plan, and the North Atlantic Treaty Organization. He did not disapprove the sending of troops to Korea, but he believed that the President had exceeded his constitutional rights in sending them without the specific authorization of Congress; also, he favored a Congressional limit on the number of American troops that could be sent to Europe. On domestic affairs, he was in general conservative, the outstanding opponent of most measures favored by the "New Deal" and the "Fair Deal." His sponsorship of the Taft-Hartley Labor Relations Act made him anathema to the labor leaders of the nation, although his triumphant re-election in 1950 had demonstrated that the rank and file of labor, at least in his own state, could not have held his record seriously against him.

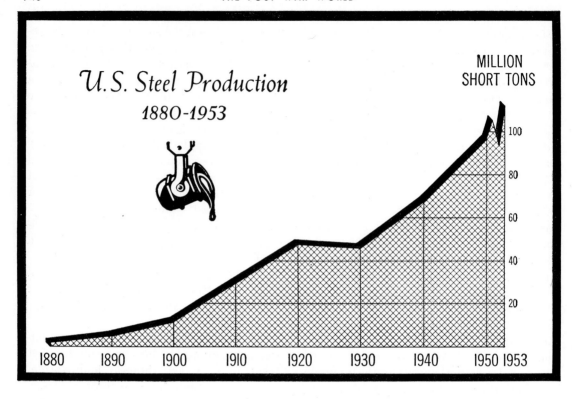

U.S. Steel Production
1880-1953

MILLION
SHORT TONS

Taft's conservatism, coupled with his ability and industry, marked him out as the leading member of his party in Congress, "Mr. Republican," as he was sometimes called. It was hard to see how the nomination for which he had tried so many times could now be denied him.

What worried some of the Republican leaders was the fear that Taft, if nominated, could not be elected. His views were too well known. Republicans who went along with Roosevelt and Truman in foreign affairs might even prefer to vote for a Democrat for President rather than for a man whose affinity for isolationism was so strong. Furthermore, the voters had seemingly accepted the New Deal point of view on many aspects of domestic policy, such, for example, as social security. Would it be wise to nominate a man who, correctly or incorrectly, could be charged with advocating a retreat to the nineteenth century? Many Republicans who were sceptical of Taft as a candidate actually shared his views, but they were

eager for a party victory, and ready to embrace the only real alternative to Taft, General Dwight D. Eisenhower. Eisenhower was known to be internationally minded, but on domestic matters a believer in the free enterprise system. His political experience was limited; as President he would have the disadvantages of the amateur in his contacts with professionals, but as a candidate he would be unbeatable.

Eisenhower was reluctant to engage in political campaigning, and refused on this account to become a candidate for the Republican nomination in 1948. But those who saw in him the only sure road to Republican victory in 1952 put tremendous pressure on him to resign his NATO command, return to the United States, and campaign against Taft. That there was a widespread demand for him to become a candidate was apparent from the results of primaries in New Hampshire, New Jersey, Massachusetts, and Pennsylvania, but the firm Taft control of the Republican organization in so many other states made it clear that only by the most heroic efforts could the General hope to win. On June 1 Eisenhower came back to the United States, and entered the lists. He was at pains to assert his devotion to the Republican Party and to its insistence on a free economy, but he supported the existing program of collective security in Europe, admitted that he had no panacea for ending the Korean War, and assured the voters that he would preserve and promote rather than destroy the social gains of the Roosevelt era. Skillful political leaders, such as Thomas E. Dewey and Senator Henry Cabot Lodge, helped devise the Eisenhower tactics, and by the time the Republican convention met in Chicago, June 7, it was clear that the General would have approximately as many votes as Taft, with the balance of power in the hands of contested delegations and delegates pledged to minor candidates.

When the Convention opened in Chicago it was apparent that the Taft forces fully expected to win. They had control of the National Committee, which chose General Douglas MacArthur, a Taft man, to be keynote speaker, and Joseph W. Martin, another Taft man, to be permanent chairman. They also secured temporary seats for most of the Taft delegates from states in which there were contests, notably from Texas, Louisiana, and Georgia, where the party machines had ignored the plainly expressed preference of the voters for Eisenhower. But the Convention itself, in no mood to be steam-rollered, and conscious of the fact that millions of voters were watching the entire spectacle on television, set aside the rule that allowed delegates temporarily seated, but whose seats were being contested, to vote on the merits of other contestants. It was this rule that had enabled Taft's father to defeat Theodore Roosevelt for the Republican nomination in 1912; its repeal assured Eisenhower's triumph in 1952. It took only three ballots for the minor candidates to give up the contest, and join with the original Eisen-

The Republican Convention

hower men to make the General the nominee. For Vice-President the Convention chose Richard M. Nixon, junior Senator from California. The platform, except in its ringing denunciation of Democratic rule, was, like most party platforms, far from explicit. The issues, as everyone knew, would be drawn by the candidates themselves rather than by the platforms on which they were supposed to stand.

The Democratic Convention, also held in Chicago, opened on July 21. The Twenty-second Amendment to the Constitution, ratified February 26, 1951, provided that no person should hold the office of President more than twice, and that no person who had acted as President "for more than two years of a term to which some other person was elected" should be chosen more than once. This latter provision would have excluded Truman from being a candidate in 1952 but for the fact that the amendment specifically excepted from its prohibitions the person who held the office of President when it was proposed. But Truman, who at the time the Convention met was 68 years of age, had announced the preceding March that he would not be a candidate to succeed himself. This left the field wide open, and although the chances of defeating Eisenhower seemed dim, there were many who were willing to try. Chief among the contenders was Senator Estes Kefauver of Tennessee, whose crime investigations had dissociated him from the corruption charges being leveled at the Truman administration, and whose popularity throughout the country had been attested by victories in many state presidential primaries. Other candidates included the venerable Vice-President, Alben W. Barkley, Senators Russell of Georgia and Kerr of Oklahoma, Mutual Security Administrator Averell Harriman, and, without his consent and against his wishes, Governor Adlai E. Stevenson of Illinois. Eager to heal the breach in the party made by the Dixiecrats in 1948, the Convention refused to bind all delegates in advance to support the party

The Democratic Convention

Adlai E. Stevenson, grandson of a Vice-President by the same name, was the Democratic standard-bearer in 1952.

nominee, and wrote into its platform moderate provisions on civil rights and minimum wages. And, primarily because Stevenson had the fewest enemies and was most acceptable to all factions, the Convention drafted him to be its nominee for President. In another move calculated to appease the South, it chose Senator John J. Sparkman of Alabama as its candidate for Vice-President.

The importance of television as a means of campaigning became immediately apparent as the contenders joined forces.

Stevenson

The whole American public, or at least a large fraction of it, expected to see Eisenhower and Stevenson in action. The people were not much interested in seeing or hearing lesser lights; the main burden of the campaign had to be carried by the candidates themselves. Both men felt obliged to travel by plane or train the country over, and in addition to scheduled speeches, to make innumerable "whistle-stop" appearances. The surprise of the campaign was Governor Stevenson. A virtual unknown in competition with a man of world renown, he made a truly remarkable showing. Just as Franklin D. Roosevelt had proved himself to be an adept in the use of the radio, so Stevenson

demonstrated an almost uncanny facility in the use of television. As a debater, his keenness of intellect, his intimate knowledge of politics, his rare gift of words, and his genial wit made him a tremendous success. While he had been nominated as a compromise candidate, he proved to be no compromiser. He stood firmly by the foreign policy of the Truman administration. He advocated federal enforcement of fair employment practices and federal control of tidelands oil, attitudes that led many states'-rights Democrats to desert him for Eisenhower. He admitted that the Taft-Hartley Act had its good points, but urged that it be entirely redrawn. He did what he could to dissociate himself from the political scandals of the Truman administration, and showed every intention of cleaning up "the mess in Washington," if given an opportunity. But the Democratic record was there, and the President helped keep it in the limelight by touring the country in a series of hard-hitting speeches against his detractors and in defense of his administration.

Up to the time of his entrance into politics Eisenhower had not seemed to be an extreme partisan; in fact, many Democrats had wanted him as their **Eisenhower's campaign** candidate both in 1948 and in 1952. He took pains when registering as a New York City voter in 1948 not to declare himself a member of any party. Furthermore, he had apparently been in fundamental agreement with the Truman administration on foreign policy, and only recently had been engaged in implementing that policy in Europe. But he now left no stone unturned to indicate his complete devotion to Republicanism, and made it his first concern to heal the breach in the party that had seemed so deep at the time of the Convention. He conferred with Taft and took his advice on many aspects of the campaign; he publicly shook hands with McCarthy; and he gave isolationist Republicans who were candidates for office the same unqualified support that he gave internationalists. He denounced the Truman administration for its "appalling and disas-

The election of 1952 aroused the country to a high pitch of excitement, although the two major parties avoided most head-on issues. In general, the independent vote favored Eisenhower for President, but was far less certain on the desirability of a Republican Congress.

REPUBLICAN CONVENTION. The 1952 meeting in Chicago had all the trappings of modern politics.

PARTIES, NOT ISSUES. On many important questions, the two major parties took similar stands.

INAUGURATION CEREMONIES. Unusual aerial view.

trous mismanagement of our foreign affairs," hinted strongly that the Truman policy of "containment" might better be replaced by a policy of "liberation," called attention to the administration's indifference to corruption in government, cast grave doubts on the soundness of its economic policies, and found fault with its record in Korea. As for the Taft-Hartley Act, he admitted, as Taft did also, that it needed some changes, but found no fault with the principles on which it was drawn. His associate on the ticket, Senator Nixon, charged the Democrats with unreasonable tenderness toward Communism, and made much of the fact that Governor Stevenson had once given a favorable deposition as a character witness for Alger Hiss. But Nixon's usefulness in the campaign was threatened when it came out that his friends in California had subscribed over $18,000

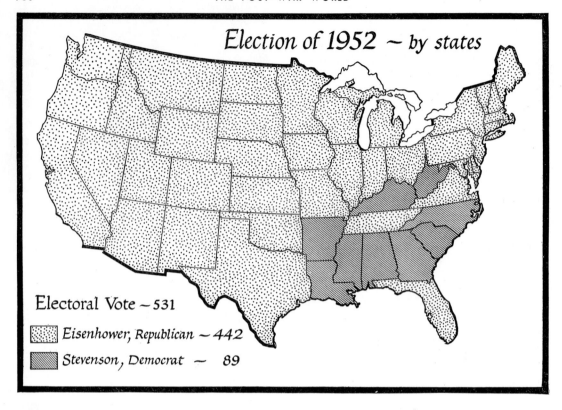

Election of 1952 ~ by states

Electoral Vote ~ 531

Eisenhower, Republican ~ 442

Stevenson, Democrat ~ 89

for his use while a United States Senator in keeping his political house in order. Nixon, however, in a well-devised television address made a good case for himself, and probably won more votes for the ticket than he lost. The public in general saw little difference between what he had done and Stevenson's admitted practice as Governor in using party funds under his control to augment the salaries of a few non-political administrative officers. On the radio and television Eisenhower was at first not nearly as effective as Stevenson, but he did better as time went on, and campaigned tirelessly. His political ten-strike was a promise he made that, if elected, he would go to Korea, a promise which was interpreted by many to mean that, if elected, he would find some speedy way to end the Korean War.

The outcome of the election could never have been in serious doubt, but Stevenson's **Election** extraordinary gifts as a cam-**results** paigner made many people think that it was. When the results came in it was apparent that Eisenhower had won

by a landslide. Stevenson carried only nine states, all southern, with a total of 89 electoral votes; while Eisenhower carried thirty-nine states, with a total of 442 electoral votes. In the popular vote, which was exceptionally heavy, Eisenhower won 33,927,-549 to Stevenson's 27,311,316. The Eisenhower landslide carried many Republican governors into office, but curiously had far less effect than previous landslides on the political complexion of Congress. The new Senate consisted of 48 Republicans, 47 Democrats, and Senator Morse of Oregon, a Republican who had broken with his party during the campaign to support Stevenson. The House of Representatives numbered 221 Republicans to 213 Democrats, and a computation of totals indicated that the number of voters who had favored Democratic candidates was slightly larger than the number who had favored Republican candidates.[1] The election could be interpreted as a strong

[1] Later a sufficient number of by-elections went against the Republicans to reduce the House majority to three.

endorsement of Eisenhower and a rebuke to the Truman administration, but hardly as a vote of confidence in the Republican Party or a complete repudiation of the Democratic record. Many splinter parties, including the fellow-travelling Progressive Party that had supported Wallace in 1948, ran candidates, but they polled only insignificant numbers of votes, and in no way affected the outcome.

Bibliography

A surprising amount of writing has already come out of the Korean War. The Navy's role in the first half-year of the war is vividly told in Walter Karig, Malcolm W. Cagle, and Frank A. Manson, *Battle Report, VI, The War in Korea* (1952). The activities of the Marines are recounted in Andrew Geer, *The New Breed: The Story of the U.S. Marines in Korea* (1952). Marguerite Higgins, *War in Korea: The Report of a Woman Combat Correspondent* (1951), is a first-rate journalistic account. S. L. A. Marshall, *The River and the Gauntlet* (1952), tells graphically the story of the unsuccessful Yalu venture. A. Wigfall Green, *The Epic of Korea* (1950); and John C. Caldwell and Lesley Frost, *The Korea Story* (1952), are both caustically critical of American handling of the Korean situation. Other aspects of the Korean venture are brought out in Robert C. North, *Moscow and the Chinese Communists* (1953); and Pauline Tompkins, *American-Russian Relations in the Far East* (1949). See also references to China and Russia for chapters 32 and 33, pp. 702, 726. On the problem of inflation due to cold war and Korean war expenditures, two excellent reports by experts were put out by the Twentieth Century Fund: A. G. Hart, *Defense without Inflation* (1951); and A. G. Hart and others, *Financing Defense* (1951).

The MacArthur dismissal attracted much attention in the newspapers and magazines, and resulted also in the writing of a number of books. Clark G. Lee and Richard Henschel, *Douglas MacArthur* (1952), is a friendly and admiring biography. John Gunther, *The Riddle of MacArthur* (1951), presents all available information with little effort at critical appraisal. Richard H. Rovere and A. M. Schlesinger, Jr., *The General and the President, and the Future of American Foreign Policy* (1951), upholds the action taken by President Truman. Louis Smith, *American Democracy and Military Power: A Study of Civil Control of the Military Power in the United States* (1951), deals with constitutional aspects of the problem.

The loyalty issue is discussed with reasonable restraint in Nathaniel Weyl, *The Battle against Disloyalty* (1951). Robert K. Carr, *The House Committee on Un-American Activities* (1952), is a critical study by a law professor whose findings are not complimentary to the Committee. Jackson Anderson and Ronald W. May, *McCarthy, The Man, the Senator, the Ism* (1952), is a devastating attack on the McCarthy methods. Alan Barth, *The Loyalty of Free Men* (1951); and Carey McWilliams, *Witch Hunt: The Revival of Heresy* (1950), call attention to the danger to liberty involved in the loyalty program. Owen Lattimore, *Ordeal by Slander* (1950), is the hard-hitting reply of one whose motives were impugned. James Oneal and G. A. Werner, *American Communism; A Critical Analysis of its Origins, Development, and Programs* (new ed., 1947), is an attempt to write the history of a movement that studiously concealed its most important sources. Benjamin Gitlow, *The Whole of Their Lives* (1948); and Louis Francis Budenz, *Men without Faces: The Communist Conspiracy in the U.S.A.* (1950), are scathing attacks on Communism by former party members. The Hiss trial and the issues it raised are discussed temperately by Alistair Cooke, *A Generation on Trial: U.S.A. v. Alger Hiss* (1950); and intemperately by Ralph De Toledano and Victor Lasky, *Seeds of Treason: The True Story of the Hiss-Chambers Tragedy* (1950). For his own story, see Whittaker Chambers, *Witness* (1952).

The candidacies of the leading participants in the campaign and election of 1952 were advertised in a variety of ways. Estes Kefauver, *Crime in America* (1951), set forth as the Senator's bid for the Presidency his report on his investigations. Robert A. Taft, *A Foreign Policy for Americans* (1951), was designed to clear the Ohioan of the charge of isolationism. Caroline T. Harnsberger, *A Man of Courage, Robert A. Taft* (1952), was a not-very-good campaign biography. Kevin McCann, *Man from Abilene* (1952); and Noel F. Busch, *Adlai E. Stevenson of Illinois* (1952), both campaign biographies, suffered from too hasty compilation, and were at their best when quoting the candidates. Unofficial offerings were somewhat better. John Gunther, *Eisenhower: The Man and the Symbol* (1952), was a lively and impressive portrait, full of colorful detail. J. B. Martin, *Adlai Stevenson* (1952), was interesting,

concise, and informative. Adlai E. Stevenson, *Major Campaign Speeches of Adlai E. Stevenson, 1952* (1953), included also an extremely illuminating description of the trials and tribulations of a candidate. An excellent pre-election study of the nature of American political parties is Samuel Lubell, *The Future of American Politics* (1952). A subject of considerable concern during the campaign and after is treated in Ernest R. Bartley, *The Tidelands Oil Controversy: A Legal and Historical Analysis* (1953).

35

The United States at Mid-Century

Eisenhower — New appointments — The Korean truce — Korean War statistics — Atomic weapons — Foreign policy — The Geneva Conference — Eisenhower and Congress — McCarthy again — Population increase — Assimilation of immigrants — Pacific Coast growth — The South — Urban growth — Changes in business — The "working classes" — Labor-saving devices — The income tax — The Negro — Women's rights — Amusements — Scientific advance — Literature

DWIGHT D. EISENHOWER (1890–   ) was born in Denison, Texas, but his parents moved to Abilene, Kansas, when he was only a year old and he grew up as a Middle Westerner. He had hoped for an appointment to the Naval Academy, but when that failed to materialize because he was overage, he sought and obtained an appointment to West Point, where he graduated in 1915, sixty-first in a class of 164. He failed to see service in the First World War, although at the time the armistice was signed he was in command of a tank battalion that was about to sail for France. He was an earnest student of military science, graduated in quick succession from the Command and General Staff School at Fort Leavenworth, the Army War College, and the Army Industrial College. For several years he served as special assistant to General Douglas MacArthur, went with him to Manila, and helped work out plans for the defense of the Philippines. During the Louisiana war maneuvers of 1941, the excellence of his planning called attention to him, and immediately after Pearl Harbor General Marshall called him to Washington, where

Eisenhower

he became head of the War Plans Division, then chief of the Operations Division. When finally it was decided that Marshall should stay in Washington, Eisenhower was the natural choice for commander of the United States forces in Europe, and in December, 1943, he became Supreme Allied Commander. His military successes in North Africa, Italy, France, and Germany, coupled with his skill in dealing with the great variety of nationalities placed under his command, marked him not only as a leading American, but as a leading world figure. After the war, President Truman appointed him Chief of Staff to succeed Marshall, a position he surrendered in 1948 to become President of Columbia University. But he was still subject to call for military duty, and in December, 1950, the President sent him on a second mission to Europe, this time as head of the NATO defense forces. Then followed the stirring events which made him first a candidate for the Presidency and eventually President of the United States.

Once the election was over Eisenhower paid his promised visit to Korea, and settled down to the task of selecting the person-

Dwight D. Eisenhower

THIRTY-FOURTH PRESIDENT OF THE United States, Eisenhower was the first regular army officer to be chosen to the Presidency since Ulysses S. Grant. His nomination and election emphasized anew the hold of the "great man tradition" on the American people in their choice of a President. An amateur in politics, Eisenhower in office took time to develop a program and to establish his leadership.

nel of his administration. Undoubtedly

New appointments

Thomas E. Dewey could have been his Secretary of State had he been willing to accept the post, but at Dewey's suggestion the President-elect chose instead John Foster Dulles, long a favored agent of the department he was called to head, and the principal author of the recent treaty of peace with Japan. Dulles's appointment made clear Eisenhower's determination to maintain an internationalist rather than an isolationist point of view on foreign affairs. Eisenhower also took Dewey's advice in choosing Herbert Brownell, Jr., to be Attorney General, and sought to placate organized labor by making Martin P. Durkin, a labor leader who had voted for Stevenson, his Secretary of Labor.[1] But in many of his other nominations he showed a strong predilection for high-salaried business executives, such, for example, as Charles E. Wil-

[1] Durkin resigned in September, 1953, because of the failure of the administration to press for changes in the Taft-Hartley Act.

son, his Secretary of Defense, formerly head of General Motors. It was apparent at once that he wished to re-establish between government and business a relationship of mutual trust and respect that had been lacking since the administration of Herbert Hoover. As President, he lost little time in making a complete sweep of the Joint Chiefs of Staff who had advised Truman on military matters, and appointed a new team headed by Admiral Arthur W. Radford. Responding to the patronage demands of a party long out of power, he also stripped civil service protection from many high ranking federal appointees so that Democrats might be replaced by Republicans.

The Far Eastern situation presented for the new administration, no less than for its predecessor, problems of the first magnitude. Eisenhower's

The Korean truce

trip to Korea supplied him with few new ideas. He withdrew the restrictions that President Truman had made on Chiang Kai-shek's freedom to attack the mainland of China, but since Chiang had not the strength to make any such attacks in force anyway, this change of policy was inconsequential. As for the truce talks in Korea, one impasse had succeeded another with disheartening regularity ever since they had begun in the summer of 1951. By the time Eisenhower took office, however, the negotiators had hammered out agreements upon most matters of fundamental importance, with the exception of the vexing problem of prisoner exchange. The United Nations representatives consistently refused to consider the return of captives who had expressed a desire not to be repatriated, whereas the Communists insisted that all prisoners should be exchanged, regardless of their wishes. The first break in this deadlock came during the spring of 1953, after Stalin's death, when the truce teams agreed to exchange sick and wounded prisoners: as a result, a few hundred United Nations prisoners held by the Chinese were exchanged for several thousand Chinese and North Korean prisoners held by the Allies.

Eventually the negotiators got together, also, on what to do with the anti-Communist Chinese and North Korean prisoners (46,380 out of 132,000) who did not wish to go home. These individuals, instead of being freed or exchanged, would be handed over to a neutral commission composed of representatives from five nations — Sweden, Switzerland, Poland, Czechoslovakia, and India. Then for a three-months period, with Indian troops standing guard, Communist agents would be given the freedom of the prison camps (seven agents for each 1000 prisoners) in order to explain away any fears the prisoners might feel about repatriation. After that, any who changed their minds and said they wished to go home, might do so, provided a majority of the neutral commission agreed. To balance matters properly, it was agreed also that United Nations prisoners who had no desire to be repatriated should go through a similar process. Then the political "peace conference" which would follow the armistice would endeavor to solve the problem of any prisoners who had not asked for repatriation, but if it failed to reach a solution in thirty days' time these prisoners, with the consent of the neutral commission, would be given the status of civilians and presumably set free. Thus, in a period of from four to six months, the anti-Communist prisoners had at least a chance to escape repatriation. The plan obviously left much to be desired, but it at least would permit United Nations spokesmen to claim that they had not yielded completely to the Communist demand for involuntary repatriation. The ink on this agreement was scarcely dry when Syngman Rhee, the Korean President, took matters into his own hands by ordering the release of over 25,000 anti-Communist North Koreans who were being guarded by South Korean troops. The indignation of the United Nations authorities, particularly those representing the United States, at this unilateral action was great, and for the time being armistice negotiations were again stalled. But eventually the plan was adopted, and on July 27, 1953, the truce was

John Foster Dulles, a favorite adviser and agent of the State Department under Truman, became Eisenhower's Secretary of State.

officially signed, two years and seventeen days after the negotiations began. The first exchange of prisoners took place on August 5, and continued until completed. The release of prisoners who refused repatriation dragged out over months; in the end only a small fraction of those held by the Allies went back to Communism, while only about twenty Allied prisoners of the Communists refused to return home.

The Korean War turned out to be a far greater venture than anyone could have foreseen when it started in June, 1950. At the outset the United States furnished the bulk of the troops on the United Nations side, but as the war went on Republic of Korea forces, armed, trained, and equipped mainly by the Americans, came to exceed those of all other participants combined:

Korean War statistics

R.O.K.	460,000
U.S.	250,000
Others	40,000

Casualties were extremely high, and followed somewhat the same proportions. They included, killed in combat:

R.O.K.	71,500
U.S.	25,000
Others	2,500

In addition, the number of wounded reached about 250,000, while those missing or captured were counted at above 83,000. Among the missing were at least 8,500 Americans, many of whom could be presumed to be dead. Estimates of civilian South Koreans who had lost their lives in the war ran as high as 400,000, with far more than that number left homeless, and perhaps 100,000 orphans. The cost of the war to the United States alone reached $22 billion, but the losses of South Korea, where, for example, 75 per cent of the mines and textile mills had been destroyed, were incalculable. North Korean losses were even greater in proportion than those suffered by the South Koreans; the population of North Korea, some said, had declined from eight to four million. Chinese casualties had probably exceeded a million. But in return for all this ghastly expenditure of "blood and treasure," it was possible to count some gains. Much had been learned about air fighting, particularly with jet planes, although at heavy cost, for each side shot down nearly a thousand of its opponent's planes. The program of preparedness in the western world, languishing when the war began, had taken on new life: now the United States alone had an army of 3,600,000 men, and the NATO forces in Europe had been substantially increased. The war, too, had proved that aggression could be costly and futile; the battle-lines came to rest in Korea about where they had started. As for the signing of the definitive treaty of peace, negotiations looking in that direction speedily broke down. Despite the constant peace protestations of the Communist governments, the evidence accumulated that they had no interest in peace except on their own terms. That too might be a lesson learned.

Throughout the Korean War both sides had refrained completely from the use of

Atomic weapons atomic weapons. Only a Presidential order would permit the American forces to resort to atomic warfare, and neither Truman nor Eisenhower was willing to give the order. It was known that Russia had staged an atomic explosion about September 1, 1949, but the Russians showed no disposition to invite American retaliation by helping the Chinese and the North Koreans stage an atomic attack. In the United States, the Korean War served greatly to accelerate the work of the Atomic Energy Commission, which rapidly increased its stockpile of fissionable materials, and added unrevealed numbers to its store of atomic bombs. Repeated tests, at Bikini and Eniwetok Atolls in the South Pacific, and at remote spots on the Nevada desert, proved alike the appalling destructiveness of the new weapons, and the capacity of the Commission to produce them. Most of the tests were apparently of bombs, but they included also an atomic cannon that could be used in tactical warfare. The Atomic Energy Commission was long divided on the wisdom of attempting to construct a hydrogen bomb, the destructive power of which would dwarf that of the atomic bomb to relative insignificance. But on January 31, 1950, President Truman gave the order that eventuated in an H-bomb explosion at Eniwetok late in 1952. Meantime the British had exploded an A-bomb somewhere in Australia, while the Russians, also known to be at work on the H-bomb, achieved similar results with that dread weapon in 1953. Grown callous to such announcements the American public showed little excitement over what had happened, but President Eisenhower put himself on record as favoring the full exploitation of American potentialities when he appointed Lewis L. Strauss to be chairman of the Atomic Energy Commission, succeeding Gordon Dean. Strauss had resigned from the Commission in February, 1950, presumably because of its reluctance to proceed more actively with work on the H-bomb. Efforts of the United Nations to establish international control over the national development of atomic energy continued, but with complete lack of results. Both the

United States and Soviet Russia claimed to favor such a program, but each nation insisted on terms that the other regarded as inadmissible.

On other aspects of foreign policy the President also had his troubles. The efforts **Foreign policy** of Secretary of State Dulles to adopt a more aggressive attitude toward the spread of Communism than the "containment" policy of the Truman administration seemed not in the least to frighten the Soviets and their satellites, but aroused the greatest anxiety among the European allies of the United States, who feared that American inexperience and ineptitude would plunge the world again into war. The growing distrust of American capacity for diplomatic leadership seemed even to threaten the system of defensive alliances the United States had built up since 1947. The French government was in a chronic condition of impotence; the Italian premier, Alcide de Gasperi, who had been consistently friendly to the United States, lost office; the European Defense Community on which the United States set such store seemed in real danger. Only the victory of the pro-American government of Konrad Adenauer in West Germany served to lighten the general gloom. At home, there was a growing resistance to foreign commitments, particularly those that cost the American taxpayer money. Moreover, many Americans were deeply resentful of the foreign criticisms leveled at the United States, and almost in an isolationist mood. If the nations to which American aid had been given so freely were dissatisfied with American leadership, it was high time, some said, for them to find other sources of help, or undertake to go it alone.

The accumulation of tensions seemed even to threaten Anglo-American accord. Winston Churchill, whom a Conservative victory had returned to power in Great Britain in 1951, had long sought to bring about a top-level conference between the Russian Premier, the President of the United States, and himself. The death of Stalin March 5, 1953,

The hydrogen bomb brought to reality a power which the public was scarcely able to grasp. Its overwhelming potentialities are illustrated by Pletcher in the Sioux City *Journal*.

and the succession to the Russian premiership of Georgi Malenkov, seemed to offer an excellent opportunity for such a meeting, but Eisenhower was unwilling to consent to it until the Soviet government should prove by deeds as well as words that it really desired peace. The President agreed, however, to meet with the British Prime Minister and the French Premier at Bermuda to discuss the problems of the Allies, a meeting that Churchill fondly hoped might lead to the conference with Malenkov through which the problems of the world could be settled. The Bermuda meeting, in spite of delays due to the illness of Churchill and the instability of the French government, took place early in December, 1953, but Eisenhower flew back to the United States after only a scant three days of discussion to deliver an address to the United Nations in which he proposed the pooling for peaceful purposes of the resources in atomic energy of both the Communist and the western worlds. The President's proposal, as he must have foreseen, drew much favorable response from the free nations, but broke down in the face of Soviet opposition. It also, to the considerable distress of Churchill, shifted attention away from the Bermuda meeting, which after Eisenhower's departure failed to accomplish anything of consequence. Russia, meantime, had agreed to a four-power conference of foreign ministers, to be held in Berlin early in 1954. During these sessions it became clear that the objective of the U.S.S.R. was principally to widen the cleavage between the United States and her principal allies, Great Britain and France. Soviet bargaining on Germany and Austria was conditioned upon the abandonment of the European Defense Community, which France no longer seemed to want, and the willingness of the western powers to deal with Red China on terms of entire equality, which, but for American opposition, both Great Britain and France might have considered. The only important result of this meeting was the calling of an-

Konrad Adenauer, German Chancellor, ably led the West German recovery program and consistently allied himself with western efforts.

other conference, to be held in Geneva, to consider the problem of peace in Korea and Indo-China. At this conference Red China was to be represented, but the western powers did not construe this to mean diplomatic recognition.

The Geneva Conference, which opened on April 27, was an impressive international gathering. Delegations repre- **The Geneva** senting all the participants in **Conference** the Korean and Indo-Chinese wars were present. Red China was represented by Chou En-lai, the Red premier; Russia by Molotov; Great Britain by Eden; France by Bidault; the United States by Dulles and Walter Bedell Smith, the Under Secretary of State. The Viet Nam Republic, the Kingdoms of Cambodia and Laos, and Thailand all sent delegations. Unfortunately, even before the Conference met, the rift between the United States and its European allies had widened. For a time the American government had insisted that Indo-China, being essential to the defense of all southeast Asia, must be saved at all cost, but public opinion at home was hesitant. In American eyes the French had delayed too long their promise of ultimate independence for the Indo-Chinese states; the American people had small interest in a war to protect colonialism. They demanded, at the very least, that there should be no such thing as unilateral intervention; the United States must not send troops to Indo-China without allied support. This end was equally desired by the Department of State, which was seeking to transform the various bilateral defense agreements it had negotiated with such Pacific powers as the Philippines, New Zealand, Australia, and South Korea into a kind of Pacific NATO, which would include both Great Britain and France. But the French, despairing of victory in Indo-China, were increasingly ready for peace at almost any price, while the British were unwilling to act on the proposed Pacific pact until after the Geneva Conference had shown what it could do. In the end the Conference accomplished nothing on Korea, for both sides laid down conditions that would insure a united Korean government satisfactory to itself but wholly unsatisfactory to its opponents. On Indo-China, the Communists demanded not only Vietnamese territory, but also parts of Laos and Cambodia, states in which there had been neither war nor rebellion until Red troops marched in. Finally the French, under a new Premier, Pierre Mendès-France, signed a humiliating armistice, July 21, 1954, which gave up all northern Viet Nam to the Communists. The United States refused to approve this arrangement, but agreed not to use force to upset it.

Meantime, President Eisenhower was having plenty of troubles at home. Possibly because of his conviction that the executive branch of the government should work with and not seek to dominate the legislative, he had made less effort than some of his predecessors to force his will on Congress. He had been slow about developing his legislative program, and had failed to take full advantage of the "honeymoon period" at the beginning of an administration, when Congress responds most readily to Presidential pressure. He had disposed of the patronage more with an eye to satisfying all elements in the Republican Party than to getting the support he needed for measures he favored. He found himself seriously handicapped also by the deep cleavage that existed between the Taft and the Eisenhower factions of the Republican party. It was possible during the campaign to overlook these differences (although Stevenson had repeatedly charged that there were two Republican parties), but with Congress in session the President needed the united support of a united party. Taft, who became majority leader in the Senate, tried hard to hold the party together, although he did not hesitate from time to time to oppose the President vigorously and openly. In both houses of Congress the number of Republicans who had supported Taft for the nomination was probably greater than the number who had supported Eisenhower, and

Eisenhower and Congress

Taft men held most of the important committee chairmanships. On foreign policy and on many domestic issues, the Democrats generally held views more in accordance with those favored by the President than did the more conservative members of the Republican party, but the President's tendency to blame the preceding Democratic administrations for most of the evils to which he had fallen heir made the Democrats somewhat less than enthusiastic about supporting him. Some issues cut across party, or even factional, lines. The attitude of a Congressman toward farm subsidies, for example, was apt to depend far more upon the nature of his constituency than upon his political affiliations. The sudden death of Senator Taft in the summer of 1953, far from aiding the Eisenhower forces, removed the man upon whom, more than any other, the President had come to depend for party unity. Taft was succeeded by a Democrat, Thomas A. Burke, thus giving the Democrats 48 senators, exactly half the total number.

Georgi Malenkov, successor to Stalin as Premier of the U.S.S.R., aroused hopes of a change in Soviet policy, but these hopes soon proved false.

During the campaign the Republicans had persistently attacked the Truman adminis-

Economy again tration for its heavy spending, its excessive taxes, and its failure to balance the national budget. It was not surprising, therefore, that President Eisenhower should attempt to prune down the budget of $79 billion that Truman had submitted to Congress just before he left office. With the assistance of his able Director of the Budget, Joseph M. Dodge, the new President proposed to make substantial reductions in these figures all along the line, but his suggestions stepped on almost as many Republican as Democratic toes, and had their opponents in both parties. Since so large a proportion of the national expendi-

The Geneva Conference brought to an end the eight-year war in Indo-China. Photo shows parts of Russian, British, and Chinese delegations.

tures went for national defense, it seemed clear that, despite the Korean War and the cold war with Russia, the armed forces would have to do with less money. To the surprise of all concerned, the President proposed, with the full support of the Secretary of Defense, to make most of the cuts at the expense of the air force, which stood to lose $5.2 billion, and to be required to lower its sights from a proposed 143 wings to only 120 wings. This, the President insisted, would be adequate for the national defense, but there were many even in his own party who thought otherwise. His decision represented a return to the "balanced forces" principle, which called for relatively equal appropriations for army, navy, and air force, and an abandonment of the idea, to which the Truman administration had been converted, that air protection was of paramount importance. A year later, however, the President reversed himself, and while lowering the totals still further, asked that more money be put on the air force than on either the army or navy.

Despite the political hazards involved, the President dashed the hopes of those who had expected an immediate cut in taxes. The existing high rates, he said, including even the excess profits tax, would be necessary until 1954, and even by retaining them the budget for 1953 could not be balanced. On the retention of the excess profits tax, Congress proved to be particularly difficult, but eventually, with much Democratic assistance, the President's recommendation won.

The determination of Congress to cut taxes, regardless of whether the budget could be balanced, could not long be restrained. It allowed the high rates levied at the outset of the Korean War to lapse in January, 1954, a reduction to income tax payers of about ten per cent, and during its second session it reduced excise taxes, including the rates on luxury items, by as much as fifty per cent, a loss to the Treasury of nearly a billion dollars. A general tax revision bill, passed in the closing days of the second session, also reduced taxes on income derived from divi-

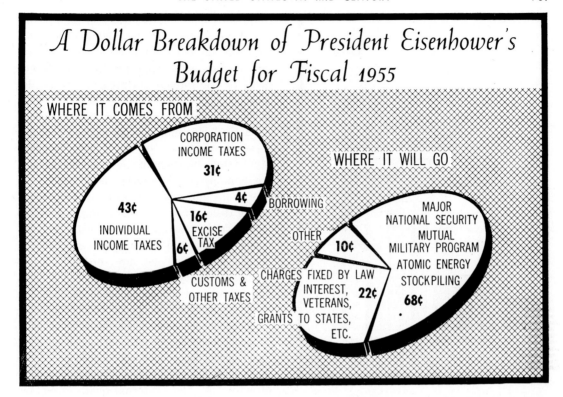

A Dollar Breakdown of President Eisenhower's Budget for Fiscal 1955

WHERE IT COMES FROM

CORPORATION INCOME TAXES
31¢

WHERE IT WILL GO

43¢
INDIVIDUAL INCOME TAXES

16¢
EXCISE TAX

4¢
BORROWING

6¢
CUSTOMS & OTHER TAXES

OTHER

10¢
CHARGES FIXED BY LAW
INTEREST, VETERANS, GRANTS TO STATES, ETC.
22¢

MAJOR NATIONAL SECURITY
MUTUAL MILITARY PROGRAM
ATOMIC ENERGY STOCKPILING
68¢

dends, permitted businessmen when making their returns more liberal application of losses against profits and greater freedom in charging off research costs, increased deductions for medical expenses, and liberalized provisions for working mothers, retired persons, and farmers. Altogether the changes lowered the estimated revenue over $1.3 billion. Yet, in spite of this, Congress refused to heed the President's request that the debt limit be raised from $275 billion to $290 billion, and permitted only a niggardly temporary increase of $6 billion. With the budget of 1954 still hopelessly out of balance, this presented the Treasury with a serious problem.

On other matters the record of the Eighty-third Congress sometimes pleased the President, but more often fell far short of the goals he had set. **The 83rd Congress** On one of the promises he had made during the campaign, the return of tidelands oil rights to the states, the Republicans were in substantial agreement, and promptly made good on the President's pledges. The Presi-

dent also obtained from the second session Congressional assent to American participation in the completion of the Great Lakes – St. Lawrence Seaway, a project for which Hoover, Roosevelt, and Truman had sought in vain to win favorable action. It is reasonable to suppose, however, that the changed attitude of Congress resulted in part from the decision of the Canadian government to construct the Seaway alone, along an all-Canadian route, if the United States continued its refusal to share in the work. Eisenhower won another victory, although negative in nature rather than positive, when he persuaded Congress not to submit for adoption the so-called Bricker Amendment to the Constitution, the purpose of which was to limit the independence of the President in the making of treaties and executive agreements. He obtained permission to admit displaced persons (DP's) from war-torn Europe to the extent of 209,000 in excess of the regular quotas during a period of three years, but the law fell into unfriendly hands

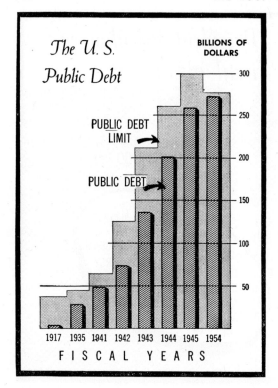

for administration, and by March, 1954, only six such refugees had been admitted, and fifty others granted visas. He failed to obtain the revision of the Taft-Hartley Act which he had promised during the campaign. On the proposals of Secretary of Agriculture Benson for more flexible price supports to replace the rigid 90 per cent of parity system he won only a partial victory, a spread of 82½ to 90 per cent of parity, instead of the 75 to 90 per cent for which he had asked. He urged Congress to provide for 140,000 new housing units in four years, but got only 35,000 in one year, and these subject to hampering building restrictions. He favored strongly the recommendations of the Randall Commission on foreign economic policy urging that the Reciprocal Trade Act should be continued and liberalized, that the President should be granted authority to reduce existing tariff rates by as much as five per cent during each of the next three years, and that other measures designed to expand rather than to contract world trade should be undertaken. But the best the President

could get from Congress was a grudging continuation on a year by year basis of the existing trade agreements policy. On many matters, including the appropriations needed to carry on the foreign aid program, which he deemed essential, he was obliged to accept the aid of large blocks of Democratic votes.

Particularly embarrassing to the President were the activities of Republican Senator McCarthy, chairman of the Senate committee on government operations and of the subcommittee investigating disloyalty. The President, hoping to restrict the investigation of loyalty and security risks to the executive branch of the government, had set up separate three-member security boards for each department and agency. Perhaps as evidence that the new system was working far better than the old, which had depended upon a centralized loyalty review board, Attorney-General Brownell revealed the seamy aspects of the record of Harry Dexter White, a former director of the International Monetary Fund, whom, he charged, Truman had kept in office long after his guilt of subversion had been established by the FBI. But McCarthy, whose largely unsubstantiated charges had already frightened many State Department employees into virtual impotence and had reduced the radio Voice of America "to a whisper," was in no mood to give up the weapon upon which so exclusively his reputation depended. When Truman took to the air to deny Brownell's charges, McCarthy replied over the same networks, not only charging the outgoing administration with laxity toward Communism, but implying that in some matters the new administration was far from vigilant. Early in 1954 a McCarthy inquiry into an alleged espionage ring at Ft. Monmouth, N.J., an army signal corps laboratory, brought the Senator into conflict with the Department of the Army, which finally in a state of desperation charged him and his chief counsel, Roy Cohn, with seeking special service favors for G. David Schine, a draftee friend and assistant of Cohn's. A prolonged and undignified

McCarthy again

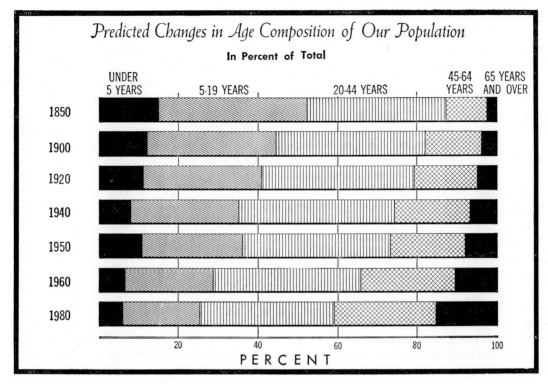

Predicted Changes in Age Composition of Our Population

In Percent of Total

| | UNDER 5 YEARS | 5-19 YEARS | 20-44 YEARS | 45-64 YEARS | 65 YEARS AND OVER |

1850
1900
1920
1940
1950
1960
1980

20   40   60   80   100

PERCENT

This chart assumed medium fertility, medium mortality, and no immigration. (From *Problems of a Changing Population*, Washington National Resources Committee, 1938.)

televised hearing resulted, with the Secretary of the Army, Robert T. Stevens, and Senator McCarthy the chief participants. Throughout these proceedings the President's irritation at McCarthy's methods and the damage they were doing the Republican Party was ill-concealed, although he scrupulously refrained from denouncing the Senator by name.

The problems which the United States had to face, whether at home or abroad, **U.S. population increase** were grave enough to invite despair; and yet, the nation could point with justifiable pride to the remarkable changes that had recently come over American society. For one thing, there were many, many more Americans. An increase in the population of the United States was not exactly news; every census since the first in 1790 had registered a spectacular advance. Nor should Americans have deemed it strange that the nation had

doubled its numbers since 1900; the same thing had happened between 1865 and 1900. What made the census report that the population had passed the one hundred and fifty million mark so interesting was that the prophets of the 1930's had been confounded. They had said that the population curve of the United States was destined shortly to level off, that the nation had reached full maturity and could not be expected to grow very much more. Instead, the decade of the 1940's had produced a phenomenal statistical spurt; when it ended there were nineteen million more Americans than when it began. Whether because of the revival of prosperity, or the outbreak of war, or both, the number of births shot sharply upward, and, with people living longer, the proportion of deaths to births lagged far behind. In the totals, the casualties due to the twin killers of the times, war and automobile traffic, could hardly be noticed. Post-war statistics were as bloated as those of the war years. According to careful estimates the country grew another ten millions in the three years following the census of 1950.[1]

Not fully appreciated by the public was the fact that this increase in population owed

Assimilation of immigrants comparatively little to immigration. In earlier years the United States could count on a steady influx of foreigners, but the restrictions imposed after the First World War virtually ended this source of population supply. The proportion of foreign-born in the United States dropped from 13.6 per cent in 1900 to 8.7 per cent in 1950, and, unless the nation's immigration policy should change, it was due almost to disappear. Moreover, the process of assimilation had made notable strides. This became increasingly clear during the Second World War when Americans, whatever their European ancestry, came to realize that they had infinitely more in common with each other than with the Old World nationalities from which they had sprung. Whatever the original immigrants may have thought, their descendants, especially after they had risen in economic status, felt little or no sense of inferiority. American surnames might represent a medley of European nations, but increasingly Americans thought of themselves only as Americans. Intermarriage among the descendants of different immigrant groups, and with the older American stock, tended also to dim transplanted nationalistic memories. Many an American citizen who on one side of his family stemmed only recently from Europe, was eligible on the other side for membership in the Sons or Daughters of the American Revolution, or even in the Society of Mayflower Descendants.

The distribution of the American population within the borders of the United States

Pacific Coast growth also showed significant changes. As had happened every decade since 1790 the center of popula-

[1] The total population of the United States, March 1, 1954, including members of the armed services overseas, had reached 161,542,000, according to U.S. Bureau of the Census estimates.

tion had pushed farther to the West, but this was no longer due to an advancing frontier. For the most part it resulted from a tremendous drive to the Pacific Coast and the Southwest. The population of California during the decade of the forties increased from about seven million to about ten million, with Washington and Oregon, New Mexico and Arizona, making comparable gains. As a result California passed both Illinois and Pennsylvania in population, and ranked second only to New York, while the other states mentioned left Eastern states previously in their population bracket far behind. The drive toward the West had begun long before the Second World War, but it was greatly accelerated during and after that struggle. It gathered momentum from the fact that many wartime industries, such as ship- and airplane-building, were located in this area, and offered high wages to induce labor to come in; also, many servicemen who had experienced the easier climates of the West returned as civilians when their terms of service came to an end.

The South, too, had undergone a remarkable transformation. Observing its economic unbalance, both within **The South** itself and in its effect on the nation as a whole, Franklin D. Roosevelt had once described it as "the nation's No. 1 economic problem." But much had happened to the South since the 1930's. As with the Pacific Coast, the war had led to a new emphasis on industrialism. Symbolic of the new trend were the expanded steel mills of Birmingham, the synthetic rubber plants of Baton Rouge, the shipyards of New Orleans, and the various manufacturing establishments of the Tennessee Valley that depended on cheap hydroelectric power. Cotton and tobacco, one or both, were still major products throughout the South, but the economic dependence of the section on its agricultural staples was far less marked than formerly. The evils of farm tenancy still existed, but with a difference in degree; also, the opportunity to flee the farm for the factory was far more readily available than ever before. Undoubtedly the greatest changes had occurred in Texas, where the tremendous new oil and gas fields that had been opened up earlier in the century had expanded to include a good share of the eastern part of the state. During the depression oil prices had been low, but with the coming of the Second World War they shot upward, while at the war's end, with the world's demand for oil still seemingly insatiable, the boom continued. The population of Texas, which had increased by twenty per cent during the decade of the forties, was by 1954 approximately eight million in spite of the fact that half the counties of the state — the rural counties — had lost steadily in population. In a sense oil had replaced cotton as the Texas staple. The number of Texas acres once planted to cotton had dropped in a generation from sixteen million to six million. Out of the riches of Texas oil the nation had produced its newest, and perhaps its richest, crop of millionaires. But for many lesser people the oil boom meant better jobs and greater security.

The drift to the West and Southwest did not mean any diminution in the persistent **Urban growth** trend toward urbanization. Indeed, cities in these regions grew even more rapidly than the cities of the East. Los Angeles, the most phenomenal of them all, started the century with a population of only a little more than 100,000, but by 1950, it was approaching two million. Houston, Texas, a city of only 250,000 in 1930, claimed 750,000 by 1954. Throughout the nation the proportion of the people that lived in the country dropped precipitately, while the proportion that lived in the city grew inordinately; in 1900, sixty per cent of the population could be classed as rural, but in 1950, only thirty-eight per cent. Suburbs, sometimes incorporated as a part of the city to which they furnished bedroom facilities, sometimes separately incorporated, and sometimes not incorporated at all, grew in leap-frog fashion around each metropolitan center. Curiously, the rapid growth of urban centers did not result in an equally rapid growth of urban political influence. In nearly every state, both for legislative and for congressional purposes, redistricting lagged far behind, and the power of the rural voters at election time was far greater than their numbers justified.

East or West, North or South, a basic feature of post-war America was the unrivaled business activity that gripped **Changes in** the nation. The last traces of **business** economic depression had disappeared, and the American people enjoyed a phenomenal prosperity. But the new business economy showed startling modifications since the days of the great American tycoons, or even since the days when Calvin Coolidge delivered his dictum: "The business of America is business." The number of stockholders in the great corporations had multiplied incredibly — in one of the greatest, for example, the American Telephone and Telegraph Company, over a million individuals held shares, and the maximum holding did not exceed one tenth of one per cent of the total. With ownership so widely diffused, the control of such companies lay not so much with a few leading stockholders as in earlier days, as with management itself. As for the business executives to whom the term management was applied, they tended more and more to be trained specialists; they might in some cases be related to the founding families, but far more likely, they were not. To a great extent the large corporation was its own banker, and so was no longer dependent on Wall Street. By building up reserves out of earnings, it provided without borrowing a large part of the funds necessary for the maintenance and retooling of its plants, and even for the expansion of its activities. Thus the stranglehold that Wall Street financiers had once exercised over the business world was materially lessened, if not broken altogether.

It was no longer Wall Street, but now government, mostly federal, and sometimes even state and local, which called the signals that corporation executives felt obliged to obey. Particularly in wartime, but by no means exclusively so, government interfered with the freedom of corporations to charge all the traffic would bear, it stated minimum wages below which they might not pay, it limited the advertising claims they could make for their products or services, and in numerous other ways it curtailed their prerogatives. Even more significant were the heavy taxes the corporations must pay — taxes on earnings, social security taxes, withholding taxes, property taxes — all involving intricate bookkeeping activities which cost the companies heavily, but which they could not possibly avoid. Business management must also keep an eye out for the attitudes of labor leaders, and of the public at large. As Frederick Lewis Allen in his arresting book, *The Big Change*, pointed out: "The limitations are so numerous and severe that to speak of [corporation managers] as engaged in 'free enterprise' is more picturesque than accurate. They are managing private institutions operating under a series of severe disciplines, and committed to doing so with an eye to the general welfare." [1] Of course, not all American business was big business, and in general the smaller the business the less the government circumscribed its freedom. But all along the line the limitations were felt. The United States had retained the capitalist system, but it was a modified capitalism quite different from the model of the nineteenth century. Freedom of competition in the original sense of the term had practically disappeared. Through trade associations — twelve thousand of them, national and local — the various types of businesses pooled their information, planned for the general interest, and, as far as anti-trust regulations would permit, reduced throat-cutting operations to a minimum.

Under the new dispensation the American working classes fared far better than ever before. In the year 1900 the American worker made on an average only four or five hundred dollars a

The "working classes"

year, and recurring unemployment, especially for the unskilled, was likely to be a chronic affair. Working time ran normally to sixty hours a week, often more, and the number of those who were "underfed, underclothed, and poorly housed" [1] was estimated at not less than ten million. Literally hundreds of thousands of children were wage earners, many of them at the expense of schooling. By mid-century the changes that had occurred in the position of labor were little short of revolutionary. The diminished value of the dollar made statistical comparison difficult, but according to the President's Council of Economic Advisers, reporting in January, 1951, only one-fifth of the "spending units" of the nation had incomes under $1,280 a year, and this included many single persons, both young and old, for whom such a sum was not necessarily inadequate. Three fifths of the "spending units" had incomes from $1,280 to $4,499, and one fifth $4,500 or over. Workers in American manufacturing establishments earned on an average $59.33 per week, or, assuming continuous employment, close to $3,000 per year, while by 1953 the average hourly wage in American factories had risen to $1.77, with a legal week of forty hours, and higher pay for overtime. The small amount of unemployment that existed was alleviated greatly by the existence of unemployment insurance, while child labor in mines and factories had practically disappeared.

Indeed, the ordinary American worker, far from harboring the proletarian sentiments radicals sought to arouse in him, thought of himself as middle class. Although housing never seemed quite to catch up with the demands of a steadily increasing population, he was usually well-housed. Housing projects in the cities, both publicly and privately financed, had eliminated most of the pestilential tenements of a half century earlier. During the decade of the forties the net gain in housing units for the nation as a whole reached 8,550,000, and the housing boom

---

[1] Frederick Lewis Allen, *The Big Change* (1952), p. 240. Quoted by permission of Harper and Brothers, New York.

[1] Robert Hunter, *Poverty* (1912), preface, p. vi, quoted in Allen, *The Big Change*, p. 56.

continued on into the fifties with new construction at the rate of about a million units a year. The FHA, established in 1934 as a New Deal agency, continued to underwrite mortgages, and much additional assistance came through such agencies as the Veterans Administration. The proportion of American working-class families who lived in respectable houses or apartments, equipped with good kitchens, central heating, adequate plumbing, electrical refrigerators, telephones, and comfortable furniture was far greater than it had ever been before; even the farm houses, except in the most primitive areas, were acquiring "all modern conveniences." No longer was the high American standard of living restricted to the favored upper classes alone. In astonishingly large numbers working-class families could afford to wear good clothes, own an automobile and a TV set, attend the movies, buy a house on the installment plan, take out insurance, enjoy vacations. The danger of revolution in the United States as long as these conditions existed was strictly theoretical. In fact, the revolution had already occurred.

The theory that assembly-line production could only be monotonous, and that work in the machine age must of necessity be deadly dull had also been seriously undermined. Certainly not every job provided entertainment for its holder, but routine tasks tended more and more to fall to machines, the operation of which required a certain amount of skill. In the building trades noisy power machines replaced hand labor to an amazing degree; in road-making, giant earth-moving devices did most of the work; in the loading of ships, great cranes lifted the crates and boxes into place. As a result of thousands of such changes the number of non-agricultural workers who could be classified as unskilled dropped precipitately, from about eleven millions in 1900 to about six millions in 1950, this in spite of the vastly increased production. Great numbers of the unskilled workers, particularly in New York City, were

Labor-saving devices

recently-arrived Puerto Ricans. Even on the farm, thanks largely to rural electrification and the gasoline engine, the back-breaking duties of an earlier generation had diminished phenomenally. In 1935, ninety per cent of the farms in the United States had no electricity; in 1954, ninety per cent of them had it. In 1935 a farmer had to pay from ten to seventeen cents per kilowatt hour for the electric current he bought; in 1954 it cost him on the average only a little over three cents. The variety of tools in use included such innovations as corn- and cotton-picking machines, milking machines, combines that harvested and threshed the grain in one operation, tractors to supply power for every variety of machine used in the fields. "Stoop-labor," as in the production of sugar beets and vegetables, still existed, much of it now furnished in the West and Southwest by Mexicans, either legal entrants or "wetbacks," but in a constantly reducing ratio to production. In fact, the nation counted only eight million farm laborers in 1950 in comparison with nine and one-half million in 1940, although during the decade agricultural production had risen twenty-five per cent.

The United States had certainly not achieved the "classless society" which some revolutionists set as their goal, but except for the "big rich," many of whom somehow contrived to retain their supremacy, the disparity of incomes between those in the upper brackets and those in the lower brackets was showing a remarkable change. High taxes accounted in very considerable part for this state of affairs. Even after the ablest lawyers had taken full advantage of every loophole in the law, a really large income tended to drop to modest proportions after the payment of taxes. For example, under the 1951 tax levies a married couple with two dependents would have to pay $18,884 in income taxes out of a $50,000 income; $56,036 out of a $100,000 income; $228,276 out of a $300,000 income; $411,228 out of a $500,000 income; and $871,456 out of a million dollar income.

The income tax

Most states also levied income taxes, graduated steeply to hit the higher income brackets, while estate taxes on inheritances, property taxes, sales taxes, and a host of "nuisance" taxes took additional tolls. There were still a few loopholes through which the "big rich" could escape, such as the low tax on capital gains (25 per cent), which were often purely speculative, tax-exempt state and municipal bonds, and the 27.5 per cent allowance for depletion of resources that kept many oil men rich. Whereas the depletion tax assumed that an oil field would be exhausted in less than four years, the actual figure was closer to fifteen. High salaries, too, could be made much higher by ultra-liberal expense accounts. But for most of those who in an earlier day would have been accounted extremely well-to-do there was, as one of them complained, "no such thing as being rich" any more, "only being poor on a much larger scale." [1]

Of necessity the standards of living of the well-to-do had to be modified to meet these new conditions. Imposing houses built in an earlier age, partly to display the owners' wealth, became a liability. Not only was the cost of upkeep prohibitive, but the servants needed to maintain such establishments simply did not exist; those few who tried to maintain the old manner of living confronted an endless procession of perplexities. The old servant class, once recruited steadily by immigration from Europe, had all but disappeared. Immigrants no longer came in numbers, and for those who came there were usually far better-paying jobs than domestic service could supply. Obliged for the most part to get along without servants, more and more American women did their own housework. They insisted on smaller houses, houses all on one floor, houses equipped with electric vacuum cleaners, washing machines, clothes dryers, ironers, dishwashers, and a hundred other labor-saving devices. Thus the houses of the rich and the houses of the poor tended to become more and more alike,

with functionalism winning most of the battles against display.

Foreign critics of the United States found their greatest satisfaction in concentrating on American treatment of the Negro, whose position on the bottom rung of the social and economic ladder had for so long remained unchallenged. Throughout the world the revolt against colonialism had been accompanied by an equally determined revolt against drawing the color line. Were Americans, as exponents of democracy, practicing what they preached? Were the much-advertised discriminations against the Negro in the United States as common as ever? Undoubtedly these questions put Americans on the defensive, but they could point, nevertheless, to remarkable changes in the status of the Negro; even he was far better off than he had ever been before. To Communist insistence that lynchings were an everyday occurrence in the United States, the statistics were a complete answer. The number of Negroes lynched each year had dropped from a humiliating total of 106 in 1900 to exactly zero in 1952. The civil and political disabilities from which Negroes had suffered were also on the decline. Negroes who had moved to the North from the time of the First World War onward had experienced little difficulty in voting, and their growing political power had much to do with breaking down the restrictions of the southern states on Negro suffrage. By the 1950's, indeed, under the impact of public opinion and judicial decisions, Negroes were permitted to vote throughout most of the South, even in the Democratic primaries, from which they had been most insistently barred. Discrimination against Negroes in the use of hotel, hospital, and restaurant facilities, and in the holding of property in "restricted" areas also were beginning to give way. Negroes participated freely in sports, including baseball and football; in 1951 the major baseball leagues counted fourteen Negroes among their most valued players. The year 1951 also saw the segregation of Negroes in the armed forces offi-

The Negro

---

[1] Quoted in Allen, *The Big Change*, pp. 215–216.

cially abandoned; thereafter the number of Negroes winning commissions and promotions in all branches of the services steadily increased. Probably most important of all, discriminations against Negroes in the field of education had received a deadly blow. Following a trend already well established, the Supreme Court ruled, March 17, 1954, that the old judicial doctrine of "separate but equal" facilities for the races would no longer satisfy the requirements of the Constitution, and that Negroes must everywhere in the nation be permitted to attend the same public schools as the whites.[1] Individual Negroes won high acclaim in many walks of life. By the elections of 1950 twenty-six of them achieved membership in state legislatures. Mrs. Edith S. Sampson became an alternate member of the United States delegation to the United Nations. Dr. Ralph J. Bunche received the Nobel Peace Prize for his effective handling of the Arab-Israeli dispute. Howard Swanson won an award of the New York Music Critics' Circle for his *Short Symphony* (1951). Peter M. Murray became vice-president of the Medical Society of the County of New York. Ethel Waters' autobiography, *His Eye Is on the Sparrow* (1951), made a notable sales record. Dorothy Maynor sang at Constitution Hall, Washington, D.C., in the spring of 1951, thus ending a long period of discrimination against Negro artists on its stage. And Negro participants in the Helsinki Olympics of 1952 set six new records.

In spite of all this, the economic status of the Negroes remained far less satisfactory than that of the whites. Whatever security the need of their labor had once given them in the rural South was undermined by the increasing use of the cotton-picker and the cotton-stripper. For thousands of them there was no alternative but flight to the industrial centers. There they soon learned that when workers were laid off the Negroes

Dr. *Ralph J. Bunche,* an American of African descent, won world-wide acclaim by arranging an armistice between Israel and the Arab states.

were likely to be the first to go; also, that when new workers were taken on they were usually the last to be hired. During the depression the relief measures of the New Deal proved to be a godsend to the Negroes, and resulted, incidentally, in a wholesale drift from the Republican Party which had freed the slaves to the Democratic Party which had fed the needy. Fortunately, the rising tide of prosperity that characterized the forties lifted the Negroes along with the rest of the population. Their incomes tended to be substantially lower than those of the whites, their living conditions less satisfactory, and their jobs less secure. But in comparison with their earlier economic status, they had gone far. No longer were they all in the lowest income brackets. Many had lifted themselves from the bottom fifth of the "spending units" to the fourth, third, and even second fifths. Their rising economic status was reflected in a variety of other ways. Illiteracy among them had declined from 44.5 per cent in 1900 to 11 per cent in 1950. More and more of them attended colleges or universities, a total of 74,526 in 1950, according to United States Office of Education statistics, but this figure was probably far too low since so many institutions kept no records that dis-

[1] This opinion, in which every member of the Court concurred, was delivered by the new Chief Justice, Earl Warren, whom President Eisenhower had chosen the year before to succeed Chief Justice Vinson, deceased.

tinguished between white and Negro students. Also, they were increasingly well organized and on guard to defend their rights, particularly through the National Association for the Advancement of Colored People, which left no stone unturned in its efforts to achieve for American Negroes full equality of treatment. The virtually complete failure of the Communists to make converts among the American Negroes was not without considerable significance. Not even among the prisoners of war captured by the Red forces in Korea were they able to make any serious headway. American Negro workers were no more ready than American white workers to classify themselves as a downtrodden proletariat.

If equality between the races had not yet been achieved, equality between the sexes **Women's** had very nearly approached the **rights** ultimate. Women won full suf-

TV. The social, industrial, and political influence of television is immeasurable. TV aerials have sprouted a new skyline across the nation. This is a transmitting antenna.

frage rights at the end of the First World War, and the number of women in politics grew greater with each succeeding election. Educational equality had long been theirs, but the numbers who availed themselves of their opportunities steadily increased. Women lawyers, women physicians, women preachers, women professors, women writers, women in business were too numerous to excite comment. Equal property rights for married women reached a maximum with the growing popularity of community property laws, laws which in California and many other western states automatically divided the family income and assets evenly between husband and wife. But in the nation as a whole the women quite outranked the men as property holders; seventy per cent of the nation's property belonged to them. Divorce was more common than ever before, and most of the divorces were granted to women; but not all who were divorced remained single, and the institution of marriage stood up remarkably well. In nearly all matters women enjoyed far greater freedom than their grandmothers, and even than their mothers. They dressed comfortably and sensibly, ignored the taboos of an earlier age, claimed for themselves, and for the most part achieved, the same standards of conduct that applied to men. Nor were these rights and privileges confined to the upper income brackets alone. Women of every class participated to a remarkable degree in the new freedom.

The pursuit of happiness, a goal set by the Declaration of Independence, was never long absent from the American mind. **Amusements** With the attainment of almost complete literacy, Americans, more than they ever had before, found amusement in reading. The number of daily newspapers diminished, but their circulation rose. Popular magazines to fit the taste of the masses were multiplied endlessly. Comic books reached not only the juveniles, but millions of adults also. Pocket books that sold for thirty-five cents or less made available to the general public a tremendous variety of reading, good and bad, and sold by the hundreds of thousands. Television, which technical and financial considerations had barred from general use until after the Second World War, at last caught on. Not until the year 1947, with twelve stations broadcasting televised programs in nine American cities, did its extensive expansion begin. From then on the growth of the industry was phenomenal. By June, 1952, it had become a three billion dollar a year business, with well over one hundred television broadcasting stations, and about eighteen million receiving sets.

The growth of television, as already noted,[1] hit the moving picture industry hard, and gave radio plenty of competition. It also affected athletics; many people who had previously bought tickets to football and baseball games preferred, when it was possible, to watch the games at home. In fact, one of the most notable results of television was the way in which it reconstructed the American family, not around the dinner table or the fireside, but around the television set. Television programs rescued vaudeville from the undeserved fate to which the movies had consigned it, brought to life good and bad films that had long been extinct, made excellent advances in broadcasting "live" plays and musical productions, and created an insatiable demand for boxing and wrestling matches. The campaign and election of 1952 introduced the television industy to politics. Hundreds of thousands of Americans watched the antics of the nominating conventions by television, and saw as well as heard the candidates address audiences in all parts of the United States. They watched, also, the coronation of Queen Elizabeth II of Great Britain, the return of the soldiers from Korea, and news events of importance all over the world. After the election, President Eisenhower made some effort to substitute communication with the country by television for the fireside chats by radio which Franklin D. Roosevelt had used so effect ively.

The same drive toward scientific achieve-

[1] See p. 526.

ment that had produced television for the amusement of the people and atomic explosions for their perturbation exhibited itself in many other ways also. Except for the secrecy, real and fancied, that for security reasons tended to surround atomic research, most scientific investigation was essentially international rather than national in character with individuals and groups from all over the world contributing toward the attainment of a given goal. In general, scientific research, both at home and abroad, depended more and more upon cooperative activities to obtain results. The costs involved were often spectacularly high, and in the United States, at least, were met in considerable part by federal funds, especially when the projects undertaken were of interest to the armed services. Congress, in May, 1950, established the National Science Foundation "to promote the welfare of science; to advance the national health, prosperity, and welfare; to secure the national defense." Operating through a National Science Board and a director, the Foundation sought to develop a national science policy, and to support basic scientific research in a variety of ways, including the awarding of graduate fellowships. The cooperative and international nature of scientific research, whether in university or n industrial laboratories, made the task of assigning credit to individuals extremely difficult. Perhaps Americans were less successful than Europeans in establishing basic principles, but at least Americans showed infinite versatility in applying the new ideas to practical ends.

Out of this composite of research came such wonder-working drugs as penicillin, aureomycin, and cortisone, blood plasma for use in the treatment of the wounded, a variety of life-saving serums, powerful insecticides such as DDT to cut down on carriers of disease, and thousands of other new products of incalculable importance to medical science. Out of it came also tremendous advances in the field of electronics, especially radar, which meant so much to ships and planes during the war in the detection of op-

Scientific advance

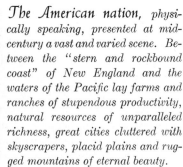

The American nation, *physically speaking, presented at mid-century a vast and varied scene. Between the "stern and rockbound coast" of New England and the waters of the Pacific lay farms and ranches of stupendous productivity, natural resources of unparalleled richness, great cities cluttered with skyscrapers, placid plains and rugged mountains of eternal beauty.*

THE ROCKY COAST. Northern New England is dotted with lights and beacons. This one is Portland Light off Portland, Maine.

THE COLUMBIA RIVER. Rich in salmon and a source of hydroelectric power, this is one of the great waterways of the Pacific Northwest.

MOUNTAINS AND PLAINS. Natural beauty and natural resources make Montana a rich and varied state. Sheep and cattle grazing are common in the plains.

posing craft; but the application of electronics to industrial uses also went forward apace, for example with the construction of electronic calculating machines able to solve problems of infinite complexity. Out of the necessities of war came the improvement and greater use of synthetic rubber, synthetic fabrics, frozen foods, and plastics, all of which could be, and were, adapted to peacetime needs. Jet-propelled aircraft broke through the sound barrier, and threatened to revolutionize commercial as well as military aviation. And so on indefinitely.

To the very considerable concern of those who called themselves humanists, American achievements in science were not fully matched in the field of literature. Of making many books there was no end, and great numbers of these books were good books. But the literary distinction of the decade following the First World War found no parallel after the Second.

Literature

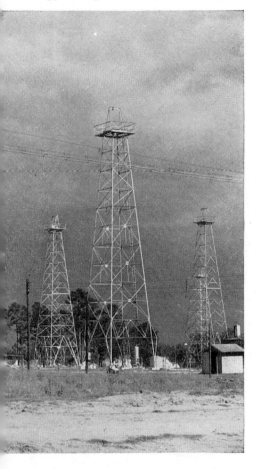

STEEL AND SKY. Oil derricks on sandy Texas soil stand against an approaching storm.

TOWERS OF MANHATTAN. The Third Avenue "El," one of the last of its kind in New York.

FERTILE FIELDS. Endless acres of wheat and corn checker the great plains. These fields are near Fergus Falls Minnesota.

Some of the writers of earlier years continued to hold the attention of the public, but the number of new writers whose works would live on seemed strangely few. Such able writers as William Faulkner and Ernest Hemingway continued to produce, but the sources of their power reached back to an earlier day. Among the best of the novels that came out of the war were Norman Mailer's *The Naked and the Dead* (1948), Irwin Shaw's *The Young Lions* (1948), James Jones's *From Here to Eternity* (1951), James A. Michener's *Tales of the South Pacific* (1947), and (on the Korean War) *The Bridges at Toko-ri* (1953).

The history of the Second World War reached the public officially through two sets of publications, Samuel Eliot Morison's *History of United States Naval Operations in World War II* (9 vols., 1947–54), and an even more voluminous series, of composite authorship, *United States Army in World War II* (21 vols., 1947–54); but far more people read biographic or autobiographic accounts such as Dwight D. Eisenhower's *Crusade in Europe* (1948), Robert Sherwood's *Roosevelt and Hopkins* (1948), and Omar N. Bradley, *A Soldier's Story* (1951). Penetrating philosophical works by American authors were

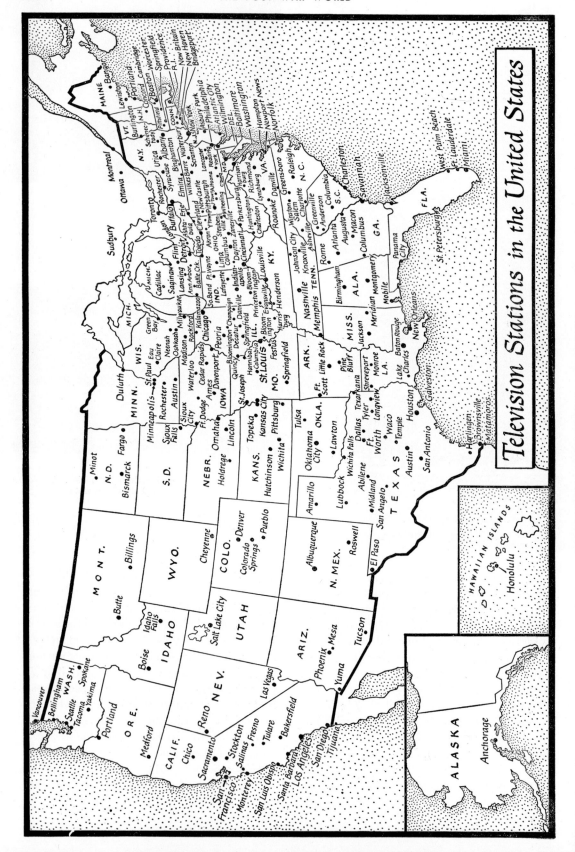

Television Stations in the United States

not much in evidence, but many American readers found food for thought in the writings of an Englishman, Arnold Joseph Toynbee, whose *A Study of History* (1946) abridged six earlier volumes on the same subject, and was soon supplemented by two still shorter books, *Civilization on Trial* (1948), and *War and Civilization* (1951). Among serious readers there was an unmistakable interest in books on religion, such as Reinhold Niebuhr's *Faith and History* (1949), Harry Emerson Fosdick's *The Man from Nazareth* (1949), and Henry Morton Robinson's *The Cardinal* (1950). Possibly the inability of human reason to provide solutions for the overwhelming problems of the age had led to a new reliance on faith. Certainly church membership was on the increase, up about fifty per cent since 1926, and had come to include some fifty-eight per cent of the population. In line with this trend, General Eisenhower after his election to the Presidency joined the Presbyterian Church, included in his inaugural address a prayer of his own composition, and set a new precedent by opening cabinet meetings with prayer.

Although the President's personal popularity long remained undimmed, the Republican party was clearly on **Elections of 1954** the defensive as the time approached for the mid-term elections of 1954. After the fighting in Korea died down, lowered expenditures for national defense brought much temporary distress to both industry and agriculture. Naturally critics of the Republican administration made good use of this situation for campaign purposes. They also criticized the Dixon-Yates contract, by which the federal government had authorized private capitalists to construct a power plant to supplement TVA needs for atomic research, as a sell-out of public to private power interests, and found fault with the harshness of the new loyalty-security program. The Republicans, particularly through Vice-President Nixon, continued the charge that the Democrats were "soft on Communism," [1] and in an effort to recover the Negro vote, most of which

they had lost during the New Deal, tended to identify the desegregation decision of the Supreme Court with the Eisenhower administration. In the end the Democrats won a majority of 29 in the House of Representatives and of 2 in the Senate, while the number of Republican governors dropped from 29 before the election to 21 after it.

In foreign affairs changes within Russia aroused new hopes for peace. After Stalin's death dissension among the **Soviet** members of the "presidium," **policy** as the ruling clique in the USSR was now called, led in December, 1953, to the summary execution of Lavrenti P. Beria, Stalin's once powerful police chief, and in February, 1955, to the resignation of Malenkov as premier.[2] The chief power then devolved upon Nicolai A. Bulganin, who became premier, and Nikita S. Khrushchev, who as first secretary of the Communist party wielded even greater power. By way of answer to NATO the new Soviet leaders soon signed at Warsaw a mutual assistance pact with the Russian satellite states, but in a dramatic reversal of policy invited Great Britain, France, and the United States to join with the Soviet government in concluding a treaty of peace with Austria. This invitation the western powers accepted with alacrity, and at Vienna in May, 1955, the long-delayed treaty, which called for the neutralization of Austria after the Swiss pattern and the withdrawal from Austrian soil of all foreign troops, was duly signed. By the end of the summer Austria was free. Bulganin and Khrushchev also paid a goodwill visit to Tito of Yugoslavia, and toured India, Burma, and Afghanistan, seeking everywhere to gain friends. They even modified the Soviet practice of news censor-

---

[1] Republican senators furnished many of the votes after the election to sustain a charge against Senator McCarthy of conduct unbecoming a senator. When McCarthy died suddenly in 1957, McCarthyism was already long since dead.

[2] Malenkov remained a member of the presidium until July, 1957, when he was removed, together with Molotov and several others who had opposed Khrushchev.

ship, permitted groups of Russians to go abroad, and allowed some foreign tourists to visit Russia.

The most outstanding result of this new conciliatory attitude was the "conference at the summit" that Winston Churchill had long sought, but had failed to obtain. Meeting at Geneva, July 25, 1955, without a formal agenda but with the understanding that their discussions should center mainly upon the abatement of European tensions, were President Eisenhower, Sir Anthony Eden, who had succeeded the aged Churchill as British prime minister, Edgar Faure, the current French premier, Bulganin and Khrushchev, besides many lesser lights. For six days the delegates debated without the bitter recriminations that had characterized earlier negotiations, but little more than this friendly "spirit of Geneva" came out of the Conference; on all the principal sources of tension there was total, if mannerly, disagreement. President Eisenhower took the Russians somewhat by surprise when he proposed that "we give each other a complete blueprint of our military establishment" and provide mutually for inspection by means of "aerial photography," but at a subsequent meeting of the "Big Four" foreign ministers, also held in Geneva, Molotov, the Russian delegate, described Eisenhower's suggestions as "not of a constructive nature." Molotov further made it clear that the Soviet Union would never accept any plan for the unification of Germany, such as western-style free elections, that would imperil the ascendancy of Communism in eastern Germany.

Another Geneva Conference

Progress toward the reduction of tension in Asia was equally unsatisfactory. Only the active intervention of the United States prevented Red China from making an all-out effort to conquer Formosa, which together with some adjacent and off-shore islands was all that remained of Chiang Kai-shek's Republic of China. By a treaty signed with Chiang, December 2, 1954, which Congress at President Eisen-

Asiatic relations

hower's insistence specifically authorized him to defend by force if necessary, the United States committed itself to the protection of Formosa and the Pescadores Islands. In addition to this "necessary link in the Far Eastern defense," Secretary Dulles soon added another, the Southeast Asia Treaty Organization (SEATO), an anti-Communist pact to which the United States, Pakistan, the Philippines, Thailand, Australia, New Zealand, France, and Great Britain subscribed at Bangkok, February 22–25, 1955. To close the Anti-Communist gap between southeastern Asia and the Mediterranean, another conference, held in Baghdad, November 21–22, 1955, created the Middle East Treaty Organization (METO), with Great Britain, Pakistan, Iran, Iraq, and Turkey as the official adherents, and the United States as an unofficial benefactor. The reaction of Red China to this program of encirclement was less bellicose than might have been expected. A visit by Dag Hammarskjöld, Secretary General of the United Nations, to Peking won a promise that American airmen and civilians imprisoned by the Chinese Communists would be freed, while at a Congress of Asian and African nations, held in Bandung, Indonesia, during April, 1955, Chou En-lai, the Red China premier, assumed a conciliatory pose, and accepted without apparent resentment the essentially neutralist rather than anti-western attitude that the conference adopted. Nevertheless, the United States steadfastly refused to recognize the Communist government of China, successfully resisted all efforts to permit Red China delegates to replace those of Chiang Kai-shek in the United Nations, and ardently opposed any lessening of the trade restrictions imposed on the Chinese mainland by many of the free nations of the world.

It was the oil-rich Middle East rather than the Far East that occupied the world's principal attention during the last half of Eisenhower's first term. Here the sources of conflict could hardly have been more numerous. Local potentates bar-

The Middle East

gained with foreign oil companies for maximum profits, and the oil companies competed vigorously among themselves along national lines. Heated antagonisms existed between East and West, an inevitable legacy of colonialism. The very existence of the state of Israel, and the way it had come into being, fanned into flames long-standing hatreds between Arabs and Jews. The Arab states persistently refused to recognize Israel, and united in what amounted to an economic war against the new state. Hundreds of thousands of displaced Arabs who had fled from Israel, leaving their property behind them, lived miserably in refugee camps. The ownership and operation of the Suez Canal by a foreign corporation was a constant thorn in the flesh for Egypt, the nation through which the Canal ran. And the importance of the Canal to world trade, particularly in oil, made it an object of solicitude to all western Europe, which had so little oil of its own.

In response to nationalistic pressure and the rising tide of anti-colonialism, the British finally withdrew from Egypt **Egypt** early in the 1950's. The strong man of the new Egyptian republic, which an army junta proclaimed in 1953, was Colonel Gamel Abdel Nasser, who sought to cover the slow progress of internal reform under his regime by a vigorous foreign policy. Claiming that the Israeli government was arming against him, and that the West would not give him arms enough to meet the challenge, he made a bargain with Czechoslovakia to exchange Egyptian cotton for Russian-type arms, thus opening his country and the whole Middle East to Communist penetration. Apparently Nasser had in mind not only the extinction of Israel, but also the creation of an all-Arab federation with himself at its head. He gave every possible aid to the nationalist movements in French North Africa, and in his propaganda developed a strongly anti-French, anti-British, anti-American line. One of Nasser's favorite projects was the Aswan High Dam on the upper Nile river, from the building of

which he expected great things for the Egyptian economy. Toward the financing of this 1.3 billion dollar undertaking, the United States had agreed to supply 56 million dollars, Great Britain 14 million dollars, and the International Bank for Reconstruction and Development 200 million dollars. But Nasser, hoping to play the East against the West in his search for additional funds, let it be known that he was considering a Soviet proposal (never firmly made) to finance the project. The United States, in consequence, withdrew its offer, after which both Great Britain and the International Bank withdrew theirs. Thereupon Nasser, in angry retaliation, announced on July 26, 1956, the nationalization of the Suez Canal. Henceforth all of the funds, assets, and obligations of the Suez Canal Company were to be the property of the Egyptian government, and the income derived from operating the Canal would be used for building the High Dam.

Most outraged by Nasser's coup were Great Britain and France. The British government owned 44% of the **Suez** Canal stock, and private French shareholders 78% of the balance, so profits were involved, although not for long, since the Canal Company's concession was due to expire in 1968. The graver dangers were that Nasser, under Soviet influence, might not only stop the flow of vital oil through the Canal to western Europe, but also by his all-Arab, anti-Israel crusade bring on a third World War. For a time American restraint kept the British and the French from military intervention, but early in November, 1956, a Franco-British force took Port Said and began to occupy all Egyptian territory adjacent to the Canal. At about the same time the Israeli launched a spectacularly successful attack on Egyptian troops in the Gaza strip and the Sinai desert, in retaliation, the Israeli claimed, for constant border outrages. The evidence of Anglo-Franco-Israeli collusion was strong, but the British and French claimed that they had acted only to maintain uninterrupted transit through the Canal, as their treaty rights permitted.

Knowing that the course of action they had chosen would deeply offend the United States, the anti-Egyptian allies had not consulted the American government in advance, assuming, apparently, that it would accept a *fait accompli.* But instead the Eisenhower administration, working mainly through the United Nations where the Soviet and neutralist blocs gave it enthusiastic support, demanded and obtained an immediate end to hostilities, together with the speedy withdrawal of all the attacking forces. In the end it was arranged that small United Nations detachments, drawn exclusively from the armies of minor powers, should police the troubled areas while the invaders got out. Meantime the Egyptian dictator, Nasser, whose forces had shown up badly in the fighting, vented his rage by blocking the Canal with sunken ships, while at the same time Arab sabotage, particularly in Syria, ended the westward flow of oil through three out of four of the Middle East's great pipe lines. Somewhat belatedly, the American government put into effect an emergency plan, worked out by the American oil companies long before, which temporarily helped supply the oil needs of western Europe. After several months the Canal was reopened strictly on Nasser's terms, the pipe-lines were in part repaired, and oil began to flow westward again.

Following his rift with the United States, Sir Anthony Eden, whose health was also **The** seriously impaired, resigned as **Eisenhower** prime minister, and was suc- **Doctrine** ceeded by Harold Macmillan. But neither the British nor the French governments would accept further responsibility for the Middle East, and the United States had no choice but to fill itself the "vacuum of power" it had helped to create. In recognition of this development, Congress, at the President's insistence, gave its approval to what was generally called the Eisenhower Doctrine, according to which the American government agreed to support against external Communist aggression any Middle East-ern power that asked for American help. Congress also granted the President, at his request, a special fund of $200,000,000 for him to use in the struggle against Communist expansion in the Middle East.

The Anglo-French-Israeli action against Egypt shared headlines in the newspapers with events of equally great moment in Central Europe. Early **Hungary** in 1956 Khrushchev had stunned the Communist world by a speech to the Party Congress in Moscow charging Stalin with the crimes of self-glorification, gross misrule, wholesale murder, mass repressions, unjustifiable deportations, and much else that the non-Communist world had taken for granted all along. A calculated result of this sudden downgrading of the once all-powerful Soviet leader was better Soviet relations with Marshal Tito of Yugoslavia, whom Stalin had attempted unsuccessfully to purge. But another result, far less palatable to the Russian leaders, was trouble in Poland and Hungary, where discontent with Russian domination came finally to a head in October and November. In Poland the Soviet leaders made terms with the revolt, permitting a Communist-type government somewhat independent of Moscow to take over. But in Hungary, where the revolt won widespread support within the Hungarian army and went to far greater extremes, there was bitter fighting and ruthless suppression. Death totals, estimated as high as 50,000, and not all Hungarian, occurred before Russian troops and tanks were able to win an uneasy peace. More than 150,000 refugees fled to neighboring Austria, from which the nations of the western world made frantic efforts to transport them as immigrants — the United States agreed at first to take 21,500, but actually took many more. By a decisive vote in which many neutralist nations joined the western bloc, the United Nations Assembly voiced in vigorous resolutions its censure of Russian behavior. But the Soviet government, unlike the invaders of Egypt, persisted in its course, blamed American propaganda for all the trouble in Hungary, and through its puppet government in Budapest refused even to grant United Nations investigators permission to enter the stricken nation. President Eisenhower publicly expressed his sympathy with the heroic fight of the Hungarians for freedom, but denied that the American government had in any way sought to promote a revolt that was foredoomed to failure. One result of the tough Russian policy in Hungary was that the NATO alliance, which had shown many signs of falling apart, began to draw together again.

Meantime the election of 1956 had come and gone. That Eisenhower would be a candidate for renomination seemed **Election of** in grave doubt after he suffered **1956** a heart attack, September 24, 1955, while on vacation at Denver, Colorado. He made an excellent recovery, however, and by Armistice Day was back in Washington. The following February 29 he announced his decision to run again, and in spite of an operation in June for ileitis, a serious intestinal disease, he did not change his mind. At the Republican convention, held in San Francisco late in August, both Eisenhower and Nixon were unanimously renominated. A week earlier the Democrats, meeting in Chicago, had renominated Stevenson, with his closest contestant, Estes Kefauver, as their choice for Vice-President. Despite platform rhetoric, there were really no basic differences, either on foreign or domestic affairs, between the President and his challenger. Two proposals that the Democratic candidate brought forward, an end to the draft and negotiations with Russia to stop further testings of the dreaded H-bomb, were denounced by the President as impracticable, and seem to have swayed few voters. Indeed, the re-election of Eisenhower, whose popularity withstood all attacks, was never in doubt. Against the charge that he was overfriendly to big business could be set the fact that in July, 1955, he had cancelled the Dixon-Yates contract, when assured that the city of Memphis would build its own municipal power plant, thus relieving TVA of its

anticipated shortage. Also, he had vetoed a bill to free natural gas producers from federal regulation, not because he opposed such legislation on principle, but because some oil interests had made improper campaign contributions to aid members of Congress known to favor the measure. The President probably gained still further support as a result of the turmoil in Egypt and Hungary; many voters hesitated to change leaders in the midst of such crises. Eisenhower's popular majority in 1956 was the largest since Roosevelt's in 1936, while the vote in the electoral college stood 457 to 73.[1] Other election results, however, virtually duplicated those of 1954. The Democrats retained control of the House by 32 votes, of the Senate by 2, and increased the number of Democratic governorships to 29. Perhaps the fundamental explanation of the split voting lay in the fact that through the years party labels had come to mean very little. Independent voters therefore considered principally the views of the men for whom they cast their ballots, and tended to ignore mere party loyalties.

While the nation's deep concern with foreign affairs long overshadowed what was happening to the domestic **Business** economy, business oscillations **Conditions** throughout the 1950's were a source of considerable anxiety to close observers. Happily the recession of 1954–55 proved to be short-lived. World trade, facilitated alike by a new three-year Trade Agreements Act and the continuance of the Truman foreign aid policy, prospered inordinately, and generous installment credits did much to promote a buying boom, especially in automobiles, housing, household appliances, and television sets. Unemployment all but disappeared, and investment seekers eagerly drove the price of stocks to unprecedented heights. Fearing an unhealthy expansion such as had preceded the Panic of 1929, the Federal Reserve Board raised its rediscount

[1] Stevenson should have received 74 votes, but an Alabama elector voted instead for Walter B. Jones of Montgomery.

rates in rapid stages from $1\frac{1}{2}\%$ to $3\frac{1}{2}\%$, with each increase immediately reflected in higher interest rates on commercial loans. New margin requirements designed to restrain stock speculation rose likewise, first from 50% to 60%, then up to 70%. As another means of restraining the boom, the federal government cut down sharply on expenditures, even for defense and foreign aid, although President Eisenhower's proposed budget for the fiscal year 1957–58 ran to $71.8 billion, and elicited from Secretary of the Treasury Humphrey the prediction of a "hair-curling depression" if such excessive appropriations continued. Congress, in ready response, began to trim down the President's requests.

Events soon proved that it was easier to put the brakes on business than to take them off. A decline in the value of stocks that set in during the summer of 1957 came to a climax on October 22, when sales on the New York Stock Exchange reached a volume of over five million shares, with losses as high as from 25% to 40%. Business fell off rapidly, and unemployment by early 1958 had risen to over five million, the highest such figure since 1941. At once government policy began to change; the rediscount rate dropped to $2\frac{1}{4}\%$, margin requirements to 50%, and government spending loosened up. What to do for the farmer, who had not shared in the boom, became an obsession with both parties. Back in 1956 Congress, under the President's urging, had enacted a soil-bank program, strongly reminiscent of the New Deal, but the payments it had authorized for acreage reductions and the withdrawal of poor lands from use had not achieved the results expected. With an election in sight, politicians of both parties looked with increasing disfavor on Secretary Benson's flexible price supports, and vehemently demanded his resignation.

During the fall and winter of 1957–58, one untoward event after another added to the **Alarums and** alarm for the future that the **Excursions** American public was beginning to feel. Scandals in the misuse of labor funds, particularly in the powerful Teamsters' Union, rocked the labor world, and imperiled the solidarity it had achieved by the A.F. of L.-C.I.O. merger of 1955. In the field of education, integration slowed down almost to a halt. When the governor of Arkansas, by calling out the national guard, circumvented a carefully-planned effort to admit nine Negro children to a white public school in Little Rock, President Eisenhower countered by placing the Arkansas guardsmen under Army control, and sending a thousand airborne regulars to the scene. The Negro pupils attended classes, but the use of Federal troops against a state revived memories of Reconstruction throughout the South, and made the North realize the depth of southern feeling on integration. Soviet launching in October of the first earth satellite (Sputnik I), followed a month later by a second (Sputnik II), jarred Americans out of their complacent assumption that western scientists led the world, and pointed up the lag in rocket and missile development that economy in defense spending had produced. Months elapsed before the Army got its "Explorer" into orbit, and the Navy its "Vanguard." Late in November the President suffered a mild stroke. His recovery was so rapid that he was able to attend a NATO conference in Paris before Christmas, but public concern for his health remained great. Soviet leaders were pressing hard for another conference at the summit; could the President effectively represent the United States? And what would happen if he became unable to perform the normal duties of his high office? Throughout the world tension was on the rise, with a rebellion against French rule in Algeria, another against British rule in Cyprus, a union of Syria with Nasser's Egypt, a civil war in Indonesia, the success of Communist propaganda almost everywhere. Truly the times were "out of joint," but the American people, despite their deep anxiety, had not lost faith; deep in their hearts they believed that they could see the crisis through, and without a surrender of the freedoms they cherished.

Bibliography

For much that has transpired since the inauguration of Eisenhower one must trust to the newspapers, periodicals, and yearbooks. There are a few good books, however, that describe the social scene. Frederick Lewis Allen, *The Big Change; America Transforms Itself, 1900–1950* (1952), finds in the first half of the twentieth century an era of remarkable progress for the ordinary man. This may be compared with Strunsky, *The Living Tradition: Change and America*, already mentioned, which surveys the social, economic, and political situation on the eve of the Second World War. Peter F. Drucker, *The New Society: The Anatomy of the Industrial Order* (1950), is an appraisal of modern industrial society and the problems it is creating. Russell W. Davenport and others, *U.S.A.: The Permanent Revolution* (1951), is an unrestrained defense of the American way of life, sponsored by the editors of the magazine, *Fortune*. Gerald W. Johnson, *Incredible Tale: The Odyssey of the Average American in the Last Half Century* (1950), is informal, provocative, and optimistic. Allan Nevins and John A. Krout, editors, *The Greater City: New York, 1898–1948* (1948), is an entertaining popular history, profusely illustrated. With regard to the increase in the nation's population, see Joseph S. Davis, *The Population Upsurge in the United States* (1949); Louis I. Dublin, *Health Progress, 1936 to 1945* (1948); R. C. Williams, *The United States Public Health Service, 1798–1950* (1951); and Louis I. Dublin and others, *Length of Life: A Study of the Life Table* (1949). Ernest R. Groves, *The American Woman: The Feminine Side of a Masculine Civilization* (1944), describes the changing status of women, especially in wartime. Gilbert V. Seldes, *The Great Audience* (1950), deals with the movies, the radio, and television. Oscar Handlin, *The American People in the Twentieth Century* (1954), pays especial attention to the immigrants and the Negroes.

On the Negro, Myrdal, *An American Dilemma*, continues to be useful. Robert C. Weaver, *Negro Labor: A National Problem* (1946), is a competent and objective analysis. Wilson Record, *The Negro and the Communist Party* (1951), provides authentic evidence as to why Communist propaganda failed among the American Negroes.

On the world in general, Hans Kohn, *The Twentieth Century: A Midway Account of the Western World* (1949), attempts to supply the data for a better understanding between the Old World and the New. W. P. Webb, *The Great Frontier* (1952), points out the significance of disappearing world opportunities for European expansion. *Propaganda in War and Crises: Materials for American Policy*, edited by Daniel Lerner (1951), discusses some of the key problems that confront the nation in times of international tension. *Mid-Century: The Social Implications of Scientific Progress*, edited by John Ely Burchard (1950), brings together the divergent opinions of forty eminent scientists. David Lilienthal, *This I Do Believe* (1949), argues that democracy has the capacity to survive any trials that may lie ahead. Vannevar Bush, *Modern Arms and Free Men* (1949), by the one-time head of the Office of Scientific Research, is too optimistic to be wholly convincing. Walter Gellhorn, *Security, Loyalty, and Science* (1950), stresses the problem created by the demand for secrecy in atomic research.

On the European situation Theodore H. White, *Fire in the Ashes: Europe in Mid-Century* (1953), is an excellent journalistic appraisal.

APPENDIX

i

THE DECLARATION OF INDEPENDENCE

In Congress, July 4, 1776.

THE UNANIMOUS DECLARATION OF THE THIRTEEN UNITED STATES OF AMERICA.

WHEN, in the course of human events, it becomes necessary for one people to dissolve the political bands which have connected them with another, and to assume, among the powers of the earth, the separate and equal station to which the laws of nature and of nature's God entitle them, a decent respect to the opinions of mankind requires that they should declare the causes which impel them to the separation.

We hold these truths to be self-evident, that all men are created equal; that they are endowed by their Creator with certain unalienable rights; that among these, are life, liberty, and the pursuit of happiness. That, to secure these rights, governments are instituted among men, deriving their just powers from the consent of the governed; that, whenever any form of government becomes destructive of these ends, it is the right of the people to alter or to abolish it, and to institute a new government, laying its foundation on such principles, and organizing its powers in such form, as to them shall seem most likely to effect their safety and happiness. Prudence, indeed, will dictate that governments long established, should not be changed for light and transient causes; and, accordingly, all experience hath shown, that mankind are more disposed to suffer, while evils are sufferable, than to right themselves by abolishing the forms to which they are accustomed. But, when a long train of abuses and usurpations, pursuing invariably the same object, evinces a design to reduce them under absolute despotism, it is their right, it is their duty, to throw off such government and to provide new guards for their future security. Such has been the patient sufferance of these colonies, and such is now the necessity which constrains them to alter their former systems of government. The history of the present King of Great Britain is a history of repeated injuries and usurpations, all having, in direct object, the establishment of an absolute tyranny over these States. To prove this, let facts be submitted to a candid world: —

He has refused his assent to laws the most wholesome and necessary for the public good.

He has forbidden his governors to pass laws of immediate and pressing importance, unless suspended in their operation till his assent should be obtained; and, when so suspended, he has utterly neglected to attend to them.

He has refused to pass other laws for the accommodation of large districts of people, unless those people would relinquish the right of representation in the legislature; a right inestimable to them, and formidable to tyrants only.

He has called together legislative bodies at places unusual, uncomfortable, and distant from the depository of their public records, for the sole purpose of fatiguing them into compliance with his measures.

He has dissolved representative houses repeatedly for opposing, with manly firmness, his invasions on the rights of the people.

He has refused, for a long time after such dissolutions, to cause others to be elected; whereby the legislative powers, incapable of annihilation, have returned to the people at large for their exercise; the state remaining, in the meantime, exposed to all the danger of invasion from without, and convulsions within.

He has endeavored to prevent the population of these States; for that purpose, obstructing the laws for naturalization of foreigners, refusing to pass others to encourage their migration hither, and raising the conditions of new appropriations of lands.

He has obstructed the administration of justice, by refusing his assent to laws for establishing judiciary powers.

He has made judges dependent on his will alone, for the tenure of their offices, and the amount and payment of their salaries.

He has erected a multitude of new offices, and sent hither swarms of officers to harass our people, and eat out their substance.

He has kept among us, in time of peace, standing armies, without the consent of our legislatures.

He has affected to render the military independent of, and superior to, the civil power.

He has combined, with others, to subject us to a jurisdiction foreign to our Constitution, and unacknowledged by our laws; giving his assent to their acts of pretended legislation:

For quartering large bodies of armed troops among us:

For protecting them by a mock trial, from punishment, for any murders which they should commit on the inhabitants of these States:

For cutting off our trade with all parts of the world:

For imposing taxes on us without our consent:

For depriving us, in many cases, of the benefit of trial by jury:

For transporting us beyond seas to be tried for pretended offences:

For abolishing the free system of English laws in a neighboring province, establishing therein an arbitrary government, and enlarging its boundaries, so as to render it at once an example and fit instrument for introducing the same absolute rule into these colonies:

For taking away our charters, abolishing our most valuable laws, and altering, fundamentally, the powers of our governments:

For suspending our own legislatures, and declaring themselves invested with power to legislate for us in all cases whatsoever.

He has abdicated government here, by declaring us out of his protection, and waging war against us.

He has plundered our seas, ravaged our coasts, burnt our towns, and destroyed the lives of our people.

He is, at this time, transporting large armies of foreign mercenaries to complete the works of death, desolation, and tyranny, already begun, with circumstances of cruelty and perfidy scarcely paralleled in the most barbarous ages, and totally unworthy the head of a civilized nation.

He has constrained our fellow citizens, taken captive on the high seas, to bear arms against their country, to become the executioners of their friends, and brethren, or to fall themselves by their hands.

He has excited domestic insurrections amongst us, and has endeavored to bring on the inhabitants of our frontiers, the merciless Indian savages, whose known rule of warfare is an undistinguished destruction of all ages, sexes, and conditions.

In every stage of these oppressions, we have petitioned for redress, in the most humble terms; our repeated petitions have been answered only by repeated injury. A prince, whose character is thus marked by every act which may define a tyrant, is unfit to be the ruler of a free people.

Nor have we been wanting in attention to our British brethren. We have warned them, from time to time, of attempts made by their legislature to extend an unwarrantable jurisdiction over us. We have reminded them of the circumstances of our emigration and settlement here. We have appealed to their native justice and magnanimity, and we have conjured them, by the ties of our common kindred, to disavow these usurpations, which would inevitably interrupt our connections and correspondence. They, too, have been deaf to the voice of justice and consanguinity. We must, therefore, acquiesce in the necessity which denounces our separation, and hold them, as we hold the rest of mankind, enemies in war, in peace, friends.

We, therefore, the representatives of the United States of America, in general Congress assembled, appealing to the Supreme Judge of the world for the rectitude of our intentions, do, in the name, and by the authority of the good people of these colonies, solemnly publish and declare, that these united colonies are, and of right ought to be, free and independent states: that they are absolved from all allegiance to the British Crown, and that all political connection between them and the state of Great Britain is, and ought to be, totally dissolved; and that, as free and independent states, they have full power to levy war, conclude peace, contract alliances, establish commerce, and to do all other acts and things which independent states may of right do. And, for the support of this declaration, with a firm reliance on the protection of Divine Providence, we mutually pledge to each other our lives, our fortunes, and our sacred honor.

THE CONSTITUTION OF
THE UNITED STATES

WE the people of the United States, in order to form a more perfect union, establish justice, insure domestic tranquillity, provide for the common defense, promote the general welfare, and secure the blessings of liberty to ourselves and our posterity, do ordain and establish this Constitution for the United States of America.

ARTICLE I

SECTION 1

All legislative powers herein granted shall be vested in a Congress of the United States, which shall consist of a Senate and House of Representatives.

SECTION 2

1. The House of Representatives shall be composed of members chosen every second year by the people of the several States, and the electors in each State shall have the qualifications requisite for electors of the most numerous branch of the State legislature.

2. No person shall be a representative who shall not have attained to the age of twenty-five years, and been seven years a citizen of the United States, and who shall not, when elected, be an inhabitant of that State in which he shall be chosen.

3. Representatives and direct taxes [1] shall be apportioned among the several States which may be included within this Union, according to their respective numbers, which shall be determined by adding to the whole number of free persons, including those bound to service for a term of years, and excluding Indians not taxed, three fifths of all other persons.[2] The actual enumeration shall be made within three years after the first meeting of the Congress of the United States, and within every subsequent term of ten years, in such manner as they shall by law direct. The number of representatives shall not exceed one for every thirty thousand, but each State shall have at least one representative; and until such enumeration shall be made, the State of New Hampshire shall be entitled to chose three, Massachusetts eight, Rhode Island and Providence Plantations one, Connecticut five, New York six, New Jersey four, Pennsylvania eight, Delaware one, Maryland six, Virginia ten, North Carolina five, South Carolina five, and Georgia three.

4. When vacancies happen in the representation from any State, the executive authority thereof shall issue writs of election to fill such vacancies.

5. The House of Representatives shall choose their speaker and other officers; and shall have the sole power of impeachment.

SECTION 3

1. The Senate of the United States shall be composed of two senators from each State, chosen by the legislature thereof,[1] for six years; and each senator shall have one vote.

2. Immediately after they shall be assembled in consequence of the first election, they shall be divided as equally as may be into three classes. The seats of the senators of the first class shall be vacated at the expiration of the second year, of the second class at the expiration of the fourth year, and of the third class at the expiration of the sixth year, so that one third may be chosen every second year; and if vacancies happen by resignation, or otherwise, during the recess of the legislature of any State, the executive thereof may make temporary appointments until the next meeting of the legislature, which shall then fill such vacancies.[1]

3. No person shall be a senator who shall not have attained to the age of thirty years, and been nine years a citizen of the United States, and who shall not, when elected, be an inhabitant of that State for which he shall be chosen.

4. The Vice President of the United States shall be President of the Senate, but shall have no vote, unless they be equally divided.

5. The Senate shall choose their other officers and also a president pro tempore, in the absence of the Vice President, or when he shall exercise the office of the President of the United States.

6. The Senate shall have the sole power to try all impeachments. When sitting for that purpose, they shall be on oath or affirmation. When the President of the United States is tried, the chief justice shall preside: and no person shall be convicted without the concurrence of two thirds of the members present.

7. Judgment in cases of impeachment shall not extend further than to removal from office, and disqualifications to hold and enjoy any office of honor, trust or profit under the United States: but the party convicted shall nevertheless be liable and subject to indictment, trial, judgment and punishment, according to law.

SECTION 4

1. The times, places, and manner of holding elections for senators and representatives, shall be prescribed in each State by the legislature thereof; but the Congress may at any time by law make or alter such regulations, except as to the places of choosing senators.

[1] Revised by the 16th Amendment.
[2] Revised by the 14th Amendment.

[1] Revised by the 17th Amendment.

2. The Congress shall assemble at least once in every year, and such meeting shall be on the first Monday in December, unless they shall by law appoint a different day.

SECTION 5

1. Each House shall be the judge of the elections, returns and qualifications of its own members, and a majority of each shall constitute a quorum to do business; but a smaller number may adjourn from day to day, and may be authorized to compel the attendance of absent members, in such manner, and under such penalties as each House may provide.

2. Each House may determine the rules of its proceedings, punish its members for disorderly behavior, and, with the concurrence of two thirds, expel a member.

3. Each House shall keep a journal of its proceedings, and from time to time publish the same, excepting such parts as may in their judgment require secrecy; and the yeas and nays of the members of either House on any question shall, at the desire of one fifth of those present, be entered on the journal.

4. Neither House, during the session of Congress, shall, without the consent of the other, adjourn for more than three days, nor to any other place than that in which the two Houses shall be sitting.

SECTION 6

1. The senators and representatives shall receive a compensation for their services, to be ascertained by law, and paid out of the Treasury of the United States. They shall in all cases, except treason, felony, and breach of the peace, be privileged from arrest during their attendance at the session of their respective Houses, and in going to and returning from the same; and for any speech or debate in either House, they shall not be questioned in any other place.

2. No senator or representative shall, during the time for which he was elected, be appointed to any civil office under the authority of the United States, which shall have been created, or the emoluments whereof shall have been increased during such time; and no person holding any office under the United States shall be a member of either House during his continuance in office.

SECTION 7

1. All bills for raising revenue shall originate in the House of Representatives; but the Senate may propose or concur with amendments as on other bills.

2. Every bill which shall have passed the House of Representatives and the Senate, shall, before it becomes a law, be presented to the President of the United States; if he approves he shall sign it, but if not he shall return it, with his objections to that House in which it shall have originated, who shall enter the objections at large on their journal, and proceed to reconsider it. If after such reconsideration two thirds of that House shall agree to pass the bill, it shall be sent, together with the objections, to the other House, by which it shall likewise be reconsidered, and if approved by two thirds of that House, it shall become a law. But in all such cases the votes of both Houses shall be determined by yeas and nays, and the names of the persons voting for and against the bill shall be entered on the journal of each House respectively. If any bill shall not be returned by the President within ten days (Sundays excepted) after it shall have been presented to him, the same shall be a law, in like manner as if he had signed it, unless the Congress by their adjournment prevent its return, in which case it shall not be a law.

3. Every order, resolution, or vote to which the concurrence of the Senate and the House of Representatives may be necessary (except on a question of adjournment) shall be presented to the President of the United States; and before the same shall take effect, shall be approved by him, or being disapproved by him, shall be repassed by two thirds of the Senate and House of Representatives, according to the rules and limitations prescribed in the case of a bill.

SECTION 8

The Congress shall have the power

1. To lay and collect taxes, duties, imposts, and excises, to pay the debts and provide for the common defense and general welfare of the United States; but all duties, imposts, and excises shall be uniform throughout the United States;

2. To borrow money on the credit of the United States;

3. To regulate commerce with foreign nations, and among the several States, and with the Indian tribes;

4. To establish a uniform rule of naturalization, and uniform laws on the subject of bankruptcies throughout the United States;

5. To coin money, regulate the value thereof, and of foreign coin, and fix the standard of weights and measures;

6. To provide for the punishment of counterfeiting the securities and current coin of the United States;

7. To establish post offices and post roads;

8. To promote the progress of science and useful arts, by securing for limited times to authors and inventors the exclusive right to their respective writings and discoveries;

9. To constitute tribunals inferior to the Supreme Court;

10. To define and punish piracies and felonies committed on the high seas, and offenses against the law of nations;

11. To declare war, grant letters of marque and reprisal, and make rules concerning captures on land and water;

12. To raise and support armies, but no ap-

propriation of money to that use shall be for a longer term than two years;

13. To provide and maintain a navy;

14. To make rules for the government and regulation of the land and naval forces;

15. To provide for calling forth the militia to execute the laws of the Union, suppress insurrections and repel invasions;

16. To provide for organizing, arming, and disciplining the militia, and for governing such part of them as may be employed in the service of the United States, reserving to the States respectively, the appointment of the officers, and the authority of training the militia according to the discipline prescribed by Congress;

17. To exercise exclusive legislation in all cases whatsoever, over such district (not exceeding ten miles square) as may, by cession of particular States, and the acceptance of Congress, become the seat of the government of the United States, and to exercise like authority over all places purchased by the consent of the legislature of the State in which the same shall be, for the erection of forts, magazines, arsenals, dockyards, and other needful buildings; and

18. To make all laws which shall be necessary and proper for carrying into execution the foregoing powers, and all other powers vested by this Constitution in the government of the United States, or in any department or officer thereof.

Section 9

1. The migration or importation of such persons as any of the States now existing shall think proper to admit, shall not be prohibited by the Congress prior to the year one thousand eight hundred and eight, but a tax or duty may be imposed on such importation, not exceeding ten dollars for each person.

2. The privilege of the writ of habeas corpus shall not be suspended, unless when in cases of rebellion or invasion the public safety may require it.

3. No bill of attainder or ex post facto law shall be passed.

4. No capitation, or other direct, tax shall be laid, unless in proportion to the census or enumeration hereinbefore directed to be taken.[1]

5. No tax or duty shall be laid on articles exported from any State.

6. No preference shall be given by any regulation of commerce or revenue to the ports of one State over those of another: nor shall vessels bound to, or from, one State be obliged to enter, clear, or pay duties in another.

7. No money shall be drawn from the treasury, but in consequence of appropriations made by law; and a regular statement and account of the receipts and expenditures of all public money shall be published from time to time.

8. No title of nobility shall be granted by the

[1] Revised by the 16th Amendment.

United States: and no person holding any office of profit or trust under them, shall, without the consent of the Congress, accept of any present, emolument, office, or title, of any kind whatever, from any king, prince, or foreign State.

Section 10

1. No State shall enter into any treaty, alliance, or confederation; grant letters of marque and reprisal; coin money; emit bills of credit; make anything but gold and silver coin a tender in payment of debts; pass any bill of attainder, ex post facto law, or law impairing the obligation of contracts, or grant any title of nobility.

2. No State shall, without the consent of the Congress, lay any imposts or duties on imports or exports, except what may be absolutely necessary for executing its inspection laws: and the net produce of all duties and imposts laid by any State on imports or exports, shall be for the use of the treasury of the United States; and all such laws shall be subject to the revision and control of the Congress.

3. No State shall, without the consent of the Congress, lay any duty of tonnage, keep troops, or ships of war in time of peace, enter into any agreement or compact with another State, or with a foreign power, or engage in war, unless actually invaded, or in such imminent danger as will not admit of delay.

ARTICLE II

Section 1

1. The executive power shall be vested in a President of the United States of America. He shall hold his office during the term of four years, and, together with the Vice President, chosen for the same term, be elected as follows:

2. Each State shall appoint, in such manner as the legislature thereof may direct, a number of electors, equal to the whole number of senators and representatives to which the State may be entitled in the Congress: but no senator or representative, or person holding an office of trust or profit under the United States, shall be appointed an elector.

The electors shall meet in their respective States, and vote by ballot for two persons, of whom one at least shall not be an inhabitant of the same State with themselves. And they shall make a list of all the persons voted for, and of the number of votes for each; which list they shall sign and certify, and transmit sealed to the seat of the government of the United States, directed to the president of the Senate. The president of the Senate shall, in the presence of the Senate and House of Representatives, open all the certificates, and the votes shall then be counted. The person having the greatest number of votes shall be the President, if such number be a majority of the whole number of electors appointed; and if there be more than one who have such majority, and have an equal number of votes, then the House of Representatives shall immediately choose by ballot one of them for President; and if no person have a majority, then from the five highest on the list the said House shall in like manner choose the President. But in choosing the President, the votes shall be taken by States, the representation from each State having one vote; a quorum for this purpose shall consist of a member or members from two thirds of the States, and a majority of all the States shall be necessary to a choice. In every case, after the choice of the President, the person having the greatest number of votes of the electors shall be the Vice President. But if there should remain two or more who have equal votes, the Senate shall choose from them by ballot the Vice President.[1]

3. The Congress may determine the time of choosing the electors, and the day on which they shall give their votes; which day shall be the same throughout the United States.

4. No person except a natural born citizen, or a citizen of the United States, at the time of the adoption of this Constitution, shall be eligible to the office of President; neither shall any person be eligible to that office who shall not have attained to the age of thirty-five years, and been fourteen years a resident within the United States.

5. In case of the removal of the President from office, or of his death, resignation, or inability to discharge the powers and duties of the said office, the same shall devolve on the Vice President, and the Congress may by law provide for the case of removal, death, resignation, or inability, both of the President and Vice President, declaring what officer shall then act as President, and such officer shall act accordingly, until the disability be removed, or a President shall be elected.

6. The President shall, at stated times, receive for his services a compensation, which shall neither be increased nor diminished during the period for which he shall have been elected, and he shall not receive within that period any other emolument from the United States, or any of them.

7. Before he enter on the execution of his office, he shall take the following oath or affirmation: — "I do solemnly swear (or affirm) that I will faithfully execute the office of President of the United States, and will to the best of my ability, preserve, protect and defend the Constitution of the United States."

Section 2

1. The President shall be the commander in chief of the army and navy of the United States, and of the militia of the several States, when called into the actual service of the United States; he may require the opinion, in writing, of the principal officer in each of the executive departments, upon any subject relating to the duties of their respective offices, and he shall have power to grant reprieves and pardons for offenses against the United States, except in cases of impeachment.

2. He shall have power, by and with the advice and consent of the Senate, to make treaties, pro-

vided two thirds of the senators present concur; and he shall nominate, and by and with the advice and consent of the Senate, shall appoint ambassadors, other public ministers and consuls, judges of the Supreme Court, and all other officers of the United States, whose appointments are not herein otherwise provided for, and which shall be established by law: but the Congress may by law vest the appointment of such inferior officers, as they think proper, in the President alone, in the courts of law, or in the heads of departments.

3. The President shall have power to fill up all vacancies that may happen during the recess of the Senate, by granting commissions which shall expire at the end of their next session.

Section 3

He shall from time to time give to the Congress information of the state of the Union, and recommend to their consideration such measures as he shall judge necessary and expedient; he may, on extraordinary occasions, convene both Houses, or either of them, and in case of disagreement between them with respect to the time of adjournment, he may adjourn them to such time as he shall think proper; he shall receive ambassadors and other public ministers; he shall take care that the laws be faithfully executed, and shall commission all the officers of the United States.

Section 4

The President, Vice President, and all civil officers of the United States, shall be removed from office on impeachment for, and conviction of, treason, bribery, or other high crimes and misdemeanors.

ARTICLE III

Section 1

The judicial power of the United States shall be vested in one Supreme Court, and in such inferior courts as the Congress may from time to time ordain and establish. The judges, both of the Supreme and inferior courts, shall hold their offices during good behavior, and shall, at stated times, receive for their services, a compensation, which shall not be diminished during their continuance in office.

Section 2

1. The judicial power shall extend to all cases, in law and equity, arising under this Constitution, the laws of the United States, and treaties made, or which shall be made, under their authority; — to all cases affecting ambassadors, other public ministers and consuls; — to all cases of admiralty and maritime jurisdiction; — to controversies to which the United States shall be a party;[1] — to controversies between two or more States; — between citizens of different States; — between citizens of the same State claiming lands under grants of different States, and between a State, or

---

[1] Voided by the 12th Amendment.

[1] Revised by the 11th Amendment.

the citizens thereof, and foreign States, citizens or subjects.

2. In all cases affecting ambassadors, other public ministers and consuls, and those in which a State shall be party, the Supreme Court shall have original jurisdiction. In all the other cases before mentioned, the Supreme Court shall have appellate jurisdiction, both as to law and to fact, with such exceptions, and under such regulations as the Congress shall make.

3. The trial of all crimes, except in cases of impeachment, shall be by jury; and such trial shall be held in the State where the said crimes shall have been committed; but when not committed within any State, the trial shall be at such place or places as the Congress may by law have directed.

Section 3

1. Treason against the United States shall consist only in levying war against them, or in adhering to their enemies, giving them aid and comfort. No person shall be convicted of treason unless on the testimony of two witnesses to the same overt act, or in confession in open court.

2. The Congress shall have power to declare the punishment of treason, but no attainder of treason shall work corruption of blood, or forfeiture except during the life of the person attainted.

ARTICLE IV

Section 1

Full faith and credit shall be given in each State to the public acts, records, and judicial proceedings of every other State. And the Congress may by general laws prescribe the manner in which such acts, records and proceedings shall be proved, and the effect thereof.

Section 2

1. The citizens of each State shall be entitled to all privileges and immunities of citizens in the several States.[1]

2. A person charged in any State with treason, felony, or other crime, who shall flee from justice, and be found in another State, shall on demand of the executive authority of the State from which he fled, be delivered up to be removed to the State having jurisdiction of the crime.

3. No person held to service or labor in one State under the laws thereof, escaping into another, shall, in consequence of any law or regulation therein, be discharged from such service or labor, but shall be delivered up on claim of the party to whom such service or labor may be due.[2]

Section 3

1. New States may be admitted by the Congress into this Union; but no new State shall be formed or erected within the jurisdiction of any other State; nor any State be formed by the junction of two or more States, or parts of States,

without the consent of the legislatures of the States concerned as well as of the Congress.

2. The Congress shall have power to dispose of and make all needful rules and regulations respecting the territory or other property belonging to the United States; and nothing in this Constitution shall be so construed as to prejudice any claims of the United States, or of any particular State.

Section 4

The United States shall guarantee to every State in this Union a republican form of government, and shall protect each of them against invasion; and on application of the legislature, or of the executive (when the legislature cannot be convened) against domestic violence.

ARTICLE V

The Congress, whenever two thirds of both Houses shall deem it necessary, shall propose amendments to this Constitution, or, on the application of the legislatures of two thirds of the several States, shall call a convention for proposing amendments, which in either case, shall be valid to all intents and purposes, as part of this Constitution when ratified by the legislatures of three fourths of the several States, or by conventions in three fourths thereof, as the one or the other mode of ratification may be proposed by the Congress; Provided that no amendment which may be made prior to the year one thousand eight hundred and eight shall in any manner affect the first and fourth clauses in the ninth section of the first article; and that no State, without its consent, shall be deprived of its equal suffrage in the Senate.

ARTICLE VI

1. All debts contracted and engagements entered into, before the adoption of this Constitution, shall be as valid against the United States under this Constitution, as under the Confederation.[1]

2. This Constitution, and the laws of the United States which shall be made in pursuance thereof; and all treaties made, or which shall be made, under the authority of the United States, shall be the supreme law of the land; and the Judges in every State shall be bound thereby, anything in the Constitution or laws of any State to the contrary notwithstanding.

3. The senators and representatives before mentioned, and the members of the several State legislatures, and all executive and judicial officers, both of the United States and of the several States, shall be bound by oath or affirmation to support this Constitution; but no religious test shall ever be required as a qualification to any office or public trust under the United States.

ARTICLE VII

The ratification of the conventions of nine States shall be sufficient for the establishment of

---

[1] Elaborated by the 14th Amendment, Sec. 1.
[2] See the 13th Amendment, abolishing slavery.

[1] See the 14th Amendment, Sec. 4, for additional provisions.

this Constitution between the States so ratifying the same.

Done in Convention by the unanimous consent of the States present the seventeenth day of September in the year of our Lord one thousand seven hundred and eighty-seven, and of the independence of the United States of America the twelfth. In witness whereof we have hereunto subscribed our names.

AMENDMENTS

First Ten Amendments submitted by Congress Sept. 25, 1789. Ratified by three-fourths of the States December 15, 1791.

ARTICLE I

Congress shall make no law respecting an establishment of religion, or prohibiting the free exercise thereof; or abridging the freedom of speech, or of the press; or the right of the people peaceably to assemble, and to petition the government for a redress of grievances.

ARTICLE II

A well regulated militia, being necessary to the security of a free State, the right of the people to keep and bear arms, shall not be infringed.

ARTICLE III

No soldier shall, in time of peace be quartered in any house, without the consent of the owner, nor in time of war, but in a manner to be prescribed by law.

ARTICLE IV

The right of the people to be secure in their persons, houses, papers, and effects, against unreasonable searches and seizures, shall not be violated, and no warrants shall issue, but upon probable cause, supported by oath or affirmation, and particularly describing the place to be searched, and the persons or things to be seized.

ARTICLE V

No person shall be held to answer for a capital, or otherwise infamous crime, unless on a presentment or indictment of a grand jury, except in cases arising in the land or naval forces, or in the militia, when in actual service in time of war or public danger; nor shall any person be subject for the same offense to be twice put in jeopardy of life or limb; nor shall be compelled in any criminal case to be a witness against himself, nor be deprived of life, liberty, or property, without due process of law; nor shall private property be taken for public use without just compensation.

ARTICLE VI

In all criminal prosecutions, the accused shall enjoy the right to a speedy and public trial, by an impartial jury of the State and district wherein the crime shall have been committed, which district shall have been previously ascertained by law, and to be informed of the nature and cause of the accusation; to be confronted with the witnesses against him; to have compulsory process for obtaining witnesses in his favor, and to have the assistance of counsel for his defense.

ARTICLE VII

In suits at common law, where the value in controversy shall exceed twenty dollars, the right of trial by jury shall be preserved, and no fact tried by a jury shall be otherwise reëxamined in any court of the United States, than according to the rules of the common law.

ARTICLE VIII

Excessive bail shall not be required, nor excessive fines imposed, nor cruel and unusual punishments inflicted.

ARTICLE IX

The enumeration in the Constitution of certain rights shall not be construed to deny or disparage others retained by the people.

ARTICLE X

The powers not delegated to the United States by the Constitution, nor prohibited by it to the States, are reserved to the States respectively, or to the people.

ARTICLE XI

Submitted by Congress March 5, 1794. Ratified January 8, 1798.

The judicial power of the United States shall not be construed to extend to any suit in law or equity, commenced or prosecuted against one of the United States by citizens of another State, or by citizens or subjects of any foreign State.

ARTICLE XII

Submitted by Congress December 12, 1803. Ratified September 25, 1804.

The electors shall meet in their respective States, and vote by ballot for President and Vice President, one of whom, at least, shall not be an inhabitant of the same State with themselves; they shall name in their ballots the person voted for as President, and in distinct ballots, the person voted for as Vice President, and they shall make distinct lists of all persons voted for as President and of all persons voted for as Vice President, and of the number of votes for each, which lists they shall sign and certify, and transmit sealed to the seat of the government of the United States, directed to the President of the Senate; — The President of the Senate shall, in the presence of the Senate and House of Representatives, open all the certificates and the votes shall then be counted; — The person having the greatest number of votes for President, shall be the President, if such number be a majority of the whole number of electors appointed; and if no person have such majority, then from the persons having the highest numbers not exceeding three on the list of those voted for as President, the House of Representatives shall choose immediately, by ballot the President. But in choosing the President, the votes shall be taken by States, the representation from each State having one vote; a quorum for this purpose shall consist of a member or members from two thirds of the States, and a majority of all the States shall be necessary to a choice. And if the House of Representatives shall not choose a President whenever the right of choice shall devolve upon them, before the fourth day of March next following, then the Vice President shall act as President, as in the case of the death or other constitutional disability of the President. The person having the greatest number of votes as Vice President shall be the Vice President, if such number be a majority of the whole number of electors appointed, and if no person have a majority, then from the two highest numbers on the list, the Senate shall choose the Vice President; a quorum for the purpose shall consist of two thirds of the whole number of Senators, and a majority of the whole number shall be necessary to a choice. But no person constitutionally ineligible to the office of President shall be eligible to that of Vice President of the United States.

ARTICLE XIII

Submitted by Congress February 1, 1864. Ratified December 18, 1865.

SECTION 1

Neither slavery nor involuntary servitude, except as punishment for crime whereof the party shall have been duly convicted, shall exist within the United States, or any place subject to their jurisdiction.

SECTION 2

Congress shall have power to enforce this article by appropriate legislation.

ARTICLE XIV

Submitted by Congress June 16, 1866. Ratified July 28, 1868.

SECTION 1

All persons born or naturalized in the United States, and subject to the jurisdiction thereof, are citizens of the United States and of the State wherein they reside. No State shall make or enforce any law which shall abridge the privileges or immunities of citizens of the United States; nor shall any State deprive any person of life, liberty, or property, without due process of law; nor deny to any person within its jurisdiction the equal protection of the laws.

SECTION 2

Representatives shall be apportioned among the several States according to their respective numbers, counting the whole number of persons in each State, excluding Indians not taxed. But when the right to vote at any election for the choice of electors for President and Vice President of the United States, representatives in Congress, the executive and judicial officers of a State, or the members of the legislature thereof, is denied to any of the male inhabitants of such State, being twenty-one years of age, and citizens of the United States, or in any way abridged, except for participation in rebellion, or other crime, the basis of representation therein shall be reduced in the proportion which the number of such male citizens shall bear to the whole number of male citizens twenty-one years of age in such State.

SECTION 3

No person shall be a senator or representative in Congress, or elector of President and Vice President, or hold any office, civil or military, under the United States, or under any State, who having previously taken an oath, as a member of Congress, or as an officer of the United States, or as a member of any State legislature, or as an executive or judicial officer of any State, to support the Constitution of the United States, shall have engaged in insurrection or rebellion against the same, or given aid or comfort to the enemies thereof. But Congress may by a vote of two thirds of each House, remove such disability.

SECTION 4

The validity of the public debt of the United States, authorized by law, including debts incurred for payment of pensions and bounties for services in suppressing insurrection or rebellion, shall not be questioned. But neither the United States nor any State shall assume or pay any debt or obligation incurred in aid of insurrection or rebellion against the United States, or any claim for the loss or emancipation of any slave; but all such debts, obligations, and claims shall be held illegal and void.

SECTION 5

The Congress shall have power to enforce, by appropriate legislation, the provisions of this article.

ARTICLE XV

Submitted by Congress February 27, 1869. Ratified March 30, 1870.

SECTION 1

The right of citizens of the United States to vote shall not be denied or abridged by the United States or by any State on account of race, color, or previous condition of servitude.

SECTION 2

The Congress shall have power to enforce this article by appropriate legislation.

ARTICLE XVI

Submitted by Congress July 12, 1909. Ratified February 25, 1913.

The Congress shall have power to lay and collect taxes on incomes, from whatever source derived, without apportionment among the several States, and without regard to any census or enumeration.

ARTICLE XVII

Submitted by Congress May 16, 1912. Ratified May 31, 1913.

The Senate of the United States shall be composed of two senators from each state, elected by the people thereof, for six years; and each senator shall have one vote. The electors in each State shall have the qualifications requisite for electors of the most numerous branch of the State legislature.

When vacancies happen in the representation of any State in the Senate, the executive authority of such State shall issue writs of election to fill such vacancies: *Provided,* That the legislature of any State may empower the executive thereof to make temporary appointments until the people fill the vacancies by election as the legislature may direct.

This amendment shall not be so construed as to affect the election or term of any senator chosen before it becomes valid as part of the Constitution.

ARTICLE XVIII [1]

Submitted by Congress December 17, 1917. Ratified January 29, 1919.

After one year from the ratification of this article, the manufacture, sale, or transportation of intoxicating liquors within, the importation thereof into, or the exportation thereof from the United States and all territory subject to the jurisdiction thereof for beverage purposes is hereby prohibited.

The Congress and the several States shall have concurrent power to enforce this article by appropriate legislation.

This article shall be inoperative unless it shall have been ratified as an amendment to the Constitution by the legislatures of the several States, as provided in the Constitution, within seven years from the date of the submission hereof to the states by Congress.

ARTICLE XIX

Submitted by Congress June 5, 1919. Ratified August 26, 1920.

The right of citizens of the United States to vote shall not be denied or abridged by the United States or by any State on account of sex.

The Congress shall have power by appropriate legislation to enforce the provisions of this article.

ARTICLE XX

Submitted by Congress March 3, 1932. Ratified January 23, 1933.

SECTION 1

The terms of the President and Vice President shall end at noon on the 20th day of January, and the terms of Senators and Representatives at noon on the 3d day of January, of the years in which such terms would have ended if this article had not been ratified; and the terms of their successors shall then begin.

[1] Repealed by the 21st Amendment.

SECTION 2

The Congress shall assemble at least once in every year, and such meeting shall begin at noon on the 3d day of January, unless they shall by law appoint a different day.

SECTION 3

If, at the time fixed for the beginning of the term of the President, the President-elect shall have died, the Vice President-elect shall become President. If a President shall not have been chosen before the time fixed for the beginning of his term, or if the President-elect shall have failed to qualify, then the Vice President-elect shall act as President until a President shall have qualified; and the Congress may by law provide for the case wherein neither a President-elect nor a Vice President-elect shall have qualified, declaring who shall then act as President, or the manner in which one who is to act shall be selected, and such person shall act accordingly until a President or Vice President shall have qualified.

SECTION 4

The Congress may by law provide for the case of the death of any of the persons from whom the House of Representatives may choose a President whenever the right of choice shall have devolved upon them, and for the case of the death of any of the persons from whom the Senate may choose a Vice President whenever the right of choice shall have devolved upon them.

SECTION 5

Sections 1 and 2 shall take effect on the 15th day of October following the ratification of this article.

SECTION 6

This article shall be inoperative unless it shall have been ratified as an amendment to the Constitution by the legislatures of three-fourths of the several States within seven years from the date of its submission.

ARTICLE XXI

Submitted by Congress February 20, 1933. Ratified December 5, 1933.

SECTION 1

The Eighteenth Article of amendment to the Constitution of the United States is hereby repealed.

SECTION 2

The transportation or importation into any State, Territory, or possession of the United States for delivery or use therein of intoxicating liquors in violation of the laws thereof, is hereby prohibited.

SECTION 3

This article shall be inoperative unless it shall have been ratified as an amendment to the Constitution by conventions in the several States, as provided in the Constitution, within seven years from the date of the submission thereof to the States by the Congress.

ARTICLE XXII

Submitted by Congress March 12, 1947. Ratified March 1, 1951.

No person shall be elected to the office of the President more than twice, and no person who has held the office of President, or acted as President, for more than two years of a term to which some other person was elected President shall be elected to the office of the President more than once.

But this article shall not apply to any person holding the office of President when this article was proposed by the Congress, and shall not prevent any person who may be holding the office of President, or acting as President, during the term within which this article becomes operative from holding the office of President or acting as President during the remainder of such term.

This article shall be inoperative unless it shall have been ratified as an amendment to the Constitution by the legislatures of three-fourths of the several states within seven years from the date of its submission to the states by the Congress.

THE STATES OF THE UNION, 1787-1954

(with dates of ratification of the Constitution or admission to the Union)

1. Delaware	Dec. 7, 1787	25. Arkansas	June 15, 1836
2. Pennsylvania	Dec. 12, 1787	26. Michigan	Jan. 26, 1837
3. New Jersey	Dec. 18, 1787	27. Florida	Mar. 3, 1845
4. Georgia	Jan. 2, 1788	28. Texas	Dec. 29, 1845
5. Connecticut	Jan. 9, 1788	29. Iowa	Dec. 28, 1846
6. Massachusetts	Feb. 6, 1788	30. Wisconsin	May 29, 1848
7. Maryland	Apr. 28, 1788	31. California	Sept. 9, 1850
8. South Carolina	May 23, 1788	32. Minnesota	May 11, 1858
9. New Hampshire	June 21, 1788	33. Oregon	Feb. 14, 1859
10. Virginia	June 25, 1788	34. Kansas	Jan. 29, 1861
11. New York	July 26, 1788	35. West Virginia	June 19, 1863
12. North Carolina	Nov. 21, 1789	36. Nevada	Oct. 31, 1864
13. Rhode Island	May 29, 1790	37. Nebraska	Mar. 1, 1867
14. Vermont	Mar. 4, 1791	38. Colorado	Aug. 1, 1876
15. Kentucky	June 1, 1792	39. North Dakota	Nov. 2, 1889
16. Tennessee	June 1, 1796	40. South Dakota	Nov. 2, 1889
17. Ohio	Mar. 1, 1803	41. Montana	Nov. 8, 1889
18. Louisiana	Apr. 30, 1812	42. Washington	Nov. 11, 1889
19. Indiana	Dec. 11, 1816	43. Idaho	July 3, 1890
20. Mississippi	Dec. 10, 1817	44. Wyoming	July 10, 1890
21. Illinois	Dec. 3, 1818	45. Utah	Jan. 4, 1896
22. Alabama	Dec. 14, 1819	46. Oklahoma	Nov. 16, 1907
23. Maine	Mar. 15, 1820	47. New Mexico	Jan. 6, 1912
24. Missouri	Aug. 10, 1821	48. Arizona	Feb. 14, 1912

OTHER GOVERNMENTAL UNITS

(with appropriate dates)

District of Columbia	Created, July 16, 1790; governmental status fixed, June 11, 1878
Alaska	Acquired by treaty, Mar. 10, 1867; becomes organized territory, Aug. 24, 1912
Hawaii	Annexed by joint-resolution, July 7, 1898; becomes organized territory, June 14, 1900
Guam	Acquired by treaty, Dec. 10, 1898; becomes unincorporated territory, Aug. 1, 1950
Philippine Islands	Acquired by treaty, Dec. 10, 1898; become independent, July 4, 1946
Puerto Rico	Acquired by treaty, Dec. 10, 1898: achieves commonwealth status, July 3, 1952
American Samoa	Acquired by treaty, Dec. 2, 1899; transferred from Navy to Interior, July 1, 1951
Panama Canal Zone	Acquired by treaty, Nov. 8, 1903; government defined, Aug. 24, 1912
Virgin Islands	Acquired by treaty, Aug. 4, 1916; U.S. takes possession, March 31, 1917

President	Vice-President	Secretary of State	Secretary of Treasury	Secretary of War
17. Andrew Johnson....1865 Unionist		W. H. Seward....1865	Hugh McCulloch.1865	E. M. Stanton ..1865 U. S. Grant.....1867 L. Thomas......1868 J. M. Schofield..1868
18. Ulysses S. Grant....1869 Republican	Schuyler Colfax.....1869 Republican Henry Wilson......1873 Republican	E. B. Washburne.1869 Hamilton Fish ...1869	Geo. S. Boutwell .1869 W. A. Richardson 1873 Benj. H. Bristow .1874 Lot M. Morrill...1876	J..A. Rawlins...1869 W. T. Sherman .1869 W. W. Belknap .1869 Alphonso Taft ..1876 J. D. Cameron..1876
19. Rutherford B. Hayes 1877 Republican	William A. Wheeler .1877 Republican	W. M. Evarts....1877	John Sherman....1877	G. W. McCrary 1877 Alex. Ramsey...1879
20. James A. Garfield...1881 Republican	Chester A. Arthur...1881 Republican	James G. Blaine..1881	Wm. Windom....1881	R. T. Lincoln...1881
21. Chester A. Arthur...1881 Republican		F. T. Frelinghuy-sen..........1881	Chas. J. Folger...1881 W. Q. Gresham..1884 Hugh McCulloch.1884	R. T. Lincoln...1881
22. Grover Cleveland....1885 Democratic	T. A. Hendricks....1885 Democratic	Thos. F. Bayard .1885	Daniel Manning..1885 Chas. S. Fairchild 1887	W. C. Endicott .1885
23. Benjamin Harrison..1889 Republican	Levi P. Morton.....1889 Republican	James G. Blaine..1889 John W. Foster ..1892	Wm. Windom....1889 Charles Foster ...1891	R. Proctor .....1889 S. B. Elkins.....1891
24. Grover Cleveland ...1893 Democratic	Adlai E. Stevenson..1893 Democratic	W. Q. Gresham ..1893 Richard Olney ...1895	John G. Carlisle..1893	D. S. Lamont...1893
25. William McKinley...1897 Republican	Garret A. Hobart...1897 Republican Theodore Roosevelt 1901 Republican	John Sherman....1897 Wm. R. Day.....1897 John Hay........1898	Lyman J. Gage...1897	R. A. Alger.....1897 Elihu Root.....1899
26. Theodore Roosevelt .1901 Republican	Chas. W. Fairbanks 1905 Republican	John Hay........1901 Elihu Root.......1905 Robert Bacon....1909	Lyman J. Gage...1901 Leslie M. Shaw...1902 G. B. Cortelyou..1907	Elihu Root.....1901 Wm. H. Taft....1904 Luke E. Wright 1908
27. William H. Taft.....1909 Republican	James S. Sherman ..1909 Republican	P. C. Knox......1909	F. MacVeagh....1909	J. M. Dickinson.1909 H. L. Stimson...1911
28. Woodrow Wilson....1913 Democratic	Thomas R. Marshall 1913 Democratic	Wm. J. Bryan....1913 Robert Lansing ..1915 Bainbridge Colby 1920	W. G. McAdoo...1913 Carter Glass.....1918 D. F. Houston...1920	L. M. Garrison..1913 N. D. Baker....1916
29. Warren G. Harding..1921 Republican	Calvin Coolidge.....1921 Republican	Chas. E. Hughes .1921	Andrew W. Mel-lon...........1921	John W. Weeks .1921
30. Calvin Coolidge.....1923 Republican	Charles G. Dawes...1925 Republican	Chas. E. Hughes .1923 Frank B. Kellogg.1925	Andrew W. Mel-lon...........1923	John W. Weeks .1923 Dwight F. Davis 1925
31. Herbert Hoover.....1929 Republican	Charles Curtis......1929 Republican	Henry L. Stimson 1929	Andrew W. Mel-lon...........1929 Ogden L. Mills...1932	James W. Good 1929 Pat. J. Hurley ..1929
32. Franklin D. Roose-velt..............1933 Democratic	John Nance Garner .1933 Democratic Henry A. Wallace...1941 Democratic Harry S. Truman...1945 Democratic	Cordell Hull.....1933 E. R. Stettinius, Jr............1944	Wm. H. Woodin .1933 Henry Morgen-thau, Jr........1934	Geo. H. Dern...1933 H. A. Woodring.1936 H. L. Stimson...1940
33. Harry S. Truman....1945 Democratic	Alben W. Barkley...1949 Democratic	James F. Byrnes .1945 Geo. C. Marshall.1947 Dean G. Acheson.1949	Fred M. Vinson..1945 John W. Snyder..1946	Robt. H. Patter-son..........1945 K. C. Royall....1947 *
34. Dwight D. Eisen-hower..........1953 Republican	Richard M. Nixon ..1953 Republican	John Foster Dulles........1953	George G. Humphrey.....1953	

* Lost cabinet status in 1947

AND CABINET MEMBERS

Attorney-General	Postmaster-General	Secretary of Navy	Secretary of Interior	Secretary of Agriculture	Other Members
James Speed.... 1865 Henry Stanbery. 1866 Wm. M. Evarts. 1868	Wm. Dennison .1865 A. W. Randall. .1866	Gideon Welles ... 1865	John P. Usher. .1865 James Harlan. . 1865 O. H. Brown- ing..........1866	Cabinet status since 1889.	*Secretary of Commerce and Labor* Established Feb. 14, 1903. George B. Cortelyou..... 1903 Victor H. Metcalf. .1904–6 O. S. Straus...1907–9 Chas. Nagel ..1909 (Department divided, 1913.)
E. R. Hoar..... 1869 A. T. Ackerman. 1870 Geo. H. Williams........1871 Edw. Pierrepont.........1875 Alphonso Taft ..1876	J. A. J. Creswell 1869 Jas. W. Marshall.......1874 Marshall Jewell.1874 James N. Tyner.......1876	Adolph E. Borie. .1869 Geo. M. Robeson.1869	Jacob D. Cox ..1869 C. Delano..... 1870 Zach. Chandler. 1875		
Chas. Devens... 1877	David M. Key .1877 Horace Maynard........1880	R. W. Thompson 1877 Nathan Goff, Jr. .1881	Carl Schurz.... 1877		
W. MacVeagh ..1881	T. L. James.... 1881	W. H. Hunt..... 1881	S. J. Kirkwood .1881		*Secretary of Commerce*
B. H. Brewster .1881	T. O. Howe.... 1881 W. Q. Gresham.1883 Frank Hatton. .1884	W. E. Chandler . 1881	Henry M. Teller.......1881		W. C. Redfield.......1913 Joshua W. Alexander. .1919 H. C. Hoover 1921 H. C. Hoover .1925
A. H. Garland ..1885	Wm. F. Vilas... 1885 D. M. Dickinson..........1888	W. C. Whitney ..1885	L. Q. C. Lamar.1885 Wm. F. Vilas ..1888	N. J. Colman .1889	
W. H. H. Miller. 1889	J. Wanamaker .1889	Benj. F. Tracy... 1889	John W. Noble. 1889	J. M. Rusk.... 1889	W. F. Whiting. 1928 R. P. Lamont. 1929 R. D. Chapin. 1932
R. Olney.......1893 J. Harmon.....1895 J. McKenna....1897 J. W. Griggs....1897 P. C. Knox..... 1901	W. S. Bissell... 1893 W. L. Wilson ..1895 James A. Gary .1897 Chas. E. Smith .1898	Hilary A. Herbert.......1893 John D. Long.... 1897	Hoke Smith.... 1893 D. R. Francis ..1896 C. N. Bliss..... 1897 E. A. Hitchcock........1899	J. S. Morton... 1893 James Wilson. .1897	D. C. Roper. .1933 H. L. Hopkins.1939 Jesse Jones... 1940 Henry A. Wallace..... 1945 W. Averell Harriman ..1946
P. C. Knox..... 1901 W. H. Moody ..1904 C. J. Bonaparte.1907	Chas. E. Smith.1901 Henry C. Payne.......1902 Robt. J. Wynne......1904 G. B. Cortelyou.........1905 G. von L. Meyer.1907	John D. Long.... 1901 Wm. H. Moody .1902 Paul Morton..... 1904 C. J. Bonaparte .1905 Victor H. Metcalf..........1907 T. H. Newberry. .1908	E. A. Hitchcock........1901 J. R. Garfield... 1907	James Wilson. .1901	Charles W. Sawyer..... 1948 Sinclair Weeks..... 1953 *Secretary of Labor* Established March 4, 1913.
G. W. Wickersham.........1909 J. C. McReynolds.........1913 Thos. W. Gregory......1914 A. M. Palmer ...1919	F. H. Hitchcock.........1909 A. S. Burleson. .1913	G. von L. Meyer .1909 Josephus Daniels 1913	R. A. Ballinger 1909 W. L. Fisher ...1911 F. K. Lane.....1913 J. B. Payne....1920	James Wilson. .1909 D. F. Houston .1913 E. T. Meredith. 1920	W. B. Wilson.1913 J. J. Davis 1921–29 W. N. Doak ..1930 Frances Perkins '33 L. B. Schwellenbach....1945
H. M. Daugherty........1921	Will H. Hays ..1921 Hubert Work ..1922 Harry S. New .. 1923	Edwin Denby.... 1921	Albert B. Fall. .1921 Hubert Work ..1923	H. C. Wallace.1921	M. J. Tobin ..1948 M. P. Durkin.1953 James P. Mitchell ...1953
H. M. Daugherty........1923 Harlan F. Stone. 1924 John G. Sargent. 1925	Harry S. New .. 1923	Edwin Denby.... 1923 Curtis D. Wilbur .1924	Hubert Work ..1923 Roy O. West... 1928	H. M. Gore.... 1924 W. M. Jardine. .1925	*Secretary of Defense* Established July 26, 1947.
Wm. D. Mitchell......1929	Walter F. Brown.......1929	Chas. F. Adams . 1929	Ray L. Wilbur .1929	Arthur M. Hyde.......1929	James V. Forrestal.....1947 Louis A. Johnson....1949 George C. Marshall...1950
H. S. Cummings.......1933 Frank Murphy. .1939 Robt. H. Jackson......1940 Francis Biddle. .1941	James A. Farley.......1933 Frank C. Walker.......1940	Claude A. Swanson...........1933 Chas. Edison..... 1940 Frank Knox..... 1940 James V. Forrestal........ 1944	Harold L. Ickes.1933	H. A. Wallace. .1933 C. R. Wickard .1940	Robert A. Lovett..... 1951 Charles E. Wilson..... 1953
Tom C. Clark... 1945 J. H. McGrath. 1949 James P. McGranery...1952 Herbert Brownell, Jr. .1953	Robt. E. Hannegan.... 1945 Jesse L. Donaldson... 1947 Arthur E. Summerfield .1953	James V. Forrestal..... 1945 *	Harold L. Ickes.1945 Julius A. Krug. .1946 O. L. Chapman.........1951 Douglas McKay......1953	C. P. Anderson.1945 C. F. Brannan .1948 Ezra T. Benson........ 1953	*Secretary of Health Education, and Welfare* Established April 1, 1953. Oveta Culp Hobby.....1953

* Lost cabinet status in 1947

JUSTICES OF THE UNITED STATES SUPREME COURT

Name Chief Justices in Boldface Type	Service		Name Chief Justices in Boldface Type	Service	
	Term	Yrs.		Term	Yrs.
John Jay, N.Y.	1789–1795	6	Stanley Matthews, Ohio	1881–1889	8
John Rutledge, S.C.	1789–1791	2	Horace Gray, Mass.	1881–1902	21
William Cushing, Mass.	1789–1810	21	Samuel Blatchford, N.Y.	1882–1893	11
James Wilson, Pa.	1789–1798	9	Lucius Q. C. Lamar, Miss.	1888–1893	5
John Blair, Va.	1789–1796	7	**Melville W. Fuller,** Ill.	1888–1910	22
Robert H. Harrison, Md.	1789–1790	1	David J. Brewer, Kan.	1889–1910	21
James Iredell, N.C.	1790–1799	9	Henry B. Brown, Mich.	1890–1906	16
Thomas Johnson, Md.	1791–1793	2	George Shiras, Jr., Pa.	1892–1903	11
William Paterson, N.J.	1793–1806	13	Howell E. Jackson, Tenn.	1893–1895	2
John Rutledge, S.C.	1795–1795	..	Edward D. White, La.	1894–1910	16
Samuel Chase, Md.	1796–1811	15	Rufus W. Peckham, N.Y.	1895–1910	14
Oliver Ellsworth, Conn.	1796–1799	4	Joseph McKenna, Calif.	1898–1925	27
Bushrod Washington, Va.	1798–1829	31	Oliver W. Holmes, Mass.	1902–1932	29
Alfred Moore, N.C.	1799–1804	5	William R. Day, Ohio	1903–1922	19
John Marshall, Va.	1801–1835	34	William H. Moody, Mass.	1906–1910	4
William Johnson, S.C.	1804–1834	30	Horace H. Lurton, Tenn.	1910–1914	5
Brock. Livingston, N.Y.	1806–1823	17	Charles E. Hughes, N.Y.	1910–1916	6
Thomas Todd, Ky.	1807–1826	19	Willis Van Devanter, Wyo.	1911–1937	26
Joseph Story, Mass.	1811–1845	34	Joseph R. Lamar, Ga.	1911–1916	6
Gabriel Duval, Md.	1811–1836	25	**Edward D. White,** La.	1910–1921	11
Smith Thompson, N.Y.	1823–1843	20	Mahlon Pitney, N.J.	1912–1922	12
Robert Trimble, Ky.	1826–1828	2	Jas. C. McReynolds, Tenn.	1914–1941	27
John McLean, Ohio	1829–1861	32	Louis D. Brandeis, Mass.	1916–1939	23
Henry Baldwin, Pa.	1830–1844	14	John H. Clark, Ohio	1916–1922	6
James M. Wayne, Ga.	1835–1867	32	**William H. Taft,** Conn.	1921–1930	9
Roger B. Taney, Md.	1836–1864	28	George Sutherland, Utah	1922–1938	16
Philip P. Barbour, Va.	1836–1841	5	Pierce Butler, Minn.	1922–1939	17
John Catron, Tenn.	1837–1865	28	Edward T. Sanford, Tenn.	1923–1930	7
John McKinley, Ala.	1837–1852	15	Harlan F. Stone, N.Y.	1925–1941	16
Peter V. Daniel, Va.	1841–1860	19	**Charles E. Hughes,** N.Y.	1930–1941	11
Samuel Nelson, N.Y.	1845–1872	27	Owen J. Roberts, Pa.	1930–1945	15
Levi Woodbury, N.H.	1845–1851	6	Benjamin N. Cardozo, N.Y.	1932–1938	6
Robert C. Grier, Pa.	1846–1870	24	Hugo Black, Ala.	1937–....	..
Benj. R. Curtis, Mass.	1851–1857	6	Stanley Reed, Ky.	1938–....	..
John A. Campbell, Ala.	1853–1861	8	Felix Frankfurter, Mass.	1939–....	..
Nathan Clifford, Me.	1858–1881	23	William O. Douglas, Conn.	1939–....	..
Noah H. Swayne, Ohio	1862–1881	20	Frank Murphy, Mich.	1940–1949	9
Samuel F. Miller, Iowa	1862–1890	28	**Harlan F. Stone,** N.Y.	1941–1946	5
David Davis, Ill.	1862–1877	15	James F. Byrnes, S.C.	1941–1942	2
Stephen J. Field, Calif.	1863–1897	34	Robert H. Jackson, N.Y.	1941–1954	13
Salmon P. Chase, Ohio	1864–1873	9	Wiley B. Rutledge, Iowa	1943–1949	6
William Strong, Pa.	1870–1880	10	Harold H. Burton, Ohio	1945–....	..
Joseph P. Bradley, N.J.	1870–1892	22	**Fred M. Vinson,** Ky.	1946–1953	7
Ward Hunt, N.Y.	1872–1882	10	Thomas C. Clark, Texas	1949–....	..
Morrison R. Waite, Ohio	1874–1888	14	Sherman Minton, Ind.	1949–....	..
John M. Harlan, Ky.	1877–1911	34	**Earl Warren,** Calif.	1953–....	..
William B. Woods, Ga.	1880–1887	7	John M. Harlan, N.Y.	1955–....	..

SPEAKERS OF THE HOUSE OF REPRESENTATIVES, 1863-1955

Schuyler Colfax, Indiana	1863–1869		Frederick H. Gillett, Massachusetts	1919–1925
James G. Blaine, Maine	1869–1875		Nicholas Longworth, Ohio	1925–1931
Michael C. Kerr, Indiana	1875–1876		John Nance Garner, Texas	1931–1933
Samuel J. Randall, Pennsylvania	1876–1881		Henry T. Rainey, Illinois	1933–1934
Joseph W. Keifer, Ohio	1881–1883		Joseph W. Byrns, Tennessee	1935–1936
John G. Carlisle, Kentucky	1883–1889		William B. Bankhead, Alabama	1936–1940
Thomas B. Reed, Maine	1889–1891		Sam Rayburn, Texas	1940–1947
Charles F. Crisp, Georgia	1891–1895		Joseph W. Martin, Jr., Massachusetts	1947–1949
Thomas B. Reed, Maine	1895–1899		Sam Rayburn, Texas	1949–1953
David B. Henderson, Iowa	1899–1903		Joseph W. Martin, Jr., Massachusetts	1953–1955
Joseph G. Cannon, Illinois	1903–1910		Sam Rayburn, Texas	1955–
Champ Clark, Missouri	1911–1919			

POPULATION OF THE UNITED STATES, 1870-1950

Division and State	1870	1880	1890	1900	1910	1920	1930	1940	1950
UNITED STATES.....	39,818,449	50,155,783	62,947,714	75,994,575	91,972,266	105,710,620	122,775,046	131,669,275	150,697,361
GEOGRAPHIC DIVISIONS									
New England......	3,487,924	4,010,529	4,700,749	5,592,017	6,552,681	7,400,909	8,166,341	8,437,290	9,314,453
Middle Atlantic....	8,810,806	10,496,878	12,706,220	15,454,678	19,315,892	22,261,144	26,260,750	27,539,487	30,163,533
South Atlantic.....	5,853,610	7,597,197	8,857,922	10,443,480	12,194,895	13,990,272	15,793,589	17,823,151	21,182,335
East South Central.	4,404,445	5,585,151	6,429,154	7,547,757	8,409,901	8,893,307	9,887,214	10,778,225	11,477,181
West South Central	2,029,965	3,334,220	4,740,983	6,532,290	8,784,534	10,242,224	12,176,830	13,064,525	14,537,572
East North Central	9,124,517	11,206,668	13,478,305	15,985,581	18,250,621	21,475,543	25,297,185	26,626,342	30,399,368
West North Central	3,856,594	6,157,443	8,932,112	10,347,423	11,637,921	12,544,249	13,296,915	13,516,990	14,061,394
Mountain........	315,385	653,119	1,213,935	1,674,657	2,633,517	3,336,101	3,701,789	4,150,003	5,074,998
Pacific............	675,125	1,114,578	1,888,334	2,416,692	4,192,304	5,566,871	8,194,433	9,733,262	14,486,527
NEW ENGLAND									
Maine...........	626,915	648,936	661,086	694,466	742,371	768,014	797,423	847,226	913,774
New Hampshire ...	318,300	346,991	376,530	411,588	430,572	443,083	465,293	491,524	533,242
Vermont..........	330,551	332,286	332,422	343,641	355,956	352,428	359,611	359,231	377,747
Massachusetts.....	1,457,351	1,783,085	2,238,947	2,805,346	3,366,416	3,852,356	4,249,614	4,316,721	4,690,514
Rhode Island......	217,353	276,531	345,506	428,556	542,610	604,397	687,497	713,346	791,896
Connecticut.......	537,454	622,700	746,258	908,420	1,114,756	1,380,631	1,606,903	1,709,242	2,007,280
MIDDLE ATLANTIC									
New York.........	4,382,759	5,082,871	6,003,174	7,268,894	9,113,614	10,385,227	12,588,066	13,479,142	14,830,192
New Jersey........	906,096	1,131,116	1,444,933	1,883,669	2,537,167	3,155,900	4,041,334	4,160,165	4,835,329
Pennsylvania......	3,521,951	4,282,891	5,258,113	6,302,115	7,665,111	8,720,017	9,631,350	9,900,180	10,498,012
SOUTH ATLANTIC									
Delaware.........	125,015	146,608	168,493	184,735	202,322	223,003	238,380	266,505	318,085
Maryland.........	780,894	934,943	1,042,390	1,188,044	1,295,346	1,449,661	1,631,526	1,821,244	2,343,001
Dist. of Columbia..	131,700	177,624	230,392	278,718	331,069	437,571	486,869	663,091	802,178
Virginia..........	1,225,163	1,512,565	1,655,980	1,854,184	2,061,612	2,309,187	2,421,851	2,677,773	3,318,680
West Virginia......	442,014	618,457	762,794	958,800	1,221,119	1,463,701	1,729,205	1,901,974	2,005,552
North Carolina....	1,071,361	1,399,750	1,617,949	1,893,810	2,206,287	2,559,123	3,170,276	3,571,623	4,061,929
South Carolina....	705,606	995,577	1,151,149	1,340,316	1,515,400	1,683,724	1,738,765	1,899,804	2,117,027
Georgia..........	1,184,109	1,542,180	1,837,353	2,216,331	2,609,121	2,895,832	2,908,506	3,123,723	3,444,578
Florida...........	187,748	269,493	391,422	528,542	752,619	968,470	1,468,211	1,897,414	2,771,305
EAST SOUTH CENTRAL									
Kentucky.........	1,321,011	1,648,690	1,858,635	2,147,174	2,289,905	2,416,630	2,614,589	2,845,627	2,944,806
Tennessee........	1,258,520	1,542,359	1,767,518	2,020,616	2,184,789	2,337,885	2,616,556	2,915,841	3,291,718
Alabama..........	996,992	1,262,505	1,513,401	1,828,697	2,138,093	2,348,174	2,646,248	2,832,961	3,061,743
Mississippi.......	827,922	1,131,597	1,289,600	1,551,270	1,797,114	1,790,618	2,009,821	2,183,796	2,178,914
WEST SOUTH CENTRAL									
Arkansas..........	484,471	802,525	1,128,211	1,311,564	1,574,449	1,752,204	1,854,482	1,949,387	1,909,511
Louisiana........	726,915	939,946	1,118,588	1,381,625	1,656,388	1,798,509	2,101,593	2,363,880	2,683,516
Oklahoma *.......			258,657	790,391	1,657,155	2,028,283	2,396,040	2,336,434	2,233,351
Texas............	818,579	1,591,749	2,235,527	3,048,710	3,896,542	4,663,228	5,824,715	6,414,824	7,711,194
EAST NORTH CENTRAL									
Ohio..............	2,665,260	3,198,062	3,672,329	4,157,545	4,767,121	5,759,394	6,646,697	6,907,612	7,946,627
Indiana..........	1,680,637	1,978,301	2,192,404	2,516,462	2,700,876	2,930,390	3,238,503	3,427,796	3,934,224
Illinois...........	2,539,891	3,077,871	3,826,352	4,821,550	5,638,591	6,485,280	7,630,654	7,897,241	8,712,176
Michigan.........	1,184,059	1,636,937	2,093,890	2,420,982	2,810,173	3,668,412	4,842,325	5,256,106	6,371,766
Wisconsin........	1,054,670	1,315,497	1,693,330	2,069,042	2,333,860	2,632,067	2,939,006	3,137,587	3,434,576
WEST NORTH CENTRAL									
Minnesota........	439,706	780,773	1,310,283	1,751,394	2,075,708	2,387,125	2,563,953	2,792,300	2,982,483
Iowa.............	1,194,020	1,624,615	1,912,297	2,231,853	2,224,771	2,404,021	2,470,939	2,538,268	2,621,073
Missouri..........	1,721,295	2,168,380	2,679,185	3,106,665	3,293,335	3,404,055	3,629,367	3,784,664	3,954,653
North Dakota.....	2,405	36,909	190,983	319,146	577,056	646,872	680,845	641,935	619,636
South Dakota.....	11,776	98,268	348,600	401,570	583,888	636,547	692,849	642,961	652,740
Nebraska.........	122,993	452,402	1,062,656	1,066,300	1,192,214	1,296,372	1,377,963	1,315,834	1,325,510
Kansas...........	364,399	996,096	1,428,108	1,470,495	1,690,949	1,769,257	1,880,999	1,801,028	1,905,299
MOUNTAIN									
Montana.........	20,595	39,159	142,924	243,329	376,053	548,889	537,606	559,456	591,024
Idaho............	14,999	32,610	88,548	161,772	325,594	431,866	445,032	524,873	588,637
Wyoming........	9,118	20,789	62,555	92,531	145,965	194,402	225,565	250,742	290,529
Colorado.........	39,864	194,327	413,249	539,700	799,024	939,629	1,035,791	1,123,296	1,325,089
New Mexico.......	91,874	119,565	160,282	195,310	327,301	360,350	423,317	531,818	681,187
Arizona..........	9,658	40,440	88,243	122,931	204,354	334,162	435,573	499,261	749,587
Utah............	86,786	143,963	210,779	276,749	373,351	449,396	507,847	550,310	688,862
Nevada...........	42,491	62,266	47,355	42,335	81,875	77,407	91,058	110,247	160,083
PACIFIC									
Washington.......	23,955	75,116	357,232	518,103	1,141,990	1,356,621	1,563,396	1,736,191	2,378,963
Oregon...........	90,923	174,768	317,704	413,536	672,765	783,389	953,786	1,089,684	1,521,341
California........	560,247	864,694	1,213,398	1,485,053	2,377,549	3,426,861	5,677,251	6,907,387	10,586,223

* Includes population of Indian territory: 1890, 180,182; 1900, 392,060.

Country	1841–50	1851–60	1861–70	1871–80	1881–90
Austria ⎰ Hungary ⎱ ··········			7,800	72,969	353,719
Belgium.............	5,074	4,738	6,734	7,211	20,177
Bulgaria.............					
Czechoslovakia.......					
Denmark............	539	3,749	17,094	31,771	88,132
Finland..............					
France..............	77,262	76,358	35,986	72,206	50,464
Germany............	434,626	951,667	787,468	718,182	1,452,970
Greece..............	16	31	72	210	2,308
Italy...............	1,870	9,231	11,725	55,759	307,309
Netherlands.........	8,251	10,789	9,102	16,541	53,701
Norway ⎰ Sweden ⎱ ··········	13,903	20,931	109,298	⎰ 95,333 ⎱ 115,922	176,586 391,776
Poland..............	105	1,164	2,027	12,970	51,806
Rumania.............				11	6,348
Russia..............	551	457	2,512	39,284	213,282
Spain...............	2,209	9,298	6,697	5,266	4,419
Portugal............	550	1,055	2,658	14,082	16,978
Switzerland.........	4,644	25,011	23,286	28,293	81,988
Turkey (in Europe)...	59	83	129	337	1,562
United Kingdom......	1,047,763	1,338,093	1,042,674	984,914	1,462,839
England...........	32,092	247,125	222,277	437,706	644,680
Ireland............	780,719	914,119	435,778	436,871	655,482
Scotland..........	3,712	38,331	38,769	87,564	149,869
Wales.............	1,261	6,319	4,313	6,631	12,640
Not Specified......	229,979	132,199	341,537	16,142	168
Yugoslavia..........					
Other Europe........	79	5	8	1,001	682
Total Europe........	1,597,501	2,452,660	2,065,270	2,272,262	4,737,046

From *Statistical Abstract of the United States.*

THE UNITED STATES, 1841-1950

1891–1900	1901–10	1911–20	1921–30	1931–40	1941–50
592,707	2,145,266	{453,649	32,868	*	24,860
		{442,693	30,680	7,861	3,469
18,167	41,635	33,746	15,846	4,817	12,189
160	39,280	22,533	2,945	938	375
		3,426	102,194	14,393	8,347
50,231	65,285	41,983	32,430	2,559	5,393
		756	16,691	2,146	2,503
30,770	73,379	61,897	49,610	12,623	38,809
505,152	341,498	143,945	412,202	117,621	226,578
15,979	167,519	184,201	51,084	9,119	8,973
651,893	2,045,877	1,109,524	455,315	68,208	57,661
26,758	48,262	43,718	26,948	7,150	14,860
95,015	190,505	66,395	68,531	4,740	10,100
226,266	249,534	95,074	97,249	3,960	10,665
96,720		4,813	227,734	17,026	7,571
12,750	53,008	13,311	67,646	3,871	1,076
505,290	1,597,306	921,201	61,742	1,356	548
8,731	27,935	68,611	28,958	3,258	2,898
27,508	69,149	89,732	29,994	3,329	7,423
31,179	34,922	23,091	29,676	5,512	10,547
3,626	79,976	54,677	14,659	737	580
659,954	865,015	487,589	550,804		
216,726	388,017	249,944	157,420	21,756	111,252
388,416	339,065	146,181	220,591	13,167	25,377
44,188	120,469	78,357	159,781	6,887	16,131
10,557	17,464	13,107	13,012	735	
67					
		1,888	49,064	5,835	1,576
122	665	8,111	22,983	8,865	7,734
3,558,978	8,136,016	4,376,564	2,477,853	348,289	621,704

* With Germany after 1938.

THE GENEALOGY OF AMERICAN POLITICAL PARTIES

	Republican	**Democratic**				**Prohibitionist**
1864 ■ Johnson–(UNION and DEM.)						
1868 ■ Grant–(REPUBLICAN)						Prohibitionist
1872 ■ Grant–(REPUBLICAN)	Liberal Republican	Anti-Monopoly (Granger)				
1876 ■ Hayes–(REPUBLICAN)		Greenback				
1880 ■ Garfield / Arthur (REPUBLICAN)						
1884 ■ Cleveland–(DEMOCRAT)						
1888 ■ Harrison–(REPUBLICAN)						
1892 ■ Cleveland–(DEMOCRAT)		Populist	Socialist-Labor			
1896 ■ McKinley–(REPUBLICAN)						
1900 ■ McKinley / Roosevelt (REPUBLICAN)			Socialist			
1904 ■ Roosevelt–(REPUBLICAN)						
1908 ■ Taft–(REPUBLICAN)						
1912 ■ Wilson–(DEMOCRAT)	Progressive (T. R.)					
1916 ■ Wilson–(DEMOCRAT)						
1920 ■ Harding / Coolidge (REPUBLICAN)				Communist (Workers)		
1924 ■ Coolidge–(REPUBLICAN)	Progressive (LaFollette)					
1928 ■ Hoover–(REPUBLICAN)						
1932 ■ Roosevelt–(DEMOCRAT)						
1936 ■ Roosevelt–(DEMOCRAT)						
1940 ■ Roosevelt–(DEMOCRAT)						
1944 ■ Roosevelt / Truman (DEMOCRAT)						
1948 ■ Truman–(DEMOCRAT)	Progressive (Wallace)					
1952 ■ Eisenhower–(REPUBLICAN)						

THE FOURTEEN POINTS

Given to Congress by President Wilson, Jan 8 1918

I. Open covenants of peace, openly arrived at, after which there shall be no private international understandings of any kind but diplomacy shall proceed always frankly and in the public view.

II. Absolute freedom of navigation upon the seas, outside territorial waters, alike in peace and in war, except as the seas may be closed in whole or in part by international action for the enforcement of international covenants.

III. The removal, so far as possible, of all economic barriers and the establishment of an equality of trade conditions among all the nations consenting to the peace and associating themselves for its maintenance.

IV. Adequate guarantees given and taken that national armaments will be reduced to the lowest point consistent with domestic safety.

V. A free, open-minded, and absolutely impartial adjustment of all colonial claims, based upon a strict observance of the principle that in determining all such questions of sovereignty the interests of the populations concerned must have equal weight with the equitable claims of the government whose title is to be determined.

VI. The evacuation of all Russian territory and such a settlement of all questions affecting Russia as will secure the best and freest cooperation of the other nations of the world in obtaining for her an unhampered and unembarrassed opportunity for the independent determination of her own political development and national policy and assure her of a sincere welcome into the society of free nations under institutions of her own choosing; and, more than a welcome, assistance also of every kind that she may need and may herself desire. The treatment accorded Russia by her sister nations in the months to come will be the acid test of their good will, of their comprehension of her needs as distinguished from their own interests, and of their intelligent and unselfish sympathy.

VII. Belgium, the whole world will agree, must be evacuated and restored, without any attempt to limit the sovereignty which she enjoys in common with all other free nations. No other single act will serve as this will serve to restore confidence among the nations in the laws which they have themselves set and determined for the government of their relations with one another. Without this healing act the whole structure and validity of international law is forever impaired.

VIII. All French territory should be freed and the invaded portions restored, and the wrong done to France by Prussia in 1871 in the matter of Alsace-Lorraine, which has unsettled the peace of the world for nearly fifty years, should be righted, in order that peace may once more be made secure in the interest of all.

IX. A readjustment of the frontiers of Italy should be effected along clearly recognizable lines of nationality.

X. The peoples of Austria-Hungary, whose place among the nations we wish to see safeguarded and assured, should be accorded the freest opportunity of autonomous development.

XI. Rumania, Serbia, and Montenegro should be evacuated; occupied territories restored; Serbia accorded free and secure access to the sea; and the relations of the several Balkan states to one another determined by friendly counsel along historically established lines of allegiance and nationality; and international guarantees of the political and economic independence and territorial integrity of the several Balkan states should be entered into.

XII. The Turkish portions of the present Ottoman Empire should be assured a secure sovereignty, but the other nationalities which are now under Turkish rule should be assured an undoubted security of life and an absolutely unmolested opportunity of autonomous development, and the Dardanelles should be permanently opened as a free passage to the ships and commerce of all nations under international guarantees.

XIII. An independent Polish state should be erected which should include the territories inhabited by indisputably Polish populations, which should be assured a free and secure access to the sea, and whose political and economic independence and territorial integrity should be guaranteed by international covenant.

XIV. A general association of nations must be formed under specific covenants for the purpose of affording mutual guarantees of political independence and territorial integrity to great and small states alike.

THE FOUR FREEDOMS

From President Roosevelt's annual message to Congress, Jan. 6, 1941

In the future days, which we seek to make secure, we look forward to a world founded upon four essential human freedoms.

The first is freedom of speech and expression — everywhere in the world.

The second is freedom of every person to worship God in his own way — everywhere in the world.

The third is freedom from want — which, translated into world terms, means economic understandings which will secure to every nation a healthy peacetime life for its inhabitants — everywhere in the world.

The fourth is freedom from fear — which, translated into world terms, means a worldwide reduction of armaments to such a point and in such a thorough fashion that no nation will be in a position to commit an act of physical aggression against any neighbor — anywhere in the world.

That is no vision of a distant millennium. It is a definite basis for a kind of world attainable in our own time and generation. That kind of world is the very antithesis of the so-called new order of tyranny which the dictators seek to create with the crash of a bomb.

To that new order we oppose the greater conception — the moral order. A good society is able to face schemes of world domination and foreign revolutions alike without fear.

Since the beginning of our American history we have been engaged in change — in a perpetual peaceful revolution — a revolution which goes on steadily, quietly adjusting itself to changing conditions — without the concentration camp or the quick-lime in the ditch. The world order which we seek is the cooperation of free countries, working together in a friendly, civilized society.

This nation has placed its destiny in the hands and heads and hearts of its millions of free men and women; and its faith in freedom under the guidance of God. Freedom means the supremacy of human rights everywhere. Our support goes to those who struggle to gain those rights or keep them. Our strength is in our unity of purpose.

To that high concept there can be no end save victory.

THE ATLANTIC CHARTER

Issued August 14, 1941

The President of the United States of America and the Prime Minister, Mr. Churchill, representing His Majesty's Government in the United Kingdom, being met together, deem it right to make known certain common principles in the national policies of their respective countries on which they base their hopes for a better future for the world.

First, their countries seek no aggrandizement, territorial or other;

Second, they desire to see no territorial changes that do not accord with the freely expressed wishes of the peoples concerned;

Third, they respect the right of all peoples to choose the form of government under which they will live; and they wish to see sovereign rights and self government restored to those who have been forcibly deprived of them;

Fourth, they will endeavor, with due respect for their existing obligations, to further the enjoyment of all States, great or small, victor or vanquished, of access, on equal terms, to the trade and to the raw materials of the world which are needed for their economic prosperity;

Fifth, they desire to bring about the fullest collaboration between all nations in the economic field with the object of securing, for all, improved labor standards, economic advancement and social security;

Sixth, after the final destruction of Nazi tyranny, they hope to see established a peace which will afford to all nations the means of dwelling in safety within their own boundaries, and which will afford assurance that all men in all lands may live out their lives in freedom from fear and want;

Seventh, such a peace should enable all men to traverse the high seas and oceans without hindrance;

Eighth, they believe that all the nations of the world, for realistic, as well as spiritual reasons, must come to the abandonment of the use of force. Since no future peace can be maintained if land, sea or air armaments continue to be employed by nations which threaten, or may threaten, aggression outside of their frontiers, they believe, pending the establishment of a wider and permanent system of general security, that the disarmament of such nations is essential. They will likewise aid and encourage all other practicable measures which will lighten for peace-loving peoples the crushing burden of armaments.

CHARTER OF THE UNITED NATIONS

WE, the peoples of the United Nations determined to save succeeding generations from the scourge of war, which twice in our lifetime has brought untold sorrow to mankind, and

To reaffirm faith in fundamental human rights, in the dignity and worth of the human person, in the equal rights of men and women and of nations large and small, and

To establish conditions under which justice and respect for the obligations arising from treaties and other sources of international law can be maintained, and

To promote social progress and better standards of life in larger freedom, and for these ends

To practice tolerance and live together in peace with one another as good neighbors, and

To unite our strength to maintain international peace and security, and

To insure, by the acceptance of principles and the institution of methods, that armed force shall not be used, save in the common interest, and

To employ international machinery for the promotion of the economic and social advancement of all peoples, have resolved to combine our efforts to accomplish these aims.

Accordingly, our respective governments, through representatives assembled in the city of San Francisco, who have exhibited their full powers found to be in good and due form, have agreed to the present Charter of the United Nations and do hereby establish an international organization to be known as the United Nations.

CHAPTER I

Purposes and Principles

ARTICLE 1

The purposes of the United Nations are:

1. To maintain international peace and security, and to that end: to take effective collective measures for the prevention and removal of threats to the peace, and for the suppression of acts of aggression or other breaches of the peace, and to bring about by peaceful means, and in conformity with the principles of justice and international law, adjustment or settlement of international disputes or situations which might lead to a breach of peace;

2. To develop friendly relations among nations based on respect for the principle of equal rights and self-determination of peoples, and to take other appropriate measures to strengthen universal peace;

3. To achieve international co-operation in solving international problems of an economic, social, cultural or humanitarian character, and in promoting and encouraging respect for human rights and for fundamental freedoms for all without distinction as to race, sex, language or religion; and

4. To be a center for harmonizing the actions of nations in the attainment of these common ends.

ARTICLE 2

The organization and its members, in pursuit of the purposes stated in Article 1, shall act in accordance with the following principles:

1. The organization is based on the principle of the sovereign equality of all its members.

2. All members, in order to ensure to all of them the rights and benefits resulting from membership, shall fulfill in good faith the obligations assumed by them in accordance with the present Charter.

3. All members shall settle their international disputes by peaceful means in such a manner that international peace and security, and justice, are not endangered.

4. All members shall refrain in their international relations from the threat or use of force against the territorial integrity or political independence of any state, or in any other manner inconsistent with the purposes of the United Nations.

5. All members shall give the United Nations every assistance in any action it takes in accordance with the present Charter, and shall refrain from giving assistance to any state against which the United Nations is taking preventive or enforcement action.

6. The organization shall ensure that states not members of the United Nations act in accordance with these principles so far as may be necessary for the maintenance of international peace and security.

7. Nothing contained in the present Charter shall authorize the United Nations to intervene in matters which are essentially within the domestic jurisdiction of any state or shall require the members to submit such matters to settlement under the present Charter; but this principle shall not prejudice the application of enforcement measures under Chapter VII.

CHAPTER II

Membership

ARTICLE 3

The original members of the United Nations shall be the states which, having participated in the United Nations Conference on International Organization at San Francisco, or have previously signed the Declaration by United Nations of Jan. 1, 1942, sign the present Charter and ratify it in accordance with Article 110.

NORTH ATLANTIC TREATY

Signed at Washington, D.C., April 4, 1949

The Parties to this Treaty reaffirm their faith in the purposes and principles of the Charter of the United Nations and their desire to live in peace with all peoples and all governments.

They are determined to safeguard the freedom, common heritage and civilization of their peoples, founded on the principles of democracy, individual liberty and the rule of law.

They seek to promote stability and well-being in the North Atlantic area.

They are resolved to unite their efforts for collective defense and for the preservation of peace and security.

They therefore agree to this North Atlantic Treaty:

ARTICLE 1

The Parties undertake, as set forth in the Charter of the United Nations, to settle any international disputes in which they may be involved by peaceful means in such a manner that international peace and security, and justice, are not endangered, and to refrain in their international relations from the threat or use of force in any manner inconsistent with the purposes of the United Nations.

ARTICLE 2

The Parties will contribute toward the further development of peaceful and friendly international relations by strengthening their free institutions, by bringing about a better understanding of the principles upon which these institutions are founded, and by promoting conditions of stability and well-being. They will seek to eliminate conflict in their international economic policies and will encourage economic collaboration between any or all of them.

ARTICLE 3

In order more effectively to achieve the objectives of this Treaty, the Parties, separately and jointly, by means of continuous and effective self-help and mutual aid, will maintain and develop their individual and collective capacity to resist armed attack.

ARTICLE 4

The Parties will consult together whenever, in the opinion of any of them, the territorial integrity, political independence or security of any of the Parties is threatened.

ARTICLE 5

The Parties agree that an armed attack against one or more of them in Europe or North America shall be considered an attack against them all; and consequently they agree that, if such an armed attack occurs, each of them, in exercise of the right of individual or collective self-defense recognized by Article 51 of the Charter of the United Nations, will assist the Party or Parties so attacked by taking forthwith, individually and in concert with the other Parties, such action as it deems necessary, including the use of armed force, to restore and maintain the security of the North Atlantic area.

Any such armed attack and all measures taken as a result thereof shall immediately be reported to the Security Council. Such measures shall be terminated when the Security Council has taken the measures necessary to restore and maintain international peace and security.

ARTICLE 6

For the purpose of Article 5 an armed attack on one or more of the Parties is deemed to include an armed attack on the territory of any of the Parties in Europe or North America, on the Algerian departments of France, on the occupation forces of any Party in Europe, on the islands under the jurisdiction of any Party in the North Atlantic area north of the Tropic of Cancer or on the vessels or aircraft in this area of any of the Parties.

ARTICLE 7

This Treaty does not affect, and shall not be interpreted as affecting, in any way the rights and obligations under the Charter of the Parties which are members of the United Nations, or the primary responsibility of the Security Council for the maintenance of international peace and security.

ARTICLE 8

Each Party declares that none of the international engagements now in force between it and any other of the Parties or any third state is in conflict with the provisions of this Treaty, and undertakes not to enter into any international engagement in conflict with this Treaty.

ARTICLE 9

The Parties hereby establish a council, on which each of them shall be represented, to consider matters concerning the implementation of this Treaty. The council shall be so organized as to be able to meet promptly at any time. The council shall set up such subsidiary bodies as may be necessary; in particular it shall establish immediately a defense committee which shall recommend measures for the implementation of Articles 3 and 5.

ARTICLE 10

The Parties may, by unanimous agreement, invite any other European state in a position to further the principles of this Treaty and to contribute to the security of the North Atlantic area to accede to this Treaty. Any state so invited may become a party to the Treaty by depositing its instrument of accession with the Government of the United States of America. The Government of the United States of America will inform each of the Parties of the deposit of each such instrument of accession.

ARTICLE 11

This Treaty shall be ratified and its provisions carried out by the Parties in accordance with their respective constitutional processes. The instruments of ratification shall be deposited as soon as possible with the Government of the United States of America, which will notify all the other signatories of each deposit. The Treaty shall enter into force between the states which have ratified it as soon as the ratifications of the majority of the signatories, including the ratifications of Belgium, Canada, France, Luxem-burg, the Netherlands, the United Kingdom and the United States, have been deposited and shall come into effect with respect to other states on the date of the deposit of their ratifications.

ARTICLE 12

After the Treaty has been in force for ten years, or at any time thereafter, the Parties shall, if any of them so requests, consult together for the purpose of reviewing the Treaty, having regard for the factors then affecting peace and security in the North Atlantic area, including the development of universal as well as regional arrangements under the Charter of the United Nations for the maintenance of international peace and security.

ARTICLE 13

After the Treaty has been in force for twenty years, any Party may cease to be a party one year after its notice of denunciation has been given to the Government of the United States of America, which will inform the Governments of the other Parties of the deposit of each notice of denunciation.

ARTICLE 14

This Treaty, of which the English and French texts are equally authentic, shall be deposited in the archives of the Government of the United States of America. Duly certified copies thereof will be transmitted by that Government to the Governments of the other signatories.

LIST OF BOOKS CITED

(With page references to original citations in chapter bibliographies)

Aaron, Daniel. *Men of Good Hope: A Story of American Progressives.* 1951. 383.

Abbott, Edith. *Historical Aspects of the Immigration Problem: Select Documents.* 1926. 203.

Abbott, Lawrence F. *Impressions of Theodore Roosevelt.* 1919. 331.

Abell, Aaron I. *The Urban Impact on American Protestantism, 1865–1900 (Harvard Historical Studies, LIV).* 1943. 264.

Acheson, Dean. *Strengthening the Forces of Freedom: Selected Speeches and Statements of Secretary of State Acheson, February, 1949–April, 1950.* 1950. 726.

Adamic, Louis. *Dynamite: The Story of Class Violence in America.* 1931. Rev. ed., 1934. 187.

—— *A Nation of Nations.* 1945. 204.

Adams, Adeline V. *The Spirit of American Sculpture.* 1923. 548.

Adams, Charles F., Jr. *Charles Francis Adams (American Statesmen, XXIX).* 1900. 53.

—— *Railroads: Their Origins and Problems.* 1878. Rev. ed., 1887. 146.

Adams, Ephraim D. *Great Britain and the American Civil War.* 2 vols. 1925. 53.

Adams, Grace K. *Workers on Relief.* 1939. 591.

Adams, Henry. *The Education of Henry Adams: An Autobiography.* 1918. 264.

—— *Henry Adams and his Friends: A Collection of his Unpublished Letters.* Edited by Harold D. Cater. 1947. 264.

Adams, James T. *Our Business Civilization: Some Aspects of American Culture.* 1929. 547.

Adams, Samuel H. *Incredible Era: The Life and Times of Warren Gamaliel Harding.* 1939. 479, 505.

Adams, William F. *Ireland and Irish Emigration to the New World from 1815 to the Famine.* 1932. 203.

Addams, Jane. *Forty Years at Hull House.* 1935. 264.

Agar, Herbert. *The Price of Union.* 1950. 126.

Alexander, DeAlva S. *Four Famous New Yorkers: The Political Careers of Cleveland, Platt, Hill, and Roosevelt.* 1923. 126.

Alexander, Thomas B. *Political Reconstruction in Tennessee.* 1950. 18.

Alger, Russell A. *The Spanish-American War.* 1901. 286.

Allen, Frederick J. *The Shoe Industry (American Business Series).* 1922. 168.

Allen, Frederick L. *The Big Change: America Transforms Itself, 1900–1950.* 1952. 775.

—— *The Great Pierpont Morgan.* 1949. 244.

—— *Only Yesterday: An Informal History of the Nineteen-Twenties.* 1931. 505, 549.

—— *Since Yesterday: The Nineteen-Thirties in America, September 3, 1929–September 3, 1939.* 1940. 547.

Allen, Gwenfread. *Hawaii's War Years, 1941–1945.* 1950. 676.

Allen, William H. *Al Smith's Tammany Hall, Champion Political Vampire.* 1928. 522.

Alsop, Joseph, and Turner Catledge. *The 168 Days.* 1938. 611.

Alsop, Joseph, and Robert Kintner. *Men Around the President.* 1939. 610.

Alter, J. Cecil. *James Bridger.* 1925. 76.

Ambler, Charles H. *A History of Education in West Virginia: From Colonial Times to 1949.* 1951. 103.

American Meat Institute. *The Packing Industry.* 1924. 168.

Anderson, Jackson, and Ronald W. May. *McCarthy: The Man, The Senator, The Ism.* 1952. 751.

Anderson, Nels. *The Right to Work.* 1938. 591.

Andrews, Elisha B. *The United States in Our Own Time.* 1903. 126.

Andrews, Kenneth R. *Nook Farm: Mark Twain's Hartford Circle.* 1950. 104.

Angell, Robert C. *The Campus: A Study of Contemporary Undergraduate Life in the American University.* 1928. 548.

Aptheker, Herbert, ed. *A Documentary History of the Negro People in the United States.* 1951. 34.

Armes, Ethel M. *The Story of Coal and Iron in Alabama.* 1910. 169.

Arnett, Alex M. *Claude Kitchin and the Wilson War Policies.* 1937. 453.

—— *The Populist Movement in Georgia (Columbia University, Studies in History, Economics and Public Law, CIV).* 1922. 228.

Arnold, Benjamin W. *History of the Tobacco Industry in Virginia from 1860 to 1894 (Johns Hopkins University, Studies in Historical and Political Science, XV, 1–2).* 1897. 17, 169.

Arnold, Henry H. *Global Mission.* 1949. 657.

Asbury, Herbert. *The Gangs of New York: An Informal History of the Underworld.* 1928. 103.

—— *The Great Illusion: An Informal History of Prohibition.* 1950. 548.

Ashley, Percy W. L. *Modern Tariff History: Germany, United States, France.* 1904. 3rd ed., 1926. 126.

Ayres, Leonard P. *The War With Germany: A Statistical Summary.* 1919. 452.

Babcock, Kendric C. *The Scandinavian Element in the United States.* 1914. 203.

Bailey, Thomas A. *America Faces Russia: Russian-American Relations from Early Times to Our Day.* 1950. 726.

—— *A Diplomatic History of the American People.* 1940. 4th ed., 1950. 53, 285.

—— *The Man in the Street: The Impact of American Public Opinion on Foreign Policy.* 1948. 658.

—— *The Policy of the United States toward the Neutrals, 1917–1918.* 1942. 452.

—— *Theodore Roosevelt and the Japanese-American Crises.* 1934. 331.

—— *Wilson and the Peacemakers.* 1947. 453.

—— *Woodrow Wilson and the Great Betrayal.* 1945. 453.

—— *Woodrow Wilson and the Lost Peace.* 1944. 453.

Baker, Newton D. *Why We Went to War.* 1936. 427.

Baker, Ray S. *American Chronicle: The Autobiography of Ray Stannard Baker.* 1945. 357.

—— *Woodrow Wilson and World Settlement.* 3 vols. 1922. 453.

—— *Woodrow Wilson, Life and Letters.* 8 vols. 1927–1939. 401.

Bakken, Henry H., and M. A. Schaars. *The Economics of Co-operative Marketing.* 1937. 478.

Balch, Emily Greene. *Our Slavic Fellow Citizens.* 1910. 203.

Baldwin, Hanson W. *Great Mistakes of the War.* 1950. 658.

Ballantine, Duncan S. *U.S. Naval Logistics in the Second World War.* 1947. 658.

Bancroft, Frederic. *The Life of William H. Seward.* 2 vols. 1900. 34.

Bancroft, Hubert H. *History of Nevada, Colorado and Wyoming, 1540–1888.* 1890. 75.

Banks, Enoch M. *Economics of Land Tenure in Georgia* (Columbia University, Studies in History, Economics and Public Law, XXIII, No. 1). 1905. 228.

Barber, Herbert L. *The Story of the Automobile.* 1917. 547.

Barck, Oscar T., Jr., and N. M. Blake. *Since 1900.* 1947. Rev. ed., 1952. 357.

Barclay, Thomas S. *The Liberal Republican Movement in Missouri, 1865–1871.* 1926. 53.

Barghoorn, Frederick C. *The Soviet Image of the United States: A Study in Distortion.* 1950. 726.

Barnard, Harry. *Eagle Forgotten, The Life of John Peter Altgeld.* 1938. 187.

Barnes, James A. *John G. Carlisle, Financial Statesman.* 1931. 126.

—— *Wealth of the American People: A History of their Economic Life.* 1949. 478.

Barr, Elizabeth S. "The Populist Uprising." In *A Standard History of Kansas and Kansans,* II. Edited by W. E. Connelley. 1918. 229.

Barrett, Don C. *The Greenbacks and Resumption of Specie Payments, 1862–1879 (Harvard University Studies, XXXVI).* 1931. 125.

Barrett, James W. *Joseph Pulitzer and His World.* 1941. 264.

Barrows, Chester L. *William M. Evarts, Lawyer, Diplomat, Statesman.* 1941. 125.

Barth, Alan. *The Loyalty of Free Men.* 1951. 751.

Bartlett, Ruhl J. *The League to Enforce Peace.* 1944. 453.

——, ed. *The Record of American Diplomacy: Documents and Readings in the History of American Foreign Relations.* 1947. 725.

Bartley, Ernest R. *The Tidelands Oil Controversy: A Legal and Historical Analysis.* 1953. 751.

Baruch, Bernard M. *American Industry in the War: A Report of the War Industries Board.* 1921. 452.

—— *The Making of the Reparation and Economic Sections of the Treaty.* 1920. 453.

Baruch, Bernard M., and J. M. Hancock. *War and Postwar Adjustment Policies.* 1944. 676.

Baskerville, Beatrice C. *The Polish Jew: His Social and Economic Value.* 1906. 204.

Bassett, John S. *Our War with Germany: A History.* 1919. 452.

Bate, H. Maclear. *Report from Formosa.* 1952. 702.

Baur, John I. H. *Revolution and Tradition in Modern American Art.* 1951. 548.

Beach, Joseph W. *American Fiction, 1920–1940.* 1941. 548.

Beale, Howard K. *Are American Teachers Free? An Analysis of Restraints upon the Freedom of Teaching in American Schools.* 1936. 548.

—— *The Critical Year: A Study of Andrew Jackson and Reconstruction.* 1930. 18.

—— *A History of Freedom of Teaching in American Schools.* 1941. 548.

Beals, Carleton. *The Crime of Cuba.* 1933. 310.

—— *Porfirio Diaz, Dictator of Mexico.* 1932. 426.

—— *The Story of Huey P. Long.* 1935. 611.

Beamish, Richard J., and F. A. Murch. *America's Part in the World War.* 1919. 452.

Bean, Walton. *Boss Ruef's San Francisco: The Story of the Union Labor Party, Big Business, and the Graft Prosecution.* 1952. 383.

Beard, Charles A. *American Foreign Policy in the Making, 1932–1940.* 1946. 702.

—— *President Roosevelt and the Coming of the War, 1941: A Study in Appearances and Realities.* 1948. 632.

Beard, Charles A., ed. *A Century of Progress.* 1933. 104.

———, ed. *Documents on the State-Wide Initiative, Referendum and Recall.* 1912. 382.

Beard, Charles A. and Mary R. *America in Midpassage.* 1939. 547.

——— *The Rise of American Civilization.* 2 vols. 1927. New ed., 1949. 17, 547.

Beard, Charles A., and G. H. E. Smith. *The Future Comes: A Study of the New Deal.* 1933. 568.

Beard, Mary R. *The American Labor Movement: A Short History.* 1924. 187.

Beardsley, Frank G. *A History of American Revivals.* 1904. 2nd ed., 1912. 104, 264.

Beasley, Norman. *The Cross and the Crown: A History of Christian Science.* 1952. 104.

Becker, Carl L. *Cornell University: Founders and the Founding.* 1943. 103.

——— *How New Will the Better World Be?* 1944. 702.

Beer, Thomas. *Hanna.* 1929. 243.

——— *The Mauve Decade: American Life at the End of the Nineteenth Century.* 1926. 264.

Bell, Herbert C. F. *Woodrow Wilson and the People.* 1945. 401.

Bellot, H[ugh] Hale. *American History and American Historians.* 1952. 264.

Bemis, Samuel F. *A Diplomatic History of the United States.* 1936. 3rd ed., 1950. 53, 285, 632.

——— *The United States as a World Power: A Diplomatic History, 1900–1950.* 1950. 632.

———, ed. *The American Secretaries of State and Their Diplomacy.* 10 vols. 1927–29. 53, 285, 286.

Benét, Rosemary, and Stephen Vincent Benét. *A Book of Americans.* 1933. 348.

Bergmann, Karl. *History of Reparations.* 1927. 522.

Berman, Edward. *Labor Disputes and the President of the United States* (Columbia University, Studies in History, Economics and Public Law, CXI). 1924. 187.

Bernheimer, Charles S., ed. *The Russian Jew in the United States.* 1905. 204.

Bernstorff, J. H. von. *My Three Years in America.* 1920. 427.

Besterman, Theodore. *UNESCO: Peace in the Minds of Men.* 1951. 725.

Bigelow, John. *The Life of Samuel J. Tilden.* 2 vols. 1895. 125.

Bigelow, John, Jr. *Reminiscences of the Santiago Campaign.* 1899. 286.

Billington, Ray A. *Westward Expansion: A History of the American Frontier.* 1949. 75.

Binkley, Robert C. *The Cultural Program of the W.P.A.* 1939. 548.

Binkley, Wilfred E. *American Political Parties: Their Natural History.* 1943. 2nd ed., 1945. 125.

Bishop, Joseph B. *Theodore Roosevelt and His Time Shown in His Own Letters.* 2 vols. 1920. 331.

Bishop, Joseph B., and Farnham Bishop. *Goethals, Genius of the Panama Canal.* 1930. 331.

Bisson, Thomas A. *American Policy in the Far East, 1931–1941.* 1941. 632.

Black, Cyril E., and E. C. Helmreich. *Twentieth Century Europe: A History.* 1950. 632.

Black, John D. *Agricultural Reform in the United States.* 1929. 505.

Blaine, James G. *Twenty Years of Congress: From Lincoln to Garfield.* 2 vols. 1884–86. 126.

Blegen, Theodore C. *Building Minnesota.* 1938. 76.

——— *Norwegian Migration to America.* 2 vols. 1931–40. 203.

Blum, John M. *Joe Tumulty and the Wilson Era.* 1951. 401.

——— *The Republican Roosevelt.* 1954. 331.

Bogart, Ernest L. *Direct and Indirect Costs of the Great World War.* 1919. 2nd ed., 1920. 452.

Bogart, Ernest L., and D. L. Kemmerer. *Economic History of the American People.* 1938. 2nd ed., 1947. 478.

Bolles, Blair. *Tyrant from Illinois: Uncle Joe Cannon's Experiment with Personal Power.* 1951. 383.

Bond, Horace Mann. *The Education of the Negro in the American Social Order.* 1934. 103.

Borchard, Edwin, and W. P. Lage. *Neutrality for the United States.* 1937. 427.

Borg, Dorothy. *American Policy and the Chinese Revolution, 1925–1928.* 1947. 479.

Bowers, Claude G. *Beveridge and the Progressive Era.* 1932. 310, 383.

——— *The Tragic Era: The Revolution after Lincoln.* 1929. 17.

Boyd, William K. *The Story of Durham, City of the New South.* 1925. 169.

Boyle, James E. *Farm Relief: A Brief on the McNary-Haugen Plan.* 1928. 522.

Boynton, Percy H. *America in Contemporary Fiction.* 1940. 548.

Bradford, Gamaliel. *D. L. Moody: A Worker in Souls.* 1927. 104.

Bradley, David J. *No Place to Hide.* 1948. 726.

Bradley, Harold W. *The American Frontier in Hawaii: The Pioneers, 1789–1843.* 1942. 285.

Bradley, Omar N. *A Soldier's Story.* 1951. 657.

Branch, E[dward] Douglas. *The Cowboy and His Interpreters.* 1926. 76.

——— *The Hunting of the Buffalo.* 1929. 76.

——— *Westward: The Romance of the American Frontier.* 1930. 75.

Brandeis, Louis D. *Other People's Money.* 1914. 401.

Brant, Irving. *Storm over the Constitution.* 1936. 611.

Brawley, Benjamin G. *A Short History of the American Negro.* 1913. 4th ed., 1939. 17.

—— *A Social History of the American Negro.* 1921. 17.

Brereton, Lewis Hyde. *The Brereton Diaries: The War in the Air in the Pacific, Middle East, and Europe.* 1946. 657.

Briggs, Harold E. *Frontiers of the Northwest: A History of the Upper Missouri Valley.* 1940. 76.

Brissenden, Paul F. *The I.W.W.: A Study in American Syndicalism* (Columbia University, Studies in History, Economics and Public Law, LXXXIII, No. 193). 1919. 401.

Brittain, Marion L. *The Story of Georgia Tech.* 1948. 104.

Brogan, Denis W. *The American Character.* 1944. 547.

—— *The Era of Franklin D. Roosevelt: A Chronicle of the New Deal and Global War* (*Chronicles of America,* LII). 1950. 567.

Brookings Institution. *The Recovery Problem in the United States.* 1936. 522.

Brooks, John G. *American Syndicalism: The I.W.W.* 1913. 401.

Brooks, Robert P. *The Agrarian Revolution in Georgia, 1865–1912* (University of Wisconsin, *Bulletin,* History series, Vol. III, no. 3). 1914. 17.

Brooks, Van Wyck. *New England: Indian Summer, 1865–1915.* 1940. 104.

Brown, Sterling A., A. P. Davis, and Ulysses Lee, eds. *The Negro Caravan: Writing by American Negroes,* 1941. 348.

Brown, William G. *The Lower South in American History.* 1902. New ed., 1930. 53.

Browne, Waldo R. *Altgeld of Illinois: A Record of His Life and Work.* 1924. 187.

Bruce, Andrew A. *The Administration of Criminal Justice in Illinois.* 1929. 548.

—— *Non-Partisan League.* 1921. 478.

Bruce, Philip A. *The Rise of the New South.* 1905. 168.

Bruntz, George G. *Allied Propaganda and the Collapse of the German Empire in 1918.* 1938. 452.

Bryan, William Jennings. *The First Battle: A Story of the Campaign of 1896.* 1897. 243.

—— *A Tale of Two Conventions.* 1912. 383.

Bryan, William J. and Mary B. *The Memoirs of William Jennings Bryan.* 1925. 243, 401

Bryce, James. *The American Commonwealth.* 2 vols. 1888. New ed., 1931–33. 187.

Bryn-Jones, David. *Frank B. Kellogg, A Biography.* 1937. 522.

Buck, Paul H. *The Road to Reunion, 1865–1900.* 1937. 34.

Buck, Solon J. *The Agrarian Crusade* (*Chronicles of America,* XLV). 1920. 146.

—— *The Granger Movement* (*Harvard Historical Studies,* XIX). 1913. 146.

Budenz, Louis Francis. *Men without Faces: The Communist Conspiracy in the U.S.A.* 1950. 751.

Buell, Raymond L. *The Washington Conference.* 1922. 479.

Bullard, Arthur. *Mobilising America.* 1917. 452.

Bullard, Robert L. *Personalities and Reminiscences of the War.* 1925. 452.

Bullitt, William O. "How We Won the War and Lost the Peace." *Life,* XXV, 83–97, August 30, 1948; 88–103, September 6, 1948. 702.

Bullock, Alan L. C. *Hitler: A Study in Tyranny.* 1952. 632, 658.

Burchard, John Ely, ed. *Mid-Century: The Social Implications of Scientific Progress.* 1950. 776.

Burgess, John W. *Reconstruction and the Constitution, 1866–1876.* 1902. 17.

Burgess, Warren R. *The Reserve Banks and the Money Market.* 1936. 591.

Burke, Robert E. *Olson's New Deal for California.* 1953. 611.

Burlingame, Merrill G. *The Montana Frontier.* 1942. 75.

Burlingame, Roger. *Peace Veterans: The Story of a Racket, and a Plea for Economy.* 1932. 505.

Burns, Eveline M. *Toward Social Security: An Explanation of the Social Security Act and a Survey of the Larger Issues.* 1936. 610.

Busbey, L. White. *Uncle Joe Cannon.* 1927. 383.

Busch, Noel F. *Adlai E. Stevenson of Illinois, A Portrait.* 1952. 751.

Bush, Vannevar. *Modern Arms and Free Men: A Discussion of the Role of Science in Preserving Democracy.* 1949. 776.

Bushnell, Sarah T. *The Truth about Henry Ford.* 1922. 547.

Buss, Claude A. *War and Diplomacy in Eastern Asia.* 1941. 632.

Butt, Archibald W. *The Letters of Archie Butt.* 1924. 331.

—— *Taft and Roosevelt: The Intimate Letters of Archie Butt.* 2 vols. 1930. 331.

Butts, R. Freeman. *The American Tradition in Religion and Education.* 1950. 264.

Byars, William V. *An American Commoner: The Life and Times of Richard Parks Bland.* 1900. 125.

Byrne, Patrick E. *Soldiers of the Plains.* 1926. 76.

Byrnes, James F. *Speaking Frankly.* 1947. 702.

Cahill, Holger. *New Horizons in American Art*. 1936. 548.

Cahill, Holger, and Alfred H. Barr, Jr., eds. *Art in America: A Complete Survey*. 1934. 548.

Caldwell, John C., and Lesley Frost. *The Korea Story*. 1952. 751.

Caldwell Robert G. *James A. Garfield, Party Chieftain*. 1931. 125.

Callahan, James M. *The Alaska Purchase and Americo-Conadian Relations*. 1908. 310.

—— *American Foreign Policy in Canadian Relations*. 1937. 611.

—— *American Foreign Policy in Mexican Relations*. 1932. 426.

Callcott, Wilfrid H. *The Caribbean Policy of the United States, 1890–1920*. 1942. 331.

Campbell, John C., and others. *The United States in World Affairs, 1948–1949*. 726.

Capek, Thomas. *The Czechs in America*. 1920. 204.

Capper, Arthur. *The Agricultural Bloc*. 1922. 505.

Carey, Jane P. *Deportation of Aliens from the United States to Europe*. 1931. 478.

Cargill, Oscar. *Intellectual America: Ideas on the March*. 1941. 102.

Carnegie, Andrew. *Autobiography of Andrew Carnegie*. 1920. 168.

Carpenter, Edmund J. *America in Hawaii: A History of United States Influence in the Hawaiian Islands*. 1899. 285.

Carr, Albert H. Z. *Truman, Stalin and Peace*. 1950. 726.

Carr, Robert K. *The House Committee on Un-American Activities, 1945–1950*. 1952. 751.

Carr, William G. *One World in the Making: The United Nations*. 1946. 2nd ed., 1947. 725.

Carroll, Henry K. *The Religious Forces of the United States*. 1896. Rev. ed., 1912. 264.

Carskadden, Thomas R. *Houses for Tomorrow*. 1944. Rev. ed., 1945. 591.

Carter, John F. *The Future Is Ours*. 1939. 610.

Carver, Thomas N. *The Present Economic Revolution in the United States*. 1925. 505.

Cary, Edward. *George William Curtis*. 1894. 103.

Cash, Wilbur J. *The Mind of the South*. 1941. 228.

Caskey, Willie M. *Secession and Restoration of Louisiana* (Louisiana State University, *Studies*, XXXVI). 1938. 18.

Casson, Herbert N. *The History of the Telephone*. 1910. 147.

Catton, Bruce. *U. S. Grant and the American Military Tradition*. 1954. 53.

Caughey, John W. *California*. 1940. 2nd ed., 1953. 611.

Cave, Floyd A., and associates. *The Origins and Consequences of World War II*. 1948. 726.

Chadsey, Charles E. *The Struggle between President Johnson and Congress over Reconstruction* (Columbia University, *Studies in History, Economics and Public Law*, VIII, no. 1). 1896. 34.

Chadwick, French E. *The Relations of the United States and Spain: Diplomacy*. 1909. 286.

—— *The Relations of the United States and Spain: The Spanish American War*. 2 vols. 1911. 286.

Chafee, Zechariah, Jr. *Free Speech in the United States*. 1941. 264.

Chaffin, Nora C. *Trinity College, 1839–1892: The Beginnings of Duke University*. 1950. 104.

Chamberlain, John R. *Farewell to Reform: The Rise, Life and Decay of the Progressive Mind in America*. 1932. 357.

Chambers, Clarke A. *California Farm Organizations: A Historical Study of the Grange, the Farm Bureau and the Associated Farmers, 1929–1941*. 1952. 611.

Chambers, Frank P., C. P. Harris, and C. C. Bayley. *This Age of Conflict: A Contemporary World History, 1914 to the Present*. 1943. Rev. ed., 1950. 632.

Chambers, Whittaker. *Witness*. 1952. 751.

Chandler, Alfred N. *Land Title Origins: A Tale of Force and Fraud*. 1945. 228.

Chapman, Charles C. *Development of American Business and Banking Thought, 1913–36*. 1936. 591.

Chase, Stuart. *Men and Machines*. 1929. 505.

—— *Prosperity: Fact or Myth*. 1929. 505.

—— *The Tragedy of Waste*. 1925. 505.

Cheney, Martha. *Modern Art in America*. 1939. 548.

Cherrington, Ernest H. *The Evolution of Prohibition in the United States of America*. 1920. 383.

Cheyney, Edward P. *History of the University of Pennsylvania, 1740–1940*. 1940. 103.

Child, Clifton J. *The German-Americans in Politics, 1914–1917*. 1939. 426.

Child, Richard W. *Battling the Criminal*. 1925. 548.

Churchill, Winston. *The Second World War*. 6 vols. 1948–53. 657.

Ciano, Galeazzo. *The Ciano Diaries*. 1946. 658.

Clapesattle, Helen. *The Doctors Mayo*. 1941. 548.

Clark, Champ. *My Quarter Century of American Politics*. 2 vols. 1920. 383.

Clark, [Charles] Badger. *Sun and Saddle Leather, Including Grass Grown Trails and New Poems*. 1917. New ed., 1936. 76.

Clark, Dan E. *The West in American History*. 1937. 75.

Clark, John B. *Populism in Alabama*. 1927. 228.

Clark, John M. *The Costs of the World War to the American People.* 1931. 452.

────── *Demobilization of Wartime Economic Controls.* 1944. 676.

Clark, John S. *The Life and Letters of John Fiske.* 2 vols. 1917. 104.

Clark, Mark W. *Calculated Risk.* 1951. 657.

Clark, Thomas B. *Hawaii, The 49th State.* 1947. 676.

Clark, Thomas D. *Pills, Petticoats, and Plows: The Southern Country Store.* 1944. 228.

Clark, Victor S., and others. *Porto Rico and Its Problems.* 1930. 310.

Clay, Lucius D. *Decision in Germany.* 1950. 702.

────── *Germany and the Fight for Freedom.* 1950. 702.

Clemen, Rudolf A. *The American Livestock and Meat Industry.* 1923. 168.

Clemens, Samuel L. (Mark Twain). *Roughing It.* 1872. 75.

Clements, Paul H. *The Boxer Rebellion.* 1915. 310.

Cleveland, Grover. *The Government in the Chicago Strike of 1894.* 1913. 187.

────── *Letters of Grover Cleveland, 1850–1908.* Edited by Allan Nevins. 1933. 126.

────── *Presidential Problems.* 1904. 243.

Cochran, Thomas C., and William Miller. *The Age of Enterprise: A Social History of Industrial America.* 1942. 102.

Cohn, David L. *Combustion on Wheels, An Informal History of the Automobile Age.* 1944. 547.

Colbert, Evelyn S. *The Left Wing in Japanese Politics.* 1952. 702.

Cole, Arthur C. *A Hundred Years of Mount Holyoke College: The Evolution of an Educational Ideal.* 1940. 104.

Cole, Arthur H. *The American Wool Manufacture.* 2 vols. 1926. 168.

Cole, Wayne S. *America First: The Battle against Intervention, 1940–1941.* 1953. 657.

Coleman, Charles H. *The Election of 1868: The Democratic Effort to Regain Control.* 1933. 53.

Coleman, James W. *The Molly Maguire Riots.* 1936. 187.

Coleman, McAlister. *Eugene V. Debs: A Man Unafraid.* 1930. 187.

Commager, Henry S. *The American Mind: An Interpretation of American Thought and Character since the 1880's.* 1950. 102.

──────, ed. *Documents of American History.* 1934. 5th ed., 1949. 34.

Commons, John R. *Races and Immigrants in America.* 1907. New ed., 1920. 203.

Commons, John R., and associates. *History of Labour in the United States.* 4 vols. *1918–35.* 187, 478.

Condit, Carl W. *The Rise of the Skyscraper.* 1952. 548.

Condliffe, John B. "Point Four and the World Economy." Foreign Policy Association, *Headline Series.* January-February, 1950. 726.

Conference on Unemployment. *Recent Economic Changes in the United States.* 2 vols. 1929. 478.

Conroy, Hilary. *The Japanese Frontier in Hawaii, 1868–1898.* (University of California, *Publications in History,* XLVI). 1953. 310.

Cook, James H. *Fifty Years on the Old Frontier.* 1923. 76.

Cooke, Alistair. *A Generation on Trial: U.S.A. v. Alger Hiss.* 1950. 751.

Coolidge, Calvin. *The Autobiography of Calvin Coolidge.* 1929. 505.

Coolidge, Louis A. *Ulysses S. Grant (American Statesmen,* XXXII). 1917. 53.

Coolidge, Mary R. *Chinese Immigration.* 1909. 187, 204

Coon, Horace. *Columbia, Colossus on the Hudson (American College and University Series).* 1947. 103.

Copeland, Melvin T. *The Cotton Manufacturing Industry of the United States (Harvard Economic Studies,* VIII). 1912. 168.

Copland, Aaron. *Our New Music: Leading Composers in Europe and America.* 1941. 548.

Corbett, Percy E. *The Settlement of Canadian-American Disputes.* 1937. 331.

Corey, Herbert. *The Truth about Hoover.* 1932. 567.

Corey, Lewis. *The House of Morgan.* 1930. 357.

Cotner, Robert C., John S. Ezell, and Gilbert C Fite, eds. *Readings in American History; 1865 to the Present.* 1952. 18.

Cortissoz, Royal. *Life of Whitelaw Reid.* 2 vols. 1921. 310.

Corwin, Edward S. *The Twilight of the Supreme Court.* 1934. 611.

────── *Court over Constitution.* 1938. 611.

Coulter, E[llis] Merton. *Civil War and Readjustment in Kentucky.* 1926. 34.

────── *The South during Reconstruction, 1865–1877 (A History of the South,* VIII). 1947. 34

Craven, Wesley F., and James L. Cate, eds. *The Army Air Forces in World War II.* 5 vols. 1948–53. 658.

Crawford, Arthur W. *Monetary Management under the New Deal.* 1940. 591.

Crawford, Jay B. *The Crédit Mobilier of America.* 1880. 53.

Creel, George. *How We Advertised America.* 1920. 452.

────── *Rebel at Large: Recollections of Fifty Crowded Years.* 1947. 452.

———— *The War, the World, and Wilson.* 1920. 452.

Croly, Herbert. *Marcus Alonzo Hanna.* 1912. 243.

———— *The Promise of American Life.* 1909. 382.

Crook, George. *General George Crook: His Autobiography.* Edited by Martin F. Schmitt. 1946. 76.

Cross, Ira B. *A History of the Labor Movement in California.* 1935. 187.

Crowell, Benedict, and R. F. Wilson, eds. *How America Went to War: An Account from Official Sources of the Nation's War Activities, 1917–1920.* 6 vols. 1921. 452.

Crowther, James G. *Famous American Men of Science.* 1937. 104.

Cubberly, Ellwood P. *Public Education in the United States.* 1919. Rev. ed., 1934. 103.

Cudahy, John. *Archangel: The American War with Russia.* 1924. 452.

Cullom, Shelby M. *Report of the Committee on Interstate Commerce* (49 Cong., 1 sess., *S. Rep.* No. 46 — serial 2356). 1886. 146.

Current, Richard N. *Old Thad Stevens: A Story of Ambition.* 1942. 34.

———— *Pine Logs and Politics: A Life of Philetus Sawyer, 1816–1900.* 1950. 382.

———— *Secretary Stimson, A Study in Statecraft.* 1954. 657.

Curti, Merle E. *Bryan and World Peace* (Smith College, *Studies in History*, XVI). 1931. 310.

———— *The Growth of American Thought.* 1943. 2nd ed., 1951. 102.

Curti, Merle E., and Vernon Carstensen. *The University of Wisconsin: A History, 1848–1925.* 2 vols. 1949. 103.

Curtin, Jeremiah. *The Memoirs of Jeremiah Curtin.* Edited by Joseph Schafer. 1940. 331.

Custer, George A. *My Life on the Plains.* 1874. 76.

Dabney, Virginius. *Below the Potomac: A Book about the New South.* 1942. 228.

Daggett, Stuart. *Chapters on the History of the Southern Pacific.* 1922. 147.

Dakin, Edwin F. *Mrs. Eddy: The Biography of a Virginal Mind.* 1929. 104.

Dale, Edward E. *Cherokee Cavaliers: Forty Years of Cherokee History (Civilization of the American Indian Series).* 1939. 76.

———— *The Range Cattle Industry.* 1930. 76.

Dana, Edward S., and others. *A Century of Science in America.* 1918. 104.

Daniels, Jonathan. *The Man of Independence.* 1950. 726.

———— *A Southerner Discovers the South.* 1938. 228.

Daniels, Josephus. *Life of Woodrow Wilson, 1856–1924.* 1924. 401.

———— *Our Navy at War.* 1922. 401.

———— *The Wilson Era: Years of Peace, 1910–1917.* 1944. 401.

———— *The Wilson Era: Years of War and After, 1917–1923.* 1946. 453.

Daugherty, Carroll R. *Labor Problems in American Industry.* 1933. Rev. ed., 1948. 187.

———— *Labor under the NRA.* 1934. 591.

David, Henry. *The History of the Haymarket Affair: A Study in the American Social-Revolutionary and Labor Movements.* 1936. 187.

Davidson, Marshall B. *Life in America.* 2 vols. 1951. 263.

Davie, Maurice R. *World Immigration, with Special Reference to the United States.* 1936. 203.

Davis, Forrest. *The Atlantic System: The Story of Anglo-American Control of the Seas.* 1941. 427.

Davis, Forrest, and E. K. Lindley. *How War Came.* 1942. 657.

Davis, Jerome. *The Russian Immigrant.* 1922. 204.

Davis, John P. *The Union Pacific Railway.* 1894. 147.

Davis, Joseph S. *On Agricultural Policy, 1926–1938.* 1939. 591.

———— *The Population Upsurge in the United States.* 1949. 776.

Davis, Oscar K. *Released for Publication: Some Inside Political History of Theodore Roosevelt and His Times.* 1925. 383.

Davis, Philip, ed. *Immigration and Americanization: Selected Readings.* 1920. 204.

Davis, Susan L. *Authentic History, Ku Klux Klan, 1865–1877.* 1924. 53.

Davis, Warren J. *The World's Wings.* 1927. 547.

Davis, William W. *The Civil War and Reconstruction in Florida* (Columbia University, *Studies in History, Economics and Public Law*, LIII). 1913. 34.

Dawes, Charles G. *A Journal of the McKinley Years.* Edited by Bascom E. Timmons. 1950. 243.

Dean, Vera Micheles. *Europe and the United States.* 1950. 726.

———— *The Four Cornerstones of Peace.* 1946. 725.

———— *The United States and Russia.* 1947. Rev. ed., 1948. 726.

Dearing, Charles L., and others. *The ABC of the NRA.* 1934. 591.

Debo, Angie. *Prairie City: The Story of an American Community.* 1944. 228

———— *Tulsa: From Creek Town to Oil Capital.* 1943. 228.

De Conde, Alexander. *Herbert Hoover's Latin American Policy*. 1951. 522.

Dennett, Tyler. *Americans in Eastern Asia*. 1922. New ed., 1941. 310.

—— *John Hay: From Poetry to Politics*. 1933. 310.

—— *Roosevelt and the Russo-Japanese War*. 1925. 331.

Dennis, Alfred L. P. *Adventures in American Diplomacy, 1896–1906*. 1928. 286, 331.

—— *The Anglo-Japanese Alliance*. 1923. 331.

Desmond, Humphrey J. *The A.P.A. Movement*. 1912. 204.

Destler, Chester McA. *American Radicalism, 1865–1901: Essays and Documents*. 1946. 229.

De Toledano, Ralph, and Victor Lasky. *Seeds of Treason: The True Story of the Hiss-Chambers Tragedy*. 1950. 751.

Deutscher, Isaac. *Stalin: A Political Biography*. 1949. 632.

De Voto, Bernard. *Mark Twain's America*. 1932. 104.

Dewey, David R. *Financial History of the United States (American Citizen Series)*. 1903. New ed., 1936. 102.

Dewey, George. *Autobiography of George Dewey*. 1916. 286.

Dewey, John. *Democracy and Education: An Introduction to the Philosophy of Education*. 1916. 548.

—— *The School and Society*. 1899. 548.

De Witt, Benjamin P. *The Progressive Movement*. 1915. 383.

Dewitt, David M. *The Impeachment and Trial of Andrew Johnson*. 1903. 34.

Dexter, Edwin G. *A History of Education in the United States*. 1904. 103.

Diamond, William. *The Economic Thought of Woodrow Wilson*. 1943. 401.

Dick, Everett. *The Sod House Frontier, 1854–1890*. 1937. 76.

—— *Vanguards of the Frontier*, 1941. 75.

Diffie, Bailey W., and J. W. Diffie. *Porto Rico: A Broken Pledge*. 1931. 310.

Dillon, Mary E. *Wendell Willkie, 1892–1944*. 1952. 657.

Dodd, William E. *Ambassador Dodd's Diary, 1933–1938*. Edited by William E. Dodd, Jr., and Martha Dodd. 1941. 632.

—— *Woodrow Wilson and His Work*. 1920. 401.

Dodge, Grenville M. *How We Built the Union Pacific Railway, and Other Railway Papers and Addresses*. 1910. 146.

Dolivet, Louis. *The United Nations: A Handbook on the New World Organization*. 1946. 725.

Donaldson, Thomas. *The Public Domain*. 1884. 76.

Donham, Wallace B. *Business Adrift*. 1931. 522.

Dorfman, Joseph. *The Economic Mind in American Civilization*. 3 vols. 1946–49. 102.

—— *Thorstein Veblen and His America*. 1934. 357.

Douglas, Paul H. *Social Security in the United States*. 1936. Rev. ed., 1939. 610.

Drucker, Peter F. *The New Society: The Anatomy of the Industrial Order*. 1950. 775.

Dublin, Louis I. *Health and Wealth*. 1928. 548.

—— *Health Progress, 1936 to 1945*. 1948. 776.

Dublin, Louis I., and others. *Length of Life: A Study of the Life Table*. 1949. 776.

Du Bois, W[illiam] E. B. *Black Reconstruction*. 1935. 17.

Duffy, Herbert S. *William Howard Taft*. 1930. 383.

Dulebohn, George R. *Principles of Foreign Policy under the Cleveland Administration*. 1941. 286.

Dulles, Foster R. *America in the Pacific: A Century of Expansion*. 1932. 2nd ed., 1938. 285.

—— *America Learns to Play: A History of Popular Recreation, 1607–1940*. 1940. 264.

—— *The American Red Cross: A History*. 1950. 452, 675.

—— *Forty Years of American-Japanese Relations*. 1937. 479.

—— *Labor in America: A History*. 1949. 187.

—— *Twentieth Century America*. 1945. 357.

Dumba, Constantin. *Memoirs of a Diplomat*. 1932. 427.

Dumke, Glenn S. *The Boom of the Eighties in Southern California*. 1944. 228.

Dummeier, Edwin F., and R. B. Heflebower. *Economics with Applications to Agriculture*. 1934. 505.

Dumond, Dwight L. *America in Our Time: 1896–1946*. 1947. 357.

Dunn, Arthur W. *From Harrison to Harding*. 2 vols. 1922. 244.

Dunning, William A. *The British Empire and the United States*. 1914. 286.

—— *Essays on the Civil War and Reconstruction*. 1904. 17.

—— *Reconstruction, Political and Economic, 1865–1877 (American Nation, XXII)*. 1907. 17.

Du Val, Miles P., Jr. *And the Mountains Will Move: The Story of the Building of the Panama Canal*. 1947. 331.

Dyer, Brainerd. *The Public Career of William M. Evarts*. 1933. 125.

Dyer, Frank L., and T. C. Martin. *Edison, His Life and Inventions*. 2 vols. 1910. New ed., 1929. 169.

Earhart, Mary. *Frances Willard: From Prayers to Politics.* 1944. 103.

Eastman, Joseph B. *Report of Federal Coordinator of Transportation* (74 Cong., 1 sess., H. Doc. no. 89 — serial 9920). 1934. 591.

—— *Report of Federal Coordinator of Transportation on Regulation of Transportation Agencies* (73 Cong., 1 sess., S. Doc. no. 152 — serial 9790). 1933. 591.

Easum, Chester V. *The Americanization of Carl Schurz.* 1929. 103.

—— *Half-Century of Conflict.* 1952. 632.

Eaton, Allen H. *The Oregon System.* 1912. 382.

Ebenstein, William. *The Law of Public Housing.* 1940. 591.

Eccles, Marriner S. *Beckoning Frontiers: Public and Personal Recollections.* 1951. 591.

Eckenrode, Hamilton J. *Rutherford B. Hayes, Statesman of Reunion.* 1930. 125.

—— *The Political History of Virginia during Reconstruction* (Johns Hopkins University, Studies in Historical and Political Science, XXII, nos. 6, 7, 8). 1904. 18.

Economist, The. *The New Deal: An Analysis and Appraisal.* 1937. 610.

Eddy, [George] Sherwood. *A Century with Youth: A History of the YMCA from 1844 to 1944.* 1944. 104.

Edmonds, Helen G. *The Negro and Fusion Politics in North Carolina, 1894–1901.* 1951. 229.

Edmonds, Walter D. *They Fought with What They Had: The Story of the Army Air Forces in the Southwest Pacific, 1941–1942.* 1951. 658.

Eggleston, Edward. *The Hoosier Schoolmaster.* 1871. 103.

Eisenhower, Dwight D. *Crusade in Europe.* 1948. 657.

Eliot, Charles W. *A Late Harvest.* 1924. 103.

Eliot, Clara. *The Farmers' Campaign for Credit.* 1927. 505.

Ellis, Elmer. *Henry Moore Teller, Defender of the West.* 1941. 243.

—— *Mr. Dooley's America: A Life of Finley Peter Dunne.* 1941. 310.

Ellis, Howard S. *The Economics of Freedom: The Progress and Future of Aid to Europe.* 1950. 726.

Ellis, John T. *The Formative Years of the Catholic University of America.* 1946. 103.

Ellis, Lewis E. *Reciprocity, 1911: A Study in Canadian-American Relations.* 1939. 383.

Epstein, Abraham. *Insecurity: A Challenge to America.* 1933. Rev. ed., 1938. 610.

Ernst, Morris L. *The Ultimate Power.* 1937. 611.

Evans, Henry C., Jr. *Chile and Its Relations with the United States.* 1927. 286.

Evans, Luther H. *The Virgin Islands: From Naval Base to New Deal.* 1945. 310.

Ewen, David. *American Composers Today.* 1949. 548.

Ewing, Cortez A. M. *Presidential Elections from Abraham Lincoln to Franklin D. Roosevelt.* 1940. 657.

Fairbank, John King. *The United States and China.* 1948. 632.

Fairchild, Henry P. *Greek Immigration to the United States.* 1911. 204.

Farley, James A. *Jim Farley's Story: The Roosevelt Years.* 1948. 568, 657.

Farrar, Victor J. *The Annexation of Russian America to the United States.* 1937. 310.

Faulkner, Harold U. *American Economic History.* 1931. 6th ed., 1949. 478.

—— *The Decline of Laissez Faire, 1897–1917* (Economic History of the United States, VII). 1951. 383.

—— *From Versailles to the New Deal: A Chronicle of the Harding-Coolidge Era* (Chronicles of America, LI). 1950. 505.

—— *The Quest for Social Justice, 1898–1914* (History of American Life, XI). 1931. 357.

Faust, Albert B. *The German Element in the United States.* 2 vols. 1909. New ed. (1 vol.), 1927. 203.

Fay, Sidney B. *The Origins of the World War.* 2 vols. 1928. Rev. ed., 1938. 426.

Federal Council of the Churches of Christ in America, Department of Research and Education. *Broadcasting and the Public.* 1938. 547.

—— *The Prohibition Situation.* 1925. 548.

Feis, Herbert. *The China Tangle: The American Effort in China from Pearl Harbor to the Marshall Mission.* 1953. 702.

—— *The Road to Pearl Harbor: The Coming of the War between the United States and Japan.* 1950. 657.

—— *The Spanish Story: Franco and the Nations at War.* 1948. 632.

Feldman, Herman. *Racial Factors in American Industry.* 1931. 204.

Ferleger, Herbert R. *David A. Wells and the American Revenue System, 1865–1870.* 1942. 53.

Ferrara, Orestes. *The Last Spanish War: Revelations in Diplomacy.* 1937. 286.

Fetter, Frank A. *The Masquerade of Monopoly.* 1931. 401.

Ficklen, John R. *History of Reconstruction in Louisiana.* (Johns Hopkins University, Studies in Historical and Political Science, XXVII, no. 1). 1910. 18.

Field, James A., Jr. *The Japanese at Leyte Gulf: The Shō Operation.* 1947. 658.

Fine, Nathan L. *Labor and Farmer Parties in the United States, 1828–1928.* 1928. 229, 382.

Finer, Herman. *Mussolini's Italy.* 1935. 632.

——— *The United Nations Economic and Social Council.* 1946. 725.

Finkelstein, Sidney W. *Jazz: A People's Music.* 1948. 548.

Fish, Carl R. *The Civil Service and the Patronage.* 1905. 126.

——— *The Path of Empire (Chronicles of America,* XLVI). 1919. 286.

Fite, Gilbert C. *George N. Peek and the Fight for Farm Parity.* 1954. 522.

Fitzgibbon, Russell H. *Cuba and the United States, 1900–1935.* 1935. 310.

Fitzpatrick, Edward A. *McCarthy of Wisconsin.* 1944. 382.

Flack, Horace E. *The Adoption of the Fourteenth Amendment* (Johns Hopkins University, *Studies in Historical and Political Science,* Extra vol. XXVI). 1908. 34.

Flanagan, John T., ed. *America Is West: An Anthology of Middlewestern Life and Literature.* 1945. 75.

Fleming, Denna F. *The United States and the League of Nations, 1918–1920.* 1932. 453.

——— *The United States and the World Court.* 1945. 479.

——— *The United States and World Organization, 1920–1933.* 1938. 479.

Fleming, Walter L. *Civil War and Reconstruction in Alabama.* 1905. New ed., 1949. 34.

——— *The Sequel of Appomattox: A Chronicle of the Reunion of the States (Chronicles of America,* XXXII). 1919. 17.

———, ed. *Documentary History of Reconstruction.* 2 vols. 1906–07. 17.

Flick, Alexander C. *Samuel Jones Tilden.* 1939. 125.

Flint, Winston A. *The Progressive Movement in Vermont.* 1941. 382.

Florinsky, Michael T. *Toward an Understanding of the U.S.S.R.* 1939. Rev. ed., 1951. 632.

Flynn, Edward J. *You're the Boss.* 1947. 568.

Flynn, John T. *Country Squire in the White House.* 1940. 610.

——— *God's Gold: The Story of Rockefeller and His Times.* 1932. 168.

——— *The Roosevelt Myth.* 1948. 610.

Foerster, Robert F. *The Italian Emigration of Our Times (Harvard Economic Studies,* XX). 1919. 204.

Folwell, William W. *A History of Minnesota.* 4 vols. 1921–30. 76.

Ford, Henry J. *The Cleveland Era (Chronicles of America,* XLIV). 1919. 126.

Ford, Henry. *My Life and Work.* 1922. 547.

Forrestal, James. *The Forrestal Diaries.* Edited by Walter Millis and Edward Duffield. 1951. 675.

Fortune, Editors of, and Russell W. Davenport. *U.S.A.: The Permanent Revolution.* 1951. 775.

Fosdick, Raymond B. *American Police Systems.* 1920. 548.

——— *The Story of the Rockefeller Foundation.* 1952. 548.

Fossum, Paul R. *The Agrarian Movement in North Dakota* (Johns Hopkins University, *Studies in Historical and Political Science,* XLIII, no. 1). 1925. 229.

Fox, Dixon R., ed. *Sources of Culture in the Middle West: Backgrounds vs. Frontier.* 1934. 263.

Frank, John P. *Mr. Justice Black: The Man and His Opinions.* 1949. 611.

Frankfurter, Felix. *The Case of Sacco and Vanzetti.* 1927. New ed., 1954. 478.

Frankfurter, Felix, and Nathan Greene. *The Labor Injunction.* 1930. 505.

Franklin, Fabian. *The Life of Daniel Coit Gilman.* 1910. 103.

Franklin, Harold B. *Sound Motion Pictures.* 1929. 547.

Franklin, John H. *From Slavery to Freedom: A History of the American Negroes.* 1947. 34.

Frederick, James V. *Ben Holladay, The Stagecoach King: A Chapter in the Development of Transcontinental Transportation.* 1940. 76.

Frederick, Justus George. *The New Deal: A People's Capitalism.* 1944. 591.

Freidel, Frank B. *Franklin D. Roosevelt.* 2 vols. 1952–54. 567.

French, John C. *A History of the University Founded by Johns Hopkins.* 1946. 103.

Fried, [John] Hans Ernest. *The Guilt of the German Army.* 1942. 632.

Friedmann, Wolfgang. *The Allied Military Government of Germany.* 1947. 702.

Fries, Robert F. *Empire in Pine: The Story of Lumbering in Wisconsin, 1830–1900.* 1951. 168.

Fritz, Percy S. *Colorado, The Centennial State.* 1941. 75.

Frothingham, Thomas G. *The American Reinforcement in the World War.* 1927. 452.

——— *The Naval History of the World War.* 3 vols. 1924–1926. 452.

Fuess, Claude M. *Calvin Coolidge, The Man from Vermont.* 1940. 505.

——— *Joseph B. Eastman, Servant of the People.* 1952. 591.

Fuller, Robert H. *Jubilee Jim: The Life of Colonel James Fisk, Jr.* 1928. 103.

Gabriel, Ralph H. *The Course of American Democratic Thought: An Intellectual History since 1815.* 1940. 102.

Gamio, Manuel. *Mexican Immigration to the United States.* 1930. 505.

Gardiner, Dorothy. *West of the River.* 1941. 76.

Garis, Roy L. *Immigration Restriction.* 1927. 204, 505.

Garner, James W. *International Law and the World War.* 1920. 427.

—— *Reconstruction in Mississippi.* 1901. 34.

Garraty, John A. *Henry Cabot Lodge.* 1953. 453.

Garwood, Darrell. *Artist in Iowa: A Life of Grant Wood.* 1944. 548.

Gaston, Herbert E. *The Nonpartisan League.* 1920. 478.

Gates, Paul W. *The Wisconsin Pine Lands of Cornell University: A Study in Land Policy and Absentee Ownership.* 1943. 103.

Gates, William B., Jr. *Michigan Copper and Boston Dollars: An Economic History of the Michigan Copper Mining Industry.* 1951. 168.

Gayer, Arthur D. *Public Works in Prosperity and Depression.* 1935. 591.

——, ed. *The Lessons of Monetary Experience.* 1937. 591.

Gee, Wilson. *The Place of Agriculture in American Life.* 1930. 505.

Geer, Andrew. *The New Breed: The Story of the U.S. Marines in Korea.* 1952. 751.

Geiger, George R. *The Philosophy of Henry George.* 1933. 228.

Geiger, Louis G. *Joseph W. Folk of Missouri.* 1953. 382.

Geismar, Maxwell D. *Writers in Crisis.* 1942. 548.

Gelber, Lionel M. *The Rise of Anglo-American Friendship: A Study in World Politics, 1898–1906.* 1938. 286.

Gellhorn, Walter. *Security, Loyalty, and Science.* 1950. 776.

Gerard, James W. *My Four Years in Germany.* 1917. 427.

Gibson, John M. *Physician to the World: The Life of General William C. Gorgas.* 1950. 331.

Gilman, Daniel C. *The Launching of a University.* 1906. 264.

Ginger, Ray. *The Bending Cross: A Biography of Eugene Victor Debs.* 1949. 187.

Gitlow, Benjamin. *The Whole of Their Lives: Communism in America.* 1948. 751.

Glass, Carter. *An Adventure in Constructive Finance.* 1927. 401.

Glasscock, Carl B. *The Big Bonanza: The Story of the Comstock Lode.* 1931. 75.

Glasson, William H. *Federal Military Pensions in the United States.* 1918. 126.

Glück, Elsie. *John Mitchell, Miner.* 1929. 357.

Glueck, Sheldon. *The Nuremberg Trial and Aggressive War.* 1946. 702.

Godkin, Edwin L. *Life and Letters of Edwin Lawrence Godkin.* Edited by Rollo Ogden. 2 vols. 1907. 103.

Goebbels, Joseph. *The Goebbels Diaries, 1942–1943.* 1948. 658.

Goerlitz, Walter. *History of the German General Staff, 1657–1945.* 1953. 632.

Going, Allen J. *Bourbon Democracy in Alabama, 1874–1890.* 1951. 125.

Goldberg, Isaac. *Tin Pan Alley: A Chronicle of the American Popular Music Racket.* 1930. 548.

Goldenweiser, Emanuel A. *American Monetary Policy.* 1951. 591.

Goldman, Eric F. *Charles J. Bonaparte, Patrician Reformer: His Earlier Career* (Johns Hopkins University, *Studies in Historical and Political Science,* LXI, no. 2). 1943. 382.

—— *Rendezvous with Destiny: A History of Modern American Reform.* 1952. 103, 382.

——, ed. *Historiography and Urbanization: Essays in American History in Honor of W. Stull Holt.* 1941. 264.

Gompers, Samuel. *American Labor and the War.* 1919. 452.

—— *Seventy Years of Life and Labor.* 2 vols. 1925. 187.

Goodrich, Leland M., and E. Hambro. *Charter of the United Nations: Commentary and Documents.* 1949. 725.

Goodspeed, Thomas W. *The Story of the University of Chicago, 1890–1925.* 1925. 103.

—— *William Rainey Harper, First President of the University of Chicago.* 1928. 264.

Gorgas, Marie D., and B. J. Kendrick. *William Crawford Gorgas, His Life and Work.* 1924. 331.

Gosnell, Harold F. *Champion Campaigner, Franklin D. Roosevelt.* 1952. 676.

Grady, Henry W. *The New South.* 1890. 169.

Graham, Frank. *Al Smith, American: An Informal Biography.* 1945. 522.

Graham, Malbone W. *American Diplomacy in the International Community.* 1948. 676.

Gratton, C[linton] Hartley. *Why We Fought.* 1929. 427.

Graves, William S. *America's Siberian Adventure, 1918–1920.* 1931. 452.

Gray, James. *The University of Minnesota, 1851–1951.* 1951. 103.

Greeley, Horace. *Recollections of a Busy Life.* 1868. 53.

Green, A[dwin] Wigfall. *The Epic of Korea.* 1950. 751.

Greene, Laurence. *The Era of Wonderful Nonsense.* 1939. 547.

Greenfield, Kent Roberts, Robert R. Palmer, and Bell I. Wiley. *The Army Ground Forces: The Organization of Ground Combat Troops.* 1947. 675.

Greenslet, Ferris. *The Lowells and Their Seven Worlds.* 1946. 103.

Greer, Thomas H. *American Social Reform Movements: Their Pattern since 1865.* 1949. 103, 187.

Gregory, Charles O. *Labor and the Law.* 1946. Rev. ed., 1949. 676.

Gresham, Matilda. *Life of Walter Quintin Gresham.* 2 vols. 1919. 229.

Grew, Joseph C. *Report from Tokyo.* 1942. 632.

——— *Ten Years in Japan.* 1944. 632.

——— *Turbulent Era: A Diplomatic Record of Forty Years, 1904–1945.* 1952. 632.

Grindrod, Muriel. *The New Italy: Transition from War to Peace.* 1947. 726.

Grinnell, George B. *The Cheyenne Indians: Their History and Ways of Life.* 2 vols. 1923. 76.

——— *The Fighting Cheyennes.* 1915. 76.

Griswold, Alfred W. *The Far Eastern Policy of the United States.* 1938. 331, 632.

Grodzins, Morton. *Americans Betrayed: Politics and the Japanese Evacuation.* 1949. 676.

Groves, Ernest R. *The American Woman: The Feminine Side of a Masculine Civilization.* 1944. 776.

Grunder, Garel A., and William E. Livezey. *The Philippines and the United States.* 1951. 702.

Guerrant, Edward O. *Roosevelt's Good Neighbor Policy* (University of New Mexico, *Inter-Americana Studies,* V). 1950. 611.

Guggenheim, Harry F. *The United States and Cuba: A Study in International Relations.* 1934. 611.

Guichard, Louis. *The Naval Blockade, 1914–1918.* 1930. 452.

Gunther, John. *Eisenhower: The Man and the Symbol.* 1952. 751.

——— *Inside U.S.A.* 1947. Rev. ed., 1951. 547.

——— *The Riddle of MacArthur.* 1951. 751.

——— *Roosevelt in Retrospect: A Profile in History.* 1950. 568.

Haas, William H., ed. *The American Empire: A Study of the Outlying Territories of the United States.* 1940. 310.

Hacker, Louis M. *American Problems of Today.* 1938. 479.

——— *A Short History of the New Deal.* 1934. 567.

Hacker, Louis M., and Helene S. Zahler. *The United States in the 20th Century.* 1952. 357.

Hackett, Alice P. *Fifty Years of Best Sellers, 1895–1945.* 1945. 548.

Hafen, LeRoy R. *Colorado: The Story of a Western Commonwealth.* 1933. 75.

Hafen, LeRoy R., and Carl Coke Rister. *Western America.* 1941. 75.

Hagedorn, Hermann. *Leonard Wood: A Biography.* 2 vols. 1931. 310.

Hall, Clifton R. *Andrew Johnson, Military Governor of Tennessee.* 1916. 17.

Hall, Walter Phelps. *Iron out of Calvary: An Interpretative History of the Second World War.* 1946. 657.

Hallgren, Mauritz A. *Seeds of Revolt: A Study of American Life and the Temper of the American People during the Depression.* 1933. 548.

Hamilton, Joseph G. de R. *Reconstruction in North Carolina* (Columbia University, *Studies in History, Economics and Public Law,* LVIII). 1914. 34.

Hamilton, Peter J. *The Reconstruction Period.* 1906. 17.

Hammond, Matthew B. *The Cotton Industry: An Essay in American Economic History.* 1897. 17, 228.

Handlin, Oscar. *The American People in the Twentieth Century.* 1954. 776.

——— *Boston's Immigrants, 1790–1865: A Study in Acculturation.* 1941. 204.

——— *The Uprooted: The Epic Story of the Great Migrations that Made the American People.* 1951. 203.

Handlin, Oscar and Mary W. "A Century of Jewish Immigration to the United States," *American Jewish Yearbook,* 1948–49, pp. 1–85. 204.

Haney, Lewis H. *A Congressional History of Railways in the United States* (University of Wisconsin, *Bulletin,* Economics and Political Science Series, III, no. 2; VI, no. 1). 2 vols. 1910. 146.

Hansen, Marcus Lee. *The Atlantic Migration, 1607–1860: A History of the Continuing Settlement of the United States.* 1940. 203.

——— *The Immigrant in American History.* 1940. 203.

Hansen, Marcus Lee, and J. B. Brebner. *The Mingling of the Canadian and American Peoples.* 1940. 204.

Harbord, James G. *The American Army in France, 1917–1919.* 1936. 452.

Harley, John Eugene. *Documentary Textbook on the United Nations.* 1947. 2nd ed., 1950. 725.

Harnsberger, Caroline T. *A Man of Courage, Robert A. Taft.* 1952. 751.

Harris, Herbert. *Labor's Civil War.* 1940. 591.

Harris, Seymour E., ed. *Economic Reconstruction.* 1945. 676.

Harrison, Carter H. *Stormy Years: The Autobiography of Carter H. Harrison.* 1935. 383.

Harrison, Francis B. *The Corner-Stone of Philippine Independence: A Narrative of Seven Years.* 1922. 310.

Hart, Albert B. *Salmon Portland Chase* (*American Statesmen,* XXVIII). 1899. New ed., 1917. 53.

———, ed. *The American Nation: A History.* 28 vols. 1904–28. 17.

Hart, Albert B., and H. R. Ferleger, eds. *Theodore Roosevelt Cyclopaedia.* 1941. 331.

Hart, Albert G. *Defense without Inflation.* 1951. 751.

Hart, Albert G., and others. *Financing Defense: Federal Tax and Expenditure Policies.* 1951. 751.

Hart, James D. *The Popular Book: A History of America's Literary Taste.* 1950. 104.

Hartwick, Harry. *The Foreground of American Fiction.* 1934. 548.

Harvey, George B. McC. *Henry Clay Frick, The Man.* 1928. 187.

Harvey, Rowland H. *Samuel Gompers: Champion of the Toiling Masses.* 1935. 187.

Haskins, Charles H., and R. H. Lord. *Some Problems of the Peace Conference.* 1920. 453.

Hatch, Alden. *Franklin D. Roosevelt, An Informal Biography.* 1947. 567.

Haworth, Paul L. *The Hayes-Tilden Disputed Presidential Election of 1876.* 1906. 125.

Hayes, Carlton J. H. *Wartime Mission to Spain, 1942–1945.* 1945. 658.

Haynes, Frederick E. *James Baird Weaver.* 1919. 229.

—— *Social Politics in the United States.* 1924. 505.

—— *Third Party Movements since the Civil War, with Special Reference to Iowa.* 1916. 125. 229.

Haynes, George H. *Charles Sumner (American Crisis Biographies).* 1909. 34.

Haynes, Williams. *Men, Money and Molecules.* 1936. 548.

Heck, Frank H. *The Civil War Veteran in Minnesota Life and Politics.* 1941. 126.

Hedges, James B. *Henry Villard and the Railways of the Northwest.* 1930. 147.

Heindel, Richard H. *The American Impact on Great Britain, 1898–1914.* 1940. 286.

Hendel, Samuel. *Charles Evans Hughes and the Supreme Court.* 1951. 611.

Henderson, Gerard C. *The Federal Trade Commission: A Study in Administrative Law and Procedure.* 1924. 401.

Hendrick, Burton J. *The Age of Big Business (Chronicles of America, XXXIX).* 1920. 168.

—— *The Jews in America.* 1923. 204.

—— *The Life and Letters of Walter H. Page.* 3 vols. 1922–25. 427.

Hepburn, Alonzo B. *A History of Currency in the United States.* 1915. Rev. ed., 1924. 243.

Hersey, John R. *Hiroshima.* 1946. 726.

Hesseltine, William B. *Confederate Leaders in the New South.* 1950. 125.

—— *The Rise and Fall of Third Parties from Anti-Masonry to Wallace.* 1948. 726.

—— *The South in American History.* 1943. 168.

—— *Ulysses S. Grant, Politician.* 1935. 53.

Hewitt, Abram S. *Selected Writings of Abram S. Hewitt.* Edited by Allan Nevins. 1937. 168.

Hibbard, Benjamin H. *Effects of the Great War upon Agriculture in the United States and Great Britain* (Carnegie Endowment for International Peace, *Economic Studies*, no. 11). 1919. 505.

—— *A History of the Public Land Policies* (*Land Economics Series*) 1924. New ed., 1939. 76.

—— *Marketing Agricultural Products.* 1921. 478.

Hibben, Paxton. *The Peerless Leader, William Jennings Bryan.* 1929. 243.

Hicks, Granville. *The Great Tradition.* 1933. 548.

Hicks, John D. *The Constitutions of the Northwest States* (University of Nebraska, *University Studies*, XXIII, Nos. 1–2). 1923. 228.

—— *The Populist Revolt.* 1931. 228.

Higgins, Marguerite. *War in Korea: The Report of a Woman Combat Correspondent.* 1951. 751.

High, Stanley. *Roosevelt — and Then?* 1937. 610.

Hill, Howard C. *Roosevelt and the Caribbean.* 1927. 331.

Hinshaw, David. *Herbert Hoover: American Quaker.* 1950. 522.

Hinton, Harold B. *Cordell Hull: A Biography.* 1942. 611.

Hoar, George F. *Autobiography of Seventy Years.* 1906. 310.

Hoffman, Paul G. *Peace Can Be Won.* 1951. 726.

Hofstadter, Richard. *The American Political Tradition and the Men Who Made It.* 1948. 383.

—— *Social Darwinism in American Thought, 1860–1915.* 1944. 102.

Hofstadter, Richard D., and C. Dewitt Hardy. *The Development and Scope of Higher Education in the United States.* 1952. 676.

Holborn, Hajo. *American Military Government: Its Organization and Policies.* 1947. 702.

—— *The Political Collapse of Europe.* 1951. 632.

Holborn, Louise W., ed. *War and Peace Aims of the United Nations, 1939–1945.* 2 vols. 1943–48. 702.

Holland, Kenneth, and F. E. Hill. *Youth in the CCC.* 1942. 591.

Hollander, Jacob H. *War Borrowing: A Study of Treasury Certificates of Indebtedness of the United States.* 1919. 452.

Holt, Rackham. *George Washington Carver: An American Biography.* 1943. 104.

Holt, W[illiam] Stull. *The Bureau of Public Roads.* 1923. 401.

—— *Treaties Defeated by the Senate.* 1933. 310.

Holzworth, John M. *The Fighting Governor: The Story of William Langer and the State of North Dakota.* 1938. 611.

Hoover, Herbert. *Addresses upon the American Road, 1933–1938.* 1938. 522.

—— *American Individualism.* 1922. 522.

——— *The Challenge to Liberty*. 1934. 522.

——— *The Memoirs of Herbert Hoover*. 3 vols. 1951–52. 522.

——— *The New Day*. 1928. 522.

——— *The State Papers and other Public Writings of Herbert Hoover*. Edited by W. S. Myers. 2 vols. 1934. 567.

Hoover, J[ohn] Edgar. *Persons in Hiding*. 1938. 548.

Hopkins, C[harles] Howard. *History of the Y.M.C.A. in North America*. 1951. 104.

Hopkins, Harry L. *Spending to Save: The Complete Story of Relief*. 1936. 591.

Hopkins, James F. *The University of Kentucky: Origins and Early Years*. 1951. 103.

Horn, Stanley F. *Invisible Empire: The Story of the Ku Klux Klan, 1866–1871*. 1939. 53.

Hoskins, Halford L. *The Atlantic Pact*. 1949. 726.

Hough, Emerson. *The Passing of the Frontier: A Chronicle of the Old West (Chronicles of America, XXVI)*. 1918. 75.

——— *The Story of the Cowboy (The Story of the West Series)*. 1897. 76.

Hourwich, Isaac A. *Immigration and Labor: The Economic Aspects of European Immigration to the United States*. 1912. 204.

House, Edward M. *The Intimate Papers of Colonel House*. Edited by Charles Seymour. 4 vols. 1926–28. 426.

House, Edward M., and Charles Seymour, eds. *What Really Happened at Paris*. 1921. 453.

Houston, David F. *Eight Years with Wilson's Cabinet*. 2 vols. 1926. 401.

Hovey, Carl. *The Life Story of J. Pierpont Morgan*. 1911. 357.

Howard, John T. *Our Contemporary Composers: American Music in the Twentieth Century*. 1941. 3rd ed., 1946. 548.

Howard, Joseph K. *Montana: High, Wide, and Handsome*. 1943. 75.

Howe, Frederic C. *The City, The Hope of Democracy*. 1905. 383.

——— *The Confessions of a Reformer*. 1925. 357.

Howe, George F. *Chester A. Arthur*. 1934. 125.

Howe, Mark A. De W. *Portrait of an Independent: Moorfield Storey*. 1932. 310.

Howells, William Dean. *Years of My Youth*. 1916. 104.

Howland, Harold J. *Theodore Roosevelt and His Times (Chronicles of America, XLVII)*. 1921. 357.

Hudnut, Joseph. *Modern Sculpture*. 1929. 548.

Hudson, Manley O. *The Permanent Court of International Justice, and the Question of American Participation*. 1925. 479.

Hütter, Jean Paul. *La Question de la Monnaie d'Argent aux États-Unis des Origines à 1900*. 1938. 125.

Hughes, Glenn. *A History of the American Theatre, 1700–1950*. 1951. 547.

Huidekoper, Frederic L. *The Military Unpreparedness of the United States*. 1915. 426.

Hull, Cordell. *The Memoirs of Cordell Hull*. 2 vols. 1948. 611, 658.

Hull, William I. *The Two Hague Conferences and Their Contributions to International Law*. 1908. 331.

Hume, Robert A. *Runaway Star: An Appreciation of Henry Adams*. 1951. 264.

Humphrey, Seth K. *Following the Prairie Frontier*. 1931. 76.

Hunter, Robert. *Poverty*. 1904. New ed., 1912. 264.

Hurwitz, Howard L. *Theodore Roosevelt and Labor in New York State, 1880–1900*. 1943. 382.

Hutchinson, William T. *Cyrus Hall McCormick*, Vol. II *Harvest, 1858–1884*. 1935. 168.

———, ed. *The Marcus W. Jernegan Essays in American Historiography*. 1937. 264.

Hutton, [David] Graham. *Midwest at Noon*. 1946. 547.

Huxley, Julian S. *TVA: Adventure in Planning*. 1943. 610.

Ichihashi, Yamato. *The Washington Conference and After*. 1928. 479.

Ickes, Harold L. *The Autobiography of a Curmudgeon*. 1943. 568.

——— *Back to Work: The Story of PWA*. 1935. 591.

——— "My Twelve Years with F.D.R.," *Saturday Evening Post*, June 5–July 24, 1948. 568.

——— *The Secret Diary of Harold L. Ickes*. 2 vols. 1953–54. 568.

Ike, Nobutaka. *The Beginnings of Political Democracy in Japan*. 1950. 702.

Iles, George. *Leading American Inventors*. 1912. 169.

Ingersoll, Robert G. *Letters*. Edited by Eva Ingersoll Wakefield. 1951. 264.

Interchurch World Movement of North America. Report on the Steel Strike of 1919. 1920. 478.

Isakoff, Jack F. *The Public Works Administration*. 1938. 591.

Ise, John. *The United States Forest Policy*. 1920. 103.

——— *The United States Oil Policy*. 1926. 505.

Isely, Jeter A., and Philip A. Crowl. *The U.S. Marines and Amphibious War*. 1951. 658.

Jackson, Robert H. *The Case against the Nazi War Criminals*. 1946. 702.

——— *The Nürnberg Case*. 1947. 702.

——— *The Struggle for Judicial Supremacy*. 1941. 611.

Jacobs, Lewis. *The Rise of the American Film*. 1939. 547.

Jacobstein, Meyer. *The Tobacco Industry in the United States.* 1907. 17.

Jaffe, Bernard. *Men of Science in America: The Role of Science in the Growth of our Country.* 1944. 104.

James, Henry. *Charles W. Eliot: President of Harvard University, 1869–1909.* 2 vols. 1930. 264.

——— *Richard Olney and His Public Service.* 1923. 286.

Janeway, Eliot. *The Struggle for Survival: A Chronicle of Economic Mobilization in World War II (Chronicles of America, LIII).* 1951. 675.

Janson, Florence E. *The Background of Swedish Immigration, 1840–1930.* 1931. 203.

Jarvis, J[ose] Antonio. *The Virgin Islands and Their People.* 1944. 310.

Jenkins, John W. *James B. Duke, Master Builder.* 1927. 169.

Jenkins, Warren. The Foreign Policy of the Chicago *Tribune*, 1914–1917. Unpublished Ph. D. Thesis, University of Wisconsin. 1942. 427.

Jenks, Jeremiah W., and W. J. Lauck. *The Immigration Problem.* 1912. 6th ed., 1926. 203.

Jenks, Jeremiah W., and W. E. Clark. *The Trust Problem.* 1900. 5th ed., 1929. 169.

Jessup, Philip C. *Elihu Root.* 2 vols. 1938. 357.

Johnson, Allen, and Allan Nevins, eds. *The Chronicles of America Series.* 56 vols. 1918–1950. 17.

Johnson Allen, and Dumas Malone, eds. *Dictionary of American Biography.* 20 vols. 1928–36. 34.

Johnson, Charles S. *The Negro in American Civilization: A Study of Negro Life and Race Relations in the Light of Social Research.* 1930. 34.

Johnson, Charles S., and others. *The Collapse of Cotton Tenancy.* 1935. 591.

Johnson, Emory R. *American Railway Transportation.* 1903. Rev. ed., 1912. 146.

Johnson, Gerald W. *Incredible Tale: The Odyssey of the Average American in the Last Half Century.* 1950. 775.

——— *Roosevelt: Dictator or Democrat?* 1941. 568.

Johnson, Hugh S. *The Blue Eagle from Egg to Earth.* 1935. 591.

Johnson, Walter. *The Battle against Isolation.* 1944. 657.

——— *William Allen White's America.* 1947. 657.

Johnston, Alexander. *Ten — and Out: The Complete Story of the Prize Ring in America.* 1927. 264.

Jones, Chester L. *Caribbean Interests of the United States.* 1916. 310, 331.

——— *The Caribbean since 1900.* 1936. 331.

——— *The United States and the Caribbean.* 1929. 331.

Jones, Eliot. *The Trust Problem in the United States.* 1921. 169.

Jones, Howard Mumford. *Ideas in America.* 1944. 547.

Jones, Jesse H. *Fifty Billion Dollars: My Thirteen Years with the RFC, 1932–1945.* 1951. 675.

Jones, John P., and P. M. Hollister. *The German Secret Service in America, 1914–1918.* 1918. 427.

Jones, Joseph M. *Tariff Retaliation: Repercussions of the Hawley-Smoot Bill.* 1934. 522.

Joseph, Samuel. *Jewish Immigration to the United States from 1881 to 1910 (Columbia University, Studies in History, Economics and Public Law, LIX, no. 4).* 1914. 204.

Josephson, Matthew. *The Politicos, 1865–1896.* 1938. 125.

——— *The President Makers: The Culture of Politics and Leadership in an Age of Enlightenment, 1896–1919.* 1940. 244.

——— *The Robber Barons: The Great American Capitalists, 1861–1901.* 1934. 168.

Joslin, Theodore G. *Hoover, Off the Record.* 1934. 567.

Joughin, George Louis, and Edmund M. Morgan. *The Legacy of Sacco and Vanzetti.* 1948. 478.

Kaempffert, Waldemar B., ed. *A Popular History of American Invention.* 2 vols. 1924. 104.

Kane, Harnett. *Louisiana Hayride: The American Rehearsal for Dictatorship, 1928–1940.* 1941. 611.

Kaplan, Abraham D. H. *The Liquidation of War Production.* 1944. 676.

Karig, Walter, and others. *Battle Report.* 6 vols. 1944–52. 658, 751.

Kavanaugh, Marcus A. *The Criminal and His Allies.* 1928. 548.

Kefauver, Estes. *Crime in America.* 1951. 751.

Keim, Jeanette. *Forty Years of German-American Political Relations.* 1919. 286.

Keith, John A. H., and W. C. Bagley. *The Nation and the Schools.* 1920. 401.

Kelly, Fred C. *The Wright Brothers.* 1943. 547.

Kelly, Robert L. *Tendencies in College Administration.* 1925. 548.

Kendrick, Benjamin B. *The Journal of the Joint Committee of Fifteen on Reconstruction, 39th Congress, 1865–1867 (Columbia University, Studies in History, Economics and Public Law, LXII).* 1914. 34.

Kennan, George. *E. H. Harriman: A Biography.* 1922. 357.

Kennan, George F. *American Diplomacy, 1900–1950.* 1951. 632.

Kennedy, John F. *Why England Slept.* 1940. 632.

Kennedy, Joseph P. *I'm for Roosevelt,* 1936. 610.

Kent, Frank R. *Political Behavior.* 1928. 547.

Key, Valdimer O., Jr. *Southern Politics in State and Nation.* 1949. 611.

Keynes, John Maynard. *The Economic Consequences of the Peace.* 1919. 453.

King, Ernest, and W. M. Whitehill. *Fleet Admiral King: A Naval Record.* 1952. 657.

Kinsley, Philip. *The Chicago Tribune: Its First Hundred Years.* 3 vols. 1943–46. 264.

Kipnis, Ira. *The American Socialist Movement, 1897–1912.* 1952. 383.

Kirk, Grayson L. *Philippine Independence: Motives, Problems, and Prospects.* 1936. 310.

Kirkland, Edward C. *A History of American Economic Life.* 1932. 3rd ed., 1951. 478.

Kirkpatrick, John. *The American College and Its Rulers.* 1926. 548.

Kirwan, Albert D. *Revolt of the Rednecks: Mississippi Politics, 1876–1925.* 1951. 125.

Kleinsorge, Paul L. *The Boulder Canyon Project: Historical and Economic Aspects.* 1941. 568.

Knauth, Oswald W. *The Policy of the United States towards Industrial Monopoly.* 1914. 401.

Knight, Edgar W. *Education in the United States.* 1929. 3d ed., 1951. 103.

—— *The Influence of Reconstruction on Education in the South.* 1913. 34.

—— *Public Education in the South.* 1922. 103.

Knoles, George H. *The Presidential Campaign and Election of 1892.* 1942. 229.

Kohlsaat, Herman H. *From McKinley to Harding: Personal Recollections of Our Presidents.* 1923. 244.

Kohn, Hans. *The Twentieth Century: A Midway Account of the Western World.* 1949. 776.

Kolbe, Parke R. *The Colleges in War Time and After.* 1919. 452.

Konefsky, Samuel J. *Chief Justice Stone and the Supreme Court.* 1945. 611.

Kraus, Michael. *The Writing of American History.* 1953. 263.

Kreider, Carl J. *The Anglo-American Trade Agreement: A Study of British and American Commercial Policies, 1934–1939.* 1943. 611.

Krout, John A. *The Origins of Prohibition.* 1925. 383.

Krutch, Joseph W. *The American Drama since 1918.* 1939. 547.

Kuhlmann, Charles B. *The Development of the Flour-Milling Industry in the United States.* 1929. 168.

Kuykendall, Ralph S., and A. Grove Day. *Hawaii: A History, from Polynesian Kingdom to American Commonwealth.* 1948. 285.

La Farge, Oliver, ed. *The Changing Indian.* 1942. 568.

LaFollette, Belle Case and Fola. *Robert M. La-Follette, 1855–1925.* 2 vols. 1953. 382.

LaFollette, Robert M. *Autobiography.* 1913. 3d ed., 1919. 382, 383.

Lane, Franklin K. *The Letters of Franklin K. Lane, Personal and Political.* Edited by A. W. Lane and L. H. Wall. 1922. 401.

Lane, Frederic C., and others. *Ships for Victory: A History of Shipbuilding under the U.S. Maritime Commission in World War II.* 1951. 675.

Lanfear, Vincent W. *Business Fluctuations and the American Labor Movement, 1915–1922.* 1924. 478.

Langer, William L. *Our Vichy Gamble.* 1947. 658.

Langer, William L., and S. E. Gleason. *The Challenge to Isolation, 1937–1940.* 1952. 632, 657.

—— *The Undeclared War, 1940–1941.* 1953. 632, 657.

Langford, Nathaniel P. *Vigilante Days and Ways.* 1912. 75.

Langsam, Walter C. *The World Since 1914.* 1933. 6th ed., 1948. 632.

Lansing, Robert. *The Big Four and Others of the Peace Conference.* 1921. 453.

—— *War Memoirs of Robert Lansing, Secretary of State.* 1935. 427.

Larkin, Oliver W. *Art and Life in America.* 1949. 263, 548.

Larson, Henrietta M. *Jay Cooke, Private Banker (Harvard Studies in Business History, II).* 1936. 102.

Laserson, Max M. *The American Impact on Russia, Diplomatic and Ideological, 1784–1917.* 1950. 453.

Lasswell, Harold D. *Propaganda Technique in the World War.* 1927. 427.

Latané, John H. *America as a World Power, 1897–1907 (American Nation, XXV).* 1907. 286.

—— *From Isolation to Leadership.* 1918. Rev. ed., 1925. 331.

Latané, John H., and D. W. Wainhouse. *A History of American Foreign Policy.* 1934. 2nd ed., 1940. 285.

Latourette, Kenneth Scott. *The American Record in the Far East, 1945–1951.* 1952. 702.

Lattimore, Owen. *Manchuria, Cradle of Conflict.* 1932. Rev. ed., 1935. 632.

—— *Ordeal by Slander.* 1950. 751.

Lauck, William Jett. *The Causes of the Panic of 1893.* 1907. 243.

Laughlin, J[ames] Laurence. *The History of Bimetallism in the United States.* 1892. 125.

Lawrence, David. *The True Story of Woodrow Wilson.* 1924. 401.

Leahy, William D. *I Was There: The Personal Story of the Chief of Staff to Presidents Roosevelt and Truman.* 1950. 675.

Lee, Clark G., and Richard Henschel. *Douglas MacArthur.* 1952. 751.

Leopold, Richard W. *Elihu Root and the Conservative Tradition.* 1954. 383.

Lerner, Daniel, ed. *Propaganda in War and Crises: Materials for American Policy.* 1951. 776.

Lester, John C., and Daniel L. Wilson. *Ku Klux Klan, Its Origin, Growth and Disbandment.* 1884. New ed., 1905. 53.

Letiche, John M. *Reciprocal Trade Agreements in the World Economy.* 1948. 611.

Leupp, Francis E. *The Indian and His Problem.* 1910. 76.

Levinger, Lee J. *The Causes of Anti-Semitism in the United States.* 1925. 204.

Levinson, Edward. *Labor on the March.* 1938. 591.

Lewis, Lloyd. *Captain Sam Grant.* 1950. 53.

Lewis, McMillan. *Woodrow Wilson of Princeton.* 1952. 401.

Lewis, Oscar. *The Big Four: The Story of Huntington, Stanford, Hopkins and Crocker.* 1938. 147.

Lewis, William Draper. *The Life of Theodore Roosevelt.* 1919. 331.

Liddell-Hart, Basil H. *The German Generals Talk.* 1948. 632.

Liggett, Hunter. *Commanding an American Army: Recollections of the World War.* 1925. 452.

Liggett, Walter W. *The Rise of Herbert Hoover.* 1932. 567.

Lilienthal, David E. *TVA: Democracy on the March.* 1944. 610.

——— *This I Do Believe.* 1949. 776.

Lind, Andrew W. *Hawaii's Japanese: An Experiment in Democracy.* 1946. 676.

Lindberg, John S. *The Background of Swedish Emigration to the United States.* 1930. 203.

Lindbergh, Charles A. *The Spirit of St. Louis.* 1953. 547.

——— *"We."* 1927. 547.

Lindley, Betty and E. K. *A New Deal for Youth.* 1938. 591.

Lindley, Ernest K. *Franklin D. Roosevelt: A Career in Progressive Democracy.* 1931. Rev. ed., 1934. 567.

——— *Half Way with Roosevelt.* 1936. 610.

——— *The Roosevelt Revolution: First Phase.* 1933. 568.

Lindsay, Charles. *The Big Horn Basin* (University of Nebraska, *University Studies,* XXVIII–XXIX). 1932. 75.

Lindsey, Almont. *The Pullman Strike.* 1942. 187

Link, Arthur S. *Wilson, The Road to the White House.* 1947. 401.

——— *Woodrow Wilson and the Progressive Era, 1910–1917.* 1954. 401.

Lippmann, Walter. *The Cold War: A Study in U.S. Foreign Policy.* 1947. 726.

——— *The Method of Freedom.* 1934. 568.

——— *A Preface to Morals.* 1929. 547.

——— *The Supreme Court, Independent or Controlled.* 1937. 611.

——— *U.S. Foreign Policy: Shield of the Republic.* 1943. 702.

——— *U.S. War Aims.* 1944. 702.

Lloyd, Caro[line] A. *Henry Demarest Lloyd, 1847–1908.* 2 vols. 1912. 357.

Lloyd, Henry D. *Wealth against Commonwealth.* 1894. New ed., 1936. 357.

Lloyd George, David. *Memoirs of the Peace Conference.* 2 vols. 1939. 453.

——— *War Memoirs of David Lloyd George.* 6 vols. 1933–37. 452.

Locklin, David P. *Economics of Transportation.* 1935. 3rd ed., 1947. 478.

Lockmiller, David A. *Magoon in Cuba: A History of the Second Intervention, 1906–1909.* 1938. 310.

Lodge, Henry Cabot. *The Senate and the League of Nations.* 1925. 453.

Lomax, John A., ed. *Songs of the Cattle Trail and Cow Camp.* 1920. New ed., 1950. 76.

Lomax, John A., and Alan Lomax, eds. *Cowboy Songs and Other Frontier Ballads.* 1945. 76.

Lombardi, John. *Labor's Voice in the Cabinet.* 1942. 357.

Long, John C. *Bryan, The Great Commoner.* 1928. 243.

Long, John D. *The New American Navy.* 2 vols. 1903. 286.

Lonn, Ella. *Reconstruction in Louisiana after 1868.* 1918. 34.

Looker, Earle. *The American Way: Franklin Roosevelt in Action.* 1933. 610.

Lorant, Stefan. *FDR: A Pictorial Biography.* 1950. 676.

——— *The Presidency: A Pictorial History of Presidential Elections from Washington to Truman.* 1951. 53.

Lord, Russell. *The Wallaces of Iowa.* 1947. 568.

Lorwin, Lewis L. *The American Federation of Labor.* 1933. 187.

——— *Youth Work Programs: Problems and Policies.* 1941. 591.

Loud, Grover C. *Evangelized America.* 1928. 264.

Lowell, Amy. *Tendencies in Modern American Poetry.* 1917. 548.

Lowes, John L. *Convention and Revolt in Poetry.* 1919. 548.

Lubell, Samuel. *The Future of American Politics.* 1952. 751.

Ludwig, Emil. *Roosevelt: A Study in Fortune and Power.* 1941. 567.

Lutz, Harley L. *Public Finance.* 1924. 4th ed., 1947. 610.

Lynch, Denis T. *"Boss" Tweed: The Story of a Grim Generation.* 1927. 103.

Lynd, Robert S. and H. M. *Middletown: A Study in Contemporary American Culture.* 1929. 548.

—— *Middletown in Transition.* 1937. 548.

Lyon, Leverett S., and others. *The National Recovery Administration: An Analysis and Appraisal.* 1935. 591.

Lyons, Eugene. *Our Unknown Ex-President: A Portrait of Herbert Hoover.* 1948. 567.

McAdoo, Eleanor Wilson. *The Woodrow Wilsons.* 1937. 401.

McAdoo, William G. *Crowded Years: The Reminiscences of William G. McAdoo.* 1931. 401.

McCain, William D. *The United States and the Republic of Panama.* 1937. 331.

McCall, Samuel W. *Thaddeus Stevens (American Statesmen, XXXI).* 1899. New ed., 1917. 34.

—— *Thomas B. Reed (American Statesmen, XXXV).* 1914. 126.

McCann, Kevin. *Man from Abilene.* 1952. 751.

McCarthy, Charles. *The Wisconsin Idea.* 1912. 382.

McCarthy, Charles H. *Lincoln's Plan of Reconstruction.* 1901. 17.

McClure, Samuel S. *My Autobiography.* 1914. 357.

McConnell, Grant. *The Decline of Agrarian Democracy.* 1953. 505.

McCulloch, Hugh. *Men and Measures of a Half Century: Sketches and Comments.* 1888. 53.

McCune, George M. *Korea Today.* 1950. 702.

Macdonald, Dwight. *Henry Wallace, The Man and the Myth.* 1948. 568.

MacDonald, William. *The Menace of Recovery: What the New Deal Means.* 1934. 568.

McElroy, Robert McNutt. *Grover Cleveland: The Man and the Statesman.* 2 vols. 1923. New ed. (1 vol.), 1925. 243.

McGinty, Garnie W. *Louisiana Redeemed: The Overthrow of Carpetbag Rule, 1876–1880.* 1941. 125.

McGrath, John S., and J. J. Delmont. *Floyd Björnsterne Olson: Minnesota's Greatest Liberal Governor.* 1937. 611.

Mack, Effie M. *Nevada: A History of the State from Earliest Times through the Civil War.* 1936. 75.

MacKay, Kenneth C. *The Progressive Movement of 1924.* 1947. 505.

McKee, Irving. *"Ben Hur" Wallace. The Life of General Lew Wallace.* 1947. 104.

Mackenzie, Catherine D. *Alexander Graham Bell, The Man Who Contracted Space.* 1928. 147.

McMaster, John B. *The United States in the World War.* 2 vols. 1918–20. 452.

McMurry, Donald L. *Coxey's Army: A Study of the Industrial Army Movement of 1894.* 1929. 187.

MacVeagh, Rogers. *The Transportation Act, 1920: Its Sources, History and Text.* 1923. 478.

McVey, Frank L. *The Populist Movement* (American Economic Association, *Economic Studies,* I, no. 3). 1896. 228.

McWilliams, Carey. *A Mask for Privilege: Anti-Semitism in the United States.* 1948. 204.

—— *Prejudice; Japanese-Americans: Symbol of Racial Intolerance.* 1944. 676.

—— *Witch Hunt: The Revival of Heresy.* 1950. 751.

Madison, Charles A. *American Labor Leaders: Personalities and Forces in the Labor Movement.* 1950. 187.

Mahan, Alfred T. *From Sail to Steam: Recollections of Naval Life.* 1907. 286.

—— *Lessons of the War with Spain, and Other Articles.* 1899. 310.

Malin, James C. *The United States after the World War.* 1930. 478.

—— *Winter Wheat in the Gold Belt of Kansas: A Study in Adaptation to Subhumid Geographical Environment.* 1944. 228.

Marshall, George C. *Biennial Report of the Chief of Staff of the United States Army.* 1941–43–45. 657.

Marshall, Samuel L. A. *The River and the Gauntlet.* 1952. 751.

Martienssen, Anthony. *Hitler and His Admirals.* 1948. 658.

Martin, John B. *Adlai Stevenson.* 1952. 751.

Martin, Ralph G. *The Best Is None Too Good.* 1948. 676.

Martin, Roscoe C. *The People's Party in Texas* (University of Texas, *Bulletin,* no. 3308). 1933. 228.

Mason, Alpheus T. *Brandeis, A Free Man's Life.* 1946. 611.

—— *Organized Labor and the Law.* 1925. 505.

Masterson, Vincent V. *The Katy Railroad and the Last Frontier.* 1952. 75.

Mathews, Basil J. *Booker T. Washington, Educator and Interracial Interpreter.* 1948. 103.

Mavor, James. *The Russian Revolution.* 1928. 632.

May, Henry F. *Protestant Churches and Industrial America.* 1949. 104, 264.

Mayer, George H. *The Political Career of Floyd B. Olson.* 1951. 611.

Mayo, Katherine. *Soldiers, What Next!* 1934. 505.

—— *"That Damn Y": A Record of Overseas Service.* 1920. 452.

Mears, Eliot G. *Resident Orientals on the American Pacific Coast.* 1927. 204.

Mecklin, John M. *The Ku Klux Klan: A Study of the American Mind.* 1924. 478.

Merriam, Charles E. *American Political Ideas: Studies in the Development of American Political Thought, 1865–1917.* 1929. 382.

Merriam, Lewis. *Relief and Social Security*, 1946. 610.

Merrill, Horace S. *Bourbon Democracy of the Middle West, 1865–1896*. 1953. 229.

———— *William Freeman Vilas: Doctrinaire Democrat*. 1954. 229.

Merz, Charles. *The Dry Decade*. 1931. 548.

Metz, Harold W. *Labor Policy of the Federal Government*. 1945. 676.

Meyer, Balthasar H. *A History of the Northern Securities Case* (University of Wisconsin, *Bulletin*, Economics and Political Science Series, I, no. 3). 1906. 357.

Mezerik, Arrahm G. *The Revolt of the South and West*. 1946. 568.

Milbank, Jeremiah, Jr. *The First Century of Flight in America: An Introductory Survey*. 1943. 547.

Miles, Nelson A. *Serving the Republic: Memoirs of the Civil and Military Life of Nelson A. Miles*. 1911. 76.

Miller, David H. *The Drafting of the Covenant*. 2 vols. 1928. 453.

———— *The Peace Pact of Paris*. 1928. 522.

Miller, Francis T. *History of World War II*. 1945. 657.

Milligan, Maurice M. *Missouri Waltz: The Inside Story of the Pendergast Machine by the Man Who Smashed It*. 1948. 676.

Millington, Herbert. *American Diplomacy and the War of the Pacific* (Columbia University, Studies in History, Economics and Public Law 535). 1948. 285.

Millis, Harry A., and Emily Clark Brown. *From the Wagner Act to Taft-Hartley: A Study of National Labor Policy and Labor Relations* 1950. 676.

Millis, Walter. *The Martial Spirit: A Study of Our War with Spain*. 1931. 286.

———— *Road to War: America, 1914–17*. 1935. 427.

———— *This Is Pearl! The United States and Japan — 1941*. 1947. 657

Milton, George F. *The Age of Hate: Andrew Johnson and the Radicals*. 1930. 17.

Mims, Edwin. *History of Vanderbilt University*. 1946. 104.

Mitchell, Alice M. *Children and Movies*. 1929. 547.

Mitchell, Broadus. *Depression Decade: From New Era through New Deal, 1929–1941* (Economic History of the United States, IX). 1947. 561.

———— *The Rise of Cotton Mills in the South*. 1921. 169.

Mitchell, Broadus, and G. S. Mitchell. *The Industrial Revolution in the South*. 1930. 169.

Mitchell, George S. *Textile Unionism and the South* (The University of North Carolina, Social Study Series). 1931. 187.

Mitchell, Wesley C. *History of the Greenbacks*,

With Special Reference to the Economic Consequences of Their Issue, 1862–65*. 1903. 53.

Mixer, Knowlton. *Porto Rico: History and Conditions — Social, Economic and Political*. 1926. 310.

Mock, James R., and Cedric Larson. *Words that Won the War: The Story of the Committee on Public Information, 1917–1919*. 1939. 452.

Mock, Elizabeth, ed. *Built in U.S.A., 1932–1944*. 1944. 548.

Moley, Raymond L. *After Seven Years*. 1939. 568.

Montague, Gilbert H. *The Rise and Progress of the Standard Oil Company*. 1903. 168.

Moody, John. *The Masters of Capital* (*Chronicles of America*, XLI). 1921. 168.

———— *The Railroad Builders* (*Chronicles of America*, XXXVIII). 1919. 146.

———— *The Truth about the Trusts*. 1904. 169.

Moore, Arthur L. *The Farmer and the Rest of Us*. 1945. 591.

Moore, Charles. *Daniel H. Burnham: Architect, Planner of Cities*. 2 vols. 1921. 263.

Moore, John Bassett. *The Principles of American Diplomacy*. 1918. 285.

Morgan, Arthur E. *Edward Bellamy* (*Columbia Studies in American Culture*, No. 15). 1944. 383.

Morgenstern, George. *Pearl Harbor: The Story of the Secret War*. 1947. 657.

Morison, Elting E. *Admiral Sims and the Modern American Navy*. 1942. 452.

Morison, Samuel E. *History of United States Naval Operations in World War II*. 9 vols. 1947–1954. 658.

———— *Three Centuries of Harvard, 1636–1936*. 1936. 103.

Morrissey, Alice M. (Mrs. McDiarmid). *The American Defense of Neutral Rights, 1914–1917*. 1939. 427.

Moseley, Philip. "The Berlin Deadlock." *American Perspective*, II, 331–339. December, 1948. 702.

Mott, Frank L. *American Journalism: A History of Newspapers in the United States*. 1941. Rev. ed., 1950. 264.

Moulton, Harold G. *Financial Organization and the Economic System*. 1938. 591.

Moulton, Harold G., and associates. *The American Transportation Problem*. 1933. 478.

Moulton, Harold G., and Leo Pasvolsky. *War Debts and World Prosperity*. 1932. 522.

———— *World War Debt Settlement*. 1926. 522.

Mowat, Robert B. *The Diplomatic Relations of Great Britain and the United States*. 1925. 286.

Mowry, George E. *The California Progressives, 1900–1920* (*Chronicles of California Series*). 1951. 382.

———— *Theodore Roosevelt and the Progressive Movement*. 1946. 382.

Munro, Dana G. *The Five Republics of Central America.* 1918. 383.

Muzzey, David S. *James G. Blaine: A Political Idol of Other Days.* 1934. 126.

—— *The United States of America.* 2 vols. 1922–24. New ed., 1933. 382.

Myers, Gustavus. *The History of Tammany Hall.* 1901. Rev. ed., 1917. 103.

—— *History of the Great American Fortunes.* 3 vols. 1910. New ed., 1936. 102.

Myers, William S. *The Foreign Policies of Herbert Hoover, 1929–1933.* 1940. 522.

Myers, William S., and W. H. Newton. *The Hoover Administration: A Documented Narrative.* 1936. 522.

Myrdal, Gunnar. *An American Dilemma: The Negro Problem and Modern Democracy.* 2 vols. 1944. 478, 776.

Nadlee, Marcus, and J. I. Bogen. *The Banking Crisis: The End of an Epoch.* 1933. 568.

National Industrial Conference Board. *The American Merchant Marine Problem.* 1929. 478.

—— *The Inter-Ally Debts and the United States.* 1925. 522.

—— *The World War Veterans and the Federal Treasury.* 1932. 505.

Nearing, Scott, and Joseph Freeman. *Dollar Diplomacy: A Study in American Imperialism.* 1925. 383.

Nelson, Bernard H. *The Fourteenth Amendment and the Negro since 1920.* 1946. 478.

Nelson, Donald M. *Arsenal of Democracy: The Story of American War Production.* 1946. 675.

Nevins, Allan. *Abram S. Hewitt: With Some Account of Peter Cooper.* 1935. 168.

—— *The Emergence of Modern America, 1865–1878* (*A History of American Life,* VIII). 1927. 102.

—— *Grover Cleveland: A Study in Courage.* 1932. 126, 243.

—— *Hamilton Fish: The Inner History of the Grant Administration.* 1936. 53.

—— *Henry White: Thirty Years of American Diplomacy.* 1930. 331.

—— *John D. Rockefeller.* 2 vols. 1940. 168.

—— *The New Deal and World Affairs: A Chronicle of International Affairs, 1933–1945* (*Chronicles of America,* LVI). 1950. 632.

—— *Study in Power: John D. Rockefeller, Industrialist and Philanthropist.* 2 vols. 1953. 168.

—— *The United States in a Chaotic World: A Chronicle of International Affairs, 1918-1933* (*Chronicles of America,* LV). 1950. 479.

Nevins, Allan, and L. M. Hacker, eds. *The United States and Its Place in World Affairs, 1918–1943.* 1943. 657.

Nevins, Allan, and John A. Krout, eds. *The Greater City: New York, 1898–1948.* 1948. 775.

Newell, Frederick H. *Irrigation in the United States.* 1902. 357.

Newman, James R., and B. S. Miller. *The Control of Atomic Energy.* 1948. 726.

Nichols, Jeannette P. *Alaska: A History of Its Administration, Exploitation and Industrial Development.* 1924. 310.

Nicolson, Harold G. *Dwight Morrow.* 1935. 426.

Nixon, Raymond B. *Henry W. Grady, Spokesman of the New South.* 1943. 228.

Noblin, Stuart. *Leonidas LaFayette Polk: Agrarian Crusader.* 1949. 228.

Nordhoff, Charles. *The Cotton States in the Spring and Summer of 1875.* 1876. 34.

Norris, George W. *Fighting Liberal: The Autobiography of George W. Norris.* Edited by James E. Lawrence. 1945. 505.

North, Robert C. *Moscow and the Chinese Communists.* 1953. 751.

Notter, Harley. *The Origins of the Foreign Policy of Woodrow Wilson.* 1937. 427.

Nourse, Edwin G. *American Agriculture and the European Market.* 1924. 478.

—— *Marketing Agreements under the AAA.* 1935. 591.

Nourse, Edwin G., and associates. *America's Capacity to Produce.* 1934. 505.

Nourse, Edwin G., and others. *Three Years of the Agricultural Adjustment Administration.* 1937. 591.

Nowlin, William F. *The Negro in American National Politics.* 1931. 34.

Noyes, Alexander D. *Forty Years of American Finance.* 1909. 125.

Nye, Russell B. *Midwestern Progressive Politics: A Historical Study of Its Origins and Development, 1870–1950.* 1951. 229, 382.

Oberholtzer, Ellis P. *A History of the United States since the Civil War.* 5 vols. 1917–1937. 17, 103, 187.

—— *Jay Cooke, Financier of the Civil War.* 2 vols. 1907. 102.

—— *The Referendum in America* (University of Pennsylvania, *Publications, Political Economy and Public Law Series,* IV). 1893. 382.

O'Connor, Harvey. *Mellon's Millions: The Biography of a Fortune.* 1933. 505.

Odegard, Peter H. *Pressure Politics: The Story of the Anti-Saloon League, 1928.* 383.

O'Gara, Gordon C. *Theodore Roosevelt and the Rise of the Modern Navy.* 1943. 286.

Ogburn, William F., ed. *Social Change and the New Deal.* 1934. 610.

Ogg, Frederic A. *National Progress, 1907–1917* (*American Nation,* XXVII). 1918. 357.

Ogle, Ralph H. *Federal Control of the Western Apaches, 1848–1886.* 1940. 76.

Olcott, Charles S. *The Life of William McKinley.* 2 vols. 1916. 126, 310.

Older, Fremont. *My Own Story.* 1925, 383.

Oliver, John W. *History of the Civil War Military Pensions, 1861–1885* (University of Wisconsin, *Bulletin, History Series,* I, no. 4). 1917. 126.

Olson, James C. *J. Sterling Morton.* 1942. 228.

Oneal, James, and G. A. Werner. *American Communism: A Critical Analysis of Its Origins, Development, and Programs,* 1927. New ed., 1947. 751.

O'Neill, Herbert C. (Strategicus). *A Short History of the Second World War.* 1950. 657.

Orcutt, William D. *Burrows of Michigan and the Republican Party.* 2 vols. 1917. 126.

Orth, Samuel P. *The Armies of Labor* (*Chronicles of America,* XL). 1919. 187.

—— *The Boss and the Machine* (*Chronicles of America,* XLIII). 1919. 126.

—— *Our Foreigners* (*Chronicles of America,* XXXV). 1920. 203.

O'Shaughnessy, Edith L. *Intimate Pages of Mexican History.* 1920. 426.

Osgood, Ernest S. *The Day of the Cattleman.* 1929. 76.

Ostrogorski, Moiseï I. *Democracy and the Organization of Political Parties.* 2 vols. 1902. 229.

Ostrolenk, Bernhard. *The Surplus Farmer.* 1932. 505.

Otken, Charles H. *The Ills of the South.* 1894. 228.

Overmyer, Grace. *Government and the Arts.* 1939. 548.

Overton, Richard C. *Burlington West: A Colonization History of the Burlington Railroad.* 1941. 147.

—— *Gulf to Rockies: The Heritage of the Ft. Worth and Denver-Colorado and Southern Railways, 1861–1898.* 1953. 147.

Packard, Francis R. *The History of Medicine in the United States.* 2 vols. 1901. New ed., 1932. 104.

Padelford, Norman J. *The Panama Canal in Peace and War.* 1942. 331.

Paine, Albert B. *Mark Twain: A Biography.* 3 vols. 1912. New ed. (2 vols), 1935. 104.

—— *Thomas Nast: His Period and His Pictures.* 1904. 103.

Painter, Floy R. *That Man Debs and His Life Work.* 1929. 187.

Palmer, Frederick. *America in France.* 1918. 452.

—— *Bliss, Peacemaker: The Life and Letters of General Tasker Howard Bliss.* 1934 453.

—— *Our Greatest Battle.* 1919. 452.

—— *Newton D. Baker: America at War.* 2 vols. 1931. 452.

—— *This Man Landon.* 1936. 610.

Palmer, Robert R., Bell I. Wiley, and William R. Keast. *The Army Ground Forces: The Procurement and Training of Ground Combat Troops.* 1947. 675.

Pao (Bau), Ming-ch'ien. *The Open Door Doctrine in Relation to China.* 1923. 310.

Parish, John Carl. *The Persistence of the Westward Movement and Other Essays.* 1943. 228.

Parker, James S. *Social Security Reserves.* 1942. 610.

Parks, E. Taylor. *Colombia and the United States, 1765–1934.* 1935. 331.

Parrington, Vernon L. *The Beginnings of Critical Realism in America, 1860–1920* (*Main Currents in American Thought,* III). 1930. 104.

Paschal, Joel F. *Mr. Justice Sutherland.* 1951. 611.

Pattee, Fred L. *A History of American Literature since 1870.* 1915. 104.

—— *The New American Literature, 1890–1930.* 1930. 548.

Patton, Clifford W. *The Battle for Municipal Reform: Mobilization and Attack, 1875–1900.* 1940. 103.

Patton, James W. *Unionism and Reconstruction in Tennessee.* 1934. 18.

Paul, Rodman W. *The Abrogation of the Gentlemen's Agreement.* 1936. 331.

—— *California Gold: The Beginnings of Mining in the Far West.* 1947. 76.

Paxson, Frederic L. *American Democracy and the World War, 1913–1923.* 3 vols. 1936–48. 401, 452, 479.

—— *The Great Demobilization and Other Essays.* 1941. 479.

—— *History of the American Frontier, 1763–1893.* 1924. 75.

—— *The Last American Frontier.* 1910. 75.

—— *When the West Is Gone.* 1930. 263

Peake, Ora Brooks. *The Colorado Range Cattle Industry,* 1937. 76.

Peck, Harry T. *Twenty Years of the Republic, 1885–1905.* 1907. 126.

Peck, Mary G. *Carrie Chapman Catt: A Biography.* 1944. 103.

Peek, George N., and Samuel Crowther. *Why Quit Our Own.* 1936. 522.

Peel, Roy V., and T. C. Donnelly. *The 1928 Campaign: An Analysis.* 1931. 522.

—— *The 1932 Campaign: An Analysis.* 1935 567.

Peffer, E. Louise. *The Closing of the Public Domain: Disposal and Reservation Policies, 1900–50.* 1951 357.

Pelzer, Louis. *The Cattlemen's Frontier: A Record of the Trans-Mississippi Cattle Industry from*

Open Trains to Pooling Companies, 1850–1890. 1936. 76.

Perkins, Dexter. *America and Two Wars.* 1944. 657.

—— *The American Approach to Foreign Policy.* 1952. 726.

—— *Hands Off: A History of the Monroe Doctrine.* 1941. 286.

—— *The Monroe Doctrine, 1867–1907.* 1937. 286.

Perkins, Frances. *The Roosevelt I Knew.* 1946. 568.

Perlman, Selig. *A History of Trade Unionism in the United States.* 1922. 187.

Pershing, John J. *My Experiences in the World War.* 2 vols. 1931. 452.

Peterson, Horace C. *Propaganda for War: The Campaign against American Neutrality, 1914–1917.* 1939. 427.

Pettigrew, Richard F. *Imperial Washington.* 1922. 310.

Phelps, Mary M. *Kate Chase, Dominant Daughter: The Life Story of a Brilliant Woman and Her Famous Father.* 1935. 53.

Pier, Arthur S. *American Apostles to the Philippines.* 1950. 310.

Pike, James S. *The Prostrate State: South Carolina under Negro Government.* 1874. New ed., 1935. 34.

Pinchot, Gifford. *The Fight for Conservation.* 1910. 383.

Pomeroy, Earl S. *Pacific Outpost: American Strategy in Guam and Micronesia.* 1951. 310.

—— *The Territories and the United States, 1861–1890: Studies in Colonial Administration.* 1947. 228.

Porteus, Stanley D. *And Blow Not the Trumpet: A Prelude to Peril.* 1947. 676.

Post, Langdon W. *The Challenge of Housing.* 1938. 591.

Potwin, Marjorie A. *Cotton Mill People of the Piedmont* (Columbia University, *Studies in History, Economics and Public Law,* no. 291). 1927. 169.

Powderly, Terence V. *The Path I Trod: The Autobiography of Terence V. Powderly.* Edited by Harry J. Carman and others. 1940. 187.

—— *Thirty Years of Labor.* 1889. 187.

Powell, Lyman P. *Mary Baker Eddy.* 1930. New ed., 1950. 104.

Pratt, Fletcher. *War for the World: A Chronicle of Our Fighting Forces in World War II* (*Chronicles of America,* LIV). 1950. 657.

Pratt, Julius W. *Expansionists of 1898: The Acquisition of Hawaii and the Spanish Islands.* 1936. 285.

President's Research Committee on Social Trends. *Recent Social Trends in the United States.* 2 vols. 1933. 547.

Pringle, Henry F. *Alfred E. Smith: A Critical Study.* 1927. 522.

—— *The Life and Times of William Howard Taft.* 2 vols. 1939. 383.

—— *Theodore Roosevelt.* 1931. 331, 357, 383.

Pritchett, C[harles] Herman. *The Roosevelt Court: A Study in Judicial Politics and Values, 1937–1947.* 1948. 611.

—— *The Tennessee Valley Authority: A Study in Public Administration.* 1943. 610.

Puleston, William D. *The Influence of Sea Power in World War II.* 1947. 658.

—— *Mahan: The Life and Work of Captain Alfred Thayer Mahan, U.S.N.* 1939. 286.

Pusey, Merlo J. *Charles Evans Hughes.* 2 vols. 1951. 611.

Pyle, Joseph G. *The Life of James J. Hill.* 2 vols. 1917. 147, 357.

Qualey, Carlton C. *Norwegian Settlement in the United States.* 1938. 203.

Quiett, Glenn C. *Pay Dirt: A Panorama of American Gold Rushes.* 1936. 76.

—— *They Built the West: An Epic of Rails and Cities.* 1934. 146.

Quick, Herbert. *One Man's Life: An Autobiography.* 1925. 103.

Quigley, Harold S., and G. H. Blakeslee. *The Far East: An International Survey.* 1939. 632.

Quinn, Arthur H. *American Fiction: An Historical and Critical Survey.* 1936. 548.

—— *A History of the American Drama from the Civil War to the Present Day.* 2 vols. 1927. New ed. (1 vol.), 1936. 547.

Quint, Howard N. *The Forging of American Socialism: Origins of the Modern Movement.* 1953. 383.

Ramsdell, Charles W. *Reconstruction in Texas* (Columbia University. *Studies in History, Economics and Public Law,* XXXVI). 1910. 34.

Randall, James G. *The Civil War and Reconstruction.* 1937. 17.

Raney, William F. *Wisconsin, A Story of Progress.* 1940. 611.

Raper, Arthur F., and Ira DeA. Reid. *Sharecroppers All.* 1941. 228.

Rappaport, Armin. *The British Press and Wilsonian Neutrality.* 1951. 427.

Rastall, Benjamin. *The Labor History of the Cripple Creek District.* 1908. 187.

Ratner, Sidney. *American Taxation: Its History as a Social Force in Democracy.* 1942. 591.

Rauch, Basil. *A History of the New Deal, 1933–38.* 1944. 567.

—— *Roosevelt: From Munich to Pearl Harbor; A Study in the Creation of a Foreign Policy.* 1950. 632.

Ravage, Marcus E. *The Story of Teapot Dome.* 1924. 505.

Record, Wilson. *The Negro and the Communist Party.* 1951. 776.

Redfield, William C. *With Congress and Cabinet.* 1924. 401.

Reeve, Joseph E. *Monetary Reform Movements: A Survey of Recent Plans and Panaceas.* 1943. 591.

Regier, Cornelius C. *The Era of the Muckrakers.* 1932. 357.

Reid, John G. *The Manchu Abdication and the Powers, 1908–1912.* 1935. 383.

Reischauer, Edwin O. *The United States and Japan.* 1950. 702.

Reuter, Bertha A. *Anglo-American Relations during the Spanish-American War.* 1924. 286.

Rhodes, James Ford. *History of the United States from the Compromise of 1850.* 9 vols. 1900–28. 17, 103, 187.

—— *The McKinley and Roosevelt Administrations, 1897–1909.* 1922. 244.

Richards, Henry I. *Cotton and the AAA.* 1936. 591.

Richardson, Leon B. *History of Dartmouth College.* 2 vols. 1932. 104.

—— *William E. Chandler, Republican.* 1940. 125.

Riegel, Robert E. *America Moves West.* 1930. Rev. ed., 1947. 75.

—— *The Story of the Western Railroads.* 1926. 146.

Ripley, William Z. *Main Street and Wall Street.* 1927. 522.

—— *Railroads: Finance and Organization.* 1915. 146.

—— *Railroads: Rates and Regulation.* 1912. 146.

—— *Trusts, Pools, and Corporations.* 1905. New ed., 1916. 169.

Rippy, J[ames] Fred. *America and the Strife of Europe.* 1938. 310.

—— *The Capitalists and Colombia.* 1931. 331.

—— *The Caribbean Danger Zone.* 1940. 331.

—— *Latin America in World Politics.* 1928. 3rd ed., 1938. 331.

—— *The United States and Mexico.* 1926. Rev. ed., 1931. 426.

Rister, Carl C. *Border Command: General Phil Sheridan in the West.* 1944. 76.

—— *Land Hunger: David L. Payne and the Oklahoma Boomers.* 1942. 228.

—— *No Man's Land.* 1948. 228.

—— *Oil! Titan of the Southwest.* 1949. 357.

—— *Southern Plainsmen.* 1938. 228.

Robbins, Roy M. *Our Landed Heritage.* 1942. 76.

Roberts, Owen J. *The Court and the Constitution.* 1951. 611.

Robinson, Edgar E. *The New United States.* 1946. 547.

—— *The Presidential Vote, 1896–1932.* 1934. 244.

—— *The Presidential Vote, 1936.* 1940. 610.

—— *They Voted for Roosevelt: The Presidential Vote, 1932–1944.* 1947. 567.

Robinson, Edgar E., and V. J. West. *The Foreign Policy of Woodrow Wilson, 1913–1917.* 1917. 427.

Robinson, Henry M. *Fantastic Interim: A Hindsight History of American Manners, Morals, and Mistakes between Versailles and Pearl Harbor.* 1943. 505.

Robinson, William A. *Thomas B. Reed, Parliamentarian.* 1930. 126.

Rollins, Philip A. *The Cowboy.* 1922. 76.

Roos, Charles F. *N.R.A. Economic Planning.* 1937. 591.

Roosevelt, Eleanor. *This I Remember.* 1949. 568.

—— *This Is My Story.* 1937. 568.

Roosevelt, Franklin D. *F.D.R.: His Personal Letters, 1905–1945.* Edited by Elliott Roosevelt. 4 vols. 1947–50. 567.

—— *The Public Papers and Addresses of Franklin D. Roosevelt.* 13 vols. 1938–50. 567.

Roosevelt, Theodore. *The Letters of Theodore Roosevelt, 1868–1919.* Edited by Elting E. Morison and others. 8 vols. 1951–54. 331.

—— *Theodore Roosevelt: An Autobiography.* 1913. New ed., 1929. 331, 357.

Roosevelt, Theodore, and Henry Cabot Lodge. *Selections from the Correspondence of Theodore Roosevelt and Henry Cabot Lodge, 1884–1918.* 2 vols. 1925. 310.

Rose, Philip M. *The Italians in America.* 1922. 204.

Rosenman, Samuel I. *Working with Roosevelt.* 1952. 568.

Rosewater, Victor. *Back Stage in 1912.* 1932. 383.

Ross, Earle D. *Democracy's College: The Land-Grant Movement in the Formative Stage.* 1942. 103.

—— *A History of Iowa State College of Agriculture and Mechanic Arts.* 1942. 103.

—— *The Liberal Republican Movement.* 1919. 53.

Rovere, Richard H., and A. M. Schlesinger, Jr. *The General and the President, and the Future of American Foreign Policy.* 1951. 751.

Rowe, Henry K. *The History of Religion in the United States.* 1924. 264.

Rubinow, Isaac M. *The Quest for Security.* 1934. 610.

Rudy, S[olomon] Willis. *The College of the City of New York: A History, 1847–1947.* 1949. 103.

Russell, Charles E. *Blaine of Maine: His Life and Times.* 1931. 126.

———— *The Story of the Nonpartisan League.* 1920. 478.

Ryden, George H. *The Foreign Policy of the United States in Relation to Samoa* (*Yale Historical Publications, Miscellany,* XXIV). 1933. 285.

Sabin, Edwin L. *Building the Pacific Railway.* 1919. 147.

Sageser A[delbert] Bower. *The First Two Decades of the Pendleton Act: A Study of Civil Service Reform* (University of Nebraska, *University Studies,* XXXIV–XXXV). 1935. 126.

Saloutos, Theodore, and John D. Hicks. *Agricultural Discontent in the Middle West, 1900–1939.* 1951. 478.

Sargeant, Winthrop. *Jazz, Hot and Hybrid.* 1939. 548.

Sargent, Herbert H. *The Campaign of Santiago de Cuba.* 3 vols. 1907. 286.

Satterlee, Herbert L. *J. Pierpont Morgan: An Intimate Portrait.* 1939. 357.

Sayre, Francis Bowes. *The Way Forward: The American Trade Agreements Program.* 1939. 611.

Schafer, Joseph. *Carl Schurz, Militant Liberal.* 1930. 103.

Schieber, Clara E. *The Transformation of American Sentiment Toward Germany, 1870–1914.* 1923. 286.

Schlesinger, Arthur M. *New Viewpoints in American History.* 1922. New ed., 1937. 383.

———— *Paths to the Present.* 1949. 547.

———— *The Rise of the City, 1878–1898* (*History of American Life,* X). 1933. 264.

Schley, Winfield S. *Forty-five Years Under the Flag.* 1904. 286.

Schmidt, Louis B., and E. D. Ross, eds. *Readings in the Economic History of American Agriculture.* 1925. 76.

Schmitt, Bernadotte E. *The Coming of the War, 1914.* 2 vols. 1930. 426.

Schneider, Herbert W. *Making the Fascist State.* 1928. 632.

———— *Religion in Twentieth Century America.* 1952. 547.

Schnier, Jacques P. *Sculpture in Modern America.* 1948. 548.

Schriftgiesser, Karl. *The Gentleman from Massachusetts: Henry Cabot Lodge.* 1944. 453.

Schubert, Paul. *The Electric Word: The Rise of the Radio.* 1928. 547.

Schuman, Frederick L. *The Nazi Dictatorship.* 1935. 632.

Schurr, Sam H., and Jacob Marshak. *Economic Aspects of Atomic Power.* 1951. 726.

Schurz, Carl. *Speeches, Correspondence and Political Papers of Carl Schurz.* Edited by Frederic Bancroft. 6 vols. 1913. 34.

Schwartz, Benjamin I. *Chinese Communism and the Rise of Mao.* 1951. 702.

Scott, James B. *The Hague Peace Conferences of 1899 and 1907.* 2 vols. 1909. 331.

Seabrook, William B. *These Foreigners.* 1938. 203.

Seabury, William M. *The Public and the Motion Picture Industry.* 1926. 547.

Seitz, Don C. *The Dreadful Decade, 1869–1879.* 1926. 102.

Seldes, Gilbert V. *The Great Audience.* 1950. 776.

———— *The Years of the Locust: America, 1929–1932.* 1933. 522.

Seligman, Edwin R. A. *The Economics of Farm Relief.* 1929. 505.

Selznik, Philip. *TVA and the Grass Roots.* 1949. 610.

Seton-Watson, Hugh. *The East European Revolution.* 1951. 726.

Seward, George F. *Chinese Immigration in Its Social and Economical Aspects.* 1881. 204.

Seymour, Charles. *American Diplomacy during the World War.* 1934. 426.

———— *American Neutrality, 1914–1917.* 1935. 427.

———— *Woodrow Wilson and the World War* (*Chronicles of America,* LXVIII). 1921. 427.

Seymour, Flora W. *The Story of the Red Man.* 1929. 76.

Shannon, Fred A. *America's Economic Growth.* 1940. 3rd ed., 1951. 478.

———— *The Farmer's Last Frontier: Agriculture, 1860–1897* (*Economic History of the United States,* V). 1945. 229.

Sharp, Frank C., and Philip G. Fox. *Business Ethics: Studies in Fair Competition.* 1937. 103.

Sheldon, William D. *Populism in the Old Dominion: Virginia Farm Politics, 1885–1900.* 1935. 228.

Sherman, John. *Recollections of Forty Years in the House, Senate and Cabinet: An Autobiography.* 2 vols. 1895. 125.

Sherman, William R. *The Diplomatic and Commercial Relations of the United States and Chile, 1820–1914.* 1924. 286.

Sherrod, Robert L. *History of Marine Corps Aviation in World War II.* 1952. 658.

Sherwood, Robert E. *Roosevelt and Hopkins: An Intimate History.* 1948. Rev. ed., 1950. 567, 658, 702.

Shinn, Charles H. *Mining Camps: A Study in American Frontier Government.* 1885. New ed., 1948. 76.

———— *The Story of the Mine, As Illustrated by the Great Comstock Lode of Nevada.* 1896. 75.

Shippee, Lester B. *Canadian-American Relations, 1849–1874.* 1939. 331.

Shirer, William L. *Berlin Diary: The Journal of a Foreign Correspondent, 1934–1941.* 1941. 632.

Shotwell, James T. *At the Paris Peace Conference.* 1937. 453.

——— *War as an Instrument of National Policy, and Its Renunciation in the Pact of Paris.* 1929. 522.

Shryock, Richard H. *American Medical Research, Past and Present.* 1947. 548.

Shugg, Roger W. *Origins of Class Struggle in Louisiana: A Social History of White Farmers and Laborers during Slavery and After, 1840–1875.* 1939. 18.

Shugg, Roger W., and H. A. De Weerd. *World War II: A Concise History.* 1946. 657.

Shulman, Milton. *Defeat in the West.* 1947. 658.

Shultz, William J. *Financial Development of the United States.* 1937. 102, 591.

Siegfried, André. *America Comes of Age.* 1927. 505.

Sievers, Harry J. *Benjamin Harrison, Hoosier Warrior, 1833–1865.* 1953. 125.

Simkins, Francis B. *Pitchfork Ben Tillman: South Carolinian.* 1944. 228.

——— *The South Old and New: A History, 1820–1947.* 1947. 34.

——— *The Tillman Movement in South Carolina.* 1926. 228.

Simkins, Francis B., and R. H. Woody. *South Carolina during Reconstruction.* 1932. 34.

Sims, William S., and B. J. Kendrick. *The Victory at Sea.* 1920. 452.

Sinclair, Upton. *I, Candidate for Governor, and How I Got Licked.* 1935. 611.

Sinclair, William A. *The Aftermath of Slavery: A Study of the Condition and Environment of the American Negro.* 1905. 53.

Slosson, Preston W. *The Great Crusade and After, 1914–1928 (History of American Life, XII).* 1937. 547.

Small, John D. *From War to Peace: Civilian Production Achievements in Transition* (United States, Civilian Production Administration, *Report to the President*). 1946. 676.

Smalley, Eugene V. *History of the Northern Pacific Railroad.* 1883. 147.

Smallwood, William M., and M. S. C. Smallwood. *Natural History and the American Mind (Columbia Studies in American Culture, no. 8).* 1941. 104.

Smith, Alfred E. *Up to Now: An Autobiography.* 1929. 522.

Smith, Arthur D. H. *Commodore Vanderbilt: An Epic of American Achievement.* 1927. 103.

Smith, Charles H. *The Coming of the Russian Mennonites: An Episode in the Settling of the Last Frontier, 1874–1884.* 1927. 76.

Smith, Darrell H., and P. V. Betters. *The United States Shipping Board: Its History, Activities and Organization.* 1931. 478.

Smith, Darrell H., and H. Guy Herring. *The Bureau of Immigration: Its History, Activities and Organization.* 1924. 204.

Smith, Henry L. *Airways: The History of Commercial Aviation in the United States.* 1942. 547.

Smith, Henry Nash, *Virgin Land: The American West as Symbol and Myth.* 1950. 104, 229.

Smith, Joseph Russell. *The Story of Iron and Steel.* 1908. 168.

Smith, Louis. *American Democracy and Military Power: A Study of Civil Control of the Military Power in the United States.* 1951. 751.

Smith, Sara R. *The Manchurian Crisis, 1931–1932.* 1948. 632.

Smith, Theodore C. *The Life and Letters of James Abram Garfield.* 2 vols. 1925. 125.

Smith, Walter Bedell. *My Three Years in Moscow.* 1950. 726.

Smythe, William E. *The Conquest of Arid America.* 1900. New ed., 1905. 357.

Somers, Herman Miles. *Presidential Agency: OWMR, The Office of War Mobilization and Reconversion.* 1950. 675.

Somerville, John. *Soviet Philosophy: A Study of Theory and Practice.* 1946. 632.

Souders, David A. *The Magyars in America.* 1922. 204.

Soule, George H. *Prosperity Decade: From War to Depression: 1917–1929 (Economic History of the United States, VIII).* 1947. 522.

Spalding, Albert G. *America's National Game.* 1911. 264.

Spero, Hubert. *Reconstruction Finance Corporation Loans to the Railroads, 1932–37.* 1939. 591.

Spiller, Robert E., and others, eds. *Literary History of the United States.* 3 vols. 1948. 104.

Sprout, Harold and Margaret. *The Rise of American Naval Power, 1776–1918.* 1939. 286.

——— *Toward a New Order of Sea Power: American Naval Policy and the World Scene, 1918–1922.* 1940. 479.

Stahl, Rose M. *The Ballinger-Pinchot Controversy (Smith College, Studies in History, XI, no. 2).* 1926. 383.

Stanton, Elizabeth Cady, and others. *History of Woman Suffrage.* 6 vols. 1881–1922. 103.

Stanton, Stephen B. *The Behring Sea Controversy.* 1892. 285.

Stanwood, Edward. *American Tariff Controversies in the Nineteenth Century.* 2 vols. 1903. 126.

——— *A History of the Presidency.* 2 vols. 1916. New ed., 1928. 53.

Staples, Henry L., and A. T. Mason. *The Fall of a Railroad Empire: Brandeis and the New Haven Merger Battle.* 1947. 401.

Staples, Thomas S. *Reconstruction in Arkansas, 1862–1874 (Columbia University, Studies in History, Economics and Public Law, CIX).* 1923. 18.

Stearns, Harold E., ed. *Civilization in the United States: An Inquiry by Thirty Americans.* 1922. 547.

Stedman, Murray S., Jr., and Susan W. Stedman. *Discontent at the Polls: A Study of Farmer and Labor Parties, 1827-1948.* 1950. 229.

Steffens, [Joseph] Lincoln. *The Autobiography of Lincoln Steffens.* 2 vols. 1931. 357.

—— *The Shame of the Cities.* 1904. 383.

Stein, Charles W. *The Third Term Tradition: Its Rise and Collapse in American Politics.* 1943. 657.

Steiner, Edward A. *On the Trail of the Immigrant.* 1906. 204.

Steiner, Harold Arthur, ed. "Report on China." *Annals of the American Academy of Political and Social Science.* September, 1951. 702.

Stephenson, George M. *A History of American Immigration, 1820-1924.* 1926. 203.

—— *John Lind of Minnesota.* 1935. 426.

—— *The Religious Aspects of Swedish Immigration.* 1932. 204.

Stephenson, Nathaniel W. *Nelson W. Aldrich: A Leader in American Politics.* 1930. 383.

Stettinius, Edward R., Jr. *Lend-Lease, Weapon for Victory.* 1944. 675.

—— *Roosevelt and the Russians: The Yalta Conference.* Edited by Walter Johnson. 1949. 702.

Steuart, Justin. *Wayne Wheeler, Dry Boss.* 1928. 383.

Steuben, John. *Labor in Wartime.* 1940. 452.

Stevenson, Adlai E. *Major Campaign Speeches of Adlai E. Stevenson, 1952.* 1953. 751.

Stewart, Frank M. *The National Civil Service Reform League: History, Activities, and Problems.* 1929. 103.

Stewart, George R. *Bret Harte: Argonaut and Exile.* 1931. 104.

Stewart, William M. *Reminiscences of Senator William M. Stewart of Nevada.* Edited by G. R. Brown. 1908. 75.

Stieglitz, Julius O., and others, eds. *Chemistry in Medicine.* 1928. 548.

Still, Bayrd. *Milwaukee, The History of a City.* 1948. 264.

Stilwell, Joseph W. *The Stilwell Papers.* Edited by Theodore H. White. 1948. 657.

Stimson, Henry L. *The Far Eastern Crisis: Recollections and Observations.* 1936. 632.

Stimson, Henry L., and McGeorge Bundy. *On Active Service in War and Peace.* 1947. 675.

Stoddard, Henry L. *Horace Greeley, Printer, Editor, Crusader.* 1946. 53.

—— *Presidential Sweepstakes: The Story of Political Conventions and Campaigns.* Edited by Francis W. Leary. 1948. 126.

Stokes, Anson P. *Church and State in the United States: Historical Development and Contemporary Problems of Religious Freedom under the Constitution.* 3 vols. 1950. 264.

Stolberg, Benjamin. *The Story of the CIO.* 1938. 591.

Stoner, John E. *S. O. Levinson and the Pact of Paris: A Study in the Techniques of Influence.* 1942. 522.

Storey, Moorfield. *Charles Sumner (American Statesmen, XXX).* 1900. New ed., 1917. 34.

Storey, Moorfield, and M. P. Lichauco. *The Conquest of the Philippines by the United States, 1898-1925.* 1926. 310.

Strachey, Rachel C. *Frances Willard: Her Life and Work.* 1912. 103.

Strakhovsky, Leonid I. *The Origins of American Intervention in North Russia, 1918.* 1937. 452.

Straus, Michael W., and Talbot Wegg. *Housing Comes of Age.* 1938. 591.

Straus, Nathan. *The Seven Myths of Housing.* 1944. 591.

Strong, Josiah. *The Twentieth Century City.* 1898. 264.

Strunsky, Simeon. *The Living Tradition: Change and America.* 1939. 547, 775.

Stryker, Lloyd P. *Andrew Johnson: A Study in Courage.* 1929. New ed., 1936. 18.

Stuart, Graham H. *Cuba and Its International Relations* (Institute of International Education, International Relations Clubs, *Syllabus,* no. XIV). 1923. 310.

Sullivan, Louis H. *The Autobiography of an Idea.* 1924. 548.

Sullivan, Mark. *The Great Adventure at Washington: The Story of the Conference.* 1922. 479.

—— *Our Times, 1900-1925.* 6 vols. 1926-35. 228, 310, 357, 426, 479, 505.

Sumner, Charles. *Memoir and Letters of Charles Sumner.* Edited by Edward L. Pierce. 4 vols. 1877-93. 34.

Sward, Keith T. *The Legend of Henry Ford.* 1948. 547.

Swearingen, Rodger, and Paul Langer. *Red Flag in Japan: International Communism in Action, 1919-1951.* 1952. 702.

Sweet, William W. *The Story of Religion in America.* 1930. 264.

Swint, Henry L. *The Northern Teacher in the South, 1862-1870.* 1941. 17.

Taft, Helen H. (Mrs. William Howard Taft). *Recollections of Full Years.* 1914. 383.

Taft, Lorado. *The History of American Sculpture.* 1903. New ed., 1930. 548.

Taft, Robert A. *A Foreign Policy for Americans.* 1951. 751.

Tallmadge, Thomas S. *The Story of Architecture in America.* 1927. Rev. ed., 1936. 548.

Tanaka, Giichi. *Japan's Dream of World Empire:*

The Tanaka Memorial. Edited by Carl Crow. 1942. 632.

Tansill, Charles C. *America Goes to War.* 1938. 427.

―――― *Backdoor to War: The Roosevelt Foreign Policy, 1933–41.* 1952. 632.

―――― *Canadian-American Relations, 1875–1916.* 1943. 331.

―――― *The Congressional Career of Thomas Francis Bayard, 1869–1885.* 1946. 126.

―――― *The Foreign Policy of Thomas F. Bayard, 1885–1897.* 1940. 126.

Tarbell, Ida M. *The History of the Standard Oil Company.* 2 vols. 1904. New ed. (1 vol.), 1937. 168.

―――― *The Life of Elbert M. Gary: The Story of Steel.* 1925. 357.

―――― *The Nationalizing of Business, 1878–1898 (History of American Life, IX).* 1936. 169.

―――― *The Tariff in Our Times.* 1911. 126.

Tasch, Henry J. *The Reciprocal Trade Policy of the United States.* 1938. 611.

Taussig, Frank W. *The Silver Situation in the United States.* 1893. New ed., 1896. 243.

―――― *The Tariff History of the United States.* 1890. 8th ed., 1931. 126.

Taylor, Alonzo E. *The New Deal and Foreign Trade.* 1935. 611.

Taylor, Alrutheus A. *The Negro in South Carolina during Reconstruction.* 1924. 17.

―――― *The Negro in Tennessee, 1865–1880.* 1941. 17.

―――― *The Negro in the Reconstruction of Virginia.* 1926. 34.

Taylor, Carl C. *The Farmers' Movement, 1620–1920.* 1953. 478.

Taylor, James M., and Elizabeth H. Haight. *Vassar (American College and University Studies).* 1915. 104.

Taylor, Paul S. *Mexican Labor in the United States* (University of California, *Publications in Economics,* VI, VII, XII). 2 vols. in 3. 1928–34. 505.

Taylor, Robert L. *Winston Churchill: An Informal Study of Greatness.* 1952. 658.

Teele, Ray P. *Irrigation in the United States.* 1915. 357.

Temperley, Harold W. V., ed. *A History of the Peace Conference of Paris.* 1924. 453.

Thayer, William R. *The Life and Letters of John Hay.* 2 vols. 1915. 310.

―――― *Theodore Roosevelt: An Intimate Biography.* 1919. 331.

Theobald, Robert A. *The Final Secret of Pearl Harbor.* 1954. 657.

Thomas, Charles M. *Thomas Riley Marshall: Hoosier Statesman.* 1939. 479.

Thomas, Dorothy S., and others. *Japanese-*

American Evacuation and Resettlement. 2 vols. 1946–52. 676.

Thomas, Norman M. *After the New Deal, What?* 1936. 568.

Thomas, Shipley. *The History of the A.E.F.* 1920. 452.

Thomas, William I., and Florian Znaniecki. *The Polish Peasant in Europe and America.* 5 vols. 1918–20. 204

Thompson, C[lara] Mildred. *Reconstruction in Georgia, Economic, Social, Political, 1865–1872* (Columbia University, *Studies in History, Economics and Public Law,* LXIV). 1915. 34.

Thompson, Holland. *The Age of Invention (Chronicles of America,* XXXVII). 1921. 169.

―――― *From the Cotton Field to the Cotton Mill: A Study of Industrial Transition in North Carolina.* 1906. 169.

―――― *The New South (Chronicles of America,* XLII). 1919. 168.

Thompson, James W. *A History of Livestock Raising in the United States, 1607–1860.* 1942. 76.

Thompson, Slason. *A Short History of American Railways.* 1925. 146.

Thwing, Charles F. *The American and the German University: One Hundred Years of History.* 1928. 103.

―――― *A History of Higher Education in America.* 1906. 103.

Timmons, Bascom N. *Garner of Texas: A Personal History.* 1948. 568.

Tippett, Thomas. *When Southern Labor Stirs.* 1931. 187.

Todd, Helen. *A Man Named Grant.* 1940. 53.

Todd, Lewis P. *Wartime Relations of the Federal Government and the Public Schools, 1917–1918* (Columbia University, Teachers College, *Contributions to Education,* no. 907). 1945. 452.

Tompkins, Pauline. *American-Russian Relations in the Far East.* 1949. 751.

Tostlebe, Alvin S. *The Bank of North Dakota: An Experiment in Agrarian Banking* (Columbia University, *Studies in History, Economics and Public Law,* CXIV, no. 1). 1924. 478.

Treat, Payson J. *Diplomatic Relations between the United States and Japan, 1895–1905.* 2 vols. 1932. New ed., 1938. 331.

Trent, William P., and others, eds. *The Cambridge History of American Literature.* 3 vols. 1936. 348.

Trevor-Roper, Hugh R. *The Last Days of Hitler.* 1947. 658.

Trimble, William J. *The Mining Advance into the Inland Empire* (University of Wisconsin, *Bulletin,* History Series, III). 1914. 75.

Truman, Harry S. *Mr. President: The First Publication from the Personal Diaries, Private Letters, Papers and Revealing Interviews of Harry S.*

Truman, *Thirty-second President of the United States of America.* Edited by William Hillman. 1952. 676.

—— *The Truman Program: Addresses and Messages of the President.* 1949. 726.

Tsuchida, William S. *Wear It Proudly: Letters.* 1947. 676.

Tugwell, Rexford G. *Industry's Coming of Age.* 1927. 505.

—— *Mr. Hoover's Economic Policy.* 1932. 522.

—— *The Stricken Land, The Story of Puerto Rico.* 1947. 611.

Tully, Grace G. *F.D.R., My Boss.* 1949. 676.

Tupper, Eleanor R., and G. E. McReynolds. *Japan in American Public Opinion.* 1937. 479.

Turner, Frederick Jackson. *The Early Writings of Frederick Jackson Turner.* 1938. 263.

—— *The Frontier in American History.* 1921. 75.

Twentieth Century Fund, Committee on Debt Adjustment, *Debts and Recovery,* 1929–37. 1938. 610.

——, Committee on Taxation. *Facing the Tax Problem.* 1937. 610.

——, Power Committee. *The Power Industry and the Public Interest.* 1944. 610.

Tyler, Alice F. *The Foreign Policy of James G. Blaine.* 1927. 126, 285.

United States, Department of State. *Documents on German Foreign Policy, 1918–1945, from the Archives of the German Foreign Ministry (Publications 3277, 3548).* Edited by R. J. Sontag and others. 2 vols. 1949. 632.

—— *Nazi-Soviet Relations, 1939–41 (Publication 3023).* Edited by R. J. Sontag and J. S. Beddie. 1948. 632.

—— *Our Foreign Policy (Publication 3972).* 1950. 726.

—— *Peace and War: United States Foreign Policy, 1931–1941 (Publication 1983).* 1943. 657.

United States, Department of the Army, Historical Division. *United States Army in the World War, 1917–1919.* 17 vols. 1948. 452.

—— *The United States Army in World War II.* 21 vols. 1947–54. 658, 675.

United States Marine Corps. *Monographs.* 14 vols. 1947–54. 658.

United States, Office of Contract Settlement. *A History of War Contract Terminations and Settlements.* 1947. 676.

Vagts, Alfred. *Deutschland und die Vereinigten Staaten in der Weltpolitik.* 2 vols. 1935. 331.

Van Alstyne, Richard W. *American Crisis Diplomacy: The Quest for Collective Security, 1918–1952.* 1952. 702.

Vance, Rupert B. *Human Factors in Cotton Culture.* 1929. 228.

—— *Human Geography of the South.* 1932. 2nd ed., 1935. 228.

Van Hise, Charles R. *The Conservation of Natural Resources in the United States.* 1910. 357.

Veblen, Thorstein. *The Theory of Business Enterprise.* 1904. 357.

—— *The Theory of the Leisure Class.* 1899. New ed., 1934. 264, 357.

Vernadsky, George. *The Russian Revolution, 1917–1931.* 1932. 632.

Vestal, Stanley. *Kit Carson.* 1928. 76.

—— *Mountain Men.* 1937. 76.

Viles, Jonas. *The University of Missouri: A Centennial History.* 1939. 103.

Villard, Henry. *Memoirs of Henry Villard: Journalist and Financier, 1835–1900.* 1904. 147.

Vinacke, Harold M. *A History of the Far East in Modern Times.* 1928. 5th ed., 1950. 479, 632.

—— *The United States and the Far East, 1945–51.* 1952. 702.

Wald, Lillian D. *The House on Henry Street.* 1915. 264.

Walker, Albert H. *History of the Sherman Law of the United States of America.* 1910. 357.

Walker, Franklin. *San Francisco's Literary Frontier.* 1939. 104.

Walker, Stanley. *Dewey: An American of This Century.* 1944. 726.

Wallace, David D. *History of Wofford College, 1854–1949.* 1951. 104.

Wallace, Henry A. *America Must Choose.* 1934. 568.

—— *New Frontiers.* 1934. 591.

Walsh, John R. *C.I.O.: Industrial Unionism in Action.* 1937. 591.

Walters, Francis P. *A History of the League of Nations.* 1952. 479.

Walton, William. *World's Columbian Exposition, MDCCCXCIII: The Art and Architecture.* 2 vols. in 3. 1893–95. 263.

Warburg, James P. *Hell Bent for Election.* 1935. 610.

—— *Still Hell Bent.* 1936. 610.

Warburg, Paul M. *The Federal Reserve System.* 2 vols. 1930. 401.

Ware, Norman J. *The Labor Movement in the United States, 1860–95.* 1929. 187.

Warne, Colston E., and others, eds. *Labor in Post-War America (Yearbook of American Labor, II).* 1949. 676.

—— *War Labor Policies (Yearbook of American Labor, I).* 1945. 676.

Warren, Charles. *Congress, Constitution, and the Supreme Court.* 1925. Rev. ed., 1935. 611.

—— *The Supreme Court in United States His-*

tory. 3 vols. 1922. Rev. ed. (2 vols.), 1937. 34.

Warren, Sidney. *American Freethought, 1860–1914* (Columbia University, *Studies in History, Economics and Public Law*, No. 504). 1943. 264.

Washington, Booker T. *Up from Slavery: An Autobiography*. 1901. New ed., 1945. 103.

Wasson, Woodrow W. *James A. Garfield: His Religion and Education*. 1952. 125.

Waters, Walter W. *B.E.F.: The Whole Story of the Bonus Army*. 1933. 567.

Weaver, Robert C. *Negro Labor: A National Problem*. 1946. 776.

Webb, Walter P. *Divided We Stand: The Crisis of a Frontierless Democracy*. 1937. New ed., 1944. 169.

——— *The Great Frontier*. 1952. 776.

——— *The Great Plains*. 1931. New ed., 1936. 75.

——— *The Texas Rangers: A Century of Frontier Defense*. 1935. 76.

Weber, Herman C. *Evangelism: A Graphic Survey*. 1929. 264.

Weberg, Frank P. *The Background of the Panic of 1893*. 1929. 243.

Webster, Noah. *Letters of Noah Webster*. Edited by Harry W. Warfel. 1953. 103.

Wecter, Dixon. *The Age of the Great Depression, 1929–1941* (*History of American Life*, XIII). 1948. 567.

——— *Sam Clemens of Hannibal*. 1952. 104.

Wecter, Dixon, and others. *Changing Patterns in American Civilization*. 1949. 547.

Wehle, Louis B. *Hidden Threads of History: Wilson through Roosevelt*. 1953. 610.

Weissman, Rudolph L. *The New Federal Reserve System*. 1936. 591.

——— *The New Wall Street*. 1939. 591.

Welles, Gideon. *Diary of Gideon Welles*. 3 vols. 1911. 34.

Welles, Sumner. *Naboth's Vineyard: The Dominican Republic, 1844–1924*. 2 vols. 1928. 53.

——— *Seven Decisions that Shaped History*. 1951. 702.

——— *The Time for Decision*. 1944. 702.

Wellman, Paul I. *Death in the Desert*. 1935. 76.

——— *Death on Horseback: Seventy Years of War for the American West*. 1947. 76.

——— *Death on the Prairie*. 1934. 76.

Werner, Morris R. *Bryan*. 1929. 243.

——— *Privileged Characters*. 1935. 505.

——— *Tammany Hall*. 1928. 522.

Wesley, Charles H. *Negro Labor in the United States, 1850–1925*. 1927. 187.

West, Richard S. *Admirals of the American Empire*. 1948. 286.

Weyand, Alexander M. *American Football: Its History and Development*. 1926. 264.

Weyl, Nathaniel. *The Battle against Disloyalty*. 1951. 751.

Weyl, Nathaniel, and Sylvia C. *The Reconquest of Mexico: The Years of Lázaro Cárdenas*. 1939. 611.

Weyl, Walter E. *The New Democracy*. 1912. New ed., 1927. 382.

Wharton, Vernon L. *The Negro in Mississippi, 1865–1890*. 1947. 17.

Wheeler, Joseph. *The Santiago Campaign*. 1898. 286.

Wheeler-Bennett, John W. *The Pipe-Dream of Peace: The Story of the Collapse of Disarmament*. 1935. 632.

——— *Munich: Prologue to Tragedy*. 1948. 632.

White, Andrew D. *A History of the Warfare of Science with Theology in Christendom*. 2 vols. 1896. New ed., 1910. 264.

White, Bouck. *The Book of Daniel Drew*. 1910. New ed., 1937. 103.

White, Edward A. *Science and Religion in American Thought: The Impact of Naturalism*. 1952. 264.

White, Horace. *Coin's Financial Fool: Or, the Artful Dodger Exposed*. 1895. 243.

——— *The Life of Lyman Trumbull*. 1913. 34.

——— *Money and Banking Illustrated by American History*. 1896. 6th ed., 1935. 243.

White, Theodore H. *Fire in the Ashes: Europe in Mid-century*. 1953. 776.

White, William A. *The Autobiography of William Allen White*. 1946. 505.

——— *Calvin Coolidge: The Man Who Is President*. 1925. 505.

——— *Masks in a Pageant*. 1928. 505.

——— *A Puritan in Babylon: The Story of Calvin Coolidge*. 1938. 505.

——— *What It's All About*. 1936. 610.

——— *Woodrow Wilson: The Man, His Times and His Task*. 1924. 401.

White, William L. *Bernard Baruch: Portrait of a Citizen*. 1950. 452.

Whitman, Willson. *Bread and Circuses: A Study of Federal Theatre*. 1937. 591.

Wickersham, George W. *Report of the National Commission on Law Observance and Enforcement* (71 Cong., 3 Sess., *H. Doc.* no. 722 — serial 9361). 1931. 548.

Wiest, Edward. *Agricultural Organization in the United States*. 1923. 478.

Wilbur, Ray Lyman, and A. M. Hyde. *The Hoover Policies*. 1937. 522.

Wilbur, Sibyl. *The Life of Mary Baker Eddy*. 1929. New ed., 1938. 104.

Wildman, Murray S. *Money Inflation in the United States*. 1905. 53, 125.

Wilgus, Horace L. *A Study of the United States Steel Corporation in Its Industrial and Legal Aspects*. 1901. 357.

Wilkerson, Marcus M. *Public Opinion and the Spanish-American War: A Study in War Propaganda.* 1932. 286.

Wilkins, Ernest H. *The Changing College.* 1927. 548.

Willard, Frances E. *Glimpses of Fifty Years.* 1889. 103.

Williams, Benjamin H. *Economic Foreign Policy of the United States.* 1929. 522.

Williams, Charles R. *The Life of Rutherford Burchard Hayes.* 2 vols. 1914. 125.

Williams, George W. *History of the Negro Race in America from 1619 to 1880.* 2 vols. 1882. 17.

Williams, Mary W. *Anglo-American Isthmian Diplomacy, 1815–1915.* 1916. 331.

Williams, Ralph C. *The United States Public Health Service, 1798–1950.* 1951. 776.

Williams, William A. *American Russian Relations: 1781–1947.* 1952. 726.

Willis, Henry P. *The Federal Reserve: A Study of the Banking System of the United States.* 1915. 401.

Willkie, Wendell. *One World.* 1943. 702.

Willoughby, William F. *Financial Condition and Operations of the National Government, 1921–30.* 1931. 505.

—— *Government Organization in Wartime and After.* 1919. 452.

—— *The National Budget System.* 1927. 505.

—— *The Problem of a National Budget.* 1918. 505.

—— *Territories and Dependencies of the United States.* 1905. 310.

Wilson, Edith Bolling. *My Memoir.* 1939. 401.

Winkler, John K. *Incredible Carnegie: The Life of Andrew Carnegie.* 1931. 168.

Winnacker, Rudolph A. "Yalta — Another Munich?" *Virginia Quarterly Review*, XXIV, 521–537. Autumn, 1948. 702.

Winston, Robert W. *Andrew Johnson, Plebeian and Patriot.* 1928. 18.

Winther, Oscar O. *The Great Northwest, A History.* 1947. Rev. ed., 1950. 75.

Wisan, Joseph E. *The Cuban Crisis as Reflected in the New York Press, 1895–1898* (Columbia University, *Studies in History, Economics and Public Law*, No. 403). 1934. 286.

Wish, Harvey. *Contemporary America: The National Scene since 1900.* 1945. 357.

—— *Society and Thought in America.* 2 vols. 1950–52. 102.

Witte, Edwin E. *The Government in Labor Disputes.* 1932. 505.

Wittke, Carl F. *German-Americans and the World War, with Special Emphasis on Ohio's German Language Press* (*Ohio Historical Collections*, V). 1936. 426.

—— *We Who Built America: The Saga of the Immigrant.* 1939. 203.

Woestemeyer, Ina Faye, and J. Montgomery Gambrill. *The Westward Movement: A Book of Readings on Our Changing Frontiers.* 1939. 75.

Wood, Clement. *Herbert Clark Hoover: An American Tragedy.* 1932. 567.

Woodbridge, George, ed. *UNRRA: The History of the United Nations Relief and Rehabilitation Administration.* 3 vols. 1951. 726.

Woodburn, James A. *The Life of Thaddeus Stevens.* 1913. 34.

Woodley, Thomas F. *Great Leveller: The Life of Thaddeus Stevens.* 1937. 34.

—— *Thaddeus Stevens.* 1934. 34.

Woodward, C[omer] Vann. *Origins of the New South, 1877–1913* (*A History of the South*, IX). 1951. 125, 228.

—— *Reunion and Reaction: The Compromise of 1877 and the End of Reconstruction.* 1951. 125.

—— *Tom Watson, Agrarian Rebel.* 1938. 228.

Woodward, William E. *Meet General Grant.* 1928. New ed., 1946. 53.

Woody, Thomas. *History of Women's Education in the United States.* 2 vols. 1929. 103.

Wright, Frank Lloyd. *An Autobiography.* 1932. New ed., 1943. 548.

—— *Modern Architecture.* 1931. 548.

Wright, Gordon. *The Reshaping of French Democracy.* 1948. 726.

Wright, Wilbur and Orville. *Miracle at Kitty Hawk: The Letters of Wilbur and Orville Wright.* Edited by Fred C. Kelly. 1951. 547.

Xenides, J. P. *The Greeks in America.* 1922. 204.

Yardley, Herbert O. *The American Black Chamber.* 1931. 479.

Yellen, Samuel. *American Labor Struggles.* 1936. 187.

Young, Desmond. *Rommel, The Desert Fox.* 1950. 658.

Young, Robert T. *Biology in America.* 1922. 548.

Zacharias, Ellis M. *Behind Closed Doors: The Secret History of the Cold War.* 1950. 726.

—— "The Inside Story of Yalta." *United Nations World*, III, 12–18. January, 1949. 702.

—— *Secret Missions: The Story of an Intelligence Officer.* 1946. 658.

Zeis, Paul M. *American Shipping Policy.* 1938. 478.

Zimmermann, Erich W. *Zimmermann on Ocean Shipping.* 1921. 478.

Zinkin, Maurice. *Asia and the West.* 1951. 702.

PICTURE CREDITS

In the following page-by-page list of credits, page numbers appear in bold face. Where there is more than one picture on a page, the pictures are referred to from left to right, top to bottom. The following abbreviations have been used for a few sources from which a great many illustrations have been obtained: *Bettmann* — The Bettmann Archive; *Brown* — Brown Brothers; *Culver* — Culver Service; *I.N P.* — International News Photos; *L. of C.* — Library of Congress; *N.Y.P.L.* — New York Public Library; *W.W.* — Wide World.

3 Civil War ruins. Bettmann. **4** both from Bettmann. **5** both from Bettmann. **9** Bettmann. **10** courtesy of Bland Gallery; Bettmann. **11** Bettmann; through the courtesy of Wildenstein & Co., Inc., N.Y. **19** Detail from Nast cartoon, "Emergence of the Solid South." *Harper's Weekly*, April 19, 1879. **20** right, Brown. **21** Brown. **28** upper right, Bettmann. **30** Bettmann; Culver. **35** "The Brains." Nast's presentation of Tweed as figure with money sack for head. *Harper's Weekly*, October 21, 1871. **36** right, National Archives. **44** upper right, middle left, Bettmann. **47** Bettmann. **50** middle left, Bettmann. **54** Detail from "Emigrants Crossing the Plains." *Appleton's Journal*, 1869. U.S. Bureau of Public Roads. **56** Bettmann; Bettmann; Old Print Shop. **57** bottom, Old Print Shop. **60** Bettmann; Colts Patent Firearms Co., Hartford; Bettmann. **64** upper left, right, and middle from Smithsonian Institution; bottom, Culver. **68** Smithsonian Institution. **70** Denver Public Library, Western Collection; Old Print Shop; Bettmann. **71** Union Pacific Railroad; Nebraska State Historical Society. **72** upper left, Swift & Company; middle left, lower left, Bettmann; middle right, Kansas State Historical Society. **78** L. of C. **80** Bettmann; Culver. **87** all from Brown. **90** middle, Johns Hopkins University; lower, Vassar College. **91** Harvard University; National Archives. **96** left, Brown. **101** Brown; L. of C. **105** The Torch of Liberty. Woodcut. Bettmann. **107** Bettmann. **113** Handy Collection. **116** Brown. **117** Brown. **119** Brown. **121** Handy Collection. **129** Early wall telephone, 1878. Am. Tel. & Tel. Co. **132** top, Metropolitan Museum; middle left, Union Pacific Railroad; lower left, Columbia University; lower right, Bettmann. **134** Museum of the City of N.Y. **136** top left, L. of C.; lower right, Montgomery Ward Co. **140** L. of C. **144** upper and middle left, Am. Tel. & Tel. Co.; lower right, N.Y. Hist. Soc. **148** Shooting an oil well. *Century Magazine*, July, 1883. **150** Chicago Historical Society. **152** right, Handy Collection. **154** top, Standard Oil Company of N.J.; center, middle

left, Brown. **162** courtesy of Thomas A. Edison, Inc. **165** all from Bettmann except lower right, courtesy of Procter & Gamble Co. **170** Section of John White Alexander murals, in Carnegie Institute, Pittsburgh. **171** lower right, L. of C. **173** L. of C. **177** Brown. **180** courtesy of National Park Service. **188** Detail from cover of sheet music, "Only an Emigrant," by Charlie Baker. Library of Congress. **190** middle right, Bettmann; all others Alexander Alland Collection. **194** Alexander Alland Collection. **196** middle left, Bettmann; lower right, N.Y. Hist. Soc. **200** in the collection of the Corcoran Gallery of Art, Washington. **205** Detail from "The Purpose of the Grange." Lithograph by Strobridge Co., 1813. **206** lower left, L. of C. **212** Baker Library, Harvard Business School. **213** upper left, Bettmann; lower left, N.Y. Hist Soc. **222** both from Brown. **224** Brown. **232** Victor in *Judge*, March 7, 1896. **234** Bettmann. **237** left, Brown; right, Bettmann. **239** Western Reserve Historical Society. **245** "Checkers Up at the Farm" by John Rogers, 1877. Bronze. **247** left, Brown; right, Chicago Historical Society. **250** Metropolitan Museum. **255** Bettmann. **258** courtesy of the Rhode Island School of Design Museum of Art, Providence, R.I. **261** Handy Studios. **262** upper left, L. of C.; middle left, Bettmann; bottom, L. of C. **273** both from Mariners Museum. **275** Mariners Museum. **276** Navy Dept.; Mariners Museum. **282** upper right, State of Vermont and Metropolitan Museum; middle, by special permission of Chief, U.S. Secret Service, Treas. Dept. Further reproduction in full or part is strictly prohibited; lower left and right, Kraushaar Galleries, N.Y. **289** *Rocky Mountain News*, Denver, 1900. **290** all from Brown. **297** Brown. **302** all from Brown. **307** National Archives. **314** *Rev. of Rev.*, Dec., 1903. **318** Brown. **319** upper left, Brown; lower left, Keystone View Co. **326** all from Brown. **332** Detail from cartoon, "Bosses of the Senate." Library of Congress. **333** Brown; Bettmann. **335** Culver. **337** courtesy *Minneapolis Journal*. **344** all courtesy of U.S. Forest Serv-

ice. **349** Brown; Culver; U.S. Forest Service; Brown. **350** Brown. **355** Brown. **358** Suffragettes as sandwichwomen. Brown Bros. **359** both from Brown. **362** State Historical Society of Wisconsin. **364** all from Bettmann. **365** both Brown. **368** Berry Rockwell. **370** Brown. **372** Brown. **380** Hull House Association. **384** The President's Flag. Photo by Abbie Rowe. National Park Service. **385** Culver. **393** courtesy of Frank C. Kirk. **394** Brown. **396** both from Brown. **398** upper right and middle, Bettmann; all others courtesy of Ford Motor Co. **405** "Coalition Turned into War." Bettmann. **408** both from Brown. **409** all from Brown. **410** I.N.P. **412** Brown. **416** upper, National Archives; middle, European Picture Service; bottom, Navy Dept. **423** National Archives. **428** U.S. Signal Corps. **432** upper left, Museum of Modern Art; bottom right, Berry Rockwell. **433** Brown. **436** all from National Archives. **438** National Archives. **439** National Archives. **442** European Picture Service. **443** I.N.P. **448** European Picture Service. **449** I.N.P. **454** Edison re-enacts invention of his light in October, 1929, at Edison Museum in Dearborn, Michigan. **458** all from the *Boston Post*. **459** all from the *Boston Post*. **460** both from Culver. **470** *Dallas News*. **473** N.Y. Hist. Soc. **476** top, Brown; bottom, W. W. **480** Detail from "Politics" cartoon. *The New York Times*, June 21, 1936. **481** Brown. **486** top, Brown. **487** Brown; I.N.P.; Brown. **489** I.N.P. **490** Brown. **494** National Gallery of Art, Washington. **495** I.N.P. **506** Detail from cartoon on Anti-Trust Act of 1890. *Harper's Weekly*, Dec. 3, 1887. **509** Brown. **514** Handy Collection. **515** Brown. **520** I.N.P. **524** courtesy of Ford Motor Company. **527** National Broadcasting Company. **530** upper and middle, Institute of Aeronautical Sciences; lower, United Air Lines. **535** Federal Bureau of Investigation. **536** N.Y. Hist. Soc. **537** Berry Rockwell; Brown; Brown; H. Armstrong Roberts; Brown; Gustav Anderson. **540** top right, Acme Newspictures; left and bottom, Theatre Collection, Harvard University. **542** left, Theatre Collection, Har-

LIST OF MAPS AND CHARTS

INDEX OF PLACE NAMES ON MAPS

INDEX OF ILLUSTRATIONS

GENERAL INDEX

Pacific
Ocean

Coast Ranges
Valley of California
Sierra Nevada
Great Basin
Great Salt
Lake
Wasatch
Mts.
Wyoming
Basin
Park Range
Rocky Mts.
Great Plains

GENERALIZED EAST